EU SHIPPING LAW

VOLUME I

LLOYD'S SHIPPING LAW LIBRARY
Series Editors: Hatty Sumption and Clare Ambrose

LLOYD'S SHIPPING LAW LIBRARY

Laytime and Demurrage
Seventh edition
John Schofield

The Law of Ship Mortgages
Second edition
David Osborne, Graeme Bowtle and Charles Buss

Berlingieri on Arrest of Ships
Sixth edition
Francesco Berlingieri

Merchant Shipping Legislation
Third edition
Aengus R.M. Fogarty

*CMR
Contracts for the International Carriage
of Goods by Road*
Fourth edition
Andrew Messent and David A. Glass

London Maritime Arbitration
Fourth edition
Clare Ambrose, Karen Maxwell and
Michael Collett

The York-Antwerp Rules
The Principles and
Practice of General Average Adjustment
Fourth edition
N. Geoffrey Hudson and Michael D. Harvey

Admiralty Jurisdiction and Practice
Fifth edition
Nigel Meeson and John A. Kimbell

General Average
Law and Practice
Third edition
F. D. Rose

The Law of Tug and Tow and Offshore Contracts
Fourth edition
Simon Rainey

EU Shipping Law
Third edition
Vincent Power

EU SHIPPING LAW

THIRD EDITION

VOLUME I

VINCENT POWER
B.C.L. (NUI), LL.M., Ph.D. (Cambridge), Solicitor
Partner, A&L Goodbody Solicitors
and
Adjunct Professor of Law, University College Cork
European Union Centre for Excellence Visiting Professor of European Union Law,
Dalhousie University, Canada

informa law
from Routledge

Third edition published 2019
by Informa Law from Routledge
2 Park Square, Milton Park, Abingdon, Oxon OX14 4RN

and by Informa Law from Routledge
711 Third Avenue, New York, NY 10017

Informa Law from Routledge is an imprint of the Taylor & Francis Group, an informa business

© 2019 Vincent Power

The right of Vincent Power to be identified as author of this work has been asserted by him in accordance with sections 77 and 78 of the Copyright, Designs and Patents Act 1988.

All rights reserved. No part of this book may be reprinted or reproduced or utilized in any form or by any electronic, mechanical, or other means, now known or hereafter invented, including photocopying and recording, or in any information storage or retrieval system, without permission in writing from the publishers.

Whilst every effort has been made to ensure that the information contained in this book is correct, neither the author nor Informa Law can accept any responsibility for any errors or omissions or any consequences arising therefrom.

Trademark notice: Product or corporate names may be trademarks or registered trademarks, and are used only for identification and explanation without intent to infringe.

First edition published by Lloyd's of London 1992
Second edition published by LLP Reference Publishing 1998

British Library Cataloguing-in-Publication Data
A catalogue record for this book is available from the British Library

Library of Congress Cataloging-in-Publication Data
A catalog record has been requested for this book

ISBN: 978-1-843-11633-2 (hbk)
ISBN: 978-1-315-62614-7 (ebk)
ISBN: 9780-367-02563-2 (volume I)

Typeset in Times New Roman
by Wearset Ltd, Boldon, Tyne and Wear

Printed and bound by CPI Group (UK) Ltd, Croydon, CR0 4YY

CONTENTS

VOLUME I

Preface		lxxiii
Table of abbreviations		lxxv
Table of cases		lxxxi
Table of legislation		xcv
CHAPTER 1	INTRODUCTION	1
CHAPTER 2	A COMMERCIAL OVERVIEW OF SHIPPING IN THE EUROPEAN UNION	26
CHAPTER 3	AN OVERVIEW OF THE EUROPEAN UNION AND EUROPEAN UNION LAW	69
CHAPTER 4	OVERVIEW OF EUROPEAN UNION TRANSPORT LAW	110
CHAPTER 5	THE HISTORICAL DEVELOPMENT OF EUROPEAN UNION SHIPPING LAW	133
CHAPTER 6	EUROPEAN UNION LAW RELATING TO THE FREEDOM OF ESTABLISHMENT OF SHIPPING BUSINESSES AND THE REGISTRATION OF SHIPS	207
CHAPTER 7	EUROPEAN UNION LAW RELATING TO FREEDOM TO SUPPLY SERVICES: INTERNATIONAL SERVICES; CABOTAGE SERVICES; AND SHIPPING SERVICES GENERALLY	281
CHAPTER 8	EUROPEAN UNION LAW RELATING TO EMPLOYMENT IN THE SHIPPING SECTOR	443

CHAPTER 9	INTRODUCTION TO LINER CONFERENCES: THE CONCEPT OF LINER CONFERENCES AND THE UNITED NATIONS CODE ON LINER CONFERENCES AND THE UNITED NATIONS LINER CODE	572
CHAPTER 10	AN OVERVIEW OF EUROPEAN UNION COMPETITION LAW GENERALLY AND HOW IT APPLIES TO THE SHIPPING SECTOR GENERALLY	601
CHAPTER 11	EUROPEAN UNION COMPETITION LAW: THE OLD REGIME RELATING TO SHIPPING – REGULATION 4056/86	671
CHAPTER 12	EUROPEAN UNION COMPETITION LAW: THE NEW REGIME RELATING TO SHIPPING – REGULATION 1419/2006	728
CHAPTER 13	EUROPEAN UNION COMPETITION LAW: PORTS	810
CHAPTER 14	EUROPEAN UNION COMPETITION LAW: CONSORTIA	855
CHAPTER 15	EUROPEAN UNION STATE AID LAW: SHIPPING AND PORTS	887
CHAPTER 16	EUROPEAN UNION MERGER CONTROL: SHIPPING, PORTS AND SHIPBUILDING	939
CHAPTER 17	REGULATION 4057/86: DUMPING OF SHIPPING SERVICES AND THE UNFAIR PRICING OF SHIPPING SERVICES	1007
CHAPTER 18	REGULATION 4058/86: CO-ORDINATED ACTION TO SAFEGUARD FREE ACCESS TO CARGOES IN OCEAN TRADE	1030

VOLUME II

CHAPTER 19	EUROPEAN UNION LAW RELATING TO THE MARITIME ENVIRONMENT: INTRODUCTION; EUROPEAN UNION MEASURES RELATING TO THE MARITIME ENVIRONMENT GENERALLY; AND PENALTIES FOR INFRINGEMENTS	1041
CHAPTER 20	EUROPEAN UNION LAW RELATING TO THE MARITIME ENVIRONMENT: ORGANOTIN	1134

CONTENTS

CHAPTER 21	EUROPEAN UNION LAW RELATING TO THE MARITIME ENVIRONMENT: THE HAZARDOUS AND NOXIOUS SUBSTANCES BY SEA CONVENTION	1143
CHAPTER 22	EUROPEAN UNION LAW RELATING TO SHIPBUILDING	1146
CHAPTER 23	EUROPEAN UNION LAW RELATING TO SHIP REPAIR	1195
CHAPTER 24	EUROPEAN UNION LAW RELATING TO SHIP DISMANTLING AND RECYCLING	1198
CHAPTER 25	EUROPEAN UNION EXTERNAL RELATIONS LAW AND SHIPPING	1227
CHAPTER 26	MARITIME SAFETY: INTRODUCTION AND EUROPEAN UNION MEASURES RELATING TO MARITIME SAFETY GENERALLY	1260
CHAPTER 27	MARITIME SAFETY: THE EUROPEAN MARITIME SAFETY AGENCY	1284
CHAPTER 28	MARITIME SAFETY: PORT STATE CONTROL	1305
CHAPTER 29	MARITIME SAFETY: SHIP INSPECTION AND SURVEY ORGANISATIONS	1349
CHAPTER 30	MARITIME SAFETY: CASUALTY AND ACCIDENT INVESTIGATION	1392
CHAPTER 31	MARITIME SAFETY: MINIMUM TRAINING OF SEAFARERS	1413
CHAPTER 32	MARITIME SAFETY: MINIMUM SAFETY AND HEALTH REQUIREMENTS FOR IMPROVED MEDICAL TREATMENT ON BOARD VESSELS	1437
CHAPTER 33	MARITIME SAFETY: INTERNATIONAL SAFETY MANAGEMENT CODE FOR THE SAFE OPERATION OF SHIPS AND FOR POLLUTION PREVENTION	1444
CHAPTER 34	MARITIME SAFETY: FERRIES AND RO-RO VESSELS	1451
CHAPTER 35	MARITIME SAFETY: ORGANISATION OF WORKING TIME OF SEAFARERS	1490

CHAPTER 36	MARITIME SAFETY: MARITIME LABOUR CONVENTION 2006	1497
CHAPTER 37	MARITIME SAFETY: MARINE EQUIPMENT	1505
CHAPTER 38	PIRACY	1537
CHAPTER 39	NAVIGATION	1554
CHAPTER 40	PILOTAGE	1585
CHAPTER 41	SHORT SEA SHIPPING	1592
CHAPTER 42	SECURITY: SHIPS AND PORTS	1606
CHAPTER 43	PORTS: GENERALLY AND THE PORT SERVICES REGULATION 2017/352	1635
CHAPTER 44	PORTS: REPORTING FORMALITIES FOR SHIPS IN EUROPEAN UNION PORTS: DIRECTIVE 2010/65	1659
CHAPTER 45	PORTS: ELECTRICITY FOR SHIPS IN PORTS	1670
CHAPTER 46	CARRIAGE OF GOODS AND PASSENGERS	1676
CHAPTER 47	EUROPEAN UNION LAW AND SHIPPING LITIGATION: THE "BRUSSELS I" REGULATION	1740
CHAPTER 48	BREXIT	1769
CHAPTER 49	CONCLUSIONS	1801
Index		1821

DETAILED CONTENTS

VOLUME I

Preface	lxxiii
Table of abbreviations	lxxv
Table of cases	lxxxi
Table of legislation	xcv

CHAPTER 1 INTRODUCTION

A. Scope of this book	1.001
B. The European Union	
Introduction	1.003
Evolution of the European Union	1.004
The EU is the world's largest economic bloc	1.008
Population	1.010
The internal market	1.011
Transport in the EU	1.013
Future of the EU	1.015
C. Shipping in the EU	1.016
Introduction	1.016
Strategic significance of shipping for the EU	1.017
Shipping has an important role in the EU's global and internal trading activities	1.019
Shipping is an important employer in the EU	1.021
Shipping is an important earner of foreign currency and an indispensable part of the EU's ability to trade globally	1.022
Open/non-protectionist policy	1.023
Internal balances	1.024
Multidimensional nature of EU shipping law and policy	1.025
Social dimension to EU shipping policy	1.026
Safety dimension to EU shipping policy	1.027
Environmental dimension to EU shipping policy	1.028
Competition dimension to EU shipping policy	1.029
International dimension to EU shipping policy	1.030
Divergent influences on the development of EU shipping policy?	1.031
Staggered or strategic development of EU shipping policy?	1.036
Should the EU have a role in shipping?	1.037
Introduction	1.037

DETAILED CONTENTS

Arguments in favour of the EU having a role to play in shipping	1.038
Arguments against the EU having a role to play in shipping	1.040
Is there a comprehensive EU shipping policy?	1.041
Who influences EU shipping law?	1.042
The EU and shipping: a brief comparative perspective in the context of international organisations and shipping generally	1.043
D. EU shipping law in the wider context of EU maritime policy	1.044
E. Outline of this book	1.046

CHAPTER 2 A COMMERCIAL OVERVIEW OF SHIPPING IN THE EUROPEAN UNION

A. Introduction	2.001
B. Commercial significance of shipping for the EU	2.004
C. Commercial philosophy of the EU relating to shipping	2.014
D. State of shipping in the EU	2.016
E. Ports in the EU	2.027
F. Passengers	2.028
G. Contribution to the EU from the shipping sector	2.029
H. Analysis of shipping in the Member States	
Austria	2.030
Belgium	2.031
Bulgaria	2.034
Croatia	2.036
Cyprus	2.038
Czech Republic	2.040
Denmark	2.042
Estonia	2.045
Finland	2.047
France	2.049
Germany	2.056
Greece	2.063
Hungary	2.073
Ireland	2.074
Italy	2.080
Latvia	2.086
Lithuania	2.089
Luxembourg	2.094
Malta	2.096
The Netherlands	2.098
Poland	2.104
Portugal	2.110
Romania	2.117
Slovakia	2.119
Slovenia	2.120
Spain	2.122
Sweden	2.129

United Kingdom	2.133
I. Conclusions	2.142

CHAPTER 3 AN OVERVIEW OF THE EUROPEAN UNION AND EUROPEAN UNION LAW

A. Introduction	3.001
B. The European Union	
Introduction	3.003
European Coal and Steel Community ("ECSC")	3.004
EAEC	3.005
EEC/EC/EU	3.006
C. History	
European integration	3.008
Marshall Aid, the Organisation for European Economic Cooperation ("OEEC") and the UN Economic Commission for Europe	3.009
Congress of Europe	3.010
Benelux Union	3.011
Council of Europe	3.012
North Atlantic Treaty Organisation ("NATO")	3.013
Schumann Declaration	3.014
ECSC	3.015
European Defence Treaty	3.016
The EEC and EAEC	3.017
European Free Trade Association ("EFTA")	3.018
UK's position at the time of the foundation of the European communities	3.019
Institutions: Merger Treaty	3.020
Customs Union	3.021
Accessions	3.022
European Monetary System	3.023
Direct elections to the European Parliament	3.024
Internal Market White Paper	3.025
Single European Act ("SEA")	3.026
Central and Eastern Europe	3.027
Internal market	3.028
EMU	3.029
Failed Constitution but the adoption of the Treaty of Lisbon	3.030
Outlook	3.031
D. Institutional and organic structure of the EU	
Introduction	3.032
Commission	3.034
Introduction	3.034
Composition	3.035
Functions	3.036
Operation	3.037
DG MOVE: Directorate-General for Mobility and Transport	3.039

DG MARE: Directorate-General for Maritime Affairs and Fisheries	3.040
DG COMP: Competition	3.041
Conclusion	3.042
The Council	3.043
Introduction	3.043
Composition	3.044
Functions	3.045
Operation and voting	3.046
The Council's Committee of Permanent Representatives ("COREPER")	3.047
General Secretariat of the Council	3.048
The Council and shipping	3.049
European Council	3.050
European Parliament	3.051
Introduction	3.051
Seat	3.052
Members	3.053
Election	3.055
Operation	3.056
Functions	3.057
The Parliament and shipping	3.058
Future	3.059
The CJEU including the General Court	3.060
Introduction	3.060
Functions	3.061
Personnel	3.062
Operation of the Court	3.068
Procedure	3.073
Jurisdiction	3.076
Other institutions	3.086
Bodies	3.087
Introduction	3.087
Economic and Social Committee	3.088
European Investment Bank	3.089
Civic Society and Lobby Groups	3.090
E. EU law	
Introduction	3.091
Sources of EU law	3.092
Primary law	3.092
Secondary law	3.101
Direct effect and direct applicability	3.113
Publication of EU law	3.114
Relationship between EU law and national laws	3.115
Interpretation of EU law	3.116
Selected fundamental principles of EU law	3.117
F. Conclusions	3.122

CHAPTER 4 AN OVERVIEW OF EUROPEAN UNION TRANSPORT LAW

A. Introduction
   Purpose of this chapter 4.001
   Importance of transport in the EU 4.002
   Need to achieve a common transport policy 4.003
   Failure to achieve a CTP 4.004
   Legal bases of EU transport law 4.005
   Adoption and administration of EU transport law 4.006
   Sources of EU transport law 4.007

B. Position of transport in the TFEU
   Introduction 4.008
   The TFEU and transport generally 4.016
   Article 4 of the TFEU 4.018
      Text 4.018
      Commentary 4.019
   Article 58 of the TFEU 4.020
      Text 4.020
      Commentary 4.021
   Article 90 of the TFEU 4.022
      Text 4.022
      Commentary 4.023
   Article 91 of the TFEU 4.028
      Text 4.028
      Commentary 4.029
   Article 92 of the TFEU 4.036
      Text 4.036
      Commentary 4.037
   Article 93 of the TFEU 4.039
      Text 4.039
      Commentary 4.040
   Article 94 of the TFEU 4.043
      Text 4.043
      Commentary 4.044
   Article 95 of the TFEU 4.045
      Text 4.045
      Commentary 4.046
   Article 96 of the TFEU 4.050
      Text 4.050
      Commentary 4.051
   Article 97 of the TFEU 4.053
      Text 4.053
      Commentary 4.054
   Article 98 of the EU Treaty 4.055
      Text 4.055
      Commentary 4.056
   Article 99 of the TFEU 4.057

Text	4.057
Commentary	4.058
Article 100 of the TFEU	4.060
Text	4.060
Commentary	4.061
C. Secondary legislation	4.071
D. European Economic Area ("EEA")	4.072
E. Conclusions	4.073

CHAPTER 5 THE HISTORICAL DEVELOPMENT OF EUROPEAN UNION SHIPPING LAW

A. Introduction	5.001
B. The 1950s: the Foundation Treaties	5.003
C. The 1960s	5.004
Introduction	5.004
1960: Memorandum from the Commission to the Council	5.005
1961: Memorandum on the basic approach to be adopted in the Common Transport Policy	5.006
1962: Action programme for a Common Transport Policy	5.007
1962: Regulations on competition and shipping	5.008
D. The 1970s	
Introduction	5.010
Bodson's proposals	5.011
The 1973 enlargement of the then EEC	5.012
Commission's Communication to Council on 25 October 1973	5.013
ECSC	5.014
1973: Oil crisis	5.015
1973: *French Seamen's* case	5.016
1974: Ports	5.018
1974: Enforcement of sanctions	5.019
1975: French initiative	5.020
Non-Member States	5.021
Code of Conduct for Liner Conferences	5.022
1976: Interim Report drawn up on behalf of the European Parliament's Committee on Economic and Monetary Affairs on the Community Shipping Industry	5.023
1977: Interim Report drawn up on behalf of the Committee on Regional Policy, Regional Planning and Transport on the Sea Transport Problems in the Community	5.024
1977: Consultation procedure: Decision 77/587	5.025
1978: Decision on relations with State trading countries: Decision 78/774	5.026
Tanker disasters: safety responses	5.027
1978: Ship's inspection proposals	5.028
1978: Decision in respect of liner trades between the Community and East Africa/Central America	5.029

1978: Pilotage	5.030
1979: Ratification of the UNCTAD Code of Conduct for Liner Conferences	5.031
1979: Parliamentary resolution on shipping accidents	5.032
1979: Parliamentary resolution on the Community's relations with the COMECON States in maritime shipping	5.033
1979: EESC opinion on Flags of Convenience	5.034
1979: International Convention for Safe Containers	5.035
Shipping crisis	5.036
E. The 1980s	
Introduction	5.037
Shipping crisis as well as port distortions	5.038
1980: Recommendation on the Torremolinos International Convention for the Safety of Fishing Vessels	5.039
1980: Draft for a Council Resolution Concerning Priorities and the Timetable for Decisions to be taken by the Council in the Transport Sector during the Period up to the End of 1983	5.040
1980: Extension of the 1978 collection of information decision	5.041
1980: Proposal on port control of pollution	5.042
1980: Parliamentary resolutions on oil pollution	5.043
1981: Accession of Greece	5.044
1981: Council resolution on its priorities in the transport sector up to 1983	5.045
1981: Decision extending the collection of information regime in respect of the Far East	5.046
1981: Netherlands and the Liner Conference Code	5.047
1981: Tankers entering into German ports	5.048
1981: Proposal on competition rules and shipping	5.049
1981: Proposals on concerted research on shore-based maritime navigation aid systems	5.050
1982: Extension of the collection of information systems	5.051
1982: Memorandum of Understanding on Port State Control	5.052
1983: EESC opinion on the Commission's proposal on the application of Articles 85 and 86 to shipping	5.053
1983: Recommendation on SAR	5.054
1983: Countermeasures decision	5.055
1983: Parliament's case against the Council for failure to elaborate proposals in the area of transport	5.056
1984: Commission Memorandum on Maritime Transport	5.057
1985: Progress towards a Common Maritime Policy: Commission Communication	5.058
Introduction	5.058
Analysis of the market	5.059
Proposals	5.060
EESC's opinion on the communication	5.068
The 1986 package	5.069

Regulation 4055/86	5.070
Regulation 4056/86	5.071
Regulation 4057/86	5.072
Regulation 4058/86	5.073
Statements on the package	5.074
Assessment of the 1986 package	5.078
The SEA	5.080
1987: Antwerp meeting	5.081
1987: Joint Committee on Maritime Transport	5.082
1987: Italy/Algeria	5.083
1987: Commission Decision 87/359 on Spanish nationals	5.084
1988: Shipbuilding talks with Japan	5.085
1988: Commission proposal on the minimum health and safety requirements for improved medical treatment on board vessels	5.086
1988: Competition procedures	5.087
1988: Commission Programme	5.088
1989: Positive measures	5.089
Proposal for a Council Regulation establishing a Community Ship Register and Providing for the Flying of the Community Flag by Sea-Going Vessels	5.090
Proposal for a Commission Recommendation on Improving the Effectiveness of Port State Control in the EU	5.091
Proposal for a Council Regulation providing for a Common Definition of a Community Shipowner	5.092
Proposal for a Council Regulation applying the Principle of Freedom to Provide Services to Maritime Transport within Member States ("Cabotage")	5.093
1990: Proposal for a Council Regulation regarding the Transfer of Ships from one Register to another within the EU	5.094
Financial and fiscal measures	5.095
F. The 1990s	
Introduction	5.096
June 1990 Resolution on Passenger Ferry Safety	5.097
1990: Proposal for a Council regulation to grant a block exemption for consortia	5.098
1991: Permanent dialogue on the maritime industry	5.099
1991: Transfer of ships between Member State registers	5.100
1991: Establishment of European Maritime Law Organisation ("EMLO")	5.101
1992: Establishment of the Maritime Industries Forum ("MIF")	5.102
1992: Radionavigation systems	5.103
1992: Council of Ministers enable consortia block exemption to be adopted	5.104
1992: Medical treatment on board vessels	5.105
1992: Maritime industries communication	5.106
1992: Cabotage regime enacted	5.107

1993: Spanish derogation to cabotage regime	5.108
1993: Safe seas	5.109
1993: Safety conventions	5.110
1993: Dangerous or polluting goods	5.111
1993: Shipbuilding directive extended	5.112
European Economic Area ("EEA") agreement with the EC	5.113
1994: *Commission v French Republic*	5.114
Protocol 19 on maritime transport	5.115
1994: Ships inspection/classification societies	5.117
1994: Seafarers' training	5.118
1994: Global Navigation System	5.119
1995: Commission regulation on application of Article 85(3) (now Article 101(3) TFEU) to consortia	5.120
1995: Port State control	5.121
1995: Short sea shipping communication	5.122
Council Regulation 3051/95 on the safety management of roll-on/roll-off passenger ferries (ro-ro ferries)	5.123
1995: Statistical return on passengers and goods	5.124
1996: Short sea shipping resolution	5.125
1996: Commission communication: "Towards a New Maritime Strategy"	5.126
1996: CEWAL before the General Court	5.127
1997: Commission communication: "External Relations in the Field of Maritime Transport"	5.128
1997: Council Resolution on a New Strategy to Increase the Competitiveness of Community Shipping	5.129
1997: Community guidelines on State aid	5.130
1998: Trans-Atlantic Conference Agreement	5.131
1990s Generally	5.132
G. The 2000s	
Introduction	5.133
2000: Consortia block exemption: Regulation 823/2000	5.134
2000: Promotion of intermodality and intermodal freight transport in the EU	5.135
2000: Promotion of short sea shipping	5.136
2000: Commission fines shipping lines for pricing agreement on the Europe/Far East trade	5.137
2001: Ports package	5.139
2002–2003: Repeal of Regulation 17/62 and adoption of Regulation 1/2003	5.140
2002: *TAA* and *FEFC*	5.141
2002: Full liberalisation of cabotage	5.142
Establishment of the European Maritime Safety Agency ("EMSA")	5.143
2004: State aid guidelines	5.144
2005: Mid-term review of the White Paper on European transport policy	5.145

Consortia block exemption extended until 2010   5.146
Green Paper on a future EU maritime policy   5.147
2006: Rejection of the port services liberalisation measures   5.149
2006: Repeal of Regulation 4056/86 and the adoption of Regulation 1419/2006   5.150
2007: An Integrated Maritime Policy for the EU   5.151
2008: Ending of the block exemption for liner conferences and the extension of the general competition regime to cabotage and tramp shipping on 18 October 2008   5.153
2008: Shipping guidelines   5.154
2008: Commission opens consultations on review of block exemption for liner shipping consortia   5.155
2009: EU Maritime Transport Policy for 2018 and Commission Strategy Plan to Establish a European Maritime Transport Space without Barriers   5.156
2009: Third maritime safety package   5.157
2000s: Tonnage taxes   5.158
2009: State aid and ship management companies   5.159
2009: Recognition of the Polish Register   5.160
2009: Entry into force of the Treaty of Lisbon   5.161
2000s: Conclusions   5.162

H. The 2010s
2010: Integrated Maritime Policy for the EU   5.163
2010: Entry into force of the new consortia block exemption   5.164
2013: Ports package   5.165
2013: Proposal to enhance seafarer's rights   5.166
2014: The Athens Declaration   5.167
Commission communication setting the strategic goals and recommendations for the EU's maritime transport policy until 2018   5.168
2014: Report on ships' formalities   5.169
2014: Decision 2014/241 concerning the ratification of, or the accession to, the Hong Kong International Convention for the Safe and Environmentally Sound Recycling of Ships, 2009, by the EU Member States in the interests of the EU   5.170
2014: Regulation on detailed rules for the imposition of fines and periodic penalty payments and the withdrawal of recognition of ship inspection and survey organisations   5.171
2014: Consortia block exemption regulation extended   5.172
2015: Regulatory Summit   5.173
2015: Portuguese Shipyard ENVC   5.174
2015: Shipment of waste: Commission guidelines for customs controls on transboundary shipments of waste   5.175

2015: Regulation 2015/757 of the European Parliament and of the Council of 29 April 2015 on the monitoring, reporting and verification of carbon dioxide emissions from maritime transport, and amending Directive 2009/16	5.176
2015–2016: Migration crisis	5.177
2016: Brexit vote	5.178
I. Conclusion	5.179

CHAPTER 6 EUROPEAN UNION LAW RELATING TO THE FREEDOM OF ESTABLISHMENT OF SHIPPING BUSINESSES AND THE REGISTRATION OF SHIPS

A. Right of establishment	
Introduction	6.001
Concept of the right of establishment	6.002
General rule on freedom of establishment	6.003
Prohibition of new restrictions	6.006
Implementation of the Treaty provisions on establishment	6.007
Freedom of establishment and registration of ships	6.009
Mutual recognition of diplomas, certificates and qualifications	6.010
Exceptions to the freedom of establishment	6.012
Introduction	6.012
Exception 1: Exercise of official authority	6.013
Exception 2: Public policy	6.015
Exception 3: Public security	6.016
Exception 4: Public health	6.017
Definition of a Community or EU Shipowner	6.018
B. Registration of ships in international law	
Introduction	6.019
Traditional home registries	6.021
Traditional open registries	6.022
Offshore registries	6.024
International registries	6.025
International law on registration	6.026
Geneva Convention on the High Seas 1958	6.027
United Nations Convention on the Law of the Sea 1982	6.031
United Nations Convention on the Registration of Ships 1986	6.033
C. EU perspective on registration of ships	
Introduction	6.035
EU reaction to the UN Convention on the Registration of Ships 1986	6.036
Commission's communication	6.036
Commission's proposal	6.043
European Parliament's report	6.044
D. Transfer of ships between EU Member State registries: Regulation 613/91 (now repealed)	
Introduction	6.045
Background to the Proposal	6.049

Legislative history	6.054
Relationship between the regulation and other rules	6.057
Legal bases of the regulation	6.058
Interpretation	6.059
Application of the regulation	6.063
Obligation on Member State to register	6.066
No additional requirements for certificates	6.070
Divergences of interpretation	6.071
Committee of maritime experts	6.074

E. Transfer of ships between EU Member State registries: Regulation 789/2004 (current regime)

Introduction	6.078
Purpose of Regulation 789/2004	6.081
Concepts in Regulation 789/2004	6.082
Scope	6.083
Transfer of register	6.084
Certificates	6.085
Refusal of transfer and interpretation	6.086
Committee procedure	6.087
Reporting	6.088

F. Parallel registries

Introduction	6.090
The *Sloman Neptun* litigation	6.094

G. Case law of establishment and registration generally

The *Commission v Greece* case	6.096
The *Factortame* litigation	6.099
Introduction	6.099
The Factortame I case	6.105
The Factortame II case	6.109
The Factortame III case	6.117

H. The *Viking* litigation

Introduction	6.118
Factual background	6.120
UK litigation	6.127
Free movement of persons	6.132
Second question: Horizontal Direct Effect and Article 49	6.134
Essence of the CJEU's ruling in *Viking*	6.139
Analysis of the ruling	6.140

I. The *Commission v Netherlands* litigation

Introduction	6.141
Legal background	6.143

J. An abandoned proposal for an EU register: EUROS

Proposal	6.152
Objective of the proposal	6.154
Legal bases	6.156
Market reaction	6.157

Establishment of the register 6.158
Eligibility to be registered 6.159
Safety on EUROS-registered ships 6.167
Advantages of being registered on EUROS 6.180
Assessment of the proposal 6.181

CHAPTER 7   EUROPEAN UNION LAW RELATING TO FREEDOM TO SUPPLY SERVICES: INTERNATIONAL SERVICES; CABOTAGE SERVICES; AND SHIPPING SERVICES GENERALLY

A. Introduction 7.001
B. Freedom to provide services in EU law 7.006
C. International shipping services: Regulation 4055/86
   Introduction 7.007
   Purpose of the Regulation 4055/86 7.008
   Commercial background to Regulation 4055/86 7.015
   Effect of Regulation 4055/86 7.016
   Entry into force of Regulation 4055/86 7.020
   Implementation of Regulation 4055/86 7.021
   Basic provision relating to freedom to provide services: Article 1 of Regulation 4055/86 7.022
   Unilateral national restrictions and the timetable: Article 2 of Regulation 4055/86 7.029
   Cargo-sharing arrangements in bilateral agreements: Articles 3 and 4 of Regulation 4055/86 7.030
   Cargo-sharing arrangements in future agreements: Article 5 of Regulation 4055/86 7.033
   Non-discrimination between EU nationals on the basis of nationality 7.035
   Non-EU nationals and Regulation 4055/86 7.036
   Temporary establishment 7.037
   Review 7.038
   Assessment of Regulation 4055/86 generally 7.039
D. Cabotage or domestic shipping services: Regulation 3577/92
   Introduction 7.040
   Concepts of cabotage 7.044
   Commercial overview of cabotage 7.047
   Merits of cabotage 7.048
     Arguments for cabotage 7.048
     Arguments against cabotage 7.049
   An historical perspective on cabotage in the Member States 7.050
     Introduction 7.050
   States which had cabotage restrictions in more recent times 7.051
     Introduction 7.051
     France 7.052
     Germany 7.053
     Greece 7.054
     Italy 7.055

Portugal	7.056
Spain	7.057
Sweden	7.058
States which did not have cabotage restrictions in more recent times	7.059
Belgium	7.059
Ireland	7.060
United Kingdom	7.061
States which had limited cabotage restrictions	7.062
Denmark	7.062
States which had no cabotage restrictions or issues	7.063
Development of the EU law on cabotage	7.064
1974: Commission v France	7.064
1984: European Parliamentary Question	7.065
1985: Communication from the Commission to the Council	7.066
1986: December package	7.067
1988: Commission Programme	7.068
1989: Positive Measures Programme	7.069
Council Regulation (EEC) 3577/92 of 7 December 1992 applying the principle of freedom to maritime transport within Member States (maritime cabotage)	7.071
Introduction	7.071
Key concepts in Regulation 3577/92	7.072
The benefits of cabotage	7.078
Legal bases of Regulation 3577/92	7.079
Beneficiaries of Regulation 3577/92	7.080
EU Member States generally	7.080
Vessels registered on the EUROS Register	7.081
Implementation of Regulation 3577/92	7.082
Introduction	7.082
General principle	7.083
Mediterranean	7.085
Suspensory effect of Regulation 3577/92	7.086
Operation of Regulation 3577/92	7.088
Public service obligations and Regulation 3577/92	7.090
Introduction	7.090
Crewing or manning of vessels engaged in cabotage	7.094
Mainland cabotage	7.094
Island cabotage	7.095
Cruise liners	7.098
Serious disturbances in the market and Regulation 3577/92	7.099
Introduction	7.099
Definition of "a serious disturbance of the internal transport market"	7.100
Member State's request to the Commission to adopt safeguard measures in the event of "a serious disturbance of the internal transport market"	7.101
Temporary provision of cabotage services	7.105

Ongoing evaluation of Regulation 3577/92 — 7.106
Monitoring of Member State/national law — 7.108
Conclusion — 7.109
    Cabotage and competition — 7.113
E. Case law relating to Regulation 4055/86 and Regulation 3577/92
    Introduction — 7.117
    1989: *Corsica Ferries* case — 7.118
    1994: *Peralta* — 7.127
    1997: *Haahr Petroleum Ltd v Åbenrå Havn and others*: taxation of cargoes — 7.138
    1985: *Commission v Council (Italo-Algerian Maritime Transport)* — 7.145
    1994: *Corsica Ferries Italia Srl v Corporazione dei piloti del Porto di Genova* — 7.157
    1994: *Commission v France*: passenger levy case — 7.160
    1993: *Cenargo: UK/Morocco* — 7.165
    1988: *Corsica Ferries France v Gruppo Antichi Ormeggiatori del Porto di Genova Coop. arl, Gruppo Ormeggiatori del Golfo di La Spezia Coop. arl and Ministero dei Trasporti e della Navigazione* — 7.166
    2001: *Analir* — 7.178
    2002: *Commission v Italy*: disembarkation of passengers — 7.189
    2002: *Geha Naftiliaki EPE and Others v NPDD Limeniko Tameio DOD/SOU and Elliniko Dimosio*: port charges — 7.191
    2002: *Inspecteur van de Belastingdienst Douane, district Rotterdam v Sea-Land Service Inc. and Nedlloyd Lijnen BV* — 7.193
    2004: *Commission v Greece* — 7.200
    Commission v Spain — 7.209
    2007: *Commission v Greece*: towage — 7.215
    2007: *Commission v Greece*: harbour dues — 7.227
    2007: *International Transport Workers' Federation and Finnish Seamen's Union v Viking Line ABP and OÜ Viking Line Eesti* — 7.230
    2006: *Agip Petroli SpA v Capitaneria di porto di Siracusa, Capitaneria di porto di Siracusa – Sezione staccata di Santa Panagia and Ministero delle Infrastrutture e dei Trasporti* — 7.239
    2010: *Commission v Spain* — 7.246
    2010: *Enosi Efopliston: Island Services* — 7.247
    2003: *Commission v Finland* — 7.251
    2014: *Alpina River Cruises GmbH v Ministero delle Infrastructure e dei trasporti* — 7.252
    2014: *Fonnship A/S v Svenska Transportarbetareförbundet and Facket för Service och Kommunikation (SEKO) and Svenska Transportarbetareförbundet v Fonnship A/S* — 7.258
    2011: *Navtiliaki Etairia Thasou AE and Amalthia I Navtiki Etairia v Ipourgos Emborikis Navtilías* — 7.271
    2000: *Commission v France* — 7.278
    2010: *Commission v Malta* — 7.283
    2009: *Presidente del Consiglio dei Ministri v Regione Sardegna* — 7.289

1999: *Commission v Belgium*	7.297
1999: *Commission v Belgium and Luxembourg*	7.301
2000: *Commission v Portugal*	7.302
2000: *Commission v Portugal*	7.303
1998: *Commission v Belgium and Luxembourg*	7.304
F. Conclusions	7.308

CHAPTER 8 EUROPEAN UNION LAW RELATING TO EMPLOYMENT IN THE SHIPPING SECTOR

A. Introduction	8.001
B. The principal provisions relating to employment in the Treaty on the Functioning of the European Union	8.008
C. International legal background on the employment of seafarers	8.013
D. Sources of EU law on employment in the shipping sector	8.014
E. Directive 2015/1794: the 2015 Directive to extend certain rights to seafarers	
Introduction	8.016
Background	8.019
2013: Proposal to extend certain EU employment rights to all seafarers	8.021
Adoption of Directive 2015/1794	8.026
Entry into force of Directive 2015/1794	8.027
Transposition of Directive 2015/1794	8.028
Background to Directive 2015/1794	8.029
Changes brought about by Directive 2015/1794	8.031
Reporting by the Commission on the directive	8.037
F. Directive 1999/63 concerning the agreement on the organisation of working time of seafarers concluded by the European Community Shipowners' Association and the Federation of Transport Workers' Unions in the European Union	
Introduction	8.038
Application of Directive 1999/63	8.047
Definitions in Directive 1999/63	8.048
Working hours	8.049
Age limits	8.050
Resources to ensure compliance	8.051
Fitness to work	8.052
G. Directive 1999/95 of the European Parliament and of the Council of 13 December 1999 concerning the enforcement of provisions in respect of seafarers' hours of work on board ships calling at Community ports	
Introduction	8.059
Background to Directive 1999/95	8.060
Purpose and scope of Directive 1999/95	8.062
Application of Directive 1999/95	8.063
Definitions of certain concepts in Directive 1999/95	8.064
Preparation of reports	8.065
Inspection and more detailed inspection	8.066
Rectification of deficiencies	8.067

Follow-up procedures	8.069
Right of appeal	8.071
Administrative co-operation	8.072
"No more favourable" treatment clause	8.073
H. Council Decision 2007/431 authorising Member States to ratify, in the interests of the EU, the 2008 Maritime Labour Convention of the ILO	8.074
I. Directive 2005/45 of the European Parliament and of the Council of 7 September 2005 on the mutual recognition of seafarers' certificates issued by the Member States and amending Directive 2001/25	
Introduction	8.081
Scope of the directive	8.084
Definitions in the directive	8.085
Operative provisions	8.087
J. Directive 2008/106 of the European Parliament and of the Council of 19 November 2008 on the minimum level of training of seafarers	
Introduction	8.091
Concepts in the directive	8.094
Scope of Directive 2008/106	8.125
Training and certification	8.126
Certificate	8.127
Certificates and endorsements	8.128
Prevention of fraud and other unlawful practices	8.131
Penalties or disciplinary measures	8.132
Quality standards	8.133
Medical standards: issue and registration of certificates	8.135
Revalidation of certificates	8.137
Simulators	8.143
Responsibilities of companies	8.157
Fitness for duty	8.161
Dispensation	8.162
Responsibilities of Member States with regard to training and assessment	8.164
On-board communication	8.165
Recognition of certificates	8.166
Non-compliance with the requirements of the STCW Convention	8.172
Reassessment	8.179
Port State control	8.180
Port State control procedures	8.181
Detention of vessels	8.185
Regular monitoring of compliance	8.186
Information for statistical purposes	8.187
Reports	8.188
Amendment and exercise of delegation	8.189
Penalties	8.192
Transitional provisions	8.193

Communication	8.194
Repeal	8.195
K. Employees and the performance of public duties	
Introduction	8.196
The *Colegio de Oficiales de la Marina Mercante Española v Administración del Estado* case	8.197
Introduction	8.197
Factual background	8.206
The second question	8.211
CJEU ruling to the Tribunal Supremo	8.214
Assessment	8.215
The *Albert Anker, Klaas Ras, Albertus Snoek v Bundesrepublik Deutschland* case	
Introduction	8.216
Essence of the dispute	8.217
Legal background	8.218
Factual background	8.219
The question referred	8.224
Ruling of the Court	8.225
L. Collective actions and seafarers	
The *International Transport Workers' Federation, Finnish Seamen's Union v Viking Line ABP* case	8.227
Introduction	8.227
Legal context	8.232
The dispute	8.233
The first question	8.240
The second question	8.241
The remaining questions	8.242
M. Seafarers remaining in a Member State after being at sea	8.244
N. Standards for seafarers: Council Recommendation 79/114 of 21 December 1978 on the ratification of the 1978 International Convention on Standards of Training, Certification and Watchkeeping for Seafarers	8.255
O. Council Directive 2009/13 of 16 February 2009 implementing the agreement concluded by the ECSA and the ETF on the Maritime Labour Convention, 2006, and amending Directive 1999/63	
Introduction	8.259
Background	8.261
P. *Commission v Italy* on an alleged failure to fulfil obligations under Directive 1999/95	8.270
Q. Minimum level of training of seafarers: Directive 2008/106	8.292
R. The *Fiamingo* case	8.293
S. The *Bakker* case	8.306
T. The *Iraklis Haralambidis v Calogero Casilli* case	8.318
The dispute in the main proceedings and the questions referred for a preliminary ruling	8.326

U. The *Jan Voogsgeerd v Navimer SA* case	8.332
V. The *Raad van bestuur van de Sociale verzekeringsbank v Wieland and Rothwangl* case	8.343
W. Directive 2013/54 concerning certain flag State responsibilities for compliance with and enforcement of the Maritime Labour Convention, 2006	8.352
X. Council Directive (EU) 2018/131 of 23 January 2018 implementing the agreement concluded by the ECSA and the ETF to amend Directive 2009/13 in accordance with the amendments of 2014 to the Maritime Labour Convention, 2006, as approved by the International Labour Conference on 11 June 2014	8.359

CHAPTER 9 INTRODUCTION TO LINER CONFERENCES: THE CONCEPT OF LINER CONFERENCES AND THE UNITED NATIONS CODE ON LINER CONFERENCES AND THE UNITED NATIONS LINER CODE

A. Introduction	9.001
B. Liner conferences	9.002
Consortia v liner conference	9.006
C. United Nations Code of Conduct for Liner Conferences	
Introduction	9.015
UNCTAD negotiations	9.016
Objectives and principles of the UNCTAD Code	9.020
Signature and entry into force of the Code	9.022
Perspectives on the Code	9.023
Application of the Code	9.026
Provisions of the Code relating to relations between conference members	9.027
Introduction	9.027
Membership	9.028
Participation	9.029
Decision-making	9.031
Sanctions	9.032
Self-policing	9.033
Conference agreements	9.034
Provisions of the Code relating to relations with shippers	9.035
Provisions of the Code relating to freight rates	9.041
D. The UNCTAD Liner Code and EU law	
Introduction	9.048
Compatibility of the Code with EU law: Regulation 954/79	9.055
Legislative history of Regulation 954/79	9.056
1974: Commission proposal	9.056
1975: Commission proposal	9.057
Code of Conduct: and the then existing EEC Treaty	9.058
Council	9.061
Contents of Regulation 954/79	9.063

Existing conferences	9.064
Cargo allocation	9.065
OECD Member States	9.066
Decision-making procedures	9.067
Reservations and interpretative reservations	9.068
E. Regulation 1490/2007	9.070
F. Implementation: ratification in certain Member States	
Introduction	9.071
The Netherlands	9.072
Germany	9.073
Denmark	9.074
Belgium	9.075
United Kingdom	9.076
France	9.077

CHAPTER 10 AN OVERVIEW OF EUROPEAN UNION COMPETITION LAW GENERALLY AND HOW IT APPLIES TO THE SHIPPING SECTOR GENERALLY

A. Introduction	10.001
B. An overview of EU competition law generally	
Introduction	10.009
Applicability of EU competition law	10.016
Direct applicability of Articles 101 and 102 of the TFEU	10.019
Market definition	10.020
Undertaking	10.027
Introduction	10.027
Definition	10.028
Consideration of whether particular entities are undertakings	10.029
C. An overview of EU competition law generally	10.051
D. Article 101 of the TFEU: anti-competitive arrangements	
Introduction	10.052
Text of Article 101 of the TFEU	10.053
Basic concepts in Article 101	10.054
Agreements, decisions and concerted practices	10.054
Object or effect of preventing, restricting or distorting competition	10.074
Preventing, restricting and distorting competition	10.077
Effect on inter-State trade	10.079
Agreements falling outside Article 101(1)	10.086
Onus of proof	10.097
Article 101(2): voidness	10.098
Article 101(3): exemption	10.102
Position before, and after, 1 May 2004	10.104
Position prior to 1 May 2004	10.104
Position since 1 May 2004	10.105
Conditions for exemption under Article 101(3)	10.106

Contribution to improving the production or distribution of goods or promoting economic or technical progress	10.106
Fair share to the consumers	10.107
No indispensable restrictions	10.108
No substantial elimination of competition	10.109
Individual exemptions	10.110
Block exemptions	10.111
Introduction	10.111
Examples	10.114
Arbitration	10.115
E. Article 102 of the TFEU: abuse of dominance	
Introduction	10.116
Text of Article 102	10.118
Importance of economic evidence	10.119
Interpretation of Article 102	10.120
Economic rationale for Article 102	10.121
Check-list for the application of Article 102	10.122
Undertakings	10.123
Concept of a dominant position or dominance and a further analysis of market definition	10.124
There is no definition of dominance in the TFEU	10.125
The definition used by the EU institutions	10.126
Introduction	10.126
Relevant product market	10.133
Relevant geographical market	10.141
Relevant temporal market	10.142
Dominance/market power	10.143
Introduction	10.143
Measuring market power	10.144
Market shares	10.145
Barriers to entry and/or barriers to expansion and/or barriers to exit	10.146
Economies of scale	10.147
Evidence of the undertakings	10.148
Price movements	10.149
Conduct	10.150
Overall strength and size of the undertaking(s)	10.151
Legal provisions	10.152
Deep pocket	10.153
Within the internal market or a substantial part of it	10.154
Concept of "abuse of a dominant position"	10.155
Definition of abuse	10.156
Effect on inter-State trade	10.159
Example of Article 102 in practice: the Doctrine of Essential Facilities	10.160
F. Enforcement of Articles 101–102 of the TFEU: competition procedure	
Introduction	10.161

Role of the Commission	10.164
Role of the Member State authorities and courts	10.168
Initiation of proceedings	10.175
Complaints	10.176
Own-initiative investigations	10.177
Sectoral investigations or studies	10.178
Conduct of proceedings	10.179
Fact-finding	10.179
Requests for information	10.180
Investigations/dawn raids	10.181
Burden of proof	10.183
Standard of proof	10.184
Legal professional privilege	10.185
Fines	10.186
Remedies	10.190
Interim measures	10.191
Termination of proceedings	10.192
Private enforcement: court actions by private parties to enforce EU competition law	10.193
National competition law dimension	10.196
International dimension to competition enforcement	10.198
G. Article 106 of the TFEU	10.199
H. Selected practices	10.206
I. Selected case law	
Introduction	10.207
The *Ferry Operators–Currency Surcharges* case	10.208
The *P&O/Stena Line* case	10.211
The *Greek Ferries* case	10.216
The *Bulk Liquids by Sea on Deep Sea Routes* case	10.219
The *Ship Classification* case	10.220
The *GT-link* case	10.224

CHAPTER 11 EUROPEAN UNION COMPETITION LAW: THE OLD REGIME RELATING TO SHIPPING – REGULATION 4056/86

A. Introduction	11.001
B. Legislative history of Regulation 4056/86	
Introduction	11.008
1981: Commission proposal	11.011
1983: EESC opinion	11.012
1984: European Parliament's report	11.013
1985: Amended Commission proposal	11.015
1986: Commission amendment	11.016
1986: Council adoption of Regulation 4056/86	11.017
C. Entry into force of Regulation 4056/86	11.020
D. Legal bases of Regulation 4056/86	11.021
E. Legal effect of Regulation 4056/86	11.023

DETAILED CONTENTS

F. Interpretation of Regulation 4056/86	11.024
G. Application of Regulation 4056/86	
Text of Article 1	11.028
Effect of Article 1	11.030
Transport services	11.031
International transport services	11.032
Maritime services	11.034
Services other than tramp services	11.035
Transport users	11.040
Agreements between providers of ancillary services	11.041
Passenger traffic	11.042
Definition of a "liner conference"	11.043
Scope of Article 1	11.044
Affecting trade between Member States	11.045
H. Technical agreements: Article 2 of Regulation 4056/86	
Introduction	11.046
Text of Article 2	11.047
The introduction of uniform application of standards or types in respect of vessels and other means of transport, equipment, supplies or fixed installations	11.051
The exchange or pooling for the purpose of operating transport services, of vessels, space on vessels or slots or other means of transport, staff, equipment or fixed installations	11.052
The organisation and execution of successive or supplementary maritime transport operations and the establishment or application of inclusive rates and conditions for such operations	11.053
The co-ordination of transport timetables for connecting routes	11.054
The consolidation of individual assignments	11.055
The establishment or application of uniform rules concerning the structure and the conditions governing the application of transport tariffs	11.056
Amendment to Article 2	11.057
Assessment	11.058
I. Block exemption for liner conferences: Article 3 of Regulation 4056/86	
Introduction	11.059
Liner conferences	11.060
Block exemption	11.061
The Article 4 condition attaching to the block exemption for liner conferences	11.069
Obligations attaching to the exemption	11.071
Introduction	11.071
Consultations	11.074
Loyalty arrangements	11.075
Services not covered by the freight charges	11.077
Availability of tariffs	11.079

Notification to the European Commission of awards at arbitration
and recommendations 11.080
Uniform or common freight rates 11.081
J. Block exemption for agreements between transport users and
conferences concerning the use of scheduled maritime transport
services 11.082
K. Monitoring of exempted agreements
Introduction 11.083
Commentary 11.084
L. Abuse of a dominant position: Article 102 of the TFEU
Introduction 11.085
Commentary 11.087
M. Conflicts of national laws
Text of Article 9 of the regulation 11.088
Commentary 11.089
N. Rules of procedure
Introduction 11.090
Complaints 11.091
Introduction and text of Article 10 11.091
Procedures on complaint or on the Commission's own initiative 11.092
Locus standi to submit a complaint 11.093
Result of procedures on complaint or on the Commission's own
initiative 11.094
Introduction 11.094
Text of Article 11 11.095
Commentary on Article 11 11.096
Opposition procedure 11.097
Introduction 11.097
Text of Article 12 11.098
Commentary 11.099
Duration and revocation of individual exemptions 11.102
Introduction 11.102
Text of Article 13 11.103
Renewal and revocation of the exemption 11.104
Amendment of the exemption 11.105
Prohibition of specified acts by the parties 11.106
Publication of the decision 11.107
Powers of the Commission 11.108
Commentary 11.109
Liaison with the authorities of the Member States 11.110
Introduction 11.110
Commentary 11.111
Commission requests for information 11.112
Introduction 11.112
Commentary 11.113

Investigations	11.114
Introduction	11.114
Commentary	11.115
Investigations by authorities of the Member States	11.116
Secrecy of information gathered	11.117
Fines and periodic penalty payments	11.118
Fines	11.118
Periodic penalty payments	11.123
Hearings of the parties and others	11.125
Introduction	11.125
Commentary	11.126
Review by the Court of Justice of the fines and periodical penalty payments	11.127
Introduction	11.127
Commentary	11.128
Publication of decisions	11.129
Implementing provisions	11.130
O. Procedure: Commission Regulation 4260/88	
Introduction	11.131
Legal basis and background	11.132
Notifications	11.133
Complaints	11.134
Applications for exemptions	11.135
Hearings	11.136
Communicating awards and recommendations to the Commission	11.137
P. Case law relating to Regulation 4056/86 and selected competition cases in the shipping sector	11.138
Q. Reform of Regulation 4056/86	11.139
R. Assessment	11.140

CHAPTER 12   EUROPEAN UNION COMPETITION LAW: THE NEW REGIME RELATING TO SHIPPING – REGULATION 1419/2006

A. Introduction	12.001
B. Debate on the old regime: Regulation 4056/86	12.002
C. Adoption of the new regime: Regulation 1419/2006	12.042
D. Effect of the new regime: Regulation 1419/2006	12.046
E. The transitional period for the new regime: Regulation 1419/2006 and procedural dimension of Regulation 1419/2006	12.053
F. An introduction to the Commission's guidelines on maritime services	
Introduction	12.056
Adoption process	12.057
Purpose of the Guidelines	12.058
Duration of the Guidelines	12.062
Place and status of the Guidelines in EU competition law generally	12.063
Limitations	12.066
Non-renewal	12.067

G. Market definition
   Introduction   12.070
   Liner shipping   12.071
   Tramp shipping   12.072
   Technical agreements   12.081
H. Information exchange
   Introduction   12.083
   What is information exchange?   12.084
   Nature of the law on information exchange   12.088
   Topicality of the issue of information exchange   12.090
   Situations where information exchange is an issue   12.092
   Types of information exchange   12.097
   Competition law has to strike the right balance   12.205
   What are the EU rules, as set out in the guidelines, on information exchange?   12.114
      Is there an anti-competitive arrangement or abuse of dominance?   12.114
      What is the structure of the market?   12.115
      What is the nature of the information being exchanged?   12.117
      Exchange of commercially sensitive data   12.118
      Exchange of public and unpublished information   12.119
      Aggregated and disaggregated data   12.122
      Age of the data   12.124
      Frequency of the exchanges   12.126
      Manner of the exchange   12.127
      Price indexes   12.128
      Exchange of information in the context of liner conferences   12.130
   Exchange of information in the context of liner consortia   12.133
      Concluding remarks and observations   12.134
I. Shipping pools   12.143
J. Self-assessment   12.152
K. Effect on trade between Member States   12.153
L. Liner shipping in the new regime
   Introduction   12.156
   Market definition   12.158
      Introduction   12.158
      Product market definition   12.159
      Geographic market definition   12.161
M. Tramp shipping in the new regime
   Introduction   12.163
   Market definition   12.165
      Introduction   12.165
      Product market definition   12.166
      Geographic market definition   12.169
   Pools between undertakings who are not actual or potential competitors   12.170
   Pools of minor importance in competition terms   12.171
   Pools between competitors limited to joint selling   12.173

Full function joint ventures	12.175
N. Cabotage under the new regime	12.180
O. Compliance with the new regime	12.182
P. The *Bulk Liquid Shipping* case	12.193
Q. The *IACS: International Association of Classification Societies* case	12.194
R. The *Baltic Max Feeder* case	12.199
S. The *Container Liner Shipping* case	12.202
T. The *Maritime Car Carriers* case	12.204
U. Outlook	12.205

CHAPTER 13 EUROPEAN UNION COMPETITION LAW: PORTS

A. Introduction	
Scope of the chapter	13.001
Relevance of competition law to ports	13.002
Competition law applies to ports	13.005
Absence of specific competition law rules in the context of ports	13.013
Examples of need to comply with competition law	13.014
Competition law rules relevant to ports	13.017
Application of competition law to undertakings: ports as undertakings	13.020
Application of the EU competition rules to ports generally	13.023
B. Obtaining access to ports	
Introduction	13.024
Anti-competitive arrangements	13.025
Abuse of dominance	13.026
Roscoff: Irish Continental Group v CCI Morlaix	13.027
C. Obtaining access to services in ports	
Introduction	13.029
Genoa: Merci Convenzionali Porto di Genova SpA v Siderurgica Gabrielli SpA	13.032
Holyhead I: B&I Line v Sealink Harbours Ltd	13.047
Holyhead II: Sea Containers v Stena Sealink	13.051
Silvano Raso	13.058
Coe Clerici Logistics SpA v Commission	13.077
D. Information exchange in the context of ports	13.081
E. Pricing in ports	
Port charges	13.088
General pricing issues	13.089
Rødby	13.090
Port of Kristiansand and Fjord Line	13.091
Harbour agreements in Sandefjord (Norway) and Strømstad (Sweden): Color Line	13.092
F. Negotiations relating to ports	13.094
G. Ports and State aid	13.096

CHAPTER 14 EUROPEAN UNION COMPETITION LAW: CONSORTIA

A. Introduction	14.001
B. Juridical nature of consortia	
Introduction	14.023
Merger control regulation	14.024
Regulation 4056/86	14.025
C. Commercial view on consortia	14.029
D. 1990 Communication on consortia	
Introduction	14.033
Background to the communication on consortia	14.034
E. The need for a block exemption	14.036
F. Adoption of consortia block exemption regimes over time	14.039
G. Background to the current consortia block exemption regime	14.043
H. Council regulations to enable the Commission to adopt block exemptions	
Conferral by the Council of the power on the commission to adopt a block exemption	14.052
Duration and amendment of the block exemption regulation	14.054
Potential retroactive effect of the block exemption regulation	14.055
Public consultation on the draft block exemption regulation	14.057
Consultation with the Advisory Committee on restrictive practices and dominant positions on the draft block exemption regulation	14.058
I. Current block exemption: Commission Regulation 906/2009 (as amended)	
Introduction	14.059
Legislative basis for the commission block exemption regulation	14.060
Duration of the block exemption regulation	14.061
Structure of the block exemption regulation	14.062
Legislative and commercial background to the block exemption regulation	14.063
European Commission perspective on the background to the 2009 changes to the consortia agreement	14.066
Changes in the new consortia block exemption regime	14.069
Overall perspective on the block exemption regulation	14.071
Scope and application of the block exemption regulation	14.072
Concept of consortium or consortia agreement	14.073
Exempted agreements	14.080
Hardcore restrictions which render Regulation 906/2009 inapplicable	14.081
Market share restrictions which potentially render Regulation 906/2009 inapplicable	14.085
Consortia agreements falling outside the scope of the block exemption	14.090
Relationship with Article 102 of the TFEU	14.091
Withdrawal from a consortium agreement	14.092
Withdrawal of the block exemption by the European Commission	14.093
Withdrawal of the block exemption by a Member State competition authority	14.094
Arrangements falling outside the scope of the block exemption	14.095
Consultation	14.096

J. 2018 Consultation 14.097
K. Conclusions 14.098

CHAPTER 15 EUROPEAN UNION STATE AID LAW: SHIPPING AND PORTS
A. Introduction 15.001
B. Concept of State aid 15.014
C. Sources of EU State aid law
  Introduction 15.017
  Treaty provisions 15.017
    Introduction 15.018
    Article 107 of the TFEU 15.019
    Article 108 of the TFEU 15.023
    Article 109 of the TFEU 15.024
    Article 106 15.026
  Commission communications 15.028
  Decisions and judgments 15.030
D. State aid and the maritime sector generally 15.031
E. European Commission guidelines on State aid in maritime transport
  Introduction 15.033
  2003/2004 Guidelines 15.034
    Introduction 15.034
    Purposes or objectives of the Guidelines 15.036
    Analysis of the Guidelines 15.037
    Part 1 of the Guidelines: "Introduction" 15.038
    Part 2 of the Guidelines: "Scope and General Objectives of the Revised State Aid Guidelines" 15.039
    Part 3 of the Guidelines: "Fiscal and Social Measures to Improve Competiveness" 15.040
    Part 4 of the Guidelines: "Crew Relief" 15.044
    Part 5 of the Guidelines: "Investment Aid" 15.045
    Part 6 of the Guidelines: "Regional Aid on the Basis of Article 107(3)(a) and (c)" 15.046
    Part 7 of the Guidelines: "Training" 15.047
    Part 8 of the Guidelines: "Restructuring Aid" 15.048
    Part 9 of the Guidelines: "Public Service Obligations and Contracts" 15.049
    Part 10 of the Guidelines: "Aid to Short Sea Shipping" 15.050
    Part 11 of the Guidelines: "Ceiling" 15.052
    Part 12 of the Guidelines: "Final Remarks" 15.053
    Part 13 of the Guidelines: "Appropriate Measures" 15.054
    Annex 15.055
  2017: Update to the 2004 communication 15.056
F. EU State aid law and the motorways of the seas 15.057
G. EU State aid law and ship management companies 15.062
H. State aid and ports: generally and under the general block exemption
  Introduction 15.071

I. State aid and ports generally
  Introduction   15.076
  Relevance of state aid rules for ports   15.080
  Some practical issues in the application of the state aid rules in the context of ports   15.095
    Introduction   15.095
    Market definition   15.096
    Is a port an "undertaking" under Article 107?   15.097
    Sale of land to ports and the purchase of land for ports   15.100
    Construction of infrastructure which would be open to all equally   15.105
    Construction of infrastructure which would be user-specific/selective   15.106
    Construction of facilities with significant state funding   15.107
    Construction of facilities which would be available on a priority basis for one operator   15.108
    What if security measures at a port are paid for by the state?   15.109
    Mergers and acquisitions   15.110
    Operation of a "public service" between ports   15.111
    What if a Member State never notifies the European Commission of the aid?   15.112
    What are the principles which can be discerned from the Commission's analysis of port cases?   15.113
  Conclusions   15.115
J. General Block Exemption Regulation   15.116
K. Tonnage tax   15.122
L. Shipping sector   15.124
M. Seafarers   15.125
N. Conclusion   15.128

CHAPTER 16   EUROPEAN UNION MERGER CONTROL: SHIPPING, PORTS AND SHIPBUILDING

A. Introduction   16.001
B. Concept of concentrations   16.011
C. Concentrations with a Union dimension   16.023
D. Notification   16.030
E. How does the Commission assess a proposed concentration? The test for approval (or otherwise) of a proposed concentration   16.137
F. Remedies   16.043
G. Market definition   16.044
H. Role of the Member States in the process   16.045
I. Ancillary restrictions   16.051
J. Minority stakes   16.052
K. Role of the CJEU   16.053
L. The MCR in the shipping sector
  Introduction   16.054
  1998: DFO/Scandlines   16.057
  1998: GE Capital/GE SeaCo   16.066

1999: Maersk/Safmarine	16.076
1999: Maersk/Sea-Land	16.087
2001: HBG/Ballast NEDAM/Baggeren JV	16.089
2002: Vopak/Van der Sluijs	16.090
2002: Wallenius Lines/Wilhelmsen/Hyundai	16.091
2003: Van Oord/BHD/Bagger Holding JV	16.093
2008: DP World/Conti 7/Rickmers/DP World Breakbulk	16.095
2008: DPWL/ZIM/Contarsa	16.096
2008: APMM/Swift Tankers Pool	16.097
2009: APMM/Broström	16.098
2008: Hutchison/Evergreen	16.110
2005: NYK Reefers/Lauritzen	16.111
2005: Maersk/PONL	16.114
2005: TUI/CP Ships	16.122
2006: Costa Crociere/Royal Caribbean/Marinvest/RCT	16.132
2005: Svitzer/Wilhelmsen Offshore/JV	16.133
2005: CMA CGM/Delmas	16.134
2006: Veolia – BCP/SNCM	16.136
2006: RREEF/Peel Port Holdings/Peel Ports	16.137
2007: Allianz/3i/Scandlines	16.138
2007: WWL/EUKOR/ARMACUP/AGENCIE	16.139
2007: PSA/IPH	16.140
2007: China Shipbuilding Industry Corporation/Wärtsilä/Mitsubishi Heavy Industries	16.141
2007: Peter Döhle Schiffahrts-KG/GE Transportation Finance Inc	16.142
2008: Eurogate/AP Moller-Maersk Joint Venture	16.143
2009: COSTA/MSC/MPCT	16.146
2009: BPH/Euroports Holding	16.147
2011: Acquisition of Douala International Terminal JV by APMM and Bollore	16.148
2011: Acquisition by Socimac and Bollore of Joint Control of Societe d'exploitation du Terminal de Vridi	16.149
2011: Arcelormittal/Atic Services	16.150
2011: Teekay/Marubeni/Maersk LNG	16.151
2013: FSI/Merit/Yildirim/CMA CGM	16.152
2013: NORDIC Capital/Unicorn	16.153
2014: CSAV/HGV/Kühne Maritime/HAPAG-LLOYD AG	16.154
2015: Acquisition of ODPR by CMA CGM	16.155
2016: Triton/KKR/EM	16.156
2016: CMA CGM/Bollore/Kribi JV	16.157
2016: CMA CGM/NOL	16.158
2016: Royal Caribbean Holdings de España, S.L. of Spain by Royal Caribbean Cruises LTD of the US and Springwater Capital LLC of Switzerland	16.159
2017: CK Hutchison/TMA HOLDING/TMA Logistics	16.160
2018: PSA/TIL/PPIT	16.161

     2018: Acquisition of Maersk Product Tankers by APMH Invest and
       Mitsui   16.162
  M. The MCR in the shipbuilding sector
     Introduction   16.163
     1999: UPM-Kymmene/STORA ENSO/Metsallito/JV   16.164
     1998: Blohm+Voss/Lisnave   16.165
     1999: Preussag/Babcock/Celsius   16.166
     2000: Aker Maritime/Kvaerner (Withdrawn)   16.167
     2005: Rabobank/IHC   16.168
     2005: ThyssenKrupp AG/Hellenic Shipyards   16.169
     2006: Aker Yards ASA/Chartiers de l'Atlantique   16.170
     2006: Thyssemkrupp/EADS/Atlas   16.171
     2006: Candover/Ferretti   16.172
     2007: Thales/DCN   16.173
     2007: Bain Capital/Bavaria Yachtbau   16.174
     2007: BAE Systems/VT/JV   16.175
     2007: Carlyle/Zodiac Marine   16.176
     2008: Aker Yards/STX   16.177
     2017: WÄRTSILÄ/CSSC/JV   16.179
  N. Conclusions   16.180

CHAPTER 17   REGULATION 4057/86: DUMPING OF SHIPPING
             SERVICES AND THE UNFAIR PRICING OF SHIPPING SERVICES
  A. Introduction   17.001
  B. Council Regulation 4057/86
     Introduction   17.002
     Legal basis   17.005
     Commercial background   17.006
     Legal history   17.007
     Entry into force   17.008
     Purpose   17.009
     Application of the regulation   17.010
        Concepts   17.011
     Role of EU institutions under the regulation   17.020
        The Commission   17.020
        The Council of Ministers   17.021
        The Court of Justice of the European Union   17.022
     Complaints   17.023
        Complaint procedure   17.023
        Who may lodge a complaint?   17.024
        Form of complaint   17.025
        Contents of the complaint   17.026
        To whom is the complaint made?   17.027
        Confidentiality of the complaint   17.028
        Withdrawal of the complaint   17.029
     Consultation   17.030

Initiation and investigation	17.031
Initiation	17.031
Contents of the investigation	17.032
Invitation to the allegedly guilty party to make their case	17.033
Co-operation	17.034
Confidentiality of information supplied	17.035
Conclusion of the first stages of investigation	17.036
Formal rights of the parties	17.037
Outcome of the Commission's investigations	17.038
Introduction	17.038
No action	17.039
Undertakings	17.040
Redressive duties	17.043
Power to impose redressive duties	17.044
Calculation of the redressive duties	17.045
Imposition of redressive duties	17.046
Collection of redressive duties	17.047
Duration of the redressive duties	17.048
Retroactivity of redressive duties	17.049
Review of redressive duties	17.050
Refunds of redressive duties	17.051
Appeals	17.052
Practice to date	17.053

CHAPTER 18　REGULATION 4058/86: CO-ORDINATED ACTION TO SAFEGUARD FREE ACCESS TO CARGOES IN OCEAN TRADE

A. Introduction	18.001
B. Application of Regulation 4058/86	18.004
C. Legal bases of Regulation 4058/86	18.005
D. Background to Regulation 4058/86	18.006
E. Legal history of Regulation 4058/86	18.008
F. Entry into force of Regulation 4058/86	18.009
G. Concepts in Regulation 4058/86	18.010
H. Triggering event	18.011
I. Requests by a Member State for co-ordinated action	
Introduction	18.012
Text of Article 3	18.013
J. Co-ordinated action	
Introduction	18.015
Text of Article 4	18.016
Diplomatic representations	18.017
K. Procedure	18.018
L. Action by Member States in default of Council action	
Individual or group action	18.020
Urgent action	18.021
Report to the Commission	18.022

M. Consultation	18.023
N. OECD Member States	
Introduction	18.024
Article 8 of the regulation	18.025
O. Application and observations	18.026
P. Conclusions	18.037

VOLUME II

CHAPTER 19   EUROPEAN UNION LAW RELATING TO THE MARITIME ENVIRONMENT: INTRODUCTION; EUROPEAN UNION MEASURES RELATING TO THE MARITIME ENVIRONMENT GENERALLY; AND PENALTIES FOR INFRINGEMENTS

A. Introduction	19.001
B. Context and factual background	
The maritime environment is a challenge for the EU and not just the Member States individually	19.008
Level of environmental cleanliness of the shipping sector	19.009
Costs	19.011
The EU in the wider international arena	19.012
C. The EU institutional dimension	19.013
D. Overview of the EU responses to marine environmental issues	
Introduction	19.014
Aims	19.015
Form of measures	19.016
Treaties	19.017
Regulations	19.018
Directives	19.019
Decisions	19.020
Recommendations and opinions	19.021
Strategy statements	19.022
White papers	19.023
E. Relationship between EU and international legislation	19.024
F. Range of maritime environmental issues	19.025
G. General measures	19.026
H. Bunkers	
Introduction	19.027
Council Decision 2002/762 of 19 September 2002 authorising the Member States, in the interest of the Community, to sign, ratify or accede to the International Convention on Civil Liability for Bunker Oil Pollution Damage, 2001	19.028
I. Oil pollution	
Introduction	19.039

Council Decision 2004/246 of 2 March 2004 authorising the Member States to Sign, Ratify or Accede to, in the Interest of the European Community, the Protocol of 2003 to the International Convention on the Establishment of an International Fund for Compensation for Oil Pollution Damage, 1992, and Authorising Austria and Luxembourg, in the Interest of the European Community, to Accede to the Underlying Instruments ... 19.040

J. Land-based pollution
Introduction ... 19.049
Council Resolution of 3 March 1975 on the Convention for the Prevention of Marine Pollution from Land-Based Sources ... 19.050
Council Decision 75/437 of 3 March 1975 concluding the Convention for the Prevention of Marine Pollution from Land-Based Sources ... 19.053

K. Port reception facilities
Introduction ... 19.058
Directive 2000/59 on port facilities ... 19.059
Legal basis and history of Directive 2000/59 ... 19.061
Purpose of Directive 2000/59 ... 19.062
Concepts in Directive 2000/59 ... 19.063
Scope of Directive 2000/59 ... 19.064
Port reception facilities ... 19.065
Waste reception and handling plans ... 19.068
Notification ... 19.070
Delivery of ship-generated waste ... 19.071
Fees for ship-generated waste ... 19.072
Exemptions ... 19.075
Delivery of cargo residues ... 19.076
Enforcement ... 19.077
Penalties ... 19.082
Committee procedure ... 19.083
Amendment procedure ... 19.084
Entry into force and implementation ... 19.085
EU evaluation of Directive 2000/59 ... 19.086

L. Discharge of hydrocarbons at sea Commission Decision 80/686 setting up an advisory committee on the control and reduction of pollution caused by oil and other harmful substances discharged at sea ... 19.087

M. Low sulphur fuels
Introduction ... 19.101
Commission Recommendation of 21 December 2009 on the safe implementation of the use of low sulphur fuel by ships at berth in Community ports ... 19.102

N. Regional measures
Introduction ... 19.112
Mediterranean ... 19.113

Mediterranean: Council Decision 77/585 of 25 July 1977 concluding the Convention for the protection of the Mediterranean Sea against pollution and the Protocol for the prevention of the pollution of the Mediterranean Sea by dumping from ships and aircraft   19.114

Mediterranean: Council Decision 83/101 of 28 February 1983 concluding the Protocol for the protection of the Mediterranean Sea against pollution from land-based sources   19.116

Mediterranean: Council Decision 2013/5 of 17 December 2012 on the accession of the European Union to the Protocol for the Protection of the Mediterranean Sea against pollution resulting from exploration and exploitation of the continental shelf and the seabed and its subsoil   19.120

Mediterranean: Council Decision 2010/631 of 13 September 2010 concerning the conclusion, on behalf of the European Union, of the Protocol on Integrated Coastal Zone Management in the Mediterranean to the Convention for the Protection of the Marine Environment and the Coastal Region of the Mediterranean   19.127

Mediterranean: Council Decision 2004/575 on the conclusion, on behalf of the European Community, of the Protocol to the Barcelona Convention for the Protection of the Mediterranean Sea against Pollution, concerning cooperation in preventing pollution from ships and, in cases of emergency, combating pollution of the Mediterranean Sea   19.132

Mediterranean: Protocol Concerning Cooperation in Preventing Pollution from Ships and, in Cases of Emergency, Combating Pollution of the Mediterranean Sea   19.137

North Sea and other areas: the Bonn Agreement   19.156

North-East Atlantic

Atlantic: the OSPAR Convention   19.182

Atlantic: Council Decision 98/249 of 7 October 1997 on the conclusion of the Convention for the protection of the marine environment of the north-east Atlantic   19.188

Atlantic: Lisbon Agreement: Council Decision 2010/655 of 19 October 2010 concerning the conclusion, on behalf of the European Union, of the Additional Protocol to the Cooperation Agreement for the Protection of the Coasts and Waters of the North-East Atlantic against Pollution   19.191

Baltic Sea: Convention on the Protection of the Marine Environment in the Baltic Sea Area of 1992 (further to the earlier version of 1974) – the Helsinki Convention   19.195

Baltic Sea: Council Decision 94/156 of 21 February 1994 on the accession of the Community to the Convention on the Protection of the Marine Environment of the Baltic Sea Area 1974 (Helsinki Convention)   19.197

DETAILED CONTENTS

  Baltic Sea: Council Decision 94/157 of 21 February 1994 on the
   conclusion, on behalf of the Community, of the Convention on
   the Protection of the Marine Environment of the Baltic Sea Area
   (Helsinki Convention as revised in 1992)   19.201
 O. Carbon dioxide emissions
  Introduction   19.205
  Regulation 2015/757 on the monitoring, reporting and verification of
   carbon dioxide emissions from maritime transport, and amending
   Directive 2009/16/EC
  Introduction   19.206
  Chapter I of Regulation 2015/757: "general provisions"   19.207
  Chapter II of Regulation 2015/757: "monitoring and reporting"   19.223
  Chapter III of Regulation 2015/757: "verification and accreditation"   19.232
  Chapter IV of Regulation 2015/757: "compliance and publication of
   information"   19.236
  Chapter V of Regulation 2015/757: "international cooperation"   19.241
  Chapter VI: "delegated and implementing powers and final provisions"   19.242
  Commission implementing Regulation (EU) 2016/1927 of 4 November
   2016 on templates for monitoring plans, emissions reports and
   documents of compliance pursuant to Regulation (EU) 2015/757
   of the European Parliament and of the Council on monitoring,
   reporting and verification of carbon dioxide emissions from
   maritime transport   19.246
  Commission implementing Regulation 2016/1928 of 4 November 2016
   on determination of cargo carried for categories of ships other
   than passenger, ro-ro and container ships pursuant to Regulation
   (EU) 2015/757 of the European Parliament and of the Council on
   the monitoring, reporting and verification of carbon dioxide
   emissions from maritime transport   19.247
 P. Flag state requirements: Directive 2009/21 of the European Parliament
   and of the Council of 23 April 2009 on compliance with flag State
   requirements   19.252
 Q. Port charges and environment-friendly maritime transport activities and
   sustainable transportation   19.262
 R. Penalties for environmental law breaches
  Introduction   19.263
  Council Framework Decision 2005/667
  Introduction   19.264
  Background   19.265
  Definitions and territorial scope   19.266
  Implementation   19.267
  Criminal offences   19.268
  Aiding, abetting and inciting   19.270
  Penalties   19.271
  Liability of legal persons   19.272
  Penalties against legal persons   19.273

Jurisdiction	19.274
Notification of information	19.275
Conclusion	19.276

Directive 2005/35 on ship-source pollution and on the introduction of penalties, including criminal penalties, for pollution offences

Introduction	19.277
Background to the directive	19.278
Purpose of the directive	19.279
Definitions	19.280
Scope of the directive	19.281
Exceptions	19.283
Criminal offences as well as inciting, aiding and abetting	19.284
Enforcement measures with respect to ships within a port of a Member State	19.286
Enforcement measures by coastal States with respect to ships in transit	19.287
Penalties	19.288
Introduction	19.288
Penalties against natural persons	19.289
Liability of legal persons	19.290
Penalties against legal persons	19.292
Compliance with international law	19.293
Accompanying measures	19.294
Feasibility study	19.296
Reporting	19.297
Committee procedure	19.298
Provision of information	19.299
Amendment procedure	19.300
Implementation	19.301
Entry into force	19.302
Directive 2005/35 and the Charter of Fundamental Rights of the European Union	19.303

The *Intertanko* litigation

Introduction	19.304
International law	19.307
EU law	19.311
Questions referred to the CJEU for a preliminary ruling	19.315
Admissibility of the preliminary reference	19.316
Consideration of the questions referred for a preliminary ruling	19.317
Questions 1 to 3	19.317

CHAPTER 20   EUROPEAN UNION LAW RELATING TO THE MARITIME ENVIRONMENT: ORGANOTIN

A. Introduction	20.001
B. Regulation 782/2003 on the prohibition of organotin compounds on ships	
Introduction	20.005
Legal basis	20.006

Legislative history	20.007
Objective of Regulation 782/2003	20.010
Concepts in Regulation 782/2003	20.011
Scope of Regulation 782/2003	20.012
Prohibition of the application of organotin compounds which act as biocides	20.013
Prohibition of the bearing of organotin compounds which act as biocides	20.014
Survey and certification	20.015
Port State control	20.016
Adaptations	20.017
Committee	20.018
Annexes	20.019
Evaluation	20.020
C. Regulation 536/2008 giving effect to Article 6(3) and Article 7 of Regulation 782/2003 on the prohibition of organotin compounds on ships and amending that Regulation	
Introduction	20.021
Purpose of the regulation	20.024
D. Conclusions	20.029

CHAPTER 21 EUROPEAN UNION LAW RELATING TO MARITIME ENVIRONMENT: THE HAZARDOUS AND NOXIOUS SUBSTANCES BY SEA CONVENTION

A. Introduction	21.001
B. Council Decision 2002/971 of 18 November 2002 authorising the Member States, in the interest of the Community, to ratify or accede to the International Convention on Liability and Compensation for Damage in Connection with the Carriage of Hazardous and Noxious Substances by Sea, 1996 (the "HNS Convention")	21.004

CHAPTER 22 EUROPEAN UNION LAW RELATING TO SHIPBUILDING

A. Introduction	
Purpose of this chapter	22.001
Overview of shipbuilding in the EU	22.004
Economic value of shipbuilding in the EU	22.007
Strategic significance for the EU of shipbuilding	22.008
Challenges for the EU shipbuilding sector	22.009
EU's legislative competence in regard to shipbuilding	22.020
EU's aims in regard to shipbuilding	22.022
Historical evolution of EU shipbuilding measures	22.024
B. The OECD dimension	22.025
OECD Agreement	22.030
EU reaction	22.031
C. Council Resolution of 19 September 1978 on the reorganisation of the shipbuilding industry	22.032

D. Regulation 2016/1035 on protection against injurious pricing of vessels
  Introduction   22.038
  Principles and definitions   22.045
  What is "injurious pricing"? How is it determined?   22.057
  The determination of "injury"   22.068
  Definition of Union industry   22.069
  Initiation of proceedings   22.070
  The investigation   22.081
  Termination without measures, imposition and collection of injurious
    pricing charges   22.088
  Injurious pricing and injury   22.089
  Alternative remedies   22.090
  Countermeasures – denial of loading and unloading rights   22.091
  Organisational issues   22.093
E. Commission Decision 98/157 of 5 November 1997 concerning aid
    Spain proposes to grant to Astilleros Zamacona SA in respect of five
    tugboats   22.098
F. Commission Decision 92/569 of 31 July 1992 concerning proposed aid
    by Germany to the Chinese shipping company Cosco for the
    construction of container vessels   22.101
G. CJEU and Commission case law on shipbuilding
  Introduction   22.106
  French guarantee scheme for financing shipbuilding   22.107
  2006: Volkswerft Stralsund shipyard in Germany   22.108
  2006: Rolandwerft shipyard in Berne in Lower Saxony   22.109
  2007: Italian oil and chemical tankers   22.110
  2007: German Peene-Werft shipyard   22.111
  2001: Spanish shipyards   22.112
  2006: German Volkswert Stralsund shipyard   22.114
  2015: Portuguese shipyard   22.115
  2018: Croatian shipyard Uljanik   22.116

CHAPTER 23   EUROPEAN UNION LAW RELATING TO SHIP REPAIR

CHAPTER 24   EUROPEAN UNION LAW RELATING TO SHIP
              DISMANTLING AND RECYCLING
A. Introduction   24.001
B. Ship dismantling   24.002
C. Ship recycling
  Introduction   24.003
  International level   24.004
  EU level   24.007
D. Regulation (EU) No 1257/2013 of the European Parliament and of the
    Council of 20 November 2013 on ship recycling and amending
    Regulation (EC) No 1013/2006 and Directive 2009/16
  Introduction   24.011

Multiple regulation of the issue internationally | 24.015
Interpretation | 24.018
Hazardous materials | 24.019
Compliance | 24.020
Subject-matter and scope of the regulation and definitions in the regulation | 24.021
Definitions | 24.024
Ships | 24.052
   Introduction | 24.052
   Control of hazardous materials | 24.053
   Inventory of hazardous materials | 24.054
   General requirements for shipowners | 24.055
   Ship recycling plan | 24.057
   Surveys | 24.061
   Issuance and endorsement of certificates | 24.062
   Duration and validity of certificates | 24.066
   Port State control | 24.067
   Requirements for ships flying the flag of a third country | 24.068
Ship recycling facilities | 24.074
   Introduction | 24.074
   Authorisation of ship recycling facilities located in a Member State | 24.079
   Ship recycling facilities located in a third country | 24.080
   Establishment and updating of the European List | 24.081
General administrative provisions | 24.082
Reporting and enforcement | 24.087
   Enforcement in Member States | 24.089
   Request for action | 24.090
Final provisions in the regulation | 24.092
   Introduction | 24.092
   Committee procedure | 24.093
   Transitional provision | 24.094
   Amendments | 24.095
   Financial incentive | 24.096
   Review | 24.097
   Annexes | 24.098
E. Commission implementing Decision (EU) 2016/2325 of 19 December 2016 on the format of the certificate on the inventory of hazardous materials issued in accordance with Regulation (EU) No 1257/2013 of the European Parliament and of the Council on ship recycling | 24.099

CHAPTER 25 EUROPEAN UNION EXTERNAL RELATIONS LAW AND SHIPPING

A. Introduction | 25.001
B. EU law generally on external relations
   Introduction | 25.004
   The Treaty on European Union | 25.005

DETAILED CONTENTS

Treaty on the Functioning of the European Union 25.036
C. Council Decision 83/573 of 26 October 1983 concerning
  counter-measures in the field of international merchant shipping 25.057
D. Council Decision of 17 September 1987 relating to maritime transport
  between Italy and Algeria 25.062
E. Cooperation agreement between the European Community and the
  Kingdom of Cambodia – joint declarations – exchange of letters on
  maritime transport 25.063
F. China: Council Decision 2009/825 of 26 October 2009 concerning the
  conclusion of the protocol amending the agreement on maritime
  transport between the European Community and its Member States,
  of the one part, and the government of the People's Republic of
  China, of the other part 25.076
G. Brazil: framework agreement for co-operation between the European
  Economic Community and the Federative Republic of Brazil
  – exchange of letters on maritime transport 25.082
H. Brazil: framework agreement for cooperation between the European
  Economic Community and the Federative Republic of Brazil –
  exchange of letters between the European Economic Community
  and the Federative Republic of Brazil on maritime transport 25.092
I. EU–African relations in shipping law 25.103
J. Canada–EU: comprehensive economic and trade agreement 25.104

CHAPTER 26   MARITIME SAFETY: INTRODUCTION AND
              EUROPEAN UNION MEASURES RELATING TO
              MARITIME SAFETY GENERALLY
A. Introduction 26.001
B. 1978: Council Recommendation 78/584 on the ratification of
  conventions on safety in shipping 26.008
C. 1993: Council Resolution of 8 June 1993 on a common policy on safe
  seas 26.010
D. Regulation (EC) No 2099/2002 of the European Parliament and of the
  Council of 5 November 2002 establishing a Committee on Safe Seas
  and the Prevention of Pollution from Ships (COSS) and amending
  the Regulations on maritime safety and the prevention of pollution
  from ships 26.011
E. Council Decision (EU) 2016/2077 of 17 October 2016 on the position
  to be adopted on behalf of the European Union at the International
  Maritime Organization (IMO) during the 70th session of the Marine
  Environment Protection Committee and the 97th session of the
  Maritime Safety Committee, on the adoption of amendments to
  MARPOL Annex VI, SOLAS Regulations II-1, SOLAS Regulations
  III/1.4, III/30 and III/37, SOLAS Regulations II-2/1 and II-2/10,
  SOLAS Regulation II-1/3–12, the STCW Convention and Code, the
  Fire Safety Systems Code and the 2011 Enhanced Survey
  Programme Code 26.021

l

F. Council Recommendation of 25 July 1983 on the ratification of or accession to the 1979 International Convention on Maritime Search and Rescue (SAR)   26.027
G. Commission Regulation (EU) No 802/2010 of 13 September 2010 implementing Article 10(3) and Article 27 of Directive 2009/16 of the European Parliament and of the Council as regards company performance   26.028
H. Commission Regulation (EU) No 801/2010 of 13 September 2010 implementing Article 10(3) of Directive 2009/16 of the European Parliament and of the Council as regards the flag State criteria   26.035
I. Council Decision 2014/826 of 10 November 2014 on the position to be adopted on behalf of the European Union within the International Maritime Organization during the 94th session of the Maritime Safety Committee on the adoption of amendments to the 2011 Enhanced Survey Programme Code   26.040
J. Council Decision 2014/280 of 8 May 2014 on the position to be adopted on behalf of the European Union at the International Maritime Organization during the 93rd session of the Maritime Safety Committee on the adoption of amendments to SOLAS Regulations II-1/29, II-2/3, 2/9.7, 2/13.4, 2/18, III/20, the Life Saving Appliances Code and the 2011 Enhanced Survey Programme Code   26.043
K. Conclusions   26.047

CHAPTER 27   MARITIME SAFETY: THE EUROPEAN MARITIME SAFETY AGENCY

A. Introduction   27.001
B. Background to the establishment of EMSA   27.003
C. Legal regime relating to EMSA   27.006
D. Location of EMSA   27.007
E. Legal status and standing of EMSA   27.008
F. Structure and governance of EMSA
    Introduction   27.011
    Administrative Board   27.012
    Chairmanship of the Administrative Board   27.016
    Voting in the Administrative Board   27.017
    Executive Director   27.018
G. Staff, privileges, liability and languages of EMSA
    Staff   27.020
    Privileges   27.021
    Liability   27.022
    Languages   27.023
H. Budget of EMSA   27.024
I. Functions of EMSA: introduction   27.025
J. Functions of EMSA: core tasks of EMSA   27.031
K. Functions of EMSA: ancillary tasks of EMSA
    Introduction   27.052

EMSA's assistance of the Commission 27.054
EMSA's assistance of the Commission and the Member States 27.061
European co-operation on coast guard functions 27.065
L. Relations with Member States 27.067
M. Relations with non-Member States 27.071
N. Relations with the public, transparency and protection of information 27.072
O. The EU's re-evaluation of EMSA 27.074
P. Conclusions 27.076

CHAPTER 28 MARITIME SAFETY: PORT STATE CONTROL
A. Introduction 28.001
B. Background to PSC 28.003
C. Directive 2009/16 on PSC
Introduction 28.004
Purpose of Directive 2009/16 28.005
Entry into force 28.006
Legal basis and history of Directive 2009/16 28.007
Scope of Directive 2009/16 28.008
Background to Directive 2009/16 28.013
Concepts in Directive 2009/16 28.030
Inspection powers 28.053
Inspection system and annual inspection commitment 28.054
Modalities of compliance with the inspection commitment 28.055
Modalities allowing a balanced inspection share within the EU 28.056
Notification of arrival of ships 28.061
Ship risk profile 28.062
Frequency of inspections 28.064
Selection of ships for inspection 28.065
Initial and more detailed inspections 28.066
Expanded inspections 28.067
Safety and security guidelines and procedures 28.068
Access refusal measures concerning certain ships 28.071
Report of inspection to the master 28.075
Complaints 28.077
Onshore Maritime Labour Convention 2006 complaint-handling
  procedures 28.078
Rectification and detention 28.082
Right of appeal 28.093
Follow-up to inspections and detentions 28.094
Professional profile of inspectors 28.096
Reports from pilots and port authorities 28.103
Inspection database 28.104
Exchange of information and co-operation 28.105
Publication of information 28.106
Publication of a list of companies with a low and very low performance 28.107
Reimbursement of costs 28.108

Data to monitor implementation   28.109
Monitoring of compliance and performance of Member States   28.110
Delegated acts   28.111
Committee   28.116
Implementing rules   28.117
Penalties   28.118
Review   28.119
Implementation and notification   28.120
Elements of the Community Port State Inspection System   28.121
D. Directive 2009/15 of 23 April 2009 of the European Parliament and of the Council on the common rules and standards for ship inspection and survey organisations and for the relevant activities of maritime administrations
    Introduction   28.122
    Purpose of the directive   28.124
    Definitions used in the directive   28.125
    Article 3: Appropriate enforcement   28.126
    Article 4: Member States may generally not refuse to authorise any of the recognised organisations to undertake certain functions   28.127
    Article 5: Working relationship   28.128
    Role of the Committee on Safe Seas and the Prevention of Pollution from Ships   28.129
    Suspension or revocation of an authorisation   28.131
    Competence of organisations   28.132
    Reporting to the Commission   28.133
    Obligations on Member States   28.134
    Vigilance   28.135
E. Council Decision 2015/873 of 18 May 2015 on the position to be adopted, on behalf of the European Union, at the 48th session of the Port State Control Committee of the Paris Memorandum of Understanding on port State control   28.136
F. Council Decision 2016/381 of 14 March 2016 on the position to be adopted, on behalf of the European Union, within the Port State Control Committee of the Paris Memorandum of Understanding on port State control   28.143
G. Commission Regulation 428/2010 of 20 May 2010 implementing Article 14 of Directive 2009/16 of the Parliament and Council as regards expanded inspections of ships   28.149
H. Commission Directive 96/40 of 25 June 1996 establishing a common model for an identity card for inspectors carrying out port State control   28.152
I. Commission Regulation 801/2010 of 13 September 2010 implementing Article 10(3) of Directive 2009/16 of the Parliament and Council as regards the flag State criteria   28.156
J. Member State having too few inspections: Commission v France   28.159

CHAPTER 29   MARITIME SAFETY: SHIP INSPECTION AND
             SURVEY ORGANISATIONS
  A. Introduction   29.001
  B. Regulation 391/2009 on common rules and standards for ship
       inspection and survey organisations
    Introduction   29.003
    Objectives of Regulation 391/2009   29.026
    Definitions of key concepts in Regulation 391/2009   29.028
    Requests for initial authorisation/recognition   29.039
    Granting initial authorisation/recognition   29.040
    Failure by a recognised organisation to comply with the minimum
       criteria in the regulation   29.041
    Fines and periodic penalties on organisations in breach   29.042
    Withdrawal of Regulation 391/2009   29.043
    Assessment of organisations   29.045
    Access to information from organisations   29.049
    Consultation   29.050
    Establishment and maintenance of an independent quality assessment
       and certification entity   29.056
    Committee on Safe Seas and the Prevention of Pollution from Ships
       (COSS) and interaction with selected other EU instruments   29.063
    Amendment of Regulation 391/2009   29.064
    Adoption and publication of criteria   29.065
    Continuation of recognition   29.068
    Verification of the holder of recognition   29.069
    Commission must keep the Parliament and the Council informed on the
       application of Regulation 391/2009   29.070
  C. Directive 2009/15 on common rules and standards for ship inspection
       and survey organisations and for the relevant activities of maritime
       administrations
    Introduction   29.072
    Objective of Directive 2009/15   29.082
    Concepts in Directive 2009/15   29.083
    Enforcement of Directive 2009/15   29.084
    Article 4: Recognition of organisations   29.087
    Article 5: Working relationships   29.088
    Article 6: assistance by COSS to the Commission   29.092
    Article 7: amendments to the regime   29.093
    Article 8: amendments to the regime   29.094
    Article 9: supervision of recognised organisations   29.095
    Article 10: Member State reports to the Commission   29.096
    Article 11: Member State obligation relating to vessels flying its flag   29.097
    Article 12: Commission reports to the Parliament and Council   29.098
    Article 13: entry into force of the directive   29.099
    Article 14: repeal   29.100

DETAILED CONTENTS

D. Commission Decision 2005/311 of 18 April 2005 on the extension of the limited recognition of "Rinave – Registro Internacional Naval"	29.101
E. Commission Regulation 788/2014 of 18 July 2014 laying down detailed rules for the imposition of fines and periodic penalty payments and the withdrawal of recognition to Articles 6 and 7 of Regulation (EC) No 391/2009 of the European Parliament and of the Council	
Introduction	29.106
General provisions	29.122
Fines and periodic penalty payments	29.125
Time limits	29.146
National competent authorities	29.147
F. Commission implementing Decision (EU) 2015/668 of 24 April 2015 on amending the recognitions of certain organisations in accordance with Article 16 of Regulation (EC) No 391/2009 of the European Parliament and of the Council	29.149
G. Commission implementing Decision 2013/765 of 13 December 2013 amending the recognition of Det Norske Veritas pursuant to Regulation (EC) No 391/2009 of the European Parliament and of the Council on common rules and standards for ship inspection and survey organisations	29.155
H. Commission implementing Decision 2014/281 of 14 May 2014 granting EU recognition to the Croatian Register of Shipping pursuant to Regulation (EC) No 391/2009 of the European Parliament and of the Council on common rules and standards for ship inspection and survey organisations	29.156
I. Commission Regulation (EU) No 428/2010 of 20 May 2010 implementing Article 14 of Directive 2009/16 of the European Parliament and of the Council as regards expanded inspections of ships	29.157

CHAPTER 30   MARITIME SAFETY: CASUALTY AND ACCIDENT INVESTIGATION

A. Introduction	30.001
B. Investigation of maritime casualties generally	30.002
C. National and international legal dimension on maritime accident investigation	30.003
D. Directive 2009/18 of the European Parliament and of the Council of 23 April 2009 establishing the fundamental principles governing the investigation of accidents in the maritime transport sector and amending Council Directive 1999/35 and Directive 2002/59 of the European Parliament and of the Council	
Introduction	30.008
Directive 2009/18 and Member State law	30.016
Purpose of Directive 2009/18	30.019
Scope of Directive 2009/18	30.023
Status of safety investigations	30.025

Obligation to investigate   30.027
Obligation to notify   30.032
Leading of, and participation in, safety investigations   30.033
Investigative bodies   30.034
Confidentiality   30.040
Costs   30.041
Review process   30.042
Permanent co-operation framework   30.043
Co-operation with substantially interested third countries   30.045
Preservation of evidence   30.046
Accident reports   30.047
Safety recommendations   30.049
European database for marine casualties   30.052
Role of COSS in the area of marine accident investigation   30.054
Amendments to the regime   30.055
Observations   30.056
Common methodology for investigating marine casualties and incidents   30.057

CHAPTER 31   MARITIME SAFETY: MINIMUM TRAINING OF SEAFARERS

A. Introduction   31.001
B. Background to Directive 2008/106   31.006
C. Definitions in Directive 2008/106   31.007
D. Scope of Directive 2008/106   31.048
E. Training and certification   31.049
F. Certificates of competency, certificates of proficiency and endorsements   31.050
G. Training requirements   31.057
H. Principles governing near-coastal voyages   31.058
I. Prevention of fraud and other unlawful practices   31.062
J. Penalties or disciplinary measures   31.063
K. Quality standards   31.064
L. Medical standards   31.065
M. Revalidation of certificates of competency and certificates of proficiency   31.066
N. Use of simulators   31.067
O. Responsibilities of companies   31.068
P. Fitness for duty   31.073
Q. Dispensation   31.074
R. Responsibilities of Member States with regard to training and assessment   31.075
S. On-board communication   31.077
T. Recognition of certificates of competency and/or certificates of proficiency   31.078
U. Non-compliance with the requirements of the STCW Convention   31.079
V. Reassessment   31.080
W. Port State control   31.081
X. Port State control procedures   31.082

Y. Detention	31.083
Z. Regular monitoring of compliance	31.084
AA. Information for statistical purposes	31.085
AB. Reports	31.086
AC. Amendment to the directive	31.087
AD. Exercise of the delegation of powers	31.088
AE. Committee procedure	31.089
AF. Penalties	31.090
AG. Transitional provisions	31.091
AH. Repeal	31.092

CHAPTER 32   MARITIME SAFETY: MINIMUM SAFETY AND HEALTH REQUIREMENTS FOR IMPROVED MEDICAL TREATMENT ON BOARD VESSELS

A. Introduction	32.001
B. Background to Directive 92/29	32.003
Legal basis	32.005
C. Basic concepts in Directive 92/29	
Antidote	32.006
Medical supplies	32.007
Owner	32.008
Vessel	32.009
Worker	32.011
D. Obligation to have medical supplies on board	32.012
E. Obligation on ships to carry antidotes	32.013
F. Allocation of responsibilities	32.014
G. Information and training	32.015
H. Medical consultations by radio	32.018
I. Inspection	32.019
J. Committee procedure	32.020
K. Entry into force	32.021
L. Conclusion	32.022

CHAPTER 33   MARITIME SAFETY: INTERNATIONAL SAFETY MANAGEMENT CODE FOR THE SAFE OPERATION OF SHIPS AND FOR POLLUTION PREVENTION

A. Introduction	33.001
B. Regulation 336/2006 on the implementation of the international safety management code within the Community and repealing Council Regulation 3051/95	
Introduction	33.003
Background	33.008
Objective of the regulation	33.013
Concepts in the regulation	33.014
Scope of regulation 336/2006	33.015
Compliance	33.017

Safety management requirements 33.018
Certification and verification 33.019
Derogation 33.020
Validity, acceptance and recognition of certificates 33.021
Penalties 33.022
Reporting 33.023
Amendments 33.024
Committee procedure 33.025
Repeal 33.026
Annexes 33.027

CHAPTER 34 MARITIME SAFETY: FERRIES AND RO-RO VESSELS
  A. Introduction 34.001
  B. Resolution of the Council and of the representatives of the governments of the Member States, meeting within the Council of 19 June 1990 on improving passenger ferry safety 34.007
  C. Council Resolution of 22 December 1994 on the safety of roll-on/roll-off passenger ferries 34.009
  D. Council Directive 1999/35 on a system of mandatory surveys for the safe operation of regular ro-ro ferry and high-speed passenger craft services
    Introduction 34.010
    Purpose of Directive 1999/35 34.012
    Concepts in Directive 1999/35 34.013
    Scope of Directive 1999/35 34.014
    Initial verifications required in relation to ro-ro ferries and high-speed passenger craft 34.015
    Initial verifications required in relation to companies and flag states 34.016
    Initial specific surveys 34.017
    Special provisions 34.018
    Regular specific surveys and other surveys 34.019
    Notification 34.021
    Prevention of operation 34.022
    Procedures related to initial and regular specific surveys 34.026
    Accompanying measures 34.030
    Co-operation between host States 34.032
    Supporting measures 34.033
    Committee procedure 34.034
    Amendment procedure 34.035
    Penalties 34.036
    Application 34.037
    Assessment of application of Directive 1999/35 34.038
    Proposed amendments 34.039
  E. Directive 2003/25 on specific stability requirements for ro-ro passenger ships
    Introduction 34.040
    Purpose of Directive 2003/25 34.043
    Concepts in Directive 2003/25 34.044

DETAILED CONTENTS

Scope of Directive 2003/25	34.045
Significant wave heights ("hs")	34.046
Sea areas	34.047
Specific stability requirements	34.048
Introduction of the specific stability requirements	34.049
Certificates	34.050
Seasonal and short-time period operations	34.051
Adaptations and committee procedure	34.052
Committee procedure	34.053
Penalties	34.054
Implementation	34.055
F. Directive 2009/45 of the European Parliament and of the Council of 6 May 2009 on safety rules and standards for passenger ships	
Introduction	34.056
Purposes of Directive 2009/45	34.061
Definitions for the purposes of Directive 2009/45	34.062
Scope of Directive 2009/45	34.063
Classes of passenger ships	34.065
Application of Directive 2009/45	34.068
Safety requirements	34.069
Stability requirements and phasing-out of ro-ro passenger ships	34.073
Safety requirements for persons with reduced mobility	34.074
Additional safety requirements, equivalents, exemptions and safeguard measures	34.078
Adaptations	34.083
COSS Committee	34.087
Surveys	34.088
Certificates	34.092
1974 SOLAS Convention regulations	34.095
Penalties	34.096
Notifications	34.097
G. Commission Decision 2003/587 of 5 August 2003 on compliance of the fire-extinguishing system used on the ro-ro ferry "Finnsailor" (IMO No 8401444) with Council Directive 1999/35 of 29 April 1999	34.098
H. 2016 Commission proposals to amend the common rules on safety of ships carrying passengers in EU waters	34.101
I. Commission implementing Decision 2013/795 of 19 December 2013 on a notification by the United Kingdom of measures it intends to adopt in accordance with Article 9(2) and (3) of Directive 2009/45 of the European Parliament and of the Council on safety rules and standards for passenger ships	34.106
CHAPTER 35 MARITIME SAFETY: ORGANISATION OF WORKING TIME OF SEAFARERS	
A. Introduction	35.001
B. Background to the directive	35.003

  C. Purpose of the directive   35.004
  D. Minimum requirements   35.005
  E. Transposition   35.006
  F. Annex to Directive 1999/63   35.007

CHAPTER 36 MARITIME SAFETY: MARITIME LABOUR CONVENTION 2006
  A. Introduction   36.001
  B. Maritime Labour Convention 2006   36.002
  C. Council Decision 2007/431 authorising Member States to ratify, in the interests of the European Community, the Maritime Labour Convention, 2006, of the International Labour Organisation   36.003
  D. Directive 2013/54 of the European Parliament and of the Council of 20 November 2013 concerning certain flag State responsibilities for compliance with and enforcement of the Maritime Labour Convention 2006   36.012
   Introduction   36.012
   Subject matter of Directive 2013/54   36.025
   Definitions in Directive 2013/54   36.026
   Monitoring of compliance with Directive 2013/54   36.027
   Personnel in charge of compliance monitoring   36.028
   On-board complaint procedures, handling of complaints and corrective measures   36.029
   Reports   36.030
   Transposition of Directive 2013/54   36.031
  E. Decision 2014/346 on the position to be adopted on behalf of the European Union at the 103rd session of the International Labour Conference concerning amendments to the Code of the Maritime Labour Convention   36.032

CHAPTER 37 MARITIME SAFETY: MARINE EQUIPMENT
  A. Introduction   37.001
  B. Directive 2014/90 of the European Parliament and of the Council of 23 July 2014 on marine equipment and repealing Council Directive 96/98
   Introduction   37.003
   Background   37.004
   Objective of Directive 2014/90   37.009
   Definitions used in Directive 2014/90   37.010
   Scope of Directive 2014/90   37.032
   Requirements for marine equipment   37.033
   Application of the directive   37.034
   Functioning of the internal market   37.035
   Transfer of a ship to the flag of a Member State   37.036
   Standards for marine equipment   37.037
   The wheel mark   37.039
   Rules and conditions for affixing the wheel mark   37.042

Electronic tag	37.043
Obligations of economic operators	37.047
Obligations of manufacturers	37.048
Obligations of authorised representatives	37.052
Other economic operators	37.053
Conformity assessment and notification of conformity assessment bodies	37.057
EU declaration of conformity	37.059
Notification of conformity assessment bodies	37.060
Notifying authorities	37.061
Information obligation on notifying authorities	37.062
Subsidiaries of, and subcontracting by, notified bodies	37.063
Changes to notifications	37.064
Challenges to the competence of notified bodies	37.065
Operational obligations of notified bodies	37.066
Obligation of notified bodies to provide information	37.067
Union market surveillance, control of products, safeguard provisions	37.068
EU market surveillance framework	37.069
Procedure for dealing with marine equipment presenting a risk at national level	37.070
EU safeguard procedure	37.076
Compliant products which present a risk to maritime safety, to health or to the environment	37.081
Formal non-compliance	37.085
Exemptions based on technical innovation	37.086
Exemptions for testing or evaluation	37.088
Exemptions in exceptional circumstances	37.089
Final provisions	37.090
Exchange of experience	37.091
Co-ordination of notified bodies	37.092
Implementing measures	37.093
Amendments	37.094
Exercise of the delegation	37.095
Committee on Safe Seas and the Prevention of Pollution from Ships ("COSS")	37.096
Transposition	37.097
Repeal	37.098
C. Commission implementing Regulation 2017/306 of 6 February 2017 indicating design, construction and performance requirements and testing standards for marine equipment	37.099
D. Commission Recommendation 2010/167 of 19 March 2010 on the authorisation of systems for mobile communication services on board vessels (MCV services)	37.103

DETAILED CONTENTS

CHAPTER 38   PIRACY
  A. Introduction   38.001
  B. European Commission Recommendation of 11 March 2010 on measures for self-protection and the prevention of piracy and armed robbery against ships
    Introduction   38.008
    Legal basis   38.009
    Essence of the recommendation   38.010
    Best practices as set out in the recommendation   38.011
    Assessment of the recommendation   38.015
  C. 2011: Strategic Framework for the Horn of Africa   38.016
  D. Judicial intervention   38.022
  E. Operation Atalanta   38.023
  F. Political and Security Committee Decision Atalanta/4/2014 of 24 July 2014 on the appointment of the EU Force Commander for the European Union military operation to contribute to the deterrence, prevention and repression of acts of piracy and armed robbery off the Somali coast (Atalanta) and repealing Decision Atalanta/1/2014 (2014/500/CFSP)   38.024
  G. Conclusions   38.025

CHAPTER 39   NAVIGATION
  A. Introduction
    Introduction   39.001
    Navigation   39.002
    Short sea shipping   39.003
  B. Council Decision 92/143 on radionavigation systems for Europe
    Introduction   39.004
    Legal background to the decision   39.005
    Factual background to the decision   39.006
    Operative provisions in the decision   39.007
  C. Navigation: repealed: Commission Decision 2004/71 on essential requirements relating to marine radio communication equipment which is intended to be used on non-SOLAS vessels and to participate in the Global Maritime Distress and Safety System (GMDSS)
    Introduction   39.010
    Legal background   39.011
    Factual background   39.012
    Scope of the decision   39.013
    Effect of the decision   39.014
  D. Navigation: Commission Decision 2013/638 of 12 August 2013 on essential requirements relating to marine radio communication equipment which is intended to be used on non-SOLAS vessels and to participate in the Global Maritime Distress and Safety System (GMDSS)   39.015

DETAILED CONTENTS

E. Commission Recommendation 2010/167 of 19 March 2010 on the authorisation of systems for Mobile Communication Services on board vessels (MCV services)	39.028
Purpose of the recommendation	39.030
F. The *Jan De Nul NV v Hauptzollamt Oldenburg* case	39.041
G. Council Decision 87/475 of 17 September 1987 relating to maritime transport between Italy and Algeria	39.049
H. Directive 2002/59 of 27 June 2002 of the European Parliament and of the Council establishing a community vessel traffic monitoring and information system and repealing Council Directive 93/75	
Introduction	39.051
Purpose of the directive	39.053
Scope of the directive	39.054
Definitions in the directive	39.055
Notification prior to entry into ports of the Member States	39.056
Monitoring of ships entering the area of mandatory ship reporting systems	39.057
Use of automatic identification systems	39.058
Use of ship's routing systems	39.060
Monitoring of the compliance of ships with vessel traffic services	39.061
Infrastructure for ship reporting systems, ships' routing systems and VTS	39.062
Voyage data recorder systems	39.063
Notification of dangerous or polluting goods on board ships (HAZMAT)	39.064
Monitoring of hazardous ships and intervention in the event of incidents and accidents at sea	39.065
Accompanying measures	39.075
I. Commission Decision (EU) 2016/566 of 11 April 2016 on Establishing the High-Level Steering Group for Governance of the Digital Maritime System and Services and Repealing Decision 2009/584	39.076

CHAPTER 40 PILOTAGE

A. Introduction	40.001
B. The 1978 North Sea Pilotage Directive	
Introduction	40.002
Legal bases	40.003
Purpose	40.004
Obligation on certain States to provide qualified pilots	40.005
Member States are obliged to encourage ships which fly their flags to use qualified pilots	40.006
Implementation	40.007
Implementation opinions	40.008
C. 1985 Commission Memorandum on shipping	40.019
D. Discrimination on the basis of nationality	40.020
E. Pilotage exemption certificates	40.021

DETAILED CONTENTS

CHAPTER 41 SHORT SEA SHIPPING
A. Introduction   41.001
B. 1996: Council Resolution on short sea shipping   41.003
C. 2000: Resolution on the promotion of short sea shipping   41.004
D. 2000: Resolution on the promotion of intermodality and intermodal
   freight transport in the European Union   41.008
E. 2004: Communication from the Commission to the Council, the
   European Parliament, the European Economic and Social
   Committee and the Committee of the Regions on short sea shipping   41.010
F. Current EU perspective on short sea shipping   41.011

CHAPTER 42 SECURITY: SHIPS AND PORTS
A. Introduction   42.001
B. Regulation 725/2004 on enhancing ship and port facility security
   Introduction   42.009
   Objectives of Regulation 725/2004   42.015
   Concepts in Regulation 725/2004   42.016
   Joint measures and scope   42.026
   Communication of information   42.033
   Alternative security agreements or equivalent security arrangements   42.037
   Provision of security information prior to entry into a port of a Member
      State   42.043
   Exemptions from the provision of security information prior to entry
      into a port   42.046
   Security checks in Member State ports   42.047
   Implementation and conformity checking   42.048
   Integration of amendments to international instruments   42.049
   Committee procedure   42.050
   Confidentiality   42.051
   Dissemination of information   42.054
   Sanctions   42.055
C. Directive 2005/65 of the European Parliament and of the Council on
   enhancing port security
   Introduction   42.056
   Subject matter of Directive 2005/65   42.070
   Scope of Directive 2005/65   42.071
   Definitions   42.072
   Co-ordination with measures taken in application of Regulation
      725/2004   42.078
   Port security authority   42.079
   Port security assessment   42.082
   Port security plan   42.084
   Security levels   42.089
   Port security officer   42.092
   Reviews   42.093
   Recognised security organisations   42.094

Focal point for port security	42.095
Implementation and conformity checking	42.096
Adaptations	42.097
Committee procedure	42.098
Confidentiality and dissemination of information	42.099
Penalties	42.100
Implementation	42.101
Evaluation report	42.102
Annexes	42.103

D. Commission Regulation (EC) No 324/2008 of 9 April 2008 laying down revised procedures for conducting Commission inspections in the field of maritime security

Introduction	42.104
Subject matter of the regulation	42.108
Definitions used in the regulation	42.109
Structure of the regulation	42.127
Member States' duty to co-operate	42.128
Exercise of Commission powers	42.129
Participation of national inspectors in Commission inspections	42.130
Technical assistance from EMSA in Commission inspections	42.131
Qualification criteria and training for Commission inspectors	42.132
Notice of inspections	42.133
Preparation of inspections	42.134
The actual conduct of inspections	42.135
Inspection report	42.136
Response from the Member State	42.137
Action by the Commission	42.138
Confidentiality of information	42.139
Commission's inspection programme	42.140
Informing Member States of major non-conformity	42.141
Review	42.142

CHAPTER 43   PORTS: GENERALLY AND THE PORT SERVICES REGULATION 2017/352

A. Introduction	43.001
B. The EU's port services Regulation 2017/352	
Introduction	43.006
Adoption of Regulation 2017/352	43.008
Essence of Regulation 2017/352	43.009
Purpose of Regulation 2017/352	43.014
The nature of the regulation	43.018
Entry into force of the regulation	43.020
Brexit and the regulation	43.024
Purpose of the regulation	43.025
Subject matter and scope of application of the regulation	43.026
Framework on market access	43.035

Organisation of port services 43.039
Minimum requirements for the provision of port services 43.042
Procedural aspects 43.049
Limiting the number of service providers 43.050
PSOs 43.056
Internal operator 43.057
Safeguarding of employees' rights 43.058
Financial transparency and autonomy 43.063
Transparency of financial relations 43.064
Port service charges 43.066
Port infrastructure charges 43.070
General provisions 43.074
   Introduction 43.074
   Training of staff 43.075
   Consultation of port users and other stakeholders 43.076
   Complaints 43.077
   Penalties 43.081
   Relevant authorities 43.082
   Review of the regulation 43.083
   Practical issues 43.084

CHAPTER 44 PORTS: REPORTING FORMALITIES FOR SHIPS IN EUROPEAN UNION PORTS: DIRECTIVE 2010/65

A. Introduction 44.001
B. Directive 2002/6 on reporting formalities for ships arriving in and/or departing from ports of the Member States of the Community 44.005
C. Directive 2010/65 on reporting formalities for ships arriving in and/or departing from ports of the Member States and repealing Directive 2002/6
Introduction 44.006
Legal basis 44.007
Entry into force 44.008
Factual background 44.009
Subject matter and scope of the directive 44.014
Harmonisation and co-ordination of reporting formalities 44.018
Notification of ships prior to their arrival into ports 44.019
Amendment procedure 44.026
Reporting on the functioning of the directive 44.027
Reporting requirements 44.029
Assessment and conclusions 44.030

CHAPTER 45 PORTS: ELECTRICITY FOR SHIPS IN PORTS

A. Introduction 45.001
B. 2002: Commission Communication on a strategy to reduce atmospheric emissions from seagoing ships 45.002
C. 2003: European Parliament Resolution on the strategy to reduce atmospheric emissions from seagoing ships 45.004

D. 2006: Commission Recommendation on the promotion of shore-side electricity for use by ships at berth in community ports	45.006
E. Conclusion	45.009

CHAPTER 46 CARRIAGE OF GOODS AND PASSENGERS

A. Introduction	46.001
B. Containers	
1979: Council Recommendation 79/487 on the ratification of the International Convention for Safe Containers (CSC)	46.003
C. Registration of persons sailing on board passenger ships	
Introduction	46.005
Council Directive 98/41 of 18 June 1998 on the registration of persons sailing on board passenger ships operating to or from ports of the Member States of the Community	46.006
Introduction	46.006
Entry into force of the directive	46.008
Legal basis of Directive 98/41	46.009
Purpose of Directive 98/41	46.010
Scope and application of Directive 98/41	46.011
Counting of passengers	46.012
Communication of passenger numbers before the vessel leaves port	46.013
Information which must be recorded for the purposes of the directive	46.014
Functional criteria for registration systems	46.017
Limitation on the number of passengers exceeding the permitted number	46.018
Obligations on companies operating passenger ships	46.019
Ships outside the EU	46.021
Relationship between Directive 98/41 and SOLAS	46.022
Aspects of the administration of Directive 98/41	46.023
Penalties for breaching the regime	46.024
D. Liability of carriers of passengers by sea in the event of accidents	
Regulation 392/2009 of the European Parliament and of the Council on the liability of carriers of passengers by sea in the event of accidents	46.025
Introduction	46.025
Adoption of the resolution	46.038
Purpose and subject matter of Regulation 392/2009	46.039
Scope of Regulation 392/2009	46.040
Liability and insurance under Regulation 392/2009	46.041
Compensation in respect of mobility equipment or other specific equipment	46.042
Global limitation of liability	46.043
Advance payment	46.044
Information to passengers	46.045
Reporting	46.046

Amendments	46.047
Role of COSS	46.048

E. Statistical returns in respect of the carriage of goods and passengers by sea

Introduction	46.049
Directive 2009/42 on statistical returns in respect of carriage of goods and passengers by sea	46.050
Introduction	46.050
Factual background	46.052
Concepts in Directive 2009/42	46.053
Collection of data	46.054
Data collection characteristics	46.055
Ports	46.056
Accuracy and processing	46.057
Transmission, reports and dissemination of data	46.059
Committee procedure	46.062
Background to the amendments	46.066

F. Passenger rights: Regulation 1177/2010 concerning the rights of passengers when travelling by sea and inland waterway and amending Regulation 2006/2004

Protection of maritime passengers	46.072
Adoption of Regulation 1177/2010	46.073
Persons with disabilities in the context of Regulation 1177/2010	46.078
Informing passengers promptly of delays/cancellations and compensation	46.079
Chapter I: General provision	46.086
Tickets and non-discriminatory contract conditions	46.091
Other performing parties	46.092
Exclusion of waiver	46.093
Chapter II: "Rights of disabled persons and persons with reduced mobility"	46.094
Chapter III: "Obligations of carriers and terminal operators in the events of interrupted travel"	46.103
Information in the event of cancelled or delayed departures	46.104
Assistance in the event of cancelled or delayed departures	46.108
Chapter IV: "General rules on information and complaints"	46.118
Chapter V: "Enforcement and national enforcement bodies"	46.121
Chapter VI: "Final provisions"	46.125

G. Decision 87/359 concerning reductions in air and sea transport fares available only to Spanish nationals resident in the Canary Islands and the Balearic Islands — 46.126

H. Council Decision 2012/22 of 12 December 2011 concerning the accession of the European Union to the protocol of 2002 to the Athens Convention relating to the carriage of passengers and their luggage by sea, 1974, with the exception of Articles 10 and 11 thereof — 46.130

I. Council Decision 2012/23 concerning the accession of the European Union to the protocol of 2002 to the Athens Convention relating to the carriage of passengers and their luggage by sea, 1974, as regards Articles 10 and 11 thereof   46.138
J. Directive 2001/96 establishing harmonised requirements and procedures for the safe loading and unloading of bulk carriers
  Introduction   46.147
  Purpose of the directive   46.149
  Scope of the directive   46.150
  Definitions used in the directive   46.151
  Requirements in relation to the operational suitability of bulk carriers   46.152
  Temporary authorisation   46.154
  Responsibilities of masters and terminal representatives   46.155
  Procedures between bulk carriers and terminals   46.156
  Role of the competent authorities   46.157
  Repair of damage incurred during loading or unloading   46.158
  Verification and reporting   46.159
K. Commission Decision 96/513 of 29 July 1996 in application, at the request of France, of Article 5(4) of Council Directive 93/75 concerning minimum requirements for vessels bound for or leaving Community ports and carrying dangerous or polluting goods   46.168
L. Commission Decision 96/710 of 27 November 1996 in application, at the request of Germany, of Article 5(4) of Council Directive 93/75 of 13 September 1993 concerning minimum requirements for vessels bound for or leaving Community ports and carrying dangerous or polluting goods   46.171
M. Commission Decision 1999/461 of 24 June 1999 on the publication of the list of existing class A and B passenger ships notified by Greece in accordance with Council Directive 98/18 for which the derogation of Article 6(3)(g) may be applied   46.174
N. Commission Decision 96/127 on the application, at the request of Germany, of Article 5(4) of Council Directive 95/75 concerning minimum requirements for vessels bound for or leaving Community ports and carrying dangerous or polluting goods   46.176
O. Commission Decision 96/710 of 27 November 1996 in application, at the request of Germany, of Article 5(4) of Council Directive 93/75 of 13 September 1993 concerning minimum requirements for vessels bound for or leaving Community ports and carrying dangerous or polluting goods   46.178
P. Directive 2009/20 of the European Parliament and of the Council of 23 April 2009 on the insurance of shipowners for maritime claims   46.181

CHAPTER 47   EUROPEAN UNION LAW AND SHIPPING LITIGATION: THE "BRUSSELS I" REGULATION
  A. Introduction   47.001
  B. Scope and application of the Recast Brussels I Regulation   47.007

C. Jurisdiction	
Introduction	47.011
Basic rule on jurisdiction	47.012
Special jurisdiction	47.017
Limitations actions	47.019
Insurance	47.020
Consumer contracts	47.026
Employment contracts	47.029
Exclusive jurisdiction	47.033
Prorogation of jurisdiction	47.034
Examination as to jurisdiction and admissibility	47.039
Lis pendens (or related articles)	47.041
Pending proceedings in a third State	47.049
Provisional and protective measures	47.052
D. Recognition and enforcement of judgments	47.053
E. Relationship between the Recast Regulation and specialised conventions	47.089
F. Conclusions	47.093

CHAPTER 48   BREXIT

A. Introduction	48.001
B. Chronology of Brexit	48.010
C. Background observations on the impact of Brexit on EU shipping law and policy	48.028
D. Freedom of establishment and registration of vessels	48.031
E. Free movement of services in the maritime sector	48.032
F. Discrimination on the basis of nationality	48.035
G. Maritime safety law	48.036
H. Employment and seafarer qualifications	48.038
I. Marine equipment	48.040
J. Ship recycling	48.041
K. Competition law generally	48.042
L. Merger control in the maritime sector	48.043
M. State aid	48.044
N. Litigation	48.045
O. Divergence between EU and UK law	48.048
P. Sanctions regime	48.049
Q. Ship finance	48.050
R. Environmental law	48.051
S. Implications of Brexit on contracts	48.052
T. Passenger rights	48.053
U. Carriage of live animals	48.055
V. Customs	48.056
W. Other issues	48.057
X. Conclusions	48.061

CHAPTER 49 CONCLUSIONS

A. Introduction	49.001
B. The EU as a force in the world generally	
Introduction	49.009
The place of the EU in world shipping	49.010
C. EU shipping law was not an early feature of EU law	49.011
D. There is hardly any limit to the possible application of EU law to shipping yet there is a limit to the possible development of EU shipping law	49.012
E. EU transport policy was slow to develop	49.014
F. EU shipping policy has not been entirely successful	49.016
G. Is shipping a public service or merely another service in the marketplace?	49.018
H. EU shipping law is only a component of international shipping law	49.019
I. The formulation of EU shipping law requires the involvement of all partners	49.020
J. EU shipping law and policy must seek to protect EU shipowners, seafarers and all those involved in the EU shipping industry	49.021
K. EU shipping law in an environment of self-regulation?	49.023
L. Is EU shipping law characterised by knee-jerk reactions?	49.024
M. Limitations to the development of EU shipping law	49.025
N. Role of the EU in shipping matters by comparison with other international organisations	49.026
O. Uneven distribution of marine resources in the EU	49.027
P. Modal isolation	49.028
Q. Informed approach	49.029
R. Open markets	49.030
S. Recurring themes	49.031
T. Short sea transport	49.032
U. SWOT analysis of EU shipping	
Introduction	49.033
Strengths	49.034
Weaknesses	49.041
Opportunities	49.045
Threats	49.049
V. Consideration of other issues	
Introduction	49.051
Do Member States act in their own self-interest?	49.052
Contrast with the USA	49.053
Contrast with the IMO	49.054
An integrated approach is essential	49.055
New areas will continue to emerge	49.056
Technology	49.057
Taxation	49.058
Role of competition law	49.059
State aid	49.060

Non-discrimination on the basis of nationality	49.061
Brussels as benefactor or bully?	49.062
Inefficiency in the industry	49.063
Role of the EU in international maritime affairs	49.064
Climate change	49.065
More legislation?	49.066
EU shipping law can be used pro-actively	49.067
Role of the Member States, institutions and industry	49.068
Role of shipping in the EU	49.069
W. Protectionism	49.070
X. Attitudes and policies of Member States	49.071
Y. The institutional dimension to the evolution of EU shipping law	49.075
Z. The future	49.076
Index	1821

PREFACE

Writing a book on European Union shipping law is like trying to paint a moving train. Since the first edition of this book was drafted, we have moved from the European Economic Community ("EEC") to the European Community ("EC") to the European Union ("EU") with all the attendant changes which occurred at each phase. Equally, within each of these phases of evolution, the law changes rapidly while developing in a way which is both complex and complicated. Given the enormous body of EU law which now exists, it is hard to believe that EU law is just over 60 years old and there are many aspects which have yet to evolve. Despite the challenges of writing this book, there is no doubt that writing it, and the previous editions, has brought its pleasures.

On the challenges, three specific challenges should be mentioned. First, terminology has been changing. For convenience, the term "European Union" (or "EU") is used throughout the book even though it would not be entirely accurate at certain earlier times because the term is a very recent one. Equally, the names of the EU's institutions have changed over time so the current names are used throughout (unless the context requires otherwise) so as to avoid confusion for readers (e.g. what was the Court of First Instance is now called the General Court so the latter (i.e. current) term is usually used in this book). Second, the numbering of EU legal provisions has also been changing. Over the last 60 years, the numbering used in the treaties has changed such that, for example, the provision on the abuse of dominance has been numbered Article 86 of the Treaty establishing the European Economic Community, Article 82 of the Treaty establishing the European Community and now Article 102 of the Treaty on the Functioning of the European Union. The current numbering is used in this book (i.e. the original numbering in quotations is replaced by the current numbering provided there is a current equivalent of the earlier provision). Third, the law on this area is complex and apparently all pervasive so it is often difficult not only to discern the rules but to decide what to include and what to omit.

On the content of this book, there is some deliberate repetition of material in different chapters but this is so that readers (particularly busy practitioners) can read material in one convenient location rather than having to cross-refer between different parts of the book. Equally, the book includes many quotations and extracts from primary sources so as to make the book more convenient for the reader.

Sadly, books these days have to contain exclusion clauses. Readers are therefore advised to seek competent professional legal advice before making any decision in respect of the matters addressed in this book. No responsibility is accepted for the contents of this book. The law is stated as I understood it to be on 1 September 2018. I have already commenced working on the next edition so that the gap between editions will not be as long and the work will be easier to complete, so I welcome comments and correspondence at vpower@algoodbody.com and 6492226@gmail.com.

On a pleasant note, there are many people who deserve my sincerest appreciation. First, the genesis of this book was very simple: I gave a lecture at a conference and the late William V Packard, who was a fellow speaker, approached me after my speech and asked would I be interested in writing a book on what was then EEC Shipping Law for Lloyd's of London Press. I was, and remain, flattered by his approach and am very grateful for his request and faith. Second, the reception to the book was equally flattering and I am very grateful to the Comité Maritime International for bestowing on the book the honour of the Albert Lilar Prize as the best shipping law book in the world over the previous five years and, in that context, I would like to pay tribute to the Irish Maritime Law Association and its then President J Niall McGovern whose idea it was to propose the book for the Prize and whose pride was palpable and touching in the ensuing victory. Third, I would like to thank everyone with whom I have come into contact over the years because of this book including lawyers, judges, European Union officials, company executives, clients and, in particular, the European Maritime Law Organisation and its wonderful Board of Directors. Fourth, I would like to thank my colleagues at A&L Goodbody who have put up with my unusual habit of writing books at weekends alongside a very busy practice. Penultimately, the publishers have been both extraordinarily professional and blessed with saintly patience throughout the gestation of this edition; hopefully, this book will be proof of my appreciation of their work. Ultimately, it is my family who deserve the greatest acknowledgment of all: to my late loving parents, John and Patricia, who taught me a love of the sea and the land respectively and moulded me into whatever I have become today; to my wife, Edwina, who has endured this project like so many others and who is the rock upon which everything is built and the North Star to guide me always; and to our two beautiful daughters, Grace and Juliet, who make it all worthwhile. To all, and especially my family, thank you and I dedicate this book to my family.

Dr Vincent J G Power
Dublin
September 2018

ABBREVIATIONS

ACP	African, Caribbean and Pacific countries
AFS-Convention	International Convention on the Control of Harmful Anti-Fouling Systems on Ships
AIDS	Acquired immune deficiency syndrome
AIS	Automatic identification systems
AJIL	American Journal of International Law
BERs	Block exemption regulations
BES	Business expansion scheme
BMP	Best management practices
CAACE	Comité des Associations d'Armateurs des Communautés Européennes
CAP	Common Agricultural Policy
CCJN	Commission's Consolidated Jurisdictional Notice
CE	Conformité Européene
CENELEC	European Committee for Electrotechnical Standardization
CENSA	Council of European and Japanese National Shipowners' Associations
CETA	Comprehensive Economic and Trade Agreement
CFSP	Common foreign and security policy
CGRT	Compensated gross registered tonnes
CGT	Compensated grt
CJEU	Court of Justice of the European Union
CLC	Commercial Law Cases
CMLR	Common Market Law Reports
CMLRev	Common Market Law Review
Cmnd	Command Paper (United Kingdom)
CO_2	Carbon dioxide
COM	Communication
COMECON	Council for Mutual Economic Co-operation
COREPER	Committee of Permanent Representatives
COSS	Committee on Safe Seas and the Prevention of Pollution from Ships
COST	Co-operation Européenne dans la domaine de la recherche Scientifique et Technique
CSC	Convention of Safe Containers

ABBREVIATIONS

CSDP	Common Security and Defence Policy
CTG CMAI	Consultative Technical Group for Cooperation in Marine Accident Investigation
CTP	Common transport policy
CYELS	Cambridge Yearbook of European Legal Studies
Dec.	Decision
DG	Directorate-General
DG COMP	Directorate General for Competition
DG Compiles	Directorate General for Competition
DG MOVE	Directorate-General for Mobility and Transport
DG TREN	Directorate General for Transport and Energy
Dir.	Directive
DSC Code	Code of Safety for Dynamically Supported Craft
Duke J. Comp. & Int'l L.	Duke Journal of Comparative and International Law
dwt	Deadweight tons
EAEC	European Atomic Energy Community (Euratom Treaty)
EATA	European Asia Trades Agreement
EC	European Community or European Communities
ECB	European Central Bank
ECHR	European Convention for the Protection of Human Rights and Fundamental Freedoms
ECJ	Court of Justice of the European Communities/European Court of Justice (now the Court of Justice of the European Union, "CJEU")
ECLI	European Case Law Identifier
ECLI:EU:C:	European Case Law Identifier: Court of Justice of the European Union
ECLI:EU:T:	European Case Law Identifier: General Court
ECLR	European Competition Law Review
ECN	European Competition Network
ECR	European Court Reports
ECSA	European Community Shipowners' Association
ECSC	European Coal and Steel Community
EC Treaty	Treaty establishing the European Community
Ed.	Edited comment
EDA	European Defence Agency
EDC	European Defence Community
EEA	European Economic Area
EEAS	European External Action Service
EEC	European Economic Community
EESC	European Economic and Social Committee
EEZ	Exclusive economic zone
EFTA	European Free Trade Association
EIB	European Investment Bank
ELAA	European Liner Affairs Association

ABBREVIATIONS

ELRev	European Law Review
EMCIP	European Marine Casualty Information Platform
EMLO	European Maritime Law Organisation
EMS	European monetary system
EMSA	European Maritime Safety Agency
EMSO	European Maritime Safety Organisation
EMU	Economic and Monetary Union
EP	European Parliament
EPC	European Political Community
ERDF	European Regional Development Fund
ESCB	European System of Central Banks
ESN	European Shortsea Network
ESPO	European Sea Ports Organisation
ETL	European Transport Law
ETS	Emission Trading System
EU	European Union
EU-15	The EU (then the European Communities) when it had 15 Member States
EU-27	The EU when it had 27 Member States
EU-28	The current EU (i.e. having 28 Member States)
EU NAVFOR – ATALANTA	European Naval Force Somalia – Operation Atalanta
Euratom	European Atomic Energy Community
Eur J Int Law	European Journal of International Law
EUSR	EU Special Representative
EUROS	Community Ship Register
EWCA Civ	England and Wales Court of Appeal Civil Division
EWHC	England and Wales High Court
FAL Convention	IMO Convention on Facilitation of International Maritime Traffic
FEFC	Far Eastern Freight Conference
FETTCSA	Far East Trade Tariff Charges and Surcharges Agreement
FOC	Flag of convenience
Fordham Int'l L J	Fordham International Law Journal
FPSOs	Floating production storage and off-loading units
FRONTEX	European Agency for the Management of Operational Cooperation at the External Borders of the Member States of the European Union
FSC	Flag State Control
FSUs	Floating storage units
FST	Federation of Transport Workers' Unions in the European Union
GATT	General Agreement on Tariffs and Trade
GBER	General Block Exemption Regulation
GDP	Gross domestic product
GDR	German Democratic Republic
GHG	Greenhouse gas
GIS	German International Shipping Register

GMDSS	Global Maritime Distress and Safety System
GNS	Global navigation system
GoA	Gulf of Aden
grt	Gross registered tonnage
GSM	Global System for Mobile Communications
gt	Gross tons
GVA	Gross value added
HHI	Herfindahl-Hirschman Index
HLSG	High-level steering group for governance of the digital maritime system and services
HMSO	Her Majesty's Stationery Office
HSC Code	High-Speed Craft Code
IACS	International Association of Classification Societies
ICCLR	International Company and Commercial Law Review
ICLQ	International and Comparative Law Quarterly
ILO	International Labour Organization
ILPr	International Litigation Procedure
IMB	International Maritime Bureau
IMCO	Intergovernmental Maritime Consultative Organization
IMDO	Irish Maritime Development Office
IMO	International Maritime Organization
IMP	Integrated Maritime Policy
Ir.Jur.(n.s.)	Irish Jurist (New Series)
IRLR	Industrial Relations Law Reports
ISM Code	International Management Code for the Safe Operation of Ships and for Pollution Prevention
ISPS Code	International Ship and Port Facility Code
ITF [ITWF]	International Transport Federation
ISO	International Organisation for Standardisation
JBL	Journal of Business Law
JCMS	Journal of Common Market Studies
JECL&P	Journal of European Competition Law & Practice
JIML	Journal of International Maritime Law
JMLC	Journal of Maritime Law and Commerce
JO	Journal Officiel
JWTL	Journal of World Trade Law
LDT	Light displacement tonnes
LMCLQ	Lloyd's Maritime and Commercial Law Quarterly
LNG	Liquefied natural gas
Lo-lo	Lift-on/lift-off
LQR	Law Quarterly Review
LRIT	Long-range identification and tracking
MARPOL	International Convention for the Prevention of Pollution by Ships
MCR	Merger Control Regulation (also abbreviated as "EUMR" or "ECMR")
MCV Services	Mobile Communication Services on Board Vessels

ABBREVIATIONS

MEIP	Market economy investor principle
MEP	Member of the European Parliament
MEPC	Marine Environment Protection Committee
MIF	Maritime Industries Forum
MLR	Modern Law Review
MOU	Memorandum of Understanding
MRV	Monitoring, reporting and verification
MSC	Maritime Safety Committee
MSCHOA	Maritime Security Centre – Horn of Africa
NACE	Nomenclature statistique des activités économiques dans la Communauté européenne
NAFTA	North American Free Trade Agreement
NATO	North Atlantic Treaty Organisation
NCAs	National competition authorities
NIEO	New International Economic Order
NIS	Norwegian International Ships Register
NLS	Noxious liquid substances
No	Number
NUMAST	UK Seafaring Officers' Union
OECD	Organisation for Economic Co-operation and Development
OEEC	Organisation for European Economic Cooperation
OJ	Official Journal of the European Union
OSPAR Convention	Convention for the Protection of the Marine Environment of the North-East Atlantic
Paris MoU	Paris Memorandum of Understanding on port State control
PM	Particulate matter
PSC	Port State control
PSO	Public Service Obligation
Reg.	Regulation
RFD	Reporting Formalities Directive
Ro-ro	Roll-on/roll-off
RPM	Resale price maintenance
SAM	State Aid Modernisation
SAR	Search and Rescue or International Convention on Maritime Search and Rescue
SEA	Single European Act
SGEIs	Services of general economic interest
SIEC	Significant impediment to effective competition
SIRP	Shipping Industry Rationalisation Plan (Korea)
SMS	Short message service
SOLAS	International Convention for the Safety of Life at Sea
SPC	Shortsea Promotion Centre
SSNIP	Significant and Non-transitory Increase in Price
STCW	International Convention on Standards of Training, Certification and Watchkeeping
TACA	Trans-Atlantic Conference Agreement

ABBREVIATIONS

TBT	Tributyltin
TEC	Treaty establishing the European Community
TEN-T	Trans-European Network – Transport
TERFN	Trans-European Rail Freight Network
TEU	Treaty on the European Union
teu	Twenty foot equivalent unit
TFEU	Treaty on the Functioning of the European Union
THETIS	The information system supporting the port State control inspection regime
TRAN	European Parliament Committee on Transport and Tourism
UK	United Kingdom
UKCLR	United Kingdom Competition Law Reports
UKIP	United Kingdom Independence Party
UKMTO	UK Maritime Trade Operations
UN	United Nations
UNCLOS	United Nations Convention on the Law of the Sea
UNCLOS III	Third United Nations Convention on the Law of the Sea
UNCTAD	United Nations Conference on Trade and Development
UNCTAD Code	UN Convention on a Code of Conduct for Liner Conferences
UNICE	Union des Industries de la Communauté européenne (now known as Business Europe)
UNODC	United Nations Office for Drugs and Crime
UNTS	United Nations Treaty Series
USA	United States of America
USSR	Union of Soviet Socialist Republics
VDR	Voyage data recorder
VOCs	Volatile organic compounds
VTS	Vessel traffic management services
WFP	World Food Programme
WSC	World Shipping Council
YEL	Yearbook of European Law

Terms

"Commission": Commission of the European Communities
"Council of Ministers": Council of Ministers of the European Union
"Economic and Social Committee": Economic and Social Committee of the European Union
"Member States": Member States of the European Union
"Parliament": European Parliament

TABLE OF CASES

Joined Cases C-3/58 to C-18/58, C-25/58, C-26/58 Barbara Erzberghau AG v High
    Authority [1960] ECR 173, ECLI:EU:C:1960:18 ....4.051
Joined Cases C-43/59 etc. Lachmuller v Commission [1960] ECR 463,
    ECLI:EU:C:1960:37 ....3.002
Joined Cases C-2/60 and C-3/60 Niederrheinische Bergwerks–AG et al. v High Authority
    [1961] ECR 133 at pp. 146–147, ECLI:EU:C:1961:15...3.043
Case C-13/61 Bosch v De Geus [1962] ECR 45, ECLI:EU:C:1962:11 ....3.109
Case C-26/62 Van Gend en Loos v Nederlandse Administratie der Belastingen [1963]
    ECR 1, ECLI:EU:C:1963:1 ....3.002, 3.115
Case C-6/64 Costa v ENEL [1964] ECR 585, ECLI:EU:C:1964:66.....................3.091, 3.115, 6.006
Joined Cases C-56/64 and C-58/64 Établissements Consten SARL and
    Grundig-Verkaufs-GmbH v Commission [1966] ECR 299,
    ECLI:EU:C:1966:41 ....10.079, 10.100, 10.106
Case C-48/65 Lütticke v Commission [1966] ECR 19 at 27, ECLI:EU:C:1966:8 ....3.077
Case C-56/65 Société Technique Minière v Maschinenbau Ulm [1966] ECR 235,
    ECLI:EU:C:1966:38 ....10.074, 10.084, 10.091, 10.100
Case C-23/67 Brasserie de Haecht v Wilkin [1967] ECR 407, ECLI:EU:C:1967:54................10.076
Case C-28/67 Molkerei-Zentrale Westfalen v Hauptzollamt Paderborn [1968] ECR 143,
    ECLI:EU:C:1968:17 ....3.115
Case C-7/68 Commission v Italy [1968] ECR 423, ECLI:EU:C:1968:51 ....3.077, 6.014
Case C-14/68 Walt Wilhelm and Others v Bundeskartellamt [1969] ECR 1 ....7.135
Case C-1/69 Italy v Commission [1969] ECR 277, ECLI:EU:C:1969:34 ....4.051, 4.052
Case C-5/69 Volk v Vervaecke [1969] ECR 295, ECLI:EU:C:1969:35.......................10.080, 10.087
Case C-7/69 Commission v Italy [1970] ECR 111 at 117, ECLI:EU:C:1970:15 ....3.077
Case C-31/69 Commission v Italy [1970] ECR 25 at 33, ECLI:EU:C:1970:10 ....3.077
Case C-41/69 ACF Chemiefarma NV v Commission [1970] ECR 661,
    ECLI:EU:C:1970:71 ....10.061
Joined Cases C-48/69, C-49/69, C-51/69 to C-57/69 ICI v Commission (Dyestuffs) [1972]
    ECR 619, ECLI:EU:C:1972:70 ....10.030, 10.070
Case C-9/70 Grad v Finanzamt Traunstein [1970] ECR 825, ECLI:EU:C:1970:78...................3.113,
    4.037, 4.051
Case C-20/70 Transports Lesage & CIE v Hauptzollamt Freiburg [1970] ECR 861,
    ECLI:EU:C:1970:84 ....4.051
Case C-22/70 Commission v Council [1971] ECR 263, ECLI:EU:C:1971:32 ....4.013, 4.014,
    4.030, 4.033, 4.035
Case C-78/70 Deutsche Grammophon v Metro [1971] ECR 487, ECLI:EU:C:1971:59 ....3.007
Case C-7/71 Commission v France [1971] ECR 1003, ECLI:EU:C:1971:121.................3.077, 3.091
Case C-15/71 Mackprang v Commission [1971] ECR 797 at 804, ECLI:EU:C:1971:98............3.081

TABLE OF CASES

Case C-22/71 Beguelin Import v GL Import-Export [1971] ECR 949,
ECLI:EU:C:1971:113 ....10.072, 10.090, 10.098
Case C-43/71 Politi [[1971] ECR 1039] 7.249
Case C-1/72 Frilli [1972] ECR 457, [ECLI:EU:C:1972:56] 8.213
Case C-6/72 Europemballage Corpn and Continental Can Co. Inc. v Commission [1973]
ECR 215, ECLI:EU:C:1973:22 ....10.120, 10.127, 10.133, 10.134, 10.136, 10.140, 10.157
Case C-8/72 Vereniging Cementhandelaren (VCH) v Commission [1972] ECR 677,
ECLI:EU:C:1972:84 ....10.069, 10.081
Joined Cases C-21/72 to C-24/72 International Fruit Company and Others v Produktschap
voor Groenten en Fruit [1972] ECR 1219 ....3.113, 7.129, 19.319
Case C-39/72 Commission v Italy [1973] ECR 101, ECLI:EU:C:1973:13 ....3.077, 9.074
Case C-81/72 Commission v Council [1973] ECR 575, ECLI:EU:C:1973:60 ....3.109
Case C-4/73 Nold v Commission [1974] ECR 491, ECLI:EU:C:1974:51 ....3.109
Joined Cases C-6/73, C-7/73 Instituto Chemioterapico Italiano SpA and Commercial
Solvents Corpn v Commission [1974] ECR 223, ECLI:EU:C:1974:18 ....10.085, 10.090,
10.120, 10.133, 10.136, 10.157, 10.159
Joined Cases C-37/73 and C-38/73 Diamantarbeiders v Indiamex [1973] ECR 1609,
ECLI:EU:C:1973:165 ....7.140
Cases C-40/73 etc. Suiker Unie v Commission (Sugar Cartel) [1975] ECR 1663,
ECLI:EU:C:1975:174 ....10.039, 10.070, 10.071, 10.095, 10.154, 10.157
Case C-127/73 Belgische Radio en Televisie (BRT) v SABAM [1974] ECR 51,
ECLI:EU:C:1974:25 ....10.019, 10.098
Case C-152/73 Sotgiu [1974] ECR 153, ECLI:EU:C:1974:13 ....8.209, 8.210, 8.225, 8.330
Case C-155/73 Italian State v Sacchi [1974] ECR 409, ECLI:EU:C:1974:40 ....10.032, 10.041
Case C-167/73 Commission v France (known as the French Merchant Seamen,
French Seafarers or the Code du Travail Maritime case) [1974] ECR 359,
ECLI:EU:C:1974:35 ....3.002, 3.022, 3.077, 3.115, 4.009, 4.013, 4.014, 4.040, 4.066,
4.068, 4.076, 5.003, 5.006, 5.016, 6.001, 7.064, 7.225, 7.228,
9.053, 9.056, 10.015, 11.008, 49.008, 49.011, 49.075
Case C-2/74 Reyner v Kingdom of Belgium [1974] ECR 631, ECLI:EU:C:1974:68 ....6.005
Case C-8/74 Procureur du Roî v Dassonville [1974] ECR 837, ECLI:EU:C:1974:82 ....3.115
Case C-15/74 Centrafarm v Sterling Drug [1974] ECR 1147 at 1167,
ECLI:EU:C:1974:114 ....10.046, 10.090
Case C-36/74 B N O Walrave & Another v Association Union Cycliste & Others [1974]
ECR 1405 (a workers and services case)..6.128, 6.133, 7.236
Case C-41/74 Van Duyn v Home Office [1974] ECR 1337, ECLI:EU:C:1974:133 ....3.115
Case C-71/74 FRUBO v Commission [1975] ECR 563..10.035
Case C-26/75 General Motors v Commission [1975] ECR 1367,
ECLI:EU:C:1975:150 ....10.123
Case C-36/75 Rutili v Commission [1974] ECR 491, ECLI:EU:C:1975:137..............................3.109
Case C-39/75 Coenen v Sociaal-Economische Raad [1975] ECR 1547,
ECLI:EU:C:1975:162 ....7.002
Case C-43/75 Defrenne [1976] ECR 455 ....3.115, 6.135, 7.237
Case C-48/75 Royer [1976] ECR 497, ECLI:EU:C:1976:57 ....6.005
Case C-51/75 EMI Records Ltd v CBS UK Ltd [1976] ECR 811 at 848–9,
ECLI:EU:C:1976:85 ....10.067
Case C-118/75 Watson and Belmann [1976] ECR 1185, ECLI:EU:C:1976:106 ....6.002
Case C-12/76 Industrie Tessili Italiana Como v Dunlop AG [1976] ECR-1473,
ECLI:EU:C:1976:133 ....47.017
Case C-13/76 Donà v Mantero [1976] ECR 1333, ECLI:EU:C:1976:115.............6.001, 6.133, 7.236

TABLE OF CASES

Case C-20/76 Schottle and Söhne OHG v Finanzamt Traunstein [1977] ECR 247,
 ECLI:EU:C:1977:26 ....4.037, 7.143
Case C-21/76 Handelskwekerij G. J. Bier BV v Mines de potasse d'Alsace SA [1976] ECR
 1735, ECLI identifier: ECLI:EU:C:1976:166..47.017
Case C-27/76 United Brands v Commission [1978] ECR 207, ECLI:EU:C:1978:22 ....10.120,
 10.126, 10.128, 10.133, 10.134, 10.135, 10.141, 10.142,
 10.143, 10.145, 10.147, 10.150, 10.153, 10.159
Case C-29/76 LTU Lufttransportunternehmen GmbH & Co. KG v Eurocontrol [1976] ECR
 1541, ECLI:EU:C:1976:137 ....47.009
Case C-46/76 Bauhuis [1977] ECR 5 ....7.143
Case C-50/76 Amsterdam Bulb [1977] ECR 137, ECLI:EU:C:1977:13 ....3.103, 3.113
Case C-71/76 Thieffry v Conseil de l'Ordre des Avocats à la Cour de Paris [1977] ECR 765,
 ECLI:EU:C:1977:65 ....6.001, 6.011, 6.148
Case C-74/76 Iannelli v Meroni [1977] ECR 557 ....7.143
Case C-85/76 Hoffmann-La Roche and Co AG v Commission [1979] ECR 461,
 ECLI:EU:C:1979:36 ....3.109, 10.022, 10.120, 10.126, 10.145, 10.151, 10.157
Case C-90/76 Van Ameyde v UCI [1977] ECR 1091, ECLL:EU:C:1977:101..........................10.028
Case C-114/76 Bela-Muhle v Grows Farm [1977] ECR 1211, ECLI:EU:C:1977:116................3.109
Case C-125/76 Cremer [1977] ECR 1593 ....7.244
Case C-11/77 Patrick v Ministre des Affaires Culturelles [1977] ECR 1199,
 ECLI:EU:C:1977:113 ....6.001, 6.005
Case C-19/77 Miller v Commission [1978] ECR 131 at 161, ECLI:EU:C:1978:19....................3.105
Case C-28/77 Tepea v Commission [1978] ECR 1391, ECLI:EU:C:1978:133 ....10.056, 10.057
Case C-58/77 Ireland v France (OJ 1977 C142/8)..3.078
Case C-61/77 Commission v Ireland [1978] ECR 417, ECLI:EU:C:1978:29 ....3.077
Case C-77/77 Benzine en Petroleum Handelsmaatschappij BV and others v Commission
 [1978] ECR 1513 ....10.154, 10.155, 10.156
Joined Cases C-103/77 and C-145/77 Royal Scholten Honig v Intervention Board [1978]
 ECR 2037 at 2072, ECLI:EU:C:1978:186..3.109
Case C-106/77 Simmenthal [1978] ECR 629, ECLI:EU:C:1978:49...3.120
Case C-156/77 Commission v Belgium [1978] ECR 1811, ECLI:EU:C:1978:180....................4.013,
 4.014, 4.040
Case C-16/78 Choquet [1978] ECR 2293, ECLI:EU:C:1978:210 ....6.001
Case C-22/78 Hugin Kassaregister AB v Commission [1979] ECR 1869 at 1899,
 ECLI:EU:C:1994:77 ....10.079, 10.136, 10.152
Case C-30/78 Distillers Company v Commission [1980] ECR 2229..10.064
Case C-83/78 Pigs Marketing Board v Redmond [1978] ECR 2347, ECLI:EU:C:1978:214.......3.116
Case C-97/78 Schumalla [1978] ECR 2311, ECLI:EU:C:1978:211 ....4.033, 4.061, 19.326
Joined Cases C-110/78 and C-111/78 Ministere Public and Chambre syndicale des agents
 artistique et impresario de Belgique v Van Wesemael and Follachio [1979] ECR 35,
 ECLI:EU:C:1979:8 ....6.001, 7.002
Case C-122/78 Buitoni v FORMA [1979] ECR 677 at 684, ECLI:EU:C:1979:43 ....3.109
Case C-159/78, Case C-36/74 Walrave and Koch v Association Union Cycliste
 Internationale et al. [1974] ECR 1405, ECLI:EU:C:1974:140..6.005
Cases C-209/78 etc. Van Landewyck v Commission [1980] ECR 3125,
 ECLI:EU:C:1980:248 ....3.109, 10.027, 10.055, 10.056, 10.057
Case C-258/78 Nungesser KG v Commission [1982] ECR 2015 ....10.031, 10.033, 10.037, 10.091
Case C-22/79 Greenwich Film Production v SACEM [1979] ECR 3275,
 ECLI:EU:C:1979:245 ....10.085
Case C-68/79 Just [1980] ECR 501 ....7.143

TABLE OF CASES

Case C-136/79 National Panasonic (UK) Ltd v Commission [1980] ECR 2033,
    ECLI:EU:C:1980:169 ....3.109, 3.116
Case C-149/79 Commission v Belgium [1980] ECR 3881, ECL1:EU:C:1982:195 ....8.210, 8.225
Case C-155/79 AM & S Europe v Commission [1982] ECR 1575, ECLI:EU:C:1982:157 ....3.116
Case C-730/79 Philip Morris [1980] ECR 2671, ECLI:EU:C:1980:209 ....22.103
Case C-812/79 Attorney General v Burgoa [1980] ECR 2787..7.303
Case C-814/79 Rüffer [1980] ECR 3807, ECLl:EU:C:1980:291..47.009
Case C-27/80 Fietje [1980] ECR 3389 at 3853, ECLI:EU:C:1980:293......................................3.061
Case C-31/80 L'Oreal NV v De Nieuwe AMCK PVBA [1980] ECR 3775;
    ECLI:EU:C:1980:289 ....10.126
Case C-61/80 Co-operative Stremsel- en Kleurselfabriek v Commission [1981] ECR 851,
    ECLI:EU:C:1981:75 ....10.034
Cases C-100/80 to C-103/80 Musique Diffusion Francaise v Commission [1983] ECR 1825,
    ECLI:EU:C:1983:158 ....10.046
Case C-122/80 Analog Devices [1981] ECR 2781, ECLI:EU:C:1981:273 ....3.116
Joined Cases C-142/80 and C-143/80 Amministrazione delle Finanze dello Stato v Essevi
    SpA et al. [1981] ECR 1413 at 1432–1433, ECLI:EU:C:1981:121 ....3.077
Case C-150/80 Elefanten Schuh GmbH v Pierre Jacqmain [1981] ECR-1671,
    ECLI:EU:C:1981:148 ....47.038
Case C-155/80 Oebel [1981] ECR 1993...7.135
Case C-158/80 Rewe v Hauptzollamt Kiel [1981] ECR 1805,
    ECLI:EU:C:1981:163 ....3.115, 3.120
Case C-169/80 Gondrand Freres [1981] ECR 1219 at 1232, ECLI:EU:C:1981:171 ....3.109
Case C-203/80 Casati [1981] ECR 2595 ....19.326
Joined Cases C-62/81 and C-63/81 Seco v EVI [1982] ECR 223..7.197
Case C-211/81 Commission v Denmark [1982] ECR 4547 at 4557,
    ECLI:EU:C:1982:437 ....3.077
Case C-283/81 CILFIT v Ministry of Health [1982] ECR 3415, ECLI:EU:C:1982:335............3.083
Case C-319/81 Commission v Italy [1983] ECR 601..7.143
Case C-322/81 Nederlandsche Banden-Industrie Michelin NV v Commission [1983] ECR
    3461, ECLI:EU:C:1983:313 ....10.120, 10.126, 10.133, 10.136, 10.150
Case C-7/82 GVL v Commission [1983] ECR 483, ECLI:EU:C:1983:52 ....10.085
Case C-96/82 etc. IAZ International Belgium NV v Commission [1983] ECR 3369,
    ECLI:EU:C:1983:310 ....10.035, 10.069, 10.075
Case C-107/82 AEG Telefunken v Commission [1983] ECR 3151, ECLI:EU:C:1983:293 ....10.046,
    10.068, 10.090
Case C-126/82 DJ Smit Transport BV v Commissie Grensoverschrijdend Beroepsvervoer
    [1983] ECR 73, ECLI:EU:C:1983:14...4.014
Joined Cases C-286/82 and C-26/83 Luisi and Carbone v Ministero del Tesoro [1984] ECR
    377, ECLI:EU:C:1984:35 ....3.116, 3.117, 7.294
Case C-292/82 Merck v Hauptzollamt Hamburg-Jonas [1983] ECR 3781,
    ECLI:EU:C:1983:335 ....3.116
Case C-319/82 Société de Vente de Ciments v Kerpen [1983] ECR 4173,
    ECLI:EU:C:1983:374 ....10.100
Case C-13/83 Parliament v Council of Ministers [1985] ECR 1513,
    ECLI:EU:C:1985:220 ....3.081, 4.006, 4.013, 4.014, 4.015, 4.033, 4.069, 4.076, 7.158
Case C-14/83 von Colson v Land Nordheim-Westfalen [1984] ECR 189,
    ECLI:EU:C:1984:153 ....3.116
Case C-18/83 Corsica Ferries Italia Srl v Corporazione del piloti del Porto di Genova [1994]
    ECR I-1783, ECLI:EU:C:1998:306..7.157

TABLE OF CASES

Joined Cases C-29/83 and C-30/83 Compagnie Royale Asturienne des Mines SA and
  Rheinzink GmbH v Commission [1984] ECR 1679, ECLI:EU:C:1971:113 .... 10.049,
  10.070, 10.071, 10.075, 10.085
Case C-35/83 BAT v Commission [1985] ECR 363, ECLI:EU:C:1985:32 .... 10.037
Case C-41/83 Italy v Commission [1985] ECR 873 .... 10.032, 10.123, 10.141, 10.144
Case C-51/83 Commission v Italy [1984] ECR 2793 at 2804, ECLI:EU:C:1984:261 .... 3.077
Case C-71/83 Partenreederei ms. Tilly Russ and Ernest Russ v NV Haven- & Vervoerbedrijf
  Nova and NV Goeminne Hout [1984] ECR-2417, ECLI:EU:C:1984:217 .... 47.036
Case C-107/83 Ordre des Avocats au Barreau de Paris v Klopp [1984] ECR 2971,
  ECLI:EU:C:1984:270 .... 6.001
Case C-123/83 BNIC v Clair [1985] ECR 391, ECLI:EU:C:1985:33 .... 10.033
Case C-170/83 Hydrotherm v Compact [1984] ECR 2999 .... 10.030
Case C-193/83 Windsurfing International Inc v Commission [1986] ECR 611,
  ECLI:EU:C:1986:75 .... 10.082
Case C-231/83 Cullet v Leclerc [1986] ECR 529, ECLI:EU:C:1985:29 .... 3.007
Case C-254/83 Commission v Italy [1984] ECR 3395, ECLI:EU:C:1984:302 .... 3.077
Case C-270/83 Commission v France [1986] ECR 273, ECLI:EU:C:1986:37 .... 6.001, 6.005
Case C-2/84 Commission v Italy [1985] ECR 1127, ECLI:EU:C:1985:151 .... 4.052
Case C-42/84 Remia BV and Verenigde Bedrijven Nutricia NV v Commission [1985] ECR
  2545; ECLI:EU:C:1985:327 .... 10.037, 10.091
Case C-44/84 Hurd v Jones (Her Majesty's Inspector of Taxes) [1986] ECR 29 .... 7.133
Case C-106/84 Commission v Denmark [1986] ECR 833 .... 7.143
Case C-152/84 Marshall v Southampton Area Health Authority [1986] ECR 723,
  ECLI:EU:C:1986:84 .... 3.113
Case C-161/84 Pronuptia v Schillgalis [1986] ECR 353, ECLI:EU:C:1986:41 .... 10.091
Case C-197/84 Steinhausser v City of Biarritz [1985] ECR 1819, ECLI:EU:C:1985:260 .... 6.001
Joined Cases C-209/84 to C-213/84 Ministere Public v Asjes (the "Nouvelles Frontières")
  [1986] ECR 1425, ECLI:EU:C:1986:188 .... 4.013, 7.123, 7.131, 7.158, 10.015
Case C-222/84 Johnston v Chief Constable of the RUC [1986] ECR 1651 at para. 53,
  ECLI:EU:C:1986:206 .... 3.116
Case C-226/84 [1986] ECR 3263, ECLI:EU:C:1986:421 .... 10.138
Case C-311/84 Centre Belge d'Etudes de Marche Tele-Marketing v CLT [1985] ECR 3261,
  ECLI:EU:C:1985:394 .... 10.123, 10.144, 13.090
Case C-66/85 Lawrie-Blum [1986] EU:C:1986:284 .... 8.330
Joined Cases C-89/85, C-104/85, C-114/85, C-116/85, C-117/85 and C-125/85 to C-129/85
  Ahlström Osakeyhtiö and others v Commission [1988] ECR 5193 .... 10.016
Joined Cases C-98/85, C-162/85 and C-258/85 Bertini [1986] ECR 1893,
  ECLI:EU:C:1986:246 .... 3.083
Case C-118/85 Commission v Italy [1987] ECR 2599, ECLI:EU:C:1987:283 .... 13.021
Case C-131/85 Gül [1986] ECR 1573, ECLI:EU:C:1986:200 .... 8.210, 8.225
Case C-168/85 Commission v Italy [1986] ECR 2945 .... 7.282
Case C-196/85 Commission v France [1987] ECR 1597 .... 7.143
Case C-221/85 Commission v Belgium [1987] ECR 719, ECLI:EU:C:1987:81 .... 6.004
Case C-225/85 Commission v Italy [1987] ECR 2625, ECLI:EU:C:1987:284 .... 8.210
Case C-272/85 Association nationale des travailleurs independants de la batellerie (Antib) v
  Commission [1987] ECR 2201, ECLI:EU:C:1987:235 .... 10.076
Case C-305/85 United Kingdom v Commission [1988] ECR 467,
  ECLI:EU:C:1988:41 .... 3.116, 3.117
Case C-60/86 Commission v United Kingdom [1988] ECR 3921, ECLI:EU:C:1988:382 .... 3.115
Case C-63/86 Commission v Italy [1988] ECR 29, ECLI:EU:C:1988:9 .... 6.005, 7.002

TABLE OF CASES

Case C-66/86 Ahmed Saeed Flugreisen v Zentrale zur Bekämpfung Unlauteren Wettbewerbs eV [1989] ECR 803, ECLI:EU:C:1989:140 ....4.014, 10.134, 11.085
Case C-74/86 Commission v Germany [1988] ECR 2139 ....7.282
Case C-80/86 Kolpinghuis Nijimegen [1987] ECR 3969, ECLI:EU:C:1987:431 ....3.113
Case C-102/86 Apple and Pear Development Council v Customs and Excise [1988] ECR 1443, ECLI:EU:C:1988:120 ....3.116
Case C-127/86 Ministère Public v Ledoux [1988] ECR 3741, ECLI:EU:C:1988:366 ....7.122
Case C-144/86 Gubisch v Guilio Palumbo [1987] ECR 4861, ECLI: EU: C: 1987: 528 ....47.044
Case C-147/86 Commission v Greece [1988] ECR 1637, ECLI:EU:C:1989:611 ....6.005
Case C-198/86 Conradi et al. v Direction de la Concurrence et des Prix des Hauts de la Seine et al. [1987] ECR 4469, ECLI:EU:C:1987:489 ....6.005
Case C-246/86 Belasco v Commission; Polypropylene [1989] ECR 2117, ECLI:EU:C:1989:301 ....10.057
Case C-263/86 Humbel and Edel [1988] ECR 5365 ....7.294
Case C-267/86 Van Eycke v ASPA [1988] ECR 4769 ....7.131
Case C-292/86 Gullung v Conseil de l'Ordre des Avocats au Barreau de Colmar et al. [1988] ECR 111, ECLI:EU:C:1988:15 ....6.001
Case C-20/87 Ministère Public v Gauchard [1987] ECR 4879, ECLI:EU:C:1987:532 ....6.005
Case C-21/87 Borowitz v Bundesversicherungsanstalt für Angestellte [1988] ECR 3715, ECLI:EU:C:1988:362 ....3.115
Case C-27/87 Erauw-Jacquery v La Hesbignonne, [1988] ECR 1919, ECLI:EU:C:1988:183 ....10.091
Case C-30/87 Corrine Bodson v Pompes Funèbres des Regions Libérées SA [1988] ECR 2479, ECLI:EU:C:1988:225 ....10.033, 10.043, 10.044
Case C-81/87 R v HM Treasury and Commissioners of Inland Revenue, ex parte Daily Mail and General Trust PLC [1988] ECR 5483, ECLI:EU:C:1988:456................6.005, 6.008, 6.138, 6.148, 7.134, 7.238, 8.243
Case C-169/87 Commission v France [1974] ECR 359, ECLI:EU:C:1988:393 ....3.113
Case C-186/87 Cowan [1989] ECR 195 [ECLI:EU:C:1989:47] 8.213
Case C-189/87 Athanasios Kalfelis v Bankhaus Schröder, Münchmeyer, Hengst and Co and others [1988] ECR-5565, ECLI:EU:C:1988:459 ....47.018
Case C-196/87 Steymann v Staatssecretaris van Justitie [1988] ECR 6159, ECLI:EU:C:1988:475 ....6.002
Case C-204/87 Bekaert v Procureur de la République de Rennes [1988] ECR 2029, ECLI:EU:C:1988:192 ....6.005
Joined Cases C-266/87 and C-267/87 R. v Royal Pharmaceutical Society of Great Britain ex parte Secretary of State for Social Services [1989] ECR 1295, ECLI:EU:C:1989:205 ....3.115
Case C-302/87 European Parliament v Council [1988] ECR 5615, ECLI:EU:C:1988:461..........4.025
Case C-344/87 Bettray [1989] EU:C:1989:226 ....8.330
Case C-355/87 Commission v Council (Italo-Algerian Maritime Transport) [1989] ECR 1517, ECLI:EU:C:1989:220 ....7.145, 7.151
Case C-360/87 Commission v Italy [1991] ECR I-791, ECLI:EU:C:1991:86..............................8.290
Case C-4/88 Lambregts Transportbedrijf v Belgian State [1989] ECR 2583, ECLI:EU:C:C:1989:320, at paras 8 and 9 ....7.123
Case C-9/88 Da Veiga v Staatssecretaris van Justitie [1989] ECR 2989, ECLI:EU:C:1989:346 ....4.009
Case C-18/88 GB-Inno-BM [1991] ECR I-5941, ECLI:EU:C:1991:474 ....13.075, 13.090
Case C-39/88 Re Fishery Price Information: Commission v Ireland [1990] ECR I-4271, ECLI:EU:C:1990:420 ....3.077
Case C-69/88 Krantz v Ontranger der Directe Belastingen [1990] ECR I-583............................7.132

Case C-131/88 Commission v Germany [1991] ECR I-825, ECLI:EU:C:1991:87 .... 8.290
Case C-49/89 Corsica Ferries France v Direction Générale des Douanes Françaises [1989]
    ECR 4441, ECLI:EU:1989:649 .... 7.001, 7.014, 7.018, 7.039, 7.118,
                                                                        7.119, 7.120, 7.143, 7.158, 7.269
Case T-51/89 Tetra Pak Rausing SA v Commission [1990] ECR II-309,
    ECLI:EU:1:1990:41 .... 10.012
Case C-93/89 Commission v Ireland [1991] ECR I-4569, ECLI:EU:C:1991:374 .... 6.098
Case C-152/89 Commission v Luxembourg [1991] ECR I-3141 .... 7.143
Case C-154/89 Commission v France [1991] ECR I-659 .... 7.135, 7.162
Case C-190/89 Marc Rich & Co. AG v Società Italiana Impianti PA [1991] ECR I-3855,
    ECLI:EU:C:1991:319 .... 47.009
Case C-209/89 Commission v Italy [1991] ECR I-1575 .... 7.143
Case C-213/89 R. v Secretary of State for Transport, ex parte Factortame (No. 2) [1990]
    ECR I-02433, ECLI:EU:C:1990:257, [1991] AC 603, [1990] 3 WLR 818, [1991]
    1 All ER 70 .... 49.012
Case C-221/89 R v Secretary of State for Transport ex parte Factortame Limited and Others
    (No. 2) [1991] 3 CMLR 589 .... 6.009, 6.098, 6.102, 6.105, 6.109, 6.110,
                                                                        6.113, 6.138, 6.148, 7.134, 7.238, 8.243
Case C-246/89 Commission v United Kingdom [1991] ECR I-4585, ECLI:EU:C:1991:375 ..... 6.098
Case C-260/89 Elliniki Radiophonia v DRP [1991] ECR I-2925, ECLI:EU:C:1991:254 .... 7.159,
                                                                                            7.174, 13.049, 13.075
Case C-288/89 Collectieve Antennevoorziening Gouda [1991] ECR I-4007 .... 7.162
Case C-300/89 Commission v Council (Titanium dioxide) [1991] ECR I-28670 .... 19.326
Case C-351/89 Overseas Union Insurance Ltd and Deutsche Ruck UK Reinsurance Ltd and
    Pine Top Insurance Company Ltd v New Hampshire Insurance Company [1991] ECR
    I-3317, ECLI:EU:C:1991:279 .... 47.013
Case C-353/89 Commission v Netherlands [1991] ECR I-4069 .... 7.294
Case C-6/90 Francovich [1991] ECR 537, ECLI:EU:C:1991:428 .... 6.117
Case C-41/90 Höfner and Elser v Macnotron GmbH [1991] ECR I-1979, [1993] 4 CMLR
    306, ECLI:EU:C:1991:161 .... 7.159, 7.174, 10.027, 49.063
Case C-76/90 Säger [1991] ECR I-4221 .... 7.176, 7.185
Joined Cases C-78/90 to C-83/90 Compagnie Commerciale de l' Ouest and Others v
    Receveur Principal des Douanes de La Pallice Port [1992] ECR I-1847 .... 7.158
Case C-179/90 Merci Convenzionali Porto di Genova v Siderurgica Gabrielli [1991] ECR
    I-5889, ECLI:EU:C:1991:464 .... 7.130, 7.158, 7.159, 7.174, 10.030, 10.033, 10.205,
                                                                                            13.032, 13.078, 13.090
Case C-208/90 Emmott [1991] ECR I-4269, ECLI:EU:C:1991:333 .... 7.140
Cases C-271/90, C-281/90 and C-289/90 .... 13.090
Case C-286/90 Poulsen and Diva Navigation [1992] ECR I-6019 .... 19.319
Case C-332/90 Steen v Deutsche Bundespost [1992] ECR I-341 .... 7.133
Case C-2/91 Meng [1993] ECR I-5751 .... 7.131
Joined Cases C-72/91 and C-73/91 Sloman Neptun Schiffahrts AG v Seebetriebsrat Bodo
    Ziesemer der Sloman Neptun Schiffahrts AG [1993] ECR I-887, ECLI:EU:C:1993:97 ..... 6.094
Case C-106/91 Ramrath [1992] ECR I-3351, paragraphs 29 and 30 .... 6.148
Case C-156/91 Hansa Fleisch Ernst Mundt [1992] ECR I-5567 .... 7.249
Case C-158/91 Levy [1993] ECR I-4287 .... 7.303
Case C-185/91 Bundesanstalt fuer den Gueterfernverkehr v Gebr. Reiff [1993]
    ECR I-5801 .... 7.131, 7.173
Case C-266/91 CELBI [1993] ECR I-4337, ECLI:EU:C:1993:334 .... 7.143
Case C-8/92 General Milk Products [1993] ECR I-779 .... 7.244

Case T-9/92 Peugeot v Commission [1993] ECR II-493, ECLI:EU:T:1993:38 ....11.025
Case C-19/92 Dieter Kraus v Land Baden-Württemberg [1993] ECR I-1663 ....6.128, 6.148, 7.185
Case C-72/92 Scharbatke [1993] ECR I-5509..7.143
Case C-93/92 CMC Motorradcenter v Pelin Baskiciogullari [1993] ECR I-5009 ....7.132
Case C-109/92 Wirth [1993] ECR I-6447 ....7.294
Case C-130/92 OTO [1994] ECR I-3281 ....7.143
Case C-364/92 SAT Fluggesellschaft v Eurocontrol [1994] ECR I-43, ECLI:EU:C:1994:7 ....13.021
Case C-379/92 Matteo Peralta [1994] ECR I-3453, ECLI:EU:C:1994:296....................7.024, 7.124,
 7.162, 7.172, 19.319
Case C-405/92 Mondiet [1993] ECR I-6133 ....19.319
Case C-406/92 Owners of the cargo lately laden on board the ship "Tatry" v Owners of the
 ship "Maciej Rataj" [1994] ECR I-05439, ECLI:EU:C:1994:400, [1995] 1 Lloyd's Rep
 302..47.005, 47.044
Case C-431/92 Commission v Germany [1995] ECR I-2189 ....7.303
Case C-18/93 Corsica Ferries v Corpo dei Piloti del Porto di Genova [1994] ECR I-1783,
 ECLI:EU:C:1994:195 ....7.135, 7.162, 7.269, 13.088, 19.326
Joined Cases T-24/93 to T-26/93 and T-28/93 CMB, CMBT and Dafra-Lines v Commission
 [1996] ECR II-1201 ....5.127
Case C-43/93 Vander Elst [1994] ECR I-3803...7.185
Case C-48/93 Factortame III, ECLI:EU:C:1996:79 ....6.117
Case C-153/93 Delta Schiffahrts- und Speditionsgesellschaft [1994] ECR I-2517 ....7.173
Case C-279/93 Schumacker [1995] ECR I-225..7.294
Case C-312/93 Peterbroeck, Van Campenhout & Cie v Belgian State [1995] ECR I-4599,
 ECLI:EU:C:1995:437 ....10.173
Case C-323/93 Centre d'Insémination de la Crespelle [1994] ECR I-5077..................................7.174
Joined Cases C-358/93 and C-416/93 Bordessa and Others [1995] ECR I-361.........................7.185
Case C-381/93 Commission v France [1994] ECR I-5145, ECLI:EU:C:1994:370 ....5.114,
 7.019, 7.027, 7.160, 7.189, 7.192, 7.197, 7.269
Case C-415/93 Union Royale Belge des Société de Football ASBL and Others v Jean-Marc
 Bosman and Others [1995] ECR I-4921 ....6.128, 6.131, 6.133, 6.138, 7.198, 7.236
Case C-434/93 Bozkurt [1995] ECR I-1475...8.250
Case C-479/93 Francovich [1995] ECR I-3843..7.197
Case C-45/94 Cámara de Comercio, Industria y Navegación, Ceuta [1995] ECR I-4385,
 ECLI:EU:C:1995:425 ....7.143
Case C-55/94 Gebhard [1995] ECR I-4165...6.138, 7.185, 7.238
Case C-61/94 Commission v Germany [1996] ECR I-3989 ....19.319
Case C-90/94 Haahr Petroleum Ltd v Åbenrå Havn and others [1997] ECR I-4085,
 ECLI:EU:C:1997:368 ....7.138
Case C-96/94 Centro Servizi Spediporto [1995] ECR I-2883 ....7.172
Case C-157/94 Commission v Netherlands [1997] ECR I-5699 ....7.174
Case C-159/94 Commission v France [1997] ECR I-5815 ....7.205
Joined Cases C-163/94, C-165/94 and C-250/94 Sanz de Lera [1995] ECR I-4821....................7.185
Case C-272/94 Guiot [1996] ECR I-1905 ....7.185
Case C-290/94 Commission v Greece [1996] ECR I-3285, ECLI:EU:C:1996:265..........8.210, 8.330
Joined Cases T-305/94 etc/94 NV Limburgse Vinyl Maatschappij v Commission [1999]
 ECR II-931, ECLI:EU:C:1999:80 ....10.073
Case C-334/94 Commission v France (French Seamen's Case) [1996] ECR I-01307,
 ECLI:EU:C:1996:90 ....3.022, 4.017, 4.069, 6.098
Case T-374/94 European Night Services Ltd v Commission [1998] ECR II-3141,
 ECLI:EU:C:1998:198 ....10.089

Case C-96/95 Commission v Germany [1997] ECR I-1653 .... 7.303
Case C-120/95 Decker [1998] ECR I-1831 .... 6.133, 7.236
Case C-242/95 GT-Link A/S v De Danske Statsbanier [1997] ECR I-4349,
    ECLI:EU:C:1997:376 .... 10.205, 10.224
Case C-265/95 Commission v France [1997] ECR I-6959 .... 6.135, 7.237
Case C-282/95P Guerin Automobiles v Commission [1997] ECR I-1503,
    ECLI:EU:C/1997:159 .... 10.019
Case C-339/95 SUNAG (no judgment) 10.004
Case C-343/95 Diego Calí & Figli Srl v Servizi ecologici porto di Genova SpA [1997] ECR
    I-1547, ECLI:EU:C:1997:160 .... 13.021
Case C-391/95 Van Uden Maritime BV, trading as Van Uden Africa Line v
    Kommanditgesellschaft in Firma Deco-Line [1998] ECR I-7091,
    ECLI:EU:C:1998:543 .... 47.009
Case C-398/95 SETTG [1997] ECR I-3091 .... 7.176
Case C-15/96 Schöning-Kougebetopoulou [1998] ECR I-47, ECLI:EU:C:1998:3 .... 6.133,
    7.236, 8.240
Case T-24/96 Compagnie maritime belge de transports [1996] ECR II-01201,
    ECLI:EU:T:1996:139 .... 11.025
Joined Cases C-51/96 and C-191/97 Deliège [2000] ECR I-2549 .... 6.133, 7.236
Case C-62/96 [1997] ECR I-6725, ECLI:EU:C:1997:565 .... 6.096
Case C-67/96 Albany [1999] ECR I-5751, ECLI, EU:C:1999:430 .... 6.129, 7.236, 8.237, 8.240
Case C-108/96 Mac Quen and Others [2001] ECR I-837 .... 7.197
Case C-129/96 Inter-Environnement Wallonie [1997] ECR I-7411 .... 7.249
Case C-151/96 Commission v Ireland [1997] ECR I-3327, ECLI:EU:C:1997:294 .... 6.098
Case C-158/96 Kohll [1998] ECR I-1931 .... 6.133, 7.236
Case C-162/96 Racke [1998] ECR I-3655 .... 19.319
Case C-163/96 Raso and Others [1998] ECR I-0000 .... 7.174
Case C-170/96 Commission v Council [1998] ECR I-2763 .... 19.326
Case C-266/96 Corsica Ferries France v Gruppo Antichi Ormeggiatori del Porto di Genova
    Coop. arl, Gruppo Ormeggiatori del Golfo di La Spezia Coop. arl and Ministero dei
    Trasporti e della Navigazione [1998] ECR I-3949, ECLI:EU:C:1998:306 .... 7.166, 7.185,
    7.197, 7.276
Case C-367/96 Kefalas and Others [1998] ECR I-2843 .... 7.244
Joined Cases C-369/96 and C-376/96 Arblade and Others [1999] ECR I-8453 .... 6.138, 7.185,
    7.197, 7.238
Joined Cases C-395/96P and C-396/96P Compagnie Maritime Belge v Commission [2000]
    ECR I-1365, [2000] 4 CMLR 1076 .... 5.127, 9.011, 10.129, 10.186
Case C-7/97 Oscar Bronner GmbH & Co. KG v Mediaprint Zeitungs-und Zeitschriftenverlag
    GmbH & Co. KG, Mediaprint Zeitungsvertriebsgesellschaft mbH & Co. KG and
    Mediaprint Anzeigengesellschaft mbH & Co KG [1998]
    ECR I-7791 .... 10.160, 13.080
Case C-35/97 Commission v France [1998] ECR I-5325, ECLI:EU:C:1998:431 .... 6.133,
    7.236, 8.240
Case C-114/97 Commission v Spain [1998] ECR I-6717, ECLI:EU:C:1998:519 .... 8.209, 8.210
Case C-126/97 Eco-Swiss China Time Ltd v Benetton International NV [1999] ECR I-3055,
    ECLI:EU:C:1999:269 .... 10.115
Joined Cases C-176/97 and C-177/97 Commission v Belgium and Luxembourg 7.304
Case C-212/97 Centros [1999] ECR I-1459, paragraph 18 .... 6.148
Case C-224/97 Ciola [1999] ECR I-2517 .... 7.197
Case C-226/97 Lemmens [1998] ECR I-3711 .... 19.326

TABLE OF CASES

Case C-336/97 Commission v Italy [1999] ECR I-3771, ECLI:EU:C:1999:272..........................8.290
Case C-346/97 Braathens [1999] ECR I-3419..39.046
Case C-373/97 Diamantis [2000] ECR I-1705 ....7.244
Joined Cases C-15/98 and C-105/99 Italy and Sardegna Lines v Commission [2000] ECR
    I-8855, ECLI:EU:C:2000:570..7.206
Case C-22/98 Jean Claude Becu, Annie Verweire, NV Smeg and NV Adia Interim [1999]
    ECR I-05665, ECLI:EU:C:1999:419..13.022
Joined Cases C-49/98, C-50/98, C-52/98 to C-54/98 and C-68/98 to C-71/98 Finalarte and
    Others [2001] ECR I-7831...6.138, 7.238
Case C-62/98 Commission v Portugal [2000] ECR I-5171, ECLI:EU:C:2000:358 ....7.302
Case C-84/98 Commission v Portugal [2000] ECR I-5215, ECLI:EU:C:2000:359 ....7.303
Case T-127/98 UPS Europe v Commission [1999] ECR II-2633 ....13.080
Case C-156/98 Germany v Commission [2000] ECR I-6857 ....7.197, 7.295
Case C-165/98 Mazzoleni and ISA [2001] ECR I-2189 ....6.138, 7.238
Case C-170/98 Commission v Belgium [1999] ECR I-5493, ECLI:EU:C:1999:411 ....7.297, 7.303
Joined Cases C-171/98, C-201/98 and C-202/98 Commission v Belgium and Luxembourg
    [1999] ECR I-05517, ECLI:EU:C:1999:412 ....7.301
Joined Cases C-180/98 to C-184/98 Pavlov and Others [2000] ECR I-6451,
    ECLI:EU:C:2000:428 ....6.129, 7.236, 8.237
Case C-222/98 Van der Woude [2000] ECR I-7111, ECLI:EU:C:475 ....6.129, 7.236, 8.237
Case C-281/98 Roman Angonese v Cassa di Risparmio di Bolzano SpA [2000] ECR I-4139
    paragraphs 1–2, 5–10 and 28–36 ....6.128, 6.133, 7.236
Case C-355/98 Commission v Belgium [2000] ECR I-1221..7.185
Case C-390/98 Banks [2001] ECR I-6117..7.198
Case C-412/98 Group Josi Reinsurance Company SA v Universal General Insurance
    Company (UGIC) [2000] ECR I-5925, ECLI:EU:C:2000:399 ....47.013
Case C-36/99 Idéal tourisme [2000] ECR I-6049..7.198
Case T-56/99 Marlines v Commission [2003] ECR I-5225, ECLI:EU:T:2003:333 .....10.095, 10.217
Case T-59/99 Ventouris v Commission [2003] ECR II-5257 [ECLI:EU:T:2003:334]..............10.017
Case C-70/99 Commission v Portugal [2001] ECR I-4845, ECLI:EU:C:2001:355 ....7.027, 7.192
Case C-71/99 Commission v Germany [2001] ECR I-5811, ECLI:EU:C:2001:433 ....8.290
Case C-143/99 Adria-Wien Pipeline and Wietersdorfer & Peggauer Zementwerke [2001]
    ECR I-8365 ....7.295
Case C-160/99 Commission v France ECR I-6155, ECLI:EU:C:2000:411..............................7.278
Case C-163/99 Portugal v Commission [2001] ECR I-2613, ECLI:EU:C:2001:189 ....8.213
Case C-205/99 Asociación Profesional de Empresas Navieras de Líneas Regulares (Analir)
    and Others and Administración General del Estado [2001] ECR I-1271,
    ECLI:EU:C:2001:107 ....7.158, 7.197, 7.205, 7.210, 7.211, 7.225, 7.228, 7.244, 7.275,
    7.276, 7.277, 7.286
Case C-283/99 Commission v Italy [2001] ECR I-4363, ECLI:EU:C:2001:307..............8.209, 8.210
Case C-309/99 Wouters v Algemene Raad van de Nederlandse Orde van Advocaten [2002]
    ECR II-2823 ....6.128, 6.133, 7.236
Case T-342/99 Airtours v Commission [2002] ECR II-2585, ECLI:EU:T:2004:192................10.130
Joined Cases C-430/99 and C-431/99 Inspecteur van de Belastingdienst Douane, district
    Rotterdam v Sea-Land Service Inc. and Nedlloyd Lijnen BV [2002] ECR I-523,
    ECLI:EU:C:2002:364 ....7.027, 7.039, 7.193, 7.269
Case C-453/99 Courage Ltd v Crehan [2001] ECR I-6297, ECLI:EU:C:2001:465......10.168, 10.193
Case C-478/99 Commission v Sweden [2002] ECR I-4147, ECLI:EU:C:2002:281 ....8.290
Case C-49/00 Commission v Italy [2001] ECR I-8575, ECLI:EU:C:2001:611..........................8.290
Case T-52/00 Clerici Logistics SpA v Commission [2003] ECLI:EU:T:2003:168 ....13.077

TABLE OF CASES

Case C-97/00 Commission v France [2001] ECR I-2053, ECLI:EU:C:2001:149 ....8.291
Case C-110/00 Commission v Austria [2001] ECR I-7545, ECLI:EU:C:2001:538 ....8.291
Case C-112/00 Schmidberger [2003] ECR I-5659 ....6.133, 6.138, 7.236
Case C-147/00 Commission v France [2001] ECR I-2387 ....7.189
Case C-208/00 Überseering [2002] ECR I-9919, paragraph 56 ....6.148
Case C-280/00 Altmark Trans GmbH v Nahverkehrs–gesellschajt [2003] ECR I-7747,
 ECLI:EU:C:2003:415 ....10.204
Case C-295/00 Commission v Italy [2002] ECR I-1737, ECLI:EU:C:2002:100..............7.189, 7.269
Case C-336/00 Huber [2002] ECR I-76990..19.326
Case C-355/00 Freskot [2003] ECR I-5263..7.294
Case C-435/00 Geha Naftiliaki EPE and Others v NPDD Limeniko Tameio DOD/SOU and
 Elliniko Dimosio [2002] ECR I-10615, ECLI:EU:C:2002:661 ....7.027, 7.191, 7.269
Case T-18/01 Goldstein v Commission [2002], not published in the ECR 13.080
Case C-142/01 Commission v Italy [2002] ECR I-4541, ECLI:EU:C:2002:302...........................8.213
Case C-198/01 Consorzio Industries Fiammiferi (CIF) v AutoritàGarante della Concorrenza
 e del Mercato [2003] ECR I-8055 ....10.172
Case C-240/01 Commission v Germany [2004] ECR I-4733; ECLI:EU:C:2004:251 ....39.046
Case C-296/01 Commission v France [2003] ECR I-13909, ECLI:EU:C:2003:626 ....8.290
Case C-352/01 Commission v Spain [2002] ECR I-10263 ....28.185
Case C-405/01 Colegio de Oficiales de la Marina Mercante Española v Administración del
 Estado [2003] ECR I-10391, ECLI:EU:C:2003:515 ....8.196, 8.197, 8.330
Case C-429/01 Commission v France [2003] ECR I-4355, ECLI:EU:C:2003:643 ....8.290
Case C-36/02 Schmidberger and Omega [2004] ECR I-9609, ECLI:EU:C:2004:614 ....6.133,
 7.236, 8.240
Case C-39/02 Maersk Oil & Gas AS [2004] ECR I-9657, ECLI:EU:C:2004:615, [2005] 1
 Lloyd's Rep 210..47.044
Case C-47/02 Albert Anker, Klaas Ras, Albertus Snoek v Bundesrepublik Deutschland
 [2003] ECR I-10447, ECLIL:EU:C:2003:516...8.196, 8.215, 8.330
Case C-116/02 Erich Gasser GmbH v MISAT Srl [2003] ECR I-14693,
 ECLI:EU:C:2003:657 ....47.005
Joined Cases C-184/02 and C-223/02 Spain and Finland v Parliament and Council [2004]
 ECR I-77890 ....19.326
Case C-255/02 Halifax and Others [2006] ECR I-1609 ....7.244
Case C-281/02 Andrew Owusu v NB Jackson trading as 'Villa Holidays Bal-Inn Villas' and
 others [2005] ECR I-1383, ECLI:EU:C:2005:120 ....6.128, 47.005
Case C-288/02 Commission v Greece [2004] ECR I-10071, ECLI:EU:C:2004:647........7.200, 7.211
Case C-299/02 Commission v Netherlands [2005] 59 AJIL 867. See 2004 EU Focus,
 No.153, page 13 ....6.141
Case C-334/02 Commission v France [2004] ECR I-2229 ....6.133, 7.236
Case C-389/02 Deutsche See-Bestattungs-Genossenschaft [2004] ECR I-3537 ....39.046, 39.047
Case C-400/02 Merida [2004] ECR I-8471, ECLI:EU:C:200:737.........................6.133, 7.236, 8.240
Case C-439/02 Commission v France [2004] EU:C:2004:380...28.159
Case C-17/03 VEMW and Others [2005] ECR I-4983, ECLI:EU:C:2005:362 ....7.210, 39.046
Case C-72/03 Carbonati Apuani [2004] ECR I-8027 ....7.294
Case C-88/03 Portugal v Commission [2006] ECR I-7115...7.295
Case C-110/03 Belgium v Commission [2005] ECR I-2801...19.322
Case C-148/03 Nürnberger Allgemeine Versicherungs AG v Portbridge Transport
 International BV [2004] ECR I-10327, ECLI:EU:C:2004:677 ....47.089
Case C-173/03 Traghetti del Mediterraneo v Repubblica Italiano [2006] ECR I-5177,
 ECLI:EU:C:2006:391 (see Ruffert (2007) 44 CMLRev 479)..3.002

Case C-176/03 Commission v Council [2005] ECR I-7879 .... 19.325, 19.326
Case C-205/03 FENIN v Commission [2006] ECR I-6295 .... 10.027, 10.028
Case C-230/03 Mehmet Sedef v Freie und Hansestadt Hamburg 8.245
Case C-323/03 Commission v Spain [2006] ECR I-2161, ECLI:EU:C:2006:159 .... 7.209,
7.256, 7.276
Case C-350/03 Schulte [2005] ECR I-9215 .... 6.131, 7.236
Case C-410/03 Commission v Italy [2007] ECLI:EU:C:2005 .... 8.270
Case C-446/03 Marks & Spencer [2005] ECR I-10837 .... 6.133, 7.236
Case C-459/03 Commission v Ireland [2006] ECR I-4635 .... 19.319
Case C-511/03 Ten Kate Holding Musselkanaal and Others [2005] ECR I-8979 .... 7.270
Case C-515/03 Eichsfelder Schlachtbetrieb [2005] ECR I-7355 .... 7.244
Joined Cases C-544/03 and C-545/03 Mobistar and Belgacom Mobile [2005]
    ECR I-7723 .... 7.294
Case C-551/03P General Motors v Commission [2006] ECR I-3173,
    ECLI:EU:C:2006:229 .... 10.076
Case C-43/04 Stadt Sundern [2005] ECR I-4491 .... 7.210
Cases C-110/04P, C-111/04P, C-112/04P and C-121/04 Strinzis Lines Shipping SA,
    Adriatica di Navigazione SpA, Marlines SA and Minoan Lines SA 10.218
Case C-150/04 Commission v Denmark [2007] ECR I-1163 .... 7.294
Case C-237/04 Enirisorse [2006] ECR I-2843 .... 7.295
Case C-251/04 Commission v Greece [2007] ECR I-00067, ECLI:EU:C:2007:5 .... 1.001,
7.215, 7.227, 7.256
Case C-255/04 Commission v France [2006] ECR I-5251 .... 7.225, 7.228
Joined Cases C-294/04 to C-298/04 Manfredi v Lloyd Adriatico Assicurazioni SpA and
    others [2006] ECR I-6619, ECLI:EU:C:2006:461 .... 10.173
Joined Cases C-295/04 to C-298/04 Manfredi [2006] ECR I-6619, ECLI:EU:C:2006:461 ..... 10.019,
10.193, 10.194, 10.196
Case C-311/04 Algemene Scheeps Agentuur Dordrecht [2006] ECR I-609 .... 19.319
Case C-344/04 IATA and ELFAA [2006] ECR I-403 .... 19.319
Case C-412/04 Commission v Italy [2008] ECR I-619 .... 7.287
Case C-456/04 [2006] ECR I-3395, ECLI:EU:C:2006:241 .... 7.239
Case C-519/04P Meca-Medina and Majcen v Commission [2006] ECR I-6991,
    ECLI:EU:C:2006:492 .... 6.133, 7.236, 8.240
Case C-76/05 Schwarz and Gootjes-Schwarz [2007] ECR I-6849 .... 7.294
Case C-178/05 Commission v Hellenic Republic [2007] ECR I-04185,
    ECLI:EU:C:2007:317 .... 19.326, 49.013
Case C-269/05 Commission v Greece [2007] ECR I-00004, ECLI:EU:C:2007:17 .... 7.227
Case C-285/05 Enosi Efopliston Aktoploïas and Others 7.249
Case C-292/05 Eirini Lechouritou and Others v Dimosio tis Omospondiakis Dimokratias tis
    Germanias [2007] ECR I-1519, ECLI:EU:C:2007:102 .... 47.009
Case C-303/05 Advocaten voor de Wereld [2007] ECR I-3633 .... 19.322
Case C-318/05 Commission v Germany [2007] ECR. I-6957 .... 7.294
Case C-341/05 Laval un Partneri v Svenska Byggnadsarbetareforbundet case [2008] All ER
    (EC) 166; [2008] IRLR 160 .... 6.119, 7.269, 8.227
Case C-391/05 Jan De Nul NV v Hauptzollamt Oldenburg [2007] ECR I-01793,
    ECLI:EU:C:2007:126 .... 39.041
Case C-438/05 International Transport Workers' Federation (ITF) and Finnish Seamen's
    Union (FSU) v Viking Line ABP and OÜ Viking Line Eesti [2008] 1 CMLR 51; [2008]
    All ER (EC) 127; [2008] IRLR 143 .... 6.118, 6.119, 6.140, 7.230, 8.227, 8.228

Case C-97/06 Navicon SA v Administración del Estado [2007] ECR I-08755,
ECLI:EU:C:2007:609 ....1.077
Case C-212/06 Government of the French Community and Walloon Government [2008]
ECR I-1683 ....7.294
Case C-250/06 United Pan-Europe Communications Belgium and Others [2007] ECR
I-11135 ....7.294
Case C-268/06 Impact [2008] EU:C:2008:223..8.302
Case C-319/06 Commission v Luxembourg [2008] ECR I-4323, ECLI:EU:C:2008:350 ....8.227
Joined Cases C-341/06P and C-342/06P Chronopost and La Poste v UFEX and Others
[2008] ECR I-4777 ....7.295
Case C-346/06 Rüffert [2008] ECR I-1989, ECLI:EU:C:2008:189......................................8.227
Joined Cases C-428/06 to C-434/06 UGT-Rioja and Others [2008] ECR I-6747......................7.295
Case C-527/06 Renneberg [2008] ECR I-7735 ....7.294
Case C-89/07 Commission v France [2008] EU:C:2008:154..8.330
Case C-169/07 Hartlauer [2009] ECR I-0000 ....7.294
Case C-185/07 Allianz SpA (formerly Riunione Adriatica di Sicurta SpA) v West Tankers
Inc (The Front Comor) [2009] 1 AC 1138, [2009] 1 Lloyd's Rep 413 ....47.006
Case C-209/07 Competition Authority v Beef Industry Development Society Ltd and Barry
Brothers (Carrigmore) Meats Ltd [2008] ECR I-8637, ECLI:EU:C:2008:643.....10.075, 10.076
Case C-222/07 UTECA [2009] ECR I-0000 ....7.294
Case C-303/07 Aberdeen Property Fininvest Alpha [2009] ECR I-0000................................7.294
Case C-550/07P Akzo Nobel Chemicals Ltd v. Commission [2010] ECR-8301. See Power,
ECLI:EU:C:2010:512 ....10.185
Case C-168/08 Hadadi [2009] ECR I-6871 ....7.287
Case C-169/08 Presidente del Consiglio dei Ministri v. Regione Sardegna [2009] ECR
I-10821, ECLI:EU:C:2009:709..7.289
Case C-211/08 Commission v. Spain [2010] ECR I-0000 ....7.287
Case C-508/08 Commission v. Malta [2010] ECR I-10589, ECLI:EU:C:2010:643.................7.283
Case C-533/08 TNT Express Nederland BV v. AXA Versicherung AG [2010] ECR I-04107,
ECLI:EU:C:2010:243 ....47.089
Case C-18/09 Commission v. Spain [2010] ECR I-00013, ECLI:EU:C:2010:58............7.246, 7.269
Case C-122/09 Enosi Efopliston Aktoploïas and Others, Ipourgos Emporikis Naftilias,
Ipourgos Aigaiou [2010] ECR I-03667, ECLI:EU:C:2010:222 ....7.247
Case C-232/09 Danosa [2010] EU:C:2010:674..8.330
Case C-338/09 Yellow Cab Verkehrsbetrieb [2010] ECR I-0000...7.276
Case C-542/09 Commission v. Netherlands [2012] EU:C:2012:346 ....8.329, 8.330
Case C-20/10 Vino [2010] EU:C:2010:677..8.304
Joined Cases C-128/10 and C-129/10 Navtiliaki Etairia Thasou AE and Amalthia I Navtiki
Etairia v. Ipourgos Emborikis Navtilías ECR I-1885, ECLI:EU:C:2011:163......................7.271
Case C-384/10 Jan Voogsgeerd v. Navimer SA [2011] ECR I-13275, ECLI:EU:C:2011:842 ...8.332
Case C-106/11 Bakker v. Minister van Financiën 8.306
Case C-251/11 Huet [2012] EU:C:2012:133 ....8.304
Case C-544/11 Petersen [2013] EU:C:2013:124 ....8.330
Case C-17/13 Alpina River Cruises GmbH and Nicko Tours GmbH v. Ministero delle
infrastrutture e dei trasporti – Capitaneria di Porto di Chioggia [2014]
ECLI:EU:C:2014:191 ....7.252
Case C-83/13 Fonnship A/S v. Svenska Transportarbetareförbundet and Facket för Service
och Kommunikation (SEKO) and Svenska Transportarbetareförbundet v. Fonnship A/S
case [2014] ECLI:EU:C:2014:2053 ....7.258
Case C-270/13 Iraklis Haralambidis v. Calogero Casilli..8.318

Joined Cases C-362/13, C-363/13 and C-407/13 Maurizio Fiamingo, Leonardo Zappalà,
   Francesco Rotondo and Others v. Rete Ferroviaria Italiana SpA 8.293, 8.302
Case C-465/14 Raad van bestuur van de Sociale verzekeringsbank v. Wieland and
   Rothwangl [2016] ECLI:EU:C:2016:820 .... 8.343
Case C-270/15P Belgium v. Commission (The TSE Case) [2016] ECLI:EU:C:2016:489 .... 15.016
Case C-383/17 Commission v. Portuguese Republic 28.132

TABLE OF LEGISLATION

Statutes

United Kingdom
Act of Accession 1972
   Protocol 2 .... 6.024
Civil Jurisdiction and Judgments Act
   1982 .... 47.002
Companies Act 2006 .... 29.150
European Communities Act 1972 .... 48.019
   art 2 .... 7.284, 7.287
   Protocol 3, art 2 .... 6.092
Industrial & Provident Societies Act
   1965 .... 29.150
Landlord and Tenant Act 1954 .... 13.095
Merchant Shipping (Liner Conferences) Act
   1982 .... 9.076
Merchant Shipping (Registration of Fishing
   Vessels) Regulations 1988 ..... 6.101, 6.103,
      6.107
Merchant Shipping Act 1894 .... 6.102, 6.103
Merchant Shipping Act 1988 .... 6.035, 6.103,
      6.114, 7.061
   Part II 6.101, 6.107
   s 14 .... 6.105, 6.107
Navigation Act 1651 .... 7.043
Rules of Procedure Court of Justice
   art 38(1)(c) 7.287

Belgium
Belgisch Staasblad 1978
   art 39 .... 8.335

Denmark
Law No 239 .... 7.139
Law No 935 .... 9.074

Finland
Constitution
   art 13 .... 7.231, 8.232

France
Charter of Paris 25.008
Commercial Code
   arts R.212–17 .... 7.160
   arts R.212–19 .... 7.161
   arts R.212–20 .... 7.161
Customs Code
   art 257(1) 7.278, 7.279, 7.281, 7.282
   art 258 .... 7.279
   art 259(1) 7.280
Merchant Seamen Code 1926
   s 3(2) 4.066

Germany
International Maritime Register (ISR)
   art 1(2) 6.094
Regulation implementing the Law on personal
   status 8.218
Ships' Crews Regulation 8.218

Greece
Code on Maritime Law
   art 5 .... 6.098
General Ports Regulations
   art 4(2)(b) 7.220
Law 2932/2001 .... 7.249, 7.274, 7.276
   art 1 .... 7.272
   art 1(1) 7.247, 7.248
   art 2(6) 7.272
   art 3 .... 7.247, 7.272
   art 3(1) 7.248
   art 4 .... 7.272
   art 4(4) 7.275, 7.277
   art 4(4)(a) 7.275, 7.276
   art 4(4)(b) 7.275, 7.276
   art 4(4)(c) 7.275, 7.277
   art 4(5) 7.275

Law No 187/73
   art 11(1)(aa) 7.220
   art 11(1)(b) 7.220
   art 188 .... 7.220
   art 188(2) 7.220
   art 188(3) 7.220
   art 189 .... 7.220
Law No 2399/1996
   art 6 .... 7.191
   art 6(2)(A) 7.191
   art 6(2)(B)(a) 7.191
Presidential Decree No 45/83
   art 1 .... 7.223, 7.228
   art 1(1) 7.220
   art 3 .... 7.220, 7.223, 7.228

Ireland
Shipping Investment Grants Act 1969 .... 2.078
Shipping Investment Grants Act 1987 .... 2.078

Italy
Codice della Navigazione (Italian Shipping
   Code) 7.170
   art 54 .... 8.325
   art 62 .... 7.170
   art 116 .... 7.170
   art 224 .... 7.189, 7.252, 7.253, 7.256
   art 318 .... 7.240
   art 325 .... 8.302
   art 326 .... 8.302
   art 332 .... 8.302
   art 374 .... 8.302
   art 633 .... 7.170
Decree No 174
   art 1(1)(b) 8.321
Decree No 20
   art 1 .... 7.170
Finance Law 2007 (Regional Law
   No 4/2006) 7.292
   art 2 .... 7.293
   art 3 .... 7.293
   art 4 .... 7.293, 7.294, 7.295, 7.296
   art 4(2)(a) 7.294
   art 4(2)(b) 7.294
Italian Code of Civil Procedure
   art 633 .... 7.169
Italian Constitution
   art 51 .... 8.319
   art 117 .... 7.291, 7.293

Law No 1369 1960
   art 1 .... 13.066
   art 1(1) 13.059, 13.067
   art 1(2) 13.067
Law No 160/89 .... 7.171
   art 9(7) 7.171
Law No 2 Region of Sardinia
   art 3(3) 7.292, 7.296
Law No 30/1998 .... 7.189
Law No 457
   art 7 .... 7.189
Law No 82/1963
   art 32(d) 7.189
Law No 84/94 .... 13.062
   art 6 .... 8.321
   art 7 .... 8.321
   art 7(3)(a) 8.330
   art 7(3)(c) 8.330
   art 8 .... 8.322, 13.079
   art 8(1) 8.326, 8.330
   art 8(2) 8.330
   art 8(3) 8.327, 8.330
   art 12 .... 8.323
   art 12(2)(a) 8.330
   art 12(2)(b) 8.330
   art 16 .... 13.078
   art 16(1) 13.064, 13.078
   art 16(3) 13.068
   art 17(1) 13.065
   art 18 .... 8.324
   art 18(1) 13.063, 13.079
   art 18(2) 13.064, 13.079
   art 18(3) 13.064
   art 21(1)(b) 13.065, 13.066, 13.068, 13.069
   art 23(3) 13.065
   art 27 .... 13.065
Law No 979/82 .... 7.127
   Annex A 7.127
   art 16 .... 7.126, 7.127
   art 20 .... 7.127
Legislative Decree No 165 .... 8.320
   art 38(1) 8.319
   art 38(2) 8.319
Legislative Decree No 174 .... 8.320
Legislative Decree No 20 .... 7.170
   art 2 .... 7.170
Legislative Decree No 271 .... 8.288
   art 11(1) 8.289
   art 11(10) 8.289
   art 11(3) 8.289

art 21(1) 8.290
art 21(3) 8.290
Legislative Decree No 29 ....8.320
Recreational Sailing Code 7.292
   art 1(2) 7.291
   art 2(1) 7.291
   art 3(b) 7.292
Regolamento per la Navigazione Marittima
   (Regulations for Maritime Navigation)
   arts 208–214 ....7.170
   art 209 ....7.170
   art 212 ....7.170
Sea and Air Navigation Code
   art 265 *et seq.* 7.292
   art 743 ....7.291
   art 743 *et seq.* 7.292
   art 874 *et seq.* 7.292

Luxembourg
Luxembourg Public Maritime Register 1990
   art 80(2) 8.335

Netherlands
Algemene Ouderdomswet (Stb. 1956, No 281)
   art 6 ....8.308
Burgerlijk Wetboek (Civil Code)
   art 8:160 ....6.145
   art 8:163 ....6.145
   art 8:169 ....6.141, 6.151
   art 8:169(1) 6.145
BVS (Stb. 1994, No 807) 7.195
   art 2(1) 7.195
   art 4(1) 7.195
   art 5(1) 7.195
Scheepvaartverkeerswet (Shipping Act)
   1988 ....7.195
Staatscourant 1995, No 8 ....7.195
SVW (Stb. 1994, No 585) 7.195
   art 1(1)(i) 7.195
   art 15c 7.195
   art 15d 7.195
Wetboek van Koophandel (Code of Commerce)
   art 311 ....6.141, 6.151
   art 311(1) 6.144

Spain
Código Civil (Civil Code)
   art 52 ....8.204
   art 722 ....8.204
   art 729 ....8.204

Código de Comercio (Commercial Code)
   art 610 ....8.203
   art 627 ....8.205
   art 700 ....8.204
   art 705 ....8.205
Law 48/2003
   art 24(5) 7.246
   art 27(1) 7.246
   art 27(2) 7.246
   art 27(4) 7.246
Law No 27/1992 ....8.199, 8.200
   art 6(1)(h) 7.181
   art 7(4) 7.180, 7.181
   art 11 ....8.202
   art 116(3)(f) 8.202
   art 77 ....8.199, 8.206
   art 77(2) 8.207
   art 83(2) 7.182
Reglamento del Registro Civil (Regulations on
   the register of births, marriages and deaths)
   art 19 ....8.205
   art 71 ....8.205
   art 72 ....8.205
Royal Decree No 1466/1997 ....7.179, 7.182,
                                              7.183
   art 4 ....7.181, 7.185
Royal Decree No 2062/1999 ....8.198
   art 8 ....8.201
   art 8(2) 8.207
   art 8(3) 8.206, 8.207, 8.208, 8.209, 8.211,
                                          8.213, 8.214

Australia
Trade Practices Act 1974 ....12.031

South Korea
Maritime Transportation Fostering Act
   art 16 ....17.043

United States
Jones Act/Merchant Marine Act 1920 ....7.015
Ocean Shipping Reform Act 12.005
Sherman Act 1890 ....9.011
Shipping Act 1916 ....9.007, 9.008, 9.011
Shipping Act 1984 ....9.008

Agreements

Agreement establishing the World Trade
    Organisation 22.044
Agreement for Cooperation between the EEC
    and Brazil 25.082, 25.090, 25.091,
                                                    25.102
    art 1 .... 25.084, 25.085, 25.093
    art 2 .... 25.094
    art 2(1) 25.085
    art 2(2) 25.085
    art 3 .... 25.086, 25.095
    art 3(4) 25.087
    art 4 .... 25.087, 25.096
    art 4(1) 25.087
    art 4(2) 25.087
    art 5 .... 25.087, 25.096
    art 6 .... 25.097
    art 7 .... 25.098
    art 8 .... 25.089, 25.099
    art 9 .... 25.100
    art 9(1) 25.090
    art 9(2) 25.090
    art 15 .... 25.101
    art 28(3) 25.085
Agreement on Maritime Transport and
    Navigation between the Italian Republic
    and the People's Democratic Republic of
    Algeria 39.049, 39.050
Agreement on Maritime Transport and
    Navigation with the People's Democratic
    Republic of Algeria 25.062
Agreement on Subsidies and Countervailing
    Measures 22.044
Anti-Dumping Agreement 1994 .... 22.044
Belgium and Zaire Agreement 7.299
    art 1(1) 7.298
    art 3(3) 7.298
    art 4 .... 7.298
    art 18 .... 7.298
    art 18(2) 7.298
Belgo-Luxembourg Economic Union and
    Malaysia Agreement 7.304
    art 1(1) 7.305
    art 2 .... 7.307
    art 2(1) 7.305
    art 3 .... 7.305, 7.307
    art 16 .... 7.305, 7.307
    art 21 .... 7.306, 7.307

BIMCO's Standard Ship Management
    Agreement (SHIPMAN 98) 15.064
Bonn Agreement 19.156, 19.157, 19.158
    Annex 19.164, 19.180
    art 1 .... 19.159, 19.161, 19.162, 19.164
    art 1(2) 19.159
    art 2 .... 19.159, 19.160, 19.176
    art 3(1) 19.161
    art 3(2) 19.161
    art 4 .... 19.162
    art 5(1) 19.163
    art 5(2) 19.163
    art 5(3) 19.163
    art 6 .... 19.165, 19.166, 19.180
    art 6(1) 19.164
    art 6(2) 19.164
    art 6(3) 19.164
    art 6(4) 19.164
    art 6A 19.161, 19.164, 19.165, 19.168
    art 7 .... 19.166
    art 8 .... 19.166
    art 8(2) 19.166
    art 8(3) 19.166
    art 9 .... 19.168
    art 9(1) 19.168
    art 9(2) 19.168
    art 9(3) 19.165, 19.168
    art 10 .... 19.168
    art 11 .... 19.168
    art 12 .... 19.169
    art 12(1) 19.169
    art 12(2) 19.169
    art 13 .... 19.170
    art 14 .... 19.170
    art 15 .... 19.171
    art 15(1) 19.171
    art 15(2) 19.171
    art 16(1) 19.172
    art 16(2) 19.172
    art 17 .... 19.172, 19.173
    art 18 .... 19.175, 19.179
    art 18(1) 19.174
    art 18(2) 19.174
    art 19(1) 19.175
    art 19(2) 19.175
    art 20(1) 19.176
    art 20(2) 19.176
    art 21(1) 19.177
    art 21(2) 19.177
    art 22 .... 19.178

art 23 .... 19.179
art 24 .... 19.180
Part I 19.160
Part II 19.160
Bretton Woods Agreement 25.068
Canada Transpacific Stabilization Agreement
 (CTSA) 12.001
Comprehensive Economic and Trade
 Agreement (CETA) 25.104, 25.105,
 25.106, 48.033
Cooperation Agreement for the Protection of
 the Coasts and Waters of the North-East
 Atlantic against Pollution ... 19.191, 19.192,
 19.193
EU and Cambodia Cooperation
 Agreement 25.063
 art 1 .... 25.065
 art 2 .... 25.066
 art 3 .... 25.067
 art 4 .... 25.068
 art 4(1) 25.068
 art 4(2) 25.068
 art 4(3) 25.068
 art 4(3)(a) 25.068
 art 4(4) 25.068
 art 4(5) 25.068
 art 4(6) 25.068
 art 5 .... 25.069
 art 6 .... 25.069
 art 15 .... 25.071
 art 15(1) 25.071
 art 15(2) 25.071
 art 16 .... 25.072
 art 17 .... 25.073
 art 18 .... 25.074
 art 19 .... 25.063, 25.075
 art 20 .... 25.063
 art 21 .... 25.063
 art 21(1) 25.063
 art 21(2) 25.063
Europe Asia Trades Agreement
 (EATA) 5.138, 12.159
Far East Trade Tariff Charges and Surcharges
 Agreement (FETTCSA) 5.137, 5.138
Free Trade Agreement between the European
 Communities and Lithuania 25.001
General Agreement on Tariffs and Trade
 (GATT) 19.318, 25.084
 art VI 22.044
Horizontal Co-operation Agreements 12.064

Interinstitutional Agreement (OLAF) 27.024
Interinstitutional Agreement on better
 law-making 29.081
Lisbon Agreement 19.191, 19.192, 19.194
Maritime Transport Agreement between EU
 and China 25.076, 25.079
Maritime Transport of Agreement on the
 European Economic Area 7.268, 7.270,
 11.006, 16.086, 39.080
 Annex XIII 7.269
 art 7(a) 7.269
 art 53 .... 12.194, 12.196, 12.203, 13.091,
 13.092
 art 53(1) 14.056
 art 54 .... 13.091, 13.092
 art 57(2)(a) 16.098
 Protocol 19 .... 4.072, 5.113, 5.116
OECD Agreement Respecting Normal
 Competitive Conditions in the Commercial
 Shipbuilding and Repair Industry ... 22.027,
 22.028, 22.031, 22.040, 22.042, 22.043,
 22.044, 22.056, 22.058, 22.087
 Annex I 22.030
 Annex II 22.030
 Annex III 22.030, 22.044
 art 1 .... 22.030
Omnibus Agreement 16.070
Paris MOU
 Annex 1 .... 28.010
Slot Charter Agreement 14.025
Stockholm Agreement ... 34.042, 34.044, 34.060
Trans-Atlantic Conference Agreement
 (TACA) 5.131, 12.002, 12.024, 12.044,
 12.153, 16.081, 16.082
Transpacific Stabilization Agreement
 (TSA) 12.001
Tripartite Agreement 48.055
Working Time Agreement ECSA and
 FST 8.061, 8.062, 15.068, 31.006,
 35.001, 35.004, 35.007
 Clause 2 .... 35.009
 Clause 3 .... 35.010
 Clause 4 .... 35.011
 Clause 5 .... 35.011, 35.012
 Clause 6 .... 35.013
 Clause 7 .... 35.011
 Clause 8 .... 35.011
 Clause 9 .... 35.016
 Clause 10 .... 35.017
 Clause 11 .... 35.018

Clause 12..35.017
Clause 13..35.017

Conventions

1969 International Convention on Civil
 Liability for Oil Pollution Damage (CLC)
 1969...26.010
Arrest Convention 1952...........................47.017
Athens Convention relating to the Carriage of
 Passengers and their Luggage by
 Sea 1974................46.026, 46.027, 46.029,
  46.030, 46.031, 46.032, 46.035, 46.039,
  46.041, 46.130, 46.132, 46.133, 46.134,
  46.136, 46.137, 46.138, 46.140, 46.141,
  46.145, 46.146
 Annex II 46.032
 art 1 ....46.040, 46.041
 art 1(b)..46.041
 art 2(2)...46.041
 art 23 ....46.047
 art 3 ....46.141
 art 3(1)...46.047
 art 3(3)...46.042
 art 4 ....46.141
 art 4(1)...46.047
 art 4b 46.141
 art 6 ....46.044
 art 7(1)...46.047
 art 8 ....46.042, 46.047, 46.047
 art 10 ....46.130, 46.138, 46.140, 46.141,
  46.142, 46.144
 art 11 ....46.130, 46.138, 46.140, 46.141,
  46.142, 46.143, 46.144
 art 15 ....46.132
 art 17 ....46.034, 46.141
 art 17(2)(b) 46.132, 46.140
 art 17(2)(c) 46.134, 46.142
 art 17(3)....................................46.134, 46.142
 art 17b 46.034, 46.141, 46.143
 art 19 ....46.132, 46.134, 46.140, 46.142
Ballast Water Management Convention
 2004..23.008
Basel Convention on the Control of
 Transboundary Movements of Hazardous
 Wastes and Their Disposal (Basel
 Convention).........................24.010, 24.076
Brussels Convention on Jurisdiction and the
 Enforcement of Judgments in Civil and
 Commercial Matters 1968................47.002

art 3 ....47.007
art 4 ....47.007
art 59 ....47.007
Codice della Navigazione (the Italian Shipping
 Code)
 art 110 ....13.033, 13.060
 art 111 ....13.060
 art 112 ....13.060
 art 203 ....13.060
Convention Establishing the Belgo-
 Luxembourg Economic Union (BLEU
 Convention)
 art 31(1).......................................7.304, 7.307
Convention Facilitation of International
 Maritime Traffic (FAL
 Convention)...........44.005, 44.010, 44.016,
  44.020, 44.031
Convention for Rhine Navigation............46.101
Convention for the Prevention of Marine
 Pollution from Land-Based Sources
 1974..........19.050, 19.051, 19.053, 19.055,
  19.057
 art 1 ....19.056
Convention for the Protection of the Marine
 Environment and the Coastal Region of the
 Mediterranean (Barcelona Convention)
 1975..........19.113, 19.114, 19.117, 19.122,
  19.122, 19.125, 19.127, 19.129, 19.130,
  19.131, 19.132, 19.133, 19.134, 19.135,
  19.136, 19.138, 19.139, 19.140, 19.141,
  19.142, 19.143, 19.144, 19.145, 19.146,
  19.147, 19.148, 19.149, 19.150, 19.151,
  19.152, 19.153, 19.182
 art 4 ....19.138
 art 4.3(3)..19.128
 art 6 ....19.138
 art 7 ....19.123
 art 9 ....19.138
 art 23 ....19.114
 art 24 ....19.114
Convention for the Protection of the Marine
 Environment of the North-East Atlantic
 (OSPAR)...............19.183, 19.185, 19.187,
  19.188, 19.189, 19.190
 Annex I..19.186
 Annex II 19.186
 art 10 ....19.190
 art 26 ....19.190
Convention on Access to Information, Public
 Participation in Decision-making and

TABLE OF LEGISLATION

Access to Justice in Environmental Matters (Aarhus Convention) 19.240
  art 9(3) 24.020
Convention on Certain Institutions Common to the Three Communities 1957 .... 3.096
Convention on Limitation of Liability for Maritime Claims 1976 .... 46.036, 46.043, 46.181, 46.184
  art 11 .... 47.019
  art 15(3b) 46.036
Convention on the Grant of European Patents 47.033
Convention on the International Regulations for Preventing Collisions at Sea 1972 (Colreg) 28.031, 37.013
Convention on the Law Applicable to Contractual Obligations (Rome Convention) 1980 .... 48.045
  art 1(1) 8.334
  art 3 .... 8.339
  art 4 .... 8.339
  art 6 .... 8.332, 8.339, 8.341
  art 6(1) 8.337
  art 6(2) 8.340, 8.342
  art 6(2)(b) 8.338
Convention on the Protection of the Marine Environment in the Baltic Sea Area (Helsinki Convention) 1992 .... 19.195, 19.196, 19.197, 19.198, 19.199, 19.201, 19.202, 19.203, 19.204
  art 26 .... 19.200
Convention on the Protection of the Marine Environment in the Baltic Sea Area 1992 .... 19.060
Convention Regarding the Regime of Navigation on the Danube 46.101
European Convention for the Protection of International Watercourses against Pollution 1974 .... 19.051
European Convention on Human Rights (EHCR) 1950 .... 3.010, 3.012, 25.050, 48.010
  art 1 .... 48.010
  art 14 .... 8.346
Freedom of Association and Protection of the Right to Organise Convention (ILO C87) 1948 .... 6.133, 6.171, 7.236
Geneva Convention on the High Seas 1958
  art 5 .... 6.028, 6.031, 6.098
  art 5(1) 6.027

Hague Convention on the Service Abroad of Judicial and Extrajudicial Documents in Civil or Commercial Matters
  art 15 .... 47.040
Hong Kong International Convention for the Safe and Environmentally Sound Recycling of Ships 2009 (Hong Kong Convention) 5.170, 24.004, 24.005, 24.006, 24.007, 24.008, 24.010, 24.012, 24.013, 24.015, 24.018, 24.019, 24.020, 24.022, 24.054, 24.058, 24.076, 24.090, 24.097
  Appendix 3 .... 24.062
  Appendix 4 .... 24.065
  Appendix 6 .... 24.078
  Appendix 7 .... 24.078
  art 1(1) 24.007
  reg 8(2) 24.019
IMCO Convention on Standards for the Training and Certification of Seafarers and Watchkeeping (STCW) 1978 .... 5.027, 6.035, 8.002, 8.053, 8.081, 8.083, 8.085, 8.088, 8.093, 8.115, 8.118, 8.119, 8.126, 8.128, 8.130, 8.131, 8.132, 8.133, 8.134, 8.136, 8.138, 8.140, 8.141, 8.143, 8.157, 8.160, 8.167, 8.172, 8.173, 8.175, 8.176, 8.178, 8.180, 8.181, 8.182, 8.188, 8.189, 8.255, 8.256, 8.257, 8.258, 8.263, 26.021, 26.024, 28.031, 31.006, 31.028, 31.049, 31.058, 31.059, 31.060, 31.063, 31.064, 31.069, 31.079, 31.082, 31.086, 31.092, 35.020, 46.078, 46.101
  Annex 31.056
  Annex I, reg V/1-1 .... 31.051, 31.051, 31.052, 31.052, 31.053, 31.053, 31.055, 31.055
  Annex, reg I/2, para 3 .... 31.050
  Annex, reg I/9 .... 31.065
  art IV, para 2 .... 31.050
  art 28 .... 8.167, 8.176
  art VII 31.028
  reg I/10 .... 31.055
  reg I/10, para 1.2 .... 31.062
  reg I/15 .... 31.028
  reg V/1-1 .... 8.166, 31.078
  reg V/1-2 .... 8.166, 31.078
  Section A-I/11 .... 31.066
  Section A-I/3 .... 31.060
  Section A-I/9 .... 31.055, 31.065
  Section B-I/9 .... 31.065

International Convention for the Prevention of
   Pollution from Ships 1973 .... 6.082
International Convention of Safe Containers
   (CSC) 1972 .... 5.035, 46.003, 46.004
International Convention on Civil Liability for
   Bunker Oil Pollution Damage
   2001 .... 46.183
International Convention on Civil Liability for
   Bunker Oil Pollution Damage 2001
   (Bunkers Convention) 19.030, 19.033,
      19.034, 19.035, 19.037, 19.038, 19.040,
                                                              28.031
   art 9 .... 19.031
   art 10 .... 19.031
International Convention on Civil Liability for
   Oil Pollution Damage 1992
   (CLC 92) 28.031
International Convention on Liability and
   Compensation for Damage in Connection
   with the Carriage of Hazardous and
   Noxious Substances by Sea (HNS
   Convention) 1996 .... 1.065, 21.001, 21.002,
      21.003, 21.004, 21.007, 21.009, 21.010,
                                                              46.183
   art 1(1) 21.008
   art 2 .... 21.008, 21.009
   art 3(1) 21.010
   art 4 .... 21.011
   art 5 .... 21.012
   art 38 .... 21.008
   art 39 .... 21.008
   art 40 .... 21.008
International Convention on Load Lines
   1966 .... 6.060, 6.065, 6.082, 20.011,
      28.031, 28.123, 28.125, 29.030, 29.076,
               29.083, 30.007, 34.062, 34.070
International Convention on Maritime Search
   and Rescue (SAR) 1979 .... 5.054, 26.027,
                                                   39.045, 46.010
International Convention on the Control of
   Harmful Anti-Fouling Systems on Ships
   (AFS Convention) 2001 ..... 20.002, 20.003,
         20.004, 20.008, 20.009, 20.011, 20.015,
               20.020, 20.023, 20.025, 28.031
   Annex 4 .... 20.024
   art 1(4)(a) 20.023
   art 10 .... 20.024
   art 11 .... 20.016, 20.017, 20.026
   art 11(1) 20.023
   art 11(2) 20.023

International Convention on the Establishment
   of an International Fund for Compensation
   for Oil Pollution Damage (FUND)
   1971 .... 26.100
International Convention on the Establishment
   of an International Fund for Compensation
   for Oil Pollution Damage (Supplementary
   Fund Protocol) 1992 .... 19.042, 19.043,
                                                   19.044, 19.048
International Convention on the Prevention of
   Pollution by Ships 1973 as modified by the
   Protocol of 1978 (MARPOL) 5.027,
         5.110, 6.060, 6.065, 6.082, 7.129, 7.136,
         19.060, 19.063, 19.106, 19.151, 19.277,
         19.300, 19.305, 19.309, 19.323, 24.028,
         25.009, 28.031, 28.031, 28.123, 28.125,
         29.030, 29.076, 29.083, 30.007, 37.013,
                               39.055, 45.005, 45.008
   Annex I 19.283, 24.027, 25.009, 39.045
   Annex II, reg 6(b) 19.269
   Annex I, reg 9 .... 19.309, 19.313, 19.317,
                                                   19.318, 19.319
   Annex I, reg 9(2) 19.309
   Annex I, reg 10 .... 19.309, 19.313
   Annex I, reg 11 .... 19.309
   Annex I, reg 11(a) 19.310, 19.313
   Annex I, reg 11(b) 19.269 19.310, 19.313,
                                          19.315, 19.317, 19.318, 19.319
   Annex I, reg 11(c) 19.310, 19.313
   Annex II 19.085, 19.283, 24.027, 39.045
   Annex II, reg 5 .... 19.310, 19.313, 19.317,
                                                   19.318, 19.319
   Annex II, reg 6(a) 19.310, 19.313
   Annex II, reg 6(b) 19.310, 19.313, 19.315,
                                          19.317, 19.318, 19.319
   Annex II, reg 6(c) 19.310, 19.313
   art 2 .... 19.280
International Convention on the Removal of
   Wrecks 2007 (Wrecks Removal
   Convention) 46.183
International Convention on the Safety of Life
   at Sea (SOLAS) 1974 .... 5.027, 5.110,
         6.060, 6.063, 6.065, 6.067, 6.082, 6.083,
         6.161, 8.116, 8.117, 8.126, 8.289, 24.006,
         25.006, 26.008, 26.024, 26.030, 26.043,
         26.045, 28.031, 28.123, 28.125, 29.030,
         29.076, 29.083, 31.026, 31.029, 31.030,
         33.002, 34.009, 34.011, 34.011, 34.013,
         34.060, 34.062, 34.069, 34.070, 34.071,
         34.072, 34.083, 34.099, 34.100, 37.007,

TABLE OF LEGISLATION

37.013, 39.005, 39.015, 39.025, 39.055, 39.059, 39.066, 41.010, 42.005, 42.009, 42.015, 42.017, 42.026, 42.027, 42.033, 42.035, 42.037, 42.038, 42.038, 42.040, 42.043, 42.045, 42.046, 42.047, 42.048, 42.049, 42.133, 46.016, 46.148, 46.151, 46.155, 46.156, 46.157
Chaper III 46.022
Chaper XI-2 .... 42.017
Chapter II-1 .... 28.049, 34.095
Chapter II-1, Part A-1, reg 3-1 .... 28.122
Chapter II-2 .... 34.095
Chapter III 34.095
Chapter IV 39.013
Chapter IV, reg 2 .... 34.062
Chapter IX 33.008
Chapter IX, reg 1(2) 39.045
Chapter IX-1 .... 42.027
Chapter V 31.077
Chapter V, reg 10 .... 39.060
Chapter V, reg 11 .... 39.057
Chapter X, reg 1 .... 34.042, 46.006
reg 14 .... 8.157, 31.069
reg 14, para 4 .... 8.165
reg 17 .... 34.069
reg 18 .... 34.069
reg 18.1 .... 34.069
reg 19 .... 34.069
reg 20 .... 34.069
reg 21 .... 34.069
reg I/21 .... 30.007
reg IB/12(a)(vi) 33.012
reg II-1/29 .... 26.001
reg II-1/B/8 .... 34.042, 34.048
reg II-2/13.4 .... 26.001
reg II-2/18 .... 26.001
reg II-2/3 .... 26.001, 34.044
reg II-2/3.18 .... 34.099
reg II-2/37.1.3 .... 34.099
reg II-2/9.7 .... 26.001
reg III/10.4 .... 31.049
reg III/20 .... 26.001
reg IX/4 .... 34.013
reg VI/7 .... 46.150
reg X/1 .... 33.012
reg X-1/2 .... 33.014
International Convention on Tonnage
 Measurement of Ships 1969 ... 6.082, 8.269, 28.031, 33.014, 39.045
 Annex I 19.212, 20.011, 24.035
International Convention relating to
 Intervention on the High Seas in Cases of
 Oil Pollution Casualties 1969 .... 39.045
International Labour Organisation
 Convention 1979 .... 15.077
International Telecommunication
 Convention 31.025
Lomé Convention 18.010, 18.026
Lugano Convention 1988 .... 46.140, 46.143, 47.002, 47.007
Maritime Labour Convention (MLC)
 2006 .... 5.159, 8.002, 8.030, 8.038, 8.047, 8.048, 8.049, 8.050, 8.051, 8.052, 8.053, 8.054, 8.055, 8.056, 8.057, 8.058, 8.074, 8.259, 8.261, 8.262, 8.268, 8.269, 8.301, 8.352, 8.353, 8.359, 8.361, 9.004, 15.068, 19.253, 28.031, 36.001, 36.002, 36.003, 36.004, 36.008, 36.009, 36.010, 36.012, 36.017, 36.018, 36.032, 36.034, 36.036, 36.037, 36.039, 36.040, 48.038
 art II, para 6 .... 36.027
 art VIII 36.016
 reg 5.1.2 .... 28.051, 28.052, 36.020, 36.030
Merchant Shipping (Minimum Standards)
 Convention (ILO C147) 1976 .... 5.027, 6.153, 8.061, 8.063, 8.073, 8.286, 25.008, 28.003
OECD Convention 1948 .... 3.009
OECD Convention 1960 .... 3.009
Seafarers' Hours of Work and the Manning
 of Ships Convention (ILO C180)
 1996 .... 8.061, 8.063, 8.073, 8.076, 8.077, 8.078, 8.079, 8.080, 8.286
Stockholm Convention on Persistent Organic
 Pollutants 24.076
UN Convention on a Code of Conduct for Liner
 Conferences (UNCTAD) 1974 .... 5.022, 5.031, 5.031, 5.047, 5.062, 5.083, 7.009, 7.045, 7.146, 7.147, 7.148, 7.150, 7.152, 7.297, 9.015, 9.021, 9.022, 9.025, 9.036, 9.049, 9.050, 9.051, 9.054, 9.056, 9.057, 9.063, 9.070, 9.072, 9.073, 9.074, 9.075, 9.076, 9.077, 11.003, 11.015, 11.018, 11.022, 11.141, 12.033, 12.044, 18.007, 18.010
 art 1 .... 9.028, 9.058
 art 2 .... 9.029, 9.058
 art 3 .... 9.031
 art 4 .... 9.032
 art 5 .... 9.033

art 6 .... 9.034
art 7 .... 9.036
art 8 .... 9.037
art 9 .... 9.038, 11.079
art 10 .... 9.039
art 11 .... 9.040
art 12 .... 9.042
art 13 .... 9.043
art 14 .... 9.044
art 15 .... 9.045
art 16 .... 9.046
art 17 .... 9.047
UN Convention on the Law Sea (UNCLOS III) 1982....... 6.030, 6.031, 7.256, 8.013, 8.210, 8.218, 8.225, 8.315, 17.007, 19.005, 19.265, 19.265, 19.281, 19.287, 19.293, 19.305, 19.306, 19.307, 19.323, 25.002, 34.042, 37.103, 37.104, 39.028, 39.032, 49.064
art 2 .... 19.308, 30.003, 30.004
art 2(1)... 8.312
art 2(3)... 19.318
arts 2–120.. 19.319
art 8 .... 7.210
art 17 .... 19.308
art 34 .... 19.308
art 42 .... 19.308
art 42(1)(b).. 19.318
art 45 .... 19.318
art 56(1)... 19.308
art 58(1)... 19.308
art 79 .... 19.308
art 79(1)... 19.308
art 86 .... 8.013
art 89 .... 19.308
art 90 .... 6.031, 19.308
art 91 .... 6.028, 6.031, 8.013
art 91 *et seq.* 6.098
art 91(1).. 6.143, 6.148
art 92 .... 8.013
art 94 .... 6.032, 6.143, 8.013, 30.005, 30.006
art 94(1)............................ 6.148, 8.274, 8.291
art 94(7)... 30.005
art 97 .... 8.013
art 116 .... 19.308
art 211 .... 19.308
art 211(1)... 19.318
art 211(5)... 19.318
art 220 .... 19.278
art 230 .... 19.267, 19.271

Part V 19.308
Part VII... 8.013
UN Framework Convention on Climate Change 1992.. 5.176
UNCTAD Convention on Conditions for Registration of Ships 1986..... 6.029, 6.030, 6.033, 6.035, 6.037, 6.043, 6.044, 6.049, 6.098
art 1 .... 6.029
art 7 .... 6.039, 6.040
art 8 .... 6.038, 6.039, 6.042, 6.043
art 9 .... 6.038, 6.040, 6.042, 6.043
art 9(2)(b).. 6.043
art 9(4).. 6.043
art 10 .... 6.038, 6.041, 6.042, 6.043
art 10(1).. 6.043
United Nations Convention on the Rights of Persons with Disabilities
art 9 .... 46.078
United States Convention on a Code of Conduct for Liner Conferences 39.049
Vienna Convention on the Law of Treaties (VCLT) 1969
art 19 .... 6.043
art 20 .... 6.043
art 21 .... 6.043
art 30(4)(b)... 7.303

Regulations

ITU Radio Regulations
art 1.28 .... 39.013, 39.025
ITU Radio Regulations
art 1.29 .... 39.013, 39.025
17/62 .... 5.008, 5.017, 5.140, 7.113, 9.050, 11.001, 11.008, 11.009, 11.018, 11.037, 11.090, 12.005, 12.048, 12.049, 12.055, 13.053, 14.037
art 2 .... 11.087
art 9(1)... 10.110
141/62 .... 5.008, 5.009, 5.017, 7.113, 9.050, 11.008, 11.018, 12.048, 12.055
art 1 .... 5.008
1017/68/EEC....... 5.009, 11.018, 11.019, 11.070, 11.090, 12.033, 14.037
art 3 .... 11.049, 11.050
1612/68/EEC... 6.153
art 1 .... 4.066, 5.017
art 1a... 8.197

art 4 .... 4.066, 4.068, 5.017, 8.197
art 7 .... 4.066, 5.017
1191/69 .... 4.042
580/70/EEC 9.074
1107/70/EEC 4.042, 5.135, 41.008
1251/70
   art 7 .... 6.096, 6.097, 6.098, 6.098
1408/71/EEC 8.306, 8.310, 8.311, 8.312,
       8.315, 8.343, 8.346, 8.347, 8.349, 8.350
   art 1(a)(i) 8.307
   art 3 .... 8.343, 8.348, 8.350
   art 13(2)(c) 6.172, 8.313, 8.316, 8.317
   art 94 .... 8.343
   art 94(1) 8.350, 8.351
   art 94(2) 8.348, 8.350, 8.351
2822/71/EEC 13.080
574/72 .... 8.343, 8.351
706/73/EEC 48.055
2988/74 .... 5.019, 10.175
1473/75 .... 4.042
954/79/EEC 5.022, 5.022, 5.031, 5.047,
       5.062, 5.069, 5.083, 7.030, 7.152, 7.297,
       9.048, 9.050, 9.051, 9.053, 9.054, 9.055,
       9.056, 9.060, 9.061, 9.070, 9.072, 9.073,
       9.074, 9.075, 9.076, 9.077, 11.008, 11.009,
       11.013, 11.018, 12.040, 12.044, 25.062,
       39.049
   art 1 .... 9.063, 9.073, 9.075, 9.077
   art 2 .... 9.064
   art 3 .... 7.152, 9.065, 9.066
   art 4 .... 7.152, 9.066, 9.072, 9.075
   art 5 .... 9.067
   art 6 .... 9.072, 9.073, 9.074, 9.075,
       9.076, 9.077
1658/82 .... 4.042
2176/84 .... 17.005, 17.015
3626/84 .... 4.047
4055/85 .... 7.066
4005/86
   art 1 .... 8.232
4055/86/EEC 1.001, 1.053, 3.103, 5.061,
       5.069, 5.070, 5.093, 5.142, 6.131, 6.132,
       6.134, 6.137, 7.001, 7.006, 7.007, 7.008,
       7.009, 7.010, 7.012, 7.013, 7.014, 7.015,
       7.016, 7.017, 7.018, 7.020, 7.021, 7.023,
       7.027, 7.036, 7.039, 7.067, 7.117, 7.118,
       7.119, 7.123, 7.124, 7.129, 7.135, 7.136,
       7.143, 7.157, 7.164, 7.165, 7.166, 7.169,
       7.171, 7.176, 7.177, 7.191, 7.194, 7.196,
       7.198, 7.219, 7.224, 7.226, 7.230, 7.236,
       7.269, 7.297, 7.298, 7.300, 8.230, 8.237,
       8.239, 11.017, 11.017, 15.039, 17.001,
       18.026, 18.027, 34.060, 48.029, 48.032,
       48.033
   art 1 .... 4.072, 5.113, 5.114, 5.116, 6.128,
       7.012, 7.022, 7.029, 7.153, 7.158, 7.160,
       7.161, 7.189, 7.190, 7.191, 7.191, 7.227,
       7.246, 7.258, 7.269, 7.298, 15.050
   art 1(1) 7.024, 7.027, 7.027, 7.035, 7.135,
       7.157, 7.158, 7.191, 7.197, 7.231, 7.258,
       7.269, 7.298, 8.232, 13.088, 48.033
   art 1(2) 7.012, 7.025, 7.027, 7.035, 7.197,
       7.258, 7.269
   art 1(3) 7.026, 7.161, 7.197, 7.258
   art 1(4) 7.067, 7.219, 7.222, 7.225, 7.227,
       7.228
   art 2 .... 7.029, 7.298
   art 2(1) 7.226
   art 3 .... 7.030, 7.298, 7.299, 7.301, 7.302,
       7.303
   art 4 .... 7.030, 7.032, 7.298
   art 4(1) 7.299, 7.299, 7.301, 7.302, 7.303
   art 4(1)(a) 7.298
   art 4(1)(b) 7.298
   art 5 .... 7.033, 7.151, 7.298, 7.298, 7.299,
       7.301, 7.304
   art 5(1) 4.072, 5.113, 5.116, 7.146, 7.147,
       7.152, 7.154, 7.307
   art 5(6) 5.116
   art 6 .... 4.072, 5.113, 7.034, 7.151
   art 6(1) 5.083, 39.049, 39.049
   art 6(2) 5.083, 5.083, 7.034, 7.146, 7.148,
       7.153, 7.154, 39.049, 39.049
   art 6(3) 7.034
   art 6(4) 7.153
   art 6(5) 7.146
   art 7 .... 4.072, 5.113, 5.116, 7.028, 7.036
   art 8 .... 7.037, 7.161, 7.197
   art 9 .... 7.035, 7.135, 7.176
   art 10 .... 7.021
   art 12 .... 7.016, 7.020
   Recital 12 .... 7.258
   Recital 7 .... 7.258
   Recital 8 .... 7.258
   Recital 9 .... 7.258
4056/86/EEC 1.029, 1.042, 1.057, 1.058,
       3.041, 3.103, 5.002, 5.009, 5.071, 5.087,
       5.133, 5.137, 5.140, 5.150, 5.153, 5.162,
       7.113, 7.131, 9.003, 9.021, 9.048, 9.070,
       10.016, 10.112, 10.113, 10.114, 10.214,

10.219, 11.001, 11.002, 11.004, 11.005, 11.006, 11.007, 11.008, 11.009, 11.010, 11.017, 11.017, 11.019, 11.020, 11.021, 11.024, 11.032, 11.036, 11.038, 11.039, 11.040, 11.050, 11.131, 11.137, 11.138, 11.139, 11.140, 11.141, 11.142, 12.001, 12.002, 12.004, 12.005, 12.007, 12.008, 12.009, 12.012, 12.012, 12.015, 12.017, 12.018, 12.021, 12.023, 12.025, 12.028, 12.030, 12.031, 12.032, 12.033, 12.034, 12.035, 12.037, 12.038, 12.041, 12.042, 12.043, 12.044, 12.044, 12.047, 12.051, 12.053, 12.055, 12.056, 12.061, 12.068, 12.082, 12.091, 12.165, 12.180, 12.181, 12.185, 12.193, 13.083, 13.090, 14.013, 14.016, 14.017, 14.020, 14.023, 14.026, 14.027, 14.037, 14.043, 14.046, 14.064, 14.067, 14.068, 14.069, 14.083, 16.084, 16.135, 17.001, 17.010, 18.026, 18.027, 46.077

art 1 ..... 5.077, 7.034, 11.028, 11.029, 11.030, 11.039, 11.044

art 1(2)............ 7.034, 11.032, 11.033, 11.035, 11.087

art 1(3)...11.035

art 1(3)(a) 12.032, 12.048, 12.180

art 1(3)(b) 5.150, 9.004, 11.003, 11.025, 11.042, 11.043, 11.060, 11.061, 11.081

art 1(3)(c) 5.150, 11.082

art 2 .... 5.077, 11.041, 11.046, 11.050, 11.053, 11.054, 11.055, 11.056, 11.058, 12.081, 14.025, 14.029, 14.034, 14.036

art 2(1)..11.047, 11.050

art 2(1)(c) 11.053

art 2(2)...11.049

art 3 ... 5.077, 11.025, 11.034, 11.059, 11.060, 11.061, 11.062, 11.066, 11.069, 11.071, 11.072, 11.077, 11.080, 11.081, 11.083, 11.084, 11.085, 11.086, 11.087, 11.097, 11.100, 14.027, 14.029

arts 3–7...5.150

art 4 .... 11.059, 11.061, 11.062, 11.063, 11.069, 11.072, 11.133

art 5 .... 11.059, 11.071, 11.072, 11.073, 11.075, 11.076, 11.079, 11.080, 11.083, 11.084, 11.118, 11.121

art 5(1)........................ 7.034, 11.074, 11.082

art 5(2)....................... 11.076, 11.082, 11.133

art 5(3)....................... 11.077, 11.078, 11.133

art 5(4)..11.079

art 5(5).......... 11.118, 11.120, 11.130, 11.132, 11.133

art 6 ... 7.033, 11.059, 11.069, 11.082, 11.082, 11.083

art 7 .... 11.083, 11.084, 11.090, 11.091, 11.092, 11.095, 11.096, 11.108, 11.109, 11.118, 11.121, 11.123, 11.124

art 7(1)....................................11.083, 11.084

art 7(2)....................................11.083, 11.084

art 7(2)(b)(i) 7.153

art 7(2)(c) 11.084

art 8 ....11.086

art 8(1)....................................11.085, 11.087

art 8(2)......................5.150, 11.085, 11.087

art 8(3)..11.087

art 9 ....11.088, 11.089

art 9(1)..11.089

art 9(2)..11.089

art 9(3)..11.089

art 10 .... 11.085, 11.086, 11.087, 11.091, 11.092, 11.093, 11.098, 11.099, 11.100, 11.110, 11.111, 11.130, 11.132, 11.134

art 11 .... 7.038, 11.094, 11.095, 11.096, 11.123, 11.124, 11.125, 11.126, 11.129

art 11(1)..11.096

art 11(2)..11.096

art 11(3)..11.096

art 11(4)........ 11.083, 11.084, 11.096, 11.099, 11.102, 11.103

art 12 .... 11.097, 11.100, 11.118, 11.120, 11.130, 11.132, 11.135

art 12(1)..11.099

art 12(2)..................... 10.211, 11.099, 11.109

art 12(3)......... 11.099, 11.100, 11.108, 11.110, 11.111, 11.125, 11.126, 11.129

art 12(4)........ 11.099, 11.102, 11.103, 11.111, 11.126

art 13 ....11.102

art 13(1)....................................11.118, 11.121

art 13(2)....................................11.100, 11.104

art 13(3)........ 11.100, 11.105, 11.106, 11.107, 11.123, 11.124, 11.126, 11.129

art 14 ....11.108, 11.109

art 15 .... 11.088, 11.089, 11.110, 11.111

art 15(1)..11.111

art 15(2)..................... 11.098, 11.099, 11.111

art 15(3)........ 11.111, 11.118, 11.122, 11.123, 11.124

art 15(4)........ 11.111, 11.118, 11.122, 11.123, 11.124

art 15(5) 11.111
art 15(6) 11.111
art 16 .... 11.112, 11.114
art 16(2) 11.113
art 16(3) 11.113, 11.118, 11.120
art 16(4) 11.113
art 16(5) 11.113, 11.118, 11.120, 11.123, 11.124
art 16(6) 11.113
art 17 .... 11.116, 11.117, 11.118, 11.120
art 17(1) 11.116
art 17(2) 11.116
art 18 .... 11.114, 11.117, 11.118, 11.120
art 18(1) 11.115, 11.116
art 18(2) 11.115
art 18(3) 11.115, 11.116, 11.118, 11.120, 11.123, 11.124
art 18(4) 11.115
art 18(6) 11.115
art 19 .... 11.118, 11.120, 11.126
art 19(1) 11.120
art 19(1)(a) 11.120
art 19(1)(b) 11.112, 11.113
art 19(1)(c) 11.114, 11.115
art 19(2) 11.121, 11.122
art 19(3) 11.122
art 19(4) 11.120, 11.122
art 20 .... 11.123, 11.124, 11.126
art 20(1) 11.124
art 20(1)(a) 11.124
art 20(1)(c) 11.112, 11.113, 11.124
art 20(1)(d) 11.114, 11.115, 11.124
art 20(2) 11.124
art 20(3) 11.124
art 21 .... 11.127, 11.128
art 22 .... 11.120
art 23 .... 11.117, 11.125
art 23(1) 11.126, 11.130, 11.132, 11.136
art 23(2) 11.126, 11.130, 11.132
art 23(3) 11.126
art 24 .... 11.117
art 24(1) 11.117
art 24(2) 11.117
art 24(3) 11.117
art 25(1) 11.096, 11.100, 11.107, 11.129
art 25(2) 11.096, 11.100, 11.107, 11.129
art 26 .... 5.150, 11.110, 11.111, 11.130, 11.132
art 27 .... 11.023
Recital 1 .... 11.008

Recital 2 .... 11.008
Recital 3 .... 11.008
Recital 8 .... 12.003, 12.009
Recital 9 .... 11.065
4057/86/EEC 1.063, 3.103, 4.072, 5.071, 5.072, 5.113, 5.116, 6.018, 11.017, 11.017, 17.001, 17.002, 17.004, 17.005, 17.007, 17.008, 17.010, 17.013, 17.015, 17.016, 17.023, 17.033, 17.053, 18.027
art 1 .... 17.001, 17.009
art 2 .... 17.043
art 2(2) 17.043
art 3(a) 17.019, 17.020, 17.024
art 3(b) 17.012
art 3(d) 17.019
art 4(2) 17.017
art 5 .... 17.032
art 5(1) 17.024, 17.025
art 5(1)(c) 17.032
art 5(2) 17.026
art 5(2)(a) 17.032
art 5(2)(b) 17.032
art 5(3) 17.027
art 5(3)(a) 17.032
art 5(4) 17.029
art 5(5) 17.026
art 5(6) 17.024
art 6 .... 17.030
art 6(1) 17.030
art 6(2) 17.030
art 6(3) 17.030
art 6(4) 17.030
art 7 .... 17.053
art 7(1) 17.030
art 7(1)(a) 17.031
art 9(1) 17.039
art 10(1) 17.040
art 12 .... 17.018, 17.043
art 15(2) 17.048
art 16 .... 17.051
art 18 .... 17.010
Recital 1 .... 17.006
Recital 3 .... 17.006
Recital 4 .... 17.006
Recital 5 .... 17.009, 17.015
Recital 6 .... 17.012
4058/86 .... 1.064, 3.103, 4.072, 5.069, 5.073, 5.116, 7.009, 11.017, 11.017, 18.001, 18.002, 18.003, 18.004, 18.005, 18.006,

18.007, 18.008, 18.009, 18.010, 18.011,
18.017, 18.026, 18.027, 18.028, 18.037
art 1 .... 18.010
art 2 .... 18.010
art 3 .... 18.012, 18.013, 18.018
art 4 .... 18.013, 18.016
art 4(1)(b) 18.018
art 4(2) 5.076
art 4(6) 5.076
art 5 .... 18.018, 18.019
art 6(1) 18.020, 18.021
art 6(2) 18.021
art 6(3) 18.022
art 6(5) 5.076
art 7 .... 18.023
art 8 .... 18.025
art 9 .... 18.009
2658/87/EEC 48.056
3975/87 .... 5.009, 11.010, 11.090
3976/87 .... 11.010
2423/88 .... 17.007
4260/88 .... 5.087, 11.130, 11.131, 11.131,
11.132
 Annex I 11.135, 11.136
 art 1 .... 11.133
 art 2 .... 11.134
 art 4 .... 11.135
 art 5 .... 11.136
 art 6 .... 11.136
 Recital 3 .... 11.134
15/89 .... 17.053
1100/89 .... 4.042
4064/89 .... 16.002, 16.073
 art 2(3) 16.038
 art 22(2) 14.024
613/91 .... 5.100, 6.045, 6.046, 6.062, 6.064,
6.065, 6.069, 6.078, 26.013, 26.020
 art 1 .... 6.061, 6.062, 6.066
 art 1(a) 6.060
 art 1(c) 6.063
 art 2 .... 6.063
 art 2(a) 6.066
 art 3 .... 6.066, 6.070, 6.072
 art 3(1) 6.067, 6.068
 art 3(3) 6.068
 art 4 .... 6.070
 art 5 .... 6.072
 art 6 .... 6.074
 art 7 .... 6.060, 6.072, 6.073, 6.075
 art 9 .... 6.077

3921/91 .... 7.256
443/92 .... 25.067
479/92/EEC 5.098, 5.104, 12.033, 14.050,
14.050, 14.060, 14.060
 art 2 .... 14.020
 Recital 1 .... 14.050
2577/92
 art 3(2) 7.243
2913/92 .... 44.020, 44.022
 art 79 .... 19.080
3577/92/EEC 5.070, 5.107, 5.108, 5.142,
6.098, 7.001, 7.006, 7.007, 7.040, 7.064,
7.071, 7.079, 7.090, 7.117, 7.161, 7.182,
7.183, 7.203, 7.204, 7.205, 7.210, 7.219,
7.224, 7.225, 7.228, 7.248, 7.249, 7.250,
7.253, 7.254, 7.255, 7.257, 7.271, 7.278,
7.283, 7.286, 7.287, 15.039, 34.060,
46.077, 48.029, 48.032
 art 1 .... 7.072, 7.083, 7.115, 7.179, 7.184,
7.185, 7.188, 7.200, 7.208, 7.209, 7.211,
7.215, 7.216, 7.217, 7.224, 7.225, 7.228,
7.242, 7.247, 7.249, 7.271, 7.277, 7.281,
7.287, 12.180
 art 1(1) 7.202, 7.205, 7.247, 7.252, 7.256,
7.256, 7.281, 7.282, 48.033
 art 1(3) 7.184
 art 2 .... 7.046, 7.179, 7.185, 7.206, 7.247,
7.249, 7.252, 7.276
 art 2(1) 7.073, 7.094, 7.215, 7.218, 7.221,
7.222, 7.224, 7.225, 7.256
 art 2(1)(a) 7.210
 arts 2(1)(a)–(c) 7.256
 art 2(1)(c) 7.181, 7.206, 7.210
 art 2(2) 7.074, 48.000
 art 2(3) 7.075, 7.092, 7.187, 7.188
 art 2(4) 7.076
 art 2(5) 7.077, 7.100
 art 3 .... 7.200, 7.208, 7.252
 art 3(1) 7.094, 7.098, 7.207, 7.242, 7.256
 art 3(2) 7.095, 7.185, 7.207, 7.241, 7.242,
7.245
 art 3(3) 7.096, 7.240, 7.240, 7.241, 7.242,
7.245
 art 3(4) 7.096
 art 3(c) 7.185
 art 4 .... 7.093, 7.179, 7.184, 7.185, 7.188,
7.209, 7.212, 7.247, 7.249, 7.277,
7.287, 15.049
 art 4(1) 7.184, 7.187, 7.188, 7.286
 art 4(2) 7.184, 7.185, 7.187, 7.277

art 5 ....5.108, 7.099, 7.111, 7.112, 7.115	307/1999/EC 8.306
art 5(1)...............................7.101, 7.102, 7.115	659/1999/EC
art 5(2)..7.101, 7.103	art 19(2)...15.054
art 6 ....7.084, 7.085, 7.200, 7.208, 7.213,	955/1999/EC 19.080
7.252, 7.278	1073/1999 ....27.024
art 6(1)....................7.115, 7.116, 7.161, 7.256	823/2000/EC 5.134, 5.146, 5.153, 5.155,
art 6(2)...7.249, 7.276	5.164, 12.003, 12.004, 12.005, 12.028,
art 6(3).......6.098, 6.098, 7.206, 7.247, 7.249,	12.044, 12.133, 12.180, 14.017, 14.018,
7.276	14.020, 14.040, 14.041, 14.042, 14.065,
art 7 ....7.080, 7.087, 7.213	14.067, 14.071, 14.083
art 8 ....7.105	art 3(2)(d)...14.070
art 9 ....7.108, 7.209, 7.214, 7.279, 7.281	art 3(2)(e) 14.070
art 10 ....7.107	art 3(2)(f)..14.070
Recital 10 ....7.099	art 6 ....12.149
Recital 11 ....7.106	2658/2000/EC 12.177
Recital 2 ....7.079	44/2001/EC 19.031, 19.041, 21.008, 21.009,
Recital 3 ....7.078, 7.216	46.140, 46.142, 47.002, 47.007, 47.091
Recital 4 ....7.078, 7.216	art 80 ....47.007
Recital 5 ....7.080, 7.088	45/2001/EC 27.073, 39.080, 44.024
Recital 6 ....7.081	68/2001/EC 15.047
Recital 8 ....7.082	1049/2001/EC 39.081, 42.054
Recital 9 ....7.091, 7.187	art 8 ....27.073
3760/92 ....6.098, 6.098	1406/2001
1836/93/EEC 19.069	art 4 ....8.187
2158/93 ....5.110	417/2002/EC 12.076, 22.110
2454/93 ....44.022	1406/2002/EC 5.143, 8.083, 8.085, 8.089,
2978/94 ....26.020, 26.103	8.093, 19.240, 19.278, 19.295, 26.029,
870/95/EEC........5.120, 14.017, 14.020, 14.040,	27.006, 28.015, 31.006, 36.022, 37.008
14.040, 14.050, 16.084	art 1 ....27.012, 27.013
art 1(1)...14.041	art 1(1).......................................27.002, 27.026
art 6 ....14.041	art 1(2).......................................27.026, 27.027
art 7 ....14.041	art 1(3)...27.027
3051/95 ....5.123, 26.013, 26.020, 33.003,	art 2 ....27.031, 27.052, 27.053, 27.065,
33.008, 33.026, 34.022	27.068
art 5(2)...33.012	art 2(2)...27.032
3094/95/EU 22.031	art 2(2)(a)..27.033
385/96 ....22.031, 22.038	art 2(2)(b).......................................27.034, 42.131
118/97/EC 8.306, 8.343, 8.351	art 2(2)(c)..27.035
543/97/EC 5.135, 41.008	art 2(2)(d)......................................27.012, 27.036
1310/97 ....16.002	art 2(3)..27.012, 27.037
75/98/EC 41.010	art 2(3)(a)..27.038
1540/98/EC 15.039, 15.045, 22.029	art 2(3)(b)..27.039
2842/98 ....13.080	art 2(3)(c)....................8.353, 27.040, 36.022
art 6 ....13.080	art 2(3)(d)..27.041
art 7 ....13.080	art 2(4)(a)..27.043
art 8 ....13.080	art 2(4)(c)..27.045
44/200 ....46.034	art 2(4)(d)...27.046
823/200/EC 12.006, 12.033	art 2(4)(e)..27.047
906/200 ....14.006	art 2(4)(f)..27.048
964/1992 ....11.139	art 2(4)(g)...27.049

art 2(4)(h)	27.050	art 13(2)	27.018
art 2(4)(i)	27.048	art 13(3)	27.015
art 2(5)	27.012, 27.071	art 13(4)	27.015
art 2(b)(i)	28.110	art 13(5)	27.015
art 2(b)(iii)	5.160	art 13(6)	27.015
art 2(e)	30.030	art 13(7)	27.015
art 21	27.012	art 14	27.017
art 22	27.025, 27.074	art 14(1)	27.017
art 24	27.006	art 14(2)	27.017, 27.018
art 2a	27.052, 27.068	art 14(3)	27.017
art 2a(1)	27.053	art 15	27.018
art 2a(2)	27.054	art 15(1)	27.018
art 2a(2)(a)	27.055	art 15(2)	27.012, 27.018
art 2a(2)(b)	27.056	art 15(3)	27.019
art 2a(2)(c)	27.057	art 16	27.012, 27.012, 27.018, 27.020
art 2a(2)(d)	27.058	art 17	27.018
art 2a(2)(e)	27.059	art 17(2)	27.014
art 2a(2)(f)	27.060	art 18	27.012, 27.018
art 2a(3)	27.061	art 19	27.012, 27.018
art 2a(3)(a)	27.062	Recital 1	27.004
art 2a(3)(b)	27.063	Recital 3	27.026
art 2a(3)(c)	27.064	Recital 4	27.028
art 2b	27.064, 27.065	Recital 5	27.029
art 3	19.295, 27.012, 27.018, 27.034, 27.040, 27.053, 27.069, 27.070	Recital 6	27.028
		Recital 7	27.072
art 3(4)	27.060	Recital 8	27.079
art 3(5)	27.060	Recital 9	27.011
art 4	27.073, 31.085	Recital 10	27.011
art 5(1)	27.008	Recital 11	27.024, 27.074
art 5(2)	27.008	Recital 12	27.024
art 5(3)	27.010	2099/2002/EC	8.184, 8.193, 26.011, 28.129, 29.063, 29.092, 29.150, 29.155, 30.054, 31.089, 34.060, 34.099, 37.096
art 5(4)	27.008, 27.018		
art 6	27.020		
art 6(2)	27.018	art 1	26.012
art 7	27.021	art 2	26.013
art 8	27.022	art 2(2)	26.012, 26.017, 26.019, 26.103
art 9(1)	27.023	art 3	6.087, 19.083, 20.018, 26.015, 28.116, 33.025, 34.010, 34.034, 34.053, 46.023, 46.162
art 9(2)	27.023		
art 10	27.012		
art 10(2)	27.065	art 3(1)	26.015
art 10(2)(c)	27.018	art 3(2)	26.015
art 10(2)(g)	27.018	art 3(3)	26.015, 26.019
art 11	27.012	art 4	26.016, 26.018
art 11(1)	27.012	art 5	6.089, 19.084, 19.300, 26.015, 26.016, 26.017, 26.018, 28.130, 29.064, 29.093, 30.055, 33.024, 34.035, 34.086, 37.033, 46.022, 46.163
art 11(2)	27.014		
art 11(3)	27.014		
art 11(4)	27.014		
art 12(1)	27.016		
art 12(2)	27.016	art 5(6)	26.015
art 13(1)	27.015	art 6	26.018

TABLE OF LEGISLATION

art 7 ....26.015, 26.019
art 8 ....26.015
2204/2002/EC 15.043
417/20028 ....16.100
1/2003/EC 5.140, 5.150, 5.153, 10.015,
       10.017, 10.019, 10.105, 10.164, 10.165,
       10.180, 10.219, 11.007, 11.008, 11.025,
       11.038, 11.039, 11.050, 11.061, 11.084,
       11.109, 12.003, 12.005, 12.012, 12.021,
       12.029, 12.030, 12.032, 12.038, 12.042,
       12.043, 12.044, 12.044, 12.048, 12.049,
       12.049, 12.051, 12.060, 12.164, 12.180,
       12.181, 12.190, 12.210, 14.021, 14.036,
       14.042, 14.064, 14.093, 14.094
   art 2 ....10.183
   art 3 ....12.153
   art 8 ....10.191
   art 9 ....12.203
   art 9(1) 10.222, 12.196
   art 11(6) 12.203
   art 14 ....14.058
   art 16(1) 12.203
   art 17 ....10.178
   art 27(4) 12.203
   art 32 ....5.150, 12.048
   art 32(a) 12.001, 12.032
   art 32(b) 12.001, 12.032
   art 35 ....10.165
782/2003/EC 20.005, 20.008, 20.009, 26.013
   Annex I 20.010, 20.024
   Annex II 20.010
   Annex III 20.010
   Annex IV 20.010
   art 1 ....20.010
   art 2 ....20.010
   art 3 ....20.012
   art 3(1) 20.013, 20.014
   art 3(1)(a) 20.013
   art 3(1)(b) 20.013
   art 3(1)(c) 20.025, 20.026
   art 3(2) 20.012
   art 4 ....20.013, 20.015
   art 5 ....20.014, 20.015, 20.024, 20.025,
                     20.025, 20.028
   art 6 ....20.015, 20.021, 20.027
   art 6(1) 20.015
   art 6(2) 20.015
   art 6(3) 20.015, 20.021
   art 7 ....20.016, 20.021, 20.027
   art 8 ....20.017, 20.021

   art 9(1) 20.018
   art 9(2) 20.015, 20.016, 20.017, 20.018
   art 9(3) 20.018
   Recital 1 ....20.001
   Recital 3 ....20.003
   Recital 5 ....20.004
   Recital 6 ....20.004
   art 10 ....20.020
   art 11 ....20.006
859/2003 ....8.346
   art 1 ....8.350
   art 2(1) 8.343, 8.351
   art 2(2) 8.343, 8.351
1382/2003/EC 15.059, 41.010
   art 5(2) 15.052
1644/2003 ....27.006
1882/2003 ....32.003
139/2004/EC 10.093, 10.094, 10.105, 10.164,
       12.175, 12.175, 14.024, 16.001, 16.002,
       16.003, 16.005, 16.007, 16.008, 16.009,
       16.010, 16.011, 16.021, 16.024, 16.034,
       16.048, 16.048, 16.054, 16.132, 16.146,
       16.168, 16.169, 16.172, 16.174, 16.179,
       48.043
   art 1 ....16.036, 16.042, 16.098
   art 1(2) 16.015, 16.025
   art 1(3) 16.026
   art 2 ....16.037
   art 2(1) 16.037, 16.038
   art 2(4) 12.175, 16.039
   art 2(5) 16.039
   art 3 ....16.012, 16.016, 16.036, 16.042
   art 3(1) 16.013, 16.018
   art 3(1)(a) 16.033, 16.036
   art 3(1)(b) 16.016, 16.033, 16.036, 16.161,
                     29.155
   art 3(2) 14.024, 16.014
   art 3(3) 16.015
   art 3(4) 12.175, 16.161
   art 3(5) 16.017
   art 4 ....16.034, 16.036, 16.042, 16.161,
                     29.155
   art 4(1) 16.032
   art 4(2) 16.033
   art 4(3) 16.034, 16.035
   art 4(4) 16.034, 16.049
   art 4(5) 16.034, 16.042, 16.097
   art 5 ....16.027
   art 6 ....16.040, 16.043
   art 6(1) 16.040

art 6(1)(a) 16.040, 16.041	42.132, 42.133, 42.135, 42.136, 42.138, 42.141, 44.010
art 6(1)(b) 16.040, 16.041, 16.042, 16.141, 16.142, 16.147, 16.148, 16.149, 16.170, 29.155	Annex I....................... 42.009, 42.017, 42.110
	Annex II 42.009, 42.017
art 6(1)(c) 16.040	Annex III.. 42.017
art 6(2).. 16.043	art 1(1)... 42.015
art 7 .... 16.042	art 1(2)... 42.015
art 8(1).. 16.040, 16.042	art 2 .... 42.016, 42.017, 42.049
art 8(2).. 16.040, 16.042	art 2(5)..................................... 42.004, 42.047
art 8(3).. 16.040, 16.042	art 2(7)... 42.047
art 8(4)... 16.040	art 3 ....42.043, 42.048
art 9 ....16.040, 16.045	art 3(1)........................28.068, 42.026, 42.049
art 9(2)... 16.049	art 3(2).......... 28.068, 42.009, 42.027, 42.032, 42.040
art 9(3)... 16.049	
art 9(5)... 16.049	art 3(3).......... 28.068, 42.009, 42.032, 42.040, 42.129
art 9(6)... 16.036	
art 9(7)... 16.036	art 3(4)................................... 42.028, 42.029
art 9(8)............................ 16.036, 16.049	art 3(5)................................... 38.009, 42.030
art 9(9)... 16.036	art 3(6)... 42.030
art 10(6)... 16.042	art 3(7)... 42.031
art 16 .... 16.053	art 3(8)... 42.032
art 17 .... 16.034	art 4(1)... 42.033
art 18 .... 16.034	art 4(2)... 42.034
art 20 .... 16.034	art 4(3)..................................... 42.035, 42.054
art 21 .... 16.049	art 5(1)... 42.037
art 22 .... 16.045	art 5(2)..................................... 42.038, 42.054
art 25 .... 16.002	art 5(3)... 42.039
art 26 .... 16.002	art 5(4)..................................... 42.040, 42.054
Recital 7 .... 16.002, 16.002	art 5(6)... 42.049
Recital 9 .... 16.023	art 6 ....42.046, 44.003
Recital 10 .... 16.021	art 6(1)..................................... 42.043, 42.044
Recital 11 .... 16.045	art 6(3)... 42.045
Recital 14 .... 16.046	art 7(1)... 42.046
Recital 15 .... 16.048	art 7(2)... 42.046
Recital 16 .... 16.047	art 7(4)... 42.046
Recital 17 .... 16.053	art 7(5)... 42.046
Recital 18 .... 16.049	art 8(1)... 42.047
Recital 19 .... 16.050	art 8(2)..................................... 42.047, 42.135
Recital 21 .... 16.051	art 9(1)... 42.048
411/2004 .... 12.081	art 9(2)... 42.048
415/2004 .... 26.011	art 9(3).....................................42.048, 42.129
463/2004/EC 12.033, 14.042, 14.065	art 9(4).......... 27.034, 42.009, 42.042, 42.048, 42.048, 42.064, 42.096, 42.105, 42.129
724/2004/EC 8.083, 27.006	
725/2004/EC 5.156, 28.105, 42.007, 42.009, 42.009, 42.009, 42.010, 42.011, 42.015, 42.016, 42.019, 42.020, 42.056, 42.057, 42.058, 42.070, 42.071, 42.078, 42.081, 42.082, 42.084, 42.092, 42.095, 42.098, 42.105, 42.106, 42.108, 42.110, 42.113, 42.115, 42.116, 42.117, 42.124, 42.129,	art 9(5)..................................... 42.042, 42.048
	art 9(6)....................... 42.042, 42.048, 42.054
	art 10 .... 42.049
	art 10(1)... 42.049
	art 10(2)... 42.049
	art 10(3)... 42.049
	art 10(4)... 42.049

TABLE OF LEGISLATION

art 10(5) 42.049, 42.049
art 10(6) 42.049
art 10(7) 42.050
art 10(8) 42.050
art 11(1) 42.048, 42.049, 42.050, 42.106, 42.125, 42.130
art 11(2) 42.048, 42.049, 42.050
art 11(3) 42.038
art 11(4) 42.049, 42.050
art 11(5) 42.049, 42.049, 42.050
art 12 .... 42.051
art 13(1) 42.054
art 13(2) 42.054, 42.105
art 13(3) 42.054, 42.105
art 14 .... 42.055
art 15 .... 42.009
Recital 2 .... 42.006, 42.014
Recital 3 .... 42.006
Recital 5 .... 42.011
Recital 7 .... 42.006
Recital 10 .... 42.012
Recital 11 .... 42.013
Recital 12 .... 42.065
Recital 13 .... 42.014
Recital 14 .... 42.014
Recital 17 .... 42.008
773/2004/EC 5.150, 12.180
789/2004 .... 6.045, 6.046, 6.077, 6.078, 6.079, 6.080, 26.013
  art 1 .... 6.081
  art 2 .... 6.082, 6.089
  art 2(b) 6.083
  art 3 .... 6.084
  art 3(1) 6.083
  art 3(2) 6.083
  art 4 .... 6.084, 6.086
  art 5 .... 6.085
  art 6 .... 6.086
  art 6(1) 6.084
  art 7 .... 6.086, 6.087
  art 7(2) 6.086
  art 7(3) 6.089
  art 8 .... 6.088
  art 9 .... 6.089
  art 10 .... 6.078
802/2004/EC 16.034, 16.043
2006/2004/EC 46.072, 46.073, 46.074, 46.085, 46.125, 48.053, 48.053
1/2005/EC 48.055, 48.055
  art 21 .... 48.055

61/2005 .... 14.043
611/2005 .... 5.146, 12.033, 14.017, 14.020, 14.042, 14.065
647/2005 .... 8.343, 8.351
725/2005 .... 42.137
768/2005 .... 27.065
884/2005 .... 42.104, 42.104, 42.105, 42.106
141/2006 .... 11.017, 11.139
149/2006 .... 12.067
336/2006 .... 26.013, 33.003, 33.004, 33.005
  Annex I 33.014, 33.027
  Annex II 33.003, 33.012, 33.020, 33.024, 33.027
  art 1 .... 33.013
  art 2 .... 33.014
  art 3(1) 33.013, 33.015, 33.018
  art 3(2) 33.016
  art 4 .... 33.017
  art 5 .... 33.018
  art 6 .... 33.019, 33.020
  art 7 .... 33.020
  art 7(1) 33.020
  art 7(2) 33.020
  art 7(3) 33.020
  art 7(4) 33.020
  art 8 .... 33.021
  art 9 .... 33.022
  art 10(1) 33.023
  art 10(2) 33.023
  art 10(3) 33.023
  art 11 .... 33.024
  art 11(1) 33.024
  art 11(2) 33.024
  art 12 .... 33.025
  art 12(2) 33.023
  art 12(2) 33.020
  art 12(3) 33.024
  art 13(1) 33.026
  art 14 .... 33.006, 33.012
  Recital 9 .... 33.007
562/2006 .... 44.020, 44.022
  art 7 .... 44.003
1013/2006/EC 5.175, 24.005, 24.007, 24.010, 24.011, 24.015, 24.094, 24.095, 24.097, 24.099
  art 1(3) 24.095
1080/2006/EC 15.067
1084/2006/EC 15.059
1367/2006/EC 19.240, 19.240, 24.090
  art 11 .... 24.090

1419/2006/EC 1.029, 1.058, 5.009, 5.150,
    5.153, 7.113, 10.016, 10.017, 11.006,
    11.007, 11.017, 11.020, 11.068, 12.001,
    12.038, 12.039, 12.040, 12.042, 12.046,
    12.047, 12.049, 12.050, 12.053, 12.058,
    12.066, 12.077, 12.081, 12.164, 12.175,
    12.180, 12.180, 12.181, 12.182, 14.018,
    14.064
  art 1 .... 5.150, 11.058
  art 2 .... 5.150, 12.055
  Recital 12 .... 12.055
  Recital 9 .... 11.058
1692/2006/EC 15.059
  art 5(1)(b) 15.059
  art 7 .... 15.059
1891/2006 .... 27.018
1907/2006 .... 24.019
2038/2006/EC 27.006, 27.012
93/2007/EC 20.023, 26.011
680/2007/EC 15.060
1393/2007/EC
  art 19 .... 47.040
1490/2007 .... 9.051, 9.070
324/2008 .... 42.104, 42.136
  art 1 .... 42.108
  art 2 .... 42.109
  art 2(11) 42.108
  art 3 .... 42.128
  art 3(1) 42.128
  art 3(2) 42.128
  art 4 .... 42.129
  art 4(1) 42.129
  art 4(2) 42.129
  art 4(3) 42.129
  art 5 .... 42.130
  art 5(1) 42.130
  art 5(2) 42.130
  art 5(3) 42.130
  art 5(4) 42.130
  art 5(5) 42.130
  art 6 .... 42.131
  art 7 .... 42.111
  art 7(1) 42.132
  art 7(2) 42.132
  art 7(3) 42.132
  art 7(4) 42.132
  art 8 .... 42.133, 42.133
  art 8(1) 42.133, 42.135
  art 8(2) 42.133
  art 8(2)(b) 42.136
  art 8(3) 42.133
  art 8(4) 42.133
  art 8(5) 42.133
  art 8(6) 42.133
  art 8(7) 42.133
  art 8(8) 42.133
  art 8(9) 42.133
  art 9 .... 42.133, 42.134
  art 9(1) 42.134
  art 9(2) 42.134
  art 9(3) 42.133, 42.134
  art 10 .... 42.135
  art 11 .... 42.135, 42.136
  art 12 .... 42.133
  art 12(1) 42.137, 42.140
  art 12(2) 42.137
  art 12(3) 42.137
  art 13 .... 42.138
  art 13(1) 42.138
  art 13(2) 42.138
  art 14 .... 42.139
  art 15 .... 42.140
  art 15(1) 42.140
  art 15(2) 42.140
  art 16 .... 42.135, 42.141
  art 17 .... 42.142
  art 18 .... 42.104
  art 19 .... 42.104
  Chapter I 42.107
  Chapter II 42.127
  Chapter III 42.127
  Chapter IV 42.127
450/2008 .... 44.022
536/2008 .... 20.021
  art 1 .... 20.024
  art 2 .... 20.025
  art 2(1) 20.025
  art 2(2) 20.025, 20.025
  art 2(3) 20.025
  art 3 .... 20.026
  art 3(1) 20.026
  art 3(2) 20.026
  art 3(3) 20.026
  art 4 .... 20.027
  art 5 .... 20.023
  art 8 .... 20.023
540/2008 .... 33.003
593/2008/EC
  art 6(1) 48.053
  art 6(2) 48.053

TABLE OF LEGISLATION

art 6(3) 48.053
art 6(4) 48.053
765/2008/EC 19.213, 19.234, 37.069
   art 2 .... 37.024, 37.025
   art 19 .... 37.051
   art 21 .... 37.071, 37.077
   art 30 .... 37.040
   Chapter III 37.009, 37.069
1033/2008 .... 16.034
1137/2008 .... 19.059, 32.003, 33.003, 34.040,
                                         46.006, 46.147
1272/2008 .... 24.019, 24.019
4/2009/EC 47.009
219/2009 .... 6.078, 6.079, 42.009, 42.056
223/2009 .... 46.059, 46.062
246/2009 .... 14.006, 14.043, 14.049, 14.050,
                                        14.052, 14.053, 14.060
   art 1 .... 14.054, 14.055, 14.056, 14.058
   art 2 .... 14.054
   art 3 .... 14.055
   art 4 .... 14.056
   art 5 .... 14.056
   art 6 .... 14.058
   art 7 .... 14.060
   art 8 .... 14.050
391/2009/EC 5.157, 5.160, 19.111, 19.256,
        24.033, 24.033, 24.036, 24.037, 26.013,
        27.040, 27.070, 28.073, 28.123, 28.125,
        29.004, 29.005, 29.006, 29.007, 29.014,
        29.033, 29.081, 29.083, 29.110, 29.111,
        29.112, 29.114, 29.116, 29.120, 29.128,
        29.131, 29.147, 29.152, 29.153, 29.154,
                                                  29.155
   Annex I 28.131, 29.039, 29.041, 29.042,
            29.043, 29.045, 29.064, 29.067, 29.071,
                              29.093, 29.124, 29.156
   Annex II 29.071
   art 1 .... 29.026, 29.027
   art 2 .... 29.028, 29.108, 29.124
   art 2(b) 29.064
   art 2(c) 29.026, 29.027, 29.028, 29.150,
                                           29.155, 48.037
   art 3 .... 29.040, 29.057, 29.124
   art 3(1) 29.039
   art 3(2) 29.039
   art 3(3) 29.039
   art 4 .... 29.040, 48.037
   art 4(1) 29.040, 29.040, 29.150, 29.155,
                                                 29.156
   art 4(2) 29.040

art 4(3) 29.040, 29.068, 29.150, 29.155
art 4(4) 29.040
art 4(5) 29.040
art 5 .... 29.041, 29.042, 29.068
art 6 ... 5.171, 26.013, 29.042, 29.043, 29.066,
      29.106, 29.106, 29.107, 29.107, 29.108,
                        29.121, 29.123, 29.134
art 6(1) 29.043, 29.124, 29.126
art 6(1)(a) 29.126
art 6(2) 29.043, 29.128
art 6(3) 29.129, 29.130, 29.132
art 7 ... 5.171, 26.013, 29.066, 29.068, 29.106,
      29.106, 29.107, 29.107, 29.108, 29.121,
                        29.123, 29.134
art 7(1) 29.043, 29.115, 29.133
art 7(1)(a) 29.132
art 7(1)(b) 29.132
art 7(1)(c) 29.132
art 7(1)(d) 29.132
art 7(1)(e) 29.132
art 7(2) 29.043, 29.132, 29.133
art 7(3) 29.044, 29.133
art 8 .... 29.133, 48.037
art 8(1) 29.042, 29.043, 29.045, 29.049,
                                                 29.069
art 8(2) 29.045, 29.046
art 8(3) 29.046
art 8(4) 29.039, 29.042, 29.048, 29.124,
                                                 29.156
art 9 .... 29.039, 29.042, 29.071, 29.124,
                                          29.140, 29.156
art 9(1) 29.049
art 9(2) 29.049
art 10 .... 29.039, 29.042, 29.124, 29.156
art 10(1) 29.050
art 10(2) 29.051
art 10(3) 29.052
art 10(4) 29.053
art 10(5) 29.054
art 10(6) 29.055
art 11 .... 29.042, 29.124, 29.156
art 11(1) 29.056, 29.071
art 11(2) 29.057
art 11(3) 29.058
art 11(4) 29.059
art 11(5) 29.060
art 11(6) 29.061
art 11(7) 29.062
art 12 .... 5.160
art 12(1) 29.048, 29.063

art 12(2)	29.042, 29.141
art 12(3)	29.039, 29.040, 29.044, 29.063, 29.067, 29.068, 29.141
art 12(4)	29.064, 29.065, 29.066
art 13(1)	29.064
art 13(2)	29.064
art 14	29.039
art 14(1)	29.065
art 14(2)	29.066, 29.109
art 14(3)	29.067
art 15	5.160, 48.037
art 15(1)	29.068, 29.150, 29.155
art 16	29.069, 29.149, 29.150, 29.155
art 17	29.070
art 18	29.071
art 19	29.003
Recital 3	29.027
Recital 4	29.008, 29.027
Recital 5	29.009
Recital 6	29.010
Recital 7	29.011, 29.040
Recital 8	29.012
Recital 9	29.012
Recital 10	29.013
Recital 12	29.015
Recital 13	29.016
Recital 14	29.016
Recital 15	29.016
Recital 17	29.018
Recital 18	29.017, 29.020
Recital 19	29.020
Recital 20	29.020
Recital 21	29.020
Recital 22	29.023
Recital 23	29.024, 29.027
Recital 24	29.025
392/2009/EC	5.157, 25.006, 26.013, 46.025, 46.028, 46.029, 46.038, 46.132, 46.132, 46.140, 46.183
Annex I	46.026, 46.039, 46.041, 46.047
Annex II	46.039, 46.041, 46.047
art 1	46.039
art 2	46.040
art 3	46.043
art 3(1)	46.041, 46.044
art 3(2)	46.041
art 4	46.042, 46.102
art 5	46.043
art 6	46.044
art 7	46.045
art 8	46.046
art 9	46.047
art 10	46.048
art 10(2)	46.047
art 11	46.027
art 12	46.027
Recital 1	46.025
Recital 3	46.030
Recital 4	46.031
Recital 5	46.044
Recital 7	46.032
Recital 8	46.032
Recital 10	46.033
Recital 12	46.035
Recital 13	46.042
Recital 16	46.046
Recital 17	46.036
Recital 19	46.037
596/2009	26.011
609/2009	14.096
Recital 12	14.093
Recital 13	14.094
906/2009/EC	5.153, 5.164, 5.172, 14.010, 14.020, 14.021, 14.021, 14.030, 14.042, 14.043, 14.053, 14.059, 14.060, 14.063, 14.064, 14.067, 14.069, 14.085, 14.086, 14.087, 14.090, 14.097
art 1	14.072
art 2(1)	9.014, 14.073
art 2(2)	14.075, 14.077
art 2(3)	14.075, 14.078
art 2(4)	14.079
art 3	14.080, 14.081, 14.085, 14.092
art 3(2)	14.080, 14.081
art 3(4)	14.070
art 4	14.081, 14.082, 14.083, 14.084
art 5	14.085, 14.089
art 6	14.092
art 7	14.017, 14.061
Recital 5	14.070
Recital 11	14.092
Recital 14	14.091
206/2010/EC	
art 12	48.055
428/2010	28.149, 29.157
art 1	28.150
art 2	28.150
697/2010	14.010
801/2010	26.035, 28.156
Annex	28.145, 28.145

art 1	26.036, 28.157	art 9(1)	46.096, 46.097
art 1(1)	28.157	art 9(2)	46.096
art 1(2)	28.157	art 9(3)	46.096
art 1(3)	28.157	art 9(4)	46.096
art 2	28.158	art 10	46.097, 46.098
art 3	26.036, 26.038	art 11	46.098
802/2010	26.028, 28.138	art 11(1)	46.098
art 1	26.030	art 11(1)(a)	46.099
art 2	26.031	art 11(2)	46.095, 46.098, 46.099
art 3	26.032	art 11(3)	46.098
art 3(1)	26.032	art 11(4)	46.098
art 3(2)	26.032	art 11(5)	46.098
art 4	26.033	art 12	46.099
1090/2010/EU	46.050, 46.066, 46.067, 46.068, 46.070, 46.071	art 12(1)	46.099
		art 12(2)	46.099
1177/2010	46.072, 46.073, 46.074, 46.075, 46.076, 46.077, 46.078, 46.079, 46.080, 46.081, 46.082, 46.083, 46.084, 46.085, 48.053	art 12(3)	46.098, 46.099
		art 13	46.097, 46.100
		art 13(1)	46.100
		art 13(2)	46.100
		art 13(3)	46.100
Annex I	46.095, 46.097	art 14	46.101
Annex II	46.100	art 15	46.102
Annex III	46.097, 46.100	art 15(1)	46.102
Annex IV	46.101	art 15(2)	46.102
art 1	46.087	art 15(4)	46.102
art 2	46.088	art 16	46.104, 46.105
art 2(1)(a)	48.053	art 16(1)	46.105
art 2(1)(b)	48.053	art 16(2)	46.088, 46.106
art 2(1)(c)	46.106, 48.053	art 16(3)	46.107
art 2(2)	46.089	art 17	46.108, 46.112, 46.116
art 2(3)	46.089	art 17(1)	46.109, 46.110, 46.112
art 2(4)	46.089, 46.121	art 17(2)	46.111, 46.112
art 2(5)	46.089	art 17(3)	46.113
art 3	46.090	art 18	46.088, 46.114, 46.116
art 3(e)	46.088, 48.053	art 18(1)	46.114
art 3(k)	46.110	art 18(2)	46.114
art 4(1)	46.090	art 18(3)	46.114
art 4(2)	46.090	art 19	46.088, 46.115, 46.116
art 5	46.092	art 19(1)	46.115
art 5(1)	46.092	art 19(2)	46.115
art 6	46.093	art 19(3)	46.115
art 7	46.094	art 19(4)	46.115
art 7(1)	46.094, 46.095	art 19(5)	46.115
art 7(2)	46.094	art 20	46.116
art 8	46.094, 46.095	art 20(1)	46.088, 46.108, 46.116
art 8(1)	46.095	art 20(2)	46.108, 46.116
art 8(2)	46.095	art 20(3)	46.116
art 8(3)	46.095	art 20(4)	46.088, 46.116
art 8(4)	46.095	art 21	46.117
art 8(5)	46.095	art 22	46.118
art 9	46.096		

art 23 ....46.119	art 5(1)..47.014
art 23(1)..46.119	art 6 ....47.015, 47.016, 47.020, 47.026,
art 23(2)..46.119	47.029
art 23(3)..46.119	art 7 ....47.017, 47.018, 47.019, 47.020,
art 24 ....46.120, 46.121	47.026, 47.029, 47.050, 47.051
art 24(1)..46.120	art 7(1)(a) 47.017
art 24(2)..46.120	art 7(3)..47.017
art 25 ....46.121, 46.122	art 7(7)..47.017
art 25(1)....................46.119, 46.121, 46.123	art 8 ....47.018, 47.020, 47.029, 47.050,
art 25(2)..46.121	47.051, 47.087
art 25(3)..46.121	art 8(1)..47.018
art 25(4)..46.121	art 9 ....47.019, 47.050, 47.051
art 26 ....46.122	art 10 ....47.020, 47.022
art 27 ....46.123	art 11 ....47.020, 47.022
art 28 ....46.124	art 12 ....47.021, 47.022
art 29 ....46.125	art 13 ....47.022, 47.087
Chapter I..46.086	art 13(3)..47.023
Chapter II 46.094	art 14 ....47.023
Chapter III...46.103	art 15 ....47.024, 47.035
Chapter V 46.121	art 15(5)..................................47.024, 47.025
Chapter VI...46.125	art 16 ....47.024, 47.025
Recital 13 ....46.112	art 17 ....47.026
Recital 2 ....46.076	art 17(1)..48.053
182/2011 ....8.184, 8.193, 19.243, 22.093,	art 17(1)(a) 48.053, 48.053
24.093, 31.089, 37.008	art 17(1)(b)..48.053
art 5 .....8.184, 8.193, 22.093, 24.093, 28.116,	art 17(3)..47.026
31.089, 37.096	art 18 ....47.027
art 5(4).........19.243, 24.093, 28.116, 31.089,	art 18(1)..................................47.015, 48.053
37.096	art 19 ....47.028, 47.035
651/2011 ....30.010, 30.044	art 20 ....47.029
205/2012 ....28.138	art 21 ....47.030
530/2012 ....26.011, 26.013, 26.023, 26.024	art 21(2)..47.015
art 5 ....26.040, 26.041, 26.045	art 22 ....47.031
art 6 ....26.040, 26.041	art 23 ....47.032, 47.035
art 65 ....26.045	art 24 ....47.015, 47.033, 47.038, 47.039
966/2012	art 24(5)..47.034
art 78 ....29.143	art 25 ....47.015, 47.035, 47.036, 47.037,
art 79 ....29.143	47.038, 47.044, 47.046
art 80 ....29.143	art 26 ....47.038, 47.044, 47.046
art 83 ....29.143	art 26(2)..47.038
1025/2012 ....37.038	art 27 ....47.039
1205/2012 ....26.028	art 28 ....47.040, 47.092
1215/2012 ....47.001, 47.002, 47.003, 47.005,	art 29 ....47.013, 47.043, 47.044
47.006, 47.011, 48.045	art 29(1)..47.044
art 1(1)..47.009	art 30 ....47.043, 47.045
art 1(2)....................................47.009, 47.010	art 31 ....47.043, 47.046, 47.047
art 2 ....47.010	art 31(2)..................................47.042, 47.044
art 3 ....47.010	art 32 ....47.043, 47.044, 47.048
art 4 ....47.012, 47.019, 47.050, 47.051	art 33 ....47.049, 47.050
art 5 ....47.014, 47.020	art 34 ....47.049, 47.051

art 35 .... 47.052
art 36 .... 47.054
art 37 .... 47.055
art 38 .... 47.056
art 39 .... 47.057
art 40 .... 47.058, 47.062
art 41 .... 47.060
art 42 .... 47.061
art 43 .... 47.062
art 44 .... 47.063
art 45 .... 47.054, 47.056, 47.060, 47.065,
47.067
art 46 .... 47.067
art 47 .... 47.068
art 48 .... 47.069
art 49 .... 47.072
art 49(1) 47.070
art 49(2) 47.070
art 50 .... 47.071, 47.072
art 51 .... 47.072
art 52 .... 47.074
art 53 .... 47.055, 47.061, 47.062, 47.075,
47.079
art 54 .... 47.076
art 55 .... 47.077
art 56 .... 47.078
art 57 .... 47.055, 47.061, 47.079
art 58 .... 47.081
art 59 .... 47.082
art 60 .... 47.079, 47.083
art 61 .... 47.085
art 62 .... 47.013
art 63 .... 47.013
art 64 .... 47.086
art 65 .... 47.087
art 66 .... 47.007
art 67 .... 47.088
art 68(1) 47.088
art 68(2) 47.088
art 69 .... 47.089, 47.090
art 70 .... 47.089, 47.090
art 71 .... 47.089, 47.089, 47.092
art 72 .... 47.007
art 73(1) 47.007
art 73(2) 47.007
art 73(3) 47.007
art 75 .... 47.007, 47.068, 47.070, 47.071
art 76 .... 47.007
art 76(1) 47.014, 47.015, 47.087, 47.089
art 76(2) 47.087, 47.089

art 79 .... 47.003
art 81 .... 47.007
Chapter V 47.084
Recital 3 .... 47.004
Recital 4 .... 47.004
Recital 5 .... 47.004
Recital 6 .... 47.004
Recital 10 .... 47.009
Recital 12 .... 47.009
Recital 17 .... 47.017, 47.020
Recital 21 .... 47.041
Recital 22 .... 47.041
Recital 23 .... 47.041
1268/2012
  arts 80–92 .... 29.143
100/2013 .... 27.006
517/2013 .... 46.130, 46.138
524/2013 .... 48.053
525/2013
  Annex I 19.245
  Annex II 19.245
  Annex III 19.245
  art 15 .... 19.245
  art 16 .... 19.245
  art 26 .... 19.243, 19.244, 19.248
576/2013 .... 48.055
952/2013 .... 48.056
1257/2013/EC 24.010, 24.011, 24.013,
24.014, 24.015, 24.016, 24.017, 24.018,
24.020, 24.026, 24.095, 24.097, 24.099,
48.041
  Annex I 24.020, 24.053, 24.054, 24.069,
24.080, 24.095, 24.098
  Annex II 24.020, 24.054, 24.070, 24.095
  Annex III 24.040
  art 1 .... 24.021, 24.099
  art 2 .... 24.011, 24.023, 24.068, 24.099
  art 2(1) 24.023, 48.041
  art 2(2) 24.023
  art 3 .... 24.024
  art 3(1) 24.024
  art 3(2) 24.047, 24.047
  art 3(3) 24.036
  art 4 .... 24.011, 24.053, 24.054, 24.068
  art 5 .... 24.011, 24.061, 24.068, 24.088,
24.099
  art 5(1) 24.054
  art 5(2) 24.011, 24.054, 24.068, 24.068,
  art 10 .... 24.066
  art 11 .... 24.011, 24.067, 24.068

art 12 .... 24.011, 24.023, 24.068, 24.068, 48.037
art 12(1)...................... 24.011, 24.068, 24.068
art 12(2)............................... 24.068, 24.069
art 12(3).. 24.068
art 12(4).. 24.070
art 12(5).. 24.071
art 12(6)............................... 24.071, 24.072
art 12(7)............................... 24.071, 24.072
art 12(8)...................... 24.011, 24.068, 24.073
art 13 .... 24.011, 24.047, 24.068, 24.068, 24.075, 24.079, 24.080, 24.081, 24.090, 24.091
art 13(1).. 24.076
art 13(2).. 24.077
art 13(3).. 24.078
art 14 .... 24.011, 24.068, 24.068, 24.081
art 14(1).. 24.079
art 14(2).. 24.079
art 14(3)............................... 24.079, 24.081
art 14(4).. 24.079
art 14(5).. 24.079
art 15 .... 24.047, 24.068, 24.081, 24.090, 24.091
art 15(1).. 24.080
art 15(2).. 24.080
art 15(2)(b).. 24.059
art 15(3).. 24.080
art 15(4).. 24.080
art 15(5).. 24.080
art 16 .... 24.047, 24.068, 24.080, 24.081, 48.041
art 16(1).. 24.081
art 16(1)(b)............................ 24.090, 24.091
art 16(2)...................... 24.054, 24.080, 24.081
art 16(3).. 24.081
art 16(4).. 24.081
art 16(5).. 24.081
art 16(6)...................... 24.011, 24.068, 24.081
art 17 .... 24.083
art 17(2).. 24.083
art 18 .... 24.011, 24.068, 24.084
art 18(1).. 24.084
art 18(2).. 24.084
art 19 .... 24.011, 24.068, 24.085
art 19(1).. 24.085
art 19(2).. 24.085
art 19(3).. 24.085
art 20 .... 24.011, 24.068, 24.086
art 21 .... 24.011, 24.068, 24.088

art 22 .... 24.068, 24.089
art 22(1).. 24.089
art 22(2).. 24.089
art 22(3).. 24.089
art 22(4).. 24.089
art 23 .... 24.090
art 23(1)................................ 24.090, 24.091
art 23(2).. 24.091
art 23(3).. 24.091
art 23(4).. 24.091
art 24 .... 24.054, 24.092
art 24(2).. 24.092
art 24(3).. 24.092
art 24(4).. 24.092
art 24(5).. 24.092
art 25 .... 24.062, 24.065, 24.068, 24.078, 24.080, 24.081, 24.093, 24.099
art 25(1).. 24.093
art 25(2).. 24.093
art 26 .... 24.068, 24.094
art 27 .... 24.095
art 28 .... 24.095
art 29 .... 24.096
art 30 .... 24.097
art 31 .... 24.011
art 32 .... 24.011, 24.068, 24.099
art 32(2)........ 24.054, 24.068, 24.073, 48.037 24.073

1257/2013/EC
art 5(2)... 48.037
art 5(3)... 24.054
art 5(4)... 24.054
art 5(5)... 24.054
art 5(5)(a)... 24.062
art 5(6)... 24.054
art 5(7)................................ 24.045, 24.054
art 5(8)................................ 24.054, 24.092
art 6 .... 24.055
art 6(1)................................ 24.055, 24.058
art 6(1)(b)... 24.060
art 6(2)... 24.056
art 6(2)(a)... 48.041
art 6(3)... 24.056
art 6(4)... 24.056
art 6(5)... 24.056
art 7 .... 24.045, 24.055, 24.061, 24.083
art 7(1)... 24.057
art 7(2)... 24.058
art 7(2)(d)... 24.047

art 7(3)..........24.056, 24.059, 24.077, 24.081, 24.081	art 3 ....29.125, 29.129, 29.144
art 7(4)...24.060	art 4 ....29.126, 29.130
art 8 ....24.061, 24.099	art 4(1)...29.126
art 8(1)...24.061	art 4(2)...29.126
art 8(2)...24.061	art 4(3)...29.126
art 8(3)...................................24.061, 24.073	art 4(4)...29.126
art 8(4)...24.061	art 5 ....29.126, 29.127, 29.129, 29.132
art 8(5)...................................24.061, 24.066	art 6 ....29.126, 29.126, 29.128, 29.129, 29.132
art 8(6)...................................24.061, 24.062	art 7 ....29.129
art 8(7)...................................24.061, 24.065	art 7(1)...29.137
art 8(8)...................................24.061, 24.062	art 7(2)...29.130
art 9 ....24.056, 24.062, 24.066, 24.067, 24.083, 24.099	art 8 ....29.126, 29.129, 29.130
	art 9 ....29.126, 29.129, 29.130, 29.131
art 9(1)...24.062	art 10 ....29.131, 29.133
art 9(3)...24.062	art 11 ....29.133
art 9(5)...24.063	art 12 ....29.133, 29.134, 29.135
art 9(6)...24.063	art 13 ....29.135
art 9(7)...24.064	art 14 ....29.136
art 9(8)...24.064	art 14(1)...29.136
art 9(9)..........24.045, 24.062, 24.065, 24.066	art 14(2)...29.136
Recital 4 ....24.005	art 14(3)...29.136
Recital 5 ....24.012	art 14(4)...29.136
Recital 6 ....24.006	art 14(5)...29.136
Recital 7 ....24.013	art 15 ....29.137, 29.144
Recital 9 ....24.014	art 16 ....29.138, 29.147
Recital 10 ....24.015	art 17 ....29.139
Recital 12 ....24.018	art 18 ....29.140, 29.147
Recital 13 ....24.017	art 19 ....29.141, 29.145
Recital 14 ....24.019	art 20 ....29.142
Title I...24.021	art 21 ....29.130, 29.143
Title II..24.052	art 22 ....29.144
Title III...24.074	art 22(2)...29.144
Title IV...24.082	art 22(3)...29.144
Title V..24.087	art 23 ....29.144, 29.145
Title VI...24.092	art 23(1)...29.144
1315/2013 ....42.030, 43.004	art 23(2)...29.145
Annex II 42.030	art 23(3)...29.145
art 20(2)...43.064	art 23(4)...29.145
651/2014 ....15.026, 15.071, 15.116, 15.128	art 24 ....29.134, 29.146, 29.147
art 4(1)...15.121	art 25 ....29.147
art 56b...15.121	art 26 ....29.148
art 56c...15.121	art 27 ....29.148
691/2014 ....14.017	Chapter IV..............................29.133, 29.134
697/2014 ....5.172, 14.017, 14.043, 14.059	Chapter V 29.148
art 1 ....14.030	Recital 2 ....29.109
702/2014 ....15.026, 15.071, 15.116	Recital 3 ....29.110
788/2014 ....5.171, 26.013, 29.106, 29.107	Recital 4 ....29.111
art 1 ....29.123	Recital 5 ....29.113, 29.115
art 2 ....29.124	Recital 6 ....29.113, 29.114

Recital 8	29.116
Recital 9	29.117
Recital 10	29.118
Recital 11	29.119
Recital 12	29.120
Recital 13	29.121
1355/2014	29.004
1257/2014	28.004
668/2015	29.149
755/2015	22.064
757/2015	5.176, 19.206, 19.214, 19.215, 19.246, 19.247, 26.023, 28.004
Annex I	19.224, 19.227, 19.228, 19.232, 19.235
Annex II	19.224, 19.227, 19.228, 19.232, 19.235, 19.248, 19.251
art 1	19.207, 19.249
art 2	19.208, 19.213, 19.249
art 2(1)	19.208
art 2(2)	19.208
art 3	19.209, 19.251
art 4	19.223, 19.247
art 4(1)	19.224
art 4(2)	19.224
art 4(3)	19.224, 19.248
art 5	19.224
art 5(2)	19.242
art 6	19.225, 19.232
art 7	19.225, 19.232
art 7(1)	19.225
art 7(2)	19.225
art 7(3)	19.225
art 7(4)	19.225
art 8	19.223, 19.226, 19.232, 19.238, 19.239
art 9	19.227, 19.232, 19.238, 19.239
art 9(1)	19.227, 19.249, 19.251
art 9(2)	19.227
art 10	19.227, 19.228, 19.232, 19.238, 19.239, 19.240
art 11	19.229, 19.230, 19.232, 19.235, 19.238, 19.239, 19.240
art 12	19.223, 19.229, 19.231, 19.232, 19.233, 19.235, 19.238, 19.239, 19.240
art 12(1)	19.231
art 12(2)	19.231
art 13	19.230, 19.232, 19.235
art 13(1)	19.225, 19.226, 19.227, 19.228
art 13(3)	19.223
art 13(4)	19.223
art 14	19.233, 19.234, 19.234, 19.235
art 15	19.234, 19.235
art 15(5)	19.242
art 16	19.234
art 16(3)	19.242
art 17	19.235, 19.240
art 17(4)	19.238
art 18	19.237, 19.239
art 19	19.238
art 20	19.239
art 20(1)	19.239
art 20(2)	19.239, 19.240
art 20(3)	19.239
art 20(4)	19.239
art 21	19.240
art 21(1)	19.238, 19.240
art 21(2)	19.240
art 21(3)	19.240
art 21(4)	19.240
art 21(5)	19.240
art 21(6)	19.240
art 22	19.241, 26.023
art 22(1)	19.241
art 22(2)	19.241
art 22(3)	19.241
art 23	19.224, 19.234, 19.234, 19.242
art 24	19.243
art 24(2)	19.225, 19.231, 19.235
2016/103	26.011
art 12	26.011
1035/2016/EU	22.002, 22.031, 22.038
art 1	22.045
art 1(1)	22.046
art 1(2)	22.047, 22.048
art 1(3)	22.048
art 1(3)(a)	22.049
art 1(3)(b)	22.050
art 1(3)(c)	22.051
art 1(3)(d)	22.052
art 1(3)(e)	22.053
art 1(3)(f)	22.054
art 1(3)(g)	22.055
art 2	22.057, 22.072
art 2(1)	22.058
art 2(11)	22.066
art 2(12)	22.067
art 2(13)	22.058
art 2(2)	22.059
art 2(3)	22.059
art 2(4)	22.060

art 2(5)	22.061	art 12	22.084, 22.086, 22.095
art 2(6)	22.062	art 13	22.096
art 2(7)	22.063	art 14	22.097
art 2(8)	22.064	art 14(1)	22.097
art 2(9)	22.064	art 14(2)	22.097
art 3	22.068	art 14(3)	22.097
art 3(3)	22.073	art 14(4)	22.097
art 3(5)	22.073	art 15	22.041, 22.042
art 3(8)	22.069	art 16(1)	22.043
art 4	22.069	art 16(2)	22.084, 22.086, 22.087
art 4(1)	22.069	art 17	22.031
art 4(3)	22.069	art 18	22.038, 22.040
art 5	22.070	art 23	22.041
art 5(1)	22.070, 22.071, 22.072, 22.074	art 207(2)	22.038
art 5(11)	22.078, 22.079	Recital 1	22.038
art 5(12)	22.084, 22.085	Recital 3	22.044
art 5(13)	22.080, 22.084, 22.085	Recital 4	22.044
art 5(2)	22.071	Recital 5	22.044
art 5(4)	22.073	1036/2016	22.044, 22.093
art 5(5)	22.074	1037/2016	22.093
art 5(6)	22.069, 22.074, 22.074, 22.075, 22.076	1624/2016	27.065
		1625/2016	27.006
art 5(8)	22.070	1927/2016	19.246
art 6	22.081	1928/2016	19.247
art 6(1)	22.080, 22.082	2071/2016	19.206
art 6(10)	22.072	306/2017	
art 6(2)	22.083	Annex	37.102
art 6(3)	22.083	art 1	37.101
art 6(3)(d)	22.076	art 2	37.102
art 6(4)	22.084, 22.084	352/2017	42.027, 42.029, 42.030, 42.031, 42.032, 42.033, 42.034, 43.004, 43.004, 43.005, 43.007, 43.009, 43.011, 43.012, 43.013, 43.015, 43.016, 43.017, 43.018, 43.019, 43.020, 43.021, 43.022, 43.023, 43.024, 43.025, 43.039, 43.040, 43.049, 43.076, 43.078, 43.085
art 6(5)	22.079, 22.084		
art 6(6)	22.084		
art 6(7)	22.084, 22.086		
art 6(8)	22.084, 22.086		
art 6(9)	22.077, 22.084, 22.086		
art 7	22.084, 22.086, 22.088, 22.091		
art 7(1)	22.084, 22.086, 22.088	art 1(1)	43.009
art 7(3)	22.068, 22.084, 22.086, 22.088	art 1(2)	43.027
art 7(4)	22.089	art 1(3)	43.028
art 8	22.090	art 1(4)	43.030
art 9	22.089, 22.091	art 1(5)	43.030
art 10	22.093	art 1(6)	42.030
art 10(1)	22.093	art 1(7)	42.032
art 10(2)	22.084, 22.086, 22.088, 22.089, 22.093	art 2(1)	43.027
		art 2(10)	43.027
art 10(5)	22.084, 22.086, 22.089	art 2(11)	43.066
art 11	22.094	art 2(12)	43.023
art 11(1)	22.094	art 2(13)	43.043
art 11(2)	22.094	art 2(14)	43.017
art 11(3)	22.094	art 2(16)	43.014, 43.026

art 2(17)	43.027
art 2(18)	42.029, 43.027
art 2(2)	43.027
art 2(3)	42.034
art 2(4)	43.028
art 2(5)	42.033
art 2(6)	43.027
art 2(7)	43.027
art 2(8)	43.027
art 2(9)	43.070
art 3	43.042
art 3(1)	43.040, 43.041
art 3(2)	43.040
art 3(3)	43.041
art 4	43.042, 43.047, 43.049, 43.054, 43.057
art 4(1)	43.042, 43.042, 43.043, 43.046, 43.052
art 4(2)	43.043, 43.046, 43.049
art 4(3)	43.043
art 4(4)	43.043, 43.044
art 4(5)	43.045
art 4(6)	43.042, 43.042, 43.046
art 4(7)	43.042, 43.047, 43.052
art 5	43.049
art 5(1)	43.049, 43.049
art 5(2)	43.049
art 5(3)	43.049
art 5(4)	43.049
art 5(5)	43.048
art 6	43.050, 43.052
art 6(1)	43.051, 43.057, 43.067
art 6(2)	43.051, 43.052
art 6(3)	43.051, 43.052
art 6(4)	43.052
art 6(5)	43.052
art 6(6)	43.053, 43.054, 43.057
art 7	43.042, 43.047, 43.051, 43.056
art 8	43.052, 43.054, 43.056, 43.057, 43.076
art 8(1)	43.054
art 9	43.058
art 9(1)	43.059
art 9(2)	43.060
art 9(3)	43.061
art 9(4)	43.062
art 10	42.038
art 10(1)	42.035
art 10(2)	42.035, 42.038
art 11	43.063, 43.064, 43.065
art 11(1)	43.065
art 11(2)	42.028, 43.064, 43.065
art 11(5)	43.082
art 12	43.063, 43.067
art 12(1)	43.067, 43.069
art 12(2)	43.068
art 12(3)	43.069, 43.082
art 13	43.063, 43.071
art 13(1)	43.071
art 13(2)	43.071
art 13(3)	43.071
art 13(4)	43.071, 43.073
art 13(5)	43.072, 43.073
art 13(6)	43.073, 43.082
art 14	43.075
art 15	43.076
art 16	43.077, 43.080
art 16(1)	43.078
art 16(2)	43.079
art 16(3)	43.080
art 16(4)	43.080
art 16(5)	43.080
art 16(6)	43.080
art 16(7)	43.080
art 16(8)	43.080
art 17	43.082
art 19	43.081
art 20	43.083
art 21	42.035, 42.038, 43.023
art 22	43.020, 43.021
Chapter I	43.010
Chapter II	42.035, 42.038, 43.010
Chapter III	43.010, 43.063
Chapter IV	43.010, 43.074
Recital 1	43.006
Recital 2	43.006
Recital 3	43.007
Recital 4	43.014
Recital 6	43.063
Recital 7	42.030
Recital 8	43.027
Recital 9	43.016
Recital 10	43.016
Recital 11	43.011
Recital 13	43.043
Recital 16	43.059
Recital 17	43.043
Recital 20	43.043
Recital 23	43.017
Recital 37	43.075

Recital 53 ....43.077
Recital 56 ....43.083
Recital 57 ....42.032
1084/2017/EU ... 15.026, 15.031, 15.071, 15.116
2321/2017 ....22.093

Directives

64/221/EEC
   art 3(1)...8.209
64/432/EEC...48.055
67/548 ....24.019
69/262/EEC (First Shipbuilding
   Directive) 22.024
72/273/EEC (Second Shipbuilding Directive)....
   22.024
73/148 ....6.008
75/34/EEC
   art 7 ....6.096, 6.097, 6.098
75/432/EEC (Third Shipbuilding Directive).......
   22.024, 22.035
   art 9 ....22.024
   Preamble 22.008, 22.015
75/439/EEC..19.079
75/442/EEC....................................7.249, 19.079
   art 1(a)..19.063
76/464 ....19.114
76/769/EEC
   Annex I..20.009
77/388 ....1.077
78/338/EEC (Fourth Shipbuilding Directive).....
   22.024
78/660/EEC
   art 5(3)...16.017
79/115/EEC........................5.030, 5.069, 40.002,
   40.009, 40.010
   art 1(1).......................40.005, 40.006, 40.010,
   40.014, 40.017
   art 1(2) 40.006, 40.017
   art 2 ....40.007, 40.009, 40.010, 40.011,
   40.012, 40.013, 40.014, 40.015, 40.016,
   40.017, 40.018
   art 3 ....40.009
   art 7 ....40.009
   Preamble 40.004
79/116 ....5.048, 5.069
81/363/EEC (Fifth Shipbuilding
   Directive) 22.024
   art 4(3) 22.100
   Recital 3 ....22.024

82/714/EEC..46.089
83/349/EEC
   art 1 ....15.040
84/450/EEC..48.053
85/577/EEC..48.053
86/167/EEC (Sixth Shipbuilding
   Directive) 22.024
86/560/EEC..48.056
87/372/EEC...................................37.103, 39.003
89/48/EEC......................6.011, 8.083, 8.218
   art 4(1)(b)..8.218
89/391/EEC.....................8.261, 34.060, 46.148
   art 5 ....8.264
   art 17a(1) 32.021
   art 17a(2) 32.021
   art 17a(3) 32.021
   art 17a(4) 32.021
89/662/EEC..5.156
89/686/EEC..37.038
90/314/EEC (Package Travel
   Directive) 46.045, 46.080, 46.117
   art 2(2)...46.090
   art 2(3)...46.090
90/425/EEC.....................................5.156, 48.055
   Annex A(I) 48.055
90/675/EEC..48.055
90/684/EEC (Seventh Shipbuilding Directive)...
   5.112, 22.015, 22.099
   art 4(2)...22.100
   art 4(3)...22.100
   art 4(4)...22.100
   art 4(7)......................................22.103, 22.104
   art 11(2)(c) 22.103
   Preamble 22.008, 22.015
   Recital 6 ....22.024
91/68/EEC..48.055
91/156/EEC..7.249
91/496/EEC
   art 4 ....48.055
   art 9 ....48.055
91/689/EEC..19.079
91/692/EEC..24.088
92/12/EEC 39.043
92/29/EEC...........5.105, 32.003, 32.005, 32.017
   Annex I......................................32.009, 32.010
   Annex II 32.007, 32.012, 32.013, 32.015
   Annex III................................32.006, 32.013
   Annex IV...32.012
   Annex V 32.015, 32.017

art 1	32.006, 32.007, 32.008, 32.009, 32.011	art 5(3)	46.169, 46.170, 46.172, 46.173, 46.176, 46.177, 46.179
art 2	32.012	art 5(4)	46.168, 46.168, 46.169, 46.171, 46.172, 46.176, 46.178, 46.179
art 2(1)(c)	32.019		
art 3	32.013	art 12	28.152, 34.011
art 3(1)	32.007	93/104/EC	8.040, 35.003
art 4	32.014	93/113/EC	5.112
art 4(1)(b)	32.015	93/115	5.112
art 5	32.015	art 1	5.112
art 6	32.018	art 3	5.112
art 7	32.019	94/9/EC	37.038
art 8	32.020	94/25/EC	37.038
art 9(1)	32.021	94/31/EEC	19.079
art 9a	32.021	94/57/EC	5.117, 5.160, 6.085, 6.182, 20.011, 28.123, 29.007, 29.008, 29.010, 29.068, 29.075, 29.081, 29.100, 29.101, 29.150, 29.155, 33.010, 33.012, 33.014
Recital 5	32.022		
92/51/EEC	8.083, 8.218		
art 4(1)(b)	8.218		
92/65/EEC	48.055	Annex	29.102, 29.103
Annex C	48.055	Annex I, Part B	28.123
art 18(2)	48.055	art 4	6.082, 33.012, 34.062, 46.151
92/81	39.041	art 4(2)	5.160, 5.160, 6.182
art 8(1)	39.043, 39.046, 39.047	art 4(3)	6.182, 29.102, 29.103, 29.105
art 8(1)(c)	39.042, 39.045, 39.046, 39.047, 39.048	art 4(5)	6.182, 29.103
		art 7	5.160, 6.182, 29.104
art 8(2)	39.043, 39.046	art 11(3)	5.160
art 8(2)(b)	39.045, 39.046	art 14(2)	34.069
art 8(2)(g)	39.047	art 15(2)	5.160
Recital 3	39.046	art 15(4)	5.160
Recital 5	39.046	art 15(5)	5.160
92/111	1.077	94/58/EC	5.118, 34.009
93/7/EEC		art 8(1)	34.009
art 1	47.017	art 8(2)	34.009
art 1(1)	47.017	94/73	
93/12/EEC	26.013, 45.007, 45.008	art 4(3)	22.099
art 4(d)(2)	26.013	94/74	39.042, 39.048
93/13/EEC	48.053	95/16/EC	37.038
93/15/EEC	37.038	95/21/EC	5.121, 5.129, 6.083, 8.093, 8.165, 8.185, 19.060, 19.077, 20.009, 20.016, 20.026, 28.004, 28.152, 28.159, 31.006, 31.077, 31.081, 31.082, 31.083, 34.011, 34.060, 34.068, 42.014, 46.151, 46.158
93/57			
art 4(2)	29.101		
art 4(3)	29.101		
93/75/EEC	5.111, 26.011, 26.013, 34.022, 39.051		
Annex I	46.169, 46.170, 46.172, 46.173, 46.176, 46.177, 46.179, 46.180	Annex I-1	39.065
		Annex V	34.026
art 2	46.180	art 2(1)	46.151
art 3	46.180, 46.181	art 2(5)	42.047
art 5	46.169, 46.172, 46.176, 46.179	art 5(1)	28.159
art 5(2)	46.169, 46.170, 46.172, 46.173, 46.176, 46.177, 46.179	art 7(1)	34.026
		art 7(4)	34.026

art 12(4) 28.152, 28.153
art 14 .... 8.072, 8.285
art 15 .... 8.072, 8.285
95/46/EC 30.040, 44.024, 46.085
95/64 .... 5.124
96/23/EC 48.055
96/39 .... 5.111
96/40/EC 5.121, 28.099, 28.152, 28.157
    Annex I 28.158
    art 1 .... 28.153
    art 2(1) 28.154
    art 2(2) 28.154
    art 3 .... 28.155
    art 10(3) 28.155
    art 10(3)(a) 28.158
    Recital 1 .... 28.155
    Recital 2 .... 28.155
    Recital 3 .... 28.155
96/67/EC 13.031
96/98/EC 6.084, 26.013, 26.013, 26.045,
    29.050, 34.060, 36.005, 37.003, 37.008,
    39.012, 39.022, 39.025
    Annex A(1) 34.069
    Annex I 34.068
    Annex III 37.008
    art 5(1) 26.045
    art 35(2) 37.098, 37.099
97/7/EC 48.053
97/23/EC 37.038
97/70 .... 26.013
97/78/EC
    Annex I 48.055
98/6/EC 48.053
98/18/EC 6.082, 6.083, 33.012, 34.013,
    34.042
    art 2 .... 7.210
    art 2(f) 33.104
    art 2(p) 7.210
    art 4 .... 33.016, 34.013, 34.014, 42.027,
    46.027, 46.033, 46.039, 46.040, 46.047
    art 6(3)(g) 46.174, 46.175
    art 7 .... 6.084
    art 11 .... 6.082
    art 17 .... 34.059
    art 18 .... 34.059
98/27/EC 48.053

98/34/EC 28.123, 28.134, 29.081,
    29.097, 34.015, 37.038, 37.038, 46.153
    art 5 .... 37.080
98/41/EC 25.006, 26.005, 26.013,
    34.102, 34.105, 44.034, 46.005, 46.006,
    46.009
    art 1 .... 46.010
    art 2 .... 46.006, 46.011, 46.012, 46.013,
    46.013, 46.014, 46.016, 46.017, 46.022
    art 3 .... 46.011
    art 4 .... 46.016, 46.019
    art 4(1) 46.012, 46.016, 46.021
    art 4(2) 46.013, 46.016, 46.021, 44.034
    art 5 .... 46.008, 46.014, 46.016, 46.019
    art 5(1) 46.016, 46.021
    art 5(2) 46.021, 44.034
    art 6 .... 46.021
    art 7 .... 46.018
    art 8 .... 46.019, 46.020
    art 9 .... 46.015, 46.016
    art 10 .... 46.020
    art 11 .... 46.017, 46.019
    art 12 .... 46.022
    art 13 .... 46.023
    art 13(2) 46.016
    art 13(3) 46.022
    art 14 .... 46.024
    art 15(1) 46.008
    art 16 .... 46.008
    Recital 1 .... 46.007
    Recital 3 .... 46.018
    Recital 4 .... 46.010
    Recital 6 .... 46.022
    Recital 7 .... 46.022
    Recital 8 .... 46.007
    Recital 9 .... 46.024
    Recital 14 .... 46.015
    Recital 17 .... 46.022
98/59/EC 5.166, 8.016, 8.019, 8.034
99/5/EC 37.104, 39.015, 39.030
    art 3(3)(e) 39.012, 39.015
99/32/EC 19.110, 26.013, 45.005
    art 2(3e) 19.106
    art 4b 19.015, 45.007, 45.008
    art 6 .... 19.104
99/35/EC 25.006, 26.005, 26.013,
    28.002, 28.027, 28.071, 30.008, 30.012,
    34.010, 34.011, 34.014, 34.035, 34.039,
    34.051, 34.099, 34.104, 34.105
    Annex I 34.016, 34.017, 34.019, 34.035

Annex II	34.022, 34.035
Annex III	34.017, 34.019, 34.020
Annex IV	34.019, 34.035
Annex V	34.013
art 1	34.012, 34.100
art 2	30.015, 34.013, 34.035, 34.100
art 2(a)	15.043, 28.068
art 2(b)	28.068
art 3(1)	34.014
art 3(2)	34.012
art 4	34.016, 34.017, 34.018, 34.021, 34.022, 34.025, 34.029, 34.045
art 4(1)	34.015
art 4(1)(d)	34.037, 39.063
art 4(1)(e)	34.042, 34.049
art 5	34.016, 34.017, 34.018, 34.021, 34.022, 34.025, 48.037
art 5(1)	34.029, 34.035
art 6	28.069, 34.013, 34.017, 34.018, 34.019, 34.021, 34.022, 34.025, 34.028, 34.035, 48.037
art 6(2)	34.017
art 7	34.018
art 7(1)	34.018
art 7(2)	34.018
art 7(3)	34.018
art 8	28.069, 34.013, 34.021, 34.022, 34.028, 34.035
art 8(1)	34.019, 34.035
art 8(2)	34.020
art 8(3)	34.019
art 9	34.021
art 10	28.070, 34.022
art 10(1)	34.022, 34.023, 34.035
art 10(2)	34.023
art 10(3)	34.024
art 10(4)	34.025
art 11(1)	34.026
art 11(2)	34.027
art 11(3)	34.028
art 11(4)	34.028
art 11(5)	34.028
art 11(6)	34.029, 34.031
art 11(7)	34.029, 34.099
art 11(8)	34.029, 34.099
art 12	30.016, 34.016
art 13	34.038
art 13(1)	34.022, 34.030
art 13(2)	34.031
art 13(3)	34.031
art 13(5)	34.022, 34.031
art 14	34.033
art 15	34.033
art 16	34.099
art 16(1)	34.017, 34.034
art 16(2)	34.015, 34.028, 34.029, 34.031, 34.034
art 16(3)	34.035
art 17	34.035
art 18	34.036
art 19	34.037
art 19(1)	34.015, 34.016, 34.017, 34.037
art 19(2)	34.037
art 19(3)	34.037
art 19(4)	34.037
art 20	34.038
art 21	34.009
99/44/EC	48.053
99/45/EC	24.019
99/63/EC	8.038, 8.047, 8.048, 8.061, 8.093, 8.153, 8.161, 8.259, 8.261, 8.263, 8.271, 8.279, 8.280, 8.281, 8.282, 8.301, 15.068, 31.006, 31.073, 35.001, 35.002, 35.003, 36.017, 36.036
Annex	35.004, 35.007
art 1	8.044, 35.004
art 2	8.045, 35.005
art 2(1)	8.045, 35.005
art 2(2)	8.045, 35.005
art 3	35.006
art 3(1)	8.046, 35.006
art 3(2)	8.040, 35.006
art 3(3)	8.040
art 4	8.040
art 4(2)	8.040
99/70/EC	8.293, 8.302
art 1	8.294
99/95	8.059, 8.270, 8.271, 8.278, 35.001
art 1	8.062, 8.279
art 1(2)	8.065
art 2	8.064
art 3	8.065, 8.272, 8.280, 8.291
art 4	8.065, 8.066, 8.069, 8.281, 8.291
art 5	8.069, 8.282, 8.291
art 5(1)	8.067
art 5(2)	8.068
art 6	8.283, 8.291
art 6(1)	8.069, 8.273, 8.274
art 6(2)	8.070
art 7	8.284, 8.291

art 7(1)	8.071
art 7(2)	8.071
art 7(3)	8.071
art 8	8.072, 8.285, 8.291
art 9	8.073, 8.286
art 10	8.059, 8.287
art 11	8.063
Recital 1	8.060
Recital 2	8.061
Recitals 3–13	8.061
2000/29/EC	5.156
2000/31/EC	48.053
2000/59/EC	5.156, 15.120, 19.007, 19.059, 19.061, 19.074, 19.278, 19.294, 26.013, 28.105, 43.027, 44.010
Annex II	19.070, 19.071
art 1	19.062, 19.081
art 2	19.062, 19.084
art 2(b)	19.084
art 2(c)	19.085
art 3	19.064
art 4	19.068
art 4(1)	19.065
art 4(2)	19.066
art 4(3)	19.067, 19.079
art 5	19.068
art 5(1)	19.068
art 5(2)	19.068
art 5(3)	19.068
art 6	19.068, 19.071, 19.075, 19.077, 19.079
art 6(1)	19.070
art 6(2)	19.070
art 7	19.068, 19.071, 19.077, 28.105
art 7(1)	19.071, 19.075
art 7(2)	19.071
art 7(3)	19.071
art 8	19.072, 19.075
art 8(1)	19.072
art 8(2)	19.072
art 8(2)(c)	19.081
art 8(3)	19.073
art 8(4)	19.073
art 9	19.066, 19.075
art 9(1)	19.075
art 9(2)	19.075
art 10	19.068, 19.076, 19.077, 28.105
art 11	19.077
art 11(2)	19.077
art 11(3)	19.078

art 12	19.068, 19.079
art 12(1)	19.079
art 12(2)	19.080
art 12(3)	19.081
art 13	19.077, 19.082
art 14(1)	19.083
art 14(2)	19.083, 19.084
art 15	19.084
art 16	19.085
art 16(1)	19.073, 19.085
art 17	19.086
art 17(1)	19.086
art 17(2)	19.086
art 18	19.085
Recital 1	19.004
2001/19/EC	8.083
2001/23/EC	5.166, 8.016, 8.019, 8.035, 43.061
2001/25/EC	8.081, 8.083, 8.086, 8.195, 31.003, 31.092, 48.039
Annex I	8.085
art 1(27)	8.085
art 5(2)	8.085
art 5(6)	8.085
art 7	8.086
art 21a	8.089
art 21b	8.089
art 4	8.085
2001/65	44.002
Recital 28	44.003
2001/81/EC	45.005
2001/96/EC	26.013, 46.147
Annex	46.163
Annex I	46.152, 46.167
Annex II	46.153, 46.167
Annex III	46.155, 46.167
Annex IV	46.155, 46.167
Annex V	46.155, 46.167
Annex VI	46.155, 46.167
art 1	46.149
art 2	46.150
art 3	46.151, 46.163
art 4	46.152, 46.153
art 5(1)	46.159
art 5(4)	46.154, 46.159
art 6	46.154, 46.159
art 7	46.155
art 7(1)(b)	46.166
art 7(1)(d)	46.166
art 7(2)	46.159

art 8 .... 46.156, 46.157, 46.159, 46.163
art 9 .... 46.157
art 9(1) 46.157
art 9(2) 46.157
art 10 .... 46.158
art 10(1) 46.158
art 10(3) 46.158
art 10(4) 46.158
art 11 .... 46.159
art 11(2) 46.159, 46.160, 46.163
art 12 .... 46.160, 46.163
art 13 .... 46.161
art 14 .... 46.162
art 14(2) 46.163
art 15 .... 46.163
art 15(1) 46.163
art 16 .... 46.164
art 17(1) 46.164
art 18 .... 46.166
Recital 1 .... 46.148
Recital 2 .... 46.148
Recital 3 .... 46.148
2002/6/EC 5.156, 44.002, 44.003, 44.003, 44.005
2002/14/EC 5.166, 8.016, 8.019, 8.033
2002/20/EC 37.103, 39.028
  art 3(2) 37.103, 39.028
  art 5 .... 37.103, 39.028
  art 5(1) 37.103, 37.104, 39.028, 39.036
  art 6(2) 37.103, 39.028
  art 14 .... 37.103, 39.028
2002/21/EC 37.103
  art 19(1) 37.103, 39.028
  art 2(c) 37.104, 39.031
  art 9(1) 37.103, 39.028
  art 9(2) 37.103, 39.028
2002/22/EC 39.028
2002/59/EC 5.156, 26.013, 27.028, 27.043, 27.062, 28.061, 28.086, 30.008, 30.013, 39.051, 44.010, 44.016, 44.020, 44.022, 44.025
  Annex I 39.057, 39.064
  Annex I(1) 39.056
  Annex I(23) 39.064
  Annex I(3) 39.064
  Annex II 39.058
  Annex II(I) 39.062
  Annex II(II) 39.063
  Annex III 39.064, 39.075, 39.078
  Annex IV 39.068

Annex XIV 28.104
art 1 .... 39.053
art 2 .... 39.054
art 3 .... 39.055, 44.018
art 3(1) 44.018
art 3(2) 44.018
art 3(s) 28.104
art 4 .... 28.061, 39.056, 39.064, 44.003, 44.019
art 4(1) 39.056, 39.064
art 4(2) 39.056
art 5 .... 39.057, 44.020
art 5(1) 39.057
art 5(2) 39.057
art 6 .... 44.003, 44.020
art 6(1) 39.058
art 6(2) 39.058
art 6a 39.058
art 6b 27.043, 39.059
art 6b(1) 39.059
art 7(1) 39.060
art 7(2) 39.060
art 9(1) 39.062
art 9(2) 39.062
art 9(3) 39.062
art 10(1) 39.063
art 11 .... 30.016
art 12 .... 39.064, 39.068
art 13 .... 39.056, 39.064, 39.074, 44.003
art 13(4) 39.064
art 14 .... 39.064, 39.075
art 15 .... 39.064
art 16 .... 39.065
art 17 .... 39.065, 39.068, 39.074
art 17(1) 39.068, 39.074
art 18 .... 39.066
art 18a 39.068
art 19 .... 39.068
art 20 .... 39.066, 39.068
art 20(1) 39.070, 39.071, 39.073
art 20(3) 39.075
art 20a 39.070, 39.071
art 20b 39.071, 39.072
art 20c 39.072
art 20d 39.073
art 21 .... 39.074
art 22 .... 39.075
art 22a 27.043, 39.075
art 23 .... 39.075

art 24	39.075
Recital	44.017
2002/62/EC	20.009
2002/65/EC	48.053
2002/84/EC	5.160, 6.182, 19.059, 20.009, 20.011, 29.101, 34.010, 46.006, 46.147
2003/3/EC	20.009
2003/10/EC	26.023
art 3	26.023
2003/25/EC	25.006, 26.013, 34.040, 34.041, 34.042, 34.060
Annex I	34.044, 34.046, 34.048, 34.049, 34.050, 34.051, 34.052
Annex II	34.048, 34.052
art 1	34.043, 34.054
art 2	34.044
art 3	34.045
art 3(1)	34.045, 34.048
art 3(2)	34.045
art 4	34.046
art 5(1)	34.047
art 5(2)	34.047
art 5(3)	34.047
art 6	6.084, 34.048, 34.050, 34.052, 34.073
art 6(1)	34.049
art 6(2)	34.049
art 6(3)	34.052
art 7	34.049
art 8	34.073
art 8(1)	34.050, 34.051
art 8(2)	34.050
art 8(3)	34.050
art 9	34.051, 34.073
art 10	34.052
art 11	34.052
art 11(1)	34.053
art 11(2)	34.052
art 13	34.055
2003/87	5.176
2003/96/EC	45.007, 45.008, 45.009
2004/17	42.032
2004/22/EC	37.038
2004/68/EC	48.055
2004/261	46.110
2005/29/EC	48.053
2005/33/EC	45.008, 45.009
2005/35/EC	19.263, 19.265, 19.277, 19.278, 19.316, 19.325, 26.013, 27.048, 46.181
art 1	19.279
art 1(1)	19.279
art 1(2)	19.279
art 2	19.266, 19.280
art 3	19.281
art 3(1)	19.282, 19.283, 19.286, 19.287, 19.311, 19.312, 19.313
art 3(1)(a)	19.274
art 3(1)(b)	19.274, 19.287
art 3(1)(c)	19.283, 19.287, 19.313
art 3(1)(d)	19.283, 19.287, 19.313
art 3(1)(e)	19.283, 19.287, 19.313
art 4	19.268, 19.282, 19.284, 19.286, 19.288, 19.304, 19.312, 19.314, 19.315, 19.317, 19.318, 19.320, 19.321, 19.322, 19.323, 19.326
art 4(1)	19.282
art 4(2)	19.282
art 5	19.268, 19.283, 19.284, 19.288, 19.304, 19.313, 19.317, 19.318, 19.326
art 5(1)	19.315
art 5(2)	19.315
art 5a	19.284
art 5a(1)	19.285, 19.289, 19.290, 19.291
art 5a(3)	19.285, 19.289, 19.290, 19.291
art 5b	19.285, 19.289, 19.290, 19.291
art 6	19.286
art 6(1)	19.286, 19.287
art 6(2)	19.286
art 7(1)	19.287
art 7(2)	19.287
art 7(3)	19.287
art 8	19.288, 19.314, 19.322
art 8(3)	19.290, 19.291
art 8a	19.289
art 8b	19.292
art 8b(1)	19.290
art 8b(2)	19.291
art 8c	19.292
art 9	19.293
art 10(1)	19.294
art 10(2)	19.295
art 11	19.296
art 12	19.296
art 13	19.300

art 14	19.299
art 15	19.300
art 16	19.301
art 17	19.300
Recital 16	19.303
2005/36/EC	8.093, 24.036, 31.006
art 3	24.041
2005/45/EC	8.081, 8.082, 8.083, 48.039
Annex I	8.081
Annex II	8.081
Annex III	8.081
art 1	8.084
art 19(2)	8.081
art 2	8.085
art 3	8.086, 48.039
art 32	8.081
art 4	8.087
art 4(2)	8.088
art 4(4)	8.089
art 5	8.090
art 5(1)	8.090
art 5(2)	8.090
art 6	8.081
2005/65/EC	42.056, 42.057, 42.058, 42.064, 42.065, 42.066, 42.071, 42.105, 42.108, 42.110, 42.113, 42.115, 42.116, 42.117, 42.124, 42.129, 42.132, 42.133, 42.135, 42.136, 42.137, 42.138
Annex I	42.083, 42.097, 42.103
Annex II	42.086, 42.097, 42.103
Annex III	42.088, 42.097, 42.103
Annex IV	42.094, 42.097, 42.103, 42.110
art 1(1)	42.070
art 1(2)	42.070
art 2(1)	42.071
art 2(2)	42.058, 42.071
art 2(3)	42.071, 42.120
art 2(4)	42.071
art 3	42.072
art 3(1)	42.073
art 3(2)	42.074
art 3(3)	42.075
art 3(4)	42.076
art 3(5)	42.077
art 4	42.078
art 5(1)	42.079
art 5(2)	42.080
art 5(3)	42.080
art 6	42.093
art 6(1)	42.082
art 6(2)	42.082
art 6(3)	42.082
art 6(4)	42.082
art 7	42.093
art 7(1)	42.084
art 7(2)	42.085
art 7(3)	42.086
art 7(4)	42.087
art 7(5)	42.087
art 7(6)	42.087
art 7(7)	42.088
art 8	42.085
art 8(1)	42.089
art 8(2)	42.089
art 8(3)	42.090
art 8(4)	42.091
art 9(1)	42.092
art 9(2)	42.092
art 9(3)	42.092
art 10(1)	42.093
art 10(2)	42.093
art 11	42.083, 42.087, 42.094
art 12	42.095, 42.096, 42.120, 42.133
art 13	42.096, 42.102
art 13(1)	42.096
art 13(2)	42.133
art 13(3)	42.096, 42.106
art 14	42.097
art 15(1)	42.098
art 15(2)	42.097, 42.098
art 15(3)	42.097, 42.098
art 16(1)	42.099
art 16(2)	42.099
art 17	42.100
art 18	42.101
art 18(1)	42.101
art 19	42.102
art 21	42.058
Recital 1	42.006
Recital 11	42.064
Recital 13	42.066
Recital 15	42.067
Recital 16	42.068
Recital 18	42.058
Recital 2	42.006
Recital 3	42.057
Recital 4	42.057
Recital 5	42.059
Recital 7	42.060

Recital 8	42.061
Recital 9	42.062, 42.063
2006/87/EC	27.060, 46.078, 46.089
2006/88/EC	48.055
2006/112/EC (the 'VAT Directive)	48.056
2006/123/EC	8.318
art 2(2)(d)	7.006
2007/23/EC	37.038
2007/30	32.003
2007/71	19.059
2008/9/EC	48.056
2008/16	8.137, 8.168, 8.170, 8.171
art 3	8.164
art 5	8.164, 8.170
art 5(6)	8.178
art 8(1)	8.131
art 8(2)	8.131
art 8(3)	8.131
art 9	8.132
art 10	8.133
art 10(2)	8.133
art 10(3)	8.134
art 11	8.135, 8.138
art 12	8.191
art 13	8.143
art 13(1)	8.143
art 14	8.158
art 14(1)	8.157
art 14(2)	8.158
art 14(3)	8.159
art 15	8.161
art 16	8.164
art 16(2)	8.164
art 17	8.164
art 18	8.165
art 19	8.166, 8.168
art 19(1)	8.167
art 19(2)	8.172
art 19(3)	8.179
art 19(6)	8.179
art 19(7)	8.132
art 20	8.168, 8.172
art 22	8.180
art 23	8.179, 8.180, 8.181
art 23(2)	8.182, 8.183
art 24	8.185
art 25	8.188
art 25a(3)	8.189
art 26	8.188
art 27	8.178, 8.189
art 28	8.184, 8.193
art 28(2)	8.187
art 29	8.192
art 30	8.190
2008/50/EC	
art 22	19.105
2008/56/EC (Marine Strategy Framework Directive)	19.125, 27.055
2008/94/EC	5.166, 8.016, 8.019
art 1(3)	8.031
2008/98	24.015, 24.015, 24.016
art 3	24.042
art 5	24.044
art 9	24.044
2008/99/EC	24.097
2008/106/EC	8.091, 8.092, 8.093, 8.292, 26.013, 26.023, 27.040, 27.047, 27.070, 31.001, 31.003, 31.004, 31.005, 31.006, 31.033, 31.043, 31.092, 48.039
Annex I	31.048, 31.055, 31.057, 31.066, 31.090, 31.092
Annex I, Chapter II	31.041
Annex I, Chapter III	31.010, 31.012, 31.041
Annex I, Chapter IV	31.037, 31.041
Annex I, Chapter VII	31.041
Annex II	31.078, 31.079, 31.080, 31.092
Annex III	31.092
Annex III, Part A	31.092
Annex III, Part B	31.006, 31.092
Annex IV	31.092
Annex V	31.056, 31.085, 31.087, 31.092
art 1	8.094, 31.007, 31.049
art 1(1)	8.095
art 1(3)	8.097
art 1(4)	8.098
art 2	8.125, 8.126, 31.048, 31.049, 31.081
art 3	8.129, 31.049, 31.057, 31.075, 31.090, 31.092, 48.039
art 3(1)	8.126, 31.049
art 3(2)	8.126, 31.049
art 4	8.127
art 5	8.127, 8.128, 8.130, 31.050, 31.075, 31.090
art 5(1)	8.128, 31.050
art 5(10)	8.128, 31.055

art 5(2)..................................8.128, 31.050	art 17..31.075, 31.090
art 5(3)...31.050	art 17(1)...31.075
art 5(3a)................................8.128, 31.050	art 17(2)...31.076
art 5(4)..................................8.128, 31.050	art 18.........................31.066, 31.076, 31.090
art 5(5)..................................8.128, 31.050	art 19.........................31.078, 31.090, 48.039
art 5(6)....................31.020, 31.078, 31.079	art 19(2)....................8.128, 31.050, 31.092
art 5(7)..................................8.128, 31.053	art 19(3)...31.080
art 5(8)..................................8.128, 31.054	art 19(4)..8.169
art 5(9)..................................8.128, 31.054	art 19(5)..8.170
art 5a..31.056	art 19(6)........................8.128, 8.170, 31.080
art 6..8.129, 31.057	art 19(7).............8.128, 8.171, 31.055, 31.063
art 7........................8.130, 31.061, 31.090	art 20..31.078, 31.079
art 7(1)..31.058	art 20(1)......................................8.172, 8.173
art 7(1)(a)..31.058	art 20(3)..8.174
art 7(2)..31.059	art 20(4)..8.175
art 7(3)..31.060	art 20(5)..8.176
art 7(3)(a)..31.060	art 20(6)..8.177
art 7(3)(b)..31.060	art 20(7)..8.178
art 7(4)..31.061	art 21..8.179, 31.080
art 75...31.060	art 22........................31.081, 31.082, 31.090
art 8..8.131, 31.062	art 23.............31.080, 31.082, 31.084, 31.090
art 9..31.063	art 24..31.083, 31.090
arts 9–15..31.090	art 25..8.186, 31.086
art 10.......................................31.064, 31.076	art 25a.....................................8.187, 31.085
art 10(1)(a)..8.133	art 25a(3)..31.087
art 10(1)(c)..8.133	art 26...31.086
art 10(1)(d)..8.133	art 27..31.087, 31.088
art 10(2)..8.134	art 27a......................................31.087, 31.088
art 10(2)(d)..8.134	art 28..31.089, 31.090
art 11.......................................31.065, 31.066	art 28(1)...31.079
art 11(1)..8.135	art 28(2)....................31.078, 31.079, 31.085
art 11(2)..8.135	art 29...31.090
art 11(4)..8.136	art 30...31.091
art 12...31.066	art 31..8.194, 31.090
art 12(2)..8.139	art 32...31.092
art 12(3)..8.140	Chapter II, Annex I.................31.045, 31.047
art 12(4)..8.141	Chapter III, Annex I.............................31.044
art 12(5)..8.142	Recital 1..31.003
art 12(l)..8.138	Recital 2..31.004
art 13...31.067	Recital 3..31.005
art 14.......................................31.069, 31.070	Recital 4..31.005
art 14(1)...31.069	Recital 6..31.006
art 14(2)...31.070	Recital 7..31.006
art 14(3)....................................31.066, 31.071	2008/118/EC..48.056
art 14(4)...31.072	2009/13/EC...........8.030, 8.038, 8.259, 8.353,
art 15...31.070	8.354, 8.359, 8.360, 8.361, 35.001, 36.018,
art 15(1)..8.161	36.036
art 16.......................................31.074, 31.075	Annex 36.017, 36.026, 36.036
art 16(1)....................................8.162, 31.074	art 1..8.262, 8.301
art 16(2)....................................8.163, 31.074	art 2..8.263

art 3 ....8.264
art 4 ....8.265
art 5 ....8.266
art 6 ....8.267
art 7 ....8.268
2009/15/EC 5.157, 8.355, 26.013,
    28.124, 29.004, 29.025, 29.073, 29.074,
        29.076, 29.098, 29.124, 36.027
Annex I, Part A 29.100
Annex I, Part B 29.100
art 1 ....29.082
art 2 ....28.125, 29.083
art 2(d).................................28.130, 29.093
art 26 ....28.122
art 3 ....28.126, 28.127, 28.128, 28.131,
        29.053, 29.084, 29.085, 29.087, 29.090,
                                                        29.094
art 3(1).........................28.130, 29.085, 29.093
art 3(2)......................28.127, 28.128, 29.132,
        29.085, 29.087, 29.088, 29.095
art 3(3)......................................29.084, 29.085
art 4 ....28.127
art 4(1)..29.087
art 4(2)..29.087
art 5 ....28.127, 28.128, 28.130, 29.087,
                                                        29.093
art 5(1)..29.088
art 5(2)......................................29.089, 29.093
art 5(2)(b).............................28.130, 29.093
art 5(3)..29.090
art 6 ....28.129
art 6(1)..29.092
art 6(2).......................28.127, 28.134, 29.087,
                                            29.092, 29.097
art 6(3)..................................28.130, 29.093
art 7 ....28.130, 29.093
art 8 ....28.127, 28.131, 29.087, 29.094
art 9 ....27.040, 28.127, 28.132
art 9(1)..................28.128, 28.132, 29.095
art 9(2)......................................28.133, 29.095
art 10 ....28.133, 29.043, 29.046, 29.096
art 11 ....28.134
art 11(1)...................................28.134, 29.097
art 11(2)....................28.126, 28.134, 29.085,
                                                        29.097
art 11(3)...................................28.134, 29.097
art 12 ....28.135, 29.098
art 12(2)...29.099
art 13 ....28.122
art 13(1)...................................28.133, 29.099

art 14 ....29.100
art 15 ....28.122, 29.072
Recital 1 ....29.075
Recital 2 ....29.075
Recital 10 ....29.001
Recital 14 ....29.079
Recital 15 ....29.080
2009/16/EC 8.030, 19.206, 19.238,
        24.005, 24.006, 24.011, 24.067, 24.099,
        26.013, 26.023, 26.029, 26.034, 27.046,
        28.002, 28.004, 28.013, 28.138, 28.144,
        28.145, 29.053, 34.039, 34.104, 34.105,
        36.036, 44.010, 46.181, 46.186, 48.037
Annex 28.150
Annex I......................28.054, 28.060, 28.121
Annex I, Part I............28.064, 28.065, 28.107
Annex I, Part I.1....................26.031, 26.037,
                                            28.062, 28.073
Annex I, Part II 2A...............................28.065
Annex I, Part II 2B...............................28.065
Annex I, Part II 3A................28.065, 28.067
Annex I, Part II 3B................28.065, 28.067
Annex I, Part IIA..................................28.064
Annex I, Part IIB..................................28.064
Annex II 28.062, 28.121
Annex III...................28.061, 28.105, 28.121
Annex IV................24.095, 28.066, 28.121,
                                                        48.037
Annex IX....................................28.075, 28.121
Annex V.....................................28.066, 28.121
Annex V, Part A..................................28.075
Annex VI....................................28.111, 28.121
Annex VII 28.041, 28.067, 28.069,
        28.072, 28.073, 28.074, 28.121, 28.121,
                                            28.149, 29.157
Annex X...................28.085, 28.121, 29.128
Annex XI....................28.096, 28.100, 28.121
Annex XII 28.104, 28.121
Annex XIII..............................28.106, 28.121
Annex XIV..............................28.109, 28.121
Annex XV..28.121
Annex XVI...28.121
art 1 ....28.005
art 2 ....28.012
art 2(18)...26.030
art 3 ....28.008
art 3(1)..28.008
art 3(2)..28.009
art 3(3).......................................28.010, 28.011
art 3(4)..28.012

art 3(5)	28.012	art 16(4)	28.074
art 4(1)	28.053	art 16(5)	28.074
art 4(2)	28.053	art 17	28.075, 28.121
art 5	28.054, 28.119, 28.121, 28.138	art 18	28.075, 28.078, 28.081
art 5(1)	28.054	art 18(4)	28.078
art 5(2)	28.054, 28.055	art 18a	28.080, 28.081
art 5(2)(a)	28.056	art 18a(1)	28.078
art 5(2)(b)	28.056	art 18a(2)	28.078
art 5(3)	28.054	art 18a(3)	28.078
art 6	28.055, 28.119	art 18a(5)	28.078
art 7	28.119	art 18a(6)	28.079
art 7(1)	28.056	art 18a(7)	28.080, 28.117
art 7(2)	28.056	art 18a(8)	28.081
art 7(3)	28.057	art 19	28.078, 28.138
art 8	28.058, 28.119	art 19(1)	28.082
art 8(1)	28.058	art 19(10)	28.092
art 8(2)	28.059	art 19(2)	28.083, 28.095
art 8(3)	28.060	art 19(2a)	28.084
art 9	28.105	art 19(3)	28.085, 28.121
art 9(1)	28.061, 28.121	art 19(4)	28.086
art 9(2)	28.061	art 19(5)	28.087
art 9(3)	28.061	art 19(6)	28.087, 28.095
art 9(4)	28.061	art 19(7)	28.089
art 10	28.062, 28.069	art 19(8)	28.090
art 10(1)	28.062	art 19(9)	28.091
art 10(2)	28.121	art 20(1)	28.093
art 10(3)	26.028, 26.029, 26.034, 26.035, 28.063, 28.116, 28.117	art 20(2)	28.093
		art 20(3)	28.093
art 10(3)(a)	26.039	art 20(4)	28.093
art 11	28.064, 28.069	art 21	28.086, 28.094, 28.138
art 12	28.054, 28.065, 28.066, 28.069	art 21(1)	28.095
art 12(a)	28.054	art 21(2)	28.095
art 12(b)	28.054	art 21(4)	28.095, 28.108
art 13	28.066, 28.078, 28.108, 48.037	art 21(6)	28.071
art 13(1)	28.039, 28.121	art 22	28.096
art 13(3)	28.040, 28.041, 28.121	art 22(1)	28.121
art 14	28.061, 28.067, 28.068, 28.121, 28.149, 28.150, 29.157	art 22(5)	28.121
		art 23	28.103, 28.105
art 14(4)	28.117, 28.149, 28.151, 29.157	art 23(5)	28.116, 28.117
		art 24	28.078, 28.104
art 15	28.068	art 24(1)	28.121
art 15(1)	28.068, 28.121	art 25	28.105
art 15(2)	28.068	art 26	28.093, 28.106, 28.121
art 15(3)	28.068	art 27	26.028, 26.029, 26.032, 28.107, 28.116, 28.117
art 15(4)	28.117		
art 16	28.067, 28.074, 28.108, 28.121, 28.138	art 28	28.108
		art 29	28.109, 28.121
art 16(1)	28.071	art 29(1)	28.095
art 16(2)	28.072	art 29(3)	28.095
art 16(3)	28.073	art 29(4)	28.095

art 29(4)(a) 28.095
art 29(4)(b) 28.095
art 30 ....28.111
art 30a............28.111, 28.112, 28.113, 28.115
art 30b 28.111
art 31 ....28.116
art 31(3) 28.063, 28.067, 28.070,
            28.080, 28.103, 28.107, 28.117
art 33 ....28.117
art 34 ....28.118
art 35 ....28.057, 28.119
art 36 ....28.120
art 37 ....28.121
art 38 ....28.006
Recital 6 ....28.014
Recital 10 ....28.012
Recital 11 ....28.016
Recital 12 ....28.017
Recital 13 ....28.018
Recital 14 ....28.019
Recital 16 ....28.021
Recital 17 ....28.022
Recital 18 ....28.023
Recital 19 ....28.024
Recital 20 ....28.025
Recital 21 ....28.026
Recital 22 ....28.027
Recital 26 ....28.027
Recital 27 ....28.029
2009/17 ....39.051
2009/18/EC 26.013, 27.045, 30.008,
            30.009, 30.010, 30.011, 30.012, 30.013,
            30.014, 30.015, 30.057, 34.010, 39.051
    Annex I...................................30.047, 30.048
    Annex II 30.052
    art 1 ....30.045
    art 1(1) 30.019
    art 1(2) 30.020
    art 2(1) 30.023
    art 2(2) 30.024
    art 3 ....30.015
    art 3(1) 30.045, 30.055
    art 3(2) 30.015
    art 3(3) 30.015
    art 3(4) 30.015
    art 3(5) 30.015
    art 3(6) 30.015
    art 3(7) 30.015
    art 4 ....30.025
    art 4(1) 30.025

art 4(2) 30.026
art 5 ....30.027
art 5(1) 30.028
art 5(1)(c) 30.034
art 5(2) 30.028, 30.057
art 5(3) 30.029
art 5(4) 30.030
art 5(5) 30.031
art 6 ....30.032
art 7 ....30.026, 30.033
art 8 ....30.028
art 8(1) 30.034
art 8(2) 30.035
art 8(3) 30.036
art 8(4) 30.037
art 8(5) 30.038
art 8(6) 30.039
art 9 ....30.040, 30.043
art 10 ....30.026, 30.043
art 11 ....30.041
art 11(1) 30.041
art 11(2) 30.041
art 13 ....30.046
art 14 ....30.047
art 15 ....30.049
art 16 ....30.043, 30.051
art 17 ....27.045, 30.052
art 17(3) 30.028
art 18 ....30.022
art 19(1) 30.054
art 19(2) 30.043
art 19(3) 30.030, 30.055
art 20 ....30.055
art 21 ....30.018
art 22 ....30.016, 30.017
art 23 ....30.042
art 25 ....30.016
art 25(1) 30.016
art 25(2) 30.016
Recital 1 ....30.002
Recital 2 ....30.002
Recital 4 ....30.004
Recital 5 ....30.006
Recital 6 ....30.006
Recital 7 ....30.006
Recital 8 ....30.006
Recital 9 ....30.022
Recital 10 ....30.040
Recital 18 ....30.033
Recital 19 ....30.041

Recital 25 ....30.050
Recital 26 ....30.021
Recital 29 ....30.055
2009/20/EC 46.181, 48.037
   Annex 46.183
   art 1 ....46.182
   art 2 ....46.183
   art 2(1)..46.183
   art 2(2)..46.183
   art 2(3)..46.183
   art 3 ....46.184
   art 4 ....46.185, 46.187
   art 4(1)...46.188
   art 4(1)...48.037
   art 5 ....46.186
   art 6 ....39.072, 46.186, 46.187
   art 7 ....46.188
   art 8 ....46.189
   art 9 ....46.190
2009/21/EC 8.354, 19.252, 26.013,
                               36.019, 36.020
   art 1(1)...19.254
   art 12 ....19.261
   art 2 ....19.255
   art 3 ....19.256
   art 4 ....19.257
   art 5 ....19.258
   art 6 ....19.259
   art 8 ....19.260
   art 9 ....8.358, 19.261, 36.030
   art 10 ....19.261
   art 11(1)...19.261
2009/22/EC
   art 4 ....48.053
2009/23/EC 37.038
2009/28/EC
   art 2 ....15.120
2009/29 ....5.176
2009/38/EC 5.166, 8.016, 8.019
2009/42/EC 46.050, 46.051, 46.052,
                   46.066, 46.067, 46.068, 46.071
   Annex I..46.055
   Annex II...46.055
   Annex III..46.055
   Annex I–IV 46.068
   Annex IV..46.055
   Annex I–VIII..46.070
   Annex V...46.055
   Annex VI..46.055
   Annex VII 46.055, 46.068
   Annex VIII 46.055, 46.056, 46.057,
                                         46.059
   art 1 ....46.054
   art 2 ....46.053
   art 3 ....46.055, 46.058, 46.059
   art 3(1)...46.055
   art 3(2)...46.055
   art 3(3)...46.055
   art 3(4)......................46.055, 46.063, 46.064,
                                    46.068, 46.070
   art 4 ....46.056
   art 4(1)...........46.056, 46.063, 46.064, 46.068
   art 4(2)...46.056
   art 4(3)...46.056
   art 5 ....46.057, 46.058, 46.063, 46.068
   art 6 ....46.058
   art 7 ....46.059
   art 7(1)...46.059
   art 7(3)...46.059
   art 8 ....46.060
   art 9 ....46.061
   art 10a..46.070
   art 10a(1)..46.069
   art 10(2).....................46.059, 46.061, 46.062
   art 10(a).....................46.056, 46.057, 46.063
   art 10(b).....................46.056, 46.057, 46.063,
                                         46.064
   art 10(c).....................46.056, 46.057, 46.063,
                                         46.065
   art 11 ....46.051
   art 13 ....46.051
2009/45/EC 26.005, 26.013, 26.023,
          26.045, 34.056, 34.057, 34.058, 34.102,
              34.105, 39.025, 46.078, 46.089
   Annex 12(3) 34.089
   Annex I......................34.062, 34.070, 34.071,
                              34.079, 34.095, 34.107
   Annex I, Regulation III/2.1 ....34.113,
                              34.114, 34.115, 34.116
   Annex II..34.092
   Annex III.................................34.074, 34.075
   art 1 ....34.061, 34.116
   art 2 ....34.062, 34.083, 34.086, 34.116
   art 3(1)...34.063
   art 3(2)...34.064
   art 4(1)...................................34.065, 34.066
   art 4(2)...................................34.062, 34.066
   art 4(3)...34.066
   art 5(1)...34.068
   art 5(3)...34.068

art 5(4)	34.068
art 6(1)	34.069
art 6(2)	34.070
art 6(2)(a)(i)	26.023
art 6(3)	34.071
art 6(4)	34.072, 34.089
art 6(5)	34.082
art 7(1)	34.073
art 7(2)	34.073
art 8(1)	34.074
art 8(2)	34.075
art 8(3)	34.076
art 8(4)	34.077
art 9(1)	34.068, 34.078
art 9(2)	34.079, 34.106, 34.108, 34.109, 34.110
art 9(3)	34.080, 34.094, 34.106, 34.107, 34.108, 34.109, 34.110
art 9(4)	34.081, 34.107, 34.108, 34.110
art 10(1)	34.083, 34.085
art 10(2)	34.084, 34.085
art 10(4)	34.086
art 11	34.087
art 11(1)	34.087
art 11(2)	34.071, 34.081, 34.082, 34.087, 34.108, 34.112
art 11(3)	34.085, 34.087
art 12	34.083, 34.088
art 12(1)	34.091, 34.092
art 12(2)	34.088, 34.091, 34.092
art 12(3)	34.091
art 12(4)	34.090
art 12(5)	34.091
art 13	34.068
art 13(1)	34.092
art 13(2)	34.092
art 13(3)	34.092
art 14(1)	34.095
art 14(2)	34.072, 34.095
art 15	34.096
art 16	34.097
2009/95	29.073
2009/105/EC	37.038
2009/111	29.073
2009/114/EC	
art 1	37.103, 39.028
2009/123	19.277
2009/138/EC	47.025
2009/156/EC	48.055
art 6	48.055
2009/158/EC	48.055
2010/6	
Recital 13	44.005
2010/36	34.056
2010/65/EU	2.012, 5.169, 26.005, 27.051, 34.102, 34.105, 40.021, 44.002, 44.003, 44.006, 44.007, 44.028, 44.030, 44.031, 44.033, 44.034, 44.034
Annex	44.029
Annex A	44.034
Annex B	44.025
art 1	44.014
art 1(1)	44.014
art 1(2)	44.014
art 1(3)	44.014
art 2	44.016
art 3	44.027
art 3(2)	39.978
art 6	44.022
art 7	44.023
art 8(1)	44.024
art 8(2)	44.024
art 9	44.025
art 10	44.026
art 11	44.026
art 12	44.026
art 13	44.026
art 14	44.008
art 15	27.063, 44.027
art 16	44.003
Recital 2	44.009
Recital 3	44.010
Recital 4	44.011, 44.012
Recital 6	44.013
Recital 8	44.010
Recital 9	44.001
Recital 10	44.016
Recital 11	44.001
Recital 12	44.021
Recital 19	44.004
Recital 24	44.015
2011/15	39.051
2011/83/EU	48.053
2012/35/EU	8.091, 8.127, 8.157, 8.292, 31.003
2013/11/EU	48.053
2013/38/EU	28.004, 36.036
2013/54/EU (Flag State Directive)	8.030, 8.352, 36.012, 36.013, 36.014, 36.015, 36.023, 36.024, 36.036

art 1 ....8.354, 36.025	art 2(15) 37.024
art 2 ....36.026	art 2(16) 37.024
art 3 ....8.352, 36.027	art 2(17) 37.026
art 3(3) 36.028	art 2(18) 37.027
art 4 ....8.356, 36.028	art 2(19) 37.028
art 5 ....8.357, 36.029	art 2(2) 37.012
art 5(1) 36.029	art 2(20) 37.028, 37.032
art 5(2) 36.029	art 2(21) 37.032
art 5(3) 36.029	art 2(22) 37.032
art 6 ....8.358, 36.030	art 2(3) 37.013
art 6(1) 36.030	art 2(5) 37.015
art 6(2) 36.030	art 2(6) 37.016
art 7(1) 36.031	art 2(7) 37.017
art 7(2) 36.031	art 2(8) 37.018
art 8 ....36.031	art 2(9) 37.018
Recital 2 ....36.014	art 3 ....37.011
Recital 3 ....36.014	art 3(1) 37.032
Recital 4 ....36.015	art 3(2) 37.032
Recital 7 ....36.016	art 4 ....37.048, 37.059, 37.073, 37.079, 37.089
Recital 8 ....36.017	
Recital 9 ....36.018	art 4(1) 37.033
Recital 10 ....36.019	art 4(2) 37.033
Recital 11 ....36.020	art 4(4) 37.033, 37.093
Recital 12 ....36.021	art 5 ....37.034
Recital 13 ....36.022	art 5(1) 37.034
Recital 14 ....36.023	art 5(2) 37.034
Recital 15 ....36.024	art 5(3) 37.034
2014/11 ....28.122	art 6 ....37.035
2014/23 ....42.032	art 7 ....37.036
2014/25	art 7(1) 37.036
art 34 ....43.051	art 7(2) 37.036
art 35 ....43.051	art 7(3) 37.036
2014/90/EU 26.013, 37.003, 37.034, 37.099, 37.100	art 7(4) 37.036
	art 8 ....37.014, 37.037, 37.095
Annex I 37.016, 37.040, 37.041	art 8(1) 37.038
Annex II 37.041, 37.048, 37.058, 37.059	art 8(2) 37.038
	art 8(3) 37.038, 37.079
Annex III 37.041, 37.060, 37.063, 37.064, 37.094	art 8(4) 37.038
	art 9 ..37.016, 37.040, 37.043, 37.048, 37.085
Annex IV 37.041	art 9(3) 37.040
Annex V 37.041, 37.061	art 10 ....37.043, 37.048, 37.085
art 1 ....37.009, 37.032	art 10(1) 37.042
art 2 ....37.010	art 10(2) 37.042
art 2(1) 37.011	art 10(3) 37.042
art 2(10) 37.019	art 10(4) 37.042
art 2(11) 37.020	art 11 ....37.016, 37.093, 37.095
art 2(12) 37.021	art 11(1) 37.043
art 2(13) 37.022	art 11(2) 37.043
art 2(14) 37.019, 37.020, 37.021, 37.022	art 11(3) 37.043, 37.046
	art 11(4) 37.044, 37.046

art 11(5)	37.045
art 11(6)	37.046
art 12	37.047, 37.048, 37.055, 37.066
art 12(1)	37.048, 37.052, 37.059
art 12(10)	37.051
art 12(2)	37.048
art 12(3)	37.048
art 12(4)	37.048
art 12(5)	37.048
art 12(6)	37.048
art 12(7)	37.049
art 12(8)	37.050
art 13	37.047, 37.052, 48.040
art 13(1)	37.052
art 13(2)	37.048, 37.052
art 13(3)	37.052
art 13(4)	37.052
art 14	37.047
art 14(1)	37.052
art 14(2)	37.054, 37.058
art 14(3)	37.055, 37.058
art 15	37.026, 37.033, 37.058, 37.066
art 15(1)	37.058
art 16	37.030, 37.048, 37.059
art 16(1)	37.059
art 16(2)	37.059
art 16(3)	37.059
art 16(4)	37.059
art 16(5)	37.059
art 17	37.017
art 17(2)	37.060
art 18	37.061
art 18(1)	37.061
art 18(2)	37.061
art 18(3)	37.061
art 18(4)	37.061
art 18(5)	37.061
art 19(1)	37.062
art 19(2)	37.062
art 20	37.061
art 20(1)	37.063
art 20(2)	37.063
art 20(3)	37.063
art 20(4)	37.063
art 21(1)	37.064
art 21(2)	37.064
art 22(1)	37.065
art 22(2)	37.065
art 22(3)	37.065
art 22(4)	37.065
art 23(1)	37.066
art 23(2)	37.066
art 23(3)	37.066
art 24(1)	37.067
art 24(2)	37.067
art 25	37.068
art 25(1)	37.069
art 25(2)	37.069
art 25(3)	37.069
art 25(4)	37.051
art 26	37.085
art 26(1)	37.070, 37.071, 37.072, 37.081
art 26(2)	37.071
art 26(3)	37.072
art 26(4)	37.072, 37.073
art 26(6)	37.074
art 26(7)	37.075
art 26(8)	37.075
art 27	37.095
art 27(1)	37.076, 37.077
art 27(2)	37.083
art 27(3)	37.076, 37.078
art 27(4)	37.076, 37.079
art 27(5)	37.079
art 27(6)	37.014, 37.079
art 27(7)	37.079, 37.080
art 27(8)	37.079
art 28(1)	37.081
art 28(2)	37.082
art 28(3)	37.082
art 28(4)	37.083
art 29(1)	37.085
art 29(2)	37.085
art 30	37.086, 37.087, 37.088
art 30(1)	37.086, 37.087
art 30(2)	37.086
art 30(3)	37.086
art 30(4)	37.087
art 30(5)	37.087
art 30(6)	37.087
art 31	37.088
art 32	37.089
art 33	37.090, 37.091
art 34	37.090
art 34(1)	37.092
art 34(2)	37.092
art 35	37.090
art 35(1)	37.093

art 35(2) 37.033, 37.038, 37.048,
          37.051, 37.093
art 35(3) 37.038, 37.051, 37.093
art 36 .... 37.094, 37.095
art 37 .... 37.038, 37.043, 37.079, 37.094,
          37.095
art 37(1) 37.095
art 37(2) 37.095
art 37(3) 37.095
art 37(4) 37.095
art 37(5) 37.095
art 38(1) 37.096
art 38(2) 37.044, 37.058, 37.079,
          37.087, 37.089, 37.093, 37.096
art 38(3) 37.045
art 38(4) 37.045
art 38(5) 37.093
art 39(1) 37.033, 37.097
art 39(2) 37.097
art 40 .... 37.098
art 41 .... 37.003
Chapter 2 .... 37.039
Recital 1 .... 37.004
Recital 2 .... 37.005
Recital 3 .... 37.005
Recital 4 .... 37.006
Recital 5 .... 37.007
2014/100 .... 39.051
2014/104/EU (Damages Directive) 3.120
2015/94
  art 8(1) 8.028
  art 8(2) 8.028
2015/230/EU
  art 18(1) 48.053
2016/844 .... 34.057
2017/306 .... 37.100
  Annex 37.099
  art 3 .... 37.099
2018/131 .... 8.359
  art 1 .... 8.360
  art 2 .... 8.361
  art 3 .... 8.362
2065/65
  Recital 17 .... 42.069
2015/1794 .... 8.015, 8.016, 8.018, 8.030
  art 1 .... 8.031
  art 2 .... 8.031
  art 3 .... 8.033
  art 4 .... 8.034
  art 5 .... 8.034

art 6 .... 8.034
art 7 .... 8.034
art 9 .... 8.027
Recital 4 .... 8.029
Recital 5 .... 8.029
Recital 6 .... 8.029
Recital 7 .... 8.030
Recital 10 .... 8.030
Recital 14 .... 8.030
2015/2087 .... 19.059
2017/2110/EU 25.006, 48.037

Treaties

Community Charter of the Fundamental Social
    Rights of Workers 1989 .... 8.237
ECSC Treaty (Treaty of Paris) 1951 .... 1.006,
    3.004, 3.015, 3.017, 4.008, 4.010, 5.003,
          10.125, 16.007, 48.011
  art 2 .... 3.004
  art 3 .... 3.004
  art 18 .... 3.004
  art 24 .... 3.004
  art 66 .... 16.007
  art 97 .... 3.017
EEC Treaty (Treaty of Rome) 1957 .... 1.006,
    1.023, 3.005, 3.026, 3.043, 4.002, 4.011,
    4.013, 5.003, 5.005, 5.056, 5.129, 5.161,
    6.043, 7.009, 7.268, 7.294, 9.054, 9.057,
    9.064, 9.068, 9.069, 15.088, 16.007,
    16.135, 21.005, 25.074, 26.027, 41.003,
    42.010, 42.104, 45.006, 46.003, 46.009,
    46.028, 46.051, 48.003, 49.041
  art 1 .... 3.006
  art 2 .... 4.014, 4.067, 6.138, 7.238, 8.242,
          19.325
  art 3 .... 4.014, 4.067, 7.166, 7.171, 7.173
  art 3(1)(c) 6.138, 7.238, 8.242
  art 3(1)(f) 4.024, 7.127
  art 3(1)(g) 7.131, 7.293
  art 3(1)(j) 6.138, 7.238, 8.242
  art 3(f) 7.127
  art 5 .... 7.131, 7.166, 7.171, 7.173, 7.175,
          8.083, 8.261, 19.253, 19.265, 29.024,
          29.027
  art 6 .... 6.096, 6.097, 6.098, 19.326
  art 6(3) 20.022
  art 7 .... 6.043, 6.105, 7.127, 46.127
  art 9 .... 7.140
  art 10 .... 7.249, 7.293, 19.319

art 12	7.140
art 16	4.065
art 18	7.140
art 23	7.142
art 24	7.142
art 28	7.127, 7.140
art 30	7.127, 7.166, 7.171, 7.172, 7.177
art 38(2)	4.067
art 39	7.127, 8.240
art 39(2)	6.128
art 39(3)	8.225
art 39(4)	8.212
art 42	35.008, 36.005
art 43	6.147, 7.127, 8.237, 8.240
art 46(1)	7.294
art 47	19.326
art 48	4.068, 5.016, 6.096, 6.097, 6.098, 6.128, 6.153, 7.127, 8.242, 40.009
art 48	40.011
arts 48–51	4.067, 6.043
art 49	6.005, 7.118, 7.127, 7.213, 7.225, 7.247, 7.249, 7.294, 8.240
art 49(1)	7.225
art 50	7.294
art 51	7.127
art 51(1)	7.225
art 52	6.105, 6.096, 6.097, 6.098, 6.128, 7.127, 40.009, 40.011
arts 52–58	6.043
art 53	6.006
art 54	7.225
art 54(3)(g)	16.017
art 55	40.009, 40.011
arts 55–58	7.022
art 56	7.176, 7.177, 7.293
arts 56–62	7.161
art 58	6.096, 6.097, 6.098, 7.128
art 59	7.127, 7.166, 7.176, 7.177, 7.185
art 61	7.185, 19.041
art 61(1)	7.087
art 61(c)	19.029, 19.041, 21.005
art 62	7.022, 7.086, 7.087, 7.127, 7.191, 7.213
art 67(1)	21.005
arts 67–71	19.041
arts 67–73	6.043
art 70	19.326
art 71	19.326
art 71(1)	19.326
art 74	4.014, 4.067
arts 74–83, Title IV	5.006
art 75	46.003
art 75(1)	4.065
art 75(3)	4.065
art 79(3)	4.047
art 80	7.118, 7.127
art 80(1)	19.326
art 80(2)	4.065, 6.079, 7.087, 7.128, 7.225, 7.276, 8.082, 8.091, 19.061, 19.325, 19.326, 20.006, 25.078, 27.006, 28.007, 28.122, 29.005, 29.073, 31.003, 33.004, 34.041, 34.057, 42.058, 46.028, 46.147
art 81	5.140, 5.150, 7.293, 12.056, 12.085, 12.101, 12.125, 12.180, 12.181, 12.203, 14.018, 14.058
art 81(1)	12.171, 14.018
art 81(3)	5.164, 12.033, 12.180, 14.018, 14.059, 14.060
arts 81–86	10.001
art 82	5.140, 10.116, 10.120, 12.180, 12.181, 12.203, 14.058
art 83	12.033, 12.042, 14.060, 16.001
art 84	5.003, 7.066, 7.127, 17.005
art 84(1)	4.067
art 84(2)	4.062, 4.064, 4.067, 5.004, 5.009, 5.011, 5.016, 5.080, 6.058, 6.156, 7.079, 7.185, 11.012, 11.021, 11.022, 25.057, 34.010, 39.005, 46.003, 46.009
art 85	5.008, 5.009, 5.017, 5.049, 5.053, 5.068, 5.071, 7.067, 7.166, 7.171, 7.173, 11.001, 11.014, 11.021, 11.068, 12.180, 46.077
art 85(1)	5.077, 6.133
art 85(3)	5.062, 5.104, 5.120
arts 85–90	10.001
arts 85–94	5.008, 46.127
art 86	5.008, 5.009, 5.017, 5.049, 5.053, 5.068, 5.071, 7.067, 7.166, 7.171, 7.173, 10.224, 11.001, 11.014, 11.021, 12.033, 12.180, 46.077
art 86(2)	15.111
art 87	7.293, 7.295, 11.012, 11.013, 11.021, 11.022, 12.033, 15.077
arts 87–89	15.007, 15.047
art 88	15.047
art 88(1)	15.054
art 90	7.142, 7.173, 46.127
art 90(1)	7.166, 7.171, 46.126, 46.127
art 90(2)	7.174, 7.176

art 90(3)	46.126
art 92(3)	6.156
art 92(3)(d)	22.024
art 95	7.141, 10.224
art 99	39.047
art 100	4.067
art 101	7.131, 7.175
arts 101–106	7.131
art 102	7.175
art 106(1)	7.175
art 107(3)(c)	15.060, 15.066
art 113	5.017, 7.140, 22.024
art 116	5.017
art 117	6.094
art 118A	32.005
art 130	7.127
art 130r	19.198, 19.202
art 130s	19.198
art 132	12.056
art 136	6.129, 6.133, 6.138, 7.235, 7.236, 8.237, 8.240, 8.242, 8.261
art 137	8.240, 8.269
art 137(5)	8.240
art 138	8.269
art 138(2)	8.261
art 138(4)	8.261
art 139	8.269
art 139(2)	8.039, 8.260, 8.261, 8.269
art 148(2)	6.073, 6.075
art 158	7.185
art 169	5.017, 6.043, 6.105
art 172	11.128
art 174	7.127, 45.005
art 175(1)	19.133
art 186	6.043
art 189	9.074
art 191	7.127, 9.074
art 195	27.073
art 211	45.006
art 214	19.100
art 221	6.096, 6.097, 6.098, 6.105
art 226	7.285, 31.084
art 228	19.198
art 230	27.073
art 234	7.303, 19.319
art 235	19.117
art 249	7.249, 8.261, 8.269, 19.320
art 251	42.009, 46.038
art 254(2)	3.105
art 285(1)	46.051
art 299(2)	7.185, 28.008
art 300	19.041
art 300(2)	19.029, 19.041, 19.133, 21.005, 25.078, 36.005
art 300(3)	19.041, 19.133, 25.078, 36.005
art 300(7)	19.319
art 308	16.001
Part 2	4.067, 7.128
Title III	6.129, 6.133, 7.236
Title IV	7.141
Title VI	6.129, 7.236
Title XI	6.129, 7.235
Euratom Treaty (EAEC) 1957	3.004, 3.006, 3.092, 4.008, 5.003
art 1	3.005
art 208	3.017
European Defence Treaty	3.016
European Social Charter 1961	8.237
European Union Charter of Fundamental Rights 2000	
art 28	7.236
European Union Charter of Fundamental Rights 2000	6.133, 8.240, 8.261, 8.318
Merger Treaty 1965	3.004, 3.006, 3.017, 3.020, 3.096
North Atlantic Treaty 1949	3.013, 25.031
Single European Act 1986	
art 1, Title I	3.098
art 16(5)	6.058
Single European Act 1986	3.006, 3.026, 3.043, 3.070, 3.096, 3.098, 4.004, 4.013, 4.065, 4.070, 5.016, 5.080, 18.013
TEU (Maastricht Treaty) 1992	3.006, 3.092, 3.096, 3.099, 22.036, 25.005, 35.003, 42.011, 42.059
art 2	48.020
art 3	4.002
art 4(3)	3.007, 7.131, 7.158, 7.247, 29.081
art 5	8.030, 36.023, 37.008, 42.069, 46.085
art 6	19.265, 46.085
art 13(2)	3.032
art 15(1)	3.050
art 15(2)	3.050
art 15(3)	3.050, 3.053
art 15(4)	3.050
art 15(5)	3.050
art 17(3)	3.035
art 18	13.035, 13.044
art 19	3.060
art 19(1)	3.061

art 19(2) 3.062	art 42(3) 25.031
art 20(2)(c) 25.023	art 42(4) 25.031
art 21 .... 19.117, 25.009, 25.041, 25.047	art 42(5) 25.031
art 21(1) 25.008	art 42(6) 25.031, 25.035
art 21(2) 25.008	art 42(7) 25.031
art 21(3) 25.008	art 43 .... 25.026, 25.029, 25.031, 25.033
art 22(1) 25.009, 25.019	art 43(1) 25.032
art 23 .... 25.011, 25.023	art 43(2) 25.032
art 23(3) 25.012	art 44 .... 25.031
art 24(1) 25.012	art 44(1) 25.033
art 24(2) 25.012	art 44(2) 25.033
art 24(3) 25.022	art 44(3) 25.034
art 25 .... 25.013	art 45(1) 25.034
art 26(1) 25.014	art 45(2) 25.034
art 26(2) 25.014	art 46 .... 25.031
art 26(3) 25.014	art 46(1) 25.035
art 27(1) 25.015	art 46(2) 25.035
art 27(2) 25.015	art 46(3) 25.035
art 27(3) 25.015	art 46(4) 25.035
art 28(1) 25.016	art 46(5) 25.035
art 28(2) 25.016	art 47 .... 3.002, 19.325, 19.326, 25.004
art 28(3) 25.016	art 49 .... 48.020
art 28(4) 25.016	art 50 .... 48.006, 48.020, 48.021, 48.039, 48.041
art 28(5) 25.016	art 50(3) 48.041
art 29 .... 19.326, 25.017	art 51 .... 25.031
art 30(1) 25.018	art 81 .... 12.193
art 30(2) 25.018	art 81(1) 12.193
art 30(3) 25.018, 48.024	art 84(2) 11.089
art 31 .... 25.019	art 87 .... 15.060
art 31(1) 25.029, 25.055	art 88 .... 15.060
art 31(1)(e) 19.325	art 100(2) 8.082
art 31(5) 25.019	Part Five 25.036
art 32 .... 25.020	Title V 25.006, 25.007
art 33 .... 25.019, 25.021	Title V, Ch 2 .... 25.049
art 34 .... 19.265	Title VI 19.325, 19.326
art 34(1) 25.022	TFEU (Treaty of Lisbon) 2007 ...... 1.023, 3.006, 3.017, 3.030, 3.046, 3.067, 3.070, 3.092, 3.100, 4.001, 4.016, 4.055, 4.056, 5.104, 5.161, 7.065, 8.008, 8.014, 8.082, 10.011, 14.072, 15.021, 16.038, 19.128, 22.020, 25.005, 35.002, 35.003, 41.006, 43.022, 44.007, 46.067
art 34(2) 25.022	
art 34(2)(b) 19.325	
art 35 .... 25.023	
art 36 .... 25.024	
art 37 .... 25.025	
art 38 .... 25.026	
art 39 .... 25.027	
art 40 .... 25.012, 25.028	art 2(1) 7.228
art 41(1) 25.029	art 3 .... 6.018
art 41(2) 25.029	art 3(2) 35.003
art 41(3) 25.029	art 3(3) 35.003
art 42 .... 25.031	arts 3–6 .... 25.028
art 42(1) 25.029, 25.031, 25.032	art 4 .... 4.018, 6.018, 35.003
art 42(2) 25.029, 25.031	art 4(2) 4.002, 4.009, 4.012, 4.018, 35.004

art 4(3) 29.024
art 5 ... 7.177, 24.020, 28.123, 29.081, 33.012,
    35.003, 46.181
art 6 .... 13.040
arts 9–13 .... 7.142
art 13 .... 3.032
art 16 .... 25.027
art 17 .... 3.117
art 18 .... 3.002, 3.117, 4.009, 4.014, 6.035,
    6.039, 6.043, 6.096, 7.035, 7.130, 7.135,
    7.154, 7.158, 8.343, 8.346, 8.348, 8.350,
    8.351, 13.022, 13.039, 15.026, 40.001,
    40.020, 48.035
art 26 .... 4.002
art 26(2) 4.002
art 28 .... 7.140, 7.143
art 28(1) 3.021
arts 28–32 .... 25.038
arts 28–37 .... 4.048
art 29 .... 7.143, 7.293
art 30 .... 7.169, 13.038, 13.042, 13.044,
art 34 .... 7.127, 7.132, 7.143, 7.171
art 36 .... 7.166, 8.212, 13.035
art 38 .... 4.024
art 39(2) 6.007
art 45 .... 4.009, 4.068, 5.016, 6.096, 6.128,
    6.133, 7.127, 7.133, 7.236, 8.009, 8.010,
    8.196, 8.197, 8.206, 8.211, 8.318, 8.328,
    8.329, 8.343, 8.346, 8.348, 8.350, 8.351,
    13.038, 13.042
art 45(1) 8.318, 8.330
arts 45(1–3) 8.210, 8.225
art 45(2) 8.213
art 45(3) 8.210, 8.212
art 45(4) 3.117, 8.209, 8.210, 8.212, 8.213,
    8.214, 8.216, 8.222, 8.223, 8.224, 8.225,
    8.226, 8.318, 8.330
arts 45–48 .... 4.067, 7.026
art 46 .... 8.010, 8.237
art 47 .... 8.011
art 48 .... 8.012, 13.045, 13.061
art 49 .... 6.003, 6.004, 6.096, 6.115, 6.116,
    6.128, 6.131, 6.132, 6.133, 6.134, 6.135,
    6.136, 6.137, 6.138, 6.139, 6.142, 6.146,
    6.148, 6.151, 7.123, 7.127, 7.134, 7.230,
    7.235, 7.236, 7.237, 7.238, 7.293, 8.229,
    8.230, 8.236, 8.237, 8.239, 8.240, 8.241,
    8.242, 8.318, 8.328
arts 49–54 .... 8.242
arts 49–55 .... 6.001, 6.043
art 50 .... 6.007
art 51 .... 6.013, 8.318, 8.328
art 52 .... 6.015, 6.016, 6.017, 6.137, 7.194,
    7.196, 7.197, 7.198, 7.236, 8.212, 8.237
art 52(1) 6.148, 7.197
art 53 .... 6.010
art 54 .... 6.003, 6.007, 6.096, 6.116, 6.138,
    6.142, 6.148, 6.151, 7.134, 7.197, 7.238,
    8.242
art 55 .... 6.096, 6.105, 6.138
art 56 .... 6.128, 6.133, 7.006, 7.024, 7.118,
    7.120, 7.123, 7.127, 7.135, 7.157, 7.158,
    7.161, 7.189, 7.191, 7.194, 7.196, 7.197,
    7.198, 7.225, 7.228, 7.235, 7.247, 7.289,
    7.296, 8.240
arts 56–62 .... 7.006
art 57 .... 7.161, 7.197, 7.236
art 58 .... 4.020, 7.079, 7.127, 7.161
art 58(1) 4.009, 4.014, 4.021, 4.067, 6.002,
    7.001, 7.006, 7.065, 7.123, 7.158, 7.225,
    7.228, 7.276
art 59 .... 13.069, 13.075
art 61 .... 7.123, 7.225, 7.228, 19.029
art 62 .... 7.123
arts 63–66 .... 6.043
art 66 .... 7.166
art 67 .... 19.029
art 67(1) 19.029
art 68 .... 19.029
art 69 .... 19.029
art 70 .... 19.029
art 71 .... 19.029, 25.055
art 73 .... 4.042
art 80 .... 4.070, 7.123
art 81 .... 46.142, 47.004
art 81(1) 46.139
art 81(2)(a) 46.139
art 81(2)(c) 46.139
art 81(3) 12.032, 14.017
art 83 .... 12.033
art 84(2) 4.061, 4.067, 7.143
art 85 .... 7.175
art 85(3) 14.050
arts 85–94 .... 13.040
art 86(1) 13.035
art 90 .... 4.014, 4.022, 4.023, 4.024, 4.026,
    4.027, 4.028, 4.038, 4.060
art 90(1) 13.040
arts 90–100 .... 1.041, 4.005, 4.009
art 91 .... 4.028, 4.029, 4.030, 4.035

TABLE OF LEGISLATION

art 91(1)..... 4.030, 4.031, 4.032, 4.036, 4.045, 46.074
art 91(1)(a) 4.033
art 91(1)(b) 4.033, 7.115
art 91(1)(c) 4.032, 4.033
art 91(2).. 4.033
art 91(3).. 4.034
art 92 .... 4.027, 4.036, 4.037, 4.038
art 93 .... 4.039, 4.040, 4.041, 4.042, 15.017
art 95 .... 4.045, 4.046, 4.047, 4.048, 7.142, 11.070
art 96 .... 4.050, 4.051
art 97 .... 4.053, 4.054, 7.191
art 98 .... 4.055, 4.056
art 99 .... 4.057, 4.058
art 100 .... 3.043, 4.013, 4.023, 4.052, 4.060, 4.061, 5.003, 7.118, 7.127, 7.129, 7.191, 28.143, 36.013, 46.135
art 100(2)... 1.041, 3.043, 3.101, 4.026, 4.052, 4.068, 4.070, 5.080, 6.058, 6.079, 6.156, 7.018, 7.066, 7.079, 7.087, 7.123, 7.128, 7.129, 7.142, 7.158, 7.185, 7.189, 7.197, 7.225, 7.228, 7.276, 8.091, 8.352, 10.015, 19.061, 25.057, 25.078, 26.023, 26.040, 26.043, 27.006, 28.007, 28.122, 28.136, 29.005, 29.073, 30.013, 31.003, 33.004, 34.010, 34.041, 34.057, 36.013, 39.005, 40.002, 42.058, 43.022, 44.007, 46.003, 46.009, 46.028, 46.074, 46.131, 46.147, 46.181
art 101 .... 1.056, 1.057, 3.120, 5.008, 5.009, 5.049, 5.053, 5.068, 5.140, 5.150, 5.154, 5.172, 7.067, 7.114, 7.153, 7.166, 7.169, 7.171, 7.173, 7.175, 7.177, 7.293, 8.240, 10.007, 10.008, 10.011, 10.019, 10.022, 10.027, 10.033, 10.044, 10.047, 10.049, 10.052, 10.053, 10.055, 10.056, 10.059, 10.060, 10.069, 10.070, 10.071, 10.072, 10.074, 10.079, 10.083, 10.084, 10.085, 10.087, 10.091, 10.092, 10.093, 10.105, 10.111, 10.115, 10.159, 10.164, 10.169, 10.191, 10.194, 10.208, 10.209, 10.210, 10.220, 11.001, 11.004, 11.006, 11.008, 11.021, 11.028, 11.032, 11.036, 11.037, 11.058, 11.085, 11.090, 11.091, 11.092, 11.094, 11.095, 11.108, 11.134, 12.001, 12.008, 12.012, 12.017, 12.031, 12.032, 12.033, 12.038, 12.044, 12.045, 12.048, 12.049, 12.053, 12.054, 12.055, 12.056, 12.059, 12.064, 12.065, 12.066, 12.067, 12.068, 12.082, 12.103, 12.104, 12.105, 12.114, 12.116, 12.119, 12.120, 12.122, 12.124, 12.126, 12.128, 12.135, 12.143, 12.146, 12.153, 12.179, 12.184, 12.185, 12.190, 12.194, 12.196, 12.199, 12.201, 12.202, 12.203, 12.204, 13.005, 13.017, 13.020, 13.022, 13.025, 13.035, 13.044, 13.080, 13.085, 13.090, 13.091, 14.018, 14.022, 14.067, 14.069, 14.076, 14.090, 14.093, 14.094, 15.092, 16.001, 16.002, 16.007, 16.009, 16.108, 16.173, 48.042
art 101(1)... 1.057, 3.043, 4.026, 5.138, 5.155, 5.164, 6.133, 7.236, 10.054, 10.058, 10.076, 10.077, 10.086, 10.088, 10.089, 10.090, 10.097, 10.183, 11.025, 11.040, 11.046, 11.047, 11.048, 11.049, 11.050, 11.052, 11.053, 11.054, 11.055, 11.056, 11.058, 11.061, 11.062, 11.063, 11.064, 11.082, 11.083, 11.087, 11.090, 11.095, 11.096, 11.098, 11.099, 11.100, 11.103, 11.108, 11.118, 11.121, 11.123, 11.124, 12.001, 12.008, 12.043, 12.044, 12.045, 12.060, 12.067, 12.072, 12.115, 12.118, 12.119, 12.122, 12.125, 12.126, 12.129, 12.131, 12.132, 12.133, 12.138, 12.139, 12.142, 12.143, 12.146, 12.148, 12.151, 12.153, 12.170, 12.171, 12.175, 12.179, 12.184, 13.015, 13.085, 14.017, 14.022, 14.033, 14.034, 14.051, 14.052, 14.053, 14.056, 14.060, 14.080, 14.083, 14.087, 14.089, 14.090, 14.091, 16.002, 16.038
art 101(2)...... 10.098, 10.099, 11.087, 11.089, 11.103, 11.104, 11.105, 11.106, 12.143, 13.015, 14.027, 16.002, 17.005, 18.005, 18.013, 18.029
art 101(3)...5.062, 5.120, 5.134, 5.150, 5.164, 10.012, 10.096, 10.102, 10.103, 10.104, 10.106, 10.110, 10.165, 10.166, 10.183, 10.213, 10.214, 11.008, 11.011, 11.015, 11.025, 11.038, 11.040, 11.061, 11.064, 11.067, 11.068, 11.069, 11.078, 11.083, 11.084, 11.085, 11.095, 11.096, 11.097, 11.098, 11.099, 11.100, 11.104, 11.108, 11.118, 11.121, 11.125, 11.126, 12.006, 12.009, 12.032, 12.033, 12.035, 12.044, 12.045, 12.064, 12.067, 12.086, 12.126, 12.132, 12.143, 12.146, 12.150, 12.151, 12.175, 12.179, 13.015, 14.017, 14.022, 14.033, 14.037, 14.040, 14.048, 14.050, 14.051, 14.052, 14.053, 14.056, 14.059,

14.060, 14.061, 14.067, 14.075, 14.080, 14.087, 14.090, 14.093, 14.094, 16.002, 16.038, 48.042
art 101(3)(b) 11.083, 11.084
arts 101–106 .... 10.001
arts 101–109 .... 5.008, 13.010, 15.026
art 102 .... 1.056, 1.057, 3.120, 5.008, 5.009, 5.049, 5.053, 5.068, 5.140, 5.150, 5.154, 7.067, 7.114, 7.153, 7.157, 7.159, 7.166, 7.169, 7.171, 7.173, 7.174, 7.177, 10.007, 10.008, 10.011, 10.012, 10.019, 10.022, 10.023, 10.027, 10.033, 10.045, 10.052, 10.079, 10.093, 10.104, 10.116, 10.117, 10.118, 10.119, 10.120, 10.121, 10.122, 10.124, 10.125, 10.144, 10.154, 10.155, 10.159, 10.164, 10.169, 10.191, 10.194, 10.224, 11.001, 11.004, 11.007, 11.011, 11.021, 11.028, 11.032, 11.036, 11.037, 11.058, 11.085, 11.086, 11.087, 11.090, 11.091, 11.092, 11.094, 11.095, 11.096, 11.108, 11.123, 11.124, 11.134, 12.001, 12.012, 12.017, 12.031, 12.032, 12.038, 12.044, 12.048, 12.049, 12.055, 12.064, 12.065, 12.114, 12.143, 12.153, 12.184, 12.190, 12.202, 12.203, 13.005, 13.016, 13.017, 13.019, 13.020, 13.022, 13.026, 13.035, 13.036, 13.038, 13.040, 13.041, 13.042, 13.044, 13.045, 13.049, 13.050, 13.051, 13.053, 13.054, 13.058, 13.061, 13.069, 13.072, 13.074, 13.075, 13.077, 13.080, 13.087, 13.090, 13.091, 13.094, 14.061, 14.067, 14.069, 14.076, 14.091, 14.093, 14.094, 15.092, 16.001, 16.002, 16.007, 16.009, 16.173, 48.042
art 102(2)(a) 13.036
art 102(2)(b) 13.036
art 102(c) 7.159
art 103 .... 3.045, 11.013, 12.042, 14.060, 16.001
arts 103–105 .... 10.011
art 104 .... 12.001
art 105 .... 3.036
art 106 .... 7.173, 7.174, 10.011, 10.033, 10.199, 10.201, 10.202, 10.205, 11.086, 13.005, 13.017, 13.020, 13.021, 13.035, 13.069, 13.072, 13.075, 13.077, 13.080, 15.026, 15.027, 15.094, 46.127
art 106(1) ... 7.157, 7.166, 7.171, 7.174, 7.177, 7.187, 10.204, 13.018, 13.022, 13.038, 13.040, 13.041, 13.042, 13.044, 13.045, 13.058, 13.061, 13.071, 13.074, 13.075, 13.080, 13.090
art 106(2) 7.174, 10.123, 10.144, 10.204, 10.224, 13.018, 13.035, 13.044, 13.045, 13.090, 15.027, 15.039, 15.056, 15.111
art 106(3) 10.204, 13.080, 13.090, 46.127
art 106(c) 7.159
art 107 .... 5.066, 6.094, 6.095, 7.194, 7.289, 7.293, 7.295, 10.033, 15.019, 15.023, 15.024, 15.043, 15.094, 15.097, 15.128, 22.020, 22.115
art 107(1) ... 5.174, 6.095, 7.196, 7.198, 7.296, 15.006, 15.016, 15.020, 15.039, 15.089, 15.113, 22.103
art 107(2) 4.042, 15.021
art 107(3) 4.042, 6.156, 15.006, 15.022, 15.039, 15.121
art 107(3)(a) 22.111, 22.114
art 107(3)(c) 15.056, 22.109, 22.110
art 107(a) 15.046
art 107(c) 15.046
arts 107–109 .... 4.040, 4.042, 5.174, 10.011, 13.017, 15.004, 15.007, 15.017, 15.018, 15.124
art 108 .... 5.066, 15.023, 15.024, 15.043, 15.128, 22.114
art 108(2) 22.099, 22.100
art 108(3) 15.024
art 109 .... 15.023, 15.024
art 110 .... 7.141, 7.143, 7.144
art 121 .... 39.047
art 136 .... 35.003
arts 136–139 .... 35.003
art 139(2) 35.003
art 151 .... 6.129, 6.133, 7.235, 7.238, 8.017, 8.240
art 153 .... 6.133, 7.236, 8.018, 8.240
art 153(1)(3) 8.017
art 153(1)(b) 8.017, 36.033
art 153(2)(b) 8.017, 36.033
art 153(5) 6.133, 7.236
art 155 .... 6.133, 35.002
art 166 .... 6.133, 27.064
art 173 .... 22.020
art 191 .... 7.136
art 192(1) 24.011
art 196(2) 19.191
art 205 .... 25.037
art 206 .... 25.038
art 206(3) 25.038

art 206(4)	25.038
art 206(5)	25.038
art 206(6)	25.038
art 207	22.020, 25.038, 25.050
art 207(1)	25.038
art 207(2)	25.038
art 207(3)	25.038
art 208	25.041
art 208(1)	25.040
art 208(2)	25.040
arts 208–211	25.044
art 209(1)	25.041
art 209(3)	25.041
art 210(1)	25.042
art 210(2)	25.042
art 211	25.042
art 212	25.050
art 212(1)	25.044
art 212(2)	25.044
art 212(3)	25.044
art 213	25.045
art 214(1)	25.047
art 214(2)	25.047
art 214(3)	25.047
art 214(4)	25.047
art 214(5)	25.047
art 214(6)	25.047
art 214(7)	25.047
art 215	25.049
art 215(1)	25.049
art 215(3)	25.049
art 216(1)	25.050
art 216(2)	25.050
art 217	25.050
art 218	19.029, 19.319, 25.038, 25.051, 25.078
art 218(1)	25.050
art 218(10)	25.050
art 218(11)	3.084, 25.050
art 218(2)	25.050
art 218(3)	25.050, 48.020
art 218(4)	25.050
art 218(5)	25.050
art 218(6)	25.050, 46.131, 46.139
art 218(6)(a)	19.191
art 218(7)	25.050
art 218(8)	25.050, 46.131, 46.139
art 218(9)	25.050, 26.023, 26.040, 26.043, 28.136, 28.138, 28.143, 28.144, 36.033, 36.038
art 219(1)	25.051
art 219(2)	25.051
art 219(3)	25.051
art 219(4)	25.051
art 220(1)	25.052
art 220(2)	25.052
art 221(1)	25.053, 25.055
art 221(2)	25.053, 25.055
art 221(3)	25.055
art 221(4)	25.055
art 235	19.054
art 237	3.046
art 238	7.225
art 238(1)	3.046
art 238(2)	3.046
art 238(3)	3.046
art 238(3)(a)	25.035
art 238(3)(b)	48.020
art 240	3.047, 25.026, 25.055
art 249	3.116, 35.003
art 251	3.069
arts 251–281	3.060
art 252	3.065
art 253	3.067
art 254	3.067
art 255	3.067
art 256	3.070
art 257	3.070
art 258	3.077, 3.104, 4.017, 5.017, 7.200, 7.215, 7.228, 7.285, 15.023, 31.084
art 259	3.078, 15.023
art 260(1)	3.077, 3.078
art 261	3.079, 11.119, 11.127, 11.128, 16.053
art 263	3.070, 3.074, 3.080, 7.151, 13.080
art 265	3.070, 3.081, 4.015, 13.080
art 267	3.083, 3.116, 6.114, 6.131, 7.194, 7.236, 7.240, 8.197, 10.167, 13.032, 13.034, 13.059, 19.319, 48.045
art 268	3.070
art 270	3.070, 3.082
art 272	3.070
art 275	25.012
art 288	3.102, 3.103, 3.104, 3.105, 3.113, 7.247
art 290	24.020, 36.008, 44.026, 46.067
art 292	19.102, 38.009
art 296	7.156
art 299	29.119, 13.045, 13.061

arts 301–304	3.088
art 314	27.018
art 335	3.002, 47.002
art 339	39.080
art 345	10.203, 13.002, 13.008, 43.016
art 346	16.050
art 349	15.022, 28.008, 43.030
art 352	16.001, 19.054
art 355	46.090, 47.088
art 356	3.017, 3.093
Part 3, Title III	4.021
Part 3, Title V	4.023
Part 3, Title VI	7.276
Part Five	25.008, 25.036
Part Five, Title I	25.037
Part Three, Title V	46.132
Protocol 14	35.003
Title IV	8.008
Title IX	6.129, 6.132
Title V	7.141
Title X	7.235

Treaty Amending Certain Budgetary Provisions 1970 .... 3.097
Treaty Amending Certain Financial Provisions 1975 .... 3.097
Treaty of Accession 1972 ... 3.019, 3.022, 4.042, 4.047, 48.010
Treaty of Accession 1979 .... 3.022
Treaty of Accession 1994 .... 27.023
Treaty of Accession 2005
   art 6(2) 25.079
Treaty of Amsterdam 1997 .... 3.006, 3.096, 3.099, 7.185, 7.191, 7.213, 8.039, 10.001, 19.265, 35.003
   art 138 .... 8.025
Treaty of Nice 2001 .... 3.006, 3.096, 8.240
United Nations Charter 1945
   art 102 .... 19.180

CHAPTER 1

Introduction

A. SCOPE OF THIS BOOK

1.001 This book is an introduction to several aspects of the law of the European Union ("EU")[1] as it relates to shipping or maritime transport.[2] Instead of being a general textbook on EU law, this book takes a specialist approach to EU law by identifying and examining many of the aspects of EU law most relevant to shipping.[3] Given the breadth of the topic, the book concentrates on issues most relevant to shipping because almost any area of EU law is potentially relevant to the sector.

1.002 EU shipping law is an important topic because, as was stated in the Athens Declaration of 7 May 2014 (more formally entitled *Mid-Term Review of the EU's Maritime Transport Policy until 2018 and Outlook to 2020*),

---

1 Although the term "European Union" ("EU" or "Union") is relatively recent in origin, it is used in this book for convenience to describe what has been variously called, over time, the European Economic Community ("EEC"), the European Community ("EC") and, most recently, the European Union ("EU").

2 In this book, "shipping" is given a wide meaning. The term "shipping" has been defined as meaning the "business of transporting goods and persons in ships from a dockside point across the sea for commercial purposes" (*Committee of Inquiry into Shipping*, Viscount Rochdale, London 1970, HMSO, Cmnd 4337). The EU's system for collating and presenting statistics (i.e., *Nomenclature statistique des activités économiques dans la Communauté européenne* ("NACE")) refers to water transport (H50) (which is then subdivided into H50.1 – sea and coastal passenger water transport; H50.1.0 – sea and coastal passenger water transport; H50.2 – sea and coastal freight water transport; and H50.2.0 – sea and coastal freight water transport) and there is also N77.3.4 – renting and leasing of water transport equipment. A similar broad approach is taken to the term in this book to cover shipping and ports. The terms "shipping" and "maritime transport" are both construed widely and used interchangeably for the purposes of this book. On the definition of maritime transport in a specific EU context, see Case C-251/04 *Commission v Greece* [2007] ECR 67, ECLI:EU:C:2007:5 where the Court of Justice of the European Union ("CJEU") had to consider the meaning of the term "maritime transport service" in the context of Regs 4055/86 (OJ 1986 L378/1 with an unofficial consolidation available at: http://eur-lex.europa.eu/legal-content/EN/TXT/HTML/?uri=CELEX:01986R4056-20061018&qid=1498255496325&from=EN) and 3577/92 (OJ 1992 L364/7 available at: http://eur-lex.europa.eu/legal-content/EN/TXT/HTML/?uri=CELEX:31992R3577&from=EN) (see chap. 7). On shipping generally, see Brodie, *Commercial Shipping Handbook* (2015); Brodie, *Dictionary of Shipping Terms* (2013); and Branch and Robarts, *Branch's Elements of Shipping* (2014). On the shipping business and the economics of the sector, see Grammenos (ed.), *The Handbook of Maritime Economics and Business* (2014) and Stopford, *Maritime Economics* (3rd ed., 2008). For a convenient location to source the international maritime conventions, see Berlingieri's, *International Maritime Conventions (Volume 1): The Carriage of Goods and Passengers by Sea* (2014), *International Maritime Conventions (Volume 2): Navigation, Securities, Limitation of Liability and Jurisdiction* (2014) and *International Maritime Conventions (Volume 3): Protection of the Marine Environment* (2015). On maritime law generally, see Baatz (ed.), *Maritime Law* (2014); Baughen, *Shipping Law* (2015); Bundock, *Shipping Law Handbook* (2011); and Mandaraka-Sheppard, *Modern Maritime Law (Volume 1): Jurisdiction and Risks* (2013) and *Modern Maritime Law (Volume 2): Managing Risks and Liabilities* (2013). On EU transportation law, see vol.1 of Jessen and Werner (eds), *EU Transportation Law* (2016) entitled *Brussels Commentary on EU Maritime Transport Law*.

3 For the benefit of readers unfamiliar with EU law, chap. 3 is an introduction to the EU and EU law.

"the EU is highly dependent on maritime transport[4] both for its internal and external trade since 75% of the Union's imports and exports and 37% of the internal trade transit through seaports[5] and that shipping is a highly mobile industry facing increasingly fierce competition from third countries".[6]

The EU is now a major source of shipping law.

B. THE EUROPEAN UNION

Introduction

1.003 Before introducing EU shipping law, it is useful to provide some background on the EU generally. The EU is the most sophisticated international organisation in the world. It comprises 28 Member States[7] who have ceded some elements of their sovereignty to create the EU. The conduct of these Member States along with other participants in the sector such as shipping companies, ports and seafarers can now be controlled in certain circumstances by the EU; in return, however, they have rights and opportunities which they would not otherwise possess (e.g. the right to establish businesses or work in other Member States on an equal footing with nationals in those Member States).[8]

Evolution of the European Union

1.004 The EU is the successor of the European Economic Community[9] ("EEC") which was founded in 1957. The EEC became the European Community ("EC") in the 1990s and is now the EU.

1.005 The EU is the product of the phenomenon known as European Integration. After the ravages of the Second World War in Europe, a plan was devised known as the Schuman Plan[10] advocating that France and Germany should form closer links between the two countries (who had fought each other three times over the previous 70 years) to place the principal weapons of war at the time (namely, coal and steel) under the supervision of a common authority[11] and in a common market[12] so as to minimise the risk of war between them and in Europe generally. This plan led to the creation of the European

---

4 Ed., the Commission had earlier stated in its communication entitled *Blue Belt, a Single Transport Area for Shipping* (COM(2013) 510 final, 8 July 2013), p. 2 that the "European Union is highly dependent on maritime transport for its trade with the rest of the world and within its internal market".

5 COM(2012) 0494 final.

6 http://ec.europa.eu/transport/modes/maritime/consultations/doc/2015-mts-review/council-conclusions-on-mid-term-review-of-eu-maritime-policy.pdf.

7 The term "Member State" refers to a State which is a member of the EU. All other States are usually referred to as "third States". The United Kingdom voted in a referendum on 23 June 2016 to leave the EU but as the terms and modalities of its exit (assuming that it proceeds to exit the EU) are not yet clear, the text assumes that the UK remains a Member State and not a third State. See chap. 48 on Brexit.

8 E.g. EU shipping companies may operate services between ports in any Member State (see chap. 7) while EU citizens may work, in most circumstances, in any Member State on the same terms as citizens of the host Member State.

9 The term "Community" was used historically to describe the phenomenon which is now known as the "Union".

10 The plan was named after the then French Foreign Minister Robert Schuman.

11 This "common authority" is now called the European Commission. In this book, the European Commission is normally referred to simply as the "Commission". On the Commission, see chap. 3.

12 The "common market" is now known as the "internal market".

Coal and Steel Community ("ECSC") in 1952. While the original plan was just to involve France and Germany, four other States (i.e. Belgium, Italy, Luxembourg and the Netherlands) also participated in the ECSC. The ECSC was successful and it was quickly realised that the successes in the context of coal and steel could be extended to other economic sectors (i.e. to the economy generally including the shipping sector). This led to the establishment of the EEC and the European Atomic Energy Community ("EAEC") in 1957.

1.006 The ECSC had come into existence in 1952 with six Member States.[13] These six States then formed the EEC and EAEC in 1957.[14] In 1973, the membership of the three Communities (i.e. the ECSC, EEC and EAEC) grew to nine States;[15] there were ten States when Greece acceded in 1981; in 1986, two Iberian States[16] joined; three States joined in 1995;[17] ten States joined in 2004 in the largest accession ever;[18] two further States joined in 2007;[19] and one State joined in 2013.[20] Today, there are therefore 28 Member States in the EU: Austria; Belgium; Bulgaria; Croatia, Cyprus; Czech Republic; Denmark; Estonia; Finland; France; Germany; Greece; Hungary; Ireland; Italy; Latvia; Lithuania; Luxembourg; Malta; Netherlands; Poland; Portugal; Romania; Slovakia; Slovenia; Spain; Sweden; and United Kingdom. Albania, Bosnia and Herzegovina, Iceland, Kosovo, Montenegro, Serbia, Turkey and Ukraine are among the potential future Member States.

1.007 The EU is an evolving phenomenon. Generally speaking, it is expanding, rather than contracting, in terms of membership, competence and activities. It has experienced dynamic development punctuated by occasional stagnation but rarely permanent reversal. It began life in the 1950s as a group of three intergovernmental organisations[21] and is now an economic, monetary[22] and political union[23] of global significance. There were times in the 1970s and 1980s when it suffered degrees of paralysis. In recent years, it suffered a crisis related to the euro currency and the Economic and Monetary Union ("EMU") but it has survived the crisis. It will face further challenges in the future including, at the time of writing, a crisis over migration and the possible exit from the EU by the United Kingdom. However, the EU is now playing a significant role in world affairs as a collective unit having diplomatic relations and standing around the world. The EU developed a special relationship with some neighbouring States by the formation of the European Economic Area ("EEA") with effect from 1994 and today those States are Iceland, Norway and Liechtenstein. Equally, the EU is forming relationships in different spheres throughout the world. The EU, as a separate entity from its Member States, has the power

---

13 Belgium, France, the then Federal Republic of Germany ("West Germany"), Italy, Luxembourg and the Netherlands. A treaty to establish the ECSC was signed on 18 April 1951. It entered into force in 1952. The treaty was signed in Paris hence it is often known as the Treaty of Paris.

14 These six States signed two treaties in Rome on 25 March 1957 to establish the EEC and the EAEC. The treaty establishing the EEC is often known as the Treaty of Rome as it was signed in Rome.

15 Denmark, Ireland and the UK acceded on 1 January 1973 to join the pre-existing six Member States.

16 Portugal and Spain.

17 Austria, Finland and Sweden.

18 Cyprus; Czech Republic; Estonia; Hungary; Latvia; Lithuania; Malta; Poland; Slovakia; and Slovenia.

19 Bulgaria and Romania.

20 Croatia joined in 2013.

21 The ECSC, the EEC and the EAEC.

22 Not all Member States have chosen to participate in the Economic and Monetary Union ("EMU"); 19 of the 28 Member States operate the euro currency and participate in the EMU.

23 It is worth noting that the EU involves a "union" of members but not "uniformity" among members so there is still some diversity.

to conclude certain types of international agreements within its sphere of competence and has concluded many such agreements to date. Ultimately, the EU evolves and acquires new powers because its Member States confer new powers upon it.

The EU is the world's largest economic bloc

1.008 The EU is the world's largest economic bloc. There is no doubt that the EU has long been forced, in the words of the European Parliament many years ago, to "speak with one voice and to adopt a common position".[24] It represents around 7% of the world's population, constitutes the top trading partner for 80 countries around the world but about 23% of the world's nominal gross domestic product ("GDP") and represents 16% of global exports and imports. It is the world's largest exporter of goods[25] and the second largest importer.[26]

1.009 The EU's *Statistical Pocketbook 2017* (the most recent available at the time of writing) puts the EU into a global context (Table 1.1).

Table 1.1 Comparison EU28 – World

	General data				
	EU28	USA	Japan	China	Russia
Population million	506.65	313.91	127.56	1,350.70	143.53
Population growth % change since previous year	0.1	0.7	–0.2	0.5	0.4
Urban population % of total	74	83	92	52	74
Area thousand km^2	4,414	9,629	378	9,597	17,075
Population density persons/km^2	115	33	338	141	8
GDP (nominal) € billion	12,971	12,644	4,623	6,378	1,562
Real GDP growth %	–0.4	2.8	1.4	7.8	3.4
Relative GDP per capita in PPP (EU28=100)	100	154	105	27	70
Exports of goods € billion	1,683	1,215	604	1,534	410
Imports of goods € billion	1,798	1,792	646	1,286	261

Source: Eurostat, World Bank. Relative GDP per capita and currency conversion rates: own calculations based on World Bank data (2012 data used).

Notes
EU28: area, population: including French overseas departments.
EU28: trade: only extra-EU trade.

Population

1.010 The EU has a population of just over 500 million. It is therefore the third most populous area in the world after China and India. It is more populous than the USA. The

---

24 The European Parliament's Committee on Regional Policy, Regional Planning and Transport, *Interim Report on the Sea Transport Problems in the Community* (1977), para. 4.
25 See European Commission's analysis at http://ec.europa.eu/eurostat/statistics-explained/index.php/International_trade_in_goods.
26 Ibid.

three largest Member States in terms of population are Germany (with 81 million people), France (with 66 million people) and the UK (with 64 million people).[27] Its Member States represent a range in terms of population from these three large States to States such as Cyprus and Malta with relatively small populations.

The internal market

1.011 One of the core elements of the EU is the notion of the internal market which means that goods and services must be able to move freely within the EU (subject to very limited exceptions, i.e. the "internal market") and there would be a common external tariff vis-à-vis the rest of the world (i.e. the customs union). This internal market (or common market) has been at the heart of the EU project since the 1950s. Initially, the notion was that States were less likely to go to war if they traded intensively with each other but now there is an inherent economic merit in having an internal market apart altogether from the prevention of war because of the efficiencies created by a large "home" market (i.e. the whole of the EU).

1.012 Establishing an internal market has always been difficult. Some Member States (or, sometimes some sectoral interests within those States) have sought to erect barriers to trade.[28] While progress was made in the 1960s, the completion of the internal market had still not been achieved by the early 1980s. So a programme, the Internal Market Programme (known colloquially as the "1992 Programme" because the aim was to complete the internal market programme by the end of 1992) was devised by the Commission in 1985. The plan devised involved 279 measures to integrate the national markets of the Member States into one single or internal market. The internal market programme achieved a great deal and today the market is largely internalised but the success of the project has not been recognised fully.[29]

Transport in the EU

1.013 Transport plays a very significant role in the EU.[30] Expenditure on transport in the EU is very high as a proportion of expenditure generally in EU households as compared to other forms of expenditure.[31] Transport in the EU has traditionally been highly regulated by Member State governments with historically significant levels of State ownership (but less so in shipping than in the railway or airline sectors), but this has changed (in large measure though not entirely) since the mid-1980s with the EU institutions becoming much more involved in regulating maritime transport, many transport

---

27 If the UK leaves the EU then Italy would become the third most populous EU Member State with 60 million people
28 E.g., see the debate on maritime cabotage (i.e. domestic trade between two ports in the same Market State) in chap. 7.
29 See Power, "The Uncelebrated Revolution: The Completion of the Internal Market" [1993] 4 ICCLR 323.
30 See chap. 4.
31 Eurostat commented in 2015 that Member State accounts data reveal "that a little over a fifth of total household consumption expenditure in the EU in 2006 was devoted to housing, water, electricity, gas and other housing fuels. Expenditure on transport and food and non-alcoholic beverages constitute the next two most important categories in the EU, at about the same level and together accounting for a little more than a quarter of total household consumption expenditure" (http://ec.europa.eu/eurostat/statistics-explained/index.php/Household_consumption_expenditure_-_background).

companies being privatised and aspects of the sector being deregulated in whole or in part. The EU's involvement in the transport sectors has been typically to eliminate anti-competitive practices, liberalise markets, standardise certain rules, improve safety, protect the environment, protect passengers and to internalise generally the EU transport market in the context of the global transport environment.

1.014 Turning from transport generally to shipping in particular, it is clear that shipping is extremely important in the EU. The Transport Council stated in their 7 May 2014 Athens Declaration:

> "RECALLING that shipping and related services are an important contributor to the European economy and to the quality of life of European citizens, providing jobs and being essential for European competitiveness; NOTING that the EU's blue economy currently represents 5,4 million jobs and a gross added value of almost €500 billion per year; RECOGNISING the potential of maritime and coastal tourism for economic growth and employment; ACKNOWLEDGING that shipping is a key element of the security of the EU supply chain, in particular as regards the importation of energy and raw materials..."[32]

Future of the EU

1.015 The EU is currently on a path of growth and development but there will be many difficulties ahead. Many Member States are committed to economic and monetary union with 19 Member States[33] adopting the euro as their currency. The EU may grow to replace the Member States in many more spheres but probably not in all spheres. It may well be the case that there are "several problems which the [EU] could tackle more effectively than individual Member States"[34] – the whole can be greater than the sum of the parts. Thus, on the level of world shipping, the EU (as an entity) could be, in certain areas, more important and influential than the individual Member States. The importance of the EU in shipping is demonstrated by the statement that "[t]hroughout Europe, a number of maritime interests have re-targeted their lobbying structures and strategies aiming to influence the development of the maritime related European Union ... policies".[35] The future of the EU and the future of shipping are therefore intertwined.

---

32 Athens Declaration, see fn. 6, recitals. The "blue economy" is slightly wider than shipping but it is effectively comparable because shipping represents such a huge proportion of the blue economy.

33 I.e. in 1999: Austria; Belgium; Finland; France; Germany; Ireland; Italy; Luxembourg; the Netherlands; Portugal and Spain; in 2001: Greece; in 2007: Slovenia; in 2008: Cyprus and Malta; in 2009: Slovakia; in 2011: Estonia; in 2014: Latvia; and in 2015: Lithuania. The euro coins and banknotes were not introduced until 2002 despite the currency existing since 1999.

34 The Commission's communication to the Council of Ministers entitled *A Future for the Community Shipping Industry: Measures to Improve the Operating Conditions of Community Shipping*, COM(89)266 final, 3 August 1989, p. 9. In this context, note the concept of subsidiarity, which posits that whatever can best be done at the level of Member States ought to be done by Member States and not by the EU. See, generally, Greaves, "EC Maritime Transport Policy and Regulation" (1992–1993) 3 Duke J. Comp. & Int'l L. 119.

35 Pallis, "Maritime Interests in the EU Policy-Making" (2007) World Maritime University Journal of Maritime Affairs 3 at 3. See Karamitsos, "EC Law and Maritime Transport: Preliminary Remarks" in Antapassis, Athanassiou and Røsæg (eds), *Competition and Regulation in Shipping and Shipping Related Industries* (2009), p. 1.

C. SHIPPING IN THE EU

Introduction

1.016 Chapter 2 contains a commercial overview of shipping in the EU. It would however be useful at this stage to outline some basic facts about shipping and the EU as part of this introductory chapter.

Strategic significance of shipping for the EU

1.017 The EU has a very long coastline which is four times that of Russia and seven times that of the USA. There are two oceans surrounding the EU: the Atlantic and the Arctic. There are four seas surrounding the EU: the Baltic; the Black Sea; the Mediterranean; and the North Sea. Indeed, the outermost regions of the EU (places such as Azores, Canaries, Guadeloupe, Guyana, Madeira, Martinique and Reunion) are surrounded by the Caribbean and the Indian Ocean. There is no doubt about the strategic significance of shipping for the EU and its Member States. Maritime-based activities represent about 3% of the EU's GDP. The maritime surface areas under the jurisdiction of Member States exceed, in extent, the land area of the Member States. Between 80% and 90% of the EU's foreign trade is carried by sea.[36] About one-third of the goods carried between the Member States are carried by sea. Shipping companies belonging to EU nationals control around one-third of the world fleet. Ships registered in Member States carry about 70% of the trade between Member States as well as 40% of the EU's external trade and there would be other ships used for this latter trade which are owned by nationals from Member States but registered outside the EU. More than 400 million passengers sail annually through the EU's ports. The EU's 23 coastal Member States have over 1,200 ports including some of the most important and largest in the world. Almost three-and-a-half billion tonnes of freight are loaded and unloaded at EU ports annually. If the EU is to maintain and grow its position in international traded goods then it must have a strong shipping and port capacity available to it.

1.018 The maritime transport sector includes shipbuilding, ship management, ship crewing, ship repair, marine insurance, ports, fishing and related industries and services. The sector clearly makes a very significant contribution to the EU. It is inevitable that the EU should recognise the significance of the sector. The Commission has written that it:

> "considers that a strong [EU] fleet is essential to the [EU] both for economic and strategic reasons. As the leading world trading entity,[37] the [EU] should not be excessively dependent on third country[38] fleets for its imports and exports, so losing control and influence on the price and quality of transport to and from its territory."[39]

---

36 See Commission, *Guidelines on State Aid to Maritime Transport* OJ 2004 C13/3. The Commission stated in its *Maritime Transport Strategy 2009–2018* (2009), p. 2 that "80% of world trade is carried by sea whilst short-sea shipping carries 40% of intra-European freight. With more than 400 million sea passengers passing through European ports each year, maritime transport has also a direct impact on the quality of life of citizens, both as tourists and inhabitants of islands and peripheral regions." While the exact figures can vary dependent on the particular metric chosen, maritime transport is significant to the EU on any method of measurement.

37 Ed., see para.1.008.

38 Ed., i.e. the States which are not EU Member States.

39 Commission, *Guidelines for the Examination of State Aids to Community Shipping Companies* (1990), p. 3.

The strategic significance of shipping to the EU means that the EU must have a shipping policy. As the EU's Economic and Social Committee ("EESC")[40] commented:

> "the [EU] needs a maritime transport policy concerned with the promotion of all maritime activities such as the carriage of goods and passengers by companies in Member States, the use of vessels registered in Member States and the employment of seafarers from Member States".[41]

The same Committee also wrote:

> "there is no disputing the fact that if Member States do not want to lose their economic independence, and if they desire to keep control over their own means of transport and maintaining jobs, they must under all circumstances have a merchant fleet at their disposal".[42]

The Commission has commented succinctly: "[a] cheap and efficient sea transport system is a basic pre-requisite for expansion of [EU] trade, especially with non-member countries".[43]

In 2009, the Commission stated:

> "[s]hipping represents one of Europe's largest export industries, providing deep sea transport services between Europe and the rest of the world, as well as in cross trades between third countries. European shipping is present in all segments of the sector in all regions of the planet. Transport of freight and passengers at sea generated € 24.7 billion in 2006 as a net contribution to the EU balance of payments. In terms of added value, traditional maritime sectors represent a share of 1.09% in the total GDP of the EU-27[44] and Norway. Maritime transport activities' related employment in Europe amounts to 1.5 million people. Some 70% of shipping related jobs are onshore – in shipbuilding, naval architecture, science, engineering, electronics, cargo-handling and logistics."[45]

The last sentence of the quotation – that so many "shipping" jobs are ashore – is striking and would be surprising to many.

Shipping has an important role in the EU's global and internal trading activities

1.019 Shipping is an indispensable element in trade between the Member States as well as between Member States and third countries.[46] Transport is therefore vital for both internal and external trade. The EU needs good transport and, preferably, its own transport fleet: as the EESC has commented: "[a] viable [EU] fleet, registered in Member

---

40 In this book, the Economic and Social Committee is normally referred to simply as the "EESC". On this committee, see chap. 3.
41 EESC, *Opinion of the Economic and Social Committee on the Communication and Proposals (II.3, II.4) by the Commission to the Council on Progress towards a Common Transport Policy: Maritime Transport*, COM(85)90 final (TRA/116), para. 1.2.
42 Commission, *EEC Shipping Policy: Flags of Convenience*, OJ 1979 C171/35.
43 *Communication from the Commission to the Council on The Community's Relations with Non-Member Countries in Shipping Matters*, COM(76)341 final, para. 2. It is submitted that the fleet must also be a safe and high quality one.
44 Ed., the abbreviation "EU-27" means the then 27 Member States of the EU.
45 MEMO/09/16 citing the ECOTEC Study prepared for DG Maritime Affairs in 2006.
46 See the commentary surrounding the failed proposal for a Council Regulation establishing a Community ship register and providing for the flying of the Community flag by seagoing vessels, contained in the Commission's communication to the Council entitled *A Future for the Community Shipping Industry: Measures to Improve the Operating Conditions of Community Shipping*, COM(89)266 final, 3 August 1989.

States is essential if services to exporters and importers in the [EU] are not to be dominated by third party shipping interests".[47]

1.020 Georgios Anastassopoulos, the then chairman of the Transport Committee of the European Parliament,[48] commented in 1987 (but the comments are equally valid today) that his Committee:

> "strongly believe[d] that one could not in fact envisage a major trading and economic power, such as the [EU], the largest in the world, ... without [an EU] fleet. That would leave the [EU] open at any time to all sorts of pressures by the other world trading and economic powers. It would deprive a wide range of other industries [of] a basic element of support. It would have meant the loss of a major source of foreign currency and of a major client of European banking and insurance institutions and perhaps the last client of the remnants of the European shipbuilding industry. It would have signified a major loss of employment. The European ports, that happen to be among the largest in the world ... would have also tremendously suffered."[49]

Anastassopoulos was therefore not only making the case that the EU needs to have a sufficient maritime resource available to the EU but the EU should also have its own fleet and infrastructure available to it. He went on to say that there were also defensive[50] and competitive reasons supporting the existence of a strong EU shipping fleet. Shipping is of strategic significance not only for the EU in terms of its relations with the rest of the world, but also in terms of its internal activities. Huge numbers of passengers are transported around the EU both on short- and long-haul services in, for example, the Baltic, the Mediterranean, North Sea, the English Channel and the Irish Sea. Shipping is the "dominant mode"[51] or even the only mode for many trades, for example, heavy goods which need to be transported internationally.

Shipping is an important employer in the EU

1.021 Shipping, port services and, to a lesser extent, shipbuilding as well as ship repairs are substantial employers in the EU. It is almost impossible to calculate all those who benefit from the shipping industry in the EU – these people would include crew, staff of shipping companies, dockers, hauliers, ships' agents, ships' providers, shipbuilders, steel makers, ship financiers, bankers, maritime lawyers as well as those people who work in businesses which have been established near ports because of the availability of shipping services. The Commission estimated that there were five million people employed in

---

47 *Opinion of the Economic and Social Committee on the Communication and Proposals (II.3, II.4) by the Commission to the Council on Progress towards a Common Transport Policy: Maritime Transport*, COM(85)90 final (TRA/116), para. 1.1.
48 In this book, the European Parliament is normally referred to simply as the "Parliament". On the Parliament, see chap. 3.
49 See his address at the Antwerp Shipping Symposium, "A Future for the Community Fleet", 6 May 1987; reprinted in (1987) 22 ETL at 197–198.
50 The absence of a fleet during wartime can cause enormous difficulties for a Member State or the EU: for example, difficulties were experienced by the UK during the Falklands Crisis where it was relatively short of merchant ships to transport support materials to the Falklands.
51 The term used by the EESC in *Opinion of the Economic and Social Committee on the Communication and Proposals (II.3, II.4) by the Commission to the Council on Progress towards a Common Transport Policy: Maritime Transport*, COM(85)90 final (TRA/116), para. 1.2 for freight and passenger traffic between some Member States.

maritime-related sectors generally in 2004–2005[52] and the figure would not be too different now[53] though estimates vary and some believe that it is as low as three million. The Member States with the largest number employed in the sector are Spain, the UK, Greece, Germany, Italy, the Netherlands and Poland but Member States such as Cyprus and Malta are also significant. It was estimated that the EU maritime transport sector (i.e. principally shipping) provided a total of 303,000 jobs in 2004/2005 on board ships flying EU, the EEA and third country flags. The largest numbers of seafarers come from Greece, Italy and Poland. Other important Member States as sources of seafarers include Cyprus, the Netherlands, Latvia and the UK. A significant part of direct shipbuilding jobs are in the UK, France and Germany. For many years, these three countries represented almost three-quarters of the total EU workforce in shipbuilding. Employment in ports throughout the EU is still significant but declining. It is a fact of life, however, that employment levels are falling in many of these industries in Europe (particularly in the case of shipbuilding) but there are other areas where it is growing (such as maritime leisure and short sea shipping). On 18 November 2013, the Commission reckoned that there were about 345,455 EU citizens working on ships worldwide with 157,561 EU citizens working as fishermen.[54] In 2015, the European Commission estimated that about 5.4 million jobs exist in the "blue economy" (i.e. the maritime economy) in the EU.[55] In July 2018, the European Maritime Safety Agency ("EMSA") published that it believed that there had been over 174,000 EU masters and officers at the end of 2016.[56] The issue of employment is considered further in chapters 2 and 8.

Shipping is an important earner of foreign currency and an indispensable part of the EU's ability to trade globally

1.022 Shipping has traditionally been an important earner of foreign currency for some Member States. Foreign currency is earned not just in terms of charter and carriage fees, but also in terms of insurance premia, interest on bank loans, shipbuilding contracts, ship-repair contracts, wages, bunkers, fuel, pilotage, harbour dues, legal fees and so on. The UK, for example, earns considerable amounts through the marine insurance as well as the financial and legal services it offers in the City of London. Using 2004 figures, shipping in the EU represented 44.1% of the world value of shipping.[57] At that time, shipbuilding represented 34.8% of the value of the world shipbuilding industry[58] while ports represented 41.9% of the turnover in ports worldwide. In January 2009, the Commission recalled that "the maritime transport system is at the forefront of the globalisation process and has provided the vehicle for an unprecedented growth of world trade and industrial and commercial interconnections in the world economy"[59] so it is clear that shipping

---

52 Commission, *Study: Employment Trends in all Sectors Related to the Sea or Using Sea Resources* (2006), http://ec.europa.eu/maritimeaffairs/studies/employment/main-report.pdf.
53 See para. 1.014.
54 IP/13/1094, 18 November 2013.
55 See Commission, http://ec.europa.eu/maritimeaffairs/policy/blue_growth/.
56 See www.emsa.europa.eu/news-a-press-centre/external-news/item/3321-seafarer-statistics-in-the-eu-statistical-review-2016-data-stcw-is.html.
57 €151,137 million in the EU out of €342,743 million.
58 €13,143 million in the EU out of €25,017 million.
59 MEMO/19/18.

plays a critical role in the EU's ability in regard to exports and trade globally. In February 2013, Maritime UK launched a series of studies on the value of the maritime services sector to the UK[60] and said that the sector contributed 262,700 direct jobs, £13.8 billion (€17.25 billion approximately) to the UK's GDP and generated £2.7 billion (€3.4 billion approximately) for the UK Exchequer. Indirectly, it created 537,000 other jobs, generated £31.7 billion (€40 billion approximately) to the UK's GDP and generated £8.5 billion (€11 billion) for the UK Exchequer. In 2017, it was estimated that the shipping industry directly supported just over £13.9 billion in business turnover, £4.3 billion in gross value added and 152,600 jobs (with 51,000 jobs for UK employees in 2015).[61]

Open/non-protectionist policy

1.023 The thrust of EU shipping policy as a whole[62] is towards encouraging and maintaining an open and free shipping market.[63] The EU is opposed generally to protectionism. According to Dimitri Petropolous, the then Head of the Maritime Transport Division in the then Transport Directorate-General of the Commission,[64] because of, among other things,

> "the direction provided by the Treaty of Rome[65] towards a policy based on market economy principles, ... the first objective for [EU] maritime transport policy must be to *safeguard free access to a free world shipping market. Indeed there is nothing to be gained by a protectionist [EU] shipping policy*. Although the [EU] is a big cargo generating area you can normally not reserve more than half of the cargo to your own ships – your trading partners can make their claims.[66] As the [EU] fleet is already carrying around 40% of the [EU's] foreign trade on vessels registered in the [EU], the possible gain, if any, would be small and could place in jeopardy the revenue which the [EU] shipping industry gets from cross-trading between third countries. Moreover, the [EU's] shipping policy cannot simply look at the position of shipowners. An essential consideration of shipping policy must be that the [EU's] foreign trade should have the advantages of freight rates arrived at in fair and free competition. Therefore the [EU] has to defend itself against protectionist measures of other countries whilst at the same time bringing its own house in order in this respect."[67]

This is a clear expression of open market economics. This openness is not surprising: first, the EU supports an open and free economy generally and, second, most shipping companies in the EU are private profit-making organisations and not State-operated concerns. The openness of EU shipping policy does not mean that the EU will never protect

---

60 See www.maritimeuk.org.

61 See Cebr's "The Economic Contribution of the UK Shipping Industry", a report for Maritime UK in September 2017, www.maritimeuk.org.

62 Aspects of the shipping policies of each Member State are examined in chap. 2.

63 On shipping policies generally, see Bredima-Savopoulou and Tzoannos, *The Common Policy of the EEC* (1990), pp. 36–37.

64 The Directorate-General for Transport was known as the Seventh Directorate-General of the European Commission or DG VII. It then became known as the Directorate General for Transport and Energy or DG TREN. It is now known as the Directorate-General for Mobility and Transport or DG MOVE. The relationship between this and other Directorates-General is considered in chap. 3.

65 Ed., this was the treaty which established the EEC. The treaty has been amended and is now the Treaty on the Functioning of the European Union ("TFEU"). The comments in the quotation linked to this footnote apply as equally to the TFEU as to the EEC Treaty.

66 Ed., see chaps 5 and 10.

67 In a speech "The European Community Transport Policy: An Overview", in *The Future of Shipping in Europe: Key Legal and Commercial Issues*, London, 28–29 June 1990, pp. 4–5 (emphasis added).

its own interests. The Parliament has said that the EU "is not faced with a stark choice between a free market and protectionism, rather there can be a balanced and pragmatic approach applying selective defensive actions where the basic viability of the shipping industry is being undermined".[68] Much of the package of measures adopted by the Council[69] in December 1986[70] was based on the free market philosophy. On the other hand, the EU has protected the interests of EU shipping on occasion. The dumping[71] measures adopted by the Council in 1986[72] were designed to protect EU shipping interests. It is true to say however that the EU has not always been as vigilant as it might have been in protecting the interests of its shipping industry so as to achieve an open and competitive market generally. Sometimes the EU does not achieve the right balance between protectionism and openness:

> "so far, the [EU] in the context of its economic and political relations with third countries has concentrated on promoting economic development and trade by providing through Conventions significant concessions concerning the free entry to its markets of industrial products and most agricultural products originating from those countries. These concessions have not, on the other hand, been reciprocated by the guarantees that the countries concerned will refrain from flag discrimination practices at the expense of the [EU] fleets.
>
> It appears that whenever the [EU] has been confronted with a conflict between trade and development interests on one hand, and shipping interests on the other, it has opted in favour of the former."[73]

Conversely, the EU may not want to engage in protectionism; instead an open policy may well be the desired course of action. It is however interesting to note that the apparent openness of EU shipping policy was out of step with the protectionism afforded by some States to their fleets.[74] Cabotage and cargo reservation have been, in the past, two instruments of such protectionism but the former should now be of no significance within the EU because of the opening of domestic routes in Member States to carriers from other Member States.

Internal balances

1.024 There is an interesting and delicate balance to be struck in the formulation of EU shipping law and policy. The interests of shipowners, seafarers, shippers,[75] port operators, passengers, governments, as well as others involved in the transport industry, are

---

68 "The European Parliament's *Opinion on the Communication and Proposals by the Commission to the Council of Ministers on Progress towards a Common Transport Policy: Maritime Transport*", reprinted in OJ 1986 C207/31 at p. 32.
69 On the Council, or as it was traditionally called the Council of Ministers, see chap. 3.
70 On the historical background to these measures, see, *inter alia*, chap. 5 generally.
71 The word "dumping" refers in this context to subsidy or trade dumping rather than environmental dumping.
72 On these measures, see chap. 17.
73 Bredima-Savopoulou and Tzoannos, "In Search of a Common Shipping Policy for the EC" (1981) 20 JCMS 95 at 97.
74 See Ademuni-Odeke, *Protectionism and the Future of International Shipping* (1984), generally and Hayman in Barston and Birnie, *The Maritime Dimension* (1980), p. 130.
75 A "shipper" is the person who sends goods to be transported by ship. The "carrier" is the shipping company which transports them.

sometimes incapable of harmonisation.[76] Shipowners could seek a protective market in which freight rates are fixed by means of agreements between the shipowners but such a policy could be contrary to the interests of shippers and consumers. Some governments could wish to protect their national fleets and are therefore willing to offer State aid[77] and this can be contrary to the wishes of other governments, shipowners from other States, the EU's policy generally and the well-being of the industry in general. There is also a balance to be struck in terms of dividing competences between the Member States and the EU itself. The EU institutions have been very anxious to have power resting with them: this is clear from a press release as long ago as 1984, in which the Commission stated: "[t]he Commission believes that the best way of serving the interests of the [EU] fleet and its users and of achieving the Treaty objectives is to maintain *a trade-orientated, multilateral Community shipping policy*".[78] The EU's former Commissioner for Fisheries and Maritime Affairs, Commissioner Borg, stated that one

> "of the most important elements for a competitive and stable shipping sector, is undoubtedly a stable regulatory framework. We believe that European shipping, along with other maritime sectors, to a large extent, already benefits from this. … We recognise, therefore, that from the industry's point of view, it is vital to have a stable legal and regulatory environment in order to, in turn, have an efficient and effective business environment. With a view to improving on what exists, the EU has already started to work towards a simpler and more consolidated regulatory regime."[79]

In some ways, the European Commission's creation of the Maritime Industries Forum in 1992 was an attempt to, depending on one's perspective, harness, harmonise or control the internal tensions which are possible.

Multidimensional nature of EU shipping law and policy

1.025 EU shipping law and policy have multiple dimensions. The dimensions involved include issues such as social protection, safety, environmental protection, competition, navigation, pilotage, shipbuilding and the employment of seafarers. There has been a more serious attempt in recent years by the EU institutions to ensure a more harmonious co-ordination of these diverse strands. An interesting comment was made by the Commissioner for Fisheries and Maritime Affairs in 2007, Commissioner Borg, when he stated:

> "responsibility for policies and actions related to the seas are divided between EU authorities, national governments, and regional and local authorities. Many rules of behaviour are then, furthermore, derived from international organisations. Therefore, if the aims of an integrated maritime policy are to be achieved, all levels of government must move towards a more integrated approach and in turn, be collectively responsible for ensuring its success."[80]

---

76 Lord Stanley Clinton Davies, a former EU Commissioner for Transport, is reported to have said that each of these interest groups "has to comprehend the problems of the other; each has to be mutually supportive": see IP(85)60. An obvious example would be the desire of many carriers to operate liner conferences and the wish of most shippers that such conferences would be outlawed.
77 On State aid, see chap. 15.
78 P-95, December 1984, emphasis added. On the principle of subsidiarity, see chap. 3.
79 Borg, Speech to Mare Forum Conference, 25 September 2006.
80 Speech/07/494 "Governance in a European Maritime Policy", Lisbon, 19 July 2007.

The EU's Transport Ministers stated in their 7 May 2014 Athens Declaration entitled *Mid-Term Review of the EU's Maritime Transport Policy until 2018 and Outlook to 2002*:

> "RECOGNISING the importance of maintaining a stable and innovation-friendly regulatory framework securing competitiveness for the fleets of EU Member States providing the legal certainty for investments and stimulating the establishment of maritime activities in the EU Member States in a context of liberalised international maritime services."[81]

Social dimension to EU shipping policy

1.026 EU shipping policy has a social dimension. For example, seafarers deserve protection. A bi-partite committee was established in 1987 to advise the Commission on how best to promote social measures for the protection of seafarers in the EU. The "*Positive Measures*" communication of 3 August 1989[82] contained a number of specific measures designed to improve the social conditions of seafarers. In the interim, the EU has adopted a series of measures which improve the position of seafarers.[83] This social dimension is an aspect of EU shipping policy which will become even more important as the EU develops its social policy in the future. The working conditions and circumstances of seafarers require special protection because the employees are away from home (often for long periods) and the operations of the vessels require round-the-clock involvement and long hours of work by the seafarers involved and often in an unsafe or potentially hazardous environment.

Safety dimension to EU shipping policy

1.027 Safety is a very important aspect of EU shipping law and policy. In part, EU maritime safety law has developed because of, and in response to, tragedies and disasters in European waters.[84] If the EU wants to ensure the highest safety standards within the EU then it faces two primary challenges: first, safety is a global issue and not just one confined to the EU so it may find it difficult (but not impossible)[85] to apply more stringent rules in the EU where those rules are not adopted at an international level and, second, there are those who would argue that safety is a matter for specialist maritime organisations such as the International Maritime Organization ("IMO") and not "general" organisations such as the EU. Irrespective of the merits of whether the EU should be involved in maritime safety issues at all, the reality is that the EU *is* involved in the area of safety and therefore the EU has adopted rules on various aspects of shipping safety including rules on passenger ferries and oil tankers.[86] It has now reached the point that the EU needs to be involved in maritime safety because most citizens around the EU would be very annoyed if the EU did not prevent (or, at the very least, respond to) maritime safety

---

81 See fn. 6.
82 On this communication, see chap. 5.
83 See, in particular, chap. 32.
84 See chaps 26–37 on safety.
85 E.g. by circumventing the flag State rules and jurisdiction by using the port State control regime (see chap. 29).
86 See chaps 26–37 on safety.

incidents which could threaten the lives, livelihood and environment of the EU's 500 million citizens.

Environmental dimension to EU shipping policy

1.028 EU shipping policy is also concerned with the environment.[87] Some of the earliest legal measures adopted by the EU in the area of shipping were in relation to the protection of the marine environment.[88] Indeed, EU environmental law developed more in the maritime sector than in many other sectors during the early years of EU environmental law but often in response to maritime environmental disasters such as oil spillages. In the last four decades or so, international concern about the environment has meant that the EU has come under substantial pressure to adopt and enforce stringent environmental controls. This pressure has been particularly strong in the context of the marine environment because marine environmental incidents (such as spillages from oil tankers) are newsworthy and can cause significant public concern which, in turn, often leads to calls for the EU and the Member States to take action.

Competition dimension to EU shipping policy

1.029 In line with the EU's general policy in favour of an open and competitive market generally as well as its open and competitive policy in the shipping sector in particular (e.g. the abolition of the block exemption for liner conferences),[89] a great deal of EU shipping law relates to competition law but the remit of EU shipping law is becoming much wider than competition law. This area of the law is designed to ensure competitive freedom and rivalry in the marketplace by prohibiting generally anti-competitive arrangements, prohibiting always the abuse of dominance, controlling State aid and supervising State conduct in the marketplace.[90]

International dimension to EU shipping policy

1.030 The EU's shipping policy must take into account the international obligations of the Member States as well as the role of the EU in the world. Many of these obligations are fulfilled through membership of various international organisations, most notably, the IMO. It is not always desirable or possible for the EU or its Member States to take unilateral or divergent positions.[91] In any event, shipping by its very nature is a sector with an international global dimension.

---

87 See chaps 19–24 on the environment.
88 See e.g. chap. 5.
89 Reg. 4056/86 OJ 1986 L378/4 has been repealed by Reg. 1419/2006 OJ 2006 L269/1 (see chap.12).
90 The issue of competition is dealt with at several points in this book including, most particularly, chaps 10–15.
91 External relations in shipping matters are examined in chap. 25.

Divergent influences on the development of EU shipping policy?

1.031 EU shipping policy does not develop in a consistent and steady way with little or no outside influences. Instead, it develops in divergent ways and subject to different influences. The influences could be seen as internal and external. It is useful to consider first some of the internal influences. For example, there are at least eight Commissioners of the 28 Commissioners whose portfolios touch on maritime or shipping matters: the transport commissioner; the commissioner for environment, fisheries and maritime affairs; the commissioner for jobs, growth, investment and competitiveness; the commissioner for research, science and innovation; the commissioner for regional policy; the commissioner for energy; and the competition commissioner. This number is apart from commissioners who may play a role in shipping matters from time to time. The EU and its Member States are parties to over 100 treaties or agreements relating to maritime matters. The EU has various agencies dealing with maritime matters including the European Maritime Safety Agency ("EMSA"), FRONTEX (the European agency for the management of operational co-operation at the external borders of the Member States), the European Defence Agency, the European Space Agency, the Community Fisheries Control Agency and the European Environment Agency. Equally, the Parliament, the Council and the EESC are all influential in the evolution of EU shipping law and policy.

1.032 Apart from these overly political institutions and bodies, there is also the CJEU which has had a significant influence on the development and evolution of EU shipping law. While the CJEU has been an important force in the development of aspects of EU shipping law, it is necessarily reactive in that the court can only deal with the particular cases which are brought before it. By contrast, the Commission, the Council and the Parliament can act more easily; of these three institutions, the Commission has been the most significant in terms of influencing the evolution and direction of EU shipping law and has done so across areas as diverse as safety, competition, employment, security, navigation and so on. The Commission's significance comes from such factors as its monopoly on the power to initiate legislation, its centrality in the EU regime and its permanent staff working on shipping and maritime matters in various directorates general but the Council and European Council as well as the Parliament are each becoming even more significant over time.

1.033 The EU has not been unique in terms of divergent approaches because the United Nations has 12 or so organisations involved in maritime policy. However, by contrast with the UN, the EU has greater potency and powers to adopt and enforce its rules. Indeed, the EU has carved out its own role despite the long-established IMO which is a specialised maritime organisation. While the IMO is specialist in maritime matters, the EU not only has specialist maritime personnel and competency, it also has a wider remit, the ability to adopt laws which are binding automatically (e.g. very often without the need for ratification)[92] as well as greater coherence among its Member States than the IMO.

1.034 Equally, there are many external influences including lobbying groups, companies, trade unions and associations of shippers, carriers and others interested in the sector (e.g. those interested in environmental issues).

---

92 In EU law, only treaties require ratification but measures such as regulations, directives and decisions do not require ratification although directives require implementation.

1.035 Clearly, there is an ongoing need for coherence and consistency among the various agencies and actors who have an influence on EU shipping law and policy.

Staggered or strategic development of EU shipping policy?

1.036 There is a choice between the development of EU shipping law and policy on a co-ordinated basis or in a piecemeal way. While there is some merit in dealing with individual issues on a piecemeal basis, there is an obvious need for a co-ordinated approach. France has traditionally favoured the comprehensive framework approach. The piecemeal approach has been favoured by the likes of the UK and Greece so as to address specific issues as they arise. While the latter approach allows considerable flexibility and freedom in respect of those areas which are not regulated by the EU, there is surely considerable merit in having a comprehensive overview within which individual issues can be tackled as and when it is appropriate. There is a need for a comprehensive and not just an incremental or modal approach to shipping and other transport areas. It is heartening to see that the EU's recent initiatives in the area of shipping have attempted to follow a more coherent and comprehensive approach but individual and specific measures should be adopted even where they do not fit within the scope of an overall or coherent pattern.

Should the EU have a role in shipping?

Introduction

1.037 It is useful to consider, in this opening chapter, whether the EU should be involved in shipping at all given that the boundaries of shipping are much broader than the EU (it is obviously one of the most global of all industries) and there are already specialist international organisations involved in the area. Whether the EU should have a role in shipping is a long-standing and controversial issue but it is now more of a theoretical rather than practical issue as the EU is firmly involved in the area of shipping and its role has been very largely accepted by all concerned.

Arguments in favour of the EU having a role to play in shipping

1.038 There are several arguments in favour of the EU becoming more involved in shipping matters.

1.039 It is useful to review a selection of the arguments in favour of the EU's involvement in this sector. First, the EU needs a strong shipping fleet and industry for the purposes of external and internal trade. It would therefore be wrong for the EU not to become involved in the regulation and operation of the sector and to simply leave it to chance as to whether or not the EU has such a fleet and how it would be regulated. It would be preferable for the EU not to be overly dependent on non-EU interests in such a strategic area; the EESC wrote that a viable EU fleet, registered in Member States, is essential if services to exporters and importers in the EU are not to be dominated by third party shipping interests. Second, "the [EU] needs to have a role in maritime transport not only from the perspective of external trade but also internal trade". Third, the EESC also wrote that the EU needs to have a role in maritime transport not only from the perspective of external trade but also internal trade.[93] This means that the "whole" or "totality" of the 28 Member States would be much stronger than the individual Member States otherwise there is a risk of inconsistency. Fourth, as mentioned above, significant numbers of passengers sail in EU waters (e.g. the Baltic, the Mediterranean, English Channel and Irish Sea). Passenger safety is extremely important and the EU would be criticised by its citizens were it to neglect the issue or leave it to non-member States who may have a different agenda (e.g. to attract tonnage and therefore income rather than to enhance safety). Fifth, given the fact that so many people in the EU are employed in the maritime sector (both directly and indirectly), it is important that the EU plays a role in the sector. Sixth, if the EU were not involved then there is a risk that there would be damaging divergence between the approaches of the Member States. Penultimately, there are other actors on the international stage who have not been as effective, as some of the EU Member States would have wanted, in terms of developing and enforcing rules on shipping. For example, Member States have adopted more rigorous rules on certain aspects of ship safety than were adopted at the time within the IMO.[94] In many ways, the relatively smaller, more nimble and less diverse EU is better able to adopt and enforce stricter rules than the larger and more diverse global organisations such as the IMO.[95] Finally, there can be defence and security reasons for the EU to have a strong maritime fleet.[96] All of this supports the notion of the EU having a role to play in the shipping sector.

Arguments against the EU having a role to play in shipping

1.040 The arguments in favour of the EU having a role in regulating shipping have held sway so the EU now has a well-established role but it is useful nonetheless to review some of the counter-arguments. First, shipping is a global industry which goes beyond the boundaries of the EU and therefore it is arguably somewhat pointless for the EU to seek to regulate it when ships move and can be registered all over the world. Put another way, the argument is that the market is global so therefore it is meaningless or even wrong to regulate it on a regional basis.[97] (If this argument were taken to its logical conclusion then there would be no point in having national laws in many sectors (e.g. steel, wheat, oil and so on).) Second, there are specialist international maritime organisations and bodies which are better able to regulate maritime matters than the generalist EU. The IMO is focused entirely on maritime matters – unlike the EU which has a variety of issues on its

---

93 Commission's communication to the Council of Ministers, *A Future for the Community Shipping Industry: Measures to Improve the Operating Conditions of Community Shipowners*, COM(89)266 final, 3 August 1989, p. 9.

94 This has meant that there could be measures adopted at the IMO which are inconsistent with EU law with the result that EU Member States may not comply with the IMO measures where they are inconsistent with EU law.

95 This ability of the EU to respond quicker and deeper than a global organisation is, in part, the response of those who support the EU having a significant role in regard to maritime transport despite the existence of specialist maritime agencies such as the IMO. While some commentators would argue that the EU lacks the technical competence of an organisation such as the IMO, this view is no longer accurate or tenable given the increase in technical competence in the likes of the European Commission and the European Maritime Safety Association ("EMSA") in maritime matters so the EU has the relevant technical competence.

96 E.g. an EU LPG tanker fleet can minimise (though not eliminate) some of the risks associated with the cutting off of pipeline supplies of gas to Europe.

97 The Parliament's Committee on Regional Policy, Regional Planning and Transport set out the argument at paras 7–9 of its interim report *Sea Transport Problems in the Community* in 1977 (Doc.5/77, 23 March 1977).

agenda and maritime matters play a small role. Equally, the IMO has global reach which would not be the case with any regional general organisation such as the EU. Third, it is often argued that there is a high level of self-regulation in the shipping sector and therefore the intervention of the EU (or any organisation) is unwelcome. Finally, some argue that shipping has such special features that it should not be subject to EU law at all. They point to the "special features" of the sector including its global nature, the expensive assets involved and the special infrastructural requirements of the sector. However, these arguments are difficult to sustain because most industries are now global in nature. Whatever may be the arguments against the EU having a role to play in the regulation of shipping, the EU's role in the sector will continue to expand. There is therefore a need to harmonise the EU and Member State dimensions to produce the optimum output given the different resources, aims and tools available to both participants in the process.[98]

Is there a comprehensive EU shipping policy?

1.041 For many years, the EU did not appear to have a uniform and comprehensive policy on shipping.[99] It is vital that such an important industry, which has suffered so badly at times (including in recent times), has an effective and well-designed policy for the short, medium and long terms. While one cannot blame the decline in the fortunes of shipping on the EU, one must however consider whether the decline might not have been so great had the Member States (and other European States not then EU members) been able to combine together and produce an effective policy. It is heartening to record that the EU's shipping policy has become much more structured and organised in recent years. This change in approach is welcome, because there is a clear need to formulate a common policy on shipping which would be both open and competitive so as to meet the challenges of the internal market, the adoption by the Central and East European States of the free market economy model, changes in maritime technology (such as high-speed passenger ferries and unmanned ships) as well as the need for safer and more environmentally friendly ships. The need for a comprehensive shipping policy was skilfully and convincingly argued in an interim report published as early as 1977 by the Parliament's Committee on Regional Policy, Regional Planning and Transport on Sea Transport Problems in the Community.[100] The Committee stated:

---

98 Commissioner Borg, the then Commissioner for Fisheries and Maritime Affairs in 2007 said: "[put simply:] an EU maritime policy will only work if Member States adopt their own arrangements, albeit in line with the subsidiarity principle, to provide for enhanced coordination of all maritime related affairs and for better collaboration at a national level. For our part, at an EU level, we can best add value to the process, not only by helping it to come about but also by developing a set of common tools which can serve to create synergies between different sectoral policies, between different government agencies and activities, and between different economic actors, which did not exist before. These are tools that can help policy makers optimise the use of marine and coastal space and the development of maritime activities in an environmentally sustainable manner. The justification for their development of one single system is vastly more cost effective than that of multiple, often contradictory, national systems." (Speech/07/494, http://europa.eu/rapid/press-release_SPEECH-07-494_en.htm).

99 It is, of course, acknowledged that the adoption of such a policy is difficult given the diversity of interests and the absence of specific Treaty provisions.

100 Doc.5/77, 23 March 1977.

"7. B... your Committee wishes to state its strong and unequivocal opposition to a number of arguments frequently advanced by those who are against the inclusion of sea transport in the [EU's] terms of reference.
8. Sea transport, it is argued, should not be included in the Common Transport Policy because it is governed by 'special conditions' and cannot be made subject to the same rules as other means of transport.

Needless to say, this report does not call for the same conditions. The principles governing land transport quite clearly cannot be applied to sea transport as they stand. No one is suggesting that locomotives should be used to pull sea-going vessels. What is needed is a dynamic concept for a common sea transport policy which allows for world-wide contingencies and developments and the specific conditions governing sea transport. But it is equally clear that certain basic principles of the common economic policy of the [EU] must also be applied to sea transport. The generally free-market basic structure of the [EU], the principle of non-discrimination and a number of other fundamental principles must surely also be applied to sea transport. There can be no progress in the discussion on this subject if some demand that different and others that the same principles be applied as to the other means of transport without saying what these principles are: basic principles such as market economy, competition, equal treatment, and non-discrimination or 'second-line principles' like those laid down in Articles [90 to 100 of the TFEU].
9. Another frequently heard argument is that since sea transport is subject to world-wide ramifications and world-wide rules, it should not be forced into the 'narrow confines' of [EU] regulations, which would only represent a step backwards compared with world-wide arrangements.

There is no logic to this argument, popular though it may be. What European industry is *not* subject to world-wide ramifications? Is it not simply true to say of the European economy, with its dependence on imports of raw materials and its vital need to export, that everything we do has world-wide ramifications? Even the cereals which grow in our fields are subject to world-wide rules, which in some respects go further than world arrangements for sea transport.

The reason why the 'world-wide ramifications' argument has found so many adherents in transport policy is perhaps that at least one major mode of transport – rail transport – does not have such ramifications. However, the railways, with their regional monopolies, are the major exception among all other sectors of the economy. The ramifications of the other modes of transport (road transport, inland waterways, pipelines) are also continental rather than world-wide; however, it is only in relation to these and not to industry and agriculture that the world-wide ramifications of sea transport are unusual.

In addition, it is perfectly clear that any [EU] policy (whether on cereals or sea transport) must take account of existing international agreements and either conform to them or, if they are seen to be inadequate, attempt to supplement or correct them.

The world-wide ramifications of sea transport cannot be used as an argument against the application of ... [of the TFEU]. The [EU] is no longer a free trade area which is not developing a common external economic policy. In view of the world-wide ramifications of the [EU's] economy as a whole it is essential for sea transport to be included in the [EU's] external economic policy.
10. A further argument, usually muted, is that sea transport policy is better left in the hands of the maritime nations and city-ports, of economic circles close to shipping and possessing the necessary expertise, than in the hands of bureaucrats in Brussels."

Whatever may have been the shortcomings in the past, and there were some, there is little doubt but EU shipping law and policy is becoming more comprehensive and integrated. It is now clear that there is a desire to have a comprehensive and coherent maritime policy; as former Commissioner Joe Borg (the then Commissioner for Fisheries and Maritime Affairs) said in a speech on 19 July 2007[101] about such concepts as "an all-embracing

---

101 Speech/07/494.

INTRODUCTION

and integrated maritime policy", "a more holistic view of the maritime sector", the "joined-up and integrated approach", it "is exactly in enhanced co-ordination and better collaboration that the very essence of the new approach to maritime affairs lies", the "desired integrated approach", a "maritime policy will also need a framework within which the necessary convergence of policies and actions of government will be housed and made to work as a dynamic and constructive process" and "joined-up policy-making". However, in the same speech, Commissioner Borg also stated that "we should not seek to draw up a one-size-fits-all solution, but to identify solutions that respond appropriately to the specific attributes of the various European maritime regions and sectors".

Who influences EU shipping law?

1.042 Stakeholder interests are an obvious source of influence on EU shipping law. Examples illustrate the point. The reaction of port workers to the two proposed (but failed) port services directives[102] helped to force the Parliament to vote against the proposal and ultimately cause its demise. Certain shipowners would have been lobbying for, and advocating, the adoption in 1986 of the liner conference block exemption.[103] Shipowners tend to seek more protectionist regimes while shippers tend to seek more liberal ones and shippers would have been pleased with the ultimate repeal of the liner conference block exemption.[104] Both shippers and the Commission however advocated tenaciously and successfully the repeal of the block exemption for liner conferences. There can be differences of approach between EU institutions; for example, the Commission did not much care for the Council's block exemption for liner conferences in Regulation 4056/86.[105] Member States have the greatest influence. They clearly influence EU shipping law in different ways. First, they may seek to be protective of their industries whether they be their shipping, shipbuilding or seafarer sectors. Second, the European Council[106] and the Council is presided over by one Member State on a rotating basis (in conjunction with the President of the Council)[107] and the Member State which holds the presidency can influence the measures adopted by the EU during the term of its presidency. Individual Member States can have a greater or lesser influence depending on their interest in shipping matters. Ultimately, EU shipping law is a product of a combination of forces and influences.

The EU and shipping: a brief comparative perspective in the context of international organisations and shipping generally

1.043 It is useful to analyse briefly the nature of the EU's role in shipping matters by contrasting it with various international organisations involved in the sector such as the IMO. Unlike those organisations dedicated to shipping, the EU has a much wider remit than shipping or maritime matters, it has a narrow membership (e.g. they are limited to some

---

102 See chap. 43.
103 See chap. 12.
104 See chap. 12.
105 OJ 1986 L378/4. See chap. 11.
106 On the European Council, see chap. 3.
107 On the President of the Council, see chap. 3.

European States), it has less of a technical focus on shipping matters than the technical shipping organisations but it has the advantage of greater resources, permanent sophisticated institutional machinery, a more effective legal machinery than any other international organisation and a more coherent or uniform membership profile than many of the more global shipping organisations. The EU can also be more nimble (in terms of reacting to events and adopting new legislation) than any other global organisation. The EU also has a more potent legal regime which can be used to enforce its regime – other international organisations lack the sophisticated institutional regime which the EU possesses.

D. EU SHIPPING LAW IN THE WIDER CONTEXT OF EU MARITIME POLICY

1.044 In recent years, there has been the welcome and important development of EU maritime[108] policy. EU shipping law forms part of that EU maritime policy but it also forms parts of other policies and areas such as EU transport policy, EU competition policy, EU employment policy and so on. The EU has been striving to achieve an integrated European maritime policy.[109]

1.045 The EU has tried in recent years not only to develop an EU maritime policy but also to develop an integrated one.[110] On 10 October 2007, the Commission adopted its so-called "Blue Book" which was entitled *An Integrated Maritime Policy for the European Union*.[111] This notion of an integrated maritime policy for the EU had followed similar exercises for Australia, Canada, New Zealand and the USA.

E. OUTLINE OF THIS BOOK

1.046 This book deals with the shipping law of the EU. It does not deal with EU law relating to internal waterway transport, that is to say, either waterway or canal transport. Nor does it deal with fisheries law[112] or offshore installations. Given the enormity of EU law and its possible impact on shipping in so many ways, the book has been deliberately selective.

1.047 This first chapter has been an introduction to the topic of EU shipping law. It should be read in conjunction with the final chapter of the book which draws a number of conclusions or impressions on the subject which is known as EU shipping law.

---

108 It has been commented that the distinction between "maritime" and "marine" policy is that: "[the word] 'maritime' [means] everything related to human activities on the seas and oceans [while] ... 'marine' means everything related to the marine environment, or to be more precise, the natural environment of seas, coasts and oceans" (Siemers, "A European Integrated Maritime Policy: An Innovative Approach to Policy-Making" (2009) 23 Ocean Yearbook 231 at 232). This book focuses on shipping which is a sub-set associated with ships. Nonetheless, shipping is part of the marine dimension.

109 Siemers, op. cit. at fn. 109, p. 233 defined the term "Integrated European Maritime Policy" as a "joined-up deliberate plan of actions developed by and for the European Union and its regions aimed at the sustainable management of activities on coasts, seas and oceans".

110 See Commission, *An Integrated Maritime Policy for the European Union* (COM(2007) 575 final). See also Siemers, op. cit. at fn. 109.

111 COM(2007) 575 final.

112 On EC fisheries law, Churchill and Owen, *The EEC Common Fisheries Policy* (2010); Holden, *The Common Fisheries Policy* (1993 and 1996); Long and Curran, *Enforcing the Common Fisheries Policy* (2000); and Munir, *Fisheries After Factortame* (1991).

INTRODUCTION

1.048 Chapter 2 is a brief commercial overview of shipping in the EU. It is imperative to understand the commercial perspective before dealing with the legal dimension to transport generally and shipping in particular.

1.049 Chapter 3 is an overview of the EU and EU law. It describes the institutions, the sources of EU law and provides an overview of many aspects of EU law. It is designed for those readers who do not have an understanding or knowledge of this area of the law and for those readers this chapter is a desirable inclusion.

1.050 Chapter 4 gives an overview of EU transport law generally. It is useful to be able to put the particular body of EU law relating to shipping into the overall context of EU transport law generally. Given the nature of the chapter, it is, of necessity, brief and somewhat elementary.

1.051 Chapter 5 traces the historical development of EU shipping law. It describes the evolution of EU law by paying attention to the phases of evolution of EU shipping law.

1.052 The next chapter, Chapter 6, describes and discusses the EU law on freedom of establishment as it relates to shipping and the registration of ships.

1.053 Chapter 7 deals with the complex but commercially vital area of freedom to provide shipping services. This chapter examines the law relating to: (a) international shipping services involving an EU port (i.e. Regulation 4055/86);[113] and (b) the controversial issue of cabotage (i.e. the carriage of goods and passengers between two ports in one and the same State).[114]

1.054 Chapter 8 outlines the EU law relating to the employment of seafarers and their social conditions. Traditionally, seafarers have been disadvantaged in terms of the level of protection which is afforded to them by EU law but there are clear signs that this situation is changing. The application of EU law to the employment of seafarers has often been controversial.

1.055 Chapter 9 looks at liner conferences generally and their relationship with competition policy generally and the United Nations Liner Code.

1.056 Chapter 10 discusses, in broad terms, the application of the competition law of the EU to shipping and then examines Articles 101 and 102 of the TFEU which are the principal rules on competition in the TFEU. Article 101 prohibits generally anti-competitive arrangements between those involved in economic activities (known in competition law as "undertakings"[115]).[116] Article 102 prohibits absolutely, without any exception, the abuse of dominance by any undertaking having a dominant position.[117]

1.057 Chapter 11 examines the old competition regime embodied in Regulation 4056/86[118] which applied Articles 101 and 102 of the TFEU to maritime transport. Regulation 4056186 contained a block exemption to exempt liner conferences from the application of Article 101(1) of the TFEU. It was a very controversial regime and has been repealed.

---

113 OJ 1986 L378/1.
114 Cabotage is controversial where the coastal State wishes to preserve for its own nationals the right to carry goods and passengers between ports in that coastal State and not allow other nationals the right to do so.
115 On the concept of "undertaking", see chap. 10.
116 On Art. 101, see chap. 10.
117 On Art. 102, see chap. 10.
118 OJ 1986 L378/4.

1.058 Chapter 12 then examines the new EU competition law regime and landscape for shipping given the entry into force of Regulation 1419/2006[119] which repealed the famous or infamous[120] Regulation 4056/86.[121]

1.059 Chapter 13 examines the application of EU competition rules to ports. This has proven to be a fascinating area of EU shipping law with the access to ports being a recurring theme.

1.060 Chapter 14 describes and discusses the competition law relating to consortia. EU law has been much more tolerant of consortia than liner conferences because consortia lack any element of price-fixing.

1.061 Chapter 15 relates to State aid in relation to both shipping and ports. State aid involves the provision of assistance on a discriminatory basis to economic operators in a way which distorts competition. Some State aid is permissible.

1.062 Chapter 16 examines the EU's merger control regime and how it applies to shipping, ports and shipbuilding.

1.063 Chapter 17 considers Regulation 4057/86.[122] This regulation, which is loosely described as the "Dumping Regulation", attempts to deal with the "dumping" of low shipping rates on the EU market by non-EU companies benefiting from unfair non-commercial advantages.

1.064 Chapter 18 deals with Regulation 4058/86[123] which concerns co-ordinated action to safeguard free access to cargoes in ocean trade.

1.065 Chapter 19 deals with the many aspects of the law of the EU relating to the marine environment. This area is in a state of flux and development. Chapters 20–21 deal with specific aspects of EU maritime environmental law, namely, organotin, the Hazardous and Noxious Substances by Sea Convention as well as penalties for infringements.

1.066 Shipbuilding is the subject-matter of Chapter 22 and is a topic which covers more than just competition issues. Chapters 23 and 24 deal with the related topics of ship repair and ship dismantling.

1.067 The external relations of the EU in shipping matters are the subject of Chapter 25.

1.068 EU maritime safety law is introduced in Chapter 26 but expanded on in Chapters 27–37 which deal with issues such as the European Maritime Safety Agency, port state control, training of seafarers, health requirements, marine equipment and so on.

1.069 Chapter 38 deals with piracy.

1.070 Chapters 39 and 40 deal with navigation and pilotage respectively.

1.071 Chapter 41 deals with short sea shipping.

1.072 Ports generally are addressed in Chapters 42–45 where topics such as the port services regulation, port security (as well as ship security because the two are linked), reporting formalities and electricity are addressed. However, ports are also addressed elsewhere in the book too.

1.073 The relatively nascent EU law on the carriage of goods and passengers forms the basis of Chapter 46.

---

119 OJ 2006 L269/1.
120 On the debate over Reg. 4056/86, see chaps 11 and 12.
121 OJ 1986 L378/4.
122 OJ 1986 L378/14.
123 OJ 1986 L378/21.

1.074 The EU law relating to shipping litigation is examined in Chapter 47. This chapter focuses on the EU rules on jurisdiction as well as the recognition and the enforcement of judgments in civil and commercial matters.

1.075 Brexit – the expected departure from the EU by the UK and Gibraltar – is the subject of chapter 48.

1.076 The final chapter involves an appraisal of EU shipping law by drawing a number of conclusions on the present state and future development of this fascinating branch of EU law.

1.077 EU law could affect almost any area of shipping; for example, the CJEU considered the concept of "chartering sea-going vessels" in the context of the sixth value added tax directive[124] in *Navicon SA v Administración del Estado*.[125] So this book, despite its length, has to be naturally selective otherwise it would have to consider every aspect of EU law which could potentially affect shipping. It is therefore important for lawyers considering and advising on EU shipping law to recall that there is no hermetically sealed body of rules called EU shipping law but rather almost any rule of EU law could potentially be relevant to shipping. Equally, rules of Member State law must be measured and validated by reference to any relevant EU law or principle to see if the Member State law is still valid vis-à-vis EU law.

---

124 Dir. 77/388 of 17 May 1977 on the harmonisation of the laws of the Member States relating to turnover taxes – Common system of value added tax: uniform basis of assessment (OJ 1977 L145/1) as amended by Council Dir. 92/111 of 14 December 1992 (OJ 1992 L384/47).
125 C-97/06 [2007] ECR I-08755, ECLI:EU:C:2007:609.

CHAPTER 2

A commercial overview of shipping in the European Union

A. INTRODUCTION

2.001 It is almost pointless to study European Union ("EU") shipping law without understanding its commercial context. This chapter is a somewhat general and non-exhaustive introduction to the commercial background to shipping and ports in the EU. The chapter relies heavily on statistics published by the EU, the United Nations[1] and various other groups.[2] It describes the picture at the EU and Member State levels. This overview relates primarily to shipping activities (in the narrow sense) but it is important to remember that shipping is not a single industry but is instead interconnected with, and related to, many other economic activities such as shipbuilding, ports, ship repair, tourism, pilotage, shipbroking, marine insurance, stevedoring, shipping finance, maritime law and so on. The data outlined in this chapter includes some historical data so as to put the whole picture into context. While some of the data vary (depending on the source of the data), the general trends are clear-cut.

2.002 Shipping is critical both to the world generally and to the EU in particular. In terms of the world generally, shipping carries around 90% of the world's trade in goods by volume. Interestingly, EU interests control around 40% of the world's tonnage. As the EU is the world's largest trading bloc, it is not surprising that shipping is an important source of employment for Europeans (e.g. in ports, shipping companies, ship management agencies, ship repairers, ship finance and shipping lawyers). In broad terms and while figures change over time, EU interests control about 60% of all container vessels, 52% of the world's multi-purpose vessels, 43% of the world's tankers and 37% of the world's offshore vessels.[3] It has been suggested that the EU shipping industry contributes about €145 billion to EU gross domestic product ("GDP"), €41 billion in taxes and 2.3

---

1 E.g. the United Nations Conference on Trade and Development ("UNCTAD") has an excellent website containing a great deal of useful data on the topic: http://unctadstat.unctad.org/wds/ReportFolders/reportFolders.aspx?IF_ActivePath=P,11&sCS_ChosenLang=en. See also UNCTAD, *Review of Maritime Transport 2017* (UNCTAD/RMT/2017).
2 E.g. an Oxford Economics report entitled *The Economic Value of the EU Shipping Industry* (2014) (https://halopublications.s3.amazonaws.com/272456/open20140710071200.pdf?AWSAccessKeyId=AKIAJEH775QE2PUYLYDA&Expires=1438799896&Signature=75D1V%2BeMft1Jh7tscGBYdlVKUnc%3D) which was prepared for the European Community Shipowners' Association ("ECSA") (this report is referred to in this chapter as the "ECSA/Oxford Economics Report"). This excellent report has since been updated: www.ecsa.eu/sites/default/files/publications/2017-02-27-Oxford-Economics-Update-2017---FINAL.pdf. Other organisations such as the European Sea Ports Organisation ("ESPO") also publish data or provide data on request: www.espo.be/fact-and-figures.
3 ECSA/Oxford Economics Report.

million jobs in the EU with 590,000 directly in the shipping sector.[4] More recently, it was suggested that the EU shipping sector had a direct value of around €54 billion, an indirect value of €57 billion and an induced value of €29 billion.[5] It has also been suggested that the EU shipping sector has a multiplier effect of creating an additional €1.60 for every €1.00 contributed by the EU to the EU GDP.[6] Employees in the EU shipping sector are regarded as more productive than their counterparts in other EU industries with the workers in the EU shipping sector generating an average of €88,000 each to the EU GDP as compared to an average of €53,000 for other workers in the EU.[7] Around 400 million passengers embark and disembark annually in EU ports.[8] In 2015, half of EU trade in goods is carried by sea and the value of EU trade in goods with third countries carried by sea was estimated at close to €1,777 billion, accounting for about 51% of EU trade in goods. Some 53% of EU imports entered the EU by sea while shipping represented 48% of EU exports to third countries. The use of maritime transport for EU trade in goods increased slightly over the last ten years: in 2006, less than half (47%) of the EU trade in goods with third countries was by sea. Portugal, Cyprus and Greece were among the leaders for international trade in goods by sea. Shipping was the main mode of transport in a majority of Member States in 2015. The highest shares of trade in goods with non-EU countries carried by sea were recorded in Portugal (81% of trade value), Cyprus (80%), Greece (77%), Spain (74%), Malta (67%), Italy (61%) and Finland (60%). Shares of over 50% were also reported by the Netherlands, Romania, Bulgaria, Denmark and Germany. Interestingly, maritime transport was less significant in the extra-EU trade in goods of the Czech Republic (12%), Luxembourg (19%), Ireland (27%), Latvia (27%), Austria (31%) and Croatia (35%). Rotterdam, Antwerp and Hamburg are the busiest cargo ports in the EU and they collectively account for almost a fifth of the gross weight of goods handled in EU ports.

2.003 In understanding the commercial background, it is useful to reflect on the different types of shipping activities. The European Parliament has categorised shipping activities in a way which is a very convenient summary for present purposes:

> "[m]aritime transport can be categorized on the basis of two criteria: service and distance. The first covers bulk shipping and liner shipping for cargo, and passenger ferries and cruise ships for carrying passengers; the second covers deep sea and short sea shipping.
> The different types of transport are distinct from one another. Bulk transport is generally organized within a free market and is labour-intensive rather than capital-intensive. Liner shipping, on the other hand, is organized in conferences, which for the most part are cartels that control the rates and market share of a specific liner shipping company or group of companies.[9] In terms of production factors, liner shipping is highly capital-intensive[10] in both tonnage and land-based infrastructures. As regards the carriage of persons, passenger ferries are generally operated as a public service, whereas cruise ships are part of the tourism sector.

---

4 Ibid.
5 Oxford Economics cited on the ECSA website homepage: www.ecsa.eu.
6 ECSA/Oxford Economics Report.
7 Ibid.
8 This figure appears to vary between commentators (e.g. 500 million is also cited) but it is enormous in any event.
9 Ed., see chap. 11 on why cartelised-liner conferences may no longer operate in the EU.
10 Ed., shipping is often a largely fixed cost business with very expensive assets (e.g. ships and terminals) with relatively low variable costs (e.g. fuel/bunkers, crew, insurance/protection and indemnity costs and harbour dues).

Deep sea transport involves long distances and is generally carried out by liner shipping services. Short sea shipping, on the other hand, covers maritime transport services between the EU Member States, other states in the Baltic Sea and the Mediterranean, and Norway and Iceland. In other words, short sea shipping does not involve an ocean crossing and includes sea/river transport by coastal vessels to and from ports in the hinterland. A significant number of bulk, cruise and ferry services which technically fall under the service criterion qualify as short sea shipping."[11]

B. COMMERCIAL SIGNIFICANCE OF SHIPPING FOR THE EU

2.004 Shipping plays an extremely important role in the commercial life of the EU generally. In terms of the EU's GDP, maritime transport is quite significant. In 2006, the transport of freight and passengers by sea generated €24.7 billion as a net contribution to the EU balance of payments. Again in 2006, the Commission stated that

> "between 3 and 5% of Europe's Gross Domestic Product (GDP) is estimated to be generated by marine based industries and services, without including the value of raw materials, such as oil, gas or fish. The maritime regions account for over 40% of GDP."

It was estimated that in 2015, the direct contribution of shipping to EU GDP in 2013 was €56 billion with an additional €61 billion being added indirectly.[12]

2.005 Shipping is also extremely important in terms of employment both directly and indirectly. There are many millions of people employed in shipping and shipping-related activities in the EU. These include both the direct and indirect jobs in areas such as shipping and ports but also indirect supply services such as shipbuilding, ship repair, ship management, stevedoring, warehousing, pilotage, ship finance, legal services and so on.

2.006 Shipping is vital in terms of the movement of cargo within the EU, to the EU and, particularly, from the EU. Some 90% (by volume) of the goods which are moved between the EU and the rest of the world are moved by sea. The main ports in the EU generally handle about twice as much inward cargo as outward cargo in terms of weight. The types of cargo would typically be, in descending amounts of weight, liquid bulk goods, dry bulk goods, large containers, ro-ro (roll-on/roll-off) mobile units and then general cargo. More than twice the cargo weight would be short sea rather than ocean traffic. The Commission has stated:

> "[s]hipping and ports are essential for international trade and commerce. 90% of the EU's external trade and over 40% of its internal trade is transported by sea. Europe's leadership in this global industry is beyond any doubt with 40% of the world fleet. 3.5 billion tonnes of cargo per year and 350 million[13] passengers pass[ing] through European seaports. Approximately 350,000 people work in ports and related services which together generate an added value of about €20 billion (and while these estimates vary, there is no doubting that they are significant). The perspectives for both these sectors are of continued growth, with world trade volume on the rise, and with the development of Short Sea Shipping and Motorways of the Sea in Europe.[14] Maritime transport is a catalyst for other sectors, notably shipbuilding and marine equipment.

---

11 Parliament, Directorate-General for Research, Working Document, Transport Series, W 14, "The Common Maritime Policy", www.europarl.europa.eu/workingpapers/tran/w14/1_en.htm, footnote omitted.
12 ECSA/Oxford Economics Report.
13 Ed., more recent estimates would put this figure higher at *c.* 400 million but a figure as high as 500 million has been cited at times.
14 Ed., on short sea shipping and motorways of the sea in Europe, see throughout this book.

Maritime ancillary services such as insurance, banking, brokering, classification and consultancy is another area where Europe should maintain its leadership."[15]

In that context, it is worth noting that marine tourism in Europe is a growing sector. This covers not only yachting and marine leisure activities but also the cruise sector.

2.007 The cruise industry has been growing steadily in recent years; for example, between 2008 and 2013, the total output of the European cruise industry increased by 22% to over €39 billion[16] while the number of European sourced passengers grew by 44% to 6.4 million in 2013. Europe is the second largest cruise market after the USA. Demand by European-based passengers for cruises worldwide represents about 30% of the world market. There were 43 cruise lines domiciled in Europe in 2013 operating 125 cruise ships with a capacity for over 145,000 passengers. Direct employment in Europe is estimated to involve around 339,000 jobs. European shipyards have been to the fore in the construction of cruise liners for the world market as they build almost all of the new larger and more sophisticated liners. All the current indications are (though there is always a risk of creating over-supply/over-capacity) that the EU cruise sector will grow in the coming years. The *2017–2018 Cruise Industry News Annual Report*[17] estimated that the European cruise capacity will grow more than 60% over the next decade. The estimated passenger capacity of the European brands was 6.8 million passengers in 2017 but would be 11.1 million by 2027, based on new ship orders and ship deployment, but excluding the capacity of North American brands also sourcing in European markets. The single largest brand in Europe is MSC Cruises with a European passenger capacity of 1.6 million, followed by Costa Crociere with 1.1 million, AIDA with nearly 950,000, and P&O with more than 550,000.

2.008 EU shipping interests invest heavily in shipping; for example, the European Community Shipowners Association ("ECSA") wrote that the total "investments by [European Economic Area ("EEA")] domiciled shipowners during 2005–2007 are prudently estimated at €110–120 billion"[18]; today, it would be even higher given the rising value of ships. In terms of the EU's role in world shipping, it is worth noting that EEA registered vessels represent around a quarter of the world merchant fleet while over 40% of the world's fleet is controlled by EEA interests. The EU's participation in a globalised world is very dependent on being able to move goods to and from the EU by ship. Shipping is an export industry for the EU as its shipping companies provide services to and from the EU as well as providing cross trading services elsewhere in the world. All of this means that there is also a related demand for financial, accounting and legal expertise within the EU.

2.009 Shipping is critical to the movement of people around the EU. Between 400 million and 500 million passengers are now transported by ship within the EU annually. It is extremely important for the peripheral regions and islands in the EU where air connections are often neither frequent nor cheap or indeed feasible in some circumstances. The EU's maritime regions account for some 40% of its GDP and population. The EU[19]

---

15 Green Paper – *Towards a Future Maritime Policy for the Union: A European Vision for the Oceans and Seas*, SEC(2006) 689, p. 7.
16 The cruise sector contributed around €39.4 billion in terms of the purchase of goods and services.
17 www.cruiseindustrynews.com/store/product/annual-reports/2017-2018-cruise-industry-news-annual-report/.
18 www.polshipowners.pl/documents/rapport_2007-2008.pdf, p. 7.
19 Leaving aside the overseas territories.

borders on two oceans (i.e. the Atlantic and the Arctic) and several seas. Indeed, as the Commission has observed:

"Europe's well-being is ... inextricably linked with the sea. Shipbuilding and shipping, ports and fisheries remain key maritime activities, but offshore energy (including oil, gas and renewables), and coastal and maritime tourism also generate massive revenues. Sea-ports and shipping allow Europe to benefit from the rapid growth of international trade and to play a leading role in the global economy, while the exploitation of mineral resources, aquaculture, blue biotech and emerging sub-sea technologies represent increasingly important business opportunities. Equally significant are the recreational, aesthetic and cultural uses we make of the seas and the ecosystem services they provide."[20]

2.010 While some Member States are landlocked – some 23 of the 28 Member States have ports[21] – the EU has some of the largest ports in the world along its 70,000 kilometres of coastline. In terms of total cargo, the largest five ports in the EU are (but this can change over time), in descending order of weight handled in recent years, Rotterdam, Antwerp, Hamburg, Marseille and Le Havre. There is a good spread of ports handling different types of goods with Rotterdam, Marseille, Bergen, Le Havre and Antwerp being the top five in terms of liquid bulk goods; Rotterdam, Amsterdam, Dunkirk, Immingham and Hamburg being the top five in terms of dry bulk cargo; Rotterdam, Antwerp, Hamburg, Bremerhaven and Algeciras were the top five in large containers; while Dover, Zeebrugge, Calais, Lubeck and London were the five largest ports in the EU in terms of ro-ro mobile units.

2.011 Short-sea shipping has a key role to play in relieving congestion on the EU's land networks and reducing the environmental impact of road transport. The development of transport networks through the trans-European transport network ("TEN-T") programme (including the Motorways of the Sea project) is important at reducing congestion on land by diverting traffic to the sea. In their 7 May 2014 Athens Declaration entitled *Mid-Term Review of the EU's Maritime Transport Policy until 2018 and Outlook to 2020*, the Council of the Economic Union stated:

"that Short Sea Shipping needs to play a stronger role in the EU to ensure the necessary accessibility and trade flows, including between the mainland and islands, and to shift long-distance transport away from roads in order to address capacity, energy and climate challenges while noting, in this context, the goals defined in the White Paper on transport policy published by the Commission in 2011;
RECOGNISING the important role of the European Shortsea Network (ESN) and its members Shortsea Promotion Centres (SPCs) to that regard;
ACKNOWLEDGING the importance of the establishment of the European Maritime Transport Space without Barriers and the Blue Belt initiative as essential elements to facilitate intra-EU maritime transport of goods, the attractiveness of Short Sea Shipping and the well-functioning of the internal market."[22]

---

20 Communication from the Commission to the European Parliament, the Council, the European Economic and Social Committee and the Committee of the Regions, *An Integrated Maritime Policy for the European Union*, COM/2007/0575 final, http://eur-lex.europa.eu/legal-content/EN/TXT/HTML/?uri=CELEX:52007DC0575&from=EN.
21 Austria, Czech Republic, Hungary, Luxembourg and Slovakia are landlocked. See http://ec.europa.eu/maritimeaffairs/documentation/studies/documents/landlocked_eu_countries_employment_trends_en.pdf.
22 See http://ec.europa.eu/transport/modes/maritime/consultations/doc/2015-mts-review/council-conclusions-on-mid-term-review-of-eu-maritime-policy.pdf.

2.012 The Ministers went on to say in the same Declaration:

"V. Exploiting the full potential of short-sea shipping and sea transportation services for business and citizens in Europe

15. CALL UPON the Commission and Member States to reinforce policy efforts regarding the promotion of Short Sea Shipping with the aim of shifting long-distance transport away from roads and ensuring the necessary accessibility and trade flows, including between the mainland and islands; and REQUEST adequate financial support, as appropriate, to promote the supply and demand for Short Sea Shipping services, in particular through the Connecting Europe Facility, allowing for better environmental performance of shipping, innovation and the integrated development of Motorways of the Sea;

16. UNDERLINE the importance of financial support, as appropriate, for the adaptation of ships to new environmental and safety requirements, in particular in the context of Short Sea Shipping;

17. RECALL that the implementation of appropriate alternative fuels infrastructure at EU ports, in particular for LNG refuelling, constitutes an issue of priority;

18. ENCOURAGE the development of more sustainable and efficient port systems to further enhance the environmental performance of ports and accommodate the ever-increasing maritime transport of goods and passengers with a view to meeting the demands of EU businesses and consumers for cost-efficient and timely transportation from door-to-door; CALL UPON the Commission to adopt State aid guidelines for seaports, with the aim of ensuring fair competition and a stable legal framework for port investment;

19. CALL for enhanced connectivity, especially through sea links and better port access as an integral part of the economic and social cohesion of Europe taking full advantage of the funding opportunities provided in the context of the current EU financial perspectives and, in particular, AGREE to promote, including through the Connecting Europe Facility and the European structural funds, better connections of islands and long-distance intra-EU passenger and freight transport through quality ferry services and appropriate port terminals, as well as appropriate hinterland connections of ports, in order to bridge existing gaps, prevent isolation and offer equal growth opportunities to small and remote islands, as well as insular Member States and promote coastal tourism;

20. URGE the Commission and the Member States to continue work on further digitalisation and simplification of administrative and operational procedures and the consequent reduction of administrative burden for the facilitation of maritime traffic, especially through the full and swift implementation of the Blue Belt including e-Manifest, the related e-Maritime services, and the development and deployment of national single windows in accordance with Directive 2010/65/EU, taking also into account the relevant IMO developments, in order to set up a European maritime transport space without barriers and to improve competitiveness."[23]

2.013 The strategic significance of shipping to the EU is well known. As the Commission has stated:

"The EU is the leading maritime power in the world, in particular with regard to shipping, shipbuilding technology, coastal tourism, offshore energy, including renewables, and ancillary services. Looking to the future, according to a study of the Irish Marine Institute, the sectors with most growth potential appear to be cruise shipping, ports, aquaculture, renewable energy, submarine telecommunications and marine biotechnology."[24]

---

23 Ibid.
24 Green Paper, *Towards a Future Maritime Policy for the Union: A European Vision for the Oceans and Seas – "How Inappropriate to Call this Planet Earth When it is Quite Clearly Ocean"*, SEC(2006) 689, p. 6, footnote omitted.

C. COMMERCIAL PHILOSOPHY OF THE EU RELATING TO SHIPPING

2.014 The EU's approach to shipping is expressed as being very open and liberal. It has abolished cabotage restrictions in Member States so any operator from any Member State may operate domestic services between ports in other Member States. It also opened the way for international maritime transport services. It repealed the block exemption for liner conferences which some saw as being price-fixing and market-sharing cartels.[25] It has championed the liberal agenda internationally and within the EU. It has fought for competition and the elimination of anti-competitive practices and arrangements. However, it is not all laissez-faire as it seeks to uphold the highest safety and environmental standards and it is somewhat protective in trying to build up shipping in the EU (for example, it has adopted a somewhat protectionist stance in regard to State aid by EU governments). The EU has also sought to respond to the attractions of flags of convenience by liberalising rules on taxation and social security payments.

2.015 The Oxford Economics/ECSA Report observed:

"• The shipping industry has a number of unique features which provide a rationale for a more favourable taxation policy than is available to other industries. The industry is, by its very nature, highly mobile and activity can easily be moved to countries which adopt more favourable taxation and regulatory regimes. A healthy and competitive shipping industry forms the core of the wider European maritime cluster and supports development of the EU's international trading linkages. It is also strategically important, for example in ensuring a secure energy supply and in providing capacity to support military operations in times of crisis or in peacekeeping missions.
• Recognising such arguments, and in response to intense international competition from third country shipping registers and global shipping centres, EU governments have introduced a range of state aid measures to support shipping, most notably in the form of tonnage tax and reduced income tax and social security contributions for seafarers. This approach has been guided by policy at the European level through the Commission's guidelines on state aid.
• Based on an illustrative counter-factual scenario using trends in fleet data for nine EU countries, it is tentatively estimated that the total economic contribution of the European shipping industry could have been around 50 per cent lower in 2012, in terms of GVA[26] and employment, if the countries in the analysis had not introduced tonnage tax regimes and other state aid measures."[27]

D. STATE OF SHIPPING IN THE EU

2.016 It is useful to begin by striking a note of caution in regard to the statistics relating to shipping in the EU. It is difficult for several reasons to present a commercial overview of EU shipping law. First, there is often a delay in the collation and publication of data. So, for example, the January 2015 Eurostat data on maritime ports freight and passenger statistics[28] utilise data from 2013.[29] Second, there are also different ways of measuring various variables. For example, in the case of a ship, weight can be expressed in terms of deadweight tons (i.e. "dwt") or gross tons (or gross tonnes) (i.e. "gt"). The term "dwt" refers to how much mass/weight a ship is carrying or can carry safely (i.e. the sum

---

25 See chap. 11.
26 Ed., i.e. gross value added.
27 Oxford Economics report, op. cit. at fn. 2.
28 http://ec.europa.eu/eurostat/statistics-explained/index.php/Maritime_ports_freight_and_passenger_statistics.
29 Even then some of the data were provisional and could be revised further.

of the weight of the cargo, passengers, water, fuel, provisions etc. but not the weight of the ship itself). The term "gt" refers to the measure of volume inside a vessel. Third, in terms of measuring a fleet, one can use different measurements. Oxford Economics has commented in the context of its report on shipping in the EU and Member States:

> "There are three main ways of measuring the EU fleet, each with its own merits and drawbacks.
>
> Firstly, the 'controlled' or 'beneficially owned' fleet includes ships whose ultimate ownership or control lies in an EU country, but which may be flagged in a different country. It is imperfect as a measure of economic activity since the country of ownership or control (to which dividends and profits flow) does not necessary align with where the direct operational activity and employment associated with the fleet takes place. Whilst imperfect, some data are available to assess the size of the EU fleet in terms of the number of vessels and tonnage on this basis.
>
> Secondly, the 'operated' fleet comprises ships operated by companies (or legal entities) based in the EU, which have substantive shore establishments within the EU, and which are subject to EU laws and taxation. The operated fleet includes ships operated under EU flags, plus non-EU flagged ships operated by EU shipping companies. The shore establishments may be a company's headquarters, but they may also be the European or national subsidiary of the company in question. Nonetheless, they are the centre of commercial management of the business that takes decisions on day-to-day operations and employment, even if all or part of their shareholding is abroad.
>
> The operated fleet is likely to align most closely with the industry's economic impact in terms of gross value added and employment. ... However, only very limited data are currently available to measure the size of the EU operated fleet.
>
> Finally, the 'flag' fleet comprises ships operating under the flag of an EU country. Flagging is an embodiment of the legal principle that every ship should belong to a state. Flag country is important since it determines which country's jurisdiction a ship and its crew falls under in terms of legal matters. The cost of complying with a flag state's legal and regulatory requirements is just one of a wide range of factors that may influence a shipowner's choice of flag state. Other factors include the type of vessel (some countries have registry practices tailored to specific sectors); a flag state's reputation for upholding safety and other standards; the provision of naval protection; and marketing considerations. A flag state, or a group of potential flag states, may also be specified by a ship's charter, financing organisation, or insurer.
>
> There may be some link between country of flag and the location of economic benefit due to reasons of cultural closeness or geographic proximity, but in many cases there may be little or no link. Nonetheless, the registration process creates very good data sets, which go back over 30 years in some cases.
>
> The EU controlled fleet ... has been chosen [in this report] as the preferred measure of the EU fleet because it provides the best balance between data availability and alignment with economic impact."[30]

2.017 So it is best to see the information which is set out below in relative, rather than absolute, terms. There are varying estimates of various factors – for example, the number of passengers travelling by sea in the EU can vary from *circa* 350 million to 500 million depending on the source. So, the following picture should not be seen as a mathematically or scientifically correct assessment but rather as a somewhat impressionistic and general overview of the situation but, however the figures are viewed, the EU is, and needs to be, a significant player in EU shipping.

2.018 The EU's *Statistical Pocketbook for 2017* (the most recently published by the EU at the time of writing) describes the EU Merchant Fleet in the following terms (Table 2.1).[31]

---

30 Oxford Economics report, op. cit. at fn. 2.
31 It also includes a number of other States as well – most notably, Norway.

Table 2.1 Profile of EU merchant fleet as of 1 January 2016

Sea: EU Merchant Fleet
Ships of 1000gt and over
On January 1st, 2016

	Total fleet controlled		National flag (¹)		Foreign flag (including other EU)		% of foreign flag in total fleet		
	Number	mio dwt	Number	mio dwt	Number	mio dwt	Number	mio dwt	
EU-28[2]	**13 340**	**625.711**	**3 300**	**139.348**	**10 040**	**486.366**			EU-28
EU-15[3]	**12 633**	**611.244**	**3 106**	**135.501**	**9 527**	**475.745**			EU-15
EU-13[4]	**707**	**14.467**	**194**	**3.847**	**513**	**10.621**			EU-13
BE[5]	196	20.068	66	7.186	130	12.883	66.3%	64.2%	BE
BG[6]	70	1.276	14	0.103	56	1.173	80.0%	91.9%	BG
CZ[7]	–	–	–	–	–	–	–	–	CZ
DK[8]	862	37.726	329	15.774	533	21.953	61.8%	58.2%	DK
DE[9]	3 456	120.793	217	11.251	3 239	109.542	93.7%	90.7%	DE
EE[10]	64	0.245	10	0.018	54	0.227	84.4%	92.7%	EE
IE[11]	86	1.433	31	0.287	55	1.146	64.0%	80.0%	IE
EL[12]	4 439	324.406	750	68.784	3 689	255.622	83.1%	78.8%	EL
ES[13]	176	2.450	90	0.501	86	1.949	48.9%	79.6%	ES
FR[14]	281	10.901	115	3.122	166	7.779	59.1%	71.4%	FR
HR[15]	92	2.731	58	1.640	34	1.091	37.0%	39.9%	HR
IT[16]	1 085	46.329	482	14.515	603	31.814	55.6%	68.7%	IT
CY[17]	151	5.315	51	1.676	100	3.639	66.2%	68.5%	CY
LV[18]	54	0.951	10	0.047	44	0.905	81.5%	95.2%	LV
LT[19]	56	0.338	19	0.168	37	0.170	66.1%	50.3%	LT
LU[20]	–	–	–	–	–	–	–	–	LU

HU[21]	–	–	–	–	–	HU
MT[22]	29	0.273	22	7	0.128	24.1%	46.99%	MT
NL[23]	908	10.764	637	271	5.201	29.8%	48.3%	NL
AT[24]	6	0.043	–	6	0.043	100.0%	100.0%	AT
PL[25]	107	2.437	8	99	2.411	92.5%	98.99%	PL
PT[26]	39	0.952	18	21	0.867	53.8%	91.1%	PT
RO[27]	80	0.883	2	78	0.859	97.5%	97.3%	RO
SI[28]	4	0.018	–	4	0.018	100.0%	100.0%	SI
SK[29]	–	–	–	–	–	–	–	SK
FI[30]	107	1.884	74	33	1.060	30.8%	56.3%	FI
SE[31]	331	6.417	84	247	5.349	74.6%	83.4%	SE
UK[32]	661	27.078	213	448	20.537	67.8%	75.8%	UK
AL[33]	22	0.082	12	10	0.043	45.5%	52.4%	AL
ME[34]	6	0.143	4	2	0.003	33.3%	2.1%	ME

Source: ISL, based on updates from Clarkson Research Services Limited (CRSL)

Notes
Russia: 1 449 ships, 21.054 mio dwt;
Monaco: 44 ships, 2.772 mio dwt;
Ukraine: 361 ships, 3.554 mio dwt;
Gibraltar: 7 ships, 0.032 mio dwt.

1 [I]ncluding international registers like NIS and DIS. Including vessels registered at territorial dependencies.
2 Ed., i.e. all 28 Member States of the EU.
3 Ed., i.e. the first 15 States to be members of the EU (i.e. the pre-2004 Member States).
4 Ed., i.e. the most recent 13 States to be join the EU (i.e. the 2004 and subsequent Member States).
5 Ed., i.e. Belgium.
6 Ed., i.e. Bulgaria.
7 Ed., i.e. Czech Republic.
8 Ed., i.e. Denmark.
9 Ed., i.e. Germany.
10 Ed., i.e. Estonia.
11 Ed., i.e. Ireland.
12 Ed., i.e. Greece.
13 Ed., i.e. Spain.
14 Ed., i.e. France.
15 Ed., i.e. Croatia.
16 Ed., i.e. Italy.
17 Ed., i.e. Cyprus.
18 Ed., i.e. Latvia.
19 Ed., i.e. Lithuania.
20 Ed., i.e. Luxembourg.
21 Ed., i.e. Hungary.
22 Ed., i.e. Malta.
23 Ed., i.e. Netherlands.
24 Ed., i.e. Austria.
25 Ed., i.e. Poland.
26 Ed., i.e. Portugal.
27 Ed., i.e. Romania.
28 Ed., i.e. Slovenia.
29 Ed., i.e. Slovakia.
30 Ed., i.e. Finland.
31 Ed., i.e. Sweden.
32 Ed., i.e. UK.
33 Ed., i.e. Albania.
34 Ed., i.e. Montenegro.
35 Ed., i.e. Turkey.
36 Ed., i.e. Iceland.
37 Ed., i.e. Norway.
38 Ed., i.e. Switzerland.

2.019 It is also interesting to see how the EU fits into the global picture. Again, the EU's *Statistical Pocketbook for 2017* (the most recently published by the EU at the time of writing) sets out the position in the terms shown in Table 2.2.

2.020 It is also interesting to see the global and EU perspectives on various types of vessels shown in Table 2.3.

2.021 The Oxford Economics/ECSA Report makes the following interesting observations:

"At the start of 2014, the EU controlled fleet (which comprises ships whose ultimate ownership or control lies in an EU country, but which may be flagged in a different country) comprised of 660 million deadweight tonnes, 450 million gross tonnes, and 23,000 vessels. For the purposes of this report, the EU includes the 28 EU countries plus Norway.

Between the start of 2005 and the start of 2014, the EU controlled fleet expanded by more than 70 per cent in terms of both gross and deadweight tonnage. The number of vessels grew at a much lower rate, reflecting the trend towards larger ships which offer greater economies of scale.

At the start of 2014, the EU controlled 40 per cent of world gross tonnage and 39 per cent of world deadweight tonnage. This is a slight decrease from 41 per cent in 2005 (on both measures), reflecting that EU shipping companies continue to face strong competitive pressure from other rapidly-growing centres of world shipping, particularly those in Asia and the Middle East.

Greece has the largest controlled fleet within Europe, equivalent to 36 per cent of gross tonnage, or 43 per cent of deadweight tonnage. Germany represents a further 21 per cent of gross tonnage, or 19 per cent of deadweight tonnage.

The EU controlled fleet is dominated by three types of vessel: bulkers (28 per cent of gross tonnage), oil tankers (25 per cent) and container ships (25 per cent). The EU controls 60 per cent of the world's container ships in gross tonnage terms.

Within the EU controlled fleet, the strongest growth between 2005 and 2014 was recorded amongst offshore vessels. The EUs share of the world offshore fleet increased from 28 per cent in 2005 to 37 per cent in 2014 (in gross tonnage terms)."[32]

2.022 Some key features of the EU shipping sector include:

- In 2014, the EU's tonnage represented about 40% of the world fleet by gross tonnage.
- EU tonnage grew by 70% between 2005 and 2014 and represented in 2014 some 660 million dwt and 23,000 vessels.
- In 2014, the EU shipping industry had about 60% of the world's container vessels, 52% of the world's multi-purpose vessels, 43% of the world's oil tankers and 37% of the world's offshore vessels.
- The EEA fleet in 2013 could be classified in terms of control and flag in the manner shown in Table 2.4.

"The EU controlled fleet has grown strongly since 2005 (the earliest year for which data are available on a consistent basis for all EU countries). Between the start of 2005 and the start of 2014, the fleet expanded by 74 per cent in gross tonnage terms, and by 72 per cent in terms of deadweight tonnage. ... Growth in the number of vessels was much lower, at 31 per cent, reflecting the trend for shipping companies to invest in larger vessels that offer greater economies of scale. It should be noted that this analysis includes all 28 EU countries and Norway for the entire duration of the time series. The growth trend shown is not, therefore, influenced by the accession of Bulgaria, Romania and Croatia to the EU during the period."[33]

---

32 Oxford Economics report, op. cit. at fn. 2.
33 Ibid.

Table 2.2 Geographical profile of world merchant fleet as of 1 January 2016

Sea: World Merchant Fleet
Total controlled fleet by world region

World region	On 1st January											
	1995	2000	2005	2008	2009	2010	2011	2012	2013	2014	2015	2016
	dwt (million)											
Europe*	311.246	350.136	400.947	480.869	507.666	518.276	552.970	601.009	669.864	696.400	739.100	773.535
of which: EU-28**	223.564	257.975	316.850	392.052	417.895	432.246	460.399	508.581	545.012	575.031	600.143	625.711
of which: EU-15	207.543	247.549	305.030	377.384	402.884	417.610	444.625	490.743		558.184	584.504	611.244
North America	51.024	49.413	45.414	49.689	52.244	50.539	56.033	62.973	69.064	70.211	82.881	91.419
Latin America	18.691	15.679	14.422	13.470	13.990	30.867	47.548	47.055	22.651	31.838	29.608	26.721
Asia/Oceania	246.722	292.722	361.311	462.661	497.788	532.446	560.390	607.475	748.366	780.826	805.594	619.712
Africa	6.742	7.121	5.142	5.070	6.981	7.586	8.818	12.753	13.640	13.451	13.689	
Unknown	37.956	38.115	52.687	59.274	67.647	86.555	116.621	126.018	8.178	3.007	4.561	7.385
Total	672.381	753.226	879.923	1 071.033	1 144.375	1 225.665	1 340.655	1 453.842	1 530.876	1 595.922	1 652.479	1 707.066
	Share of EU in Total and of Foreign Flag in EU											
EU-28** control of total	33.2%	34.2%	36.0%	36.6%	36.5%	35.3%	34.3%	35.0%	35.6%	36.0%	36.3%	37.6%
EU-15 control of total	30.9%	32.9%	34.7%	35.2%	35.2%	34.1%	33.2%	33.8%		35.0%	35.4%	35.8%
EU-28**: Foreign flag share***	56.5%	68.1%	67.8%	68.6%	69.4%	69.4%	69.1%	70.6%		74.0%	75.5%	77.7%
EU-15: Foreign flag share***	57.7%	67.7%	67.0%	68.7%	69.3%	69.3%	69.1%	70.6%		74.2%	75.6%	77.8%

Source: ISL, up to 2011 based on quarterly updates from IHS Fairplay, since 2012 on Clarkson Research Services Limited (CRSL).

Notes
Only ships of 1000 gt and over.
*: In this table Europe includes EU-28, EFTA, Monaco, Gibraltar, Andorra, Turkey, Western Balkan countries, Russia, Ukraine and Moldavia
**: EU-28 since 2012
***: foreign flag share includes ships registered by EU countries in other EU countries.

Table 2.3 Functional profile of world merchant fleet as of 1 January 2016

Sea: World Merchant Fleet						
For transport of goods and passengers: fleet by type of ship and country of domicile, numbers and deadweight						
On January 1st, 2016 (ships of 1000 gt and over)	Number World	EU-28	%	dwt (1000) World	EU-28	%
Total fleet	**41 822**	**13 340**	32%	**1 707 066**	**625 711**	37%
Tankers of which	**11 511**	**3 514**	31%	**597 131**	**217 969**	37%
Crude oil and oil product tankers	5 402	1 461	27%	441 854	158 768	36%
Oil/chemical tankers	4 564	1 604	35%	101 033	45 576	45%
Liquid gas tankers	1 545	449	29%	54 244	13 625	25%
Bulk carriers	**10 507**	**3 123**	30%	**752 104**	**233 550**	31%
Container ships	**5 226**	**2 768**	53%	**244 165**	**140 298**	57%
General cargo of which	**12 383**	**3 198**	26%	**107 566**	**31 514**	29%
Conventional cargo	8 647	2 099	24%	47 462	13 471	28%
Special cargo (*)	1 380	513	37%	36 340	10 939	30%
Pure car carriers	781	105	13%	12 358	1 527	12%
Reefer	697	197	28%	4 353	1 819	42%
Ro-Ro cargo	878	284	32%	7 052	3 758	53%
Passenger and passenger cargo	**2 195**	**737**	34%	**6 110**	**2 382**	39%
For transport of goods and passengers: passenger and passenger/cargo ships by registered flag, numbers and gross tons						
On January 1st, 2016 (ships of 300 gt and over)	Number World	EU-28	%	gt (1000) World	EU-28	%
Total	**4 316**	**1 295**	30%	**37 374**	**15 797**	42%
Cargo passenger and Ro-Ro passenger ships	2 641	875	33%	17 180	9 448	55%
Passenger (not Ro-Ro)	1 675	420	25%	20 194	6 349	31%
Cruise ships by registered flag, numbers and gross tons						
Up to December 2016(**) (ships of 1000 gt and over)	Number World	EU-28	%	gt (1000) World	EU-28	%
	301	97	32%	19 759	6 316	32%

Source: Institute for Shipping Economics and Logistics, Bremen.

Notes
(*) Including open hatch carriers.
(**) No deadweight figure is given for cruise ships, since dwt is a measure of the weight admissible in the vessel.
Ro-Ro: vehicles roll on to embark, vehicles roll off to disembark.

Table 2.4 Flag State/controlling State profile as of 1 January 2016

	Number of vessels	Gross tonnage	Deadweight tonnage
EEA-controlled/EEA-flagged	7%	7%	7%
EEA-controlled/Non-EEA-flagged	39%	53%	54%
Non-EEA controlled/EEA-flagged	54%	40%	39%

On 1 January 2014, the number of vessels totalled around 23,000 representing around 450 million gt or 660 million dwt.

- The Oxford Economics Report found that world fleet has also grown over the ... decade up to 2014, and

"at a slightly higher rate than the EU fleet, reflecting that other centres of world shipping, particularly in Asia and the Middle East, continue to expand rapidly. As a result, the EU controlled share of the global fleet has declined slightly from 41 per in 2005 to 40 per cent in 2014 in gross tonnage terms, or to 39 per cent by deadweight tonnage. ... Nonetheless, the EU controls 26 per cent of the world's vessels, the same proportion as in 2005. The fact that the EU controlled share of the number of vessels has remained constant whilst its share of tonnage has decreased slightly reflects that growth elsewhere has been particularly concentrated on very large vessels."[34]

2.023 Indeed, it is interesting to note some of the highlights of the sector as recorded in the Oxford Economics Update 2017[35] including the following facts:

"The EU shipping industry directly employed 640,000 people and supported a €57 billion contribution to GDP in 2015.

- Once supply chain and worker spending multiplier impacts are taken into account the shipping industry's employment contribution rises to 2.1 million.
- The total GDP contribution of the industry, including supply chain and worker spending impacts, is estimated to have been €140 billion in 2015.
- At €89,000 per worker in 2015, productivity in the EU shipping industry remains above the EU average, as well as that of sectors such as manufacturing and healthcare."

The Update also recorded that in terms of the people employed in the EU shipping industry, there were 374,000 employed in freight transport (including towage and dredging), 191,000 employed in passenger transport, 68,000 employed in service and offshore support vessels with 7,000 employed in chartering, renting and leasing. Interestingly 81% (516,000 people) of the EU shipping industry employees were at sea while 19% (124,000 people) were shore-based. Officers account for 42% (216,000 people) while 58% (300,000 people) were ratings; this means that EU seafarers tend to be better qualified than seafarers generally. Interestingly, of the 516,000 seafarers in the EU, 207,000 were EU/EEA nationals in 2015.

2.024 There was a steady and significant growth in the world shipping industry for many years until the end of the 1970s – from 1957 and 1990, the number of ships worldwide doubled and the gross tonnage quadrupled. Growth within the EU was not however

---
34 Ibid.
35 www.ecsa.eu/sites/default/files/publications/2017-02-27-Oxford-Economics-Update-2017---FINAL.pdf.

as dramatic as it was elsewhere in the world,[36] the Far East, the former USSR, China and the Open Registry States[37] grew much more significantly. During the 1980s, however, the world experienced a severe shipping crisis. The EU suffered more deeply and earlier[38] than the rest of the world during this crisis. Between 1975 and 1983, the absolute size of the merchant fleet under the flags of the EU Member States decreased only slightly. Nonetheless its share of world tonnage fell from 29% to 23.3% during the same period. Conversely, the former socialist states, the open registry states and developing countries' fleets grew during the same period. While world shipping capacity fell by some 8% between 1981 and 1987, total EU-owned capacity (including ships registered outside the EU) fell by some 28%.[39] In 1989, the EU Member States had only 50% of the gross tonnage and 73% of the number of ships they had in 1980. EU-flagged tonnage represented some 32.7% of the world total in 1967 but this had fallen to 14.7% by 1989. The decline in the EU's fortunes was dramatic. For example, in the five-year period between 1984 and 1989, the EU-flagged fleet fell by one-third in terms of tonnage and in the 1981–1989 period, the EU registered fleet fell (in terms of world tonnage) from 29% to 15%. The EU fleet, in September 2006, comprised 8,690 ships under European flags which represented 225 million deadweight tons and 23% of the world's tonnage. There were also in September 2006, around 3,500 ships flying non-EU Member State flags but owned by EU interests. There were also 190,000 European seafarers. So why did the EU suffer more than other regions? Writing in 1989, the Commission stated that the:

> "prolonged recession in world trade with the accompanying excess shipping capacity, the erosion of comparative advantage of Community shipping and the growth of protectionist practices adopted by third countries have been the major causes of the decline of the [EU] fleet relative to world tonnage over the last decade. During the same period, open registry and other third country fleets, including those of developing countries, have continued to expand. The expansion of non-[EU] merchant fleets has, inter alia, been based on the comparative advantage deriving from specific fiscal treatment and low manning, including social costs. This loss of the [EU] share of the world fleet shows that the competitive disadvantages of operating under [EU] flags have proved too great for many [EU]shipowners."[40]

2.025 In essence, there were two reasons: the EU is a relatively high-cost and regulatory base from which to operate; and second, some other countries were more protectionist (i.e. supportive of their shipping sector) than the EU in their shipping policies. Undoubtedly, greater aid was given by some non-EU governments towards the acquisition and operation of ships than their EU counterparts. It is equally clear that many jurisdictions worldwide have lower taxes and social security payments for shipping operations than EU jurisdictions. Indeed, the tolerance by some non-EU Member States of

---

36 Bredima-Savopoulou and Tzoannos, *The Common Policy of the EEC* (1990) comment (p. 8) that prior to 1980 the "total size of the combined [EU] fleets grew by a much smaller percentage than the corresponding size of the world total would or the other principal fleets, indicating that the decline in the relative position of the [EU] fleet had started long before the recent crisis".
37 Such as the Bahamas, Bermuda, Liberia and Panama.
38 See Bredima-Savopoulou and Tzoannos, op. cit. at fn. 2, p. 8. See also "Call for Action to Halt Fleet Decline", Lloyd's List, 7 May 1987, p. 1.
39 See Petropolous, "The European Community Transport Policy: An Overview", at *The Future of Shipping in Europe: Key Legal and Commercial Issues*, London, 28–29 June 1990, p. 4.
40 "Guidelines for the Examination of State Aids to Community Shipping Companies", Annex I to Commission of the European Communities, *Financial and Fiscal Measures Concerning Shipping Operations with Ships Registered in the Community*, SEC (89)921 final, 3 August 1989.

sub-standard ships flying their flags[41] has meant that some non-EU operators have had an unfair and unsafe advantage over their EU counterparts.

2.026 Nonetheless, the difficulties facing the EU in the 1980s also prompted it into action. The depression in the EU stimulated joint action by the Member States of the EU – indeed the December 1986 package of measures would probably not have been adopted had it not been for the shipping crisis just beforehand. It is also true to say that the package of positive measures published by the Commission in August 1989[42] and the subsequent stimulus measures would probably not have emerged either but for the decline which prompted a response. Indeed, generous regimes on tonnage tax permitted in recent years is also a result of the EU feeling under pressure from non-EU regimes which are generous to shipping companies and therefore attracting some EU shipowners. The EU has sought to respond to the difficulties faced by shipping generally as well as by shipbuilding. It is noteworthy that these somewhat protectionist responses by the EU have all been in the 1980s, 1990s and 2000s rather than more recently. Nonetheless, there are limits to what the EU can do; for example, first, it cannot legally do more than it is permitted to do by virtue of international law[43] and, second, commercially, the cyclical nature of the industry must be recognised because it did rebound and has only recently suffered a decline (albeit a very dramatic one) in the aftermath of the Credit Crunch in late 2008 and 2009.

E. PORTS IN THE EU

2.027 The EU has some of the biggest ports in the world. It is interesting to see the gross weight of goods handled in all ports in the EU. In March 2018, Eurostat, published[44] the following table (Table 2.5).

F. PASSENGERS

2.028 The EU's *Statistical Pocketbook for 2017* describes the number of passengers travelling through the major EU seaports in the terms shown in Table 2.6.

G. CONTRIBUTION TO THE EU FROM THE SHIPPING SECTOR

2.029 The 2014 Oxford Economics/ECSA Report makes the following observations:

"*Direct impact*
- In 2012, the EU shipping industry is estimated to have directly contributed €56 billion to EU GDP, employed 590,000 people, and generated tax revenues of €6 billion.
- It is estimated that around four-fifths of posts, or 470,000 jobs, are based at sea. It is tentatively estimated that around 40 per cent of these seafarers are EU or EEA nationals.

---

41 See Opinion of the Economic and Social Committee on the Communication and Proposals (II.3, II.4) by the Commission to the Council on *Progress towards a Common Transport Policy: Maritime Transport*, COM (85)90 final (TRA/116), para. 1.8.
42 On this package, see chap. 5.
43 E.g. by virtue of the World Trade Organization ("WTO") arrangements.
44 http://ec.europa.eu/eurostat/statistics-explained/index.php/Maritime_ports_freight_and_passenger_statistics.

Table 2.5 Profile of top 20 ports in the EU

Rank 2016	Port	*	2011	2012	2013	2014	2015	By direction		
			Total	Total	Total	Total	Total	Inwards	Outwards	Total
1	Rotterdam (NL)	=	404.4	409.8	411.9	418.6	436.9	298.3	1337	**431.9**
2	Antwerp (BE)	=	168.5	164.5	172.0	180.4	190.1	103.3	95.4	**198.7**
3	Hamburg (DE)	=	114.4	113.5	120.6	126.0	120.2	70.0	50.4	**120.3**
4	Amsterdam (NL)	=	88.4	91.7	92.3	96.3	98.8	62.3	34.0	**96.3**
5	Algeciras (ES)	=	68.9	72.3	67.6	75.6	79.4	46.0	37.4	**83.4**
6	Botas (TR)	=	65.5	61.2	56.1	57.0	78.1	14.6	63.8	**78.4**
7	Marseille (FR) (^{1})	=	84.5	81.8	76.2	74.4	77.5	56.0	20.4	**76.4**
8	Izmit (TR)	=	55.0	60.6	60.7	58.6	64.2	47.9	18.1	**66.0**
9	Le Havre (FR)(^{2})	=	63.4	59.2	64.4	61.4	62.9	43.3	16.8	**60.0**
10	Valencia (ES)	+1	54.2	54.2	53.5	55.0	57.6	26.9	31.4	**58.3**
11	Immingham (UK)	−1	57.2	60.1	62.6	59.4	59.1	38.9	15.5	**54.4**
12	Bremerhaven (DE)	=	55.9	58.2	54.5	53.6	49.8	23.3	29.0	**52.3**
13	London (UK)	+2	48.8	43.7	43.2	44.5	45.4	43.2	7.2	**50.4**
14	Allaga (TR)	=	37.6	42.6	39.5	42.0	48.4	33.3	16.9	**50.1**
15	Trieste (IT)	−2	41.8	42.1	46.0	47.3	49.1	43.3	6.0	**49.3**
16	Sines (PT)	+2	24.9	27.4	34.6	35.1	41.2	28.7	19.3	**48.1**
17	Genova (it)	+2	42.4	42.5	40.8	43.4	43.4	27.9	17.2	**45.0**
18	Bergen (NO)	−2	52.3	54.6	51.8	42.1	43.6	9.6	35.1	**44.7**
19	Piraeus (EL)	+1	23.5	35.2	40.2	41.1	38.3	20.9	20.1	**41.0**
20	Goteborg (SE)	+2	41.3	41.1	38.4	36.8	37.8	21.9	19.1	**41.0**
Total top 20 ports (^{3})		–	1 637.7	1 634.2	1 634.1	1 658.3	1 723.4	1 059.5	686.7	1 746.2
EEA + ME + TR (all ports) (^{4})		–		4 330.9	4 313.8	4 377.8	4 454.5	2 600.7	1 895.2	4 495.9

Notes
(*) Column indicates number of positions lost or gained compared to 2015. (:) not available. (−) not applicable.
(^{1}) 2010–2014: partially estimated by Eurostat.
(^{2}) 2010–2014: partially estimated by Eurostat.
(^{3}) Total figure for the ports being part of the top 20 ports during the reference year concerned.
(^{4}) All ports in the EU, EFTA and candidate countries reporting gross weight of goods.

By type of cargo handled (%)				Other cargo	Growth rate 2015–2016 (%)	Growth rate 2011–2016 (%)
Liquid bulk goods	Dry bulk goods	Large containers	Ro-Ro mobile units			
50	18	25	3	5	−1.1	+6.8
34	6	51	3	5	+4.5	+17.9
12	25	61	0	1	+0.1	+5.2
47	45	0	1	6	−2.5	+9.0
33	2	60	1	4	+5.1	+21.1
85	14	0	0	1	+0.4	+19.7
65	17	12	3	3	−1.4	−9.5
39	32	18	0	11	+2.8	+20.0
63	3	33	1	0	−4.6	−9.5
7	4	76	3	11	+1.3	+7.6
35	29	4	30	2	−8.0	−4.9
1	0	89	7	2	+5.1	−6.4
30	30	22	16	3	+10.9	+3.2
49	33	12	0	5	+3.6	+33.2
77	2	9	8	4	+0.4	+18.0
51	12	36	0	0	+16.6	+93.2
36	3	42	17	2	+3.7	+6.3
91	6	0	0	2	+2.5	−14.6
1	1	86	11	0	+7.0	+74.6
58	0	18	23	1	+8.4	−0.8
43	16	32	4	4	+1.3	+6.6
:	:	:	:	:	+0.9	

Table 2.6 Top 60 passenger ports in the EU

Sea: Passenger traffic at major EU seaports
Passengers embarked and disembarked

Rank	Port	Country	2000	2001	2002	2003	2004	2005	2006
1	Dover	UK	16 197	15 957	16 449	14 770	14 429	13 501	13 987
2	Helsinki	R	9 251	9 010	8 871	8 549	8 747	8 854	8 548
3	Stockholm	SE	7 746	7 001	6 826	7 294	7 823	8 211	8 054
4	Calais	FR	15 066	14 370	14 991	13 729	13 259	11 695	11 460
5	Tallinn	EE		5 740	5 136	5 172	6 452	6 701	6 447
6	Piraeus	EL	7 289	8 237	8 639	9 315	10 713	11 076	11 539
7	Heisingborg	SE	13 525	11 771	11 666	11 693	11 808	11 102	10 776
8	Helsingør (Elsinore)	DK	13 322	11 513	11 609	11 646	11 612	11 023	10 721
9	Paloukie Salamines	EL		3 624	12 133	12 541	11 568	11 663	11 981
10	Perama	EL		3 624	12 133	12 541	11 568	11 663	11 981
11	Messina	IT	11 898	11 612	10 256	9 833	10 128	9 802	10 834
12	Napoli	IT	6 748	7 056	6 708	6 811	6 801	6 084	6 084
13	Puttgadgen	DE	5 430	5 984	6 592	6 422	6 741	6 760	6 789
14	Radby (Færgehavn)	DK	5 430	6 028	6 508	6 421	6 744	6 761	6 789
15	Reggio Calabria	IT	11 839	11 511	10 137	9 698	9 992	9 645	10 669
16	Palma Mallorca	ES	1 864	1 873	2 286	2 537	3 742	4 817	4 942
17	Algeciras	ES	4 261	4 402	4 286	4 542	4 648	4 829	5 166
18	Cirkewwa	MT			3 320	3 388	3 512	3 463	3 555
19	Mgarr, Gozo	MT			3 320	3 388	3 512	3 463	3 555
20	Capri	IT	5 404	5 546	5 028	4 749	4 771	3 860	4 940
21	Santa Cruz de Tenerife	ES	4 927	4 910	4 861	5 011	4 941	4 249	4 343
22	Split	HR	1 952	2 135	2 456	2 788	2 902	3 267	3 476
23	Plombino	IT	3 161	3 501	3 675	3 716	3 702	3 277	3 948
24	Turku	FL	3 514	4 074	4 025	4 039	3 828	3 697	3 620
25	Dunkerque	FR	96	331	460	563	598	813	1 535
26	Marlehamn	FI	1 885	2 377	2 311	2 389	2 843	3 192	3 099
27	Portoferralo	IT	2 641	3 036	3 176	3 120	3 195	2 829	3 198
28	Rostock	DE	1 767	1 962	2 099	2 332	2 253	2 417	2 557
29	Porto D'Ischia	IT	3 686	3 844	3 576	3 494	3 535	3 169	3 443
30	Sjaellands Odde	DK	2 283	2 211	2 191	2 294	2 381	2 310	2 270
31	Olbia	IT	2 359	2 458	2 683	2 764	2 908	3 253	3 665
32	Hirtshals	DK	1 855	1 693	1 734	1 709	1 743	1 959	1 916
33	Århus	DK	1 143	1 250	1 376	1 572	1 763	1 710	1 686
34	Igoumenitsa	EL	933	958	2 202	2 467	2 221	2 338	2 531
35	Norddelch	DE	2 253	2 281	2 285	2 332	2 267	2 257	2 322
36	Genova	IT	2 444	2 390	2 820	2 961	2 507	2 406	2 320
37	Barcelona	ES	1 424	1 442	1 473	1 869	2 039	1 575	1 927
38	Civitavecchia	IT	2 241	2 136	1 975	1 932	2 145	2 099	2 500
39	Nordemey L	DE	2 015	2 038	2 017	2 055	2 016	1 990	2 056
40	Bastla	FR	1 916	1 968	2 123	2 123	2 052	2 208	2 162
41	Livomo	IT	1 886	1 706	1 792	1 907	2 013	2 166	2 789
42	Ceuta	ES	2 498	2 445	2 353	2 091	2 138	2 129	2 385
43	Ystad	SE	1 136	1 285	1 436	1 472	1 612	1 815	1 937
44	Holyhead	UK	2 518	2 380	2 371	2 333	2 262	2 173	2 057
45	Kiel	DE	1 108	1 050	1 152	1 212	1 225	1 486	1 474
46	Portsmouth	UK	3 270	3 393	3 469	3 169	3 127	2 679	2 208
47	Frederikshavn	DK	3 726	3 427	3 597	3 537	3 449	3 004	2 859
48	Zadar – passenger port	HR	1 376	1 421	1 621	1 629	1 742	1 924	1989
49	Sorrento	IT	2 071	2 412	2 195	2 046	1 966	1 558	2 101
50	Dublin	UK	1 415	1 404	1 446	1 426	1 364	1 200	1 245
51	Thasos	GR		291	1 460	1 362	1 306	1 326	1 454
52	Dagebüll	DE	1 658	1 579	1 575	1 557	1 485	1 459	1 571
53	Trelleborg	SE	2 086	1 853	1 855	2 100	1 941	1 691	1 697
54	La Maddalena	IT	2 025	2 026	1 895	1 965	2 068	1 843	3 371
55	Palau	IT	2 106	2 085	1 940	2 007	2 067	1 843	3 371
56	Supetar	HR	794	813	921	1 048	1 144	1 303	1 417
57	Korcula	HR	453	526	648	653	1 137	1 133	922
58	Visby	SE	1 291	1 294	1 377	1 422	1 456	1 460	1 472
59	Göteborg	SE	2 937	2 658	2 747	2 750	2 608	2 267	2 188
60	Esbjerg	DK	1 896	1 860	1 841	1 829	1 824	1 796	1 805

2007	2008	2009	2010	2011	2012	2013	2014	2015	Change 14/15 %
14 433	14 006	13 265	13 361	12 918	12 076	12 898	13 381	13 082	−2.2
8 561	8 976	9 085	9 849	10 326	10 637	10 756	10 942	11 214	2.5
8 127	8 677	0 089	9 147	9 184	9 108	8 889	9 933	9 887	−0.5
11 519	11 002	10 158	10 237	10 063	9 345	10 372	10 703	9 757	−8.8
6 220	6 870	6 841	7 523	8 043	8 417	8 727	9 098	9 299	2.2
11 063	11 079	10 444	10 944	9 182	7 918	7 704	8 136	8 169	0.4
10 966	10 911	9 415	8 540	8 339	7 841	7 763	7 656	7 670	0.2
10 966	10 912	9 415	8 534	8324	7 822	7 721	7 634	7 644	0.1
13 066	13 063	12 821	12 705	11 662	11 430	10 724	7 016	7 050	0.5
13 066	13 063	12 821	12 705	11 662	11 430	10 724	7 016	7 050	0.5
10 603	10 380	10 441	10 765	8 060	8 126	7 256	6 988	7 021	0.5
6 598	6 185	6 932	8 356	7 859	7 964	7 360	7 652	6 484	−15.3
7 069	6 768	6 305	6 261	6 028	5 963	5 944	6 002	6 141	2.3
7 058	6 756	6 305	6 261	6 028	6 000	5 944	6 003	6 139	2.3
10 336	10 116	11 047	9 891	7 704	7 760	6 758	6 187	6 053	−2.2
5 275	5 048	4 692	4 496	4 610	4 292	4 756	4 939	5 496	11.3
5 227	4 988	4 608	4 663	4 504	4 849	4 812	5 386	5 473	1.6
3 795	3 942	3 792	4 031	4 125	4 093	4 395	4 643	4 740	2.1
3 795	3 942	3 792	4 031	4 125	4 093	4 395	4 643	4 740	2.1
5 421	7 169	6 944	6 517	6 576	6 744	6 488	6 054	4 355	−28.1
4 592	4 191	3 887	4 110	4 305	3 923	4 546	4 245	4 320	1.8
3 726	3 733	3 558	3 523	3 698	3 769	3 807	3 506	3 992	13.9
3 982	5 036	4 987	3 477	3 972	3 618	3 532	3 386	3 517	3.9
3 480	3 488	3 520	3 498	3 306	3 224	3 452	3 426	3 256	0.3
1 939	2 203	2 422	2 533	2 601	2 499	2 302	2 518	3 198	27.0
3 125	3 306	3 394	3 302	3 220	3 191	3 011	2 981	3 043	2.1
3 155	3 927	3 971	2 769	2 899	2 981	2 839	2 872	2 945	2.5
2 585	2 713	2 431	2 195	2 249	2 344	2 300	2 477	2 863	15.6
2 812	2 342	2 364	2 589	2 605	1 964	2 089	2 597	2 789	6.6
2 233	1 911	1 782	1 777	1 903	2 038	2 463	2 525	2 690	6.5
3 487	3 567	3 785	3 863	3 703	2 514	2 458	2 502	2 598	3.8
1 838	1 888	2 063	2 178	2 247	2 246	2 345	2 479	2 567	3.5
1 583	1 443	1 277	1 284	1 345	1 509	2 182	2 350	2 532	7.7
2 683	2 631	2 741	2 726	2 567	2 262	2 471	2 544	2 532	−0.5
2 312	2 267	2 394	2 287	2 439	2 437	2 410	2 526	2 497	−1.1
2 639	2 510	3 454	2 991	2 573	2 502	2 358	2 196	2 344	6.7
2 090	2 314	2 405	2 358	2 498	2 310	2 373	2 606	2 327	−10.7
2 285	2 677	2 837	2 440	2 474	2 376	2 524	2 099	2 236	6.5
2 023	1 971	2 056	2 093	2 182	2 309	2 408	2 550	2 162	−15.2
2 200	2 312	2 495	2 524	2 282	2 173	2 162	2 065	2 048	−0.8
3 251	3 273	2 782	2 637	1 923	1 923	1 923	1 898	2 001	5.4
2 567	2 422	2 126	1 897	1 812	1 874	1 876	1 959	1 985	1.45
1 878	1 857	1 823	1 770	1 913	1 962	1 934	1 953	1 983	1.5
2 138	1 996	1 942	2 073	2 020	1 898	1 954	2 013	1 970	−2.1
1 559	1 761	1 772	1 854	1 904	1 964	1 882	2 002	1 956	−2.3
2 127	2 132	2 187	2 260	2 130	1 943	1 948	1 958	1 950	−0.4
2 894	2 258	2 102	1 999	2 011	1 964	1 966	1 996	1 937	−3.0
2 098	2 228	2 230	2 145	2 247	2 144	2 136	1 792	1 873	4.5
2 361	1 887	1 967	1 637	1 992	1 968	1 580	1 822	1 844	1.2
1 287	1 335	1 497	1 768	1 671	1 595	1 610	1 699	1 798	5.8
1 706	1 791	1 732	1 586	1 577	1 511	1 588	1 717	1 743	1.5
1 526	1 542	1 613	1 624	1 584	1 587	1 697	1 713	1 729	0.9
1 816	1 821	1 556	1 569	1 564	1 538	1 618	1 681	1 713	1.9
2 918	2 374	2 333	2 064	1 808	1 616	1 744	1 724	1 700	−1.4
2 907	2 364	2 366	2 064	1 811	1 616	1 760	1 724	1 700	−1.4
1 509	1 509	1 532	1 383	1 470	1 558	1 611	1 552	1 688	8.8
986	1 618	1 583	1 474	1 386	1 467	1 620	1 680	1 672	−0.5
1 565	1 583	1 629	1 474	1 386	1 467	1 620	1 680	1 672	−0.5
2 091	1 845	1 722	1 691	1 637	1 605	1 647	1 719	1 642	−4.6
1 827	1 796	1 809	1 790	1 775	1 723	1 685	1 710	1 631	−4.6

- Shipping is a high productivity industry: each worker is estimated to have generated €88,000 of GDP, significantly above the EU average of €53,000.
- The skills and experience of seafarers are vital to the smooth functioning of the shipping industry, and are also highly valued by firms in the wider maritime cluster and beyond.
- Indicative estimates suggest there were approximately 38,000 students/cadets in maritime academy-type training in 2012, an 11 per cent increase from 2004.

Indirect and induced impacts
- The shipping industry indirectly supported an estimated €59 billion contribution to GDP and 1.1 million jobs through its European supply chain in 2012.
- The spending of wages by those employed in the shipping industry and its supply chain supported an estimated additional €30 billion of GDP and jobs for 550,000 people.

Total economic impact
- Taking all of the impacts together, direct, indirect and induced, the total GDP contribution of the European shipping industry in 2012 is estimated to have been €145 billion.
- For every €1 million the European shipping industry contributes to GDP itself, it creates another €1.6 million elsewhere in the European economy.
- The industry also supported employment for an estimated 2.3 million people and tax revenues estimated at €41 billion."[45]

H. ANALYSIS OF SHIPPING IN THE MEMBER STATES[46]

Austria

2.030 As Austria is landlocked, one would not expect it to be relevant in the context of EU shipping law. However, on 1 January 2007, there were eight ships of 1,000 grt (gross registered tonnage) or more controlled by Austrian shipowners amounting 0.048 million dwt. It had six vessels on the national flag amounting to 0.038 million dwt with the balance of two vessels amounting to 0.01 million dwt being on foreign flags (i.e. 25% of the fleet was flagged out and those vessels amounted to 20.8% of the Austrian tonnage). It also had some people employed in boat building and has a strong marine equipment sector with over 7,000 people employed in the sector. By 1 January 2012, Austrians had control of only two vessels of more than 1,000 grt and both were foreign flagged. The United Nations Conference on Trade and Development (UNCTAD) reported in 2017 that Austria had no flagged national fleet, no shipbuilding, no ship scrapping and no container port traffic. There was however 320,000 dwt of tonnage owned by Austrian interests. The total carrying capacity by type of ship (by thousands of dwt) of the Austrian fleet was 44,000 in 2005 (divided between general cargo (38,000) and container ships (other types of ships) but in 2010, the fleet (then only 11,700 dwt) comprised solely general cargo in nature.

---

45 Oxford Economics report, op. cit. at fn. 2.
46 This short section gives an overview of shipping in the Member States. Further information is available from various sources including the ECSA website (e.g. its annual reports), the EU websites as well as websites dedicated to particular Member States and their shipping registries. Historical information is also included so as to contextualise the evolution of shipping in Member States over time.

Belgium

2.031 The Belgian fleet continued to grow (both in tonnage and ship numbers) from 1957 until 1986 – indeed, the tonnage quadrupled during that period. In 1948, the Belgian fleet was only 435,000 grt. In 1970, the Belgian fleet had 230 ships (representing 0.4% of the world total and almost 3% of the then EU total). In 1970, the Belgian fleet was almost 1,100,000 grt. In 1975, the number of vessels had risen to 252 (representing 0.4% of the world total and 2.1% of the then EU total). By 1975, the fleet was almost 1,300,000 grt. In 1987, this figure had risen to 350 ships (representing 0.5% of the world total and 2.5% of the then EU total). However, by 1989, the increases made in the 1957–1986 period in both numbers and tonnage had been virtually eliminated. Between 1984 and 1989 the gross tonnage registered had fallen from 2,406,714 to 2,043,594. By 1991, only 314,198 grt were registered in Belgium given the shift to, in particular, the Luxembourg registry. On 1 January 2007, the gross tonnage was 12,014,000 with 169 vessels. Of these 169, 52 were flying the Belgian flag with 117 flagged out (i.e. over 69% in volume or 47% in terms of tonnage). On 1 January 2012, Belgium had 173 ships of more than 1,000 grt under the control of Belgians with 65 flagged under the Belgian flag and 108 under foreign flag (with slightly more than half of the tonnage flagged out).

2.032 Some further points are worth noting. In 1986, there were 2,928 persons employed in the merchant marine (representing 0.09% of the total Belgian civilian labour force in 1986) and 3,871 persons employed in shipbuilding (representing 0.1% of the total civilian labour force in 1986). In 2002, Belgium introduced an integrated shipping policy which led since 2004 to flagging in and growth in the size of the fleet managed in Belgium.

2.033 UNCTAD reported that in 2017 that the national flagged fleet had 8,322,000 dwt but the national owned fleet had 22,098,000 dwt, there had been 6,642 grt of ship scrapping and 11,061,400 teu (twenty foot equivalent unit) in terms of container port throughput. Of the 8,322,000 dwt, some 4,381,700 dwt were oil tankers, 2,372,600 dwt were bulk carriers, 2,372,600 dwt was composed of general cargo and 99,400 dwt were container ships. Belgium would take some encouragement from the fact that its fleet grow in dwt terms from 6,815,000 in 2005 to 6,575,100 in 2010, 8,658,000 in 2015 to 8,322,000 in 2016.

Bulgaria

2.034 On 1 January 2007, the Bulgarian-controlled fleet of 1,000 dwt or more vessels numbered 107 with a dwt of 1,749,000. Most were flying the Bulgarian flag (74% in number and 70% in tonnage) with 68 ships amounting to 1,211,000 dwt being on the Bulgarian register. As of 1 January 2012, there were 69 ships under the control of Bulgarian interests and they represented 1,460,000 dwt. Sixteen of them were flying the national flag (representing 352,000 dwt) with 53 flagged under foreign flags (representing 1,108,000 dwt).

2.035 UNCTAD reported some interesting statistics in 2017 that the national flagged fleet had 109,000 dwt but the national owned fleet had 1,278,000 dwt, no ship scrapping and 195,800 teu in terms of container port throughput. Of the 109,000 dwt in 2017, some 7,000 dwt were oil tankers, 33,600 dwt were bulk carriers, 46,300 dwt were general cargo and 22,500 dwt were other types of ships. It is notable how the fleet had fallen from 1,151,000 dwt in 2005 to 686,800 dwt in 2010, 145,500 in 2015 and 109,400 in 2016.

Croatia

2.036 As of 1 January 2012, there were 106 ships under the control of Croatian interests and they represented 3,456,000 dwt. Of these, 73 were flying the national flag (representing 2,489,000 dwt) with 31 flagged under foreign flags (representing 963,000 dwt) – one of the few States to have more flagged at home rather than under foreign flags.

2.037 UNCTAD reported some interesting statistics in 2017 that the national flagged fleet had 1,996,000 dwt, the national owned fleet had 2,751,000 dwt and 211,900 teu in terms of container port throughput. Of the 1,995,700 dwt, some 1,066,400 dwt were oil tankers, 866,000 dwt was in bulk carriers, 20,000 dwt was in general cargo and 42,500 dwt was in other types of ships. The fleet had grown from 2005 (1,522,000 dwt) to 1,995,700 dwt in 2016 which had shown a fall from 2,277,100 in 2010 and 2,096,700 in 2015.

Cyprus

2.038 Cypriot shipping has enjoyed a period of prosperity over the last quarter century. While suffering a decline in the late 1970s and early 1980s, Cyprus enjoyed a period of considerable prosperity during the 1980s with a doubling in ship numbers and a multifold increase in gross tonnage. As at 1 January 2007, the Cypriot-controlled fleet amounted to 186 ships totalling 5,028,000 dwt. Just a little over half (51% by number and 52% by tonnage) of these vessels were flagged outside Cyprus. As of 1 January 2012, there were 204 ships under the control of Cypriot interests and they represented 6,802,000 dwt. Fifty-eight of them were flying the national flag (representing 2,060,000 dwt) with 146 flagged under foreign flags (representing 4,742,000 dwt). It now has one of the largest fleets in the EU and the world. It has, by some measurements, the largest third party ship management business in the world. It has achieved this success by being competitive and attractive to shipowners. In return, shipping contributes around 4% to the GDP of Cyprus. There have also been a considerable number of jobs created both ashore and at sea in the shipping sector. Cyprus is on the "White Lists" of both the Paris and Tokyo Memoranda of Understanding on Port State Control.

2.039 UNCTAD reported some interesting statistics in 2017 that the national flagged fleet had 33,178,400 dwt, the national owned fleet however was 9,050,000 dwt showing the attractiveness of the Cypriot flag and only (relative to other maritime States) 307,661 teu in terms of container port throughput. Of the 33,178,400 dwt, some 4,196,200 dwt were oil tankers, 21,339,800 dwt were bulk carriers, 1,301,900 dwt were represented by general cargo, 4,705,000 dwt were represented by container ships and 1,635,500 dwt were represented by other types of ships. Over the period 2005–2016, the Cypriot fleet was quite stable: the national fleet hardly moved over that timeframe – from 34,180,000 in 2005, 31,305,200 in 2010, 33,123,400 in 2015 and 33,178,400 in 2016.

Czech Republic

2.040 The Czech Republic, a landlocked State, had one vessel controlled by Czech interests on 1 January 2007 and she was flagged outside the Czech Republic. As of 1 January 2012, there was one ship of more than 1,000 dwt and it was flagged out. There were some people employed in boat repair and building in the Republic. There are under 1,000 seafarers living in the Republic.

2.041 UNCTAD reported some statistics on the position in 2017 and they showed that there was no shipbuilding, no flagged fleet, no owned fleet and no container port traffic – all of which is not surprising.

Denmark

2.042 The number of ships in the Danish fleet in 1970 was 1,210 (representing 2.3% of the then world total). In 1970, the Danish fleet was almost 3,400,000 grt. By 1975, the fleet was almost 4,500,000 grt. By 1980, the tonnage reached 5,500,000 grt and by 1989, the tonnage had fallen to 5,000,000. On 1 January 2007, its tonnage amounted to 21,251,000 dwt in terms of Danish interests or 9,674,000 in terms of Danish flagged tonnage. On 1 May 2008, the tonnage of the Danish fleet was 9,500,000 grt. On 19 March 1990, of 591 ships owned by Danish parent companies, 123 were less than four years old, 171 were between five and nine years old, 106 were between 10 and 14 years old, 59 were between 15 and 19 years old, 27 were between 20 and 24 years old with 20 being 25 years or older. In 1991, the Danish fleet was the youngest in the EU. The age profile was due in part to the Danish government granting loan subsidies and loan guarantees. In 1986, there were 9,779 persons employed in the merchant marine (representing 0.4% of the total civilian Danish labour force in 1986) and 12,260 persons employed in shipbuilding (representing 0.5% of the total civilian labour force in 1986). In 1975, this figure had risen to 1,371 (representing 2.15% of the world total and 11.6% of the then EU total). In 1987, this figure had fallen back to 1,256 ships (representing 1.6% of the world total and 10.7% of the then EU total). Shipping represented 2.7% of the Danish GDP in 1992. On 1 January 2007, Danish interests controlled 684 vessels amounting to 21,251,000 dwt. Almost two-thirds by number (62.7%) and just over half by tonnage (54.5%) is flagged out of Denmark. On 1 May 2008, the Danish fleet numbered 514. As of 1 January 2012, there were 3,916 ships under the control of Danish interests and they represented 125,496,000 dwt. Of these, 390 were flying the national flag (representing 17,495,000 dwt) with 3,526 flagged under foreign flags (representing 108,001,000 dwt). The fleet is largely involved in cross-trading as Danish trade alone would not support such a fleet. It is estimated that Danish shipowners account for a significant portion of the world fleet: the ECSA's Annual Report 2007–2008 stated that

> "Danish shipowners maintain an impressive international position: they own a total of 3% of the world merchant fleet and are responsible for 5% of international newbuilding orders. Adding hereto the large amount of tonnage controlled by other means, the total consolidated fleet is estimated to account for 7–8% of the world merchant fleet. Given the concentration of Danish shipowners in advanced, high value shipping sectors such as container, product and gas tanker and special transport, Danish shipowners transport goods of relatively high value. This implies that Danish shipping companies account for about 10% of overall world trade measured by value."

2.043 Denmark has a diverse range of ports which collectively handle over 100 million tonnes of cargo and around 60 million passengers per annum. Shipping is a very large export industry. The Danish government has been to the forefront of many debates in the EU on shipping issues. Denmark has not only its own registry but has had since 1988 an international registry as well (i.e. the Danish International Registry). The Faroe Islands also have a registry. Of the 591 ships owned by Danish parent companies on 19 March 1990, 118 (i.e. 20%) were registered on the Danish registry and 235 (i.e. 40%) were registered on the Danish International Registry with the rest being registered around the world (in particular, in the Bahamas, Liberia and Singapore). The K/S partnership scheme[47] encouraged investment in shipping by providing tax savings for the investors. In Denmark, the DSB is the State-owned railway company and it operates a fleet of vehicle and train ferries. It was one of the few State-owned shipping companies in the EU but in 1984 it started to work in a way which was largely independent of government control. Under Danish tax law, it has been possible to create tax-free reserves from operating profits or from book profits resulting from the sale of a ship and these reserves may then be used for the purchase of new ships. The Danish fleet is strong in the container sector and is, within the EU, second only to the German fleet. The Danish company Maersk is the largest in the EU and in the world. The Danish shipbuilding sector was second only to Germany in terms of the tonnage launched in EU Member States between 1984 and 1990. The Danish Shipowners' Association has been a very powerful advocate of the interests of the Danish shipping industry. The Danish shipping industry has prospered enormously in recent years. The Danish government published an action plan in 2006 with 60 specific initiatives aimed at improving the competitiveness of Danish shipping. The fleet grew 10% between 2007 and 2008. In 2007, Danish shipping contributed DKK 175 billion to the Danish balance of payments. As at 1 January 2008, Danish shipowners had placed orders for 350 vessels representing 15 million dwt with a value of DKK 85 billion which in turn represents about 5% of the international new building orders. Danish shipping companies carry out around 10% of overall world trade measured by value. Less than 20% of the total turnover of the Danish fleet comes from voyages calling at European ports and most comes from voyages elsewhere in the world (particularly, the USA, China and Japan). There has been considerable vibrancy and vitality in the Danish shipping sector with new companies being founded or listed on stock markets. Danish shipowners have placed orders for newbuilds with Danish interests representing around 5% of newbuilds worldwide in recent years. It has been estimated that Danish shipping accounts for around 8% of world tonnage but accounts for around 10% of the global maritime turnover in terms of the money spent on the movement of goods by sea. There are significant numbers of people employed in shipping, marine equipment and shipbuilding. Moreover, Denmark has "punched above its weight" in influencing maritime policy issues both in the EU and beyond.

2.044 UNCTAD reported some statistics in 2017 that the national flagged fleet had 17,154,000 dwt, the national owned fleet had 38,315,000 dwt, 13,074 gt of ship scrapping and there was 744,000 teu in terms of container port throughput. Of the 17,153,600 dwt, some 3,473,900 dwt were oil tankers, 357,600 dwt were bulk carriers, 262,400 dwt were

---

[47] For further details on the K/S partnership in the context of shipping, see https://samfundsansvar.dk/sites/default/files/partnerships_in_the_danish_shipping_industry.pdf.

in general cargo, 262,400 dwt were container ships and 1,661,800 dwt were other types of ships. The Danish fleet has grown steadily from 2005 (9,033,000 dwt), to 13,813,800 in 2010, 16,453,800 in 2015 to 17,153,600 in 2016.

Estonia

2.045 On 1 January 2007, Estonia had 234 vessels of more than 1,000 dwt each. However, 47% of the vessels (in terms of numbers) were flagged outside Estonia. The 234 vessels of more than 1,000 dwt each on the Estonian register on 1 January 2007 amounted to 4,443,000 dwt. However, 80.7% of this tonnage was flagged outside Estonia. The majority in number (124 of the 234) of Estonian controlled vessels are flagged in Estonia but the majority in tonnage terms (3,584,000 dwt of 4,443,000 dwt) is flagged out. As of 1 January 2012, there were 81 ships under the control of Estonian interests and they represented 307,000 dwt. Nineteen of them were flying the national flag (representing 60,000 dwt) with 62 flagged under foreign flags (representing 247,000 dwt). There has been limited State aid for Estonian cargo vessels. Estonian shipping is stronger in terms of ferries than cargo vessels. Some of the vessels had been flagged out to Latvia.

2.046 UNCTAD reported in 2017 that the national flagged fleet had 79,700 dwt, the national owned fleet had 249,000 (showing that two-thirds of its fleet was flagged out) and 260,293 teu in terms of container port throughput. Of the 79,700 dwt, some 12,400 dwt were oil tankers, 16,400 dwt were in general cargo and 50,900 dwt were other types of ships.

Finland

2.047 As at 31 December 1995, the average age of the Finnish fleet was 26 years. This has improved since. As at 31 December 1995, of the 274 ships registered in Finland: 170 were cargo vessels and 104 were vessels of other types. There were 13 oil tankers included in that 274. There were 31 ro-ro cargo ships, 35 ro-ro/passenger vessels and 14 passenger vessels. On 1 January 2007, over a third (37%) of the Finnish vessels were flagged out and they amounted to almost two-thirds of the tonnage (63%). As of 1 January 2012, there were 126 ships under the control of Finnish interests and they represented 1,973,000 dwt. Of these, 82 were flying the national flag (representing 889,000 dwt) with 44 flagged under foreign flags (representing 1,084,000 dwt). Finnish vessels transport about a third of all exports and imports from, or to, Finland which travel by sea. Finnish trade unions are strong and there is a very high proportion of Finnish nationals crewing Finnish vessels.

2.048 UNCTAD reported some interesting statistics in 2017, namely, that the national flagged fleet had 1,177,000 dwt, the national owned fleet had 2,121,000 dwt and 1,440,350 teu in terms of container port throughput. Of the 1,176,600 dwt, some 330,000 dwt were oil tankers, 200,900 dwt were bulk carriers, general cargo amounted to 457,000 dwt, container ships amounted to 13,700 and other types of ships amounted to 174,900 dwt. Over time, the fleet has remained constant – the changes have been immaterial from 1,113,000 dwt in 2005, to 1,171,300 dwt in 2010, 1,194,000 in 2015 and 1,176,000 dwt in 2016.

France

2.049 In 1970, the French fleet had over 1,400 ships. In 1975, the fleet had not changed in numerical strength. However, by 1980, the number had fallen to around 1,230 and, by 1989, the number had fallen to around 950. By 1 January 2007, it had 208 vessels of more than 1,000 dwt with just over half of these vessels flagged outside France. The French-flagged fleet represented about 0.5% of the world fleet but French shipowners represented around 2% of the world fleet. The rate of growth in the French controlled fleet between 2005 and 2014 was even stronger than the EU average, at 169% over this period.[48]

2.050 In 1970, the French fleet was almost 6,500,000 grt but by 1978, this rose dramatically to over 12,000,000 grt but had fallen even more dramatically to just over 4,500,000 grt by 1989 having been in "free-fall" since 1980. By 1991, it has fallen to less than 4,000,000 grt. By 1 January 2007, it had tonnage amounting to 5,724,000 dwt with just over half of the tonnage flagged out. The controlled fleet was believed to amount to over 26,000,000 dwt.

2.051 On 19 March 1990, of 298 ships owned by French parent companies, 22 were less than four years old, 60 were between five and nine years old, 104 were between 10 and 14 years old, 64 were between 15 and 19 years old, 14 were between 20 and 24 years old with 16 being 25 years old or older. It was estimated by the ECSA in its 2007–2008 annual report that the average age of the French fleet then was 7.3 years which is relatively young.

2.052 In terms of employment, in 1986 there were 6,807 persons employed in the merchant marine (representing 0.03% of the total French civilian labour force in 1986) and 20,916 persons employed in shipbuilding (representing 0.06% of the total French civilian labour force in 1986).

2.053 Several points are worth mentioning in regard to France and shipping. First, shipbuilding is quite important – for example, many of the largest liners in recent times have been built in France. The French government has consistently sought to encourage its shipping companies to build in France and thereby bolster French shipbuilding. This encouragement has given rise to complaints to the Commission about unlawful State aid to some French operators. Second, the government offered grants towards the acquisition of ships and operating subsidies. Third, there have been accelerated depreciation allowances in respect of shipping activities. Fourth, it was possible to create tax-free reserves from operating profits or from book profits resulting from the sale of a ship and these reserves may then be used for the purchase of new ships.

2.054 As of 1 January 2012, there were 255 ships under the control of French interests and they represented 10,091,000 dwt. Of these, 116 were flying the national flag (representing 3,213,000 dwt) with 139 flagged under foreign flags (representing 6,878,000 dwt).

2.055 UNCTAD reported some interesting statistics in 2017 about the French maritime sector. The French national flagged fleet had 6,905,000 dwt, the national owned fleet had 42,084,000 dwt, there had been 11,775 gt of ship scrapping and 5,207,128 teu in terms of container port throughput. Of the 6,905,400 dwt, some 3,563,400 dwt was represented by oil tankers, there were no bulk carriers, 111,400,000 dwt was represented by general cargo, 2,341,200 dwt was represented by container ships and 889,400 dwt was represented by other types of ships.

---

48 Oxford Economics report, op. cit. at fn. 2.

Germany

2.056 The German fleet is very significant in both EU and global terms. The vessels are also relatively young. The German shipping fleet is particularly strong in terms of container vessels with traditionally over a third of the EU's container vessel fleet.

2.057 It is interesting to review the number of ships. In the late 1950s, the Federal Republic of Germany had about 2,200 ships flying its flag; by the late 1960s, this had risen to over 2,800; but by the late 1970s, it had fallen to about 1,850 and by the late 1980s, it had fallen to around 1,200. On 1 January 2007, the reunified German fleet of 1,000 dwt or more vessels numbered 2,942. Of these, 87% were flagged out. It was reported that

> "[a]t the end of 2007, the German merchant fleet consisted of 3,232 vessels, totalling 66.4 million gt, its largest size ever. During the last four years, the fleet has doubled in size. Since 1998, it has achieved a growth rate of 15.6% a year on average. Due to the high inflow of new, modern tonnage, Germany has become the third largest shipping nation in the world. In its core business – container shipping – it even leads the global market with 36% of the controlled container vessel fleet."[49]

Germany has about 21% of the EU gross tonnage or 19% of the EU deadweight tonnage. The rate of growth in the German controlled fleet between 2005 and 2014 was even stronger at 128% over this period than the EU average.

2.058 At the start of 1990, the tonnage registered under the Federal Republic of Germany's flag was only marginally better than it was in 1957. It had about four million gross tons of ships flying its flag but this is less than half the tonnage flying the flag during the mid-1970s. On 1 January 2007, the total tonnage of German controlled vessels of more than 1,000 dwt amounted to 85,330,000 dwt. Of this, 85% was flagged out.

2.059 As of 1 January 2012, there were 3,916 ships under the control of German interests and they represented 125,496,000 dwt. Of these, 390 were flying the national flag (representing 17,495,000 dwt) with 3,526 flagged under foreign flags (representing 108,001,000 dwt).

2.060 In 1986, there were 20,470 persons employed in the merchant marine (representing 0.08% of the total civilian labour force in 1986) and 38,118 persons employed in shipbuilding (representing 0.02% of the total civilian labour force in 1985).

2.061 Germany's fleet has also been rejuvenated by a very high number of newbuilds – these newbuilds have centred on container traffic. The German government has offered grants towards the acquisition of ships. Shipbuilding is very important because Germany has a large shipbuilding industry. Of the 1,025 ships of over 1,000 grt owned by German parent companies on 19 March 1990, 53.7% were registered there with the bulk of the others registered in Cyprus, Antigua, Liberia and Panama. It has been possible to create tax-free reserves from operating profits or from book profits resulting from the sale of a ship and these reserves may then be used for the purchase of new ships. Germany established a second register in April 1989, the so-called German International Register (the "GIS"). German seafaring unions opposed it. Nonetheless shipping companies there regard it as a success because it has halted the flight of ships from the traditional German register to offshore registries around the world. In March 1990, it was reckoned that about

---

49 Oxford Economics report, op. cit. at fn. 2.

40% of the ships of the (then) Federal Republic of Germany were on the GIS. The Court of Justice of the European Union ("CJEU") upheld the second register in terms of its compatibility with EU State aid law. By October 1990, the GIS fleet amounted to 427 vessels of 2.8 million grt. Part of the traffic from what was East Germany (or the German Democratic Republic) flows through Hamburg which is, after all, one of the largest ports in Europe.

2.062 UNCTAD reported some interesting statistics in 2017 that, in 2016, the German national flagged fleet had 11,020,000 dwt but the owned fleet amounted to 119,181,000 dwt, there has been 2,541 dwt of ship scrapping and a very significant 19,866,700 teu in terms of container port throughput. Of the 11,020,100 dwt, some 476,200 dwt were oil tankers, 322,400 dwt were bulk carriers, 210,400 dwt was general cargo tonnage, 9,793,200 dwt were container ships and 217,900 dwt were other types of ships. It is clear that container vessels represent a very large proportion of the tonnage. The German fleet has varied in size from 9,381,000 dwt in 2005 to 17,570,200 in 2010 to 12,537,800 in 2015 and then down further to 11,020,100 in 2016.

Greece

2.063 Greece acceded to the EU in 1981. In general terms, Greece is the most important shipping nation within the EU at present – at various times, it has always represented a very significant part of the EU shipping sector. In 2016, it had over 4% of the world's fleet in terms of Greek flagged vessels but it had 16% of the world's fleet in terms of ownership.

2.064 In terms of the number of ships, the growth in the number of ships under the Greek flag has been spectacular. In 1957, there were fewer than 400 ships under the Greek flag but by 1980 this figure had reached almost 4,000. Unfortunately, this figure fell back by 1991 to just under 1,900 but the growth was still significant. On 1 January 2007, the Greek controlled fleet numbered 3,041 which would be equivalent to 28.8% of the EU fleet. Of the Greek controlled fleet on 1 January 2007, 77% was flagged out. Greece has the largest controlled fleet within the EU with about 36% of the EU gross tonnage or 43% of dwt. The rate of growth in the Greek controlled fleet between 2005 and 2014 was broadly in line with the EU average.[50]

2.065 In terms of tonnage, just as the growth in the number of ships was spectacular, so too was the growth in the tonnage under the Greek flag. In 1957, there were less than two million grt under the Greek flag but by 1980, this had risen over 20-fold to over 41 million grt. By 1991, this had fallen back to 22.8 million grt. It has capacity of around 7.5 million dwt. On 1 January 2007, the Greek controlled fleet represented 46.2% of the EU fleet in terms of tonnage. Of the Greek controlled tonnage on 1 January 2007, 71.1% was flagged out.

2.066 As of 1 January 2012, there were 3,214 ships under the control of Greek interests and they represented 217,149,000 dwt. Of these, 737 were flying the national flag (representing 64,897,000 dwt) with 2,477 flagged under foreign flags (representing 152,252,000 dwt). Greece is therefore the largest shipowning Member State.

---

50 Oxford Economics report, op. cit. at fn. 2.

2.067 In 1986, there were 31,934 persons employed in the merchant marine (representing 0.9% of the total Greek civilian labour force in 1986) and 6,328 persons employed in ship-building (representing 0.2% of the total Greek civilian labour force in 1986). The proportion of marine jobs to total civilian jobs is higher in Greece than any other Member State.

2.068 Greece has specialised in the tramp or bulk markets and now has one of the largest bulk carrier fleets in the world. The Greek government has offered grants towards the purchase of ships. It is also very strong in ferries. Of the 2,423 ships owned by Greek parent companies on 19 March 1990, only about 40% were registered on the Greek registry with large numbers registered in Cyprus (24%), Panama (12%), Liberia (6.6%) and Malta (6.6%). The move to open registries intensified during the 1980s and 1990s. A significant portion of Greece's external trade is carried on board Greek ships. The Greek tax regime is particularly attractive for shipping. The European Commission in its August 1989 publication, "Financial and Fiscal Measures Concerning Shipping Operations with Ships Registered in the Community", analysed the tax regimes of each of the Member States as they relate to shipping and concluded that the Greek system, whereby shipping companies are subject only to a tonnage tax, is advantageous at times of medium and high profit. Greece has supported open liner conferences but closed cabotage services. Free movement of EU seafarers has applied to Greece since 1 January 1988. The accession of Greece to the EU had a huge impact on shipping in the EU. Beyer de Ryke, a Member of the European Parliament, asked the Commission: "can the Commission provide a full report on the economic effects in [the maritime chartering] sector of Greece's entry into the common market and its consequences for chartering in other Member States?" Commissioner Contogeorgis answered:

> "[as] at April 1st 1981, the Greek merchant fleet, at 38.4 million grt represented about 10% of the world fleet and about 36.5% of the [EU] fleet. The accession of Greece increased the [EU] fleet by some 57%. The [EU] fleet now represents rather over 27% of the world fleet. It is difficult to evaluate the consequences of this addition to the Community's merchant fleet, as the Greek merchant fleet, unlike those of many of the other Member States, is mainly engaged in transport of bulk cargoes. This is a worldwide transport market in which shipowners may generally participate freely, without regard to nationality, and in which there is little flag discrimination. As far as the method of chartering vessels is concerned, membership of the Community is not likely to lead to any major changes in this particular sector of the shipping market. This is especially true as far as the allocation of cargoes and freight rates are concerned."

2.069 On the other hand, it is clear that the importance of the Greek merchant fleet lends added weight to the EU in all international negotiations concerning shipping matters, especially those on the open registry and bulk shipping questions within the framework of UNCTAD and the Organisation for Economic Co-operation and Development ("OECD"), in the work on shipping safety in IMO (International Maritime Organization) and in the current discussions connected with the establishment of a second Hague Memorandum on Port State Control.

2.070 The accession of some Balkan countries to the EU and changes in the energy market (e.g. new pipelines in the region) has further enhanced the role and strategic significance of Greece as a shipping location.

2.071 Shipping is Greece's primary economic sector employing thousands of seafarers including many highly trained personnel. The maritime cluster generally employs even more people, representing about 5% of the country's workforce.

2.072 UNCTAD reported some interesting statistics in 2017 that the national flagged fleet had 73,445,000 dwt, the national owned fleet had 293,087,000 (four times more than the flagged fleet) and it had 3,934,713 teu in terms of container port throughput. Of the 77,445,300 dwt, some 45,848,800 dwt were oil tankers, 24,612,900 dwt were bulk carriers, 173,000 dwt was general cargo, 819,600 dwt were container ships and 1,990,900 dwt were other types of ships.

Hungary

2.073 Hungary is a landlocked state and it is, therefore, not relevant in the case of EU shipping law. Nonetheless, there is a small number of seafarers living in Hungary with the majority being officers rather than ratings.

Ireland

2.074 Ireland acceded to the EU in 1973 along with Denmark and the UK and is one of the smaller shipping States in the EU. Shipping is however of considerable strategic significance for Ireland (an island) as the vast bulk of its imports and exports of goods are carried by sea.

2.075 Ireland has more ships now than it did in 1957 when the European Economic Community ("EEC") was founded or in 1973 when it acceded. Indeed, Ireland has seen a consistent growth in ship numbers since the mid-1970s, after a period of remarkable consistency in numbers during the period 1957 to 1977.

2.076 While Ireland has had good fortune in terms of ship numbers over the 1957–1989 period, it has not been so fortunate in terms of tonnage during that same period. While it has almost doubled the tonnage under its flag during that period, it has lost the gains made during the 1970s. At mid-1989 the gross tonnage of ships registered in Ireland was 167,000.

2.077 As of 1 January 2012, there were 54 ships under the control of Irish interests and they represented 492,000 dwt. Of these, 24 were flying the national flag (representing 158,000 dwt) with 30 flagged under foreign flags (representing 334,000 dwt).

2.078 Ireland's fleet is, in relative terms, small compared to its EU counterparts. The fleet comprises mainly fishing vessels, ferries and small freighters. The Irish government has offered grants towards the purchase of ships. The Shipping Investment Grants Act 1987 provided some funding towards the acquisition of certain types of ships less than seven years old. This Act was a successor to an earlier Act of 1969. Of the 51 ships owned on 19 March 1990 by Irish parent companies, 42 (i.e. 82%) were registered on the Irish flag with only a few almost evenly divided between the Bahamas, the UK and Panama. The Irish taxation regime is particularly favourable towards the shipping industry. The Business Expansion Scheme ("BES") – a tax scheme whereby the purchase of shares in certain types of, *inter alia*, shipping companies attracts tax relief – helped foster some shipping companies. Ireland now has a tonnage tax regime. In recent years, impressive work has been done by the Irish Maritime Development Office ("IMDO")[51] in trying to develop the Irish maritime sector.

---

51 www.imdo.ie.

2.079 UNCTAD reported in 2017 some interesting statistics relating to 2016, namely, that the national flagged fleet had 305,000 dwt, the national owned fleet had 1,883,000 dwt and there was a container port throughput of 793,105 teu. Of the 305,100 dwt, the vast majority were bulk carriers (200,700 dwt) and general cargo (95,900 dwt) with a tiny amount in terms of oil carriers and other types of ships. The ferries operating to and from Ireland are all flagged abroad.

Italy

2.080 Italy, one of the founder members of the EU, has always been a strong maritime nation. In terms of tonnage, it has traditionally been second only to Greece. The gross registered tonnage registered under its flag fell from 9,157,867 in 1984 to 7,602,032 in 1989. The ports of Genoa and Venice are bustling and significant ports. Cruising has become even more significant in Italian waters.

2.081 The number of ships under the Italian flag was quite consistent during the 1957–1989 period with only marginal variation over that time frame. In the late 1950s, it had around 1,250 ships and, in 1989, it had around 1,500 ships. On 1 January 2007, there were 677 Italian controlled vessels of more than 1000 grt according to the EU but the ECSA reported that:

"[a]t the end of 2007, the Italian owned merchant fleet consisted 1,535 ships, with a total of 13,970,38 gt, distributed as follows: over 1,000 gt, 738 vessels totalling 13,712,746 gt; from 100 to 999 gt, 797 vessels totalling 257,601 gt. ... The units entered in the Italian International Register number 606 totalling 12,465,231 gt, equal to 89% of the Italian-owned merchant fleet. The ships entered in the Ordinary Register number 922 with a total of 1,475,700 gt, while the number of Italian-owned ships temporarily flying a foreign flag (bare-boat charter registration) currently number only 6, totally 27,930 gt.

The part of the fleet controlled by nationals whose capital is all or predominantly private is equal to more than 95.6% of the total, while the portion controlled by the public sector shows a constant decline. The Italian fleet is young, both in absolute terms and compared to the world-wide average: approximately 57% of vessels are less than 10 years old and 33% less than 5 years old. During the period 1998–2007, delivery was made of 481 units totalling 6.9 mn gt, while, at the end of 2007, there were 97 units under construction in Italian and foreign shipyards, totalling 1.4 mn tons.

... The maritime cluster produces about €38,850 mn, equivalent to 2.7% of GDP, and the same as to the agricultural sector...

Without doubt, the competitive revival of the Italian fleet can be traced to the reform of international navigation undertaken in 1998, with the approval of Law no. 30. This established the Italian International Register."

2.082 In 1957, the gross registered tonnage was around 4,500,000, by 1970 this had risen to 7,000,000 grt, by 1979 this had risen to the high of over 11,500,000 grt but, by 1989, it had fallen back to 7,500,000 grt. On 1 January 2007, the 677 Italian controlled vessels amounted to 15,364,000 dwt.

2.083 As of 1 January 2012, there were 755 ships under the control of Italian interests and they represented 24,415,000 dwt. Of these, 533 were flying the national flag (representing 18,106,000 dwt) with 202 flagged under foreign flags (representing 6,309,000 dwt).

2.084 Italian shipowners are relatively hesitant to flag out their vessels. Of the 722 vessels over 1,000 grt owned by Italian parent companies on 19 March 1990, 679 (i.e.

94%) were on the Italian register. Of the 677 Italian controlled vessels on 1 January 2007, less than a quarter in terms of number (22.6%) and tonnage (24.7%) was flagged out. The Italian government has offered grants towards the purchase of ships. There are accelerated depreciation allowances in respect of shipping activities. The fleet is dominated by tankers and bulk carriers as well as passenger vessels.

2.085 UNCTAD reported in 2017 some interesting statistics for 2016 that the national flagged fleet had 16,433,000 dwt, the national owned fleet had 22,739,000 dwt and there had been 10,260,00 teu in terms of container port throughput. Of the 16,432,700 dwt, some 5,692,200 dwt were oil tankers, 5,846,000 dwt were bulk carriers, 1,665,800 dwt was in general cargo, container ships represented 623,400 dwt and 2,605,200 dwt involved other types of ships.

Latvia

2.086 Latvia acceded to the EU in 2004. The maritime sector then accounted for around 60,000 jobs in Latvia. The traditional maritime sectors accounted for more than two-thirds of those jobs. Shipbuilding and marine equipment have been important. As at 1 January 2007, shipping was significant with 132 ships (over 1,000 dwt) controlled amounting to 1.63 million dwt but only 18 of those were registered on the national flag. The fleet grew considerably in tonnage but declined in number. It consisted mainly of micro dry bulk carriers. There were around 18,000 Latvian seafarers. Its ports employed just over 11,000 people. As of 1 January 2012, there were 68 ships under the control of Latvian interests and they represented 1,159,000 dwt. Of these, three were flying the national flag (representing only 10,000 dwt) with 65 flagged under foreign flags (representing 1,149,000 dwt).

2.087 The main port is Riga which is located in the southern part of the Gulf of Riga on the Baltic Sea at the estuary of the river Daugava. It is a multifunctional port which handles all types of cargo except for crude oil. In 2014, cargo turnover at the port reached 41.1 million tons and it grew by 8.4% per year on average during the previous decade. Around 80% of cargo handled at Riga is transit traffic. Riga is currently the biggest port in the Baltic States handling approximately 27% of the region's total cargo turnover in 2014. The Freeport of Riga, which is the main port, is engaged in a major relocation project, the Krievu Sala project which involves developing a new port infrastructure measuring 56 hectares and increasingly attracting cruise ships.

2.088 UNCTAD reported in 2017 some interesting statistics for 2016 that the national flagged fleet had 103,000 dwt, the national owned fleet had 969,000 dwt and 391,200 teu was handled in terms of container port throughput. The bulk of the flagged tonnage was general cargo vessels (75,000 dwt) with the rest divided between oil tankers (8,900 dwt) and other types of vessel (19,400 dwt).

Lithuania

2.089 Lithuania acceded to the EU in 2004. Transport and logistics accounted for about 13% of the country's GDP and employed about 4% of the population.

2.090 On 1 January 2007, the Lithuanian controlled fleet amounted to 57 vessels. Of these, the vast majority, 71.9%, were on the Lithuanian flag. The ECSA Annual Report for 2007–2008 reported a slightly different picture but the trend of growth and dynamism was mirrored in the report: "[a]ll in all, 155 ships with a total of 436,934 gt were registered with the Register of Seagoing Ships of the Republic of Lithuania at the beginning of 2008". The ECSA Annual Report for 2007–2008 reported that the age of the majority of ships on the Lithuanian register was 18–20 years.

2.091 As of 1 January 2012, there were 55 ships under the control of Lithuanian interests and they represented 331,000 dwt. Thirty-three of them were flying the national flag (representing 251,000 dwt) with 22 flagged under foreign flags (representing 80,000 dwt).

2.092 Lithuania has introduced a tonnage tax system and reduced its social contribution taxes so as to stimulate shipping activity. The tonnage tax regime was approved in 2007. The social security tax changes were agreed in 2006 and approved by the European Commission.

2.093 UNCTAD reported in 2017 some interesting statistics about the situation in 2016 that the national flagged fleet had 258,000 dwt, the national owned fleet had 288,000 dwt (meaning a strong correlation between the size of the owned and flagged fleets) and 450,400 teu in terms of container port throughput. Of the 258,200 dwt, some 4,600 dwt were in oil tankers, 93,600 dwt were in bulk carriers, 83,100 dwt in general cargo, 21,000 dwt in container ships and the balance (55,900 dwt) were other types of ships. The fleet was fluctuated somewhat in size over time (412,000 dwt in 2005, 364,200 dwt in 2010, 268,900 in 2015 and 258,200 in 2016).

Luxembourg

2.094 It may appear strange in a book about shipping in the EU to include a section on Luxembourg, a landlocked Member State, but this State is important in a number of respects for present purposes. Luxembourg registered its first ship in 1988 and its second in 1989. At the end of 1989, there were two ships registered in Luxembourg with a gross tonnage of around 35,000. The creation of the register was an important development. It has been equivalent to a second registry for Belgium. Some companies may decide to register there because of the generous fiscal regime, well-established financial services centre, low administration costs and an efficient mortgage registration system. A proportion of the Belgian bulk carrier and tanker fleet moved to the Luxembourgeois register. As of 1 January 2012, there were 20 ships under the control of Luxembourgeois interests and they represented 1,331,000 dwt. Two of them were flying the national flag (representing 14,000 dwt) with 20 flagged under foreign flags (representing 1,331,000 dwt).

2.095 UNCTAD reported in 2017 some interesting statistics relating to 2016 that the national flagged fleet and the national owned fleet was exactly the same – 3,726,500 dwt. It had no container traffic (not surprisingly being inland). Of the 3,072,500 dwt, the largest component was container ships (1,447,600 dwt) with the rest made of bulk carriers (661,200 dwt), general cargo (115,300 dwt), oil tankers (14,900 dwt) and other ships (833,400 dwt). More significantly, the fleet grew from 919,000 dwt in 2005, to 1,099,800 dwt in 2010, 3,621,300 dwt in 2015 and 3,072,000 dwt in 2016.

Malta

2.096 Malta joined the EU in 2004. It is extremely important in maritime transport globally. On 1 January 2007, the Maltese controlled fleet comprised 17 ships with a total tonnage of 57,000 dwt. Of these, four were flagged out amounting to 20,000 dwt. As of 1 January 2012, there were 16 ships under the control of Maltese interests and they represented 53,000 dwt. Fourteen of them were flying the national flag (representing 45,000 dwt) with two flagged under foreign flags (representing 8,000 dwt). These statistics underestimate the role of Malta in shipping. This is because the Malta International Ship Register has an enormous number of ships on it. The register has grown over time. The register has grown due to its various advantages including efficiency, level of intervention, sophisticated maritime legislation, dynamic amendment of legislation, responsiveness, absence of nationality restrictions for masters/officers and crew, a network of impressive professions as well as Malta's membership of the EU. There are restrictions on older vessels from being registered at all or having to undergo further inspections. It is now one of the largest registers in the world and the second largest in the EU. Malta is on the White List of the Paris and Tokyo Memoranda of Understanding as well as the Low Risk Ship List of the Paris Memorandum of Understanding. It is a member of the Council of the IMO. It has been particularly strong also in terms of cruise liners visiting Malta (particularly Valletta) as well as container lines using Malta as a transhipment point. Malta is one of the largest registries in the EU. Indeed, it had the eighth largest fleet in the world on 1 June 2013 in terms of gross tonnage and was the largest of the EU Member States – ahead of Greece, Cyprus, the UK, Italy, Germany and so on. There are over 3,000 people employed in shipping in Malta with over 5,000 employed in ports and over 1,700 employed in shipbuilding.

2.097 UNCTAD reported in 2017 some interesting statistics relating to 2016, namely, that the national flagged fleet had 94,824,300 dwt, the national owned fleet had 1,399,000 dwt (demonstrating the power of the Maltese flag) and it had 2,949,036 teu in terms of container port throughput. Of the deadweight tonnage, some were oil tankers, some were bulk carriers, some were general cargo, some were container ships and some were other types of ships. The fleet has grown very significantly over time: from 36,101,000 dwt in 2005, 56,156,100 dwt in 2010, 86,379,300 dwt in 2015 and 94,823,300 dwt in 2016.

The Netherlands

2.098 The Netherlands has long been a strong maritime nation. The Dutch have traditionally been very strong in the liner (as opposed to tramp) sector. Today, it is particularly strong in the container sector. The Dutch fleet fell almost consistently in the period between 1957 and 1989: it fell from a level of about 1,900 ships in the late 1950s to about 1,250 in the late 1980s. Of the 656 ships (greater than 1,000 grt) registered on 19 March 1990, six were oil tankers, 48 were chemical and product carriers, 19 were liquid gas carriers, 25 were ore and bulk carriers, 29 were pure container ships, 350 were cargo ships, 17 were passenger ships and the remaining 162 were of various types. On 1 January 2007, the EU estimated that the Dutch controlled fleet was 620 of which 30.8% were flagged outside the Netherlands. The ECSA Annual Report for 2007–2008 estimated that at 1 January 2008, the total number in the Dutch fleet (i.e. the merchant navy and the seagoing towage industry) amounted to 748 ships with a total gross tonnage of 5.3 million.

2.099 The tonnage under the Dutch flag remained quite consistent for many years after 1957 despite the gyrations of the shipping market during that period. There were about 4,500,000 grt under the Dutch flag in the late 1950s and just under 4,000,000 grt by the end of the 1980s – although there were more than 5,000,000 tons registered under the Dutch flag throughout the 1960s and 1970s. In 1991, this was 3,900,000 tons. On 1 January 2007, the EU estimated that the Dutch controlled fleet amounted to 7,631,000 dwt of which 50.5% was flagged outside the Netherlands.

2.100 As of 1 January 2012, there were 725 ships under the control of Dutch interests and they represented 8,841,000 dwt. Of these, 531 were flying the national flag (representing 5,052,000 dwt) with 194 flagged under foreign flags (representing 3,789,000 dwt).

2.101 In 1986, there were 14,218 persons employed in the merchant marine (representing 0.3% of the total civilian labour force in 1986) and 15,300 persons employed in shipbuilding (representing 0.3% of the total civilian labour force in 1985). The ECSA Annual Report for 2007–2008 estimated that there were then only around 4,500 Dutch seafarers. The European Commission's Directorate General for Fisheries and Maritime Affairs believed that there were over 25,000 employed in ports directly and over 10,000 employed indirectly while there are almost 20,000 employed in shipping directly and over 5,000 employed indirectly. There are also over 10,000 employed directly in shipbuilding and 10,000 employed indirectly.

2.102 The Netherlands is very strong in terms of port services with Rotterdam being one of the world's busiest ports. The Netherlands is reasonably strong in terms of cargo ships but was relatively weak in terms of oil tankers and passenger ships. Of the 656 ships owned by Dutch parent companies on 19 March 1990, some 442 (i.e. 67%) were registered in the Netherlands and 37 (i.e. 5.6%) were registered in the Netherlands Antilles. It has been possible to create tax-free reserves from operating profits or from book profits resulting from the sale of a ship and these reserves may then be used for the purchase of new ships. The world's largest salvage operator is based in the Netherlands. The Netherlands has introduced measures to reduce the cost of employing Dutch seafarers by granting relief on personal taxation and social security. The Dutch government has a liberal approach to maritime transport. It adopted a policy which operated since 1996 which helped to promote shipping in the Netherlands but it has since adopted a policy entitled "Responsible Shipping and a Vital Fleet" for the timeframe 2008–2013. Rotterdam is the EU's largest port and around 70,000 people are employed in the port area.

2.103 UNCTAD reported in 2017 some interesting statistics about the position in 2016. The national flagged fleet had 7,992,100 dwt but the national owned fleet had 17,441,000 dwt showing a very high level of flagging out, 6,825 dwt of ship scrapping and, very significantly, 12,671,464 teu in terms of container port throughput. Of the 7,992,100 dwt, general cargo was the largest type of ship (4,397,700 dwt) with 217,500 dwt devoted to oil tankers, 217,500 dwt being bulk carriers, container ships amounted to 925,200 dwt and 1,830,900 dwt were other types of ships.

Poland

2.104 Poland is very significant in EU maritime matters. It acceded to the EU in 2004. In terms of the number of ships, the EU believed that on 1 January 2007, Polish interests controlled 108 vessels of 1,000 grt or more. Very few, ten, of these were registered on the Polish national register and these were the smaller vessels with the rest being registered abroad. The ECSA Annual Report for 2007–2008 estimated that at 1 January 2008, the total Polish controlled fleet amounted to 136 ships with a total gross tonnage of 1,839,300 or 2,482,000 dwt. Of these 136, 121 were ocean-going vessels and 15 were passenger vessels. However, only 17 of the 136 vessels recorded by the ECSA were Polish registered.

2.105 In terms of tonnage, the EU believed that on 1 January 2007, Polish interests controlled vessels amounting to 1,903,000 dwt. Of this tonnage, 97.7% (or 1,859,000 dwt) was registered abroad.

2.106 As of 1 January 2012, there were 110 ships under the control of Polish interests and they represented 2,776,000 dwt. Seven of them were flying the national flag (representing 15,000 dwt) with 103 flagged under foreign flags (representing 2,761,000 dwt, i.e. 99.5% by tonnage).

2.107 In terms of employment, the ECSA Annual Report for 2007–2008 estimated that at 1 January 2008 there were as many as 4,800 seafarers/officers employed by Polish shipowners. Employment in the shipbuilding sector has fallen over time.

2.108 The Polish Tonnage Tax Law of 24 August 2006 which had been enacted by the Polish Sejm and approved by the President proved controversial because the European Commission was concerned about it.

2.109 UNCTAD reported in 2017 that in 2016, the national flagged fleet had 101,900 dwt, the national owned fleet 2,593,000 dwt and 2,139,616 teu in terms of container port throughput. Of the 101,900 dwt, oil tankers (7,500 dwt), bulk carriers (0 dwt), general cargo (21,300 dwt) and container ships (7,600 dwt) were a small part but other types of ships (e.g. ferries) were the most significant (64,600 dwt). The size of the Polish fleet has been quite stable from 2005 to 2016 (101,000 dwt in 2005, 130,900 dwt in 2010, 107,400 dwt in 2015 and 100,900 dwt in 2016).

Portugal

2.110 In 1988, the Commission estimated that between 85% and 90% of the capacity of the Portuguese fleet belonged to companies under State control.

2.111 The number of ships under the Portuguese flag in 1989 was virtually identical to the number under that flag in 1957. Apart from a dramatic increase in numbers during the mid-1970s, the number of ships under the Portuguese flag had remained consistent at around 350 from the mid-1950s to the mid-1980s. The ECSA estimated that at the beginning of 2008, Portuguese shipowners controlled 50 ships. Of this total of 50, only 15 (i.e. 30%) were flying the conventional Portuguese flag, 21 (i.e. 42%) were flying the Madeira International Register flag and the balance of 14 were flagged out. A large proportion of the fleet (in terms of tonnage) consisted of oil tankers and large bulk tankers. The majority of the vessels registered were fishing vessels.

2.112 The tonnage registered under the Portuguese flag rose dramatically between the late 1950s (when it was just over 0.5 million gt) and the mid-1980s (when it reached over 1.5 million gt). It suffered a considerable decline in the late 1980s during which time the tonnage was more than halved. By 1991, the tonnage had fallen to less than one million gt. The ECSA estimated that at the beginning of 2008, Portuguese shipowners controlled ships totalling 485,413 grt. Of this total of 50, only 66,544 gt was under the conventional Portuguese flag, 70,129 gt was under the Madeira International Register flag and the balance of 348,740 gt (i.e. 72%) was flagged out.

2.113 As of 1 January 2012, there were 33 ships under the control of Portuguese interests and they represented 71,000 dwt. Four of them were flying the national flag (representing 22,000 dwt) with 29 flagged under foreign flags (representing 688,000 dwt).

2.114 In terms of employment, in 1985, there were 2,913 persons employed in the merchant marine (representing 0.07% of the total civilian labour force in 1986) and 14,150 persons employed in shipbuilding (representing 0.4% of the total civilian labour force in 1985).

2.115 Portugal is often underestimated as a maritime nation. Portugal has undergone an extensive privatisation programme and shipping companies such as Portline and Transinsular were prepared for sale. Portugal established an offshore registry in Madeira in 1989 but it has not been very successful in attracting tonnage. Of the 125 ships over 1,000 grt owned by Portuguese parent companies on 19 March 1990, 90 (i.e. 72%) were registered in Portugal with the balance registered mainly in Panama. The Portuguese government provides operating subsidies. There are also accelerated depreciation allowances in respect of shipping activities. There has been a long delay in the introduction of a tonnage tax regime for Portuguese shipping companies. The ECSA reported that at the beginning of 2008, Portuguese shipowners controlled 50 ships. The ECSA Annual Report 2007–2008 reported that, at the beginning of 2008, Portuguese shipowners controlled ships of a collective tonnage of 485,000,413 gt. Of the 50 ships reportedly controlled by Portuguese shipowners at the beginning of 2008, 15 were flying the conventional Portuguese flag, 21 were flying the Madeira international registers flag and 14 were flagged out. Of these, 42% in terms of tonnage were under the Madeira flag, 30% under the conventional flag and 28% were flagged out.

2.116 UNCTAD reported in 2017 some interesting statistics relating to 2016: the national flagged fleet had 8,889,900 dwt, the national owned fleet had 968,000 dwt (representing a very significant amount of flagging in) and there were 2,500,300 teu in terms of container port throughput. Of the 8,888,900 dwt, some 514,000 dwt were oil tankers, 2,574,000 dwt were bulk carriers, 256,000 dwt were general cargo, 256,700 dwt were container ships and 385,200 dwt were other types of ships. What is of more significance is how the size of the fleet has grown: the flagged fleet has grown from 1,757,000 in 2005, fell to 1,288,300 in 2010 but grew to 5,249,400 by 2015 and rose again to 8,888,900 in 2016.

Romania

2.117 On 1 January 2007, there were 60 vessels of 1,000 grt or more controlled by Romanian interests. They amounted to 855,000 tonnes. Most, 47 (78%), were registered outside Romania and the larger vessels were registered outside Romania (82.5% of the tonnage). As of 1 January 2012, there were 31 ships under the control of Romanian interests and they represented 554,000 dwt. Three of them were flying the national flag (representing 33,000 dwt) with 28 flagged under foreign flags (representing 521,000 dwt).

2.118 UNCTAD reported in 2017 that in 2016 the national flagged fleet had 58,400 dwt, the national owned fleet had 936,000 dwt (representing significant flagging out), 822,010 gt of shipbuilding and 668,349 teu in terms of container port throughput. Of the 58,400 dwt, some 6,400 dwt were oil tankers, general cargo represented 34,800 dwt and 17,200 dwt were other types of ships. More significantly for Romania, the fleet has fallen in size from 481,000 dwt in 2005, 244,10 dwt in 2010, to 55,000 dwt in 2015 and then 58,400 dwt in 2016.

Slovakia

2.119 Slovakia is landlocked. Nonetheless, there are reported to be around 1,500 people employed in the maritime sector. As of 1 January 2012, there were no ships owned by, or registered to, Slovakian interests. UNCTAD reported in 2017 that there was no fleet in 2016.

Slovenia

2.120 Slovenia acceded to the EU in 2004. It has a very short coastline of only 46 kilometres but it has 16 harbours on that coast. The Port of Koeper receives around 2,000 vessels annually handling around 12 million tonnes of cargo and is growing in significance for cruise liner traffic. Slovenia adopted a tonnage tax act in 2007. As of 1 January 2012, there were 27 ships under the control of Slovenian interests and they represented 936,000 dwt. All of them were flagged under foreign flags.

2.121 UNCTAD reported in 2017 that in 2016 the national owned fleet had 586,000 dwt but the national flagged fleet was tiny and there were 647,000 teu in terms of container port throughput. The fleet has remained small in size.

Spain

2.122 In terms of the number of ships, the Spanish fleet almost doubled in terms of ship numbers during the 1957–1989 period. In the late 1950s, there were just over 1,200 ships on the Spanish registry but by the late 1980s this reached just under 2,400. Spain, in common with a number of States, reached a high point (in terms of ship numbers) during the mid-1970s but then went into sustained decline. In 1979, 8.3 million gt were registered in Spain and just 3.6 million gt were registered in 1991. In 1988, it was estimated by the Commission that some 25% of the tonnage of the Spanish fleet was in the hands of the State.

2.123 Many of the ships were flagged out to flags of convenience. On 1 January 2008, the Spanish controlled fleet comprised 289 ships. On 1 January 2008, the Spanish controlled fleet amounted to 4,302,332 gt and 5,012,506 dwt. On 1 January 2008, 57.1% of the ships and 54.9% of the gross tonnage controlled by Spanish shipping companies sailed under the Spanish flag.

2.124 In terms of tonnage, in spite of a large number of ships, the tonnage registered under the Spanish flag is relatively low. At present, about four million gt are registered under the Spanish flag. This is more than twice the figure in the late 1950s but less than half of the amount registered in the late 1970s when Spanish tonnage was at its highest. Almost half of the tonnage was represented by oil tankers.

2.125 As of 1 January 2012, there were 228 ships under the control of Spanish interests and they represented 4,307,000 dwt. Ninety-six of them were flying the national flag (representing 1,315,000 dwt) with 132 flagged under foreign flags (representing 2,992,000 dwt).

2.126 In terms of employment, in 1986, there were 19,873 persons employed in the merchant marine (representing 0.2% of the total civilian labour force in 1986) and 22,996 persons employed in shipbuilding (representing 0.2% of the total civilian labour force in 1986).

2.127 Of the 535 ships of over 1,000 grt owned by Spanish parent companies on 19 March 1990, 445 (i.e. 83%) were registered in Spain with the bulk of the remainder registered in the Canary Islands or Panama. Spanish ships were used quite significantly in respect of the import of goods into Spain but not so much in respect of exports from Spain. The Spanish government offered grants towards the acquisition of ships. Traditionally, Spain was somewhat protectionist in its approach. The government provided operating subsidies. There were accelerated depreciation allowances in respect of shipping activities. It was possible to create tax-free reserves from operating profits or from book profits resulting from the sale of a ship and these reserves may then be used for the purchase of new ships. Spain had been very insistent about reserving cabotage traffic to Spanish registered vessels and thus resisted EU liberalisation measures. Spain argued for a long time against liberalisation of cabotage services and delayed liberalisation. The Canary Islands special register is seen as being particularly attractive. There have been several new bills in recent years. Ports are very important in Spain and provide considerable employment, particularly in regard to container traffic but also passenger traffic.

2.128 UNCTAD reported in 2017 that as of 2016, the national flagged fleet had 1,823,800 dwt, the national owned fleet had 2,409,000 dwt, there had been 980 gt of ship scrapping and an impressive 14,245,488 teu in terms of container port throughput. Of the 1,823,800 dwt, some 443,400 dwt were oil tankers, 10,900 dwt were bulk carriers, 181,500 dwt were general cargo, there was no container ship tonnage and 1,187,900 dwt were other types of ships.

Sweden

2.129 As at 31 December 1995, there were 621 ships registered under the Swedish flag. As at 1 January 2007, there were 327 ships controlled by Swedish entities but only 154 were flying the Swedish flag which amounted to just under 48% of the total number. More than 170 million tonnes of goods passed through Swedish ports in 2005. The turnover of the industry in 2004 was more than 33 billion SEK. Around 30 million passengers travel by ferries to and from Sweden. Shipping accounts for over 14,000 jobs with ports employing another 6,500 and shipbuilding representing around 2,500 jobs.

2.130 In terms of tonnage, as at 31 December 1995, the gross registered tonnage on the Swedish flag was 2,995,425. As at 1 January 2007, there were 327 ships controlled by Swedish entities amounting to 6,255,000 dwt.

2.131 As of 1 January 2012, there were 287 ships under the control of Swedish interests and they represented 6,262,000 dwt. Eighty-eight of them were flying the national flag (representing 1,049,000 dwt) with 199 flagged under foreign flags (representing 5,212,000 dwt).

2.132 UNCTAD reported in 2017 that as of 2016, the national flagged fleet had 1,352,000 dwt, the national owned fleet had 6,104,000 dwt (representing significant flagging out) and there had 1,446,200 teu in container port throughput. Of the 1,352,200 dwt, 22,900 dwt was represented by oil tankers, 504,000 dwt was represented by general cargo and 825,400 dwt was represented by other types of ship. The Swedish fleet has fallen in size over the period of 2005 (2,191,000 dwt)/2010 (2,206,300 dwt) to 2015 (1,456,800 dwt)/2016 (1,352,200 dwt).

United Kingdom

2.133 As is well known, the UK (with the longest coastline in the EU) has a fine record in shipping. Estimates of the value of the sector vary but it is, by any measure, a huge contributor to the UK economy. However, since the late 1950s, the UK has sadly seen a steady decline.[52] Large-scale shipbuilding ended in the 1980s. The number of ships registered under its flag has declined too. The UK's ports are no longer as relatively significant to global trade as they once were. The decline is probably due to several factors: (a) the structural changes in shipping worldwide; (b) the decline of the UK in relative terms in global trade (e.g. with the emergence of other States and trading blocs worldwide); and (c) the lack of government subsidies at times coupled with high labour costs and standards in the UK. Around 95% of international trade to, and from, the UK passes through ports. The turnover of those ports is significant. The short sea traffic through UK ports is the highest of any Member State. A major report published in September 2015, entitled *Maritime Growth Study: Keeping the UK Competitive in a Global Market*,[53] estimated that in 2013, shipping alone directly contributed around £1.8 billion to the UK's trade balance which represented about 2% of the UK's overall surplus in services trade while ports and related services in the UK accounted for over 40,000 jobs. Shipbuilding and marine equipment accounts for more jobs and while the latter has grown, the former has fallen. Offshore gas and oil is important and the UK is home to over a third of all employees in the EU in that sector. The City of London earns a considerable amount from shipping activities. The City is the location of a third of all maritime service related jobs in the EU and generates enormous sums in overseas earnings. The owners of about 20% of the world's tonnage have offices in London. The City is seen as the centre of activity for maritime finance, law, brokerage and certification of vessels.

2.134 In 2017, a report for UK Maritime estimated that the shipping industry made a substantial macroeconomic contribution to the UK economy: £13.9 billion in business turnover, £4.3 billion in gross value added and 152,000 jobs (with 51,000 jobs for UK employees) in 2015.[54]

---

52 E.g. see "Britain's Maritime Industry under Pressure to Heighten its Profile" in *International Shipping News*, 8 September 2015.

53 www.gov.uk/government/uploads/system/uploads/attachment_data/file/458265/maritime-growth-study-keeping-UK-competitive.pdf.

54 *The Economic Contribution of the UK Shipping Industry: A Report for Maritime UK* (2017) which was prepared by Cebr.

2.135 In terms of the number of ships, on 19 March 1990, of 998 ships (greater than 1,000 grt) owned by UK parent companies, 99 were oil tankers, 87 were chemical and product carriers, 36 were liquid gas carriers, five were combination carriers, 85 were ore and bulk carriers, 78 were pure container ships, 240 were cargo ships, 81 were passenger ships and the remaining 287 were of various types. The size of the UK registered fleet is not a true indicator of the real involvement of the UK in shipping. About half of the UK owned tonnage was registered on other British flag registries (e.g. Isle of Man and Hong Kong) and one-fifth was registered in non-British registries. The UK fleet represented about one-tenth of the EU registered fleet. On 1 January 2007, UK interests controlled 652 vessels of more than 1,000 grt and they amounted to 24.97 million dwt. Some 269 of those were registered in the UK.

2.136 In terms of tonnage, in 1975 the gross tonnage was around 32,200,000 grt; this was the highest tonnage in the entire 1957–1989 period. In 1984, the tonnage was 15,874,062 grt. By 1989, this had fallen to 7,200,000 grt and, by 1991, to 6,600,000 grt. On 1 January 2007, UK interests controlled 652 vessels of more than 1,000 grt and they amounted to 24.97 million dwt. Some 269 of those were registered in the UK which was around 36% of the total UK controlled tonnage.

2.137 As of 1 January 2012, there were 748 ships under the control of UK interests and they represented 40,280,000 dwt. Of these, 330 were flying the national flag (representing 13,172,000 dwt) with 418 flagged under foreign flags (representing 27,108,000 dwt).

2.138 In terms of employment, in 1976 there were 58,333 UK nationals employed as seafarers. In 1986, there were 29,781 persons employed in the merchant marine (representing 0.1% of the total civilian labour force in 1986) and 11,694 persons employed in shipbuilding (representing 0.5% of the total civilian labour force in 1986). By 1989, only 17,838 UK nationals were employed as seafarers with 7,892 being officers and 9,946 being ratings.

2.139 UNCTAD reported in 2017 some interesting statistics relating to 2016: the national flagged fleet had 37,421,000 dwt, the national owned fleet was higher with 51,614,000 dwt, there had been 2,876 gt of ship scrapping and 9,417,570 teu in terms of container port throughput. Of the 37,421,000 dwt, some 9,889,000 dwt were oil tankers, 11,928,000 dwt were bulk carriers, 1,009,000 dwt was in general cargo, 9,301,400 dwt was in container ships and 5,293,800 dwt were other types of ships. The UNCTAD data also shows that the UK's fleet has grown in tonnage from 2005 (23,161,000 dwt) to 2016 (37,421,700 dwt). It has remained stable in size between 2010 (36,887,200 dwt) to 2015 (38,863,800 dwt).

2.140 The UK government reported that the gross tonnage on the UK's ship register grew 7% in the year to the end of 2017 and was 16,200,000 gt at the end of 2017. This represented three years of consecutive growth (i.e. 18% growth since the end of 2014). However, the UK represented only 0.8% of the world fleet on a deadweight tonnage basis and 1.2% on a gross tonnage basis. The UK registered fleet was the eighteenth largest in the world on a deadweight tonnage basis while the wider "red ensign" group[55] amounted to the tenth largest fleet.

---

55 I.e. the shipping registers of the UK, the Crown Dependencies and the Overseas Territories.

2.141 The penultimate chapter of this book deals with Brexit – the expected departure of the UK and Gibraltar from the EU – and it is quite likely that the impact of Brexit will be material and significant for UK shipping and ports – views differ whether the impact will be positive or negative but it will be both material and significant.

I. CONCLUSIONS

2.142 Despite being one of the oldest trades in human history, there is no sign whatsoever that it is in terminal decline; on the contrary, the globalisation of trade means that there is an increase in shipping activity. One of the challenges facing the EU in the years ahead is to strike a balance between a desire to have its own fleet (despite strong world competition) and a desire to have an effective competition policy. The EU's Economic and Social Committee commented as long ago as 1986 that ships registered in

> "Member States are important cross-traders between other Member States and third countries and between third countries only. They face strong competition from flag of convenience shipping under other flags, and are threatened by the increasing trend towards cargo reservation and the desire of many non-[EU] States to build up their fleets."[56]

The position is still accurate more than three decades later.

---

56 http://aei.pitt.edu/41822/1/A5965.pdf.

CHAPTER 3

An overview of the European Union and European Union Law

A. INTRODUCTION

3.001 This chapter provides a general overview of the law, legal system, policies and institutions of the European Union ("EU").[1] An understanding of EU law is vital to understand fully the subsequent chapters. The inclusion of such a chapter is useful because many readers could be maritime or non-EU lawyers who are unfamiliar with this area of law.

3.002 The legal consequences for each Member State of its involvement in the EU are very significant. The EU is, in the words of the Court of Justice of the European Union ("CJEU"), "a new legal order of international law".[2] Every citizen of a Member State has acquired new rights and duties.[3] A Member State is liable to citizens where it breaches EU law; for example, a Member State may even be liable to pay damages to an individual resulting from a manifest infringement of EU law by a Member State court.[4] There is hardly a sector of the economy which is not affected: be it agriculture, banking, energy or transport.[5] The consequences of EU membership are equally significant through social, environmental, employment and regional development policies; for example, there is a prohibition on discrimination in terms of pay on the basis of gender and obligations on employers to treat employees in accordance with standards which are higher than those which might have otherwise operated in Member State law. And, politically, the EU represents a transfer of some aspects of sovereignty by the Member States to the Union.[6]

---

1 On EU law generally, see Chalmers, Davies and Monti, *European Union Law: Text and Materials* (3rd ed., 2014); Craig and De Búrca, *EU Law: Text, Cases and Materials* (6th ed., 2015); Hartley, *The Foundations of European Union Law* (7th ed., 2010); Foster, *Foster on EU Law* (5th ed., 2015); Mathijsen, *A Guide to European Union Law* (11th ed., 2013); Steiner and Woods, *EU Law* (11th ed., 2014); as well as Wyatt and Dashwood, *The Substantive Law of the EEC* (6th ed., 2011).

2 Case 26/62 *Van Gend en Loos v Nederlandse Administratie der Belastingen* [1963] ECR 1, ECLI:EU:C:1963:1.

3 E.g. there may be no discrimination in matters covered by the Treaty on the Functioning of the European Union ("TFEU") between citizens of Member States (TFEU, Art. 18). *Cf.* Case 167/73 *Commission v France* [1974] ECR 359, ECLI:EU:C:1974:35 (on discrimination between EU seafarers in terms of nationality).

4 Case C-173/03 *Traghetti del Mediterraneo v Repubblica Italiano* [2006] ECR I-5177, ECLI:EU:C:2006:391 (see Ruffert (2007) 44 CMLRev 479).

5 See chap. 4 for the effects of EU law generally on transport.

6 See Case 26/62 *Van Gend en Loos v Nederlandse Administratie der Belastingen* [1963] ECR 1, ECLI:EU:C:1963:1. The EU has legal personality and legal capacity: see Treaty on the European Union ("TEU"), Art. 47 and TFEU, Art. 335 and Joined Cases 43/59 etc. *Lachmuller v Commission* [1960] ECR 463, ECLI:EU:C:1960:37.

B. THE EUROPEAN UNION

Introduction

3.003 The EU is an international organisation of the most extraordinary variety. Apart from the EU, there is also the European Atomic Energy Community ("EAEC") which is separate from the EU but is, in practical terms, interlinked by shared institutions organs and resources. The EAEC and the EU are collectively referred to as the EU for present purposes though the EAEC is not often relevant for those in the shipping sector and hence will not be addressed much in this book. The EU operates principally in the political, economic, social and financial spheres while the EAEC's activities are confined to the field of nuclear energy. Before examining the EU in more depth, it is useful to place them in their overall and historical contexts.

European Coal and Steel Community ("ECSC")

3.004 Before the European Economic Community ("EEC") and the EAEC were created in 1957, the ECSC had been established and was seen by its six Member States to be working successfully.[7] The ECSC was founded on 18 April 1951 under the Treaty of Paris which was signed by Belgium, the (then) Federal Republic of Germany (i.e. West Germany), France, Italy, Luxembourg and the Netherlands.[8] Over time, other States joined the ECSC at the same time as they joined the EAEC and what is now the EU. However, the ECSC's practical significance declined over time as coal and steel became, in relative terms, less significant given that the EU covered every economic sector (other than nuclear energy which is within the remit of the EAEC). The ECSC is now defunct as its 50 year mandate, under the ECSC Treaty, has expired. The operation of the ECSC was confined to the coal and steel sectors[9] – two economic sectors which were critical in the European economy and political world of the early 1950s. The ECSC had as its task

> "to contribute, in harmony with the general economy of the Member States and through the establishment of a common market [in coal and steel], to economic expansion, growth of employment and a rising standard of living in the Member States".[10]

It had to

> "progressively bring about conditions which will of themselves ensure the most rational distribution of production at the highest possible level of productivity, while safeguarding continuity of employment and taking care not to provoke fundamental and persistent disturbances in the economies of Member States".[11]

---

7 On the ECSC, see, in particular, Reuter, *La CECA* (1953).

8 Cmnd 7460; 261 UNTS 141. The Treaty entered into force on 25 July 1952. An annotated text is published in Simmonds (ed.), *Encyclopedia of Community Law*, vol. BI.

9 This is in contrast to the EEC (later, the European Community ("EC")) or the EU which applied (or apply) to virtually all sectors of the economy (other than coal and steel while the ECSC Treaty operated, or nuclear power which is regulated, for the most part, by the EAEC Treaty).

10 ECSC Treaty, Art. 2. The term "common market" has now been replaced by the term "internal market" in EU law.

11 ECSC Treaty, Art. 2. Cf. ECSC Treaty, Art. 3, for the objectives of the ECSC institutions.

When first drafted, the ECSC Treaty contemplated a High Authority (a permanent executive supra-national body),[12] a Special Council of Ministers (to harmonise the actions of the High Authority and Member States), a Common Assembly (or Parliament, with no legislative powers but with some supervisory functions)[13] and a Court of Justice (to resolve legal disputes). Under Article 97 of the ECSC Treaty, the ECSC would exist for 50 years only and so the ECSC came to an end in 2002. Coal and steel were then subsumed into the general (then) EC regime (and now the EU regime).[14] It is not too surprising that the ECSC had little significance for shipping (it was relevant to shipping only in so far as the ECSC was interested in shipping rates for the transport of coal and steel) so there will be little reference to the ECSC elsewhere in this book.

EAEC

3.005 The EAEC was founded by the Treaty of Rome (a separate treaty from the one which established the EEC but also signed on 25 March 1957), which became effective on 1 January 1958. Initially, the EAEC or Euratom was composed of the "Six" (i.e. Belgium, France, the (then)[15] Federal Republic of Germany, Italy, Luxembourg and the Netherlands), but has since been joined by all the other States which joined the EU. The task of the EAEC is to contribute to raising of the standard of living in the Member States and to the development of relations with each other by creating the conditions necessary for the speedy establishment and growth of nuclear industries.[16] Its sphere of operation is limited to the nuclear energy sector and is not of any great significance to shipping companies.[17]

EEC/EC/EU

3.006 The EEC was established by Article 1 of the Treaty of Rome (a treaty separate to the EAEC Treaty) which was also signed in Rome[18] on 25 March 1957 which became effective on 1 January 1958 and has been amended by a number of other treaties.[19] Initially, it was also composed of the "Six" (i.e. Belgium, France, the (then) Federal Republic of Germany, Italy, Luxembourg and the Netherlands), but now has 28 Member States (i.e. Austria, Belgium, Bulgaria, Croatia, Cyprus, Czech Republic, Denmark, Estonia, Finland, France, Germany, Greece, Hungary, Ireland, Italy, Latvia, Lithuania, Luxembourg, Malta, Netherlands, Poland, Portugal, Romania, Slovakia, Slovenia, Spain, Sweden and the United Kingdom). Following the entry into force of the Treaty on the European Union ("TEU") signed at Maastricht on 7 February 1992, the "EEC" became

---

12 ECSC Treaty, Art. 18 (in its original form). The High Authority was abolished in 1967 by the Merger Treaty. The High Authority became the Commission.
13 ECSC Treaty, Art. 24 (as originally drafted).
14 There is no time limit on the EU.
15 I.e. excluding the German Democratic Republic or East Germany.
16 EAEC Treaty, Art. 1. The hopes and ambitions in the 1950s for the nuclear energy sector would be difficult to understand today.
17 Except nuclear-powered ships in an indirect way.
18 Hence, it was often known as the Treaty of Rome.
19 E.g. the Merger Treaty, the Single European Act, the Maastricht Treaty, the Treaty of Amsterdam, the Treaty of Nice and the Treaty of Lisbon.

the EC. On 1 December 2009, on the entry into force of the Treaty of Lisbon, the EC became the EU. Now the EC has disappeared and been replaced by the EU. While the change from the EC to the EU was cosmetic in some respects, the symbolism of a "Union" (as opposed to a community) and its increased powers were substantial changes for many observers.

3.007 The EU now has a wide range of objectives and competences spanning many areas including transport, competition, the environment, safety, employment, social security, taxation and so on. Member States are obliged to "take all appropriate measures, whether general or particular, to ensure fulfilment of the obligations arising out of [the TFEU] or resulting from action taken by the institutions of the [EU]. They shall facilitate the achievement of the [EU's] task."[20] States must

> "[p]ursuant to the principle of sincere co-operation, the Union and the Member States shall, in full mutual respect, assist each other in carrying out tasks which flow from the Treaties. The Member States shall take any appropriate measure, general or particular, to ensure fulfilment of the obligations arising out of the Treaties or resulting from the acts of the institutions of the Union. The Member States shall facilitate the achievement of the Union's tasks and refrain from any measure which could jeopardise the attainment of the Union's objectives".[21]

They must co-ordinate their respective policies to the extent necessary to attain the objectives of the Treaties. This obligation to uphold EU law even where it might conflict with Member State law or policy is at the heart of the EU's legal structure and the relationship between the EU and Member States; this is the principle that EU law has *supremacy* over Member States' law but only where EU law applies. Unlike the EAEC, the EU's competence is not limited to a particular economic sector but covers virtually all economic activities so the extent of the EU's powers is very significant and has grown very substantially over time.

C. HISTORY

European integration

3.008 The story of how the EU developed is fascinating.[22] The EU is the product of the spirit of European Integration. The notion of European integration is not new but it has gathered momentum since the end of the Second World War. Thinkers and talkers such as Henry IV of France 400 years ago (with his "Great Republic of Europe" concept); William Penn 300 years ago (with his "European Parliament" concept); as well as Kant, Saint-Simon and Cattaneo 200 years ago each advanced notions of European integration. The first half of the twentieth century saw politicians such as Coudenhove-Kalergi and Briand advocate the doctrine. Progress was however slow and stumbling. The Second

---

20 Cf. Case 78/70 *Deutsche Grammophon v Metro* [1971] ECR 487, ECLI:EU:C:1971:59 and Case 231/83 *Cullet v Leclerc* [1986] ECR 529, ECLI:EU:C:1985:29.
21 TEU, Art. 4(3).
22 See Gilbert, *European Integration: A Concise History* (2012); Judt, *Postwar: A History of Europe Since 1945* (2007); Hoggart and Johnson, *An Idea of Europe* (1987); Kennedy, *The Rise and Fall of the Great Powers* (1988); Nicoll and Salmon, *Understanding the European Communities* (1990), chap. 1; Stone, *Goodbye to all That? The Story of Europe since 1945* (2014); Urwin, *Western Europe Since 1945* (4th ed., 1989); van Middelaar, *The Passage to Europe* (English ed., 2014, translated by Waters); and Vaughan, *Post-War Integration in Europe* (1976).

World War convinced many people of the dire need for European unity and the need for an international organisation to avoid the worst excesses of the nation state. The Second World War and its attendant calamity impressed on everyone the need to avoid another war. In 1946, Winston Churchill spoke at Zurich University of the need to

> "recreate the European family, or as much of it as we can[23] and provide it with a structure under which it can dwell in peace, in safety and in freedom. We must build a kind of United States of Europe ... The first step in the recreation of the European family must be a partnership between France and Germany."

There was therefore already a movement towards European integration and the germ of what became the EU today. The need to unify France and Germany meant that it was imperative to pool coal and steel – the weapons of war at the time and which would have been used by France and Germany in any war against each other or any other entity. Integration, in this context, was undertaken both for positive reasons (e.g. so as to achieve both economic growth and political stability) as well as negative or defensive reasons (e.g. avoiding war and domination by the Stalinist USSR).

Marshall Aid, the Organisation for European Economic Cooperation ("OEEC") and the UN Economic Commission for Europe

3.009 In June 1947 at Harvard University, General George Marshall, the then US Secretary of State, announced a plan for European relief (a plan which became known as the "Marshall Plan") under which the USA would offer cash aid to individual European States on condition that Europe worked out a common programme for the relief of poverty and for economic reconstruction.[24] Sixteen Western European States participated in a conference on the plan. The Central and Eastern European States largely ignored the aid on offer as they were now largely within the orbit of the then Union of Soviet Socialist Republics ("USSR"). Thirteen billion dollars was given by the USA to Europe in so-called Marshall Aid. The Marshall Plan led to the establishment of the OEEC in 1948.[25] This was an intergovernmental organisation consisting of a Council of Ministers, an Executive Committee and a Secretariat.[26] Its members were States and it operated along the classic lines of an international organisation: unanimity of Member States was required before action could be taken.[27] One of its early functions was to administer Marshall Aid efficiently. The organisation constituted the first major attempt to achieve *economic* co-operation throughout modern Europe. The name of this organisation was changed in 1961[28] to the Organisation for Economic Co-operation and Development ("OECD") when the USA and Canada (i.e. non-European States) joined. Today, it has a wide and large membership. The EU (in its corporate capacity) is now a de facto member

---

23 Ed., by 1946, it was clear that some Central and European States were unlikely to join the Western European alliance contemplated by Churchill because they were already under the influence of the USSR.
24 The plight of Europe at the time is difficult to understand today – there were parts of Europe suffering near famine conditions while the destruction of property and industry was dramatic in the extreme.
25 Convention of 16 April 1948, TS59 (1949) (UK), p. 13.
26 It was much less ambitious than the ECSC, EEC or EAEC; it was intergovernmental in nature.
27 Such an approach limits the possibility for progress because the organisation could not act on the basis of only a majority view.
28 Convention of 14 December 1960, TS21 (1962); Cmnd 1646.

of OECD.[29] The OECD has proved particularly important in recent years in the context of liner conferences[30] and shipbuilding.[31] It is worth noting that, simultaneously with the establishment of the OECD, the United Nations ("UN") also established an Economic Commission for Europe in 1947 with the purpose of exchanging information on coal, electricity and transport in Western Europe.

Congress of Europe

3.010 A Congress of Europe was held in The Hague in May 1948. This was a gathering of many people who were influential either then or later in European politics, including such figures as Churchill, Eden, Macmillan and Mitterrand. The Congress called for a European Parliament to be established. This did not happen – largely because it was too ambitious. Instead, less representative institutions were established which lay within the control of the European States involved and these institutions formed part of the Council of Europe which proved to be significant in the context of human rights although its significance for shipping has been marginal.[32]

Benelux Union

3.011 Also in 1948, the Benelux Union was established between Belgium, the Netherlands and Luxembourg whereby customs barriers were removed and closer co-operation was established between those three States. This was to prove instrumental in the establishment in the EEC (now the EU). It proved a partial, but not perfect, model for what would emerge as the ECSC, EEC and EAEC.

Council of Europe

3.012 Along with the OEEC,[33] another organisation, the Council of Europe was created at this time – it was largely born out of the Congress of Europe.[34] It still survives today. It is an intergovernmental organisation consisting of States throughout Western, Central and Eastern Europe.[35] It has been largely unsuccessful in achieving its remit in the area of political co-operation but it has succeeded very well in the areas of the protection of human rights as well as co-operation in the field of culture. Its failure to achieve all of its goals is due in no small way to the limits placed on it by the Statute establishing

---

29 In a Supplementary Protocol to the OECD Convention, the signatory states decided that the EU's Commission "shall participate in the work" of the Organisation. The OECD believes that this participation goes well beyond that of a mere observer, and, in fact, gives the Commission quasi-Member status (www.oecd.org/pages/0,3417,en_36734052_36761800_1_1_1_1_1,00.html).
30 See chap. 9.
31 See chap. 22.
32 A limited exception would be the case of *Pressos Compania Naviera S.A. and Others v Belgium* which involved a claim under the European Convention on Human Rights in respect of ships where the applicants were shipowners, mutual shipping insurance associations and, in one case, an insolvency administrator whose ships were involved in casualties in Belgian or Netherlands territorial waters (A 332 (1995), 21 EHRR 301 (merits); 1997-IV p. 1292, 24 EHRR CD 16 (just satisfaction).
33 See para. 3.010.
34 On the Congress of Europe, see para. 3.010.
35 The constitutive instrument is the Statute of the Council of Europe TS51 (1949); Cmnd 7779.

it, the fact that its Member States were not willing to cede much power to it and the extraordinary breadth of its membership. It is interesting to note that the opening up of Central and Eastern Europe in recent years has proven to be a blessing for the Council of Europe because these States have joined. It has little significance for shipping but its European Convention on Human Rights may well provide comfort for some companies which suffer loss.[36]

North Atlantic Treaty Organisation ("NATO")

3.013 NATO was established in 1949.[37] It is a collective security pact: armed aggression against one member of NATO constitutes armed aggression against all of the members. It traditionally consisted of the non-neutral Western European states along with the USA and Canada. The existence of NATO has probably meant that the EU has not had a significant military dimension up to this time; however, the EU is now developing a military and security dimension. NATO has no particular relevance for shipping in the context of EU shipping law.

Schumann Declaration

3.014 All of this organisation and reorganisation of Europe in the aftermath of the Second World War led many to believe that further integration was not only possible, but necessary, for European peace and prosperity even if such integration was on a smaller scale. On 9 May 1950, Robert Schumann, the then French Foreign Minister, stated that a united Europe was essential for world peace. He argued that such a united Europe would not come about until there was a coming together of France and Germany.[38] He proposed that the coal and steel production of those two former adversaries should be pooled under a common High Authority.[39] The purpose was two-fold: first, to avoid the possibility that either State could build up a war industry (coal and steel being the significant raw materials for war at that time) and, second, to create economic growth through an enlarged market, albeit in limited economic sectors initially. France needed access to the German market so as to sell agricultural products. Conversely, Germany needed the French market as an outlet for German manufactured goods. The Schumann Proposal led to the foundation of the ECSC. Schumann's proposal was described at the time by President Truman of the US as "an act of constructive statesmanship". The work of Schumann should always be seen in the context of the great work of Jean Monnet, the French businessman who championed the cause of European Integration and influenced Schumann and others to act.

---

36 A shipping company may seek to invoke the European Convention on Human Rights to vindicate, for example, property or procedural rights where such rights have been violated by States which are parties to the European Convention on Human Rights (see fn. 31).
37 The North Atlantic Treaty was signed in Washington DC on 4 April 1949, TS56 (1949 (UK)).
38 It should not be forgotten that only five years earlier, France and Germany were at war with each other.
39 The High Authority would later be named the European Commission.

ECSC

3.015 The ECSC was founded in 1951 by means of a treaty signed in Paris (sometimes known as the Treaty of Paris) which entered into force in 1952. The ECSC proved to be an immediate success. This was the stimulus for the later birth of the EEC (later known as the EC or EU). The new organisation had a High Authority (later called the Commission), a Council of Ministers, an Assembly (later known as the Parliament) and a Court of Justice. The ECSC was a success – had it been a failure then in all probability neither the EEC/EU nor the EAEC would ever have been created. The ECSC ceased to exist in 2002 when its 50 year mandate (under the Treaty of Paris) expired and its activities were subsumed under the EC (now EU) regime.

European Defence Treaty

3.016 In 1952, it was proposed that a European Defence Community ("EDC") would be established under the proposed European Defence Treaty. This Community was stillborn because of opposition on the part of some States (notably France). The impetus for this community came, in large measure, from fear of the USSR and the success of the ECSC. While the EDC was a failure, the Member States were not deterred and they went on to found the EEC which had much greater significance than any defence community. A similar notion of a European Political Community ("EPC") did not succeed largely because it was too ambitious for its time and circumstances. Both the EDC and the EPC are proof that the EU evolves through periods of both success and failure – the occasional setback has not proven fatal for the EU overall.

The EEC and EAEC

3.017 The Benelux countries[40] proposed the establishment of a common market in products other than coal and steel as well as services generally.[41] A conference was held in Messina in June 1955 to discuss the proposals. Spaak (the then Belgian Foreign Minister) was asked to report on the feasibility of a general economic union and the joint development and peaceful use of atomic energy. The Spaak Report was discussed in Venice in May 1956. The Foreign Ministers of the Six (i.e. the Benelux along with France, Germany and Italy) decided at that meeting to establish two new Communities (i.e. the EEC and EAEC). The Foundation Treaties for both the EEC and EAEC were drafted speedily[42] and later signed on 25 March 1957. Unlike the ECSC Treaty which was designed to last for 50 years,[43] the EEC and EAEC Treaties were of unlimited duration.[44] The EEC and EAEC both came into existence on 1 January 1958. The institutional framework was amended in the 1960s when a convention on certain institutions common to the

---

40 The Benelux countries consisted of Belgium, the Netherlands and Luxembourg. Belgium and Luxembourg had earlier formed an economic union in 1921 and a later one after the Second World War.
41 Although invited, Britain did not take part in the three new Communities because of (among other things) its British Commonwealth responsibilities and its special link with the US.
42 It is remarkable that much of the work done at that time, at great speed, is largely intact today in the Treaty on the Functioning of the European Union ("TFEU") with relatively minimal amendment.
43 ECSC Treaty, Art. 97.
44 See TFEU, Art. 356 and Euratom Treaty, Art. 208.

Communities entered into force on the same day as the EEC and Euratom Treaties.[45] The organisations have been changed over time by amending treaties including the Treaty of Lisbon which entered into force on 1 December 2009.

European Free Trade Association ("EFTA")

3.018 In 1959, EFTA was founded by Austria, Denmark, Norway, Portugal, Sweden, Switzerland and the UK. This was an organisation of some non-EEC European States and was designed to create a free trade area (but not a customs union)[46] between them. Austria, Denmark, Finland, Sweden and the UK left EFTA when they joined the Communities. The economic relationship between the EEC and EFTA deepened with the creation of the European Economic Area ("EEA"). Some sceptics would have seen the EFTA as being an attempt to emulate, but only in part, the EEC.

UK's position at the time of the foundation of the European communities

3.019 The position of the UK during the formation of the ECSC, EEC and EAEC is interesting. The UK had opposed even the earliest plans for European federation put forward in 1929 by Astrid Briand at the General Assembly of the League of Nations.[47] The UK believed that its relationship with the then British Commonwealth of Nations prevented it from joining such a European alliance.[48] Nonetheless, it should not be forgotten that Lord Salisbury, the British Prime Minister, said in 1897:

> "[t]he federated action of Europe, if we can maintain it, is our sole hope of escaping from the constant terror and calamity of war, the constant pressure of the burdens of an armed peace, which weigh down the spirits and darken the prospect of every Nation in this part of the world. The Federation of Europe is the only hope we have."[49]

While the UK decided not to join the ECSC, the EEC or the EAEC when they were established, the UK did seek to join later.[50] The UK applied to join the three European Communities in 1961. While it did not join because it was prevented from doing so by De Gaulle's France, it was really a somewhat reluctant applicant at that time. Nevertheless, it renewed its applications in 1967 and 1970. Ultimately, the UK signed a Treaty of Accession to the three Communities on 22 January 1972 and joined on 1 January 1973. It had chosen to join by way of a vote in Parliament rather than after a vote of its people. In 1975, after two years of membership, the UK held a referendum on its continued membership of the Communities and the people voted to remain in the Communities. The relationship between the EU and the UK has been somewhat tempestuous over the years because of disputes over the level of integration, budgetary contributions by the UK,

---

45 The Merger Treaty was signed on 8 April 1965 and entered into force on 29 June 1967.
46 The distinction between a free trade area and a customs union is that a customs union also has an external trade regime. The customs union is therefore much more advanced and sophisticated than the free trade area.
47 See Nicoll and Salmon, op. cit. at fn. 22, p. 4.
48 See Joll (ed.), *Britain and Europe: Pitt to Churchill 1793–1940* (1961) generally.
49 Cited by Macmillan in *Tides of Fortune 1945–1955* (London, 1969), p. 151.
50 This phenomenon of not joining at the time the development was occurring but seeking to join later is like not participating in the planning of the house but once it is built, announcing that one wants to live in it provided certain changes are made – whether such changes can be made depends on the circumstances.

social policy, economic and monetary union, migration, welfare payments for migrant workers as well as fisheries. The relationship showed some signs of stabilising with the election of the Blair Labour government in 1997. Now, the question of continued membership or, at least the terms of continued membership, is at the centre of political debate in the UK and a slim majority of voters decided (by way of a referendum held on 23 June 2016) that the UK should leave the EU. It is anticipated that the UK would leave the EU on 29 March 2019.. EU shipping policy has been influenced positively by the UK and it is also fair to say that EU shipping policy has been positive for the UK but whether that will continue rests with the UK politicians and people.

Institutions: Merger Treaty

3.020 It was clear by the mid-1960s that the three Communities had an inherent inefficiency due to their overlapping institutions – each had a commission, a court and so on. The Merger Treaty of 8 April 1965[51] established a single Council of Ministers and a single Commission. Thus, from mid-1967 (when the Merger Treaty entered into force) there was one Council of Ministers and one Commission for all three Communities (as well as one Parliament and one Court of Justice).

Customs Union[52]

3.021 The EU

"shall comprise a customs union which shall cover all trade in goods and which shall involve the prohibition between Member States of customs duties on imports and exports and of all charges having their equivalent effect, and the adoption of a common customs tariff in their relations with third countries".[53]

The Customs Union became fully operative on 1 July 1968 (18 months ahead of the timetable laid down in the original Treaty). A common external tariff was put in place vis-à-vis trade with the rest of the world.

Accessions

3.022 What is now the EU has grown in time by way of accessions: from six founding States to the now 28 Member State body. For example, the Treaty of Brussels was signed on 22 January 1972 by which Denmark, Ireland, Norway and the UK acceded to the EU. This treaty allowed the signatories to accede to the EEC, EAEC and the ECSC. Three of these four States ratified the Treaty but Norway did not – in a subsequent referendum, the Norwegian people voted against joining, largely because of concerns over the then EEC's fishing polices.[54] Thus Ireland, the UK and Denmark joined the three Communities on

---

51 JO 152/2 (1967).
52 A customs union involves the abolition of internal trade barriers and the creation of a common customs tariff towards the rest of the world. This latter element, the common customs tariff, is missing from a free trade area.
53 See TFEU, Art. 28(1).
54 There is no doubt that had Norway joined the EEC in 1973, shipping would have had a greater impact on EU policy even earlier.

1 January 1973. The accession of Denmark and the UK (as well as Ireland to a very much lesser extent) brought shipping to the forefront and led to the Commission instituting proceedings against France over its Maritime Code because the Commission believed that the Code discriminated in favour of French nationals and against the nationals of other Member States.[55] The Communities then had two island Member States having been entirely continental up to that time. On 12 June 1975, Greece applied for membership of the then Communities and joined on 1 January 1981 by means of the Accession Treaty of 28 May 1979. Its accession dramatically altered the shipping profile of the then EC and its fleet today accounts for a substantial part of the EU's fleet. The accession of the three States in 1973 and Greece in 1981 had an enormous impact on the development of a shipping policy: until 1973, 90% of transportation between the then six Member States was by means of inland transport but after enlargement to ten States, 90% of the trade between the old six and the new four was carried by sea – a direct reversal of position for shipping. Expansion also took place in the west of the continent: Spain and Portugal applied for membership in 1977[56] and became members on 1 January 1986. Austria, Finland and Sweden joined in 1995. Cyprus, Czech Republic, Estonia, Hungary, Latvia, Lithuania, Poland, Slovakia and Slovenia joined on 1 May 2004 – the accession of States such as Cyprus, Malta and Poland was particularly significant for EU shipping law and policy. Bulgaria and Romania became members on 1 January 2007. Croatia joined on 1 July 2013. There is a number of other candidate and possible Member States but it proving to be a challenge to manage the already very large EU!

European Monetary System

3.023 The Member States decided to establish the European Monetary System (the so-called "EMS"). It was designed to create closer monetary co-operation leading to European monetary stability. It was introduced on 13 March 1979. This was a significant step on the road to the full economic and monetary union which has since been created among many (but not all) Member States. EMS may not have been entirely successful but it helped the EU learn about what was possible.

Direct elections to the European Parliament

3.024 While there had been a European Assembly (or, as it is now called, European Parliament) since the inception of the European Communities, the members of the institution were originally nominated by their respective national governments or parliaments and they were not elected by the people until 1979. It was widely believed that the European Parliament would gain prestige and power by being directly elected by the people. Following the 1976 Act concerning the Election of the Representatives of the Assembly by Direct Universal Suffrage,[57] the first direct elections took place in June 1979 and now

---

55 See Case 167/73 *Commission v France* [1974] ECR 359, ECLI:EU:C:1974:35. See also Case C-334/94 *Commission v France* [1996] ECR I-01307, ECLI:EU:C:1996:90.
56 See Bull. 7/8–1977, 6 and Suppl. 9/78 in respect of Spain, and Bull. 3–1977, 8 and Suppl. 5/78 in respect of Portugal.
57 OJ 1976 L278/1.

take place every five years with the most recent election in June 2009. The percentage turnout has fallen from 61.99% in 1979 to 42.61% in 2014.

Internal Market White Paper

3.025 In June 1985, the Commission published its White Paper on the Completion of the Internal Market. This is one of the most important documents in the entire catalogue of EU documents. It set the objective that the internal market would be achieved by 31 December 1992. It was an important stimulus for economic activity in the EU.

Single European Act ("SEA")

3.026 The SEA[58] which was signed in Luxembourg on 17 February 1986 and in The Hague on 28 February 1986 constitutes one of the most significant documents in EU law and special attention must be paid to it. The SEA was agreed upon by a meeting of the European Council in December 1985. The SEA amended the then EEC Treaty quite extensively, particularly in the area of foreign policy. The SEA also enhanced the role of the Parliament. The most significant change was however relating to voting – traditionally, the Council of Ministers had to adopt legislation by way of a unanimous vote (which meant that any State could veto a proposal) but the SEA allows for the adoption of many matters, including some quite controversial ones, by way of a majority vote.

Central and Eastern Europe

3.027 The opening up of Central and Eastern Europe was a process of huge significance for the EU as a whole. The unification of Germany expanded the EU. The conclusion of numerous joint ventures with Eastern European companies created both promise and problems for the EU. Ultimately, in 2004, Latvia, Lithuania, Poland, Slovakia and Slovenia joined the EU. Bulgaria and Romania joined in 2007. The EU shipping fleet expanded (particularly, through the accession of Poland) and employment issues became even more important as many Central and Eastern European citizens are seafarers.

Internal market

3.028 Following on from the Internal Market White Paper, the internal market was established formally on 1 January 1993 when a programme of 279 measures was due to be adopted and the vast majority was adopted. The programme contemplated the abolition of physical, technical, fiscal and other barriers. The programme was designed to create a market without internal barriers. It was possible to adopt many of these measures because the SEA had been adopted.

---

58 Despite being called an "act", the SEA was a treaty. See Campbell, "The Single European Act and the Implications" (1985) 34 ICLQ 359, and Murphy, The "Single European Act" (1985) 30 Ir.Jur.(n.s.) 17, at p. 239.

EMU

3.029 A majority (but not all) of the Member States have agreed to establish and operate among themselves an economic and monetary union ("EMU"). This involves a common economic and monetary policy (including uniform interest rates being set by the European Central Bank (or "ECB")) as well as a single currency (the "euro"). Such a union facilitates trade between Member States and may well have a positive impact on shipping in the coming years. There have been several crises relating to the EMU since *circa* 2008 with the crisis related to Greece being the most significant. While many commentators, market participants and politicians have expressed views (sometimes views which supporting their political or financial circumstances), EMU has proved very resilient.

Failed Constitution but the adoption of the Treaty of Lisbon

3.030 A plan to adopt a new constitutional Treaty to replace the then existing treaties was thwarted after the people of France and the Netherlands voted in referenda not to allow their countries to ratify it but a new amended treaty, the Treaty of Lisbon, was adopted on 13 December 2007 and entered into force on 1 December 2009. The Constitution was seen by some commentators and citizens as "going too far" in giving the EU some of the characteristics and emblems of a State (including an anthem) while others saw it as only an incremental step in the EU's evolution – either way, it does not matter because the Constitution was rejected. Much of what was in the draft Constitution was included in a less ambitious Treaty of Lisbon. While less ambitious than the Constitution, the Treaty of Lisbon abolished the EC and converted the entire project into the EU, established new institutions, altered voting patterns and developed new or expanded areas of policy.

Outlook

3.031 The outlook for the EU is quite positive. However, it has become more of a two-speed Europe than many would have expected because of issues such as EMU. The EU has various failures and setbacks from time to time but there is no doubting that the EU has helped to avoid wars between Member States and has instead facilitated peace and prosperity for its citizens. Recent setbacks have included the financial and migrant crises which have challenged many aspects of the EU including the basic fundamental freedoms. The planned exit of the UK would be significant for the EU were it to occur. Overall, it appears to overcome the challenges which it faces eventually though often in a way which is characterised by drama and political intrigue.

D. INSTITUTIONAL AND ORGANIC STRUCTURE OF THE EU

Introduction

3.032 The EU's organs are classified under EU law as either "institutions" (which are capable of taking decisions binding on Member States) or "bodies" (which are not capable of taking such binding decisions).[59] The seven institutions[60] are the European Commission, the Council, the European Council, the European Parliament, the CJEU, the ECB and the Court of Auditors. The bodies, offices and agencies are too numerous to enumerate here but include the Economic and Social Committee ("EESC") and the Committee of Regions. There are other bodies including the Maritime Industries Forum which also have a role to play in the EU because they provide, among other things, a more informal opportunity to exchange ideas and information among industry participants. The European Maritime Safety Agency ("EMSA") is considered at various points throughout this book. All institutions, bodies, agencies and offices must act within the powers conferred on them under EU law.[61] There is criticism that some of the organs are remote from the citizens of the EU but this may be an inevitable consequence of the scale of the project.[62]

3.033 The Council, the European Council and the Commission are politically the most significant of the institutions because they comprise the Member State's politicians in the case of the first two as well as, in the case of the Commission, the institution which proposes new EU laws and has the power to implement EU law and policy. However, the Parliament has a growing role to play and is more significant politically than it has ever been before – there is little doubt but that the Parliament's role will become stronger over time. The CJEU has an obviously critically important role in adjudicating on disputes between various parties[63] relating to EU law but also develops the law in various cases (sometimes in ways which would not be possible for the Member States to agree politically) and establishes or enunciates various key principles (e.g. the supremacy of EU law over conflicting Member State law or that Member States are liable in damages to citizens where the Member States breach EU law).

Commission

Introduction

3.034 The Commission is the central cog in the EU wheel. It is not just very much the permanent civil service of the EU but has a wider role. It is the EU's executive organ. One Commission serves the EU and the EAEC. It is responsible for executing the decisions of the EU. It sends to the Council various proposals which may ultimately find their way into regulations, directives and so on (i.e. it proposes new EU laws). It also makes key decisions in areas such as competition where it has the ability to block or permit (conditionally or unconditionally) mergers and joint ventures as well as the power to

---

59 There are also offices and agencies (e.g. the European Maritime Safety Agency).
60 See TFEU, Art. 13.
61 TEU, Art. 13(2): "Each institution shall act within the limits of the powers conferred on it in the Treaties, and in conformity with the procedures and conditions set out in them. The institutions shall practice mutual sincere co-operation."
62 See Mackenzie Stuart (1979) 39 NILQ 95, at p. 98.
63 The CJEU typically deals with disputes on EU law between Member States as well as those where an EU institution is involved. Disputes on EU law involving private parties are not typically matters which come before the CJEU (except where the Member State court or tribunal refers questions of EU law to the CJEU by way of a preliminary reference) but are dealt with by Member State courts or tribunals. Even when an issue is dealt with by a Member State court or tribunal, the latter is invariably mindful of the jurisprudence of the CJEU in deciding the matter.

impose fines on those businesses (known as "undertakings") which breach competition law.[64]

Composition

3.035 The Commission's 28 members are appointed by agreement between the governments of the Member States on the basis of their general competence and European commitment. Each Member State nominates one person to be a Commissioner but that person does *not* represent the Member State but rather must represent the EU if appointed. All Commissioners must be persons whose independence is beyond doubt and they must be completely independent in the performance of their functions.[65] Commissioners are appointed for five-year renewable periods.[66] The Commission has a President[67] and a number of Vice-Presidents. Apart from the President of the Commission, each Commissioner has responsibility for particular portfolios (e.g. competition, transport, maritime affairs and fisheries as well as trade) with each Commissioner heading up a department (known as a Directorate General) with responsibility for that area of activity.

Functions

3.036 The functions of the Commission fall into three broad categories: first, the guardian of the Treaties; second, the initiator and guardian of the EU policy; and third, the EU's executive organ. The Commission ensures that the Treaties and measures taken pursuant to them are complied with by all Member States, institutions and the general public; it formulates recommendations or delivers opinions on matters dealt with in the Treaties, if the Treaties provide or if the Commission considers it necessary; the Commission has its own power of decision and participation in the shaping of measures taken by the Council and by the European Parliament in the manner provided for in the Treaties; and exercises the powers conferred on it by the Council for the implementation of the rules laid down by the latter. Thus, for example, a Commission regulation may well implement a Council of Ministers regulation.[68] The Commission has the power to initiate legislation by proposing opinions or recommendations to the Council for adoption. It does so either because the Treaties require it or because the Commission considers it necessary. It is worth noting that the Commission has the power to take its own decisions in some areas but they are limited with the notable exception of competition where it has the ability and has imposed enormous fines. The Treaties specifically charge the Commission with the task of enforcing EU competition law.[69] The Commission is independent of the Member States and thus it is

---

64 See chap. 9 as well as chaps 11–16.
65 TEU, Art. 17(3).
66 Ibid.
67 The President of the Commission is extremely influential and his or her work can set the tone for the entire EU. As Siemers records: the "project to develop an Integrated Maritime Policy for the European Union is not without antecedents. The [then] President of the European Commission, Mr José Manuel Barroso, is the former Prime Minister of Portugal. During his tenure, Mr Barroso led the development of an integrated oceans policy for his country, the first of its kind in Europe, and brought this experience with him to the European Commission" (in "A European Integrated Maritime Policy: An Innovative Approach to Policy-Making" (2009) 23 Ocean Yearbook 231 at 233). The current President of the European Commission is Jean Claude Juncker.
68 This is quite common in the area of competition law and policy.
69 TFEU, Art. 105.

independent in the exercise of its functions. This independence gives the Commission greater authority. The Commission can sometimes irritate Member States by forcing them to change conduct (e.g. to open up markets). It can also act, though it is sometimes reluctant to do so, as a form of "honest broker" in disputes – an example is to be found in *B & I Line plc v Sealink Harbours* where it intervened to try to solve a dispute between an Irish shipping company and a UK harbour company but did so not to be some form of "business dispute resolution service" but to promote and protect competition (which is one of its formal functions).[70] The Commission may grant interim measures (which are comparable to injunctions or conservatory measures in Member State law): these are unusual but it has done so in the case of a number of port cases. The Commission also has the power to impose enormous fines to punish breaches of EU competition law and has also sought to change competition law in various ways (for example, the reform of the competition law relating to liner conferences was spearheaded by the Commission much to the chagrin of those who wanted to retain the block exemption regime for liner conferences).[71]

Operation

3.037 The Commission is very much based in Brussels but has representative information offices in the Member States. The Commission maintains delegations in a number of cities throughout the world. The collegiate Commission typically meets weekly (normally on Wednesdays) but individual Commissioners may make decisions on their own in certain circumstances (e.g. in competition matters). The Commission has a Secretary-General and over several thousands of employees.[72] It operates through Directorates-General – a concept like Government Departments or Ministries. A Director-General presides over each Directorate-General. Some of these Directorates-General are sub-divided into Directorates. A selection of the Directorates-General relevant to EU shipping law includes:

Mobility and Transport and Energy;
Competition;
Fisheries and Maritime Affairs;
External Relations;
Economic and Financial Affairs;
Internal Market and Industrial Affairs;
Employment, Social Affairs and Education;
Information, Spokesman's Group;
Environment, Consumer Protection and Nuclear Safety;
Science, Research and Development, Joint Research Centre;
Energy;
Financial Institutions and Taxation;
Regional Policy;
Trade; and
Taxation and Customs.

---

70 Case No IV/33.045 [1992] 5 CMLR 255 and http://ec.europa.eu/competition/antitrust/cases/dec_docs/34174/34174_2_2.pdf.
71 See chaps 11 and 12.
72 Many of these employees are engaged in language translation activities.

3.038 These Directorates-General are assisted by a centralised Commission Legal Service which advises the Commission on legal matters, determines the legality of all its decisions and represents it in proceedings before the CJEU (including the General Court). Of all the Directorates-General, the Directorates-General for Transport, Maritime Affairs and Fisheries as well as Competition are the most significant from the perspective of shipping. The Commissioner with responsibility for fisheries and maritime affairs has responsibility for developing a maritime policy. However, there are at least seven Commissioners with responsibilities relating to shipping including the Commissioners for transport; fisheries and maritime affairs; environment, science and research; regional policy; enterprise and industry; and energy. Commissioners with responsibility for climate action and energy, trade, employment, social affairs, labour markets, the internal market, industry and so on could also be relevant. There is no uniformity of views on which Directorates-General matter most – for example, it has been observed:

> "[a]s regards the Commission Directorate Generals (DGs), the main focus is on the DG dealing with [t]ransport. However, the groups representing maritime interests names other DGs as lobbying targets as well, due to (a) an apparent institutional and cultural fragmentation of the Commission and (b) the existing variations between DGs with respect to policy frames. When asked about their list of lobbying targets, [maritime] interest groups mention more frequently the DGs dealing with the Environment, Research, and Enterprises, than those DGs dealing with Competition, Employment and Social Affairs, Enlargement, Fisheries and Regional Development."[73]

However, one views the issue, the Commission is extremely important in the area of shipping.

DG MOVE: Directorate-General for Mobility and Transport

3.039 The Directorate-General for Transport (sometimes known by the acronym "DG MOVE") deals with transport matters generally. It is responsible for the development of EU transport policy as well as its implementation. It used to deal (until 2010) with State aid in transport matters but the competence to deal with that has now been transferred to the Directorate-General for Competition.[74] It also exercises political scrutiny over the maritime safety agency and various initiatives including the Galileo Joint Undertaking. Since 1 November 2014, the Commissioner is Violeta Bulc who is a Slovenian entrepreneur and politician.

DG MARE: Directorate-General for Maritime Affairs and Fisheries

3.040 The Directorate-General for Maritime Affairs and Fisheries is of growing significance in this context. It has responsibility for, among other matters (principally, fisheries) the EU's Integrated Maritime Policy.[75] Since 1 November 2014, Karmenu Vella has been Commissioner for Environment, Maritime Affairs and Fisheries. He is a Maltese national.

---

73 Pallis, "Maritime Interests in the EU Policy-Making" (2007) World Maritime University Journal of Maritime Affairs 3 at 12.
74 See chap. 15.
75 See http://ec.europa.eu/maritimeaffairs/index_en.htm.

DG COMP: Competition

3.041 Directorate-General Competition ("DG COMP") (formerly known as DG IV pronounced "DG4") deals with competition. It deals with anti-competitive arrangements, abuses of dominance, State aid, State authorities as well as concentrations (i.e. mergers, acquisitions and some joint ventures). It was central to the debate over the abolition of Council Regulation 4056/86 and its block exemption on liner conferences.[76] It has also proposed that the Commission impose very heavy fines on various shipping companies in breach of competition law. Since 1 November 2014, Margrethe Vestager has been Commissioner for Competition. She is a Danish national.

Conclusion

3.042 There is no doubt that the Commission is a central feature of the EU's institutional machinery and while not as powerful as sometimes portrayed, it is extremely important for the shipping sector not only in terms of regulation and competition but also stimulation of the sector.

The Council

Introduction

3.043 The Council comprises a government minister from each Member State. It is the institution through which the Member States primarily act and decide.[77] It is an EU institution and not just an intergovernmental organ. One Council serves the EU and the EAEC. Given the regime established by Article 100 of the TFEU, the Council was historically accorded an extensive role to play in shipping matters. Article 100(1) of the TFEU provides that the Title[78] relating to transport in that Treaty shall apply to transport by rail, road and inland waterway. However, Article 100(2) provides:

> "[t]he European Parliament and the Council, acting in accordance with the ordinary legislative procedure, may lay down by a qualified majority, appropriate provisions for sea and air transport. They shall act after consulting the committee of the Regions and the Economic and Social Committee."

The Council was thus given the power to determine the way in which the TFEU's Title on transport applied to shipping. Indeed, until the SEA, unanimity was needed in the Council hence matters were slowed down considerably – the framers of the original EEC Treaty could have allowed for the Title on transport to apply in full to maritime transport but the founding Member States chose otherwise.[79] In practice, the adoption of major steps in regard to EU transport law and policy has been dependent on the Council agreeing to the changes.

---

76 See chaps 11 and 12.
77 On the balance between the Member States upholding their own nationalistic interests and the interests of the EU as a whole, see Cases 2 and 3/60 *Niederrheinische Bergwerks-AG et al. v High Authority* [1961] ECR 133, at pp. 146–147, ECLI:EU:C:1961:15.
78 A title is a section of the TFEU which is devoted to a particular topic (e.g. transport).
79 On this issue, see chap. 4.

Composition

3.044 The Council is composed of one *representative* from each Member State, that is to say, each of the members of the Council acts, not on his/her own initiative, but on the instructions of his or her State.[80] Each government delegates one of its members to sit on the Council. These representatives are the Foreign Ministers of the Member States but States may send other Ministers (e.g. agriculture, finance or transport) instead of the Foreign Minister because of the subject-matter under discussion. Shipping matters are typically discussed by Marine or Transport Ministers. Occasionally, the Council will act with Ministers from different disciplines such as in the aftermath of the *Braer* tanker disaster, there was a joint Council of Ministers[81] meeting comprised of Environment and Transport/Marine/Shipping Ministers.

Functions

3.045 The Council exercises the powers and functions conferred on it by the Treaties. It has the duty of ensuring that the objectives of the Treaties are attained. It also has the task of ensuring co-ordination of the general economic objectives of the Member States. It must also ensure co-ordination of the general economic policies of the Member States. It has the power to take decisions and confer on the Commission, in the acts which the Council adopts, powers for the implementation of the rules which the Council lays down. The Council has a representative role in international affairs. The Council is largely (but by no means entirely) the EU's legislature in that it adopts legislation and not, as might be expected, the European Parliament alone. The Council now shares that legislative role with the European Parliament. This legislation is usually embodied in regulations and directives. Typically, the Council can only act on a proposal from the Commission and does not usually have the power to initiate legislation but it can invite the Commission to bring forward proposals. The Treaties oblige the Council to adopt appropriate regulations and directives to deal with particular matters in a number of special situations.[82]

Operation and voting

3.046 The Council is bound to act on the basis of the treaties (i.e. it cannot act without a legislative basis to do so). It operates in accordance with its own rules of procedure.[83] A general Council meeting involves the President of the Council and the Foreign Ministers of the Member States. The Council is presided over by the President. The Presidency rotates among the Member States in the alphabetical order of the name of the State on a six-monthly basis. The President has the formal functions of notifying the members of meetings of the Council, putting issues to a vote as well as signing. In practice, the presidency plays a much more important role as it sets the tone for the EU in many ways during its term of office, seeks to resolve disputes and often acts as an honest broker. The

---

80 This is in contrast to the Commission whose members are independent and may not take instructions from Member States or third parties.
81 The Council was known at that time as the Council of Ministers.
82 E.g. competition (TFEU, Art. 103).
83 TFEU, Art. 240(3).

meetings are convened at the request of the President of the Council, a member of the Council or the Commission.[84] Instead of one State–one vote, there is a more complex voting system in operation.

The Council's voting regime is somewhat complicated. First, there are matters which are decided by way of a simple majority. A simple majority is reached if at least 15 Council members vote in favour (this would become 14 if Brexit occurs). The Council takes decisions by simple majority: (a) in procedural matters, such as the adoption of its own rules of procedure and organisation of its secretariat general, the adoption of the rules governing the committees foreseen in the treaties; and (b) to request the Commission to undertake studies or submit proposals. Second, there are matters which are decided by way of a qualified majority. If the Council is voting on a proposal by the Commission or the High Representative of the Union for Foreign Affairs and Security Policy then a qualified majority is reached if two conditions are met: (a) 55% of Member States vote in favour – in practice this means 16 out of 28; and (b) the proposal is supported by Member States representing at least 65% of the total EU population (this is the so-called "double majority" rule). There can be a block minority but it must include at least four Council members representing more than 35% of the EU population. There are also special cases. Whenever not all Council members participate in the vote, for example due to an opt-out in certain policy areas, a decision is adopted if 55% of the participating Council members, representing at least 65% of the population of the participating Member States, vote in favour. Whenever the Council votes on a proposal not coming from the Commission or the High Representative a decision is adopted if: (a) at least 72% of Council members vote in favour; and (b) they represent at least 65% of the EU population. An abstention under qualified majority voting counts as a vote against. Abstention is not the same as not participating in the vote. A Member State may abstain at any time. Third, there are some matters which require unanimity and all members must vote in favour of the proposal or abstain. Unanimity is required on such matters as accession of new Member States, aspects of common foreign and security policy, aspects of citizenship, EU finance and aspects of justice and home affairs. There is a rotating presidency of the Council. However, since the Lisbon Treaty, there has been a full-time President of the European Council which is discussed below.

The Council's Committee of Permanent Representatives ("COREPER")

3.047 A discussion of the Council would be incomplete without mention of COREPER. Its legal basis is Article 240 of the TFEU which provides that a "committee consisting of the Permanent Representatives[85] of the Governments of the Member States shall be responsible for preparing the work of the Council and for carrying out the tasks assigned to it by the latter". It prepares and trims the agenda for the Council. It is a medium for the interchange of information between the Member States and helps prepare the way for agreement at Council meetings. It is important to stress that COREPER has no powers of decision but it is nonetheless powerful.

---

84 TFEU, Art. 237.
85 Ed., these Permanent Representatives are in the nature of Ambassadors from the Member States to the EU.

OVERVIEW OF THE EU AND EU LAW

General Secretariat of the Council

3.048 The General Secretariat of the Council, under a Secretary-General, is a permanent service to the Council acting as a liaison between the Council and COREPER.

The Council and shipping

3.049 While proposals are made by the Commission, the Council plays the central role in adopting the proposal as legislation. It is therefore important in various areas of EU shipping law including safety, the marine environment, employment and competition. The Council was more favourably disposed towards liner conferences than the Commission but often acts at the behest of, or on the basis of proposals made by, the Commission.

European Council

3.050 The European Council consists of the Heads of State or of Government of the Member States with the President of the Commission.[86] The European Council was not established by the original Foundation Treaties in the EEC. In the past, summit meetings were arranged as the occasion demanded but since the early 1970s they are held at least twice yearly. Article 15(3) of the TEU provides that they shall meet at least quarterly. The European Council is politically very important. It is the final court of political appeal. Matters which have not been resolved at the Council of Ministers or Commission levels are often resolved at the European Council meetings.[87] The European Council shall "provide the Union with the necessary impetus for its development and shall define the general political directions and priorities thereof. It shall not exercise legislative functions".[88] Unless the Treaties provide otherwise, the decisions of the European Council are taken by consensus.[89] The President of the European Council is elected by the Council, by a qualified majority, for a term of two-and-a-half years which is renewable once.[90] It is not directly relevant for shipping but could become involved in, for example, the aftermath of a major shipping disaster where political action was required.

European Parliament

Introduction

3.051 The European Parliament[91] traditionally had a modest and limited role. Its profile has increased in significance since the first direct elections in 1979 but it has not yet reached its full potential and it is not entirely analogous to parliaments in the Member

---

86 TEU, Art. 15(2).
87 Sometimes this is done for effect – the political clout of a European Council meeting outweighs that of an "ordinary" Council meeting.
88 TEU, Art. 15(1).
89 TEU, Art. 15(4).
90 TEU, Art. 15(5).
91 Although originally called the "Assembly" in the Treaties, that body resolved that it be called the "European Parliament": Resolution of 30 March 1962 (JO 1962, 1045).

States. Nonetheless, its role has increased significantly and it is has a co-legislative role now in many areas.

Seat

3.052 The Parliament holds sessions in Brussels, Strasbourg and Luxembourg which is not very efficient.

Members

3.053 The Parliament's members are elected in elections held throughout the EU every five years.[92] The members are representatives of the peoples of the Member States. These members are arranged not in national delegations but are instead gathered in groups according to political outlook (e.g. socialists are grouped together as one). The members elect a President and officers from among themselves.

3.054 There are 751 members of the European Parliament ("MEPs") divided among Member States as shown in Table 3.1.

Election

3.055 Prior to 1979, the members of the Parliament were nominated principally by the parliaments of the Member States. Since 1979, members of the Parliament have been elected directly by voters throughout the EU on the basis of universal suffrage. The direct elections in 1979 (at which 110 million people voted throughout the then EC) heightened public awareness in many Member States of the workings of the Parliament.

Operation

3.056 The Parliament has a Bureau composed of the President of the Parliament, Vice-Presidents and Questors. These Questors are officials who have special responsibility for financial and administrative matters relating to the Parliament. The Parliament's Secretariat is in charge of the organisational and administrative aspects of the Parliament. The Parliament has various standing committees. Each of these Committees specialises in a particular area of EU policy. These standing committees prepare reports which form the bases of debates in the Parliament. The Transport Committee is extremely important in the context of shipping.

Functions

3.057 The functions of the Parliament have traditionally been advisory and supervisory but it now has a legislative function as well. It can question the Commission and ultimately dismiss it by motion of censure. The Parliament has some control over the Community's budget; it can reject the EU budget and it has done so. It can institute

---

[92] TEU, Art. 14(3) provides that the "Members of the European Parliament shall be elected for a term of five years by direct universal suffrage in a free and secret ballot."

Table 3.1 Allocation of MEPs to each Member State

Member State	Number of MEPs
Austria	18
Belgium	21
Bulgaria	17
Croatia	11
Cyprus	6
Czech Republic	21
Denmark	13
Estonia	6
Finland	13
France	74
Germany	96
Greece	21
Hungary	21
Ireland	11
Italy	73
Latvia	8
Lithuania	11
Luxembourg	6
Malta	6
Netherlands	26
Poland	51
Portugal	21
Romania	32
Slovakia	13
Slovenia	8
Spain	54
Sweden	20
United Kingdom	73

proceedings in the CJEU and it did so in respect of, among other matters, transport. The Parliament normally acts by an absolute majority of the votes cast and in accordance with its own rules of procedure. The Parliament has some control over the Commission and the Council. Both institutions must answer questions put to them by MEPs. The Parliament adopts resolutions on issues which it feels to be important. Its resolutions on competition policy, agriculture and budgetary matters carry considerable weight within the EU. The Parliament has been the forum for various questions on shipping posed by MEPs to the Commission; such questions are usually answered by the Transport, Maritime Affairs and Competition Commissioners. The Parliament meets throughout the year. It may meet in extraordinary sessions at the request of a majority of its members, the Council or the Commission.

The Parliament and shipping

3.058 The Parliament has had an important role to play in regard to EU shipping law. Its role was limited but is growing. It encouraged the Commission to adopt guidelines on the application of competition law to the maritime transport sector. It has had an important role in regard to safety and employment issues in shipping as well as the maritime environment.

Future

3.059 Many commentators believe that the Parliament will become more important as a political forum in the future, but this is a matter of debate. It has grown in status but it is not yet a parliament in the conventional sense.

The CJEU including the General Court

Introduction

3.060 The CJEU (including the General Court) is the judicial institution of the EU.[93] They provide a system of "checks and balances" in the institutional system of the EU by monitoring the conduct of the Member States and the other institutions to ensure that they act in accordance with law. The CJEU has existed since the foundation of the EEC. The General Court (originally called the Court of First Instance), which was established to cope with the huge backlog of work facing the CJEU, commenced operations in 1989.[94] The General Court has primary responsibility in the EU's judicial framework for competition matters but appeals from the General Court judgments lie to the CJEU. The General Court has therefore proven to be the first court of appeal in maritime competition cases from Commission decisions.

Functions

3.061 The principal function of the CJEU (including the General Court) is to ensure that in the interpretation and application of the Treaties "the law is observed".[95] Unlike some English courts (such as the High Court) which have an inherent jurisdiction, the CJEU must act within the limits of the powers conferred upon it by the Treaties. The court is, in part, a law-maker[96] because the nature of EU law constantly requires creation,[97] refinement and adaptation.[98]

Personnel

Judges

3.062 The CJEU and the General Court are each composed of 28 judges. Each Member State appoints one judge to each court. The judges are appointed by the common accord of the governments of the Member States for a renewable period of six years. The

---

93 TEU, Art. 19 and TFEU, Arts 251 to 281.
94 On the Court of First Instance, see Millett, *The Court of First Instance* (1990). See also Kennedy, "The Essential Minimum: The Establishment of the Court of First Instance" (1989) 14 ELRev 7.
95 TEU, Art. 19(1).
96 This allows the CJEU to be judicially active in terms of developing EU law.
97 The Treaties are somewhat skeletal in nature and need a great degree of interpretation.
98 Case 27/80 *Fietje* [1980] ECR 3389 at 3853, ECLI:EU:C:1980:293.

judges are guaranteed independence in the exercise of their functions and are in no way representatives of their States.[99]

President of the Court

3.063 The President of each court holds office for a renewable period of three years and is appointed by the judges from among their own number by a majority vote by way of a secret ballot. Each of the chambers of each court has a President who holds office for a renewable term of three years.

Registrar

3.064 Each court appoints its own registrar who is in charge of the court's administration and is responsible for the conduct of cases. The registrar's duties are enumerated in the Protocol on the Statute of the Court and the Rules of Procedure.

Advocates-General

3.065 The CJEU is assisted by 11 Advocates-General[100] who are similar in nature to the *Commissaire du Gouvernement* of the French *Conseil d'Etat*. (The General Court does not have Advocates-General.) These advocates are equal to judges in order of precedence but they are not judges. It is the duty of the Advocates-General "acting with complete impartiality and independence, to make, in open court, reasoned submissions on cases". One Advocate-General normally acts in each case before the CJEU. The Advocate-General summarises the arguments of the parties and makes reasoned arguments to the Court on the merits of the case and the options facing the Court, much in the manner of an *amicus curiae*. These opinions are highly influential and are usually followed by the Court. The opinions are also typically more detailed and longer than the ultimate judgment of the CJEU. There have been advocates-general with particular expertise and experience in EU shipping matters including, most notably, Advocates-General Gordon Slynn and Francis Jacobs.

Legal secretaries

3.066 Each judge and Advocate-General is assisted by "legal secretaries" or referendaires. These legal secretaries assist in the drafting of opinions and judgments. They are not secretaries in the traditional English sense of the term but are well-qualified lawyers who play an important role in the preparation of judgments. They are somewhat similar to clerks in the Supreme Court in the United States of America.

Appointment process of Judges and Advocates-General

3.067 Both judges and Advocates-General are chosen from

> "persons whose independence is beyond doubt and who possess the qualifications required for appointment to the highest judicial offices in their respective countries or who are jurisconsults of recognised competence; they shall be appointed by common accord of the Governments of the Member States for a term of six years".[101]

---

99 TEU, Art. 19(2).
100 TFEU, Art. 252.
101 TFEU, Art. 253.

Since the entry into force of the Treaty of Lisbon on 1 December 2009, their appointment requires consultation with a panel of former members of the CJEU and the General Court, national supreme courts and lawyers of recognised competence including one proposed by the European Parliament.[102] Instead of all the judges and advocates being replaced at one time, there is instead a partial replacement every three years.[103] As only some of the judges leave office, this ensures continuity. Judges and Advocates may be re-elected.[104] Judges and Advocates-General can also be dismissed or resign.

Operation of the Court

Seat

3.068 The Court has its seat in Luxembourg.

Plenary and chamber sessions

3.069 As a general rule, the Court sits in plenary session (i.e. a significant number of judges would sit on each case).[105] In some specific circumstances, namely, in cases brought by a Member State or an EU institution, or in a preliminary reference, the Court must sit in a larger format (i.e. more judges than the normal chamber). But, the Court may, and mostly does, sit in chambers of judges. The chamber system means that more cases can be dealt with by the Court as a whole and specialisation is possible. Chambers typically have a relatively small number of judges. Irrespective of the composition, one judge typically acts as the reporting judge and it is that judge who prepares a report for the other judges. The chamber or court issues a single judgment and there are no dissenting or separate opinions, which leads to uniformity or consistency.

General Court (formerly the Court of First Instance)

3.070 The SEA amended the Treaties so as to provide for a Court of First Instance (now called the General Court since the Treaty of Lisbon entered into force) to hear some classes of cases (such as competition), subject to an appeal to the CJEU itself but only on points of law.[106] It has expedited proceedings and developed enormous experience – particularly in the area of competition. The jurisdiction of the General Court has been expanded over time and it now has extensive jurisdiction.[107] It is very important in the context of competition law.

Lawyers

3.071 Any lawyer who is a member of the Bar of a Member State is entitled to appear before the Court.

---

102 TFEU, Art. 255.
103 TFEU, Art. 254.
104 Ibid.
105 TFEU, Art. 251.
106 TFEU, Art.256.
107 It has jurisdiction to hear and determine at first instance actions or proceedings under Arts 263, 265, 268, 270 and 272 TFEU with the exception of those assigned to a specialised court under Art. 257 and those reserved to the CJEU but these are not relevant to EU shipping law.

Languages

3.072 French is the working language of the Court but it also functions in the other official languages of the EU. The choice of language is determined by such factors as the Member State involved and the choice of language made by the applicant.

Procedure

3.073 The rules on practice and procedure generally of the Court are laid down in its Statute and rules of procedure.[108] The Court relies heavily on the written and inquisitorial procedures. The parties to the case initially submit written arguments to the Court. Typically the applicant submits an application to which the defendant files a Defence and there can then be a Reply and Rejoinder. The Court appoints a judge to investigate the case more fully. This judge collects evidence and starts considering the legal and factual issues involved. The Court then hears short oral arguments from the parties' lawyers. These arguments are not presented in an accusatorial way because there is, typically, no cross-examination of witnesses. Some time after the oral stage, the Advocate-General in the CJEU (but not in the General Court) usually delivers an opinion which is public. The Advocate-General proposes a decision to the problem at issue and sets out the legal position. This opinion (which is much longer than the eventual judgment of the Court) is often very important in outlining the current state, and sometimes predicting the future state, of EU law. The Court delivers its judgment some time after the Advocate-General's opinion and the judgment is normally short and consists of two parts: the *motifs* (the reasons for the decision) and the *dispositif* (the ruling). The Court usually follows the opinion of the Advocate-General. The Court often adopts a teleological approach in its interpretation. (The General Court does not have Advocate-General or an Advocate-General like procedure.)

Locus standi

3.074 Historically, as a general rule, only Member States, the Commission, the Council of Ministers or the Parliament may bring actions in the Court. Others may always bring cases on many aspects of EU law before the courts in each of the Member States. Parties other than Member States and EU institutions have limited rights before the CJEU. However, they may institute proceedings under Article 263 of the TFEU where the decision is of direct concern to them.[109] So, for example, an undertaking such as a shipping company fined by way of a Commission decision for breaching EU competition law may appeal the Commission decision to the General Court and, if need be, to the CJEU. Article 263 is examined below.

Effect and enforcement of judgments

3.075 A judgment has binding force from the date of its delivery. If the CJEU gives judgments against a body or an individual in the form of a fine then the fine is enforceable as a judgment debt.

---

108 See http://curia.europa.eu/jcms/upload/docs/application/pdf/2012-10/rp_en.pdf.
109 The action must be brought within typically two months of the decision.

Jurisdiction

Introduction

3.076 The jurisdiction of the CJEU (in the broadest sense of that term) may be classified under the following broad headings: (a) the Commission contending that a Member State has failed to fulfil a Treaty obligation; (b) a Member State contends that another Member State has failed to fulfil a Treaty obligation; (c) unlimited jurisdiction with respect to penalties; (d) actions to annul EU measures (e.g. Commission decisions imposing fines for breaches of competition law); (e) actions for inactivity; (f) pleas of illegality; (g) staff disputes; (h) preliminary references; and (i) opinions on external relations. It is useful to review a selection of headings of jurisdiction.

Article 258: Commission contending that a Member State has failed to fulfil a Treaty obligation

3.077 Article 258 of the TFEU provides:

"If the Commission considers[110] that a Member State has failed to fulfil an obligation under the Treaties, it shall deliver a reasoned opinion on the matter after giving the State concerned the opportunity to submit its observations.

If the State concerned does not comply with the opinion within the period laid down by the Commission, the latter may bring the matter before the Court of Justice of the European Union."

This provision[111] allows the Commission to fulfil more easily its function as watchdog of the Treaty. It is a necessary function: for example, the Commission issues hundreds of warnings to Member States each year. The Commission initiates the process by sending a letter[112] to the Member State concerned which must fully[113] set out the case against that State. If the Commission is not satisfied with the response (if any) to its letter then it may issue a non-legally binding opinion on the matter.[114] The Commission may then decide, if there has been no response to the opinion which is satisfactory to the Commission, to pursue the matter in the CJEU. If the Court "finds" that the Member State has failed to comply with the relevant provision then that State "shall be required to take the necessary measures to comply with the judgment of the Court".[115] An individual may not force the Commission to bring such proceedings.[116] Nor may the Member State defend the action by pleading internal circumstances (e.g. costs or lack of personnel).[117]

---

110 Ed., the Commission does not have to demonstrate a legal interest: Case 167/73 *Commission v France* [1974] ECR 359 at 368–369, ECLI:EU:C:1974:35.

111 On Art. 258 see e.g. Case 7/71 *Commission v France* [1971] ECR 1003, ECLI:EU:C:1971:121 and Case 61/77 *Commission v Ireland* [1978] ECR 417, ECLI:EU:C:1978:29.

112 See Case 211/81 *Commission v Denmark* [1982] ECR 4547 at 4557, ECLI:EU:C:1982:437.

113 See Case 31/69 *Commission v Italy* [1970] ECR 25 at 33, ECLI:EU:C:1970:10; Case 7/69 *Commission v Italy* [1970] ECR 111 at 117, ECLI:EU:C:1970:15; and Case 51/83 *Commission v Italy* [1984] ECR 2793 at 2804, ECLI:EU:C:1984:261.

114 See Cases 142 and 143/80 *Amministrazione delle Finanze dello Stato v Essevi SpA et al.* [1981] ECR 1413, at 1432–1433, ECLI:EU:C:1981:121.

115 TFEU, Art. 260(1).

116 Case 48/65 *Lütticke v Commission* [1966] ECR 19 at 27, ECLI:EU:C:1966:8; Case 7/68 *Commission v Italy* [1968] ECR 423 at 428 ECLI:EU:C:1968:51; and Case 7/71 *Commission v France* [1971] ECR 1003 at 1016, ECLI:EU:C:1971:121.

117 See Case 254/83 *Commission v Italy* [1984] ECR 3395, ECLI:EU:C:1984:302; Case 39/72 *Commission v Italy* [1973] ECR 101, ECLI:EU:C:1973:13; and Case C-39/88 *Re Fishery Price Information: Commission v Ireland* [1990] ECR I-4271, ECLI:EU:C:1990:420.

Article 259: A Member State contends that another Member State has failed to fulfil a Treaty obligation

3.078 Under Article 259 of the TFEU:

"A Member State which considers that another Member State has failed to fulfil an obligation under the Treaties may bring the matter before the Court of Justice of the European Union.

Before a Member State brings an action against another Member State for an alleged infringement of an obligation under the Treaties, it shall bring the matter before the Commission.

The Commission shall deliver a reasoned opinion after each of the States concerned has been given the opportunity to submit its own case and its observations on the other party's case both orally and in writing.

If the Commission has not delivered an opinion within three months of the date on which the matter was brought before it, the absence of such opinion shall not prevent the matter from being brought before the Court."

Article 259 is an alternative to the Article 258 procedure. Article 259 is invoked rarely. Ireland was the first State to invoke the procedure though the case was later withdrawn.[118] If the Court "finds" that the Member State has failed to comply with the relevant Treaty then that State "shall be required to take the necessary measures to comply with the judgment of the Court".[119]

Article 261: Unlimited jurisdiction with respect to penalties

3.079 Article 261 of the TFEU provides:

"[r]egulations adopted jointly by the European Parliament and the Council, and by the Council, pursuant to the provisions of the Treaties, may give the Court of Justice of the European Union unlimited jurisdiction with regard to the penalties provided for in such regulations".

Article 263: Actions to annul EU measures

3.080 Under Article 263 of the TFEU, the CJEU/General Court have extensive powers of annulment. The article provides:

"The Court of Justice of the European Union shall review the legality of legislative acts, of acts of the Council, of the Commission and of the European Central Bank, other than recommendations and opinions, and of acts of the European Parliament and of the European Council intended to produce legal effects vis-à-vis third parties. It shall also review the legality of acts of bodies, offices or agencies of the Union intended to produce legal effects vis-à-vis third parties.

It shall for this purpose have jurisdiction in actions brought by a Member State, the European Parliament, the Council or the Commission on grounds of lack of competence, infringement of an essential procedural requirement, infringement of the Treaties or of any rule of law relating to their application, or misuse of powers.

The Court shall have jurisdiction under the same conditions in actions brought by the Court of Auditors, by the European Central Bank and by the Committee of the Regions for the purpose of protecting their prerogatives.

Any natural or legal person may, under the conditions laid down in the first and second paragraphs, institute proceedings against an act addressed to that person or which is of direct and individual concern to them, and against a regulatory act which is of direct concern to them and does not entail implementing measures.

---

118 Case 58/77 *Ireland v France* (OJ 1977 C142/8).
119 TFEU, Art. 260(1).

Acts setting up bodies, offices and agencies of the Union may lay down specific conditions and arrangements concerning actions brought by natural or legal persons against acts of these bodies, offices or agencies intended to produce legal effects in relation to them.

The proceedings provided for in this Article shall be instituted within two months of the publication of the measure or of its notification to the plaintiff, or, in the absence thereof, of the day on which it came to the knowledge of the latter, as the case may be."

This article is normally used in seeking annul Commission decisions.

Article 265: Actions for inactivity

3.081 A remedy must be available not only where an institution *acts* unlawfully but also where it fails to act. Under Article 265 of the TFEU:

"[s]hould the European Parliament, the European Council, the Council, the Commission or the European Central Bank, in infringement of the Treaties, fail to act, the Member States and the other institutions of the Union may bring an action before the Court of Justice of the European Union to have the infringement established. This Article shall apply, under the same conditions, to bodies, offices and agencies of the Union which fail to act.

The action shall be admissible only if the institution concerned has first been called to act. If, within two months of being so called upon, the institution concerned has not defined its position, the action may be brought within a further period of two months.

Any natural or legal person may, under the conditions laid down in the preceding paragraphs, complain to the Court of Justice of the European Union that an institution, body, office or agency of the Union has failed to address to that person any act other than a recommendation or an opinion."

Thus, the CJEU can be asked to declare that the failure of an EU institution or body to act, where it was legally obliged to do so, constitutes a breach of EU law. An action for failure to act may be brought by the European Parliament.[120] A natural or legal person may bring proceedings under this procedure against an institution or body which fails to issue a binding act only when that person would have been the addressee.[121]

Article 270 TFEU: Staff disputes

3.082 The judicial tribunals of many international organisations have jurisdiction over disputes relating to staff within the organisations. Under Article 270 of the TFEU, the CJEU has jurisdiction in any dispute between the Union and its servants within the limits and under the conditions laid down in the Staff Regulations of Officials and the Conditions of Employment of other servants of the Union. These matters are now heard by a special labour court or Civil Service Tribunal.[122]

Article 267 TFEU: Preliminary references

3.083 Perhaps the most interesting procedural provision in the TFEU is Article 267 of the TFEU which provides the CJEU with the competence to give preliminary rulings concerning, *inter alia*, the interpretation of the Treaties.[123] The article states:

---

120 E.g. Case 13/83 *Parliament v Council* OJ 1983 C49/9.
121 Case 15/71 *Mackprang v Commission* [1971] ECR 797 at 804, ECLI:EU:C:1971:98.
122 http://curia.europa.eu/jcms/jcms/T5_5230/.
123 On the preliminary reference See Gray, "Advisory Opinions and the European Court of Justice" (1983) 8 ELRev 24 and Arnull, "Article 177 and the Retreat from *Van Duyn*" (1983) 8 ELRev 365. The original numbering of treaty provision relating to preliminary references was Art. 177 of the EEC Treaty.

"The Court of Justice of the European Union shall have jurisdiction to give preliminary rulings concerning:

(a) the interpretation of the Treaties;
(b) the validity and interpretation of acts of the institutions, bodies, offices or agencies of the Union.

Where such a question is raised before any court or tribunal of a Member State, that court or tribunal may, if it considers that a decision on the question is necessary to enable it to give judgment, request the Court to give a ruling thereon.

Where any such question is raised in a case pending before a court or tribunal of a Member State against whose decisions there is no judicial remedy under national law, that court or tribunal shall bring the matter before the Court.

If such a question is raised in a case pending before a court or tribunal of a Member State with regard to a person in custody, the Court of Justice of the European Union shall act with the minimum of delay."

Thus, where an issue arises in the course of litigation in a Member State court or tribunal involving an interpretation of the Treaties then the national court or tribunal *may*[124] request the CJEU to give a preliminary ruling on the point at issue. A reference *must* be made by any court or tribunal against whose decisions there is no judicial remedy. Article 267 has been used by the courts in Member States on numerous occasions. The CJEU deals, as a general rule, in "abstract questions" with the final judgment being left for the Member State court or tribunal.

Opinions on external relations

3.084 Article 218(11) of the TFEU provides in the context of international agreements concluded by the EU:

"A Member State, the European Parliament, the Council or the Commission may obtain the opinion of the Court of Justice as to whether an agreement envisaged is compatible with the Treaties. Where the opinion of the Court of Justice is adverse, the agreement may not enter into force unless it is amended or the Treaties are revised."

Interim measures

3.085 It is also possible that the CJEU or the General Court may grant interim measures which are comparable to injunction in English law. It should be stressed that their grant is unusual and requires high standards to be met.

Other institutions

3.086 There are two other institutions, namely, the ECB and the Court of Auditors. The ECB, established in 1999, is the central bank for Europe's single currency, the euro. The ECB's main task is to maintain the euro's purchasing power and price stability in the euro area. The euro area comprises the 19 Member States. A single Court of Auditors has

---

124 The decision to refer is a critical one (given the cost, delay and other implications of a referral) and is for the national court to make the decision (see Cases 98, 162 and 258/85 *Bertini* [1986] ECR 1893, ECLI:EU:C:1986:246). Ultimately, it is a matter for the CJEU to decide on whether or not a reference should be made: Case 283/81 *CILFIT v Ministry of Health* [1982] ECR 3415, ECLI:EU:C:1982:335.

served all three Communities since 1 June 1977. Its function is to ensure that the EU's financial resources are properly spent.

Bodies

Introduction

3.087 There are several agencies or bodies (i.e. entities less than an institution) which deal with maritime matters including FRONTEX (the European agency for the management of operational co-operation at the external borders of the Member States), the European Defence Agency, the EMSA, the Community Fisheries Control Agency and the European Environmental Agency.

Economic and Social Committee

3.088 The EESC[125] is an advisory body which delivers advisory reports on proposed regulations and draws up reports on matters such as competition. It assists the Council and the Commission acting in an advisory capacity. The Committee has played a very significant role in shipping matters.

European Investment Bank

3.089 The non-profit making European Investment Bank ("EIB") is established with the task of contributing, by having recourse to the capital market and utilising its own resources, to the balanced and steady development of the internal market in the interest of the Union. Its members are the Member States. It grants loans and gives guarantees which facilitate the financing of: (a) projects for developing less-developed regions; (b) projects for modernising or converting undertakings or for developing fresh activities called for by the progressive establishment or functioning of the internal market, where these projects are of such a size or nature that they cannot be entirely financed by the various means available in the individual Member States; (c) projects of common interest to several Member States which are of such a size or nature that they cannot be entirely financed by the various means available in the individual Member States. It is different from the ECB which is the monetary and policy authority for the Member States which are part of the EMU. The EIB lends money to finance certain port projects; for example, in 2003, the EIB announced that it was fronting a €22.4 million loan to the Port of Brussels as part of a larger €50 million agreement for financing port projects (namely, the clean-up and rehabilitation of a site, refurbishment and expansion of a multimodal logistics centre as well as the construction of warehousing).

Civic Society and Lobby Groups

3.090 There is now a well-established network of associations and lobbyists seeking to influence the EU and its institutions. There can be no doubt that these associations have some influence over the EU's institutions and their output. Among the better known

---

125 TFEU, Arts 301–304.

associations are the European Community Shipowners' Association,[126] the World Shipping Council,[127] the European Tugowners' Association,[128] the European Dredging Association,[129] the Cruise Lines International Association,[130] Interferry[131] and the European Community Association of Ship Brokers and Agents.[132] There is no doubt that both sides gain something by learning from each other's perspectives.

E. EU LAW

Introduction

3.091 The laws enacted by the EU have a unique character and quality. Unlike most other international organisations, the EU has the power to make law which is binding on Member States and even persons in those States. EU law is supreme and overrides any national law of the Member States which may be in conflict.[133] In essence, there has been a transfer of some of the powers of the Member States to the EU.[134]

Sources of EU law

Primary law

Foundation Treaties (including annexes and protocols)
3.092 The primary sources of EU law are the TEU, the TFEU and the EAEC. A number of other treaties and agreements have been concluded between the Member States which supplement the regime.

Duration
3.093 The treaties are of unlimited duration.[135]

Territorial application
3.094 The Treaties apply to both the land mass and the territorial sea of the Member States. The Treaties apply to various territories of Member States outside Europe as well. As this area is involved and evolving, regard should be had to the position in regard to each territory at any one point in time. They may have extra-territorial effect in certain cases.

Accession Treaties
3.095 There were six founding States. Twenty-two States have joined since the foundation of the EU and each State has acceded to the Foundation Treaties. Thus, there

---

126 www.ecsa.eu/.
127 www.worldshipping.org/.
128 www.eurotugowners.com/.
129 www.european-dredging.eu/.
130 www.cruising.org/.
131 www.interferry.com/.
132 www.fonasba.com/fonasba-member/ecasba.
133 Case 6/64 *Costa v ENEL* [1964] ECR 585, ECLI:EU:C:1964:66.
134 See Case 7/71 *Commission v France* [1971] ECR 1003, at p. 1018, ECLI:EU:C:1971:121. See also Ussher, *European Community Law and National Law: The Irreversible Transfer?* (1981).
135 TFEU, Art. 356.

have been several so-called Accession Treaties. Each made significant changes to the Foundation Treaties. One area, namely Greenland, has left the EU. Thus there is one secession treaty, called the "Treaty amending, with regard to Greenland, the Treaties establishing the European Communities". The implications of this latter treaty are understandably marginal.

Institutional treaties and measures

3.096 The institutional treaties include the Convention on Certain Institutions Common to the Three Communities,[136] the Treaty Establishing a Single Council and a Single Commission (the so-called Merger Treaty),[137] the Act of the Council concerning Direct elections to the European Parliament, the SEA, the TEU, the Treaty of Amsterdam and the Treaty of Nice.

Financial treaties

3.097 There are treaties and other measures relating to financial and budgetary matters. These include the Decision Creating the Communities' Own Resources, the Treaty Amending Certain Budgetary Provisions and the Treaty Amending Certain Financial Provisions.

SEA

3.098 The SEA was adopted by the Member States as part of their desire "to continue the work undertaken on the basis of the Treaties establishing the European Communities and to transform relations as a whole among their States into a European Union".[138] Title I, Article 1 of the SEA provides that the "European Communities and European Political Co-operation shall have as their objective to contribute together to making concrete progress towards European Unity".

Maastricht Treaty

3.099 A TEU was signed in Maastricht on 7 February 1992. The Treaty provides for the establishment of a European Union involving an EMU. The TEU was supplemented by the Treaty of Amsterdam in 1997.

Failed Constitution

3.100 The proposal to have a constitution for the EU was defeated by virtue of the fact that the people of France and the Netherlands rejected ratification by their countries of the proposed Constitution. The project for the Constitution was abandoned. After a period of reflection, a new treaty, the Treaty of Lisbon, was agreed by the Member States. The Treaty of Lisbon was rejected by the Irish people in a referendum but after Ireland was given certain commitments, Ireland voted in favour of ratification. Ultimately, the Treaty of Lisbon entered into force on 1 December 2009. In all probability, the Constitution was seen as too ambitious for the EU and sought to displace the Member States.

---

136 1957.
137 1965.
138 Preamble to the SEA.

Secondary law

3.101 Secondary legislation is very important in the context of shipping because maritime transport is mentioned only once in the context of primary legislation (i.e. Article 100(2) of the TFEU). Secondary legislation is as binding as primary legislation but is secondary in so far as if it conflicts with primary legislation then it is "secondary" to the primary legislation. Secondary legislation has full legal effect. It is published in the *Official Journal of the European Union*.[139] In simple terms, the different instruments of secondary EU law are shown in Table 3.2.

Table 3.2 EU sources of law and policy

Primary Law	EC Treaty
Secondary Laws	Regulations
Secondary Laws	Directives
Secondary Laws	Decisions
Non-Binding	Opinions
Non-Binding	Recommendations

3.102 Article 288 of the TFEU provides:

"To exercise the Union's competences, the institutions shall adopt regulations, directives, recommendations and opinions.

A regulation shall have general application. It shall be binding in its entirety and directly applicable in all Member States.

A directive shall be binding, as to the result to be achieved, upon each Member State to which it is addressed, but shall be binding in its entirety. A decision which specifies those to whom it is addressed shall be binding only on them.

Recommendations and opinions shall have no binding force."

Regulations

3.103 A regulation[140] is adopted by (a) the European Parliament acting jointly with the Council, (b) the Council itself or the Commission. The Council/Parliament act on the basis of a provision or provisions in a Treaty while the Commission normally acts on the basis of powers delegated to it from the Council. A regulation is general in application. It binds all the Member States from the date of its adoption or entry into force (whichever is specified in the regulation). It must be published in the *Official Journal of the European Union*.[141] A regulation is binding in its entirety and is directly applicable in all Member States.[142] It has the same effect as if it were a national law but is superior to any conflicting national law where the regulation is adopted validly. Regulations do not require implementing legislation[143] but they may have supplementary legislation in such matters as a means of enforcing the regulation. A regulation has the purpose of achieving

---

139 The *Official Journal* (referred to as the OJ) is published almost daily principally in two forms: the first referred to as the "L" version contains legislation and other matters whose publication is compulsory as well as the "C" version which contains notices and matters whose publication is not compulsory (such as certain Commission proposals).
140 On regulations see TFEU, Art. 288.
141 In the "L" series of the OJ.
142 TFEU, Art. 288.
143 See Case 50/76 *Amsterdam Bulb* [1977] ECR 137, ECLI:EU:C:1977:13.

uniformity between the Member States; this is achieved in part by the fact that Member States have no implementing legislation to adopt so there is less chance of interference with the EU aims which are embodied in the regulation itself. It must be reasoned and based on a provision in the relevant Treaty (normally the TFEU). A regulation is presumed to be valid unless and until it is struck down/annulled by the CJEU. Any national legislation which conflicts with a regulation is invalid and of no effect. Regulations have been used on a number of occasions in regard to shipping matters, most notably, in the cases of Regulations 4055/86,[144] the now repealed 4056/86[145] as well as the still extant 4057/86[146] and 4058/86.[147]

Directives

3.104 Not everything is capable of, or suitable for, uniform treatment throughout the EU by way of a regulation. Directives require Member States to achieve a particular *result* but leave the *form and method* to the individual Member State.[148] Thus, Member States are obliged to amend their laws so as to bring them into line with directives. The Member States must implement the directive *in full* within the specified time limits – failure to do so exposes the Member State to possible enforcement proceedings being instituted by the Commission in the CJEU.[149] Directives must be based on a provision of the Foundation Treaties, normally, the TFEU. The purpose of a directive is to achieve approximation and harmonisation of the laws between the Member States but not uniformity. Directives are addressed to Member States but may still create rights for individuals. Directives have been used in shipping matters, such as in the area of safety but they are relatively uncommon as compared to regulations and decisions in this area.

Decisions

3.105 A decision is binding in its entirety on the State or the person to whom it is addressed.[150] Decisions must be reasoned and based on a provision of the Treaties (most normally, for present purposes, on a provision of the TFEU). While publication is not obligatory,[151] they are usually published in the *Official Journal of the European Union*. Decisions are important in regard to the application of competition law to shipping in that a decision may be taken against an undertaking breaching EU competition law. A decision is the legal instrument used to impose fines or condemn behaviour.

Recommendations

3.106 Occasionally, EU institutions merely *recommend* a course of action rather than order it. For example, the Council made a recommendation in respect of passenger ferry safety and the Commission proposed a recommendation on improving the effectiveness

---

144 OJ 1986 L378/1.
145 OJ 1986 L378/3.
146 OJ 1986 L378/14.
147 OJ 1986 L378/21.
148 TFEU, Art. 288.
149 Note, in particular, the possibility of Art. 258 proceedings.
150 TFEU, Art. 288. Advocate-General Warner said in Case 19/77 *Miller v Commission* [1978] ECR 131 at 161, ECLI:EU:C:1978:19 that decisions were not "law creating".
151 EC, Art. 254(2). The Commission decision in *Irish Continental Group plc v CCI de Morlaix (Interim Measures)* was not published in the OJ but it has been published elsewhere (e.g. [1995] 5 CMLR 177).

of Port State Control.¹⁵² Recommendations are not legally binding in themselves but may lay the foundation for future action by the EU.

Resolutions

3.107 Bodies such as the European Parliament occasionally adopt resolutions on particular topics. These resolutions are not legally binding in themselves but express the "resolve" of the institution adopting the resolution.

Agreements

3.108 The EU, in its international capacity, frequently adopts agreements with other international organisations (which have the legal capacity to conclude such agreements) and States. They are of growing significance in shipping and international legal matters.

General principles of EU law

3.109 Some principles of law common to all or many of the legal systems in Member States have been used by the CJEU and the Commission in reaching its decisions. It has used, for example, the principles of legitimate expectation,¹⁵³ proportionality,¹⁵⁴ legal certainty,¹⁵⁵ the principles of human rights¹⁵⁶ as well as equality and non-discrimination.¹⁵⁷

Case law of the CJEU

3.110 Unlike the system of *stare decisis* operated by the English, American, Commonwealth and Irish courts, the CJEU is not obliged to follow its previous decisions and may depart freely from them without having to provide an explanation. In practice, it rarely departs from its own previous decisions. Case law is therefore cited regularly as a source of law.

Soft law

3.111 Despite the TFEU setting out the sources of law, there are some instruments and principles which are not legally binding but are referred to as so-called "soft law" because while not hard law they are persuasive to some extent.

Opinions of the Advocates-General

3.112 The opinions of the Advocates-General are not binding in themselves but they can be persuasive in present and future cases.

---

152 On the Commission proposal, see OJ 1989 C263/15.
153 I.e. the EU will not act in any way contrary to the expectations legitimately held by those affected by the proposed action: see Case 81/72 *Commission v Council* [1973] ECR 575, ECLI:EU:C:1973:60.
154 I.e. EU action should not exceed what is actually necessary so as to achieve the objectives sought. Cf. Case 114/76 *Bela-Muhle v Grows Farm* [1977] ECR 1211, ECLI:EU:C:1977:116 and Case 122/78 *Buitoni v FORMA* [1979] ECR 677 at 684, ECLI:EU:C:1979:43.
155 See Case 13/61 *Bosch v De Geus* [1962] ECR 45, ECLI:EU:C:1962:11; Case 85/76 *Hoffmann-La Roche v Commission* [1979] ECR 461, at 510, ECLI:EU:C:1979:36; Case 169/80 *Gondrand Freres* [1981] ECR 1219, at 1232, ECLI:EU:C:1981:171; Case 4/73 *Nold v Commission* [1974] ECR 491, ECLI:EU:C:1974:51; and Cases 209/78 etc., *Van Landewyck v Commission* [1980] ECR 3125 at 3248, ECLI:EU:C:1980:248.
156 Cf. Case 36/75 *Rutili v Commission* [1974] ECR 491, ECLI:EU:C:1975:137 and Case 136/79 *National Panasonic v Commission* [1979] ECR 2033, ECLI:EU:C:1980:169.
157 Cases 103 and 145/77 *Royal Scholten Honig v Intervention Board* [1978] ECR 2037 at 2072, ECLI:EU:C:1978:186.

Direct effect and direct applicability

3.113 In accordance with the doctrine of direct applicability as set out in Article 288 of the TFEU, regulations have direct applicability in Member States. Directives or decisions do not have direct applicability under the TFEU. This means that regulations do not need to be re-enacted in the legislation of the Member States.[158] Directives and decisions are not given direct applicability under the TFEU and require national legislation so as to implement them generally.[159] The CJEU has held, in a series of judgments,[160] that these measures may have direct effect. Direct effect means that a measure creates rights which may be relied upon by persons in litigation before the courts of the Member States and those courts must give effect to these measures. Directly effective measures may only be invoked *against* a Member State[161] (or an emanation of the State) but not *by* a Member State[162] (i.e. it only has "vertical effect" (i.e. person ↔ State) but not horizontal effect (i.e. person ↔ person) which regulations have). The CJEU adopted this reasoning because Member States have often failed to adopt laws to implement those measures. The Court is of the view that it would be illogical and inconsistent with the binding nature of the EU legal system not to allow persons to rely on these measures against Member States in so far as they establish clear, precise and legally complete obligations just because the Member States or the Institutions have failed to implement the measure.

Publication of EU law

3.114 The secondary legislation, as well as many other instruments, is published in the EU's *Official Journal of the European Union*. Since 1 January 1968, the *Official Journal* has been divided into two separate series, the "L" series which contains legislation and the "C" series which contains notices, proposals, information, as well as various communications.

Relationship between EU law and national laws

3.115 The EU is an independent legal order which is capable of creating rights and duties affecting not only the Member States but individuals and other undertakings. EU law is part of the national law of each of the Member States. EU law is superior to national law but only in so far as EU law applies. Provisions of EU law which confer rights and duties on individuals and so on are said to have direct effect.[163] Any measure

---

158 See Case 50/76 *Amsterdam Bulb* [1977] ECR 137, ECLI:EU:C:1977:13. See Arnull, "The Direct Effect of Directives: Grasping the Nettle" [1986] 35 ICLQ 932.
159 See Case 169/87 *Commission v France* [1974] ECR 359, ECLI:EU:C:1988:393.
160 E.g. see Case 9/70 *Grad v Finanzant Traunstein* [1970] ECR 825, ECLI:EU:C:1970:78.
161 See Cases 21–4/72 *International Fruit Co v Produktschap* [1972] ECR 1219, ECLI:EU:C:1972:115, and Case 152/84 *Marshall v Southampton Area Health Authority* [1986] ECR 723, ECLI:EU:C:1986:84.
162 See Case 80/86 *Kolpinghuis Nijimegen* [1987] ECR 3969, ECLI:EU:C:1987:431.
163 Winter, "Direct Applicability and Direct Effect: Two Distinct and Different Concepts in Community Law", 9 CMLRev 425; Pescatore, "The Doctrine of 'Direct Effect': An Infant Disease of Community Law", 8 ELRev 155. Cf. Case 26/62 *Van Gend en Loos* [1963] ECR 1, ECLI:EU:C:1963:1; Case 6/64 *Costa v ENEL* [1964] ECR 585, ECLI:EU:C:1964:66; Case 28/67 *Molkerei-Zentrale Westfalen v Hauptzollamt Paderborn* [1968] ECR 143, ECLI:EU:C:1968:17; Case 41/74 *Van Duyn v Home Office* [1974] ECR 1337, ECLI:EU:C:1974:133; Case 43/75 *Defrenne v Sabena* [1976] ECR 455, 474, ECLI:EU:C:1976:56.

which has direct effect is superior to any Member State law. EU law takes precedence over the national law of the Member States irrespective of when the laws were adopted.[164] This rule applies to civil and criminal[165] law as well as, in certain case, the rules of professional organisations.[166] Member State legislation which is incompatible with EU law is of no effect and should be "repealed" – if only for good legal order.[167] If an area of law has been made subject to EU legislation exclusively then the Member States may no longer legislate in respect of that area.[168] Member States may continue to legislate where the EU has done no more than co-ordinate national legislation on a topic.[169] The courts of the Member States are obliged to ensure the effectiveness of EU law.[170]

Interpretation of EU law

3.116 The interpretation of EU law is a fascinating study. There are four primary interpretative techniques or methods used by the CJEU and others involved in construing EU law: the literal; the historical; the comparative; and the teleological. The literal method involves examining the obvious meaning in the literary context of the document. The historical method involves an analysis of the legislative history of the provision at issue. This is rarely used in practice.[171] The comparative approach involves a comparison of the laws of the various legal systems of the Member States[172] – while using this approach, the Court does not look for the lowest common denominator between the laws. The teleological approach involves looking at the broad aims and goals of the legislators in enacting the provision. The CJEU is flexible in its approach to interpretation but must not be too flexible.[173] The context of the legislation must be examined.[174] This approach is assisted by the use of recitals as preambular statements in the measures.[175] Juristic writings are far more important in the CJEU than in the British or Irish courts. EU laws are multilingual,[176] being published in all of the official languages.[177] Each text is equally authentic. If there is a divergence between the texts then each text must be interpreted in the light of the other texts.[178] Both the Advocates-General and the judges have examined words and expressions used in several languages to elucidate meanings of provisions in various measures. The interesting problem of how to interpret national legislation which has been enacted

---

164 See Case 6/64 *Costa v ENEL* [1964] ECR 585, ECLI:EU:C:1964:34.
165 See Case 8/74 *Procureur du Roi v Dassonville* [1974] ECR 837, ECLI:EU:C:1974:82.
166 See Cases 266 and 267/87 *R. v Royal Pharmaceutical Society of Great Britain ex p. Secretary of State for Social Services* [1989] ECR 1295, ECLI:EU:C:1989:205.
167 See Case 167/73 *Commission v France (the French Seafarers' case)* [1974] ECR 359, ECLI:EU:C:1974:35.
168 Case 60/86 *Commission v United Kingdom* [1988] ECR 3921, ECLI:EU:C:1988:382.
169 See Case 21/87 *Borowitz v Bundesversicherungsanstalt für Angestellte* [1988] ECR 3715, ECLI:EU:C:1988:362.
170 See Case 158/80 *Rewe v Hauptzollamt Kiel* [1981] ECR 1805, ECLI:EU:C:1981:163.
171 See Case 136/79 *National Panasonic (UK) Ltd v Commission* [1980] ECR 2033, ECLI:EU:C:1980:169.
172 See Case 155/79 *AM & S Europe v Commission* [1982] ECR 1575, ECLI:EU:C:1982:157.
173 See Case 122/80 *Analog Devices* [1981] ECR 2781, ECLI:EU:C:1981:273.
174 See Case 292/82 *Merck v Hauptzollamt Hamburg-Jonas* [1983] ECR 3781, ECLI:EU:C:1983:335.
175 E.g. Case 83/78 *Pigs Marketing Board v Redmond* [1978] ECR 2347, ECLI:EU:C:1978:214.
176 See e.g. Cases 286/82 and 26/83 *Luisi and Carbone v Ministero del Tesoro* [1984] ECR 377, ECLI:EU:C:1984:35; and Case 305/85 *United Kingdom v Commission* [1988] ECR 467, ECLI:EU:C:1988:41.
177 Some measures are also published in the Irish language, but this is not an official language.
178 This is a frequent problem in international law.

because of, or on the basis of, EU legislation was discussed by the CJEU in *Johnston v Chief Constable of the RUC* when the Court said:

> "in applying national law, and in particular the provisions of national legislation specifically introduced in order to implement [d]irective[s] ... national courts are required to interpret their national law in the light of the wording and the purpose of the directive in order to achieve the result referred to in the third paragraph of Article [249] of the [TFEU]".[179]

Article 267 of the TFEU facilitates a uniform interpretation by allowing the CJEU to adopt a common approach to the interpretation of a particular provision in a measure.[180]

Selected fundamental principles of EU law

Non-discrimination between EU nationals on the basis of nationality

3.117 It is a fundamental general[181] principle of EU law that there may be no discrimination between nationals of Member States in any area of EU law.[182] This could be quite useful in the context of EU shipping law because sometimes Member States seek to adopt measures which protect their own nationals to the prejudice of nationals of other Member States. Article 18 of the TFEU provides:

> "Within the scope and application of the Treaties, and without prejudice to any special provisions contained therein, any discrimination on grounds of nationality shall be prohibited.
>
> The European Parliament and the Council, acting in accordance with the ordinary legislative procedure, may adopt rules designed to prohibit such discrimination."

Proportionality

3.118 The doctrine of proportionality[183] provides that an action or course of conduct must be proportionate or appropriate to the objective to be achieved.

Legitimate expectation

3.119 The doctrine of legitimate expectation is recognised in EU law. This means that EU law will protect the interests of someone who acted to his or her detriment on the basis of a "legitimate expectation".

Enforcement of EU law in the Courts of Member States

3.120 All the courts in the Member States are obliged to apply EU law.[184] EU law may be raised as an issue in any court in the EU.[185] In the English courts, tort actions might be brought in relation to the breach of EU law on grounds such as breach of statutory duty or

---

179 Case 222/84 [1986] ECR 1651 at para. 53, ECLI:EU:C:1986:206. See also Case 14/83 *von Colson v Land Nordheim-Westfalen* [1984] ECR 189, ECLI:EU:C:1984:153.
180 See e.g. Case 102/86 *Apple and Pear Development Council v Customs and Excise* [1988] ECR 1443, ECLI:EU:C:1988:120.
181 Exceptions are permitted, see e.g. TFEU, Art. 45(4).
182 TFEU, Art. 17. See e.g. Cases 286/82 and 26/83 *Luisi and Carbone v Ministero del Tesoro* [1984] ECR 377, ECLI:EU:C:1984:35 and Case 305/85 *United Kingdom v Commission* [1988] ECR 467, ECLI:EU:C:1988:41.
183 See *Garden Cottage Foods v Milk Marketing Board* [1984] AC 130.
184 See Case 106/77 *Simmenthal* [1978] ECR 629, ECLI:EU:C:1978:49.
185 See Case 158/80 *Rewe v Hauptzollamt Kiel* [1981] ECR 1805, ECLI:EU:C:1981:163.

perhaps misfeasance in a public office.[186] Injunctions may be granted in those courts to restrain breaches of EU law.[187] Claims for damages for breach of EU competition law (e.g. Articles 101 or 102 of the TFEU) may also be instituted in the courts of any Member States and have been made somewhat easier by virtue of the adoption of the so-called "Damages Directive".[188]

Freedoms

3.121 It is worth highlighting briefly at this juncture, as the issue is explored further in other parts of this book, the four basic freedoms in EU law. As a general principle, goods may move freely around the Member States (i.e. the free movement of goods principle), persons (e.g. workers) may move freely around the EU (i.e. the free movement of persons principle), services may move and EU business may establish freely in other Member States (i.e. the freedom of establishment and free movement of services principle) and, finally, capital may move freely around the EU (i.e. the free movement of capital principle).

F. CONCLUSIONS

3.122 This chapter is a very basic introduction to some aspects of EU law and has been designed to give readers an overview of some aspects of EU law. It is impossible to encapsulate in a single chapter all the richness and complexities of EU law. It is useful to recall in construing and applying EU law the flexibility, malleability and adaptability of EU law but also the fact that it is relatively new – it is just over 50 years old – so it is constantly developing and evolving.

---

186 See *Bourgoin v Ministry of Agriculture* [1985] 3 WLR 1027.
187 See *Garden Cottage Foods v Milk Marketing Board* [1984] AC 130.
188 Dir. 2014/104 of the European Parliament and of the Council of 26 November 2014 on certain rules governing actions for damages under national law for infringements of the competition law provisions of the Member States and of the European Union OJ L349/1, 5 December 2014, http://eur-lex.europa.eu/legal-content/EN/TXT/PDF/?uri=CELEX:32014L0104&from=EN.

CHAPTER 4

An overview of European Union transport law

A. INTRODUCTION

Purpose of this chapter

4.001 This chapter examines selected aspects of the law of the European Union ("EU") as it relates to transport[1] generally.[2] An understanding of the EU law relating to transport in general is useful in trying to understand the EU law relating to shipping in particular. This short chapter therefore forms a backdrop to the discussion of EU shipping law which follows in later chapters. In particular, this chapter examines the provisions relating to transport in the Treaty on the Functioning of the European Union ("TFEU").

Importance of transport in the EU

4.002 Transport is an inherent part of any economic community – it is, however, particularly important in the EU's economy. First, it accounts for about 6.3% of the EU's gross domestic product ("GDP")[3] and this is more than agriculture – indeed, agriculture and transport were the only economic sectors which had Titles devoted to them in the original EEC Treaty. Transport is the subject of a common policy under Article 3 of the EU

---

1 In the context of this chapter, "transport" is taken to mean the carriage of persons or goods from one place to another other than by pipeline. So it covers road, rail, inland waterway, air and sea/maritime transport.

2 On EU transport law and policy generally see, Abbati, *Transport and European Integration* (1986); Commission, *The European Community's Transport Policy*, Periodical 3/1984; Commission, *The Community and Transport Policy*, European File 10/85; Greaves, *Transport Law of the European Community* (1991); Greaves, *EC Transport Law* (2000); Handley, *Transport Policy in the European Union* (2003); Kapteyn and Van Themaat, *Introduction to the Law of the European Communities* (2nd ed., 1989, ed. Gormley), p. 705 *et seq.*; Karsten, "Passengers, Consumers, and Travellers: The Rise of Passenger Rights in EC Transport Law and its Repercussions for Community Consumer Law and Policy" (2007) 30 Journal of Consumer Policy 117; and Simons, *Recht en Onrecht in het Europees Vervoerbeleid* (1986). See also Close, "Article 84 EEC: The Development of Transport Policy in the Sea and Air Sectors" (1980) 5 ELRev 188; Close, "Inland Transport Services: Recent Developments in Community Policy" (1985) 22 CMLRev 587; Greaves, "EC Transport Law and Policy: A Status Report" (1999) 2 CYELS 261; and Xuereb (1989) 38 ICLQ 697. See also the Report of a Conference held on 4 and 5 March 1963 on "The Legal Provisions Relating to Transport in the Common Market" (British Institute of International and Comparative Law, Special Publication No 2 (1963)).

On EU transport generally, see Despicht, *Policies for Transport in the Common Market* (1964); Feige, "Transport in the European Community", *EIU European Trends*, 1990, No 2, p. 42; and Gwilliam, *Co-ordination of Investments in Transport Infrastructures*, Studies, Transport Series, No 3 (1973).

On specific modes, see e.g. Adkins, *Air Transport and EC Competition Law* (1994); Dagtoglou, *Air Transport and the European Union: Essays and Comments* (1994); Dempsey, *European Aviation Law* (2004); and Goh, *European Air Transport Law and Competition* (2007).

3 The Commission has said that the "transport industry directly employs more than 10 million people, accounting for 4.5% of total employment, and represents 4.6% of Gross Domestic Product (GDP). Manufacture of transport equipment provides an additional 1.7% GDP and 1.5% employment" and that "13.2% of every household's budget is spent on average on transport goods and services", http://ec.europa.eu/transport/strategies/facts-and-figures/transport-matters/index_en.htm.

Treaty. Under Article 4(2) of the TFEU, there is shared competence between the EU and the Member States in regard to transport. Second, the opening up of the Central and Eastern European markets as well as the completion of the EU's internal market requires a common transport policy and legislative regime.[4] Third, it is worth remembering that transport is a huge employer around the EU with many millions of people employed in the transport sector in the EU. Fourth, the development of such freedoms as free movement of goods, services and persons presupposes a transport system. Ultimately, the integration of the EU requires the development of a transport system: there is an ongoing need to have a low-cost, highly efficient, competitive and optimum transport system, allowing transport users a reasonable choice and transport operators a fair return on investment.

Need to achieve a common transport policy

4.003 Transport is one of the foundations of the TFEU: a common transport policy ("CTP") is a necessary pre-requisite if the internal market is ever to be achieved and maintained. A common policy envisages national policies being recast into one single EU policy: the national becoming supranational. The need to adopt such a policy was identified as early as the Spaak Report which was adopted even before the EEC was established.[5] The TFEU provides for the adoption of such a policy. The CTP is vital for the EU given its size and population. There is a need to integrate all areas of transport policy: for example, there is a need to co-ordinate road and rail networks with the building and operation of ports and ferry ports. The CTP needs to be not only coherent in itself, but also integrated with many of the EU's other policies such as agriculture (e.g. the carriage of food aid), the environment (e.g. pollution), competition (e.g. prohibition of unfair pricing practices) and social policy (e.g. dealing with unemployment among shipbuilding workers made redundant). The CTP must also take into account what is happening in other European organisations (such as the Central Commission for the Navigation of the Rhine, the Moselle Commission, the European Conference of Ministers for Transport, the Council of Europe and the Economic Commission for Europe) as well as international bodies (such as the International Maritime Organization and the United Nations Conference on Trade and Development). Sadly, neither internal nor external integration has taken place fully despite much work being done. The CTP needs to be not only a common policy but also a coherent one.

Failure to achieve a CTP

4.004 Despite the need for a CTP, a comprehensive policy remains somewhat elusive. The elements of the policy which have been adopted so far are somewhat unconnected and incomplete: it has been a "policy of steps". The lack of achievement in achieving an EU transport policy is due, for the most part, to the lack of a common will on the part of the Member States because of their differing interests and attitudes. It has also been

---

4 On the internal market programme, see Art. 26 of the TFEU. Art. 26(2) TFEU provides that the "internal market shall comprise an area without internal frontiers in which the free movement of goods, person, services and capital is endures in accordance with the provisions of the Treaties".
5 See Abbati, op. cit. at fn. 2, para. 2.3.1.

difficult because of the differences and divergences between the transport systems in Member States. The Common Agricultural Policy ("CAP") has been, despite its many critics, a remarkable achievement – the diversity of interests, the plethora of products and the complexity of the politics involved have all been overcome to produce a common agricultural policy. The CTP is not as integrated as the CAP but progress can be reported, indeed substantial progress in recent years can be reported. Various commentators have discussed the reasons for the failure of the EU to adopt an effective CTP for many years. Lowe has argued that the:

> "reason that no great progress in this area has been made is that Member States have their own divergent views as to the priorities of transport as well as their own quite individual geographic, economic and cultural considerations. Certain states have adopted strict interventionist policies while others have adopted a much more liberal approach to government participation in transport. In particular, for example, we have seen the desire of some individual Member States to adopt and maintain protectionist policies towards their railway systems, waterways and ports. In other cases protection of road systems is important because of the inherent dependence of the smaller countries of Europe on their road networks. To date there has been no definable incentive for these considerations to be pushed aside in the common good but the implementation of the Single European Act now changes this position and the new vision of a single market provides the incentive."[6]

It should be stressed that considerable progress has been achieved since his comments two decades ago but the picture is not yet complete. Other commentators have written that the reason for the non-achievement of this policy is that the transport system developed in each Member State was designed to serve *national* needs (often military ones) rather than a wider territorial unit. Member States take differing views on the degree to which States should intervene in transport affairs. It is anticipated that the future development of EU transport law on a global rather than modal basis will hopefully stimulate development. However, there has been considerable progress in recent times particularly since the late 1980s in the area of air transport law but there has also been progress in regard to maritime transport as well. EU transport law is continuously being developed.

Legal bases of EU transport law

4.005 The legal bases of EU transport law and the CTP are: first, the general rules of the EU Treaties (in particular, Articles 90 to 100 of the TFEU); second, the legislation adopted under those Treaties (e.g. regulations and directives); and, third, the case law of the Commission and the Court of Justice of the European Union ("CJEU") (including the General Court).

Adoption and administration of EU transport law

4.006 The adoption of measures relating to EU transport lies mainly in the hands of the Council, the Parliament and the Commission. The Council is by far the most politically significant and is principally involved in the *adoption* rather than the *administration* of EU transport law and policy. The Council was stimulated into action in the 1980s after

---

6 *The Transport and Distribution Manager's Guide to 1992* (1989), pp. 19–20.

the CJEU condemned it for its inactivity in the area.[7] The administration of EU transport law and policy lies largely in the hands of the Commission. The work of the Commission in the area of transport has been discussed earlier.[8] The work of these institutions is also undertaken by various bodies such as the European Maritime Safety Agency.

Sources of EU transport law

4.007 The sources of EU transport law are the same as the sources of EU law generally but it is useful to examine these sources in the specific context of transport. The sources of EU law are traditionally divided into primary and secondary sources. The secondary sources are no less legally binding (when they are legally binding) than the so-called primary sources but the *secondary* sources must be compatible with the superior (or *primary*) legislation. The primary sources are the treaties while the secondary sources of law are regulations, directives and decisions. Both the primary and secondary sources are supplemented by non-binding measures (such as recommendations and opinions) which are instructive and important in building the framework of EU transport law but are not binding in their own right. All of these sources are construed and clarified by the case law of the CJEU.

B. POSITION OF TRANSPORT IN THE TFEU

Introduction

4.008 What is the position of transport in the treaties (i.e. the primary source of EU transport law)? Transport was dealt with in the European Coal and Steel Community ("ECSC") Treaty but as this Treaty has now expired, it is no longer relevant. The topic of "transport" does not appear explicitly in the European Atomic Energy Community ("EAEC") Treaty. However, transport is dealt with by the TFEU. So this section analyses the provisions in the TFEU as it relates to transport.[9]

4.009 The TFEU contains special[10] but limited[11] provisions. These provisions are principally contained in Articles 90–100 which constitute Title V of Part Three[12] of the TFEU. Article 4(2) of the TFEU states that the EU and the Member States share competence in the area of transport. Article 58(1) of the TFEU also explicitly mentions transport (but in the context of freedom to provide services).[13] Transport is also to be seen in the

---

7 Case 13/83 *Parliament v Council* [1985] ECR 1513, ECLI:EU:C:1988:461 (see para. 4.15).
8 See chap. 3.
9 As the ECSC Treaty no longer operates, the coal and steel sectors (including the transport of coal and steel) are now regulated by the TFEU.
10 Apart from agriculture, transport was the only economic sector which had a special title in the original EEC Treaty. However, the terms of the Transport Title are vague by contrast with the Agricultural Title.
11 The provisions in the TFEU relating to transport are quite limited in terms of specifics and leave a great deal to be adopted by the Council. This degree of discretion is at its greatest in the case of air and sea transport provisions. See Fennel, "The Transport Policy Case" (1980) 10 ELRev 264.
12 Part Three of the TFEU is entitled "Union Policies and Internal Actions".
13 Art. 58(1) of the TFEU provides that "freedom to provide services in the field of transport shall be governed by the provisions of the Title relating to transport".

wider context of the other provisions of the TFEU itself[14] in so far as they are not expressly disapplied.[15]

4.010 The modes of transport contemplated by the transport provisions of the TFEU are rail, road, inland waterway, sea transport and air transport.[16] The TFEU relates to the carriage of all persons as well as all goods. In essence, the TFEU envisages the adoption of a comprehensive and ambitious common transport policy covering all modes,[17] and all cargoes[18] and persons.[19]

4.011 It is significant that while the original EEC Treaty contained provisions relating to transport from the outset (the Treaty was signed on 25 March 1957), it was not until the mid-1980s that there were significant measures adopted so as to give content to, what is now, EU transport law. The stimuli for this period of activity in the 1980s included the renewed efforts to create a single internal market, enthusiasm by some members of the Commission (such as Lord Cockfield and Peter Sutherland), developments in competition and deregulation generally and the desire in some quarters (including some members of the Parliament) to have measures adopted by the Council and the Commission). Despite this slow start, it is significant that even in 1957 considerable attention was paid to the transport sector by the framers of the then EEC Treaty and transport was given a specific chapter to itself in the Treaty.

4.012 The TFEU sets out the objective of a common policy for the transport sector. Such a common policy would replace the essential elements of Member State policies. However, what emerged was an EU policy which largely co-ordinated and supplemented national policies in many areas, and it is only in some areas, that there is an EU-wide policy. There are some EU-wide measures in relation to, for example, maritime safety and port State control. This shared competence is embodied in Article 4(2) of the TFEU which recognises that this is an area of shared competence rather than being an area of exclusive competence for either the Member States or the EU.

4.013 The EEC Treaty (as originally drafted) did not in itself oblige the speedy and thorough adoption of a common transport policy: there was ambiguity in the text, a lack of an agreed approach to transport issues generally and there was a requirement for unanimity in the Council which was (and still is) always difficult to obtain in controversial matters. This situation has now changed (at least in part): the situation has been improved by the amendment of what is now Article 100 of the TFEU[20] by the Single European Act ("SEA") as well as the decisions and rulings of the CJEU in such cases as *Commission v*

---

14 E.g. the provisions relating to nationality (TFEU, Art. 18) (see e.g. Case 167/73 *Commission v France* [1974] ECR 359, ECLI:EU:C:1974:35) and free movement of workers (TFEU, Art. 45) (see e.g. Case 9/88 *Da Veiga v Staatssecretaris van Justitie* [1989] ECR 2989, ECLI:EU:C:1989:346).

15 E.g. TFEU, Art. 58(1). See Case 167/73 *Commission v France* [1974] ECR 359, ECLI:EU:C:1974:35.

16 It does not specifically mention pipelines.

17 Apparently, other than pipelines and vacuum tubes – but there is no clear indication in the Treaty of this viewpoint.

18 While the ECSC Treaty would have dealt with coal and steel, those two cargoes are now absorbed into the TFEU.

19 Nonetheless the articles and aims of the provisions in the TFEU relating to transport are more limited in scope than the provisions in the now expired ECSC Treaty relating to transport.

20 See para. 4.060.

Council,²¹ *Commission v France*,²² *Commission v Belgium*,²³ *Parliament v Council* ²⁴ and *Ministere Public v Asjes*.²⁵

4.014 In reviewing the specific provisions on transport in the TFEU, it is worth bearing in mind that the general provisions of the TFEU also apply to transport. This principle has been confirmed²⁶ by the CJEU in *Commission v France*²⁷ when the court said:

> "When Article [90 of the TFEU (ex Article 74 of the original EEC Treaty)] refers to the objectives of the Treaty, it means the provisions of Articles 2 and 3 [of the original EEC Treaty], the attainment of which the fundamental provisions applicable to the whole complex of economic activities seek to ensure. Far from involving a departure from these fundamental rules, the object of the rules relating to the common transport policy is to implement and complement them by means of common action. Consequently the said general rules must be applied in so far as they can achieve these objectives."

This principle was confirmed in *Parliament v Council of Ministers*.²⁸ Thus, such provisions of the TFEU as those relating to competition,²⁹ non-discrimination on the basis of nationality,³⁰ freedom of establishment,³¹ the common commercial policy, free movement of goods and so on apply to transport. It is worth noting however that the free movement of services in the field of transport is dealt with by the Title in the Treaty relating to transport and not by the ordinary provisions on freedom to provide services.³²

4.015 In *Parliament v Council* ³³ the CJEU held, in an action brought by the Parliament against the Council, that the Council had failed in its duty under the TFEU to ensure freedom to provide services in the sphere of international transport and to lay down conditions under which carriers not resident in one Member State could provide services in another Member State. This was the first case taken under Article 265 of the TFEU brought to the CJEU by one EU institution against another. The ambiguity of the Treaty provisions caused considerable (and unnecessary) doubt before the CJEU resolved some of the difficulties in various cases.

---

21 Case 22/70 [1971] ECR 263 ECLI:EU:C:1971:32.
22 Case 167/73 [1974] ECR 359, ECLI:EU:C:1974:35.
23 Case 156/77 [1978] ECR 1811, ECLI:EU:C:1978:180.
24 Case 13/83 [1985] ECR 1513, ECLI:EU:C:1985:220.
25 Cases 209–213/84 [1986] ECR 1425, ECLI:EU:C:1986:188.
26 The historical background to this debate is interesting but need not detain the present discussion. For the historical debate, see Abbati, op. cit. at fn. 2, para. 2.3.6.
27 Case 167/73 [1974] ECR 359, ECLI:EU:C:1974:35 (known as the *French Merchant Seamen, French Seafarers* or the *Code du Travail Maritime* case). See also Case 22/70 *Commission v Council* [1971] ECR 263, ECLI:EU:C:1971:32; Case 156/77 *Commission v Belgium* [1978] ECR 1811, ECLI:EU:C:1978:180; Case 13/83 *Parliament v Council* [1985] ECR 1513, ECLI:EU:C:1985:220; Cases 209–213/84 *Ministère Public v Asjes (the "Nouvelles Frontières")* [1986] ECR 1425, ECLI:EU:C:1986:188; Case 66/86 *Ahmed Saeed Flugreisen v Zentrale zur Bekämpfung Unlauteren Wettbewerbs eV* [1989] ECR 803, ECLI:EU:C:1989:140.
28 Case 13/83 [1985] ECR 1513, ECLI:EU:C:1985:220.
29 See also Cases 209–213/84 *Ministere Public v Asjes* [1986] ECR 1425 ECLI:EU:C:1986:188; and Case 66/86 *Ahmed Saeed Flugreisen and Silver Line Reisebüro GmbH v Zentrale zur Bekämpfung Unlauteren* [1989] ECR 803, ECLI:EU:C:1989:140. In regard to state aid: see Case 156/77 *Commission v Belgium* [1978] ECR 1811, ECLI:EU:C:1978:180.
30 See TFEU, Art. 18 and see also Case 126/82 *DJ Smit Transport BV v Commissie Grensoverschrijdend Beroepsvervoer* [1983] ECR 73, ECLI:EU:C:1983:14.
31 See the General Programme for the Abolition of Restrictions on Freedom of Establishment, OJ English Special Edition (2nd Series), IX, p. 7. In the case of free movement of workers, see Case 167/73 *Commission v France* [1974] ECR 359, ECLI:EU:C:1974:35.
32 TFEU, Art. 58(1).
33 Case 13/83 [1985] ECR 1513, ECLI:EU:C:1985:220.

The TFEU and transport generally

4.016 The TFEU contemplated the creation of a common transport policy thus the Treaty contains provisions dealing specifically with transport. The fact that the provisions were both few in number and relatively weak in effect and that the TFEU did not contemplate very much activity by the EU is indicative of the desire, at the time the Treaty was first drafted in the 1950s, for transport matters to remain very much within the remit of the Member States. This approach by Member States was due in large measure to the fact that transport was very much State owned and regulated without any contemplation of the benefits which could flow from deregulation and liberalisation. In some ways, the TFEU is less than ambitious when it came to the CTP. It only laid down a timetable and some procedural structures for such a policy. The Founding States were reluctant to develop the situation very much. Nonetheless, to elaborate on what has been said above,[34] transport was dealt with in the Treaty for several reasons. First, the success of so many elements of the Treaty was dependent on a successful transport policy. Second, an internal market would result in increased transport activity. Third, transport costs and practices could prove an obstacle to trade within the EU and therefore there was a need to curb any anti-competitive practice. Fourth, transport represented about 40 per cent of public investment in the Member States.

4.017 Given that there are specific provisions in the TFEU relating to transport, the natural question is the extent to which some or all of the other provisions of the Treaty apply to transport. The CJEU has confirmed in judgments such as *Commission v France (French Seamen's Case)*[35] that the provisions of the Treaty generally applied to the transport sector and not just those provisions which dealt specifically with the transport sector. In this case, the CJEU held the rights of nationals from another Member State to seek employment on French-registered ships. The Commission instituted proceedings under Article 258 of the TFEU against France. The case is dealt with throughout this chapter.

Article 4 of the TFEU

Text

4.018 Article 4 of the TFEU allocates competences between the EU and the Member States. Article 4(2) provides: "*Shared competence between the Union and the Member States applies in the following principal areas:... (g) transport; ...*".

Commentary

4.019 This provision recognises the reality that competence has to be shared between the EU and the Member States. It is very unlikely that the EU would have exclusive competence for transport (at least in the near term) and it is no longer feasible to reverse the trend such that the EU would merely support the Member States – it is now an area of shared competence with the EU having an increasing role.

---

34 Para. 4.002.
35 [1996] ECR I-01307, ECLI:EU:C:1996:90.

Article 58 of the TFEU

Text

4.020 Article 58 of the TFEU provides:

"1. Freedom to provide services in the field of transport shall be governed by the provisions of the Title relating to transport.
2. The liberalisation of banking and insurance services connected with movements of capital shall be effected in step with the progressive liberalisation of movement of capital."

Commentary

4.021 Article 58(1) removes transport from the ambit of the general provisions in the Chapter[36] on Services in Title III[37] of Part 3[38] of the TFEU.[39] This area will be examined more thoroughly in Chapter 7.[40] It means that anyone seeking to avail of the right to provide services must rely on specific transport related provisions rather than the general regime.

Article 90 of the TFEU

Text

4.022 Article 90 of the TFEU provides: "The objectives of the Treaties shall, in matters governed by this Title, be pursued by Member States within the framework of a common transport policy".

Commentary

4.023 This article, as part of Title V of Part Three of the TFEU, contemplates the establishment and operation of the CTP. The initial and controversial question which arose was whether Article 100 required: (a) only a CTP as such; or (b) a CTP which involved a common market for transport services. This means that the objectives of the Treaty such as free movement of goods, services, people and capital are to be achieved "*within the framework* of a common transport policy" (italics added) so there are limitations on the achievement of those aims.

4.024 Greaves has commented that the "wording of the Article has ... been relied in argument to show that it is the [EU], rather than each individual member state, that has a mandate to act in transport matters, including perhaps the conclusion of international agreements". She also comments, in the context of Articles 3(1)(f) of the old EC Treaty and Article 90 of the TFEU that "apart from this requirement [in Article 90 TFEU] of coherence in action and cooperation on the part of the member states, nothing more can be concluded from the provision as to what is meant by CTP". Article 90 is much less

---

36 I.e. chap. 3.
37 This Title is entitled: "Free Movement of Persons, Services and Capital".
38 The Part is entitled: "Union Policies and Internal Actions".
39 I.e. the Title on free movement of persons, services and capital.
40 Chap. 7 of this book deals with freedom to provide services.

ambitious than the comparable Article 38 of the TFEU on the CAP. The CTP is radically different from the CAP in several respects. First, the CTP is much less interventionist than the CAP. Second, the proportion of the budget allocated to the CTP is a fraction of that allocated to the CAP. Third, the CAP supports the income of some market participants such as farmers while the CTP does not engage in such protectionism.

4.025 There was a long delay in adopting the CTP. Commission proposals were discussed but not adopted. Ultimately, the CJEU condemned the inactivity of the Council of Ministers. This was in *Parliament v Council* case.[41] The CTP gained impetus by the adoption of the 1992 or Internal Market Programme.

4.026 It is worth noting while reviewing Article 90 of the TFEU that Article 100(1) of the same Treaty specifically provides that the provisions of the Transport Title are to apply only to rail, road and inland waterway while Article 100(2) provides that the Council of Ministers "may, acting by a qualified majority, decide whether, to what extent and by what procedure appropriate provisions may be laid down for sea and air transport". In effect, Articles 90 to 100 do not automatically apply to sea transport.

4.027 In accordance with Articles 90 and 92,[42] the Council[43] adopted a decision on 21 March 1962 (which has since been amended)[44] to institute a procedure for the prior examination and consultation on certain laws, regulations and administrative provisions proposed by Member States relating to rail, road and inland waterway transport which are liable to substantially interfere with the implementation of the CTP. The procedure is two-fold: first, a Member State must notify the Commission and inform the other Member States of the proposed measure; and, second, the Commission must address an opinion or recommendation to the relevant Member State and inform the other Member States of this opinion or recommendation.

Article 91 of the TFEU

Text

4.028 Article 91 of the TFEU provides:

"1. For the purpose of implementing Article 90, and taking into account the distinctive features of transport, the European Parliament and the Council[45] shall, acting in accordance with the ordinary legislative procedure and after consulting the Economic and Social Committee[46] and the Committee of the Regions[47] lay down:

   (a) common rules applicable to international transport to or from the territory of a Member State or passing across the territory of one or more Member States;
   (b) the conditions under which non-resident carriers may operate transport services within a Member State;
   (c) measures to improve transport safety;
   (d) any other appropriate provisions."

---

41 Case 302/87 *European Parliament v Council* [1988] ECR 5615, ECLI:EU:C:1988:461.
42 On Art. 92 of the TFEU, see below.
43 On the Council, see chap. 3.
44 Dec. 73/402, OJ 1973 L347/48.
45 Ed., on the Council, see chap. 3.
46 Ed., on the Economic and Social Committee, see chap. 3.
47 Ed., on the Committee of the Regions, see chap. 3.

Commentary

4.029 Article 91[48] is the legal basis for most of the secondary legislation in the area of transport. It is the means for the implementation of the CTP in relation to rail, road and inland waterway. It gives the Council the power to elaborate and implement the CTP. The article "contains indisputably the most important provisions on transport in the whole of [the] Title".[49]

4.030 In *Commission v Council*[50] the CJEU ruled that in those areas where the EU had developed a common transport policy, it was the EU which was competent to negotiate international agreements as opposed to the Member States. Article 91 represents an element of this legal authority to negotiate international agreements. Article 91(1) refers to the measures which may be enacted.

4.031 Article 91(1) refers to the "distinctive features of transport". This is a phrase which has considerable significance and is often used in the secondary legislation relating to transport. The use of the phrase would tend to indicate that the framers of the Treaty recognised that there would be limitations or hindrances to the development of the CTP (i.e. the development of the CTP would be limited by virtue of these distinctive features). The distinctive features include the heavy investment, significant State investment, divergent modes, the role of the transport industry in facilitating other industrial activity, the varying size of transport operators, the public service role of many transport services, transport services are not capable of being stocked and used later, differences in transport needs and approaches between the Member States, the role of transport in the economic and social policies of Member States, the use of so-called public service obligation contracts, the diversity of transport operators (e.g. large and small or local and global), the international dimension to many transport modes and evolving forms of regulation. Other distinctive characteristics include: the division of ownership in the infrastructure and the means of transport; competition between modes; international dimension; dependence on infrastructure; the demand-led nature of the sector; high fixed costs; the large-scale nature of the industry; high employment levels; the role of transport in servicing other industries; the social function of the industry; and impossibility of storing up supply.

4.032 Article 91(1) contemplates that it is the Council which would take action in regard to the development of the CTP. Ironically, the Council is the institution with the least incentive for developing a liberal or deregulated transport market because many of the members of the Transport Council are, at least nominally, owners of many transport interests who may not welcome such liberalisation and deregulation which would lead to enhanced competition. Article 91(1) obliges the Council to consult with the Economic and Social Committee ("EESC") and the Committee of the Regions. Article 91(1)(c) makes specific reference to laying down "measures to improve transport safety" which has proved significant. Given the principle of subsidiarity, it may be that measures to promote safety should be adopted at either the EU or Member State level.

4.033 Article 91(1)(a) relates to "international transport operations applying both in the case of carriage between Member States and in the case of carriage from a Member

---

48 See Bellieni, "Comments on Article 75", *Jupiter*, No 1, 1973.
49 Abbati, op. cit. at fn. 2, para. 2.3.5.
50 Case 22/70 [1971] ECR 263, ECLI:EU:C:1971:32. See also Opinion 1/76 *Laying-Up Fund* [1977] ECR 741, ECLI:EU:C:1977:63.

State to a third country".[51] Article 91(1)(b) is simple: it relates to the situation where transport services are provided by non-resident carriers entirely within a Member State (i.e. cabotage). The measures contemplated by Article 91(1)(a) and Article 91(1)(b) were both to have been adopted during the transitional period[52] but not all the measures were adopted.[53] It has been through Article 91(1)(c), the residual clause, that the Council has been able to develop the notion of transport policy.[54] This is a very broad residual power.

4.034 Article 91(3) is an unusual and important derogation because it permits a Member State to invoke its particular circumstances so as to prevent the adoption of a common transport policy. The circumstances in which such a provision could be exercised would have to be limited.

4.035 Close has succinctly analysed Article 91 in the context of international agreements in the following terms:

"The legislative power[55] of the [EU Council] for the purposes of the common transport policy extends to the conclusion of agreements with one or more third countries or an international organisation where the agreements form the subject of transport policy.[56] The power to enter into international commitments exists not only where internal measures have been adopted to attain the common transport policy, but also where the Community's participation in an international agreement is necessary for the attainment of one of the Community's objectives. The Community may also co-operate in the setting up of an international organism in order to attain the common transport policy, and for this purpose to give it appropriate powers of decision and to define, in a manner appropriate to the objectives pursued, the nature, elaboration, implementation and effects of the provisions to be adopted within the organism. In so doing, however, the Community must respect its internal constitution."[57]

Article 92 of the TFEU

Text

4.036 Article 92 of the TFEU provides:

"Until the provisions referred to in Article 91(1) have been laid down, no Member State may, unless the Council has unanimously adopted a measure granting a derogation, make the various provisions governing the subject on 1 January 1958 or, for acceding States, the date of their accession, less favourable in their direct or indirect effect on carriers of other Member States as compared with carriers who are nationals of that State."

Commentary

4.037 The essence of Article 92 is that until the CTP has become a reality, no Member State may, as a general rule,[58] make the various national provisions[59] governing transport

---

51 See Case 22/70 *Commission v Council* [1971] ECR 263, ECLI:EU:C:1971:32 and Close, op. cit. at fn. 2, para. 18.21.
52 TFEU, Art.91(2).
53 See Case 13/83 *Parliament v Council* [1985] ECR 1513, ECLI:EU:C:1985:220.
54 Case 97/78 *Schumalla* [1978] ECR 2311, ECLI:EU:C:1979:14.
55 Ed., i.e. under Art. 91 TFEU.
56 Case 22/70 *Commission v Council* [1971] ECR 263, ECLI:EU:C:1971:32.
57 *Opinion 1/76 (draft agreement establishing a European laying-up fund for inland waterway vessels)* [1977] ECR 741, ECLI:EU:C:1977:63.
58 The principal exception was where the Council unanimously allowed otherwise.
59 Other than the right of establishment.

when the TFEU entered into force, less favourable on carriers of other Member States than on its own nationals. It is a standstill provision. Article 92 attempted to crystallise the position[60] in respect of the original Member States as of 1 January 1958 for the original six Member States and the date of accession in respect of the newer States. It is a standstill clause.

4.038 In accordance with Articles 90 and 92, the Council adopted a decision on 21 March 1962 (which has since been amended) to institute a procedure for the prior examination and consultation on certain laws, regulations and administrative provisions proposed by Member States relating to rail, road and inland waterway transport which are liable to interfere substantially with the implementation of the common transport policy. The procedure is two-fold: first, a Member State must notify the Commission and inform the other Member States of the proposed measure; and, second, the Commission must address an opinion or recommendation to the relevant Member State and inform the other Member States of this opinion or recommendation. The better view is that Article 92 is directly applicable.

Article 93 of the TFEU

Text

4.039 Article 93 of the TFEU provides: "Aids shall be compatible with the Treaties if they meet the needs of co-ordination of transport or if they represent re-imbursement for the discharge of certain obligations inherent in the concept of a public service."

Commentary

4.040 Aid granted by States to transport is common and needs to be tightly controlled.[61] Article 93 is not an exception to the provisions contained in Articles 107 to 109 of that same Treaty on state aid[62] – instead it sets out two further forms of State aid which are permissible under the TFEU,[63] namely: (a) aid which meet the needs of co-ordination of transport and (b) aid which represents reimbursement for the discharge of certain obligations inherent in the concept of a public service. Thus, Article 93 should be read in conjunction with the other provisions of the TFEU as it relates to State aid.[64]

4.041 Article 93 complements the general provisions on State aid in the EU generally. It provides two exceptions to the prohibition on State aid. The first is aid which meets the needs of co-ordination of transport. This is a term which is undefined. The second exception relates to situations where aid is a "reimbursement for the discharge of certain obligations inherent in the concept of a public service". The CJEU has held that the aid is compatible where it represents the reimbursement for the discharge of certain obligations inherent in the concept of a public service function.

---

60 See Case 9/70 *Grad v Finanzamt Traunstein* [1970] ECR 825, ECLI:EU:C:1970:78 and Case 20/76 *Schottle and Söhne OHG v Finanzamt Traunstein* [1977] ECR 247, ECLI:EU:C:1977:26.
61 See chap. 15.
62 Case 156/77 *Commission v Belgium* [1978] ECR 1881, ECLI:EU:C:1978:180.
63 On Article 107 TFEU, see chap. 15.
64 Case 167/73 *Commission v France* [1974] ECR 359, ECLI:EU:C:1974:35; Case 156/77 *Commission v Belgium* [1978] ECR 1881, ECLI:EU:C:1978:180.

4.042 Kapteyn and Van Themaat make an interesting observation on what is now Article 93:

> "[t]he applicability to transport of Articles [107–109 of the TFEU] relating to aids was always assumed in the practice of the Commission and follows moreover from Article [93 of the TFEU] according to which state aids are deemed to be compatible with the Treaty if they meet the needs of co-ordination of transport or if they represent reimbursement for the discharge of certain obligations inherent in the concept of a 'public service'. It would of course be unnecessary to deem such aids compatible if Article [109 of the TFEU], according to which aids are in principle deemed incompatible with the common market, were not applicable. Article [93], therefore, is to be considered as a supplement to the exceptions to incompatibility mentioned in Article [107](2) and (3) [of the TFEU]."[65]

Article 93 is extended by means of secondary legislation. Regulation 1191/69[66] is a limitation on the public service obligations dimension to Article 73.[67] Articles 107 to 109 were applied by Regulation 1107/70[68] to road, rail and inland waterway transport.[69] It helped to clarify, in part, Regulation 1191/69.

Article 94 of the TFEU

Text

4.043 Article 94 of the TFEU provides: "Any measures taken within the framework of the Treaties in respect of transport rates and conditions shall take account of the economic circumstances of carriers."

Commentary

4.044 Article 94 is an unusual provision. It is very protective of the sector. It is widely acknowledged that, to date, this provision has been of little practical significance.

Article 95 of the TFEU

Text

4.045 Article 95 of the TFEU provides:

"1. In the case of transport within the Union, discrimination which takes the form of carriers charging different rates and imposing different conditions for the carriage of the same goods over the same transport links on grounds of the country of origin or of destination of the goods in question shall be prohibited.
2. Paragraph 1 shall not prevent the European Parliament and the Council from adopting other measures in pursuance of Article 91(1).

---

65 Op. cit. at fn. 2, pp. 713–714, footnote omitted.
66 JO 1969, L156/1; OJ 1969, 276.
67 This has been amended by the 1972, 1979 and 1985 Treaties of Accession as well as by Dec.73/101 (OJ L2/1, 1 January 1973).
68 JO 1970, L130/1, 15 June 1970; OJ 1970, 360. See Reg. 1107/70.
69 This was both derogated from and extended by the 1972 Treaty of Accession; supplemented by Reg. 1658/82 (OJ L184/1, 29 June 1982); as well as amended by Reg. 1473/75 (OJ 1975, L152/1, 12 June 1975) and Reg. 1100/89 (OJ L116, 28 April 1989, p. 24).

3. The Council shall, on a proposal from the Commission and after consulting the Parliament and the Economic and Social Committee, lay down rules for implementing the provisions of paragraph 1.

   The Council may in particular lay down the provisions needed to enable the institutions of the Union to secure compliance with the rule laid down in paragraph 1 and to ensure that users benefit from it to the full.
4. The Commission shall, acting on its own initiative or on application by a Member State, investigate any cases of discrimination falling within paragraph 1 and after consulting any Member State concerned, shall take the necessary decisions within the framework of the rules laid down in accordance with the provisions of paragraph 3."

Commentary

4.046 Article 95 sets out the general principle that in intra-EU trade, all discrimination taking the form of carriers charging different rates and imposing different conditions for the carriage of the same goods over the same transport links on the bases of the country of origin or the country of destination must be abolished. Such discrimination was to be abolished by the end of the second stage of the transitional period. In essence, it required the abolition of discrimination in freight rates and conditions of EU transport.

4.047 In order to ensure the implementation of Article 95, the Council adopted Regulation 11 of 27 June 1960[70] so as to oblige undertakings to notify their governments of any discriminatory practices (within the meaning of Article 95) and to further oblige the governments to notify the Commission. Smit and Herzog were of the opinion that Regulation 11 enabled the Commission to impose upon carriers the burden of showing that their actions do not violate Article 95.[71] It is to be presumed that this prohibition is directly applicable.[72,73]

4.048 The article provides that discrimination in rates and conditions for transport of goods must be eliminated. It does not relate to the transport of passengers. Regulation 11[74] represents the discharge of the duties of Article 95. It covers State owned or operated railways. Article 95 contemplates Articles 28 to 37 of the TFEU. These latter Articles set out the rules of free movement of goods.

4.049 In regard to Consultation, the EESC is mentioned but the Committee of Regions is not referred to as a body which must be consulted.

Article 96 of the TFEU

Text

4.050 Article 96 of the TFEU provides:

"1. The imposition by a Member State, in respect of transport operations carried out within the Union, of rates and conditions involving any element of support or protection in the interest

---

70 OJ English Special Edition, 1959–1962, p. 60. OJ No 52, 16 August 1960, p.1121. This regulation was extended by the 1972 Treaty of Accession and amended by Reg. 3626/84 (OJ L335/4, 22 December 1984). See also the Commission Recommendation to the Member States on the application of Reg. 11 concerning the abolition of discrimination in transport rates and conditions, in implementation of Art. 79(3) of the EEC Treaty (OJ No 50, 22 July 1961, p. 975).
71 In *The Law of the European Community: A Commentary on the EEC Treaty* (1976), vol. 2, para. 74.04.
72 On the concept of direct applicability, see chap. 3.
73 See Gaudet and Bayens (1969) ETL 42; and Kapteyn and Van Themaat, op. cit. at fn. 2, p. 715, fn.169.
74 OJ 1960 p.1121.

of one or more particular undertakings or industries shall be prohibited unless authorised by the Commission.
2. The Commission shall, acting on its own initiative or on application by a Member State, examine the rates and conditions referred to in paragraph 1, taking account in particular of the requirements of an appropriate regional economic policy, the needs of underdeveloped areas and the problems of areas seriously affected by political circumstances on the one hand, and of the effects of such rates and conditions on competition between the different modes of transport on the other.

After consulting each Member State concerned, the Commission shall take the necessary decisions.
3. The prohibition provided for in paragraph 1 shall not apply to tariffs fixed to meet competition."

Commentary

4.051 Article 96 of the TFEU[75] prohibits Member States imposing, in regard to transport operations carried out in the EU, rates and conditions[76] involving any element of support or protection in the interest of one or more particular undertakings or industries as and from the beginning of the second stage of the transitional period. This support or protection differs from State aid in that the benefit is a reduced transport bill rather than the direct payment of money. In essence, a Member State may not impose rates and conditions involving support or protection of undertakings.

4.052 Article 100(2) provides that the Commission may however authorise the imposition of such support tariffs in exceptional cases. The exercise of this power is a matter of considerable significance.[77] In examining the rates and conditions, the Commission must take into account, on the one hand, the requirements of an appropriate regional policy and the needs of underdeveloped areas as well as, on the other hand, the problems of areas seriously affected by political circumstances. It is to be presumed that Article 100 of the TFEU is directly applicable.[78]

Article 97 of the TFEU

Text

4.053 Article 97 of the TFEU provides:

"Charges or dues in respect of the crossing of frontiers which are charged by a carrier in addition to the transport rates shall not exceed a reasonable level after taking the costs annually incurred thereby into account.

Member States shall endeavour to reduce these costs progressively.

The Commission may make recommendations to Member States for the application of this Article."

---

[75] On Art. 96 of the TFEU, see, in particular, Case 1/69 *Italy v Commission* [1969] ECR 277, ECLI:EU:C:1969:34.

[76] See Joined Cases 3–18, 25, 26/58 *Barbara Erzberghau AG v High Authority* [1960] ECR 173, ECLI:EU:C:1960:18; Case 9/70 *Grad v Finanzamt Traunstein* [1970] ECR 825, ECLI:EU:C:1970:78; and Case 20/70 *Transports Lesage & CIE v Hauptzollamt Freiburg* [1970] ECR 861, ECLI:EU:C:1970:84.

[77] Case 1/69 *Italy v Commission* [1969] ECR 277, ECLI:EU:C:1969:34 and Case 2/84 *Commission v Italy* [1985] ECR 1127, ECLI:EU:C:1985:151.

[78] On the concept of direct applicability, see chap. 3. See Gaudet and Bayens (1969) ETL 42; and Kapteyn and Van Themaat, op. cit. at fn. 2, p. 715, fn.169.

Commentary

4.054 Charges or dues in respect of crossing frontiers which are charged by a carrier in addition to the transport rates must not exceed a reasonable level and must be reduced progressively. It is important to note that the application of Article 97 is left to the Member States and thus the Commission has only the power to make recommendations. In practice, given the changes introduced as part of the Internal Market Programme, the changes which would now be imposed (if any) for crossing borders are very low or non-existent. Article 97 is to be read in the context of the TFEU which deals with the elimination of custom duties by reason of crossing frontiers. It is assumed that no charges now exist.

Article 98 of the EU Treaty

Text

4.055 Article 98 of the TFEU provides:

"The provisions of this Title shall not form an obstacle to the application of measures taken in the Federal Republic of Germany to the extent that such measures are required in order to compensate for the economic disadvantages caused by the division of Germany to the economy of certain areas of the Federal Republic affected by that division. Five years after the entry into force of the Treaty of Lisbon, the Council, acting on a proposal from the Commission, may adopt a decision repealing this Article."

Commentary

4.056 Article 98 was a special provision in relation to Germany because of the divided nature of that country before reunification in 1990. It permitted State aid to be provided in certain circumstances. It permits the provision of aid without the need for notification and authorisation of the aid. Clearly, this provision has geographically limited significance. Moreover, as an exception it is to be construed narrowly. The Treaty of Lisbon amended the article to recognise that it is no longer of such significance given the passage of time so, five years after the Treaty of Lisbon enters into force (i.e. 1 December 2014), the Council may adopt a decision repealing it. (From the perspective of law making, it is interesting that the Council may repeal a provision of the Treaty rather than the Member States having to do so.)

Article 99 of the TFEU

Text

4.057 Article 99 of the TFEU provides: "An Advisory Committee consisting of experts designated by the Governments of Member States, shall be attached to the Commission. The Commission, whenever it considers it desirable, shall consult the Committee on transport matters."

Commentary

4.058 Article 99 allows for the establishment of a Transport Advisory Committee consisting of experts designated by the governments of the Member States. It would be attached to the Commission. This specific Treaty reference to the formation of an Advisory Committee (of which there are very few established under the Treaty) is indicative of the significance attached to transport by the framers of the Treaty. It is independent of the EESC . The function of the Transport Committee would be more in the preparation of proposals rather than in the consideration of published proposals.

4.059 The rules of the Transport Committee were adopted in 1958[79] and amended since 1964.[80] It gives advice to the Commission. Council Decision 78/174 instituted a consultation procedure and set up a committee in the field of transport infrastructure.[81] Commission Decision 80/991 set up a Joint Committee on Inland Navigation.[82] Commission Decision 85/13 related to the setting up of a Joint Committee on Railways.[83] Commission Decision 85/516 set up a Joint Committee on Road Transport.[84] This decision was later amended.[85] Commission Decision 87/467 set up a Joint Committee on Maritime Transport.[86] Commission Decision 90/449 set up a Joint Committee on Civil Aviation.[87]

Article 100 of the TFEU

Text

4.060 Article 100 of the TFEU provides:

"1. The provisions of this Title shall apply to transport by rail, road and inland waterway.
2. The European Parliament and the Council, acting in accordance with the ordinary legislative procedure, may lay down appropriate provisions for sea and air transport. They shall act after consulting the Committee of the Regions and the Economic and Social Committee."

Commentary

4.061 Article 100 is the critical provision in the development of EU shipping law. It has been written that the specific mention of air, inland waterway, rail, road and sea in what was Article 84[88] excluded other forms of transport (such as pipelines) from the application of the Title on Transport.[89]

4.062 The original Article 84(2) of the EEC Treaty was an empowering provision. It prima facie excluded sea and air transport from the CTP. It allowed for provisions to be

---

79 OJ No 25, 27 November 1958, p. 509; OJ 1957–1958, p. 72 (as amended).
80 See Dec.64/390, OJ P102, 29 June 1964, p. 1602.
81 OJ L54/16, 25 February 1978.
82 OJ L297/28, 6 November 1980.
83 OJ L8/26, 10 January 1985.
84 OJ L317/33, 28 November 1985.
85 See Dec. 87/447 (OJ L240/37, 22 August 1987).
86 OJ L253/20, 4 September 1987.
87 OJ L230/22, 24 August 1990.
88 See Close, "Article 84 EEC: The Development of Transport Policy in the Sea and Air Sectors" (1980) 5 ELRev 188.
89 See Close, "The Development of Transport Policy in the Sea and Air Sectors" (1980) 5 ELRev 189. See also Case 97/78 *Schumalla* [1978] ECR 2311, ECLI:EU:C:1978:211.

laid down for sea and air transport by the Council acting unanimously. The paragraph was inserted due to the wishes of the Netherlands at the time of the drafting of the then EEC Treaty, who sought to have very little (if any) involvement by the EEC in shipping matters. If the UK had been part of the original members of the EEC then it would have been interesting to have seen its reaction to the inclusion of the second paragraph.

4.063 The second paragraph (as originally drafted) was a curiously drafted and novel provision in the then EEC Treaty. It did not follow the pattern of similar provisions – they provide for the adoption[90] of measures by the Council after a proposal by the Commission and the giving of opinions by the Parliament as well as the EESC – but this paragraph spoke simply of the Council acting unanimously to decide whether, to what extent and by what procedure appropriate provisions may be laid down for sea and air transport.

4.064 The Parliament's Committee on Regional Policy, Regional Planning and Transport published an Interim Report on the *Sea Transport Problems in the Community* in 1977 in which it said:

> "The [EEC] Treaty ... excludes sea and air transport from the common transport policy. ... There is no point in asking why the authors of the Treaty left sea transport out of the Common Transport policy during the negotiations at Val Duchesse in 1957. ... It may be that they simply could not agree on rules for sea transport or that they intended to draw up special rules for sea transport but did not have the time before the Treaty was pronounced ready for signature by the Heads of Government, or they had specific reasons for excluding sea transport which are unknown to us."[91]

4.065 Article 80(2) of the EEC Treaty, before its amendment by Article 16 of the SEA, was described as a "notorious paragraph" which gave rise "to diametrically opposed interpretations".[92] After its amendment by the SEA, it reads: "The Council may, acting by a qualified majority, decide whether, to what extent and by what procedure appropriate provisions may be laid down for sea and air transport. The procedural provisions of Article 75(1) and (3) shall apply."

4.066 Prior to 1974, it was believed by many commentators that air and sea transport fell outside the scope of the Treaty altogether because of the then Article 84(2). This restrictive view was adopted by many of the Member States for their own strategic reasons. Not surprisingly, the Commission adopted a broader perspective. The article fell to be considered by the CJEU in *Commission v France*.[93] The case came about because of the accession to the then EEC of Ireland and the UK – two islands – which prompted the Commission to bring a test case to test the point. The net point was whether the rest of the then Treaty (e.g. the provisions on free movement) applied to maritime transport. In that case, the Commission brought an action before the CJEU against France for a declaration that by not repealing, in so far as it affects the nationals of other Member States, the provisions of section 3(2) of the French Merchant Seamen Code of 13 December 1926 (as amended by Order No 581358 of 27 December 1958), the French Republic had not complied with its obligations under the provisions of the Treaty relating to freedom of movement for workers generally and Articles 1, 4 and 7 of Council Regulation 1612/68 of

---

90 Initially by unanimous vote and later by a qualified majority.
91 Working Documents; Doc. 5/77, 23 March 1977, Rapporteur: Mr H Seefeld, paras 1 and 3.
92 Bird, "Further Debate on the Treaty of Rome, Article 84, Paragraph 2 as it may affect Maritime Transport" (1966) 2 ETL 24 at p. 24.
93 Case 167/73 [1974] ECR 359, ECLI:EU:C:1974:35.

15 October 1968 on the freedom of movement of workers within the EU. Section 3(2) of the French Act had provided that such proportion (as may be laid down by the French Minister of the Merchant Marine) of the crew of a French ship must be of French nationality.

4.067 The French Minister of the Merchant Marine had made an Order on 21 November 1960 (as amended on 12 June 1969) that, apart from special exemptions granted by particular competent local administrative authorities, the employment of seafarers on the bridge and in the engine rooms of merchant ships, fishing vessels or pleasure cruisers was reserved for French nationals and the employment generally was limited in the ratio of three-to-one. The Commission argued that such restrictions were incompatible with EU law. France argued, *inter alia*, that the rules of the Treaty regarding freedom of movement for workers did not apply to transport and, in any event, not to maritime transport so long as the Council had not so decided under Article 84(2). It is interesting to read the essence of the CJEU's judgment on the point:

"17. To determine whether, in the sphere of transport, Member-States are bound by the obligations provided in Articles 48 to 51[94] of the Treaty, it is proper to consider the place of Title IV of Part Two of the ... Treaty, relating to transport, in the general system of the Treaty, and the place of Article 84(2)[95] within Title IV.

18. Under Article 2 of the [EEC] Treaty, which is placed at the head of the general principles which govern it, the Community has as its task to promote throughout the Community a harmonious development of economic activities by establishing a Common Market and progressively approximating the economic policies of member-States.

19. The establishment of the Common Market thus refers to the whole of the economic activities in the Community.

20. The basic object of Part Two of the Treaty, devoted to the foundations of the Community, is to establish the basis of the Common Market, i.e. free movement of goods (Title I) and free movement of persons, services and capital (Title III).

21. Conceived as being applicable to the whole complex of economic activities, these basic rules can be rendered inapplicable only as a result of express provision in the Treaty.

22. Such exemption is provided, in particular, by Article 38(2) under which the rules laid down for the establishment of the Common Market shall apply to agricultural products save as provided in Title II of this part of the Treaty.

23. As regards transport, which is the subject of Title IV of this part, it is proper to enquire, viewing Article 84(2)[96] in the framework of this Title, whether the provisions of the Title contain a similar exemption.

24. When Article 74[97] refers to the objectives of the Treaty, it means the provisions of Articles 2 and 3, for the attainment of which the fundamental provisions applicable to the whole complex of economic activity are of prime importance.

25. Far from involving a departure from these fundamental rules, therefore, the object of the rules relating to the common transport policy is to implement and complement them by means of common action.

26. Consequently the said general rules must be applied in so far as they can achieve these objectives.

27. Since transport is basically a service, it has been found necessary to provide a special system for it, taking into account the special aspects of this branch of activity.

28. With this object, a special exemption has been provided by Article [58(1) of the TFEU],

---

94 Ed., now Arts 45 to 48 TFEU.
95 Ed., now Art. 100 TFEU.
96 Ed., now Art. 100 of the TFEU but with amendment.
97 Ed., now Art. 90 of the TFEU but with amendment.

under which freedom to provide services in the field of transport 'shall be governed by the provisions of the Title relating to transport', thus confirming that the general rules of the Treaty must be applied insofar as they are not excluded.

29. Article 84(1)[98] provides that the provisions of the Title relating to transport shall apply to transport by rail, road and inland waterway.
30. Article 84(2)[99] provides that as regards maritime transport, the Council may decide whether, to what extent and by what procedure appropriate provisions may be laid down.
31. Far from excluding the application of the Treaty to these matters, it provides only that the special provisions of the Title relating to transport shall not automatically apply to them.
32. Whilst under Article 84(2),[100] therefore, sea and air transport, so long as the Council has not decided otherwise, is excluded from the rules of Title IV of Part Two of the Treaty relating to the common transport policy, it remains, on the same basis as the other modes of transport, subject to the general rules of the Treaty.
33. It thus follows that the application of Articles 48 to 51[101] to the sphere of maritime transport is not optional but obligatory for member-States."

4.068 The CJEU went on to state that in maintaining unamended the provisions of section 3(2) of the Merchant Seamen Code as regards the nationals of other Member States, France had failed to fulfil its obligations under, what is now, Article 45 of the TFEU and Article 4 of Regulation 1612/68.[102] The CJEU's decision clearly demonstrated that the general principles of the TFEU applied to maritime transport despite the views of some Member States that Article 100(2) somehow insulated maritime transport from the full force of EU law.

4.069 Despite the "green light" presented by the CJEU in the *French Seamen's* case, the EU (particularly, the Council) was slow to act in terms of adopting CTP. Eventually, the Parliament instituted proceedings in the CJEU against the Council for failure to act.[103]

4.070 It is clear that air and sea transport were given a special and protected status by Article 100(2). There are three observations which are appropriate in this case. First, even in the limited CTP contemplated by the Treaty, air and sea transport were being excluded. Second, this exclusion was probably due to the very significant Member State involvement in these two modes (particularly, in regard to air transport) and they had defence and sovereign dimensions. The exclusion may also be due to the much higher level of international regulation associated with air and sea transport than with most other modes. It would have been interesting to speculate as to whether the EEC would have been able to deal with the international dimension to transport in the late 1950s and 1960s – for example, would the former USSR have recognised the competence of the EEC to deal with such issues? Third, the provision which is now Article 100(2) required unanimity among the members of the Council before any provisions could be laid down for air and sea transport before the entry into force of the SEA and this requirement of unanimity effectively vetoed radical or significant developments in the area of EU transport law. Article 80 does not prevent the application of the general principles of the TFEU to sea and air transport despite Article 100(2). There is little doubt that the conversion of the

---

98 Ed., now Art. 100 of the TFEU.
99 Ed., now Art. 100 of the TFEU.
100 Ed., now Art. 100 of the TFEU.
101 Ed., now Arts 45 to 48 of the TFEU.
102 See Case 167/73 *Commission v France* [1974] ECR 359, ECLI:EU:C:1974:35 in the context of Art. 48 EC.
103 Case 13/83 *Parliament v Council* [1985] ECR 1513, ECLI:EU:C:1985:220.

voting requirement from qualified majority to simple majority would allow the Commission to propose more ambitious transport measures and thereby overcome some of the residual power held by Member States in this area. Article 100(2), as originally drafted, showed how reluctant Member States were to entrust matters to the EU.

C. SECONDARY LEGISLATION

4.071 There is an enormous body of secondary legislation relating to transport. It is beyond the scope of this chapter to consider all of the legislation but it relates to all modes and takes all forms. Thus, there are regulations, directives and decisions relating to, for example, air, rail, road and maritime transport. Much of the legislation falls into the categories of liberalisation/deregulation measures, safety measures, competition measures as well as specific technical measures. The rest of this book considers the secondary EC legislation relating to shipping.

D. EUROPEAN ECONOMIC AREA ("EEA")

4.072 It is worth recalling that Norway, Iceland and Liechtenstein have an arrangement with the EU called the EEA and that many of the rules of EU law (including many of the rules of EU transport law) apply to the EEA as well. In particular, Protocol 19 on maritime transport of the agreement on the EEA provides:

> "The Contracting Parties shall not apply between themselves the measures referred to in Council Regulations (EEC) Nos 4057/86 (OJ No L378, 31.12.1986, p. 14) and Nos 4058/86 (OJ No L378, 31.12.1986, p. 21) and Council Decision 83/573/EEC (OJ No L332, 28.11.1983, p. 37) or any other similar measures, provided that the acquis on maritime transport included in the Agreement is fully implemented.
>
> The Contracting Parties will coordinate their actions and measures towards third countries and third country companies in the area of maritime transport according to the following provisions:
>
> 1. if a Contracting Party decides to monitor the activities of certain third countries in the field of cargo shipping it shall inform the EEA Joint Committee and may propose to other Contracting Parties that they participate in this action;
> 2. if a Contracting Party decides to make diplomatic representations to a third country in response to a restriction or a threat to restrict free access to cargoes in ocean trades, it shall inform the EEA Joint Committee. The other Contracting Parties may decide to join in such diplomatic representations;
> 3. if any of the Contracting Parties intends to take measures or action against a third country and/or third-country shipowners in order to respond, inter alia, to unfair pricing practices by certain third-country shipowners engaged in international cargo-liner shipping or to restrictions or threats to restrict free access to cargoes in ocean trades, it shall inform the EEA Joint Committee. Whenever appropriate, the Contracting Party initiating the procedures may request the other Contracting Parties to cooperate in these procedures.
>
>   The other Contracting Parties may decide to take the same measures or actions for their own jurisdictions. Where measures or actions taken by a Contracting Party are evaded through the territory of other Contracting Parties which have not adopted such measures or actions, the Contracting Party whose measures or actions are evaded may take appropriate measures to remedy the situation.
> 4. if any of the Contracting Parties intends to negotiate cargo-sharing arrangements as described in Articles 5(1) and 6 of Council Regulation (EEC) No 4055/86 (OJ No L378, 31.12.1986, p. 1) or to extend the provisions of this Regulation to nationals of a third country as foreseen in Article 7 thereof, it shall inform the EEA Joint Committee.

If one or more of the other Contracting Parties object to the intended action, a satisfactory solution will be sought within the EEA Joint Committee. If the Contracting Parties do not reach agreement, appropriate measures may be taken. If no other means are available, such measures may include the revocation between Contracting Parties of the principle of freedom to provide maritime transport services, established in Article 1 of the Regulation;

5. whenever possible, the information referred to in paragraphs 1 to 4 shall be given in good time to allow the Contracting Parties to coordinate their actions;
6. at the request of a Contracting Party, consultations shall take place between Contracting Parties on questions concerning shipping matters and dealt with in international organizations and on the various aspects of development which have taken place in relations between Contracting Parties and third countries in shipping matters, and on the functioning of bilateral or multilateral agreements concluded in this sphere."

E. CONCLUSIONS

4.073 EU transport law has evolved on at least two planes or levels: the modal or sectoral basis (e.g. road, rail and maritime) as well as on a universal basis (e.g. issues which transcend all modes or sectors). This was necessary and efficient because of, on the one hand, the sector specific issues that often arise, as well as, on the other hand, beneficial because of the efficiencies to be gained by one measure across different sectors.

4.074 EU transport law has not always evolved in a planned or methodical manner. It has reacted to developments or events such as when various maritime safety or environmental measures have been adopted or expedited because of the occurrence of disasters or collisions. It would be wrong however to say that all or most of EU transport law has evolved in a haphazard manner – there has been a great deal of contemplation and planning, particularly on the part of the Commission.

4.075 The Commission has published various working papers and communications on transport issues including various plans and programmes. While it has not been as successful as it may have wanted, the Commission has convinced Member States to adopt most of what it proposed. Indeed, the delay has often been at the Member State level. Some Member States were protectionist or conservative in their approach to various matters particularly where the Commission sought progress. Examples would include the resistance of Greece to the liberation of cabotage services.[104]

4.076 EU transport law has also developed in response to the jurisprudence of the CJEU. The most notable example would be the commencement of work in response to the *Commission v France (French Seafarers)* case[105] and *Parliament v Council.*[106]

4.077 There is no entirely harmonious approach to transport in the EU. The failure to adopt a common transport policy is regrettable. A document published by the Commission has described the costs of non-adoption in the following terms:

"1. it is in the interest of Member States to make the most of the substantial private and public investment in transport. Divergences in national policies damage effectiveness, profitability and productivity. The Community could monitor the compatibility of national programmes, harmonise them where desirable and create economies of scale. It could also give technical and financial aid to projects involving more than one Member State;

---

104 See chap. 7.
105 Case 167/73 [1973] ECR 359, ECLI:EU:C:1974:35.
106 Case 13/83 [1985] ECR 1513, ECLI:EU:C:1985:220.

2. the success of other Community policies (agriculture, industry, regional development, energy, environment and tourism) relies heavily on the quality of Community transport services;
3. the elimination of distortions of competition and discriminations affecting transport undertakings is an indispensable pre-condition to the genuine achievement of one of the basic principles of the common market: the free movement of people and goods."[107]

4.078 The internalisation of the EU market as well as the integration of Western, Central and Eastern Europe will inevitably lead to transport having an even higher profile and importance in the EU. This greater profile and importance increases more than ever the need for accelerated progress on the adoption of a common transport policy. It will be fascinating to see how EU transport law develops in the future and how EU shipping law will be part of this phenomenon.

---

107 Commission, *The Community and Transport Policy*, European File 16/83 (October 1983).

CHAPTER 5

The historical development of European Union shipping law

A. INTRODUCTION

5.001 The purpose of this chapter is to provide an historical overview of the development of European Union ("EU") shipping law.[1] While there is an obvious overlap with other chapters, a separate chapter providing an historical overview is valuable to provide a background and a context to the rest of the book and to convey a sense of how the law on this area has evolved. It is proposed to analyse the development of EU shipping law using seven time-periods: (a) the 1950s; (b) the 1960s; (c) the 1970s; (d) the 1980s; (e) the 1990s; (f) the 2000s; and (g) the 2010s. While there is an obvious limitation to presenting the issues using the rubric of decades, it has a certain simplicity which facilitates the narrative.

5.002 A number of general trends emerge from an historical review of shipping in the EU. First, the fortunes of the EU have varied enormously during the last half century.[2] For the most part, the EU's fortunes have declined over time relative to the emergence of new powers in global shipping but the EU has also grown exponentially in terms of its tonnage and in certain specialist areas (e.g. containerised traffic). The last decade or so, until the financial and economic crises of 2008–2010, saw enormous growth in the fortunes of EU shipping. Second, the EU has essentially approached the issue in terms of free market or open market economics and espoused a policy of competition but has also, for many years until recently, protected the position of liner conferences by granting them a block exemption.[3] Third, despite the aspiration to have a comprehensive system of EU shipping

---

1 See Aspinwall, *Moveable Feast* (1995); Bredima-Savopoulou, *The Common Shipping Policy of the EC* (1990); Hart, Ledger, Roe and Smith, *Shipping Policy in the European Community* (1993); and Pallis, *The Common EU Maritime Transport Policy: Policy Europeanisation in the 1990s* (2002). See also Bredimas and Tzoannos, "In Search of a Common Shipping Policy for the EC" (1981) 20 JCMS 95; Cafruny, "Towards a Maritime Policy" in Hurwitz and Lequesne (eds), *The State of the European Community: Policies, Institutions and Debates in the Transition Years* (1991); Jenisch, "EU Maritime Transport: Maritime Policy, Legislation and Administration" (2004) 3(1) World Maritime University Journal of Maritime Affairs 67; Paixao and Marlow, "A Review of the European Union Shipping Policy" (2001) 28 Maritime Policy & Management 187; Power in Aspden (ed.), *Shipping Law Faces Europe: European Policy, Competition, and Environment* (1995), p. 43 *passim*; Power, "The Historical Evolution of European Union Shipping Law" (2014) 38 Tulane Maritime Law Journal 311; Tzoannos, "The EEC Common Maritime Policy and the Liberalisation of World Shipping Markets" in Yannopoulos (ed.), *Shipping Policies for an Open World Economy* (1989); and Urrutia, "The EU Regulatory Action in the Shipping Sector: A Historical Perspective" (2006) 8 Jo of Maritime Economics and Logistics 202; See also Ortiz Blanco, "Personal Reflections on the Development of EC Maritime Competition Policy: Past and Future" at the EMLO Conference, 2008.
2 See chap. 2.
3 See chaps 11 and 12.

law, it will be impossible to achieve this aim because the world of shipping is wider than the world of the EU. Fourth, there have been some inter-institutional tensions between, for example, the Council of Ministers which granted a block exemption for liner conferences in Regulation 4056/86[4] and the Commission which waged what can only be described as a battle to have the block exemption repealed; the Commission eventually succeeded.[5] Fifth, the EU has become involved in areas of shipping such as safety and environmental issues which would not have been seriously contemplated even in the 1970s. Competition law proved centre stage in many ways in the evolution of EU shipping law but this may have been a factor, in part, of the Commission's unease with the block exemption in Regulation 4056/86.[6] Sixth, progress in this area (as in so many other areas) has been slow because of the diversity of approaches and regimes between the Member States. Finally, the evolution of EU shipping law has been partly planned in terms of the Commission adopting strategy and partly reactive to events such as safety and environmental shortcomings. Some of these safety and environmental disasters enabled legislative proposals which had been lying in wait to be adopted because politicians needed to be seen to react to events.

B. THE 1950s: THE FOUNDATION TREATIES

5.003 Shipping (or, more accurately, "maritime transport") was mentioned only once in the original European Economic Community ("EEC") Treaty. It was not mentioned at all in the European Atomic Energy Community ("EAEC") Treaty. It was not expressly mentioned at all in the European Coal and Steel Community ("ECSC") Treaty. The net effect of Article 84 of the then EEC Treaty (the only treaty provision expressly referring to maritime transport) was that sea transport (like air transport) was excluded from the normal rules for formulating the common transport policy (or CTP).[7] Nonetheless, the general rules of the then EEC Treaty have always applied to sea and air transport.[8] Why was shipping treated differently from other economic sectors? It is worth recalling that the European Parliament's Committee on Regional Policy, Regional Planning and Transport published in 1977 an "Interim Report on the Sea Transport Problems in the Community" which stated:

"There is no point in asking why the authors of the [EEC] Treaty left sea transport out of the Common Transport Policy during the negotiations at Val Duchesse in 1957[9] ... It may be that they simply could not agree on rules for sea transport or that they intended to draw up special rules for sea transport but did not have the time before the Treaty was pronounced ready for signature by the Heads of Government, or they had specific reasons for excluding sea transport which are unknown to us. In any case the situation is now completely different."[10]

---

4 See chap. 11.
5 See chap. 12.
6 See chap. 11.
7 Art. 84 of the then EEC Treaty is now known as, after amendment, Art. 100 of the TFEU. See chap. 4.
8 This was confirmed in the case of sea transport by Case 167/73 *Commission v France* [1974] ECR 359, ECLI:EU:C:1974:35.
9 Ed., these negotiations were part of the negotiations which led to the EEC Treaty.
10 Working Documents, Doc. 5/77, 23 March 1977, Rapporteur: Mr H Seefeld, para. 3.

Maritime transport was therefore, for whatever reason, given a special legislative position – a position apparently outside the general Treaty regime on transport – which took some time to be eroded. Indeed, the notion that shipping is still somewhat special, or apart from the rest of EU law, is still prevalent to this day in some quarters in the shipping sector. The 1950s therefore did not represent a period of great hope or expectation for shipping even though five of the six Member States were coastal States and all of them (apart from Luxembourg at that time) had significant maritime fleets and interest in maritime matters. In the short period between 25 March 1957 (when the EEC Treaty was signed) and the remainder of the decade, the Communities had other priorities and shipping was not one of them. It is also worth recalling that shipping was still, in relative terms, an area of national jurisdiction rather than international co-operation (there had been some international co-operation, but the levels of such co-operation were much less in the 1950s than they are today).

C. THE 1960s

Introduction

5.004 The 1960s amounted to a barren period for the development of EU shipping law. This sterility was largely inevitable given the attention being paid to other economic sectors (particularly, agriculture), the need to develop the internal market generally and the cumbersome legislative process embodied in the then Article 84(2) of the EEC Treaty which required unanimity among the Member States before any proposal could be agreed.

1960: Memorandum from the Commission to the Council

5.005 In November 1960, the Commission sent a memorandum to the Council of Ministers on the applicability of the competition rules of the then EEC Treaty and the interpretation of the Treaty's application to sea and air transport.[11] At point 29 of the memorandum, the Commission contended that maritime transport should be included in the measures adopted in the field of transport in furtherance of the Treaty's objectives. This is perhaps symptomatic of a trend which was to develop across many sectors with the Commission proposing measures and the expansion of the Community's remit but the Council being relatively slow to act.

1961: Memorandum on the basic approach to be adopted in the Common Transport Policy

5.006 This memorandum is an important document because it sets out the Commission's position at the beginning of the 1960s on shipping. The Commission believed that the general rules of the then EEC Treaty (but not the specific provisions of Articles 74 to 83, i.e. Title IV on Transport) applied to maritime transport. The Commission's view was ultimately vindicated in the Court of Justice of the European Union's ("CJEU") decision

---

11 Doc. VII/S/05230, Final of 12 November 1960.

in *Commission v France*.[12] This was a somewhat revolutionary principle because the belief was that the Treaty rules generally did not apply to maritime transport because not even the full rules of the CTP (which was part of the Treaty) applied to maritime transport so it was somewhat unusual that other parts of the Treaty would apply.

1962: Action programme for a Common Transport Policy

5.007 This grandly titled document was a communication from the Commission to the Council of Ministers. It did not however contain any specific proposal which would be relevant for present purposes. It merely confirmed the approach of the Commission in its 1960 Memorandum from the Commission to the Council and 1961 Memorandum on the Basic Approach to be Adopted in the Common Transport Policy.

1962: Regulations on competition and shipping

5.008 The then Articles 85 to 94 of the EEC Treaty (now Articles 101 to 109 of the Treaty on the Functioning of the European Union, "TFEU") which relate to competition were implemented for the economy generally (including shipping) by Regulation 17/62.[13] Regulation 17/62 enabled the Commission to apply EEC competition law. Some Member States opposed the application of Regulation 17/62 to transport generally (including shipping) (i.e. they did not want to allow the full rigours of competition law to apply to the shipping sector). So on 14 June 1962, the Council requested the Commission to submit a proposal on excluding transport including sea transport from the scope of Regulation 17/62. These States argued that the underdeveloped state, at that time, of the EEC's transport policy was such that the full application of Community competition law would not be appropriate. The Commission then submitted a proposal for a Council regulation regarding the Temporary[14] Non-Application of Articles 85 to 94 of the (then) EEC Treaty to Sea and Air Transport. This proposal was adopted by the Council on 26 November 1962 in the form of Regulation 141/62.[15] Regulation 141/62 exempted all modes of transport from the scope of Regulation 17/62 and hence disapplied the easiest way for the Commission to apply Articles 85 and 86 (now Articles 101 and 102 of the TFEU). Article 1 of Regulation 141/62 provided that Regulation 17 would not apply to agreements, decisions or concerted practices in the transport sector which have as their object or effect the fixing of transport rates and conditions, the limitation or control of the supply of transport or the sharing of transport markets; nor would it apply to the abuse of a dominant position.

5.009 Regulation 141/62 therefore enhanced paradoxically the special status of maritime transport as embodied in Article 84(2) of the then EEC Treaty because not only was maritime transport outside the scope of the CTP, it was effectively outside the scope of the competition regime as well because the Commission lost the power to enforce the

---

12 Case 167/73 *Commission v France* [1974] ECR 359, ECLI:EU:C:1974:35.
13 OJ 13, 21 February 1962, pp. 204–211 (DE, FR, IT, NL). English special edition of the OJ: Series I Chapter 1959–1962, p. 0087.
14 This temporary measure was not fully reversed for 46 years until 2008 when EC (now, EU) competition law became fully applicable to maritime transport (see chaps 11–12).
15 OJ 124, 28 November 1962, pp. 2751–2751.

competition regime in the context of shipping. The effects of Regulation 141/62 were eventually reversed in respect of road, rail and inland waterway transport by means of Regulation 1017/68 adopted on 19 July 1968.[16] These modes were easier than air and sea transport because they were primarily national in nature and operation – the Preamble to Regulation 141/62 stated that

> "it is impossible to foresee whether and at what stage the Council will adopt appropriate provisions [for air and sea transport]; whereas ... a limit to the period during which Regulation 17 shall apply can be set only for transport by rail, road and inland waterway".

Indeed, it was not until the adoption of Regulation 4056/86,[17] which was adopted on 22 December 1986 (which repealed Regulation 141/62 in respect of shipping), that Articles 85 and 86 of the EEC Treaty (now Articles 101 and 102 of the TFEU) applied to shipping at all in terms of the Commission being able to apply the competition rules to the sectors. (The special position of air transport was also diminished by the adoption of Regulation 3975/87).[18] The exclusion from the Commission's remit in regard to competition of shipping by Regulation 141/62 was largely unchallenged for more than two decades until Regulation 4056/86[19] was adopted and it was not until 2008 that the Commission acquired full powers in the application of competition law to shipping when Regulation 1419/2006[20] entered into force. Again, like the 1950s, the 1960s involved relatively little by way of concrete developments but some consideration was given to the issues involved. It is worth noting that Articles 101 and 102 always applied to maritime transport, it was just that the Commission did not have the implementing legislation to apply the provisions easily.

D. THE 1970s

Introduction

5.010 The 1970s saw the beginning of some serious work on the development of an EU shipping policy.[21] Work which began in the 1970s bore fruit throughout the 1970s but blossomed most spectacularly in the mid-1980s. Why the change from the 1960s? Bredima-Savopoulou and Tzoannos identified seven factors:

> "– the first enlargement of the EC [European Community] in 1973 brought sea transport more to the fore, in that not only were the United Kingdom and Denmark both important shipping nations but also that the United Kingdom and Ireland were both islands,
> – the world-wide shipping crisis and the concomitant tonnage surpluses getting worse since 1973,
> – the expansion of flag discrimination and protectionist practices,
> – the expansion of state trading country shipping,[22] particularly in the liner trades,
> – several tanker disasters which led to extensive oil spillages such as the accident of the *Amoco Cadiz* in March 1978 and to sensitizing of public opinion on marine pollution matters,

---

16 OJ 1968 L175/1.
17 OJ 1986 L378/4.
18 OJ 1987 L374/1.
19 See chap. 11.
20 OJ 2006 L269/1.
21 See Editorial, "Towards a Shipping Code" in *The Economist*, 26 March 1977, p. 89.
22 Ed., these were the Communist or Socialist States such as Poland (at that time) and the then USSR.

- the increasing number of questions, covering a wide range of shipping matters, submitted for the European Parliament and reflecting the revival of interest in shipping,
- the second enlargement of the Community in 1981 with the accession of Greece, a leading international maritime power."[23]

These factors demonstrate how the EU's shipping law and policy often *reacted* to events rather than anticipated them but this has changed quite considerably in recent times with the Commission and, to some extent, Parliament being more proactive.

Bodson's proposals

5.011 Victor Bodson attended his last Council of Ministers meeting as Commissioner for Transport on 4 June 1970. At that meeting, he presented a report on the action to be taken at Community level on both sea and air transport.[24] Abbati has written:

"[i]n the Bodson report the Commission was not proposing that the Council adopt a full and proper policy on shipping. In view of the [then] unanimity provision of Article 84(2) of the [EEC] Treaty[25] it instead listed a number of problems on which a swift Community decision would be desirable. These can be summarized as:

(i) the need to establish proper links between the Community's commercial policy and action on shipping when it comes to negotiations on agreements with non-member countries, … a particularly important point in respect of those non-Community countries which reserve cargo for ships of their own flag;
(ii) the adoption of a common approach towards international economic organizations like UNCTAD and the OECD …;
(iii) the establishment of a procedure for co-operation between Member States in order better to protect their interests against flag discrimination by non-Community countries against the fleets of Member States;
(iv) the adoption of a common policy (harmonized at Community level) to policy on State aid for shipping aimed at improving the competitiveness of the fleets of the Member States and maintaining services felt to be essential;
(v) the standardisation of working conditions of crews."[26]

The Parliament adopted a resolution on 12 April 1972 based on the Seefeld Report[27] accepting the Commission's objectives. This report pointed out the need for the then Community to develop a common shipping policy given the impending enlargement of the Community on 1 January 1973 by the accession of three coastal States, namely, Denmark, Ireland and the UK. (Norway had planned to accede to the Communities at that time but did not; one can only speculate on how the pace of development might have been even faster had Norway, a major maritime nation, acceded to the Communities. The "Norwegian Effect" might have been comparable to, and earlier, than the "Greek Effect" in the 1980s but with Norway being less protectionist than Greece in certain respects.)

---

23 *The Common Shipping Policy of the EEC* (1990), pp. 74–75. It is interesting to re-read these sentiments in the light of Brexit (see chap. 48).
24 See Bodson, "Le prospettive della politica commune di transporti" in Automolisimo e Automobilismo industriale, Nos 5–6, 1970.
25 Ed. the unanimity requirement was removed by the Single European Act ("SEA").
26 *Transport and European Integration* (1986) at para. 7.1. See also *Fourth General Report on the Activities of the EEC* (1970), point 302.
27 EP Working Document No 10/1972.

The 1973 enlargement of the then EEC

5.012 On 1 January 1973, three new States, namely Denmark, Ireland and the UK – all of which were maritime nations (to varying degrees) – ensured that shipping would be an issue of growing significance in the then EEC. Norway had intended joining but, following a referendum, that State did not join. Even without Norway, the UK and Denmark were still important shipping States to bring about a change in the EU. The UK and Denmark accounted for half of the EC's fleet in 1973.[28] It has been estimated that prior to the accession of Denmark, Ireland and the UK, some 90% of then EEC transport was by road, rail and inland waterway and, after their accession, some 90% of the exports and imports between the three new and pre-existing six Member States were carried by sea.[29] The UK's trading relations with the rest of the world (e.g. the Americas and Australasia) meant that there was a greater emphasis on shipping than there might otherwise have been without the UK.

Commission's Communication to Council on 25 October 1973

5.013 The Commission Communication of 25 October 1973 to the Council on the Development of the Common Transport Policy explained the functions of transport within the EEC framework and reiterated the importance of maritime transport within the framework of the new approach to the common transport policy.

ECSC

5.014 On 23 May 1973, the Commission adopted Decision 73/152 obliging undertakings in the steel industry to publish schedules of transport charges for routes involving intra-Community sea links.[30] Also in 1973, the Commission and the UK agreed that the ECSC Rail Tariff No 1001 be extended to cover rail transport by ferry.[31] This was of limited significance to shipping generally and now of historical significance only.

1973: Oil crisis

5.015 The oil crisis of 1973 (as well as the later oil crisis in 1978) caused considerable difficulties for the economies of the Member States. It culminated in a major and prolonged recession. The oil tanker sector was particularly badly affected because of the reduced demand for oil. The European Parliament's Committee on Economic and

---

28 See "Communication from the Commission to the Council on the Community's Relations with Non-Member Countries in Shipping Matters", COM(76)341 final, 30 June 1976, para. 2.3.
29 The Commission stated in its 1976 *Communication to the Council of Ministers on the Community's Relations with Non-Member Countries in Shipping Matters* (COM(76)314 final, para. 2.3) that the "importance of sea transport to the Community has increased following the accession of the three new Member States, since two of these States (the United Kingdom and Denmark) have very large merchant marine fleets (more than half the Community total) which make an important contribution to their balance of payments. Furthermore, the bulk of trade between these countries and the rest of the Community is carried by sea, so that 25% of trade within the Community now goes by sea, compared with 8% in the six-nation Community."
30 OJ 1973 L172/20.
31 *Seventh General Report on the Activities of the Communities* (1973), point 403.

Monetary Affairs in its Interim Report on the Community Shipping Industry in 1976 recorded that by then:

> "[a] vast number of tankers [had] been laid up, which cuts the shipowner's costs considerably but by no means entirely. At the beginning of 1975, 45 tankers with a total deadweight of 1.6 million grt were laid up. By October [1976] these were 426 tankers of 34.9 million deadweight grt, representing almost 15% of the world tanker fleet. And 54% of this laid-up tonnage is composed of ships less than five years old."[32]

1973: *French Seamen's* case

5.016 As mentioned above, on 1 January 1973, Denmark, Ireland and the UK joined the EU. Ireland and the UK were the first ever island states to be members of the EU. Denmark and the UK were significant maritime nations. This made shipping a more important issue than before. The Commission took the opportunity to take a test case against France to determine whether or not the general provisions of the EEC Treaty applied to shipping notwithstanding the then Article 84(2) of the EEC Treaty which meant that the provisions of the chapter on transport in the Treaty only applied to maritime transport where the Council of Ministers agreed unanimously. On 4 April 1974, the CJEU delivered its judgment in *Commission v France* (the *French Seamen's* case).[33] This is still one of the most important, if not the most important, EU cases on shipping. The CJEU held that Article 48 of the then EEC Treaty (i.e. the key provision on free movement of workers in the Treaty)[34] was directly applicable and, thus, France was in breach of its Treaty obligation by restricting certain ranks on French registered vessels to French nationals. More importantly perhaps, the judgment confirmed that sea transport was subject to the general rules of the Treaty even in the absence of a decision taken pursuant to Article 84(2) of the pre-SEA[35] EEC Treaty. This judgment implied, according to the 1974 Annual Report on the General Activities of the Communities, "the applicability to sea and air transport of the rules of competition, of State aids, of social policy, of taxation and of freedom of movement". The CJEU did not at that stage specifically identify those rules. Nonetheless it was abundantly clear that the CJEU had delivered a very major judgment with wide implications. The Commission brought the case against France as a test case so as to determine whether or not Article 48 of the Treaty (which related to free movement of workers)[36] applied to the employment of seafarers but the implications were wider than just employment.

5.017 It is useful to examine the case in more specific detail. The Commission instituted the proceedings on the basis of the then Article 169 of the EEC Treaty.[37] The Commission sought a declaration that by not repealing, in so far as it affected the nationals of other Member States, the provisions of Section 3(2) of the French Merchant Seamen Code of 13 December 1926 (as amended by Order No 58-1358 of 27 December 1958), France had not complied with its obligations under the provisions of the then EEC Treaty

---

32 Doc. 479/76, Rapporteur: Mr J L Prescott, para. 14, citing *Finanstidende*, Copenhagen, 31 December 1975. On the report generally, see chap. 5.
33 [1974] ECR 359, ECLI:EU:C:1974:35.
34 This is now Art. 45 of the TFEU.
35 The SEA removed the obligation of unanimity from the then Art. 84(2) of the EEC Treaty.
36 See chap. 8.
37 Now Art. 258 of the TFEU.

relating to free movement of workers and, in particular, Articles 1, 4 and 7 of Regulation 1612/68 of 15 October 1968 on the free movement of workers within the Community. Section 3(2) of France's 1926 Code (as amended) required that a proportion of the crew of a French ship be French nationals with the exact proportion being laid down by way of a Ministerial Order. The Ministerial Order adopted (on 21 November 1960 and later amended on 12 June 1969, i.e. well after the formation of the Community) required that, apart from where special exemptions applied, employment on the bridge as well as in the engine and wireless rooms on board merchant ships, fishing vessels and pleasure cruisers was reserved for French nationals. Bredima-Savopoulou and Tzoannos have commented that the judgment:

> "was important not only for its legal implications but also for its political implications because it incorporated maritime transport in the process of European integration. Although a Court's judgment cannot be a substitute for a common policy – it cannot be an 'ersatz' of a common policy in the absence of acts of secondary law or of provisions of the Treaties – nevertheless the ... judgment triggered actions; it had practical implications within 48 hours.[38] The judgment was delivered on 4 April 1978 and two days later the final act of the UN Conference on Trade and Development (UNCTAD IV Session) was initialled in Geneva. During the course of the Conference, the Commission had not appeared as representing the Community and had not negotiated on behalf of the Member States. The European Court's judgment, however, was such that the Community had no alternative but to seek a common position two days before signature of the final act of the Code. That was the effect of the judgment upon Articles 113 and 116 of the EEC Treaty, which were considered to be enlisted among the general rules of the Treaty that applied to shipping. Instead of that, and in spite of the Commission's efforts to establish a common view 'a la recherche du temps perdu', three Member States (France, Germany and Belgium) signed the Code. With regard to voting: France, Germany and Belgium voted in favour; the United Kingdom and Denmark voted against; Italy, the Netherlands and Greece abstained; Ireland and Luxembourg did not participate in the Conference."

The judgment had another effect as well. The Eighth General Report on the Activities of the European Communities (1974) records that:

> "in view of the special characteristics of sea and air transport, which operate chiefly on the world market, the Commission has begun a series of informal consultations with shipowners and airlines in the Community in order to examine the possible practical implications of the application of the general rules of the [EEC] Treaty. The Commission intends to hold appropriate consultations with national experts."[39]

In some respects, the CJEU's judgment was not surprising. While the case concerned free movement of workers, the implications of the case spanned all areas of EU law. Had not the Council already conceded the point many years before in adopting Regulation 141 of 1962 disapplying the then Articles 85 and 86 of the then EEC Treaty to maritime transport? Had Articles 85 and 86 (i.e. part of the general provisions of the Treaty) not applied to sea transport; if they had not then why did the Council bother to adopt Regulation 141/62? Presumably, the Council accepted that the general rules of the Treaty as those rules related to competition must apply to shipping otherwise it would not have adopted

---

38 As the *Eighth General Report on the Activities of the European Communities* states at point 355: "[t]he adoption by UNCTAD ... of [the] Convention ... necessitated rapid intervention by the Commission in order to safeguard the Community's interests". This case demonstrated again the effect which a CJEU judgment can have on the development of EU law.

39 Point 355.

Regulation 17/62 and then had to adopt Regulation 141/62. In essence, the case held that the competition provisions in the Treaty applied to maritime transport. The judgment in 1974 is traditionally seen as the starting point for the EU's involvement in maritime matters.[40]

1974: Ports

5.018 The second exchange of views with the representatives of the principal EU ports took place on 19 February 1974. It was agreed that before deciding what EU action to take on ports, it was necessary to obtain a clearer picture of the management of the various ports from the institutional, structural and administrative angles, and also to define certain concepts relating to ports. It is remarkable how similar a sentiment is being expressed today more than 35 years later. The Commission chaired a working party composed of representatives of the ports which investigated these issues and which planned to report in 1975. In June 1977, the representatives of the major ports approved the Report on the Current Situation of the Major Ports of the Community. The representatives also examined a Commission staff report on the then current situation on traffic links between the ports and their hinterlands.[41] The Ports Working Group met six times during 1978 in pursuance of the instructions it received at the third plenary meeting of port authorities in June 1977.[42] During 1979, the Ports Working Group met a total of five times in pursuance of the instructions it received at the third plenary meeting of port authorities in June 1977.[43]

1974: Enforcement of sanctions

5.019 On 26 November 1974, the Council adopted Regulation 2988/74 concerning limitation periods in proceedings and the enforcement of sanctions under the rules of the EEC relating to transport and competition.[44]

1975: French initiative

5.020 On 8 December 1975, the French government presented to the Council a memorandum on the development of Community action on shipping.[45] The memorandum suggested "several lines of action both for harmonisation within the Community and for the protection of the Member States' economic interests against discrimination from outside the Community".[46] It proposed the "harmonisation of intra-Community sea transport from

---

40 Pallis, "Maritime Interests in the EU Policy-Making" (2007) World Maritime University Journal of Maritime Affairs 3 at 16: "[s]ince 1974, the EU has moved into the maritime transport policy field and has progressively expanded the common European policy dimensions".
41 *Eleventh General Report on the Activities of the European Communities*, point 382.
42 *Twelfth General Report on the Activities of the European Communities*, point 373.
43 Bull. EC 6–1977, point 2.1.117. See also *Thirteenth General Report on the Activities of the European Communities*, point 382.
44 OJ 1974 L319/1.
45 *Tenth General Report on the Activities of the European Communities*, para. 451.
46 Ibid.

the point of view of intra-Community trade". The memorandum also stated that the French government:

> "feels that a common policy on sea transport cannot be achieved through scattered efforts, which might weaken the competitiveness of Member States' merchant fleets in the world. It considers it essential that a coherent whole be shaped starting from a clear-cut definition of the content of this common policy."

Non-Member States

5.021 In June 1976, the Commission sent a report to the Council of Ministers a communication on the Community's relations with non-Member States in shipping matters. There was a growing tension between the EEC and the then Socialist States; the EEC and South-East Asia; and between the EEC and the Flags of Convenience States. (Ironically, some of the then Socialist States are now members of the EU.)

Code of Conduct for Liner Conferences

5.022 In November 1976, the Council "turned its attention for the first time to the general problems of shipping and agreed that a common stance should be adopted on the Code of Conduct for Liner Conferences and on possible action at Community level".[47] France, Germany and Belgium had voted in favour of the convention. In July 1976, the Commission decided not to initiate legal proceedings in the CJEU against the three States who had signed the convention because they had undertaken not to ratify the Code for the moment and to seek a common approach among the Member States.[48] In December 1986, the Commission sent to the Council of Ministers a proposal for a regulation in respect of accession to the UN Convention on a Code of Conduct for Liner Conferences.[49] The aim of this proposal was said to be "to avoid discrimination for reasons of nationality between the shipping lines of the Member States and, within the OECD, to maintain the principle of sharing cargoes among members of the liner conferences".[50] It was not until 15 May 1979 that the Council adopted the regulation concerning the accession of the Member States to the UN Convention on a Code of Conduct for Liner Conferences (i.e. Regulation 954/79).[51] The Thirteenth General Report on the Activities of the European Communities recorded that the adoption of this regulation

> "marked the achievement of a common approach which not only complied with the wishes of developing countries for access to liner conferences and cargo sharing but also maintained commercial arrangements for cargo sharing between OECD shipping lines and in liner trades between OECD countries".[52]

---

47 *Tenth General Report on the Activities of the European Communities*, para. 439.
48 Ibid., para. 451.
49 Bull. EC 12–1977, point 2.1.160.
50 *Eleventh General Report on the Activities of the European Communities*, para. 379.
51 Reg. 954/79, OJ 1979 L121/1; Bull. EC 5–1979, para. 2.1.120. See para. 5.028.
52 Point 378.

1976: Interim Report drawn up on behalf of the European Parliament's Committee on Economic and Monetary Affairs on the Community Shipping Industry

5.023 On 23 December 1976, the European Parliament's Committee on Economic and Monetary Affairs published its Interim Report on the Community Shipping Industry.[53] The report emphasised the need for further co-ordination in the shipping and shipbuilding fields among the Member States.[54] It also recognised the need for new ideas and policies in shipping and shipbuilding[55] – two industries which it rightly saw as being interdependent.[56] The report canvassed the traditional reasons why shipping is important for the EU: the carriage of exports of EU goods; the carriage of basic raw materials and energy into the EU; and the employment of persons on board ships as well as in ports and shipyards.

1977: Interim Report drawn up on behalf of the Committee on Regional Policy, Regional Planning and Transport on the Sea Transport Problems in the Community

5.024 The European Parliament's Committee on Regional Policy, Regional Planning and Transport published an Interim Report on the Sea Transport Problems in the Community.[57]

1977: Consultation procedure: Decision 77/587

5.025 In June 1976, a communication was issued by the Commission to the Council on the Community's relations with third countries in shipping matters.[58] The principal purpose of the paper was, according to the Commission, to stimulate debate in the Community on the possible scope and content of a Community shipping policy.[59] This communication outlined the main problems in the EU's relations with non-member countries in shipping. On 13 September 1977, the Council adopted, by way of Decision 77/587, a consultation procedure on relations between Member States and third countries and to facilitate action within international organisations.[60] This measure was designed to facilitate exchanges of information, where appropriate, on shipping matters of common interest. Such a common approach would, it was believed, allow the EU to combine the strengths of each of its Member States into one single bloc. Abbati commented:

> "[e]ven though this Decision reflected only part of the Commission's proposal – the Commission wanted prior consultation in respect both of bilateral shipping agreements concluded between Member States and non-Community countries and of shipping matters discussed in international organisations, whereas the Council authorized consultation only in respect of the former, and

---

53 Doc. 479/76, Rapporteur: Mr J L Prescott.
54 Ibid., para. 1.
55 Ibid.
56 Ibid., para. 2.
57 Working documents; Doc. 5/77; 23 March 1977; Rapporteur: Mr H Seefeld.
58 Bull. EC 6–1976, para. 2274.
59 *Progress*, p. 9.
60 See Council Dec. 77/587 of 13 September 1977 setting up a consultation procedure on relations between Member States and third countries in shipping matters and on action relating to such matters in international organisations (OJ 1977 L239/23). See also Bull. EC 9–1977, para. 2.1.64.

after the event at that[61] – it nevertheless constituted the legal instrument which would serve as a basis, at Community level, for discussion of the most urgent problems facing sea transport without raising the thorny matter of the unanimous decisions required under [the then] Article 84(2). There is no denying that from 1978 onwards the fact that the Community had this institutionalised instrument for consultation between Member States went some way towards speeding up Community action on the major shipping problems facing the Member States."[62]

The Consultation Procedure worked well – especially in the context of the then ongoing negotiations by the Community with the US and Japan.[63]

1978: Decision on relations with State trading countries: Decision 78/774

5.026 A number of Council for Mutual Economic Assistance ("COMECON")[64] States, in particular, the USSR, the German Democratic Republic (i.e. the former East Germany) and Poland were, during the late 1970s, posing a considerable threat to EEC Member State fleets because they were able to offer very competitive rates. The Commission's analysis, contained in *Les transports maritimes des pays a commerce d'Etat et la Communaute*[65] clearly showed the penetration of the Eastern Bloc fleets into the then EEC liner market. The study showed that the Netherlands' share of bilateral trade with the COMECON countries was about 5% in 1976. The study also showed that of the bilateral liner trade between the USSR and the EEC Member States, the USSR accounted for 64% of the trade with the UK in 1976, 75% with Germany in the same year and 83% with Belgium in the previous year. State-planned economies could offer long-term freight rates at a very competitive level. The Commission's solution was a proposal that channels of communication be established which would provide regular information on market penetration by COMECON fleets and such communication would allow an effective response by the EEC. This solution was embodied in a proposal for a decision forwarded by the Commission to the Council in April 1978. This proposal envisaged the Council requesting each Member State to monitor the liner trade of the State trading countries and allowing each Member State to adopt national retaliatory legislation. The Commission's proposal was adopted, for the most part by the Council in a decision adopted on 19 September 1978. This was Decision 78/774 of 19 September 1978 concerning the activities of certain third countries in the field of cargo shipping.[66] The decision referred, in general terms, to collecting information on the activities of third countries whose practices are harmful to the shipping interests of the Member States and did not refer specifically to the State trading countries – this was so as to placate the French representative on the Council who did not want to strain Soviet–French relations.[67] This provided a system of data collection in regard to such routes as East Africa, Central America and the Far East.

---

61 And in fact came in for criticism from the European Parliament: see the Seefeld Report on the present state and progress of the common transport policy, Doc. EP No 512/78 of 5 January 1979, p. 54.
62 Abbati, *Transport and European Integration* (1986), para. 7.1.
63 See *Eleventh General Report on the Activities of the European Communities*, point 380.
64 The COMECON was an association of States which were aligned with the USSR. It was often likened to, but was radically different from, the EEC.
65 Brussels, 1978.
66 OJ 1978 L258/35.
67 See Abbati, op. cit. at fn. 62.

Tanker disasters: safety responses

5.027 There were several disasters involving oil tankers during the 1970s. These disasters, many of which occurred on the coasts of Member States (including the *Amoco Cadiz*), concentrated the minds of the then Community on the need for action. The European Council discussed the matter in 1978.[68] On 26 June 1978, the Council adopted a Recommendation on the Ratification by the Member States of the International Convention on the Safety of Life at Sea (the so-called SOLAS 1974) and the International Convention on the Prevention of Pollution by Ships (the so-called MARPOL 1973), together with their 1978 protocols as well as the International Labour Organization's ("ILO") Convention No 147 concerning minimum standards in merchant ships.[69] The Council also adopted a Declaration on the need for better enforcement of international measures for the prevention of marine pollution by ships and to ensure the safety of ships and the competence of crews.[70] On 23 November 1978, the Council adopted a statement on the subject of the Memorandum of Understanding of 2 March 1978 between certain North Sea maritime authorities on the maintenance of standards on board merchant vessels.[71] On 21 December 1978, the Council adopted a number of other measures, namely, a recommendation[72] that the Member States sign the 1978 Intergovernmental Maritime Consultative Organisation ("IMCO") Convention on standards for the training and certification of seafarers and watchkeeping by 1 April 1979 and ratify it by 31 December 1980 at the latest; a directive aimed at raising qualification standards for North Sea and Channel pilots and encouraging vessels to make use of such pilots; and a directive setting out minimum rules for certain tankers entering or leaving Member State ports. (The then EEC was therefore willing to invoke the "soft law" tool of the recommendation to pursue its aims.)

1978: Ship's inspection proposals

5.028 During the 1970s, there was a growing concern by the Community and the Member States over ship safety. It is an interesting turn of events because it marked part of the move by the Community, rather than just the Member States, into this area which is wider than just the pure economic issues that the European *Economic* Community might have been concerned with; obviously, there was an economic dimension but it was also a regulatory, safety and transportation issue. On 13 November 1978, the Commission sent a proposal to the Council for a binding "decision" rendering mandatory the procedures for ship inspection forming the subject of resolutions by the IMCO (which later became the International Maritime Organization ("IMO")).[73] The Parliament delivered its opinion.[74] The Economic and Social Committee ("EESC") also delivered its opinion.[75]

---

68 Bull. EC 4–1978, point 1.4.3.
69 OJ 1978 L194/17.
70 See *Twelfth General Report on the Activities of the European Communities*, point 370.
71 Bull. EC 11–1978, point 2.1.91.
72 OJ 1979 L33/31.
73 OJ 1978 C284.
74 OJ 1979 C39.
75 OJ 1979 C128.

1978: Decision in respect of liner trades between the Community and East Africa/Central America

5.029 On 21 December 1978, the Council adopted a decision on the application of the monitoring system established under Decision 78/774 to the activities of carriers operating in liner trades between the EEC and East Africa as well as the EEC and Central America.

1978: Pilotage

5.030 On 21 December 1978, the Council adopted Directive 79/115 concerning pilotage of vessels by deep-sea pilots in the North Sea and English Channel.[76] Again, this was an interesting, if somewhat gentle, step into the waters of maritime legislation rather than pure economic legislation.

1979: Ratification of the UNCTAD Code of Conduct for Liner Conferences

5.031 The adoption of the United Nations Conference on Trade and Development ("UNCTAD") Code of Conduct for Liner Conferences forced the then EEC to think further about shipping law than it had previously done so. The Council adopted Regulation 954/79 on 15 May 1979 on the ratification of the UNCTAD Code of Conduct for Liner Conferences.[77] This measure was the most important of the early Community acts in shipping. The regulation ultimately led to the Commission having to adopt an opinion on the legal position of various States on the accession (or otherwise) to the UNCTAD Liner Code.[78] Ortiz Blanco has recalled that the

> "UNCTAD Code was the pretext and the catalyst for Community maritime transport policy, which until then had been non-existent. Given the need to reply in a united manner to the threat posed by the UNCTAD Code, the European Commission proposed and finally (after making many concessions) obtained Council Regulation 954/79, where the reservations that Member States should make to the Convention on the UNCTAD Code were agreed, in the event of their acceding to or ratifying it (something that certain countries, such as Greece, declared that they would never do)."[79]

1979: Parliamentary resolution on shipping accidents

5.032 In February 1979, the European Parliament adopted a resolution on the best means of preventing shipping accidents.[80]

1979: Parliamentary resolution on the Community's relations with the COMECON States in maritime shipping

5.033 In May 1979, the Parliament adopted a resolution on the Community's relations with the COMECON countries in maritime shipping matters.[81]

---

76 OJ 1979 L33/32. See also Commission Opinion in OJ 1980 L176/39 and OJ 1980 L267/32.
77 OJ 1979 L121/1.
78 E.g. Opinion 81/326 in regard to the Netherlands (OJ 1981 L129/68) and Opinion 82/508 in regard to the UK (OJ 1982 L229/28).
79 See Wareham and Power (eds), *Competition Law and Shipping: The EMLO Guide to EU Competition Law in the Shipping and Port Industries* (2010), p. 9.
80 OJ 1979 C67, Bull. EC 2–1979, point 2.3.10.
81 OJ 1979 C140; Bull. EC 5–1979, point 2.3.20.

1979: EESC opinion on Flags of Convenience

5.034 The EESC adopted an opinion on Flags of Convenience.[82] The EESC has long been interested in flags of convenience especially from the perspective of the employment conditions of seafarers working on ships flying flags of convenience.

1979: International Convention for Safe Containers

5.035 On 15 May 1979, the Council adopted Recommendation 79/487 on the ratification of the International Convention of Safe Containers ("CSC").[83] It is interesting how the Community had, by the end of the 1970s, already started to use a wide range of legal instruments such as binding regulations and decisions as well as the non-legally binding resolutions, opinions and recommendations.

Shipping crisis

5.036 The shipping crisis which commenced in the 1970s continued on through the early and mid-1980s. This crisis would have an impact on the content of measures which would be taken in the 1980s including the 1986 package which will be considered below.

E. THE 1980s

Introduction

5.037 If shipping was to be regulated by the EC then there was a need to adopt concrete and wide-ranging measures on the topic. The 1980s witnessed the adoption of concrete but somewhat controversial measures including the December 1986 package. The accession during the 1980s of such a major maritime power as Greece brought shipping to even greater prominence; the effect was similar to the accession of Denmark and the UK in 1973 but there was now the compounded impact of having several major maritime nations as members.

Shipping crisis as well as port distortions

5.038 The shipping crisis which commenced in the 1970s continued on through the early and mid-1980s. On 13 December 1984, the Commission presented a proposal designed to eliminate distortions of competition between ports arising from the variations in the national regulation of hinterland traffic.[84] The decline in the fortunes of the EC's fleet continued throughout the 1980s.

---

82 OJ 1868 C17; Bull. EC 4–1979, point 2.3.67.
83 OJ 1978 L125/18.
84 OJ 1985 C14; Bull. EC 12–1984, point 2.1.203.

1980: Recommendation on the Torremolinos International Convention for the Safety of Fishing Vessels

5.039 On 23 September 1980, the Council adopted a recommendation[85] calling on Member States to ratify or accede to the 1977 Torremolinos International Convention for the Safety of Fishing Vessels by 31 July 1982.

1980: Draft for a Council Resolution Concerning Priorities and the Timetable for Decisions to be taken by the Council in the Transport Sector during the Period up to the End of 1983

5.040 On 24 October 1980, the Commission submitted to the Council a draft for a Council Resolution Concerning Priorities and the Timetable for Decisions to be taken by the Council in the Transport Sector during the Period up to the End of 1983.[86] The annex outlined the proposed priorities of the Council in the area of shipping. Those priorities were:

- a system for monitoring the activities of certain third countries in sea transport;
- verifying the fulfilment of international safety standards by ships in EC ports, bringing EC interests to bear in relations between the Member States and third countries;
- State aids for shipping;
- rules on maritime transport; and
- social regulation in maritime transport.

1980: Extension of the 1978 collection of information decision

5.041 The application of the decision of 19 December 1978 on the collection of information concerning the activities of carriers participating in cargo liner traffic in certain areas of operation[87] was extended for a further two years on 4 December 1980.[88] It was also extended to include transport services between the Community and the Far East.

1980: Proposal on port control of pollution

5.042 On 2 July 1980, the Commission transmitted to the Council a proposal for a directive on the enforcement, in respect of vessels using EU ports, of international standards governing the safety of shipping and the prevention of pollution.[89] Discussions on the proposals were suspended during 1981 pending completion of the work of the second European conference which was scheduled for 1982. Meanwhile, however, on 15 December 1981, the Council adopted a resolution asserting the need for Member States to take effective action as port States to ensure that international standards for shipping safety and pollution prevention are correctly observed by all vessels.[90]

---

85 OJ 1980 L255/29.
86 COM(80)582 final. Reprinted in OJ 1980 C294/6.
87 OJ 1979 L5/31.
88 OJ 1980 L350/44.
89 Bull. EC 6–1980, point 2.1.136.
90 See Bull. EC 12–1981.

1980: Parliamentary resolutions on oil pollution

5.043 The Parliament adopted resolutions on aid for areas polluted by oil slicks and on a code of conduct for oil tankers and other vessels carrying noxious substances.[91]

1981: Accession of Greece

5.044 The accession of Greece in 1981 was a significant event in the development of EU shipping law. Greece is undoubtedly one of the major states in the shipping world. Its significance for present purposes lies at different levels such as in regard to short-sea shipping and cabotage as well as in terms of shipping globally.

1981: Council resolution on its priorities in the transport sector up to 1983

5.045 On 26 March 1981, the Council adopted a resolution on its priorities in the transport sector up to 1983. It did not take the opportunity to add further areas.

1981: Decision extending the collection of information regime in respect of the Far East

5.046 On 26 March 1981, the Council adopted a decision establishing detailed rules for the collection of information concerning the activities of carriers participating in cargo liner traffic between the Member States and the Far East. This decision[92] extended the system already in existence in two other areas.

1981: Netherlands and the Liner Conference Code

5.047 On 24 April 1981, the Commission addressed an opinion to the Netherlands regarding the implementation of Regulation 954/79 concerning the ratification by Member States of the UN Convention on a Code of Conduct for Liner Conferences.[93]

1981: Tankers entering into German ports

5.048 On 25 May 1981, the Commission adopted an opinion addressed to the government of the Federal Republic of Germany on the implementation of Council Directive 79/116 concerning minimum requirements for certain tankers entering or leaving Community ports.[94]

1981: Proposal on competition rules and shipping

5.049 On 16 October 1981, the Commission transmitted to the Council a proposal for a regulation laying down detailed rules on competition (i.e. Articles 85 and 86 of the then

---

91 OJ 1980 C85; OJ 1980 C117; OJ 1980 C147.
92 OJ 1982 L5; Bull. EC 12–1981.
93 OJ 1981 L129/68.
94 OJ 1981 L158/23.

EEC Treaty (now Articles 101 and 102 of the TFEU)) in sea transport.[95] This was to be the initiation of a controversial journey for the EU which involved the adoption of wide-ranging measures, imposition of fines and ultimate repeal of the Council regulation dealing with the issue.

1981: Proposals on concerted research on shore-based maritime navigation aid systems

5.050 On 24 September 1981, the Commission sent to the Council a proposal for a decision on a three-year concerted research project in the field of shore-based maritime navigation aid systems. Again on 24 September 1981, the Commission sent to the Council a proposal for a decision authorising the Commission to negotiate an agreement on the proposed three-year concerted research project in the field of shore-based maritime navigation aid systems between the Community and other States participating in European co-operation in the field of scientific and technical research ("COST").[96] The Parliament delivered its opinion on the proposals.[97] In the light of this opinion, the Commission amended its proposals for the decision adopting a concerted Community research project in the field of shore-based maritime navigation aid systems. On 13 December 1982, the Council finally adopted the decision.[98]

1982: Extension of the collection of information systems

5.051 In 1982, the Council extended the system for the collection of information concerning the activities of carriers participating in cargo liner traffic between the Member States and East Africa, Central America as well as the Far East for a further two years.[99]

1982: Memorandum of Understanding on Port State Control

5.052 A Memorandum of Understanding on Port State Control was signed at the Ministerial Conference on Maritime Safety in Paris on 26 January 1982.[100]

1983: EESC opinion on the Commission's proposal on the application of Articles 85 and 86 to shipping

5.053 The EESC delivered its opinion on the Commission's proposal on the Application of the then Articles 85[101] and 86[102] to shipping on 27 January 1983[103] having adopted it on 10 November 1982. This followed a request from the Council on 3 November

---

95 See OJ 1981 C282; Bull. EC 9–1981, point 2.1.27. See also the *Fifteenth General Report on the Activities of the European Communities*, points 206 and 487.
96 Bull. EC 9–1981, point 2.1.117.
97 OJ 1982 C238.
98 OJ 1982 L378.
99 See OJ 1982 L368; Bull. EC 12–1982.
100 Bull. EC 1–1982, point 2.1.74.
101 Art. 85 of the EEC Treaty is now Art. 101 of the TFEU.
102 Art. 86 of the EEC Treaty is now Art. 102 of the TFEU.
103 CES 73/83.

1981.[104] On 12 November 1981, the bureau of the EESC had instructed the Section for Transport and Communications to draw up an opinion on the proposal.[105]

1983: Recommendation on SAR

5.054 On 25 July 1983, the Council recommended that Member States ratify or accede to the 1979 International Convention on Maritime Search and Rescue ("SAR").[106]

1983: Countermeasures decision

5.055 On 26 October 1983, the Council adopted a decision whereby Member States which had taken or intended to take countermeasures against non-Member States in connection with shipping matters were to consult with the other Member States and the Commission.[107]

1983: Parliament's case against the Council for failure to elaborate proposals in the area of transport

5.056 On 22 January 1983, the Parliament instituted proceedings in the CJEU against the Council alleging inaction in respect of the transport sector. The CJEU declared that, in breach of the then EEC Treaty, the Council had failed to ensure freedom to provide services in the sphere of international transport and to lay down the conditions under which non-resident carriers may operate transport services in a Member State. The court was of the view that the Commission was obliged to elaborate proposals in the transport area. The Parliament's action provoked Commission reaction: the Commission published policy papers on inland transport in February 1983, civil aviation in March 1984 and maritime transport in March 1985.[108] While work had been progressing within the Commission to some extent, it was this CJEU judgment which stimulated action. It was an interesting and important example of how progress was accomplished by one institution forcing others to act.

1984: Commission Memorandum on Maritime Transport

5.057 In December 1984, the Commission sent a communication to the Council laying down the main lines of action for a Community shipping policy.[109] Up to then, neither the Commission nor the Council had clearly defined the general framework and it now had started to develop a "coherent approach".[110]

---

104 OJ 1981 C282/4.
105 CES 211/82.
106 OJ 1983 L237, Bull. EC 7/8–1983, point 2.1.1980.
107 Bull. EC 6–1983, point 2.1.227.
108 COM(85)90 final, 14 March 1985; reprinted in Bulletin of the EC, Supp. 5/85 and OJ 1985 C212, pp. 2–21 (proposals only). The case, Case 13/83 has been reported at [1985] ECR 1513 and [1986] CMLR 138.
109 COM(84)668 final.
110 See Commission's Information Memo P–95 of December 1984, p. 1.

1985: Progress towards a Common Maritime Policy: Commission Communication

Introduction

5.058 In many ways, EU shipping law really began in 1985.[111] In March 1985, the Commission published its *Progress towards a Common Maritime Policy: Maritime Transport* document[112] which was a communication and a set of proposals which the Commission forwarded to the Council. This was the first "systematic"[113] attempt by the Commission at defining a Community shipping policy. It was the real beginning of EU shipping law because some of the Commission's most important proposals were adopted as law by the Council at the end of 1986 which was the first serious series of shipping measures. The background to the communication was, according to Bredima-Savopoulou and Tzoannos that it:

> "was officially approved by the Commission in collegium in December 1984 under the Greek Transport Commissioner, Mr G. Contogeorgis. Thereafter, in January '85 the Transport portfolio was entrusted to the British Commissioner, Mr S. Clinton Davis. From the outset, Mr Clinton Davis made it publicly known that he had certain misgivings about the Memorandum and that he would wish it to be more pronounced over labour issues, flags of convenience and, thus, in its overall approach less liberal. Taking advantage of the fact that in the 'interregnum' between the two Commissioners – over Christmas 1985 – the versions in all languages were not ready, the new Commissioner proceeded with some amendments in the texts of the Memorandum, not in the legislative proposals."[114]

It was believed by the Commission, that the then EC had by that time reached a stage in the development of its shipping policy which required a more coherent approach. The objective was said by the Commission to be to provide an overall concept for a Community shipping policy, to review, in the light of these principles, policy developments so far and to propose the new measures which the Commission felt were required for the furtherance of the Community's trading and shipping interests.[115] This was the first inci-

---

111 Bredima-Savopoulou and Tzoannos comment (op. cit. at fn. 1): "[t]he year 1985 must be considered a turning point for policy making in the European Community (EC) with respect to its maritime sector, since it was then that the Commission submitted to the Council for the first time a comprehensive memorandum and set of proposals for interlinked measures in support of that sector".
112 COM(85)90 final, 14 March 1985; reprinted in Bulletin of the EC, Supp. 5/85 and OJ 1985 C212/2 (proposals only). Referred to later in this chapter as "*Progress*" or the "*Communication*".
113 Petropolous, "The European Community Transport Policy: An Overview" at *The Future of Shipping in Europe: Key Legal and Commercial Issues*, London, 28–29 June 1990, p. 4.
114 Op. cit. at fn. 1, pp. 113–114. The authors record these amendments thus: the "wording of the Memorandum concerning open registries has been toned down without it being coupled, however, with a change in the overall policy on open registries. Thus, there are changes to the effect that open registry shipping is considered as having 'undesirable effects' and in some respects may 'not be in conformity with international conventions' and that measures should be taken to eliminate 'unacceptable practices'. In the paragraphs concerning manpower and social aspects there is a series of presentational changes designed to adjust the tone of the section and to stress that social and employment issues are closely linked to international policy. More particularly, attention is drawn to the adverse consequences for the EEC of a reduction in the number of available seafarers. Moreover, an official dialogue between the social partners should be established to promote a greater consensus on general problems in shipping. The new text also calls for a detailed study on the problems of non-domiciled seafarers to be undertaken in this area, whilst the previous text gave a degree of acceptance to EEC owners employing non-EEC nationals. There are also some other changes, such as adding to the list of major long-term factors affecting the structure of Community shipping the following factors: major takeovers, diversification by shipping companies into non-maritime activities and increased influence of financial institutions as beneficial owners of ships. Finally, reference is made to the need for concerted action on hydrography."
115 *Progress*, p. 9.

sive analysis of the sector and the first comprehensive package of measures to be proposed in the area. Most importantly, this communication led to the first package of measures to be adopted in the sphere – in December 1986. The Commission believed that after a number of policy proposals on specific shipping policy matters, the time had come to develop a "more coherent framework" for a Community shipping policy and this document was designed to set out that framework. The Commission believed that this Paper, together with the February 1983 policy paper on inland transport[116] and the March 1984 policy paper on civil aviation[117] met the Parliament's request for a comprehensive approach to the common transport policy.[118]

Analysis of the market

5.059 The Maritime Transport Paper recognised the decline of the Community's fleet relative to world tonnage and attributed this decline to the prolonged recession in world trade, a loss of comparative advantage on the part of Community shipping interests, the competition from State trading (i.e. Socialist or Communist) entities and cargo reservation by developing countries in the case of liner trades, changing patterns of trade and the growth of protectionist practices adopted by other countries. There was not just a decline in numbers and tonnage but there was also an increase in the age of the EC's fleet. This decline was in spite of the fact that the EC was the leading trading area in the world: its trade in 1982 with third countries represented 21% by value of world imports and 20% by value of world exports with some 95% of the total trade (in terms of quantity) between the EU and third countries being carried by sea and some 30% (again in terms of quantity) of intra-EU traffic being carried by sea. The Commission's solution was not to adopt an insular or parochial view but rather to take a broader perspective – it wrote:

> "in view of the Community's dependence on world trade and the dependence of its shipping interests on international shipping markets, the Commission is of the opinion that the maintenance of a multilateral and commercially orientated Community shipping policy is still in the best interests of the Community's shipping industry, as well as of its user industries and is still the best way of achieving the objectives of the Treaty".[119]

In terms of bulk shipping operations, the Commission concluded that the pursuance of a market-orientated policy was in line with the economic interests of the Community and that open registry shipping are important economic facts for the Community fleet. While recognising these facts, the Commission also believed that they had undesirable effects as well and that in some respects they were not in conformity with international conventions. It thus argued that measures should be taken to eliminate unacceptable practices and conduct (such as substandard or unsafe ships).

---

116 OJ 1983 C154; Bull. EC 2–1983, point 2.1.128.
117 OJ 1984 C182; Bull. EC 2–1984, point 2.1.149.
118 *Progress*, Summary.
119 P. 7.

Proposals

5.060 The Paper made a number of specific proposals. First, the Commission proposed in respect of all forms of shipping a regulation permitting Community action against cargo reservation practices which would damage, or threaten to damage, Community interests.[120] The Commission believed that this was

> "one of the areas where Community action is likely to be more effective because of the greater trading weight of the Community and because only Community action can ensure that such countermeasures do not merely result in the diversion of cargo from one Community port to another".[121]

5.061 Second, the Commission also proposed a Council regulation on freedom to provide maritime services.[122] Such a regulation would apply the principle of freedom to provide services as regards offshore supply services, Member States' trades with third states, the carriage of cargo wholly or partly reserved for the national flag and, with certain specific exceptions, the carriage of passengers or goods by sea between ports in a Member State (including overseas departments of that Member State) (i.e. cabotage).

5.062 On 15 May 1979, the Member States adopted a regulation (i.e. Regulation 954/79) on the ratification of the UNCTAD Code of Conduct for Liner Conferences.[123] The UNCTAD Code was adopted subject to a number of reservations designed to preserve a market-orientated system as between the industrialised countries and as between Organisation for Economic Co-operation and Development ("OECD") liner shipping companies. This left a gap. The gap which had to be filled was a joint definition or interpretation of the "concept of national shipping line" which confers, in Code-based trades, important rights on liner shipping companies. In *Progress*, the Commission proposed a number of criteria for such a definition.[124] The Commission hoped that its criteria would avoid "any discrimination between shipping lines of the Member States and, subject to reciprocity, shipping lines of other OECD countries, without taking away from each Member State the flexibility to take into account its particular national circumstances".[125] The Commission dealt at some length in *Progress* on the issue of liner conferences and competition. It summarised its position thus:

> "[w]hile Regulation 954/79 also acknowledges the stabilising role of liner conferences, guaranteeing regular and reliable services to transport users, the Commission undertook at the same time to submit a draft Regulation on the basis of Article 85(3)[126] applying the competition rules of the Treaty to maritime transport. The Commission submitted a draft in 1981,[127] and in the light of the ensuing discussions in the Council and elsewhere has somewhat modified its original ideas. ... The Commission is concerned about the increasing trend to exclude outside competition from trades in which closed conferences operate. These cases are most serious where a State at one end of the trade route precludes non-conference competition. The Commission's proposal is designed in particular to deal with this problem."[128]

---

120 *Progress*, p. 47.
121 *Progress*, p. 7.
122 *Progress*, pp. 7 and 49. (This became, in part, Reg. 4055/86, see chap. 7.)
123 OJ 1979 L121/1.
124 *Progress*, pp. 7 and 53.
125 *Progress*, p. 7.
126 Ed., Art. 85(3) EEC is now Art. 101(3) of the TFEU.
127 OJ 1983 C282.
128 Set out in *Progress*, at p. 54.

5.063 The Commission proposed complementing that proposal with another which attempted to ensure that EU liner shipping could compete with third countries' liner shipping companies on the basis of fair and commercial principles and thus proposed that the Commission should be able to act against unfair practices where they cause or threaten material injury to EU liner conferences.[129]

5.064 In 1977, the Council had adopted a decision on EU consultation in regard to Member States' relations with third countries and relating to shipping matters in international organisations.[130] In *Progress*, the Commission proposed a Council decision amending that decision so as to allow *ex-ante* consultation on Member States' shipping relations with third States.[131]

5.065 The Commission reiterated its enthusiasm for remaining active in the area of maritime safety. To this end, the Commission said that it would pay particular attention to: (a) the development and co-ordination of the system of port State control within the European region and, in particular, the control of substandard ships and crew conditions; (b) the study of the need for and, if established, the implementation of a coastal navigational system to improve the safety of navigation around the coasts of the Community, including concerted action on hydrography; and (c) the use of the Community's relationship with developing countries to help in the training of their masters, crew and maritime administrations. Similarly, the Commission reiterated its enthusiasm for remaining active in the area of pollution prevention.

5.066 The Commission also dealt with the issue of ports. It stated that it was essential that matters relating to ports be taken into account in the context of the development of both the common inland and maritime transport policies.[132] Building on its 1984 proposal designed to eliminate distortions of competition between ports arising from the variations in the national regulation of hinterland traffic,[133] the Commission stated that it would, first, re-examine the State aid applied to ports and would deal with specific aid on the basis of what are now Articles 107 and 108 of the TFEU and, second, increase its co-operation with the ports concerning the development of common standards for the exchange of information between ports.[134]

5.067 As part of the Paper, the Commission expressed its willingness to intensify and develop its co-operation in shipping matters with the ACP (African, Caribbean and Pacific) States which was indicative of a wider external dimension to the EC's work in the area of shipping.

EESC's opinion on the communication

5.068 On 1 April 1985, the Council decided to consult the EESC on the Commission's communication and, on 26 July 1985, the Council asked the Committee to deliver its opinion on four of the six annexes, namely the Draft Council Regulation concerning co-ordinated action to safeguard Free Access to Cargoes in Ocean Trades (Annex II.1), the

---

129 *Progress*, p. 58.
130 OJ 1977 L239.
131 *Progress*, pp. 7 and 52.
132 *Progress*, p. 8.
133 OJ 1985 C14; Bull. EC 12–1984, point 2.1.203.
134 *Progress*, p. 8.

Draft Council Regulation applying to the Principle of Freedom to Provide Services to Maritime Transport,[135] amendments to the Proposal for a Council Regulation laying down detailed rules for the application of Articles 85 and 86 of the then EEC Treaty to Maritime Transport[136] and the Draft Council Regulation on Unfair Pricing Practices in Maritime Transport.[137] The EESC delivered its opinion on the communication and some of the proposals on 21 May 1986.[138] The Committee welcomed:

> "the publication of this long-awaited document on maritime transport policy because it indicates that at last the Commission has begun to regard maritime transport as an industry in its own right. Until now the Community has lacked a coherent and comprehensive policy for the transport sector and it is now crucial that such a policy should address the means of the Member States' fleets decline, if not reversing it."[139]

Nonetheless, the Committee was scathing in its view of the Commission's proposals:

> "[a]lthough the Commission has made a useful attempt to translate the principles of the ... Treaty into shipping terms, the analysis and policy have a number of deficiencies and the Commission's proposals will not halt the fleet's decline unless these proposals are amended and improved. The situation in the shipping industry is clearly deteriorating yet the Commission does not appear to appreciate fully the seriousness of the situation. The Commission's analysis is confined to a static review of the situation, failing to assess the most recent trends and the outlook for various sectors or to consider the effects of the fundamental change taking place in the level and pattern of world trade."[140]

Instead, it called for a pragmatic and realistic maritime policy which would recognise the international dimension of the industry and its relationship with other maritime industries as well as serve the social, economic and political interests of the EU enabling a prompt and effective response to any threat to these interests.

The 1986 package[141]

5.069 As compared to the first three decades of the EU, there was a frenzy of activity in the area of shipping during the 1980s and the latter half of the decade in particular. The cornerstone of this activity was the package of regulations adopted during the UK Presidency of the Council in December 1986 on freedom to provide services,[142] competition,[143] unfair pricing practices[144] and free access to cargoes and ocean trades.[145] These regulations "completed the foundations for a European shipping policy, following the steps

---

135 *Progress*, Annex II.2.
136 *Progress*, Annex II.5. These are now Arts 101 and 102 of the TFEU.
137 *Progress*, Annex II.6.
138 TRA/116.
139 TRA, para. 2.1.
140 TRA, para. 2.2.
141 See Bredima-Savopoulou and Tzoannos, op. cit. at fn. 1, chap. 8. See Aspinwall, *Moveable Feast* (1995), chap. 4.
142 Reg. 4055/86, OJ 1986 L378/1.
143 Reg. 4056/86, OJ 1986 L378/4.
144 Reg. 4057/86, OJ 1986 L378/14.
145 Reg. 4058/86, OJ 1986 L378/21.

taken since 1977 (consultation procedure,[146] monitoring system,[147] safety at sea[148] and 'Brussels Package'[149])".[150] The regulations had been proposed in the Commission's communication to the Council entitled *Progress Towards a Common Transport Policy: Maritime Transport*.[151] The adoption of these measures owed a great deal to the work of the British Presidency of the Council and the influence of Greece at the Council. The package of measures consisted of four regulations. It is worth considering the extent to which these measures are protectionist[152] and therefore out of step with the EU's avowed open shipping policy. While it is often referred to as the "22 December 1986" package, it was agreed on 16 December 1986 but only adopted on 22 December after it was put into legislative form and translated.

Regulation 4055/86

5.070 Regulation 4055/86[153] applied the principle of freedom to provide services to maritime transport between Member States and between Member States and third countries. The measure was not as broad as the Commission or the British Presidency of the Council desired: it did not extend to cabotage (i.e. services between ports in one and the same Member State). The Council asked the Committee of Permanent Representatives ("COREPER") to work towards the adoption of a measure to deal with this thorny issue.[154] It was not until the 1990s that this issue was finally resolved with the adoption of Regulation 3577/92.

Regulation 4056/86

5.071 Regulation 4056/86[155] laid down detailed rules for the application of the then Articles 85 and 86 of the EEC Treaty to certain forms of maritime transport. Regulation 4056/86 did not boldly and baldly apply the two articles to maritime transport. The regulation recognised the distinctive characteristics of the maritime transport sector, including its international character and thus allowed for negotiations with third states on matters arising. It was remarkable that the then EEC did not have a competition regime for shipping until 1986 – almost 30 years after the establishment of the EEC[156] and even then it was an incomplete regime (e.g. Regulation 4056/86 did not apply to cabotage and tramp shipping). It was a controversial measure that provoked dispute and debate between the Commission, shippers and carriers almost immediately. Regulation 4056/86 dealt with

---

146 Council Dec. 77/587, OJ 1977 L239/23.
147 Council Dec. 78/774, OJ 1978 L258/35.
148 Council Dirs 79/115 and 79/116 OJ 1979 L33/32, OJ 1979 L33/33.
149 Council Reg. (EEC) No 954/79, OJ 1979 L121/1.
150 Report from the Commission to the Council of Ministers on the Implementation of the four Regulations in the field of maritime transport adopted by the Council of Ministers on 22 December 1986, para. 1.
151 COM(85)90 final.
152 See the comments of UNICE in Agence Europe, *Business Brief*, No 1135 at p. 4.
153 On Reg. 4055/86, see chap. 7.
154 On cabotage, see chap. 7.
155 On Reg. 4055/86, OJ L378/4, see chap. 11.
156 See Hart et al., *Shipping Policy in the European Community* (1994), p. 12.

competition issues while Regulation 4057/86[157] dealt with unfair pricing practices in maritime transport.

Regulation 4057/86

5.072 Regulation 4057/86 deals with unfair pricing practices in maritime transport. This regulation related to dumping of maritime services.[158]

Regulation 4058/86

5.073 Regulation 4058/86[159] concerned co-ordinated action to safeguard free access to cargoes in ocean trades.

Statements on the package

5.074 The Council, the Commission and some national delegations made a number of statements on shipping which were entered into the minutes of the Council. These are non-binding in themselves but they give an interesting insight into the thinking of those involved in the adoption of the measure.

5.075 The first statement concerned Community shipping policy generally and was made by the Council. The Council declared that:

> "its adoption of the present Regulations marks only a first stage in the elaboration of a Community shipping policy whose aims are to maintain and develop an efficient competitive shipping industry to ensure the provision of competitive shipping services for the benefit of Community trade".

The Council recognised that for these aims to be achieved, an effort was needed to reduce the disparities in operating conditions and costs between the Community fleets as a whole and their foreign competitors. It went on to welcome the Commission's programme of proposals[160] relating to fiscal, social and technical aspects of shipping. The Council then went on to invite the Commission to submit "appropriate proposals as rapidly as possible, with a view to contributing to the completion of the internal market by 1992". Bredima-Savopoulou and Tzoannos comment that this statement "delineates the framework and purposes for future measures to be taken by the EC in the second phase of its common shipping policy".[161]

5.076 The second statement, which was made by the Commission, related to the Consultation Procedure in relation to Articles 4(2), 4(6) and 6(5) of Regulation 4058/86. The statement "requests the Council to take up as a matter of priority its proposals to amend the consultation procedure established by Council Decision 77/587/EEC".

5.077 The third statement was one by the Council on tramp shipping and consortia. It related to Articles 1 and 3 of Regulation 4056/86. In it the Council invited the

---

157 On Reg. 4057/86, see chap. 7.
158 OJ L378/14.
159 On Reg. 4058/86, OJ L378/21, see chap. 11.
160 Contained in Annex I to Doc. 8107/86 MAR 48.
161 Op. cit. at fn. 1, p. 174.

Commission "to study the situation regarding competition in the sectors of passenger shipping, tramp shipping, joint ventures, consortia and agreements between transport users to consider whether it is necessary to submit new proposals". The Council said that it regarded joint ventures and consortia which had as their object or effect the achievement of technical improvement or co-operation (within the meaning of Article 2 of Regulation 4056/86) or where the consortia only covered a minor market as falling outside the then Article 85(1) of the EEC Treaty. The Statement then went on, in the words of Bredima-Savopoulou and Tzoannos:

> "The Commission undertakes to submit within one year from the date of adoption of the Regulation a report to the Council on whether to provide for block exemptions for passenger transport services, joint ventures and consortia,[162] and to submit proposals to that effect if necessary. The Commission will meanwhile examine carefully any request for individual exemption relating to passenger transport services. In doing so, it will examine, *inter alia*, 'the extent to which such agreements are conducive to facilitating services in this area and favour their continuity and their optimum operation'."[163]

It is notable that the issues were not resolved for two decades!

Assessment of the 1986 package

5.078 The 1986 package is important but it was only a beginning. Its importance is not to be underestimated – as Dimitri Petropolous, the then Head of Division: Maritime Transport in the European Commission, has said: "[w]ith the adoption of a shipping package of four Council Regulations in December 1986, the Community has now at its disposal the legal instruments that it can use to preserve free and fair competition in world shipping".[164]

5.079 To what extent were the four regulations successful in stemming the tide of flagging out, ageing of vessels as well as scrapping or selling but not replacing? Georgios Anastassopoulos, the then Chairman of the Transport Committee of the European Parliament, speaking to the Antwerp Shipping Symposium, "A Future for the Community Fleet", on 6 May 1987, said that the four regulations

> "won't suffice to halt the decline. We have welcomed them as a first step towards a Community maritime policy. But the regulations have not prevented the continuance of flagging out and I am not the only one to fear that they won't prevent it in the future."[165]

On reflection, it is safer to assume that while the regulations did little harm, they did not do enough (nor could they be expected to do enough) to reverse the trend of the EU

---

162 "With regard to the future treatment of consortia, it has been proposed by some shipowner quarters to make the following distinction: the activities of consortia operating within conferences lie within the intent of Regulation 4056. The few consortia operated as single commercial activities should be treated in the same manner as individual shipping companies and should therefore require no special treatment under the competition rules. In the rare cases where a consortium operates outside a conference and is under single company operation it will be obliged to have a rate fixing role and should be subject to a similar group exemption as that provided under Regulation 4056."Alan Bott in "The EEC and Shipping", Institute of Maritime Law, Conference 11 February 1988, London.

163 Op. cit. at fn. 1, p. 175.

164 "The European Community Transport Policy: An Overview", at *The Future of Shipping in Europe: Key Legal and Commercial Issues*, London, 28–29 June 1990, p. 2 (personal views).

165 Reprinted in (1987) XXII ETL 200.

shipping fleet and fortune. The Select Committee of the House of Lords on the European Communities has said that the December 1986 package has "worked well. But they have not stopped the decline in the Community merchant fleet. The haemorrhage of economic and potential military resources continues."[166] The 1986 package was a compromise between the liberal and conservative views within the Council with the UK (holding the presidency of the Council) acting as the arbitrator. However, it should be recalled that the 1986 package did not come about by chance. Pallis has commented:

> "[t]he 1986 Regulations, and the initial failure to liberalise cabotage [until 1992], were outputs of a two-year debate (1984–1986) involve all ... policy actors [e.g. private interests, national governments and EU institutions]. Interest groups advocated divergent views on the dimensions of a common policy. The European Community Shipowners Association ("ECSA") offered clear support, the European Shippers Council ("ESC") believed the EU had failed to rightly interpret the situation and the International Transport Workers Federation ("ITF") judged the proposals inadequate."[167]

The SEA

5.080 The SEA was a treaty which amended the founding treaties. In particular, it reduced the number of situations where unanimity was required to adopt legislation. By abolishing the need for unanimity within the Council in maritime matters, the SEA facilitated future development in regard to shipping. Rabe commented:

> "[a] major step towards the definition of a common Community policy in the sphere of maritime transport was the adoption of the Single European Act. It has had and will have a significant impact on the EEC legislative procedure. Article 84(2) EEC Treaty[168] now clearly spells out that also for sea transport the respective instruments will generally be adopted by a majority vote. This will certainly speed up the process of establishing a common maritime transport policy of the Community."[169]

1987: Antwerp meeting

5.081 In May 1987, a gathering of representatives of the European Parliament and Commission as well as national shipowners, seafarers and administrations took place in Antwerp.[170] The meeting heard about the decline in the fortunes of EU shipping. But interestingly, for present purposes, the meeting also heard about ways of solving it – while many of these ways have not yet been adopted, some may provide a path for the future. The then Transport Commissioner, Stanley Clinton Davis, said that positive measures were needed to counter the competitive pressures on shipowners to flag out.[171] Many speakers favoured Member State governments granting a special tax and social security status for the shipping industry so as to combat the shipping crisis by allowing EU-based shipping companies to compete.[172] There were many calls for an EU-led approach.

---

166 See *Community Shipping Measures*, Session 1989–1990, 28th Report, para. 2.
167 Pallis, op. cit. at fn. 40, p. 5.
168 Ed., this provision is now Art. 100(2) of the TFEU.
169 "Recent Developments in EEC Legislation Pertaining to Maritime Transport", at the IBA Conference in Strasbourg, October 1989, Paper No SG328/A, at p. 2.
170 For the press coverage, see Lloyd's List, 7 May 1987, p. 1; 8 May 1987, p. 3.
171 Ibid., 7 July 1987, p. 1.
172 Ibid., 8 May 1987, p. 3.

1987: Joint Committee on Maritime Transport

5.082 On 31 July 1987, the Commission adopted Decision 87/467 to establish a Joint Committee on Maritime Transport.[173]

1987: Italy/Algeria

5.083 On 17 September 1987, the Council adopted Decision 87/475 on maritime transport between Italy and Algeria.[174] The decision was addressed to Italy and stated that Italy was entitled to ratify an agreement on maritime transport and navigation with Algeria on the understanding that Italy: (a) would take the necessary steps to accede as soon as possible, in accordance with Regulation 954/79, to the United Nations Convention on a Code of Conduct for Liner Conferences;[175] (b) would reiterate to Algeria that the provisions of the agreement will be implemented in accordance with Community law; and (c) would report to the Member States and the Commission, within not later than one year of notification of this decision, on the implementation of the agreement.[176]

1987: Commission Decision 87/359 on Spanish nationals

5.084 On 22 June 1987, the Commission adopted Decision 87/359 concerning reductions in air and sea transport fares available only to Spanish nationals resident in the Canary Islands and the Balearic Islands.[177]

1988: Shipbuilding talks with Japan

5.085 In July 1988, the EU and Japan discussed their differences over shipbuilding. They agreed that both sides would work together to raise prices so as to avoid a further decline in the fortunes of EU shipbuilding due to cheap prices in Japanese yards.[178]

---

173 OJ 1987 L253/20.
174 OJ 1987 L272/37.
175 On the Code, see chap. 11.
176 The background is reasonably clear from the recitals: "Having regard to Council Regulation (EEC) No 4055/86 of 22 December 1986 applying the principle of freedom to provide services to maritime transport between Member States and between Member States and third countries (1), and in particular Article 6 (2) thereof, Having regard to the proposal from the Commission, Whereas the question of Algerian practices of cargo reservation was raised by the Italian delegation in July 1985 in the context of the consultation procedure on shipping matters established by Council Decision 77/587/EEC (2) and led to a Community demarche in October 1985; Whereas the Italian Government submitted to the Commission on 17 March 1987 the text of an Agreement on Maritime Transport and Navigation between the Italian Republic and the People's Democratic Republic of Algeria which was signed on 28 February 1987 but has not been ratified; Whereas this submission is exceptionally to be treated as information for the purposes of Article 6 (1) of Regulation (EEC) No 4055/86; Whereas Article 6 (2) of Regulation (EEC) No 4055/86 provides that the Council shall decide on the necessary action where a Member State's nationals or shipping companies do not have an effective opportunity to ply for trade to and from a particular third country; Whereas Algeria recently ratified the United Nations Convention on a Code of Conduct for Liner Conference, which entered into force for that country on 12 June 1987; Whereas the provisions of the aforementioned Agreement need to be applied in such a way as to avoid a conflict with the obligations of the Member States under Community law, in particular with respect to fair, free and non-discriminatory access to cargoes by Community nationals or shipping companies, including independent lines; Whereas Italy may in these circumstances ratify the Agreement."
177 OJ 1987 L194/28.
178 See Lloyd's List, 14 July 1988.

1988: Commission proposal on the minimum health and safety requirements for improved medical treatment on board vessels

5.086 The Commission proposed a measure on minimum health and safety requirements for improved medical treatment on board vessels. This will be examined in chapter 33.

1988: Competition procedures

5.087 On 16 December 1988, the Commission adopted Regulation 4260/88 on the communications, complaints and applications and the hearings provided for in Council Regulation 4056/86.[179]

1988: Commission Programme

5.088 The Commission in its Programme for 1988 promised that after the first year of application of the 1986 package, positive measures would be taken to strengthen the position of EU fleets and national shipowners and to allow the use of an EU (as opposed to a Member State) flag. The Commission had hoped to make progress on cabotage, safety and the carriage of dangerous goods. These measures were eventually published in 1989.

1989: Positive measures

5.089 In an effort to improve the operating conditions of EU shipping and to complete the Common Shipping Policy, the Commission published on 3 August 1989 a communication by it to the Council. This document, entitled "A Future for the Community Shipping Industry: Measures to Improve the Operating Conditions of Community Shipping"[180] proposed various measures. These proposals, which were long awaited,[181] related to the establishment of an EU shipping register, the effectiveness of port State control, the common definition of an EU shipowner and the application of the freedom to provide services to maritime transport within the Member States. It was the second stage of EU shipping policy. It was largely unsuccessful in terms of the actual measures which were eventually adopted.[182]

Proposal for a Council Regulation establishing a Community Ship Register and Providing for the Flying of the Community Flag by Sea-Going Vessels

5.090 The Commission proposed a Council regulation to establish a European Community Shipping Register (the EUROS Register). This was not adopted but is examined in chapter 6. The EUROS proposal has now been officially dropped having been opposed

---

179 OJ 1988 L376/1.
180 COM(89)266 final; 3 August 1989. See the EESC Opinion (OJ 1990 C56/70).
181 See the comments of Rabe in "Recent Developments in EEC Legislation Pertaining to Maritime Transport", at the IBA Conference in Strasbourg, October 1989, Paper No SG328/A, at p. 2. The proposals of the Commission resulted from an invitation by the Council of Ministers.
182 See Aspinwall, op. cit. at fn. 141, p. viii.

by both shipowners and unions.[183] It is unlikely that such a proposal will be adopted at least in the near future.

Proposal for a Commission Recommendation on Improving the Effectiveness of Port State Control in the EU

5.091 The Commission was anxious to promote and strengthen the effectiveness of port State control and this matter is examined in chapter 29. Port State control is an important tool in ensuring safety as it provides Member States with a means to control the safety levels of vessels which are flagged abroad (and, in particular, ships which are flying flags of convenience).

Proposal for a Council Regulation providing for a Common Definition of a Community Shipowner

5.092 It was thought necessary to define a Community Shipowner for a variety of purposes (including the possible EUROS Register) and thus the Commission proposed a defining regulation. This matter is discussed in chapter 6.

Proposal for a Council Regulation applying the Principle of Freedom to Provide Services to Maritime Transport within Member States ("Cabotage")

5.093 The remaining loophole after the adoption of Regulation 4055/86[184] was cabotage. Regulation 4055/86 dealt only with international maritime services and not cabotage. Cabotage is the transport of cargo or passengers between two ports in the same country. The Commission proposed a regulation to deal with this loophole but the regulation was not adopted until 1992. The regulation is examined in chapter 7.

1990: Proposal for a Council Regulation regarding the Transfer of Ships from one Register to another within the EU

5.094 The Commission proposed a regulation to facilitate the transfer of ships between Member State registers. This regulation has been adopted and is discussed in chapter 6. It facilitates the transfer of ships from one Member State to the register of another Member State.

Financial and fiscal measures

5.095 On 3 August 1989, the Commission published a second communication entitled "Financial and Fiscal Measures Concerning Shipping Operations with Ships Registered in the Community".[185] The communication included a series of "Guidelines for the examination of State aids to Community Shipping Companies". This was a document

---

183 Pallis, op. cit. at fn. 40, p. 6 observes that their opposition was for different reasons.
184 OJ 1986 L378/1, see chap. 7.
185 SEC(89)921 final.

produced for the information of the Council. The document is noteworthy in that it did not contain any draft legislation.

F. THE 1990s

Introduction

5.096 The 1990s represented an important decade in the evolution of EU shipping law because the competition and free market measures adopted in the 1980s were coming into their own in the 1990s. Equally, new measures were adopted in several new areas including the environment, safety, employment and so on.[186]

June 1990 Resolution on Passenger Ferry Safety

5.097 Safety was becoming an even more prominent issue in the 1990s. On 19 June 1990, the Council and the Representatives of the Governments of the Member States, meeting within the Council adopted a resolution on Improving Passenger Ferry Safety.[187] There had been a number of ferry disasters in Europe over the previous few years including the *Herald of Free Enterprise* in 1987. The resolution called on the Member States and the Commission, in their capacity as members or as an observer (in the case of the Commission) of the IMO of the United Nations and the Memorandum of Understanding on Port State Control to press for the urgent identification, elaboration, adoption and implementation of measures which would improve safety of passenger ferries on an international basis in the framework of the IMO and Port State Control Memorandum. The Council and the Representatives of the Governments of the Member States were aware of: (a) the large number of passengers who travel by passenger ferries in European waters; (b) the essentially international nature of such operations; (c) the necessity of crews being able to function in a satisfactory manner in the event of an emergency; (d) the dangers which can arise from management and communication failures; (e) the potentially large-scale intervention which could be required in the event of an accident involving a passenger ferry; and (f) the fact that the transport of passengers in European waters is carried out by vessels registered both inside and outside the EU, thus requiring any necessary improvement of passenger ferry safety, including the question of crewing, to take place in a broad international context.

1990: Proposal for a Council regulation to grant a block exemption for consortia

5.098 The Council adopted a regulation on 25 February 1992 to enable the Commission to issue a block exemption to consortia. This ultimately became Regulation 479/92 and has since been updated.[188] The Commission has favoured consortia over liner conferences.

---

186 On the 1990s, see Pallis, op. cit. at fn. 1.
187 OJ 1980 C206/02.
188 See chap. 14.

1991: Permanent dialogue on the maritime industry

5.099 On 18 September 1991, the Commission announced the creation of a permanent forum for discussion on the shape of the EU's maritime policy.[189] Having recognised the huge importance of the maritime sector for the EU – the fishing, shipbuilding, offshore and shipping industries provide millions of jobs in the EU – the Commission decided to establish a permanent dialogue between all the parties concerned. This forum was to report to the Commission by summer 1992. The Commission recognised the need for a coherent response in areas such as: safety (the Commission was preparing a White Paper on such issues as ferry safety and oil tanker design); research and development; transport; international competition; and the environment. In September 1991, the Commission published a communication entitled "New Challenges for Maritime Industries".[190] This Maritime Industries Forum was a useful initiative.

1991: Transfer of ships between Member State registers

5.100 On 4 March 1991, the Council adopted Regulation 613/91 on the transfer of ships from one register to another within the Community.[191]

1991: Establishment of European Maritime Law Organisation ("EMLO")

5.101 In 1991, the EMLO was established. While it is an association and not part of the EU regime, it has proved to be a very useful forum for discussion and debate on EU shipping law matters.[192] Its website, www.emlo.org, contains very useful information and past conference papers on the subject of EU shipping law.

1992: Establishment of the Maritime Industries Forum ("MIF")

5.102 The MIF was established in 1992. It was largely a Commission driven initiative. The MIF involves the coming together of divergent industries and administrations.

1992: Radionavigation systems

5.103 On 25 February 1992, the Council adopted Decision 92/143 on radionavigation systems for Europe.[193] Article 1(1) provides that without prejudice to existing radionavigation systems, Member States which participate in or join regional agreements on Loran-C must do so in a way which fulfils international objectives. With regard to their participation in the regional agreements referred to in Article 1(1), Member States must seek to achieve the radionavigation configurations which cover the widest possible geographical area in Europe and in neighbouring waters.

---

189 Commission Information Memo P(91)64 of 18 September 1991.
190 COM(91)335 final, 20 September 1991.
191 OJ 1991 L68/1.
192 See www.emlo.org.
193 OJ 1992 L59/17.

1992: Council of Ministers enable consortia block exemption to be adopted

5.104 On 25 February 1992, the Council adopted Regulation 479/92 on the application of the then Article 85(3) of the EC Treaty[194] to consortia (referred to in the title of the regulation as "certain categories of agreements, decisions and concerted practices between liner shipping companies (consortia)").[195] This regulation enabled the Commission to adopt a block exemption on consortia.

1992: Medical treatment on board vessels

5.105 On 31 March 1992, the Council adopted Directive 92/29 on the minimum safety and health requirements for improved medical treatment on board vessels.[196]

1992: Maritime industries communication

5.106 On 18 November 1992, a communication was published by the Commission entitled "The European Maritime Industries: Further Steps for Strengthening their Competitiveness". The communication was sent to the Council, the European Parliament as well as the EESC.

1992: Cabotage regime enacted

5.107 The abolition of cabotage restrictions was a difficult task because some Member States in the Mediterranean opposed the liberalisation of cabotage services. Finally, after failures in 1986 and 1989, on 7 December 1992, the Council adopted Regulation 3577/92 applying the principle of freedom to provide services to maritime transport within Member States ("Maritime Cabotage").[197] In essence, it took seven years of "on and off" negotiation to achieve agreement on this issue.[198]

1993: Spanish derogation to cabotage regime

5.108 Council Regulation 3577/92 established a regime for the abolition of cabotage restrictions.[199] Article 5 of the regulation provided for "safeguards" in limited circumstances. Spain applied for and obtained such safeguards.[200]

1993: Safe seas

5.109 On 8 June 1993, the Council adopted a resolution on a Common Policy on Safe Seas.[201] The resolution followed on from the *Braer* in January 1993 when a tanker ran

---

194 Now Art. 101(3) of the TFEU.
195 OJ 1992 L55/3.
196 OJ 1992 L113/19.
197 OJ 1992 L364/7.
198 OJ 1992 L364/7. See Pallis, op. cit. at fn. 40, p. 5.
199 OJ 1992 L364/7.
200 See Comm. Dec. 93/125 OJ 1993 L49/88 and Comm. Dec. 93/396 OJ 1993 L173/33.
201 OJ 1993 C271/1.

aground off the Shetland Islands with over 80,000 tonnes of oil on board and similar-type incidents.

1993: Safety conventions

5.110 On 28 July 1993, the Commission adopted Regulation 2158/93 concerning the application of amendments: to (a) the International Convention for the Safety of Life at Sea 1974; and (b) the International Convention for the Prevention of Pollution from Ships 1973.[202]

1993: Dangerous or polluting goods

5.111 On 13 September 1993, the Council adopted Directive 93/75 concerning minimum requirements for vessels bound for or leaving Community ports and carrying dangerous or polluting goods.[203]

1993: Shipbuilding directive extended

5.112 On 16 December 1993, the Council adopted Directive 93/115[204] to extend the life of Directive 90/684 until 31 December 1994.[205]

European Economic Area ("EEA") agreement with the EC

5.113 On 13 December 1993, Protocol 19 on maritime transport was adopted as part of the EEA agreement between the then EC Member States and three States forming the EEA. The protocol stated:

"The Contracting Parties shall not apply between themselves the measures referred to in Council Regulations (EEC) Nos 4057/86 (OJ No L378, 31.12.1986, p. 14) and Nos 4058/86 (OJ No L378, 31.12.1986, p. 21) and Council Decision 83/573/EEC (OJ No L332, 28.11.1983, p. 37) or any other similar measures, provided that the acquis on maritime transport included in the Agreement is fully implemented.

The Contracting Parties will coordinate their actions and measures towards third countries and third country companies in the area of maritime transport according to the following provisions:

1. if a Contracting Party decides to monitor the activities of certain third countries in the field of cargo shipping it shall inform the EEA Joint Committee and may propose to other Contracting Parties that they participate in this action;
2. if a Contracting Party decides to make diplomatic representations to a third country in response to a restriction or a threat to restrict free access to cargoes in ocean trades, it shall inform the EEA Joint Committee. The other Contracting Parties may decide to join in such diplomatic representations;
3. if any of the Contracting Parties intends to take measures or action against a third country and/or third-country shipowners in order to respond, inter alia, to unfair pricing practices

---

202 OJ 1993 L194/5.
203 OJ 1993 L247/19. As amended by Dir. 96/39 OJ 1996 L196/7.
204 Council Dir. 93/113 of 16 December 1993 amending Dir. 90/684 on aid to shipbuilding. Dir. 93/115 entered into force on 1 January 1994 (Art. 3).
205 Dir. 93/115, Art. 1.

by certain third-country shipowners engaged in international cargo-liner shipping or to restrictions or threats to restrict free access to cargoes in ocean trades, it shall inform the EEA Joint Committee. Whenever appropriate, the Contracting Party initiating the procedures may request the other Contracting Parties to cooperate in these procedures.

The other Contracting Parties may decide to take the same measures or actions for their own jurisdictions. Where measures or actions taken by a Contracting Party are evaded through the territory of other Contracting Parties which have not adopted such measures or actions, the Contracting Party whose measures or actions are evaded may take appropriate measures to remedy the situation;

4. if any of the Contracting Parties intends to negotiate cargo-sharing arrangements as described in Articles 5(1) and 6 of Council Regulation (EEC) No 4055/86 (OJ No L378, 31.12.1986, p. 1) or to extend the provisions of this Regulation to nationals of a third country as foreseen in Article 7 thereof, it shall inform the EEA Joint Committee.

If one or more of the other Contracting Parties object to the intended action, a satisfactory solution will be sought within the EEA Joint Committee. If the Contracting Parties do not reach agreement, appropriate measures may be taken. If no other means are available, such measures may include the revocation between Contracting Parties of the principle of freedom to provide maritime transport services, established in Article 1 of the Regulation;

5. whenever possible, the information referred to in paragraphs 1 to 4 shall be given in good time to allow the Contracting Parties to coordinate their actions;

6. at the request of a Contracting Party, consultations shall take place between Contracting Parties on questions concerning shipping matters and dealt with in international organizations and on the various aspects of development which have taken place in relations between Contracting Parties and third countries in shipping matters, and on the functioning of bilateral or multilateral agreements concluded in this sphere."

1994: *Commission v French Republic*

5.114 On 5 October 1994, the CJEU declared that,

"by maintaining in force a system for levying charges on the disembarkation and embarkation of passengers in the case of vessels using port installations situated on its continental or island territory and arriving from ports situated in another Member State or travelling to them, whereas in the case of passenger transport between two ports situated on [the] national territory [of the French Republic] those charges are levied only on embarkation for departure from the continental or island port, and by applying higher rates of charges when passengers arrive from or embark for ports situated in another Member State than when they travel to a port situated on national territory, the French Republic has failed to fulfil its obligations under Article 1 of ... Regulation ... 4055/86 ... applying the principle of freedom to provide services to maritime transport between Member States and between Member States and third countries".[206]

Protocol 19 on maritime transport

5.115 The EEA was developed as an adjunct to the EU. Many of the elements of the EU apply to those States which are in the EEA but not in the EU.

5.116 Protocol No 19 of the EEA Agreement[207] provided:

"PROTOCOL 19 on maritime transport
The Contracting Parties shall not apply between themselves the measures referred to in Council

---

206 C-381/93 *Commission v France* [1994] ECR I-05145.
207 OJ 1994 L1/180.

Regulations (EEC) Nos 4057/86 (OJ No L378, 31.12.1986, p. 14) and Nos 4058/86 (OJ No L378, 31.12.1986, p. 21) and Council Decision 83/573/EEC (OJ No L332, 28.11.1983, p. 37) or any other similar measures, provided that the *acquis* on maritime transport included in the Agreement is fully implemented.

The Contracting Parties will coordinate their actions and measures towards third countries and third country companies in the area of maritime transport according to the following provisions:

1. if a Contracting Party decides to monitor the activities of certain third countries in the field of cargo shipping it shall inform the EEA Joint Committee and may propose to other Contracting Parties that they participate in this action;
2. if a Contracting Party decides to make diplomatic representations to a third country in response to a restriction or a threat to restrict free access to cargoes in ocean trades, it shall inform the EEA Joint Committee. The other Contracting Parties may decide to join in such diplomatic representations;
3. if any of the Contracting Parties intends to take measures or action against a third country and/or third-country shipowners in order to respond, inter alia, to unfair pricing practices by certain third-country shipowners engaged in international cargo-liner shipping or to restrictions or threats to restrict free access to cargoes in ocean trades, it shall inform the EEA Joint Committee. Whenever appropriate, the Contracting Party initiating the procedures may request the other Contracting Parties to cooperate in these procedures.

    The other Contracting Parties may decide to take the same measures or actions for their own jurisdictions. Where measures or actions taken by a Contracting Party are evaded through the territory of other Contracting Parties which have not adopted such measures or actions, the Contracting Party whose measures or actions are evaded may take appropriate measures to remedy the situation;
4. if any of the Contracting Parties intends to negotiate cargo-sharing arrangements as described in Articles 5(1) and 6 of Council Regulation (EEC) No 4055/86 (OJ No L378, 31.12.1986, p. 1) or to extend the provisions of this Regulation to nationals of a third country as foreseen in Article 7 thereof, it shall inform the EEA Joint Committee.

    If one or more of the other Contracting Parties object to the intended action, a satisfactory solution will be sought within the EEA Joint Committee. If the Contracting Parties do not reach agreement, appropriate measures may be taken. If no other means are available, such measures may include the revocation between Contracting Parties of the principle of freedom to provide maritime transport services, established in Article 1 of the Regulation;
5. whenever possible, the information referred to in paragraphs 1 to 4 shall be given in good time to allow the Contracting Parties to coordinate their actions;
6. at the request of a Contracting Party, consultations shall take place between Contracting Parties on questions concerning shipping matters and dealt with in international organizations and on the various aspects of development which have taken place in relations between Contracting Parties and third countries in shipping matters, and on the functioning of bilateral or multilateral agreements concluded in this sphere."

1994: Ships inspection/classification societies

5.117 On 22 November 1994, the Council adopted Directive 94/57 on common rules and standards for ship inspection and survey organisations and for the relevant activities of maritime administrations.[208] Commission Decision 96/587 of 30 September 1996 involved the "publication of the list of recognized organizations which have been notified by Member States in accordance with Council Directive 94/57".[209]

---

208 OJ 1994 L319/20.
209 OJ 1996 L257/43.

1994: Seafarers' training

5.118 On 22 November 1994, the Council adopted Directive 94/58 on the minimum level of training for seafarers.[210] Again, the EU became involved in an area such as the treatment of seafarers which would typically fall within the scope of the IMO and the ILO.

1994: Global Navigation System

5.119 On 15 December 1994, the Council adopted a resolution on the European contribution to the development of a Global Navigation System ("GNS").[211]

1995: Commission regulation on application of Article 85(3) (now Article 101(3) TFEU) to consortia

5.120 On 20 April 1995, the Commission adopted Regulation 870/95 on the application of, what is now, Article 101(3) of the TFEU to certain categories of agreements, decisions and concerted practices between liner shipping companies (consortia).[212]

1995: Port State control

5.121 On 19 June 1995, the Council adopted Directive 95/21 concerning "the enforcement in respect of shipping using Community ports and sailing in the waters under the jurisdiction of the Member States, of international standards for ship safety, pollution prevention and shipboard living and working conditions (Port State Control)".[213] Commission Directive 96/40 of 25 June 1996 established a common model of an identity card of inspectors carrying out port state control.[214] Port State control is essential in those circumstances particularly when flag State control is inadequate.

1995: Short sea shipping communication

5.122 In July 1995, the Commission published a communication on short sea hipping. There is no doubt that short sea shipping is vitally important for logistics in Europe given the congested and polluting land-based modes. The EU has become increasingly interested in the area of short sea shipping. This led, in part, to a resolution on the issue of short sea shipping in 1996.

Council Regulation 3051/95 on the safety management of roll-on/roll-off passenger ferries (ro-ro ferries)

5.123 On 8 December 1995, the Council adopted Council Regulation 3051/95 on the safety management of roll-on/roll-off passenger ferries (ro-ro ferries).[215]

---

210 OJ 1994 L319/1.
211 OJ 1994 C379/2.
212 OJ 1995 L89/7.
213 OJ 1005 L157/1.
214 OJ 1996 L196/8.
215 OJ 1995 L320/14.

1995: Statistical return on passengers and goods

5.124 On 8 December 1995, the Council adopted Directive 95/64 on statistical returns in respect of carriage of passengers and goods by sea.[216] This was a first step towards the recording of names of passengers. The stimulus for such measures was the fact that the identification of victims in ferry disasters took much longer than comparable air accident victims because there was no comparable manifest identifying individual ferry passengers.

1996: Short sea shipping resolution

5.125 On 11 March 1996, the Council adopted a resolution on short sea shipping.[217] It was non-binding as is the nature of a resolution. It followed on from the Commission's communication on the subject in 1995. It was a prelude to the more detailed one on 14 February 2000 which is considered below. The 1996 resolution read:

"THE COUNCIL OF THE EUROPEAN UNION,
A. Having regard to the Treaty establishing the European Community,
   Considering the White Paper on the future development of the common transport policy, of 2 December 1992,[218] which was welcomed by the Council at its meetings held on 7 and 8 June and 19 June 1993;
   Considering the Commission communication on short sea shipping, of 5 July 1995;[219]
   Considering the importance of transport for the economy of the European Union;
   Considering the increasing degree of congestion in general and the high costs which characterize land transport infrastructure;
   Considering the potential contribution that short sea shipping could make to the achievement of sustainable mobility;
   Considering that, in view of the foregoing, efforts are called for both at Community level and at the level of Member States to promote or improve short sea shipping, while respecting the free choice of users;
   Considering that, where obstacles prevent the development of short sea shipping, remedial action should be taken by regional, local or port authorities and by the maritime industries themselves;

B. NOTES:
1. the considerable advantages presented by short sea shipping for the European Union in comparison with land transport, in particular:

   (a) the general availability of space capacity in short sea shipping;
   (b) lower energy consumption and lower levels of emission of pollutants into the atmosphere;
   (c) potential contribution to the development of peripheral regions of the European Union;
   (d) possibility to extend short sea shipping further with few infrastructure costs;

2. the reports and the agreed multiannual work programmes adopted by various Conferences on shipping in different areas, such as the Baltic Sea, the Black Sea and the Mediterranean Sea;
3. the reports and proposals by the Maritime Industries Forum on the advisability of promoting

---
216 OJ 1995 L320/25.
217 OJ 1996 C99/1.
218 COM(92) 494 final.
219 COM(95) 317 final.

short sea shipping as a viable alternative, in economic, energy, safety and environmental terms, to land transport;

C. STATES that the main objectives of short sea shipping policy are:
1. to achieve a balanced growth of this mode of transport; and
2. positive and active integration of short sea shipping, including feeder services, into the intermodal transport chain,

D. INTENDS to pursue these objectives by encouraging the following actions:
1. developing further the environmental benefits of short sea shipping;
2. promoting, in the interest of the users, free and fair competition between modes of transport in which all modes bear their full costs, including external costs;
3. fostering of free and fair competition between Community ports and between shipping lines;
4. improving port efficiency in order to reduce the costs of, and time spent in, port operations;
5. making use of combined transport for the development of short sea shipping;
6. promoting the confidence of shippers and transport undertakings in the possibilities of short sea shipping;
7. streamlining and, where appropriate, coordinating, harmonizing and simplifying customs procedures and other related administrative formalities which arise in harbours;
8. encouraging initiatives by shipping undertakings involved in short sea shipping;
9. drawing up and implementing pilot projects concerning short sea shipping, where these do not distort competition between transport modes or between shipping companies or ports of all Member States, and disseminating the results;
10. supporting training, research and development in the area of short sea shipping and port activities;
11. supporting and expanding electronic data interchange (EDI),

E. IN THE LIGHT OF THE ABOVE:
1. welcomes in general the action programme contained in the Communication by the Commission;
2. notes that the Commission will submit as soon as possible its Green Paper on the internalization of external costs in transport;
3. notes that the Commission will develop as soon as possible guidelines on State aid to shipping and to ports and will consult the Member States and the maritime industries on these guidelines;
4. agrees that the promotion of short sea shipping should continue to be an important element in ongoing Community and Member States' activity such as the trans-European transport network plan and the Fourth Framework Programme on Research and Development;

F. INVITES THE COMMISSION to propose to the Council or to develop, as soon as possible, the measures necessary to attain the objectives stated in part C taking into account its action programme and the subsidiarity principle, and in particular measures which:

1. prevent distortion of competition between ports;
2. promote the increased use of short sea shipping among its potential users;
3. simplify and streamline existing customs procedures and other related administrative formalities which arise in ports, with regard to short sea shipping;
4. encourage initiatives by shipping undertakings involved in short sea shipping;
5. support programmes of training, research and development in this transport sector;
6. encourage the use of information technology for the best development of this mode of transport,

G. INVITES THE MEMBER STATES:
1. to support the objectives and the means stated in parts C and D;
2. to cooperate with the Commission in setting a Community framework to promote the short sea shipping sector;

3. to carry out actions to stimulate short sea shipping, taking into account the proposed action programme of the Commission's communication and to encourage their regional, local and port authorities and maritime industries to do likewise;
4. to promote practical consultations, for example through round tables such as those of the Maritime Industries Forum in which the maritime industries and regional, local and port authorities are represented."

1996: Commission communication: "Towards a New Maritime Strategy"

5.126 On 13 March 1996, the Commission published a communication entitled "Towards a New Maritime Strategy".[220] The communication was sent by the Commission to the Council, the European Parliament, the EESC as well as the Committee of the Regions. The Commission wrote that the communication

"introduces a new approach of the Commission to maritime strategy. It has been prepared to re-assess Community maritime policy and to set further goals towards establishing a common maritime purpose. Not all aspects of maritime safety of the Community are already established. The external maritime relations policy of the Community is also well on its way. Of course, more remains to be done in both areas. But a common answer to the problems of the competiveness of EC shipping has not yet been founded."[221]

The 1989 proposal for an EU registry of shipping was later withdrawn.

1996: CEWAL before the General Court

5.127 The General Court confirmed the substance of the *CEWAL* (the Central West Africa Conference) decision of the Commission.[222] The CJEU was to go on to do so in 2000 in terms of the substance though it annulled the fines as the Statement of Objections had been served defectively on the parties.[223]

1997: Commission communication: "External Relations in the Field of Maritime Transport"

5.128 On 14 March 1997, the Commission adopted a communication on external relations. The communication was entitled "External Relations in the Field of Maritime Transport". The Commission proposed co-operation with third countries, bilateral arrangements and consultation with third countries, redressing third countries' discriminatory practices and action to ensure fair competition.

1997: Council Resolution on a New Strategy to Increase the Competitiveness of Community Shipping

5.129 On 24 March 1997, the Council adopted a resolution on a New Strategy to Increase the Competitiveness of Community Shipping.[224] This resolution arose out of the

---

220 COM(96)81 final, 13 March 1996.
221 Ibid., p. 1.
222 Cases T-24-26/93 and T-28/93 *CMB, CMBT and Dafra-Lines v Commission* [1996] ECR II-1201.
223 Cases C-395/96P and C-396/96P *CMB, CMBT and Dafra Lines v Commission* [2000] ECR I-1365.
224 OJ 1997 C109/1.

Kinnock Report "Towards a New Maritime Strategy". The resolution was long on generalities and short on detail, concentrating on hortatory remarks on employment, training and so on. It stated:

> "Council Resolution of 24 March 1997 on a new strategy to increase the competitiveness of Community shipping
> The Council of the European Union,
>
> 1. WELCOMES the general structure and the policy direction of the Commission communication 'Towards a new maritime strategy' aiming at promoting a Community fleet and employment of Community seafarers and focusing, in particular, on a parallel and balanced development in the key areas identified by the Commission of:
>   - international competitiveness of the Community fleet,
>   - open markets,
>   - fair competition,
>   - safety;
> 2. NOTES that the key areas mentioned above are interrelated, since policy measures in one area can affect one or more of the other areas;
> 3. SEEKS to capture the economic benefits of the growing market for shipping services and to promote both the employment of Community seafarers and the employment of shore-based personnel and maritime know-how;
> 4. RECOGNIZES that the shipping market is a global market where Community shipowners have to compete internationally and that the Community's policies and rules will have to take account of this fact;
> 5. RECOGNIZES that shipping should be developed, since it is an environment-friendly alternative or complement to other modes of transport and since short-sea shipping, including regular ferry services, plays a vital role in intra-Community trade and in providing feeder services for trans-ocean traffic;
> 6. IS OF THE OPINION that the shipping industry itself has a key role to play in the face of increasing international competition in adapting to change within the legal framework of shipping while having regard to the objectives set out in this resolution;
> 7. RECOGNIZES that positive measures are needed to pursue Community objectives in the key areas outlined above and, in particular, to foster the competitiveness of the Community fleet and the employment of Community seafarers as well as to secure open markets;
> 8. CONCURS with the Commission that safety at sea is an important factor and that unacceptable competitive advantages can be obtained in shipping by the neglect of safety and environmental considerations; therefore, measures should be taken, where justified, to:
>   - strengthen everyone's commitment to quality and safety at all levels of the shipping sector,
>   - ensure that non-compliance with binding international and Community safety and quality standards does not lead to competitive and economic disadvantages for 'compliance culture' operators[225];
>
> AGREES that action should be undertaken in the following areas and pursuant to the following principles:
>
> A. 1. Helping Community shipping to continue striving for high quality and to improve its competitiveness by:
>
>   (a) ensuring the continued high-quality training of Community seafarers of all ranks and of shore-based personnel, by making optimum use of the resources of the Member States and the Community instruments;

---

[225] See also Council Resolution of 8 June 1993 on a common policy on safe seas, OJ No C271, 7. 10. 1993, p. 1.

(b) ensuring that maritime transport plays an enhanced role in Community Research and Development programmes (such as Euret, MAST, Maris) and that these programmes are properly coordinated among themselves and with national programmes, paying special attention to the need to use financial resources most effectively;
(c) developing short-sea shipping as an environment-friendly alternative or complement to other modes of transport[226];
(d) ensuring clarity in the application of the Community's competition rules, taking into account the special nature of shipping;
(e) upholding the competitive position of Community shipowners vis-à-vis their international competitors;
(f) ensuring that regulatory measures and administrative procedures concerning shipowners and shipping are always proportionate.

2. The principle that Member States should consider the prospect of ratifying the ILO Conventions adopted at the 84th (maritime) conference of the ILO, held in Geneva in October 1996.
3. Urgent adoption by the Commission of revised guidelines for State aids in accordance with Article 92 of the Treaty establishing the European Community, and noting the specific Commission statement on the matter.

B. 1. Submission by the Commission, as soon as possible, of its communication on external relations, on the basis of which a specific policy debate will be held.
2. Continuation of the multilateral and bilateral measures leading to a liberalization of international trade, with regard to both shipping and shipping-related services, so as to afford the Community industry the same opportunities as those enjoyed by the enterprises of third countries within the Community.

C. 1. Support by the Member States and the Community for the development by IMO of internationally binding quality criteria for flag administrations and ship registers.
2. If appropriate:

   – adopting a Community instrument ensuring the proper uniform implementation of those criteria, laying down principles for the safe operation of Member States' ship registers,
   – addressing in due course the questions of defining transparent liability, ownership, control and management requirements as well as of the genuine and economic link, while respecting the rules of the aforementioned Treaty.

3. Strengthening compliance with international standards by ships of the Community and third countries through effective application of Council Directive 95/21/EC of 19 June 1995 concerning the enforcement, in respect of shipping using Community ports and sailing in the waters under the jurisdiction of the Member States, of international standards for ship safety, pollution prevention and shipboard living and working conditions (port State control),[227] so as to maximize its deterrent effect; in particular, the harmonized application of detentions and effective transparency are key elements of this action.
4. Consider, in consultation with the industry, whether to extend the commitment to safe operation in shipping to cargo owners under certain circumstances.
5. Support initiatives of the industry aimed at improving the quality standard of shipping."

Such measures are, in themselves, not binding but they sometimes provide a useful weapon to be cited and used later against the EU institutions when the words are not acted upon.

---

226 See also Council Resolution of 11 March 1996 on short-sea shipping, OJ No C99, 2. 4. 1996, p. 1.
227 OJ No L157, 7. 7. 1995, p. 1.

1997: Community guidelines on State aid

5.130 In 1997, the Commission published guidelines on State aid in the maritime sector.[228] These guidelines were more flexible than the 1989 guidelines.

1998: Trans-Atlantic Conference Agreement

5.131 In 1998, the European Commission imposed fines totalling €273 million on 15 participants in the Trans-Atlantic Conference Agreement ("TACA"). The Commission later granted exemption to a more limited or restricted form of TACA where there were only seven participants and limitations on the type of information which could be exchanged between members.

1990s Generally

5.132 First, the 1990s generally witnessed intensive and imaginative intervention in the marketplace by the Commission's Directorate General for Competition as well as the General Court and the CJEU. Much of this intervention centred on competition in ports but the Commission then became very closely involved in the area of liner conferences. Second, the EU became more involved in safety issues largely due to the highly visible ferry and tanker casualties in European waters; this involvement was criticised in different quarters for different reasons – some said that it was not enough and that it is often mere resolutions while others believe that the EU should not be involved in safety at all given the existence of specialist bodies such as the IMO. Third, the CJEU became more active in terms of developing the competition law issues involved. Fourth, the EU had not solved – nor should it be expected to – the European shipping malaise but the economic boom of the early part of the twenty-first century solved the malaise.

G. THE 2000s

Introduction

5.133 The first decade of the twenty-first century witnessed a further development of EU shipping law. The block exemption for liner conferences (embodied in Regulation 4056/86) was repealed; competition law was applied extensively in the shipping sector; safety and environmental rules were extended; and there was further integration between the various strands of EU shipping and maritime policies.

2000: Consortia block exemption: Regulation 823/2000

5.134 Consortia are clearly advantageous in that they often provide shipping services in an efficient manner which meets consumer needs. However, there are some aspects of consortia arrangements which are potentially anti-competitive so an exemption mechanism is therefore vital. Commission Regulation 823/2000 granted a block exemption

---

228 OJ 1997 C205/5.

under what is now Article 101(3) of the TFEU to liner shipping consortia in certain circumstances.[229] The block exemption has been amended since.[230]

2000: Promotion of intermodality and intermodal freight transport in the EU

5.135 On 14 February 2000, the Council adopted the resolution on the promotion of intermodality and intermodal freight transport in the European Union.[231] The resolution:

"(1) WELCOMES the Commission Communication on Intermodality and Intermodal Freight Transport in the European Union of October 1999 and the Communication on the Progress of the Implementation of the Action Programme of June 1997 contained therein.

(2) NOTES with satisfaction that most projects in the action programme have been launched and encourages the Commission to continue its implementation.

(3) IS OF THE OPINION that functional and logistically efficient freight transport systems contribute to the development of economic activity within the Community for the benefit of its citizens and enterprises.

(4) ENDORSES the objective set by the Commission to develop Intermodal Freight Transport, i.e. an optimal integration of different transport modes enabling an efficient and cost-effective use of the transport system through seamless, customer-oriented door-to-door services, whilst favouring competition between transport operators.

(5) RECALLS that the Council strategy of 6 October 1999 on the integration of environment and sustainable development into the transport policy 'underlines that further progress is required, notably in the … promotion of … intermodal and combined transport … the standardisation and harmonisation of intermodal transport units … the competitiveness and the quality of services of ports and other intermodal terminals and railways, e.g. by the increased use of telematics … (and the study of) the different liability regimes'.

(6) EMPHASISES, the need determined by the same strategy 'to continue to analyse the relationship between transport (demand) and … the organisation of industrial production and services (globalisation, market deregulation, just-in-time logistics, electronic commerce)' with a view to developing actions consistent with the general goal of sustainable mobility.

(7) REAFFIRMS its determination to promote transport modes contributing to sustainable transport, in particular rail transport, short sea shipping and inland navigations; RECALLS, in this context, its conclusions of 6 October 1999 on the revitalisation of the European railways referring, in particular, to the establishment of a Trans-European Rail Freight Network (TERFN) and its Resolution of 11 March 1996 on short sea shipping,[232] Conclusions of 18 June 1997 and Resolution of 14 February 2000 on the promotion of short sea shipping.[233]

(8) RECALLS the importance of the revision of the relevant legal framework of the Community as well as the importance of research, development and demonstration on intermodal transport and notes with satisfaction the role of studies in this field in key actions of the Fifth RTD Framework Programme established by Decision No 182/1999/EC.[234]

(9) INVITES all parties concerned to work actively towards a sound operational market environment for intermodal transport, so as to make intermodality, where feasible, a viable and environmentally friendly alternative to single mode road transport.

(10) NOTES that further work must be concentrated on identifying obstacles to intermodal transport in competing successfully in the market.

---

229 OJ 2000 L100/24. It was later amended. See chap. 14.
230 See chap. 14.
231 OJ C56/1, 29 February 2000.
232 Ed., OJ C99/1, 2 April 1996.
233 Ed., OJ C56/1, 29 February 2000.
234 Ed., OJ L26/1, 1 February 1999.

(11) INVITES the Commission, in cooperation with the Member States, to continue and intensify its work for the promotion of intermodal transport including combined transport, in particular, by:

    (a) including intermodality in its revision of the TEN-T through reference to concrete actions with a view to achieving sustainable mobility, such as:

- setting up new tools for assessing the ability of planned infrastructures and actions to transfer some road transport demand towards more environmentally friendly modes,
- alleviating the bottlenecks for intermodalism, including those in the context of TERFN,
- developing and optimising terminals for intermodal transport;

    (b) taking account of intermodalism with a view to creating a level playing field in the transport market when submitting, during the year 2000, a proposal for a revision of Regulation (EEC) No 1107/70 of the Council of 4 June 1970 on the granting of aids for transport by rail, road and inland waterway[235] with regard to aid to combined transport;

    (c) integrating the information society into the European transport system, e.g. by submitting proposals for establishing an open architecture for data transfer and transport telematics;

    (d) contributing to the realisation of an open and efficient real-time information and transaction systems, as a tool for shippers and intermodal transport operators;

    (e) continuing, together with the Member States, the industry and relevant international organisations, its efforts to promote an appropriate liability regime in that area, inter alia, by exploring the aspects of a liability regime for intermodal transport and by presenting a report on the economic analysis of the consequences of the absence of a generally accepted intermodal liability regime and on the work being undertaken with the industry on the legal and economic advantages of the different solutions for a liability regime for intermodal transport;

    (f) presenting a communication on 'Benchmarking in Transport' and developing key performance indicators for freight intermodalism; in this context, demonstrating the potential cost-effectiveness of intermodal transport projects and publishing examples and information on best practices, particularly taking into account the experience gained from the Pilot Actions for Combined Transport (PACT)-programme and the different projects under the Fifth RTD Framework Programme,

    (g) directing, when proposing measures in the field of transport, the measures to the logistic and transport system as a whole and not solely to the individual modes of transport, focusing, inter alia, on harmonising the standards related to transport units and on technologies for cheaper, more efficient and environmentally friendly freight handling; to this end, presenting a communication on Supply Chain Management, logistics and intermodal transport by the end of year 2001;

    (h) planning for an appropriate follow-up to the PACT programme, focussing on innovative projects;

    (i) extending the action programme on intermodality to more integrated Intelligent Transport System applications, electronic commerce applications and demonstration projects and

    (j) bolstering the role of research and development projects on intermodal transport in the RTD framework programmes.

(12) INVITES the applicant countries to follow the above objectives and actions when formulating national and local strategies.

---

235 Ed., OJ L130/1, 15 June 1970. Regulation as last amended by Reg. (EC) No 543/97 (OJ L84/6, 26 March 1997).

(13) INTENDS to follow regularly the development in intermodality and intermodal freight transport in the European Union.
(14) INVITES the Commission to transmit to the Council, in 2001, its next progress report on intermodality and intermodal freight transport in the European Union, with possible proposals."

2000: Promotion of short sea shipping

5.136 On 14 February 2000, the Council adopted a resolution on the promotion of short sea shipping.[236] Given the importance of short sea shipping, but conscious that the issue is not dealt extensively elsewhere in the book, it is useful to cite the resolution in full:

"THE COUNCIL OF THE EUROPEAN UNION,
(1) WELCOMES the second Commission communication on the development of short sea shipping in Europe and notes that it incorporates the second two-yearly report on progress in the development of short sea shipping requested by the Council in its Conclusions of 18 June 1997.
(2) NOTES with satisfaction that the Commission communication presents a thorough review of the development of the short sea shipping, identifies the main problem areas where further action is needed in order to promote short sea shipping, outlines a comprehensive long term approach for the development of short sea shipping and makes recommendations for a number of actions to be undertaken by all parties concerned.
(3) RECONFIRMS the objectives and recommendations for action contained in the Council Resolution of 11 March 1996 on short sea shipping[237] and in the Council Conclusions of 18 June 1997 and NOTES that actions have already been undertaken and initiated on the basis of these recommendations.
(4) RECALLS that short sea shipping is an environmentally friendly transport mode which contributes to the sustainability of transport, strengthens the cohesion of the Community and contributes to an increased efficiency of the Community's transport system.
(5) EMPHASISES as a priority objective of the Council the development of short sea shipping into a dynamic part and a viable option in the intermodal door-to-door transport chain between all regions of the Community.
(6) CONSIDERS that the promotion of short sea shipping in all its aspects, such as container and bulk transport, is an on-going process, which needs to be accelerated with short, medium and long term actions, while respecting the Community rules, amongst others those governing maritime cabotage.
(7) RECONFIRMS its view that it is primarily up to the industries themselves to develop short sea shipping and that the Council, the Member States and the Commission have an essential role to play, in particular concerning the framework conditions.
(8) RECALLS that, in its report to the European Council of Helsinki on a strategy on the integration of environment and sustainable development into the transport policy, the Council addresses the need of 'promoting short sea shipping, focusing in particular on the removal of obstacles for its development as an environmentally friendly transport mode' and INVITES the Member States and the Commission to take measures in several areas, which equally lead to promoting short sea shipping.
(9) CONSIDERS, that the comprehensive approach presented in the Commission Communication forms a good and constructive basis for the future work on reaching the abovementioned priority objective and WELCOMES in general the recommendations for the development of short sea shipping included in that Communication.

---

236 OJ C2000 C56/3. On the same day, the Council adopted a resolution on the promotion of intermodality and intermodal freight transport in the EU OJ 2000 C56/1.
237 OJ C99, 2 April 1996, p. 1.

(10) IS OF THE VIEW that it is essential to find practical solutions to existing bottlenecks which hamper the development of short sea shipping and, at this stage of the development process, to focus on certain fields of action and, in particular, on:

(a) improving the efficiency of the maritime loading and unloading points in the logistics chain (i.e. intermodal connection points such as ports, terminals etc.) by streamlining the administrative procedures and by developing services and technical infrastructures (i.e. land-based facilities, hinterland connections, loading units etc.);

(b) promoting door-to-door package solutions with integrated facilities, such as one-stop shops, through the cooperation between the different transport modes and the different players in the logistic management of the supply chain, through the establishment of best practices, through the examination, with a view to their introduction, of measures such as benchmarking and key performance indicators, through the collection and dissemination of data and information on short sea shipping, amongst others using Eurostat, and through the active use of the cooperation framework provided by the round-tables and the focal points of the Member States and other national initiatives to promote short sea shipping such as national short sea shipping information offices;

(c) creating and testing new technical and market opportunities for short sea shipping, also over distances shorter than its current average distance, by promoting research and development, in particular in respect of land-based facilities, information technologies and ships specially adapted for short sea shipping; in addition, it is recommended to study possibilities for short term financial support for new projects and for the further development of existing projects in this field;

(d) creating a level playing field for short sea shipping by achieving further progress in fair and efficient pricing for infrastructure, taking into account the work of the Commission's High Level Group on transport infrastructure charging.

(11) INVITES the parties concerned, including the industries, the transport users, the Member States and the Commission to work actively towards fulfilling the priority objectives and the tasks identified under point 10, and to cooperate towards finding concrete solutions to obstacles standing in the way of the development of short sea shipping.

(12) INVITES the Commission to continue and intensify its work for the promotion of short sea shipping, in particular by:

(a) initiating urgently an exercise of compiling, with input from the focal points and other interested parties, a detailed list of bottlenecks and other specific problems and their potential solutions, such as best practices;

(b) examining and consulting the parties concerned as soon as possible with a view to presenting proposals and/or encouraging the introduction of codes of conduct to simplify and streamline transport-related administrative formalities and documentation in short sea shipping, in particular as regards the uniform application of IMO FAL forms in the Community;

(c) presenting its inventory of the public financial support to ports and proposals on the access to the market for port services, while taking into account the diversity of circumstances prevailing in the Community ports, such as their peripheral location, as well as public service obligations and the need to maintain a high level of safety;

(d) examining the possibility of earmarking more existing Community financial resources to the promotion of short sea shipping, of finding further possibilities for such funding, and of creating, in accordance with the rules of the Treaty on State aid and competition, a framework enabling the participation of national resources in initiating new short sea projects;

(e) developing tools to measure emissions from door-to-door transport chains containing a short sea leg in comparison with transport in one single mode, in order to facilitate a reasoned choice of transport modes;

(f) following short sea shipping market developments and collecting and disseminating factual information on short sea shipping and its potential;

(g) studying, in coordination with Short Sea Shipping Focal Points, the competitiveness of door-to-door transport chains containing a short sea leg as compared with other transport modes in relation to transport price in a segmented market;

(h) taking the needs of short sea shipping constantly into consideration in the application and planning of Community actions and in regional cooperation with the third countries concerned.

(13) INVITES the Commission to transmit to the Council its next progress report in 2001 and to extend this report to passenger transport in addition to cargo transport."

Ultimately, these resolutions are a useful benchmark against which later actions can be judged but they are fundamentally just words.

2000: Commission fines shipping lines for pricing agreement on the Europe/Far East trade

5.137 On 16 May 2000, the Commission imposed fines on 15 shipping lines for an illegal pricing agreement on the Europe/Far East trade ("FETTCSA").[238] It was an agreement not to offer discounts from their published tariffs. The companies were members of the Far East Trade Tariff Charges and Surcharges Agreement ("FETTCSA"). The fines amounted in total to just under €7 million. The Commission described the size of the fine as "a modest amount explained by the fact that an agreement not to discount is less damaging than a price-fixing cartel".[239] Competition Commissioner Monti said

"shipping lines operating within liner conferences benefit from an exceptionally generous exemption from the normal European competition rules.[240] It is important that a conference is faced by effective competition from independent shipping lines operating outside the conference. The FETTCSA case shows that the Commission will act firmly where conference and non-conference shipping lines conspire together as a cartel." [241]

5.138 The facts were summarised by the Commission in the following terms:

"the Far East Trade Tariff Charges and Surcharges Agreement ('FETTCSA') came into force on 4 June 1991 but was abandoned in 1994 following Commission action. The FETTCSA related to charges additional to the basic ocean freight. Charges and surcharges can represent a significant proportion of the total transport cost to shippers. The parties to the FETTCSA were the members of the Far Eastern Freight Conference ('FEFC') liner shipping conference and the FEFC's principal competitors. The parties to the FETTCSA were also essentially the same as those who were party to the Europe Asia Trades Agreement ('EATA') which was prohibited by Commission decision in 1999. The parties to the FETTCSA had a combined market share of over 80% between northern Europe and the Far East. Under the FETTCSA, the companies discussed possible ways of aligning their commercial practices concerning charges and surcharges. The companies' discussions led to an agreement not to discount from published tariffs for charges and surcharges. That agreement infringed the cartel prohibition contained in Article [101(1) TFEU]. In its decision the Commission rejects the companies' contention that the FETTCSA was merely a 'technical agreement' which is permitted under the competition rules applicable to shipping

---

238 IP/00/486.
239 Ibid. This reasoning may not be followed today because arrangements to keep prices low can be anti-competitive in some circumstances.
240 Ed., this was a reference to the block exemption in Reg. 4056/86 (see chap. 11).
241 IP/00/486.

services. Under the competition rules applicable to shipping services, liner conferences benefit from an exemption from the cartel prohibition contained in Article [101(1) TFEU]. Under the exemption, members of a liner conference may fix maritime transport rates. As a liner conference, the members of the FEFC also agree on the levels of charges and surcharges that were the subject of the FETTCSA. The Commission's decision in the FETTCSA case deals with the extension to the non-conference lines of the FEFC lines' price-fixing activities and the decision not to offer discounts."[242]

2001: Ports package

5.139 On 13 February 2001, the Commission adopted its first legislative "Ports Package". This included a communication entitled *Reinforcing Quality Service in Sea Ports: A Key for European Transport* and a proposal for a directive of the European Parliament and of the Council on Market Access to Port Services. The proposal met with a hostile reaction in some quarters. Ultimately, on 20 November 2003, after almost three years of sectoral and institutional disagreements, the European Parliament voted in plenary session to reject the compromise text of the proposed directive.

The Commission was not deterred. On 1 October 2004, the Commission made another proposal for a directive of the European Parliament and of the Council on market access to port services. However, on 18 January 2006, that proposal was also rejected at first reading by the European Parliament so the Commission withdrew that proposal.

On 18 October 2007, following a consultation with stakeholders, the Commission adopted a *Communication on the European Ports Policy* which identified the main causes of the challenges faced by the sector.

2002–2003: Repeal of Regulation 17/62 and adoption of Regulation 1/2003

5.140 Competition law generally had long been applied by the Commission under Regulation 17/62.[243] This regulation applied to most economic sectors but not shipping which was regulated, in part,[244] by Regulation 4056/86.[245] Regulation 17/62 involved a complicated system of notifications being made by businesses to benefit from exemptions or negative clearances but the system did not work because the Commission was unable to cope with the deluge of notifications (e.g. it received over 33,000 notifications while the system operated but granted no more than a dozen or so formal decisions annually) so it had to issue informal responses (so-called "comfort letters" and "discomfort letters") so reform was needed. This process of reform was cleverly[246] labelled "modernisation" and ultimately found expression in Regulation 1/2003[247] which changed the nature of the way in which EU competition law is enforced. Undertakings (i.e. the parties subject to competition law) had to decide for themselves (i.e. "self-assess") whether their arrangements complied with EU competition law and could not notify their arrangements to the

---

242 IP/00/486, footnote omitted.
243 OJ Sp. Ed. 1959–1962, 87.
244 E.g. cabotage and tramp services were not covered by any implementing regulation.
245 OJ 1986 L378/4.
246 If a reform is called "modernisation" then it is difficult to object to it.
247 OJ 2003 L1/1.

Commission anymore.[248] Member States had acquired a greater role in the enforcement of EU competition law through the so-called "European Competition Network" or "ECN".

2002: *TAA* and *FEFC*

5.141 On 28 February 2002, the General Court upheld the *TAA* and *FEFC* decisions in terms of the essence of the decisions.

2002: Full liberalisation of cabotage

5.142 Despite freedom of *international* maritime services having being established by Regulation 4055/86,[249] and the adoption of Regulation 3577/92[250] prohibiting cabotage restrictions generally, it was not until 2002 that the cabotage regulation (i.e. Regulation 3577/92)[251] was fully implemented and cabotage restrictions removed in their entirety.

Establishment of the European Maritime Safety Agency ("EMSA")

5.143 The EMSA was established under Regulation 1406/2002.[252] EMSA describes its work in the following terms:

"[t]he Agency's main objective is to provide technical and scientific assistance to the European Commission and Member States in the proper development and implementation of EU legislation on maritime safety, pollution by ships and security on board ships. To do this, one of EMSA's most important supporting tasks is to improve cooperation with, and between, Member States in all key areas. In addition, the Agency has operational tasks in oil pollution preparedness, detection and response. As a body of the European Union, the Agency sits at the heart of the EU maritime safety network and collaborates with many industry stakeholders and public bodies, in close cooperation with the European Commission."[253]

2004: State aid guidelines

5.144 In 2004, the Commission adopted guidelines relating to the EU State Aid Rules as applied to the shipping sector. These guidelines were extremely helpful, in so far as they specified matters, given the dearth of guidance on the issue generally.

2005: Mid-term review of the White Paper on European transport policy

5.145 In 2005, the Commission conducted its mid-term review of the White Paper on the European transport policy for 2010. The Commission had to take into account the fact that there were accessions to the EU which altered the situation somewhat.

---

248 This relates to notifications under the then Arts 81 and 82 of the EC Treaty (now Arts 101 and 102 TFEU) because notifications under the EU's Merger Control Regulation (see chap. 16) still operate.
249 OJ 1986 L378/1.
250 OJ 1992 L364/7.
251 OJ 1992 L364/7.
252 OJ 2002 L208/1. See chap. 27.
253 www.emsa.europa.eu/end173.html.

Consortia block exemption extended until 2010

5.146 On 20 April 2005, the Commission adopted Regulation 611/2005[254] to extend the Consortia block exemption (i.e. Regulation 823/2000)[255] by a further five years until 25 April 2010.[256] The block exemption has been extended further.[257]

Green Paper on a future EU maritime policy

5.147 On 7 June 2006, the Commission adopted the Green Paper on a future EU maritime policy.[258] It was entitled *Towards a Future Maritime Policy for the Union: A European Vision for the Oceans and Seas*.[259] It is interesting to understand the background to this move because it marked a departure in that the EU stated to develop a "maritime" policy rather than a separate policy for each of shipping, fisheries, the marine environment and so on. The background has been described in the following terms by Siemers:

"It is [the] perception ... that maritime affairs need more attention and that the maritime sectors can no longer be seen and dealt with in isolation which led to the decision to change the paradigm according to which maritime affairs had been dealt with so far in the European Union. So let us examine the history of this development.

The initiative was taken by the European Commission headed by President Barroso, upon its entry into office after the 2004 enlargement of the EU, with then 10 Member States to 25 Member States. The newly appointed Maltese Commissioner Joe Borg had taken on the Common Fisheries Policy portfolio, and was asked by the Commission President to lead the process of developing a new integrated maritime policy. In March 2005, the President of the European Commission and Commissioner Joe Borg, then Commissioner for Fisheries, presented a Communication to the European Commission entitled: *Towards a Future Maritime Policy for the Union: A European Vision for the Oceans and Seas*. The main objective was the development of an integrated approach, and thus the work was to be taken on not only by one Commissioner, but by a group of seven Commissioners in charge of various portfolios with maritime links. This group was to be called a Steering Group, to be chaired by the Commissioner in charge of Maritime Affairs. Its work was to be supported by a small team of Commission officials, a so-called Task Force, who would be working together with representatives of all relevant services within the Commission in developing this new approach. The seven Commissioners who were Members of the Steering Group were the Commissioners for: Industry, Environment, Regional Policy, Transport, Energy, Fisheries and Research.

The Task Force was attached to the Directorate-General for Fisheries, whose name was changed to Directorate-General for Fisheries and Maritime Affairs, and consisted of a team of 15 officials and national experts, headed by a senior Commission official, the former Head of the Commission Delegation to the United Nations in New York. A group of services' officials (Interservice Group) who were to support the work of the Task Force was set-up in April 2005, and was composed of representatives of almost all Commission Directorates-General. After about a year of pre-consultation and intensive preparations with the services and the Steering Group of Commissioners, the Green Paper on a Maritime Policy for the European Union was adopted on 7 June 2006, and with it, a one-year consultation period on the shape of this new policy was launched. Three Commissioners, who had become increasingly involved in important

---

254 OJ 2005 L101/10.
255 OJ 2000 L100/24.
256 OJ 2005 L101/10.
257 See chap. 14.
258 Green Paper, *A Future Maritime Policy of the Union: A European Vision of the Oceans and Seas*, COM(2006) 275.
259 COM(2006) 275 final.

aspects of maritime policy, joined the Steering Group at this time. They were the Commissioners for: External Relations, Employment and Justice, and Home Affairs."[260]

5.148 The Green Paper set out the "way forward":

"Principles of good governance suggest the need for a European maritime policy that embraces all aspects of the oceans and seas. This policy should be integrated, intersectoral and multidisciplinary, and not a mere collection of vertical sectoral policies. It should look at the oceans and seas based on sound knowledge of how they work and how the sustainability of their environment and ecosystems may be preserved. It should aim to provide answers as to how decision-making and the conciliation of competing interests in marine and coastal areas can result in a climate more conducive to investment and to the development of sustainable economic activities. To achieve this, it is necessary to increase cooperation and to promote effective coordination and integration of ocean and sea-related policies at all levels."[261]

The paper recognised the strategic importance of the seas and oceans for the EU and the EU economy. The reaction to the paper and the process was positive with several hundred submissions and contributions being made (for example, there were over 490 written submissions to the Commission and 230 events relating to the paper). This consultation process ended on 30 June 2007 and led to the adoption on 10 October 2007 of the Blue Book for an Integrated European Maritime Policy. The EU recognised the need for an integrated maritime policy rather than unconnected sectoral policies. The Commission wrote in its Staff Working Document which was an accompanying document to the 10 October 2007 Blue Book for an Integrated European Maritime Policy:

"[t]aking account of these reactions, the Commission has therefore proposed an overarching Maritime Policy with the following goals: (1) maximising the sustainable use of the oceans and seas; (2) building a knowledge and innovation base for the maritime policy; (3) delivering the highest quality of life in coastal regions; (4) promoting Europe's leadership in international maritime affairs; and (5) raising the visibility of Maritime Europe".[262]

The Commission Staff Working Document also stated that the

"new integrated maritime policy will truly encompass all aspects of the oceans and seas in a holistic, integrated approach: we will no longer look only at compartmentalised maritime activities, but we will tackle all economic and sustainable development aspects of the oceans and seas, including the marine environment, in an overarching fashion. The integrated approach is not only innovative, it is also strongly endorsed by all stakeholders who participated in the wide debate throughout Europe, during the consultation process following the launching of the Green Paper on a Future Maritime Policy for the Union."[263]

2006: Rejection of the port services liberalisation measures

5.149 After five years of debate across the EU, the European Parliament rejected the proposed directive on port services liberation in 2006. The Commission had proposed a port services directive on two occasions. However, the measures which involved, among other

---

260 Siemers, "A European Integrated Maritime Policy: An Innovative Approach to Policy-Making" (2009) 23 Ocean Yearbook 231 at 236–237.
261 COM(2006) 275 final, p. 5 (of the paper version (not the brochure version)).
262 Executive Summary, p. 2.
263 P. 4.

reforms, self-handling of cargo[264] and greater liberalisation of port services, evoked a hostile reaction in certain quarters with protests on the streets of Brussels by port workers. The measures were too controversial and therefore were dropped by the Commission.[265]

2006: Repeal of Regulation 4056/86 and the adoption of Regulation 1419/2006

5.150 Regulation 1419/2006[266] repealed Regulation 4056/86[267] and amended Regulation 1/2003.[268] Regulation 1419/2006 amended Regulation 1/2003[269] so that the latter measure applies to cabotage and international tramp services; this means that the Commission now has the power to enforce Articles 101 and 102 in these areas.[270] Regulation 1419/2006 provided that Regulation 4056/86 was repealed on the twentieth day following the publication of Regulation 1419/2006.[271] However, Article 1 of Regulation 1419/2006 goes on to provide that while Regulation 4056/86 was repealed,

> "Article 1(3)(b) and (c), Articles 3 to 7, Articles 8(2) and Article 26 of Regulation (EEC) No 4056/86 shall continue to apply in respect of liner shipping conferences satisfying the requirements of Regulation (EEC) No 4056/86 on 18 October 2006, for a transitional period of two years from that date."

The Commission later summarised the effect of Regulation 1419/2006 in the following terms:

> "3. Regulation (EC) No 1419/2006 extended the scope of Council Regulation (EC) No 1/2003 of 16 December 2002 on the implementation of the rules on competition laid down in Articles [101] and [102] of the [TFEU] ... and Commission Regulation (EC) No 773/2004 of 7 April 2004 relating to the conduct of proceedings by the Commission pursuant to Articles [101] and [102] of the [TFEU] ... to include cabotage and tramp vessel services. Consequently, as of 18 October 2006, all maritime transport services sectors are subject to the generally applicable procedural framework.
>
> 4. Regulation (EC) No 1419/2006 also repealed Council Regulation (EEC) No 4056/86 of 22 December 1986 on the application of Articles 85 and 86 [now 101 and 102] of the Treaty to maritime transport ... containing the liner conference block exemption which allowed shipping lines meeting in liner conferences to fix rates and other conditions of carriage, as the conference system no longer fulfils the criteria of Article [101](3) of the Treaty. The repeal of the block exemption [took] effect as of 18 October 2008. Thereafter, liner carriers operating services to and/or from one or more ports in the European Union must cease all liner conference activity contrary to Article [101] of the Treaty. This is the case regardless of whether other jurisdictions allow, explicitly or tacitly, rate fixing by liner conferences or discussion agreements. Moreover, conference members should ensure that any agreement taken under the conference system complies with Article [101] as of 18 October 2008...
>
> 9. Liner shipping services, cabotage and tramp services are the maritime transport sectors directly affected by the changes brought about by Regulation (EC) No 1419/2006."[272]

---

264 I.e. ships could load and discharge their own cargo without the use of dock workers.
265 The proposals are considered in depth in chap. 25.
266 OJ 2006 L269/1.
267 OJ 1986 L378/4.
268 OJ 2003 L1/1.
269 Ibid.
270 Art. 32 of Reg. 1/2003 has been deleted by Art. 2 of Reg. 1419/2006.
271 I.e. on 18 October 2006 that there was a transition period of two years (see chap. 12).
272 Guidelines on the application of Art. 81 of the EC Treaty to maritime transport services, OJ 2008 C245/2, para. 3.

2007: An Integrated Maritime Policy for the EU

5.151 On 10 October 2007, the Commission adopted a communication setting out its vision for an Integrated Maritime Policy ("IMP") for the EU, together with a detailed action plan setting out an ambitious work programme for the years ahead.[273] It has become known as either a "blue paper" or a "blue book". It followed "a unique consultation process".[274] The paper consisted of communications on an integrated overall maritime policy including an action plan and conclusions from the consultation process. It contained a list of 30 actions which were proposed for 2008 and later. The European Council endorsed the 2007 document at its meeting on 14 December 2007. It would lead to a White Paper in 2008 on maritime matters.[275] The Commission has stated that an

> "Integrated Maritime Policy will enhance Europe's capacity to face the challenges of globalisation and competitiveness, climate change, degradation of the marine environment, maritime safety and security, and energy security and sustainability. It must be based on excellence in marine research, technology and innovation, and will be anchored in the Lisbon agenda for jobs and growth, and the Gothenburg agenda for sustainability."[276]

The proposals followed a public consultation which ended in June 2007 and the work of a Steering Group of ten Commissioners chaired by Joe Borg (the Commissioner for Fisheries and Maritime Affairs). The communication and action plan were accompanied by a report on the results of the consultation which revealed strong stakeholder support for the Commission's initiative. The Commission believed that the different activities and policies relating to the seas were being managed on largely sectoral lines. An integrated maritime policy would change the way policy is formulated and decisions taken in the maritime sectors. The communication and Action Plan listed a range of actions to be launched during the mandate of the then Commission. These actions included initiatives such as: a European maritime transport space without barriers; a European strategy for marine research; national integrated maritime policies to be developed by Member States; an integrated network for maritime surveillance; a roadmap towards maritime spatial planning by Member States; elimination of pirate fishing and destructive high seas bottom trawling; promotion of a European network of maritime clusters; a review of EU labour law exemptions for the shipping and fishing sectors; a European marine observation and data network; and a strategy to mitigate the effects of climate change on coastal regions. There was a review of labour law exemptions in the maritime sectors commenced as part of the initiative. The Blue Book stated, quite emphatically but correctly:

> "An EU Integrated Maritime Policy will:
>
> - Change the way we make policy and take decisions – at every level compartmentalised policy development and decision-making are no longer adequate. Interactions must be understood and taken into account; common tools developed; synergies identified and exploited; and conflicts avoided or resolved.

---

273 COM(2007) 575 final. It was published as *An Ocean of Opportunity*. See IP/07/1463, http://ec.europa.eu/maritimeaffairs/index_en.html and http://europa.eu/rapid/pressReleasesAction.do?reference=MEMO/07/403&format=HTML&aged=0&language=EN&guiLanguage=en. The full package as well as further information on maritime affairs can be found at: http://ec.europa.eu/maritimeaffairs/index_en.html. See also MEMO/07/403.
274 *ECSA Annual Report 2007–2008*, p. 8.
275 See http://europa.eu/rapid/press-release_IP-09-84_en.htm?locale=en.
276 Commission, *An Ocean of Opportunity* (2008), p. 2.

- Develop and deliver a programme of work – action under the different sectoral policies must develop in a coherent policy framework. The Action Plan accompanying this communication gives a clear idea of the variety and magnitude of the work ahead. The following projects are of particular importance:

    - A European Maritime Transport Space without barriers
    - A European Strategy for Marine Research
    - National integrated maritime policies to be developed by Member States
    - An European network for maritime surveillance
    - A Roadmap towards maritime spatial planning by Member States
    - A Strategy to mitigate the effects of Climate Change on coastal regions
    - Reduction of CO_2 emissions and pollution by shipping
    - Elimination of pirate fishing and destructive high seas bottom trawling
    - An European network of maritime clusters
    - A review of EU labour law exemptions for the shipping and fishing sectors.

    This Communication lays the foundation for the governance framework and cross-sectoral tools necessary for an EU Integrated Maritime Policy and sets out the main actions that the Commission will pursue during the course of this mandate. These actions will be guided by the principles of subsidiarity and competitiveness, the ecosystem approach, and stakeholder participation."[277]

5.152 A useful overview is provided by the Commission's own press release on the day the policy was published:

"An ocean of opportunity: Commission proposes Integrated Maritime Policy for the EU

Today the Commission adopted a Communication setting out its vision for an Integrated Maritime Policy for the EU, together with a detailed action plan setting out an ambitious work programme for the years ahead. Scientific discoveries, huge strides in technological development, globalisation, climate change, and marine pollution are rapidly altering Europe's relationship with the seas and oceans, with all the opportunities and challenges that this presents. An integrated maritime policy will enable the Union to meet the challenges head on. This proposal is grounded in an extensive public consultation which ended last June, and represents the work of a Steering Group of 10 Commissioners chaired by Joe Borg. The Communication and Action Plan are accompanied by a report on the results of the consultation which revealed strong stakeholder support for the Commission's initiative.

Commission President, José Manuel Barroso, who initiated the new approach to maritime policy, said, 'I am convinced that a great part of our future lies in the untapped potential of the oceans. Our proposal for an integrated maritime policy has been designed to generate growth, jobs and sustainability. We conceived it to promote our common European interest and to seize all opportunities that the oceans offer, while acting in a sustainable manner. It is part and parcel of our strategy to modernise Europe and prepare it for the globalised world'.

Commissioner for Fisheries and Maritime Affairs, Joe Borg, added: 'Our stakeholders have spoken and we have listened. This is a crucial first step for Europe's oceans and seas – unlocking the potential and facing the challenges of a Maritime Europe will be our common goal. It will allow us to make the most of our maritime assets and will help Europe face some of the major challenges before it'.

Until now, the different activities and policies relating to the seas have been managed on largely sectoral lines. An integrated maritime policy will change the way policy is formulated and decisions taken in the maritime sectors, in full respect of the principle of subsidiarity. It will enable the relevant authorities to analyse interactions between the various sectors and policy areas concerned and to take them into account at every level so as to develop common tools to exploit synergies and avoid conflicts.

---

277 P. 3.

The new policy will build on Europe's strengths in marine research, technology and innovation. It will be anchored in the Lisbon agenda for more and better jobs and growth, and in the EU's overarching commitment to ensuring that economic development does not come at the price of environmental sustainability.

The Communication and accompanying Action Plan list a range of concrete actions to be launched during the mandate of this Commission. These actions cover a wide spectrum of issues ranging from maritime transport to the competitiveness of maritime businesses, employment, scientific research, fisheries and the protection of the marine environment. They include:

- A European Maritime Transport Space without barriers
- A European Strategy for Marine Research
- National integrated maritime policies to be developed by Member States
- An integrated network for maritime surveillance
- A Roadmap towards maritime spatial planning by Member States
- Elimination of pirate fishing and destructive high seas bottom trawling
- Promotion of a European network of maritime clusters
- A review of EU labour law exemptions for the shipping and fishing sectors
- A European Marine Observation and Data Network
- A Strategy to mitigate the effects of Climate Change on coastal regions
- Delivery of the Action Plan has already begun today, with Commissioner Spidla presenting a review of labour law exemptions in the maritime sectors and Commissioner Piebalgs publishing a report on the inter-linkages between the EU energy policy and the new integrated maritime policy.

An integrated maritime policy will only succeed with the continued engagement and support of all the actors and stakeholders concerned. The Commission will continue to work with stakeholders and authorities at European, national and regional levels in order to translate its vision into reality."[278]

2008: Ending of the block exemption for liner conferences and the extension of the general competition regime to cabotage and tramp shipping on 18 October 2008

5.153 On 18 October 2008, by virtue of Regulation 1419/2006,[279] the block exemption for liner conferences in Regulation 4056/86 ended and, also on that date, all shipping services (including cabotage[280] and tramp services[281]) became subject to the same competition law regime (principally applied by Regulation 1/2003) as all other economic sectors (i.e. EU competition law applies in full to the sector and to liner conferences for shipping lines operating on trade to and from the EU). This means that liner conferences which have as their object or effect the fixing of prices (i.e. tariffs) or conditions of competition to and from the EU are now prohibited. It also means that any undertakings exchanging information could be in breach of EU competition law. The full benefits of the block exemption in Regulation 4056/86 had been eroded over time anyway and the Commission had long been uncomfortable with the exemption for a price-fixing arrangement. Tramp shipping and cabotage services became fully subject to EU competition law on that date. So as to assist maritime operators, the Commission adopted guidelines on the

---

278 IP/07/1463, 10 October 2007.
279 Reg. 1419/2006 (OJ 2006 L269/1) entered into force on 18 October 2006 but provided for a two-year transitional period.
280 I.e. the transport of goods or passengers between two ports in the same country without them calling at the port of another country.
281 I.e. unscheduled maritime transport of non-containerised bulk cargo.

application of competition law to shipping. Following the repeal of Regulation 4056/86, there was only one block exemption regulation relating to maritime transport specifically and that was the consortia block exemption (i.e. Regulation 823/2000) but that was to expire in April 2010 so it had to be replaced and was replaced by Regulation 906/2009.[282]

2008: Shipping guidelines

5.154 Following the repeal of the block exemption for liner conferences in October 2008, shipping companies would have to "self-assess" to see whether their arrangements and practices complied with EU competition law as they could no longer rely on the block exemption. So as to assist such companies, the Commission (following prompting by the Parliament) has adopted guidelines. In September 2007, the Commission published draft guidelines on competition law and the shipping sector for consultation.[283] After receiving submissions from 15 interested parties and wider consultation, on 1 July 2008, these guidelines were adopted.[284] The guidelines are a helpful summary of the Commission's thinking on a limited number of issues of competition law as they relate to the shipping sector. In particular, the guidelines relate to market definition, information exchange and shipping pools.[285] The guidelines address Article 101 issues only and not Article 102 issues. The European Community Shipowners Association said that it "appreciated the guidelines [and they] take into account the specific character of the tramp sector and will be useful in the continued self assessment exercise by the operators".[286] The Commission has stated that the section dealing with the liner sector will apply for a period of five years starting from 18 October 2008 which is the effective date of repeal of the liner conference block exemption.

2008: Commission opens consultations on review of block exemption for liner shipping consortia

5.155 On 22 October 2008, the Commission opened consultations on a draft regulation[287] to revise and renew the exemption that liner shipping consortia[288] enjoy from Article 101(1) of the TFEU.[289] The consortia block exemption, Regulation 823/2000 as amended, allowed shipping lines to enter into cooperation for the purpose of providing a

---

282 OJ 2009 L256/31.
283 See http://eur-lex.europa.eu/LexUriServ/LexUriServ.do?uri=CELEX:52007XC0914(01):EN:NOT and http://europa.eu/rapid/pressReleasesAction.do?reference=IP/07/1325&format=HTML&aged=1&language=EN&guiLanguage=en.
284 OJ C2008 245/2. See also http://europa.eu/rapid/pressReleasesAction.do?reference=IP/08/1063&format=HTML&aged=0&language=EN&guiLanguage=en and http://europa.eu/rapid/pressReleasesAction.do?reference=MEMO/08/460&format=HTML&aged=0&language=EN&guiLanguage=en.
285 Shipping pools are operational co-operation agreements between tramp operators (i.e. unscheduled maritime transport of non-containerised bulk cargo).
286 ECSC Annual Report 2007–2008, p. 5.
287 http://eur-lex.europa.eu/LexUriServ/LexUriServ.do?uri=OJ:C:2008:266:0001:0006:EN:PDF.
288 Interestingly, the Commission press release stated: "A consortium is a grouping of shipping lines which co-operate to provide joint maritime cargo transport services. Such agreements usually allow shipping lines to rationalise their activities and achieve economies of scale. If consortia are faced with sufficient competition, the users of the services provided by consortia usually benefit from improvements in productivity and service quality."
289 IP/08/1566.

joint service (so-called "consortia"). The new draft regulation proposed to continue to allow for such co-operation within a new legislative and economic environment. Interested parties were invited to make their views known in the public consultation before 21 November 2008. The Commission would then consult Member States in 2009 before adopting the final block exemption regulation before the regulation expired on 25 April 2010. Competition Commissioner Neelie Kroes said: "[i]t is time to adjust the block exemption for liner shipping consortia to current market practices in the liner industry and to current antitrust law".[290] The Commission also issued a technical paper explaining the proposed changes in detail.[291]

2009: EU Maritime Transport Policy for 2018 and Commission Strategy Plan to Establish a European Maritime Transport Space without Barriers

5.156 On 21 January 2009, the Commission presented a ten-year strategy plan to promote safe, secure, clean and efficient shipping.[292] It was entitled: "Communication from the Commission to the European Parliament, the Council, the European Economic and Social Committee and the Committee of the Regions – Communication and action plan with a view to establishing a European maritime transport space without barriers". The plan contemplates a new European Integrated Maritime Policy reflecting the core principles of sustainable development, economic growth and open markets in fair competition and high environmental and social standards. The plan was embodied in a document entitled "Communication on the EU Maritime Transport Strategy 2018". The work also included a prospective study (entitled "Benchmarking strategic options for European shipping and for the European maritime transport system in the horizon 2008–2018")[293] analysing trends and signals of change in the maritime sector (the so-called "shipping scenarios" for 2018). It also involved consulting with experts from maritime administrations in the Member States and Norway, as well as taking advice from a group of senior industry leaders representing different interests within the maritime transport industries. The three possible scenarios for 2018 were the "Asian Phoenix", "Break Point" and "Global Fissures". The recommendations of the group of senior shipping professionals[294] presented an interesting insight on the issues which were pressing for the industry.[295] The Commission summarised the conclusions of the overall exercise in the following terms:

---

290 The Commission Press Release also stated: "The proposed changes take into account the necessary amendments due to the repeal of the liner conference block exemption Regulation in 2006 (see IP/06/1249). They also aim at better reflecting the current market practice through a broader definition of a consortium and by aggregating, under certain circumstances, the market shares of inter-linked consortia. In order to align the consortia block exemption Regulation with the general EU competition rules it is proposed that only consortia with a market share below 30% should benefit from the exemption."
291 See http://ec.europa.eu/comm/competition/antitrust/legislation/maritime/technical_paper.pdf.
292 COM(2009) 11final. See IP/09/84, 21 January 2009. http://ec.europa.eu/transport/strategies/2018_maritime_transport_strategy_en.htm.
293 http://ec.europa.eu/transport/maritime/studies/index_en.htm.
294 See IP/08/760, 19 May 2008.
295 See http://ec.europa.eu/transport/maritime/policy/index_en.htm.

"Several important conclusions come from this strategic review exercise. First of all, the recovery of the world economy from the current financial crisis would lead to a growth in international trade and will require a maritime transport system able to deliver advanced logistic solutions. Moreover, in a recession period, short sea shipping is a perfect vehicle for stimulating intra-EU trade exchanges and thus supporting recovery of growth in the EU and its neighbouring countries.

Overall, the next ten years may offer a unique opportunity to reinforce the competitiveness of European shipping, and to strengthen its contribution to the objectives of a sustainable European transport policy.

The strategic recommendations concern seven main issues:

- Competitive European shipping: The priority is to achieve and maintain an attractive framework for quality shipping and quality operators in Europe including financial measures. This will help maritime transport achieve sustainable development goals. Such a framework would also help the sector adapt to adverse financial conditions and to the slow-down in growth of the world's sea-borne trades.
- Human Factor: There is a genuine European interest in making maritime professions more attractive to young people and thus improving employment of seafarers. Positive measures may include facilitating life-long career prospects in the maritime clusters; enhancing the image of shipping; supporting the work of international organisation (IMO and ILO) on fair treatment of seafarers; and implementing simplification measures which aim at reducing the administrative burden on masters and senior ship officers.
- Greener Maritime Transport: The EU should encourage all actors to promote green solutions in maritime transport. The Commission, the Member States and the European maritime industry should be working together towards the long-term objective of "zero-waste, zero-emissions". The measures announced in the Greening Transport Package should be fully implemented.
- A safe and secure system: We should give priority to the enforcement of existing Community and international rules and the speedy implementation of measures introduced with the 3rd maritime safety package. The work already started should be completed by establishing a comprehensive framework for security measures in terms of prevention, reaction capacity and resilience.
- International Scene: The global challenges faced by the shipping and maritime industries demand convincing answers from the international community. The Commission and the Member States may be a real driving force for change towards a comprehensive international regulatory framework for shipping, adapted to the challenges of the 21st century.
- Short Sea Shipping and Ports: Further economic integration of the EEA Member States and of the neighbouring countries will have positive impact on maritime transport connections within the EU. It should be noted that sea-trade normally grows even in periods of business contraction. In the 2018 horizon, the European economy should recover from the current stagnation. Positive measures in support of short sea shipping should also help intensify sea-exchanges in all the European maritime façades. These measures will include the creation of a European Maritime Transport Space without Barriers the full deployment of the Motorways of the Seas but also the implementation of measures for port investment and performance. In all cases, the principles of open markets, fair competition and greening transport should be respected.
- Innovation and technological development: The competitiveness of the European maritime industries and their capacity to meet the environmental, energy, safety and human challenges is positively influenced by increased efforts in research and innovation. There is wide scope for improving energy efficiency in ships, reducing environmental impact, minimising the risks of accidents or providing better quality of life at sea. In the years to come, innovation and technological research and development in shipping should be further promoted. A framework of reference should be introduced for the deployment of 'e-Maritime' services at European and global levels.

The Communication on the EU Maritime Transport Strategy 2018 is addressed to the European Parliament and the Council. In the light of their opinion and conclusions, the Commission will continue to look for concrete ways to implement the recommendations. This work will involve close cooperation with all interested parties."[296]

On the related issue of establishing a barrier-free maritime transport sector within the EU, the Commission recalled:

"In maritime transport, voyages from one port of an EU Member State to another are always considered international even when the cargo transported consist of goods in free circulation ('Community goods').

A vessel is considered to leave the customs territory when it leaves a Community port for another Member State port with a consequence that maritime transport of goods is subject to complex administrative procedures that decrease its attractiveness for the transport of Internal Market goods.

The European maritime transport space without barriers is a concept which extends the Internal Market wider to intra-EU maritime transport through the elimination or the simplification of administrative procedures in intra-EU maritime transport, in order to enhance its attractiveness and reinforce its efficiency and competitiveness, and contribute to a higher protection of environment.

To implement this concept, the Commission identified a series of measures, which are described in the parallel Communication 'establishing an EU Maritime Transport Space without barriers'. Those measures are:

- Elimination of systematic controls and documentary requests by Customs for goods carried by sea between EU ports in line with inland transport. The measure will require a modification of the implementing provision of the Community customs code early in 2009 and should be in force by 2010.
- Concerning the legislation on veterinary and phytosanitary products, guidelines should be adopted in 2009 in order to speed up the documentary checks in Directives 89/662/EEC, 90/425/EEC and 2000/29/EC.
- Rationalisation of vessel-related and goods-related reporting and forms required by Directives 2002/6/EC (formalities for vessels at the arrival/departure of ports), 2000/59/EC (waste and residue reception), 2002/59/EC (vessel monitoring) and Regulation (EC) No 725/2004 (maritime security) through a proposal for a directive of the European Parliament and the Council attached to the Communication.
- Further enabling measures would also need to be implemented, namely:
- Examining the possibility to grant facilitation to ships sailing between Community ports but making a call in a port located in a third country or a free zone;
- Enhancing the electronic transmission of administrative data through the deployment of e-maritime systems;
- Setting-up an administrative single window;
- Evaluating the feasibility to recognise the equivalence of maritime rules and rules for road/rail for the carriage of dangerous goods in view to facilitate intermodal transport.

In addition, recommendations should be given that Member States implement further enabling measures, each time the local conditions permit to do it in an efficient manner, namely:

- To coordinate the inspections carried out in the ports by the various administrative services;
- To extend the scope of Pilot Exemption Certificates;
- To facilitate administrative communication;
- To create areas in ports dedicated to Short Sea Shipping where that can facilitate the operations for this mode.

---

296 MEMO/09/16, 21 January 2009.

The administrative simplification is expected to reduce costs for undertakings and to induce a significant modal shift from land to short sea shipping which will bring environment benefits and reduce energy consumption and greenhouse gases emissions. The benefits for undertakings was estimated at 2.4 billion €, which is probably an underestimated figure as it does not take into account the effect of modal shift." [297]

2009: Third maritime safety package

5.157 On 11 March 2009, the third maritime safety package was adopted by the European Parliament. The Third Package covers such issues as quality of flags, classification societies, port State control, traffic monitoring, accident investigation, liability of carriers (in the context of the Athens convention) and insurance generally. The process had taken several years but it was generally seen as an important step in the development of EU maritime safety law. In specific terms, the following measures were adopted: (a) Regulation 392/2009 of the European Parliament and of the Council of 23 April 2009 on the liability of carriers of passengers by sea in the event of accidents;[298] (b) Regulation 391/2009 of the European Parliament and of the Council of 23 April 2009 on common rules and standards for ship inspection and survey organisations;[299] (c) Directive 2009/15 of the European Parliament and of the Council of 23 April 2009 on common rules and standards for ship inspection and survey organisations and for the relevant activities of maritime administrations.[300]

2000s: Tonnage taxes

5.158 Throughout the 2000s, the Commission has had to consider various attempts by various Member States to operate so-called tonnage tax schemes. These attempts have been aimed at easing the burden on shipping companies by calculating their tax liability by reference to their tonnage. The Commission has been generally supportive of such schemes but has occasionally[301] refused to authorise some schemes.

2009: State aid and ship management companies

5.159 On 10 June 2009, the Commission adopted new rules on state aid to ship management companies.[302] The rules complemented the 2004 guidelines on state aid to maritime transport.[303] Under the new guidance, the tonnage tax may be applied to all ship managers, as long as they contribute to the development of the European maritime cluster and, more importantly, that they make a commitment to implement the Maritime Labour Convention 2006 ahead of its entry into force.

---

297 MEMO/09/16, 21 January 2009.
298 OJ 2009 L131/24.
299 OJ 2009 L131/11.
300 OJ 2009 L131/47.
301 E.g. IP/09/934, 17 June 2009 where the Commission refused to authorise under State aid rules, an amendment to the Danish tonnage tax scheme.
302 IP/09/900.
303 Under 2004 guidelines; see chap. 15.

2009: Recognition of the Polish Register

5.160 While it is now of historical significance only as Poland has become a Member State of the EU, it is noted for completeness that on 30 September 2009, the Commission adopted Decision 2009/728 of 30 September 2009 extending without limitations the Community recognition of the Polish Register of Shipping.[304]

> "Having regard to Regulation (EC) No 391/2009 of the European Parliament and of the Council of 23 April 2009 on common rules and standards for ship inspection and survey organisations (1), and in particular Article 15 thereof,
> Whereas:
>
> (1) By Decision 2006/660/EC (2), the Commission granted the Polish Register of Shipping a limited recognition for a period of three years. This recognition is granted to organisations known as classification societies, which fulfil all criteria other than those set out under paragraphs 2 and 3 of the 'General Minimum Criteria' section A of the Annex to Council Directive 94/57/EC of 22 November 1994 on common rules and standards for ship inspection and survey organisations and for the relevant activities of maritime administrations (3). The effects of this recognition were limited to the Czech Republic, Cyprus, Lithuania, Malta, Poland and Slovakia.
> (2) The Commission assessed the Polish Register of Shipping in accordance with Article 11(3) of Directive 94/57/EC. The assessment was based on the results of four fact-finding inspections performed in 2007 by experts of the European Maritime Safety Agency in accordance with Article 2(b)(iii) of Regulation (EC) No 1406/2002 of the European Parliament and of the Council (4). The Czech, Cypriot, Lithuanian, Maltese, Polish and Slovak administrations were invited to take part in the assessment. The Commission has also taken into consideration the findings of two further inspections carried out by the European Maritime Safety Agency in April and May 2009 in order to examine the activities of the Polish Register of Shipping in the supervision of new ship construction and to verify the corrective action implemented by the Polish Register of Shipping in response to the Commission's assessment.
> (3) Where shortcomings have been identified, the Polish Register of Shipping has promptly implemented appropriate and sufficient corrective action in most cases. The outstanding shortcomings mainly concern the implementation of its rules and procedures, particularly as regards the control of the quality of shipyards and verification of new constructions, the training and qualification of surveyors and transfer of class. The Polish Register of Shipping has therefore been invited to implement further corrective action in this respect. Despite their seriousness, these shortcomings do not at present warrant calling into question the overall quality of the organisation's main systems and control mechanisms.
> (4) In the meantime, Regulation (EC) No 391/2009 has entered into force. It provides that the organisations which, at the date of its entry into force, have been granted recognition in accordance with Directive 94/57/EC shall retain their recognition. Those recognitions have to be examined by the Commission by 17 June 2010, with a view to deciding whether the limitations are to be replaced by others or removed.
> (5) The information available to the Commission based on the assessment and inspections made shows that the Polish Register of Shipping in general complies with the requirements and obligations laid down in Regulation (EC) No 391/2009 in all trades and for all kinds of ships.
> (6) Based on the data last published by the Paris Memorandum of Understanding on Port State control, which concern the inspections carried out by the signatory parties until 2008, the rate of detention of ships for reasons relating to the certificates delivered to them by the Polish Register of Shipping in the period 2006–2008 remained at 0,77% of the total number of inspections, while the average rate for recognised organisations was 0,34%.

---

304 OJ L258/34, 1 October 2009.

(7) An extension of the Community recognition of the Polish Register of Shipping should enter into force on 29 September 2009 in order to ensure its continuity.

(8) The measures provided for in this Decision are in accordance with the opinion of the COSS Committee set up by Article 12 of Regulation (EC) No 391/2009,

HAS DECIDED AS FOLLOWS:

Article 1

The Community recognition of the Polish Register of Shipping is hereby extended without limitations with effect from 29 September 2009.

(1) OJ L131, 28.5.2009, p. 11.
(2) OJ L272, 3.10.2006, p. 17.
(3) OJ L319, 12.12.1994, p. 20.
(4) OJ L208, 5.8.2002, p. 1."

This followed on Commission Decision 2006/660:

"3.10.2006
EN
Official Journal of the European Union
L 272/17

COMMISSION DECISION
of 29 September 2006
granting Community limited recognition to the Polish Register of Shipping
(notified under document number C(2006) 4107)
(Text with EEA relevance)
(2006/660/EC)

THE COMMISSION OF THE EUROPEAN COMMUNITIES,

Having regard to the Treaty establishing the European Community,

Having regard to Council Directive 94/57/EC of 22 November 1994 on common rules and standards for ship inspection and survey organisations and for the relevant activities of maritime administrations (1), and in particular Article 4(2) thereof,

Having regard to the letters of 10 March 2004 from the Polish authorities, of 4 July 2005 from the Czech authorities, of 10 March 2006 from the Cypriot authorities, of 13 March 2006 from the Maltese authorities, of 30 March 2006 from the Lithuanian authorities and of 11 April 2006 from the Slovak authorities requesting the Commission to grant Community recognition to the Polish Register of Shipping (hereinafter PRS) pursuant to Article 4(2) of Directive 94/57/EC,

Whereas:

(1)
The limited recognition pursuant to Article 4(2) of Directive 94/57/EC is a recognition granted to organisations known as classification societies, which fulfil all criteria other than those set out under paragraphs 2 and 3 of the 'General' section A of the Annex thereto, but limited in time and scope in order for the organisation concerned to gain further experience.

(2)
The Commission has verified that the PRS meets all criteria of the Annex to Directive 94/57/EC other than those set out under paragraphs 2 and 3 of the 'General' section A of that Annex.

(3)
The PRS has undertaken to comply with the provisions of Article 15(2), (4) and (5) of Directive 94/57/EC.

(4)
The organization's safety and pollution performance records, albeit slightly below the average of recognised organisations, are satisfactory and show a positive evolution, particularly in the area of the Paris Memorandum of Understanding on Port State Control where a sustained improvement has been achieved since 2000.

(5)
The measures provided for in this Decision are in accordance with the opinion of the COSS Committee set up by Article 7 of Directive 94/57/EC,

HAS ADOPTED THIS DECISION:
Article 1
The 'Polish Register of Shipping' is recognised pursuant to Article 4(2) of Directive 94/57/EC for a period of three years as from the date of adoption of this Decision.

Article 2
The effects of the recognition are limited to the Czech Republic, Cyprus, Lithuania, Malta, Poland and the Slovak Republic.

Article 3
This Decision is addressed to the Member States.
Done at Brussels, 29 September 2006.
For the Commission
Jacques BARROT
Vice-President
(1) OJ L319, 12.12.1994, p. 20. Directive as last amended by Directive 2002/84/EC of the European Parliament and of the Council (OJ L324, 29.11.2002, p. 53)."

2009: Entry into force of the Treaty of Lisbon

5.161 After the proposed constitution had been rejected, the EU set about dealing with the constitutional difficulties which remained and the Member States adopted the Treaty of Lisbon, otherwise known as the Reform Treaty, on 13 December 2007. It did not make any change to the provisions on maritime transport but did confer new or expanded competences on the EU including in the area of climate change. The treaty finally entered into force on 1 December 2009 and most of the changes contained in the Treaty entered into effect on that day. Since then, the EC (historically, the EEC) Treaty was no more because the EC became the EU.

2000s: Conclusions

5.162 The 2000s witnessed the further development of EU shipping law. It developed areas which were already initiated such as safety. It further developed areas such as employment and the protection of seafarers. There were significant changes in how competition law is applied to the shipping sector with the abolition of the liner conference block exemption which was contained in Regulation 4056/86 and the extension of the Commission's power to apply the competition rules to cabotage and tramp shipping. There was a certain maturing of EU shipping law but the economic and financial crises which commenced at the end of the decade would prove a challenge for all involved in the shipping sector in Europe but it could also be a challenge for the EU to demonstrate its potential. The Commission ultimately achieved its objective in seeking the repeal of the liner conference block exemption in Regulation 4056/86.[305]

---

305 Curiously, EU shipping companies may still engage in liner conferences outside the EU where the trade had no effect on trade between Member States.

H. THE 2010s

2010: Integrated Maritime Policy for the EU

5.163 In 2010, the Commission published a progress report on the achievements of the EU's IMP over the previous two years. The EU's attempts at integrating maritime policy are extremely important but progress has been slow.

2010: Entry into force of the new consortia block exemption

5.164 Commission Regulation 906/2009[306] entered into force on 26 April 2010 and would apply until 25 April 2015. It recognised a number of changes in the legislative and commercial backdrop to consortia agreements. The regulation revised the regime under Regulation 823/2000. An exemption for liner conferences was extended for five years. Some changes were made to the regime under Regulation 823/2000, notably, (a) a reduction of the market share threshold from 35% to 30% (which means that there is now no automatic exemption above 30% and an individual self-assessment has to be made to determine whether Article 101(1) or Article 101(3) of the TFEU is applicable); (b) an elaboration and clarification of the method of calculating the market share threshold; (c) an extension of the scope of the exemption to all cargo liner shipping services (i.e. whether containerised or not); and (d) a prolongation of the exit clauses and lock-in periods (should a member wish to leave).

2013: Ports package

5.165 On 23 May 2013, the Commission adopted its second ports package. This package included a proposal for a regulation establishing a framework on market access to port services and financial transparency of ports. It is part of the key action on maritime transport announced in the Single Market Act II adopted by the Commission in October 2012. On 8 October 2014, the Transport, Telecommunications and Energy Council adopted a general approach on the proposal. The next step would be for the European Parliament Committee on Transport and Tourism ("TRAN") to adopt a report on the proposal. It is slowly making its way through the EU system!

2013: Proposal to enhance seafarer's rights

5.166 On 19 November 2013, the Commission proposed a directive to enhance seafarers' rights. Technically, the proposal was entitled: "Proposal for a Directive of the European Parliament and of the Council on seafarers amending Directives 2008/94/EC, 2009/38/EC, 2002/14/EC, 98/59/EC and 2001/23/EC".[307] The proposal was to give seafarers the same rights as enjoyed by workers based on land (i.e. shore workers). The proposal involved making amendments to five employment/labour law directives which currently either exempt seafarers, or allow Member States to exempt seafarers from the

---

306 Reg. 906/2009 of the European Parliament and the Council on the Application of Art. 81(3) of the EC Treaty to certain categories of agreements, decisions and concerted practices between liner shipping companies (consortia) OJ 2009 L256/31.
307 http://data.consilium.europa.eu/doc/document/ST-16472-2013-INIT/en/pdf.

scope of these directives without any express justification. On 13 May 2015, the Council's COREPER announced it had confirmed a compromise text for the new directive (i.e. approved the Council and European Parliament agreement on amending the directive improving seafarers' labour rights). If the measure is adopted, which looks increasingly likely,[308] it should improve employment rights for seafarers. The compromise text was already informally agreed between the Council and the Parliament in a so-called "trialogue" meeting on 6 May 2015. This trialogue meeting followed the adoption of the Council's General Approach in December 2014 and the position adopted by the European Parliament's Employment Committee position in April 2015.

2014: The Athens Declaration

5.167 On 7 May 2014, there was an Informal Meeting of the EU Ministers for Maritime Transport in Athens.[309] It was organised by the then Greek Presidency of the Council of the European Union. At this meeting, the Ministers signed the so-called "Athens Declaration" or, as it was more formally entitled, ""Mid-Term Review of the EU's Maritime Transport Policy until 2018 and Outlook to 2020".[310] The Declaration was aimed at revising the EU's shipping policies until 2018 and includes the conclusions to be presented at the formal Council meeting on 7 June 2014.

Commission communication setting the strategic goals and recommendations for the EU's maritime transport policy until 2018

5.168 On 21 January 2009, the Commission adopted a communication setting the strategic goals and recommendations for the EU's maritime transport policy until 2018.[311] On 5–6 June 2014, the Transport, Telecommunications and Energy Council adopted conclusions on the Mid-Term Review of the EU's Maritime Transport Policy until 2018 and Outlook to 2020 and invited the Commission to present a mid-term review of the EU's Maritime Transport Policy while taking into account the Athens Declaration adopted in May 2014.[312] On 28 January 2015, the Commission commenced a public consultation on the EU's Maritime Transport Strategy to feed into the mid-term review of the Strategy.[313] The consultation closed on 22 April 2015. It will be interesting to see the impact of the consultation and review on EU shipping policy.

---

308 It is noteworthy though that the proposal would be adopted under the ordinary legislative procedure which means that the Council and the Parliament must agree on the same final text.
309 The Commissioner for Transport was also present.
310 It was entitled the "Mid-Term Review of the EU's Maritime Transport Policy until 2018 and Outlook to 2020". For a copy of the Declaration and the background, see http://gr2014.eu/news/press-releases/athens-declaration-sets-eu-future-maritime-transport-policy-priorities.
311 http://eur-lex.europa.eu/legal-content/EN/TXT/PDF/?uri=CELEX:52009DC0008&from=EN.
312 http://gr2014.eu/sites/default/files/ATHENS%20DECLARATION_FINAL.pdf.
313 http://ec.europa.eu/transport/modes/maritime/consultations/2015-mts-review_en.htm.

2014: Report on ships' formalities

5.169 Directive 2010/65 deals with the reporting formalities for ships arriving in and/or departing from ports of EU Member States.[314] Its aim was to simplify and harmonise some of the reporting procedures by establishing a standard electronic transmission of information and by rationalising reporting formalities for ships arriving in, and ships departing from, EU Member State ports thereby reducing the administrative burden for all concerned. On 25 June 2014, the European Commission adopted a report on the functioning of Directive 2010/65.[315] The report dealt with the following five issues: (a) the progress made towards harmonisation and co-ordination of reporting formalities (the implementation of the so-called "National Single Window"); (b) the availability of data concerning ship traffic/movement within the EU, and/or calling at third country ports; (c) the feasibility of avoiding or simplifying formalities for ships that have called at a port in a third country or free zone; (d) the compatibility of the River Information Services with the electronic data transmission process; and (e) the possibility of extending the simplification introduced by Directive 2010/65 to inland waterway transport.

2014: Decision 2014/241 concerning the ratification of, or the accession to, the Hong Kong International Convention for the Safe and Environmentally Sound Recycling of Ships, 2009, by the EU Member States in the interests of the EU

5.170 On 14 April 2014, the Council adopted Decision 2014/241 concerning the ratification of, or the accession to, the Hong Kong International Convention for the Safe and Environmentally Sound Recycling of Ships, 2009, by the EU Member States in the interests of the EU.[316] The decision authorises Member States to ratify or accede to, for the parts falling under the EU's exclusive competence, the Hong Kong Convention. (The EU itself may not accede to the Hong Kong Convention, as only States may be Parties but this did not stop the EU from guiding Member States on how they should act.) Member states which have ratified or acceded to the Hong Kong Convention must notify the Commission within six months of the date of deposit of their instruments of ratification or accession. The Council will review the progress of the ratification by 31 December 2018.

2014: Regulation on detailed rules for the imposition of fines and periodic penalty payments and the withdrawal of recognition of ship inspection and survey organisations

5.171 On 18 July 2014, the Commission adopted Regulation 788/2014 laying down detailed rules for the imposition of fines and periodic penalty payments and the withdrawal of recognition of ship inspection and survey organisations pursuant to Articles 6 and 7 of Regulation 391/2009 of the European Parliament and of the Council.[317]

---

314 See Commission, Report on the functioning of Dir. 2010/65 on reporting formalities for ships arriving in and/or departing from ports of the Member States (COM (2014) 320) (25 June 2014), http://ec.europa.eu/transport/modes/maritime/ports/doc/com(2014)320.pdf.

315 See the Commission's Press release, "Maritime Transport: Continuous Efforts Needed to Establish Harmonised Reporting Procedures for Vessels" (IP/14/742, 25 June 2014).

316 OJ 2014 L128/45.

317 OJ 2014 L214/12. See corrigendum published on 7 August 2014, OJ 2014 L234/15.

2014: Consortia block exemption regulation extended

5.172 Consortia agreements typically allow liner shipping carriers to rationalise their activities and achieve economies of scale. If consortia face sufficient competition and are not used to fix prices or share the market then users of services provided by consortia are usually able to benefit from improvements in productivity and service quality. However, consortia agreements are potentially anti-competitive. However, the Commission exempted consortia agreements in 1995[318] and then prolonged the regime several times.[319] A market investigation by the Commission, conducted in 2013, showed that the main tenets of the Commission's approach are still valid. This has been confirmed by a public consultation conducted by the Commission in early 2014.[320] The Commission thus decided that the exemption has worked well, providing legal certainty to agreements which bring benefits to customers and do not unduly distort competition, and that current market circumstances warrant a prolongation. On 24 June 2014, the European Commission decided to extend for another five years the validity under Article 101 of the TFEU of the European Commission's block exemption regime for liner shipping consortia until April 2020.[321] The Commission's renewed consortia block exemption regulation allows shipping lines with a combined market share of below 30% to enter into co-operation agreements to provide joint cargo transport services. The Commission commented, at the time of the extension, that for

"consortia and alliances exceeding the market share threshold established in the block exemption regulation, it is the responsibility of the companies themselves to make sure that their agreements comply with Article 101 TFEU, and the Commission can decide to intervene if necessary. The Commission will continue to closely monitor market developments and the conduct of companies to ensure that markets remain open and competitive. In particular, in the context of the recent developments in the sector, the Commission will remain vigilant as regards any risks for competition that may arise from the implementation of maritime consortia and might intervene if necessary."[322]

2015: Regulatory Summit

5.173 On 8 May 2015, the European Commission announced that DG Competition will host the second Global Maritime Regulatory Summit on 18 June 2015 in Brussels.[323] It will be a follow-up to the first Summit in Washington in December 2013. Representatives of the Chinese Ministry of Transport, the United States' Federal Maritime Commission and the European Commission will convene to discuss current market and regulatory developments in the maritime transport sector. The discussions are expected to centre on the global trend towards increased co-operation and market consolidation in liner shipping as well as on regulatory and policy issues related to ports.

---

318 See chap. 16.
319 See chap. 16.
320 See IP/14/196, http://ec.europa.eu/competition/consultations/2014_maritime_consortia/index_en.html.
321 Commission Reg. 697/2014 of 24 June 2014 amending Reg. (EC) No 906/2009 as regards its period of application OJ L184/3, 25 June 2014.
322 http://europa.eu/rapid/press-release_IP-14-717_en.htm.
323 MEX/15/4952.

2015: Portuguese Shipyard ENVC

5.174 On 7 May 2015, the European Commission decided that the Portuguese shipyard operator Estaleiros Navais de Viana do Castelo, S.A. ("ENVC") had received €290 million of State aid from Portugal which was incompatible with Articles 107–109 of the TFEU. The Commission went further and also ordered Portugal to recover the aid from ENVC (but not, interestingly, from the new operator of the yard, namely, WestSea).[324] ENVC was founded in 1944. It used to operate the largest Portuguese shipyard in Viana do Castelo. It was nationalised by Portugal in 1975. ENVC made heavy losses since 2000. Portugal, directly and indirectly, granted various subsidies to ENVC via various measures, including: (a) a capital increase in 2006; (b) several loans, between 2006 and 2011, to cover operating costs; and (c) comfort letters and guarantees to underwrite financing agreements between ENVC and commercial banks. The Commission valued the aid element as being *circa* €290 million. In January 2013, the Commission opened an in-depth State aid investigation to examine whether these aid measures were compatible with the State aid rules. In December 2013, Portugal decided to liquidate ENVC and to start selling its assets. The yard was then acquired by WestSea following an open and competitive tender. The Commission found that there had been State aid provided to ENVC. The Commission found that the market economy investor principle (the "MEIP")[325] was not respected[326] and that the State aid was not granted in accordance with the conditions in the Commission's 2004 Guidelines on Rescue and Recovery Aid for Firms in Difficulty.[327] The Commission first examined whether the aid was granted in accordance with the MEIP. If the aid measures were granted on terms that a private operator would have accepted under market conditions then the measures would not involve State aid within the meaning of Article 107(1) of the TFEU. The Commission has concluded that the MEIP test was not fulfilled because no private investor would have agreed to subsidise a loss-making company for over 13 years in these circumstances. The measures were therefore not granted on "market terms" and therefore amounted to State aid. The Commission then considered the issue from the perspective of the 2004 Guidelines on Rescue and Restructuring Aid for Firms in Difficulty. The Commission concluded that the conditions of the Guidelines were not satisfied as: (a) ENVC, at the time, had no realistic restructuring programme to ensure the company's long-term viability without further State support; and (b) ENVC received repeated State aid, at least over the last ten years, in breach of the "one time last time" principle, which allows the grant of rescue or restructuring aid only once in a ten-year period. The Commission, therefore, concluded that the measures amounted to incompatible State aid. Moreover, the Commission ordered Portugal to recover the aid from ENVC. The Commission ordered ENVC to repay the State aid but in considering who should be responsible for repaying the aid, the Commission had to take into account the fact that ENVC was in the process of being wound up and that part of its assets (including a sub-concession of the land on which ENVC

---

324 Commission press release IP/15/4940. Case number SA.35546.
325 This principle is also known as the Market Economy Operator Principle.
326 I.e. a market economy operator or market economy investor would not have concluded a comparable deal on comparable terms in comparable circumstances. In such a scenario, the extra assistance would amount to State aid. For example, if a private investor would have paid €20 million for an asset but the Member State paid €30 million for it then the difference (i.e. €10 million) would potentially be State aid.
327 OJ C244/2, 1 October 2004.

operated) has been acquired by WestSea (owned by Martifer and Navalria). The background was that in December 2013, Portugal decided to liquidate ENVC and to start selling its assets. A private operator, WestSea, acquired some of EVNC's assets. So, would the Commission order recovery from WestSea? To establish whether State aid has been passed on to new owners in an asset sale, the Commission would assess whether there is economic continuity between the new owner and the previous one or, put another way, whether the economic link had been broken. The Commission deploys various tests to examine the economic reality (e.g. the scope of the assets sold, the sale price/consideration, the identity of the buyer and the economic logic of the transaction). Interestingly, the Commission found that there was no economic continuity between ENVC and WestSea because the assets were bought by WestSea at market conditions following an open and competitive tender and are therefore free of State aid. The Commission also found that WestSea is not the economic successor of ENVC so the obligation to repay the incompatible aid remained with ENVC. This case highlights the importance, in the maritime sector as in all economic sectors, of buying assets from Member States at market conditions and as part of an open and competitive process.

2015: Shipment of waste: Commission guidelines for customs controls on transboundary shipments of waste

5.175 On 12 May 2015, the Commission published a public summary of non-binding Guidelines for customs controls on transboundary shipments of waste in the *Official Journal*.[328] The Guidelines are aimed at supporting the EU Member States' customs authorities and national competent authorities to carry out controls on waste shipments and to support compliance with Regulation 1013/2006 of 14 June 2006 on shipments of waste.[329] The Guidelines apply to shipments of waste into, through and out of the territory of the EU. Movements of waste between Member States (i.e. cabotage shipments) are not addressed in the Guidelines. They are aimed at improving co-operation methods and developing good administrative practice. Interestingly, all the Commission has published is a summary so as to minimise the risk that the controls would be circumvented if the rules themselves were published.

2015: Regulation 2015/757 of the European Parliament and of the Council of 29 April 2015 on the monitoring, reporting and verification of carbon dioxide emissions from maritime transport, and amending Directive 2009/16

5.176 On 19 May 2015, Regulation 2015/757 of the European Parliament and of the Council of 29 April 2015 on the monitoring, reporting and verification of carbon dioxide emissions from maritime transport and amending Directive 2009/16 was published in the EU's *Official Journal*.[330] Regulation 2015/757 will enter into force on 1 July 2015. It will apply to the carbon dioxide (i.e. CO_2) emissions from ships over 5,000 grt during voyages

---

328 OJ C2015 157/1.
329 I.e. Reg. 1013/2006 of the European Parliament and of the Council of 14 June 2006 on shipments of waste provides for detailed control procedures in order to ensure the protection of the environment and EU citizens OJ L190/1, 12 July 2006.
330 OJ L123/55, 19 May 2015.

to, from and between EU ports. The regulation will not apply to warships, naval auxiliaries, fish-catching or fish-processing ships, primitive-build wooden ships, ships not propelled by mechanical means or government ships used for non-commercial purposes. It will oblige shipowners or operators to monitor, verify and report on CO_2 emissions every year from 1 January 2018. The regulation provides for expulsion orders to be made refusing ships entry to EU ports until the shipowner or operator submits its emissions reports. The background to the regulation lies in the EU's Emission Trading System ("ETS") Amending Directive 2009[331] which required that the EU include greenhouse gas ("GHG") emissions from the maritime sector in its 2020 GHG emissions reduction target if no international agreement on reducing shipping emissions had been reached by 31 December 2011. The amount of CO_2 and other GHG emissions of EU-related maritime transport activities is not known because of a lack of monitoring, reporting and verification ("MRV") of these emissions. The Commission therefore proposed in 2013 a regulation to require MRV of shipping GHG emissions. Regulation 2015/757 is the resultant measure. The Commission's impact assessment contemplates that the MRV system should reduce CO_2 emissions by up to 2% compared with a "business as usual" situation. The final regulation differed to some extent from the original proposal but the Commission was able to support the measure because it was sufficiently close to the Commission's original proposal. Separately, the EU's negotiations with the IMO towards a global MRV system to reduce shipping emissions have not made much progress but it is likely that maritime GHG emissions was be a feature of negotiations at the next UN Framework Convention on Climate Change conference in Paris in December 2015.

2015–2016: Migration crisis

5.177 As is well known, there is a serious crisis in the Mediterranean relating to migrants from Africa to Europe. The EU has paid increased attention to this migration crisis in the Mediterranean. The EU's High Representative for Foreign Affairs and Security Policy, Federica Mogherini, has said that

> "not one single action will be effective alone [to address the crisis]. All different parts of our action are relevant: saving lives at sea, working on the root causes with our partners and dismantling criminal networks that are smuggling people."

One action which has been taken was instituted on 18 May 2015 when the Council established an EU naval operation to disrupt the business model of human smugglers in the Mediterranean, EUNAVFOR Med. Under the Council's plan, EUNAVFOR Med will be conducted in sequential phases and in accordance with the requirements of international law. The first phase involves surveillance and assessment of human smuggling and trafficking networks in the Southern Central Mediterranean. The second and third phases of the operation would work to search, seize and disrupt the assets of smugglers, based on international law and in partnership with Libyan authorities.

---

331 Dir. 2009/29 of the European Parliament and of the Council of 23 April 2009 amending Dir. 2003/87 so as to improve and extend the greenhouse gas emission allowance trading scheme of the Community OJ L190/1, 12 July 2006.

2016: Brexit vote

5.178 As will be discussed in chapter 48, the UK and Gibraltar voted on 23 June 2016 by a margin of 52% to 48% to leave the EU (i.e. Brexit). This is scheduled to occur on 29 March 2019 subject to there being an implementation/transition period until 31 December 2020. However, there is a great deal of uncertainty about the terms on which the UK would leave (assuming that it does leave) and the arrangements between the EU and the UK post-Brexit. While the topic will be discussed in chapter 48, suffice it to say for present purposes that Brexit will have a considerable impact on issues such as customs and trading relations between the UK and the EU. It is also likely that the liberal approach of the UK to markets will be missed by those seeking to open up markets in the EU.

I. CONCLUSION

5.179 This chapter has been a chronological account of many, but not all, of the key developments in EU shipping law. It is proposed to delay drawing the conclusions on this process until the final chapter because the purpose of this chapter has been simply to describe the evolution of the subject.

CHAPTER 6

European Union law relating to the freedom of establishment of shipping businesses and the registration of ships

A. RIGHT OF ESTABLISHMENT

Introduction

6.001 This chapter examines the twin but related issues of: (a) right of establishment of shipping companies and operations; and (b) registration of ships under European Union ("EU") law.[1] Articles 49–55 of the Treaty on the Functioning of the European Union ("TFEU") deal with the right of establishment generally. It is clear, in the light of the Court of Justice of the European Union's ("CJEU") judgment in *Commission v France (French Seafarers)*,[2] that the rules on freedom of establishment contained in Articles 49 to 55 of the TFEU are applicable in the context of maritime transport and hence shipping. Thus, national rules of Member States restricting the right of establishment of shipping companies in a Member State to nationals/citizens or companies of that Member State are inapplicable vis-à-vis nationals or companies from other Member States; in other words, nationals in any one Member State are entitled to establish operations and register ships elsewhere in the EU on the same basis as nationals of the host Member State in question. Nationals of Member States are also able to vindicate their rights in regard to establishment in other Member State courts.[3]

Concept of the right of establishment

6.002 The right of establishment involves the entitlement of a person who is a national of a Member State to enter another Member State and "establish" there for the purpose of

---

1 On the right of establishment generally, see White, *Workers, Establishment, and Services in the European Union* (2004). On the registration of ships, see Coles and Watt, *Ship Registration Law & Practice* (2nd ed., 2009). On the *Viking* case discussed in this chapter, see Blanpain and Swiatkowski, *The Laval and Viking Cases: Freedom of Services and Establishment v Industrial Conflict in the European Economic Area and Russia* (2009).

For the case law, see, *inter alia*, Case 13/76 *Donà v Mantero* [1976] ECR 1333, ECLI:EU:C:1976:115; Case 197/84 *Steinhausser v City of Biarritz* [1985] ECR 1819, ECLI:EU:C:1985:260; Case 270/83 *Commission v France* [1986] ECR 273, ECLI:EU:C:1986:37; Case 71/76 *Thieffry v Conseil de l'Ordre des Avocats à la Cour de Paris* [1977] ECR 765, ECLI:EU:C:1977:65; Case 11/77 *Patrick v Ministre des Affairs Culturelles* [1977] ECR 1199, ECLI:EU:C:1977:113; Case 16/78 *Choquet* [1978] ECR 2293, ECLI:EU:C:1978:210; Case 110–111/78 *Ministère Public et al. v Van Wesemael and Follachio* [1979] ECR 35, ECLI:EU:C:1979:8; Case 107/83 *Ordre des Avocats au Barreau de Paris v Klopp* [1984] ECR 2971, ECLI:EU:C:1984:270; and Case 292/86 *Gullung v Conseil de l'Ordre des Avocats au Barreau de Colmar et al* [1988] ECR 111, ECLI:EU:C:1988:15.

2 Case 167/73 [1973] ECR 359, ECLI:EU:C:1974:35.

3 Bredima-Savopoulou and Tzoannos, "In Search of a Common Shipping Policy for the EC" (1981) 20 JCMS 95 at 103.

carrying on an economic activity other than under a contract of employment or for the provision of services on a temporary basis.[4] The right of establishment, as understood in EU law, includes the right to take up and pursue activities as a self-employed person or company as well as to set up and manage undertakings[5] in a Member State. Freedom of establishment is closely linked to the freedom to provide services.[6] However, establishment involves a more permanent presence in the host State than merely providing services to undertakings in that second or host State[7] on a non-permanent basis.[8] For most purposes and most economic sectors, it does not matter whether an activity involves the right of establishment or the right to provide services (as the rules relating to establishment and services are so similar) so long as the entity may operate in the other Member State. On the other hand, in the context of transport, the matter may be material because Article 58(1) of the TFEU provides that freedom to provide *services* in the field of transport is governed by the provision of the Title in the Treaty relating to transport rather than the general provisions of the Treaty on freedom of establishment – the chapter in the TFEU on freedom of establishment does not have a similar provision and therefore the Treaty's general provisions on establishment apply to the transport sector in that context.

General rule on freedom of establishment

6.003 Article 49 of the TFEU provides:

"Within the framework of the provisions set out below,[9] restrictions on the freedom of establishment of nationals of a Member State in the territory of another Member State shall be prohibited. Such prohibition shall also apply to restrictions on the setting up of agencies, branches or subsidiaries by nationals of any Member State established in the territory of any Member State.

Freedom of establishment shall include the right to take up and pursue activities as self-employed persons and to set up and manage undertakings, in particular companies or firms within the meaning of the second paragraph of Article 54, under the conditions laid down for its own nationals by the law of the country where such establishment is effected, subject to the provisions of the Chapter relating to capital."

6.004 The purpose of Article 49 is to ensure that self-employed nationals of one Member State are treated in the same way in another Member State as are nationals of that second State.[10] Or, put another way, a national of Member State X may pursue his or her freedom of establishment in Member State Y on the same basis as a national of Member State Y. The right is to be treated on the same basis as *host* State nationals.

6.005 Article 49 has direct effect.[11] In the case of the original six Member States, the equivalent article in the European Economic Community ("EEC") Treaty had direct effect from the end of the transitional period.[12] In the case of newer Member States, the article

---

4 If it were a temporary provision of services then it would be the freedom to provide services rather than the freedom of establishment which would be the relevant concept. Equally, if the person were entering the other Member State as a worker then the relevant regime would be the free movement of workers regime.
5 In essence, an undertaking is any entity carrying on an economic activity.
6 On the freedom to provide services see chap. 7.
7 See Case 118/75 *Watson and Belmann* [1976] ECR 1185, ECLI:EU:C:1976:106.
8 See Case 196/87 *Steymann v Staatssecretaris van Justitie* [1988] ECR 6159, ECLI:EU:C:1988:475.
9 Ed., i.e. Arts 49–55 of the TFEU.
10 See Case 221/85 *Commission v Belgium* [1987] ECR 719, ECLI:EU:C:1987:81.
11 See Case 2/74 *Reyner v Kingdom of Belgium* [1974] ECR 631, ECLI:EU:C:1974:68.
12 I.e. 1 January 1970. See Case 2/74 *Reyner v Kingdom of Belgium* [1974] ECR 631, ECLI:EU:C:1974:68.

had direct effect from their dates of accession.[13] The freedom of establishment under the TFEU may be enjoyed by nationals of Member States and their families, notwithstanding that some or all of the family members are not nationals of a Member State.[14] In the case of companies, freedom of establishment means that a company has a right to transfer its registered office to another Member State after the first Member State has given its consent.[15] Article 49 allows for freedom of establishment in relation to incidental matters as well such as the establishment of agencies, branches or subsidiaries.[16] It deals not merely with the establishment of the self-employed or companies but also with the exercise of a profession or management of undertakings. It is clear from the decision of the CJEU in *Commission v Italy*[17] that Article 49 does not restrict the duty of a Member State to abolish any national rule which is discriminatory. Discrimination by professional bodies is prohibited under the TFEU[18] provided there is the EU dimension: Article 49 may not be invoked to deal with purely domestic matters (i.e. within one and the same Member State) which have no EU dimension[19] (i.e. a national of Member State may not invoke the freedom of establishment rules to move elsewhere in the same Member State). Article 49 is implemented by means of a general programme as well as by directives in particular areas.

Prohibition of new restrictions

6.006 There used to be a provision, which was Article 53 of the European Community ("EC") Treaty, which prohibited Member States from introducing any new restriction on the right of establishment after they joined the then EC. It provided: "Member States shall not introduce any new restrictions on the right of establishment in their territories of nationals of other Member States, save as otherwise provided in this Treaty." It was clear from *Costa v ENEL*[20] that Article 53 had direct effect. This provision is now unnecessary because there is a general prohibition on restrictions on the freedom of establishment.

Implementation of the Treaty provisions on establishment

6.007 Article 50 of the TFEU provides for the implementation of the provisions in the TFEU on freedom of establishment by means of a General Programme and the enactment of directives. Article 50 provides:

---

13 Case 11/77 *Patrick v Ministre des Affaires Culturelles* [1977] ECR 1199, ECLI:EU:C:1977:113.
14 Case 48/75 *Royer* [1976] ECR 497, ECLI:EU:C:1976:57. There are specific rules relating to the availability of the right to non-EU nationals.
15 Case 81/87 *R v HM Treasury et al., ex p. Daily Mail and General Trust PLC* [1988] ECR 5483, ECLI:EU:C:1988:456.
16 Case 270/83 *Commission v France* [1986] ECR 273, ECLI:EU:C:1986:37.
17 Case 159/78 [1979] ECR 3247, ECLI:EU:C:1979:243.
18 Case 159/78, Case 36/74 *Walrave and Koch v Association Union Cycliste Internationale et al.* [1974] ECR 1405, ECLI:EU:C:1974:140.
19 Case 198/86 *Conradi et al. v Direction de la Concurrence et des Prix des Hauts de la Seine et al* [1987] ECR 4469, ECLI:EU:C:1987: 489; Case 20/87 *Ministère Public v Gauchard* [1987] ECR 4879, ECLI:EU:C:1987:532; Case 204/87 *Bekaert v Procureur de la République de Rennes* [1988] ECR 2029, ECLI:EU:C:1988: 192; Case 63/86 *Commission v Italy* [1988] ECR 29, ECLI:EU:C:1988:9 and Case 147/86 *Commission v Greece* [1988] ECR 1637, ECLI:EU:C:1989:611.
20 Case 6/64 [1964] ECR 585, ECLI:EU:C:1964:66.

"1. In order to attain freedom of establishment as regards a particular activity, the European Parliament and the Council, acting in accordance with the ordinary legislative procedure and after consulting the Economic and Social Committee, shall act by means of directives.
2. The European Parliament, the Council and the Commission shall carry out the duties devolving upon them under the preceding provisions, in particular:

(a) by according, as a general rule, priority treatment to activities where freedom of establishment makes a particularly valuable contribution to the development of production and trade;
(b) by ensuring close co-operation between the competent authorities in the Member States in order to ascertain the particular situation within the Union of the various activities concerned;
(c) by abolishing those administrative procedures and practices, whether resulting from national legislation or from agreements previously concluded between Member States, the maintenance of which would form an obstacle to freedom of establishment;
(d) by ensuring that workers of one Member State employed in the territory of another Member State may remain in that territory for the purpose of taking up activities therein as self-employed persons, where they satisfy the conditions which they would be required to satisfy if they were entering that State at the time when they intended to take up such activities;
(e) by enabling a national of one Member State to acquire and use land and buildings situated in the territory of another Member State, in so far as this does not conflict with the principles laid down in Article 39(2);
(f) by effecting the progressive abolition of restrictions on freedom of establishment in every branch of activity under consideration, both as regards the conditions for setting up agencies, branches or subsidiaries in the territory of a Member State and as regards the subsidiaries in the territory of a Member State and as regards the conditions governing the entry of personnel belonging to the main establishment into managerial or supervisory posts in such agencies, branches or subsidiaries;
(g) by co-ordinating to the necessary extent the safeguards which, for the protection of the interests of members and others, are required by Member States of companies or firms within the meaning of the second paragraph of Article 54 with a view to making such safeguards equivalent throughout the Union.
(h) by satisfying themselves that the conditions of establishment are not distorted by aids granted by Member States."

6.008 The General Programme was adopted in 1962.[21] Directive 73/148[22] provided that nationals,[23] and specified relatives[24] of nationals of the Member States must be admitted to any Member State on presentation of a passport or national identity card. A large number of directives has been adopted so as to deal with the freedom of establishment in a number of professions and occupations.

Freedom of establishment and registration of ships

6.009 There is a connection between the registration of a vessel and the concept of the freedom of establishment; as the CJEU stated in *Factortame*:

---

21 OJ 1962 2/36.
22 OJ 1973 L172/14. This replaced Dir. 64/220, OJ 1964 56/845.
23 This right does not extend to companies: see Case 81/87 *R v HM Treasury and Commissioners of Inland Revenue, ex p. Daily Mail and General Trust PLC* [1988] ECR 5483, ECLI:EU:C:1988:456.
24 The relatives do not have to be nationals of a Member State.

"19. At the hearing, the Commission argued that the registration of a vessel constituted in itself an act of establishment within the meaning of ... the Treaty and that therefore the rules on freedom of establishment were applicable.
20. It must be observed in that regard that the concept of establishment within the meaning of ... the Treaty involves the actual pursuit of an economic activity through a fixed establishment in another Member State for an indefinite period.
21. Consequently, the registration of a vessel does not necessarily involve establishment within the meaning of the Treaty, in particular where the vessel is not used to pursue an economic activity or where the application for registration is made by or on behalf of a person who is not established, and has no intention of becoming established, in the State concerned.
22. However, where the vessel constitutes an instrument for pursuing an economic activity which involves a fixed establishment in the Member State concerned, the registration of that vessel cannot be dissociated from the exercise of the freedom of establishment.
23. It follows that the conditions laid down for the registration of vessels must not form an obstacle to freedom of establishment within the meaning of ... the Treaty."[25]

Therefore, there is a connection in certain circumstances (i.e. those outlined in paragraph 22 of the Judgment) between registration of vessels and freedom of establishment.

Mutual recognition of diplomas, certificates and qualifications

6.010 It would frustrate the possibility of the freedom of establishment in host Member States if Member States were easily able to refuse to recognise qualifications granted by other Member States. Article 53 of the TFEU therefore provides:

"1. In order to make it easier for persons to take up and pursue activities as self-employed persons, the European Parliament and the Council, acting in accordance with the ordinary legislative procedure, [shall] issue directives for the mutual recognition of diplomas, certificates and other evidence of formal qualifications and for the co-ordination of the provisions laid down by law, regulation or administrative action in Member States concerning the taking-up and pursuit of activities as self-employed persons.
2. In the case of the medical and allied and pharmaceutical professions, the progressive abolition of restrictions shall be dependent upon coordination of the conditions for their exercise in the various Member States."

6.011 It had been held that in the absence of directives on mutual recognition of qualifications, where a person who is a national of one Member State wishes to practise his or her profession in another Member State and passes the professional examination in that second Member State then that person must be admitted to practice.[26] Directive 89/48[27] altered the situation somewhat by providing for a general system for the recognition of higher education diplomas where there has been at least three years' professional education and training towards a profession.

Exceptions to the freedom of establishment

Introduction

6.012 It would be surprising if the freedom of establishment was an entirely unfettered right. The TFEU therefore provides for some exceptions.

---

25 Case C-221/89 [1991] ECR I-3905, ECLI:EU:C:1991:320.
26 Case 71/76 *Thieffry v Conseil de l'Ordre des Avocats* [1977] ECR 765, ECLI:EU:C:1977:65.
27 OJ 1989 L19/16.

Exception 1: Exercise of official authority

6.013 Article 51 of the TFEU is an exception to the freedom of establishment. It provides:

"The provisions of this Chapter shall not apply, so far as any given Member State is concerned, to activities which in that State are connected, even occasionally with the exercise of official authority.

The European Parliament and the Council, acting in accordance with the ordinary legislative procedure may rule that the provisions of this Chapter shall not apply to certain activities."

6.014 This provision must be construed narrowly as are all exceptions to the fundamental freedoms.[28] It relates to *activities* and not entire professions unless the public activities constitute so much of the profession that the two are inseparable. However, it is noteworthy that even occasional exercise of official authority is included in the exception so there is no need for the exercise of official authority to be continuous.

Exception 2: Public policy

6.015 Article 52 of the TFEU provides:

"1. The provisions of this Chapter and measures taken in pursuance thereof shall not prejudice the applicability of provisions laid down by law, regulation or administrative action providing for special treatment for foreign nationals on grounds of public policy, public security or public health.
2. The European Parliament and the Council shall, acting in accordance with the ordinary legislative procedure, issue directives for the co-ordinators of the above-mentioned provisions."

This exception is again construed narrowly and is of relatively limited significance in shipping but could relate to, for example, individuals or cargo.

Exception 3: Public security

6.016 Article 52 of the TFEU, just cited, provides an exception relating to public security. This exception is again construed narrowly and is of relatively limited significance in shipping but could relate to, for example, individuals or cargo.

Exception 4: Public health

6.017 Article 52 of the TFEU, just cited, provides for an exception relating to public health. This exception is again construed narrowly and is of relatively limited significance in shipping but could relate to, for example, individuals or cargo.

Definition of a Community or EU Shipowner

6.018 The Commission made a proposal for a Council of Ministers Regulation on a Common Definition of a Community Shipowner.[29] The proposed regulation was never adopted but it is interesting to see how the debate unfolded. The proposal stated:

---

28 Case 7/68 *Commission v Italy* [1968] ECR 423, ECLI:EU:C:1968:51.
29 COM(89)266 final. Reprinted in OJ 1989 C263/17.

"Article 1
This Regulation lays down criteria establishing a common definition of a Community shipowner.

Article 2
Unless otherwise stated, all references to 'Community shipowner', in regulations, directives and decisions of the Council are to be interpreted in accordance with Articles 3 and 4.

Article 3
For the purpose of this Regulation 'a shipowner' means: a natural or legal person providing a liner or tramp service in the field of maritime transport of passengers or goods by one or more sea-going vessels which he or it owns or has chartered on the basis of a bare-boat charter, time charter or voyage charter.

Article 4
The following shipowners are regarded as Community shipowners:

1a a national of a Member State, who has his domicile or usual residence in a Member State;
1b a company or firm which is formed in accordance with the law of a Member State and which complies with the following conditions:

    (i) the principal place of business is situated and the effective control exercised in a Member State and
    (ii) a majority of the members of the board or of the directors are nationals of Member States having their domicile or usual residence in the Community or
       In which nationals of Member States participate by more than 50% or are company shareholders controlling more than 50% of the overall company capital;

2a a national of a Member State who has his domicile or usual residence outside the Community if he is the owner of a vessel registered in a Member State in accordance with its legislation;
2b a company or firm formed in accordance with the law or a third country in which nationals of Member States participate by more than 50% or are shareholders controlling more than 50% of the overall company capital provided that it is the owner of a vessel registered in a Member State in accordance with its legislation.

Article 5
This Regulation shall enter into force on 1 July 1991."

The proposal was dropped. In a communication from the Commission dated 13 March 1996 the following comments were made:

"The Commission will, after informing the Council and Parliament accordingly withdraw its 1989 proposal for a Council regulation defining the notion of a Community ship owner. However, appropriate definitions of the notion of Community ship owner will be provided in individual instruments for example when considering the beneficiaries of Regulation 4057/86, the Regulation concerning unfair pricing in maritime transport and in the determination of beneficiaries of State aid."

Despite the proposal not being adopted, it is useful in indicating what would be meant by the concept of an EU shipowner and therefore the beneficiary of the freedom of establishment.

B. REGISTRATION OF SHIPS IN INTERNATIONAL LAW

Introduction

6.019 The choice of the State in which to register a ship is an important strategic decision.[30] Flagging out to "flags of convenience"[31] is an everyday phenomenon in world shipping. It is done for a variety of reasons,[32] including, the possibility of lower taxes or no taxes as well as reduced crewing costs and possibly lower regulation and standards.[33] The Commission stated in its communication "Towards a New Maritime Strategy"[34] that many nationals

> "of the traditional shipping nations have seen their shipowners take advantage of the international capital and labour markets, as well as the increasing variety of ship registers now in place. In a highly competitive market, shipping registered in EU Member States and the number of EU seafarers has been constantly shrinking. While this trend predates the mid-eighties, its effects on the EU maritime industry have been a cause of common concern only since that time."[35]

6.020 The registration of ships and the choice of registry is now a very sophisticated and somewhat complex process. There are now at least four types of registry:

(a) traditional home registries;
(b) traditional open registries;
(c) offshore registries; and
(d) international registries.

Traditional home registries

6.021 The traditional home registries require the ships which are registered on those registries to be owned and/or managed and/or manned by persons resident in the State of registry.

Traditional open registries

6.022 Traditional open registries include such registries as the Bahamas, Bermuda, Cayman Islands, Costa Rica, Honduras, Hong Kong, Lebanon, Liberia, Maldives, Netherlands Antilles, Panama, Seychelles, Singapore and Somalia. The qualifications for registration on such registries are relatively lax. Almost any shipowner may register on these registries by creating a link (even a loose one) with such a registry, as, for example, by buying a shelf company incorporated in that jurisdiction. There are very few restrictions

---

30 Burns, "Registration of EC Vessels: Offshore, International or Euroregistry", at *The Future of Shipping in Europe: Key Legal and Commercial Issues*, London, 28–29 June 1990.
31 The Select Committee of the House of Lords on the European Communities defined "flags of convenience" as "States operating ship registries open to all shipowners regardless of nationality" (see *Community Shipping Measures*, 28th Report, para. 1).
32 See UNCTAD Secretariat report, *Economic Consequences of the Existence or Lack of a Genuine Link between Vessel and Flag Registry*, TD/B/C.4/168.
33 See Rabe, "Recent Developments in EEC Legislation Pertaining to Maritime Transport", IBA Conference, Strasbourg 1990, pp. 3–4.
34 COM(96)81 final, 13 March 1996.
35 Ibid., p. 1.

in such matters as safety, the environment or employment imposed on the shipowner by such registries. There may also be tax advantages to registration under such flags. The Committee of Inquiry into Shipping (the so-called "Rochdale Report")[36] describes the attributes of a registry of convenience in the following terms:

> "(a) the country of registry allows ownership and/or control of its merchant vessels by non-citizens;
> (b) access to the register is easy; a ship may usually be registered at a Consul's office abroad. Equally important, transfer from the registry at the owner's option is not restricted;
> (c) taxes on the income from the ships are not levied locally or are low. A registry fee and an annual fee, based on tonnage, are normally the only charges made. A guarantee or acceptable understanding regarding future freedom from taxation may also be given;
> (d) the country of registration is a small power with no national requirement under any foreseeable circumstances for all the shipping registered, but receipts from very small charges on a large tonnage may produce a substantial effect on its national income and balance of payments;
> (e) manning of ships by non-nationals is freely permitted;
> (f) the country of registry has neither the power nor the administrative machinery effectively to impose any government or international regulations; nor has the country the wish to control the companies themselves."

6.023 Boczek has defined a flag of convenience as: "a flag of any country allowing the registration of foreign owned and foreign controlled vessels under conditions which, for whatever reasons, are convenient and opportune for the persons who are registering the vessels".[37] The Maritime Transport Committee of the Organisation for Economic Co-operation and Development ("OECD") has in its *Study of the Expansion of the Flags of Convenience and of Various Aspects Thereof*, defined a flag of convenience as:

> "the flag of such countries whose law allows – and indeed makes it easy – for ships owned by foreign nationals or companies to fly those flags in contrast to the practice in the maritime countries where the right to fly the national flag is subject to stringent conditions and involves far-reaching obligations".

Offshore registries

6.024 The offshore registries are registries based in dependencies or colonies and are designed to attract the fleets of a particular State.[38] Shipowners are attracted to such registries by a package of advantages, including choice of crew[39] and tax privileges, as well as maintaining the right to fly the flag of the State. Examples include Bermuda (UK), the Cayman Islands (UK), the Isle of Man (UK),[40] Kerguelen (France)[41] and the Netherlands Antilles (the Netherlands). For example, a ship registered in the Cayman Islands or the Isle of Man has fewer restrictions placed on it than a ship registered in the UK itself, but the ship may still fly the Red Ensign of the UK. Thus, historically, a ship registered in the

---

36 Cmnd 4337.
37 *Flags of Convenience* (1962), p. 2.
38 On new registries generally, see Bredima-Savopoulou and Tzoannos, *The Common Shipping Policy of the EEC* (1990), pp. 52–54. On the dangers of offshore registries, see the comments of Commissioner Clinton Davies, Lloyd's List, 1 April 1987, p. 1.
39 Sometimes this includes the right to choose officers as well.
40 On the Isle of Man, see *Fairplay*, 25 January 1990, p. 24.
41 Kerguelen is often used for dry bulk carriers.

Cayman Islands may have a master, officers and crew of any nationality and still fly the Red Ensign, provided that it never visited a UK port. Other offshore registries can be more restrictive but they still remain quite flexible, for example, the Isle of Man has allowed a shipowner to register there and choose crew from anywhere in the world and still fly the Red Ensign. British shipowners are particularly attracted to such offshore registries – at some points in time, as much as one-third of the total gross tonnage in British ownership was registered on one of the British offshore registries. There are disadvantages to flagging out one's vessels to such an offshore registry and the most significant is the possibility of having one's ship boycotted unless the agreements relating to the crew's pay and conditions meet the International Transport Federation's standards. The legal status of such registries in the light of EU law is largely an open question. Another important issue is whether or not ships registered in such locations can benefit from the freedoms embodied in the Treaties. Protocol No 2 to the Act of Accession of the UK states that persons on the Isle of Man or the Channel Islands "shall not benefit from Community provisions relating to the free movement of persons and services". Cases would have to be judged on their individual circumstances.

International registries

6.025 An international register allows ships registered on it to fly the domestic flag (e.g. ships registered on the Danish International Register may still fly the Danish flag) but are still subject to detailed rules on such matters as ownership, management,[42] manning[43] and operation.[44] The Norwegian International Ships Register ("NIS") has been one of the most successful to date.[45] In the EU, for example, Denmark and Germany both have international registers.

International law on registration

6.026 International law is concerned largely with the concept of a "genuine link" between the ship and the State whose flag the ships fly. The term "genuine link" is an imprecise term which defies exact definition. Nonetheless, it involves a number of factors, which have been summarised by Marston in the following terms:

"(a) the fact of registration; (b) a substantial share of beneficial ownership in the vessel by nationals (individuals or legal entities) of the flag-State; (c) the principal place of business and effective management of the legal entity which has the beneficial ownership of the vessel should be in the flag-State; (d) the principal officers of the legal entity beneficially owning the vessel should be nationals of the flag-State; together with the further factors of national legislation to control effectively the administrative, social, technical, safety and environmental matters as well as adequate national arrangements for the implementation and supervision of such legislation".[46]

It is clear that certain registries around the world do not impose such obligations.

---

42 E.g. the NIS has required a representative office in Norway.
43 E.g. the NIS has allowed a ship on the register to have officers or crew from any State. The master may be from a foreign State provided that he or she has a dispensation from the Norwegian Maritime Directorate.
44 On new registries generally, see Bredima-Savopoulou and Tzoannos, op. cit. at fn. 3, pp. 52–54.
45 In part, the success of the NIS is attributable to the K/S system of limited partnership.
46 (1986) JWTL 575 at p. 576.

Geneva Convention on the High Seas 1958

6.027 Article 5(1) of the Geneva Convention on the High Seas 1958 dealt with the issue of "the genuine link" in the following terms:

> "Each State shall fix the conditions for the granting of its nationality to ships, for the registration of ships in its territory, and for the right to fly its flag. Ships have the nationality of the State whose flag they are entitled to fly. There must exist a genuine link between the State and the ship; in particular, the State must effectively exercise its jurisdiction and control in administrative, technical and social matters over ships flying its flag."

6.028 The United Nations Conference on Trade and Development ("UNCTAD") Secretariat responded by preparing a report which was entitled "Economic Consequences of the Existence or Lack of a Genuine Link between Vessel and Flag Registry"[47] which was published in 1977. This report pointed out that Article 5 of the Geneva Convention on the High Seas 1958[48] did not provide "an effective remedy to deal with the practice of registering merchant vessels in countries which may not be in a position to exercise effective jurisdiction and control over such vessels". After the publication of the report, an ad hoc intergovernmental working group was established. It adopted a unanimous resolution to the effect that "the expansion of open-registry fleets has adversely affected the development and competitiveness of fleets of countries which do not offer open-registry facilities, including those of developing countries".

6.029 In 1981, the UN's Committee on Shipping resolved to recommend the holding of a conference on the adoption of an international agreement on the conditions for registration of ships. The General Assembly of the United Nations ("UN") took up the Committee's call for a conference and on 20 December 1982 resolved that a plenipotentiary conference be held in 1984.[49] The purpose of the conference was to consider the adoption of an international agreement concerning the conditions under which vessels should be accepted on national shipping registers. The Conference opened in July 1984 and was attended by 93 States and a large number of international organisations. A total of 109 States were involved in the drafting of the convention. The position of States such as Liberia was obvious: they opposed any substantial change in the status quo. The United Nations Convention on the Registration of Ships[50] was eventually signed on 7 February 1986. The purpose of the convention was to deal with the enormous numbers of ships which are being registered under various flags of convenience, such as Liberia and Panama. The European Parliament later summarised the aims of the convention (by reference to Article 1 of the convention) as relating to:

> "– definition of the powers and responsibilities of national shipping authorities with respect to a number of problems concerning exercise of their jurisdiction and supervision over ships registered in the State whose flag they fly;
> – mandatory updating of national shipping registers and documents specifying the identity of the owner, operator, or other persons in charge;
> – specifying the proportions of owning interests and/or crew complements to be accounted for by nationals;

---

47 TD/B/C.4/168.
48 Art. 5 is comparable to Art. 91 of UNCLOS III (United Nations Convention on the Law of the Sea).
49 UN GA Res. 37/209.
50 TD/RS/CONF/23. On the convention, see Marston (1986) 29 JWTL 575.

- definition of the role of the flag State, especially as regards involvement of nationals in the management of shipowning companies;
- detailed guidelines on conditions of charter of ships, joint ventures between shipowning companies from different countries, and protection of the interests of countries that supply labour."[51]

6.030 The United Nations Convention on Conditions for the Registration of Ships 1986 tried to give some further meaning to the concept. A "genuine link" means, according to the convention, that nationals of the flag State participate in the ownership, crewing or management of the ship. In the words of one commentator:

"[a]re these just empty words? The answer so far appears to be yes. One of the fastest growing registries in the world is that of the Bahamas. The Bahamas are a signatory to the 1982 Convention,[52] and indeed are one of the few nations which has ratified it. Yet, under Bahamas law, anyone, of whatever nationality, can register a ship under Bahamas flag; he can manage his ship from wherever he likes, and he can employ officers and crew of whatever nationality he likes."[53]

United Nations Convention on the Law of the Sea 1982

6.031 The United Nations Convention on the Law of the Sea (UNCLOS III), which is now the leading treaty on the law of the sea and was opened for signature on 10 December 1982, deals with, among other things, the issue of registration of ships. Article 90 recognises the right of every State, whether coastal or land-locked,[54] to sail ships flying its own flag on the high seas. Article 91 of UNCLOS III goes on to deal with the nationality of ships. It provides:

"1. Every State shall fix the conditions for the grant of its nationality to ships, for the registration of ships in its territory, and for the right to fly its flag. Ships have the nationality of the State whose flag they are entitled to fly. There must exist a genuine link between the State and the ship.
2. Every State shall issue to ships to which it has granted the right to fly its flag documents to that effect."

This is really no more than what was already contained in Article 5 of the Geneva Convention on the High Seas 1958 which predated UNCLOS III.

6.032 Article 94 of UNCLOS III deals more particularly with the duties of the flag State. It reads:

"1. Every State shall effectively exercise its jurisdiction and control in administrative, technical and social matters over ships flying its flag.
2. In particular every State shall:

    (a) maintain a register of ships containing the names and particulars of ships flying its flag, except those which are excluded from generally accepted international regulations on account of their small size; and

---

51 The European Parliament's Committee on Transport published a report on the Commission's proposal for a Council decision on the common position to be adopted by Member States when signing and ratifying the United Nations Convention on Conditions for the Registration of Ships (COM(86)523 final); Doc. A2-53/88; Rapporteur: Mr D Romera I Alcazar.
52 I.e. UNCLOS III.
53 Burns, "Registration of EC Vessels: Offshore, International or Euroregistry", at *The Future of Shipping in Europe: Key Legal and Commercial Issues*, London, 28–29 June 1990, p. 5.
54 E.g. Luxembourg.

(b) assume jurisdiction under its internal law over each ship flying its flag and its master, officers and crew in respect of the administrative, technical and social matters concerning the ship.

3. Every State shall take such measures for ships flying its flag as are necessary to ensure safety at sea with regard, *inter alia*, to:

   (a) the construction, equipment and seaworthiness of ships;
   (b) the manning of ships, labour conditions, and the training of crews, taking into account the applicable international instruments;
   (c) the use of signals, the maintenance of communications and the prevention of collisions.

4. Such measures shall include those necessary to ensure:

   (a) that each ship, before registration and thereafter at appropriate intervals, is surveyed by a qualified surveyor of ships, and has on board such charts, nautical publications and navigational equipment and instruments as are appropriate for the safe navigation of the ship;
   (b) that each ship is in the charge of a master and officers who possess appropriate qualifications, in particular in seamanship, navigation, communications and marine engineering, and that the crew is appropriate in qualification and numbers for the type, size, machinery and equipment of the ship;
   (c) that the master, officers and, to the extent appropriate, the crew are fully conversant with and required to observe the applicable international regulations concerning the safety of life at sea, the prevention of collisions, the prevention, reduction and control of marine pollution, and the maintenance of communications by radio.

5. In taking measures called for in paragraphs 3 and 4 each State is required to conform to generally accepted international regulations, procedures and practices and to take any steps which may be necessary to secure their observance.

6. A State which has clear grounds to believe that proper jurisdiction and control with respect to a ship have not been exercised may report the facts to the flag State. Upon receiving such a report, the flag State shall investigate the matter and, if appropriate, take any action necessary to remedy the situation.

7. Each State shall cause an inquiry to be held by or before a suitably qualified person or persons into every marine casualty or incident of navigation on the high seas involving a ship flying its flag and causing loss of life or serious injury to nationals of another State or serious damage to ships or installations of another State or to the marine environment. The flag State and the other State shall co-operate in the conduct of any inquiry held by that other State into any such marine casualty or incident of navigation."

United Nations Convention on the Registration of Ships 1986

6.033 The UNCTAD's Committee on Shipping adopted Resolution 22(VI) on Economic Co-operation in Merchant Shipping on 9 August 1974. Paragraph 3 of the resolution read:

> "The Committee of Shipping ... [c]onsiders ... that the following matters of shipping policy may also be suitable and ripe for harmonisation: the economic consequences for international shipping of the existence or lack of a genuine link between vessel and flag of registry as explicitly defined in international conventions in force, and requests the UNCTAD secretariat to undertake an examination of this matter as soon as possible."

6.034 Having reviewed the international dimension for the registration of ships, it is now appropriate to review the EU perspective on this important topic.

C. EU PERSPECTIVE ON REGISTRATION OF SHIPS

Introduction

6.035 Many EU-based shipowners are flagging out their ships on various registries. Traditionally, there were no specific EU rules on registration generally, but the general rules of EU law apply with appropriate modifications. There can be no restrictions based on discrimination between nationals of the EU in matters falling within the remit of EU law.[55] This applies, in particular, to the freedom of establishment. Yet the registries of most of the Member States discriminate against foreigners (including EU nationals) in some way or other, for example, the historical rule that more than one-half of a ship had to be British-owned before it could be registered on the British registry.[56] A similar rule existed in France and Belgium. Other Member States require offices, shareholders, directors or principal places of business to be in the State of registration. These restrictions, in so far as they discriminate between an EU Member State's own nationals and the nationals of another EU Member State, are illegal under EU law in respect of matters covered by EU law. The Commission, the institution charged with the task of enforcing EU law, has been more vigilant in bringing to task the Member States which impose such illegal restrictions. In 1986, Sir James Scott-Hopkins, a Member of the European Parliament for the UK, asked the Commission the following question:

> "[D]oes the Commission not agree that legislation is needed, as a matter of urgency, to enable Member States to co-ordinate the policing of abuses such as the use of flags of convenience to employ sub-standard ships and inadequately trained and underpaid crews?"[57]

The then Transport Commissioner Stanley Clinton Davies responded:

> "As far as the use of open registry shipping is concerned the Member States coordinate, on the basis of Commission proposals and using the consultation procedure set up in 1977,[58] their position together with other states of Group B in the UNCTAD Conference on registration of ships, which has just held its final session in Geneva. The aim is to strengthen the link between ship and flag in order to eliminate abuses of using open registries. The Commission, which shares the Honourable Member's concerns in this field, has given its full support to all the international measures designed to eliminate the abuses associated with some of the open registry fleets.
>
> In addition Member States have coordinated their efforts to eliminate sub-standard shipping and to check on the adequacy of crews through the Memorandum on Port State Control signed in Paris in January 1982. The Memorandum was based on the Commission's proposed directive of June 1980.[59] The Memorandum will be revised at a Ministerial meeting in The Hague in April 1986. In the Commission's view, Port State Control has proved an increasingly effective means of dealing with the problems mentioned by the Honourable Member, particularly in view of the controls undertaken with respect to the IMO Convention on Standards of Seafarers' Training. As the Memorandum is applied also by non-Member States further legislation and in particular Community legislation does not at present seem necessary or appropriate."

---

55 Art. 18 TFEU provides: "[w]ithin the scope of the application of the Treaties, and without prejudice to any special provisions contained therein, any discrimination on grounds of nationality shall be prohibited."
56 Merchant Shipping Act, 1988.
57 Written Question No 1955/85.
58 OJ L239 of 17 September 1977.
59 OJ C192/8, 30 July 1980.

EU reaction to the UN Convention on the Registration of Ships 1986

Commission's communication

6.036 Having reviewed the UN Convention, it is now more appropriate to look more specifically at how the EU reacted to that convention.

6.037 On 25 September 1986, the Commission sent to the Council: (a) a Communication on the United Nations Convention on Conditions for the Registration of Ships; and (b) a Proposal for a Council Decision on the Common Position to be adopted by Member States when signing and ratifying the United Nations Convention on Conditions for the Registration of Ships.[60]

6.038 During the negotiations in Geneva on the convention, the European Commission alerted the Member States of the EU that there was a discrepancy between the UN Convention and the then EC Treaty. Articles 8, 9 and 10 of the convention conflicted with certain provisions of then EC Treaty. These incompatibilities are discussed in the next three paragraphs. The Commission's objections were not taken into account by the negotiating parties and the Commission then informed the Member States that, in the absence of a textual guarantee of compatibility between the convention and the provisions of the then EC Treaty, they were debarred under EU law from signing or ratifying the convention. The Dutch delegation, representing the Member States present at the Conference, informed the States gathered at the Conference that the Member States could not sign the convention. The Commission followed this statement by informing the Member States by way of a letter on 4 March 1986 to the effect that no Member State should sign the convention until an agreed form of reservation for Member States had been agreed. The Commission was thus of the view that the Member States could enforce the convention in a manner consistent with their obligations under EU law if, and only if, they make an appropriately worded reservation when signing and ratifying the convention.

6.039 Article 8 of the convention relates to ownership of ships. It provides:

"*Ownership of Ships*
1. Subject to the provisions of Article 7, the flag State shall provide in its laws and regulations for the ownership of ships flying its flag.
2. Subject to the provisions of Article 7, in such laws and regulations the flag State shall include appropriate provisions for participation by that State or its nationals as owners of ships flying its flag or in the ownership of such ships and for the level of such participation. These laws and regulations should be sufficient to permit the flag State to exercise effectively its jurisdiction and control over ships flying its flag."

It is believed that this provision is contrary to provisions in the TFEU that there should be no discrimination on grounds of nationality,[61] and there should be freedom of establishment and free movement of capital.

6.040 Article 9 of the convention relates to hiring of crews. It provides:

"*Manning of Ships*
1. Subject to the provisions of Article 7, a State of registration, when implementing this Convention, shall observe the principle that a satisfactory part of the complement consisting of officers and crew of ships flying its flag be nationals or persons domiciled or lawfully in permanent residence in that State.

---

60 COM(86)523 final.
61 Now see TFEU, Art. 18.

2. Subject to the provisions of Article 7 and in pursuance of the goal set out in paragraph 1 of this Article, and in taking necessary steps to this end, the State of registration shall have regard to the following:

   a. the availability of qualified seafarers within the State of registration;
   b. multilateral or bilateral agreements or other types of arrangements valid and enforceable pursuant to the legislation of the State of registration;
   c. the sound and economically viable operation of its ships.

3. The State of registration should implement the provision of paragraph 1 of this Article on a ship, company or fleet basis.
4. The State of registration, in accordance with its laws and regulations, may allow persons of other nationalities to serve on board ships flying its flag in accordance with the relevant provisions of this Convention.
5. In pursuance of the goal set out in paragraph 1 of this Article, the State of registration should, in accordance with shipowners, promote the education and training of its nationals or persons domiciled or lawfully in permanent residence within its territory.
6. The State of registration shall ensure:

   a. that the manning of ships flying its flag is of such a level and competence as to ensure compliance with applicable international rules and standards, in particular those regarding safety at sea;
   b. that the terms and conditions of employment on board ships flying its flag are in conformity with applicable international rules and standards;
   c. that adequate legal procedures exist for the settlement of civil disputes between seafarers employed on ships flying its flag and their employers;
   d. that nationals and foreign seafarers have equal access to appropriate legal processes to secure their contractual rights in their relations with their employers."

It was believed that this provision is contrary to the provisions on free movement of workers in the TFEU.

6.041 Article 10 of the convention relates to the role of flag States in the management of shipowning companies. It provides:

"Role of Flag States in respect of the Management of Shipowning Companies and Ships
1. The State of registration, before entering a ship in its register of ships, shall ensure that the shipowning company or a subsidiary shipowning company is established and/or has its principal place of business within its territory in accordance with its laws and regulations.
2. Where the shipowning company or a subsidiary shipowning company or the principal place of business of the shipowning company is not established in the flag State, the latter shall ensure, before entering a ship in its register of ships, that there is a representative or management person who shall be a national of the flag State, or be domiciled therein. Such a representative or management person may be a natural or juridical person who is duly established or incorporated in the flag State, as the case may be, in accordance with its laws and regulations, and duly empowered to act on the shipowner's behalf and account. In particular, this representative or management person should be available for any legal process and to meet the shipowner's responsibilities in accordance with the laws and regulations of the State of registration.
3. The State of registration should ensure that the person or persons accountable for the management and operation of a ship flying its flag are in a position to meet the financial obligations that may arise from the operation of such a ship to cover risks which are normally insured in international maritime transportation in respect of damage to third parties. To this end the State of registration should ensure that ships flying its flag are in a position to provide at all times documents evidencing that an adequate guarantee, such as appropriate insurance or any other equivalent means, has been arranged. Furthermore, the State of

registration should ensure that an appropriate mechanism, such as a maritime lien, mutual fund, wage insurance, social security scheme, or any governmental guarantee provided by an appropriate agency of the State of the accountable person, whether that person is an owner or operator, exists to cover wages and related moneys owed to seafarers employed on ships flying its flag in the event of default of payment by their employers. The State of registration may also provide for any other appropriate mechanism to that effect in its laws and regulations."

It was believed that this provision is contrary to the provisions on the freedom of establishment in the TFEU.

6.042 The Commission proposed the following reservation:

"[The Member State concerned] will apply Articles 8, 9 and 10 [of the UN Convention] in conformity with its obligations under the Treaty establishing the European Economic Community, and in particular with those requiring equal treatment of the nationals of the Member States of the Community."

As of 1 April 1991, the Council had still not acted on the proposal. However, in case the Council does act then a review of the communication and the proposed decision would be useful at this juncture.

Commission's proposal

6.043 To understand the background fully, it is useful to study an extract of the Commission's communication:

"1. In order to eliminate abuses of ship regulations that may become possible through the failure of flag States to meet their international obligations, the Commission fully supports the adoption of measures which aim at strengthening the link between ship and flag State. However, during the conference which led to the [Registration] Convention, the Commission made it clear to the Member States of the Community that they would not be free under Community law to sign or ratify the Convention unless they obtained a clause which rendered the Convention compatible with the EEC Treaty or found another equivalent solution.
2. COREPER[62] decided unanimously on 7 February 1986 that the text of the clause for this purpose which was being negotiated at Geneva was not acceptable as it did not meet the requirements of Community law. It made certain suggestions for the improvement of the clause, but added that if a satisfactory clause could not be negotiated, the delegation holding the Presidency [of the Council of Ministers] should make a declaration on behalf of the Member States to the effect that they would only be able to sign the Convention in conformity with the EEC Treaty. In Geneva the delegations of the Member States decided that they would not be able to renegotiate a satisfactory Community clause. The clause was, accordingly, withdrawn and the Dutch delegation made a declaration on the lines laid down by COREPER.
3. Following the conclusion of the conference at Geneva and the adoption of the text of the Convention, the Commission sent a letter of 4 March 1986 to the Member States. The letter pointed out that the conference had ended without it having been determined whether, and if so how, the Convention could be reconciled with the obligations of Member States under Community law. The letter confirmed that the Commission considered that it would be contrary to the obligations of the Member States under the EEC Treaty for them to sign or ratify the Convention without an appropriate reservation. The letter asked the Member States, therefore, to do nothing that could prejudice a final approach to be adopted by the Council

---

62 This is the Committee of the Permanent Representatives (i.e. ambassadors from the Member States to the EU).

[of Ministers] and in particular that the Member States should not sign the Convention until the Council had decided on a common form of reservation to be used by all Member States when signing and ratifying the Convention.

4. The problem of incompatibility between the Convention and the EEC Treaty arises essentially because the Convention requires that:

– the State where a ship is registered must ensure *either* that there is a sufficient participation by its nationals as owners of ships flying its flag or in the ownership of such ships (Article 8) *or* that a satisfactory part of the complement of ships flying its flag consists of officers and crew who are nationals or persons domiciled or lawfully in permanent residence (Article 9);

– the State of registration must ensure that the shipowning company or a subsidiary is established and/or has its principal place of business within its territory and makes further provision for a representative presence (Article 10).

5. Article 8 (ownership) and Article 9 (manning) are alternatives. For those Member States which wish to comply with Article 8, however, the problem arises of reconciling its provisions with the principle of non-discrimination on the ground of nationality (Article 7 of the EEC Treaty),[63] the right of establishment (Articles 52 to 58)[64] and the principle of the free movement of capital (Articles 67 to 73 of the EEC Treaty).[65] For those Member States which wish to comply with the manning provisions of Article 9, the problem arises of reconciling those provisions with the principle of the free movement of workers (Articles 48 to 51 of the EEC Treaty).[66] Finally, Article 10(1) raises questions with respect to the right of establishment (Articles 52 to 58 of the EEC Treaty).[67]

6. As the Commission has pointed out on several occasions these problems necessitated common action by the Member States in order to find a solution. The preferred solution from a Community point of view, given that it was impossible to improve the wording of the Articles in question, would have been a satisfactorily worded clause, which preserved the rights of the Member States to observe their obligations under the EEC Treaty. Another way of achieving the same degree of legal security would have been the negotiation of a protocol of signature to the same effect. Unfortunately neither of these results was achieved.

7. In order to find a solution to the problem which the Community and the Member States now face it becomes necessary to look in some detail at the Articles of the Convention in question. As regards Article 8 (ownership) the Commission notes that the Convention contains no rules on how the concept of nationality shall be defined for the purposes of the application of its provisions. It also notes that the purpose of the ownership provision is to permit the flag State to exercise effectively its jurisdiction and control over ships flying its flag. In the circumstances the Commission considers that Member States, which wish to apply the provisions of Article 8, should do so in applying the extended definition of nationality provided by the EEC Treaty for economic activities coming within its scope. Given the institutional and legal framework of the Community this will not weaken the jurisdiction and control exercised over the ship. A similar approach may be applied in respect of the manning provisions in Article 9. In addition to the arguments mentioned above, it is to be noted that Article 9(2)(b) [of the Convention] allows the State of registration to have regard to multilateral agreements and also that Article 9(4) provides that it may allow persons of other nationalities to serve on board ships flying its flag. Article 10(1) requires the State of registration, before entering a ship on its register, to ensure that the shipowning company or a subsidiary shipowning company is established and/or has its principal place of business within its territory in accordance with its laws and regulations. The Commission considers that it is legitimate to interpret this provision as meaning that the concept of establishment may be interpreted, as far as the Member States are concerned, in accordance with the

---

63 Ed., see chap. 3. Now Art. 18 of the TFEU.
64 Ed., see chap. 3. Now Arts 49–55 of the TFEU.
65 Ed., see chap. 3. Now Arts 63–66 of the TFEU.
66 Ed., see chap. 3. Now Arts 45–48 of the TFEU
67 Ed., see chap. 3. Now Arts 49–55 of the TFEU.

relevant law, that is to say Articles 52 to 58 of the EEC Treaty.[68] On the basis of this approach the application of Article 10 [of the Convention] and the relevant Treaty provisions may be reconciled.

8. In accordance with the above analysis, the Commission considers that Member States can apply the Convention in such a way as to comply with their obligations under Community law, if, but only if, they make a common reservation in appropriate terms, when they sign and ratify this Convention.
9. Under Article 19 of the Vienna Convention [on the Law of Treaties], a State may, when signing or ratifying a treaty, formulate a reservation, in a case other than where reservations are prohibited or only specified reservations are allowed, if the reservation is compatible with the object and purpose of the Treaty. For the reasons explained in paragraph 7 the Commission considers that, to the extent that the common act should be regarded as a reservation, it may be strongly argued that it is compatible with the object and purpose of the Convention on conditions for the registration of ships.
10. It is to be noted, moreover, that reservations may be accepted by other contracting States. Acceptance may be either made expressly or implicitly. In the latter case silence for a period of 12 months suffices. However, a contracting party may object to a reservation and may prevent the Convention from entering into force as between it and the State making the reservation. On the other hand, where the objecting State has not opposed the entry into force of the Treaty between itself and the reserving State, the provisions to which the reservation relates do not apply as between the two States to the extent of the reservation (Articles 20 and 21 of the Vienna Convention).
11. It is inherent in the nature of the common action which must now be adopted, in the absence of a more legally secure solution, that there will be a risk of objection. The Commission would not expect this risk to be serious given:

    – the interests which third countries have in the participation of Member States in the Convention, taking into account the importance of the Member States' fleets in world shipping;
    – the preparatory work to alert the contracting parties to the Member State's obligations under the EEC Treaty, including the declarations made at the Conference at the time of the adoption of the Convention (ref. para. 2 above),
    – the arguments which justify the statement on the basis of the particular obligations of the Member States arising from the Treaty, and
    – the rather unattractive results to an objecting State of an objection.

    Whatever the assessment of the risk, however, it is a risk that cannot be avoided.
12. To give effect to the approach described above, the Commission proposes the annexed Council Decision. This proposal is, in effect, that the Council should adopt a decision whereby on signing and ratifying the Convention, the Member States will be obliged to make a reservation in the following terms:
    '[The Member State concerned] will apply Articles 8, 9 and 10 in conformity with its obligations under the Treaty establishing the European Economic Community, and in particular with those requiring equal treatment of the nationals of the Member States of the Community.'

    The Commission wishes to make it clear, moreover, that for a Member State to sign or become a party to the Convention without making an appropriate common reservation would be a violation of Community law, and the Commission would use the possibilities provided by Articles 169 and 186 of the EEC Treaty[69] to prevent this, if necessary.

    If the Convention does not receive enough ratification to bring it into force, or if, contrary to expectations, there are substantial objections to Member States signing and ratifying it on

---

68 Ed., now Arts 49–55 of the TFEU.
69 Ed., see chap. 3. Now Arts 258 and 279 of the TFEU

European Parliament's report

6.044 On 18 May 1988, the European Parliament's Committee on Transport published a report on the Commission's proposal for a Council decision on the common position to be adopted by Member States when signing and ratifying the United Nations Convention on Conditions for the Registration of Ships (COM(86)523 final).[70]

D. TRANSFER OF SHIPS BETWEEN EU MEMBER STATE REGISTRIES: REGULATION 613/91 (NOW REPEALED)

Introduction

6.045 It is useful to consider two measures which recognised the reality of national registers and provides a mechanism to facilitate the transfer of ships between Member State registers. It was often very difficult to transfer ships from one national register to another. This part, Part D, deals with the repealed Regulation 613/91 while Part E deals with the current regulation regime (namely Regulation 789/2004).

6.046 On 1 June 1990, the Commission published its Proposal for a Council Regulation on the Transfer of Ships from one Register to another within the Community.[71] It was adopted as Regulation 613/91 on 4 March 1991.[72] Regulation 613/91 was repealed by Regulation 789/2004 of the European Parliament and of the Council of 21 April 2004 on the transfer of cargo and passenger ships between registers within the Community and repealing Council Regulation 613/91.[73]

6.047 Such a measure was very much needed. It was problematical as well as expensive to transfer ships from a register in one Member State to another because of the different national rules relating to such matters as safety, pollution and so on. States did not generally recognise certificates relating to local requirements issued by each other. These different national rules existed – despite the existence of international conventions – for two reasons: first, such conventions often allow considerable unharmonised discretion to the State parties; and, second, some States impose rules over and above the rules laid down in the conventions. The net effects of such rules are: first, the need for tests and surveys to be conducted when a ship was transferring registry so as to ensure that the ship could be re-registered; second, new equipment which may not be any better but did meet the transferee State's requirements had, on occasion, to be purchased; third, equipment sometimes had to be modified to meet the transferee State's requirements. The Commission has commented that the

> "delays and additional costs to the shipowner arising from these formalities are reflected in the ship's operating costs. It is obvious that such practices are not in accordance with the aims of the

---

70 See Doc. A2-53/88. Rapporteur: Mr D Romera I Alcazar.
71 COM(90)219 final, C3-0186/90, 1 June 1990.
72 OJ 1991 L68/1.
73 OJ 2004 L138/19.

Single Market. Moreover, the shipping industry has long since sought the abolition of these obstacles to trade in ships."[74]

6.048 In its Competitiveness and Employment Impact Statement accompanying the proposal, the Commission was of the opinion that the proposed measures would not impose any additional obligations on businesses directly and there would be no indirect obligations on businesses imposed by national, regional or local authorities.[75] In fact, the Commission believed that the competitiveness of EU shipping would be enhanced through the elimination of unnecessary costs involved in the transfer of ships.[76]

Background to the Proposal

6.049 The Commission, in its communication "A Future for the Community Shipping Industry",[77] identified the need to facilitate the transfer of ships from one register to another. The Commission was of the opinion that the facilitation of such transfer would improve the operating conditions for EU shipping.[78] The Commission wrote:

> "[a]s a parallel measure to setting up a Community Register, the Commission advocated the mutual recognition of ships' technical equipment on the basis of the 'new approach' to technical harmonisation and standardisation adopted by the Council[79] having regard to IMO[80] Conventions.
>
> The Commission considers that, without prejudice to the safety standards laid down at international level or to the general level of maritime safety, no technical requirements should be imposed which would impede the transfer of a Community-registered vessel from one Community shipowner or flag to another. Consequently, the Commission has suggested that, during the period of time required to set up the Community Register, steps should be taken to abolish nationally imposed technical standards.
>
> Accordingly, in its proposal for the establishment of a Community Register, the Commission proposed that any vessel for which classification documents and certificates have been issued and which complies with the basic technical standards to be adopted by the Council before 1 July 1991, as provided for in the Treaty, may be transferred to the register of another Member State without having to comply with additional technical requirements."[81]

6.050 The Commission had earlier written in a very interesting passage:

> "At present, if a ship is transferred from one Community register to another, it tends to be re-examined by the regulatory authorities responsible for ship safety and it is by no means uncommon for the new owner to be required to replace equipment already certified by the authorities of the original flag state. This happens because the regulatory authorities tend to have their own lists of approved equipment which owe as much to a wish to erect non-tariff barriers in favour of their own equipment industry as they do to the needs of safety. In the Commission's view this

---

74 *Proposal*, Explanatory Memorandum, p. 1. The Preamble to the proposed Regulation thus provides: "measures to facilitate the transfer of ships within the Community are required to free European shipowners from unnecessary costs and administrative procedures involved in a change of register within the Community and also to improve the operating conditions and the competitive position of Community shipping".
75 Explanatory Memorandum to the proposed Regulation, p. 14.
76 Ibid., p. 14.
77 COM(89) 266 final, 3 August 1989.
78 According to the August 1989 document: "A Future for the Community Shipping Industry: Measures to Improve the Operating Conditions of Community Shipping".
79 Council Regulation of 7 May 1985 (OJ 1985 C138).
80 Ed., the International Maritime Organisation.
81 *Proposal*, Explanatory Memorandum, p. 2. Footnote omitted.

places an unnecessary burden on shipowners. It will, therefore, following up on an idea developed by Germany, establish a Community-wide list of approved equipment as meeting IMO standards, and it will propose a Directive to the effect that ships registered under Community flags may be equipped with any of the items contained on that list. It will not itself seek to approve or disapprove such equipment; this function should remain with the regulatory authorities of the Member States who have the responsibility for implementing the relevant international conventions in pursuance of which the equipment is certified."[82]

6.051 The Council at its meeting on 4–5 December 1989 called on the Commission to present a proposal to facilitate transfer of ships between registers, as soon as possible, based on the principles of mutual recognition of existing international standards.[83] The Commission now believes that the best way of meeting the Council's request is through the means of a short and general regulation.[84]

6.052 In its Explanatory Memorandum to the Proposal, the Commission declared that it:

"is aware that the full free movement of goods will only be reached through the principle of technical harmonisation of ship equipment and certification as defined in the ... 'new approach'. The Commission is of the opinion that in the meantime a first and positive step in this direction could be reached through the proposed procedure allowing for the free transfer of ships within the Community.

Starting from the principle of compliance with the international Conventions on safety and the prevention of marine pollution, the Commission proposes mutual recognition of the safety level attested to by international certificates when a vessel flying the flag of a Member State of the Community is re-registered in another Member State. Where the vessel concerned complies with international standards, the Member States should undertake not to impose their national technical regulations which sometimes differ from those laid down in international conventions."

6.053 It is interesting to note that the Commission, in the Preamble to the proposed regulation, draws a connection between the facilitation of the transfer of ships and the completion of the internal market. It wrote:

"[w]hereas the establishment and functioning of the internal market involves the elimination of technical barriers to the transfer of ships between the national registers while safeguarding a high level of safety of ships and environmental protection in conformity with international regulations".

Legislative history

6.054 The European Parliament's Committee on Transport and Tourism in its report[85] on the Commission proposal stated:

"1. The transfer of a ship from the register of one Member State to the register of another currently entails a number of difficulties. Member States do not normally recognize certificates issued by other Member States.

---

82 Commission to the Council on *Progress towards a Common Transport Policy: Maritime Transport*, COM (85)90 final (TRA/116), para. 97. It is interesting on several levels: the erection of non-tariff barriers by some States but that the Commission believed itself powerless to deal with the issue; the desire by Germany to have a larger and freer market for its products; and the recognition of the role of the Member States.
83 Conclusions of the Council Meeting of 4–5 December 1989.
84 Explanatory Memorandum to the Proposed Regulation, p. 4.
85 Doc. A3-0345/90 (Rapporteur: Mrs Ursula Braun-Moser).

2. The technical standards required by the Member States for safety and environmental reasons are based on the current conventions (the IMO standards) but often differ on questions of detail, partly because the scope for interpreting and assessing international standards is exercised differently by the Member States, partly because for various reasons a number of Member States lay down additional technical requirements. In its proposal for a regulation setting up a Community ship register,[86] the Commission proposed that the Council shall take a decision on the harmonisation of technical standards by 1 July 1991.
3. In these circumstances the straightforward and practical solution would seem to be to facilitate the transfer of a ship from one register to another by mutual recognition of certificates issued by the Member States. This is in keeping with the Council's new approach to technical harmonisation and standardisation[87] and does not entail any safety problems, as it complies with IMO standards on all points.
4. Article 1(c) of the Commission proposal takes into account the fact that the job of issuing the required government certificates has largely been handed over to non-governmental classification societies. For historical reasons, these societies have taken over both the classification proper, that is, guaranteeing the strength of the hull and the reliability of the engines, and the issuing of maritime safety certificates on behalf of the government.
5. There must, however, be some means of ensuring that the classification companies to which government duties have been transferred meet the same requirements throughout the Community in order to guarantee that work vital to maritime safety continues to be of high quality. In particular, classification companies should have sufficient experience of and experience in carrying out technical inspections and a worldwide net of surveyors and should be capable of devising and administering recognized technical rules."

6.055 The Economic and Social Committee (or "EESC") issued its unanimous opinion on 18 December 1990.[88] The body of its opinion stated:

"*4. General Comments*

4.1 The Committee endorses the Commission proposal, since it clearly facilitates the extension of the single market to the shipping industry. It also addresses questions relating to compatibility with safety and environment-orientated action.
4.2 The process of liberalization is not, however, entirely without problems.

4.2.1 The Commission proposal would, in the medium-term, appear to run counter to the ESC approach. The proposal envisages mutual recognition of certificates until such times as Community requirements are laid down. The ESC has however stated its preference for Community recognition of international standards.
4.2.2 The Committee of course endorses the position expressed in earlier Opinions, adding that international standards should be adopted in such a way that no Community Member State applying particularly high standards of work-place safety should be compelled to lower them.

The Committee also considers that in cutting costs, care must be taken not to compromise safety considerations or generate environmental hazards, at either the national or Community level.

To this end, the Community should, within the international organizations, lobby for the fulfilment of such requirements. If this objective is to be secured, regulations and national responsibilities must be clarified, so as to avoid differences of interpretation.

In any case, and in line with the Committee's stated views, steps should be taken to enhance safety conditions at national level.

---

86 COM(89)266 final – the Sarlis Report.
87 Resolution of 7 May 1985, OJ C136, 4 June 1985.
88 TRA/202.

4.2.3 The Committee notes the exclusion of passenger vessels and urges the Commission to propose, as soon as possible, a regulation permitting the free transfer of such vessels while ensuring a high level of safety.

4.2.4 The Committee also agrees with the establishment of a committee of experts, but would wish to see consultative machinery similar to that set up by the IMO, involving employers, trade unions, conservationists and consumers, for the resolution of safety issues."

6.056 The European Parliament also delivered a favourable opinion.[89]

Relationship between the regulation and other rules

6.057 The Commission stressed in its Explanatory Memorandum to the proposed regulation that the proposal for the regulation is without prejudice to: (a) the application by the Member States of the International Maritime Organization or other international conventions; (b) the application of EU rules pursuant to existing or subsequent legislation; and (c) the role of the IMO in drafting and interpreting international conventions on safety and the prevention of marine pollution.

Legal bases of the regulation

6.058 The legal basis of the regulation was the EC Treaty generally but also, in particular, Article 84(2)[90] thereof. This means that in the light of the amendment made to Article 84(2)[91] of the EC Treaty by Article 16(5) of the Single European Act that the Council needed only a qualified majority to adopt the regulation. It was duly adopted.

Interpretation

6.059 Article 1 of the regulation was merely an interpretative provision. It defined, for the purposes of the regulation, three terms, namely, "conventions", "requirements" and "certificates".

6.060 The regulation defines "conventions" as meaning three conventions (as well as their related resolutions[92] adopted by the IMO),[93] namely: (a) the 1974 International Convention for the Safety of Life at Sea (1974 "SOLAS"); (b) the International Convention on Load Lines 1966 ("LL66"); (c) the International Convention for the Prevention of Pollution from Ships 1973 (as modified by its 1978 Protocol ("MARPOL" 73/78)). These conventions are read (as amended) on 4 March 1991 together with related resolutions of mandatory status adopted by the IMO. Article 1(a) of the regulation provided that without prejudice to the procedures for amending the conventions, the application, for the purposes of this regulation, of subsequent amendments thereto which have entered into force shall be decided upon in accordance with the provisions laid down in Article 7 of the regulation.

---

89 OJ C19, 28 January 1991.
90 On Art. 84(2), see chap. 4. This is now effectively Art. 100(2) TFEU.
91 On Art. 84(2), see chap. 4.
92 Resolutions, in this context, do not have the same meaning as the term in EU law.
93 On the IMO, see chap. 1.

6.061 The term "requirements" when used in the regulation meant "the safety and pollution prevention requirements as laid down in the Conventions".[94]

6.062 In the context of the regulation, the term "certificates" meant

"certificates issued by or on behalf of a Member State in accordance with the Conventions as well as certificates issued for chemical tankers and gas carriers built before 1 July 1986, in accordance with the Bulk Chemical Code [IMO Resolution A.212 (VIII)] or the Bulk Gas Code [IMO Resolution A.328 (IX)]".[95]

Application of the regulation

6.063 Article 2 of the regulation provided:

"This Regulation shall apply to cargo ships of 500 grt gross tonnage and upwards which:

(a) were built on or after 25 May 1980, or were built before that date, but:
compliance of which the requirements for new ships defined in the 1974 Solas Convention and in the case of chemical tankers and gas carriers, compliance with the standards codes referred to in Article 1(c) for ships built on or after 25 May 1980, is certified by or on behalf of a Member State and
(b) have been flying the flag of, and registered in, a Member State, and in active service under that flag for at least six months; and
(c) carrying valid certificates."

6.064 In its Explanatory Memorandum to the proposed regulation, the Commission commented:

"The Commission, supported by government experts, considers that passenger ships should not, at this stage, be covered by this Regulation, in view of their distinctive features and their uses: they are often constructed to meet additional requirements other than those laid down in the international conventions since they have to sail in waters affected by particular weather conditions. Furthermore, where these vessels (especially the older ones) are concerned, there are differences in the way in which the conventions are interpreted, particularly as regards the structural rules on fire protection and accident prevention, health and hygiene. Nevertheless the Commission undertakes to examine as soon as possible with the experts the possibility of including passenger vessels in the scope of the regulation, offering all the necessary guarantees on the safety level."[96]

6.065 The Explanatory Memorandum[97] stated:

"Since application of the SOLAS (1974), LL66 and MARPOL 73/78 Conventions ensures a high level of maritime safety and prevention of pollution by ships which is acceptable within the Community and without prejudice to the application of other international conventions and Community rules, the recognition of certificates is limited to the abovementioned Conventions.

The tonnage limit is that laid down in the Conventions in respect of cargo vessels providing international transport services.

The introduction of an age limit and a requirement that vessels be covered by valid certificates will help to increase the level of safety at sea and the prevention of marine pollution within the Community. Passenger liners are excluded on the grounds of their distinctive characteristics. The conditions governing registration mean that only vessels flying the flag of a Member State of the

---

94 Art. 1.
95 Art. 1.
96 Proposed Regulation, Explanatory Memorandum, p. 3.
97 Ibid., p. 5.

Community can reap the benefit of this Regulation and ensure that standards of safety and pollution prevention are complied with before transfer."

Obligation on Member State to register

6.066 Article 3 of the regulation embodied the general obligation on the other Member State to register a ship (within the meaning of Article 1 of the regulation) which was being transferred from another registry. Article 3 provided:

> "1. Member States shall not withhold from registration, for technical reasons arising from the Conventions, a cargo ship registered in another Member State complying with the requirements and carrying valid certificates and fittings and equipment approved or type-approved in the ship's country of origin.
>
> In so far as on the date of entry into force of this Regulation they are bound by regional agreements for the protection of the marine environment, Member States may impose additional rules which conform with the requirements of the optional annexes to the Conventions.
> 2. Upon the transfer of the ship, the receiving flag Member State shall issue certificates under the same conditions as under the flag previously flown.
> 3. Where the certificates are issued by an organization on behalf of a Member State, the latter must ensure that the qualifications, technical experience and staffing of the said organization are such as will enable it, in applying the Conventions, to issue certificates guaranteeing a high level of safety.
>
> The organization must be in a position to develop and update rules and regulations having the quality of accepted technical standards, and must operate with qualified and experienced surveyors so as adequately to assess a ship's condition.
> 4. Nevertheless, on transfer, a ship may be subjected to inspection by the receiving flag Member State to confirm that the actual condition of the ship and its equipment corresponds with its certificates and with the statements of compliance referred to in Article 2(a)."

6.067 Under Article 3(1) of the regulation, Member States would not have been entitled to withhold from registration a cargo ship[98] registered in another EU Member State complying with the requirements and carrying valid certificates. However, Member States parties to the Convention on the Protection of the Marine Environment in the Baltic Sea area may have imposed such additional requirements as provided for in that convention. Any new certificates issued would be on the same basis.

6.068 It would however be wrong to imagine that the transfer of a ship from a registry in a Member State to another registry would be entirely straightforward. Article 3(3) provided a minor sting in the tail to Article 3(1). Article 3(3) provided that, on transfer, a ship may be subjected to inspection by the receiving Member State to confirm that the actual condition of the ship and its equipment corresponded with its certificates.

6.069 The Commission in its Explanatory Memorandum to the proposed regulation wrote:

> "The non-application of national technical rules, combined with an acceptable level of safety and pollution prevention, makes it easier for vessels which comply with international standards to be transferred from one register to another within the Community without barriers to trade. The

---

98 Such a cargo ship would be a ship of 500 grt gross tonnage and upwards which will be: (a) built on or after 25 May 1980 or built before that date but certified by a Member State as complying with the regulations for new ships as defined in the 1974 SOLAS Convention; (b) flying the flag of, and registered in, a Member State and in active service under that flag; and (c) carrying valid certificates.

issue of new certificates include the acceptance of the interpretations and methods of implementation of the conventions of other Member States made for the purposes of the ships' design and equipment, in so far as they are in compliance with the provisions of the conventions, and of the approvals of particular fittings, materials, appliances or apparatuses, or type thereof, fitted on board the ship. The national governments are responsible for issuing the international certificates relating to the safety of, and the prevention of pollution by vessels and their equipment. The Member State to whose register the vessel is being transferred should retain a limited right of inspection in order to ensure that vessels flying the flag of a Member State of the Community meet with the standard of safety and prevention of marine pollution set by the abovementioned conventions."

No additional requirements for certificates

6.070 The regulation incorporates a prohibition on additional requirements being embodied in certificates and thus attempts to ensure compliance with the principles underlying the regulation when the certificates issued pursuant to Article 3 are renewed, extended or revised. Article 4 provided:

"In so far as requirements remain unchanged for existing receiving flag ships, at the times of renewal, extension or revision of the certificates issued under Article 3, Member States shall not impose requirements other than those initially prescribed for the full term certificates."

Divergences of interpretation

6.071 Articles 5 and 7 set up an appeal procedure to safeguard the objectives of the transfer of ships which comply with the international safety and pollution prevention requirements, without barriers to trade and unnecessary costs.

6.072 Article 5 provided:

"1. Member States shall immediately notify to the Commission any refusal to issue new certificates for reasons based on divergences of interpretation of the requirements or of the provisions which the Conventions leave to the discretion of the Parties.
    Unless the Commission is informed of an agreement between the Member States concerned within one month, it shall initiate proceedings in order to take a decision in accordance with the procedure laid down in Article 7.
2. Where a Member State considers that a ship cannot be registered under Article 3 for reasons of serious danger to safety or the environment outside the scope of certificates, registration may be suspended for a period not exceeding three months, and the Member State shall without delay bring the matter before the Commission, giving the reasons therefor. The suspension shall be confirmed or revoked in accordance with the procedure laid down in Article 7."

6.073 Article 7 provided:

"Where the procedure laid down in this article is to be followed, the representative of the Commission shall submit to the committee a draft of the measures to be taken. The committee shall deliver its opinion on the draft within a time limit which the chairman may lay down according to the urgency of the matter. The opinion shall be delivered by the majority laid down in Article 148(2) of the EEC Treaty in the case of decisions which the Council is required to adopt on a proposal from the Commission. The votes of the representatives of the Member States within the committee shall be set out in that Article. The chairman shall not vote.
    The Commission shall adopt the measures envisaged if they are in accordance with the opinion of the committee.

If the measures envisaged are not in accordance with the opinion of the committee, or if no opinion is delivered, the Commission shall, without delay, submit to the Council a proposal relating to the measures to be taken. The Council shall act by a qualified majority.

If, on the expiry of eight weeks from the date of referral to the Council, the Council has not acted, the proposed measures shall be adopted by the Commission."

Committee of maritime experts

6.074 The Commission proposed the establishment of a committee of experts. Article 6 of the regulation provided that the Commission would be assisted by a committee composed of representatives of the Member States and chaired by a representative of the Commission. Its functions were to resolve any conflict of interpretation which might arise from divergences of interpretation of the requirements of the international safety and pollution prevention conventions or recognition of certificates issued by classification societies.

6.075 Article 7 laid down a procedure. It is wiser to cite Article 7 again in its entirety so as to demonstrate the full impact of the procedure:

"Where the procedure defined in this Article is to be followed the representative of the Commission shall submit to the committee a draft of the measures to be taken. The committee shall deliver its opinion on the draft within a time limit which the chairman may lay down according to the urgency of the matter. The opinion shall be delivered by the majority laid down in Article 148(2) of the EEC Treaty in the case of decisions which the Council is required to adopt on a proposal from the Commission. The votes of the representatives of the Member States within the committee shall be weighted in the manner set out in that Article. The Chairman shall not vote.

The Commission shall adopt the measures envisaged if they are in accordance with the opinion of the committee.

If the measures envisaged are not in accordance with the opinion of the committee, or if no opinion is delivered, the Commission shall, without delay, submit to the Council a proposal relating to the measures to be taken. The Council shall act by a qualified majority.

If, on the expiry of eight weeks from the date of referral to the Council, the Council has not acted, the proposed measures shall be adopted by the Commission."

6.076 This procedure was, according to the Commission, in accordance with the Council Decision 87/373 of 13 July 1987 on the exercise by the Commission of implementing powers conferred by the Council of Ministers.[99]

6.077 Article 9 of the regulation stated that the regulation entered into force on 1 January 1992. However, it was repealed by Regulation 789/2004.

E. TRANSFER OF SHIPS BETWEEN EU MEMBER STATE REGISTRIES: REGULATION 789/2004 (CURRENT REGIME)

Introduction

6.078 On 21 April 2004, the European Parliament and the Council adopted Regulation 789/2004 on the transfer of cargo and passenger ships between registers within the Community and repealing Council Regulation 613/91.[100] This regulation has since been

---
99 Explanatory Memorandum to the proposed Regulation, p. 6.
100 OJ 2004 L138/19.

amended by Regulation 219/2009.[101] By virtue of Article 10, Regulation 613/91 was repealed.

6.079 Regulation 789/2004 was amended by Regulation 219/2009 of 11 March 2009.[102] The legal basis was the Treaty establishing the European Community ("TEC") and, in particular, Article 80(2) (which is now Article 100(2) of the TFEU). The legal history included a proposal from the Commission, an opinion of the EESC and a consultation with the Committee of the Regions.

6.080 The background to Regulation 789/2004 was clear from the recitals. The first recital recalled that the establishment and functioning of the internal market involve the elimination of technical barriers to the transfer of cargo and passenger ships between the registers of Member States and measures to facilitate the transfer of cargo and passenger ships within the EU are also required to reduce the costs and administrative procedures involved in a change of register within the EU, thereby improving the operating conditions and the competitive position of EU shipping.

Purpose of Regulation 789/2004

6.081 Article 1 sets out the purpose of the regulation. The article states that the purpose of the regulation is to eliminate technical barriers to the transfer of cargo and passenger ships flying the flag of a Member State between the registers of the Member States while, at the same time, ensuring a high level of ship safety and environmental protection, in accordance with international conventions.

Concepts in Regulation 789/2004

6.082 Article 2 sets out some key definitions for the purposes of the regulation. The term "conventions" means SOLAS 1974, LL66, the 1969 International Convention on Tonnage Measurement of Ships and MARPOL 73/78, in their up-to-date versions, and related codes of mandatory status adopted in the framework of the IMO, together with protocols and amendments thereto in their up-to-date versions. The word "Requirements" means the safety, security and pollution-prevention requirements relating to the construction and equipment of ships laid down in the conventions and, for passenger ships engaged on domestic voyages, those set out in Council Directive 98/18 of 17 March 1998 on safety rules and standards for passenger ships. The word "certificates" means certificates, documents and statements of compliance issued by a Member State or by a recognised organisation on its behalf in accordance with the conventions, and for passenger ships engaged on domestic voyages, those issued in accordance with Article 11 of Directive 98/18. The phrase "passenger ship" means a ship carrying more than 12 passengers. The word "passenger" means every person other than: (i) the master and the members of the crew or other persons employed or engaged in any capacity on board a ship on the business of that ship; and (ii) a child under one year of age. The term "domestic voyage" means a voyage in sea areas from a port of a Member State to the same or another port within that Member State. The phrase "international voyage" means a voyage by sea from

---

101 OJ 2009 L87/109.
102 OJ L2009 L87/109.

a port of a Member State to a port outside that Member State, or conversely a voyage from a port in a Member State to a port outside that Member State. The term "cargo ship" means a ship which is not a passenger ship. The term "recognised organisation" means an organisation recognised in accordance with Article 4 of Directive 94/57.

Scope

6.083 Article 3(1) provides that the regulation shall apply to:

"(a) cargo ships, carrying valid certificates, which:

(i) were built on or after 25 May 1980, or
(ii) were built before that date, but have been certified by a Member State or by a recognised organisation acting on its behalf as complying with the regulations for new ships defined in 1974 SOLAS, or, in the case of chemical tankers and gas carriers, with the relevant Standard codes for ships built on or after 25 May 1980;

(b) passenger ships engaged on domestic and/or international voyages, carrying valid certificates, which:

(i) were built on or after 1 July 1998, or
(ii) were built before that date, but have been certified by a Member State or by a recognised organisation acting on its behalf as complying with the requirements set out for ships built on or after 1 July 1998:

– in Directive 98/18/EC, for ships engaged on domestic voyages,
– in 1974 SOLAS, for ships engaged on international voyages".

Article 3(2) goes on to provide that the regulation shall not apply to:

"(a) ships following delivery after completion of their construction that do not carry valid full-term certificates from the Member State of the losing register;
(b) ships that have been refused access to Member States' ports in accordance with Directive 95/21/EC during the three years preceding application for registration and to ships that have been detained following inspection in the port of a State signatory to the Paris Memorandum of Understanding of 1982 on Port State Control and for reasons relating to the requirements defined in Article 2(b), more than once during the three years preceding application for registration. Member States shall nevertheless give due and timely consideration to applications in respect of such ships;
(c) ships of war or troopships, or other ships owned or operated by a Member State and used only on government non-commercial service;
(d) ships not propelled by mechanical means, wooden ships of primitive build, pleasure yachts not engaged in trade or a fishing vessel;
(e) cargo ships of less than 500 gross tonnage".

Transfer of register

6.084 Article 4 of Regulation 789/2004 deals with the transfer of register:

"1. A Member State shall not withhold from registration, for technical reasons arising from the Conventions, a ship registered in another Member State which complies with the requirements and carries valid certificates and equipment approved or type-approved in accordance with Council Directive 96/98/EC of 20 December 1996 on marine equipment.[103]

---

[103] OJ L46/25, 17.2.1997.

In order to fulfil their obligations under regional environmental instruments ratified before 1 January 1992, Member States may impose additional rules in accordance with the optional Annexes to the Conventions.

2. This Article shall apply without prejudice, where applicable, to any specific requirements laid down for the operation of a ship under Article 7 of Directive 98/18/EC and Article 6 of Directive 2003/25/EC of the European Parliament and of the Council of 14 April 2003 on specific stability requirements for ro-ro passenger ships.[104]
3. Upon receiving the request for transfer, the Member State of the losing register shall provide the Member State of the receiving register, or make available to the recognised organisation acting on its behalf, all relevant information on the ship, in particular, on her condition and equipment. This information shall contain the history file of the vessel and, if applicable, a list of the improvements required by the losing register for registering the ship or renewing her certificates and of overdue surveys. The information shall include all the certificates and particulars of the ship as required by the Conventions and relevant Community instruments as well as Flag State inspection and Port State control records. The Member States shall cooperate to ensure proper implementation of this paragraph.
4. Before registering a ship, the Member State of the receiving register, or the recognised organisation acting on its behalf, may subject the ship to an inspection to confirm that the actual condition of the ship and her equipment correspond to the certificates referred to in Article 3. The inspection shall be performed within a reasonable time frame.
5. If, following the inspection and having given the ship owner a reasonable opportunity to rectify any deficiencies, the Member State of the receiving register, or the recognised organisation acting on its behalf, is unable to confirm correspondence with the certificates, it shall notify the Commission in accordance with Article 6(1)."

Certificates

6.085 Article 5 of Regulation 789/2004 deals with the topic of certificates:

"1. Upon the transfer and without prejudice to Directive 94/57/EC, the Member State of the receiving register, or the recognised organisation acting on its behalf, shall issue certificates to the ship under the same conditions as those under the flag of the Member State of the losing register, provided the reasons or the grounds on the basis of which the Member State of the losing register imposed any condition or granted any exemption or waiver continue to apply.
2. At the time of renewal, extension or revision of the certificates, the Member State of the receiving register, or the recognised organisation acting on its behalf, shall not impose requirements other than those initially prescribed for the full-term certificates insofar as requirements for existing ships and conditions remain unchanged."

Refusal of transfer and interpretation

6.086 Article 6 provides:

"1. The Member State of the receiving register shall immediately notify the Commission of any refusal to issue, or to authorise the issuing of, new certificates to a ship for reasons based on divergences of interpretation of the requirements or of the provisions which the Conventions or relevant Community instruments leave to the discretion of the Parties.

Unless the Commission is informed of an agreement between the Member States concerned within one month, it shall initiate proceedings in order to take a decision in accordance with the procedure referred to in Article 7(2).

---

104 OJ L123/22 17.5.2003.

2. Where a Member State considers that a ship cannot be registered under Article 4 for reasons relating to serious danger to safety, security or to the environment, other than those referred to in paragraph 1, registration may be suspended.

The Member State shall immediately bring the matter to the attention of the Commission, stating the reasons for the suspension of the registration. The decision not to register the ship shall be confirmed or not in accordance with the procedure referred to in Article 7(2).

3. The Commission may consult the Committee referred to in Article 7 on any matter related to the interpretation and implementation of this Regulation, in particular in order to ensure that standards of safety, security and environmental protection are not reduced."

Committee procedure

6.087 The committee procedure is addressed in Article 7. The first paragraph provides that the Commission shall be assisted by the Committee on Safe Seas and the Prevention of Pollution from Ships ("COSS") set up by Article 3 of Regulation 2099/2002 of the Parliament and of the Council.[105]

Reporting

6.088 Article 8 deals with reporting:

"1. Member States shall transmit to the Commission a succinct yearly report on the implementation of this Regulation. The report shall provide statistical data on the transfer of ships carried out in accordance with this Regulation and list any difficulties encountered in its implementation.

2. By 20 May 2008 the Commission shall submit a report to the European Parliament and the Council on the implementation of this Regulation, based in part on the reports submitted by the Member States. In this report, the Commission shall assess, inter alia, whether it is appropriate to amend the Regulation."

6.089 Article 9 deals with amendments

"1. In order to take account of developments at international level, in particular in the International Maritime Organisation (IMO), and to improve the effectiveness of this Regulation in the light of experience and technical progress, the Commission may amend the definitions in Article 2 insofar as such amendments do not broaden the scope of the Regulation. Those measures, designed to amend non-essential elements of this Regulation, shall be adopted in accordance with the regulatory procedure with scrutiny referred to in Article 7(3).

2. Any amendment to the Conventions may be excluded from the scope of this Regulation, pursuant to Article 5 of Regulation (EC) No 2099/2002."

F. PARALLEL REGISTRIES

Introduction

6.090 A number of Member States operate parallel registries. Bredima-Savopoulou and Tzoannos commented:

"[t]hese registries enable a shipowner to register his vessels under the national flag but operate it with a high degree of flexibility concerning choice and conditions of employment of factors of production, including labour. Thus, whilst the government of the particular state retains

---

105 OJ L324/1, 29 November 2002.

administrative control over the ships in the parallel register, the shipowner can operate under conditions similar to those found in the traditional open registries ... many European countries are turning in increasing numbers to the invention of a parallel register for the operation of vessels under 'off-shore' conditions as an answer to the loss of competitive advantage vis-à-vis third country fleets. This practice is creating a two-tier regime for the operation of ships under the flag of the countries concerned; one with strict control of ship management including employment conditions, and a second with a high degree of flexibility in ship management."[106]

6.091 For example, Denmark has an offshore registry. France has established an "offshore" or parallel registry in the Kerguelen Islands. Luxembourg has a parallel registry. The Netherlands has an offshore registry in the Dutch Antilles. The UK has an offshore registry in the Isle of Man.

6.092 A matter of critical concern is the status of each of these "dependent territories" and so on. Article 2 of Protocol No 3 of the Act of Accession of the UK to what is now the EU provides that the residents of the Isle of Man shall not benefit from EU provisions relating to the free movement of persons and services.

6.093 Speaking to the Antwerp Shipping Symposium, "A Future for the Community Fleet", on 6 May 1987, Georgios Anastassopoulos, the then Chairman of the Transport Committee of the European Parliament, stated that the European Parliament:

"has taken a very strong position against flagging out. And naturally it has never favoured open registries with all their negative for the Community implications [*sic*]. But the question is not a theoretical one. It cannot be resolved by exorcisms. The shipowners have reiterated to us that their conversion to the open registries is the lesser of evils and that it represents for them the only way of survival in a very competitive world environment. They have argued that whilst all other costs don't make a very substantial difference, the difference in manning costs for a bulk carrier or a tanker between a normal European and an open registry amount to half a million dollars a year ... There could be no question ... [t]he European Parliament would welcome the incentives to prevent flagging out. We have to stop it before it is too late. ... The development of a European flag has aroused much enthusiasm ... Its time may later come,[107] but it seems ... that we have still a long way to go. A Community emblem would be a different question, but with more psychological than substantial repercussions."[108]

The *Sloman Neptun* litigation

6.094 It is worth noting that a preliminary reference was made to the CJEU by the *Arbeitsgericht* (Labour Court) of Bremen, which were received in 1991, in the actions between Sloman Neptun Schiffahrts AG and Bodo Ziesemer, *Seebetriebsrat* (the seamen's representative),[109] on the following question:

"The Court of Justice is requested to give a preliminary ruling on the question whether it is compatible with Articles [107 of the TFEU] and [117 of the EEC Treaty] that Article 1(2) of the Gesetz zur Einführung eines zusätzlichen Schiffregisters für Seeschiffe unter der Bundesflagge im internationalen Verkehr (Internationales Seeschiffahrtsregister – ISR) [Law on the introduction of an additional shipping register for ships flying the Federal German flag in international trade (International Shipping Register – ISR)] of 23 March 1989, BGBl. 1, p. 550, makes it

---

106 *The Common Shipping Policy of the EEC* (1990), p. 53.
107 The euros register has not yet happened.
108 (1987) XXII ETL, at p. 199.
109 Joined Cases C-72/91 and C-73/91 *Sloman Neptun Schiffahrts AG v Seebetriebsrat Bodo Ziesemer der Sloman Neptun Schiffahrts AG* [1993] ECR I-887, ECLI:EU:C:1993:97, 17 March 1993.

possible for foreign seamen with no permanent abode or residence in the Federal Republic of Germany not to be covered by German collective agreements and thus to be employed at lower 'home country' rates and on less favourable employment conditions than comparable German seamen."

6.095 The matter was decided by the CJEU. The Court opined that a system established by a Member State, such as that applicable to the International Shipping Register, which enables contracts of employment concluded with seafarers who are nationals of non-member countries and have no permanent abode or residence in that Member State to be subjected to conditions of employment and rates of pay which are not covered by the law of that Member State and are considerably less favourable than those applicable to seafarers who are nationals of that Member State, does not constitute State aid within the meaning of Article 107 of the TFEU, and

> "by the national court, and to the potential loss of tax revenue because of the low rates of pay, referred to by the Commission, are inherent in the system and are not a means of granting a particular advantage to the undertakings concerned.
> 22. It follows that a system such as that applicable to the ISR is not a State aid within the meaning of Article [107(1) TFEU]."

G. CASE LAW OF ESTABLISHMENT AND REGISTRATION GENERALLY

The *Commission v Greece* case

6.096 On 27 November 1997, the CJEU[110] gave judgment in *Commission v Greece*.[111] The proceedings involved the Commission applying for a declaration that, by maintaining in force legislative provisions which restricted the right to registration in the Greek shipping registers to vessels more than half the shares in which are owned by Greek nationals or owned by Greek legal persons more than half of whose capital is held by Greek nationals, Greece had failed to fulfil its obligations under Articles 6, 48, 52, 58 and 221 of the EC Treaty,[112] Article 7 of Regulation 1251/70 of the Commission of 29 June 1970 on the right of workers to remain in the territory of a Member State after having been employed in that State[113] and Article 7 of Council Directive 75/34 of 17 December 1974 concerning the right of nationals of a Member State to remain in the territory of another Member State after having pursued therein an activity self-employed capacity.[114]

6.097 It was not difficult for the CJEU to declare that, by maintaining in force legislative provisions which restrict the right to registration in the Greek shipping registers to vessels more than half the shares in which are owned by Greek nationals or owned by Greek legal persons more than half of whose capital is held by Greek nationals, the Hellenic Republic had failed to fulfil its obligations under Articles 6, 48, 52, 58 and 221 of the EC Treaty, Article 7 of Regulation 1251/70 of the Commission of 29 June 1970 on the right of workers to remain in the territory of a Member State after having been employed in that State and Article 7 of Council Directive 75/34 of 17 December 1974

---

110 Fifth Chamber composed of: Judges Wathelet (President of the Chamber), Moitinho de Almeida, Edward, Jann (Rapporteur) and Sevón with Advocate-General Tesauro.
111 Case C-62/96, [1997] ECR I-6725, ECLI:EU:C:1997:565.
112 With some amendments, these are Arts 18, 45, 49, 54 and 55 of the TFEU but with some amendments.
113 OJ, English Special Edition 1970 (II), p. 402.
114 OJ 1975 L14, p. 10.

concerning the right of nationals of a Member State to remain in the territory of another Member State after having pursued therein an activity in a self-employed capacity.

6.098 Key aspects of the judgment are worth analysing. The judgment recalled Article 5 of the Greek Code, entitled "Nationality of the Vessel", which provided as follows:

"Conditions for granting Greek nationality

1. Without prejudice to specific legislation, Greek nationality shall be granted to vessels more than half the shares in which are owned by Greek nationals or owned by Greek legal persons more than half of whose capital is held by Greek nationals, upon application by their owner and upon submission of the document of title.
2. If the document transferring title to a vessel was drawn up abroad, a certificate from the consular authority is required in order to enter the vessel in the registers.
3. The conditions for recognition of Greek vessels as vessels for the transport of passengers shall be determined by presidential decree issued on a proposal from the minister following consultation of the Council for the merchant navy."

The Commission claimed that the conditions for granting Greek nationality to fishing vessels and commercial vessels, laid down by that provision, are contrary to EU law and, in particular, to Articles 6, 48, 52, 58 and 221 of the EC Treaty. In regard to pleasure craft which did not constitute a means for pursuing an economic activity, the Commission took the view that Article 5 of the Code was in breach of Articles 6, 48 and 52 of the Treaty, Article 7 of Regulation 1251/70 and Article 7 of Directive 75/34. Greece considered, first of all, that, in the light of *Factortame and Others*,[115] it was entitled to apply Article 5 of the 1958 Geneva Convention on the High Seas and Article 91 et seq. of UNCLOS III, which provide that each State is to fix the conditions for the grant of its nationality to ships, for the registration of ships in its territory and for the right to fly its flag, to ensure the existence of a genuine link between the State and the ship. The reason why such a link is required is that States must meet a large number of obligations with regard to ships flying their flag. The chief criterion for granting the right to fly a flag is the nationality of the shipowner. In that connection Greece also referred to the 1986 United Nations Convention on Conditions for Registration of Ships which, in Articles 7 to 10 thereof, gives a very clear definition of the factors constituting a genuine link. It argued that the Greek legislation was in line with Article 8, which listed the criteria for the determination of ownership of ships. Second, Greece contended that Greek law did not prevent nationals of other Member States from acquiring and using Greece vessels flying the flag of another State. Greece also argued that there were certain activities which are reserved to ships flying the national flag, as provided for by Regulation 3760/92 of 20 December 1992 establishing a Community system for fisheries and aquaculture[116] and Regulation 3577/92 of 7 December 1992 applying the principle of freedom to provide services to maritime transport within Member States (maritime cabotage).[117] Although it concerned the provision of services, the latter regulation, it was argued, also had an impact on freedom of establishment if it is to have any effect at all. Greece also argued that special arrangements were provided for Greece in Article 6(3) of Regulation 3577/92 for reasons of socio-economic cohesion.[118] Finally, Greece argued that the rules on registration were

---

115 Case C-221/89 [1991] ECR I-3905, ECLI:EU:C:1991:320, para.17.
116 OJ1992 L389/1.
117 OJ 1992 L364/7.
118 See chap. 7.

justified by the requirements of its military defence organisation, which were of a specific character for historical and geo-political reasons, and that the State must be able to requisition ships where necessary. By contrast, the Commission disputed Greece's arguments. The Commission counter-argued that in the judgment in *Factortame and Others*, the CJEU did not accept an argument similar to that advanced by Greece in this case. The Commission also took the view that the provisions of Regulation 3577/92, which Greece relied on to justify reserving the exercise of the activity in question to ships flying the Greek flag, were intended to apply the principle of the free movement of maritime transport services within Member States but did not affect the rights of natural and legal persons under the Treaty. Similarly, the Commission argued that Article 5 of the Code did not affect the area governed by Regulation 3760/92 which, in any event, did not authorise Member States unilaterally to adopt measures in breach of the Treaty. The Commission also contested the view that Greece could maintain in force legislation allowing derogations from the principle of freedom of movement on the ground that it must be able to requisition ships for reasons of national defence because all owners of ships flying the Geek flag could be made subject to the same obligations as Greek nationals and there was no need to restrict freedom of movement for this purpose. The CJEU opined as follows:

> "17. In this connection the first point to note is that national legislation similar to the Greek legislation in issue is the subject of well-established case-law of the Court (see, primarily, *Factortame and Others*, cited above, and Case C-93/89 *Commission v Ireland* [1991] ECR I-4569, Case C-246/89 *Commission v United Kingdom* [1991]ECR I-4585, Case C-334/94 *Commission v France* [1996] ECR I-1307 and Case C-151/96 *Commission v Ireland* [1997] ECR I-3327).
> 18. It is clear from those decisions that as regards vessels used for the pursuit of an economic activity, each Member State must, in exercising its powers for the purpose of defining the conditions for the grant of its 'nationality' to a vessel, comply with the prohibition of discrimination against nationals of Member States on grounds of nationality, and that a condition which stipulates that where a vessel is owned or chartered by natural persons they must be of a particular nationality and, in the case of a company, the shareholders and directors must be of that nationality is contrary to Article 52 of the Treaty. A condition relating to registration or management of a vessel in the case of a secondary establishment such as an agency, branch or subsidiary is contrary to Articles 52 and 58 of the Treaty (see, in particular, *Commission v Ireland*, cited above, paragraph 12).
> 19. As regards vessels not used for the pursuit of an economic activity, the Court held in *Commission v Ireland*, cited above, paragraph 13, that, under Community law, every national of a Member State is assured of freedom both to enter another Member State in order to pursue an activity as employed or self-employed person and to reside there after having pursued such an activity. Access to leisure activities available in that State is a corollary to freedom of movement.
> 20. In paragraph 14 of that judgment, the Court concluded that registration by such a national of a pleasure craft in the host Member State falls within the scope of the Community provisions relating to freedom of movement for persons.
> 21. An appraisal of the arguments relied on by the Hellenic Republic in the light of that case-law is thus called for.
> 22. In that connection, the first point to note is that the argument of the Hellenic Government based on the international law of the sea is not supported by the judgment in *Factortame and Others*, cited above, paragraph 17. In that judgment the Court expressly stated that, in exercising their power to determine the conditions which must be fulfilled in order for a vessel to be entered in their registers and granted the right to fly their flag, Member States

must comply with the rules of Community law. Although this finding related only to Article 5 of the 1958 Geneva Convention, it cannot be invalidated by the two United Nations Conventions of 1982 and 1986, both signed after the accession of the Hellenic Republic to the Communities.

23. Secondly, the argument of the Hellenic Government that its legislation is not an obstacle to the activities of nationals of other Member States is not relevant under the second paragraph of Article 52 of the Treaty. As the Court found in its judgment in *Factortame and Others*, cited above, at paragraph 25, freedom of establishment includes, in the case of nationals of a Member State, 'the right to take up and pursue activities as self-employed persons ... under the conditions laid down for its own nationals by the law of the country where such establishment is effected...'

24. As for the argument of the Hellenic Republic based on Regulation ... 3760/92, suffice it to note that the purpose of national legislation on the registration of vessels, such as that in issue, is not to determine the arrangements for the use of quotas or access to waters at the disposal of fishermen from a Member State. Moreover, national legislation concerning the registration of all vessels cannot be justified by the existence of a Community fisheries system authorizing reserved national zones.

25. As regards Regulation ... 3577/92, which in Article 6(3) grants a temporary exemption to the Hellenic Republic, it should be pointed out that that exemption cannot be taken to authorize discriminatory conditions for the registration of vessels. Whilst the regulation defers until January 2004 the application of the principle of freedom to provide services to certain maritime transport services, it cannot constitute a basis for imposing additional restrictions on freedom of establishment.

26. Finally, as regards organization of the military defence of the Hellenic Republic, suffice it to note that the Greek authorities could decide to requisition for military purposes any ship flying the Greek flag, whatever the nationality of its owner.

27. It follows from the foregoing that, by maintaining in force legislative provisions which restrict the right to registration in the Greek shipping registers to vessels more than half the shares in which are owned by Greek nationals or owned by Greek legal persons more than half of whose capital is held by Greek nationals, the Hellenic Republic has failed to fulfil its obligations under Articles 6, 48, 52, 58 and 221 of the EC Treaty, Article 7 of Regulation ... 1251/70 and Article 7 of Directive 75/34."

With the greatest of respect to the arguments put forward by the Greek government, the CJEU's conclusions were the only proper conclusions.

The *Factortame* litigation

Introduction

6.099 One of the most important phases of the development of EU shipping law generally and of the EU law relating to registration of ships in particular was the so-called *Factortame* litigation.[119] It is useful to analyse the evolution of the *Factortame* litigation.

6.100 "Quota hopping" was a phenomenon whereby a fishing boat owner would transfer registration of a vessel from one Member State to another Member State or

---

119 On the litigation, see Aragones, "*Regina v Secretary of State for Transport ex parte Factortame Ltd:* The Limits of Parliamentary Sovereignty and the Rule of Community Law" (1990–1991) 14 Fordham Int'l L J 778; Craig, "Sovereignty of the United Kingdom Parliament after *Factortame*" (1991) 11(1) YEL 221; Toner, "Thinking the Unthinkable? State Liability for Judicial Acts after *Factortame III*" (1997) 17 YEL 165; and Vajda, "Liability for Breach of Community Law: A Survey of the ECJ Cases Post *Factortame*" (2006) 17 European Business Law Review 257. See also Churchill's incisive analysis at (1992) 29 CMLRev 405; Oliver's analysis at (1997) 34 CMLRev 635; and Toth's analysis at (1990) 27 CMLRev 573.

acquire a vessel registered in another Member State so as to acquire fishing quotas of the second Member State.

6.101 The UK statutory regime relating to the registration of British fishing vessels was altered by Part II of the Merchant Shipping Act 1988 and the Merchant Shipping (Registration of Fishing Vessels) Regulations 1988. The UK had amended the pre-existing legislation so as to try to end "quota hopping" because, for example, some Spanish owners were acquiring UK boats or transferring their boats to the UK to acquire UK quotas.

6.102 The *Factortame* case related to the owners or operators of 95 fishing vessels which were registered on the Register of British Vessels under the UK's Merchant Shipping Act 1894. Of those vessels, 53 were originally registered in Spain and flew the Spanish flag but on various dates from 1980, they were registered on the British Register. The remaining 42 vessels had always been registered in the UK. They were purchased by the companies in question on various dates since 1983.

6.103 The 1988 Act provided for the establishment of a new register in which all British fishing vessels were to be registered, including those which had been on the old register maintained under the 1894 Act. Section 14 of the 1988 Act provided that only vessels fulfilling certain criteria could be satisfied. These criteria included (subject to dispensations to be determined by the Secretary of State for Transport) that: (a) the vessel was British owned; (b) the vessel was managed and its operations were directed or controlled from within the United Kingdom; and (c) any charterer, manager or operator of the vessel is a qualified person or company. Interestingly, Section 14(2) provided that a fishing vessel was deemed to be British owned if the legal title to the vessel was vested wholly in one or more qualified persons or companies and if the vessel was beneficially owned by one or more qualified companies or, as to not less than 75%, by one or more qualified persons. Section 14(7) provided that a qualified person meant a person who is a British citizen resident and domiciled in the United Kingdom while a "qualified company" meant a company incorporated in the United Kingdom and having its principal place of business there with at least 75% of its share being owned by one or more qualified persons or companies and at least 75% of its directors being qualified persons. While the 1988 Act and 1988 Regulation were entered into force on 1 December 1988, Section 13 of the 1988 Act provided that the validity of registrations effected under the previous act were extended for a transitional period until 31 March 1989.

6.104 The Spanish fishermen behind the boats in question claimed that the UK had breached EU law by requiring that the vessels could only be UK registered (and therefore entitled to fish part of the UK quota) where the vessels were majority owned by UK subjects. The litigation lasted from 1989 to 2000. Aspects of the case are not relevant for present purposes. For example, much of the litigation turned on the relationship between EU law and Member State law generally as well as issues relating to the sovereignty of the British Parliament under UK constitutional law. This section will review *Factortame I*, *Factortame II* and *Factortame III*. *Factortame IV* involved a UK House of Lords judgment on damages being awarded against a Member State which caused losses for breach of EU law and *Factortame V* decided that certain claims were statute barred because claims against a Member State were like other claims in UK tort law capable of being statute barred.

The **Factortame I** *case*

6.105 On 4 August 1989, the Commission brought an action before the CJEU under Article 169 (as it then was) of the EC Treaty for a declaration that, by imposing the nationality requirements laid down in Section 14 of the 1988 Act, the UK had failed to fulfil its obligations under Articles 7, 52 and 221 of the then EEC Treaty.[120] The Commission also sought from the CJEU an interim order requiring the UK to suspend the application of those nationality requirements as regard the nationals of other Member States in respect of fishing vessels which until 31 March 1989 were carrying out fishing activity under the British flag and under British fishing licence. By order of 10 October 1989, the President of the European Court of Justice ("ECJ") (now the CJEU) granted that application. Pursuant to the order of the President of CJEU, the UK made an Order in Council amending Section 14 of the 1989 Act with effect from 2 November 1989.

6.106 On 18 May 1989, the House of Lords referred to the CJEU for preliminary ruling two questions on the interpretation of Community law. Those questions related to the extent of the power of Member State Courts to grant interim relief where rights claimed under EC law were at issue.

6.107 Of the 95 vessels, none of them satisfied the conditions for registration under Section 14 of the 1988 Act and could not be registered in the new register. The owners of those vessels then sought an application by judicial review before the English Courts challenging the compatibility of Part II of the 1988 Act with EC law. They also applied for the grant of interim relief until such time as the final judgment was given on their application for judicial review. On 10 March 1989, the Divisional Court of the Queen's Bench Division (i) decided to stay the proceedings and to make a preliminary reference to the CJEU; and (ii) ordered that, by way of interim relief, the application of Part II of the 1988 Act and the 1988 Regulation should be suspended was regards the applicants. On 13 March 1989, the Secretary of State for Transport appealed to the English Court of Appeal.

6.108 On 22 March 1989, the English Court of Appeal held that under national law, the Courts had no power to suspend, by way of interim relief, the application of the Acts of Parliament and therefore set aside the Order of the Divisional Court. The House of Lords gave judgment on 18 May 1989. It held that the English Courts had no power to grant interim relief in a case such as the present one. In particular, it held that an interim injunction may not be granted against the Crown (i.e. government) in conjunction with the presumption that an Act of Parliament is in conformity with EU law until such time as a decision on its compatibility with that law had been given. The House of Lords then referred various questions to the CJEU. The CJEU characterised the question as essentially being one as to "whether a national court which, in a case before it concerning Community law, considers that the sole obstacle which precludes it from granting interim relief as a rule of national law must disapply that rule". The CJEU held that

> "Community law must be interpreted as meaning that a national court which, in a case before it concerning Community law, considers that the sole obstacle which precludes it from granting interim relief as a rule of national law must set aside that rule."

---

120 I.e. the provision on discrimination on the basis of nationality and freedom of establishment. Art. 221 of the EEC Treaty is now Art. 55 of the TFEU.

The **Factortame II** *case*

6.109 Proceedings were instituted in the English High Court against the Secretary of State for Transport by Factortame Limited and other companies incorporated under UK law.

6.110 On 25 July 1991, the CJEU delivered its judgment in *R v Secretary of State for Transport ex parte Factortame Limited.*

6.111 The English High Court referred on 10 March 1989 four questions by way of preliminary ruling reference to the CJEU. These questions related to the right of establishment and the principles of proportionality and non-discrimination on the grounds of nationality with a view to determining the compatibility with Community law of national legislation laying down the conditions for registration of fishing vessels. While the questions related to fishing vessels, the principles would equally apply to other vessels as well.

6.112 The first question asked was whether EC law affects the conditions under which a Member State lays down the rules for determining which vessels are entitled to register in that State to fly its flag and carry its nationality.

6.113 The *Factortame* litigation[121] was important for many reasons including its analysis of the relationship between municipal law and EU law, the impact of EU law on the power of the UK Parliament to legislate and fishing law generally. However, in some ways, the lessons to be learned from the perspective of EU shipping law are relatively few and somewhat obvious.

6.114 The background to the litigation was relatively simple. The UK enacted the Merchant Shipping Act 1988. This Act established the grounds on which an owner could be eligible to register a ship on the British registry. In essence, owners had to be resident and domiciled in Britain besides being of British nationality. It appeared that its real aim was to restrict Spanish fishing vessels re-registering in Britain and thereby having the right to fish in waters reserved under the EU's fisheries policy to British-registered vessels. Factortame Ltd and some other companies which were incorporated in the UK instituted proceedings against the UK Secretary of State for Transport. Most of the directors and shareholders in the company were Spanish nationals. The matter was referred to the CJEU by way of a preliminary reference under Article 267 of the TFEU. The CJEU held in 1991 that the legislation infringed EU law because it discriminated on the basis of nationality between EU nationals. This result was somewhat obvious and inevitable. The CJEU stated:

> "17. ... as [EU] law stands at present, it is for the Member States to determine, in accordance with the general rules of international law, the conditions which must be fulfilled in order for a vessel to be registered in their registers and granted the right to fly their flag, in exercising that power, the member-States must comply with their rules of Community law."

6.115 The CJEU continued:

> "20. It must be observed in that regard that the concept of establishment within the meaning of Article [49] *et seq.* involves the actual pursuit of an economic activity through a fixed establishment in another Member State for an indefinite period.

---

121 See, in particular, Case C221/89 *R v Secretary of State for Transport ex parte Factortame Limited and Others (No. 2)* [1991] 3 CMLR 589.

21. Consequently, the registration of a vessel does not necessarily involve establishment within the meaning of the Treaty, in particular where the vessel is not used to pursue an economic activity or where the application for registration is made by or on behalf of a person who is not established, and has no intention of becoming established, in the State concerned.
22. However, where the vessel constitutes an instrument for pursuing an economic activity which involves a fixed establishment in the Member State concerned, the registration of that vessel cannot be dissociated from the exercise of the freedom of establishment.
23. It follows that the conditions laid down for the registration of vessels must not form an obstacle to freedom of establishment within the meaning of Article [49] *et seq.* of the Treaty."

6.116 In regard to nationality, the CJEU stated:

"27. ... it must be observed that the concept of the 'nationality' of ships, which are not persons, is different from that of the 'nationality' of natural persons.
28. The prohibition of discrimination on grounds of nationality, which is set out in particular, as regards the right of establishment, in Article [49] of the Treaty, is concerned with differences of treatment as between natural persons who are nationals of member-States and as between companies who are treated in the same way as such persons by virtue of Article [54].
29. Consequently, in exercising its powers for the purposes of defining the conditions for the grant of its 'nationality' to a ship, each Member State must comply with the prohibition of discrimination against nationals of Member States on grounds of nationality.
30. It follows from the foregoing that a condition of the type at issue in the main proceedings which stipulates that where a vessel is owned or chartered by natural persons they must be of a particular nationality and where it is owned or chartered by a company the shareholders and directors must be of that nationality is contrary to Article [49 TFEU].
31. Such a condition is also contrary to [the Treaty rule] under which member-States must accord nationals of the other member-States the same treatment as their own nationals as regards participation in the capital of companies or firms within the meaning of [the Treaty provisions on freedom of establishment].
32. As for the requirement for the owners, charterers, managers and operators of the vessel and, in the case of a company, the shareholders and directors to be resident and domiciled in the Member State in which the vessel is to be registered, it must be held that such a requirement, which is not justified by the rights and obligations created by the grant of a national flag to a vessel, results in discrimination on grounds of nationality. The great majority of nationals of the Member State in question are resident and domiciled in that State and therefore meet that requirement automatically, whereas nationals of other Member States would, in most cases, have to move their residence and domicile to that State in order to comply with the requirements of its legislation. It follows that such a requirement is contrary to Article [49 TFEU].
33. It follows from the foregoing that it is contrary to the provisions of Community law and, in particular, to Article [49 TFEU] for a Member State to stipulate as conditions for the registration of a fishing vessel in its national register: (a) that the legal owners and beneficial owners and the charterers, managers and operators of the vessel must be nationals of that member-State or companies incorporated in that member-State, and that, in the latter case, at least 75 per cent. of the shares in the company must be owned by nationals of that member-State or by companies fulfilling the same requirements and 75 per cent. of the directors of the company must be nationals of that member-State; and (b) that the said legal owners and beneficial owners, charterers, managers, operators, shareholders and directors, as the case may be, must be resident and domiciled in that member-State ...
34. ... it is sufficient to point out that a requirement for the registration of a vessel to the effect that it must be managed and its operations directed and controlled from within the member-State in which it is to be registered essentially coincides with the actual concept of establishment within the meaning of Article [49] *et seq.* of the Treaty, which implies a fixed

establishment. It follows that those Articles, which enshrine the very concept of freedom of establishment, cannot be interpreted as precluding such a requirement.

35. Such a requirement, however, would not be compatible with those provisions if it had to be interpreted as precluding registration in the event that a secondary establishment or the centre for directing the operations of the vessel in the member-State in which the vessel was to be registered acted on instructions from a decision-taking centre located in the member-State of the principal establishment.

36. Consequently, the reply to the national court must be that it is not contrary to Community law for a member-State to stipulate as a condition for the registration of a fishing vessel in its national register that the vessel in question must be managed and its operation directed and controlled from within that member-State."

The **Factortame III** case

6.117 The *Factortame III* case involved the CJEU hold that a Member State "must be liable for loss and damage caused to individuals as a result of breaches" of EU law.[122] This case built on the *Francovich* judgment which had just been delivered.[123] The case primarily relates to the conditions for the granting of compensation to persons whose EU legal rights have been infringed.

H. THE *VIKING* LITIGATION

Introduction

6.118 The *Viking* litigation is at the epicentre of the EU law relating to the re-registration or reflagging of vessels and the associated employment law issues.[124] While the case has implications for employment law in the EU generally,[125] this analysis concentrates on the shipping law dimension.

6.119 The case centres on the CJEU's ruling in *International Transport Workers' Federation (ITF) and Finnish Seamen's Union (FSU) v Viking Line ABP and OÜ Viking Line Eesti*.[126] The sensitivity of the case is illustrated by the fact that 15 governments[127] and the Commission made observations to the CJEU in the case.

---

122 Case C-48/93 ECLI:EU:C:1996:79.
123 Case C-6/90 [1991] ECR 537, ECLI:EU:C:1991:428.
124 Case C-438/05 [2007] ECR I-10779, ECLI:EU:C:2007:772, [2008] 1 CMLR 51, [2008] All ER (EC) 127, [2008] IRLR 143. For commentary, see Novtiz, "Resistance to Re-Flagging: A Restricted Right to Strike" [2008] LMCLQ 266. See also Davies, "The Right to Strike Versus Freedom of Establishment in EC Law: The Battle Commences" (2006) 35 Industrial Law Journal 75 and Novitz, "The Right to Strike and Re-flagging in the European Union: Free Movement Provisions and Human Rights" [2006] LMCLQ 242.
125 Novtiz ([2008] LMCLQ 266 at 266) sees the case as relating to the "potential conflict between domestic labour law and free movement provisions set out in the European Community (EC) Treat [and this case now provides] some legal guidance on this matter, although it may not be sufficient to allay entirely any concerns".
126 Case C-438/05 [2008] 1 CMLR 51, [2008] All ER (EC) 127, [2008] IRLR 143. For commentary, see Novtiz, op. cit. at fn. 124. The case should be read in conjunction with Case C-341/05 *Laval un Partneri v Svenska Byggnadsarbetareforbundet* case [2008] All ER (EC) 166, [2008] IRLR 160. See also Novitz, "The Right to Strike and Re-flagging in the European Union: Free Movement Provisions and Human Rights" [2006] LMCLQ 242.
127 I.e. Austria, Belgium, the Czech Republic, Denmark, Estonia, Finland France, Germany, Ireland, Italy, Latvia, Norway Poland, Sweden and the UK.

Factual background

6.120 The dispute was between, on the one hand, the ITF and the Finnish Seamen's Union (Suomen Merimies-Unioni ry, the "FSU" and, on the other hand, Viking Line ABP ("Viking") and its subsidiary OÜ Viking Line Eesti ("Viking Eesti").

6.121 The dispute concerned actual or threatened collective action liable to deter Viking (a Finnish ferry company) from reflagging one of its vessels (the *Rosella*) from the Finnish flag to that of another Member State. The vessel plied between Tallinn (Estonia) and Helsinki (Finland).

6.122 The FSU was a Finnish union of seafarers which had about 10,000 members. The crew of the *Rosella* were members of the FSU. The FSU was affiliated to the ITF, which is an international federation of transport workers' unions with its headquarters in the UK. The ITF represented 600 unions in 140 States. One of the ITF's best known policies is its 'Flag of Convenience' ("FOC") policy. The CJEU stated that the

> "primary objectives of this policy are, on the one hand, to establish a genuine link between the flag of the ship and the nationality of the owner and, on the other, to protect and enhance the conditions of seafarers on FOC ships. [The] ITF considers that a vessel is registered under a flag of convenience where the beneficial ownership and control of the vessel is found to lie in a State other than the State of the flag. In accordance with the ITF policy, only unions established in the State of beneficial ownership have the right to conclude collective agreements covering the vessel concerned. The FOC campaign is enforced by boycotts and other solidarity actions amongst workers."

6.123 Under Finnish law, so long as the *Rosella* was under the Finnish flag then Viking was obliged under Finnish law and the terms of a collective bargaining agreement to pay the crew wages at the same level as those applicable in Finland. The *Rosella* was running at a loss as a result of direct competition from Estonian vessels operating on the same route with lower wage costs which were possible on Estonian registered vessels.

6.124 In October 2003, Viking decided, as an alternative to selling the vessel, to reflag her in either Estonia or Norway, in order to be able to enter into a new collective agreement with a trade union established in one of those States. In accordance with Finnish law, Viking gave notice of its plans to the FSU and to the crew of the *Rosella*. The FSU stated their opposition to the plan. In November 2003, FSU communicated with the ITF about the plan to reflag the *Rosella*. The FSU stated that "the *Rosella* was owned beneficially in Finland and that FSU therefore kept the right to negotiate with Viking". FSU asked ITF to pass this information on to all affiliated unions and to request them not to enter into negotiations with Viking. The ITF sent a circular ('the ITF circular') to its affiliates asking them to refrain from entering into negotiations with Viking or Viking Eesti. The affiliates were expected to follow this recommendation because of the principle of solidarity between trade unions and the sanctions which they could face if they failed to comply with that circular. The manning agreement for the *Rosella* expired on 17 November 2003 and therefore FSU was, as from that date, no longer under an obligation to follow a path of "industrial peace" under Finnish law. The FSU then gave notice of a strike requiring Viking, on the one hand, to increase the manning on the *Rosella* by eight and, on the other, to abandon its plans to reflag the *Rosella*. Viking conceded the extra eight crew but refused to abandon its plans to reflag. The CJEU continues the story:

"15. FSU was still not prepared, however, to agree to a renewal of the manning agreement and, by letter of 18 November 2003, it indicated that it would only accept such renewal on two conditions: first, that Viking, regardless of a possible change of the *Rosella's* flag, gave an undertaking that it would continue to follow Finnish law, the collective bargaining agreement, the general agreement and the manning agreement on the *Rosella* and, second, that the possible change of flag would not lead to any laying-off of employees on any Finnish flag vessel belonging to Viking, or to changes to the terms and conditions of employment without the consent of the employees. In press statements FSU justified its position by the need to protect Finnish jobs."

6.125 Legal proceedings then ensued:

"16. On 17 November 2003, Viking started legal proceedings before the employment tribunal (Finland) for a declaration that, contrary to the view of the FSU, the manning agreement remained binding on the parties. On the basis of its view that the manning agreement was at an end, FSU gave notice, in accordance with Finnish law on industrial dispute mediation, that it intended to commence strike action in relation to the *Rosella* on 2 December 2003.

17. On 24 November 2003, Viking learnt of the existence of the ITF circular. The following day it brought proceedings before the Court of First Instance of Helsinki (Finland) to restrain the planned strike action. A preparatory hearing date was set for 2 December 2003.

18. According to the referring court, FSU was fully aware of the fact that its principal demand, that in the event of reflagging the crew should continue to be employed on the conditions laid down by Finnish law and the applicable collective agreement, would render reflagging pointless, since the whole purpose of such reflagging was to enable Viking to reduce its wage costs. Furthermore, a consequence of reflagging the *Rosella* to Estonia would be that Viking would, at least as regards the *Rosella*, no longer be able to claim State aid which the Finnish Government granted to Finnish flag vessels.

19. In the course of conciliation proceedings, Viking gave an undertaking, at an initial stage, that the reflagging would not involve any redundancies. Since [the] FSU nevertheless refused to defer the strike, Viking put an end to the dispute on 2 December 2003 by accepting the trade union's demands and discontinuing judicial proceedings. Furthermore, it undertook not to commence reflagging prior to 28 February 2005."

6.126 There was then a material change of events. On 1 May 2004, Estonia became a member of the EU. But the *Rosella* continued to run at a loss so Viking pursued its intention to reflag the vessel to Estonia. Because the ITF circular remained in force, on account of the fact that the ITF had never withdrawn it, the request to affiliated unions from the ITF in relation to the *Rosella* consequently remained in effect.

UK litigation

6.127 To address the issue of the ITF's circular, Viking then sued in the UK courts because the ITF was based there.[128]

---

128 Novtiz commented (op. cit. at fn. 124, p. 267): "[o]n 1 May 2004, Estonia became a member of the ... EU ... and this changed the complexion of the dispute. The issue of employers' rights to free movement between EU Member States thereby arose, and it was on this basis that Viking sought an injunction again, not this time through the potentially unsympathetic Finnish courts, but before the High Court of England and Wales Queen's Bench Division (Commercial Court), on the basis that the ITF had its registered office in London". See Chuah, "Freedom of Establishment and Threats of Industrial Action by Unions of Maritime Workers" [2005] 11 JIML 298.

6.128 On 18 August 2004, Viking brought an action before the High Court (Commercial Court) in London requesting it to declare that the action taken by ITF and FSU was contrary to what is now Article 49 of the TFEU, to order the withdrawal of the ITF circular and to order the FSU not to infringe the rights which Viking enjoys under EU law. Viking also sought injunctions to retrain the ITF from organising boycotts in other jurisdictions. Viking made three key arguments: (a) the ITF action would be contrary to Article 49 of the TFEU; (b) the ITF action would be contrary to the principle of the free movement of workers; and (c) the ITF action was contrary to Article 1 of Regulation 4055/86[129] applying the principle of freedom to provide services to maritime transport between Member States as well as between Member States and third States. The ITF argued that the English courts lacked jurisdiction. Ten months later, on 16 June 2005, the English court held that it had jurisdiction[130] and granted the form of order sought by Viking, on the grounds that the actual and threatened collective action by the ITF and FSU imposed restrictions on freedom of establishment contrary to Article 49 of the TFEU and, in the alternative, constituted unlawful restrictions on freedom of movement for workers and freedom to provide services under Articles 45 of the TFEU and 56 of the TFEU.[131] The High Court was clearly mindful that Viking's rights under EU law were threatened or potentially threatened. Interestingly, Gloster J declined the request to refer questions to the CJEU stating that the case was fact dependent and the EU law was already well established. The High Court also believed that a preliminary reference would cause a considerable delay which would be injurious to the interests of Viking. Examining the High Court's judgment, Chuah commented incisively on the question of to whom was the "right to establish" owing as a matter of EU law:

> "It is conventional law that the freedom of establishment right is one owed by a Member State to the enterprise or undertaking. The question here was, however, whether that was a right owed to Viking by [the] ITF and [the] FSU, which are clearly not emanations of the state. This is perhaps the more interesting question – and one which, perhaps, the court should have made a reference to the [CJEU]. Be that as it may, it was held that there was horizontal direct effect in Article [49 of the TFEU]. That means a private entity can claim those rights against another private entity. The court accepted Viking's argument that the [CJEU] establishes that the free movement rules apply not only to the action of public authorities but also to 'rules of any other nature aimed at regulating gainful employment in a collective manner'.[132] Indeed, in *Wouters*,[133] the [CJEU], in ruling that Article [49] could extend to professional rules imposed by the Netherlands Bar Council to lawyers, despite the fact that those rules are not public nature, held that those rules were obviously designed to regulate, collectively, self-employment and the provision of services. Article [49] should not be defeated simply by the contention that associations or organisations

---

129 OJ 1986 L378/1. See chap. 7.

130 It had been argued by the ITF that the English court should not accept jurisdiction because any order granted by the English court would not be enforced in Finland. However, the English court rejected that contention because under the EU mutual recognition and enforcement of judgments regime, the Finnish courts would recognise and enforce the English judgment. The English court accepted jurisdiction notwithstanding that the case essentially involved an English court considering the content of Finnish law and whether Finnish law was compatible with EU law (see Case C-281/02 *Andrew Owusu v NB Jackson trading as "Villa Holidays Bal-Inn Villas" and others* [2005] ECR I-1383, ECLI:EU:C:2005:120.

131 *International Transport Workers' Federation v Viking Line Abp* [2005] EWHC 1222, [2005] 1 CLC 951, [2005] 3 CMLR 29, [2005] ELR 1036, [2006] ILPr 4.

132 Case C-415/93 *Union Royale Belge des Société de Football ASBL and Others v Jean-Marc Bosman and Others* [1995] ECR I-4921 as applied in Case C-309/99 *Wouters v Algemene Raad van de Nederlandse Orde van Advocaten* [2002] ECR II-2823.

133 Ibid.

which imposed restrictive and/or discriminatory measures are not governed by public law. Gloster J was persuaded by the argument that the ITF's measures, applied by the ITF and invoked by the FSU, constituted a set of 'rules' enforced by sanctions. The court also gave some emphasis to the fact that the FSU actually performed a quasi-public function in regulating employment terms and conditions in accordance with Finnish legislation.

This approach seems consistent with the wider legislative aim of Article [49] to enable corporate entities established in one Member State to establish themselves in another Member State without being hindered by non-governmental measures which have a significant and considerable influence over the industrial sector or profession in question. [CJEU] case law has extended the proscription in Article [49] to sporting associations and professional bodies and there seems to be no good reason to exclude trade unions from the remit of Article [49], especially in the maritime sector where trade unions wield so much power on the employment of workers which is central to the right of establishment for maritime undertakings."[134]

The Court also considered the issue whether Article 39 of the EC Treaty (i.e. now Article 45 of the TFEU) on the free movement of workers had horizontal direct effect. The trial judge in London said:

"115. A third, and further alternative, submission put forward by Viking under this head, was that, according to established case-law, Article [45 of the TFEU][135] (formerly Article 48 of the EC Treaty) and Article [49 of the TFEU][136] (formerly Article 52 of the EC Treaty) pursue the same objective, i.e. the free movement of persons: see Case C-19/92 *Dieter Kraus v Land Baden-Württemberg* [1993] ECR I-1663 paragraph 29. Thus the [CJEU] has consistently applied the same case law on horizontal application to workers, establishment and services; see, for example, Case 36/74 *B N O Walrave & Another –v– Association Union Cycliste & Others* [1974] ECR 1405 (a workers and services case); Case C-415/93 *Bosman* [[1995] ECR I-4921] paragraphs 82–84 (a workers case); Case C-309/99 *Wouters* (above) (an establishment case). In Case C-281/98 *Roman Angonese v Cassa di Risparmio di Bolzano SpA* [2000] ECR I-4139 paragraphs 1–2, 5–10 and 28–36, the [CJEU] held that Article [45 TFEU] (freedom of movement of workers) applies as between private parties. The dispute there was between a private individual and a private bank in relation to a recruitment condition imposed by the bank that candidates for admission possess a specified certificate of competence in German and Italian. Thus, it was submitted, that since, in the context of Article [45], the [CJEU] had held that the Article was enforceable between private parties, it logically followed that Article [49] EC must also apply as between private parties, although this issue has not yet been decided by the [CJEU]. The Defendants contend that the facts of the present case are distinguishable from *Angonese* and that the latter case is worker specific. I do not agree. *Angonese* itself invokes the principles recognised in *Walrave* and *Bosman*; see, in particular, paragraphs 30–36. If the principle is that Articles [45] and [49] pursue the same objective, then I see no reason in principle why the decision encapsulated in paragraph 36 of the judgment in *Angonese*, namely that 'the prohibition of discrimination on grounds of nationality ... must be regarded as applying to private persons as well', should not equally apply to a freedom of establishment claim under Article [49]. The Defendants sought to argue that there was a fundamental difference in principle between an Article that governed the freedom 'of the labour market' and one that governed the freedom of an entity to establish itself, or for individuals to be self-employed, anywhere in the [EU]. I do not consider that such distinction, if any, provides any rational explanation for the non-application of the relevant article between private persons. The freedom of establishment likewise impacts

---

134 (2005) 11 JIML 298 at 301.
135 Ed., now Article 45 of the TFEU.
136 Ed., now Article 49 of the TFEU.

directly on the labour market. Accordingly, in my judgment, Viking can invoke Article [49] in this case."[137]

The English court considered whether the measures taken by the ITF were discriminatory. The trial judge was in no doubt that they were discriminatory.

6.129 On 30 June 2005, the ITF and FSU brought an appeal against that decision before the English Court of Appeal. The CJEU summarised some of the arguments of the ITF and FSU:

> "24. ... In support of their appeal they claimed, inter alia, that the right of trade unions to take collective action to preserve jobs is a fundamental right recognised by Title XI of the EC Treaty[138] and, in particular, Article 136 EC,[139] the first paragraph of which provides that '[t]he Community and the Member States, having in mind fundamental social rights such as those set out in the European Social Charter signed at Turin on 18 October 1961 and in the 1989 Community Charter of the Fundamental Social Rights of Workers, shall have as their objectives the promotion of employment, improved living and working conditions, so as to make possible their harmonisation while the improvement is being maintained, proper social protection, dialogue between management and labour, the development of human resources with a view to lasting high employment and the combating of exclusion'.
> 25. It was argued that the reference to the European Social Charter and the Community Charter of the Fundamental Social Rights of Workers incorporated a reference to the right to strike recognised by those legal instruments. Consequently, the trade unions had the right to take collective action against an employer established in a Member State to seek to persuade him not to move part or all of his undertaking to another Member State.
> 26. The question therefore arises whether the Treaty intends to prohibit trade union action where it is aimed at preventing an employer from exercising his right of establishment for economic reasons. By analogy with the Court's rulings regarding Title VI of the Treaty (Case C-67/96 *Albany* [1999] ECR I-5751; Joined Cases C-180/98 to C-184/98 *Pavlov and Others* [2000] ECR I-6451; and Case C-222/98 *Van der Woude* [2000] ECR I-7111), it is argued that Title III of the Treaty and the articles relating to free movement of persons and of services do not apply to 'genuine trade union activities'."

6.130 These were difficult issues of EU law. On 23 November 2005, the English Court of Appeal, not surprisingly, decided to stay proceedings and refer ten questions to the CJEU for a preliminary ruling. The English Court of Appeal also lifted the injunction.[140]

6.131 On 23 May 2007, Advocate-General Poiares delivered his opinion. On 11 December 2007, the CJEU delivered its ruling. It is proposed to analyse each question and each answer given by the Court but it is useful first to examine some general observations made by the CJEU in regard to the questions asked by the Court of Appeal and how the EU was not in a position to answer some of them; in particular, the CJEU stated:

---

137 Chuah commented ((2005) 11 JIML 298 at 301): "[t]hat said, it might be submitted that although the two articles promoted and pursued the same single market objectives, those objectives are expressed in a general way. Indeed, most of the free movement provisions in the Treaty promoted the same convergence objectives of the single market. Nevertheless, it must be said that this was a supplemental argument to the central thesis that trade unions, by and large, have immense powers to control the labour market, thereby affecting the freedom of establishment and as such, should be subject to free movement provisions of the Treaty. Strong non-governmental bodies such as trade unions, sporting associations, professional bodies and trade associations, should not be allowed to claim the free movement rights without being subject [to] the duties implicit in those rules."
138 Ed., now Title IX of the TFEU – relating to social policy.
139 Ed., now Art. 151 of the TFEU.
140 *International Transport Workers' Federation v Viking Line Abp* [2005] EWCA Civ 1299, [2006] 1 Lloyd's Rep 303, [2005] 2 CLC 720, [2006] 1 CMLR 27, [2006] ELR 509.

"28. It must be borne in mind that, in accordance with settled case-law, in the context of the cooperation between the Court and the national courts provided for in Article [267 of the TFEU], it is solely for the national court before which a dispute has been brought, and which must assume responsibility for the subsequent judicial decision, to determine in the light of the particular circumstances of the case both the need for a preliminary ruling in order to enable it to deliver judgment and the relevance of the questions which it submits to the Court. However, the Court has regarded itself as not having jurisdiction to give a preliminary ruling on a question submitted by a national court where it is quite obvious, inter alia, that the interpretation of Community law sought by that court bears no relation to the actual facts of the main action or its purpose or where the problem is hypothetical (see Case C-415/93 *Bosman* [1995] ECR I-4921 and Case C-350/03 *Schulte* [2005] ECR I-9215, paragraph 43).

29. In the present case, the reference for a preliminary ruling concerns the interpretation, first, of provisions of the Treaty on freedom of establishment, and secondly, of Regulation No 4055/86 applying the principle of freedom to provide services to maritime transport.

30. However, since the question on freedom to provide services can arise only after the reflagging of the *Rosella* envisaged by Viking, and since, on the date on which the questions were referred to the Court, the vessel had not yet been re-flagged, the reference for a preliminary ruling is hypothetical and thus inadmissible in so far as it relates to the interpretation of Regulation No 4055/86.[141]

31. In those circumstances, the questions referred by the national court can be answered only in so far as they concern the interpretation of Article [49 of the TFEU]."

Free movement of persons

6.132 The first question asked of the CJEU related to the scope of the free movement provisions. The question was:

"Where a trade union or association of trade unions takes collective action against a private undertaking so as to require that undertaking to enter into a collective bargaining agreement with a trade union in a particular Member State which has the effect of making it pointless for that undertaking to re-flag a vessel in another Member State, does that action fall outside the scope of Article [49 of the TFEU] and/or Regulation No 4055/86 by virtue of the [EU's] social policy including, inter alia, Title [IX] of the [TFEU] and, in particular, by analogy with the Court's reasoning in ... *Albany* (paragraphs 52 to 64)?"

6.133 The CJEU answered:

"32. By its first question, the national court is essentially asking whether Article [49 of the TFEU] must be interpreted as meaning that collective action initiated by a trade union or a group of trade unions against an undertaking in order to induce that undertaking to enter into a collective agreement, the terms of which are liable to deter it from exercising freedom of establishment, falls outside the scope of that article.

33. In this regard, it must be borne in mind that, according to settled case-law, Articles [45 of the TFEU], [49 of the TFEU] and [56 of the TFEU] do not apply only to the actions of public authorities but extend also to rules of any other nature aimed at regulating in a collective manner gainful employment, self-employment and the provision of services (see Case 36/74 *Walrave and Koch* [1974] ECR 1405, paragraph 17; Case 13/76 *Donà* [1976] ECR 1333, paragraph 17; *Bosman*, paragraph 82; Joined Cases C-51/96 and C-191/97 *Deliège* [2000] ECR I-2549, paragraph 47; Case C-281/98 *Angonese* [2000] ECR I-4139, paragraph 31; and Case C-309/99 *Wouters and Others* [2002] ECR I-1577, paragraph 120).

34. Since working conditions in the different Member States are governed sometimes by

---

141 Ed., on Reg. 4055/86, see chap. 7.

provisions laid down by law or regulation and sometimes by collective agreements and other acts concluded or adopted by private persons, limiting application of the prohibitions laid down by these articles to acts of a public authority would risk creating inequality in its application (see, by analogy, *Walrave and Koch*, paragraph 19; *Bosman*, paragraph 84; and *Angonese*, paragraph 33).

35. In the present case, it must be stated, first, that the organisation of collective action by trade unions must be regarded as covered by the legal autonomy which those organisations, which are not public law entities, enjoy pursuant to the trade union rights accorded to them, inter alia, by national law.
36. Secondly, as FSU and ITF submit, collective action such as that at issue in the main proceedings, which may be the trade unions' last resort to ensure the success of their claim to regulate the work of Viking's employees collectively, must be considered to be inextricably linked to the collective agreement the conclusion of which FSU is seeking.
37. It follows that collective action such as that described in the first question referred by the national court falls, in principle, within the scope of Article [49 of the TFEU].
38. This view is not called into question by the various arguments put forward by FSU, ITF and certain Member States which submitted observations to the Court to support the position contrary to that set out in the previous paragraph.
39. First of all, the Danish Government submits that the right of association, the right to strike and the right to impose lock-outs fall outside the scope of the fundamental freedom laid down in Article [49 of the TFEU] since, in accordance with Article [153(5) of the TFEU],[142] the [EU] does not have competence to regulate those rights.

---

142 Ed., Art. 153 of the TFEU provides:
"1. With a view to achieving the objectives of Article 151, the Union shall support and complement the activities of the Member States in the following fields:
    (a) improvement in particular of the working environment to protect workers' health and safety;
    (b) working conditions;
    (c) social security and social protection of workers;
    (d) protection of workers where their employment contract is terminated;
    (e) the information and consultation of workers;
    (f) representation and collective defence of the interests of workers and employers, including co-determination, subject to paragraph 5;
    (g) conditions of employment for third-country nationals legally residing in Union territory;
    (h) the integration of persons excluded from the labour market, without prejudice to Article 166;
    (i) equality between men and women with regard to labour market opportunities and treatment at work;
    (j) the combating of social exclusion;
    (k) the modernisation of social protection systems without prejudice to point (c).
2. To this end, the European Parliament and the Council:
    (a) may adopt measures designed to encourage cooperation between Member States through initiatives aimed at improving knowledge, developing exchanges of information and best practices, promoting innovative approaches and evaluating experiences, excluding any harmonisation of the laws and regulations of the Member States;
    (b) may adopt, in the fields referred to in paragraph 1(a) to (i), by means of directives, minimum requirements for gradual implementation, having regard to the conditions and technical rules obtaining in each of the Member States. Such directives shall avoid imposing administrative, financial and legal constraints in a way which would hold back the creation and development of small and medium-sized undertakings.

    The European Parliament and the Council shall act in accordance with the ordinary legislative procedure after consulting the Economic and Social Committee and the Committee of the Regions.

    In the fields referred to in paragraph 1(c), (d), (f) and (g), the Council shall act unanimously, in accordance with a special legislative procedure, after consulting the European Parliament and the said Committees.

    The Council, acting unanimously on a proposal from the Commission, after consulting the European Parliament, may decide to render the ordinary legislative procedure applicable to paragraph 1(d), (f) and (g).

40. In that respect it is sufficient to point out that, even if, in the areas which fall outside the scope of the [EU's] competence, the Member States are still free, in principle, to lay down the conditions governing the existence and exercise of the rights in question, the fact remains that, when exercising that competence, the Member States must nevertheless comply with [EU] law (see, by analogy, in relation to social security, Case C-120/95 *Decker* [1998] ECR I-1831, paragraphs 22 and 23, and Case C-158/96 *Kohll* [1998] ECR I-1931, paragraphs 18 and 19; in relation to direct taxation, Case C-334/02 *Commission v France* [2004] ECR I-2229, paragraph 21, and Case C-446/03 *Marks & Spencer* [2005] ECR I-10837, paragraph 29).

41. Consequently, the fact that Article [153 of the TFEU] does not apply to the right to strike or to the right to impose lock-outs is not such as to exclude collective action such as that at issue in the main proceedings from the application of Article [49 of the TFEU].[143]

42. Next, according to the observations of the Danish and Swedish Governments, the right to take collective action, including the right to strike, constitutes a fundamental right which, as such, falls outside the scope of Article [49 of the TFEU].

43. In that regard, it must be recalled that the right to take collective action, including the right to strike, is recognised both by various international instruments which the Member States have signed or cooperated in, such as the European Social Charter, signed at Turin on 18 October 1961 – to which, moreover, express reference is made in Article [151 of the TFEU] – and Convention No 87 concerning Freedom of Association and Protection of the Right to Organise, adopted on 9 July 1948 by the International Labour Organisation – and by instruments developed by those Member States at Community level or in the context of the European Union, such as the Community Charter of the Fundamental Social Rights of Workers adopted at the meeting of the European Council held in Strasbourg on 9 December 1989, which is also referred to in Article 136 EC, and the Charter of Fundamental Rights of the European Union proclaimed in Nice on 7 December 2000 (OJ 2000 C364, p. 1).[144]

44. Although the right to take collective action, including the right to strike, must therefore be recognised as a fundamental right which forms an integral part of the general principles of [EU] law the observance of which the Court ensures, the exercise of that right may none the less be subject to certain restrictions. As is reaffirmed by Article 28 of the Charter of Fundamental Rights of the European Union, those rights are to be protected in accordance with Community law and national law and practices. In addition, as is apparent from paragraph 5 of this judgment, under Finnish law the right to strike may not be relied on, in

---

3. A Member State may entrust management and labour, at their joint request, with the implementation of directives adopted pursuant to paragraph 2, or, where appropriate, with the implementation of a Council decision adopted in accordance with Article 155.

    In this case, it shall ensure that, no later than the date on which a directive or a decision must be transposed or implemented, management and labour have introduced the necessary measures by agreement, the Member State concerned being required to take any necessary measure enabling it at any time to be in a position to guarantee the results imposed by that directive or that decision.

4. The provisions adopted pursuant to this Article:
    - shall not affect the right of Member States to define the fundamental principles of their social security systems and must not significantly affect the financial equilibrium thereof,
    - shall not prevent any Member State from maintaining or introducing more stringent protective measures compatible with the Treaties.

5. The provisions of this Article shall not apply to pay, the right of association, the right to strike or the right to impose lock-outs."

143 Ed., Novitz (op. cit. at fn. 126, p. 268) commented that the ECJ's response to the Danish Government's argument "is hardly contentious, but does suggest that, unless EU Member States make Treaty provision for legislative competence relating to the right to strike, there is scope for the rights protected under domestic labour legislation and even domestic constitutions to be eroded by the emphasis placed by the ECJ on the supremacy of the free movement rights set out in the EC Treaty".

144 Ed., this paragraph represents the first time that the CJEU recognised the right to strike as being part of EU law.

particular, where the strike is *contra bonos mores* or is prohibited under national law or [EU] law.

45. In that regard, the Court has already held that the protection of fundamental rights is a legitimate interest which, in principle, justifies a restriction of the obligations imposed by [EU] law, even under a fundamental freedom guaranteed by the Treaty, such as the free movement of goods (see Case C-112/00 *Schmidberger* [2003] ECR I-5659, paragraph 74) or freedom to provide services (see Case C-36/02 *Omega* [2004] ECR I-9609, paragraph 35).

46. However, in *Schmidberger* and *Omega*, the Court held that the exercise of the fundamental rights at issue, that is, freedom of expression and freedom of assembly and respect for human dignity, respectively, does not fall outside the scope of the provisions of the Treaty and considered that such exercise must be reconciled with the requirements relating to rights protected under the Treaty and in accordance with the principle of proportionality (see, to that effect, *Schmidberger*, paragraph 77, and *Omega*, paragraph 36).

47. It follows from the foregoing that the fundamental nature of the right to take collective action is not such as to render Article [49 of the TFEU] inapplicable to the collective action at issue in the main proceedings.

48. Finally, FSU and ITF submit that the Court's reasoning in *Albany* must be applied by analogy to the case in the main proceedings, since certain restrictions on freedom of establishment and freedom to provide services are inherent in collective action taken in the context of collective negotiations.

49. In that regard, it should be noted that in paragraph 59 of *Albany*, having found that certain restrictions of competition are inherent in collective agreements between organisations representing employers and workers, the Court nevertheless held that the social policy objectives pursued by such agreements would be seriously undermined if management and labour were subject to Article 85(1) of the EC Treaty (now, Article [101(1) of the TFEU]) when seeking jointly to adopt measures to improve conditions of work and employment.

50. The Court inferred from this, in paragraph 60 of *Albany*, that agreements concluded in the context of collective negotiations between management and labour in pursuit of such objectives must, by virtue of their nature and purpose, be regarded as falling outside the scope of Article [101(1) of the TFEU].

51. The Court must point out, however, that that reasoning cannot be applied in the context of the fundamental freedoms set out in Title III of the Treaty.

52. Contrary to the claims of FSU and ITF, it cannot be considered that it is inherent in the very exercise of trade union rights and the right to take collective action that those fundamental freedoms will be prejudiced to a certain degree.

53. Furthermore, the fact that an agreement or an activity are excluded from the scope of the provisions of the Treaty on competition does not mean that that agreement or activity also falls outside the scope of the Treaty provisions on the free movement of persons or services since those two sets of provisions are to be applied in different circumstances (see, to that effect, Case C-519/04 P *Meca-Medina and Majcen v Commission* [2006] ECR I-6991).

54. Finally, the Court has held that the terms of collective agreements are not excluded from the scope of the Treaty provisions on freedom of movement for persons (Case C-15/96 *Schöning-Kougebetopoulou* [1998] ECR I-47; Case C-35/97 *Commission v France* [1998] ECR I-5325; and Case C-400/02 *Merida* [2004] ECR I-8471).

55. In the light of the foregoing, the answer to the first question must be that Article [49 of the TFEU] is to be interpreted as meaning that, in principle, collective action initiated by a trade union or a group of trade unions against an undertaking in order to induce that undertaking to enter into a collective agreement, the terms of which are liable to deter it from exercising freedom of establishment, is not excluded from the scope of that article."

Second question: Horizontal Direct Effect and Article 49

6.134 The second question referred by the English court concerned so-called horizontal direct effect. The CJEU was asked:

"Do Article [49 of the TFEU] and/or Regulation No 4055/86 have horizontal direct effect so as to confer rights on a private undertaking which may be relied on against another private party and, in particular, a trade union or association of trade unions in respect of collective action by that union or association of unions?"

6.135 The CJEU responded (addressing only Article 49 of the TFEU):

"56. By that question, the referring court is asking in essence whether Article [49 of the TFEU] is such as to confer rights on a private undertaking which may be relied on against a trade union or an association of trade unions.

57. In order to answer that question, the Court would point out that it is clear from its case-law that the abolition, as between Member States, of obstacles to freedom of movement for persons and freedom to provide services would be compromised if the abolition of State barriers could be neutralised by obstacles resulting from the exercise, by associations or organisations not governed by public law, of their legal autonomy (*Walrave and Koch*, paragraph 18; *Bosman*, paragraph 83; *Deliège*, paragraph 47; *Angonese*, paragraph 32; and *Wouters and Others*, paragraph 120).

58. Moreover, the Court has ruled, first, that the fact that certain provisions of the Treaty are formally addressed to the Member States does not prevent rights from being conferred at the same time on any individual who has an interest in compliance with the obligations thus laid down, and, second, that the prohibition on prejudicing a fundamental freedom laid down in a provision of the Treaty that is mandatory in nature, applies in particular to all agreements intended to regulate paid labour collectively (see, to that effect, Case 43/75 *Defrenne* [1976] ECR 455, paragraphs 31 and 39).

59. Such considerations must also apply to Article [49 of the TFEU] which lays down a fundamental freedom.

60. In the present case, it must be borne in mind that, as is apparent from paragraphs 35 and 36 of the present judgment, the collective action taken by FSU and ITF is aimed at the conclusion of an agreement which is meant to regulate the work of Viking's employees collectively, and, that those two trade unions are organisations which are not public law entities but exercise the legal autonomy conferred on them, inter alia, by national law.

61. It follows that Article [49 of the TFEU] must be interpreted as meaning that, in circumstances such as those in the main proceedings, it may be relied on by a private undertaking against a trade union or an association of trade unions.

62. This interpretation is also supported by the case-law on the Treaty provisions on the free movement of goods, from which it is apparent that restrictions may be the result of actions by individuals or groups of such individuals rather than caused by the State (see Case C-265/95 *Commission v France* [1997] ECR I-6959, paragraph 30, and *Schmidberger*, paragraphs 57 and 62).

63. The interpretation set out in paragraph 61 of the present judgment is also not called into question by the fact that the restriction at issue in the proceedings before the national court stems from the exercise of a right conferred by Finnish national law, such as, in this case, the right to take collective action, including the right to strike.

64. It must be added that, contrary to the claims, in particular, of ITF, it does not follow from the case-law of the Court referred to in paragraph 57 of the present judgment that that interpretation applies only to quasi-public organisations or to associations exercising a regulatory task and having quasi-legislative powers.

65. There is no indication in that case-law that could validly support the view that it applies only to associations or to organisations exercising a regulatory task or having quasi-legislative powers. Furthermore, it must be pointed out that, in exercising their autonomous power, pursuant to their trade union rights, to negotiate with employers or professional organisations the conditions of employment and pay of workers, trade unions participate in the drawing up of agreements seeking to regulate paid work collectively.

66. In the light of those considerations, the answer to the second question must be that Article [49 of the TFEU] is capable of conferring rights on a private undertaking which may be relied on against a trade union or an association of trade unions."

6.136 Thus an employer may rely on its rights under Article 49 of the TFEU in an action against a trade union or an association of trade unions.

6.137 The English court then asked a series of questions which the CJEU grouped together for the purposes of responding. The English court asked:

"Questions on the existence of restrictions on free movement

(3) Where a trade union or association of trade unions takes collective action against a private undertaking so as to require that undertaking to enter into a collective bargaining agreement with a trade union in a particular Member State, which has the effect of making it pointless for that undertaking to re-flag a vessel in another Member State, does that action constitute a restriction for the purposes of Article [49 of the TFEU] and/or Regulation No 4055/86?

(4) Is a policy of an association of trade unions which provides that vessels should be flagged in the registry of the country in which the beneficial ownership and control of the vessel is situated so that the trade unions in the country of beneficial ownership of a vessel have the right to conclude collective bargaining agreements in respect of that vessel, a directly discriminatory, indirectly discriminatory or non-discriminatory restriction under Article [49 of the TFEU] or Regulation No 4055/86?

(5) In determining whether collective action by a trade union or association of trade unions is a directly discriminatory, indirectly discriminatory or non-discriminatory restriction under Article [49 of the TFEU] or Regulation No 4055/86, is the subjective intention of the union taking the action relevant or must the national court determine the issue solely by reference to the objective effects of that action?"

"Questions on establishment/services

(6) Where a parent company is established in Member State A and intends to undertake an act of establishment by reflagging a vessel to Member State B to be operated by an existing wholly owned subsidiary in Member State B which is subject to the direction and control of the parent company:

  (a) is threatened or actual collective action by a trade union or association of trade unions hich would seek to render the above a pointless exercise capable of constituting a restriction on the parent company's right of establishment under Article [49 of the TFEU], and
  (b) after reflagging of the vessel, is the subsidiary entitled to rely on Regulation No 4055/86 in respect of the provision of services by it from Member State B to Member State A?"

Questions on Justification

"Direct discrimination

(7) If collective action by a trade union or association of trade unions is a directly discriminatory restriction under Article [49 of the TFEU] or Regulation No 4055/86, can it, in principle, be justified on the basis of the public policy exception set out in Article [52 of the TFEU] on the basis that:

  (a) the taking of collective action (including strike action) is a fundamental right protected by Community law; and/or
  (b) the protection of workers?

The policy of [ITF]: objective justification

(8) Does the application of a policy of an association of trade unions which provides that vessels should be flagged in the registry of the country in which the beneficial ownership and control of the vessel is situated so that the trade unions in the country of beneficial ownership of a

vessel have the right to conclude collective bargaining agreements in respect of that vessel, strike a fair balance between the fundamental social right to take collective action and the freedom to establish and provide services, and is it objectively justified, appropriate, proportionate and in conformity with the principle of mutual recognition?

FSU's actions: objective justification

(9) Where:

- a parent company in Member State A owns a vessel flagged in Member State A and provides ferry services between Member State A and Member State B using that vessel;
- the parent company wishes to re-flag the vessel to Member State B to apply terms and conditions of employment which are lower than in Member State A;
- the parent company in Member State A wholly owns a subsidiary in Member State B and that subsidiary is subject to its direction and control;
- it is intended that the subsidiary will operate the vessel once it has been re-flagged in Member State B with a crew recruited in Member State B covered by a collective bargaining agreement negotiated with an ITF affiliated trade union in Member State B;
- the vessel will remain beneficially owned by the parent company and be bareboat chartered to the subsidiary;
- the vessel will continue to provide ferry services between Member State A and Member State B on a daily basis;
- a trade union established in Member State A takes collective action so as to require the parent and/or subsidiary to enter into a collective bargaining agreement with it which will apply terms and conditions acceptable to the union in Member State A to the crew of the vessel even after reflagging and which has the effect of making it pointless for the parent to re-flag the vessel to Member State B, does that collective action strike a fair balance between the fundamental social right to take collective action and the freedom to establish and provide services and is it objectively justified, appropriate, proportionate and in conformity with the principle of mutual recognition?

(10) Would it make any difference to the answer to [Question] 9 if the parent company provided an undertaking to a court on behalf of itself and all the companies within the same group that they will not by reason of the reflagging terminate the employment of any person employed by them (which undertaking did not require the renewal of short term employment contracts or prevent the redeployment of any employee on equivalent terms and conditions)?"

6.138 The CJEU replied in the following terms:

"The third to tenth questions

67 … the national court is essentially asking the Court of Justice whether collective action such as that at issue in the main proceedings constitutes a restriction within the meaning of Article [49 of the TFEU] and, if so, to what extent such a restriction may be justified.

The existence of restrictions

68. The Court must first point out, as it has done on numerous occasions, that freedom of establishment constitutes one of the fundamental principles of the [EU] and that the provisions of the Treaty guaranteeing that freedom have been directly applicable since the end of the transitional period. Those provisions secure the right of establishment in another Member State not merely for [EU] nationals but also for the companies or firms referred to in Article [54 of the TFEU] (Case 81/87 *Daily Mail and General Trust* [1988] ECR 5483, paragraph 15).

69. Furthermore, the Court has considered that, even though the provisions of the Treaty concerning freedom of establishment are directed mainly to ensuring that foreign nationals and

companies are treated in the host Member State in the same way as nationals of that State, they also prohibit the Member State of origin from hindering the establishment in another Member State of one of its nationals or of a company incorporated under its legislation which also comes within the definition contained in Article [54 of the TFEU]. The rights guaranteed by Articles [49 of the TFEU] to [55 of the TFEU] would be rendered meaningless if the Member State of origin could prohibit undertakings from leaving in order to establish themselves in another Member State (*Daily Mail and General Trust*, paragraph 16).

70. Secondly, according to the settled case-law of the Court, the definition of establishment within the meaning of those articles of the Treaty involves the actual pursuit of an economic activity through a fixed establishment in another Member State for an indefinite period and registration of a vessel cannot be separated from the exercise of the freedom of establishment where the vessel serves as a vehicle for the pursuit of an economic activity that includes fixed establishment in the State of registration (Case C-221/89 *Factortame and Others* [1991] ECR I-3905, paragraphs 20 to 22).

71. The Court concluded from this that the conditions laid down for the registration of vessels must not form an obstacle to freedom of establishment within the meaning of Articles [49 of the TFEU] to [55 of the TFEU] (*Factortame and Others*, paragraph 23).

72. In the present case, first, it cannot be disputed that collective action such as that envisaged by FSU has the effect of making less attractive, or even pointless, as the national court has pointed out, Viking's exercise of its right to freedom of establishment, inasmuch as such action prevents both Viking and its subsidiary, Viking Eesti, from enjoying the same treatment in the host Member State as other economic operators established in that State.

73. Secondly, collective action taken in order to implement ITF's policy of combating the use of flags of convenience, which seeks, primarily, as is apparent from ITF's observations, to prevent shipowners from registering their vessels in a State other than that of which the beneficial owners of those vessels are nationals, must be considered to be at least liable to restrict Viking's exercise of its right of freedom of establishment.

74. It follows that collective action such as that at issue in the main proceedings constitutes a restriction on freedom of establishment within the meaning of Article [49 of the TFEU].

Justification of the restrictions

75. It is apparent from the case-law of the Court that a restriction on freedom of establishment can be accepted only if it pursues a legitimate aim compatible with the Treaty and is justified by overriding reasons of public interest. But even if that were the case, it would still have to be suitable for securing the attainment of the objective pursued and must not go beyond what is necessary in order to attain it (see, inter alia, Case C-55/94 *Gebhard* [1995] ECR I-4165, paragraph 37, and *Bosman*, paragraph 104).

76. ITF, supported, in particular, by the German Government, Ireland and the Finnish Government, maintains that the restrictions at issue in the main proceedings are justified since they are necessary to ensure the protection of a fundamental right recognised under Community law and their objective is to protect the rights of workers, which constitutes an overriding reason of public interest.

77. In that regard, it must be observed that the right to take collective action for the protection of workers is a legitimate interest which, in principle, justifies a restriction of one of the fundamental freedoms guaranteed by the Treaty (see, to that effect, *Schmidberger*, paragraph 74) and that the protection of workers is one of the overriding reasons of public interest recognised by the Court (see, inter alia, Joined Cases C-369/96 and C-376/96 *Arblade and Others* [1999] ECR I-8453, paragraph 36; Case C-165/98 *Mazzoleni and ISA* [2001] ECR I-2189, paragraph 27; and Joined Cases C-49/98, C-50/98, C-52/98 to C-54/98 and C-68/98 to C-71/98 *Finalarte and Others* [2001] ECR I-7831, paragraph 33).

78. It must be added that, according to Article 3(1)(c) and (j) EC, the activities of the Community are to include not only an 'internal market characterised by the abolition, as between Member States, of obstacles to the free movement of goods, persons, services and capital', but also 'a policy in the social sphere'. Article 2 EC states that the Community is to have as

its task, inter alia, the promotion of 'a harmonious, balanced and sustainable development of economic activities' and 'a high level of employment and of social protection'.

79. Since the Community has thus not only an economic but also a social purpose, the rights under the provisions of the Treaty on the free movement of goods, persons, services and capital must be balanced against the objectives pursued by social policy, which include, as is clear from the first paragraph of Article 136 EC, inter alia, improved living and working conditions, so as to make possible their harmonisation while improvement is being maintained, proper social protection and dialogue between management and labour.

80. In the present case, it is for the national court to ascertain whether the objectives pursued by FSU and ITF by means of the collective action which they initiated concerned the protection of workers.

81. First, as regards the collective action taken by FSU, even if that action – aimed at protecting the jobs and conditions of employment of the members of that union liable to be adversely affected by the reflagging of the *Rosella* – could reasonably be considered to fall, at first sight, within the objective of protecting workers, such a view would no longer be tenable if it were established that the jobs or conditions of employment at issue were not jeopardised or under serious threat.

82. This would be the case, in particular, if it transpired that the undertaking referred to by the national court in its 10th question was, from a legal point of view, as binding as the terms of a collective agreement and if it was of such a nature as to provide a guarantee to the workers that the statutory provisions would be complied with and the terms of the collective agreement governing their working relationship maintained.

83. In so far as the exact legal scope to be attributed to an undertaking such as that referred to in the 10th question is not clear from the order for reference, it is for the national court to determine whether the jobs or conditions of employment of that trade union's members who are liable to be affected by the reflagging of the *Rosella* were jeopardised or under serious threat.

84. If, following that examination, the national court came to the conclusion that, in the case before it, the jobs or conditions of employment of the FSU's members liable to be adversely affected by the reflagging of the *Rosella* are in fact jeopardised or under serious threat, it would then have to ascertain whether the collective action initiated by FSU is suitable for ensuring the achievement of the objective pursued and does not go beyond what is necessary to attain that objective.

85. In that regard, it must be pointed out that, even if it is ultimately for the national court, which has sole jurisdiction to assess the facts and interpret the national legislation, to determine whether and to what extent such collective action meets those requirements, the Court of Justice, which is called on to provide answers of use to the national court, may provide guidance, based on the file in the main proceedings and on the written and oral observations which have been submitted to it, in order to enable the national court to give judgment in the particular case before it.

86. As regards the appropriateness of the action taken by FSU for attaining the objectives pursued in the case in the main proceedings, it should be borne in mind that it is common ground that collective action, like collective negotiations and collective agreements, may, in the particular circumstances of a case, be one of the main ways in which trade unions protect the interests of their members (European Court of Human Rights, *Syndicat national de la police belge v Belgium*, of 27 October 1975, Series A, No 19, and *Wilson, National Union of Journalists and Others v United Kingdom* of 2 July 2002, 2002-V, § 44).

87. As regards the question of whether or not the collective action at issue in the main proceedings goes beyond what is necessary to achieve the objective pursued, it is for the national court to examine, in particular, on the one hand, whether, under the national rules and collective agreement law applicable to that action, FSU did not have other means at its disposal which were less restrictive of freedom of establishment in order to bring to a successful conclusion the collective negotiations entered into with Viking, and, on the other, whether that trade union had exhausted those means before initiating such action.

88. Secondly, in relation to the collective action seeking to ensure the implementation of the policy in question pursued by ITF, it must be emphasised that, to the extent that that policy results in shipowners being prevented from registering their vessels in a State other than that of which the beneficial owners of those vessels are nationals, the restrictions on freedom of establishment resulting from such action cannot be objectively justified. Nevertheless, as the national court points out, the objective of that policy is also to protect and improve seafarers' terms and conditions of employment.

89. However, as is apparent from the file submitted to the Court, in the context of its policy of combating the use of flags of convenience, ITF is required, when asked by one of its members, to initiate solidarity action against the beneficial owner of a vessel which is registered in a State other than that of which that owner is a national, irrespective of whether or not that owner's exercise of its right of freedom of establishment is liable to have a harmful effect on the work or conditions of employment of its employees. Therefore, as Viking argued during the hearing without being contradicted by ITF in that regard, the policy of reserving the right of collective negotiations to trade unions of the State of which the beneficial owner of a vessel is a national is also applicable where the vessel is registered in a State which guarantees workers a higher level of social protection than they would enjoy in the first State.

90. In the light of those considerations, the answer to the third to tenth questions must be that Article [49 of the TFEU] is to be interpreted to the effect that collective action such as that at issue in the main proceedings, which seeks to induce an undertaking whose registered office is in a given Member State to enter into a collective work agreement with a trade union established in that State and to apply the terms set out in that agreement to the employees of a subsidiary of that undertaking established in another Member State, constitutes a restriction within the meaning of that article. That restriction may, in principle, be justified by an overriding reason of public interest, such as the protection of workers, provided that it is established that the restriction is suitable for ensuring the attainment of the legitimate objective pursued and does not go beyond what is necessary to achieve that objective."

Essence of the CJEU's ruling in *Viking*

6.139 The CJEU itself summarised its ruling in the following terms:

"1. Article [49 of the TFEU] is to be interpreted as meaning that, in principle, collective action initiated by a trade union or a group of trade unions against a private undertaking in order to induce that undertaking to enter into a collective agreement, the terms of which are liable to deter it from exercising freedom of establishment, is not excluded from the scope of that article.
2. Article [49 of the TFEU] is capable of conferring rights on a private undertaking which may be relied on against a trade union or an association of trade unions.
3. Article [49 of the TFEU] is to be interpreted to the effect that collective action such as that at issue in the main proceedings, which seeks to induce a private undertaking whose registered office is in a given Member State to enter into a collective work agreement with a trade union established in that State and to apply the terms set out in that agreement to the employees of a subsidiary of that undertaking established in another Member State, constitutes a restriction within the meaning of that article.

That restriction may, in principle, be justified by an overriding reason of public interest, such as the protection of workers, provided that it is established that the restriction is suitable for ensuring the attainment of the legitimate objective pursued and does not go beyond what is necessary to achieve that objective."

Analysis of the ruling

6.140 Novitz has commented on the ruling in the following terms:

"[f]or the first time, we have a statement by the European Court of Justice that the right to take collective action, including the right to strike, is to be regarded as a fundamental principle under EU law. Workers and their unions are to be regarded as entitled to take industrial action which seeks to resist the re-flagging of vessels, as in the case of *Viking*. However, at the same time, this judgment severely limits their capacity to do so. This is achieved by the application of horizontal direct effect of free movement provisions to trade unions exercising their right to strike, requiring thereby that, not only the state defend the legislation that enables such action to be taken, but that the trade union concerned defend their actions under EU law, regardless of whether they are *prima facie* lawful under domestic labour law.

To defend collective action in the face of re-flagging, it seems that the trade union must demonstrate that the jobs of union members and their terms and conditions of employment are at risk. An enforceable undertaking from an employer that they will remain unaffected is enough to render action unjustifiable, even if broader issues of undercutting wage costs are at issue. Moreover, international solidarity action in support of the dispute over re-flagging would results from re-registration of the vessel in question. One might expect the ITF to amend its 'flags of convenience' policy accordingly; although any future court proceedings may still enable the ITF to provide reasons and evidence for the policy as it currently stands.

Finally, the requirement that any action is proportionate is likely to create considerable difficulties. It will be for national courts ultimately to determine whether trade unions that initiate industrial action are doing so in the least disruptive manner possible and have tried to resolve the dispute in an appropriate manner before taking the action in question. This poses problems for trade unions, given the ease of gaining an interlocutory injunction under the *American Cyanamid* principle,[145] and the uncertainty as to whether legal liability will arise once the action is already underway. A solution may be for trade unions to seek a declaration as to the legality of their actions under EU law before initiating a strike,[146] although the costs will be high."[147]

I. THE *COMMISSION V NETHERLANDS* LITIGATION

Introduction

6.141 On 14 October 2004, the CJEU held in *Commission v Netherlands*[148] that the Netherlands was in breach of EU law in respect of the Dutch regime on the registration of ships. The Commission had sought a declaration from the CJEU alleging that the Netherlands was in breach of EU law by adopting and maintaining Article 311 of the Wetboek van Koophandel (Code of Commerce) and Article 8:169 of the Burgerlijk Wetboek (Civil Code), under which certain conditions were fixed concerning:

- the nationality of the shareholders and directors of companies owning seagoing ships which they wish to register in the Netherlands; and
- the nationality and residence of the directors of shipping companies owning seagoing ships registered in the Netherlands and of the natural persons responsible for the day-

---

145 *American Cyanamid Co (No.1) v Ethicon Ltd* [1975] AC 396. For the application of a balance of convenience test under UK law, see *British Telecommunications Plc v Communications Workers' Union* [2003] EWHC 937 (QB).

146 Note the application made by the British Airline Pilots' Association in March 2008 for a High Court declaration as to whether Art. 43 EC applied to the industrial action proposed.

147 Op. cit. at fn. 126, p. 273.

148 Case C-299/02. See 2004 *EU Focus*, No 153, p. 13. See Kan, *Commission v Netherlands*, Case C-299/02, (2005) 59 AJIL 867.

to-day management of the place of business from which the shipping business which is necessary for registration of a ship in the Netherlands registers is carried out in the Netherlands,

6.142 The CJEU held that the Netherlands had failed to fulfil its obligations under Articles 49 and 54 of the TFEU by virtue of the provisions which it had incorporated into the Dutch Commercial Code and Civil Code concerning nationality requirements on the directors, shareholders and managers of shipowning companies registered in the Netherlands.

Legal background

6.143 In examining the legal framework, the CJEU recalled first the international law background. Article 91(1) of the UNCLOS III to which the EU acceded by Council Decision 98/392 of 23 March 1998,[149] provided that

> "[e]very State shall fix the conditions for the grant of its nationality to ships, for the registration of ships in its territory, and for the right to fly its flag. … There must exist a genuine link between the State and the ship".

Article 94 of the UNCLOS III also provided in paragraph 1 that "[e]very State shall effectively exercise its jurisdiction and control in administrative, technical and social matters over ships flying its flag", and set out in the following paragraphs a series of measures which the flag State is required to take to that effect.

6.144 The CJEU then considered the Dutch legal provisions. According to Article 311(1) and (3) of the Wetboek van Koophandel:

> "1. A ship has Netherlands nationality where the following conditions are fulfilled:
>
>   (a) the ship belongs as to at least two thirds to one or more natural persons or companies having the nationality of a Member State of the European Communities ['Community nationality'] or of another State Party to the Agreement on the European Economic Area ['EEA nationality'];
>   (b) the person or persons referred to in subparagraph (a) carry on a shipping business in the Netherlands through an undertaking established in that country or having a secondary place of business there … and manage the ship mainly from the Netherlands;
>   (c) the day-to-day management of the place of business referred to in subparagraph (b) is carried out by one or more natural persons having [Community] or [EEA] nationality;
>   (d) the natural person or persons referred to in subparagraph (c) have powers of representation in all matters relating to the management of the ship and concerning the ship, its captain and the other members of the crew.
>   …
>
> 3. For the purposes of this article, 'legal person having [Community] or [EEA] nationality' means a legal person constituted in accordance with the legislation of a Member State of the European Communities or of another State Party to the Agreement on the European Economic Area … and having its registered office, its central administration or its principal place of business on the territory of a Member State of the European Communities or of another State Party to the Agreement on the European Economic Area, provided that:
>
>   (a) shares representing at least two thirds of the subscribed capital are registered in the name of natural persons having [Community] or [EEA] nationality or of companies

---

[149] OJ 1998 L179/1.

within the meaning of this paragraph *ab initio*, and the majority of the directors have [Community] or [EEA] nationality, or that
(b) all the directors have [Community] or [EEA] nationality."

6.145 Under Article 8:160 of the Burgerlijk Wetboek, a shipping company is a specific form of co-ownership of a ship which enables natural persons to be co-owners of a ship without the intermediary of a legal person. Article 8:163 of the Burgerlijk Wetboek provides that "any ... company may engage an accountant [director]". Article 8:169(1) of the Burgerlijk Wetboek provides that

"the function of accountant [administrator] shall cease if ... he no longer has [Community] or [EEA] nationality or if he establishes his residence outside the territory of a Member State of the European Communities ['Community residence'] or of another State Party to the Agreement on the European Economic Area ['EEA residence']".

6.146 The Commission made three arguments contending that the Netherlands was in breach of EU law. First, it contended that the requirements to be satisfied before a ship can be registered in that Member State were in breach of EU law ("the ship registration scheme"). Those complaints derive from the incompatibility with Article 49 of the TFEU of the condition that:

- a proportion of the shareholders of a Community company owning a ship must be of EU or EEA nationality;
- the directors of a company owning a ship must be of Community or EEA nationality; and/or
- the natural persons responsible for the day-to-day management of the Netherlands place of business ("the local representatives") of a Community shipowner must be of EU or EEA nationality.

6.147 The Commission put forward two further complaints relating to the conditions which the Netherlands required to be satisfied concerning the management of ships by a company ("the ship management scheme"). Those complaints are based on the incompatibility with Article 43 EC of the condition that: the director of a shipping company must be of Community or EEA nationality; and the director of a shipping company must have a Community or EEA residence.

6.148 In regard to the first three complaints, the Commission argued that the Dutch scheme constituted a restriction of freedom of establishment. It argued that although the scheme may be justified on grounds of general interest linked with the exercise of effective control, it must be regarded as disproportionate to the aim pursued. The Netherlands replied that the ship registration scheme did not restrict the right to freedom of movement and that, even on the assumption that the scheme did entail a restriction of freedom of establishment, it would be justified on grounds of general interest relating to the need to exercise effective control and jurisdiction over ships flying the Dutch flag. The CJEU was clear in its view:

"15. It is settled case-law that Article [49 of the TFEU] precludes any national measure which, even though it is applicable without discrimination on grounds of nationality, is liable to hamper or to render less attractive the exercise by Community nationals of the freedom of establishment guaranteed by the Treaty (see, to that effect, Case C-19/92 *Kraus* [1993] ECR I-1663, paragraph 32).

16. It follows from Article [54 of the TFEU] that the right to freedom of establishment is guaranteed not only to [EU] nationals but also to companies formed in accordance with the legislation of a Member State and having their registered office, central administration or principal place of business within the [EU] (see, to that effect, Case 81/87 *Daily Mail and General Trust* [1988] ECR 5483; Case C-212/97 *Centros* [1999] ECR I-1459, paragraph 18; and Case C-208/00 *Überseering* [2002] ECR I-9919, paragraph 56).
17. Freedom of establishment may, however, in the absence of [EU] harmonisation measures, be limited by national regulations justified by the reasons stated in Article [52(1) of the TFEU] or by pressing reasons of general interest (see, to that effect, Case 71/76 *Thieffry* [1977] ECR 765, paragraphs 12 and 15, and *Kraus*, cited above, paragraph 32).
18. In that context, it is for the Member States to decide on the level at which they intend to ensure the protection of the objectives set out in Article [52(1) of the TFEU] and of the general interest and also on the way in which that level must be attained. However, they can do so only within the limits set by the Treaty and, in particular, they must observe the principle of proportionality, which requires that the measures adopted be appropriate for ensuring attainment of the objective which they pursue and do not go beyond what is necessary for that purpose (see, to that effect, Case C-106/91 *Ramrath* [1992] ECR I-3351, paragraphs 29 and 30, and *Kraus*, paragraph 32).
19. In this case, the ship registration scheme has the effect of restricting the freedom of establishment of shipowners. When shipowner companies wishing to register their ships in the Netherlands do not satisfy the conditions in issue, their only course of action is to alter the structure of their share capital or of their boards of directors; and such changes may entail serious disruption within a company and also require the completion of numerous formalities which have financial consequences. Likewise, shipowners must adjust their recruitment policies in order to ensure that their local representatives are not nationals of a State which is not a Member State of the Community or of the EEA.
20. In that regard, the Netherlands Government's argument that, unlike a nationality condition linked with a Member State, a condition requiring Community or EEA nationality cannot constitute a 'restriction' for the purposes of Article [49 of the TFEU] cannot be upheld. In the absence of a harmonised rule valid for the entire Community, a condition of Community or EEA nationality, like a condition of nationality of a specific Member State, may constitute an obstacle to freedom of establishment.
21. A restriction such as the one in issue cannot be justified by grounds of the exercise of effective control and jurisdiction over ships flying the Netherlands flag. The Netherlands registration scheme is not apt to ensure the attainment of its objectives and goes beyond what is necessary to attain them. It is difficult to imagine how the structure of the share capital or the boards of directors of the shipowning companies or the nationality of the local representative may affect the exercise of effective control of the ship by the flag State. Those circumstances are not material to the adoption of measures such as the inspection of the ship, the registration of the details concerning it, verification of the qualification and the working conditions of the crew, and also the opening and conduct of an inquiry in the event of an accident or navigation incident on the high seas.
22. In that regard, the argument whereby the Netherlands Government seeks to demonstrate that the registration scheme is proportionate cannot be upheld.
23. As regards the argument that the Kingdom of the Netherlands is required to adopt the scheme in question by Articles 91(1) and 94(1) of the Montego Bay Convention, it is sufficient to state that, as the Advocate General has shown at points 51 to 59 of his Opinion, those provisions of the Convention do not impose such an obligation on the Kingdom of the Netherlands.
24. As concerns the argument that the Community itself lays down that requirement in its secondary law, it must be held that, while conditions of Community or EEA nationality might be accepted in the context of a harmonised Community scheme, they cannot be established unilaterally by Member States in their national rules.
25. As regards the argument that, in order to ensure effective control, it is necessary to ensure a link with the actual owner (the ultimate beneficiary in the property of the ship), it must be

observed that, for the purposes of such a control, it is sufficient to provide that the management of the ship must be carried out from a place of business in the Netherlands by a person with powers of representation (see, to that effect, Case C-221/89 *Factortame and Others* [1991] ECR I-3905, paragraph 36). Thus, the Member State may deal directly with the representative of the shipowner.

26. As regards the argument that the nationality condition considerably increases the prospects of jurisdiction being effectively exercised, the possibility for a State to exercise its jurisdiction over a person depends primarily on the practical accessibility of the person concerned and not on his nationality. That test is already met when the management of the ship must be carried out from a place of business in the Netherlands by a person authorised to represent the shipowner.
27. In those circumstances, the first three complaints are well founded."

6.149 In regard to the fourth and fifth complaints, the Commission argued that the ship management scheme constituted a restriction of freedom of establishment. It further contended that although the scheme may be justified by the grounds of general interest associated with the exercise of effective control, it must be regarded as disproportionate to the aim pursued. By contrast, the Netherlands claimed that the ship management scheme did not restrict freedom of establishment but in any event, even on the assumption that the scheme did entail a restriction, it would be justified by grounds of general interest relating to the need to exercise effective control and jurisdiction over ships flying the Dutch flag.

6.150 The CJEU was again clear in its views:

"32. In the present case, the ship management scheme has the effect of restricting the freedom of establishment of the owners of the ships. Community nationals wishing to operate in the form of a shipping company with a director who is a national of or is resident in a non-member country are prevented from doing so.
33. A restriction such as the one in issue cannot be justified by the need to exercise effective control and jurisdiction over ships flying the Netherlands flag. The Netherlands ship management scheme is not appropriate for ensuring the attainment of those objectives and goes beyond what is necessary for that purpose. It is difficult to understand how the nationality and residence of the director of a shipping company which owns the ship is capable of affecting the exercise of effective control over the ship by the flag State.
34. In that regard, as concerns the nationality condition, it follows from paragraphs 23 to 26 of this judgment that the arguments whereby the Netherlands Government seeks to show that the scheme is proportionate must be rejected.
35. As regards the residence condition, the Netherlands Government's argument cannot be upheld.
36. As regards the argument that the residence condition considerably increases the prospects of jurisdiction being effectively exercised, it must be held that the possibility for a State to exercise its jurisdiction over a person depends primarily on the practical accessibility of that person and not on his residence. That test is already satisfied when the management of the ship must be carried out from a place of business in the Netherlands by a person who is authorised to represent the shipowner.
37. As regards the argument that, regard being had to the geographical situation of the Netherlands, a person whose residence is outside the Community or one of the States Parties to the Agreement on the European Economic Area cannot properly undertake the day-to-day management for which the director of a shipping company is responsible, it is appropriate to recall once again that the possibility for a State to exercise its jurisdiction over a person depends primarily on his practical accessibility and not on his residence. In that context, it is sufficient to require that the management of the ship be carried out from a place of business in the Netherlands by a person who is authorised to represent the shipowner.
38. In those circumstances, the fourth and fifth complaints are well founded."

6.151 The CJEU therefore found that the Netherlands was in breach of EU law, in particular Articles 49 and 54 of the TFEU, by adopting and maintaining in its legislation Article 311 of the Wetboek van Koophandel and Article 8:169 of the Burgerlijk Wetboek, under which certain conditions are fixed concerning:

- the nationality of the shareholders of companies owning seagoing ships which they wish to register in the Netherlands;
- the nationality of the directors of companies owning seagoing ships which those companies wish to register in the Netherlands;
- the nationality of the natural persons responsible for the day-to-day management of the place of business from which the shipping business which is necessary for registration of a ship in the Netherlands registers is carried out in the Netherlands;
- the nationality of the directors of shipping companies owning seagoing ships registered in the Netherlands; and
- the residence of the directors of shipping companies owning seagoing ships registered in the Netherlands.

The CJEU was clear that the scheme had the effect of restricting the freedom of establishment of shipowners. If a shipowner wishes to register its ships there the shipowner would have to alter the structure of its board of directors and share capital which would have been disruptive. The Court was convinced that such requirements were not proportionate and involved a breach of the freedom provisions.

J. AN ABANDONED PROPOSAL FOR AN EU REGISTER: EUROS

Proposal

6.152 This section considers the abandoned proposal to establish an EU register known as "EUROS". The proposal has been officially shelved and it is unlikely to be of any practical significance in the foreseeable future but it is of historical significance. This section is therefore of largely historical significance only. The Commission proposed in its August 1989 document "A Future for the Community Shipping Industry: Measures to Improve the Operating Conditions of Community Shipping"[150] the establishment of a Community ship register and for the flying of the Community flag by some seagoing vessels.[151] This proposal was embodied in a proposal for a Council regulation entitled Draft Council Regulation concerning the Establishment of a Community Ship Register and providing for the flying of the Community Flag by Sea-going Vessels. It would operate in parallel with the national registries in each Member State. Rabe, addressing the International Bar Association's Section on Business Law in Strasbourg, in 1989, said:

"[t]he proposal to establish a Community Ship Register (EUROS) is intended to reverse both

---

150 COM(89)266 final, 3 August 1989. On 5 July 1988, Manfred Ebel MEP proposed a European flag.
151 See ibid. For the amended proposal, see OJ C73/11, 19 March 1991. See "EC Attacked over New Euros Register", Lloyd's List, 13 December 1991, p. 1; "Improved leadership urged for EC shipping", Lloyd's List, 10 February 1992, p. 1. Note the moves in South America to adopt a Latin American register (noting the differences): "Latin American register planned", Lloyd's List, 25 November 1991, p. 1. The Commission issued a revised proposal on 13 December 1991 (COM (91)483 final) but the comments in this chapter relate to the amendment submitted on 27 February 1991.

these trends. Its objectives are to present an incentive to Community shipowners to register their ships within the Community and simultaneously to secure the employment of European seafarers in highly-skilled functions and as far as possible of those in other functions. To achieve this the Commission – correctly may I say – does regard as insufficient steps taken by individual Member States, where in some instances already second ship registers have been introduced. In view of the target of establishing a single internal market, the idea is to set up a harmonized system of operating conditions providing for high quality, reliability and safety of the transport services rendered evidenced by the Community flag. This would in the Commission's opinion also lead to a higher degree of convenience of the conditions of competition among Member States."

6.153 The Select Committee of the House of Lords on the European Communities has said that the EUROS proposal is "an imaginative idea. But given the long centuries in which law on the high seas has been that of the 'separate flags of nations' it is also fraught with dangers and complexities."[152] The Register would be an additional one to the Member States' registries and is not in substitution of them. There would be no obligation to register on it. Vessels registered on EUROS would also remain registered on the national registry. The Preamble to the proposed regulation is instructive:

"Whereas the availability of a high quality competitive fleet depends on the availability of a maritime infrastructure within the Community allowing for the preservation of a sufficient number of nationals of Member States to serve as seafarers and a cost level which is competitive;

Whereas the comparative advantage of Community shipping has been eroded over the years, and the fleet flying Member States' flags has suffered a considerable decline, and to the extent that ships have been transferred to third country registers, there has been a severe loss of employment for Community nationals; and as a result the invisible earnings of the Member States' of the Community have declined;

Whereas the efforts to meet the problem through national measures, either by the establishment of second national registers, to which more favourable conditions are attached, or by granting operating subsidies or aid to related sectors, tend to disperse the effects of the actions undertaken and risk a distortion of competition;

Whereas it is in the Community interest to aim at a structural development of a fleet of vessels, registered in Member States' registers but also identifiable as Community vessels which meet the standards laid down by international maritime conventions and to man these vessels, to the highest possible proportion, with Community seafarers;

Whereas this aim cannot be attained without a reduction of the cost level;

Whereas the establishment of a Community ship register should serve the purpose of creating a channel through which national efforts can be converged, a focus for the employment of Community seafarers, and a trade mark guaranteeing shippers a high quality service;

Whereas the Community ship register will be additional to the national register and should be introduced without delay in order to discourage the trend towards setting up secondary registers;

Whereas the right to register vessels in the Community register should be reserved for natural and legal persons having a genuine link with the Community; whereas, however, this right should also be given under certain conditions and terms to persons who have a genuine link with third countries;

Whereas the vessel to be registered in the Community register should comply with certain conditions; whereas, in particular, the vessel should be and remain registered in a national register; whereas the decisions on the admission to the national register must be taken in compliance with the provisions of the Treaty;

Whereas registration in, and continued membership of, the Community register should depend on compliance with the safety measures required by the international conventions in this respect and any rules in respect of vessels, personnel and seamen established at Community level;

---

152 See Community Shipping Measures, Session 1989–1990, 28th Report, para. 2 (footnote omitted).

Whereas the number of qualified seafarers from Member States on board vessels registered in this register should be sufficient to meet present and future requirements of the Community fleet, bearing in mind that in order to ensure passengers' safety and to safeguard employment among seafarers of the Member States, the crews of passenger vessels and ferries operating in European waters must consist entirely of Community seafarers;

Whereas seafarers from non-Community countries on vessels registered in this register should be employed on conditions which have been agreed on by their representative organizations and, in the absence of such an agreement, on conditions which comply with internationally agreed standards;

Whereas in order to ensure uniform crew composition for each category of vessel and degree of automation, in view of the substantial divergences that exist between national legislations on this matter, guidelines for the composition of the crews of vessels registered in Euros must be laid down by the Commission on the basis of the principles set out in Resolution A 481 (XII) of the International Maritime Organization and ILO Convention 147 concerning minimum standards in merchant shipping which are internationally recognized and accepted;

Whereas all seafarers on vessels registered in this register should at least benefit from the social security schemes to which they are entitled in the country where they are resident;

Whereas vessels, while remaining on this register, should be able to transfer between the national registers of Member States without technical hindrance, when they comply with the essential technical requirements to be laid down by the Council;

Whereas the right of free movement under Article 48 of the Treaty as implemented by Council Regulation 1612/68[153] applies to employment of nationals of Member States on board vessels registered in the Member States; whereas therefore this right applies to vessels registered in Euros; whereas, however, the effective exercise of that right may be hindered by differences between qualifications and licences issued in the Member States; whereas it is appropriate to provide for recognition of such qualifications and licences for seafarers for the purposes of employment on board vessels in the Community register subject to minimum requirements laid down by the Council;

Whereas registration in this register should be reflected in the right and obligation to fly the European flag which should be afforded a similar degree of protection to that enjoyed by the flags of Member States and third countries;

Whereas the Commission should, in application of the provisions of this regulation, be enabled to adopt implementing provisions concerning the establishment of the register and concerning procedures of registration and deregistration;

Whereas there should be cooperation between the Community register and the national ship registers, including an exchange of information;

Whereas the Member States should take the necessary measures to control and enforce compliance with the provisions of this Regulation;

Whereas the Commission will report annually to the European Parliament and Council on the number of vessels registered in the Community register and the number of Community seafarers employed in those vessels, thus enabling the effectiveness of this regulation to be assessed, and whereas the Commission will if necessary propose any modifications and improvements required."

Objective of the proposal

6.154 The objective of the proposed regulation was set out in Article 1 of the proposed regulation. This provision states that the regulation provides for: (a) the establishment of an EU ship register for seagoing merchant vessels; (b) the conditions for registration; (c) the provision of certain facilities accruing from such registration; (d) the right to fly

---

153 OJ No L257/2, 19,10, 1968.

the EC (now the EU) flag on these vessels in addition to the national flag;[154] and (e) associated measures aimed at ensuring the maintenance of social standards and at improving environmental and safety standards.

6.155 An advantage of the EUROS system is that such a scheme would facilitate the Commission's review of State aid because the ships registered on it would already have met the conditions set down by the Commission.

Legal bases

6.156 The legal bases of the proposed regulation was, according to the preamble to the proposal put forward by the Commission, the EC Treaty generally and, in particular, the then Articles 84(2)[155] and 92(3)(d)[156] thereof. It is noteworthy that Article 92(3)(d)[157] was added in on the amended proposal.

Market reaction

6.157 NUMAST (the UK seafaring officers' union) stated in its submission to the UK Department of Transport that the union was "not yet convinced that a Community register which, as proposed, would in essence be a dual register is the only, or even the most effective, means of achieving the objective". It also expressed concern about the criterion suggested for entry to the EUROS and expressed total opposition to the inclusion on the register of bareboat chartered tonnage. The proposals are regarded by many in the industry as falling short of their aims and geared more towards internal harmonisation than improving the general welfare of shipping within the EU.[158] Many carriers were, at best, sceptical or, at worst, very critical of the proposal. The European Parliament called for tax concessions. The Commission's revised draft provides that the income of seafarers on EUROS-registered ships would be exempt of tax normally levied in Member States and this tax would be paid over to the shipowners. The European Community Shipowners Association ("ECSA") rejected the concession on seafarers' taxation. ECSA argued that the proposal is not attractive enough to encourage ships away from flags of convenience because, among other reasons, the tax exemption relates only to EU seafarers on the EUROS Register and travelling outside the EU and when they are not involved in cabotage as well as the fact that the exemption only relates to tax and not social welfare. ECSA wanted more: in particular, they wanted a package of positive measures to attract ships. The Member States were not enthusiastic about the Commission's proposals.

Establishment of the register

6.158 EUROS would have been an additional register, i.e. a register which would operate in addition to the registers in each of the Member States. Article 2 of the proposed regulation provides for the establishment of a Community ship register (to be called

---

154 Ships registered on EUROS would also have a distinctive marking on their sterns.
155 TFEU, Art. 100(2).
156 TFEU, Art. 107(3)(d).
157 TFEU, Art. 107(3)(d).
158 General Council of British Shipping, *Shipping, 1992 and Beyond* (1990), p. 15.

"EUROS") on which seagoing merchant vessels may be registered in addition to their national registration in a Member State of the EU.

Eligibility to be registered

6.159 Registration is not automatic and a number of requirements must be met. According to the regulation, the Commission shall register a seagoing merchant vessel when the conditions laid down in Articles 3, 4 and 5 of the proposed regulation are met.[159]

6.160 Article 3 of the proposed regulation describes a community vessel owner in the following terms:

> "1. The following who are owners of a vessel registered in the national register of a Member State may apply for registration of the vessel in Euros:
>
>   (a) nationals of the Member States;
>   (b) companies formed in accordance with the law of a Member State and having their principal place of business in, and effective control exercised within, the Community, provided that a majority of the members of the board or of the directors of these companies are nationals of the Member States having their domicile or usual residence in the Community;
>   (c) companies formed in accordance with the law of a Member State or of a third country in which nationals of Member States participate by more than 50% or are company shareholders controlling more than 50% of the overall company capital.
>
> For the purpose of this regulation, a natural or legal person mentioned above will hereafter be referred to as a 'Community vessel owner';
> 2. Where it has been agreed between a third country and the Community that registration of vessels in the register of that third country and in Euros shall be permitted, the term 'nationals of the Member States' shall, for the purposes of paragraph 1(a) and (b), include nationals of the third country concerned."

6.161 Article 4 sets out the criteria for vessels eligible for registration:

> "Eligible for registration in Euros is any sea-going merchant vessel with a tonnage of at least 500 grt, built or under construction, which is already registered in a Member State and is used or to be used for the transport of cargo or passengers or any other commercial purpose, if it fulfils the following conditions:
>
> (a) the vessel must be and remain registered in the national ship register for the duration of its registration in Euros;
> (b) the vessel must be owned, and for the duration of its registration in Euros remain owned, by a Community vessel owner;
> (c) the vessel shall not be more than 20 years old at the time of its registration in Euros unless it has been completely refurbished and certified by a Member State as complying with the regulations for new ships defined in the 1974 Solas Convention."

6.162 Article 5 described registration:

> "1. The Community vessel owner shall apply to the Commission for the registration of a vessel in Euros. He shall submit this application either directly to the Commission or through the competent national authorities which shall forward the application to the Commission.
> This application shall be accompanied by:

---

159 Proposed Regulation, Art. 2, para. 2.

(a) A certificate of ownership of the vessel issued by the national registration authority;
(b) The measurement certificate of the vessel;
(c) A certified copy of the vessel's certificate of nationality;
(d) If the vessel is mortgaged, a written statement by the mortgage creditors that they consent to the registration of the vessel in Euros.

The Commission may stipulate other documents or certificates that must be submitted in order for a vessel to be registered in Euros.

2. Registration in Euros shall be completed when the following data is recorded in the relevant entry of the vessel:

   (a) the name or title of the Community vessel owner and his or its other particulars;
   (b) the name, the international call letters, the dimensions, the gross and net registered tonnage, the type and power of the engine and the age of the vessel;
   (c) the type of the vessel, its number and port of national registration.

The Commission may also lay down other data concerning the vessel which must be recorded in Euros.

3. The following data shall also be recorded in the register:

   (a) changes of ownership or national flag of the vessel;
   (b) the deregistration of the vessel.

4. Third parties shall be entitled to receive information of the data concerning a vessel registered in Euros on payment of a reasonable fee."

6.163 Article 6 dealt with notification:

"1. Where a vessel is registered in or deregistered from Euros the Commission shall notify its national registration authority.
2. Where, for any reason, a vessel is deregistered from the national register, the national register authority shall immediately notify the Commission."

6.164 Article 7 referred to certificates and documents of vessels:

"The following certificates or documents must be kept on board the vessel for the entire duration of its registration in Euros:

(a) The certificates or documents which the vessel is required to have on board under the legislation of the Member State in whose national register the vessel is registered;
(b) The certificate granting the right to fly the European flag;
(c) The certificate of minimum crew composition;
(d) The 'sea-worthiness' certificate issued by a Member State in whose register the vessel is registered."

6.165 Article 8 dealt with deregistration:

"1. A vessel registered in Euros shall be deleted:

   (a) by the Commission, acting *ex officio*, where the vessel ceases to comply with the provisions of this regulation or,
   (b) by an application from the Community vessel owner.

2. The deletion of a vessel from the national register of a Member State and its registration in the national register of another Member State at the same time, shall not affect its registration in Euros."

6.166 *Bare-boat charters.* Vessels operated by EU vessel owners on the basis of bare-boat charters[160] for a period of at least 12 months could have been registered in EUROS during the period of that charter where four conditions are fulfilled: first, the vessel is registered as a bare-boat chartered vessel in a national ship register of a Member State;[161] second, the laws of the vessel's initial flag in EUROS allow the registration of a bare-boat chartered vessel in the national register of a Member State;[162] third, the consent of the owner of the vessel and of all mortgage creditors for the registration of the bare-boat in EUROS is obtained;[163] and fourth, the bare-boat charter has been duly recorded in the register of the vessel's initial flag State.[164]

Safety on EUROS-registered ships

6.167 Article 10 of the proposed regulation provided that throughout the period of registration the vessel must be provided with all certificates required by the Member State in whose national register it is registered. Article 11 dealt with the manning of EUROS registered ships:

> "1. Guidelines concerning the manning of vessels registered in Euros shall be laid down by the Commission on the basis of the principles set out in Resolution No A 481 (XII) of 19 November 1981 of the Assembly of the International Maritime Organization (IMO), after consultation with the Joint Committee on Maritime Transport and Member States. The Commission shall adopt the guidelines within the time limit mentioned in Article 24.
> 2. The Commission shall include in the guidelines provisions ensuring that insofar as requirements concerning safe manning are met and the necessary automation exists, seafarers with multiple qualifications certificates may be employed, provided that specific reference is made to this fact in the minimum manning certificate.
> 3. Member States shall issue minimum manning certificates in conformity with paragraphs 1 and 2 and shall deliver them to the persons requesting the registration of a vessel in Euros. The Member State shall specify in the minimum manning certificate a language or languages of the crew.
> 4. At the request of the Community vessel owner concerned or seafarers employed on the vessel who consider that the minimum manning certificate issued by a Member State is not in conformity with the guidelines laid down by the Commission, the Commission will carry out an investigation and will take a decision after consultation with the Member State concerned. The Commission will take the decision within two months of the date of request.
> 5. The decision of the Commission shall lay down the minimum manning scale of the vessel. The Member State concerned shall issue immediately a new certificate in conformity with the Commission decision.
> 6. The national authorities shall monitor compliance with the provisions of the minimum manning certificate and impose sanctions where appropriate."

6.168 Article 12 dealt with the nationality of the crew:

> "1. On vessels registered in Euros all officers and at least half of the rest of the crew referred to in their minimum manning certificates shall be nationals of a Member State.
> Trainees do not count towards meeting the requirements above.

---

160 A bare-boat charter (also termed a charter-party by demise or a demise charter-party) is one whereby the owner simply provides the ship and the charterer supplies its own crew, stores and fuel. The possession and control of the vessel are normally vested in the charterer and are not retained by the owner.
161 Proposed Regulation, Art. 9(1).
162 Ibid.
163 Ibid.
164 Ibid.

2. In particular, on passenger vessels or ferries registered in Euros which operate regular lines for passengers or vehicles between the ports of the same Member State or between (1) Mediterranean ports or (2) North Sea and Baltic ports or (3) European Atlantic ports or operate cruises with embarkation and disembarkation at any of the above ports, all the officers and the remaining crew referred to in the minimum manning certificate of vessels shall be nationals of the Member States."

6.169 Article 13 related to availability of seafarers:

"1. The Member States shall provide for monitoring on a permanent basis of the availability of seafarers who are nationals of Member States in their ports, and make the information so obtained available to interested parties.
2. Where seafarers who are nationals of the Member States are not available for employment in a vessel registered in Euros that lies in the port of a Member State, under the terms and conditions of the collective wage agreements concluded with their representative organizations, the Member State may grant permission to the master of the vessel to sail on the forthcoming voyage with fewer seafarers who are nationals of the Member States than those provided in Article 12."

6.170 Interestingly, there is a provision (Article 14) dealing with wages, working hours and further labour conditions:

"1. Labour conditions and working hours of seafarers, who are not nationals of a Member State, on board vessels registered in Euros, shall be in accordance with the laws and regulations of the Member State in whose national register the vessel is registered and the Community regulations if any.
2. Wages and any other remuneration of seafarers who are not nationals of a Member State on board vessels registered in Euros shall be at least in accordance with the ILO Wages, Hours of Work and Manning (Sea) Recommendation (No 109), 1958, subject to any arrangement on collective wages agreed upon with organizations as referred to in Article 15."

6.171 Article 15 related to collective wage agreements:

"1. Seafarers who are not nationals of a Member State may be employed only on the basis of collective wage agreements concluded with trade unions representing the above seafarers.
2. No collective wage agreement may be concluded with a trade union on behalf of nationals of a third country if such union does not satisfy the conditions of ILO Convention No 87 concerning the freedom of association and protection of the right to organize.
3. The law of the Member State of registration of the vessel or, if explicitly referred to in the agreement, any other Member State, shall apply to such collective wage agreements. The courts of the Member States shall be competent to hear and determine disputes arising out of such agreements and from individual labour contracts drawn up in accordance with and in implementation of such a collective wage agreement.
4. Collective agreements must not contain discriminatory rules based on sex."

6.172 Article 16 related to social security:

"Without prejudice to Article 13(2)(c) of Council Regulation (EEC) No 1408/71[165] and in the absence of a contrary agreement at the level of governments or social partners, social security for seafarers on board vessels registered in Euros shall be the responsibility of the country in which the seafarer has his usual residence unless the legislation of that country expressly provides otherwise, in which case the Member State in whose national register the vessel is registered shall be responsible but in accordance with the legislation generally applicable to seafarers of the country of usual residence.

---

165 OJ No L149/2, 5.7.1971.

For the purpose of this provision residence means residence on shore and employment on board a vessel registered in a Member State shall not, of itself, be considered as being residence in that State."

6.173 Article 17 states that Articles 14, 15 and 16 shall apply subject to any right conferred or obligations imposed by any other Community legislative act except where such act expressly provides otherwise. Section 4 of the proposed regulation entitled "Facilities attached to registration in Euros" provides in Article 18 for the transfer of vessels. Article 18 provides:

> "Any vessel registered in Euros and having valid certificates and classification and meeting the essential technical requirements to be laid down by the Council according to the provisions of the Treaty before 31 December 1991, may be transferred to the register of another Member State without the imposition of additional technical requirements."

6.174 Article 19 dealt with the recognition of seafarers' qualifications:

> "The qualifications and licences of seafarers who are nationals of a Member State shall be recognized by the competent authorities of each Member State for the purposes of employment on any vessel registered in Euros, subject to minimum requirements for professional training and experience in the function concerned as required in Directives adopted or to be adopted by the Council, according to the provisions of the Treaty, before 31 December 1991."

6.175 Section 5 of the proposed regulation entitled "European flag, port of registration" deals with the flag. Article 20 ("European Flag") provided:

> "1. Vessels registered in Euros are entitled and obliged to fly the European flag in addition to their national flag.
> 2. Upon registration a certificate conveying the right to fly the European flag will be delivered by the Commission to the applicant for registration."

6.176 Article 21 related to the port of registration of the ship and a vessel registered in EUROS shall bear a relevant identification on its stern under the name of the port of registry in its national registration.

6.177 Article 22 related to rights *in rem* and provides that where a vessel flies the European flag this shall not affect the rights *in rem* and maritime liens on this vessel and/or matters of public, administrative or criminal law which shall continue to be governed by the laws of the national flag Member State.

6.178 Article 23 was important and novel. It relates to the calculation of the age of a vessel. For the purpose of the regulation the age of a vessel shall be calculated from 1 January of the year following the year in which the vessel was delivered by the shipyards ready for commercial use.

6.179 Section 6 related to some final matters. First, Article 24 deals with implementing measures:

> "The Commission shall, within six months after the adoption of this Regulation, adopt the necessary implementing measures concerning the establishment and functioning of Euros, the procedures for registration and deregistration, the system for monitoring compliance with the provisions of this Regulation and the sanctions in case of failure to observe them and lay down the form and content of the documents concerned, including the certificate concerning the right to fly the European flag, the form of, and rules governing the flying of the flag, and the minimum manning certificate."

Second, Article 25 dealt with cooperation:

"1. National authorities and the Commission shall assist each other in applying this Regulation and in checking compliance therewith.
2. Within the framework of this mutual assistance they shall communicate to each other the necessary information."

Third, Article 26 dealt with the transitional period. It provides:

"1. Member States shall, within 12 months of the adoption of this Regulation and after consultation with the Commission:

   (a) adopt measures to protect the European flag and take the necessary measures to enable those vessels registered in Euros to exercise their right to fly it;
   (b) take the necessary measures effectively to control compliance with the relevant provisions of Sections 2, 3 and 5 of this Regulation and of the decisions implementing these provisions which shall be issued by the Commission and to introduce the procedure for imposing sanctions.

2. Such measures shall make express reference to this regulation.
3. Member States shall forthwith communicate to the Commission the measures adopted."

Fourth, Article 27 discussed reports and review. It states:

"The Commission shall make an annual report to the European Parliament and Council, beginning on 1 July 1993, on the number of vessels registered in Euros and the composition of their crews. It shall also propose to the Council any amendments to this Regulation which may be required."

Finally, while Article 28 provided: "By 31 December 1995 at the latest the Council shall decide on a review of this Regulation on the basis of a proposal from the Commission which shall be submitted by 1 July 1995."

Advantages of being registered on EUROS

6.180 A vessel which would be registered on EUROS could be registered to the register of another Member State without having additional technical requirements imposed. There would be a mutual recognition of qualifications and licences of EU national seafarers employed on EUROS registered vessels. Such qualifications and licences would however have to conform with certain minimum requirements laid down by existing legislation as well as those adopted before 1 July 1991.

Assessment of the proposal

6.181 The Commission had been bullish about the prospects of such a Register. The Commission wrote that the "proposal will make a major contribution to the objective of furthering the common interest by reinforcing the image and the commercial attractiveness of a high quality service Community fleet".[166] However, there was no appetite for the proposal among Member States, shipowners or unions so the proposal did not proceed.

---

166 "Examination of State Aids to Community Shipping Companies", p. 3 (contained in Annex I to Commission of the European Communities, *Financial and Fiscal Measures Concerning Shipping Operations with Ships Registered in the Community*, SEC (89)921 final, 3 August 1989).

6.182 For completeness, mention is made of Commission Decision 2005/311 RINAVE.

"19.4.2005
EN
Official Journal of the European Union
L 99/15

COMMISSION DECISION
of 18 April 2005
on the extension of the limited recognition of 'RINAVE – Registro Internacional Naval, SA'
(notified under document number C(2005) 1156)
(Only the Portuguese text is authentic)
(Text with EEA relevance)
(2005/311/EC)

THE COMMISSION OF THE EUROPEAN COMMUNITIES,
Having regard to the Treaty establishing the European Community,
Having regard to Council Directive 94/57/EC of 22 November 1994 on common rules and standards for ship inspection and survey organisations and for the relevant activities of maritime administrations (1), and in particular Article 4(3) thereof,
Having regard to the letters dated 25 March 2003 and 8 May 2003 from the Portuguese Authorities, requesting the extension of the limited recognition of 'RINAVE – Registro Internacional Naval, SA' (hereafter RINAVE) as per Article 4(2) and (3) of the abovementioned Directive, for unlimited time,
Whereas:
(1)
The limited recognition under Article 4(3) of Directive 94/57/EC is a recognition granted to organisations (classification societies) which fulfil all criteria other than those set out under paragraphs 2 and 3 of the section 'General' of the Annex, but which is limited in time and scope in order for the organisation concerned to further gain experience.
(2)
Commission Decision 2000/481/EC (2) recognised RINAVE on the basis of Article 4(3) for Portugal, for a period of three years.
(3)
The Commission has verified that RINAVE meets all criteria of the Annex of the abovementioned Directive other than those set out under paragraphs 2 and 3 of the section 'General' of the Annex, including the new provisions referred to in Article 4(5).
(4)
The assessment carried out by the Commission has furthermore revealed the organisation's dependence on the technical rules of another recognised organisation.
(5)
During the period 2000 to 2003, the safety and pollution prevention performance records of RINAVE as published by the Paris Memorandum of Understanding have consistently been of the highest level.
(6)
The measures provided for in this Decision are in accordance with the opinion of the Committee set out in Article 7 of Directive 94/57/EC,

HAS ADOPTED THIS DECISION:
Article 1
The limited recognition of 'RINAVE – Registro Internacional Naval, SA' is extended pursuant to Article 4(3) of Directive 94/57/EC for a period of three years as from the date of adoption of this Decision.

Article 2
The effects of the extended recognition are limited to Portugal.

Article 3
This Decision is addressed to the Portuguese Republic.
Done at Brussels, 18 April 2005.
For the Commission
Jacques BARROT
Vice-President

(1) OJ L319, 12.12.1994, p. 20. Directive as last amended by Directive 2002/84/EC of the European Parliament and of the Council (OJ L324, 29.11.2002, p. 53).
(2) OJ L193, 29.7.2000, p. 91."

CHAPTER 7

European Union law relating to freedom to supply services: international services; cabotage services; and shipping services generally

A. INTRODUCTION

7.001 One of the fundamental[1] principles of European Union ("EU") law is that, as a general principle,[2] nationals of each Member State are legally entitled to provide services to persons in all other Member States; while conversely, nationals in any Member State are generally entitled to receive services from persons in all other Member States. It is an entitlement which is of enormous significance in many areas of the economy including shipping. However, the general rules of EU law relating to freedom to provide services do not apply to maritime transport[3] so a special regime had to be established for the transport sector. This regime is embodied primarily in Regulation 4055/86[4] and Regulation 3577/92[5] – the former deals with *international* maritime services while the latter deals with cabotage or *domestic* services. Services in ports are dealt with in the general EU regime relating to services but services between ports are dealt with by either Regulation 4055/86 or Regulation 3577/92. The principle of "freedom to provide services" has therefore been applied to the maritime transport sector by way of special secondary legislation but it does not differ too much from the general principles of the Treaty on the Functioning of the European Union ("TFEU").

7.002 The significance of the possibility of providing services in shipping throughout the EU should not be underestimated.[6] Even if a national of, for example, France decides not to provide services in another Member State, that is not the end of the matter – a

---

1 The fundamental nature of the principle is demonstrated by the comment by the CJEU in, for example, Case 49/89 *Corsica Ferries France v Direction Générale des Douanes Françaises* [1989] ECR 4441, ECLI:EU:C:1989:649, para. 8, that: "[a]s the Court has decided on various occasions, the Articles of the [TFEU] concerning the free movement of goods, persons, services and capital are fundamental [EU] provisions and any restriction, even minor, of that freedom is prohibited".
2 It is not an unqualified or absolute right and there are limitations laid down in the TFEU but these limitations must be construed narrowly.
3 TFEU, Art. 58(1).
4 OJ 1986 L378/1.
5 OJ 1992 L364/7.
6 On freedom to provide maritime services, see Aussant, "Cabotage and the Liberalisation of the Maritime Services Sector", European Maritime Law Organisation conference, 23–24 October 1992; Aussant, "Cabotage and the Liberalisation of the Maritime Services Sector" (1993) ETL 347; Aussant, "Freedom to Provide Services in Shipping in the European Communities" [1989] Il Diritto Marittimo 59; Aussant, "Freedom to Provide Services in Shipping in the European Communities" [1988] 23 ETL 556; Greaves, "The Provision of Maritime Transport Services in the European Community" [2004] LMCLQ 104; Le Bihan and Lebullenger, "Common Maritime Transport Policy: Bilateral Agreements and the Freedom to Provide Services" (1988) 9 YEL 209; and Nesterowicz, "Freedom to Provide Maritime Transport Services in European Community Law" (2003) 34 JMLC 629.

national from one of the other Member States could well decide to offer services to French customers and thereby seek to "steal" the French national's own customers. When the EU rules apply then the services are supplied in the host State on the same conditions that would apply to nationals of that State so Member States may not discriminate in favour of their own nationals.[7] Freedom to provide services is an issue which has been particularly controversial in traditionally closed markets such as the Greek island traffic market. Indeed, the notion that there would be freedom to provide services in ports led to rioting in Brussels while the two failed proposals for port services directives were being debated.

7.003 The issue of freedom to provide services may be categorised into:

(a) the freedom to provide *international* shipping services;
(b) the freedom to provide *domestic* shipping services (this latter freedom relating to domestic services, known as "cabotage", is more controversial than the freedom to provide international services because it involves an intrusion into areas traditionally the preserve of national service providers); and
(c) freedom to provide related services such as services in ports and services to shipping companies.

7.004 Karamitsos has observed that unlike

"air or rail, maritime transport had a long tradition of freedom well before the creation of the [EU]. Therefore, Europe's tasks in the creation of the internal market have been simpler, perhaps with the exception of cabotage in some jurisdictions."[8]

The observation is correct but it could also be said that ports are often not subject to or much competition as one might imagine.

7.005 There is a correlation or overlap between the area of freedom to provide services, which is considered in this chapter, with the freedom of establishment which was considered in the previous chapter. Many of the principles between freedom of establishment and freedom to provide services are similar. The distinction between establishment and services is really one of the degree of permanence with establishment involving more permanence and a base in the host State from which to offer the services.

B. FREEDOM TO PROVIDE SERVICES IN EU LAW

7.006 As mentioned at the outset of this chapter, freedom to provide services is a fundamental principle of EU law.[9] While Articles 56–62 of the TFEU relate to the

---

7 E.g. Case 39/75 *Coenen v Sociaal-Economische Raad* [1975] ECR 1547, ECLI:EU:C:1975:162; Cases 110–111/78 *Ministere Public and Chambre syndicale des agents artistique et impresario de Belgique v Van Wesemael and Follachio* [1979] ECR 35, ECLI:EU:C:1979:8 and Case 63/86 *Commission v Italian Republic* [1988] ECR 29, ECLI:EU:C:1988:9.
8 "EC Law and Maritime Transport: Preliminary Remarks" in Antapassis, Athanassiou and Røsæg (eds), *Competition and Regulation in Shipping and Shipping Related Industries* (2009), 1 at 1.
9 See e.g. Steiner, Woods and Twigg-Flesner, *EU Law* (10th ed., 2010), chap. 22. See also Aussant, "Freedom to Provide Services in the EC" (1988) 23 Journal of Law and Economics 556. For the EU provisions on freedom to provide services to apply, the services must be normally provided for remuneration. Art. 56 of the TFEU provides in its first paragraph: "[w]ithin the framework of the provisions set out below, restrictions on freedom to provide services within the Union shall be prohibited in respect of nationals of Member States who are established in a Member State other than that of the person for whom the services are intended. The European Parliament and the Council, acting in accordance with the ordinary legislative procedure may extend the provisions of the Chapter to nationals of a third country who provide services and who are established within the Union."

provision of services in EU law generally, the position is different in the context of transport because Article 58(1) of the TFEU which provides: "[f]reedom to provide services in the field of transport shall be governed by the provisions of the Title relating to transport". Thus, a special regime had to be established for shipping services within the transport title in the TFEU. (The special position of transport is also reflected in Article 2(2)(d) of Directive 2006/123 (the so-called "Services Directive" which deals with services in the economy generally) because the directive does not apply to "services in the field of transport, including port services, falling within the scope" of the title on transport in the Treaty.)[10] As the general rules on freedom to provide services are not applicable to maritime transport by virtue of Article 58(1) of the TFEU then the question arises as to which system applies. There is therefore a special regime relating to the freedom to provide services as it relates to maritime transport. This specialist maritime services regime includes Regulation 4055/86[11] and Regulation 3577/92.[12] The beneficiaries of the freedom to provide services are nationals of Member States (whether physical or legal persons) established in a Member State. As the general principles relating to freedom to provide services are inapplicable to maritime transport, the rest of this chapter concentrates on the specific regime relating to maritime transport. (It should be stressed that the general rules on freedom to provide services apply to situations other than the transport of goods or passengers (i.e. shipping) and would apply in the context of services in ports or other land-based services.)[13] The rest of this chapter therefore considers primarily the freedom to provide international maritime services under Regulation 4055/86 (Part C), the freedom to provide domestic or cabotage services under Regulation 3577/92 (Part D) and then reviews the case law on the issue (Part E).

C. INTERNATIONAL SHIPPING SERVICES: REGULATION 4055/86

Introduction

7.007 As the general regime relating to freedom to provide services was inapplicable to transport, a special regime for transport (or, at least, in this context, maritime transport) had to be enacted. This was ultimately achieved, after almost three decades had elapsed since the establishment of the European Economic Community ("EEC"), by the adoption on 22 December 1986 of Regulation 4055/86 which applies the principle of freedom to provide services to maritime transport between Member States as well as between Member States and third countries.[14] The regulation therefore deals only with *international* services involving at least one Member State. It does not deal with services between ports within one Member State (i.e. cabotage) – cabotage is dealt with by a separate regulation (i.e. Regulation 3577/92[15]) and is considered below in Part D. Nor does

---

10 Commercial services in ports are covered by the Services Directive but not maritime transport or ports services (e.g. a car hire desk at a ferry port would be covered by the Services Directive but not port services as such) (see Commission, *Handbook on the Implementation of the Services Directive* (2007), p. 11).
11 OJ 1986 L378/1.
12 OJ 1992 L364/7.
13 Recourse should therefore be had to the general works on the EU law relating to freedom to provide services. See also Arts 56–62 TFEU.
14 OJ 1986 L378/1.
15 OJ 1992 L364/7.

Regulation 4055/86 deal with services involving only non-Member States (e.g. a service between China and the USA).

Purpose of the Regulation 4055/86

7.008 Regulation 4055/86[16] was adopted to enable shipowners to overcome the restrictions imposed by some Member States on the freedom to provide services. It provided a uniform regime across the Member States. It prohibits the imposition of restrictions on international maritime services but dealt with the issue in three stages – the change towards full freedom was believed to be too radical to be achieved in one phase. The first stage, which ended on 31 December 1989, saw the phasing out of such restrictions on the carriage between Member States by ships flying a Member State flag. The second stage, which ended on 31 December 1991, involved services between Member States and third countries provided by ships flying a Member State flag. The third stage, which ended on 1 January 1993, involved any ship providing transport between Member States and between Member States and third countries.

7.009 According to Dimitri Petropolous in 1990, the then "Head of Division: Maritime Transport" at the then Commission's Transport Directorate General, in the light of, among other things:

"the direction provided by the Treaty of Rome[17] towards a policy based on market economy principles, ... the first objective for [Union] maritime transport policy must be to *safeguard free access to a free world shipping market*. Indeed there is nothing to be gained by a protectionist [Union] shipping policy. Although the [Union] is a big cargo generating area you can normally not reserve more than half of the cargo to your own ships – your trading partners can make their claims.[18] As the [EU] fleet is already carrying around 40% of the [Union]'s foreign trade on vessels registered in the [EU], the possible gain, if any, would be small and could place in jeopardy the revenue from which the [EU] shipping industry gets from cross trading between third countries. Moreover the [EU's] shipping policy cannot simply look at the position of shipowners. An essential consideration of shipping policy must be that the [EU's] foreign trade should have the advantages of freight rates arrived at in fair and free competition. Therefore the [EU] has to defend itself against protectionist measures of other countries whilst at the same time bringing its own house in order in this respect. This is the purpose of the two [EU] Regulations adopted in December 1986 on *freedom to provide international shipping services* (EEC No. 4055/86) and on *free access to ocean trades* (EEC No. 4058/86)."[19]

7.010 The Preamble to Regulation 4055/86 reiterates the anti-protectionist (i.e. open) approach of the EU towards cargo-sharing between some Member States and non-Member States. The Preamble states:

"Whereas the structure of the [EU] shipping industry is such as to make it appropriate that the provisions of the Regulation should also apply to nationals of the Member States established

---

16 OJ 1986 L378/1.
17 Ed., i.e. the EEC Treaty now, following amendments, the TFEU.
18 Ed., i.e. under the UN Convention on a Code of Conduct for Liner Conferences ("UNCTAD Code"); see chap. 9.
19 "The European Community Transport Policy: An Overview", at *The Future of Shipping in Europe: Key Legal and Commercial Issues*, London, 28–29 June 1990, pp. 4–5 (personal comments, emphasis added). This statement embodies several key principles including setting the balance in favour of open competition and away from protectionism, recognising that the interests of shippers and consumers must be borne in mind as well as those of carriers.

outside the [EU] and to shipping companies established outside the [EU] and controlled[20] by nationals of a Member State, if their vessels are registered in that Member State in accordance with its legislation..."

7.011 Commenting on this recital, Bredima-Savopoulou and Tzoannos wrote that:

"[this] statement implies that accommodation of the Greek registration system has necessitated the provision of an alternative category of beneficiaries of the freedom to provide services in maritime transport. It implies acceptance by the [EU] of the notion of nationality of ships strengthened with the additional caveat that the shipowning company established outside the [EU] will be majority owned by [EU] nationals."[21]

7.012 Greaves has also commented incisively on the issue in the following terms:

"in so far as [Regulation 4055/86] applies to shipping undertakings established outside the [EU] but controlled by [EU] nationals, the condition as to registration of the ship is not clear. There is no definition of 'control' for the purposes of the Regulation. According to the Regulation's penultimate recital, this Article[22] was introduced to take account of the structure of the [EU] shipping industry. The nationals controlling a shipping undertaking appear to have to be nationals of the Member State in which the ship is registered. Thus, it is not clear whether a shipping undertaking established in Switzerland, controlled by United Kingdom and Dutch nationals and with ships registered in the UK would be covered by Art.1. The wording of Art 1(2) seems to cover only the situation where the control of a shipping undertaking established outside the [EU] is in the hands of nationals of only one Member State. It is submitted, however, that since the [EU] should be regarded as a whole, the Regulation applies in this case as long as the ship is registered in the UK or in the Netherlands, ie, in one of the Member States whose nationality the controllers possess. However, it is unlikely the wording of Art.1(2) would be interpreted more widely to cover a situation where the ship was not registered in the UK or in the Netherlands but in Spain."[23]

7.013 Regulation 4055/86 provides that the freedom to provide maritime transport services between Member States and between third States applies in respect of: (a) nationals of Member States who are established in a Member State other than that of the person for whom the services are provided; and (b) nationals of a Member State established outside the EU and shipping companies established outside the EU and controlled by nationals of a Member State provided their vessels are registered in that Member State.

7.014 In order to understand the legal position prior to the entry into force of Regulation 4055/86, it is useful to consider *Corsica Ferries France v Direction Générale des Douanes Françaises*[24] which is considered below.

Commercial background to Regulation 4055/86

7.015 Markets where market participants are free to provide services (i.e. competitive markets) usually tend to be more efficient and characterised by lower prices and greater choice. The introduction or maintenance of restrictions would affect seriously the trading

---

20 Ed., the term "control" is not defined in the regulation but should be given its ordinary meaning.
21 *The Common Shipping Policy of the EEC* (1990), p. 176.
22 Ed., i.e. Art. 1.
23 Greaves, op. cit. at fn. 6, p. 107. One wonders however whether the last sentence might not be challenged on the basis that it would be contrary to the spirit of EU law for such discrimination between Member States to be tolerated. See para. 7.015.
24 Case C-49/89 [1989] ECR 4441, ECLI:EU:C:1989:649.

interests of all countries by increasing transport costs and limiting choice. However, some Member States[25] have traditionally sought to restrict access to their markets (particularly, their coastal traffic (i.e. cabotage trade)) so as to prevent competition and reserve services and jobs for domestic carriers and seafarers. Theory, and practice in many situations, would indicate that opening markets would reduce rates while improving service and quality but can mean that traditional providers could not be able to survive unless they are efficient.

Effect of Regulation 4055/86

7.016 Being a regulation, Regulation 4055/86 is applicable in its entirety and is directly applicable in all Member States (as a regulation).[26] It applies to nationals of Member States, whether natural or legal persons, who are established in a Member State other than that of the person, for whom the services are intended (i.e. it permits *international* services to be provided). Nationals of Member States established outside the EU and shipping companies established outside the EU and controlled by nationals of a Member State are also covered, if their vessels are registered in that Member State.

7.017 Regulation 4055/86 prohibits not only legislation limiting the freedom to provide such services but it seeks to avoid any discrimination[27] or hindrance which prevents the exercise of the right.

7.018 The Court of Justice of the European Union ("CJEU") confirmed in *Corsica Ferries France v Direction générale des douanes françaises*[28] that there was no explicit EU provision on freedom to provide maritime services before Regulation 4055/86 so it was clearly a watershed measure:

> "12. With regard in particular to maritime transport, Article [100(2)] of the [TFEU] provides that the Council may decide whether, to what extent and by what procedure appropriate provisions may be laid down for that kind of transport.
> 13. It was only in Regulation No 4055/86 of 22 December 1986 applying the principle of freedom to provide services to maritime transport between Member States and between Member States and third countries (Official Journal 1986, L378, p. 1), which entered into force on 1 January 1987, that the Council adopted, on the basis of Article [100(2)] of the Treaty, the measures necessary to achieve freedom to provide services in maritime transport between Member States.
> 14. It must therefore be concluded that in 1981 and 1982, the period at issue in the main proceedings, freedom to provide services in maritime transport had not yet been implemented and that consequently the Member States were entitled to apply provisions such as those at issue in the main proceedings."

7.019 It also clear from *Commission v France*[29] that Regulation 4055/86 prohibits not only discrimination on the basis of nationality but also other restrictions on the freedom to provide maritime services so it is much broader than simply a measure prohibiting discrimination on the basis of nationality. The effect of Regulation 4055/86 is that there is

---

25 Indeed, some non-Member States do so as well – the USA has done so through the Jones Act/Merchant Marine Act 1920.
26 Reg. 4055/86, Art. 12.
27 E.g. discrimination on the basis of nationality.
28 Case C-49/89 [1989] ECR 4441, ECLI:EU:C:1989:649.
29 Case C-381/93 [1994] ECR I-5145, ECLI:EU:C:2002:661.

no further requirement than being established in the EU to benefit from the right to provide maritime services between the EU and third States or between Member States – the vessels did not have to fly the flag of a Member State.

Entry into force of Regulation 4055/86

7.020 Regulation 4055/86 entered into force, in accordance with Article 12 of the regulation, on the day following its publication in the *Official Journal*, namely, it entered into force on 1 January 1987.

Implementation of Regulation 4055/86

7.021 A regulation does not need implementation into Member State law because it forms part of Member State law. However, Member States may adopt laws to supplement a regulation. In regard to Regulation 4055/86, Member States are obliged, under Article 10 of the regulation, to consult with the Commission before adopting laws, regulations or administrative provisions implementing the regulation. The Member States are also obliged under the provision to communicate to the Commission any such measure.

Basic provision relating to freedom to provide services: Article 1 of Regulation 4055/86

7.022 The essence of Regulation 4055/86 is embodied in Article 1 of the regulation:

"1. Freedom to provide maritime transport services between Member States and between Member States and third countries shall apply in respect of nationals of Member States who are established in a Member State other than that of the person for whom the services are intended.
2. The provisions of this Regulation shall also apply to nationals[30] of the Member States established outside the Community[31] and controlled by nationals of a Member State, if their vessels are registered in that Member State in accordance with its legislation.
3. The provisions of Articles 55 to 58 and 62 of the Treaty of the [EEC] Treaty shall apply to the matters covered by this Regulation.
4. For the purpose of this Regulation, the following shall be considered 'maritime transport services between Member States and between Member States and third countries' where they are normally provided for remuneration:

   (a) *intra-Community shipping services*:
   the carriage of passengers or goods by sea between any port of a Member State and any port or off-shore installation of another Member State;
   (b) *third-country traffic*:
   the carriage of passengers or goods by sea between the ports of a Member State and ports or off-shore installations of a third country."

7.023 It is thus clear that the regulation does not apply to services within a Member State, that is to say, cabotage. This was despite the Commission's proposal seeking to include such services within the scope of the proposed regulation. However, cabotage

---

30 Ed., this includes both natural and legal persons.
31 Ed., i.e. now the EU.

was removed from the eventual regulation because it was impossible to secure political agreement for the regulation (particularly, as Greece (as a major maritime nation) was opposed to liberalising cabotage services).

7.024 The beneficiaries of Article 1(1) are essentially the same as those who benefit from Article 56 of the TFEU. This was confirmed in *Peralta*[32] where the CJEU stated:

> "37. As the Court finds in paragraph 13 of this judgment, ... Regulation No 4055/86 was applicable at the time of the events in question.
> 38. Article 1(1) of that regulation provides:
> 'Freedom to provide maritime transport services between Member States and between Member States and third countries shall apply in respect of nationals of Member States who are established in a Member State other than that of the person for whom the services are intended.'
> 39. It is clear, first, from the very wording of that article that it applies to maritime transport operations between Member States of the kind in question in the main proceedings. It defines the persons enjoying freedom to provide services in terms which are substantially the same as those used in Article [56] of the [TFEU]."

7.025 The effect of Article 1(2) is to give the benefit of the regulation to those EU nationals who are established outside the EU and provide such services to others in a Member State. Shipping companies established outside the EU may also benefit provided those companies are controlled by nationals of a Member State and the ship used is registered in that Member State.

7.026 The effect of Article 1(3) is that Articles 45–48 of the TFEU apply in this context. This means, for example, that companies incorporated in a Member State and established in the EU are to be treated as if they were nationals of that Member State.

7.027 The CJEU confirmed in *Geha Naftiliaki EPE and Others v NPDD Limeniko Tameio DOD/SOU and Elliniko Dimosio*[33] that these rules apply in relation to trade from a Member State to a non-Member State:

> "20. Since Regulation No 4055/86 has rendered applicable to the sphere of maritime transport between Member States the totality of the Treaty rules governing the freedom to provide services (see *Commission v France*,[34] ... paragraph 13), it precludes the application of any national legislation whose effect is to make the provision of services between Member States more difficult than that of purely domestic services within a Member State, unless that legislation is justified by compelling reasons of public interest and the measures enacted thereby are necessary and proportionate (see *Commission v Portugal*,[35] ... paragraph 28).
> 21. Since Article 1(1) of Regulation No 4055/86 has extended the principle of the freedom to provide services as regards intra-[EU] traffic to traffic between a Member State and a third country, the rules established in relation to the former must be applied to the latter.
> 22. Consequently, the provision of maritime transport services between the port of Rhodes [in Greece] and a Turkish port cannot, in the absence of objective justification (see *Commission v France*, ... paragraph 16), be subject to more onerous conditions than those to which the provision of comparable services between the port of Rhodes and ports in Greece or other Member States are subject."

---

32 Case C-379/92 [1994] ECR I-3453, ECLI:EU:C:1994:296.
33 Case C-435/00 [2002] ECR I-10615, ECLI:EU:C:2002:661.
34 Ed., Case C-381/93 *Commission v France* [1994] ECR I-5145, ECLI:EU:C:1994:370.
35 Ed., Case C-70/99 *Commission v Portugal* [2001] ECR I-4845, ECLI:EU:C:2001:355.

The CJEU had earlier stated in *Inspecteur van de Belastingdienst Douane, District Rotterdam v Sea-Land Service Inc. and Nedlloyd Lijnen BV*:

> "25. ... as regards the matters covered by Regulation No 4055/86, the wording of Article 1(1) makes it clear that it applies to maritime transport services between the Member States and between the latter and third countries.
> 26. As regards the persons covered by Regulation No 4055/86, under Articles 1(1) and (2), freedom to provide maritime transport services applies to nationals of Member States who are established in a Member State other than that of the person for whom the services are intended, to nationals of Member States established outside the [EU] and to shipping companies established outside the [EU] and controlled by nationals of a Member State, if their vessels are registered in that Member State in accordance with its legislation."[36]

7.028 The Council is empowered, under Article 7 of Regulation 4055/86, to extend the provisions of the regulation to nationals of a third country (i.e. a non-Member State) which provide maritime transport services and are established in the EU.[37] It has been commented:

> "[t]his provision is basically intended to be used in order to extend the benefit of the liberalization process to other OECD [Organisation for Economic Co-operation and Development] countries which are not Member States. ... It is remarkable, however, that this provision is unduly vague: it does not specify when, how, under what criteria such a Council decision may be taken. This provision may open the door to misinterpretation and claims by nationals of other countries apart from the above group."[38]

This provision would allow some flexibility by way of bilateral or multilateral agreements.

Unilateral national restrictions and the timetable: Article 2 of Regulation 4055/86

7.029 In specific terms, Article 2 of Regulation 4055/86 states:

> "By way of derogation from Article 1, unilateral national restrictions in existence before 1 July 1986 on the carriage of certain goods wholly or partly reserved for vessels flying the national flag, shall be phased out at the latest in accordance with the following timetable:
>
> – carriage between Member States by vessels flying the flag of a Member State: 31 December 1989
> – carriage between Member States and third countries by vessels flying the flag of a Member State: 31 December 1991
> – carriage between Member States and between Member States and third countries in other vessels: 1 January 1993."

This phased process was needed because of the relatively dramatic impact of the changes.

---

36 Cases C-430 and 431/99 [2002] ECR I-5235, ECLI:EU:C:2002:364.
37 Art. 7 provided: "The Council, acting in accordance with the conditions laid down in the Treaty, may extend the provisions of this Regulation to nationals of a third country who provide maritime transport services and are established in the Community." Reg. 4055/86 applies to European Economic Area nationals.
38 Bredima-Savopoulou and Tzoannos, op. cit. at fn. 21, pp. 116–117.

Cargo-sharing arrangements in bilateral agreements: Articles 3 and 4 of Regulation 4055/86

7.030 The phasing out or adjustment of cargo-sharing arrangements contained in existing bilateral agreements concluded by Member States with third countries was provided for in Articles 3 and 4 of Regulation 4055/86.

7.031 Article 3 simply provides that cargo-sharing arrangements contained in existing[39] bilateral agreements concluded by Member States with third countries had to be phased out or adjusted in accordance with the provisions of Article 4 of the regulation. Article 3 states succinctly: "Cargo-sharing arrangements contained in existing bilateral agreements concluded by Member States with third countries shall be phased out or adjusted in accordance with the provisions of Article 4."

7.032 Article 4 of Regulation 4055/86 provides that:

"1. Existing cargo-sharing arrangements not phased out in accordance with Article 3 shall be adjusted in accordance with [Union] legislation and in particular:

   (a) where trades governed by the United Nations Code of Conduct for Liner Conferences are concerned, they shall comply with this Code and with the obligations of Member States under Regulation (EEC) No. 954/79;[40]
   (b) where trades not governed by the United Nations Code of Conduct for Liner Conferences are concerned, agreement shall be adjusted as soon as possible and in any event before January 1, 1993, so as to provide for fair, free and non discriminatory access by all [Union] nationals, as defined in Article 1, to the cargo-shares due to the Member State concerned.

2. National action in pursuance of paragraph 1 shall be notified immediately to the Member States and the Commission. The consultation procedure established by Council Decision 77/587/EEC shall apply.
3. Member States shall report to the Commission on progress made on the adjustments referred to in paragraph 1(b), initially[41] every six months and subsequently every year.
4. When difficulties arise in the process of adjusting agreements to bring them into conformity with paragraph 1(b), the Member State concerned shall inform the Council and the Commission. In cases where agreements are incompatible with paragraph 1(b), and where the Member State concerned so asks, the Council shall, acting on a proposal from the Commission, take appropriate action."

The effective date for determining whether an agreement is an "existing one" for the purposes of the regulation is 1 January 1987.

Cargo-sharing arrangements in future agreements: Article 5 of Regulation 4055/86

7.033 Article 5 of Regulation 4055/86 prohibits explicitly new cargo-sharing arrangements in future agreements except in the most exceptional of circumstances. It provides:

"1. Cargo-sharing arrangements in any future agreements with third countries are prohibited other than in those exceptional circumstances where [Union] liner shipping companies would not otherwise have an effective opportunity to ply for trade to and from the third country concerned. In those circumstances such arrangements may be permitted in accordance with the provisions of Article 6.

---

39 I.e. existing at the time of the regulation entering into force (i.e. 1 January 1987).
40 Ed., see chap. 10.
41 Ed., the word "initially" is somewhat vague.

2. In cases where a third country seeks to impose cargo sharing arrangements on Member States in liquid or dry bulk trades, the Council shall take the appropriate action in accordance with Regulation (EEC) No. 4056/86 concerning co-ordinated action to safeguard free access to cargoes in ocean trades."[42]

7.034 Article 6 of Regulation 4055/86 is in the nature of a standstill clause. It goes on to provide that where a Member State's nationals or shipping companies, as defined in Article 1, paragraphs 1 and 2, are experiencing, or are threatened by, a situation where they do not have an effective opportunity to ply for trade to and from a particular third country, the Member State concerned must inform the other Member States and the Commission as soon as possible. The Council acting by qualified majority on a proposal of the Commission, must decide on the necessary action. Such action may include, in the circumstances envisaged in Article 5(1), the negotiation and conclusion of cargo-sharing arrangements.[43] If the Council has not decided on the necessary action within six months of a Member State providing information under Article 5(1), the Member State concerned may take such action as may for the time being be necessary to preserve an effective opportunity to ply for trade in accordance with Article 5(1).[44] Article 6 of Regulation 4055/86 provides:

> "4. Any action taken under paragraph 3 shall be in accordance with [Union] law and provide for fair, free and non-discriminatory access to the relevant cargo-shares by nationals or [Union] shipping companies as defined in Article 1(1) and (2).
> 5. National action in pursuance of paragraph 3 shall be notified immediately to the Member States and the Commission. The consultation procedure established by Council Decision 77/587/EEC shall apply."

Non-discrimination between EU nationals on the basis of nationality

7.035 As long as restrictions on freedom to supply services have not been abolished, each Member State must apply such restrictions without discrimination on grounds of nationality or residence to all persons providing services within the meaning of Article 1(1) and (2) of Regulation 4055/86.[45] This amplifies the principle of non-discrimination on the basis of nationality enshrined in Article 18 of the TFEU.[46]

Non-EU nationals and Regulation 4055/86

7.036 As mentioned above, the Council is empowered to extend the provisions of the regulation to nationals of a third country who provide maritime transport services and are

---

42 In respect of the exceptional circumstances outlined in Art. 5(1), see Bredima-Savopoulou and Tzoannos, op. cit. at fn. 21, pp. 178–179.
43 Reg. 4055/86, Art. 6(2).
44 Reg. 4055/86, Art. 6(3).
45 Reg. 4055/86, Art. 9.
46 Art. 18 of the TFEU provides:

> "Within the scope of application of the Treaties, and without prejudice to any special provisions contained therein, any discrimination on grounds of nationality and embodied in EU law generally shall be prohibited.
> The European Parliament and the Council, acting in accordance with the ordinary legislative procedure, may adopt rules designed to prohibit such discrimination."

established in the EU.⁴⁷ This is an open-ended provision which confers a great deal of discretion on the Council. However, where the Council has not acted to extend the provisions of Regulation 4055/86 to third State nationals then such nationals would not have the ability to rely on the regulation as such.

Temporary establishment

7.037 Article 8 of Regulation 4055/86 provides:

"Without prejudice to the provisions of the [TFEU] relating to right of establishment, a person providing a maritime transport service may, in order to do so, temporarily pursue his activity in the Member State where the service is provided, under the same conditions as are imposed by that State on its own nationals."

Review

7.038 The Council was charged under Article 11 of the regulation to review, acting in accordance with the provisions of the TFEU, the regulation before 1 January 1995.⁴⁸ Regulation 4055/86 has remained unaltered for three decades (i.e. since its adoption).

Assessment of Regulation 4055/86 generally

7.039 Regulation 4055/86 was very welcome because it opened the market to greater competition and allowed shipowners to have greater access to a larger market. As is clear from the case law of the CJEU considered in this chapter, there was no freedom to provide services before the entry into force of the regulation. However, the regulation is vague in many instances; for example, what is meant by the phrase "fair, free and non-discriminatory access"? And what is indeed meant by the term "cargo-sharing arrangement"? The freedom embodied in Regulation 4055/86 may be removed in cases where there is objective justification by reason of public interest and the legislation is objectively necessary and proportionate to its aims.⁴⁹ Nonetheless, it represented a significant and welcome change in the law.⁵⁰

D. CABOTAGE OR DOMESTIC SHIPPING SERVICES: REGULATION 3577/92

Introduction

7.040 Cabotage is the provision of a shipping service between ports in any one State, including the overseas territories of that State.⁵¹ Cabotage restrictions would be an

---

47 Reg. 4055/86, Art. 7.
48 Reg. 4055/86, Art. 11.
49 See Cases C-430/99 and C-431/99 *Inspecteur van de Belastingdienst Douane, district Rotterdam v Sea-Land Service Inc. and Nedlloyd Lijnen BV* [2002] ECR I-523, ECLI:EU:C:2002:364.
50 Case 49/89 *Corsica Ferries France v Direction Générale des Douanes Françaises* [1989] ECR 4441, ECLI:EU:1989:649.
51 See "Reforms of Cabotage Urged", Lloyd's List, 1 April 1987, p. 3. See Migliorino, "Mediterranean Cabotage after 1992", paper presented at RORO Conference in Trieste in May 1990. See also the periodic reports by the Commission on cabotage. See Fourth Report on Maritime Cabotage COM(2002) 203 final.

impediment to trade within the EU because the possibility of trading in another Member State would not be open to EU carriers. The single market or internal market so ardently desired by the Commission in its June 1985 White Paper (the "1992 Programme") would be incomplete without the abolition of cabotage restrictions because there would not be an internal market but a series of home markets which are not open to others in the EU. Cabotage restrictions are exceptions to the free open and competition policy espoused by the Member States and championed by the Commission. Cabotage restrictions are an obstacle to the free movement of services within the EU: it is one of the cardinal principles of EU law that nationals of one EU Member State should be legally entitled to provide services to persons in other Member States on the same terms as persons in the host Member State so cabotage restrictions are inherently contrary to EU law on first impression.

7.041 The abolition of cabotage restrictions was a divisive issue among the Member States. These States which regarded it as a controversial issue can be categorised (in simple terms) into two groups: the "Northern States" which favoured the abolition of restrictions (because they had little to lose by its abolition, could instead gain from the new services which have opened up and saw a value in competitive markets) and the "Southern States" (many of which favoured the retention of cabotage restrictions either in whole or in part because they had so much to lose from their abolition (and perhaps very little to gain)).

7.042 The implications of the abolition of cabotage must not be underestimated. The Greek island traffic, the Spanish and Italian coastal traffic as well as a multitude of small routes in France, Greece, Italy, Portugal and Spain would finally be opened up. More generally, the freedom to provide services in shipping must not be underestimated. Even if a national of, for example, Greece decides not to provide services to nationals of other Member States (in Italy or wherever), that is not the end of the matter – a national from one of the other Member States might well decide to offer services to Greek residents and thereby take the Greek national's own customers.

7.043 Cabotage is a limited form of flag discrimination. It is not a new concept. Tudor England pioneered flag discrimination and Cromwell enacted the Navigation Act in 1651. The effect of these laws is summarised by Farthing in the following terms:

> "trade to and from British colonies, which at a much later stage began to expand significantly, had to be carried in British ships. No foreign-built ships were to be used. Commodities of all sorts, particularly strategic commodities had to be enumerated and their carriage regulated and controlled so that no one else got a look in. There was also general encouragement in the form of grants to British shipowners for the carriage of specified exports such as corn and other agricultural products."[52]

Concepts of cabotage

7.044 It is useful to define certain terms in this debate before proceeding further. "Cabotage" is the carriage of passengers and/or goods by sea between ports in any one Member State, including the overseas territories of that State. "State cabotage" involves

---

52 *International Shipping: An Introduction to the Policies, Politics and Institutions of the Maritime World* (1987), pp. 9–10.

restrictions which have been imposed by individual States such as, historically, France, Greece, Italy, Portugal and Spain.

7.045 A concept which is not widely known is the concept of "EU Cabotage", that is to say, that the EU as a whole could become a cabotage region, within which national restrictions would be abolished and a single internal EU market would be established. Cabotage on an EU level does not really exist because there is no cargo reservation at EU level except for the UNCTAD Code of Conduct on Liner Conferences. The idea of EU cabotage was proposed by France in a Working Paper submitted after the 11 November 1985 Council Meeting. While the idea is attractive in its simplicity, the danger is that if the EU were to adopt such a patently protectionist approach within its own borders then it would lose its moral right to advocate to others the desirability of free trade in shipping services. It is also not likely to be feasible in an increasingly globalised world.

7.046 Cabotage may also be classified, as Article 2 of Regulation 3577/92 does, into: (a) mainland cabotage; (b) offshore supply cabotage; and (c) island cabotage. Mainland cabotage involves the carriage of passengers or goods by sea between ports situated on the mainland or the main territory of one and the same Member State without calls at islands. Offshore supply services cabotage involves the carriage of passengers or goods by sea between any port in a Member State and installations or structures situated on the continental shelf of that Member State. Island cabotage involves the carriage of passengers or goods by sea between ports situated on the mainland and on one or more of the islands of one and the same Member State, and ports situated on the islands of one and the same Member State.

Commercial overview of cabotage

7.047 The volume of cabotage trade within the EU is quite significant. This trade is, for obvious reasons, clustered in the Mediterranean with historically Greece having, on an annual basis, about 20 million tonnes of cabotage cargo, Spain with about 40 million tonnes and Italy with about 55 million tonnes. Nonetheless the UK has the largest cabotage trade in the EU having historically over 65 million tonnes annually. In general, cabotage activities involve almost all shipping activities, including the transport of cargo (both wet and dry), passengers (including cruising) and offshore supplies. Among the southern Member States, dry bulk cargo is the most important as far as Greece is concerned but liquid cargoes are more important for France, Italy, Spain and Portugal. Apart from France, the amount of cargo and passengers carried on cabotage services is rising, albeit slowly. Around the EU, the bulk of cabotage trade is between the mainland and the islands as well as between two ports on the mainland. Only a small proportion is between islands and then when it is between islands, it is mainly passengers rather than cargo. The number of passengers transported on cabotage services in the cabotage States in the EU was reckoned at the time when the debate was at its most intensive to be around 50 million but growing. Some of these services are short ferry crossings and so the real figure could be higher. Greece has a significant ferry and cruise cabotage passenger business which is not equalled by any of the other cabotage states. Malta has significant inter-island traffic as well. Some passengers and workers are carried out to offshore installations throughout the EU but this is negligible in terms of the number of passengers transported in the EU.

Merits of cabotage

Arguments for cabotage

7.048 The arguments offered by some Member States for cabotage restrictions were mainly strategic ones, involving national security, the need for "public service" routes to islands and remote regions, as well as the need to preserve national fleets and seafarers' jobs. It has also been argued that goods and passengers are being carried to islands and remote regions where it is not economically viable to do so but there are government subsidies/cabotage restrictions in place which make such operations feasible.[53] On occasion, Greece has supported cabotage restrictions on the grounds of national security because of its long-standing dispute with Turkey. Greece believed that some of its islands are in dangerous proximity to Turkey and for security reasons only Greek ships should be servicing such islands. The European Parliament has said that national security is a reason why Member States should be able to restrict national services to national vessels. Spain and Italy supported the continuance of cabotage restrictions on the grounds that their removal would have adverse consequences for the jobs and welfare of its seafarers. The European Parliament's Committee on Economic and Monetary Affairs in its 1976 Interim Report on the Community Shipping Industry wrote:

> "16. In cabotage, or coastal trading, within the [EU], there is also some flag discrimination to be found. For example, some Community States' vessels have been excluded from certain Cross-Channel passenger services. The effects of such a practice, may, however, prove to be beneficial, especially where such trade is heavily seasonal. Established shipping companies may use a high revenue during the summer to help finance under-utilised shipping in the winter months, thus providing a service of considerable social and economic benefit."[54]

The abolition of cabotage was expected to reduce profits for the shipping companies (which benefit from the restriction) in those southern Member States, result in a loss of jobs as well as ships for those national fleets and could result in some services currently being offered having to be withdrawn.

Arguments against cabotage

7.049 On the other hand, cabotage had few friends north of the Mediterranean. Studies indicate that cabotage restrictions resulted in higher costs in terms of freight and passenger rates. Protected or anti-competitive markets almost invariably lead to higher prices. It is true to say that even if the rates charged for the shipment of cargo and passengers on particular cabotage routes are not higher than open routes, they may in fact be kept artificially low because of subsidies from the States involved. A protected environment almost always leads to inefficiencies. The protected environment of cabotage has meant that some protected routes were probably serviced by inefficient and old ships. Most particularly, cabotage breaches the concept of equality embodied in such provisions

---

[53] The weakness in this argument is that a Member State could still have such services provided on the basis of a "public service obligation"-type competition open to all EU nationals or indeed all providers.

[54] Doc. 479/76, Rapporteur: Mr J L Prescott, para. 14, citing *Finanstidende*, Copenhagen, 31 December 1975. On the report generally, see chap. 5.

of the TFEU: why should Greek ships be entitled to offer cabotage services along the UK coast but not the other way around?

An historical perspective on cabotage in the Member States

Introduction

7.050 In broad terms, France, Greece, Italy, Portugal and Spain favoured the retention of cabotage restrictions (of these, only Greece had been a hardliner in the final negotiations at the Council meetings) and Belgium, Denmark, Germany, Ireland, the Netherlands and the UK favoured its abolition. The matter was not of much direct interest to Luxembourg! In more specific terms, Member States may be classified into four groups of States for the purposes of cabotage: (a) States which had cabotage restrictions; (b) States which did not have cabotage restrictions; (c) States which had limited cabotage restrictions; and (d) States for which the issue did not arise.

States which had cabotage restrictions in more recent times

Introduction

7.051 The States with cabotage restrictions shared some general characteristics, namely, they have more islands (e.g. Greece (Aegean), Spain (the Balearics), France (Corsica), Italy (Sicily and Sardinia)) and long coastlines (e.g. Italy and Greece) or remote regions which are difficult to get to otherwise than by sea or air (e.g. Greece). These were the States which resisted changes.

France

7.052 France maintained some cabotage restrictions. It had *petit cabotage* which involves trade between French ports as well as *grand cabotage* which involved trade between the ports of Mediterranean France and ports in France's overseas territories such as Guadeloupe and Martinique.

Germany

7.053 Cabotage in Germany was historically restricted to ships flying the flag of any Member State.

Greece

7.054 Greece maintained cabotage restrictions for many years. The archipelago with its multitude of islands meant that Greek opposition to the abolition of cabotage was not too surprising. National trade in goods loaded and unloaded was some 40% of the total international trade in goods loaded and unloaded. Greece supported the retention of cabotage restrictions because of the public service needs of remote islands, the seasonal demand of some services, national security issues relating to the Greece–Turkey disputes and the need to protect existing Greek-operated services from competition.

Italy

7.055 National trade in goods loaded and unloaded was about a quarter of the total international trade in goods loaded and unloaded thus it is a matter of some concern. The long Italian coastline means that cabotage trade can be quite attractive. Italy maintained cabotage restrictions for a variety of protectionist reasons. The Italian cabotage trade was attractive to many shipowners. Cabotage in Italy became restricted to ships flying the flag of a Member State.

Portugal

7.056 While Portugal traditionally maintained some cabotage restrictions, there were significant moves towards liberalisation since 1988. Cabotage in Portugal was later opened to ships flying the flag of any Member State.

Spain

7.057 National trade in goods loaded and unloaded was historically more than half of the total international trade in goods loaded and unloaded. Spain had an extensive range of cabotage restrictions. Cabotage in Spain was then restricted to ships flying the flag of a Member State.

Sweden

7.058 Cabotage in Sweden was restricted to ships flying the flag of a Member State.

States which did not have cabotage restrictions in more recent times

Belgium

7.059 Belgium did not have any cabotage restrictions because cabotage there was almost unheard of in the light of its short coastline.

Ireland

7.060 Ireland did not have any cabotage restrictions. Indeed, national trade in goods loaded and unloaded was a tiny fraction of the total international trade in goods loaded and unloaded (and then mainly oil products) thus it was a matter of little concern.

United Kingdom

7.061 National trade in goods loaded and unloaded was about a third of the total international trade in goods loaded and unloaded. The UK had the largest cabotage traffic in the EU. The British pressed hard for the abolition of cabotage. British Shipping Ministers spoken out on many occasions on the issue. Mrs Thatcher (then Prime Minister) mentioned the issue in her famous Bruges Speech. They championed the adoption of EU legislation on the abolition of cabotage for many years. In 1988, the UK enacted the

Merchant Shipping Act. The Act allows the UK to retaliate against other Member States which preserved cabotage restrictions in favour of their own national shipowners and refuse to allow UK shipowners access to domestic routes. The restrictions imposed by the UK could include restrictions on the carriage of goods and passengers between ports in the UK, between British ports and offshore installations on the UK Continental Shelf and between offshore installations on the UK Continental Shelf.

States which had limited cabotage restrictions

Denmark

7.062 National trade in goods loaded and unloaded was a small portion of the total international trade in goods loaded and unloaded. Denmark had cabotage restrictions in relation to trade with the Faroe Islands. Denmark also restricted trade involving vessels up to 500 grt to national flag carriers. Nonetheless it was quite anxious to see the abolition of cabotage in the EU.

States which had no cabotage restrictions or issues

7.063 For much of this debate, Luxembourg was the only landlocked Member State but, over time, other landlocked States joined. For them, the issue was not of direct relevance.

Development of the EU law on cabotage

1974: **Commission v France**

7.064 The judgment of the CJEU in *Commission v France*[55] is important in that it emphasised that the general rules of the now TFEU applied to the maritime transport sector and therefore cabotage should be, at least in principle, unlawful under EU law. However, it was not until the adoption of the 1992 Regulation discussed below that the matter resolved itself.

1984: European Parliamentary Question

7.065 On 6 September 1984, Commissioner Giorgios Contogeorgis set out the views of the Commission at that time in regard to cabotage. He was asked the following question in the European Parliament by Robert Moreland MEP:

"Coastal Shipping
The requirement that coastal cargoes be carried in national flag vessels is included in the legislation of Denmark, France, the Federal Republic of Germany, Greece and Italy.

1. Is there any commitment in Community legislation or by Member States to end this requirement?
2. Will the Commission make proposals to ensure that coastal cargoes in any Member States are open to the ships of all Member States?"

---

55 Case 167/73 [1974] ECR 359, ECLI:EU:C:1974:35 (see chap. 5).

Commissioner Contogeorgis responded:

"In accordance with Art. [58](1) of the [TFEU], the freedom to provide services in the field of transport is governed by Title IV of the Treaty which, in respect of maritime transport, does not include any specific provisions, but leaves it open to the Council to decide whether, to what extent and by what procedure appropriate provisions may be laid down in this field.

The Commission has not to date elaborated proposals in the sense desired by the Honourable Member, taking into account, inter alia, that:

- this type of traffic constitutes a relatively modest part of maritime transport as far as most Member States are concerned;
- some Member States automatically grant dispensation to applicants of another nationality offering coastal transport services;
- the reservation of coastal transport is justified by certain Member States by their concern to ensure the continuity of a service – very often showing a deficit – for social, regional development or other reasons.

The Commission has tried to solve problems in this field, where they arose, by recommending parties concerned to avail themselves of the right of establishment.

Nevertheless, the Commission is considering the possibility of an overall approach to the question of when and how the freedom to provide services might be put into effect in respect of maritime transport services."

1985: Communication from the Commission to the Council

7.066 In its communication to the Council in 1985 on "Progress Towards a Common Transport Policy: Maritime Transport",[56] the Commission proposed the application of the principle of freedom to provide services to the maritime transport sector. This proposal ultimately became Regulation 4055/85.[57] The proposal included in Annex II-2, a draft Council regulation applying the principle of freedom to provide services in sea transport. The Council of European and Japanese National Shipowners' Associations ("CENSA") described this proposal as the cornerstone of the 1985 package. The legislative basis for the draft regulation was the then Article 84, paragraph 2, of the EEC Treaty (now, largely, Article 100(2) of the TFEU). Article 1(1) of the draft regulation provided that restrictions on freedom to provide sea transport services[58] within the EU were to be abolished by 1 July 1986 in respect of nationals of Member States who are established in a State of the EU other than that of the person for whom the services are intended. Article 1(2) immediately qualified this general principle by establishing a timetable which provided that in the case of certain sea transport services specified in Article 3(1), restrictions which existed before 1 July 1986 might be retained, but should

---

56 COM(85)90.
57 OJ 1986 L378/1.
58 The term "freedom to provide sea transport services" included the provision of sea transport services between a Member States and a third country (Art. 2 of the draft Regulation). Services were considered to be "sea transport services" where they are normally provided for remuneration and shall in particular include: (a) the carriage of passengers or goods by sea between ports in any one Member State, including overseas territories of that State (cabotage); (b) the carriage of passengers or goods by sea between any port in a Member State and installations or structures on the continental shelf of that Member State (offshore supply services); (c) the carriage of passengers or goods by sea between any port in a Member State and any port in another Member State (intra-Community shipping services); and (d) the carriage of passengers or goods by sea by a shipping company established in a Member State between the ports of another Member State and ports in a third country (cross-trading).

be progressively abolished during a period of five years after the adoption of the regulation – however, in the case of cabotage, a period of ten years was allowed. In the case of cabotage between specific regions, however, the ten-year period would not apply where its application would cause "particular difficulties". In such cases, the Member States concerned were to inform the Commission, which would before the end of the tenth year after the adoption of the regulation present specific proposals which would take account of those difficulties, for the progressive abolition of the relevant restrictions. Article 4 of the draft regulation provided that notwithstanding the application of the principle of freedom to provide services to sea transport services, a Member State may, where necessary in order to maintain sufficient sea transport services in the case of cabotage between the mainland and its islands and between its islands, impose public service obligations as a condition for the right to provide the service. It is important to remember that Article 5 of the draft regulation provided that the Council might, acting unanimously on a proposal from the Commission, extend the provisions of the draft regulation (were it enacted) to nationals of a third country which provides sea transport services and are established in the EU.

1986: December package

7.067 In December 1986, the Council adopted four regulations:[59] Regulation 4055/86 applying the principle of freedom to provide services to maritime transport between Member States and between Member States and third countries; Regulation 4056/86 laying down detailed rules for the application of, what were then, Articles 85 and 86 of the EEC Treaty (now Articles 101 and 102 of the TFEU) to maritime transport; Regulation 4057/86 on unfair pricing practices in maritime transport; and Regulation 4058/86 concerning co-ordinated action to safeguard free access to cargoes in ocean trades. Collectively, these are known as the "December 1986 Package". Cabotage restrictions proved to be the major impediment to agreement on the Council Regulation applying the Principle of Freedom to Provide Services in Sea Transport. Member States were divided along the North–South line. Most States were prepared to accept the maintenance of cabotage restrictions in respect of the ordinary services to islands and remote geographical regions (especially, where such services were unprofitable and offered only for public services reasons). There was however a gulf between Member States on the issue of whether or not cabotage restrictions should be lifted in the case of cruising operations. The gap was too wide to be bridged and therefore agreement on cabotage was postponed and a regulation on freedom to provide international services between Member States and between Member States and third countries (Regulation 4055/86) was adopted[60] instead, leaving cabotage for another day. If the opponents of cabotage had stuck to their case, Regulation 4055/86 might not have been adopted at all. As the Commission later wrote:

---

59 See chap. 5.
60 Art. 1(4) which provides that: "For the purposes of this Regulation, the following shall be considered 'maritime transport services between Member States and between Member States and third countries' where they are normally provided for remuneration."

"[i]n agreeing to the package of four regulations in the field of transport in December 1986, the Council did not find it possible to decide at that stage on the application of the principle of freedom to provide services in respect of shipping services within the Member States; it therefore agreed that further consideration of this part of the Commission proposal was necessary."[61]

1988: Commission Programme

7.068 The Commission in its Programme for 1988[62] hoped for progress on cabotage.

1989: Positive Measures Programme

7.069 In its August 1989 "Package of Positive Measures" for EU shipping, the Commission wrote:

"[i]n the context of measures being proposed with the aim of maintaining a more competitive Community fleet, with converging conditions of operation, through the instrument of a parallel [EU] register, the Commission considers it necessary to make progress with the application to Member States' internal maritime transport of the principle of the freedom to provide services, in view of the completion of the internal market by 1993."[63]

It went on to say that:

"[i]n this context, the Commission considers appropriate that the removal of restrictions on the freedom to provide services in Member States' internal maritime transport in respect of nationals and maritime companies of the Member States should be accompanied by conditions in respect of the vessels used to provide the service, so as to ensure a degree of approximation of operating conditions, always taking also due account of the special requirements of certain public services of cabotage which the Member States make in the general interest. The Commission therefore proposes that removal of restrictions is subject to the use of vessels registered in the [EU] ship register and which operate in short-sea trades."[64]

7.070 The Commission then appended a proposal for a Council regulation concerning the application to Member States' internal maritime transport of the freedom to provide services, which incorporated the considerations outlined above by the Commission.[65] This new proposal superseded the earlier one in 1985. The Commission's proposal was amended and submitted to the Council.[66]

Council Regulation (EEC) 3577/92 of 7 December 1992 applying the principle of freedom to maritime transport within Member States (maritime cabotage)

Introduction

7.071 Ultimately, on 7 December 1992, the Council adopted Regulation 3577/92 to apply the principle of freedom to provide services to maritime transport between ports within one and the same Member State.[67] Regulation 3577/92 is a measure which was

---

61 Positive Measures, para. 113.
62 Bull. EC Supp. 1/88, p. 50.
63 Positive Measures, para. 114.
64 Ibid., para. 115.
65 Ibid., Annex 4.
66 OJ C73/27, 19 March 1991.
67 OJ L364/7, 12 December 1992.

long in gestation[68] but will be slow in implementation.[69] Cabotage restrictions were thus to be abolished within the EU in accordance with this regulation.

Key concepts in Regulation 3577/92

The concept of "cabotage"

7.072 Cabotage is the right to provide transport services between two points within one and the same State. In the EU context, Article 1 of Regulation 3577/92 defines cabotage as the "freedom to provide maritime transport services within a Member State".

The concept of "maritime transport services"

7.073 What are "maritime transport services"? Article 2(1) of Regulation 3577/92 defines "maritime transport services within a Member State (maritime cabotage)" as:

"services normally provided for remuneration and shall in particular include:

(a) mainland cabotage: the carriage of passengers or goods by sea between ports situated on the mainland or the main territory of one and the same Member State without calls at islands;
(b) off-shore supply services: the carriage of passengers or goods by sea between any port in a Member State and installations or structures situated on the continental shelf of that Member State;
(c) island cabotage: the carriage of passengers or goods by sea between:

– ports situated on the mainland and on one or more of the islands of one and the same Member State,
– ports situated on the islands of one and the same Member State;

Ceuta and Melilla shall be treated in the same way as island ports".

The concept of "Community shipowner"

7.074 What is a "Community shipowner" for the purposes of Regulation 3577/92? Article 2(2) of Regulation 3577/92 defines the term "Community shipowner" as:

"(a) nationals of a Member State established in a Member State in accordance with the legislation of that Member State and pursuing shipping activities; or
(b) shipping companies established in accordance with the legislation of a Member State and whose principal place of business is situated, and effective control exercised, in a Member State; or
(c) nationals of a Member State established outside the Community or shipping companies established outside the Community and controlled by nationals of a Member State, if their ships are registered in and fly the flag of a Member State in accordance with its legislation".[70]

---

68 The long gestation was linked entirely to the controversial nature of the proposal as far as some Member States were concerned; it was reported in *Fairplay* on 11 July 1991 in an article entitled "ECSA Split on Cabotage Issue" that the "European Community Shipowners' Associations (ECSA) has expressed support for a two-stage movement towards liberalising cabotage in EU waters. But the Spanish and Italian shipowners' associations have dissented from the common viewpoint."

69 The regulation entered into force on 1 January 1993 but the full implementation of the regulation will take longer. See http://ec.europa.eu/transport/modes/maritime/news/doc/com(2014)232_en.pdf.

70 It is assumed that the term "Community" should now read as "Union" given the entry into force of the TFEU.

Now, the term "Community" shipowner would be an EU or Union Shipowner.

The concept of "a public service contract"

7.075 What is a "public service contract" for the purposes of Regulation 3577/92? Article 2(3) of Regulation 3577/92 defines the term "a public service contract" as meaning:

> "a contract concluded between the competent authorities of a Member State and a Community shipowner in order to provide the public with adequate transport services.
> A public service contract may cover notably:
>
> – transport services satisfying fixed standards of continuity, regularity, capacity and quality,
> – additional transport services,
> – transport services at specified rates and subject to specified conditions, in particular for certain categories of passengers or on certain routes,
> – adjustments of services to actual requirements."

The concept of "public service obligations"

7.076 What are "public service obligations" for the purposes of Regulation 3577/92? Article 2(4) of Regulation 3577/92 defines the term "public service obligations" as meaning: "obligations which the Community shipowner in question, if he were considering his own commercial interest, would not assume to the same extent or under the same conditions".

The concept of "a serious disturbance of the internal transport market"

7.077 What is "a serious disturbance of the internal transport market" for the purposes of Regulation 3577/92? Article 2(5) of Regulation 3577/92 defines the term as meaning:

> "the appearance on the market of problems specific to that market and which:
>
> – are likely to lead to a serious and potentially lasting excess of supply over demand,
> – are due to, or aggravated by, maritime cabotage operations, and
> – pose a serious threat to the financial stability and survival of a significant number of Community shipowners,
>
> provided that the short-term and medium-term forecasts for the market in question do not indicate any substantial and lasting improvements".

This is an "escape hatch". As with all exceptions to the fundamental principles of EU law, it should be construed narrowly.

The benefits of cabotage

7.078 The third and fourth recitals to Regulation 3577/92 provide:

> "Whereas the abolition of restrictions on the provision of maritime transport services within Member States is necessary for the establishment of the internal market; whereas the internal market will comprise an area in which the free movement of goods, persons, services and capital is ensured;
> Whereas therefore freedom to provide services should be applied to maritime transport within Member States…"

Legal bases of Regulation 3577/92

7.079 Freedom to provide transport services is subject to the Title on transport in the Treaty and not the general Treaty regime on freedom to provide services.[71] The principal legal basis of Regulation 3577/92 was the then EEC Treaty generally and the then Article 84(2) thereof in particular.[72]

Beneficiaries of Regulation 3577/92

EU Member States generally

7.080 The fifth recital of Regulation 3577/92 provides: "Whereas the beneficiaries of this freedom [to provide cabotage services] should be Community shipowners operating vessels registered in and flying the flag of a Member State whether or not it has a coastline..." Thus, all Member States (including landlocked ones) are entitled to benefit from Regulation 3577/92.

Vessels registered on the EUROS Register

7.081 The sixth recital of Regulation 3577/92 provides: "Whereas this freedom [to provide cabotage services] will be extended to vessels also registered in EUROS once that register is approved..." Thus, all vessels registered on the EUROS Register[73] would have benefited from the right to offer cabotage services. However, the EUROS Register was never adopted so this provision is now otiose.

Implementation of Regulation 3577/92

Introduction

7.082 The implementation of Regulation 3577/92 was a long-involved process. The eighth recital to the regulation provides:

"Whereas the implementation of this freedom should be gradual and not necessarily provided for in a uniform way for all services concerned, taking into account the nature of certain specific services and the extent of the effort that certain economies in the Community showing differences in development will have to sustain..."

General principle

7.083 Article 1 of Regulation 3577/92 provides:

"1. As from 1 January 1993, freedom to provide maritime transport services within a Member State (maritime cabotage) shall apply to Community shipowners who have their ships registered in, and flying the flag of a Member State, provided that these ships comply with all conditions for carrying out cabotage in that Member State, including ships registered in EUROS, once that Register is approved by the Council.

---

71 TFEU, Art. 58. See also Reg. 3577/92, Recital 2.
72 This is now largely Art. 100(2) of the TFEU.
73 On the EUROS Register, see chap. 6.

2. By way of derogation, the application of paragraph 1 requiring that ships fulfil all conditions for carrying out cabotage in the Member State in which they are registered at that time shall be temporarily suspended until 31 December 1996."

7.084 This general principle was limited by Article 6 which provided for a special regime for maritime transport services carried out in the Mediterranean and along the coast of France, Portugal and Spain. As the provision of cabotage is most controversial in the case of this area, Article 6 means that the entry into force of the regulation was delayed.

Mediterranean

7.085 Cabotage was a lively issue in the Mediterranean Member States (particularly, Greece). Article 6 of Regulation 3577/92 thus provided a special regime for the implementation of the regulation:

"1. By way of derogation, the following maritime transport services carried out in the Mediterranean[74] and along the coast of Spain, Portugal and France shall be temporarily exempted from the implementation of this Regulation:

  - cruise services, until 1 January 1995,
  - transport of strategic goods (oil, oil products and drinking water), until 1 January 1997,
  - services by ships smaller than 650 gt [gross tonnes], until 1 January 1998,
  - regular passenger and ferry services, until 1 January 1999.

2. By way of derogation, island cabotage in the Mediterranean and cabotage with regard to the Canary, Azores and Madeira archipelagos, Ceuta and Melilla, the French islands along the Atlantic coast and the French overseas departments shall be temporarily exempted from the implementation of this Regulation until 1 January 1999.
3. For reasons of socio-economic cohesion, the derogation provided for in paragraph 2 shall be extended for Greece until 1 January 2004 for regular passenger and ferry services provided by vessels less than 650 gt."

Suspensory effect of Regulation 3577/92

7.086 Article 62 of the then EEC Treaty provided: "Save as otherwise provided in this Treaty, Member States shall not introduce any new restrictions on the freedom to provide services which have in fact been attained at the date of entry into force of this Treaty."
Article 7 of Regulation 3577/92 provides: "Article 62 of the Treaty shall apply to the matters covered by this Regulation."

7.087 The purported effect of Article 7 is that no new restrictions will be imposed in regard to cabotage. An unresolved question remains however as to the validity of Article 7 invoking Article 62 of the EEC Treaty: Article 62 of the Treaty formed part of Title III of the Treaty (i.e. Free Movement of Persons, Services and Capital) and Article 61(1) of the EEC Treaty stated that freedom to provide services in the field of transport shall be governed by the provisions of the Title relating to transport (i.e. Title IV) and not, by implication, Title III so how may the regulation relating to transport services invoke a

---

74 Ed., there is no definition in the regulation of the Mediterranean.

Title III provision? One solution may be that the regulation is based not just on Article 80(2) of the then EEC Treaty (largely now Article 100(2) of the TFEU) but the Treaty as a whole.

Operation of Regulation 3577/92

7.088 The seventh recital to Regulation 3577/92 provides:

"Whereas in order to avoid distortion of competition, Community shipowners exercising the freedom to provide cabotage services should comply with all the conditions for carrying out cabotage in the Member State in which their vessels are registered; whereas Community shipowners operating ships registered in a Member State who do not have the right to carry out cabotage in that State should nevertheless be beneficiaries of this Regulation during a transitional period…"

7.089 A feature of this debate which appears to have been overlooked is the assumption that there was a link between the need to provide public services and the need to provide those services by ships registered in the coastal State – some would argue that those services could just as easily be provided by ships registered elsewhere in the EU.

Public service obligations and Regulation 3577/92

Introduction

7.090 One of the justifications for coastal States restricting and controlling cabotage services is the need to fulfil various public service obligations. Public service obligations have traditionally been important in Greece and Italy. The regulation aims to ensure transparency and competition between EU shipowners when allocating public services contracts.

7.091 The ninth recital to Regulation 3577/92 provides:

"Whereas the introduction of public services entailing certain rights and obligations for the shipowners concerned may be justified in order to ensure the adequacy of regular transport services to, from and between islands, provided that there is no distinction on the grounds of nationality or residence…"

7.092 Article 2(3) of Regulation 3577/92 defines the term "a public service contract" as meaning:

"a contract concluded between the competent authorities of a Member State and a Community shipowner in order to provide the public with adequate transport services.
  A public service contract may cover notably:

  – transport services satisfying fixed standards of continuity, regularity, capacity and quality,
  – additional transport services,
  – transport services at specified rates and subject to specified conditions, in particular for certain categories of passengers or on certain routes,
  – adjustments of services to actual requirements."

7.093 Article 4 of Regulation 3577/92 provides:

"1. A Member State may conclude public service contracts with or impose public service obligations as a condition for the provision of cabotage services, on shipping companies participating in regular services to, from and between islands.

Whenever a Member State concludes public service contracts or imposes public service obligations, it shall do so on a non-discriminatory basis in respect of all Community shipowners.
2. In imposing public service obligations, Member States shall be limited to requirements concerning ports to be served, regularity, continuity, frequency, capacity to provide the service, rates to be charged and manning of the vessel. Where applicable, any compensation for public service obligations must be available to all Community shipowners.
3. Existing public service contracts may remain in force up to the expiry date of the relevant contract."

Crewing or manning of vessels engaged in cabotage

Mainland cabotage

7.094 Article 3(1) of Regulation 3577/92 provides:

"For vessels carrying out mainland cabotage[75] and for cruise liners, all matters relating to manning shall be the responsibility of the State in which the vessel is registered (flag state), except for ships smaller than 650 gt, where host State conditions may be applied."

In respect of the State exercising its powers, the State must exercise its powers in accordance with EU law (e.g. States must not discriminate between EU citizens).

Island cabotage

7.095 Article 3(2) of Regulation 3577/92 provides: "For vessels carrying out island cabotage,[76] all matters relating to manning shall be the responsibility of the State in which the vessel is performing a maritime transport service[77] (host State)."

7.096 Article 3(3) of Regulation 3577/92 provides an exception:

"However, from 1 January 1999, for cargo vessels over 650 gt carrying out island cabotage, when the voyage concerned follows or precedes a voyage to or from another State, all matters relating to manning shall be the responsibility of the State in which the vessel is registered (flag State)."

---

75 Ed., Art. 2(1) of Reg. 3577/92 defines "mainland cabotage" as "the carriage of passengers or goods by sea between ports situated on the mainland or the main territory of one and the same Member State without calls at islands".

76 Ed., Art. 2(1) defines "island cabotage" as "the carriage of passengers or goods by sea between:

– ports situated on the mainland and on one or more of the islands of one and the same Member State,
– ports situated on the islands of one and the same Member State;

Ceuta and Melilla shall be treated in the same way as island ports."

77 Ed., Art. 2(1) of Reg. 3577/92 defines "maritime transport services within a Member State (maritime cabotage)" as:

"(a) mainland cabotage: the carriage of passengers or goods by sea between ports situated on the mainland or the main territory of one and the same Member State without calls at islands;
(b) off-shore supply services: the carriage of passengers or goods by sea between any port in a Member State and installations or structures situated on the continental shelf of that Member State;
(c) island cabotage: the carriage of passengers or goods by sea between:
   – ports situated on the mainland and on one or more of the islands of one and the same Member State,
   ports situated on the islands of one and the same Member State;

Ceuta and Melilla shall be treated in the same way as island ports."

7.097 Island cabotage is an important change in terms of the European shipping economy. Article 3(4) of Regulation 3577/92 thus provides:

"The Commission shall make an in-depth examination of the economic and social impact of the liberalization of island cabotage and shall submit a report to the Council before 1 January 1997 at the latest.
  On the basis of this report, the Commission shall submit a proposal to the Council which may include adjustments to the manning nationality provisions laid down in paragraphs 2 and 3 so that the definitive system shall be approved by the Council in due time and before 1 January 1999."

Cruise liners

7.098 Article 3(1) of Regulation 3577/92 provides:

"For vessels carrying out mainland cabotage[78] and for cruise liners, all matters relating to manning shall be the responsibility of the State in which the vessel is registered (flag state), except for ships smaller than 650 gt, where host State conditions may be applied."

In respect of the State exercising its powers, the State must exercise its powers in accordance with EU law (e.g. States must not discriminate between EU citizens).

Serious disturbances in the market and Regulation 3577/92

Introduction

7.099 The liberalisation of the cabotage market could have a dramatic effect on the relevant national markets. This effect of liberalisation is accentuated whenever there is serious disturbance in the market. Article 5 of Regulation 3577/92 attempted to deal with serious disturbances. The tenth recital to Regulation 3577/92 provides:

"Whereas provision should be adopted so that safeguard measures can be taken as regards maritime transport markets affected by a serious disturbance or in the event of an emergency; whereas, for this purpose, suitable decision-making procedures should be introduced..."

Definition of "a serious disturbance of the internal transport market"

7.100 The concept of "a serious disturbance of the internal transport market" is defined by Article 2(5) of Regulation 3577/92:

"the appearance on the market of problems specific to that market and which:

- are likely to lead to a serious and potentially lasting excess of supply over demand,
- are due to, or aggravated by, maritime cabotage operations, and
- pose a serious threat to the financial stability and survival of a significant number of Community shipowners,

provided that the short-term and medium-term forecasts for the market in question do not indicate any substantial and lasting improvements".

---

78 Ed., for the definition of "mainland cabotage" see above.

Member State's request to the Commission to adopt safeguard measures in the event of "a serious disturbance of the internal transport market"

7.101 What if there is a serious disturbance such that the liberalisation of cabotage might no longer be justified? A Member State may request the Commission to act under Article 5(1) of Regulation 3577/92. Article 5(2) of Regulation 3577/92 provides for the Commission to adopt safeguard measures on its own initiative after consulting the Member States.

7.102 Article 5(1) of Regulation 3577/92 provides that in the event of a serious disturbance of the internal transport market *due to*[79] cabotage liberalisation, a Member State may request the Commission to adopt "safeguard measures". After consulting the other Member States,[80] the Commission must decide where appropriate on the necessary safeguard measures, within 30 working days of receipt of the relevant request from a Member State.[81] Such measures may involve the temporary exclusion, not exceeding 12 months, of the area concerned from the scope of the regulation.[82] The Commission must communicate to the Council and the Member States any decision on its safeguard measures.[83] If after the period of 30 working days the Commission has taken no decision on the subject, the Member State concerned must be entitled to apply the measures requested until the Commission has taken its decision.[84] What if there is an emergency of such proportions that action needs to be taken immediately?[85] Article 5(1) of the regulation provides that in the event of an emergency, Member States may unilaterally adopt the appropriate provisional measures which may remain in force for no more than three months. In such an event, Member States must immediately inform the Commission of the adoption of such measures. The Commission may abrogate the measures or confirm them with or without modification until it takes its final decision in accordance with the procedures set out in the second subparagraph of Article 5(1).[86] This obligation to consult other Member States would be obligatory.

7.103 Article 5(2) of Regulation 3577/92 provides that the Commission may also adopt safeguard measures on its own initiative, after consulting the Member States.

7.104 It is clear that only a Member State and the Commission may take (directly or indirectly) safeguard measures – for example, individual companies and ports or local authorities may not take measures. The reservation of the right of action to the Commission and, in limited circumstances, to Member States is appropriate because the adoption of such measures should be very much the exception.

---

79 The use of the words "due to" is noteworthy. This means that the disturbance must be due to the cabotage liberalisation. So, for example, Greece could not re-impose cabotage restrictions to boost the Greek economy because the cause of the issue would have to be within the confines of Article 5(1).
80 This obligation to consult other Member States would be obligatory.
81 Reg. 3577/92, Art. 5(1).
82 Ibid.
83 Ibid.
84 Ibid.
85 A fair and reasonable construction should be given to the term "emergency".
86 The second sub-paragraph of Art. 5(1) provides: "After consulting the other Member States, the Commission shall decide where appropriate on the necessary safeguard measures, within 30 working days of receipt of the relevant request from a Member State. Such measures may involve the temporary exclusion, not exceeding 12 months, of the area concerned from the scope of the Regulation."

Temporary provision of cabotage services

7.105 Article 8 of Regulation 3577/92 provides for temporary services. It provides:

"Without prejudice to the provisions of the Treaty relating to the right of establishment and to this Regulation, a person providing a maritime transport service may, in order to do so, temporarily pursue his activity in the Member States where the service is provided, under the same conditions as are imposed by that State on its own nationals."

Ongoing evaluation of Regulation 3577/92

7.106 The eleventh recital to Regulation 3577/92 provides:

"Whereas, in view of the need to ensure the proper functioning of the internal market and of possible adaptations in the light of experience, the Commission should report on the implementation of this Regulation and if necessary submit additional proposals..."

7.107 This is amplified by Article 10 of the regulation which provides that: "The Commission shall submit to the Council, before 1 January 1995, and thereafter every two years, a report on the implementation of this Regulation and, if appropriate, shall also put forward any necessary proposals."
On 22 April 2014, the "Fifth Report on the Implementation of Council Regulation (EEC) No 3577/92 applying the principle of freedom to provide services to maritime cabotage (2001–2010)" was published.[87] It concluded:

"5. CONCLUSIONS

   5.1. *The impact of liberalisation* Almost all cabotage services in the EU have been liberalised from 1 January 1999. The Greek market, which was the last to be partly protected, has been opened up since 1 November 2002. Until 2007, the maritime cabotage market was generally stable, recording a continuous increase in volumes of goods and numbers of passengers transported in several countries. Since 2008 it has experienced a considerable decline, due to the impact of the economic crisis. As in previous years, the greatest market for cargo traffic is that of the United Kingdom, followed by that of Spain and Italy. Liquid bulk continues to lead in terms of cargo transported. Regarding passengers, Greece has the greatest traffic, followed by Italy. The penetration of the national markets by vessels flying non-national flags has increased in the cabotage of cargo, while it remains limited in the cabotage of passengers. It is apparent from the consultations conducted by the Commission that the liberalisation has had an overall modest but positive impact leading in some Member States to the modernisation of national fleets which have been faced with the increased risk of competition.
   5.2. *Further actions* Following the consultations of 2009 and 2012 mentioned in section 4 of this report, and drawing on the experience gained during several years of application of the Regulation the Commission believes that the Regulation is fit for its purpose and does not require revision. However, the Commission recognises that several questions raised in the submissions witness problems of interpretation and implementation. Therefore, the Commission has addressed these issues in its new interpretative communication on maritime cabotage. Given that the available statistical information on maritime cabotage has become scarce and as the liberalisation has now been completed and the market is stabilised, the Commission proposes to report on the economic and legal progress of liberalisation only in the case of significant

---

[87] http://ec.europa.eu/transport/modes/maritime/news/doc/com(2014)231_en.pdf.

developments in this field and in any case not later than by 2018, in order to fully assess the impact of liberalisation of maritime cabotage in Croatia, which benefits from the temporary derogation from certain provisions of the Regulation until 31 December 2014."[88]

Monitoring of Member State/national law

7.108 In an attempt to monitor the operation of national cabotage regimes, Article 9 of Regulation 3577/92 provides: "Before adopting laws, regulations or administrative provisions in implementation of this Regulation, Member States shall consult the Commission. They shall inform the latter of any measures thus adopted."

Conclusion

7.109 Overall, despite the protestation and consternation in certain quarters about the abolition of cabotage restrictions, the change was not so dramatic in practice. In large measure, this was due to the phased nature of the regulation and a relatively limited take up of the opportunities presented by the abolition of the cabotage restrictions.

7.110 Before examining the case law on the freedom to provide services, it is useful to examine a specific issue relating to Spain.

7.111 Article 5 of Regulation 3577/92 permits Member States to request the Commission to adopt safeguard measures where there was a serious disturbance of the internal transport market due to cabotage liberalisation or in the case of an emergency.

7.112 Spain invoked the safeguard clause in the main regulation. On 13 July 1993, the Commission adopted Decision 93/396 on Spain's request for adoption by the Commission of a prolongation of safeguard measures pursuant to Article 5 of Regulation 3577/92 applying the principle of freedom to provide services to maritime transport within Member States (maritime cabotage).[89] This involved giving Spain a six-month exemption from the liberalisation of the cabotage restrictions. Article 1 of Commission Decision 93/396 provided:

> "The following maritime transport services carried out in mainland Spain shall be exempted from the implementation of Regulation (EEC) No. 3577/92 for a period of six months as from 17 August 1993: transport of break-bulk general cargo, transport of dry bulk cargo (except for the transport of cement or clinker in specialized cement carriers) and transport of chemical products in specialized tankers."

Cabotage and competition

7.113 While competition law will be considered in greater depth later in the book, it is convenient to note briefly the application of competition law in the context of cabotage. Before 2006, cabotage services were excluded from the general EU competition law

---

88 Footnote omitted.
89 OJ L173/33, 16 July 1993. See also Comm. Dec. 93/125, OJ 1993 L49/88.

regime operated by the Commission.⁹⁰ Since the entry into force on 18 October 2006 of Regulation 1419/2006, cabotage services are now subject to the EU competition law regime in full where there is an effect on trade between Member States. It should be assured, unless proven opposite, that EU competition law applies to cabotage services even though they are domestic activities.⁹¹

7.114 The competition rules⁹² apply to cabotage where appropriate. Article 101 of the TFEU applies to cabotage services where there is an effect on trade between Member States so it is possible that Article 101 may be applicable because there could be an effect on trade between Member States even in the case of cabotage services. Article 102 of the TFEU also applies to cabotage where there is an abuse of dominance and there is an effect on trade between Member States. Trade within a single Member State may trigger the cross-border effect in certain circumstances (e.g. where service supplies would enter from elsewhere in the EU).

7.115 On 13 July 1993, the Commission made its decision on Spain's request for a prolongation of safeguard measures pursuant to Article 5 of the regulation. The Commission recalled that on 17 February 1993 the Commission adopted Decision 93/125 on Spain's request for adoption by the Commission of safeguard measures pursuant to Article 5 of Regulation 3577/92 by which it granted an exclusion of the Spanish mainland area from the scope of the regulation with the exception of feeder services and for a period of six months expiring on the 17 August 1993. (Decision 93/125⁹³ dealt with

---

90 Reg. 17/62 was disapplied by Reg. 141/62 while Reg. 4056/86 did not extend to cabotage.
91 E.g. carried from other countries could have provided the services, and the "effect on trade" between Member States is an easily satisfied test.
92 See chap. 9.
93 OJ 1993 L49/88. Commission Dec. 93/125 of 17 February 1993 on Spain's request for adoption by the Commission of safeguard measures under Art. 5 of Reg. (EEC) No 3577/92 against applying the principle of freedom to provide services to maritime transport within Member States (maritime cabotage) provided in the first five articles:

"Article 1
The unilateral safeguard measure adopted by Spain on 23 December 1992, is hereby abrogated and the competent Spanish authorities shall take the necessary administrative measures to implement the abrogation.

Article 2
An exclusion of the Spanish mainland area during six months from the scope of Regulation (EEC) No 3577/92 is hereby granted to Spain as from the date of notification of the present Decision.

Article 3
The abovementioned exclusion shall not apply to feeder services.

Article 4
In the event that no Spanish vessel is available at a given moment to meet the demand for mainland cabotage transport services, the Spanish authorities will allow other Member States' vessels to offer such services.

Article 5
Two independent experts shall be appointed, one by the Commission and one by the Spanish authorities, in order to prepare a joint study on the possible economic impact on the Spanish shipping sector of the liberalization of mainland cabotage. On the basis of the result of this study which shall be presented to the Commission at least 45 working days before the expiry date of the six months' derogation, the Commission will, on request from Spain, review the situation."

concessions for Spain as did Decision 93/396.[94]) The Commission recalled the background:

"Whereas, in particular, Article 5 of Decision 93/125/EEC, established that two independent experts would be appointed, one by the Commission and one by the Spanish authorities in order to prepare a joint study on the possible economic impact on the Spanish shipping sector of the liberalization of mainland cabotage, on the basis of which the Commission would, on request from Spain, review the situation;

Whereas, in accordance with the above provision, a study was submitted to the Commission on the 14 June 1993;

Whereas on 21 June 1993 Spain formally requested the Commission to prolong the safeguard measures in the same terms for an additional period of six months as from 17 August 1993;

Whereas a meeting was organized by the Commission on 24 June 1993 to consult the other Member States on this request in accordance with Article 5 (1) of the abovementioned Regulation;

Whereas on the basis of an analysis of traffic structure it was decided for the purpose of the study to pursue the analysis of the impact of cabotage liberalization through the segmentation of the cabotage market by vessel types and by market trades rather than by geographic areas, as the effects of liberalization will be geographically uniform;

Whereas each of the eight sectors into which the cabotage market was partitioned (supply services, transport of cement of clinker in bulk by specialized cement carriers, transport of reefer cargo, roll-on, roll-off transport services, transport of general cargo in containers, transport of break-bulk general cargo, transport of dry bulk cargo and transport of chemical products in specialized tankers) was analysed as to the expected impact of immediate liberalization on its international competitive position and the expected impact of the prolongation of the derogation;

Whereas the study has demonstrated the relatively unfavourable competitive position of the Spanish cabotage fleet under the Spanish Ordinary Register's conditions and under the Canary Island Special Register's present conditions as compared with representative foreign competitors;

Whereas the Royal Decree authorizing the registration of vessels and companies operating in cabotage trade in the Special Canaries Register has been approved on 11 June 1993 and will come into force on 1 July 1993, giving rise initially to a considerable labour adjustment and associated expenditure in view of new manning rules;

---

94 OJ 1993 L173/33. Commission Dec. 93/396 of 13 July 1993 on Spain's request for adoption by the Commission of a prolongation of safeguard measures pursuant to Art. 5 of Reg. (EEC) No 3577/92 applying the principle of freedom to provide services to maritime transport within Member States provided in the first four articles:

"Article 1
The following maritime transport services carried out in mainland Spain shall be exempted from the implementation of Regulation (EEC) No 3577/92 for a period of six months as from 17 August 1993: transport of break-bulk general cargo, transport of dry bulk cargo (except for the transport of cement or clinker in specialized cement carriers) and transport of chemical products in specialized tankers.

Article 2
The remaining mainland cabotage trades, with the exception of those foreseen in Article 6 (1) of Regulation (EEC) No 3577/92 which are subject to special derogations, shall be liberalized as from 17 August 1993.

Article 3
The exclusion contained in Article 1 shall not apply to feeder services.

Article 4
In the event that no Spanish vessel is available at a given moment to meet the demand for mainland cabotage transport services, the Spanish authorities will allow other Member States' vessels to offer such services."

Whereas additional legislation on manning scales and increased flexibility in the nationality requirements for manning (introduced by the Law on Ports and Merchant Marine of 25 November 1992 for the Canary Islands Special Register), needs still to be implemented;

Whereas the fiscal and social security advantages for the shipowners and vessels registered in the Canary Islands Special Register will not be introduced until the Law on the Economic and Fiscal Regime for the Canary Islands is adopted;

Whereas the Canary Islands Special Register, when fully implemented, is expected to considerably reduce operating costs of vessels registered in it;

Whereas, therefore, registration in the Canary Islands Special Register will only bring part of the expected advantages to the Spanish shipowners in the short term, i.e. within the six months which could still be granted at the most under the safeguard mechanism of Regulation ... 3577/92;

Whereas the study has demonstrated that, nevertheless, for five, out of the eight cabotage sectors (supply services, transport of cement or clinker in bulk by specialized cement carriers, transport of reefer cargo, roll-on, roll-off transport services and transport of general cargo in containers), no serious disturbance is to be expected from the immediate liberalization as from the expiry of the temporary exclusion on 17 August 1993;

Whereas the study also demonstrated that for the remaining three cabotage sectors: namely, transport of break-bulk general cargo, transport of dry bulk cargo (except for the transport of cement or clinker in bulk by specialized cement carriers) and transport of chemical products in specialized tankers, a serious disturbance may result from the immediate liberalization, inter alia because of the geographical position of Spain as a gateway between the Atlantic and the Mediterranean and as an attractive market for consecutive cabotage which could be carried out at marginal freight rates by other Community operators;

Whereas the evidence available to the Commission indicates that there has been a decline in the demand for mainland cabotage services in Spain in two of the three abovementioned sectors and, in particular, that this decline has been of 37,6% in the sectors of break-bulk general cargo and of dry bulk cargo between 1985 and 1989 whilst there has been a very slight increase in demand of 3,7% in the same period for the chemical products sector;

Whereas the combination of lower demand and lower freight rates offered by other Community shipowners entering the Spanish market will cause an excess of supply over demand in these sectors;

Whereas, in particular, shipowners in the three abovementioned sectors, representing 50% of the total number of Spanish shipowners engaged in mainland cabotage would suffer as a result of immediate liberalization;

Whereas this percentage constitutes a significant number of shipowners engaged in mainland cabotage;

Whereas the financial position of these shipowners demonstrates their dependency on mainland cabotage services and that their profit margins have declined over the years;

Whereas immediate liberalization of the three abovementioned sectors will endanger the financial stability of these shipowners and such liberalization will cause many of them to disappear from these markets;

Whereas it is expected that the competitive position of Spanish shipowners in the three sectors concerned will improve once the registration in the Special Canary Islands Register yields the advantages it is intended to produce;

Whereas transport of goods from a port in another Member State or in a third country to a continental port in Spain where they are transhipped on a vessel of the same company to be carried on to the other mainland ports in Spain or vice versa (feeder services) should, however, not benefit from any such derogation, in order not to hinder an optimal operation of deep sea services by Community carriers between Spain and other countries, and should be completely free for other Member States' shipowners as defined in Article 1 of Regulation ... 3577/92;

Whereas in the event that no Spanish vessel is available to carry out mainland cabotage services no serious disturbance can derive from the possibility for other Member States' vessels to carry out such services."

FREEDOM TO PROVIDE SERVICES

Before deciding:

"Article 1
The following maritime transport services carried out in mainland Spain shall be exempted from the implementation of Regulation ... 3577/92 for a period of six months as from 17 August 1993: transport of break-bulk general cargo, transport of dry bulk cargo (except for the transport of cement or clinker in specialized cement carriers) and transport of chemical products in specialized tankers.

Article 2
The remaining mainland cabotage trades, with the exception of those foreseen in Article 6 (1) of Regulation ... 3577/92 which are subject to special derogations, shall be liberalized as from 17 August 1993.

Article 3
The exclusion contained in Article 1 shall not apply to feeder services.

Article 4
In the event that no Spanish vessel is available at a given moment to meet the demand for mainland cabotage transport services, the Spanish authorities will allow other Member States' vessels to offer such services."

Article 91(1)(b) of the TFEU establishes the conditions under which non-resident carriers may operate within Member States.

7.116 This exclusion did not apply to feeder services.[95] The remaining cabotage trades, with the exception of those foreseen in Article 6(1) of Regulation 3577/92 which were subject to special derogations,[96] were liberalised from 17 August 1993.[97] Article 4 of Decision 93/396 provided that if "no Spanish vessel is available at a given moment to meet the demand for mainland cabotage transport services, the Spanish authorities will allow other Member States' vessels to offer such services".[98]

E. CASE LAW RELATING TO REGULATION 4055/86 AND REGULATION 3577/92

Introduction

7.117 Having considered Regulations 4055/86 and 3577/92, it is now useful to review the case law which has developed on the regulations and on the broader topic of freedom to provide services in the shipping context. There have been a number of cases relating to the regulations. Some have related mainly to historical restrictions imposed by some (but not all) States. It is proposed not to examine the case law in strict chronological order but in a more thematic manner.

1989: *Corsica Ferries* case

7.118 *Corsica Ferries France v Direction Générale des Douanes Françaises*[99] is an interesting judgment on Regulation 4055/86. The CJEU in a succinct and lucid judgment

---

95 Dec. 93/396, Art. 3.
96 I.e. relating to France, Italy, Portugal and Spain.
97 Dec. 93/396, Art. 2.
98 See (1997) 9 *International Maritime Lawyer* 288.
99 Case C-49/89 [1989] ECR 4441, ECLI:EU:C:1989:649.

dealt with a preliminary reference to it from the French Cour de Cassation on the interpretation of Articles 49 and 80 of the EC Treaty (now, Articles 56 and 100 of the TFEU).

7.119 There had been proceedings between Corsica Ferries France ("Corsica Ferries") and the Direction Générale des Douanes in regard to charges levied on the shipowner in 1981 and 1982 (i.e. *before* the entry into force of Regulation 4055/86) in respect of passengers embarked, disembarked or transferred in Corsican ports. In regard to those ports, section R.212–20 of the French Code des Ports Maritimes, as amended by the Decree of 12 May 1981, levied a charge on all passengers travelling to Corsica from mainland France or Sardinia and a charge at an identical rate on all passengers travelling to or from a port situated elsewhere in Europe or North Africa. There was thus an element of discrimination in that these charges applied to passengers going to, or coming from, other Member States but not to passengers travelling between ports in a single Member State (i.e. France).

7.120 Corsica Ferries argued that this provision was contrary to the EU law (in particular, what is now Article 56 *et seq.* of the TFEU) inasmuch as it discriminated between ships plying between Corsica and ports in mainland France, who are not required to pay tax in respect of passengers who embark at a Corsican port, and ships, such as those of Corsica Ferries, plying between Corsica and ports in another Member State, which were subject to tax both on arrival in and departure from the Corsican port.

7.121 The Cour de Cassation stayed the proceedings until the CJEU had given a preliminary ruling on the following question:

> "Must the [TFEU] ... be interpreted as meaning that a member-State is authorised, in connection with the use by a ship of harbour installations situated in its island territory, to levy charges on the embarkation and disembarkation of passengers when travelling to or arriving from a port situated in another member-State, whilst in the case of travel between two ports situated within national territory those charges are levied only on embarkation at the island port?"

7.122 The CJEU first pointed out that the French legislation could constitute a restriction on freedom to provide services within the EU in so far as it discriminated between persons providing transport services between a port situated in national territory and a port situated in another Member State and persons providing transport services between two ports situated in national territory. The CJEU reiterated that the articles of the Treaty concerning the free movement of goods, persons, services and capital "are fundamental Community provisions and any restriction, even minor, of that freedom is prohibited".[100] The CJEU repeated that in the area of freedom to provide services such a restriction may, as the CJEU pointed out in *Ministère Public v Ledoux*,[101] result from national tax measures which affect the trader's exercise of that right.

7.123 The CJEU then construed the matter carefully:

> "10. Although Article [56 of the TFEU], guaranteeing freedom to provide services within the [EU], has been directly and unconditionally applicable since the expiry of the transitional period provided for in ... the Treaty, under Article [58(1)] of the Treaty freedom to provide services in the field of transport is to be governed by the provisions of the title relating to

---

100 Judgment, para. 8.
101 Case 127/86 [1988] ECR 3741, ECLI:EU:C:1988:366.

transport (see Joined Cases 209-213/84, *Ministère Public* v. *Asjes*[102] and Case 4/88, *Lambregts Transportbedrijf* v. *Belgian State)*.[103]

11. It follows, as the Court pointed out in *Asjes*,[104] that in the transport sector the objective ... of the Treaty of abolishing during the transitional period restrictions on freedom to provide services should have been attained in the framework of the common [transport] policy ...

12. With regard in particular to maritime transport, Article [100](2) of the Treaty provides that the Council may decide whether, to what extent and by what procedure appropriate provisions may be laid down for that kind of transport.

13. It was only in Regulation 4055/86 applying the principle of freedom to provide services to maritime transport between member-States and between member-States and non-member countries, which entered into force on 1 January 1987, that the Council adopted, on the basis of Article [100](2) of the Treaty, the measures necessary to achieve freedom to provide services in maritime transport between member-States.

14. It must therefore be concluded that in 1981 and 1982, the period at issue in the main proceedings, freedom to provide services in maritime transport had not yet been implemented and that consequently the member-States were entitled to apply provisions such as those at issue in the main proceedings.

15. That conclusion is not weakened by the fact that those rules were reintroduced into the French Code des Ports Maritimes in 1981 after having been repealed in 1969. In the light of the existence of Article [56(1)] of the Treaty, [the Treaty also] prohibits the member-States from introducing any new restrictions on the freedom to provide services which had in fact been attained at the date of the entry into force of the Treaty, does not apply.

16. The answer to the question referred to the Court by the Cour de Cassation of the French Republic should therefore be that the [TFEU] Treaty, in particular Articles [49, 61, 62 and 80], did not before the entry into force of ... Regulation 4055/86, ... prevent a member-State from levying, in connection with the use by a ship of harbour installations situated within its island territory, charges on the embarkation and disembarkation of passengers arriving from or going to a port situated in another member-State, whilst in the case of travel between two ports situated within national territory those charges were levied only on embarkation at the island port."

Thus, because the events in question pre-dated the entry into force of Regulation 4055/86, Member States were able to apply national law even though it would have the effect of restricting the freedom to provide maritime transport services.

1994: *Peralta*

7.124 The next case worth considering on the topic of freedom to provide maritime services is an Italian criminal case in which a preliminary reference was made to the CJEU. It was the *Matteo Peralta* case.[105] In essence, the CJEU held that the then EC Treaty (now the TFEU) and Regulation 4055/86 do not prevent Member States adopting laws prohibiting all vessels from discharging harmful chemical substances into its territorial or internal waters but, in regard to vessels on the high seas, only imposing the same prohibition on vessels flying the Member State's flag.

---

102 Ed., [1986] ECR 1425, ECLI:EU:C:1986:188.
103 Ed., [1989] ECR 2583, ECLI:EU:C:C:1989:320, at paras 8 and 9.
104 Ed., at para. 37.
105 Case C-379/92 [1994] ECR I-3453, ECLI:EU:C:1994:296. The Chamber comprised: Judge Mancini (President of Chamber) as well as Judges Joliet, Schockweiler, Rodríquez Iglesias, Grévisse (Rapporteur), Zuleeg and Murray. The Advocate-General was AG Lenz.

7.125 The CJEU held that the rules in regard to the internal and territorial waters were applied without discrimination and the rules in regard to the high seas were the result of public international law. The CJEU also held that the difference in treatment between vessels on the high seas flying the Italian flag and vessels on the high seas not flying the Italian flag was not prohibited by the Treaty because Italian legislation can only apply to Italian vessels anyway on the high seas.

7.126 Criminal proceedings were brought against Peralta for alleged breach of Law No 979 of 31 December 1982 laying down provisions for the protection of the sea.[106] Article 16 of Law No 979 provided:

> "In territorial waters and internal maritime waters, including ports, it shall be prohibited for any vessel, regardless of nationality, to discharge into the sea or to cause to be discharged into the sea hydrocarbons or hydrocarbon mixtures or any other substances harmful to the marine environment mentioned in List A annexed to this Law.
>
> Vessels flying the Italian flag shall also be prohibited from discharging the substances referred to in the foregoing paragraph even outside territorial waters."

7.127 Criminal proceedings were brought against Peralta for alleged breach of Law No 979 of 31 December 1982. Infringements were penalised by fines and imprisonment. Professional sanctions were also possible. Masters of vessels who were Italian nationals could be suspended for a period of up to two years. Masters who were not Italian nationals could be prohibited from mooring at Italian ports for a period determined by the Minister for the Merchant Navy. Mr Peralta, an Italian national, was the master of a tanker registered in Italy which was specially equipped for the transport of chemicals. The shipowner was a company governed by Italian law. Mr Peralta repeatedly ordered the discharge into the sea of water which had been used to flush tanks which had previously contained caustic soda at a time when the vessel was outside the limit of Italian territorial waters (in most cases, in an area lying between 12 and 24 miles from Italian baselines). Caustic soda was one of the harmful substances mentioned in Annex A to Law No 979. After hearing the appeal against the criminal sanctions imposed on Mr Peralta, the trial court stayed proceedings and referred the following somewhat complicated questions to the CJEU for a preliminary ruling:

> "(1) Do the provisions of Articles 16 and 20 of Law No 979/82 constitute restrictions within the meaning of Articles 7,[107] 48,[108] 52[109] and 59[110] of the EEC Treaty and are they consequently prohibited by Article 62[111] of the same Treaty in so far as they are not justified by objective reasons relating to the protection of the public interests of the State in question?
>
> (2) Under Community law as it now stands and in the light of the Community provisions referred to in Question 1, is a rule of a Member State compatible with Community law if it prescribes treatment even a criminal penalty (for the nationals of that State) by reason of their nationality, but not for nationals of the other Member States for identical conduct; and is such a rule of criminal law compatible with the principle of proportionality guaranteed by Community law inasmuch as it entails, *inter alia*, for the master of the vessel the

---

106 GURI No 16, of 18 January 1983, Ordinary Supplement, p. 5.
107 Ed., later Arts 14–16 EC.
108 Ed., later Art. 39 EC (now Art. 45 TFEU).
109 Ed., later Art. 43 EC (now Art. 49 TFEU).
110 Ed., later Art. 49 EC (now Art. 56 TFEU).
111 Ed., then Art. 51 EC (now Art. 58 TFEU).

automatic and mandatory additional penalty of the temporary suspension of the exercise of his professional activity and work?

(3) Under Community law as it now stands, can the Member States' retention of competence for matters concerning criminal law affect the fundamental liberties guaranteed by the Treaty, such as the free movement of goods and the freedom of movement of persons and, in particular, do the provisions of Articles 16 and 20 of Law No 979/82 constitute an obstacle to the exercise of those liberties?

(4) Do the principles defended by the Community legal order in the field of the environment, in particular the principle of prevention laid down in Article 130r et seq. of the Treaty,[112] preclude a law of a Member State which, by imposing on national vessels an absolute prohibition against discharging hydrocarbons and harmful substances into the high seas, has, in practice, the effect of forcing such vessels to use an alternative method of discharge, which is inefficient from every point of view and, in any case, contrary to the obligations which that State has undertaken at an international level and in respect of which the Community has adopted implementing measures?

(5) Do the Community principles designed to guarantee that competition between persons supplying shipping and port services in the Community is free but at the same time fair and not artificially distorted and that the demand for services is satisfied with the least possible damage to the environment, and in particular Articles 3f[113] and 84[114] of the EEC Treaty, preclude a national rule such as the one laid down in Articles 16(17) and 20 of Law No 979/82, which, by imposing an absolute prohibition against the discharge of tank-flushing liquids into the high seas only on vessels registered in the State in question, even though those vessels are equipped with the extremely expensive decontamination equipment prescribed by international agreements ratified by the Community, distorts competition among seaports and shipping companies in the Community?

(6) Is Article 30[115] of the Treaty compatible with a rule of a Member State which, by imposing an absolute prohibition against discharging hydrocarbons and harmful substances into the high seas exclusively on national vessels, even though they are equipped with the extremely expensive technologies prescribed by the agreements applicable in that field, forces those vessels to utilize special technologies and to use an alternative method of discharge, which is inefficient, costly and, in any case, in breach of the obligations which that State has undertaken at the international level and in respect of which the Community has adopted implementing measures? In particular, can the criminal penalties in question and the economic burdens which fall exclusively on the national fleet, in a way which is manifestly discriminatory and entirely irrational, be regarded as measures having an effect equivalent to quantitative restrictions on imports since those burdens give rise to additional costs with consequences for the price of the goods transported, as well as affecting imports?"

7.128 The CJEU stated that it appeared

"from all the documents before the Court that the [Italian court] is essentially asking the Court whether Community law precludes legislation like the Italian legislation in question in so far as it impedes the activities of national undertakings engaged in sea transport, like the undertaking employing Mr Peralta. Such legislation could have the effect of, in particular, slowing down cleaning operations by tankers which could be carried out at sea in compliance with the relevant international agreements which Italy has signed, or of making them more difficult or costly than for vessels of other Member States."[116]

---

112 Ed., then Art. 174 EC (now Art. 191 TFEU).
113 Ed., then Art. 3(1)(f) EC (no equivalent provision in the TFEU).
114 Ed., then Art. 80 EC (now Art. 100 TFEU).
115 Ed., then Art. 28 EC (now Art. 34 TFEU).
116 Para. 9 of the Judgment.

The CJEU continued by recalling that in Part Two of the EC Treaty, transport is the subject of a separate title, Title IV and in Title IV, Article 80(2)[117] provided that the Council may decide whether appropriate provisions may be adopted for sea transport but by virtue of Article 58 of the Treaty, such particular provisions concern in particular "freedom to provide services".

7.129 The CJEU then states:

"13. On the basis of Article [100(2) of the TFEU] the Council adopted Regulation ... 4055/86. ... It was therefore applicable at the time of the events in question.

14. However, Article [100] does not exclude the application of the Treaty to transport, and marine transport remains, on the same basis as the other modes of transport, subject to the general rules of the Treaty (see the judgment in Case 167/73 *Commission v France* [1974] ECR 359, paragraphs 31 and 32).

    Observance of international conventions on the discharge of harmful substances into the sea

15. From the papers in the case it appears that, although its order for reference does not state a question in these terms, the national court is asking this Court about the compatibility of the Italian legislation with the International Convention for the Prevention of Pollution from Ships, called 'the Marpol Convention' (United Nations Treaty Series, Volume 1341, No 22484). It appears to consider that this Convention produces effects in the Community legal order.

16. In so far as the Italian court raises the question of the compatibility of the Italian legislation with the Marpol Convention, it is sufficient to find that the Community is not a party to that convention. Moreover, it does not appear that the Community has assumed, under the ... Treaty, the powers previously exercised by the Member States in the field to which that convention applies, nor, consequently, that its provisions have the effect of binding the Community (see the judgment in Joined Cases 21/72 to 24/72 *International Fruit Company and Others v Produktschap voor Groenten en Fruit* [1972] ECR 1219, paragraph 18).

17. Whether a national provision adopted by a Member State is compatible with a convention such as the Marpol Convention is not therefore a matter on which the Court may rule."

7.130 The CJEU then considered what is now Article 18 of the TFEU:

"18. It must be borne in mind that Article [18] of the [TFEU], ... which lays down as a general principle a prohibition of discrimination on grounds of nationality, applies independently only to situations governed by Community law in regard to which the Treaty lays down no specific rules prohibiting discrimination (see the judgment in Case C-179/90 *Merci Convenzionali Porto di Genova v Siderurgica Gabrielli* [1991] ECR I-5889, paragraph 11). The question whether legislation of the kind in question in the main proceedings is compatible with the Treaty must therefore be examined with reference to the specific rules implementing that principle."

7.131 The CJEU then considered what was Article 3(1)(g) of the EC Treaty[118] (which has no direct parallel in the TFEU):

"19. The national court enquires whether the principles of Community law for ensuring undistorted competition preclude national legislation like the Italian legislation in question. According to the national court, the legislation causes distortions of competition between ports and shipowners in the Community.

20. The competition rules laid down in the Treaty, and, in particular, Articles [101 to 106], apply to the transport sector (see the judgment in Joined Cases 209 to 213/84 *Ministère*

---

117 Now, largely, Art. 100(2) TFEU.
118 Art. 3(1)(g) of the EC Treaty provided: "For the purposes set out in Article 2, the activities of the Community shall include, as provided in this Treaty and in accordance with the timetable set out therein: ... (g) a system ensuring that competition in the internal market is not distorted."

Public v Asjes and Others [1986] ECR 1425, paragraph 45, and the judgment in Case C-185/91 *Bundesanstalt fuer den Gueterfernverkehr v Gebr. Reiff* [1993] ECR I-5801, paragraph 12). The same is true, in particular, for the field of sea transport (see in particular ... Regulation ... 4056/86 ...).

21. It must be pointed out that, for the purposes of the interpretation of Articles 3[(1)(g)], the second paragraph of Article 5[119] and Article [101] of the Treaty, Article [101] of the Treaty, taken on its own, is concerned only with the conduct of undertakings and not with legislative or regulatory measures of the Member States. However, according to settled case-law, Article [101], read in conjunction with Article [4(3)] of the [Treaty on the European Union], requires the Member States not to introduce or maintain in force measures, even of a legislative or regulatory nature, which may render ineffective the competition rules applicable to undertakings. Such is the case, according to that case-law, if a Member State requires or favours the adoption of agreements, decisions or concerted practices contrary to Article [101] or reinforces their effects, or deprives its own legislation of its official character by delegating to private traders responsibility for taking decisions affecting the economic sphere (see the judgment in Case 267/86 *Van Eycke v ASPA* [1988] ECR 4769, paragraph 16, and the judgment in Case C-2/91 *Meng* [1993] ECR I-5751, paragraph 14).

22. However, those provisions may not be relied upon as against legislation like the Italian legislation. That legislation does not require or foster anti-competitive conduct since the prohibition which it lays down is sufficient in itself. Nor does it reinforce the effects of a pre-existing agreement (see, to this effect, the judgment in *Meng*, cited above, paragraphs 15 and 19)."

7.132 The CJEU then considered what is now Article 34 of the TFEU:

"23. The national court enquires about the compatibility of the Italian legislation with Article [34] in so far as it requires Italian vessels to carry costly equipment. It asks itself whether this makes imports of chemical products into Italy more expensive and therefore creates an obstacle prohibited by that article.

24. On this point, it is sufficient to observe that legislation like the legislation in question makes no distinction according to the origin of the substances transported, its purpose is not to regulate trade in goods with other Member States and the restrictive effects which it might have on the free movement of goods are too uncertain and indirect for the obligation which it lays down to be regarded as being of a nature to hinder trade between Member States (see the judgment in Case C-69/88 *Krantz v Ontranger der Directe Belastingen* [1990] ECR I-583, paragraph 11, and the judgment in Case C-93/92 *CMC Motorradcenter v Pelin Baskiciogullari* [1993] ECR I-5009, paragraph 12).

25. Article [34] does not therefore preclude legislation like the national legislation in question."

7.133 The CJEU then considered what is now Article 45 of the TFEU:

"26. The national court enquires about the compatibility with Article [45] of a system of sanctions such as that laid down in the Italian legislation in question, which, by providing for the suspension of the professional qualifications of Italian masters who fail to observe the prohibition of discharging harmful substances into the sea, punishes Italian masters more severely than masters of any other nationality.

27. The Court has consistently held that the provisions of the Treaty concerning the free movement of workers may not be applied to a situation purely internal to a Member State. In particular, the mere fact that, under the legislation of a Member State, a foreign worker is in a more favourable situation than a national of that Member State is not sufficient to

---

119 Ed., Art. 5 EC provided in the second para.: "[i]n areas which do not fall within its exclusive competence, the Community shall take action, in accordance with the principle of subsidiarity, only if and insofar as the objectives of the proposed action cannot be sufficiently achieved by the Member States and can therefore, by reason of the scale or effects of the proposed action, be better achieved by the Community."

confer on that national the benefit of the Community rules on the free movement of workers if all the circumstances characterizing his situation are confined within a single Member State of which he is a national (see, to this effect, the judgment in Case 44/84 *Hurd v Jones (Her Majesty's Inspector of Taxes)* [1986] ECR 29, paragraphs 55 and 56, and the judgment in Case C-332/90 *Steen v Deutsche Bundespost* [1992] ECR I-341, paragraphs 5, 9 and 10).

28. According to the information provided in the present case, Mr Peralta is an Italian national employed by an Italian shipowner having command of a vessel which flies the Italian flag. He is therefore in a purely internal situation and cannot rely on Article [45].

29. It follows that Article [45] does not preclude legislation like the Italian legislation, which lays down provisions under which Italian masters who have failed to observe the prohibition which it lays down may have their professional qualifications suspended."

7.134 The CJEU then considered what is now Article 49 of the TFEU:

"30. It is not possible to ascertain from the order for reference the reasons for which the national court enquires about the relationship of the Law in question to Article [49] of the Treaty. In the absence of such an explanation, it should be noted that, according to Mr Peralta, the Law in question deprives Italian marine transport undertakings operating vessels flying the Italian flag of the possibility to establish themselves in other Member States and compels them to use cabotage in Italian territorial waters. He also points out that the ports of other Member States do not have the plant for treating flushing liquids which such undertakings need in order to be able to comply with the Italian legislation.

31. Even though, according to their wording, the provisions of the Treaty guaranteeing freedom of establishment are directed in particular to ensuring that foreign nationals and companies are treated in the host Member State in the same way as nationals of that State, they also prohibit the Member State of origin from hindering the establishment in another Member State of one of its nationals or of a company incorporated under its legislation which comes within the definition contained in Article [54]. For the rights guaranteed by Article [49] et seq. would be rendered meaningless if the Member State of origin could prohibit undertakings from leaving in order to establish themselves in another Member State (see the judgment in Case 81/87 *The Queen v Treasury and Commissioners of Inland Revenue, ex parte Daily Mail and General Trust* [1988] ECR 5483, paragraph 16).

32. However, legislation like the Italian legislation does not contain any provision which can be an obstacle to the establishment of Italian transport undertakings in Member States other than Italy.

33. It should also be recalled that, according to the judgment in Case C-221/89 *The Queen v The Secretary of State for Transport, ex parte Factortame and Others* [1991] ECR I-3905, paragraph 23, the conditions laid down for the registration of vessels must not form an obstacle to freedom of establishment. The legislation of the kind in question does not, however, concern the registration of vessels.

34. In the absence of Community harmonization, a Member State may certainly impose, directly or indirectly, technical rules which are specific to it and which are not necessarily to be found in the other Member States on maritime transport undertakings which, like the undertaking employing Mr Peralta, are established on its territory and which operate vessels flying its flag. But the difficulties which might arise for those undertakings from that situation do not affect freedom of establishment within the meaning of Article [49] of the Treaty. Fundamentally, those difficulties are no different in nature from those which may originate in disparities between national laws governing, for example, labour costs, social security costs or the tax system.

35. Article [49] does not therefore preclude legislation like the Italian legislation."

7.135 The CJEU then considered Article 56 of the Treaty which relates to freedom to provide services:

"36. The national court is enquiring about a situation in which an Italian master put in command of a vessel flying the Italian flag by a provider of services of Italian nationality claims that Italy, the Member State in which that provider of services is established, is infringing the freedom to provide maritime transport services.

Whether the freedom to provide maritime transport services may be relied upon

37. As the Court finds in paragraph 13 of this judgment, Regulation ... 4055/86 was applicable at the time of the events in question.
38. Article 1(1) of that regulation provides:
'Freedom to provide maritime transport services between Member States and between Member States and third countries shall apply in respect of nationals of Member States who are established in a Member State other than that of the person for whom the services are intended.'
39. It is clear, first, from the very wording of that article that it applies to maritime transport operations between Member States of the kind in question in the main proceedings. It defines the persons enjoying freedom to provide services in terms which are substantially the same as those used in Article 56 of the Treaty.
40. Second, in a judgment delivered on 17 May 1994 in Case C-18/93 *Corsica Ferries v Corpo dei Piloti del Porto di Genova*, ...[120] paragraph 30, the Court held that the freedom to provide maritime transport services between Member States may be relied on by an undertaking as against the State in which it is established, if the services are provided for persons established in another Member State.
41. Furthermore, the Court has held that the purpose of Article 56 of the Treaty was to abolish restrictions on the freedom to provide services offered by persons not established in the State in which the service was to be provided and that, consequently, the provisions of Article 56 had to apply in all cases in which a person providing services offers those services in a Member State other than that in which he is established (judgment in Case C-154/89 *Commission v France* [1991] ECR I-659, paragraphs 9 and 10).
42. Since the vessel which he commands performs deliveries intended for other Member States, Mr Peralta may rely, as against Italy, on an alleged infringement of the freedom to provide maritime transport services recognized by Community law.

The existence of discrimination between vessels owing to the different flags which they fly

43. Under Article 9 of Regulation ... 4055/86, which refers to the principle laid down in Article [18] of the Treaty, the minimum requirement applying to legislation such as that in question in the main proceedings is that it must not discriminate on grounds of nationality between persons providing maritime transport services.
44. On this point, legislation of the kind in question meets the requirement of non-discrimination as regards the rules applicable to vessels crossing territorial sea and internal Italian waters. All vessels, whichever flag they fly and whichever the nationality of the undertakings operating them, are subject to the prohibition on discharging harmful substances.
45. Outside territorial sea limits, the Italian legislation distinguishes between foreign vessels and vessels flying the national flag, which are the only ones subject to the prohibition on discharging harmful substances.
46. According to the Italian Government's and Commission's answers to a question asked by the Court, Italy has not established an exclusive economic zone in the Mediterranean Sea. Consequently, under the rules of public international law, it may exercise its jurisdiction beyond territorial sea limits only over vessels flying its flag.
47. It follows that the difference in treatment arising under legislation such as that in question between vessels flying the Italian flag and vessels not flying the Italian flag, adversely affecting only Italian vessels, does not constitute discrimination prohibited by the Treaty since the Italian legislation cannot be applicable on the high seas to vessels not flying the Italian flag. The legislation of a Member State cannot be open to objection on the ground

---

120 Ed., [1994] ECR I-1783, ECLI:EU:C:1994:195.

that it covers only vessels over which that State is entitled to exercise its jurisdiction, beyond the territorial limits of its jurisdiction.

48. Moreover, as the Court repeated in its judgment in Case 155/80 *Oebel* [1981] ECR 1993, paragraph 9, the application of national legislation cannot be held contrary to the principle of non-discrimination merely because other Member States allegedly apply less strict rules (see also the judgment in Case 14/68 *Walt Wilhem and Others v Bundeskartellamt* [1969] ECR 1, paragraph 13).

The existence of restrictions on the freedom to provide maritime transport services

49. The national court indicates that under the Italian legislation restrictions arise on the freedom to provide maritime transport services to other Member States, even if that legislation could not be held to be discriminatory.
50. It must be emphasized that the obstacle to exploitation of which Mr Peralta complains does not arise from the legislation of a Member State on whose territory a transport service is performed but from the legislation of the Member State in which the undertaking has registered the vessel under Mr Peralta's command and in which it is established, namely Italy. The situation of that undertaking in relation to its own Member State of establishment cannot therefore be compared to that of a maritime transport undertaking established in a Member State other than Italy, operating temporarily in that latter State and therefore having to satisfy simultaneously the requirements imposed by the legislation of the Member State whose flag its vessel flies and those laid down by the Italian legislation.
51. However, legislation like the Italian legislation, which prohibits the discharge of harmful chemicals at sea, applies objectively to all vessels without distinction, whether carrying products within Italy or to other Member States. It does not make any distinction regarding services for exported products and for products marketed in Italy. It does not afford any particular advantage to the domestic Italian market, to Italian transport operations or to Italian products.
52. Mr Peralta complains, on the contrary, of the indirect advantages enjoyed by carriers in other Member States who are not subject, on the same conditions, to the prohibition on discharging residues of caustic soda into the sea. However, in the absence of harmonization of the laws of the Member States in this field, those restrictions are merely the result of the national rules of the country of establishment to which the trader remains subject.
53. It follows from the foregoing that Regulation ... 4055/86 does not preclude the contested provisions of a Law such as the Italian Law relating to the discharge of harmful substances into the sea by merchant ships.
54. Consequently, the reference made by the national court ... does not call for a specific response."

7.136 The CJEU then had to finally consider Article 191 of the Treaty:

"the national court enquires whether Article [191] et seq. precludes legislation of the same kind as the contested legislation which has the effect of requiring Italian vessels to use an alternative system for treating flushing water, which, in its view, is inefficient and contrary to the international obligations which Italy has assumed.

56. On this point, it should be recalled that, as the Court held at paragraph 17, ... it is not for the Court to rule on the compatibility of a national provision adopted by a Member State with a convention such as the Marpol Convention. Nor may it interpret Article [191] in the light of an international convention which is not binding on the Community and to which, moreover, not all the Member States are parties.
57. Secondly, Article [191] is confined to defining the general objectives of the Community in the matter of the environment. Responsibility for deciding what action is to be taken is conferred on the Council. ... Moreover, ... the protective measures adopted pursuant to [the Treaty] are not to prevent any Member State from maintaining or introducing more stringent protective measures compatible with the Treaty.

58. Article [191] does not therefore preclude legislation of the kind in question in the main proceedings.
59. The answer to be given to the national court must therefore be that ... the Treaty and Regulation ... 4055/86 do not preclude the legislation of a Member State from prohibiting all vessels, regardless of the flag which they fly, from discharging harmful chemical substances into its territorial waters and its internal waters, or from imposing the same prohibition on the high seas only on vessels flying the national flag, or, finally, in the event of infringement, from penalizing masters of vessels who are nationals of that Member State by suspending their professional qualification."

7.137 This case demonstrates how EU law can be invoked in national criminal proceedings. It also analyses the sometimes complicated relationship between EU and public international law. Ultimately, it shows that Member States do reserve the power to legislate to impose harsher regimes than other Member States in circumstances where EU law does not apply. It also highlights that purely internal matters may fall outside the scope of review of some EU laws.

1997: *Haahr Petroleum Ltd v Åbenrå Havn and others*: taxation of cargoes

7.138 On 17 July 1997, the CJEU delivered its judgment in *Haahr Petroleum Ltd v Åbenrå Havn and others*.[121] The case related to import surcharge and goods duty. The CJEU was asked, by the Østre Landsret (Eastern Regional Court) in Denmark, for a preliminary ruling. The case concerned proceedings between Haahr Petroleum (a company which sold petroleum products) and the Danish commercial ports of Åbenrå, Ålborg, Horsens, Kastrup, Næstved, Odense, Struer and Vejle. The case turned on the charging by those ports of an import surcharge of 40% which until 31 March 1990 was levied in Denmark in addition to goods duties on all imported goods loaded, unloaded or otherwise taken on board or landed within Danish commercial ports or in the deep-water approach channels to those ports. In Denmark, authorisation to establish a commercial port, that is to say, a harbour used for the commercial transport of goods, vehicles and persons, was granted by the Minister for Transport. In accordance with the system of ownership and control, a distinction may be drawn between ports under local authority control, which were independent bodies answerable to the local authority, the port of Copenhagen, which had its own special legal status, the State-owned ports, operated by the Ministry of Transport, and private ports, which were operated by their owners in accordance with the conditions laid down in the relevant authorisation. Part of the ports' revenue came from duties paid for their use by users. Thus shipping and goods duties had to be paid for berthing, and for embarking and disembarking goods, vehicles or persons. Special duties were charged for the use of cranes, warehouses and storage facilities.

7.139 Under Law No 239 of 12 May 1976 on commercial ports (the "1976 Law"), which applied until 31 December 1990, the competent minister was responsible for setting the rate of shipping and goods duties after negotiations with the management of the commercial ports. It was ministerial practice to calculate the rates on the basis of the economic conditions obtaining in the 22 provincial ports regarded as being the most

---

121 Case C-90/94 [1997] ECR I-4085, ECLI:EU:C:1997:368. The chamber was composed of: Mancini (President of the Chamber) as well as Judges Murray and Kapteyn (Rapporteur). The Advocate-General was AG Jacobs.

important in terms of commercial traffic volume and to set them so as to enable the ports to cover their operating and maintenance expenditure and to ensure a reasonable degree of self-financing for necessary extensions and modernisation. The duties were set out in regulations for each port drawn up in accordance with the common regulations prepared by the competent minister for all commercial ports. Under the regulations applicable at the material time, shipping duty was payable by all ships and craft and all floating installations berthing in the port or in the deep-water approach channels. It was calculated as a fixed amount according to deadweight tonnage or gross registered tonnage either each time the vessel put into port or as an amount payable monthly. Vessels of under 100 deadweight or gross registered tonnes were exempt from payment of shipping duty. Goods duty was payable on all goods loaded, unloaded or otherwise taken on board or landed within the port or in the deep-water approach channels. It represented a certain amount per tonne. There were exemptions and special rates for certain goods. In accordance with those rules, goods duty was to be paid by the vessel or its local agent before the ship's departure, but was ultimately borne by the recipient and sender respectively of the goods from whom reimbursement could be claimed. During the period relevant to the case in the main proceedings, a surcharge of 40% was added to the goods duty levied on goods imported from abroad. It appears that the import surcharge of 40% was introduced in the context of a general adjustment to the level of port duties made in 1956 in the light of a report by the committee on rates of duty for ports and bridges set up by the Ministry of Public Works in 1954.

7.140 By an application lodged in 1991 at the Østre Landsret, Haahr Petroleum sought an order for the defendant ports to refund all import surcharges levied on it from 1 January 1984 to 31 March 1990, totalling DKR 9.6 million. In support of its application, Haahr Petroleum claimed on the basis of Articles 9 and 12 of the EEC Treaty[122] that the import surcharge in dispute was tantamount to a charge having effect equivalent to a customs duty and that, as from 1 January 1973, Denmark was not entitled to levy customs duties or charges having equivalent effect. Haahr Petroleum relied on *Diamantarbeiders v Indiamex*,[123] concerning Articles 18 to 28 and 113 of the EEC Treaty.[124] Haahr Petroleum maintained that subsequent to the introduction of the Common Customs Tariff, all Member States are prohibited from introducing, on a unilateral basis, any new charges or from raising the level of those already in force. Haahr Petroleum also objected to the time-barring of its action under the relevant national rules (which provide for a limitation period of five years), on the ground that a claim based on EU law cannot be time-barred either where the delay in making the claim was due to late transposition of a provision of EU law into the national legal order[125] or where the claim is based on the delayed abolition of a provision of national law incompatible with EU law.

7.141 The defendant ports considered that the import surcharge should be assessed under Title IV of the EEC Treaty,[126] which relates to transport, as argued by the Ministry of Transport which intervened in their support, or under Article 95 of the Treaty,[127] since

---

122 I.e. Art. 9 EEC is now Art. 28 of the TFEU. Art. 22 EEC does not have a modern equivalent.
123 Joined Cases 37/73 and 38/73 [1973] ECR 1609, ECLI:EU:C:1973:165.
124 These do not have direct equivalents in the TFEU.
125 Relying on Case C-208/90 *Emmott* [1991] ECR I-4269, ECLI:EU:C:1991:333.
126 I.e. Title V of the TFEU.
127 I.e. Art. 110 of the TFEU.

the 40% surcharge was a constituent part of the goods duty which, in its turn, formed part of a general system of domestic charges under which differentiation in the rates of duty was compatible with the Treaty provisions. Furthermore, they claimed that Haahr Petroleum's application was time-barred as regards duties paid five years or more before the action was brought before the Østre Landsret and that the circumstances of the case revealed no factor capable of justifying departure from the general rules of relevant national law. The Ministry also claimed that the duties pursued a transport policy objective in so far as, first, uniformity of duties was intended to maintain competition between the ports and road transport within Denmark and to ensure that ports did not compete with one another by means of those duties and, second, the import surcharge was supposed to guarantee the financing of the ports without diverting goods traffic to road or rail. As evidence that the objective of the import surcharge was not to affect imports of goods but rather concerned the means of transport, it pointed out that the largest port in terms of international trade, the port of Copenhagen, did not charge that duty.

7.142 The Østre Landsret referred the following questions to the Court for a preliminary ruling:

> "1. Is the special 40% import surcharge on the goods duty ordinarily levied to be regarded as coming under the ... Treaty rules on the Customs Union, including Articles 9 to 13, or under Article 95 of that Treaty?
> 2. Are the ... Treaty rules on the Customs Union, including Articles [EC 23 to 24], or Article [EC 90] of that Treaty to be understood as meaning that it is incompatible with those provisions to impose a special 40% import surcharge on the goods duty ordinarily levied if that import surcharge is imposed exclusively on goods imported from outside Denmark?
> 3. If Question 2 is answered in the affirmative, in what circumstances can such a duty be justified on the ground that it represents consideration for a service provided or on grounds of transport policy (Article [100(2)] of the [TFEU] Treaty)?
> 4. If the special import surcharge is held to be incompatible with the ... Treaty, does that finding apply to the whole of the surcharge levied since Denmark's accession to the [EU] ... or does it apply only to the increase in the import surcharge which came into effect thereafter?
> 5. If it is held that the import surcharge is incompatible with [EU] law, will the fact that a claim for reimbursement may be time-barred under national rules on limitation periods have the full or partial effect that the import surcharge cannot be reimbursed?"

In this chapter, we are more interested in the first four questions and how they impact on the freedom to provide services.

7.143 The CJEU combined questions 1, 2, 3 and 4. The CJEU said that the referring court was essentially seeking clarification of the notion of a charge having an effect equivalent to a customs duty and of the notion of discriminatory internal taxation, where a Member State levies an import surcharge of 40% on goods imported by ship from another Member State in addition to the general goods duty payable on all goods loaded, unloaded or otherwise taken on board or landed within the ports of the first Member State or in the deep-water approach channels to those ports. The CJEU recalled that it had consistently held[128] that provisions relating to charges having equivalent effect and those relating to discriminatory internal taxation cannot be applied together, so that under the Treaty the same imposition cannot belong to both categories at the same time. The Court recalled

---

128 E.g. Case C-266/91 *CELBI* [1993] ECR I-4337, ECLI:EU:C:1993:334, para. 9.

that it had consistently held[129] that any pecuniary charge, whatever its designation and mode of application, which is imposed unilaterally on goods by reason of the fact that they cross a frontier, and which is not a customs duty in the strict sense, constitutes a charge having equivalent effect within the meaning of Articles 28 and 29 of the TFEU. However, such a charge may not be so characterised if it forms part of a general system of internal dues applying systematically to categories of products according to objective criteria applied without regard to the origin of the products, in which case it falls within the scope of Article 110 of the TFEU. The CJEU stated:

> "21. ... first, ... a duty such as the general goods duty at issue in the main proceedings, forms part, together with shipping duty in particular, of a general system of internal taxes payable for the use of commercial ports and their facilities.
> 22. Second, it should be noted that with the exception of certain classes of exempt goods that tax is payable on all goods loaded, unloaded, or otherwise taken on board or landed within commercial ports, whether those goods arrive in port from another Member State or from another commercial port in the same Member State.
> 23. Third, it should be observed that that duty is imposed on goods, both domestic and imported, at the same time and in accordance with the same objective criteria, namely when they are taken on board or put ashore and according to the type of goods and their weight.
> 24. Fourth, an import surcharge such as that in issue in the main proceedings, which increases the general goods duty levied on imported goods, is an integral part of the duty itself and is not a separate duty, since the amount of the surcharge is expressed as a percentage of the duty and the surcharge and the duty are levied on the same legal basis, at the same time, in accordance with the same criteria and through the same authorities and the revenue raised thereby is paid to the same recipients.
> 25. That being so, the fact that the import surcharge is payable ex hypothesi solely on imported goods and that the origin of the goods determines the amount of the duty to be levied cannot remove the tax in general or the surcharge in particular from the scope of Article [110] of the Treaty; accordingly, their compatibility with [EU] law must be assessed in the light of that provision and not Articles [28 to 29] of the Treaty.
> 26. Here, it should first be stated that the Court has consistently held that Article [110] of the Treaty applies only to products from the Member States and, where appropriate, to goods originating in non-member countries which are in free circulation in the Member States. It follows that that provision is not applicable to products imported directly from non-member countries (Case C-130/92 OTO [1994] ECR I-3281, paragraph 18).
> 27. Next, Article [110] of the Treaty provides that no Member State is to impose, directly or indirectly, on the products of other Member States internal taxation in excess of that imposed on similar domestic products or of such a nature as to afford indirect protection to other domestic products. It is therefore beyond question that application of a higher charge to imported products than to domestic products or application to imported products alone of a surcharge in addition to the duty payable on domestic and imported products is contrary to the prohibition of discrimination laid down in Article [110].
> 28. The defendant ports claim, however, that the import surcharge is equivalent to a differential goods duty compatible with Article [110] of the Treaty as interpreted by the Court, in so far as such differentiation is based on objective criteria. They argue in particular that that differential rate of taxation is justified on the two grounds that, in the context of competition with other means of transport, international maritime transport is better able to bear the burden of the surcharge and that such transport is in general carried out by larger vessels making greater use of port facilities than the smaller vessels used in domestic transport. From the same point of view, the Ministry of Transport considers that the surcharge does

---

129 E.g. Case C-45/94 *Cámara de Comercio, Industria y Navegación, Ceuta* [1995] ECR I-4385, ECLI:EU:C:1995:425, para. 28.

not constitute unlawful discrimination, since it represents payment for the general extra costs involved for the ports in supplying services to the larger vessels used for importing goods.

29. It is true that, as the Court has consistently held (Case 196/85 Commission v France [1987] ECR 1597, paragraph 6), at its present stage of development [EU] law does not restrict the freedom of each Member State to lay down tax arrangements which differentiate between certain products, even products which are similar within the meaning of the first paragraph of Article [110] of the Treaty, on the basis of objective criteria, such as the nature of the raw materials used or the production processes employed. Such differentiation is compatible with [EU] law, however, only if it pursues objectives of economic policy which are themselves compatible with the requirements of the Treaty and its secondary legislation, and if the detailed rules are such as to avoid any form of discrimination, direct or indirect, in regard to imports from other Member States or any form of protection of competing domestic products.

30. The Court has earlier held that a criterion for the charging of higher taxation which by definition can never be fulfilled by similar domestic products cannot be considered to be compatible with the prohibition of discrimination laid down in Article [110] of the Treaty. Such a system has the effect of excluding domestic products in advance from the heaviest taxation (Case 319/81 Commission v Italy [1983] ECR 601, paragraph 17). Likewise, the Court has held that such differential taxation is incompatible with [EU] law if the products most heavily taxed are, by their very nature, imported products (Case 106/84 Commission v Denmark [1986] ECR 833, paragraph 21).

31. The same applies, a fortiori, to differential taxation where the criterion for charging a higher rate is the importation itself and where therefore domestic products are by definition excluded from the heaviest taxation.

32. In any event, the discriminatory nature of differential taxation cannot be justified by general considerations based on the differences between international and domestic transport as regards their respective abilities to bear a given fiscal charge without diverting maritime transport to other means of transport and as regards the size of the vessels used depending on whether the transport is domestic or international.

33. Even if such considerations were capable of justifying differential taxation, the fact remains that in a system such as that in question in the main proceedings they are not applied objectively, inasmuch as under that system, domestic transport carried out under the same conditions as international transport is excluded in advance from liability to the same taxation as international transport, and vice versa.

34. It is clear from the Court's case-law (in particular, Case C-152/89 Commission v Luxembourg [1991] ECR I-3141, paragraphs 20 to 25) that a system of taxation can be considered compatible with Article [110] of the Treaty only if it is proved to be so arranged as to exclude any possibility of imported products being taxed more heavily than domestic products, so that it cannot in any event have discriminatory effect.

35. As for the question of whether a discriminatory duty, such as that in issue in the main proceedings, may escape the prohibition laid down in Article [110] on the ground that it represents consideration for a service, it suffices to recall that, in accordance with the case-law relied on by the defendant ports and the Ministry of Transport (in particular Case 46/76 Bauhuis [1977] ECR 5, paragraph 11, and Case C-209/89 Commission v Italy [1991] ECR I-1575, paragraph 9), the fact that a pecuniary charge constitutes consideration for a service actually supplied to traders and is of an amount commensurate with that service merely enables it to escape classification as a charge having equivalent effect within the meaning of Article [34] et seq. of the Treaty, and does not mean that it escapes the prohibition of all discriminatory internal taxation laid down in Article [110].

36. The defendant ports and the Ministry of Transport claim also that a duty such as that in issue in the main proceedings falls outside the scope of Article [110] of the Treaty and the prohibition which it lays down since that duty pursues legitimate transport policy objectives, namely the financing of commercial ports and charging long-distance sea transport proportionately more than short-distance traffic. They add that it is clear from Case C-49/89

Corsica Ferries France [1989] ECR 4441 that charges pursuing a transport policy objective must be assessed in the light of the Treaty rules on transport, in particular Article 84(2), and of Council Regulation ... 4055/86 of 22 December 1986 applying the principle of freedom to provide services to maritime transport between Member States and between Member States and third countries (OJ 1986 L378, p. 1).

37. It is to be noted that the fact that a tax or levy is a special charge or is appropriated for a specific purpose cannot prevent its falling within the field of application of Article [110] of the Treaty (see Case 74/76 Iannelli v Meroni [1977] ECR 557, paragraph 19) nor, where appropriate, the prohibition laid down by that provision.
38. Next, it should be pointed out that a charge such as that in issue in the main proceedings is imposed on products and is borne by the recipient or sender of goods, even where it has been levied on the transport of goods or the use of commercial ports and has first to be paid by the vessel or its local agent.
39. It follows that neither Corsica Ferries France, cited above, which concerned charges levied on all passengers embarked, disembarked or transferred in certain sea-ports and which were borne by the shipowner, nor Regulation ... 4055/86 on the principle of freedom to provide services in maritime transport between Member States and between Member States and third countries, can preclude application of Article [110] of the Treaty.
40. Furthermore, the Court has already ruled that a charge imposed on the transport of goods according, inter alia, to the weight of the goods falls within the scope of Article [110] of the Treaty and, in so far as it has an immediate effect on the cost of national and imported products, must be applied in a manner which is not discriminatory to imported products (Case 20/76 Schöttle v Finanzamt Freudenstadt [1977] ECR 247, paragraphs 15 and 16).
41. As regards the question whether the incompatibility of the charge in issue with Article [110] of the Treaty affects the import surcharge in toto or only the increase in the surcharge occurring after the accession of ... Denmark to the European Communities, the Act concerning the conditions of accession of ... Denmark and the adjustments to the Treaties ... contains no transitional or derogating provision concerning application of Article [110] of the Treaty. Consequently, that provision was applicable to Denmark as soon as it acceded to the European Communities.
42. The Court has consistently held that if a charge is incompatible with Article [110] of the Treaty, it is prohibited to the extent to which it discriminates against imported products (see, to this effect, Case 68/79 Just [1980] ECR 501, paragraph 14, and Case C-72/92 Scharbatke [1993] ECR I-5509, paragraph 10).
43. It follows that a charge such as that in issue in the main proceedings is to be considered to be incompatible with Article [110] and prohibited by it only to the amount of the surcharge levied on imported goods.
44. That being so, the answer to be given to the first four questions must be that it is contrary to Article [110] of the Treaty for a Member State to impose a 40% import surcharge on a general duty levied on goods loaded, unloaded, or otherwise taken on board or landed within its ports or in the deep-water approach channels to its ports where goods are imported by ship from another Member State."

7.144 In essence, the CJEU found that it is contrary to Article 110 of the TFEU for a Member State to impose a 40% import surcharge on a general duty levied on goods loaded, unloaded or otherwise taken on board or landed within its ports or in the deep-water approach channels to its ports where goods are imported by ship from another Member State.[130]

---

130 On the procedural aspect, the CJEU held that an application to a claim for repayment based on breach of Art. 110 TFEU of a rule of national law under which proceedings for recovery of charges unduly paid are time-barred after a period of five years is not contrary to EU law, even if the effect of that rule is to prevent, in whole or in part, the repayment of those charges.

1985: *Commission v Council (Italo-Algerian Maritime Transport)*

7.145 In July 1985, Italy informed the other Member States and the Commission that it was experiencing difficulties in its trade relations with Algeria because Algeria was demanding that about 80% of goods shipped on liner services between Italy and Algeria be carried on the Algerian state shipping line. The then EEC and the Member States made representations to Algeria but to little avail. Italy, acting on its own behalf, then negotiated with Algeria an "Agreement on Maritime Transport and Navigation between the Italian Republic and the People's Democratic Republic of Algeria". This draft agreement was initialled and signed but not ratified. Article 4 of the draft Italy–Algeria agreement provided:

> "Shipowners will be responsible for taking the measures necessary for the organisation and sharing of trade in the framework of a conference or other organisation of shipowners for the most effective operation of lines, in accordance with the trade-sharing principle laid down in the Code of Conduct for Liner Conferences and subject to compliance with the international obligations of each party."

7.146 Incidentally, Italy had not acceded to the UNCTAD Liner Code.[131] On 17 March 1987, Italy notified the draft agreement to the European Commission in accordance with Article 6(5) of Regulation 4055/86. The Commission believed that Article 4 of the draft agreement had to be considered in the light of Articles 5(1) and 6(2) of Regulation 4055/86. It will be recalled that Article 5(1) of the regulation provides:

> "Cargo-sharing arrangements in any future agreements with any third countries are prohibited other than in those exceptional circumstances where Community liner shipping companies would not otherwise have an effective opportunity to ply for trade to and from the third country concerned. In these circumstances such arrangements may be permitted in accordance with the provisions of Article 6."

It will also be recalled that Article 6(2) of the regulation provides:

> "The Council, acting by qualified majority on a proposal of the Commission, shall decide on the necessary action. Such action may include, in the circumstances envisaged in Article 5(1), the negotiation and conclusion of cargo-sharing arrangements."

7.147 The Commission believed that the restrictive condition in Article 5(1) of the regulation was not met because

> "Italy would have had an effective opportunity to ply for trade to and from Algeria if it had acceded to the Convention on a Code of Conduct for Liner Conferences adopted at Geneva on 6 April 1974 ... which would, pursuant to Article 2(4) of the Code, have given its shipping companies access to the traffic in question."[132]

Article 2(4) of the Code provides:

> "When determining a share of trade within a pool of individual member lines and/or groups of national shipping lines in accordance with Article 2, paragraph 2, the following principles regarding their right to participation in the trade carried by the conference shall be observed, unless otherwise mutually agreed:

---

131 On this code, see chap. 9.
132 Judgment, para. 8.

(a) The group of national shipping lines of each of two countries the foreign trade between which is carried by the conference shall have equal rights to participate in the freight and volume of traffic generated by their mutual foreign trade and carried by the conference,

(b) Third-country shipping lines, if any, shall have the right to acquire a significant part, such as 20 per cent in the freight and volume of traffic generated by that trade."

7.148 The Commission believed that the proposed agreement could not be operated for so long as Italy was not a party to the UNCTAD Liner Conferences Code. The Commission therefore submitted to the Council a draft decision pursuant to Article 6(2) of the regulation. The decision would authorise the agreement subject to the condition that Italy would accede to the Code as quickly as possible. The agreement would cease to have effect as soon as the Code of Conduct became applicable to trade between Italy and Algeria or, at the very latest, three years after the adoption of the Council decision. The draft agreement would have to be amended in some respects however in advance so as to ensure freedom to provide services and the maintenance of effective competition.

7.149 On 17 September 1987, the Council adopted Decision 87/475[133] relating to maritime transport between Italy and Algeria. The Preamble to the decision stated:

"the provisions of the aforementioned Agreement need to be applied in such a way as to avoid a conflict with the obligations of the Member States under Community law, in particular with respect to fair, free and non-discriminatory access to cargoes by Community nationals or shipping companies, including independent lines."

7.150 Article 1 of the decision granted unconditional authorisation to ratify the agreement "on the understanding" that Italy will accede to the Liner Code as soon as possible.

7.151 On 25 November 1987, the Commission instituted proceedings before the CJEU under, what is now, Article 263 of the TFEU to annul Council Decision 87/475.[134] The Commission raised a number of arguments. First, the Commission maintained that the decision is contrary to Articles 5 and 6 of the regulation because: (a) it authorised the conclusion of a cargo-sharing arrangement although the requisite conditions were not met; and (b) the agreement was contrary to EU law in several respects. Did Article 4 of the draft agreement contain a cargo-sharing arrangement? This was the Commission's argument but the Council asserted that it simply provided for the establishment of a liner conference (i.e. a group of vessel-operating carriers which provide international liner services for the carriage of cargo and has arrangements on freight rates and other conditions of transport).

7.152 The CJEU held that it constituted a cargo-sharing arrangement. That said, was there a breach of Articles 5 and 6 of Regulation 4055/86? The CJEU said:

"17. With regard to the breach of Article 5(1) of [Regulation 4055/86], the first branch of its submission, the Commission argues that there were no 'exceptional circumstances' within the meaning of that provision such as to justify the conclusion of a cargo-sharing arrangement unlimited in its duration. Such circumstances exist only where there is no means less restrictive of freedom to provide services by which the member-State concerned can obtain access to the trade in question. In this case, Italy could have acceded to the Code of Conduct.

---

133 OJ 1987 L272/37.
134 Case 355/87 *Commission v Council (Italo-Algerian Maritime Transport)* [1989] ECR 1517, ECLI:EU:C:1989:220.

18. According to the Commission, such accession would at the same time have brought Italy under Council Regulation 954/79 of 15 May 1979, concerning the ratification by member-States of, or their accession to, the United Nations Convention on a Code of Conduct for Liner Conferences (hereinafter referred to as 'the regulation on ratification of the Code of Conduct').[135] Under Article 3 of that regulation, cargoes allocated to Italian members of the liner conference would have had to be redistributed fairly among all the Community lines which were members of that conference. The simple reference in Article 4 of the draft agreement between Italy and Algeria to the trade-sharing principle in the Code of Conduct did not make the redistribution rule in Article 3 of the regulation applicable. The draft agreement, says the Commission, thus does not guarantee freedom to provide services to the same degree as the accession of Italy to the Code of Conduct would have done.

19. The regulation on ratification of the Code of Conduct simply lays down certain obligations which Member States that accede to the Code must observe in order to ensure that the Code is applied in a manner consistent with Community law. Contrary to what the Commission proposed, the regulation does not set a time limit within which accession must take place. The regulation thus does not oblige the Member States to accede to the Code of Conduct.

20. Nor can Italy's accession to the Code of Conduct be required on the ground that it would guarantee freedom to provide services to a greater extent than the application of the agreement between Italy and Algeria. The agreement may provide the same guarantees in that respect as accession to the Code if it contains appropriate clauses guaranteeing freedom to provide services. The question whether that is the case must be considered in connection with the second branch of this submission.

21. Consequently, the Council was entitled to refrain from making authorisation to ratify the draft agreement between Italy and Algeria subject to the condition that Italy should accede to the Code of Conduct."

7.153 The first branch of the submission was therefore rejected. In the second branch of the submission, the Commission argued that the contested decision is contrary to Article 6(2) of Regulation 4055/86 because under that provision, the Council of Ministers could authorise only measures consistent with Community law; the contested decision is contrary to EU law in two respects:

"24. The Commission argues first of all that the Council could authorise ratification of the agreement only if it ensured fair, free and non-discriminatory access for companies from other member-States to shares in the traffic between Italy and Algeria. It relies in that regard on Article 6(4) of the regulation on freedom to provide services, according to which member-States which themselves negotiate a cargo-sharing arrangement, after the Council has failed to act for a prolonged period, must ensure such freedom of access. The same requirement necessarily applies to Council decisions authorising a cargo-sharing arrangement.

25. The Commission goes on to argue that the Council can authorise a cargo-sharing arrangement only if it gives Community companies which are not members of the conference effective access to cargoes transported by the conference. That obligation follows from Article 7(2)(b)(i) of Council Regulation 4056/86 of 22 December 1986, laying down detailed rules for the application of Articles [101] and [102] of the Treaty to maritime transport,[136] which requires that effective competition be maintained.

26. A comparison of the two claims set out above indicates that the first concerns the redistribution of the Italian share of the trade in question between [EU] companies which are members of the conference other than Italian companies and the second concerns access to that share of trade on the part of [EU] companies, from whatever member-State, which are not members of the conference.

---

135 OJ 1979 L121/1.
136 OJ 1986 L378/4.

27. With regard to the first claim, it should be observed that Italy is bound to ensure that all [EU] companies which are members of the conference have access to the trade share allocated to Italian shipowners by the agreement. That obligation follows from Article 1 of the regulation on freedom to provide services, which makes the freedom to provide services applicable to maritime transport.[137] It is confirmed in Article 6(4) of that regulation, which is relied on by the Commission. With regard to the second claim, it should be observed that Article 7(2)(b)(i) of Council Regulation 4056/86 does require that the agreement should preserve the possibility of access by [EU] companies which are not members of the conference to the trade share allocated to Italian shipowners by the agreement.

28. According to the Commission, the draft agreement between Italy and Algeria does not meet those two requirements because it contains no specific provisions in that respect.

29. The Commission argues first of all that the reference to Italy's international obligations contained in Article 4 of the draft agreement is too vague to ensure observance of freedom to provide services and freedom of competition.

30. Article 4 of the draft agreement is made more specific by Article 1(b) of the contested decision, under which Italy 'will reiterate to Algeria that the provisions of the agreement will be implemented in accordance with Community law'. The second to last recital in the preamble to the contested decision states that the obligations imposed by [EU] law include the obligation to ensure 'fair, free and non-discriminatory access to cargoes by Community nationals or shipping companies, including independent lines'. Italy's obligation to ensure observance of freedom to provide services and freedom of competition is thus stated in a sufficiently precise manner.

31. The Commission also objects that the international obligations referred to in Article 4 of the draft agreement cannot be relied on against private parties, that is to say the shipowners that are responsible for applying the agreement.

32. The fact that the application of the agreement is delegated to private parties cannot prejudice observance of [EU] law. Italy must adopt the necessary internal measures to ensure that its shipowners grant other [EU] companies rights of access in accordance with Italy's [EU] obligations.

33. Since the Commission has not shown that the agreement, as supplemented by the requirements set out in the contested decision, is contrary to [EU] law, the second branch of the submission must also be rejected.

34. Consequently, the first submission must be dismissed."

7.154 Turning to the breach of the prohibition of discrimination, the CJEU said:

"35. This submission is made in the alternative to the first submission, in the event that Articles 5(1) and 6(2) of the Regulation on freedom to provide services did not in themselves prevent the Council from authorising the contested agreement. The Commission submits that in that case these provisions should be implemented in such a manner as to ensure observance of the prohibition of discrimination laid down in Article [18] of the [TFEU] ... According to the Commission, that was not done in this case. However, it does not put forward arguments in that respect separate from those which it made in arguing that the contested decision is contrary to the regulation on freedom to provide services.

36. Consideration of the first submission has shown that the agreement between Italy and Algeria, as supplemented by the requirements set out in the contested decision, ensures non-discriminatory access on the part of shipping lines from other member-States to cargoes allocated to Italy under the agreement.

37. Consequently, this submission must also be dismissed."

7.155 Then turning to the alleged breach of the obligation to state reasons, the CJEU said:

---

137 Ed., i.e. Reg. 4055/86.

"38. The Commission submits that by failing, in the contested decision, to state that Article 4 of the draft agreement contained a cargo-sharing arrangement and to state what were the 'exceptional circumstances' within the meaning of Article 5(1) of the regulation on freedom to provide services which justified the conclusion of such an arrangement the Council failed to comply with its obligation to state reasons pursuant to ... the Treaty.

39. It is apparent from the first recital in the preamble to the contested decision that Algerian practices of cargo reservation were at the root of the problem. The second recital shows that the purpose of the draft agreement between Italy and Algeria was to counteract the effects of those practices. The contested decision thus gave a sufficient indication of the type of problem with which the agreement whose ratification it authorises was intended to deal. A separate, express statement that this was a cargo-sharing arrangement was therefore nugatory.

40. With regard to the existence of 'exceptional circumstances' justifying authorisation to ratify the agreement it should be emphasised that the fourth recital in the preamble to the contested decision states that its legal basis is Article 6(2) of the regulation on freedom to provide services and points out that that provision authorises the adoption of measures 'where a member-State's nationals or shipping companies do not have an effective opportunity to ply for trade to and from a particular third country'. It is apparent from that recital that the Council considered that the Algerian practices of cargo reservation had created a situation in which Italy no longer had effective access to trade with that non-member country. The contested decision therefore contains a sufficient explanation of the exceptional circumstances justifying its adoption.

41. It follows from the foregoing that the submission based on breach of the obligation to state reasons must also be rejected."

7.156 Finally, turning to the alleged breach of, what is now, Article 296 of the TFEU, the CJEU said:

"42. In its final submission the Commission argues that in adopting the contested decision the Council went beyond the limits of its right of amendment under ... the ... Treaty. Under that provision, it says, the Council can adopt a measure only if it has the same subject-matter and objective as the Commission's proposal. Otherwise the Council's measure must be considered to have been adopted without any proposal. In this case the Commission proposed that the Council should refuse authorisation to ratify the agreement if specific amendments were not made. The Council, on the other hand, granted unconditional authorisation to ratify the agreement. By so doing it completely altered the objective of the Commission's proposal and thus disregarded the limits to its right of amendment.

43. Article 1 of the proposal submitted by the Commission to the Council with a view to the adoption of the contested decision provided that 'Italy may ratify its Agreement on Maritime Transport and Navigation with Algeria, signed on 28 February 1987, on condition that...' The conditions set out in the proposal were intended to make the agreement consistent with Community law. The contested decision also authorises Italy to ratify the agreement, but makes that authorisation subject to certain requirements which, as has been established above, ensure observance of [EU] law.

44. It is not therefore necessary for the Court to rule generally on the limits of the right of amendment provided for in Article [296] of the Treaty; it is sufficient to hold that in this case, and contrary to what the Commission maintains, the Council did not in any event depart from the subject-matter of the Commission's proposal and did not alter its objective, that is to say, to ensure that the agreement was applied in compliance with [EU] law.

45. Consequently, the submission based on breach of Article [296] of the Treaty cannot be upheld.

46. It follows from all the foregoing that the action is unfounded and must be dismissed."

1994: *Corsica Ferries Italia Srl v Corporazione dei piloti del Porto di Genova*

7.157 On 17 May 1994, the CJEU gave its preliminary ruling on *Corsica Ferries Italia Srl v Corporazione del piloti del Porto di Genova*.[138] The case concerned freedom to provide services and the application of competition rules to public undertakings. The CJEU ruled that the notion to provide services in maritime transport, as embodied in Regulation 4055/86, is identical with one developed in Article 56 of the TFEU. The CJEU advised that different pilotage dues or charges which are dependent on the flag being flown by the vessel would breach EU law, being discrimination on the basis of nationality (where there is discrimination between EU nationals). The CJEU held that Article 1(1) of Regulation 4055/86 precludes the application in a Member State of different tariffs for identical piloting services, depending on whether or not the undertaking which provides maritime transport services between two Member States operates a vessel authorised to engage in maritime cabotage, which is reserved to vessels flying the flag of that State. Article 106(1) and Article 102 of the TFEU prohibit a national authority from inducing an undertaking which has been granted the exclusive right of providing compulsory piloting services in a substantial part of the common market, by approving the tariffs adopted by it, to apply different tariffs to maritime transport undertakings, depending on whether they operate transport services between Member States or between ports situated on national territory, in so far as trade between Member States is affected.

7.158 In particular, the CJEU considered the issues raised in the case in the context of the freedom to provide maritime transport services and concluded that Article 1(1) of Regulation 4055/86 precludes the application in a Member State of different tariffs for identical piloting services, depending on whether or not the undertaking which provides maritime transport services between two Member States operates a vessel authorised to engage in maritime cabotage, which is reserved to vessels flying the flag of that State:

> "17. In questions 1 and 3 the Tribunale essentially wishes to know whether [EU] law precludes the application in a Member State, for identical piloting services, of different tariffs depending on whether or not the undertaking which provides shipping services between two Member States operates a vessel which is authorized for maritime cabotage, that being reserved to vessels flying the flag of that State.
>
> 18. The Court notes to begin with that Article [4(3) of the Treaty on the European Union], referred to in question 1, which provides that Member States must ensure fulfilment of their obligations arising out of the Treaty, is worded so generally that there can be no question of applying it autonomously when the situation concerned is governed by a specific provision of the Treaty (see the judgment in Joined Cases C-78/90 to C-83/90 Compagnie Commerciale de l'Ouest and Others v Receveur Principal des Douanes de La Pallice Port [1992] ECR I-1847, paragraph 19).
>
> 19. Secondly, the Court has consistently held that Article [18] of the [TFEU], ... which lays down the general principle of the prohibition of discrimination on grounds of nationality, applies independently only to situations governed by [EU] law in respect of which the Treaty lays down no specific prohibition of discrimination (see the judgment in Case C-179/90 Merci Convenzionali Porto di Genova v Siderurgica Gabrielli [1991] ECR I-5889, paragraph 11).
>
> 20. In the field of freedom to provide services, the principle of the prohibition of discrimination is given specific expression in ... the Treaty.

---

138 Case C-18/83 [1994] ECR I-1783, ECLI:EU:C:1998:306.

21. As regards the determination of the services to which ... the Treaty is to be applied, it should be noted that a system of differential tariffs for piloting services affects a transport undertaking such as Corsica Ferries in two ways. Piloting services are services provided for consideration to the shipping undertakings by the corporation, and differences in tariffs affect those undertakings as recipients of the services. However, the differences in tariffs affect the undertakings primarily in their capacity as providers of maritime transport services, in so far as they have an effect on the cost of those services and thus place them at a disadvantage in comparison with economic operators who benefit from the preferential tariffs.
22. In assessing the tariff system at issue before the national court from the point of view of the freedom to provide maritime transport services, the Court must consider, firstly, to what extent the principle of non-discrimination laid down in ... the Treaty applies in the maritime transport sector and, secondly, whether such a system causes discrimination on the grounds of nationality.
23. Article [58(1)] of the Treaty provides that freedom to provide services in the field of transport is to be governed by the provisions of the title of the Treaty relating to transport (see in particular the judgments in Case 13/83 Parliament v Council [1985] ECR 1513, paragraph 62, and Case C-49/89 Corsica Ferries France v Direction Générale des Douanes Françaises [1989] ECR 4441, paragraph 10).
24. It follows that, as the Court held in its judgments in Corsica Ferries France, cited above, paragraph 11, and in Joined Cases 209 to 213/84 Ministère Public v Asjes [1986] ECR 1425, paragraph 37, in the transport sector the objective laid down in Article [56] of the Treaty of abolishing during the transitional period restrictions on freedom to provide services should have been attained in the framework of the common policy provided for in ... the Treaty.
25. With regard in particular to maritime transport, Article [100(2)] of the Treaty provides that the Council may decide whether, to what extent and by what procedure appropriate provisions may be laid down for that kind of transport.
26. Thus the Council, on the basis of those provisions, adopted Regulation (EEC) No 4055/86.
27. Article 1(1) of that regulation provides that:

'Freedom to provide maritime transport services between Member States and between Member States and third countries shall apply in respect of nationals of Member States who are established in a Member State other than that of the person for whom the services are intended.'

28. As regards the substantive scope of Regulation ... 4055/86, the wording of Article 1 makes it clear that the regulation applies to maritime transport services between Member States of the kind at issue in the main proceedings.
29. As to the persons covered by Regulation ... 4055/86, Article 1 refers to nationals of Member States who are established in a Member State other than that of the person for whom the services are intended, and does not mention the registration of or the flag flown by the vessels operated by the transport undertakings.
30. Moreover, the freedom to provide maritime transport services between Member States, and in particular the prohibition of discrimination on grounds of nationality, may be relied on by an undertaking as against the State in which it is established, if the services are provided for persons established in another Member State. In a case such as that in point in the main proceedings, an undertaking established in one Member State and operating a liner service, covered by Regulation ... 4055/86, to another State, provides those services, by reason of their very nature, inter alia for persons established in the latter State.
31. Consequently, the situation at issue in the main proceedings is not a purely national matter, and the Italian Government's argument on this point must be rejected.
32. In considering next whether the tariff system at issue in the main proceedings is compatible with Regulation ... 4055/86, it should be noted that paragraphs 6 and 7 of this judgment show that the system gives preferential treatment to vessels permitted to engage in maritime cabotage, in other words, those flying the Italian flag.

33. Such a system indirectly discriminates between economic operators according to their nationality, since vessels flying the national flag are generally operated by national economic operators, whereas transport undertakings from other Member States as a rule do not operate ships registered in the State applying that system.
34. That finding is not affected by the fact that the class of less favourably treated economic operators may also include national transport undertakings which operate vessels not registered in their State, or by the fact that the class of operators given favourable treatment may include transport undertakings from other Member States which operate vessels registered in the aforesaid State, since the class receiving favourable treatment consists essentially of nationals of that State.
35. It follows that Article 1(1) of Regulation ... 4055/86 prohibits a Member State from applying different tariffs for identical piloting services, depending on whether or not an undertaking, even one from that Member State, which provides maritime transport services between that Member State and another Member State operates a vessel authorized to engage in maritime cabotage, which is reserved to vessels flying the flag of that State.
36. The corporation and the Italian Government are wrong in attempting to justify the different tariffs on grounds of navigational safety, national transport policy or protection of the environment. Even if those objectives were capable of justifying intervention by the public authorities in the transport sector, a discriminatory tariff system such as that at issue before the national court does not appear necessary for attaining those objectives.
37. The answer to questions 1 and 3 must therefore be that Article 1(1) of Regulation ... 4055/86, which gives effect to the principle of freedom to provide services, and in particular to the prohibition of discrimination, in the field of maritime transport between Member States, precludes the application in a Member State of different tariffs for identical piloting services, depending on whether or not the undertaking which provides maritime transport services between two Member States operates a vessel authorized to engage in maritime cabotage, which is reserved to vessels flying the flag of that State."

7.159 Turning to the issue of competition, the CJEU concluded that Article 106(1) and Article 102 of the TFEU prohibit a national authority from inducing an undertaking which has been granted the exclusive right of providing compulsory piloting services in a substantial part of the internal market, by approving the tariffs adopted by it, to apply different tariffs to maritime transport undertakings, depending on whether they operate transport services between Member States or between ports situated on national territory, in so far as trade between Member States is affected. The CJEU's reasoning was interesting:

"38. By question 5(1) and (2) the national court essentially wishes to know whether Articles [106(1) and 102] of the Treaty prohibit a national authority from enabling an undertaking which has the exclusive right of providing compulsory piloting services in a substantial part of the common market to apply different tariffs to maritime transport undertakings, depending on whether they operate transport services between Member States or between ports situated on national territory.
39. It should be noted that the corporation, the defendant in the main proceedings, has received from the public authorities the exclusive right to provide compulsory piloting services in the port of Genoa.
40. An undertaking which has a legal monopoly in a substantial part of the [internal] market may be regarded as occupying a dominant position within the meaning of Article [102] of the Treaty (see the judgments in Case C-41/90 Hoefner and Elser v Macrotron [1991] ECR I-1979, paragraph 28; Case C-260/89 ERT v DEP and Kouvelas [1991] ECR I-2925, paragraph 31; and Merci Convenzionali Porto di Genova, cited above, paragraph 14).
41. The market in question is that of piloting services in the port of Genoa. Having regard in particular to the volume of traffic in that port and its importance in relation to maritime import and export operations as a whole in the Member State concerned, that market may

be regarded as constituting a substantial part of the common market (see the judgment in Merci Convenzionali Porto di Genova, cited above, paragraph 15).

42. The mere fact of creating a dominant position by granting exclusive rights within the meaning of Article [106(1)] is not in itself incompatible with Article [102] of the Treaty.

43. However, a Member State infringes the prohibitions in those two articles if, by approving the tariffs adopted by the undertaking, it induces it to abuse its dominant position inter alia by applying dissimilar conditions to equivalent transactions with its trading partners, within the meaning of Article [102(c)] of the Treaty.

44. Inasmuch as the discriminatory practices referred to in the order for reference affect undertakings providing transport services between two Member States, they may affect trade between Member States.

45. The answer to question 5(1) and (2) must therefore be that Article [106(1)] and Article [102] of the Treaty prohibit a national authority from inducing an undertaking which has been granted the exclusive right of providing compulsory piloting services in a substantial part of the [internal] market, by approving the tariffs adopted by it, to apply different tariffs to maritime transport undertakings, depending on whether they operate transport services between Member States or between ports situated on national territory, in so far as trade between Member States is affected."

1994: *Commission v France*: passenger levy case

7.160 On 5 October 1994, the CJEU decided *Commission v France*.[139] The case related to Article R.212–17 of the French Code which provided for charges on passengers embarking, disembarking or transhipping the maritime ports of metropolitan France. The CJEU declared that:

"by maintaining in force a system for levying charges on the disembarkation and embarkation of passengers in the case of vessels using port installations situated on its continental or island territory and arriving from ports situated in another Member State or travelling to them, whereas in the case of passenger transport between two ports situated on national territory those charges are levied only on embarkation for departure from the continental or island port, and by applying higher rates of charges when passengers arrive from or embark for ports situated in another Member State than when they travel to a port situated on national territory, the French Republic has failed to fulfil its obligations under Article 1 of Regulation ... 4055/86 applying the principle of freedom to provide services to maritime transport between Member States and between Member States and third countries".[140]

7.161 The judgment was very succinct and it is useful to consider parts of it. It began by considering the legal background.

"the Commission ... brought an action ... for a declaration that, by maintaining in force a system for levying charges on the disembarkation and embarkation of passengers in the case of vessels using port installations situated on its continental or island territory and arriving from ports situated in another Member State or travelling to them, whereas in the case of transport between two ports situated in national territory, those charges are levied only on embarkation for departure from the continental or island port, and by applying higher rates of charges when passengers arrive from or embark for ports situated in another Member State than when they travel to a port situated on national territory, the French Republic has failed to fulfil its obligations under Article 1 of ... Regulation ... 4055/86 ...

2. Under Article R.212–17 of the French Code governing maritime ports a charge is levied on

---

139 Case C-381/93 [1994] ECR I-5145, ECLI:EU:C:1994:370.
140 Declaration of the CJEU, 5 October 1994.

each passenger disembarking, embarking or transshipping in the maritime ports of metropolitan France. That charge, which is borne by the shipowner, may be recovered from the passengers.

3. Article R.212–19 of that code, as contained in Decree No 92/1089 of 1 October 1992 altering the rates of tax on passengers of commercial vessels collected by way of port dues (Official Journal of the French Republic, 7 October 1992), provides as follows:

'In the maritime ports of continental France, charges at the following rate shall be imposed on passengers of commercial vessels by way of port dues for passengers travelling on a hovercraft or any other vessel:

1. Passengers bound for a continental French port or Corsica: F 8.28 (with a 50% reduction for fourth class passengers). For the purpose of levying the charge, passengers of hovercrafts or single-class vessels shall be deemed to be second-class passengers;
2. Passengers arriving from or travelling to a port of the British Isles or the Channel Islands: F 17.52;
3. Passengers arriving from or travelling to a port situated in Europe (with the exception of those mentioned at 1 and 2 above) or in any Mediterranean country: F 21.01;
4. Passengers arriving from or travelling to all other ports: F 74.81.
…'

4. Article R.212–20 goes on to provide:

'In the maritime ports of Corsica, the following rates of charge shall be imposed on passengers of commercial vessels by way of port duty where they travel on a hovercraft or any other vessel:

1. Passengers travelling to a port in Corsica, continental France or Sardinia: F 8.28 (with a 50% reduction for fourth class passengers);
2. Passengers arriving from or travelling to a port situated in Europe (with the exception of those mentioned at 1 above) or in North Africa: F 8.28;
3. Passengers arriving from or travelling to all other ports: F 49.88 …'"

7.162 The CJEU then considered the detail:

5. The Commission considers that this system of charges is discriminatory in two ways: on the one hand, the rate of tax is lower for the transport of passengers whose destination is a French port than for the transport of passengers whose destination is a port of another Member State (except for passengers travelling to Sardinia from Corsica); in addition, for transport between French ports the charge is levied only on embarkation, whereas for transport between a French port and a port of another Member State (except for journeys between Corsica and Sardinia), the charge is levied on both embarkation and disembarkation.
6. The Commission considers that, even if the French rules do not discriminate on the basis of the nationality of the provider of the transport services in question, they constitute an impediment to the freedom to provide services contrary to Article 1 of Regulation … 4055/86 owing to the fact that they distinguish between transport services within France and those performed to or from another Member State, although the port services covered by the charge are the same in both cases.
7. In its defence the French Government maintains that Regulation … 4055/86 does not fully implement the freedom to provide services in maritime transport, inasmuch as it concerns only maritime transport between Member States and between Member States and third countries and not maritime transport within the Member States, namely maritime cabotage. In that connection it stresses that … Regulation … 3577/92 … which entered into force on 1 January 1993 provides in Article 6(1) that the freedom to provide services in the case of regular passenger and ferry services in the Mediterranean and along the coast of France are to be applicable only from 1 January 1999.

8. Therefore, according to the French Government, the observance by France of the rules concerning the freedom to provide services must be assessed separately for each of these two types of services. In both cases France satisfies the requirements of Community law, inasmuch as there is no discrimination as between French operators and operators from other Member States in intra-Community maritime transport from or to a French port; in the case of cabotage all operators from the other Member States are placed in the same situation with regard to the applicable French legislation.

10. As the Court held in its judgment in Case C-379/92 Peralta [1994] ECR I-3453 at paragraph 39, that provision defines the beneficiaries of the freedom to provide maritime transport services between Member States and between Member States and third countries in terms which are substantially the same as those used in Article [56] of the Treaty.

11. By providing, further, that 'Without prejudice to the provisions of the Treaty relating to right of establishment, a person providing a maritime transport service may, in order to do so, temporarily pursue his activity in the Member State where the service is provided, under the same conditions as are imposed by that State on its own nationals', Article 8 of Regulation ... 4055/86 transposes the principle laid down in the third paragraph of Article [57] of the Treaty to the sphere of maritime transport between Member States.

12. Finally, under Article 1(3) of Regulation ... 4055/86, the provisions of Articles [56 to 62 of the EC Treaty] and [58 of the TFEU] are to apply to those types of maritime transport.

13. Paragraph 13 of Regulation ... 4055/86 thus renders applicable to the sphere of maritime transport between Member States the totality of the Treaty rules governing the freedom to provide services.

14. In pursuance of those rules the freedom to provide services may be relied on not only by nationals of Member States established in a Member State other than that of the recipient of the services but also by an undertaking against the State in which it is established where the services are provided to recipients established in another Member State (see judgment in Case C-18/93 Corsica Ferries Italia [1994] ECR I-1783,[141] paragraph 30, and more generally whenever a provider of services offers services in a Member State other than the one in which he is established (see judgment in Case C-154/89 Commission v France [1991] ECR I-659, paragraphs 9 and 10, and the abovementioned Peralta judgment, at paragraph 41).

15. Not only are intra-[EU] maritime transport services frequently supplied to recipients established in a different Member State from that of the provider of the services, but those services are also by definition offered at least in part on the territory of a Member State other than that in which the provider of the services is established.

16. Once the provision of services at issue in the present action is established as falling within Article [56] of the Treaty, under the Court's consistent case-law Article [56] precludes the application of any national legislation which without objective justification impedes a provider of services from actually exercising that freedom (see judgment in Case C-288/89 Collectieve Antennevoorziening Gouda [1991] ECR I-4007).

17. In the perspective of [an internal] market and in order to permit the realization of its objectives, that freedom likewise precludes the application of any national legislation which has the effect of making the provision of services between Member States more difficult than the provision of services purely within one Member State.

18. Consequently, the provision of maritime transport services between Member States cannot be subject to stricter conditions than those to which analogous provisions of services at domestic level are subject.

19. In this connection the fact, invoked by the French Government, that under Regulation ... 3577/92 the freedom to provide services applies to maritime transport within the Member States only progressively and within the time-limits laid down therein is without relevance. In fact, that regulation concerns only the access to maritime cabotage by providers of services from other Member States and does not lay down rules governing intra-[EU] maritime transport.

---

141 Ed., annotated by Slot (1995) 32 CMLRev 1287–1294.

20. To accept that the Member States might on that ground be justified in charging intra-[EU] maritime transport more heavily than internal transport would be tantamount to rendering the extension of the freedom to provide services to intra-Community maritime transport provided for in Regulation ... 4055/86 to a substantial extent nugatory.
21. Where national legislation, though applicable without discrimination to all vessels whether used by national providers of services or by those from other Member States, operates a distinction according to whether those vessels are engaged in internal transport or in intra-[EU] transport, thus securing a special advantage for the domestic market and the internal transport services of the Member State in question, that legislation must be deemed to constitute a restriction on the freedom to provide maritime transport services contrary to Regulation ... 4055/86.
22. The contested French legislation undeniably operates a scheme of charges which in the case of transport services between a French port and a port in another Member State is less favourable than that applicable to transport services provided between French ports.
23. Under those circumstances the Commission's application for a declaration of a failure to fulfil obligations must be granted in the terms sought."

7.163 In essence, the tax was lower when the destination port was French. Equally, if the journey was between French ports then the tax was only imposed on embarkation. The Commission's concern was not there was discrimination based on the nationality of the provider of the service but on the difference in treatment; as Greaves has put it succinctly: "[t]he French system of charges distinguished between maritime transport services between French ports and those performed to and from another Member State, although the port services covered by the charge were the same in both cases".[142] France argued that there was no discrimination between French and non-French carriers. The CJEU however rejected that view. The fact that there was no discrimination on the basis of nationality was irrelevant. Instead, the CJEU was concerned because the level of charges varied according to whether the ships were involved in cabotage or inter-Member State travel.

7.164 Paragraph 13 of the judgment is interesting because it confirms that Regulation 4055/86 "renders applicable to the sphere of maritime transport between Member States the totality of the Treaty rules governing the freedom to provide services".

1993: *Cenargo: UK/Morocco*

7.165 Cenargo, a UK ferry operator, planned in 1993 to operate a ferry service between Spain and Morocco. Spain opposed the plan. Spain invoked a 1979 agreement between Morocco and Spain with some of the ports to be used by Cenargo not being designated ports. The UK intervened on behalf of Cenargo. The UK argued that Regulation 4055/86 obliged Spain to phase out such bilateral agreements or amend them so that other Member States could benefit from the arrangement. Eventually, in 1994, Cenargo was able to open the service. However, the difficulties experienced by Cenargo demonstrated that despite the adoption of a measure such as Regulation 4055/86, there may be practical difficulties in seeking to invoke the legal rights.

---

142 Greaves, *EC Transport Law* (1990), pp. 108–109.

1988: *Corsica Ferries France v Gruppo Antichi Ormeggiatori del Porto di Genova Coop. arl, Gruppo Ormeggiatori del Golfo di La Spezia Coop. arl and Ministero dei Trasporti e della Navigazione*

7.166 On 18 June 1988, the CJEU dealt with a preliminary reference from an Italian court in *Coriscia Ferries France SAV. Gruppo Antichi Ormeggiatori del Porto di Genova Coop. arl, Gruppo Ormeggiatori del Golfo di la Spezia Coop. arl, and Ministero dei trasporti e della Navigazione* on the interpretation of Articles 3, 5, 30, 59, 85, 86 and 90(1) of the EC Treaty and Regulation 4055/86.[143]

7.167 The questions to the CJEU arose in proceedings between Corsica Ferries France SA "Corsica Ferries" and Gruppo Antichi Ormeggiatori del Porto diGenova Coop. arl (the mooring group of the Port of Genoa ("the Genoa mooring group")) and the Gruppo Ormeggiatori del Golfo di La SpeziaCoop. arl (the mooring group of the Port of La Spezia ("the La Speziamooring group")) and the Ministero dei Trasporti e della Navigazione ("Ministry").

7.168 The French Company, "Corsica Ferries" had since 1 January 1994, been provided, in its capacity as a shipping company, a regular liner service by car ferry between Corsica and various Italian ports, including Genoa and La Spezia. For this purpose it used ferries flying the Panamanian flag on time charter from Tourship Ltd (established in Jersey). Corsica Ferries and Tourship Ltd were both controlled by Tourship SA, a company incorporated under Luxembourg law and established in Luxembourg. Over the period from 1994 to 1996 Corsica Ferries paid to the Genoa and La Spezia mooring groups various sums in respect of mooring services (mooring and unmooring of vessels) to which port stops made by vessels operated by it had given rise. Corsica Ferries always attached express reservations to its payments, indicating that the requirement to avail itself of the services of the mooring groups constituted an impediment to the free movement of goods and to freedom to provide services and that the sums it was being charged were calculated on a tariff which bore no relation to the actual services provided and had been adopted in breach of the competition rules of EU law.

7.169 In 1996 on the basis of Article 633 of the Italian Code of Civil Procedure, Corsica Ferries applied to the Tribunale di Genova for orders enjoining the Genoa mooring group to pay a sum of LIT[144] 669,838,425, the La Spezia mooring group a sum of LIT 188,472,802, and, jointly and severally, the Ministry of Transport and Shipping a sum of LIT 858,311,227, each sum to be paid with interest. According to Corsica Ferries, such an order was justified because there was no legal cause for the payments it had made. It put forward two lines of argument in this connection: (a) first, the tariffs charged for mooring operations in the ports in point in the main proceedings bore no relation to the cost of the services actually provided to vessels by the mooring groups and, furthermore, varied from one port to another. This meant that there was an impediment both to the freedom to provide services, which is guaranteed in the maritime transport sector by Regulation 4055/86, and to the free movement of goods guaranteed by Article 30 of the TFEU; and (b) second, those payments had been imposed in breach of the Treaty's

---

143 Case C-266/96 [1998] ECR I-3949, ECLI:EU:C:1998:306. The Court was composed of Judges Gulmann (President of the Chamber) Wathelet (Rapporteur), Moitinho de Almeida, Puissochet and Sevón. Arts 30, 59, 85, 86 and 90(1) EC are now, very largely, Arts 36, 66, 101, 102 and 106(1) TFEU.

144 I.e. Italian lira.

competition rules. Not only were the tariffs the result of an agreement between associations of undertakings, prohibited by Article 101 of the TFEU, but also the Genoa and La Spezia mooring groups were abusing their dominant position in a substantial part of the common market, in breach of Article 102 of the Treaty, by charging unfair tariff rates, by preventing shipping companies from using their own qualified staff to carry out mooring operations, and by setting tariffs that varied from one port to another for identical services provided to identical vessels.

7.170 In support of its application for an order that Italy be made jointly and severally liable for the payment of the sums which it claims are owed to it, Corsica Ferries claimed that the State was liable because it did not intervene in order to bring to an end the breaches of EU law of which it considered itself a victim. The CJEU reviewed the legislation applicable to the case and found that it appeared that mooring services are governed by the Codice della Navigazione (the "Code"), the Regolamento per la Navigazione Marittima (the "regulation") and, for each port, by the provisions adopted by the competent local maritime authority. Under Articles 62 and 63 of the Code, the Port Harbour Master regulated and supervised vessels' entry into and departure from the port as well as their movements, anchorage and mooring, orders berthing and unmooring manoeuvres, if need be orders, on his own initiative, the manoeuvres specified to be carried out at the vessel's own expense, and lastly orders the mooring ropes to be cut in an extreme emergency. Under Article 116 of the Code, mooring operatives formed part of the personnel assigned to port services. The rules specifically applicable to them were contained in Chapter VI (Articles 208 to 214) of the regulation. Article 209 entrusted regulating of the mooring service to the Port Harbour Master, who was to ensure that it was properly run in accordance with the needs of the port and may, among others, set up a mooring group in ports where there is such a need. Lastly, Article 212 of the regulation provides that, in each port, tariffs relating to mooring services are to be fixed by the Head of the Maritime District. The specific legislation applicable in Genoa consists of Regulation 759 of 1 June 1953, adopted by the President of the Consorzio Autonomo del Portodi Genova (the Independent Consortium of the Port of Genoa), who set up the Genoa mooring group, and the Regulation on Shipping Services and Port Police adopted on 1 March 1972, Article 13 of which states:

> "use of the services of mooring operatives for the mooring and unmooring of vessels is optional … Nevertheless, where a vessel does not request the services of mooring operatives, mooring operations must be carried out solely by the crew of the vessel."

According to the national court, the second paragraph of that provision renders use of the services of the Genoa mooring group de facto compulsory. The rules specifically applicable to the port of La Spezia were contained in Decree No 20 of 16 July 1968 of the Head of the Maritime District of La Spezia. Article 1 of that decree set up a group of operators responsible for mooring operations. According to Article 2, that group

> "shall carry out berthing and unmooring services for vessels and ensure safety in the port. The service in question is compulsory for vessels with a gross registered tonnage of more than 500 tonnes. Vessels with a lower tonnage may carry out the manoeuvre in question using its own crew provided they do not hinder traffic and do not compromise either the safety of the port or staff. It is strictly prohibited to use any other operative not belonging to the above group of operatives to provide mooring services."

7.171 According to the order for reference to the CJEU, there is no legislative text determining the criteria to which the head of each maritime district must conform in fixing the tariffs for mooring services. Those tariffs are sometimes fixed after agreements have been reached between undertakings in the sector and are made enforceable by an administrative measure. According to the Genoa and La Spezia mooring groups, Italy and the Commission, however, account must be taken of Law No 160/89 of 5 May 1989, which provides, in Article 9(7), that the Minister for the Merchant Navy is to adopt the rules harmonising tariffs for port services and operations at national level, after consultation with the trade unions most representative in the sector at national level, the other sides of the industry and the companies concerned. The tariff restructuring thus provided for was in particular regulated by Circular No 8/1994 of 19 September 1994 of the Minister for the Merchant Navy, who determines the criteria to which the port authorities must conform in fixing tariffs. According to those parties, the tariffs were thus calculated on the basis of a formula the purpose of which is to apportion the charges connected with performance of the mooring service between the various classes of port users. For the purpose of applying the tariffs, users were allotted to different categories on the basis of the gross tonnage of the vessel, and may claim reductions for certain categories of vessel, such as car ferries, or reductions linked to the frequency of berthing. The level of the tariff, which was valid for two years, is calculated on the basis of projected overall turnover for each mooring group, which itself depends on the volume of traffic in the port. Before the decision of the port authority laying down the tariff for each port is adopted, those concerned, on both the supply and demand sides, may make known their point of view. According to the Tribunale di Genova, the Genoa and La Spezia mooring groups provided services to Corsica Ferries, which itself offers services falling under Regulation 4055/86, and those groups constitute undertakings, for the purposes of Article 106(1) of the TFEU, with exclusive rights in a substantial part of the internal market. Since it entertained doubts as to whether the nature of the exclusive rights, the compulsory nature of the service, the basis on which tariffs were drawn up and the amounts charged might constitute a barrier to intra-EU trade in goods and services and induce undertakings vested with those rights to abuse their dominant position to the detriment of trade between Member States as a result of the costs borne by the undertakings engaged in transport operations between Member States, the national court decided to stay proceedings and refer to the CJEU for a preliminary ruling on the following questions:

> "(1) Must Article 30 of the Treaty[145] be interpreted as precluding legislation and/or administrative practice in a Member State which debars shipping companies established in other Member States from berthing their vessels on entry to docks in the first-mentioned State, or unmooring those vessels on departure, unless they use the services provided by a local undertaking by virtue of its exclusive concession in respect of berthing and unmooring facilities, which entails paying to that undertaking dues which may not be commensurate with the actual cost of the services provided?
> (2) Does ... Regulation ... 4055/86 of 22 December 1986 in conjunction with Article 59 of the Treaty preclude the imposition in a Member State of a requirement whereby berthing services are obligatory and shipping companies established in another Member State are charged tariffs which are fixed not by law but merely by administrative discretion in respect of the arrival or departure of their vessels in or from the first-mentioned Member State?

---

145 Ed., this is now Art. 34 of the TFEU.

(3) Do Articles 3, 5, 90(1),[146] 85[147] and 86[148] of the Treaty, in conjunction, preclude legislation and/or administrative practice in a Member State which confers on an undertaking established in that State an exclusive right to provide berthing services such as to enable those services to be made compulsory, dues to be charged which may not be commensurate with the actual cost of the services provided, tariffs to be applied which have been determined by agreement and/or administrative discretion, and tariff conditions to be imposed which vary from one port to another, even for like services?"

7.172 The CJEU considered Question 1 first:

"29. By its first question the national court asks, essentially, whether Article 30 of the Treaty precludes legislation of a Member State which requires shipping companies which are established in other Member States and whose vessels make port stops in the first-mentioned State to use the services of mooring groups holding exclusive concessions, for a charge higher than the actual cost of the service provided. The national court asks whether, although not directly concerning goods, the legislation at issue in the main proceedings is contrary to Article 30 of the Treaty, inasmuch as its effect is to render transport more costly and therefore to impede imports of goods from other Member States.

30. It should be noted that, in the case in the main proceedings, the legislation applies without distinction to any vessel, Italian or otherwise, making a port stop in one of the ports in question. The requirement it lays down is that, for a charge, local mooring services holding an exclusive concession for berthing and unmooring are to be used. As far as any effects of that requirement on the free movement of goods are concerned, it must be observed that, on the one hand, essentially what is involved in this case is the provision of a maritime transport service concerning persons as well as goods. On the other hand, even if only the transport of goods were involved, the file on the case shows that, for a vessel, the price of mooring services represents less than 5% of port costs which, in total, represent 12 to 14% of the cost of transport, making up from 5 to 10% of the cost of transported products. The use of mooring services represents an additional cost for transported products of approximately 0.05%.

31. Consequently, legislation such as that at issue in the main proceedings makes no distinction according to the origin of the goods transported, its purpose is not to regulate trade in goods with other Member States and the restrictive effects which it might have on the free movement of goods are too uncertain and indirect for the obligation which it imposes to be regarded as being capable of hindering trade between Member States (Case C-379/92 Peralta [1994] ECR I-3453, paragraph 24, and Case C-96/94 Centro Servizi Spediporto [1995] ECR I-2883, paragraph 41).

32. The answer to the first question must therefore be that Article 30 of the EC Treaty does not preclude legislation of a Member State, such as that at issue in this case, which requires shipping companies which are established in other Member States and whose vessels make port stops in the first-mentioned Member State to have recourse to the services of local mooring groups holding exclusive concessions, for a charge higher than the actual cost of the service provided."

7.173 The CJEU then considered the third question:

"33. By its third question, which it is appropriate to examine before the second question in order to make the best possible use of the information concerning the factual and legal context given in the file, the national court asks, essentially, whether Articles 3, 5, 85,[149] 86[150] and

---

146 Ed., this is now Art. 106(1) of the TFEU.
147 Ed., this is now Art. 101 of the TFEU.
148 Ed., this is now Art. 102 of the TFEU.
149 Ed., Art. 101 of the TFEU.
150 Ed., Art. 102 of the TFEU.

90[151] of the Treaty preclude legislation in a Member State which confers on undertakings established in that State an exclusive right to provide mooring services, requires those services to be used for a charge higher than the actual cost of the services provided, and provides for tariffs that vary from one port to another for equivalent services.

34. The rules on competition laid down in the Treaty apply to the transport sector (Case C-185/91 Reiff [1993] ECR I-5801, paragraph 12, and Case C-153/93 Delta Schiffahrts- und Speditionsgesellschaft [1994] ECR I-2517, paragraph 12).

35. Articles [101] and [102] of the [TFEU] are, in themselves, concerned solely with the conduct of undertakings and not with laws or regulations adopted by Member States. However, it is settled law that Articles [101] and [102], read in conjunction with Article 5 of the [EC] Treaty, require the Member States not to introduce or maintain in force measures, even of a legislative or regulatory nature, which may render ineffective the competition rules applicable to undertakings (Centro ServiziSpediport, cited above, paragraph 20, and the case-law cited therein)."

7.174 The CJEU considered Articles 102 and 106 of the TFEU:

"36. The national court asks whether there is an abuse, on the part of the Genoa and La Spezia mooring groups, of their dominant position on a substantial part of the common market by virtue of the exclusive rights conferred upon them by the Italian public authorities.

37. There are three aspects to the abuse alleged in this case. It is said to reside in the grant of exclusive rights to local mooring groups, preventing shipping companies from using their own staff to carry out mooring operations, in the excessive nature of the price of the service, which bears no relation to the actual cost of the service provided, and in the fixing of tariffs that vary from port to port for equivalent services.

38. As regards the definition of the market in question, it appears from the order for reference that it consists in the performance on behalf of third persons of mooring services relating to container freight in the ports of Genoa and La Spezia. Having regard inter alia to the volume of traffic in those ports and their importance in intra-Community trade, those markets may be regarded as constituting a substantial part of the common market (Case C-179/90 Merci Convenzionali Porto di Genova [1991] ECR I-5889, paragraph 15, and Case C-163/96 Raso and Others [1998] ECR I-0000, paragraph 26).

39. As far as the existence of exclusive rights is concerned, it is settled law that an undertaking having a statutory monopoly in a substantial part of the common market may be regarded as having a dominant position within the meaning of Article [102 of the TFEU] (Case C-41/90 Höfner and Elser v Macrotron [1991] ECRI-1979, paragraph 28; Case C-260/89 ERT v DRP [1991] ECR I-2925, paragraph 31; Merci Convenzionali Porto di Genova, cited above, paragraph 14; and Raso and Others, cited above, paragraph 25).

40. Next, it should be pointed out that although merely creating a dominant position by granting exclusive rights within the meaning of Article [106(1) of the TFEU] is not in itself incompatible with Article [102 of the TFEU], a Member State is in breach of the prohibitions contained in those two provisions if the undertaking in question, merely by exercising the exclusive rights granted to it, is led to abuse its dominant position or if such rights are liable to create a situation in which that undertaking is led to commit such abuses (Case C-41/90 Höfner and Elser v Macrotron, cited above, paragraph 29; Case C-260/89 ERT v DRP, cited above, paragraph 37; Merci Convenzionali Porto di Genova, cited above, paragraph 17; Case C-323/93 Centre d'Insémination de la Crespelle [1994] ECR I-5077, paragraph 18; Raso and Others, cited above, paragraph 27).

41. It follows that a Member State may, without infringing Article [102] of the [TFEU], grant exclusive rights for the supply of mooring services in its ports to local mooring groups provided those groups do not abuse their dominant position or are not led necessarily to commit such an abuse.

---

151 Ed., Art. 106 of the TFEU.

42. In order to rebut the existence of such abuse, the Genoa and La Spezia mooring groups rely on Article [106(2) of the TFEU], which provides that undertakings entrusted with the operation of services of general economic interest are to be subject to the competition rules contained in the Treaty only in so far as their application does not obstruct the performance, in law or in fact, of the particular tasks assigned to them. Article [106(2) of the TFEU] further provides that, in order for it to apply, the development of trade must not be affected to such an extent as would be contrary to the interests of the Community.

43. They maintain that the tariffs applied are indispensable if a universal mooring service is to be maintained. On the one hand, the tariffs include a component corresponding to the additional cost of providing a universal mooring service. On the other hand, the differences in the tariffs from one port to another, which, according to the file, result from account being taken, when the tariffs are calculated, of corrective factors reflecting the influence of local circumstances – which would tend to indicate that the services provided are not equivalent – are justified by the characteristics of the service and the need to ensure universal coverage.

44. It must therefore be considered whether the derogation from the rules of the Treaty provided for in [Article 106(2) of the TFEU] may fall to be applied. To that end, it must be determined whether the mooring service can be regarded as a service of general economic interest within the meaning of that provision and, if so, first, whether performance of that particular task can be assured only through services for which the charge is higher than their actual cost and for which the tariff varies from one port to another, and, secondly, whether the development of trade is not affected to such an extent as would be contrary to the interests of the Community (see, to that effect, Case C-157/94 Commission v Netherlands [1997] ECR I-5699, paragraph 32).

45. It is evident from the file on the case in the main proceedings that mooring operations are of general economic interest, such interest having special characteristics, in relation to those of other economic activities, which is capable of bringing them within the scope of Article 90(2) of the Treaty. Mooring groups are obliged to provide at any time and to any user a universal mooring service, for reasons of safety in port waters. At all events, the Italian Republic could properly have considered that it was necessary, on grounds of public security, to confer on local groups of operators the exclusive right to provide a universal mooring service.

46. In those circumstances it is not incompatible with Articles [102 and 106(1) of the TFEU] to include in the price of the service a component designed to cover the cost of maintaining the universal mooring service, inasmuch as it corresponds to the supplementary cost occasioned by the special characteristics of that service, and to lay down for that service different tariffs on the basis of the particular characteristics of each port.

47. Consequently, since the mooring groups have in fact been entrusted by the Member State with managing a service of general economic interest within the meaning of Article [106(2) of the TFEU], and the other conditions for applying the derogation from application of the Treaty rules which is laid down in that provision are satisfied, legislation such as that at issue does not constitute an infringement of Article [102 of the TFEU], read in conjunction with Article [106(1)]."

7.175 The CJEU considered Articles 101 of the TFEU:

"The national court asked whether the process whereby the tariffs for the mooring services are fixed is compatible with Article 101 of the TFEU.

49. The Court has already held that Articles 5 and 85 are infringed where a Member State requires or favours the adoption of agreements, decisions or concerted practices contrary to Article 85 or reinforces their effects, or where it deprives its own rules of the character of legislation by delegating to private economic operators the responsibility for taking decisions affecting the economic sphere (*Centro Servizi Spediporto*, cited above, paragraph 21, and the case-law cited therein).

50. In that connection it must be pointed out, first, that the file on the case in the main proceedings does not reveal the existence of an agreement, decision or concerted practice within the meaning of Article 85 of the Treaty.
51. Although the mooring groups do constitute undertakings for the purposes of that provision, any agreement there may be between those groups at national level does not result in fixing a common price for all ports, since the tariff is calculated on the basis of a mathematical formula to which are applied various corrective factors linked to the characteristics of each port. Moreover, even if it were shown that the ports compete with each other in a single geographical market, which is presumed to be the case in the order for reference, it remains difficult to discern the restrictive effects of any agreement, inasmuch as exclusive rights are granted in each of the ports concerned and there is therefore no potential competitor to the local mooring group. Consequently, it is not evident from the file on the case in the main proceedings that there is an agreement between undertakings the purpose or effect of which is to restrict competition.
52. Nor, on the other hand, is it evident from the file that the Italian authorities have delegated their powers with respect to the fixing of tariffs to the Genoa and La Spezia mooring groups. In each of the ports concerned the tariffs for mooring services have been fixed by the local maritime authority, pursuant to Article 212 of the Regulation, on the basis of a general formula determined at national level by the public authorities after consultation, not only with the mooring groups concerned, but also with the representatives of users and shipping agents in the ports of Genoa and La Spezia. The participation of the mooring groups in the administrative procedure for drawing up the tariffs cannot be regarded as an agreement, decision or concerted practice between economic operators which the public authorities have required or favoured or the effects of which they have reinforced.

Accordingly, Article 101 of the TFEU does not preclude legislation such as that at issue in the main proceedings.

54. In the light of the foregoing considerations, the answer to be given to the third question must be that the combined provisions of Articles [5], 101, 102 and 106(1) of the Treaty do not preclude legislation of a Member State, such as that at issue in this case,

- which confers on undertakings established in that State an exclusive right to provide a mooring service,
- which requires the service to be used at a price which, in addition to the actual cost of the service provided, includes a supplement to cover maintenance of a universal mooring service, and
- which provides for tariffs that vary from one port to another in order to take into account each port's particular characteristics."

7.176 The CJEU considered Question 2:

"55. By its second question, the national court asks, essentially, whether the combined provisions of Regulation 4055/86 and Article 59 of the Treaty preclude legislation of a Member State from requiring shipping companies established in other Member States, when their vessels make a port stop in the first-mentioned Member State, to use, for a charge, the services of local mooring groups holding exclusive concessions.
56. According to settled case-law, Article 59 of the Treaty requires not only the elimination of all discrimination against a person providing services on the ground of his nationality but also the abolition of any restriction, even if it applies without distinction to nationals providing services and to those of other Member States, when that restriction is liable to prohibit or otherwise impede the activities of a provider of services established in another Member State where he lawfully provides similar services (Case C-76/90 Säger [1991] ECR I-4221, paragraph 12, and Case C-398/95 SETTG [1997] ECR I-3091, paragraph 16).
57. As the Advocate General pointed out at paragraph 35 of his Opinion, the impugned legislation would not appear to contain any overt or covert discrimination contrary to Article 59 of the Treaty and Article 9 of Regulation ... 4055/86.

58. On the one hand, in the Port of Genoa the obligation to use the mooring services provided by the Genoa mooring group applies to all shipping companies without distinction. On the other hand, in the port of La Spezia, all operators of vessels whose gross tonnage exceeds 500 must have recourse to the services of the La Spezia mooring group. A company such as Corsica Ferries, which operates car-ferries, is therefore subject to the same obligation to use the mooring services as Italian transport companies using vessels of equivalent size.

59. As a preliminary point it should be noted that, as far as any impediment to the freedom to provide mooring services is concerned, reference need merely be made to the Court's reasoning, earlier in this judgment, regarding the application of the derogation from the rules of the Treaty which is provided for in Article 90(2) of the Treaty, to conclude that such an impediment, if it exists, is not contrary to Article 59 of the Treaty since the conditions for application of Article 90(2) are satisfied.

60. With regard to the possible existence of a restriction on freedom to provide maritime transport services, it must be observed that the mooring service constitutes a technical nautical service which is essential to the maintenance of safety in port waters and has the characteristics of a public service (universality, continuity, satisfaction of public-interest requirements, regulation and supervision by the public authorities). Accordingly, provided that the price supplement in relation to the actual cost of the service does indeed correspond to the additional cost occasioned by the need to maintain a universal mooring service, the requirement to have recourse to a local mooring service, even if it were capable of constituting a hindrance or impediment to freedom to provide maritime transport services, could be justified, under Article 56 of the EC Treaty, by the considerations of public security relied on by the mooring groups, on the basis of which the national legislation on mooring was adopted.

61. Consequently, the answer to the second question must be that the provisions of Regulation … 4055/86 and Article 59 of the EC Treaty do not preclude legislation of a Member State, such as that at issue in this case, which requires shipping companies established in another Member State, when their vessels make port stops in the first Member State, to have recourse to the services which local mooring groups holding exclusive concessions supply for a charge. Such legislation, even if it constituted an impediment to freedom to provide maritime transport services, would, in fact, be justified by considerations of public security within the meaning of Article 56 of the EC Treaty."

7.177 Ultimately, the CJEU responded to the Tribunale di Genova:

"1. Article 30 of the EC Treaty does not preclude legislation of a Member State, such as that at issue in this case, which requires shipping companies which are established in other Member States and whose vessels make port stops in the first-mentioned Member State to have recourse to the services of local mooring groups holding exclusive concessions, for a charge higher than the actual cost of the service provided.

2. The combined provisions of Articles [5], 101, 102 and 106(1) of the TFEU do not preclude legislation of a Member State, such as that at issue in this case,

   – which confers on undertakings established in that State an exclusive right to provide a mooring service,
   – which requires the service to be used at a price which, in addition to the actual cost of the service provided, includes a supplement to cover maintenance of a universal mooring service, and
   – which provides for tariffs that vary from one port to another in order to take into account each port's particular characteristics.

3. The provisions of … Regulation … 4055/86 and Article 59 of the EC Treaty do not preclude legislation of a Member State, such as that at issue in this case, which requires shipping companies established in another Member State, when their vessels make port stops in the first Member State, to have recourse to the services which local mooring groups holding exclusive concessions supply for a charge. Such legislation, even if it constituted an impediment to freedom to provide maritime transport services, would, in fact, be justified by considerations of public security within the meaning of Article 56 of the EC Treaty."

2001: *Analir*

7.178 On 20 February 2001, the CJEU delivered an opinion in *Asociación Profesional de Empresas Navieras de Líneas Regulares (Analir) and Others v Administración General del Estado*.[152]

7.179 The Spanish Supreme Court referred for a preliminary ruling three questions on the interpretation of Articles 1, 2 and 4 of Regulation 3577/92. Those questions had been raised in four sets of proceedings between Asociación Profesional de Empresas Navieras de Líneas Regulares (Analir), Isleña de Navegación SA (Isnasa), Fletamientos de Baleares SA and Unión Sindical Obrera (USO) ("Analir and Others"), respectively, on the one hand, and Administración General del Estado, on the other, concerning applications by the applicants for annulment of Royal Decree No 1466/1997 of 19 September 1997 on the legal rules governing regular maritime cabotage lines and public-interest shipping ("Royal Decree No 1466") on the ground that it is contrary to EU legislation.

7.180 Article 7(4) of Spanish Law No 27/1992 of 24 November 1992 concerning State and Merchant Navy Ports (BOE No 283 of 25 November 1992, p. 39953) defines "public-interest shipping" as that which is regarded as necessary in order to provide essential maritime connections for the peninsula, between the peninsula and the non-peninsular Spanish territories, and between the latter territories. Furthermore, under that provision, it is for the government to determine which shipping is of public interest and to specify the means of ensuring that that interest is protected.

7.181 Article 4 of Royal Decree No 1466 stated:

"Pursuant to Article 7(4) in conjunction with Article 6(1)(h) of the Law concerning State and Merchant Navy Ports services on regular island cabotage lines, meaning services for the carriage of passengers or goods by sea between ports situated on the peninsula and the non-peninsular territories and between ports of those territories, in accordance with Article 2(1)(c) of Regulation (EEC) No 3577/92, are declared to be public-interest shipping.

The provision of regular shipping services of public interest shall be subject to prior administrative authorisation, the validity of which is conditional on the fulfilment of public service obligations imposed by the Directorate General of the Merchant Navy. Exceptionally, the competent administrative authorities may enter into public-interest contracts in order to ensure the existence of adequate services for the maintenance of maritime connections."

7.182 The administrative authorisation provided for in Royal Decree No 1466 is subject to two types of conditions. First, Article 6 of that decree, entitled "Conditions for authorisation", provides:

"Authorisation to operate a regular island cabotage line shall be issued subject to the following conditions:

(a) the applicant must be a shipowner or shipping company having no outstanding tax or social security debts;

(b) in the case of hiring or chartering, it must be shown that the owner or the charterer has no outstanding tax or social security debts;

...

(e) the undertaking which owns the ships assigned to the line must have no outstanding tax or social security debts;

---

152 Case C-205/99 [2001] ECR I-1271, ECLI:EU:C:2001:107. The court was composed of: Judges Rodríguez Iglesias (President), Gulmann and Wathelet (Presidents of Chambers), Edward, Jann, Sevón, Schintgen, Macken, Colneric, von Bahr and Timmermans (Rapporteur). The Advocate-General was AG Mischo.

(f) the applicant must, within the first 15 days of June and December of each year, renew the documents provided for under (a), (b) and (e) above, proving that there are no outstanding tax or social security debts;

...

1. Only the following may be regarded as public service obligations: conditions for authorisation to operate a regular line concerning the regularity and continuity of the service, the capacity to provide it, the manning of the vessel or vessels and, where appropriate, the ports to be served, the frequency of the service and where relevant the rates.

   The imposition of public service obligations must in any event be based on objective public-interest reasons which are duly justified by the need to ensure an adequate regular maritime transport service.

   In order to prevent distortion of competition the obligations must be imposed in such a way as not to discriminate between undertakings providing the same or similar services on lines which cover the same or similar routes.

2. Exceptionally, economic compensation may be granted for the public service obligations. The compensation may not discriminate in any way between similar services on lines which cover the same routes.

   The right to economic compensation in respect of the fulfilment of public service obligations may be afforded at the request of the party concerned, or by the Ministry of Public Works after a general call for tenders has been issued for the purpose of establishing services on a regular line with public service obligations.

   Where the person concerned requests that that right be afforded, the undertaking which seeks authorisation to operate a regular line must first demonstrate to the Directorate General of the Merchant Navy that that line would be profitable in itself if it were not subject to public service obligations.

   The undertaking making the request must automatically submit the relevant documentary proof at the same time as those which it must submit in order to obtain the authorisation.

   The Directorate General of the Merchant Navy shall base its assessment on, in particular, the level of competition which the requested line will provide for other existing lines and it shall also take account of the rates to be charged.

3. In addition to the public service obligations which are set out in Regulation (EEC) No 3577/92 and referred to in the authorisation, the Directorate General of the Merchant Navy may, in accordance with Article 83(2) of the Law concerning State and Merchant Navy Ports, impose on shipping undertakings providing cabotage services specific public service obligations concerning rescue, maritime safety, pollution control, health standards and other essential matters of public or social interest. This shall, where appropriate, entitle the undertakings concerned to receive appropriate economic compensation for the supplementary costs they have incurred."

7.183 Analir and Others brought separate actions, which were subsequently joined, before the Tribunal Supremo, which in this case is the court with jurisdiction at first and last instance, for annulment of Royal Decree No 1466. They submitted, in support of their claims, that Royal Decree No 1466 was inconsistent with Community law, in particular Regulation 3577/92.

7.184 Since it considered that the outcome of the proceedings before it depended on the interpretation of that regulation, the Tribunal Supremo decided to stay proceedings and to refer the following questions to the Court for a preliminary ruling:

"1. May Article 4, in conjunction with Article 1, of ... Regulation ... 3577/92 ... be interpreted as permitting the provision of island cabotage services by undertakings covering regular shipping lines to be made subject to prior administrative authorisation?

2. If so, may the grant and continuation of such administrative authorisation be made subject to conditions, such as having no outstanding tax or social security debts, other than those set out in Article 4(2) of the regulation?
3. May Article 4(1) of Regulation ... 3577/92 be interpreted as permitting public service obligations to be imposed on some shipping companies and public service contracts within the meaning of Article 1(3) of the regulation to be concluded with others at the same time for the same line or route, in order to ensure the same regular traffic to, from or between islands?"

7.185 The CJEU considered the first question:

"13. Analir and Others claim that the combined provisions of Articles 1 and 4 of Regulation ... 3577/92 do not permit the provision of island cabotage services to be made subject to prior administrative authorisation, as required by Royal Decree No 1466. In their submission, it is sufficient to indicate when the activity is first undertaken on the basis of a system of licences by category and of declaration procedures, without prejudice to the option for the administrative authorities to impose public service obligations.

14. They are supported by the Norwegian Government and the Commission, which consider that a system of prior administrative authorisation which, without any real connection with the public-service need, is generally applicable to any carriage between the peninsula and the Spanish islands and between those islands, does not meet the requirements of Articles 2 and 4 of Regulation ... 3577/92. The implementation of Article 4 requires, in the Commission's submission, that the existence of such a need be determined separately in each case and for each line.

15. On the other hand, the Spanish Government submits that the requirement of prior administrative authorisation does not constitute an obstacle to the liberalisation of maritime island cabotage. It has proved impossible in practice to provide detailed justification for each line, and on other economic markets which are also liberalised, such as telecommunications, the provision of services is still subject to an authorisation scheme. Extending by analogy the justifications which may be relied upon in connection with telecommunications to the field of maritime cabotage services, the fact that islands are involved should enable the Member States to impose universal service obligations by means of prior administrative authorisation.

16. The Spanish Government is supported by the Greek Government, which submits that it is precisely with the aim of protecting the public interest that Article 4 of Regulation ... 3577/92, which must be construed in the light of the generally liberal spirit of that regulation, provides for the possibility of imposing public service obligations by means of prior administrative authorisation.

17. The first point to be noted here is that, under Article 3(c), ... the activities of the Community are to include an internal market characterised, in particular, by the abolition, as between Member States, of obstacles to the free movement of services.

18. Under Article 61, ... freedom to provide services in the field of transport is to be governed by the provisions of the title of that treaty relating to transport, which include Article 84(2) of the EEC Treaty,...[153] which permits the Council of the European Union to lay down appropriate provisions for sea transport.

19. On the basis of Article 84(2) of the Treaty,[154] the Council adopted Regulation ... 3577/92, the aim of which is to implement freedom to provide services for maritime cabotage under the conditions and subject to the exceptions which it lays down.

20. To that end, Article 1 of that regulation clearly establishes the principle of freedom to provide maritime cabotage services within the Community. The conditions governing the application of the principle of freedom to provide services which is laid down inter alia in Article 59 of the EEC Treaty ... and Article 61 of the Treaty have thus been defined in the maritime cabotage sector.

---

153 Ed., now Art. 100(2) TFEU.
154 Ed., now Art. 100(2) TFEU.

21. It is settled case-law that freedom to provide services requires not only the elimination of all discrimination on grounds of nationality against providers of services who are established in another Member State, but also the abolition of any restriction, even if it applies without distinction to national providers of services and to those of other Member States, which is liable to prohibit, impede or render less attractive the activities of a provider of services established in another Member State where he lawfully provides similar services (see, in particular, Case C-76/90 Säger [1991] ECR I-4221, paragraph 12; Case C-43/93 Vander Elst [1994] ECR I-3803, paragraph 14; Case C-272/94 Guiot [1996] ECR I-1905, paragraph 10; Case C-266/96 Corsica Ferries France [1998] ECR I-3949, paragraph 56; and Joined Cases C-369/96 and C-376/96 Arblade and Others [1999] ECR I-8453, paragraph 33).

22. It is clear that national legislation, such as Article 4 of Royal Decree No 1466, which makes the provision of maritime cabotage services subject to prior administrative authorisation, is liable to impede or render less attractive the provision of those services and therefore constitutes a restriction on the freedom to provide them (see, to that effect, Vander Elst, paragraph 15; and Case C-355/98 Commission v Belgium [2000] ECR I-1221, paragraph 35).

23. However, the Spanish Government argues that Article 4 of Regulation ... 3577/92 permits Member States to impose public service obligations as a condition for the provision of maritime cabotage services and establish a prior administrative authorisation scheme to that end.

24. In that regard, it should be noted, first, that the wording of Article 4 of Regulation ... 3577/92 provides no indication as to whether a prior administrative authorisation scheme may be used as a means of imposing the public service obligations to which that article refers.

25. Second, it is important to note that freedom to provide services, as a fundamental principle of the Treaty, may be restricted only by rules which are justified by overriding reasons in the general interest and are applicable to all persons and undertakings pursuing an activity in the territory of the host Member State. Furthermore, in order to be so justified, the national legislation in question must be suitable for securing the attainment of the objective which it pursues and must not go beyond what is necessary in order to attain it (see, to that effect, Säger, paragraph 15; Case C-19/92 Kraus [1993] ECR I-1663, paragraph 32; Case C-55/94 Gebhard [1995] ECR I-4165, paragraph 37; and Guiot, paragraphs 11 and 13).

26. Accordingly, it is necessary to consider whether the establishment of a prior administrative authorisation scheme may be justified as a means of imposing public service obligations.

27. First, it cannot be denied that the objective pursued, namely to ensure the adequacy of regular maritime transport services to, from and between islands, is a legitimate public interest.

28. The possibility of imposing public service obligations for maritime cabotage with, and between, islands was expressly afforded by Article 4 of Regulation ... 3577/92. The Treaty, as amended by the Treaty of Amsterdam, also takes into account, in the conditions which it lays down, the particular nature of island regions, as is clear from the second paragraph of Article 158 EC and Article 299(2) EC. That particular nature was further referred to in Declaration No 30 on island regions, annexed to the Final Act of the Treaty of Amsterdam.

29. However, it cannot be inferred from those provisions that all maritime cabotage services with, or between, islands within a Member State must, by reason of the fact that islands are involved, be regarded as public services.

30. Second, the question thus arises of whether a prior administrative authorisation scheme is necessary having regard to the objective pursued.

31. The first point to note in that respect is that the purpose of imposing public service obligations is to ensure adequate regular transport services to, from and between islands, as the ninth recital in the preamble to Regulation ... 3577/92 states.

32. Furthermore, public service obligations were defined in Article 2(4) of that regulation as obligations which the Community shipowner in question, if he were considering his own commercial interest, would not assume or would not assume to the same extent or under the same conditions.

33. Moreover, the aim of the public service contract provided for in Article 4 of Regulation ... 3577/92 was expressly defined in Article 2(3) thereof as being to provide the public with adequate transport services.
34. It follows that the application of a prior administrative authorisation scheme as a means of imposing public service obligations presupposes that the competent national authorities have first been able to determine, for specific routes, that the regular transport services would be inadequate if their provision were left to market forces alone. In other words, it must be possible to demonstrate that there is a real public service need.
35. Second, for a prior administrative authorisation scheme to be justified, it must also be demonstrated that such a scheme is necessary in order to be able to impose public service obligations and that it is proportionate to the aim pursued, inasmuch as the same objective could not be attained by measures less restrictive of the freedom to provide services, in particular a system of declarations ex post facto (see, to that effect, Joined Cases C-163/94, C-165/94 and C-250/94 Sanz de Lera [1995] ECR I-4821, paragraphs 23 to 28).
36. It is possible that prior administrative authorisation is a sufficient and appropriate means of enabling the content of the public service obligations to be imposed on an individual shipowner to be specified, taking account of his particular circumstances, or of enabling a prior check to be made on his ability to fulfil such obligations.
37. However, such a scheme cannot render legitimate discretionary conduct on the part of the national authorities which is liable to negate the effectiveness of provisions of Community law, in particular those relating to a fundamental freedom such as that at issue in the main proceedings (see, to that effect, Joined Cases C-358/93 and C-416/93 Bordessa and Others [1995] ECR I-361, paragraph 25; and Sanz de Lera, paragraph 25).
38. Therefore, if a prior administrative authorisation scheme is to be justified even though it derogates from a fundamental freedom, it must, in any event, be based on objective, non-discriminatory criteria which are known in advance to the undertakings concerned, in such a way as to circumscribe the exercise of the national authorities' discretion, so that it is not used arbitrarily. Accordingly, the nature and the scope of the public service obligations to be imposed by means of a prior administrative authorisation scheme must be specified in advance to the undertakings concerned. Furthermore, all persons affected by a restrictive measure based on such a derogation must have a legal remedy available to them.
39. It is for the national court to consider and determine whether the prior administrative authorisation scheme at issue in the case before it satisfies those conditions and those criteria.
40. In the light of the foregoing, the answer to the first question must be that the combined provisions of Articles 1 and 4 of Regulation ... 3577/92 permit the provision of regular maritime cabotage services to, from and between islands to be made subject to prior administrative authorisation only if:

 – a real public service need arising from the inadequacy of the regular transport services under conditions of free competition can be demonstrated;
 – it is also demonstrated that that prior administrative authorisation scheme is necessary and proportionate to the aim pursued;
 – such a scheme is based on objective, non-discriminatory criteria which are known in advance to the undertakings concerned."

7.186 The second question was considered by the CJEU:

"41. By its second question, the national court asks, in the event of the first question being answered in the affirmative, whether the grant and continuation of prior administrative authorisation may be made subject to conditions, such as having no outstanding tax or social security debts, other than those set out in Article 4(2) of Regulation ... 3577/92.
42. Analir and Others, supported by the Norwegian Government, claim that the obligation of having no outstanding tax or social security debts has no specific connection with the maritime traffic which is the subject-matter of the prior administrative authorisation.

Furthermore, such an obligation does not fall within the public service obligations set out in Article 4(2) of that regulation. They infer that national legislation making the grant and continuation of prior administrative authorisation subject to conditions other than those set out in Regulation ... 3577/92 is a national measure which constitutes a new restriction on the freedom already in fact attained, within the meaning of Article 62 of the EEC Treaty (repealed by the Treaty of Amsterdam), and which is, accordingly, contrary to the EC Treaty.

43. The Spanish Government submits that the conditions relating to the absence of outstanding tax or social security debts set out in Article 6 of Royal Decree No 1466 constitute general conditions for the grant of prior administrative authorisation and are not 'public service obligations' within the meaning of Regulation ... 3577/92. Accordingly, in its submission, that national provision does not go beyond the requirements of Article 4(2) of the regulation and is thus compatible with Community law.

44. The Commission, for its part, submits that the conditions mentioned in Article 6 of Royal Decree No 1466 may be regarded as covered by the reference to 'capacity to provide the service' in Article 4(2) of Regulation ... 3577/92, which includes not only the economic capacity of the Community shipowner, but also his financial capacity.

45. The first point to be noted here is that it follows from the answer to the first question that the public service obligations imposed by Member States for certain maritime cabotage services by means of prior administrative authorisation may be compatible with Community law provided that certain conditions are satisfied.

46. The national court is essentially asking, by its second question, whether in such a case a Member State may, where it intends to impose public service obligations for maritime cabotage to, from and between islands, make authorisation relating to such a service subject to the condition that the shipowner have no outstanding tax or social security debts.

47. In that regard, it must be borne in mind that the public service obligations which may be imposed under Article 4(2) of Regulation ... 3577/92 relate to requirements concerning ports to be served, regularity, continuity, frequency, capacity to provide the service, rates to be charged and manning of the vessel. No condition according to which the shipowner must have no outstanding tax or social security debts is expressly mentioned among those requirements. Clearly, such a condition, taken in isolation, cannot itself be characterised as a public service obligation.

48. However, where public service obligations for maritime cabotage are imposed on Community shipowners by means of prior administrative authorisation, the checks carried out by a Member State in order to ascertain whether the shipowners have any outstanding tax or social security debts may be regarded as being a requirement coming within the notion of 'capacity to provide the service', as mentioned in Article 4(2) of the regulation.

49. Where a Community shipowner is subject to public service obligations, such as ensuring the regularity of the maritime cabotage service to be supplied, the fact that he is in a precarious financial position – of which failure to pay his tax or social security debts could be an indication – may show that he would not be capable, in the more or less long term, of providing the public services imposed on him.

50. It follows that the Member State may take account of the solvency of a Community shipowner who performs public service obligations in the field of maritime cabotage in order to assess that shipowner's financial capacity to supply the services which have been entrusted to him, by requiring that he have no outstanding tax or social security debts. It goes without saying that such a condition must be applied on a non-discriminatory basis.

51. Accordingly, the answer to the second question must be that Community law permits a Member State to include in the conditions for granting and maintaining prior administrative authorisation as a means of imposing public service obligations on a Community shipowner a condition enabling account to be taken of his solvency, such as the requirement that he have no outstanding tax or social security debts, thus giving the Member State the opportunity to check the shipowner's 'capacity to provide the service', provided that such a condition is applied on a non-discriminatory basis."

7.187 The third question was then considered by the CJEU:

"52. By its third question, the national court asks whether Article 4(1) of Regulation … 3577/92 is to be interpreted as permitting a Member State to impose public service obligations on some shipping companies and, at the same time, to conclude public service contracts within the meaning of Article 2(3) of the regulation with others for the same line or route, in order to ensure the same regular traffic to, from or between islands.

54. As regards this question, Analir and Others claim, essentially, that concluding a public service contract or imposing public service obligations on economic operators under Article 4 of Regulation … 3577/92 are alternative options available to the Member States, which cannot be exercised simultaneously. Having a 'public service contract' for certain lines whilst imposing 'public service obligations' on other economic operators serving the same lines is contradictory, and constitutes a distortion of free competition under the relevant Treaty provisions.

55. More specifically, Analir and Others submit that the operator which concludes a 'public service contract' with the competent authorities receives, unlike the other operators, specific subsidies in respect of the transport services provided. In view of the fact that, in addition, the operators which enter into such 'public service contracts' are either public operators or undertakings which formerly enjoyed monopolies, the resulting situation constitutes a breach of Article [106(1) of the TFEU] on the ground of discrimination and distortion of the rules of free competition.

56. On the other hand, the Spanish Government submits that the two methods by which maritime cabotage services may be carried out, namely the 'public service contract' and 'public service obligations', mentioned in Article 4 of Regulation … 3577/92, may be used concurrently. The two systems which make it possible to ensure the provision of the public service, namely the conclusion of a contract or the imposition of public service obligations on the shipowner, have very different purposes. According to the Spanish Government, the Member State imposes public service obligations in order to ensure a minimum provision of a specific public service. It could, where appropriate, supplement that regime by concluding a contract

…

59. The Commission considers that, in principle, there is nothing to prevent a Member State from deciding to impose public service obligations generally and from concluding a public service contract in respect of one or more lines subject to those obligations in order to ensure an adequate level of service. However, where the two methods are used at the same time, the Commission submits that the level of the public service obligations should be as low as possible in order not to create obstacles which might result in distortion of competition.

60. In that regard, it must be noted that Article 4(1) of Regulation … 3577/92 does not expressly indicate whether the two methods of performing the public service laid down in those provisions, namely the public service contract or the imposition of public service obligations on the shipowners, may be used by Member States at the same time or only as alternatives.

61. Furthermore, the two methods pursue the same objective, namely to ensure an adequate level of regular maritime transport services to, from and between islands, as stated in the ninth recital in the preamble to Regulation … 3577/92.

62. However, it is important to specify that those two methods differ both in nature and degree.

63. First, use of the contractual method enables the public authority to obtain an undertaking from the shipowner to provide the transport services stipulated in the contract. Second, the shipowner will generally be prepared to be bound by such stipulations only if the Member State agrees to grant him a quid pro quo, such as financial compensation.

64. On the other hand, where public service obligations are imposed in the absence of a contract, the shipowner remains generally free to withdraw from the provision of the transport services in question. It is only if he wishes to provide those services that he must comply with the obligations imposed. Moreover, that method could also be combined with a

scheme of financial compensation under the second subparagraph of Article 4(2) of Regulation ... 3577/92, as evidenced by the Spanish legislation at issue in the main proceedings.

65. It therefore follows from a comparison of the features of the two methods of performing the maritime cabotage service that the contract gives more guarantees to the State that that service will actually be provided. Furthermore, as the Spanish Government rightly pointed out, the contractual method makes it possible to ensure that, if the contract is terminated, the provider will continue to carry out the service until a new contract is concluded, assuming that such a guarantee will normally be obtained only by granting a quid pro quo.

66. In the light of the features of the two methods in question and their shared purpose, there is no reason why they should not be used concurrently in respect of one line or transport route in order to ensure a certain level of public service. For the reasons given by the Advocate General in points 109 to 111 of his Opinion, where the level of service attained, even after public service obligations have been imposed on the shipowners, is not regarded as adequate or where there are still specific gaps, complementary services could be provided by concluding a public service contract, as laid down in the Spanish legislation.

67. Therefore, although Regulation ... 3577/92, and more specifically Article 4 thereof, does not preclude national legislation such as that at issue in the main proceedings, which allows the public service contract method to be employed where the public service obligations imposed on the shipowner in respect of the regular maritime cabotage transport services on a certain line or route to, from and between islands have proved to be insufficient to ensure an adequate level of transport, such application of those two methods concurrently in a concrete case will be compatible with Community law only if a number of specific conditions are met.

68. In the first place, it is clear from paragraph 34 of this judgment that Member States may impose public service obligations on Community shipowners only if a real public service need can be demonstrated. The same must also be true of the conclusion of a public service contract. Any combination of the two methods in respect of one line or route would be justified only if the same condition were met.

69. Second, as is also clear from Article 4(1) and (2) of Regulation ... 3577/92, any application of the two methods concurrently must be on a non-discriminatory basis in respect of all [EU] shipowners.

70. Third, as an obstacle to the freedom to provide maritime cabotage services is involved, any application of the two methods concurrently must, if it is to be justified and compatible with Article 1 in conjunction with Article 4(1) and (2) of that regulation, be consistent with the principle of proportionality. In other words, the combination of the two methods of having those services performed must be such as to ensure an adequate level of the services and not have restrictive effects on the freedom to provide maritime cabotage services which would go beyond what is necessary in order to attain the objective pursued.

71. Accordingly, the answer to the third question must be that Article 4(1) of Regulation ... 3577/92 is to be interpreted as permitting a Member State to impose public service obligations on some shipping companies and, at the same time, to conclude public service contracts within the meaning of Article 2(3) of the regulation with others for the same line or route in order to ensure the same regular traffic to, from or between islands, provided that a real public service need can be demonstrated and in so far as that application of the two methods concurrently is on a non-discriminatory basis and is justified in relation to the public-interest objective pursued."

7.188 In summary, the CJEU therefore responded:

"1. The combined provisions of Article 1 and Article 4 of ... Regulation ... 3577/92 permit the provision of regular maritime cabotage services to, from and between islands to be made subject to prior administrative authorisation only if:

- a real public service need arising from the inadequacy of the regular transport services under conditions of free competition can be demonstrated;
- it is also demonstrated that that prior administrative authorisation scheme is necessary and proportionate to the aim pursued;
- such a scheme is based on objective, non-discriminatory criteria which are known in advance to the undertakings concerned.

2. Community law permits a Member State to include in the conditions for granting and maintaining prior administrative authorisation as a means of imposing public service obligations on a Community shipowner a condition enabling account to be taken of his solvency, such as the requirement that he have no outstanding tax or social security debts, thus giving the Member State the opportunity to check the shipowner's 'capacity to provide the service', provided that such a condition is applied on a non-discriminatory basis.

3. Article 4(1) of Regulation ... 3577/92 is to be interpreted as permitting a Member State to impose public service obligations on some shipping companies and, at the same time, to conclude public service contracts within the meaning of Article 2(3) of the regulation with others for the same line or route in order to ensure the same regular traffic to, from or between islands, provided that a real public service need can be demonstrated and in so far as that application of the two methods concurrently is on a non-discriminatory basis and is justified in relation to the public-interest objective pursued."

2002: *Commission v Italy*: disembarkation of passengers

7.189 The CJEU considered the issue of freedom to provide services further in *Commission v Italy*.[155] This case related to a charge payable by passengers embarking or disembarking at Genoa, Naples or Trieste when arriving from, or travelling to, ports in another State (whether Member State or a non-Member State). No such charges were payable in respect of cabotage services (i.e. services from other Italian ports).[156] The Commission challenged Italy.[157] Italy did not contest the Commission's case against it. The CJEU therefore dealt with the issue very briefly. In essence, it decided that, by having a tax applicable to passengers embarking and disembarking in Italian ports when arriving

---

155 Case C-295/00 [2002] ECR I-1737, ECLI:EU:C:2002:100. The judges were Judges Macken (President of the Chamber), Gulmann and Puissochet (Rapporteur), the Advocate-General was AG Alber. See Power [2002] ICLR N-83.

156 The CJEU recalled in its judgment: that Italian Law No 82/1963 of 9 February 1963 revising maritime taxes and duties (GURI No 52 of 23 February 1963, hereinafter Law No 82/1963) imposes a special tax on the embarkation or disembarkation of passengers in the ports of Genoa, Naples and Trieste. That tax, which varies in amount depending on the class of travel and destination, is in principle payable by all passengers. However, Article 32(d) of Law No 82/1963 exempts from that tax passengers travelling to or arriving from another national port. Since the amendment of Art. 224 of the Italian Navigation Code by Art. 7 of Decree-Law No 457 of 30 December 1997, converted into a statute by Law No 30/1998 of 27 February 1998 (GURI No 49 of 28 February 1998), which authorised vessels registered in a Member State other than Italy to operate between Italian ports, that exemption has applied to the latter vessels as well as to Italian vessels.

157 The Commission sought a declaration that, by maintaining in force a tax applicable to passengers embarking and disembarking in the ports of Genoa, Naples and Trieste (Italy) when arriving from or travelling to ports in another Member State or a third country, but not in the case of carriage between two ports located on Italian territory, the Italian Republic has failed to fulfil its obligations under Art. 1 of Reg. 4055/86.

from or travelling to ports in another Member State or a third country, but not in the case of carriage between two ports located on Italian territory, then Italy had failed to fulfil its obligations under Article 1 of Regulation 4055/86. The key part of the judgment stated:

> "9. It should be recalled that Regulation ... 4055/86, which was adopted on the basis of Article [100(2) of the TFEU], lays down measures for the application in the maritime transport sector of the principle of freedom to provide services laid down in Article [56 of the TFEU]. Moreover, the Court has decided to that effect by ruling that Article 1(1) of the regulation defines the beneficiaries of the freedom to provide maritime transport services between Member States and between Member States and third countries in terms which are substantially the same as those in Article [56] of the Treaty (Case C-381/93 *Commission v France* [1994] ECR I-5145, paragraph 10).
> 10. The freedom laid down by Article [56] of the Treaty precludes the application of any national legislation which has the effect of making the provision of services between Member States more difficult than the provision of services purely within one Member State (Commission v France, cited above, paragraph 17).
> 11. Consequently, the provision of maritime transport services between Member States cannot be subject to stricter conditions than those to which analogous provisions of services at domestic level are subject (Commission v France, cited above, paragraph 18).
> 12. Furthermore, it must be recalled that the question whether a Member State has failed to fulfil its obligations must be determined by reference to the situation prevailing in the Member State at the end of the period laid down in the reasoned opinion (see, in particular, Case C-147/00 Commission v France [2001] ECR I-2387, paragraph 26).
> 13. In the present case it is not disputed that the Italian Republic did not take the measures necessary to comply with the reasoned opinion within the period prescribed.
> 14. Accordingly, it must be held that, by maintaining in force a tax applicable to passengers embarking and disembarking in the ports of Genoa, Naples and Trieste when arriving from or travelling to ports in another Member State or a third country, but not in the case of carriage between two ports located on Italian territory, the Italian Republic has failed to fulfil its obligations under Article 1 of Regulation ... 4055/86."

7.190 The CJEU then declared that, by maintaining in force a tax applicable to passengers embarking and disembarking in the ports of Genoa, Naples and Trieste (Italy) when arriving from or travelling to ports in another Member State or a third country, but not in the case of carriage between two ports located on Italian territory, the Italian Republic has failed to fulfil its obligations under Article 1 of Regulation 4055/86.

2002: *Geha Naftiliaki EPE and Others v NPDD Limeniko Tameio DOD/SOU and Elliniko Dimosio*: port charges

7.191 *Geha Naftiliaki EPE and Others v NPDD Limeniko Tameio DOD/SOU and Elliniko Dimosio*[158] also concerned port charges. It involved a preliminary reference to the CJEU from a Greek court on the meaning of Article 1 of Regulation 4055/86. The case arose out of proceedings before the Greek courts on the setting, under Greek legislation,

---

158 Case C-435/00 [2002] ECR I-10615, ECLI:EU:C:2002:661. The judges were Judges Puissochet (Rapporteur and President of the Chamber), Gulmann, Macken, Colneric and Cunha Rodrigues. The Advocate-General was AG Alber. On the case, see Chuah, "*GEHA Naftiliaki EPE and Others v NPDD Limeniko Tamio Dodekanisou*. Case C-435/00, CJEU, 14 November 2002. Harbour dues and the freedom to provide services" [2003] 9(2) JIML 153.

of higher harbour dues for passengers travelling to third countries.[159] In essence, the CJEU stated Article 1 of Regulation 4055/86 does not permit the imposition, for journeys to ports in third countries, of harbour dues that vary according to criteria relating to the distance of those ports or their geographical location if the difference in the dues is not objectively justified by differences in the way passengers are treated on account of their destination or the place from which they have come.

7.192 The CJEU began by reviewing the facts at issue. Geha Naftiliaki EPE and Total Scope NE were the respective owners of the hydrofoils *Fl. Marianna* and *Fl. Zeus*. Messrs Anastasios Charalambis, Sarlis, Kattidenios, Antonios Charalambis and Dimitrakopoulos were co-owners of the hydrofoil *Iviskos*, the shipping agent for which was Charalambis Bros OE. The three vessels were used for day excursions from the port of Rhodes to Turkey and back. In June 1996, they carried 4,067 day-trippers and 3,703 transit passengers. By way of an assessment on 1 August 1996, the Dodecanese Harbour Fund found that there was a shortfall in the harbour dues payable by, amongst others, Mr Georgiou, representing Geha Naftiliaki EPE and Total Scope NE, and Charalambis Bros OE. That finding was approved on 5 August 1996 by the regional director for the Dodecanese. By the action brought before the national court, the applicants in the main proceedings requested that these decisions be annulled and that certain sums paid in harbour dues be refunded. In support of their action, they submitted that the amounts of the harbour dues at issue in the main proceedings were calculated unlawfully. They took the view that the harbour dues should have been calculated on the basis of Article 6(2)(A) of Law No 2399/1996, that is to say at 5% on the price of the ticket, and not on the basis of Article 6(2)(B)(a) of that Law, that is to say at GRD 5,000 for each passenger, since the vessels

---

159 The CJEU recalled in its judgment: "4 Article 6 of Law No 2399/1996 (FEK, A 90), in the version in force when the measures contested in the main proceedings were adopted (hereinafter 'Law No 2399/1996'), provides as follows: '1. Every passenger who boards a means of marine transport for a destination within Greece or abroad shall be charged special dues in favour of the public body administering and operating the port of embarkation, for the modernisation and improvement of harbour works and facilities, for the use of the port and for other connected objectives relating to improvement of the service to the travelling public. 2. The dues shall consist of a percentage increase in the price of the ticket or a fixed sum in drachmas, depending on the passenger's port of destination, the kind of journey in accordance with the class of vessel and so forth, and shall be determined as follows: A. For passengers of every kind of passenger vessel, passenger/car vessel and hydrofoil on domestic routes, 5% on the price of tickets. B. For passengers of passenger and passenger/car vessels flying the Greek or a foreign flag on international routes: (a) fixed dues of GRD 5 000 for each passenger with a destination of any port of a foreign country, with the exception of the countries of the European Union, Cyprus, Albania, Russia, Ukraine, Moldova and Georgia on the Black Sea; ... (e) 30% of the revenue from the fixed dues which are provided for in the preceding subparagraphs of this paragraph shall be paid by the harbour funds concerned to the Merchant Seamen's Fund in accordance with the procedures laid down in the relevant provisions applicable to that fund. C. For passengers who partake in tourist trips (cruises) on tourist passenger vessels (cruise ships) flying the Greek or a foreign flag: (a) fixed dues of GRD 50 for each passenger who partakes in a day trip between Greek ports, for every port at which the vessel calls. If the day trip also extends to a port abroad, the fixed dues provided for in paragraph B(a), (b) and (c) above shall, as the case may be, be paid at the last port. ... 4. The dues shall be indicated on the tickets and their collection shall be the responsibility of the persons who issue the tickets, that is to say shipping agencies, tourist bureaux and similar undertakings. The sum collected in respect of each calendar month must be deposited by the persons responsible for collection, within the first 10 days of the following month, in the special account for the public body administering and operating the port entitled to that sum, which bears the sole reference 'Execution of works serving the travelling public' and is held at the Bank of Greece, together with a return indicating the number of tickets issued for each class and the sum of money due. Those sums shall be allocated exclusively to works serving passengers. 5. The undertakings responsible for collection shall be jointly and severally liable with the passengers for payment of the dues in full. ... 6. Sums owing by way of harbour dues shall be assessed by act of the board of the public body administering and operating the port."

were chartered under a full charter by tourist agencies for the purpose of day excursions from Rhodes to Turkey and back, and the final destination of those vessels was Rhodes, a domestic port, and not Turkey. The applicants in the main proceedings also contended that hydrofoils were not subject to the dues provided for in Article 6(2)(B)(a) of Law No 2399/1996, because they are not specifically referred to in that provision, but to the dues provided for in Article 6(2)(A) of that Law. They claimed that calculating harbour dues by reference to the vessel's destination gives rise to discrimination not only against them but also against passengers. In their submission that discrimination is prohibited by Greece's international obligations, they argued that it was above all, incompatible with Article 56 of the TFEU, Article 62 of the EEC Treaty (repealed by the Treaty of Amsterdam) and Article 100 of the TFEU, and with Regulation 4055/86. The CJEU stated:

"12. The national court takes the view that the amount of harbour dues found owing under the assessment of 1 August 1996 by the Dodecanese Harbour Fund was lawfully calculated in accordance with Article 6(2)(B)(a) of Law No 2399/1996 because Article 6(2)(C)(a) of that Law is applicable in the main proceedings inasmuch as they relate to day trips.
13. The national court considers that it was correct to apply the dues provided for in Article 6(2)(B)(a) of Law No 2399/1996 to passengers transported by the hydrofoils Fl. Marianna, Fl. Zeus and Iviskos.
14. It furthermore points out that the harbour dues in question in the main proceedings are collected for the use of ports and for the modernisation and improvement of harbour facilities. The dues are levied in return for a specific service provided to vessels which call at the ports and to their passengers on the occasion of the use of those facilities, and they are paid to the public body administering and operating the port.
15. The national court observes that Regulation ... 4055/86 applies the principle of freedom to provide services to maritime transport between Member States and between Member States and third countries, with effect from 1 January 1987.
16. Taking the view that application of that regulation to the main proceedings gives rise to difficulties, the Diikitiko Protodikio Rodou has referred the following questions to the Court for a preliminary ruling:

'(1) Is Article 1 of Council Regulation ... 4055/86 to be interpreted as prohibiting national legislation of a Member State from imposing restrictions in respect of the provision of maritime transport services between Member States and third countries generally, even if those restrictions are imposed without distinction on all vessels, whether they are used by its own nationals providing services or by nationals of other Member States, and on all passengers irrespective of nationality, or is it to be interpreted as prohibiting national legislation of a Member State from introducing restrictions only in respect of the provision of services between another Member State and a third country, reserving in that way more favourable treatment to domestic carriers who provide maritime transport to third countries compared with carriers who are nationals of the other Member States?
(2) May a Member State impose different (higher) harbour dues for the passengers of vessels which call at, or have as their final destination, a port of a third (non-European Union) country than the dues which are imposed on passengers whose destinations are domestic ports or ports in the other Member States of the European Union, even if those dues in both the above cases are imposed on all passengers irrespective of their nationality or that of the vessels, or does a provision of that kind constitute a restriction on the freedom to transport passengers to third countries because the higher dues might have an effect on the choice of routes, so that that provision is inconsistent with Article 1 of Regulation ... 4055/86?
(3) If the answer is in the negative, is it possible for the harbour dues which are imposed on passengers whose destinations are ports of third countries to be differentiated still

further, according to the third country, on the basis of the criterion of the distance of the ports or their geographical location, or is a national legislative provision of that kind also contrary to the abovementioned regulation, because it constitutes discrimination as regards maritime transport to a particular third country (or particular third countries) and therefore a restriction on maritime transport provided to that country (or those countries)?'

The first question

17. By its first question, the national court is essentially asking whether Article 1 of Regulation ... 4055/86 precludes a Member State from imposing, by virtue of national law, any restriction on the supply of services in the area of maritime transport between Member States and third countries, or whether that provision prohibits only restrictions that discriminate between domestic carriers and carriers who are nationals of other Member States engaging in maritime transport to third countries.

18. The Dodecanese Harbour Fund states that the harbour dues at issue in the main proceedings are payable not by maritime transport companies but by the passengers whom they carry and that they therefore do not fall within the scope of Regulation ... 4055/86. It claims that the harbour dues are intended to cover construction and maintenance expenses of harbour facilities and the provision of harbour services in general. Accordingly, they constitute fees that are compatible with Article [97 of the TFEU], and their validity cannot be called into question by a provision of secondary [EU] law such as Article 1 of Regulation ... 4055/86.

19. However, as the Commission points out, increasing harbour dues affects the price of the journey in a direct and mechanical way, so that a difference in the fees borne by passengers automatically affects the costs of the journey. The Court has held that the application of harbour charges which differ according to whether a journey is undertaken within one Member State or between Member States constitutes an infringement of the principle of the freedom to provide services, which is prohibited under Regulation ... 4055/86 (see Case C-381/93 Commission v France [1994] ECR I-5145, paragraph 21, and, in regard to airport taxes, Case C-70/99 Commission v Portugal [2001] ECR I-4845).

20. Since Regulation ... 4055/86 has rendered applicable to the sphere of maritime transport between Member States the totality of the Treaty rules governing the freedom to provide services (see Commission v France, cited above, paragraph 13), it precludes the application of any national legislation whose effect is to make the provision of services between Member States more difficult than that of purely domestic services within a Member State, unless that legislation is justified by compelling reasons of public interest and the measures enacted thereby are necessary and proportionate (see Commission v Portugal, cited above, paragraph 28).

21. Since Article 1(1) of Regulation ... 4055/86 has extended the principle of the freedom to provide services as regards intra-Community traffic to traffic between a Member State and a third country, the rules established in relation to the former must be applied to the latter.

22. Consequently, the provision of maritime transport services between the port of Rhodes and a Turkish port cannot, in the absence of objective justification (see Commission v France, cited above, paragraph 16), be subject to more onerous conditions than those to which the provision of comparable services between the port of Rhodes and ports in Greece or other Member States are subject.

23. With regard to Article [97 of the TFEU], on which the Dodecanese Harbour Fund has relied, that provision in no way precludes the application of Regulation ... 4055/86. Article [97 of the TFEU] permits the collection by the carrier, when frontiers are crossed, of charges or dues taking into account 'the costs actually incurred thereby'. The Harbour Fund has not demonstrated that those costs differ according to destination in the same proportions as the harbour dues at issue in the main proceedings.

24. The reply to the first question must therefore be that Article 1 of Regulation ... 4055/86 precludes the application in a Member State of different harbour dues for domestic or intra-Community traffic and traffic between a Member State and a third country if that difference is not objectively justified.

The second question

25. By its second question the national court is essentially asking whether, in the light of Article 1 of Regulation ... 4055/86, a Member State may impose on passengers of vessels that call at or whose final destination is a port in a third country harbour dues different from those imposed on passengers of vessels whose destination is domestic or in another Member State, where those dues apply irrespective of the nationality of the passengers or of the flag flown by the vessels.

26. Having regard to the considerations set out at paragraphs 19 to 24 of this judgment, the reply to this question must be that the imposition on passengers of vessels that call at or whose final destination is a port in a third country of different harbour dues from those imposed on passengers of vessels whose destination is domestic or in another Member State, without there being any correlation between that difference and the cost of the harbour services enjoyed by those categories of passengers, amounts to a restriction on the freedom to provide services contrary to Article 1 of Regulation ... 4055/86.

The third question

27. By its third question, the national court is essentially asking whether Article 1 of Regulation ... 4055/86 permits the imposition, for journeys to ports in third countries, of harbour dues that vary according to criteria relating to the distance of those ports or their geographical location.

28. A criterion based on the distance or geographical location of the port of destination cannot in itself justify the imposition of different harbour dues. Such a difference may be justified only where there are objective differences in the services provided to passengers by the carriers (see to that effect Commission v France, cited above, paragraph 16, and Commission v Portugal, cited above, paragraph 36).

29. The reply to the third question must therefore be that Article 1 of Regulation ... 4055/86 does not permit the imposition, for journeys to ports in third countries, of harbour dues that vary according to criteria relating to the distance of those ports or their geographical location if the difference in the dues is not objectively justified by differences in the way passengers are treated on account of their destination or the place from which they have come ...

1. Article 1 of ... Regulation ... 4055/86 precludes the application in a Member State of different harbour dues for domestic or intra-[EU] traffic and traffic between a Member State and a third country if that difference is not objectively justified.

2. The imposition on passengers of vessels that call at or whose final destination is a port in a third country of different harbour dues from those imposed on passengers of vessels whose destination is domestic or in another Member State, without there being any correlation between that difference and the cost of the harbour services enjoyed by those categories of passengers, amounts to a restriction on the freedom to provide services contrary to Article 1 of Regulation ... 4055/86.

3. Article 1 of Regulation ... 4055/86 does not permit the imposition, for journeys to ports in third countries, of harbour dues that vary according to criteria relating to the distance of those ports or their geographical location if the difference in the dues is not objectively justified by differences in the way passengers are treated on account of their destination or the place from which they have come."

FREEDOM TO PROVIDE SERVICES

2002: *Inspecteur van de Belastingdienst Douane, district Rotterdam v Sea-Land Service Inc. and Nedlloyd Lijnen BV*

7.193 The CJEU delivered an interesting judgment in *Inspecteur van de Belastingdienst Douane, district Rotterdam v Sea-Land Service Inc. and Nedlloyd Lijnen BV*[160] on charges for vessel traffic services.

7.194 The CJEU was asked four questions by way of Article 267 of the TFEU preliminary reference on Articles 52, 56 and 107 of the TFEU and Regulation 4055/86. Those questions were raised in two proceedings between the Inspecteur van de Belastingdienst Douane, Rotterdam district (the "Inspector") and Sea-Land Service Inc. ("Sea-Land"), on the one hand, and Nedlloyd Lijnen BV ("Nedlloyd"), on the other, with respect to payment of a charge for vessel traffic services.

7.195 The national legislation at issue provided, according to the CJEU:

> "8. The Scheepvaartverkeerswet (Shipping Act), as amended by the law of 7 July 1994 (Staatsblad 1994, No 585, hereinafter the SVW), which entered into force on 1 October 1995, provides, in the framework of the vessel traffic services system (verkeersbegeleidingssysteem, hereinafter the VTS system), for the introduction of a tariff for those services (hereinafter the VTS tariff). Previously, the costs of those services were covered by dues for pilotage, a service which was privatised in the Netherlands in 1995. At the relevant time, the VTS tariff was paid only by sea-going vessels.
>
> 9. Article 1(1)(i) of the SVW defines vessel traffic services as the bringing about and maintenance of safe and smooth shipping traffic by means of a system of personnel and infrastructural facilities on a systematic and interactive basis.
>
> 10. Pursuant to the first paragraph of Article 15c of the SVW, the master, owner or bareboat charterer of a ship coming under the VTS system is required to pay the VTS tariff and to provide the information necessary to determine its amount.
>
> 11. Article 15d of the SVW states:
>
>> 1. The VTS tariff serves as payment for vessel traffic services rendered by the State, in so far as those services constitute an individual provision of services.
>> 2. The tariff referred to in paragraph 1 shall be paid to the State. An administrative decree shall determine the shipping lanes to which the tariff applies, the criteria for applying that tariff and derogations.
>> 3. The tariff referred to in paragraph 1 shall be set by ministerial decree. This shall also define the rules relating to collection and methods of payment.
>
> 12. The provisions of Article 15d of the SVW were implemented by the Besluit verkeersbegeleidingstarieven scheepvaartverkeer (Decree on vessel traffic services tariffs for shipping traffic) of 4 November 1994 (Staatsblad 1994, No 807, hereinafter the BVS). Pursuant to Article 2(1) of the BVS, the VTS tariff, set by ministerial decree, is payable for navigation of a sea-going vessel in the following areas:
>
>> (a) Eems;
>> (b) Den Helder;
>> (c) Noordzeekanaal;
>> (d) Nieuwe Waterweg; and
>> (e) Westerschelde.

---

160 Cases C-430/99 and 431/99 [2002] ECR I-5235, ECLI:EU:C:2002:364. The Chamber was composed of Judges Macken (President of the Chamber) as well as Judges Gulmann (Rapporteur), Puissochet, Schintgen and Cunha Rodrigues. The Advocate-General was AG Alber.

13. Under Article 4(1) of the BVS, the basis for and amount of the VTS tariff are determined according to the length of the ship, rounded up to the whole metre, with only whole metres being taken into consideration.
14. Under Article 5(1) of the BVS, the VTS tariff is not payable for ships belonging to the following categories:

  (a) ships whose length does not exceed 41 metres;
  (b) Netherlands warships;
  (c) other ships owned or used by the State;
  (d) warships of countries other than the Netherlands, where that has been agreed with the flag State of the ships concerned;
  (e) ships coming from a port, an anchorage or a mooring in an area subject to the tariff which leave the channel in order to navigate at sea and then return to the point of departure by the same channel;
  (f) ships which come into a port, an anchorage or a mooring in the Netherlands without carrying out an economic activity in that connection.

15. The third paragraph of Article 15d of the SVW was implemented by the Regeling verkeersbegeleidingstarieven scheepvaartverkeer (Regulation on vessel traffic services tariffs for shipping traffic) of 14 September 1995 (Nederlandse Staatscourant 1995, No 8). It provides that a tariff of NLG 250 is payable for ships of between 41 and 100 metres in length, while each additional metre entails a supplementary tariff of NLG 17, with a maximum of NLG 2 800 for ships whose length is equal to or greater than 250 metres."

7.196 The CJEU recalled the factual background. The Inspector issued invoices to Sea-Land (a United States company) and to Nedlloyd (a Dutch company) for collection of the VTS tariff. The two shipping companies objected to those invoices. The Inspector rejected those objections. The Arrondissementsrechtbank (District Court) in Rotterdam ruled that the actions brought against those decisions were well founded and, accordingly, annulled them. The Inspector appealed against those judgments to the Raad van State. The Raad van State decided to stay proceedings and to submit to the Court for a preliminary ruling the following questions, set out in identical terms in the two main proceedings:

"1. (a) Does a system such as VTS, in so far as it provides for mandatory participation in vessel traffic services, constitute an obstacle to freedom to provide services for the purposes of Regulation ... 4055/86 in conjunction with Article [56] ... of the [TFEU]?
   (b) If not, is the position otherwise if participants in the system are charged for services provided?
   (c) Must Question 1(b) be answered differently if that charge is levied on shipping whose participation in the system is mandatory, but not on other users, such as inland waterway or sea-going vessels the length of which does not exceed 41 metres?
2. (a) If a system such as VTS and its associated tariff constitute an obstacle to freedom to provide services, does that obstacle come under the exceptions in Article [52] ... of the [TFEU] for provisions justified on grounds of public security?
   (b) Is it material to the reply to Question 2(a) whether the tariff is greater than the actual cost of the service provided to a given ship?
3. If a system such as VTS and its associated tariff constitute an obstacle to freedom to provide services, and if that obstacle is not justified under Article [52] ... of the [TFEU], can it be justified either because it is merely a non-discriminatory selling arrangement, as referred to in Keck and Mithouard, or because it fulfils the conditions which the Court has laid down in other judgments, in particular in Gebhard?

4. (a) Must a system of a Member State such as VTS be deemed to constitute aid within the meaning of Article [107(1) of the TFEU] ... inasmuch as it exempts certain categories of participants in that system, in particular inland waterway vessels, from the requirement to pay the tariff?
   (b) If so, does that aid come within the prohibition laid down in that provision?
   (c) If Question 4(b) must also be answered affirmatively, does the classification as aid prohibited under [EU] law also have consequences under [EU] law for the tariff which participants, apart from those exempted, are required to pay?"

7.197 The CJEU then dealt with these questions in the following terms:

"The first three questions

24. By its first three questions, the national court is essentially asking whether Regulation ... 4055/86, in conjunction with Articles [52 and 56] of the Treaty, precludes a vessel traffic services system such as the VTS system at issue, which requires payment of a tariff by seagoing vessels longer than 41 metres which participate in that system on a mandatory basis, while other vessels, such as inland waterway vessels, are exempt from that tariff.
25. First of all, as regards the matters covered by Regulation ... 4055/86, the wording of Article 1(1) makes it clear that it applies to maritime transport services between the Member States and between the latter and third countries.
26. As regards the persons covered by Regulation ... 4055/86, under Articles 1(1) and (2), freedom to provide maritime transport services applies to nationals of Member States who are established in a Member State other than that of the person for whom the services are intended, to nationals of Member States established outside the Community and to shipping companies established outside the Community and controlled by nationals of a Member State, if their vessels are registered in that Member State in accordance with its legislation.
27. Article [54] of the [TFEU] ... which, in accordance with Article 1(3) of Regulation ... 4055/86, applies to the matters covered by that regulation, provides, in its first paragraph, that companies or firms formed in accordance with the laws of a Member State and having their registered office, central administration or principal place of business within the Community are to be treated in the same way as natural persons who are nationals of Member States.
28. It is for the national court to determine whether the situations at issue in the main proceedings do in fact fall within the scope of Regulation ... 4055/86 as set out in paragraphs 25 and 26 of the present judgment.
29. The arguments which follow are based on the premise that such is in fact the case, if only for one of the abovementioned situations.
30. Regulation ... 4055/86, adopted on the basis of Article [100(2)] of the [TFEU], lays down measures for the application in the maritime transport sector of the principle of freedom to provide services laid down in Article [56] of that Treaty. Moreover, the Court held to that effect by ruling that Article 1(1) of that regulation defines the beneficiaries of freedom to provide maritime transport services between Member States and between Member States and third countries in terms which are substantially the same as those in Article [56] of the Treaty (Case C-381/93 Commission v France [1994] ECR I-5145, paragraph 10).
31. Moreover, it follows from Articles 1(3) and 8 of Regulation ... 4055/86 that the regulation makes applicable to the matters covered by the regulation the whole of the Treaty rules relating to freedom to provide services (see, to that effect, Commission v France, paragraphs 11 to 13).
32. It is settled case-law that freedom to provide services, as referred to in Article [56] of the [TFEU], requires not only the elimination of all discrimination on grounds of nationality against providers of services who are established in another Member State, but also the abolition of any restriction, even if it applies without distinction to national providers of services and to those of other Member States, which is liable to prohibit, impede or render less attractive the activities of a provider of services established in another Member State

where he lawfully provides similar services (see, inter alia, Case C-266/96 Corsica Ferries France [1998] ECR I-3949, paragraph 56; Joined Cases C-369/96 and C-376/96 Arblade and Others [1999] ECR I-8453, paragraph 33; and Case C-205/99 Analir and Others [2001] ECR I-1271, paragraph 21). Pursuant to that rule, freedom to provide services may also be relied on by an undertaking as against the State in which it is established, if the services are provided for persons established in another Member State (see, inter alia, Commission v France, cited above, paragraph 14, and Case C-224/97 Ciola [1999] ECR I-2517, paragraph 11).

33. It must be held that the VTS system, in requiring payment of a tariff by sea-going vessels longer than 41 metres and exempting inland waterway vessels, whatever their national flag and the nationality of the companies which operate them, does not constitute discrimination based directly on nationality.

34. Sea-Land and Nedlloyd, supported by the Commission, claim that the VTS system indirectly discriminates against them on the grounds of nationality, since the overwhelming majority of inland waterway traffic, which is exempt from the VTS tariff, takes place under the Netherlands flag. Ships flying the flag of a Member State are generally operated by national economic operators, whereas shipping companies from other Member States as a rule do not operate vessels registered in the former State.

35. Those arguments cannot be upheld.

36. While it is true that Article [56] and the third paragraph of Article [57] of ... Treaty ... prohibit all forms of disguised discrimination which, although based on criteria which appear to be neutral, in practice lead to the same result (see, inter alia, Joined Cases 62/81 and 63/81 Seco v EVI [1982] ECR 223, paragraph 8), it is also true that a difference of treatment cannot constitute discrimination unless the circumstances in question are comparable (see, inter alia, Case C-479/93 Francovich [1995] ECR I-3843, paragraph 23, and Case C-156/98 Germany v Commission [2000] ECR I-6857, paragraph 84).

37. As is apparent from the orders for reference, there are in this case objective differences between sea-going vessels longer than 41 metres and inland waterway vessels, in particular as concerns their respective markets – differences which reveal, moreover, that those two categories of means of transport are not comparable.

38. None the less, the VTS system at issue in the main proceedings, in that it requires the payment of a tariff by sea-going vessels longer than 41 metres, is liable to impede or render less attractive the provision of those services and therefore constitutes a restriction on their free circulation (see, to that effect, Analir, cited above, paragraph 22).

39. It is important to note that freedom to provide services, as a fundamental principle of the Treaty, may be restricted only by rules which are justified by overriding reasons in the general interest and are applicable to all persons or undertakings pursuing an activity in the territory of the host Member State. Furthermore, in order to be so justified, the national legislation in question must be suitable for securing the attainment of the objective which it pursues and must not go beyond what is necessary in order to attain it (see, to that effect, Analir, paragraph 25).

40. First, as noted above, the VTS system is not applied in a discriminatory manner.

41. Next, with regard to the question whether there are overriding reasons based on the general interest which may justify the restriction on freedom to provide services resulting from that system, it must be remembered that the protection of public security is one of the reasons which may, under Article [52(1)] of the Treaty, justify restrictions resulting from special treatment for foreign nationals. Protection of public security is therefore, in principle, also capable of justifying a national measure which applies indiscriminately, as in the cases in the main proceedings (see, to that effect, Case C-108/96 Mac Queen and Others [2001] ECR I-837, paragraph 28).

42. Vessel traffic services supplied within the framework of the VTS system constitute a nautical service essential to the maintainence [sic] of public security in coastal waters as well as in ports, and the VTS tariff to which sea-going vessels longer than 41 metres are subject, as users of that service, contributes to the general interest in public security in those waters.

43. Lastly, as regards proportionality, the VTS system, in that it requires the payment of a VTS tariff by sea-going vessels longer than 41 metres, fulfils that criterion in so far as there is in fact a correlation between the cost of the service from which those vessels benefit and the amount of that tariff. This would not be the case where that amount included cost factors chargeable to categories of ships other than sea-going vessels longer than 41 metres, such as, in particular, inland waterway vessels.
44. The answer to the three first questions must therefore be that, as regards situations falling within the scope of Regulation ... 4055/86, that regulation, in conjunction with Articles [52 and 56] of the Treaty, does not preclude a vessel traffic services system, such as the VTS system at issue in the main proceedings, which requires the payment of a tariff by sea-going vessels longer than 41 metres which participate in that system on a mandatory basis, while other vessels, such as inland waterway vessels, are exempt from that tariff, in so far as there is in fact a correlation between the amount of that tariff and the cost of the service from which those sea-going vessels benefit.

7.198 The CJEU then considered the possible application of State aid law (the fourth question):

"The fourth question
45. By its fourth question, the national court in essence asks whether a vessel traffic services system such as the VTS system at issue in the main proceedings constitutes a State aid within the meaning of Article [107(1)] of the Treaty, inasmuch as, while it requires payment of a tariff by sea-going vessels longer than 41 metres which participate in that system on a mandatory basis, it exempts other vessels from that tariff, in particular inland waterway vessels.
46. In that respect, it must be recalled that, according to settled case-law, it is solely for the national court before which the dispute has been brought and which must assume responsibility for the subsequent judicial decision to determine, in the light of the particular circumstances of the case, both the need for a preliminary ruling in order to enable it to deliver judgment and the relevance of the questions which it submits to the Court (see, inter alia, Case C-415/93 Union Royale Belge des Sociétés de Football Association and Others v Bosman and Others [1995] ECR I-4921, paragraph 59). Nevertheless, the Court has held that it cannot give a preliminary ruling on a question submitted by a national court where it is quite obvious that the ruling sought by that court on the interpretation or validity of Community law bears no relation to the actual facts of the main action or its purpose, where the problem is hypothetical, or where the Court does not have before it the factual or legal material necessary to give a useful answer to the questions submitted to it (see, inter alia, Case C-36/99 Idéal tourisme [2000] ECR I-6049, paragraph 20).
47. It must be held that the fourth question is of no relevance to the outcome of the main proceedings, which concern the requirement for Sea-Land and Nedlloyd to pay the VTS tariff. In this case, the persons liable to pay an obligatory contribution cannot rely on the argument that the exemption enjoyed by other persons constitutes State aid in order to avoid payment of that contribution (see Case C-390/98 Banks [2001] ECR I-6117, paragraph 80).
48. There is therefore no need to answer the fourth question ... in answer to the questions referred to it by the Raad van State ... hereby rules: As regards situations falling within the scope of ... Regulation ... 4055/86, ... that regulation, in conjunction with Articles [52 and 56] of the ... Treaty, ... does not preclude a vessel traffic services system, such as the verkeersbegeleidingssysteem system at issue in the main proceedings, which requires the payment of a tariff by sea-going vessels longer than 41 metres which participate in that system on a mandatory basis, while other vessels, such as inland waterway vessels, are exempt from that tariff, in so far as there is in fact a correlation between the amount of that tariff and the cost of the service from which those sea-going vessels benefit."

7.199 In many ways, the CJEU's preliminary ruling was not surprising provided there was a genuine correlation between the tariff and the cost of the service. This requirement of a genuine correlation element could prove important in later cases.

2004: *Commission v Greece*

7.200 On 21 October 2004, the CJEU delivered judgment in *Commission v Greece*[161] which was an interesting case about freedom to provide maritime services and maritime cabotage. It was Article 258 of the TFEU case in that the Commission alleged that Greece had failed to fulfil its obligations under EU law. The CJEU held that, by regarding the Peloponnese as an island and applying to EU cruise liners exceeding 650 gt which carry out island cabotage its national rules as host State on manning conditions, Greece had failed to fulfil its obligations under Articles 1, 3 and 6 of Regulation 3577/92 applying the principle of freedom to provide services to maritime transport within Member States. The CJEU then dismissed the remainder of the action.

7.201 The Commission brought an action for a declaration that:

"– by requiring from [EU] ships entered in a second or international register a certificate issued by the competent authority of the flag State declaring that that ship is authorised to provide cabotage services;
– by considering that the Pelopennese constitutes an island;
– by applying to [EU] tankers, freighters, passenger ships and tourist ships, and to [EU] cruise liners which carry out maritime transport by way of cabotage its national rules as host State relating to manning conditions."

7.202 The relevant EU law provisions included Article 1(1) of Regulation 3577/92 which, from 1 January 1993, provided that cabotage restrictions within the EU should be lifted.

7.203 In terms of Greek legislation, the Ipourgio Emborikis Naftilias (the Greek Ministry of the Merchant Navy) published three circulars addressed to the inland port authorities in 1998. First, Circular No 1151.65/1/98, entitled "Activities of cargo vessels and tankers flying Community flags which carry out maritime cabotage", stated that Regulation 3577/92 formed an integral part of Greek legislation and prevailed over any conflicting provision. Furthermore, point 2.1.1 of that circular lists the ports of the Peloponnese as island ports. Point 2.1.2 provided that, in order to be able to carry out cabotage in Greek waters, an operator using vessels entered in a second register or international register was required to furnish proof that the vessel in question is able to carry out transport activities in the flag country of origin. Second, Circular No 1151.65/2/98 entitled "Activities of passenger and tourist vessels and cruise liners flying Community flags which operate tours (cruises) in Greek waters" repeated the provisions of the previous circular so far as concerns the Peloponnese. Point 2.4.1 stated:

"In general, Greek legislation (as the legislation of the host State) is to apply to the composition of the crews of Community passenger and tourist vessels and cruise liners which are authorised to carry out cruises between mainland ports and the islands or between island ports of our country, whilst the legislation of the flag State is to apply to cruises between ports situated on the mainland."

---

161 Case C-288/02 [2004] ECR I-10071, ECLI:EU:C:2004:647. The Chamber of the Court comprised Judges Timmermans (Rapporteur and President of the Chamber), Gulmann and Schintgen.

Third, Circular No 2311.10/10/98 entitled "Manning of cargo vessels, tankers and cruise liners flying Community flags which carry out maritime cabotage" provided for the application of the provisions of the Greek navy as far as concerns manning conditions.

7.204 After an exchange of correspondence and a meeting concerning the implementation of Regulation 3577/92 by Greece, the Commission decided to bring the present action.

7.205 In regard to the complaint that by requiring from EU ships entered in a second or international register a certificate issued by the competent authority of the flag State declaring that that ship is authorised to provide cabotage services. The CJEU stated:

> "29. It should be noted that Article 1 of the Regulation clearly establishes the principle of freedom to provide maritime cabotage services within the Community (Case C-205/99 *Analir and Others* [2001] ECR I-1271, paragraph 20).
> 30. A national measure which requires from [EU] ships entered in a second or international register a certificate issued by the competent authority of the flag State declaring that that ship is authorised to provide cabotage services is liable to impede or render less attractive the provision of those services and therefore constitutes a restriction on the freedom to provide them (see, to that effect, Analir, cited above, paragraph 22).
> 31. As regards the admissibility of that restriction, it should be noted, first, that the wording of Article 1(1) of the Regulation does not itself provide any indication as to whether a certificate may be demanded in order to determine whether, as that provision requires, a ship complies with all conditions for carrying out cabotage in the flag State (see, to that effect, Analir, cited above, paragraph 24).
> 32. Secondly, it is important to note that freedom to provide services, as a fundamental principle of the ... Treaty, may be restricted only by rules which are justified by overriding reasons in the general interest and are applicable to all persons and undertakings pursuing an activity in the territory of the host Member State. Furthermore, in order to be so justified, the national legislation in question must be suitable for securing the attainment of the objective which it pursues and must not go beyond what is necessary in order to attain it (see Analir, cited above, paragraph 25, and case-law cited).
> 33. The Commission's second complaint falls within that context of the proportionality of the national legislation in question. The Commission complains that the Hellenic Republic requires from [EU] ships a certificate issued by the flag State while there are measures less restrictive of freedom to provide services in order to attain the objective, which is to determine whether that ship complies with all conditions for carrying out cabotage in that State.
> 34. However, as the Advocate General explains in paragraphs 27 to 37 of his Opinion, the alternative solutions proposed by the Commission either do not serve to fully attain the objective sought or in practice turn out to be more complex or more restrictive of freedom to provide services than the certificate system currently in existence.
> 35. In those circumstances, the Commission, which has the burden of proof in proceedings for failure to fulfil obligations (see, inter alia, Case C-159/94 Commission v France [1997] ECR I-5815, paragraph 102, and case-law cited), has not been able to show that the Hellenic Republic, by requiring that certificate, has failed to fulfil its obligations under the Regulation.
> 36. It follows that the ... complaint should be dismissed."

7.206 The next complaint related to Greece considering that the Pelopennese constitutes an island. The Commission submitted that the Greek authorities wrongly contend, relying only on the etymology of the name, that the Peloponnese constitutes an island, thereby artificially extending the derogation in Article 6(3) of the regulation to maritime cabotage services between the ports of the Peloponnese and between the ports situated on the mainland and the ports of the Peloponnese. The Commission noted that the

Peloponnese was formerly linked to the Greek mainland, from which it was separated by a man-made canal. In addition, communication between the Peloponnese and Greece is by means of a railway line and a national road above the Corinth Canal. Greece submitted that the regulation applies criteria other than the fact of actually being surrounded by water for ports to be regarded as island ports. It refers in that connection to Ceuta and Melilla which are regarded as island ports by Article 2(1)(c) of the regulation, although they are clearly mainland ports in so far as they are situated on the coast of mainland Africa.[162] The CJEU decided:

> "42. Since the Regulation does not contain a definition of the term 'island', resort must be had to the common meaning of that term under which an island is defined, in a maritime context, as an area of dry land elevated permanently from the sea.
> 43. As the Advocate General observes in paragraph 44 of his Opinion, there is no doubt that the Peloponnese is, from a geographical point of view, a peninsula. It was separated from the rest of Greece only by a man-made canal a few tens of metres wide. In those circumstances, it cannot be classified as an island for the purpose of the Regulation.
> 44. Nor does the fact that Article 2 of the Regulation put the ports of Ceuta and Melilla in the category of island ports run counter to such an interpretation.
> 45. Those two ports constitute island ports solely because they have been categorised as island ports by Article 2 of the Regulation. They are not island ports by nature. Therefore, a comparison between Ceuta and Melilla, on the one hand, and the ports of the Peloponnese, which have not been categorised as island ports by Article 2 of the Regulation, on the other, invalidates rather than bears out the argument of the Greek Government that the Peloponnese constitutes an island.
> 46. Moreover, as the Advocate General maintains in paragraph 45 of his Opinion, although in relation to mainland Africa the ports of those towns are mainland ports, the fact remains that in relation to mainland Europe and in particular to the Iberian peninsular, those ports are comparable to island ports because they have no land links with Spain.
> 47. As far as concerns the judgment referred to by the Greek Government in Italy and Sardegna Lines v Commission,[163] ... it suffices to state that in that case the Court did not express a view on the term 'island'.
> 48. Finally, the broad interpretation of Article 6(3) of the Regulation which the Greek Government suggests is at odds with the fact that that provision, as a derogation from the general rules provided for by the Regulation on freedom to provide maritime transport services within a Member State, must be interpreted strictly.
> 49. It follows from the foregoing that the Commission's ... complaint is well founded."

7.207 The CJEU then considered the last complaint, namely that, under point 2.4.1 of Circular No 1151.65/2/98, the Greek legislation on the manning of ships applies to EU cruise liners exceeding 650 gt which carry out island cabotage. The Commission argued that the provision infringed Article 3(1) of the regulation, which provides that all matters relating to manning are to be the responsibility of the flag State, except for ships smaller than 650 gt, where host State conditions may be applied. According to the Commission, it was apparent from the wording of that provision that it applies to all cruise liners whether they carry out mainland cabotage or island cabotage. The CJEU found that because of the wording of Article 3(1) of the regulation, that provision applies to vessels carrying out

---

162 Greece citing Joined Cases C-15/98 and C-105/99 *Italy and Sardegna Lines v Commission* [2000] ECR I-8855, ECLI:EU:C:2000:570 contended that the decisive criterion for determining whether or not a geographic area constitutes an island lies in a statistical analysis of trade carried out by sea.
163 Ed., Joined Cases C-15/98 and C-105/99 *Italy and Sardegna Lines v Commission* [2000] ECR I-8855, ECLI:EU:C:2000:570.

mainland cabotage and to cruise liners. Article 3(2) applies to vessels carrying out island cabotage. Therefore, the CJEU believed that the absence of any classification of "cruise liners" in Article 3(1) of the regulation means that that provision applies to all cruise liners, irrespective of the nature of the cabotage they carry out.[164] The CJEU then concluded:

> "56. ... as regards cruise liners exceeding 650 gt which carry out island cabotage, all matters relating to manning are the responsibility of the flag State. Since point 2.4.1 of Circular No 1151.65/2/98 provides the contrary, the Hellenic Republic has failed to fulfil its obligations under the Regulation.
> 57. It follows that the ... complaint is well founded."

7.208 Ultimately, therefore the court decided that by regarding the Peloponnese as an island and applying to Community cruise liners exceeding 650 gt which carry out island cabotage its national rules as host State on manning conditions, Greece had breached its obligations under Articles 1, 3 and 6 of Regulation 3577/92 and then dismissed the remainder of the action.

Commission v Spain

7.209 On 9 March 2006, the CJEU found in *Commission v Spain*[165] that Spain had infringed Articles 1, 4 and 9 of Regulation 3577/92 by maintaining in force legislation which: (a) allowed a concession for maritime transport services in the Vigo estuary to be granted to a single operator for a period of 20 years and which included as a criterion for the award of that concession experience in transport acquired in that estuary; (b) allowed the imposition of public service obligations on seasonal transport services with the islands and regular transport services between mainland ports; and (c) was not the subject of any consultation with the Commission prior to being approved.

7.210 Before examining the Commission's complaints pleaded by the Commission, the Court had to first address the Spanish government's argument that, in any event, the action was not well founded on the ground that that regulation does not apply to the maritime transport services in the Vigo estuary. Spain had argued that "maritime cabotage" must be understood as the carriage of passengers and goods by sea between ports and that maritime transport in the Vigo estuary was neither carriage by sea nor carriage between ports in the sense given to those terms in the context of Regulation 3577/92. It is worth reviewing the CJEU's comments on the question because they elucidate some of the circumstances in which the regulation is applicable:

> "19. First, as regards the meaning of carriage by sea, the Spanish Government submits that the [EU] legislature, when it regulated maritime transport, was referring to external sea and not to internal waters. External sea corresponds to territorial sea, as defined by international

---

164 The CJEU stated in para. 55: "That interpretation is borne out by the fact that, as the Advocate-General notes in paragraph 54 of his Opinion, if cruise liners carrying out island cabotage were to be regarded as being covered by Article 3(2) of the Regulation, the reference to cruise liners in Article 3(1) would no longer have any meaning since the words 'vessels carrying out mainland cabotage' already cover cruise liners carrying out that type of cabotage."
165 Case C-323/03 [2006] ECR I-2161, ECLI:EU:C:2006:159. Second Chamber: Timmermans (Rapporteur), President of the Chamber as well as Judges Makarczyk, Silva de Lapuerta, Kūris and Klučka. The Advocate-General was AG Tizzano.

treaties and, more specifically, by Article 8 of the United Nations Convention on the Law of the Sea of 10 December 1982 ('the Montego Bay Convention') which distinguishes it from internal waters which are waters on the landward side of the baseline of the territorial sea.

20. Furthermore, the Spanish Government argues, Regulation ... 3577/92 is based on the principle that cabotage is both an essential component of the [EU] transport network and an instrument necessary for establishing the internal market. Unlike external shipping or shipping in territorial sea, shipping entirely within internal waters has a very limited economic and social impact and has little effect on the objective of establishing the internal market in the [EU] context.

21. Second, the Spanish Government argues that shipping in the Vigo estuary does not constitute shipping between ports since, on the one hand, according to the applicable national rules the whole of that estuary forms part of the Vigo port services zone and, on the other, the Cíes Isles do not have a port, but only a quay for the disembarkation of passengers with limited berthing capacity.

22. Lastly, in the Spanish Government's view, it also follows from the definition of 'sea area' and 'port area' in Article 2 of Council Directive 98/18/EC of 17 March 1998 on safety rules and standards for passenger ships (OJ 1998 L144, p. 1) that the 'port area' includes all the waters of the Vigo estuary. Thus, the [EU] rules themselves do not regard that area as a sea area.

23. In interpreting a provision of [EU] law it is necessary to consider not only its wording but also the context in which it occurs and the objects of the rules of which it is part (Case C-17/03 VEMW and Others [2005] ECR I- 4983, paragraph 41, and the case-law cited).

24. It follows that, in order to interpret the term 'carriage ... by sea between ports' which is part of the definitions of mainland and island cabotage in Article 2(1)(a) and (c) of Regulation ... 3577/92, account must be taken of the objective of that provision, which is to implement freedom to provide services for maritime cabotage under the conditions and subject to the exceptions which it lays down (see Case C-205/99 Analir and Others [2001] ECR I-1271, paragraph 19).

25. Equating 'sea' within the meaning of Regulation ... 3577/92 with 'territorial sea' within the meaning of the Montego Bay Convention is likely to undermine that objective. The application of that regulation solely to territorial sea, within the meaning of that convention, would preclude the liberalisation intended by that regulation of potentially significant maritime transport services where they operate on the landward side of the baseline of the territorial sea that States may draw, in accordance with that convention, across the natural entrance points of a bay.

26. Furthermore, it does not follow from Regulation ... 3577/92 that the [EU] legislature intended to limit its scope to territorial sea within the meaning of the Montego Bay Convention.

27. Therefore, it is not permissible to equate the two terms.

28. The argument that shipping in an estuary such as the Vigo estuary has little effect on the objective of establishing the internal market is also irrelevant. There is nothing in Regulation ... 3577/92 to suggest that its scope depends on the impact that shipping in a specific area would have, in economic and social terms, on the establishing of the internal market.

29. It follows that the points raised by the Spanish Government do not show that an estuary, that is to say a river valley inundated by the sea, such as the Vigo estuary, is not part of the sea for the purposes of Regulation ... 3577/92.

30. Furthermore, the argument that maritime transport services in the Vigo estuary are not 'between ports' within the meaning of Regulation ... 3577/92 cannot be accepted either.

31. Unlike Directive 98/18 which in Article 2(p) defines, 'port area' as 'an area other than a sea area, as defined by the Member States ...', Regulation ... 3577/92 does not contain any reference to the law of those States for the purpose of defining the term 'port'.

32. It follows from the need for uniform application of [EU] law and the principle of equality that the terms of a provision of [EU] law which makes no express reference to the law of the Member States for the purpose of determining its meaning and scope must normally be

given an autonomous and uniform interpretation throughout the [EU], having regard to the context of the provision and the objective pursued by the legislation in question (Case C-43/04 Stadt Sundern [2005] ECR I-4491, paragraph 24, and the case-law cited).

33. In that connection, given the context of Regulation ... 3577/92 and the objective it pursues, namely to implement freedom to provide services for maritime cabotage, the term 'port' in that regulation encompasses infrastructure, albeit small-scale, the function of which is to enable goods to be loaded and unloaded or passengers to be embarked and disembarked for conveyance by sea. Therefore, the infrastructures that exist in the Cíes Isles must be regarded as ports within the meaning of Regulation ... 3577/92.

34. Furthermore, an autonomous and uniform interpretation of 'port' for the purposes of that regulation leads to the conclusion that the infrastructures that exist in Vigo, Cangas and Moaña are covered by that definition, since those towns each have infrastructures permitting the embarkation and disembarkation of persons and the loading and unloading of goods for conveyance by sea.

35. It is clear from all of the foregoing considerations that the maritime passenger transport services in the Vigo estuary governed by Law 4/1999 constitute transport services by sea between ports for the purposes of Regulation ... 3577/92. Consequently, that regulation is applicable to those services."

7.211 The first complaint alleged that the Spanish law constituted an infringement of Article 1 of Regulation 3577/92 in two respects: first, by reserving maritime passenger transport services in the Vigo estuary to a single undertaking by the grant of an administrative concession for a period of 20 years, thereby paralysing access to the market for the duration of that concession; and, second, by making experience in operating transport services in the Vigo estuary a criterion for the selection of the undertaking to be granted the concession, thus favouring the existing operator and leading to discrimination against operators from other Member States. The CJEU found that the complaint was well founded. First, the court noted that Article 1 of Regulation 3577/92 clearly establishes the principle of freedom to provide maritime cabotage services within the EU.[166] Second, the CJEU stated that a national measure which reserves maritime transport services in the Vigo estuary to a single undertaking by means of an administrative concession for a duration of 20 years, renewable for a period of ten years, is liable to impede or even prohibit the provision of those services by undertakings in other Member States and therefore constitutes a restriction on freedom to provide services. The same is true of the selection criterion relating to experience in maritime transport in the Vigo estuary. Third, as regards the determination of whether those restrictions may be permitted, it must be pointed out that the freedom to provide services, as a fundamental principle of the Treaty, may be restricted only by rules which are justified by overriding reasons in the public interest and are applicable to all persons and undertakings pursuing an activity in the territory of the host Member State. Furthermore, in order to be so justified, the national legislation in question must be suitable for securing the attainment of the objective which it pursues and must not go beyond what is necessary in order to attain it but that was not, however, the case in these proceedings according to the CJEU. Fourth, in regard to the need to limit visitors, the CJEU stated that measures which are less restrictive than that concession, such as the organisation of a system of advance booking and sale of the available places, could be introduced in order to adapt the traffic to those islands to environmental

---

166 Para. 43 citing Case C-205/99 *Analir and Others* [2001] ECR I-1271, ECLI:EU:C:2001:107, para. 20 and Case C-288/02 *Commission v Greece* [2004] ECR I-10071, ECLI:EU:C:2004:647, para. 29.

requirements and the limited capacity of the quay referred to by the Spanish government. Fifth, as regards the requirements relating to the organisation of traffic in the geographical area of Vigo and the Morrazo Peninsula, the CJEU observed that Spain had failed to show that passenger transport services across the Vigo estuary which serve 1,300,000 passengers per year, must be subject to a concession granted to a single operator for a duration of 20 years, which may be extended to 30 years, in order to avoid becoming unprofitable and disappearing. Penultimately, the court found that Spain had failed to show that the intensity of maritime traffic in the Vigo estuary would give rise to difficulties preventable only by the introduction of a measure as restrictive as that concession, or, even assuming that substantial investments are required in order to maintain the maritime connections in question, that such investments could be amortised only over a period of 20 or even 30 years. Finally, the CJEU stated that as regards the selection criterion relating to experience in the transport sector in the Vigo estuary, it was sufficient to observe that Spain did not plead overriding reasons to justify the restriction which results from that criterion. Therefore the complaint was well founded.

7.212 The second complaint alleged an infringement of Article 4 of Regulation 3577/92. Article 4 of the regulation provided that a Member State may conclude public service contracts with or impose public service obligations on shipping companies only if they participate in regular services to, from and between islands. The CJEU found that transport services in the Vigo estuary are not regular transport services to or between islands. The court was satisfied of this for several reasons. First, regular services such as those of the Vigo–Cangas and Vigo–Moaña routes are not island services and, second, the services to the Cíes Isles are not regular, but seasonal tourist services. The court stated that even assuming that Article 4 of Regulation 3577/92 may apply in exceptional cases to certain maritime transport services other than those to or between islands, it must be observed that the towns of Vigo, Cangas and Moaña have, in addition to the sea connections, a road network linking them directly and affording ready access to them. In those circumstances, the regular maritime transport services between those towns cannot, in any event, be treated as maritime transport services to or between islands. The CJEU therefore found that the second complaint was well founded.

7.213 The third complaint alleged an infringement of Article 7 of Regulation 3577/92. This complaint was rejected as unfounded and therefore the CJEU's analysis deserves review because the other complaints were accepted:

> "61. According to the Commission, Article 7 of Regulation ... 3577/92 prohibits Member States from introducing more restrictive arrangements than those applicable at the date of the entry into force of the regulation, that is to say 1 January 1993. The arrangements existing before the adoption of Law 4/1999 were less restrictive than those introduced by that law.
>
> 62. In that connection, it must be pointed out that Article 7 of Regulation ... 3577/92 must be interpreted in the light of the provision which immediately precedes it. Although Article 6 allows Member States to maintain after 1 January 1993 and for a period expiring at the latest on 1 January 2004 existing restrictions in a number of specific cases, Article 7 provides, in substance, that those States may not introduce restrictions that are new in relation to the existing situation. The two provisions therefore complement one another and constitute in fact the two sides to a system of progressive liberalisation.
>
> 63. That interpretation of Articles 6 and 7 of Regulation ... 3577/92 is supported by the fact that the repeal, by the Treaty of Amsterdam, of Article 62 of the EC Treaty, to which Article 7 refers, which prohibited Member States from introducing any new restrictions on

the freedom to provide services, coincided with the disappearance, in the text of Article 49 EC, of the reference to the progressive abolition, during the transitional period, of restrictions on freedom to provide services within the [EU].

64. It follows that, as the Advocate General observed in point 75 of his Opinion, Article 7 of Regulation ... 3577/92 is only meaningful in a context of progressive liberalisation of the services referred to in the regulation.

65. Therefore, the question whether ... Spain has failed to fulfil its obligations under Article 7 of Regulation ... 3577/92, on account of the adoption of Law 4/1999 by the Autonomous Community of Galicia, arises only if the maritime transport services in the Vigo estuary were covered by Article 6 of that regulation at the date on which the period laid down in the reasoned opinion expired.

66. Since that was not the case, the third complaint must be dismissed as unfounded."

7.214 The fourth complaint alleged an infringement of Article 9 of Regulation 3577/92. The Commission submitted that the Spanish law was not the subject of any consultation before it was adopted, in breach of the obligation laid down in Article 9 of Regulation 3577/92. Article 9 provides that "[b]efore adopting laws, regulations or administrative provisions in implementation of ... Regulation, Member States shall consult the Commission". The CJEU was able to find, quite succinctly, that as the law constituted such a provision, and Spain did not deny that the Commission was not consulted with regard to that law then the fourth complaint was well founded.

2007: *Commission v Greece*: towage

7.215 On 11 January 2007, in *Commission v Greece*,[167] the CJEU opined on the meaning of the phrase "maritime transport". The case involved an action by the Commission, under Article 258 of the TFEU alleging a failure by Greece to fulfil its obligations under Articles 1 and 2(1) of Regulation 3577/92.[168] The case concerned towage services on the open sea within Greek waters but the principles are clearly transferable elsewhere. The case was heard by the Second Chamber of the CJEU.[169] Advocate-General Sharpston had delivered her opinion in the case on 14 September 2006.

7.216 The only vessels which Greece allowed to provide towage services on the open sea within Greek national waters were vessels flying the Greek flag. The Commission believed that Greece had thereby failed to fulfil its obligations under Article 1 of Regulation 3577/92. It will be recalled that the third and the fourth recitals of Regulation 3577/92 state:

> "the abolition of restrictions on the provision of maritime transport services within Member States is necessary for the establishment of the internal market; ... the internal market will comprise an area in which the free movement of goods, persons, services and capital is ensured; ... therefore freedom to provide services should be applied to maritime transport within Member States".

7.217 Article 1 of Regulation 3577/92 provides that freedom to provide maritime transport services within a Member State has to apply, since 1 January 1993, "to Community shipowners who have their ships registered in, and flying the flag of a Member

---

167 Case C-251/04 [2007] ECR I-00067, ECLI:EU:C:2007:5.
168 OJ 1992 L364/7.
169 Judges Timmermans (President of the Chamber), Schintgen, Kūris, Klučka (Rapporteur) and Bay Larsen.

State, provided that these ships comply with all conditions for carrying out cabotage in that Member State".

7.218 Article 2(1) of the regulation defines "maritime transport services within a Member State (maritime cabotage)" as:

"services normally provided for remuneration [which] shall in particular include:

(a) 'mainland cabotage': the carriage of passengers or goods by sea between ports situated on the mainland or the main territory of one and the same Member State without calls at islands;
(b) 'off-shore supply services': the carriage of passengers or goods by sea between any port in a Member State and installations or structures situated on the continental shelf of that Member State;
(c) 'island cabotage': the carriage of passengers or goods by sea between:

– ports situated on the mainland and on one or more of the islands of one and the same Member State,
– ports situated on the islands of one and the same Member State."

7.219 It will be recalled that Regulation 3577/92 was designed to fill the gap which was left by Regulation 4055/86[170] which only dealt with *international* maritime transport services but not cabotage services.[171] Under Article 1(4) of Regulation 4055/86:

"the following shall be considered 'maritime transport services between Member States and between Member States and third countries' where they are normally provided for remuneration:

(a) intra-Community shipping services: the carriage of passengers or goods by sea between any port of a Member State and any port or off-shore installation of another Member State;
(b) third-country traffic: the carriage of passengers or goods by sea between the ports of a Member State and ports or off-shore installations of a third country."

7.220 Turning to Greek law at issue, Article 11(1)(b),(aa) and (bb) of Decree Law No 187/73, which constituted the Greek code of public maritime law, reserved towage operations of any kind, specified in Article 188 of the Code, as well as assistance at sea and maritime rescue operations, defined in Article 189 of that code, in national waters was reserved to vessels flying the flag of Greece, when they are effected in and between Greek territorial waters. In accordance with Article 188(2) of the Code, port authorities are to adopt port regulations setting out the conditions for granting a port towage licence, the regulation of towage, circumstances in which towage services must be provided, towage rights in port and mooring waters and all other necessary details. According to Article 188(3) of the Code, the extent of the right to tow, occasional or emergency towage by other vessels, related rights of tugs or other vessels flying the flag of a State other than Greece, as well as all other related details, are to be laid down by presidential decree. The CJEU noted in its judgment:

"8. The granting of such licences is governed in particular by Article 1(1) of Presidential Decree No 45/83 on the towage of vessels which specifies that 'the carrying out of professional towage

---

170 OJ 1986 L378/1.
171 AG Sharpston in her opinion stated at para. 7: "the Commission originally proposed to the Council a single draft regulation applying the principle of freedom to provide services to sea transport services within the Community. Subject to certain limitations, it was intended to apply to sea transport services within Member States, between Member States and between Member States and third countries. However, that draft regulation was not adopted" (footnote omitted).

between two points within Greek waters as well as the provision of all services directly relating to such an operation are reserved to Greek vessels classed as tugs under the legislation in force, licensed by the competent port authority...', as well as by Article 4(2)(b) of General Ports Regulations, issued by the Chief of Greek Port Police, which requires the vessel owner applying for such a licence to produce to the port authority a certificate of nationality.

9. Under Article 3 of Presidential Decree No 45/83, tugs or other vessels flying the flag of a State other than Greece are authorised:

> '(a) to moor at any Greek port or at any point on the Greek coast when they are towing a vessel, an auxiliary boat or other floating object the towage of which commenced in a foreign port or at any other point on the coast of a foreign State or on open sea;
>
> (b) to take over the towage, from any Greek port or any place on the Greek coast, of a vessel or any other floating object bound for a foreign port or any place on the coast of a foreign State or the open sea;
>
> (c) to cross Greek territorial waters when, coming from a foreign port or any point on the coast of a foreign State or from the open sea, they are towing a vessel, an auxiliary boat or any other floating object and are bound for a foreign port or for any place on the coast of a foreign State or the open sea'."

7.221 The parties focused on three issues, namely: (a) whether or not the list in Article 2(1) of Regulation 3577/92 is exhaustive; (b) the legal nature of towage in Greek law; and (c) the usefulness of distinguishing between towage in the port area and towage outside that area for the purposes of determining the scope of the regulation.

7.222 The first issue was whether or not the list in Article 2(1) of Regulation 3577/92 is exhaustive. On whether the list is exhaustive, although the Commission accepted that the service of towage is not expressly mentioned in Article 2(1) as a "maritime transport service", it considered that the list is only indicative, since it is introduced by the term "in particular". Greece argued, conversely, that the term "in particular", used in Article 2(1), must be understood as "more particularly", with the effect of introducing an exhaustive list. Furthermore, the term "maritime transport service" is expressly defined in Article 1(4) of Regulation 4055/86. Greece also argued that the definition of that term is identical in Regulations 3577/92 and 4055/86. It includes, according to Greece, the purpose of the transport, namely the carriage of passengers or goods, and is, in both cases, exhaustive. Greece added that maritime assistance services did not constitute a form of transport in the usual sense and that vessels which have suffered damage cannot be regarded as goods which must be transported. The Commission replied that, although the definition of "maritime transport services" in Article 1(4) of Regulation 4055/86 also includes, in its view, towage, that definition should not, in any event, apply in this case because that regulation governs only international maritime transport services.

7.223 The second issue to be considered is the nature of towage. The Commission submitted that it follows from Article 3 of Presidential Decree No 45/83 that towage is not always regarded in Greek law as a service auxiliary to maritime cabotage, since the similarity between maritime transport services and the cases of towage for which it provides led the Greek authorities to authorise, in derogation from Article 1 of that decree, albeit under strict conditions, the carrying out of towage operations by tugs flying the flag of a State other than Greece. In response, Greece argued that towage and maritime assistance constitute, in Greek law, auxiliary services which contribute solely to the proper functioning of maritime transport services. The judgment recites the Greek argument in the following terms:

"[t]he mere fact of moving a vessel under tow or a floating construction without means of propulsion does not suffice to deprive that service of its auxiliary character or to confer on it the status of maritime transport. Towage thus falls outside the scope of Regulation … 3577/92 in the absence of a direct link between what is being transported and the tug. Moreover, in considering that Article 3 of Presidential Decree No 45/83 constitutes an exception to Article 1 of that decree, the Greek Government considers that the Commission wrongly interpreted the respective scopes of those two articles. The Greek Government specifies in that respect that Article 1 of that decree governs professional towage between two points situated in Greek territorial waters, whereas the scope of Article 3 of the decree is limited to situations with a foreign element."

7.224 The third issue was the possible distinction between towage in the port area and towage outside that area. The Commission argued that Greece did not distinguish between towage services provided within the port area and those provided outside the port, contrary to what appeared in the Commission proposals for a directive on market access to port services. As those proposals did not relate to cabotage outside the port area, it is thus Regulation 3577/92 which applied in the present case according to the Commission. Conversely, Greece considered that there is no reason to subject towage services to different legal rules, depending on whether they are carried out within or outside the port area. The distinction made on the basis of the place of provision of that service is arbitrary, without any legal basis and likely to create legal uncertainty in the application of Regulation 3577/92. There is one aspect of Advocate-General Sharpston's very succinct opinion which deserves noting. This is where she crystallised the issue and recognised the limited nature of the Commission's claim against Greece:

"24. It is to be noted that the Commission has based its application exclusively on Regulation … 3577/92. Importantly, it has *not* asked the Court to declare in the alternative that the Greek legislation to which it objects, which clearly differentiates between vessels on the basis of nationality, regulates services that are *not*, on a proper analysis, maritime *transport* services, and therefore infringes the normal Treaty provisions governing freedom to provide services … and/or any other rule of Community law … read in conjunction with those provisions. The sole question raised in the pre-litigation procedure and in the application before the Court is whether the contested national legislation infringes Article 1 of Regulation … 3577/92. The Court must therefore confine its assessment to that question. In what follows, I expressly do not address the question of whether towage services provided on the open sea, if they are *not* covered by Regulation … 3577/92, nevertheless fall within the scope of other provisions of Community law.

25. It is likewise settled law that Article 1 of Regulation … 3577/92 establishes the principle of freedom to provide maritime cabotage services within the Community – provided, of course, that the services in question fall within the scope of the regulation. The conditions governing the application of that principle as laid down in [the TFEU] have thus been defined in the maritime cabotage sector. Similarly, the Court has already applied the rules deriving from [the Treaty] in the context of both Regulation … 4055/86 and Regulation … 3577/92.

26. It seems clear to me – and indeed Greece does not seriously contend the contrary – that if towage services on the open sea are covered by Regulation … 3577/92, application of that case-law should lead the Court to grant the declaration sought.

27. The single issue on which the present application stands or falls is therefore whether towage services on the open sea fall within the scope of Regulation … 3577/92, as defined by Article 2(1) thereof."[172]

---

172 Footnotes omitted.

7.225 The Court agreed. The relevant part of the Court's judgment, which was again succinct, deserves being cited in full:

"23. As a preliminary point, it should be noted that, under Article [58(1) TFEU], freedom to provide services in the field of transport is governed by the provisions of the title of the ... Treaty relating to transport, which include Article [100(2)], permitting the Council of the European Union to lay down appropriate provisions for sea transport.[173]

24. On the basis of Article [100(2)], the Council adopted Regulation ... 3577/92, the aim of which is to implement freedom to provide services in respect of maritime cabotage under the conditions and subject to the exceptions which it lays down.

25. To that end, Article 1 of that regulation establishes the principle of freedom to provide maritime cabotage services within the [EU]. The conditions governing the application of the principle of freedom to provide services, which are laid down in particular in Article [56 of the TFEU], have thus been extended to include maritime cabotage (see Case C-205/99 Analir and Others ECR I-1271, paragraph 20).

26. On the other hand, it follows from Article [58(1) of the TFEU], read in conjunction with Article [100(2) of the TFEU] that services falling within the sea transport sector, but not within the scope of Regulation ... 3577/92 or other rules adopted on the basis of Article [100(2) of the TFEU], remain governed by the legislation of Member States, in compliance with Article [61 of the TFEU] and other general provisions of the Treaty (see, to that effect Case 167/73 Commission v France [1974] ECR 359, paragraph 32).

27. In the present case, since the Commission based its application only on the complaint of infringement of Article 1 of Regulation ... 3577/92, it is appropriate solely to examine whether towage services in open sea, which fall under sea transport for the purposes of Article [100(2) of the TFEU], are covered by that regulation and constitute 'maritime transport services within a Member State (maritime cabotage)' as defined in Article 2(1) thereof. It is not for the Court to give a ruling that goes beyond the grounds for complaint and form of order sought in the Commission's application under Article [238 of the TFEU] (see, to that effect, Case C-255/04 Commission v France [2006] ECR I-5251, paragraph 24, and case-law cited).

28. In that regard, it is clear that Article 2(1) of Regulation ... 3577/92 does not expressly mention towage. However, since the list of 'maritime cabotage services' for the purposes of that article is introduced by the term 'in particular', it cannot in principle be regarded as exhaustive.

29. Despite the non-exhaustive nature of the list given in Article 2(1) of Regulation ... 3577/92, it follows from that provision, construed as a whole, that the services falling within its scope are, firstly, normally provided for remuneration and, secondly, as the essential characteristics of the examples of maritime cabotage in that article illustrate, serve the purpose of transporting passengers or goods by sea between two places in the territory of a single Member State.

30. That interpretation is confirmed, as the Greek Government rightly argues, by the wording of Article 1(4) of Regulation ... 4055/86, according to which services are to be considered maritime transport services where they are provided for consideration for the purpose of

---

173 Ed. in this context, AG Sharpston had stated in her opinion: "2. Within Title III of Part Three of the EC Treaty ('Free movement of persons, services and capital'), Articles 49 to 55 concern services. 3. Article 49(1) EC states: 'Within the framework of the provisions set out below, restrictions on freedom to provide services within the Community shall be prohibited in respect of nationals of Member States who are established in a State of the Community other than that of the person for whom the services are intended.' 4. Article 51(1) EC provides that freedom to provide services in the field of transport are to be governed by the provisions of the title relating to transport. 5. Article 54 EC states: 'As long as restrictions on freedom to provide services have not been abolished, each Member State shall apply such restrictions without distinction on grounds of nationality or residence to all persons providing services within the meaning of the first paragraph of Article 49.' 6. Article 80(2) EC, part of Title V of Part Three of the Treaty ('Transport') states that the Council may, acting by a qualified majority, decide whether, to what extent and by what procedure appropriate provisions may be laid down for sea and air transport."

transporting passengers or goods by sea between any port of a Member State and any ports or off-shore installation of another Member State or a third country.

31. As the Advocate General pointed out in points 45 to 47 of her Opinion, the nature and characteristics of towage are different from those of cabotage, as defined in Article 2(1) of Regulation ... 3577/92. Although towage is a service normally provided for remuneration, it does not in principle entail a straightforward carriage of goods or passengers by sea. Rather, it involves assisting the movement of a vessel, rig, platform or buoy. A towing vessel that is assisting another vessel to manoeuvre, or supplementing that vessel's own propulsive machinery, or substituting for it in cases of failure or breakdown, is assisting the vessel by which the passengers or goods are transported but is not itself the transporting vessel.

32. In those conditions, to infer from the term 'in particular' in Article 2(1) of Regulation ... 3577/92 that it can extend the scope of that provision to any service related, incidental or ancillary to the provision of maritime transport services within the Member States, whether or not that service has the essential characteristics of maritime cabotage as expressly defined therein, would be contrary not only to the purpose of that regulation, but also to legal certainty as to the scope of that regulation.

33. It follows that towage cannot be regarded as falling within the scope of Article 2(1) of Regulation ... 3577/92."

7.226 It is interesting to reflect on what Advocate-General Sharpston had said about "maritime transport":

"38. ... To my mind, the words 'maritime transport' naturally connote carriage of passengers and/or freight by sea between a point of departure and a point of destination. That perception of what is meant by maritime transport is also borne out by the nature of the maritime transport services explicitly mentioned in Regulation ... 4055/86 and in the earlier draft regulation (which was not adopted) applying the principle of freedom to provide services to sea transport.

39. Other situations that satisfy those criteria (i.e., carriage of passengers or goods by sea between two points in the same Member State) may, I think, legitimately be subsumed within the definition in Article 2(1) of the regulation in reliance upon the words 'in particular'. But that is as far as the natural substantive scope of the definition, as drafted, extends."[174]

The case is interesting on several levels. It gives us an insight into the meaning of "maritime transport" and the approach to the construction of EC legislation. More particularly, it demonstrates the narrow line between maritime and non-maritime matters which means that it may be useful to plead matters "in the alternative".

2007: *Commission v Greece*: harbour dues

7.227 On 11 January 2007, the CJEU delivered its judgment in *Commission v Greece*.[175] The case related to a failure by Greece to fulfil obligations under Article 1 of Regulation 4055/86. The case related to harbour dues levied on passenger vessels or cargo vessels and harbour dues levied on vehicles aboard ferries. A lower level of dues

---

174 Footnote omitted.
175 Case C-269/05 [2007] ECR I-00004, ECLI:EU:C:2007:17. See also Case C-251/04 *Commission v Greece* [2007] ECR I-00067, ECLI:EU:C:2007:5 in similar terms; see Chuah, "Whether Towage in Ocean Seas Subject to Maritime Cabotage Rules" (2007) 13 JIML 63. In Case C-251/04 *Commission v Greece* [2007] ECR I-67, ECLI:EU:C:2007:5, the CJEU held that the provision "maritime transport services" and the phrase "in particular" was not meant to be exhaustive.

was imposed when transport was between two ports within national territory. Harbour dues were levied on vehicles aboard ferries but dues were not levied on vehicles travelling between ports in national territory. The CJEU declared that by maintaining in force: (a) the harbour dues levied on passenger vessels (including cruise ships) or on cargo vessels when they enter into harbour, berth and anchor in the ports of Piraeus and Thessaloniki, applying a lower level of dues when transport is between two ports within Greece as compared with cases where transport is to a destination outside Greece; (b) harbour dues for the benefit of the harbour funds of the Port Authorities AE, set up by Law No 2932/2001, and of the ports of Piraeus and Thessaloniki, which are levied on vehicles aboard ferries on international routes, while similar dues are not levied on routes between Greek ports; (c) the right to levy dues on vehicles aboard vehicle ferries with a foreign port destination for the benefit of municipalities and communities; (d) Greece has failed to fulfil its obligations under Article 1 of Regulation 4055/86. The CJEU recalled:

> "5. Under Article 1(4) of Council Regulation ... 4055/86 ... '... the following shall be considered "maritime transport services between Member States and between Member States and third countries" where they are normally provided for remuneration:
>
>   (a) intra-Community shipping services: the carriage of passengers or goods by sea between any port of a Member State and any port or off-shore installation of another Member State;
>   (b) third-country traffic: the carriage of passengers or goods by sea between the ports of a Member State and ports or off-shore installations of a third country.'"

7.228 The CJEU then considered the concept of "maritime transport service" and the arguments on the concept before reaching conclusions:

> "16. Furthermore, the term 'maritime transport service' is expressly defined in Article 1(4) of Regulation ... 4055/86.
> 17. According to the Greek Government, the definition of that term is identical in the Regulations in question, Nos 3577/92 and 4055/86. It includes, apart from the elements already mentioned by the Commission, the purpose of the transport, namely the carriage of passengers or goods, and is, in both cases, exhaustive. The Greek Government adds that maritime assistance services do not constitute a form of transport in the usual sense and that vessels which have suffered damage cannot be regarded as goods which must be transported.
> 18. The Commission replies that, although the definition of 'maritime transport services' in Article 1(4) of Regulation ... 4055/86 also includes, in its view, towage, that definition should not, in any event, apply in this case because that regulation governs only international maritime transport services.
> 19. Secondly, the Commission submits that it follows from Article 3 of Presidential Decree No 45/83 that towage is not always regarded in Greek law as a service auxiliary to maritime cabotage, since the similarity between maritime transport services and the cases of towage for which it provides led the Greek authorities to authorise, in derogation from Article 1 of that decree, albeit under strict conditions, the carrying out of towage operations by tugs flying the flag of a State other than Greece.
> 20. In response, the Greek Government submits that towage and maritime assistance constitute, in Greek law, auxiliary services which contribute solely to the proper functioning of maritime transport services. The mere fact of moving a vessel under tow or a floating construction without means of propulsion does not suffice to deprive that service of its auxiliary character or to confer on it the status of maritime transport. Towage thus falls outside the scope of Regulation ... 3577/92 in the absence of a direct link between what is being transported and the tug. Moreover, in considering that Article 3 of Presidential Decree No 45/83 constitutes an exception to Article 1 of that decree, the Greek Government considers that

the Commission wrongly interpreted the respective scopes of those two articles. The Greek Government specifies in that respect that Article 1 of that decree governs professional towage between two points situated in Greek territorial waters, whereas the scope of Article 3 of the decree is limited to situations with a foreign element.

21. Thirdly, it is the view of the Commission that the Greek authorities do not distinguish between towage services provided within the port area and those provided outside the port, contrary to what appeared in the recent Commission proposals for a directive on market access to port services. As those proposals do not relate to cabotage outside the port area, it is thus Regulation ... 3577/92 which applies in the present case.

22. The Greek Government considers that there is no reason to subject towage services to different legal rules, depending on whether they are carried out within or outside the port area. The distinction made on the basis of the place of provision of that service is arbitrary, without any legal basis and likely to create legal uncertainty in the application of Regulation ... 3577/92.

Findings of the Court

23. As a preliminary point, it should be noted that, under Article [58(1) of the TFEU], freedom to provide services in the field of transport is governed by the provisions of the title of the ... Treaty relating to transport, which include Article [100(2) of the TFEU], permitting the Council of the European Union to lay down appropriate provisions for sea transport.

24. On the basis of Article [100(2) of the TFEU], the Council adopted Regulation ... 3577/92, the aim of which is to implement freedom to provide services in respect of maritime cabotage under the conditions and subject to the exceptions which it lays down.

25. To that end, Article 1 of that regulation establishes the principle of freedom to provide maritime cabotage services within the [EU]. The conditions governing the application of the principle of freedom to provide services, which are laid down in particular in Article [56 of the TFEU], have thus been extended to include maritime cabotage (see Case C-205/99 Analir and Others ECR I-1271, paragraph 20).

26. On the other hand, it follows from Article [58(1) of the TFEU], read in conjunction with Article [100(2) of the TFEU], that services falling within the sea transport sector, but not within the scope of Regulation ... 3577/92 or other rules adopted on the basis of Article [100(2) of the TFEU], remain governed by the legislation of Member States, in compliance with Article [61 of the TFEU] and other general provisions of the Treaty (see, to that effect Case 167/73 Commission v France [1974] ECR 359, paragraph 32).

27. In the present case, since the Commission based its application only on the complaint of infringement of Article 1 of Regulation ... 3577/92, it is appropriate solely to examine whether towage services in open sea, which fall under sea transport for the purposes of Article [100(2) of the TFEU], are covered by that regulation and constitute 'maritime transport services within a Member State (maritime cabotage)' as defined in Article 2(1) thereof. It is not for the Court to give a ruling that goes beyond the grounds for complaint and form of order sought in the Commission's application under Article [258 of the TFEU] (see, to that effect, Case C-255/04 Commission v France [2006] ECR I-5251, paragraph 24, and case-law cited).

28. In that regard, it is clear that Article 2(1) of Regulation ... 3577/92 does not expressly mention towage. However, since the list of 'maritime cabotage services' for the purposes of that article is introduced by the term 'in particular', it cannot in principle be regarded as exhaustive.

29. Despite the non-exhaustive nature of the list given in Article 2(1) of Regulation ... 3577/92, it follows from that provision, construed as a whole, that the services falling within its scope are, firstly, normally provided for remuneration and, secondly, as the essential characteristics of the examples of maritime cabotage in that article illustrate, serve the purpose of transporting passengers or goods by sea between two places in the territory of a single Member State.

30. That interpretation is confirmed, as the Greek Government rightly argues, by the wording of Article 1(4) of Regulation ... 4055/86, according to which services are to be considered

maritime transport services where they are provided for consideration for the purpose of transporting passengers or goods by sea between any port of a Member State and any ports or off-shore installation of another Member State or a third country.

31. As the Advocate General pointed out in points 45 to 47 of her Opinion, the nature and characteristics of towage are different from those of cabotage, as defined in Article 2(1) of Regulation ... 3577/92. Although towage is a service normally provided for remuneration, it does not in principle entail a straightforward carriage of goods or passengers by sea. Rather, it involves assisting the movement of a vessel, rig, platform or buoy. A towing vessel that is assisting another vessel to manoeuvre, or supplementing that vessel's own propulsive machinery, or substituting for it in cases of failure or breakdown, is assisting the vessel by which the passengers or goods are transported but is not itself the transporting vessel.

32. In those conditions, to infer from the term 'in particular' in Article 2(1) of Regulation ... 3577/92 that it can extend the scope of that provision to any service related, incidental or ancillary to the provision of maritime transport services within the Member States, whether or not that service has the essential characteristics of maritime cabotage as expressly defined therein, would be contrary not only to the purpose of that regulation, but also to legal certainty as to the scope of that regulation.

33. It follows that towage cannot be regarded as falling within the scope of Article 2(1) of Regulation ... 3577/92.

34. ... the application must be dismissed."

7.229 The Court therefore declared that, by maintaining in force:

"– the harbour dues levied on passenger vessels (including cruise ships) or on cargo vessels when they enter into harbour, berth and anchor in the ports of Piraeus and Thessaloniki, applying a lower level of dues when transport is between two ports within Greece as compared with cases where transport is to a destination outside Greece,
– harbour dues for the benefit of the harbour funds of the Port Authorities AE, set up by Law No 2932/2001, and of the ports of Piraeus and Thessaloniki, which are levied on vehicles aboard ferries on international routes, while similar dues are not levied on routes between Greek ports,
– the right to levy dues on vehicles aboard vehicle ferries with a foreign port destination for the benefit of municipalities and communities, the Hellenic Republic has failed to fulfil its obligations under Article 1 of Council Regulation ... 4055/86."

2007: *International Transport Workers' Federation and Finnish Seamen's Union v Viking Line ABP and OÜ Viking Line Eesti*

7.230 The so-called *Viking Line* judgment of the Grand Chamber of the CJEU on 11 December 2007 is an important judgment[176] on employment law and the registration of vessels in the context of EU shipping law but it also has an importance in the context of the freedom to provide services. The case involved a preliminary reference from the English Court of Appeal. The reference concerned the interpretation of Article 49 of the TFEU and Regulation 4055/86. The reference was made in connection with a dispute between the International Transport Workers' Federation ("ITF") and the Finnish Seamen's Union ("FSU"), on the one hand, and Viking Line ABP ("Viking") and its

---

176 Case C-438/05 [2007] ECR I-10779, ECLI:EU:C:2007:772. The Chamber comprised President Skouris as well as Judges Jann, Rosas, Lenaerts, Lõhmus, Bay Larsen, Schintgen (Rapporteur), Silva de Lapuerta, Schiemann, Makarczyk, Kūris, Levits and Ó Caoimh. The Advocate-General was Poiares Maduro. On the case, see Davies "One Step Forward, Two Steps Back? The Viking and Laval Cases in the ECJ" (2008) 37 Industrial Law Journal 126.

subsidiary OÜ Viking Line Eesti ("Viking Eesti"), on the other, concerning actual or threatened collective action liable to deter Viking from reflagging one of its vessels from the Finnish flag to that of another Member State.

7.231 In describing the legal background, the CJEU referred to Article 1(1) of Regulation 4055/86 which established the basic principle of freedom to provide services and Article 13 of the Finnish constitution, which confers on all individuals the freedom to form trade unions and freedom of association in order to safeguard other interests (a provision which has been interpreted as allowing trade unions to initiate collective action against companies in order to defend workers' interests). The CJEU recalled that in Finland, however, the right to strike is subject to certain limitations. Thus, according to Finland's Supreme Court, it may not be relied on, *inter alia*, where the strike is *contra bonos mores* or is prohibited under national law or under EU law.

7.232 In describing the factual background, the CJEU recalled that Viking, a company incorporated under Finnish law, was a large ferry operator with seven vessels, including the *Rosella* which, under the Finnish flag, plied between Tallinn (Estonia) and Helsinki (Finland). FSU was a Finnish union of seamen. The crew of the *Rosella* were members of the FSU. FSU was affiliated to the ITF, which was an international federation of transport workers' unions with its headquarters in London (United Kingdom). According to the order for reference, one of the principal ITF policies was its "Flag of Convenience" ("FOC") policy. The primary objectives of this policy were, on the one hand, to establish a genuine link between the flag of the ship and the nationality of the owner and, on the other, to protect and enhance the conditions of seafarers on FOC ships. ITF considered that a vessel is registered under a flag of convenience where the beneficial ownership and control of the vessel is found to lie in a State other than the State of the flag. In accordance with the ITF policy, only unions established in the State of beneficial ownership have the right to conclude collective agreements covering the vessel concerned. The FOC campaign was, according to the CJEU, "enforced by boycotts and other solidarity actions amongst workers".[177] So long as the *Rosella* was under the Finnish flag, Viking was obliged under Finnish law and the terms of a collective bargaining agreement to pay the crew wages at the same level as those applicable in Finland. Estonian crew wages are lower than Finnish crew wages. The *Rosella* was running at a loss as a result of direct competition from Estonian vessels operating on the same route with lower wage costs. As an alternative to selling the vessel, Viking sought in October 2003 to reflag it by registering it in either Estonia or Norway, in order to be able to enter into a new collective agreement with a trade union established in one of those States. In accordance with Finnish law, Viking gave notice of its plans to the FSU and to the crew of the *Rosella*. The FSU opposed those plans. The FSU wrote to the ITF stating that "the *Rosella* was beneficially owned in Finland and that FSU therefore kept the right to negotiate with Viking". The FSU asked ITF to pass this information on to all affiliated unions and to request them not to enter into negotiations with Viking. The ITF then sent a circular (the "ITF circular") to its affiliates asking them to refrain from entering into negotiations with Viking or Viking Eesti. The affiliates were expected to follow this recommendation because of the principle of solidarity between trade unions and the sanctions which they could face if they failed to comply with that circular. The manning agreement for the *Rosella* expired on

---

[177] Judgment, para. 8.

17 November 2003 and therefore FSU was, as from that date, no longer under an obligation of industrial peace under Finnish law. Consequently, it gave notice of a strike requiring Viking, on the one hand, to increase the manning on the *Rosella* by eight and, on the other, to give up its plans to reflag the *Rosella*. Viking conceded the extra eight crew but refused to give up its plans to reflag. FSU was still not prepared, however, to agree to a renewal of the manning agreement and, by letter of 18 November 2003, it indicated that it would only accept such renewal on two conditions: first, that Viking, regardless of a possible change of the *Rosella*'s flag, gave an undertaking that it would continue to follow Finnish law, the collective bargaining agreement, the general agreement and the manning agreement on the *Rosella* and, second, that the possible change of flag would not lead to any laying-off of employees on any Finnish flag vessel belonging to Viking, or to changes to the terms and conditions of employment without the consent of the employees. In press statements, FSU justified its position by the need to protect Finnish jobs.

7.233 Legal proceedings then commenced. On 17 November 2003, Viking started legal proceedings before the employment tribunal in Finland for a declaration that, contrary to the view of the FSU, the manning agreement remained binding on the parties. On the basis of its view that the manning agreement had ended, the FSU gave notice, in accordance with Finnish law on industrial dispute mediation that it intended to commence strike action in relation to the *Rosella*. Meanwhile, Viking learnt of the existence of the ITF circular. The following day it brought proceedings before the Court of First Instance of Helsinki (Finland) to restrain the planned strike action. A preparatory hearing date was set. The CJEU stated that:

> "18. According to the referring court, FSU was fully aware of the fact that its principal demand, that in the event of reflagging the crew should continue to be employed on the conditions laid down by Finnish law and the applicable collective agreement, would render reflagging pointless, since the whole purpose of such reflagging was to enable Viking to reduce its wage costs. Furthermore, a consequence of reflagging the Rosella to Estonia would be that Viking would, at least as regards the Rosella, no longer be able to claim State aid which the Finnish Government granted to Finnish flag vessels.
>
> 19. In the course of conciliation proceedings, Viking gave an undertaking, at an initial stage, that the reflagging would not involve any redundancies. Since FSU nevertheless refused to defer the strike, Viking put an end to the dispute on 2 December 2003 by accepting the trade union's demands and discontinuing judicial proceedings. Furthermore, it undertook not to commence reflagging prior to 28 February 2005."

7.234 Meanwhile, on 1 May 2004, Estonia became a member of the EU. However, the *Rosella* continued to run at a loss, and Viking pursued its intention to reflag the vessel to Estonia. Because the ITF circular remained in force, on account of the fact that the ITF had never withdrawn it, the request to affiliated unions from the ITF in relation to the *Rosella* consequently remained in effect.

7.235 On 18 August 2004, Viking brought an action before the English High Court, requesting it to declare that the action taken by ITF and FSU was contrary to Article 49 of the TFEU, to order the withdrawal of the ITF circular and to order FSU not to infringe the rights which Viking enjoys under Community law. The English court granted the form of order sought by Viking, on the grounds that the actual and threatened collective action by the ITF and FSU imposed restrictions on freedom of establishment contrary to Article 49 of the TFEU and, in the alternative, constituted unlawful restrictions on freedom of movement for workers and freedom to provide services under Articles 49 and 56 of the TFEU. The ITF and FSU then appealed that decision before the referring court. In support of their appeal they claimed that the right of trade unions to take collective action to preserve jobs is a fundamental right recognised by Title XI of the EC Treaty (now Title X of the TFEU) and, in particular, Article 151 of the TFEU.[178] It was also argued that the reference to the European Social Charter and the Community Charter of the Fundamental Social Rights of Workers incorporated a reference to the right to strike recognised by those legal instruments. Consequently, the trade unions had the right to take collective action against an employer established in a Member State to seek to persuade him not to move part or all of his undertaking to another Member State.

7.236 At this stage, given the somewhat intricate nature of the judgment, it is useful to cite much of the remainder of it in full. The CJEU continued:

> "26. The question therefore arises whether the Treaty intends to prohibit trade union action where it is aimed at preventing an employer from exercising his right of establishment for economic reasons. By analogy with the Court's rulings regarding Title VI of the Treaty[179] (Case C-67/96 *Albany* [1999] ECR I-5751; Joined Cases C-180/98 to C-184/98 *Pavlov and Others* [2000] ECR I-6451; and Case C-222/98 *Van der Woude* [2000] ECR I-7111), it is argued that Title III of the Treaty[180] and the articles relating to free movement of persons and of services do not apply to 'genuine trade union activities'.
>
> 27. In those circumstances, since it considered that the outcome of the case before it depended on the interpretation of Community law, the Court of Appeal (England and Wales) (Civil Division) decided to stay proceedings and refer the following questions to the Court for a preliminary ruling:
>
> 'Scope of the free movement provisions
>
> > (1) Where a trade union or association of trade unions takes collective action against a private undertaking so as to require that undertaking to enter into a collective bargaining agreement with a trade union in a particular Member State which has the effect of making it pointless for that undertaking to re-flag a vessel in another Member State, does that action fall outside the scope of Article [49 of the TFEU] and/or Regulation ... 4055/86 by virtue of the EC's social policy including, inter alia, [the Title on Social Policy in the TFEU] and, in particular, by analogy with the Court's reasoning in ... Albany (paragraphs 52 to 64)?
>
> Horizontal direct effect
>
> > (2) Do Article [49 of the TFEU] and/or Regulation ... 4055/86 have horizontal direct effect so as to confer rights on a private undertaking which may be relied on against another private party and, in particular, a trade union or association of trade unions in respect of collective action by that union or association of unions?

---

178 The first paragraph of Art. 136 EC (as it then was) provides that "[t]he Community and the Member States, having in mind fundamental social rights such as those set out in the European Social Charter signed at Turin on 18 October 1961 and in the 1989 Community Charter of the Fundamental Social Rights of Workers, shall have as their objectives the promotion of employment, improved living and working conditions, so as to make possible their harmonisation while the improvement is being maintained, proper social protection, dialogue between management and labour, the development of human resources with a view to lasting high employment and the combating of exclusion".

179 Ed., Title VI of the EC Treaty was entitled "Common rules on competition, taxation and approximation of laws".

180 Ed., Title III of the EC Treaty was entitled "Free movement of persons, services and capital".

Existence of restrictions on free movement

(3) Where a trade union or association of trade unions takes collective action against a private undertaking so as to require that undertaking to enter into a collective bargaining agreement with a trade union in a particular Member State, which has the effect of making it pointless for that undertaking to re-flag a vessel in another Member State, does that action constitute a restriction for the purposes of Article [49 of the TFEU] and/or Regulation ... 4055/86?

(4) Is a policy of an association of trade unions which provides that vessels should be flagged in the registry of the country in which the beneficial ownership and control of the vessel is situated so that the trade unions in the country of beneficial ownership of a vessel have the right to conclude collective bargaining agreements in respect of that vessel, a directly discriminatory, indirectly discriminatory or non-discriminatory restriction under Article [49 of the TFEU] or Regulation ... 4055/86?

(5) In determining whether collective action by a trade union or association of trade unions is directly discriminatory, indirectly discriminatory or non-discriminatory restriction under Article [49 of the TFEU] or Regulation ... 4055/86, is the subjective intention of the union taking the action relevant or must the national court determine the issue solely by reference to the objective effects of that action?

Establishment/services

(6) Where a parent company is established in Member State A and intends to undertake an act of establishment by reflagging a vessel to Member State B to be operated by an existing wholly owned subsidiary in Member State B which is subject to the direction and control of the parent company:

(a) is threatened or actual collective action by a trade union or association of trade unions which would seek to render the above a pointless exercise capable of constituting a restriction on the parent company's right of establishment under Article [49 of the TFEU], and

(b) after reflagging of the vessel, is the subsidiary entitled to rely on Regulation ... 4055/86 in respect of the provision of services by it from Member State B to Member State A?

Justification
Direct discrimination

(7) If collective action by a trade union or association of trade unions is a directly discriminatory restriction under Article [49 of the TFEU] or Regulation ... 4055/86, can it, in principle, be justified on the basis of the public policy exception set out in Article [52 of the TFEU] on the basis that:

(a) the taking of collective action (including strike action) is a fundamental right protected by [EU] law; and/or
(b) the protection of workers?

The policy of [ITF]: objective justification

(8) Does the application of a policy of an association of trade unions which provides that vessels should be flagged in the registry of the country in which the beneficial ownership and control of the vessel is situated so that the trade unions in the country of beneficial ownership of a vessel have the right to conclude collective bargaining agreements in respect of that vessel, strike a fair balance between the fundamental social right to take collective action and the freedom to establish and provide services, and is it objectively justified, appropriate, proportionate and in conformity with the principle of mutual recognition?

FSU's actions: objective justification

(9) Where:

- a parent company in Member State A owns a vessel flagged in Member State A and provides ferry services between Member State A and Member State B using that vessel;
- the parent company wishes to re-flag the vessel to Member State B to apply terms and conditions of employment which are lower than in Member State A;
- the parent company in Member State A wholly owns a subsidiary in Member State B and that subsidiary is subject to its direction and control;
- it is intended that the subsidiary will operate the vessel once it has been re-flagged in Member State B with a crew recruited in Member State B covered by a collective bargaining agreement negotiated with an ITF affiliated trade union in Member State B;
- the vessel will remain beneficially owned by the parent company and be bare-boat chartered to the subsidiary;
- the vessel will continue to provide ferry services between Member State A and Member State B on a daily basis;
- a trade union established in Member State A takes collective action so as to require the parent and/or subsidiary to enter into a collective bargaining agreement with it which will apply terms and conditions acceptable to the union in Member State A to the crew of the vessel even after reflagging and which has the effect of making it pointless for the parent to re-flag the vessel to Member State B,

does that collective action strike a fair balance between the fundamental social right to take collective action and the freedom to establish and provide services and is it objectively justified, appropriate, proportionate and in conformity with the principle of mutual recognition?

(10) Would it make any difference to the answer to [Question] 9 if the parent company provided an undertaking to a court on behalf of itself and all the companies within the same group that they will not by reason of the reflagging terminate the employment of any person employed by them (which undertaking did not require the renewal of short term employment contracts or prevent the redeployment of any employee on equivalent terms and conditions)?'

The questions referred
Preliminary observations

28. It must be borne in mind that, in accordance with settled case-law, in the context of the cooperation between the Court and the national courts provided for in Article [267 of the TFEU], it is solely for the national court before which a dispute has been brought, and which must assume responsibility for the subsequent judicial decision, to determine in the light of the particular circumstances of the case both the need for a preliminary ruling in order to enable it to deliver judgment and the relevance of the questions which it submits to the Court. However, the Court has regarded itself as not having jurisdiction to give a preliminary ruling on a question submitted by a national court where it is quite obvious, inter alia, that the interpretation of Community law sought by that court bears no relation to the actual facts of the main action or its purpose or where the problem is hypothetical (see Case C-415/93 Bosman [1995] ECR I-4921 and Case C-350/03 Schulte [2005] ECR I-9215, paragraph 43).

29. In the present case, the reference for a preliminary ruling concerns the interpretation, first, of provisions of the Treaty on freedom of establishment, and secondly, of Regulation … 4055/86 applying the principle of freedom to provide services to maritime transport.

30. However, since the question on freedom to provide services can arise only after the reflagging of the Rosella envisaged by Viking, and since, on the date on which the questions were referred to the Court, the vessel had not yet been re-flagged, the reference for a preliminary ruling is hypothetical and thus inadmissible in so far as it relates to the interpretation of Regulation … 4055/86.
31. In those circumstances, the questions referred by the national court can be answered only in so far as they concern the interpretation of Article [49 of the TFEU].

The first question

32. By its first question, the national court is essentially asking whether Article [49 of the TFEU] must be interpreted as meaning that collective action initiated by a trade union or a group of trade unions against an undertaking in order to induce that undertaking to enter into a collective agreement, the terms of which are liable to deter it from exercising freedom of establishment, falls outside the scope of that article.
33. In this regard, it must be borne in mind that, according to settled case-law, Articles [45, 49 and 56 of the TFEU] do not apply only to the actions of public authorities but extend also to rules of any other nature aimed at regulating in a collective manner gainful employment, self-employment and the provision of services (see Case 36/74 Walrave and Koch [1974] ECR 1405, paragraph 17; Case 13/76 Donà [1976] ECR 1333, paragraph 17; Bosman, paragraph 82; Joined Cases C-51/96 and C-191/97 Deliège [2000] ECR I-2549, paragraph 47; Case C-281/98 Angonese [2000] ECR I-4139, paragraph 31; and Case C-309/99 Wouters and Others [2002] ECR I-1577, paragraph 120).
34. Since working conditions in the different Member States are governed sometimes by provisions laid down by law or regulation and sometimes by collective agreements and other acts concluded or adopted by private persons, limiting application of the prohibitions laid down by these articles to acts of a public authority would risk creating inequality in its application (see, by analogy, Walrave and Koch, paragraph 19; Bosman, paragraph 84; and Angonese, paragraph 33).
35. In the present case, it must be stated, first, that the organisation of collective action by trade unions must be regarded as covered by the legal autonomy which those organisations, which are not public law entities, enjoy pursuant to the trade union rights accorded to them, inter alia, by national law.
36. Secondly, as FSU and ITF submit, collective action such as that at issue in the main proceedings, which may be the trade unions' last resort to ensure the success of their claim to regulate the work of Viking's employees collectively, must be considered to be inextricably linked to the collective agreement the conclusion of which FSU is seeking.
37. It follows that collective action such as that described in the first question referred by the national court falls, in principle, within the scope of Article [49 of the TFEU].
38. This view is not called into question by the various arguments put forward by FSU, ITF and certain Member States which submitted observations to the Court to support the position contrary to that set out in the previous paragraph.
39. First of all, the Danish Government submits that the right of association, the right to strike and the right to impose lock-outs fall outside the scope of the fundamental freedom laid down in Article [49 of the TFEU] since, in accordance with Article [153(5) of the TFEU], the [EU] does not have competence to regulate those rights.
40. In that respect it is sufficient to point out that, even if, in the areas which fall outside the scope of the [EU's] competence, the Member States are still free, in principle, to lay down the conditions governing the existence and exercise of the rights in question, the fact remains that, when exercising that competence, the Member States must nevertheless comply with [EU] law (see, by analogy, in relation to social security, Case C-120/95 Decker [1998] ECR I-1831, paragraphs 22 and 23, and Case C-158/96 Kohll [1998] ECR I-1931, paragraphs 18 and 19; in relation to direct taxation, Case C-334/02 Commission v France [2004] ECR I-2229, paragraph 21, and Case C-446/03 Marks & Spencer [2005] ECR I-10837, paragraph 29).

41. Consequently, the fact that Article [153 of the TFEU] does not apply to the right to strike or to the right to impose lock-outs is not such as to exclude collective action such as that at issue in the main proceedings from the application of Article [49 of the TFEU].

42. Next, according to the observations of the Danish and Swedish Governments, the right to take collective action, including the right to strike, constitutes a fundamental right which, as such, falls outside the scope of Article [49 of the TFEU].

43. In that regard, it must be recalled that the right to take collective action, including the right to strike, is recognised both by various international instruments which the Member States have signed or cooperated in, such as the European Social Charter, signed at Turin on 18 October 1961 – to which, moreover, express reference is made in Article 136 EC[181] – and Convention No 87 concerning Freedom of Association and Protection of the Right to Organise, adopted on 9 July 1948 by the International Labour Organisation – and by instruments developed by those Member States at Community level or in the context of the European Union, such as the Community Charter of the Fundamental Social Rights of Workers adopted at the meeting of the European Council held in Strasbourg on 9 December 1989, which is also referred to in Article 136 EC, and the Charter of Fundamental Rights of the European Union proclaimed in Nice on 7 December 2000 (OJ 2000 C364, p. 1).

44. Although the right to take collective action, including the right to strike, must therefore be recognised as a fundamental right which forms an integral part of the general principles of [EU] law the observance of which the Court ensures, the exercise of that right may none the less be subject to certain restrictions. As is reaffirmed by Article 28 of the Charter of Fundamental Rights of the European Union, those rights are to be protected in accordance with Community law and national law and practices. In addition, as is apparent from paragraph 5 of this judgment, under Finnish law the right to strike may not be relied on, in particular, where the strike is contra bonos mores or is prohibited under national law or Community law.

45. In that regard, the Court has already held that the protection of fundamental rights is a legitimate interest which, in principle, justifies a restriction of the obligations imposed by Community law, even under a fundamental freedom guaranteed by the Treaty, such as the free movement of goods (see Case C-112/00 Schmidberger [2003] ECR I-5659, paragraph 74) or freedom to provide services (see Case C-36/02 Omega [2004] ECR I-9609, paragraph 35).

46. However, in Schmidberger and Omega, the Court held that the exercise of the fundamental rights at issue, that is, freedom of expression and freedom of assembly and respect for human dignity, respectively, does not fall outside the scope of the provisions of the Treaty and considered that such exercise must be reconciled with the requirements relating to rights protected under the Treaty and in accordance with the principle of proportionality (see, to that effect, Schmidberger, paragraph 77, and Omega, paragraph 36).

47. It follows from the foregoing that the fundamental nature of the right to take collective action is not such as to render Article [49 of the TFEU] inapplicable to the collective action at issue in the main proceedings.

48. Finally, FSU and ITF submit that the Court's reasoning in Albany must be applied by analogy to the case in the main proceedings, since certain restrictions on freedom of establishment and freedom to provide services are inherent in collective action taken in the context of collective negotiations.

49. In that regard, it should be noted that in paragraph 59 of Albany, having found that certain restrictions of competition are inherent in collective agreements between organisations representing employers and workers, the Court nevertheless held that the social policy objectives pursued by such agreements would be seriously undermined if management and labour were subject to Article [101(1)] of the [TFEU] ... when seeking jointly to adopt measures to improve conditions of work and employment.

---

181 Ed., this would now be Art. 151 TFEU

50. The Court inferred from this, in paragraph 60 of Albany, that agreements concluded in the context of collective negotiations between management and labour in pursuit of such objectives must, by virtue of their nature and purpose, be regarded as falling outside the scope of Article [101(1) of the TFEU].
51. The Court must point out, however, that that reasoning cannot be applied in the context of the fundamental freedoms set out in Title III of the Treaty.
52. Contrary to the claims of FSU and ITF, it cannot be considered that it is inherent in the very exercise of trade union rights and the right to take collective action that those fundamental freedoms will be prejudiced to a certain degree.
53. Furthermore, the fact that an agreement or an activity are excluded from the scope of the provisions of the Treaty on competition does not mean that that agreement or activity also falls outside the scope of the Treaty provisions on the free movement of persons or services since those two sets of provisions are to be applied in different circumstances (see, to that effect, Case C-519/04 P Meca-Medina and Majcen v Commission [2006] ECR I-6991).
54. Finally, the Court has held that the terms of collective agreements are not excluded from the scope of the Treaty provisions on freedom of movement for persons (Case C-15/96 Schöning-Kougebetopoulou [1998] ECR I-47; Case C-35/97 Commission v France [1998] ECR I-5325; and Case C-400/02 Merida [2004] ECR I-8471).
55. In the light of the foregoing, the answer to the first question must be that Article [49 of the TFEU] is to be interpreted as meaning that, in principle, collective action initiated by a trade union or a group of trade unions against an undertaking in order to induce that undertaking to enter into a collective agreement, the terms of which are liable to deter it from exercising freedom of establishment, is not excluded from the scope of that article.

7.237 The second question essentially asked whether Article 49 of the TFEU is such as to confer rights on a private undertaking which may be relied on against a trade union or an association of trade unions. The CJEU replied:

"57. In order to answer that question, the Court would point out that it is clear from its case-law that the abolition, as between Member States, of obstacles to freedom of movement for persons and freedom to provide services would be compromised if the abolition of State barriers could be neutralised by obstacles resulting from the exercise, by associations or organisations not governed by public law, of their legal autonomy (*Walrave and Koch*, paragraph 18; *Bosman*, paragraph 83; *Deliège*, paragraph 47; *Angonese*, paragraph 32; and *Wouters and Others*, paragraph 120).
58. Moreover, the Court has ruled, first, that the fact that certain provisions of the Treaty are formally addressed to the Member States does not prevent rights from being conferred at the same time on any individual who has an interest in compliance with the obligations thus laid down, and, second, that the prohibition on prejudicing a fundamental freedom laid down in a provision of the Treaty that is mandatory in nature, applies in particular to all agreements intended to regulate paid labour collectively (see, to that effect, Case 43/75 Defrenne [1976] ECR 455, paragraphs 31 and 39).
59. Such considerations must also apply to Article [49 of the TFEU] which lays down a fundamental freedom.
60. In the present case, it must be borne in mind that, as is apparent from paragraphs 35 and 36 of the present judgment, the collective action taken by FSU and ITF is aimed at the conclusion of an agreement which is meant to regulate the work of Viking's employees collectively, and, that those two trade unions are organisations which are not public law entities but exercise the legal autonomy conferred on them, inter alia, by national law.
61. It follows that Article [49 of the TFEU] must be interpreted as meaning that, in circumstances such as those in the main proceedings, it may be relied on by a private undertaking against a trade union or an association of trade unions.
62. This interpretation is also supported by the case-law on the Treaty provisions on the free movement of goods, from which it is apparent that restrictions may be the result of actions by individuals or groups of such individuals rather than caused by the State (see Case

C-265/95 Commission v France [1997] ECR I-6959, paragraph 30, and Schmidberger, paragraphs 57 and 62).

63. The interpretation set out in paragraph 61 of the present judgment is also not called into question by the fact that the restriction at issue in the proceedings before the national court stems from the exercise of a right conferred by Finnish national law, such as, in this case, the right to take collective action, including the right to strike.

64. It must be added that, contrary to the claims, in particular, of ITF, it does not follow from the case-law of the Court referred to in paragraph 57 of the present judgment that that interpretation applies only to quasi-public organisations or to associations exercising a regulatory task and having quasi-legislative powers.

65. There is no indication in that case-law that could validly support the view that it applies only to associations or to organisations exercising a regulatory task or having quasi-legislative powers. Furthermore, it must be pointed out that, in exercising their autonomous power, pursuant to their trade union rights, to negotiate with employers or professional organisations the conditions of employment and pay of workers, trade unions participate in the drawing up of agreements seeking to regulate paid work collectively.

66. In the light of those considerations, the answer to the second question must be that Article [49 of the TFEU] is capable of conferring rights on a private undertaking which may be relied on against a trade union or an association of trade unions.

7.238 The third to tenth questions were grouped together. By those questions, which can be examined together, the national court is essentially asking the CJEU whether collective action such as that at issue in the main proceedings constitutes a restriction within the meaning of Article 49 of the TFEU and, if so, to what extent such a restriction may be justified. The CJEU responded:

"The existence of restrictions

68. The Court must first point out, as it has done on numerous occasions, that freedom of establishment constitutes one of the fundamental principles of the Community and that the provisions of the Treaty guaranteeing that freedom have been directly applicable since the end of the transitional period. Those provisions secure the right of establishment in another Member State not merely for Community nationals but also for the companies or firms referred to in Article [54] (Case 81/87 Daily Mail and General Trust [1988] ECR 5483, paragraph 15).

69. Furthermore, the Court has considered that, even though the provisions of the Treaty concerning freedom of establishment are directed mainly to ensuring that foreign nationals and companies are treated in the host Member State in the same way as nationals of that State, they also prohibit the Member State of origin from hindering the establishment in another Member State of one of its nationals or of a company incorporated under its legislation which also comes within the definition contained in Article [54 of the TFEU]. The rights guaranteed by Articles [49 to 54 of the TFEU] would be rendered meaningless if the Member State of origin could prohibit undertakings from leaving in order to establish themselves in another Member State (Daily Mail and General Trust, paragraph 16).

70. Secondly, according to the settled case-law of the Court, the definition of establishment within the meaning of those articles of the Treaty involves the actual pursuit of an economic activity through a fixed establishment in another Member State for an indefinite period and registration of a vessel cannot be separated from the exercise of the freedom of establishment where the vessel serves as a vehicle for the pursuit of an economic activity that includes fixed establishment in the State of registration (Case C-221/89 Factortame and Others [1991] ECR I-3905, paragraphs 20 to 22).

71. The Court concluded from this that the conditions laid down for the registration of vessels must not form an obstacle to freedom of establishment within the meaning of Articles [49 EC to 54 of the TFEU] (Factortame and Others, paragraph 23).

72. In the present case, first, it cannot be disputed that collective action such as that envisaged by FSU has the effect of making less attractive, or even pointless, as the national court has pointed out, Viking's exercise of its right to freedom of establishment, inasmuch as such action prevents both Viking and its subsidiary, Viking Eesti, from enjoying the same treatment in the host Member State as other economic operators established in that State.

73. Secondly, collective action taken in order to implement ITF's policy of combating the use of flags of convenience, which seeks, primarily, as is apparent from ITF's observations, to prevent shipowners from registering their vessels in a State other than that of which the beneficial owners of those vessels are nationals, must be considered to be at least liable to restrict Viking's exercise of its right of freedom of establishment.

74. It follows that collective action such as that at issue in the main proceedings constitutes a restriction on freedom of establishment within the meaning of Article [49 of the TFEU].

Justification of the restrictions

75. It is apparent from the case-law of the Court that a restriction on freedom of establishment can be accepted only if it pursues a legitimate aim compatible with the Treaty and is justified by overriding reasons of public interest. But even if that were the case, it would still have to be suitable for securing the attainment of the objective pursued and must not go beyond what is necessary in order to attain it (see, inter alia, Case C-55/94 Gebhard [1995] ECR I-4165, paragraph 37, and Bosman, paragraph 104).

76. ITF, supported, in particular, by the German Government, Ireland and the Finnish Government, maintains that the restrictions at issue in the main proceedings are justified since they are necessary to ensure the protection of a fundamental right recognised under [EU] law and their objective is to protect the rights of workers, which constitutes an overriding reason of public interest.

77. In that regard, it must be observed that the right to take collective action for the protection of workers is a legitimate interest which, in principle, justifies a restriction of one of the fundamental freedoms guaranteed by the Treaty (see, to that effect, Schmidberger, paragraph 74) and that the protection of workers is one of the overriding reasons of public interest recognised by the Court (see, inter alia, Joined Cases C-369/96 and C-376/96 Arblade and Others [1999] ECR I-8453, paragraph 36; Case C-165/98 Mazzoleni and ISA [2001] ECR I-2189, paragraph 27; and Joined Cases C-49/98, C-50/98, C-52/98 to C-54/98 and C-68/98 to C-71/98 Finalarte and Others [2001] ECR I-7831, paragraph 33).

78. It must be added that, according to Article 3(1)(c) and (j) EC, the activities of the Community are to include not only an 'internal market characterised by the abolition, as between Member States, of obstacles to the free movement of goods, persons, services and capital', but also 'a policy in the social sphere'. Article 2 EC states that the Community is to have as its task, inter alia, the promotion of 'a harmonious, balanced and sustainable development of economic activities' and 'a high level of employment and of social protection'.

79. Since the Community has thus not only an economic but also a social purpose, the rights under the provisions of the Treaty on the free movement of goods, persons, services and capital must be balanced against the objectives pursued by social policy, which include, as is clear from the first paragraph of Article [151 of the TFEU], inter alia, improved living and working conditions, so as to make possible their harmonisation while improvement is being maintained, proper social protection and dialogue between management and labour.

80. In the present case, it is for the national court to ascertain whether the objectives pursued by FSU and ITF by means of the collective action which they initiated concerned the protection of workers.

81. First, as regards the collective action taken by FSU, even if that action – aimed at protecting the jobs and conditions of employment of the members of that union liable to be adversely affected by the reflagging of the Rosella – could reasonably be considered to fall, at first sight, within the objective of protecting workers, such a view would no longer be tenable if it were established that the jobs or conditions of employment at issue were not jeopardised or under serious threat.

82. This would be the case, in particular, if it transpired that the undertaking referred to by the national court in its 10th question was, from a legal point of view, as binding as the terms of a collective agreement and if it was of such a nature as to provide a guarantee to the workers that the statutory provisions would be complied with and the terms of the collective agreement governing their working relationship maintained.

83. In so far as the exact legal scope to be attributed to an undertaking such as that referred to in the 10th question is not clear from the order for reference, it is for the national court to determine whether the jobs or conditions of employment of that trade union's members who are liable to be affected by the reflagging of the Rosella were jeopardised or under serious threat.

84. If, following that examination, the national court came to the conclusion that, in the case before it, the jobs or conditions of employment of the FSU's members liable to be adversely affected by the reflagging of the Rosella are in fact jeopardised or under serious threat, it would then have to ascertain whether the collective action initiated by FSU is suitable for ensuring the achievement of the objective pursued and does not go beyond what is necessary to attain that objective.

85. In that regard, it must be pointed out that, even if it is ultimately for the national court, which has sole jurisdiction to assess the facts and interpret the national legislation, to determine whether and to what extent such collective action meets those requirements, the Court of Justice, which is called on to provide answers of use to the national court, may provide guidance, based on the file in the main proceedings and on the written and oral observations which have been submitted to it, in order to enable the national court to give judgment in the particular case before it.

86. As regards the appropriateness of the action taken by FSU for attaining the objectives pursued in the case in the main proceedings, it should be borne in mind that it is common ground that collective action, like collective negotiations and collective agreements, may, in the particular circumstances of a case, be one of the main ways in which trade unions protect the interests of their members (European Court of Human Rights, Syndicat national de la police belge v Belgium, of 27 October 1975, Series A, No 19, and Wilson, National Union of Journalists and Others v United Kingdom of 2 July 2002, 2002-V, § 44).

87. As regards the question of whether or not the collective action at issue in the main proceedings goes beyond what is necessary to achieve the objective pursued, it is for the national court to examine, in particular, on the one hand, whether, under the national rules and collective agreement law applicable to that action, FSU did not have other means at its disposal which were less restrictive of freedom of establishment in order to bring to a successful conclusion the collective negotiations entered into with Viking, and, on the other, whether that trade union had exhausted those means before initiating such action.

88. Secondly, in relation to the collective action seeking to ensure the implementation of the policy in question pursued by ITF, it must be emphasised that, to the extent that that policy results in shipowners being prevented from registering their vessels in a State other than that of which the beneficial owners of those vessels are nationals, the restrictions on freedom of establishment resulting from such action cannot be objectively justified. Nevertheless, as the national court points out, the objective of that policy is also to protect and improve seafarers' terms and conditions of employment.

89. However, as is apparent from the file submitted to the Court, in the context of its policy of combating the use of flags of convenience, ITF is required, when asked by one of its members, to initiate solidarity action against the beneficial owner of a vessel which is registered in a State other than that of which that owner is a national, irrespective of whether or not that owner's exercise of its right of freedom of establishment is liable to have a harmful effect on the work or conditions of employment of its employees. Therefore, as Viking argued during the hearing without being contradicted by ITF in that regard, the policy of reserving the right of collective negotiations to trade unions of the State of which the beneficial owner of a vessel is a national is also applicable where the vessel is registered in a State which guarantees workers a higher level of social protection than they would enjoy in the first State.

90. In the light of those considerations, the answer to the third to tenth questions must be that Article [49 of the TFEU] is to be interpreted to the effect that collective action such as that at issue in the main proceedings, which seeks to induce an undertaking whose registered office is in a given Member State to enter into a collective work agreement with a trade union established in that State and to apply the terms set out in that agreement to the employees of a subsidiary of that undertaking established in another Member State, constitutes a restriction within the meaning of that article. That restriction may, in principle, be justified by an overriding reason of public interest, such as the protection of workers, provided that it is established that the restriction is suitable for ensuring the attainment of the legitimate objective pursued and does not go beyond what is necessary to achieve that objective...

On those grounds, the Court (Grand Chamber) hereby rules:

1. Article [49 of the TFEU] is to be interpreted as meaning that, in principle, collective action initiated by a trade union or a group of trade unions against a private undertaking in order to induce that undertaking to enter into a collective agreement, the terms of which are liable to deter it from exercising freedom of establishment, is not excluded from the scope of that article.
2. Article [49 of the TFEU] is capable of conferring rights on a private undertaking which may be relied on against a trade union or an association of trade unions.
3. Article [49 of the TFEU] is to be interpreted to the effect that collective action such as that at issue in the main proceedings, which seeks to induce a private undertaking whose registered office is in a given Member State to enter into a collective work agreement with a trade union established in that State and to apply the terms set out in that agreement to the employees of a subsidiary of that undertaking established in another Member State, constitutes a restriction within the meaning of that article.

   That restriction may, in principle, be justified by an overriding reason of public interest, such as the protection of workers, provided that it is established that the restriction is suitable for ensuring the attainment of the legitimate objective pursued and does not go beyond what is necessary to achieve that objective."

The CJEU's judgment was controversial but it also leaves the door ajar for construction and interpretation. One senses that it may have been a compromise judgment (the CJEU delivers a single judgment) but it is an important judgment for all that.

2006: *Agip Petroli SpA v Capitaneria di porto di Siracusa, Capitaneria di porto di Siracusa – Sezione staccata di Santa Panagia and Ministero delle Infrastrutture e dei Trasporti*

7.239 On 6 April 2006, the CJEU gave its preliminary ruling in *Agip Petroli SpA v Capitaneria di porto di Siracusa, Capitaneria di porto di Siracusa – Sezione staccata di Santa Panagia and Ministero delle Infrastrutture e dei Trasporti*.[182] The case, relating to cabotage, centred on the meaning of the phrase "voyage which follows or precedes a voyage to or from another State". At issue was a law applicable to the manning of vessels over 650 gt carrying out island cabotage.

7.240 The case involved a reference for a preliminary ruling under Article 267 of the TFEU from the Tribunale amministrativo regionale per la Sicilia in Italy. The case considered the meaning of Article 3(3) of Regulation 3577/92 (i.e. the maritime cabotage regulation). There had been a dispute between Agip Petroli and the Capitaneria di porto

---

182 Case C-456/04 [2006] ECR I-3395, ECLI:EU:C:2006:241.

di Siracusa (Port of Syracuse Harbour Office), the Capitaneria di porto di Siracusa – Sezione staccata di Santa Panagia (Port of Syracuse Harbour Office – Santa Panagia Division) (the "Harbour Office") and the Ministero delle Infrastrutture e dei Trasporti (Department of Infrastructure and Transport). The case concerned a decision by which the Harbour Office refused a Greek-registered tanker permission to carry out island cabotage between Magnisi and Gela. Agip Petroli chartered the Greek-registered tanker *Theodoros IV* to ship a cargo of crude oil from Magnisi to Gela, both in Sicily. In order to justify the derogation from the legislation of the host State, Italy, and the application instead of the legislation of the flag State, Greece, Agip Petroli relied on Article 3(3) of the regulation. In its application for permission to carry out this island cabotage, Agip Petroli stated that the vessel had subsequently to make a voyage directly to a foreign State without cargo on board (i.e. a voyage in ballast). The Harbour Office refused the *Theodoros IV* the permission on the ground that the crew of the vessel included, contrary to Article 318 of the Codice delle navigazione (Italian Shipping Code), sailors who were nationals of the Philippines. In its decision, the Harbour Office justified the application of Italian law, having regard to Circular No TMA3/CA/0230 of 31 January 2000 of the Ministero dei Trasporti et della Navigazione (Department of Transport and Shipping), according to which Article 3(3) of the regulation, providing for the application, by way of exception, of the law of the flag State, applies only to cases in which "the voyage which follows or precedes the cabotage ... is functionally and commercially autonomous, that is to say, the vessel has cargo on board destined for or coming from a foreign port". That provision could not, consequently, be invoked if "the ship has already completed or will complete after the voyage of island cabotage ... a voyage in ballast or a voyage with a cargo of goods which, in terms of quality and quantity, cannot render the voyage autonomous".

7.241 Agip Petroli brought an action against that decision before the referring court. The court took the view that two interpretations of Article 3(3) of Regulation 3577/92 are possible. According to that court, the need to prevent circumvention of Article 3(2) of the regulation by means of consecutive sham cabotage voyages argues in favour of a restrictive interpretation. However, there is nothing in the wording of these provisions to indicate that their scope is limited to voyages with cargo on board. Under these circumstances, the Tribunale amministrativo regionale per la Sicilia decided to stay the proceedings and to refer the following question to the Court for a preliminary ruling:

> "Does 'voyage which follows or precedes the cabotage voyage' in Article 3(3) of [Regulation 3577/92] mean only a voyage which is 'functionally and commercially autonomous, that is to say, with cargo on board destined for or coming from a foreign port', as stated in the measures at issue in the [main proceedings], or does it also include a voyage without cargo on board (that is, a 'voyage in ballast')?"

7.242 The CJEU recalled, as a preliminary point, that Regulation 3577/92's objective of liberalisation, as described in the third and fourth recitals in the preamble in particular, and which is to abolish restrictions on the provision of maritime transport services within Member States, had not yet been fully achieved. One of the limits to the liberalisation provided for by Regulation 3577/92 concerns island cabotage. While Articles 1 and 3(1) of the regulation specify that, in principle, the law of the flag State applies, Article 3(2) of the regulation lays down an exception in respect of island cabotage, providing that, for vessels carrying out that type of transport, all matters relating to manning come under the law of the host State. The principle of the application of the law of the flag State to the composition of the crew is however laid down in Article 3(3) of the regulation, when the island cabotage is preceded or followed by an international voyage carried out by a cargo vessel over 650 gt.

7.243 On the meaning of "international voyage", Article 3(2) of Regulation 2577/92 only requires that the cabotage voyage be preceded or followed by an international voyage, without giving any guidance as to what is meant by "voyage" or as to the presence or not of cargo on vessels over 650 gt.

7.244 The CJEU then reached its decision in the following way:

> "15. Under these circumstances, and as the regulation contains no definition of 'voyage' and nothing to indicate that the Community legislator intended to allow other factors to be taken into account, such as the requirement that there be cargo on board or that the international voyage be functionally and commercially autonomous, it must be understood as covering, in principle, all voyages whether or not the vessel has cargo on board.
>
> 16. This interpretation is moreover in accordance with the objective of the regulation, which is to implement freedom to provide services for maritime cabotage under the conditions and subject to the exceptions which the regulation lays down (see, in particular, Case C-205/99 Analir and Others [2001] ECR I-1271, paragraph 19). In fact, it allows the full application of Article 3(3) of the regulation which, by stipulating for its part the application of the law of the flag State, is directly in line with that objective.
>
> 17. Moreover, this interpretation is also supported by the fact that, in the area of maritime transport, it is not uncommon for voyages in ballast to take place.
>
> 18. However, in spite of that finding, it is not possible to accept sham voyages in ballast carried out to circumvent Article 3 of the regulation and the objective of the regulation itself, as recalled at paragraph 13 of this judgment.
>
> 19. It should be noted in this respect that, according to settled case-law, [EU] law cannot be relied on for abusive or fraudulent ends (see, in particular, Case C- 367/96 Kefalas and Others [1998] ECR I-2843, paragraph 20; Case C-373/97 Diamantis [2000] ECR I-1705, paragraph 33, and Case C-255/02 Halifax and Others [2006] ECR I-1609, paragraph 68).
>
> 20. The scope of [EU] law must in no case be extended to cover abuses on the part of a trader, that is to say, activities which are not carried out in the context of normal commercial transactions, but only with the aim of circumventing the rules of Community law (see to this effect, in particular, Case 125/76 Cremer [1977] ECR 1593, paragraph 21; Case C-8/92 General Milk Products [1993] ECR I-779, paragraph 21, and Halifax, paragraph 69).
>
> 21. The national courts may, consequently, on the basis of objective evidence, take account of abuse on the part of the persons concerned in order, where appropriate, to deny them the benefit of the provision of Community law on which they seek to rely. In that respect, they must nevertheless take into account the objectives pursued by that provision (see Diamantis, paragraph 34, and the case-law cited).
>
> 22. Consequently, shipowners cannot be allowed to have set up artificially an international voyage in ballast in order that Article 3(3) of the regulation, and therefore the legislation of the flag State, instead of Article 3(2) of the regulation, and therefore the legislation of the host State, be applicable.
>
> 23. Such an abuse can be found to exist only if, first, notwithstanding that technically the conditions laid down by Article 3(3) of the regulation apply, the result of the international voyage in ballast is that the shipowner benefits, for all matters relating to manning, from the application of the law of the flag State, frustrating the aim of Article 3(2) of the regulation, which is to allow the application of the law of the host State to all matters relating to manning in the case of island cabotage. Second, there must also be objective evidence to show that the essential aim of the international voyage in ballast is to avoid the application

of Article 3(2) of the regulation, in favour of Article 3(3) (see, to this effect, Halifax, paragraph 86).

24. It is for the national court, however, to verify in accordance with the rules of evidence of national law, provided that the effectiveness of Community law is not undermined, whether action constituting an abusive practice has taken place in the case before it (Case C-515/03 Eichsfelder Schlachtbetrieb [2005] ECR I-7355, paragraph 40, and Halifax, paragraph 76).

25. Having regard to the foregoing considerations, the reply to the question referred must be that an international voyage, as referred to in Article 3(3) of the regulation, means in principle any voyage to or from another State, whether or not the vessel has cargo on board. However, sham voyages without cargo on board carried out to circumvent the rules laid down in the regulation cannot be permitted. Such an abuse can be found to exist only if, first, notwithstanding that technically the conditions laid down by Article 3(3) of the regulation apply, the result of the international voyage in ballast is that the shipowner benefits, for all matters relating to manning, from the application of the law of the flag State, frustrating the aim of Article 3(2) of the regulation, which is to allow the application of the law of the host State to all matters relating to manning in the case of island cabotage. Second, there must also be objective evidence to show that the essential aim of the international voyage in ballast is to avoid the application of Article 3(2) of Regulation ... 3577/92, in favour of Article 3(3) those parties, are not recoverable."

7.245 The Court summarised its ruling in the following way:

"A 'voyage which follows or precedes' the cabotage voyage, as referred to in Article 3(3) of ... Regulation ... 3577/92 ... means in principle any voyage to or from another State, whether or not the vessel has cargo on board. However, sham voyages without cargo on board carried out to circumvent Regulation ... 3577/92 cannot be permitted. Such an abuse can be found to exist only if, first, notwithstanding that technically the conditions laid down by Article 3(3) of the regulation apply, the result of the international voyage in ballast is that the shipowner benefits, in respect of all matters relating to manning, from the application of the law of the flag State, frustrating the aim of Article 3(2) of the regulation, which is to allow the application of the law of the host State to all matters relating to manning in the case of island cabotage. Second, there must also be objective evidence to show that the essential aim of the international voyage in ballast is to avoid the application of Article 3(2) of Regulation ... 3577/92, in favour of Article 3(3)."

2010: *Commission v Spain*

7.246 On 14 January 2009, the Commission instituted proceedings against Spain with a judgment of the CJEU on 4 February 2010[183] seeking an order to declare that, by maintaining in force Ley 48/2003, de regimen económico y de prestación de servicios de los puertos de interés general (Law 48/2003 of 26 November 2003 on the economic rules and supply of services for ports of general interest) and, in particular Article 24(5) and Article 27(1), (2) and (4) thereof, which establish a system of rebates and exemptions for harbour dues, Spain has failed to fulfil its obligations under EU Law and, in particular, Article 1 of Regulation 4055/86. The Commission argues that Spanish law provides for a series of exemptions and rebates relating to harbour dues and those exemptions and rebates depend on the ports of departure or destination of the vessels with the consequence that more favourable tariffs are applied, first, to traffic between the Spanish archipelagos and Ceuta and Melilla, second, to traffic between those ports and ports of the EU and, third, between ports of the EU. The Commission takes the view that that legislation is discriminatory. Spain, which invoked the

---

183 Case C-18/09, *Commission v Spain* [2010] ECR I-00013, ECLI:EU:C:2010:58.

particular geographic situation of the ports concerned, has not justified either the need for or the proportionality of that measure. Despite having promised to amend the legislation at issue, the Commission instituted the case because as far as it was aware, no legislation had been adopted to end the infringement. The Court declared that, by maintaining in force Article 24(5) and Article 27(1), (2) and (4) of Law 48/2003 of 26 November 2003 on the economic rules and supply of services for ports of general interest, which establishes a system of rebates and exemptions for harbour dues, the Kingdom of Spain has failed to fulfil its obligations under Article 1 of Regulation 4055/86.

2010: *Enosi Efopliston: Island Services*

7.247 On 22 April 2010, in *Enosi Efopliston Aktoploïas and Others, Ipourgos Emporikis Naftilias, Ipourgos Aigaiou*,[184] the CJEU had to deal with a preliminary reference from a Greek court concerning Greek rules on maritime cabotage. This case is yet another instalment in a long-running saga relating to freedom to provide maritime services and the resistance of some countries, including Greece, to the extension of the application of the freedom. The reference concerned the interpretation of Articles 4(3) of the Treaty on the European Union as well as Article 56 and 288 of the TFEU as well as Articles 1, 2, 4 and 6(3) of Regulation 3577/92.[185] The case originated in proceedings brought by Enosi Efopliston Aktoploïas (i.e. the Association of Coastal Shipowners) and four public limited coastal shipping companies (ANEK, Minoïkes Grammes, LE Leseau and Blue Star Ferries) against the Minister for Merchant Shipping (i.e. Ipourgos Emporikis Naftillaias) and the Minister for the Aegean (Ipourgos Aigaiou). The proceedings concerned the validity of two decisions adopted by the two Ministers making maritime cabotage subject to certain conditions. Article 1(1) of Regulation 3577/92 provided that from 1 January 1993, freedom to provide maritime transport services within a Member State would apply to EU shipowners who have their ships registered in, and flying the flag of a Member State, provided that those ships complied with all conditions for carrying out cabotage in that Member State. There was, however, a derogation to Article 1 of Regulation 3577/92. This derogation was contained in Article 6 which stated that for reasons of socio-economic cohesion, the derogation in the case of Greece would last until 1 January 2004 for regular passenger and ferry services and services provided by vessels less than 650 gt. The Greek national law, Law No 2932/2001 entitled "Freedom to Provide Maritime Cabotage Services, etc."[186] states at Article 1(1):

> "As from 1 November 2002 freedom to provide services shall exist in respect of maritime transport services which: (a) are provided for remuneration by a shipowner of a Member State of the European Community (EC), the European Economic Area (EEA) or the European Free Trade Association (EFTA), except for Switzerland, and (b) are carried out between ports situated on the mainland and the islands or between ports situated on the islands by passenger/vehicle, passenger or cargo ships operating a regular passenger and ferry service, and by ships of a tonnage of up to 650 gt ... provided that the ships are registered in, and fly the flag of, Greece or another State in the EC, the EEA or EFTA, except for Switzerland."

---

184 Case C-122/09 [2010] ECR I-03667, ECLI:EU:C:2010:222. The Court was composed of Judges Bonichot (President of the Chamber) Toader, Timmermans (Rapporteur) Schiemann and Kūris. The Advocate-General was AG Cruz Villalón but he did not deliver an opinion in the case.
185 OJ 1992 L364/7.
186 FEK (Official Gazette) A 145/27.6.2001.

Article 3 of that national law also stated that "the operation of a passenger/vehicle, passenger or cargo ship shall be for a period of one year starting in 1 November (regular operation)". The applicants in the proceedings before the Greek courts brought two actions. First they sought annulment of the decision of the Minister for Merchant Shipping which was a letter of guarantee of proper fulfilment of the conditions regarding a ship's operation and, second, the annulment of a joint decision of the Minister for Merchant Shipping and the Minister for the Aegean entitled "Determination of the form, content and other required elements and documents and of related preconditions for the declaration of a ship's regular operations". In essence, the applicant submitted that the relevant provisions of the Greek law, on the basis of those decisions were invalid because they were contrary to Article 49 of the EC Treaty (i.e. Article 56 of the TFEU) and to certain provisions of Regulation 3577/92.

7.248 By way of derogation from Regulation 3577/92,

"island cabotage in the Mediterranean and cabotage with regard to the Canary, Azores and Madeira archipelagoes, Ceuta and Melilla, the French islands along the Atlantic coast and the French overseas departments shall be temporarily exempted from the implementation of this Regulation until 1 January 1999. For reasons of socio-economic cohesion, the derogation provided for in paragraph 2 was extended for Greece until 1 January 2004 for regular passenger and ferry services and services provided by vessels less than 650 gt."

The national legislation was summarised:

"5. Law No 2932/2001, entitled 'Freedom to provide maritime cabotage services etc.' (FEK (Official Gazette) A 145/27.6.2001), states as follows in Article 1(1):

'As from 1 November 2002 freedom to provide services shall exist in respect of maritime transport services which: (a) are provided for remuneration by a shipowner of a Member State of the European Community (EC), the European Economic Area (EEA) or the European Free Trade Association (EFTA), except for Switzerland, and (b) are carried out between ports situated on the mainland and the islands or between ports situated on the islands by passenger/vehicle, passenger or cargo ships operating a regular passenger and ferry service, and by ships of a tonnage of up to 650 gt ... provided that these ships are registered in, and fly the flag of, Greece or another State in the EC, EEA or EFTA, except for Switzerland.'

6. Pursuant to Article 3(1) of Law No 2932/2001:

'The operation of a passenger/vehicle, passenger or cargo ship shall be for a period of one year, starting on 1 November (regular operation).'

The actions in the main proceedings and the questions referred for a preliminary ruling."

7.249 The CJEU stated:

"7. The applicants in the [Greek] proceedings have brought two actions before the referring court. By the first, the applicants are seeking the annulment of Decision No 3332.3/1 of the Minister for Merchant Shipping of 19 October 2001, entitled 'Letter of guarantee of proper fulfilment of the conditions regarding a ship's operation' (FEK B 1448/22.10.2001), and by the second, the annulment of Joint Decision No 3332.3/3 of the Minister for Merchant Shipping and the Minister for the Aegean of 19 October 2001, entitled 'Determination of the form, content and other required elements and documents and of related preconditions for the declaration of a ship's regular operation' (FEK B 1448/22.10.2001).

8. The applicants submit, inter alia, that the relevant provisions of Law No 2932/2001, on the basis of which those decisions were adopted, are invalid because they are contrary, in particular, to Article 49 EC and to certain provisions of Regulation ... 3577/92.

9. The main proceedings gave rise to an initial reference for a preliminary ruling, which was replied to by order of 28 September 2006 in Case C-285/05 Enosi Efopliston Aktoploïas and Others. By the first question in that case, the referring court asked, in essence, whether Regulation ... 3577/92 could confer rights on individuals before 1 January 2004 when, for the type of cabotage in question, the regulation was applicable in Greece only from that date.

10. In answering that question, the Court stated as follows in paragraphs 17 to 19 of the order in Case C-285/05:

> '17.... [W]here the regulation concerned grants a Member State a specified period in which to comply with the obligations resulting from it, the regulation may not be relied on by individuals before the expiry of the period in question (see, to that effect, Case C-156/91 *Hansa Fleisch Ernst Mundt* [1992] ECR I-5567, paragraph 20).
>
> 18. In the case of Regulation ... 3577/92, it is apparent from Article 6(2) and (3) that Greek island cabotage, as regards regular passenger and ferry services and services provided by vessels less than 650 gt, is exempted from the implementation of the regulation until 1 January 2004. The wording of that provision is such that derogations from the temporary exemption are not permitted. It follows that, in this particular cabotage sector, the regulation did not begin to have effects until 1 January 2004 and can therefore confer rights on individuals only from that date (see also, to that effect, [Case 43/71] *Politi* [[1971] ECR 1039], paragraph 10).
>
> 19. That interpretation cannot be invalidated on the basis of the reasoning followed by the Court in Case C-129/96 *Inter-Environnement Wallonie* [1997] ECR I-7411, paragraph 45, where it was held that, although the Member States were not obliged to adopt measures before the end of the period prescribed for transposition, it followed from the second paragraph of Article 10 EC in conjunction with the third paragraph of Article 249 EC and from Council Directive 91/156/EEC of 18 March 1991 amending Directive 75/442/EEC on waste (OJ 1991 L78, p. 32) that during that period they had to refrain from taking any measures liable seriously to compromise the result prescribed by the directive. Even if the temporary derogation laid down by Regulation ... 3577/92 can be equated with the period for transposing a directive, it is not in any event apparent from the order for reference that it is alleged in the main proceedings that the Hellenic Republic took measures liable seriously to compromise the application of that regulation from 1 January 2004.'

11. Having regard to paragraph 19 of the order in Case C-285/05, the referring court considered that the answer to the first question referred in Case C-285/05 would possibly be different if each of the following two conditions were met, namely: (a) the Court of Justice takes the view that while the Hellenic Republic's exemption until 1 January 2004 from the implementation of Regulation ... 3577/92 was in force the Greek legislature had to refrain from adopting provisions liable seriously to compromise the full and effective application of that regulation in Greece from 1 January 2004; and (b) the Court of Justice considers that provisions such as the Greek provisions adopted before 1 January 2004 that are relevant to the outcome of the main proceedings seriously compromise the full and effective application of Regulation ... 3577/92 in Greece from 1 January 2004 onwards.

12. Taking the view that the resolution of the disputes before it required further interpretation of Articles 10 EC, 49 EC and 249 EC and of certain provisions of Regulation ... 3577/92, the Simvoulio tis Epikratias (Council of State) decided to stay the proceedings and refer the following questions to the Court for a preliminary ruling:

> '1. In accordance with the second paragraph of Article 10 EC and the second paragraph of Article 249 EC:
>
> > (a) was the Greek legislature obliged, for the duration of the temporary exemption until 1 January 2004 from the implementation of ... Regulation ... 3577/92 ... which was introduced by Article 6(3) of that regulation and

relates to Greece, to refrain from adopting provisions liable seriously to compromise the full and effective application of the regulation in Greece from 1 January 2004 onwards?

    (b) are individuals entitled to rely on that regulation to contest the validity of provisions adopted by the Greek legislature before 1 January 2004 in the event that those national provisions seriously compromise the full and effective application of the regulation in Greece from 1 January 2004?

2. If the first question referred for a preliminary ruling is answered in the affirmative, is the full application from 1 January 2004 of Regulation ... 3577/92 in Greece seriously compromised by reason of the adoption by the Greek legislature, before 1 January 2004, of provisions which are exhaustive and permanent in nature, do not lay down that they cease to have force from 1 January 2004 and are contrary to provisions of that regulation?

3. If the answers to the first two questions referred for a preliminary ruling are in the affirmative, do Articles 1, 2, and 4 of Regulation ... 3577/92 permit the adoption of national rules under which shipowners may provide maritime cabotage services only on specific operational routes determined each year by a national authority competent for that purpose and after first obtaining an administrative licence granted under an authorisation scheme having the following characteristics:

    (a) it relates to all operational routes, without exception, which serve islands, and
    (b) the competent national authorities may approve an application submitted for the grant of a licence to operate a service by unilaterally amending, in the exercise of their discretion and without prior definition by a rule of law of the criteria applied, the elements of the application which relate to the frequency and the period of interruption of the service and to the fare tariff?

4. If the answers to the first two questions referred for a preliminary ruling are in the affirmative, is a restriction on the freedom to provide services that is impermissible for the purposes of Article 49 EC introduced by national legislation which provides that a shipowner to whom the administration has granted a licence to operate a ship on a specified route (either after his application in that regard has been approved as it stands, or after it has been approved with amendments to certain of its elements, which he accepts) is in principle obliged to work the particular operational route continuously for the entire duration of the annual operational period, and that to secure compliance with this obligation imposed on him he must deposit, before the operational service commences, a letter of guarantee all or part of whose amount will be forfeited if the obligation in question is not complied with or not complied with precisely?'

Consideration of the questions referred
The second question

13. By its second question, which it is appropriate to consider first, the referring court asks in essence whether, assuming that the Greek legislature was required, for the duration of the exemption in Greece from implementation of Regulation ... 3577/92, to refrain from adopting provisions liable seriously to compromise the full and effective application of the regulation from 1 January 2004, the date on which that period of exemption expired, such full and effective application is seriously compromised because the Greek legislature adopted before 1 January 2004 provisions contrary to the regulation which are exhaustive and permanent in nature and do not lay down that they cease to apply from 1 January 2004.

14. The applicants in the main proceedings take the view that this question should be answered in the affirmative, whereas the Greek Government and the European Commission suggest, in essence, that it be answered in the negative.

FREEDOM TO PROVIDE SERVICES

15. The mere fact that a Member State adopted, in 2001, legislation such as Law No 2932/2001 – assuming that the latter is not consistent with Regulation ... 3577/92 – cannot be considered, in itself, seriously to compromise the application of the regulation after the end of the period of temporary exemption, fixed at 1 January 2004, irrespective, moreover, of the exhaustive nature of that legislation. A fact of that kind is not, in itself, such as to prevent the regulation from applying fully after the end of the period of temporary exemption.

16. The same is true of the fact that legislation such as Law No 2932/2001 is permanent in nature. As the Greek Government and the Commission rightly point out, there is nothing to prevent that legislation from being repealed before the end of the period of temporary exemption.

17. Consequently, the answer to the second question referred is that, assuming that the Greek legislature was required, for the duration of the exemption in Greece from implementation of Regulation ... 3577/92, to refrain from adopting provisions liable seriously to compromise the full and effective application of the regulation from 1 January 2004, the date on which that period of exemption expired, such full and effective application is not seriously compromised simply because in 2001 the Greek legislature adopted provisions contrary to the regulation which are exhaustive and permanent in nature and do not lay down that they cease to apply from 1 January 2004.

The first, third and fourth questions

18. In view of the answer given to the second question, it is unnecessary to reply to the first question. Moreover, since the third and fourth questions have been asked should the answers to the first two questions be in the affirmative, it is also unnecessary to answer those questions."

7.250 The Court ruled:

"Assuming that the Greek legislature was required, for the duration of the exemption in Greece from implementation of ... Regulation ... 3577/92, ... to refrain from adopting provisions liable seriously to compromise the full and effective application of the regulation from 1 January 2004, the date on which that period of exemption expired, such full and effective application is not seriously compromised simply because in 2001 the Greek legislature adopted provisions contrary to the regulation which are exhaustive and permanent in nature and do not lay down that they cease to apply from 1 January 2004."

2003: *Commission v Finland*

7.251 On 11 November 2003, the Commission announced that it was taking Finland to the CJEU[187] in respect of discriminatory charges on vessels. Finnish legislation on the taxes levied on vessels using maritime navigation routes failed to comply with EU law because it allowed cabotage services between two Finnish ports to be taxed differently from international maritime transport services. The Commission decided to issue a reasoned opinion to Finland on the grounds that its legislation on fairway dues fails to comply with the European rules on the freedom to provide maritime transport services. The Commission believed that the Finnish scheme breaches the European rules on the freedom to provide maritime transport services. In particular, it makes international operations in Finnish waters more difficult and more costly than purely national services. If no satisfactory response was received from the Finnish authorities within two months, the Commission reserved the right to refer this matter to the CJEU. Although the services

---

187 IP/03/1532.

provided to vessels are the same, Finnish legislation imposes higher fees for use of waterways on international traffic than on vessels performing cabotage operations between two ports in Finland. The fairway charge is calculated differently in each case. Vessels performing cabotage operations are liable to payment of an annual lump sum calculated on the basis of the net tonnage of the vessels and entitling them to an unlimited number of voyages. No account is taken of their "ice class" for this purpose. By contrast, vessels entering a Finnish port from another country must pay a charge based on both net tonnage and ice class for each of their first ten or 32 voyages, depending on the type of vessel. The Commission believed that although the Finnish legislation does not discriminate on grounds of the nationality of the provider of the services, it creates an obstacle to the freedom to provide services since it draws a distinction between international and domestic traffic, even though the services provided are the same. It therefore hampers operation of the internal market. The matter appears to have been resolved without court action.

2014: *Alpina River Cruises GmbH v Ministero delle Infrastructure e dei transporti*

7.252 On 27 March 2014, the CJEU[188] confirmed in *Alpina River Cruises GmbH and Nicko Tours GmbH v Ministero delle infrastrutture e dei trasporti – Capitaneria di Porto di Chioggia*[189] that Regulation 3577/92 applies to maritime cruises. The case related to proceedings between, on the one hand, Alpina River Cruises GmbH (a Swiss company) and Nicko Tours GmbH (a German company) and the Ministero delle infrastrutture e dei trasporti – Capitaneria di Porto di Chioggia (Senior Ministry for Infrastructure and Transport – Chioggia Port Authority (Italy)) relating to the authority's refusal to allow Alpina and Nicko Tours to sail a tourist vessel flying the Swiss flag through Italian territorial sea. The CJEU considered Articles 1(1), 2, 3 and 6 of Regulation 3577/92. The court also considered the relevant Italian law – under Article 224 of the Italian Shipping Code (Royal Decree No 327 of 30 March 1942, as amended) ("the ISC"):

> "1. The provision of cabotage services between the ports of the Republic is reserved, pursuant to [Regulation 3577/92], for Community shipowners who have their ships registered in, and flying the flag of, a Member State of the European Union, provided that these ships comply with all conditions for carrying out cabotage in that Member State.
> 2. The provisions of point 1 shall apply to vessels providing port, estuary and coastal maritime services."

7.253 Alpina and Nicko Tours were the shipowner and user company of the tourist vessel *MS Bellissima* which flew the Swiss flag. The companies organised a cruise to depart from Venice (Italy) which would involve crossing the Venetian lagoon to Chioggia (Italy), crossing territorial sea between Chioggia and Porto Levante (Italy), travelling for approximately 60 kilometres up the river Po (Italy) to the town of Polesella (Italy) and returning to Venice following the reverse itinerary.[190] Before the cruise, Alpina and Nicko

---

188 Third Chamber: Judges Ilešič (Rapporteur and President of the Chamber), Fernlund, Ó Caoimh, Toader and Jarašiūnas. Advocate-General was P Cruz Villalón.
189 Case C-17/13 ECLI:EU:C:2014:191. See (2014) 319 EU Focus 37.
190 Crossing the stretch of Italian territorial sea between the ports of Chioggia and Porto Levante was necessary due to the size of the *MS Bellissima*, which prevented it from navigating the canal connecting Chioggia with the river Po.

Tours had submitted to the Ministero delle infrastrutture e dei trasporti – Capitaneria di Porto di Chioggia an application for authorisation to cross that stretch of sea. The authority rejected the application on the ground that maritime cabotage was reserved for ships flying the flag of a Member State. Alpina and Nicko Tours contested that decision before the Tribunale amministrativo regionale per il Veneto (Veneto Regional Administrative Court). The latter dismissed the action by judgment of 12 April 2012, finding that the service at issue falls within the concept of "maritime cabotage" referred to in Regulation 3577/92 and is therefore subject to the reservation of cabotage services "for Community shipowners who have their ships registered in, and flying the flag of, a Member State of the European Union", stated in Article 224 of the ISC. Alpina and Nicko Tours appealed against that judgment to the Consiglio di Stato (Council of State), claiming that the concept of "maritime cabotage" applies only to services that involve true sea transport. They argued that the cruise at issue did not involve such transport for, with the exception of the short passage through territorial sea between Chioggia and Porto Levante, it would take place in internal waters. The Consiglio di Stato stayed enforcement of that judgment. For the rest, it decided to stay the proceedings and to refer the following question to the Court of Justice for a preliminary ruling:

> "Must [Regulation 3577/92] be interpreted as applying to cruises carried out between ports within a Member State without different passengers embarking and disembarking in those ports, in that those cruises start and end with the same passengers embarking and disembarking in the same port within that Member State?"

7.254 The CJEU reformulated the question as, in essence, whether a cruise which starts and ends, with the same passengers, in the same port of the Member State in which it takes place, is covered by the term "maritime cabotage" within the meaning of Regulation 3577/92.

7.255 Italy and the European Commission argued that the question should be answered in the affirmative, Alpina and Nicko Tours argued that a reply was unnecessary noting that Regulation 3577/92 related to sea transport and that, consequently, that regulation did not apply to a river cruise such as that at issue in the main proceedings. Therefore, instead of giving the interpretation sought by the referring court, Alpina and Nicko argued that it would be appropriate to find that Regulation 3577/92 does not at all events concern cruises whose itinerary takes place mainly in non-maritime waters.

7.256 The CJEU opined:

> "17. In that regard, it is true that it is apparent from Article 1(1) of Regulation ... 3577/92 that that regulation relates only to transport services within a Member State (cabotage) which are of a maritime nature. Consequently, as Alpina and Nicko Tours correctly note, inland waterway transport services provided within a Member State and not of a maritime nature are not governed by that regulation. By contrast, those services fall within the scope of Council Regulation ... 3921/91 of 16 December 1991 laying down the conditions under which non-resident carriers may transport goods or passengers by inland waterway within a Member State (OJ 1991 L373, p. 1).
> 18. However, contrary to what Alpina and Nicko Tours claim, it does not appear that the cruise which is the subject of the dispute in the main proceedings has a mainly non-maritime nature.
> 19. The term 'sea' referred to by Regulation ... 3577/92 is not limited to territorial sea within the meaning of the United Nations Convention on the Law of the Sea, signed in Montego Bay (Jamaica) on 10 December 1982, entered into force on 16 November 1994 and

approved on behalf of the European Community by Council Decision 98/392/EC of 23 March 1998 (OJ 1998 L179, p. 1), but also covers internal maritime waters which are on the landward side of the baseline of the territorial sea (see, to that effect, Case C-323/03 Commission v Spain EU:C:2006:159, paragraphs 25 to 27).

20. Consequently, even if Alpina and Nicko Tours are correct in claiming that the crossing of the stretch of sea between Chioggia and Porto Levante is in itself too short to confer a maritime nature on the cruise at issue in the main proceedings, their argument that that cruise has a mainly non-maritime nature appears, subject to verification by the referring court, at all events to be unfounded in that, besides that stretch, other sections of the itinerary, such as the areas of navigation in the Venetian lagoon and in the mouth of the river Po, form part of the internal maritime waters of the Italian Republic.

21. The relevance of the interpretation of Regulation ... 3577/92 sought by the referring court is not, moreover, affected by the fact that the vessel used for the cruise at issue in the main proceedings flies the Swiss flag.

22. The solution to that dispute depends on whether the reservation of the cabotage services between the Italian ports 'for Community shipowners who have their ships registered in, and flying the flag of, a Member State of the European Union' set out in Article 224 of the ISC, was lawfully applied against Alpina and Nicko Tours in relation to the cruise using the vessel flying the Swiss flag. As the order for reference confirms, it is apparent from Article 224 that the reservation which it sets out relates only to cabotage services covered by Regulation ... 3577/92. Consequently, in order for it to determine whether a cruise which starts and ends in the same port constitutes a cabotage service within the meaning of Article 224 of the ISC, the referring court must first know whether such a cruise comes under the cabotage services covered by Regulation ... 3577/92.

23. In the light of the foregoing considerations, it is appropriate for the Court to provide the interpretation sought by the referring court without its being necessary to amend or extend the scope of the question referred for a preliminary ruling in the way suggested by Alpina and Nicko Tours.

24. In order to reply to the question referred, it is necessary to note at the outset that it is unambiguously apparent from the reference to 'cruise liners' in Article 3(1) of Regulation ... 3577/92 and from the derogation provided until 1 January 1995 for some cruise services in Article 6(1) of that regulation that cruises are among the types of transport covered by that regulation.

25. However, since Regulation ... 3577/92 concerns 'maritime cabotage' alone, only cruises covered by that concept fall within the ambit of that regulation.

26. That concept being defined, in Article 1(1) and Article 2(1) of Regulation ... 3577/92, by the phrase 'maritime transport services within a Member State', it must be considered that all cruise services normally provided for remuneration in the maritime waters of a Member State fall within the ambit of that regulation.

27. When such a cruise starts and ends, with the same passengers, in the same port, the fact that the departure and arrival ports are one and the same and that the passengers are the same throughout the itinerary cannot render Regulation ... 3577/92 inapplicable.

28. It is true that the transport services listed in Article 2(1)(a) to (c) of Regulation ... 3577/92 are described as having different departure and arrival ports. However, that list, which is introduced by the term 'in particular', is not exhaustive and cannot have the effect of excluding from the scope of that regulation transport services having all the essential characteristics of maritime cabotage contained in the above-mentioned phrase 'maritime transport services within a Member State' (see, to that effect, Case C-251/04 Commission v Greece EU:C:2007:5, paragraphs 28 and 32)."

7.257 The CJEU therefore ruled that a maritime transport service consisting of a cruise which starts and ends, with the same passengers, in the same port of the Member State in which it takes place, is covered by the term "maritime cabotage" within the meaning of Regulation 3577/92.

2014: *Fonnship A/S v Svenska Transportarbetareförbundet and Facket för Service och Kommunikation (SEKO) and Svenska Transportarbetareförbundet v Fonnship A/S*

7.258 On 8 July 2014, the Grand Chamber of the CJEU delivered a very important preliminary ruling in the *Fonnship A/S v Svenska Transportarbetareförbundet and Facket för Service och Kommunikation (SEKO) and Svenska Transportarbetareförbundet v Fonnship A/S* case.[191] In essence, the CJEU ruled that Article 1 of Regulation 4055/86 must be interpreted as meaning that a company established in a State that is a party to the European Economic Area ("EEA") Agreement and which is proprietor of a vessel flying the flag of a third country, by which maritime transport services are provided from or to a State that is a party to the EEA Agreement, may rely on the freedom to provide services, provided that it can, due to its operation of that vessel, be classed as a provider of those services and that the persons for whom the services are intended are established in States that are parties to the EEA Agreement other than that in which that company is established.

7.259 The request to the CJEU for a preliminary ruling arose in proceedings between (i) on the one hand, the Norwegian company Fonnship A/S[192] and, on the other hand, Svenska Transportarbetareförbundet (the Swedish Transport Workers' Union, "ST") and Facket för Service och Kommunikation (Union for Service and Communication; "SEKO"), which were two unions incorporated under Swedish law, on the other, and (ii) ST and Fonnship, concerning industrial action which allegedly disrupted the provision of services provided using a vessel owned by Fonnship and flying the Panamanian flag.

7.260 After considering relevant EEA Agreement provisions, the CJEU considered various provisions of Regulation 4055/86 (including Recitals 7–9 and 12 as well as Articles 1(1) to (3)) as well as the relevant Swedish law (including the Swedish Constitution which guaranteed the right to take industrial action, subject to the limitations laid down by law). It then considered the facts. According to Fonnship, the crew members' wages on the relevant vessel were governed by a collective agreement concluded between Fonnship and a Russian trade union. According to Fonnship, the wages, which were approximately US$550 per month for the seamen, were equal to, or even better than, the wages recommended by the ITF.

7.261 In October 2001, when the vessel lay at the port of Holmsund (Sweden), ST, believing that the wages of the *Sava Star* crew were not equitable, called on Fonnship to enter into a collective agreement approved by the ITF a so called ("Special Agreement"). Following the rejection of that demand by Fonnship, industrial action took place which consisted of, *inter alia*, preventing the loading and unloading of that vessel.

7.262 A few days later, a collective agreement in the form of a "Special Agreement" was signed by Fonnship and ST ("the 2001 Agreement"). Fonnship paid US$1,794 to ST, in accordance with a provision of that agreement relating to membership fees and welfare fund contributions. The *Sava Star*'s captain prepared a letter of protest and the crew

---

191 Case C-83/13 ECLI:EU:C:2014:2053. See (2014) 322 *EU Focus* 36.
192 At the relevant time owned the vessel *Sava Star* which was a bulk carrier, which during that period, principally sailed between States that are parties to the EEA Agreement. It was registered on the Panamanian Ship Registry and therefore flew the Panamanian flag. Its crew consisted of four Polish officers and two Russian seamen. Fonnship was the crew's employer.

members signed a document stating that they did not approve of the measures taken by ST. The vessel was subsequently able to leave the port of Holmsund.

7.263 In 2002, Fonnship brought legal proceedings against ST before the Arbetsdomstolen (Labour Court) seeking an order that ST, first, repay it US$1,794 and, second, pay it damages of approximately US$10,000 for the economic loss caused by the abovementioned industrial action. ST then brought legal proceedings against Fonnship before the Arbetsdomstolen seeking an order that Fonnship pay it US$10,000 in damages for breach of the 2001 Agreement. According to ST, when the vessel lay in port at Reykjavik (Iceland), Fonnship had refused, in breach of the 2001 Agreement, to send certain documents to a person appointed by a trade union federation and had prevented that person from contacting the crew.

7.264 In 2003, the vessel was in port at Köping (Sweden). At that time, the 2001 Agreement had expired. SEKO required, in the same way that ST had done in 2001, that Fonnship sign a "Special Agreement". After industrial action had been taken, such a collective agreement was signed on 19 February 2003 ("the 2003 Agreement"). Fonnship paid, in accordance with the 2003 Agreement, US$1,794 to SEKO for "service fees" and welfare-fund contributions. The crew members signed a protest document. The vessel was subsequently able to leave that port.

7.265 On 11 March 2003, Fonnship brought legal proceedings against SEKO before the Arbetsdomstolen seeking an order that the union, first, repay it US$1,794 and, second, pay damages of €6,000 for the economic loss caused by the industrial action.

7.266 ST later brought legal proceedings against Fonnship before the Arbetsdomstolen seeking an order that that company pay it damages of approximately US$256,000, on the ground that it had not paid, during the period covered by the 2001 Agreement, the wages stipulated. The amount corresponds to the difference between the wages paid by Fonnship to the crew and the wages stipulated under the agreement.

7.267 In the context of the four cases pending before the Arbetsdomstolen, Fonnship claimed that it was not bound by the 2001 and 2003 Agreements and that ST and SEKO must pay it damages and not the other way round. In this regard, it submitted, first, that those two agreements are invalid, on the grounds of the lack of consent and the existence of unfair terms, and, second, that the industrial action giving rise to the signing of those agreements was unlawful.

7.268 The Arbetsdomstolen considered that the question of the lawfulness of that industrial action is of decisive importance for the outcome of the disputes in the main proceedings and that, to answer that question, it had to rule on whether Swedish law on industrial action is compatible with the rules of EU law on the freedom to provide services. Since the parties are, however, in dispute as to whether those rules may be relevant in a situation such as that in those disputes, in which the vessel at issue flies the Panamanian flag, it is necessary, according to that court, first to examine the question of the applicability of EU law. The Arbetsdomstolen therefore decided to stay the proceedings and to refer the following question for a preliminary ruling:

> "Is the rule in the EEA Agreement on free movement of services, maritime transport services – which rule has an equivalent in the EC Treaty – applicable to a company with its seat in an EFTA State [European Free Trade Association] as regards its activity in the form of transport services to an [European Community] Member State or an EFTA State using a vessel which is registered and flagged in another country outside the [European Community] and/or [the] EEA?"

7.269 The CJEU then considered the issues:

"24. ... Regulation ... 4055/86 [forms] an integral part of the legal order of all of the States that are parties to the EEA Agreement by virtue of Article 7(a) of the EEA Agreement and Annex XIII thereto. That regulation and those provisions of the EEA Agreement contain rules relating to the applicability of the freedom to provide services in the shipping industry between States that are parties to the EEA Agreement and between those States and third countries (see, to that effect, *Corsica Ferries (France)*, C-49/89, EU:C:1989:649, paragraph 13; *Commission v Italy*, C-295/00, EU:C:2002:100, paragraph 9; and *Sea-Land Service and Nedlloyd Lijnen*, C-430/99 and C-431/99, EU:C:2002:364, paragraph 30).

25. Article 1(1) and (2) of that regulation determines which operators enjoy the freedom to provide services.

26. Therefore, by its question, the referring court asks, in essence, whether Article 1 of Regulation ... 4055/86 must be interpreted as meaning that a company established in a State that is a party to the EEA Agreement and which is proprietor of a vessel flying the flag of a third country, by which maritime transport services are provided from or to a State that is a party to the EEA Agreement, may rely on the freedom to provide services in carrying out that economic activity.

27. Fonnship, the Greek Government and the European Commission consider that that question must be answered in the affirmative. The EFTA Surveillance Authority endorses that position but states that it is necessary to ensure that the company relying on the freedom to provide services, in this case Fonnship, is in fact the provider of the services at issue.

28. According to ST and SEKO, the question must be answered in the negative. Where a vessel flies the flag of a third country, the employment conditions of the crew of that vessel and the industrial action taken to improve them do not have any connecting factor with EU law and cannot therefore be examined in the light of that law.

29. Furthermore, ST and SEKO dispute that Fonnship may be considered to be a provider of maritime transport services established in the EEA. They claim to have information according to which Fonnship had, in essence, conferred the running of Sava Star to another company which, while being a company incorporated under Norwegian law, was controlled by a company established in Panama.

30. According to the Swedish Government, Article 1 of Regulation ... 4055/86 must be interpreted with caution with regard to companies established in the EEA and using flags of third countries to avoid the employment conditions which are normal in the EEA.

31. Where the crew members of the vessel at issue are nationals of a third country, that fact could, according to the Swedish Government, also render Regulation ... 4055/86 inapplicable to transport using that vessel.

32. It should be noted, first, that it is apparent from the wording and structure of Article 1 of Regulation ... 4055/86 that, in defining the scope ratione personae of the freedom to provide services in the shipping industry from or to States that are parties to the EEA Agreement, that article identifies two categories of persons who enjoy, if certain conditions are satisfied, that freedom to provide services, namely, first, nationals of a State that is a party to the EEA Agreement who are established in the EEA and, second, nationals of a State that is a party to the EEA who are established in a third country, as well as shipping companies established in a third country and controlled by nationals of a State that is a party to the EEA Agreement.

33. Next, it is apparent from the seventh to ninth and twelfth recitals of Regulation ... 4055/86 and from the travaux préparatoires thereof, as set out in the observations submitted to the Court, that, by including in that scope ratione personae the nationals of a Member State established in a third country or controlling a shipping company there, the EU legislature wished to ensure that a significant part of the commercial fleets owned by nationals of a Member State come under the liberalisation of the shipping industry established by that regulation, so that Member States' shipowners could better face, inter alia, the restrictions imposed by third countries.

34. Finally, the legislature set out a requirement that there be a connection by providing – in using the words 'if their vessels are registered in that [State that is a party to the EEA Agreement] in accordance with its legislation' in Article 1(2) of Regulation ... 4055/86 – that the nationals of a State which is a party to the EEA Agreement who operate from an establishment situated in a third country are excluded from the freedom to provide services if their vessels do not fly the flag of that State.

35. The absence in Article 1(1) of a similar requirement for the nationals of a State that is a party to the EEA Agreement who operate from an establishment situated in the EEA shows that the legislature considered that that category of persons displays in itself a sufficiently close connection with the law of the EEA to be included in the scope ratione personae of that regulation, and regardless of the flag flown by their vessels (see, to that effect, Corsica Ferries, C-18/93, EU:C:1994:195, paragraph 29).

36. In the light of that distinction, it is necessary, in cases where a national of a State that is a party to the EEA Agreement who is established in the EEA or a company established in the EEA rely on Article 1(1) of Regulation ... 4055/86 in a dispute relating to the question whether maritime transport services carried out using a vessel flying the flag of a third country fall within the scope of the freedom to provide services, to ascertain whether that national or that company may be considered to be a service provider.

37. Situations should not exist in which a shipping company established in a third country and providing maritime transport services from or to States that are parties to the EEA Agreement using vessels flying the flag of a third country enjoys, despite not meeting the connection requirement laid down in Article 1(2) of Regulation ... 4055/86, the freedom to provide services by claiming that benefit through a company established in the EEA which it controls, under the pretext that that company is a provider of the services at issue, where, in reality, it is the company established in the third country which provides them.

38. As the Advocate General noted at points 44 to 50 of his Opinion, for a company to be classed as a provider of maritime transport services, it must operate the vessel by which the transport is carried out.

39. In this case, Fonnship claimed, in reply to ST's and SEKO's contentions referred to in paragraph 29 above, that it operated the Sava Star itself during the relevant period. It is within the exclusive jurisdiction of the referring court to assess the truth of that assertion.

40. Assuming that its assessment shows that Fonnship must be classed as a provider of the maritime transport services at issue in the disputes in the main proceedings and, since it is not disputed that the persons for whom the services were intended were, in this case, established in a Member State which is a party to the EEA Agreement other than the Kingdom of Norway, the referring court would be led to conclude that that company falls, for the purposes of the outcome of those proceedings, within the scope ratione personae of Regulation ... 4055/86, pursuant to Article 1(1) thereof.

41. In that case, any restriction which, without objective justification, is liable to prohibit, impede or render less attractive the provision of those services must be declared incompatible with EU law. Where it is applicable, Regulation ... 4055/86 transposes, in essence, the rules of the treaty relating to the freedom to provide services and the case-law relating thereto (Commission v France, C-381/93, EU:C:1994:370, paragraphs 13 and 16; Commission v Italy, EU:C:2002:100, paragraphs 9 and 10; Sea-Land Service and Nedlloyd Lijnen, EU:C:2002:364, paragraphs 31 and 32; Geha Naftiliaki and Others, C-435/00, EU:C:2002:661, paragraphs 20 and 21; and Commission v Spain, C-18/09, EU:C:2010:58, paragraph 12). That case-law includes the judgment in Laval un Partneri (C-341/05, EU:C:2007:809) relating to the compatibility of industrial action with the freedom to provide services.

42. The application of Regulation ... 4055/86 is in no way affected by the fact that the vessel carrying out the maritime transport at issue, and on which the workers in whose favour that industrial action was taken are employed, flies the flag of a third country, nor by the fact that the crew members of the vessel are, as in the present case, third country nationals.

43. For Article 1(1) of Regulation ... 4055/86 to be applicable, it is sufficient for a provider of the maritime transport service to be a national of a State that is a party to the EEA

Agreement who is established in a State that is a party to the EEA Agreement other than that of the person for whom the services are intended.

44. In the light of all of the foregoing considerations, the answer to the question is that Article 1 of Regulation ... 4055/86 must be interpreted as meaning that a company established in a State that is a party to the EEA Agreement and which is proprietor of a vessel flying the flag of a third country, by which maritime transport services are provided from or to a State that is a party to the EEA Agreement, may rely on the freedom to provide services, provided that it can, due to its operation of that vessel, be classed as a provider of those services and that the persons for whom the services are intended are established in States that are parties to the EEA Agreement other than that in which that company is established.

7.270 The CJEU therefore ruled that Article 1 must be interpreted as meaning that a company established in an EEA State and which is proprietor of a vessel flying the flag of a third country, by which maritime transport services are provided from or to a State that is a party to the EEA Agreement, may rely on the freedom to provide services, provided that it can, due to its operation of that vessel, be classed as a provider of those services and that the persons for whom the services are intended are established in States that are parties to the EEA Agreement other than that in which that company is established.

2011: *Navtiliaki Etairia Thasou AE and Amalthia I Navtiki Etairia v Ipourgos Emborikis Navtilías*

7.271 On 17 March 2011, the CJEU delivered its ruling in *Navtiliaki Etairia Thasou AE and Amalthia I Navtiki Etairia v Ipourgos Emborikis Navtilías*.[193] The case concerned prior administrative authorisation for cabotage services and Regulation 3577/92. The case involved a reference for a preliminary ruling from the Simvoulio tis Epikratias in Greece. The references had been made in proceedings between Navtiliaki Etairia Thasou AE ("Navtiliaki Etairia Thasou") and Amalthia I Navtiki Etairia, on the one hand, and Ipourgos Emborikis Navtilías (Minister for Merchant Shipping), on the other, concerning the validity of decisions adopted by Ipourgos Emborikis Navtilías, making maritime cabotage subject to certain conditions.

7.272 The Greek national law was summarised by the CJEU as follows:

"9. Article 1 of Law 2932/2001 on the freedom to provide maritime cabotage services (FEK A' 145/27.6.2001), in the version applicable to the facts in the main proceedings ('Law 2932/2001'), provides:

'1. As from 1 November 2002, freedom to provide services shall exist in respect of maritime transport services which:

(a) are provided for remuneration by a shipowner of a Member State of the ... Community, ... and
(b) are carried out between ports situated on the mainland and the islands or between ports situated on the islands by passenger/vehicle, passenger or cargo vessels operating a regular passenger and ferry service, and by vessels of a tonnage of up to 650 gt ... provided that these vessels are registered in, and fly the flag of, Greece or another [Member] State ...

...'

---

193 Cases C-128/10 and C-129/10. The court was composed of Judges Schiemann (President of the Chamber), Bay Larsen and Toader (Rapporteur). The Advocate-General was AG Cruz Villalón.

10. Article 2(6) of Law 2932/2001 provides:

'By decision of the Minister, after consultation of the Simvoulio Aktoploïkon Syngkoinonion, public service obligations may be imposed on shipowners interested in operating a vessel on one or more routes. Those obligations shall be imposed in furtherance of reasons of public interest and shall include, without giving rise to discrimination, conditions which concern the ports to be served, the regularity of the service, the continuity, frequency and adequacy of the transport services proposed, fare tariffs and the manning of the vessels…'

11. Article 3 of Law 2932/2001, headed 'Regular operation – Conditions', provides:

'1. The operation of a passenger/vehicle, passenger or cargo vessel shall be valid for a period of one year, starting on 1 November (regular service).…
2. In order to operate services:

   (a) the vessel must satisfy all the statutory conditions for effecting cabotage in the Member State in which it is registered and in Greece, have all the shipping documents required by the provisions in force, safety and conservation of the marine environment certificates and a class certificate issued by a recognised classification society, when it is followed by it…;
   (b) the vessel must be suited to the facilities of the port installations and to any special demands of the particular route to be served…

…'

12. Article 4 of Law 2932/2001, headed 'Procedure for the operation of a regular service', provides:

'1. In order to operate one or more vessels on a particular route, a shipowner shall submit to the Ministry a declaration stating his name and the location of his seat or residence as well as, in the case of a natural person, his surname, first name and nationality. … He shall also state the vessel's designation, the services it will carry out on one or more routes within the network, the ports of departure, the final destination and the intermediate ports in order of call, the days and times of departure and arrival, the highest charge for the service in economy class or a single class … during the period of operation and the other details indicated in the decision referred to in the next paragraph.

…

3. The operating declaration shall be submitted no later than 31 January. The competent department shall publish, no later than 10 February, a press release in at least two daily newspapers distributed throughout the country which refers to the declarations which have been submitted, and, up until 20 February, any person concerned can supplement, amend or withdraw its declaration. The competent department shall communicate those amendments, no later than 28 February, by publishing a press release and indicating them on the Ministry's web page, if one exists. The department shall notify the person concerned in writing, no later than 31 March, that the declaration has been accepted, except in cases where the following paragraph applies.
4. The Minister may, to the extent necessary, amend the schedule declaration submitted if he has reason to believe that

   (a) the conditions in one or more ports do not, for reasons concerning the vessel's safety or order in the port, permit the schedules requested to be carried out,
   (b) the vessel cannot enter the port unhindered and cannot effect the transportation to a particular area of the port and at the time declared or

(c) the frequency of the services or the planned period of their interruption fails to satisfy the settled requirements as to the regular provision of services during the period of operation or, as regards the fare tariff, if he has reason to believe that the highest charge proposed, in accordance with paragraph 1, on a particular route is excessive and contrary to the public interest.

5. ... In the cases specified in paragraph 4(a) and (b), the shipowners shall be invited to adapt their timetables by mutual agreement by providing for the intervals required to solve those problems. In the absence of agreement within five days, the Minister shall adopt the necessary amendments to the timetables after consultation of the Simvoulio Aktoploïkon Syngkoinonion.

...'."

7.273 On 30 January 2006, Navtiliaki Etairia Thasou, a Greek shipping company, submitted regular service operating declarations to Ipourgos Emborikis Navtilías, attaching a table of itineraries, for the period from 1 November 2006 to 31 October 2007 concerning its ships which operate the service between the mainland and the island of Thasos, more precisely, the routes from Kavala to Prinos Thasou and from Keramoti to Thasos. Ipourgos Emborikis Navtilías sought an opinion on those declarations from the Kavala port authority and the Simvoulio Aktoploïkon Syngkoinonion, which was the collective body responsible for matters relating to cabotage, and consisted of representatives of all the social and professional bodies involved in cabotage. In March 2006, the Kavala port authority sent Ipourgos Emborikis Navtilías an opinion which indicated, in substance, first, that the simultaneous or almost simultaneous arrival or departure of vessels jeopardised the safety of shipping and, second, that another timetable for those arrivals and departures would ensure a better public service, and amendments to the timetable proposed by Navtiliaki Etairia Thasou were recommended. As various consultation meetings held at the Kavala Central Port Authority and the Ministry of Merchant Shipping failed to result in an agreement, in particular with regard to the timetable for services, the Simvoulio Aktoploïkon Syngkoinonion issued an opinion in October 2006 in which it endorsed the amendments suggested by the Kavala port authority. Ipourgos Emborikis Navtilías then imposed, by five decisions in October 2006, the following amendments to Navtiliaki Etairia Thasou's declaration:

- As regards the route from Kavala to Prinos Thasou, it amended by half an hour the operation of the service and thus decided that, for the period from 1 July to 31 August 2007, Navtiliaki Etairia Thasou's vessels would depart from the port of Prinos Thasou at 19:00 instead of 18:30 as initially declared.
- As regards the route from Keramoti to Thasos, Ipourgos Emborikis Navtilías decided that:

    (a) the times for operating services established for the ships of Navtiliaki Etairia Thasou remain those established for corresponding services for the previous operating period from 1 November 2005 to 31 October 2006,
    (b) for the period from 1 July to 31 August 2007, given the size of the Keramoti port and for safety reasons, the services must be carried out at 30 minute intervals.

7.274 Navtiliaki Etairia Thasou contested the validity of the amendments imposed by Ipourgos Emborikis Navtilías before the referring court and argued that the provisions of

Law 2932/2001, pursuant to which the decisions at issue imposed unilateral amendments to the timetables, are invalid because they are contrary to the provisions of the regulation.

7.275 The referring court took the view that the acceptance of the shipowners' declarations by Ipourgos Emborikis Navtilías constituted authorisation in Greek law. It argued that, as follows from Article 4(4) of Law 2932/2001, that law makes maritime cabotage services subject to a system of prior administrative authorisation which pursues in particular the objectives, first, of verifying, in accordance with Article 4(4)(a) and (b), whether, in light of the situation prevailing in a specific port, the schedules declared by the shipowner can be carried out under conditions which ensure the safety of the ship and the maintenance of order in the port and also that there will be no hindrance to entering the port, and, second, of imposing, as provided for by Article 4(4)(c), possible public service obligations relating to *inter alia* the frequency of services and, more generally, adequate services on the route concerned. The Greek referring court also highlighted that Article 4(5) of Law 2932/2001 in its original version provided that, where several shipowners requested access at the same time to a port which did not have enough capacity and the shipowners were unable to coordinate their arrival by mutual agreement, the administration was to issue an invitation to tender in order to determine the berth and anchor priority. Interestingly, by reference to paragraph 34 of *Analir and Others*,[194] the referring court furthermore observes that the system of prior authorisation established by Article 4(4)(c) of Law 2932/2001 concerns without exception all shipping routes to the islands, although it does not appear that, before adopting those rules, the competent national authorities determined, for each of those routes, that the regular transport services would be likely to be inadequate if their provision were left to market forces alone. In view of those considerations, the Simvoulio tis Epikratias (the Greek Council of State) decided to stay the proceedings and to refer the following question to the CJEU for a preliminary ruling:

> "Do the provisions of Articles 1, 2 and 4 of [the regulation], interpreted in accordance with the principle of freedom to provide services, allow national schemes to be adopted, whereby shipowners cannot provide cabotage services without a prior administrative authorisation, when:
>
> (a) the purpose of the authorisation system in question is to allow verification of whether, in light of the prevailing conditions in a specific port, the schedules declared by the shipowner can be implemented under conditions of safety for the ship and maintenance of order in the port and verification of the ability of the scheduled vessel to enter a specific port unhindered at the time declared by the shipowner as the preferred time for a specific service without, however, determination in advance in a legal rule of the criteria on the basis of which the authorities rule on such questions, especially in a case where more than one shipowner is interested in entering the same port at the same time;
> (b) at the same time, the authorisation system in question constitutes a means of imposing public service obligations, inasmuch as it has in that respect the following features:
>
>   (i) it applies without exception to all scheduled shipping routes to the islands,
>   (ii) it grants the administrative authority responsible for issuing authorisations the broadest discretionary powers in terms of imposing public service obligations, without determining in advance in a legal rule the criteria for the exercise of those powers and without determining in advance the content of the public service obligations which may be imposed?"

---

194 Case C-205/99 [2001] ECR I-1271, ECLI:EU:C:2001:107.

7.276 The CJEU began by making a number of preliminary observations:

"32. First, it should be noted that, under Article 58(1) TFEU, freedom to provide services in the field of transport is to be governed by the provisions of Title VI of Part Three of that treaty, relating to transport, which include Article 100(2) TFEU, which enables the European Parliament and the Council to adopt appropriate provisions for sea transport.

33. On the basis of Article 80(2) EC, now Article 100(2) TFEU, the European legislature adopted the Regulation which has as its aim, as stated in Article 1 thereof, the application to Community shipowners of the principle of freedom to provide services in maritime transport within the territory of each Member State (Analir and Others, paragraph 20, and Case C-323/03 Commission v Spain [2006] ECR I-2161, paragraph 43).

34. Pursuant to the eighth recital in the preamble to the Regulation, the implementation of the freedom to provide maritime cabotage services was to be gradual. Pursuant to Article 6(2) and (3) of the Regulation, the Hellenic Republic was exempted from the application of the Regulation until 1 January 2004. At the time that the ministerial acts in question were adopted, the Regulation was, according to Article 6(2) and (3) thereof, already applicable in Greece ratione temporis.

35. Second, the Court must consider, as a further preliminary point, whether the rules laid down by Greek law actually establish a system of prior authorisation.

36. In that regard, it should be noted that it is clear from the contents of the file that the decisions in the two sets of main proceedings concerned the imposition of amendments to the hours of departure proposed by the shipowners because of, first, the safety of ships and order in the ports and, second, the need to ensure a certain frequency on the routes served.

37. The observations submitted to the Court reveal a divergence of views on the interpretation of the applicable national law. The Greek Government and the European Commission do not agree on whether that law establishes a system of authorisation.

38. The Commission, like the referring court, considers that the system established by Law 2932/2001, under which Ipourgos Emborikis Navtilías can accept or reject the scheduled service operating declarations made by owners of ships, constitutes an authorisation system such as that at issue in Analir and Others.[195]

39. By contrast, the Greek Government submits that the procedure for examining those operating declarations submitted by shipowners does not empower the administration to carry out a review of the substance of the declarations, but merely allows it to carry out a formal review and that accordingly that procedure is not an authorisation system.

40. In that respect, it should be recalled that, as regards the interpretation of provisions of national law, the Court is in principle required to base its consideration on the description given in the order for reference. It is settled case-law that the Court of Justice does not have jurisdiction to interpret the internal law of a Member State (Case C-511/03 Ten Kate Holding Musselkanaal and Others [2005] ECR I-8979, paragraph 25 and case-law).

41. In the present case, since, according to the orders for reference, the Greek administration does not just accept the shipowners' operating declarations, but can also amend the transport plans proposed by the shipowners, particularly with regard to the departure times of the ships, the legal effects of such an amendment are equivalent to those of an authorisation. It follows that Law 2932/2001 in fact establishes a system of prior authorisation for the provision of maritime cabotage services.

42. Third, in so far as the referring court, by its questions, does not seek the interpretation of the concepts referred to in Article 2 of the Regulation, the Court finds that the appropriateness of ruling on that article is not established."

The CJEU then turned to the Greek measures to review the safety of ships and order in ports:

"43. As regards the question whether the Regulation, and in particular Article 1 thereof, precludes a system, such as that at issue in the main proceedings, liable to culminate in the

---

195 Ed., Case C-205/99 [2001] ECR I-1271, ECLI:EU:C:2001:107.

imposition of timeslots for reasons of the safety of ships and order in ports, it is important to note that national rules, which make the provision of maritime cabotage services subject to prior administrative authorisation, are liable to impede or render less attractive the provision of those services and therefore constitute a restriction on the freedom to provide them (see *Analir and Others*,[196] paragraph 22, and *Commission v Spain*, paragraph 44).

44. In the present case, the Court finds that the amendments to the shipowners' timetable proposals for reasons relating to the safety of ports and ships can constitute a restriction on the freedom to provide services which applies to the field of maritime cabotage for the purposes of Article 1 of the Regulation.

45. Such a restriction may, however, be justified by overriding reasons in the public interest. As is clear from settled case-law, the aim of ensuring safety in port waters constitutes such an overriding reason in the public interest (see to that effect, Case C-266/96 Corsica Ferries France [1998] ECR I-3949, paragraph 60).

46. In order for a measure based on reasons of safety in port waters to be justified, it must nevertheless satisfy the conditions of proportionality and non-discrimination.

47. As regards, in particular, the examination of proportionality, it should, first, be acknowledged that the introduction of a system of prior authorisation seeking, as the system at issue in the main proceedings does, to ensure that the presence at the same time of several ships in a port does not give rise to risks to the safety of those ships is an appropriate and a necessary means of pursuing the objective of safety in port waters.

48. Second, it follows from the case-law of the Court that a prior authorisation scheme cannot render legitimate discretionary conduct on the part of the national authorities which is liable to negate the effectiveness of provisions of European Union law, in particular those relating to a fundamental freedom such as that at issue in the main proceedings. Therefore, if a prior authorisation scheme is to be justified even though it derogates from that freedom, it must be based on objective, non-discriminatory criteria known in advance, in such a way as adequately to circumscribe the exercise of the national authorities' discretion (see Case C-338/09 Yellow Cab Verkehrsbetrieb [2010] ECR I-0000, paragraph 53 and the case-law cited).

49. The need to circumscribe the exercise of the administration's power by those criteria also applies when, in a situation such as that in the main proceedings, which concerns the sharing of timeslots between a number of interested shipowners in competition with each other, the national administration decides between the candidates where reasons of safety of ships and ports prevent a number of departures at the same time or require spacing between them.

50. In the present case, pursuant to Article 4(4)(a) and (b) of Law 2932/2001, the amendment to the timeslots proposed by shipowners may be based on requirements relating to the safety of ships and order in ports. In addition, those provisions provide that the Minister may amend the shipowner's declaration only 'to the extent necessary' and by a duly reasoned decision. Even though those general criteria do not define in detail the safety and order reasons which can justify a change in timeslots, they seem to provide an objective framework of a sufficiently precise nature known in advance for the exercise of the national authorities' discretion.

51. It is for the referring court to carry out the necessary checks in relation to its national legislation."[197]

7.277 The CJEU then considered the Greek national measures imposing public service obligations:

"52. As regards the question whether the Regulation and in particular Articles 1 and 4 thereof preclude a system of prior authorisation imposing public service obligations, which consists

---

196 Ed., Case C-205/99 [2001] ECR I-1271, ECLI:EU:C:2001:107.
197 Para. 51 is perfectly normal as the CJEU does not decide the proceedings before the Member State referring institution but rather only advises on the EU legal position and then leaves it to the Member State institution to decide the matter so it is not that the CJEU was shirking responsibility.

in fixing certain timeslots, it has to be noted that, in accordance with Article 4(2), a Member State can impose on shipowners such obligations relating to frequency for regular cabotage services.

53. Furthermore, according to the case-law of the Court, a prior administrative authorisation system can be a means of imposing public service obligations (see Analir and Others, paragraph 34).

54. Given that all cabotage services are not necessarily services requiring public service obligations, such a system is permitted only if the competent national authorities have determined, for each route in question, that the regular transport services would be inadequate if their provision were left to market forces alone and if that system is necessary and proportionate to the aim of ensuring the adequacy of regular transport services to and from the islands (see, to that effect, the ninth recital in the preamble to the Regulation and Analir and Others, paragraphs 29 and 34).

55. Finally, such a system of prior authorisation cannot render legitimate discretionary conduct on the part of the national authorities which is liable to negate the effectiveness of the provisions of the Regulation. Consequently, it must be based on objective, non-discriminatory criteria which are known in advance to the undertakings concerned, in such a way as to circumscribe the exercise of the national authorities' discretion, so that it is not used arbitrarily (see, to that effect, Analir and Others, paragraphs 37 and 38).

56. In its orders for reference, the Simvoulio tis Epikratias observes in particular that, in the national legislation at issue in the main proceedings, there are no objective criteria to which the administration must adhere during the procedure leading to the adoption of authorisation decisions. For their part, the Greek Government and the Commission observe that Article 4(4) of Law 2932/2001 transposes Article 4(2) of the Regulation, by reproducing the criteria contained therein.

57. As the Court has already stated in paragraph 55 of this judgment, the prior authorisation system must be based on rules known in advance, which are objective, proportionate and non-discriminatory.

58. Similarly, it is essential that the content of the public service obligations which can be imposed is also determined in a measure of a general nature so that the details and the scope of those obligations are known in advance.

59. As regards the criteria for imposing public service obligations, Article 4(2) of the Regulation, which determines the requirements to which the Member States must be limited in imposing public service obligations, namely ports to be served, regularity, continuity, frequency, capacity to provide the service, rates to be charged and manning of the ship, must be regarded as establishing an exhaustive list.

60. Such requirements may be regarded as objective criteria to which the administration must adhere in the exercise of its discretion for the imposition of public service obligations, particularly in cases where more than one shipowner is interested in entering the same port at the same time.

61. As regards the national legislation at issue in the main proceedings, it should be noted, in particular, that Article 2(6) of Law 2932/2001 lists the various requirements which may justify imposing public service obligations provided for under Article 4(2) of the Regulation. In addition, Article 2 states that such obligations must be imposed 'in furtherance of reasons of public interest' and 'without giving rise to discrimination'. For its part, Article 4(4)(c) of the same law states that the amendments to the shipowners' declarations relating to the imposition of such obligations may be justified to guarantee regularity in the provision of the services. That same provision provides lastly that such amendments may in that regard be decided on only 'to the extent necessary' and if the Minister has 'reason' to believe.

62. It is for the referring court to establish whether, on the basis of those factors, the provisions of the legislation at issue in the main proceedings fulfil the conditions referred to in paragraphs 54 and 55 above.

63. Having regard to all of the foregoing considerations, the answer to the questions referred is that the provisions of Article 1 in conjunction with Article 4 of the Regulation must be

interpreted as not precluding national legislation which establishes a system of prior authorisation for maritime cabotage services providing for the adoption of administrative decisions imposing compliance with certain timeslots for reasons relating, first, to the safety of ships and order in ports and, second, to public service obligations, provided that such a system is based on objective, non-discriminatory criteria which are known in advance, particularly in cases where more than one shipowner is interested in entering the same port at the same time. With respect to the administrative decisions imposing public service obligations, it is also necessary that a genuine public service need arising from the inadequacy of the regular transport services under conditions of free competition can be demonstrated. It is for the national court to determine whether in the main proceedings those conditions are met."

This was a very pragmatic but correct construction of the EU regime: balancing safety and operational considerations with the freedom to provide services but the regime must be operated in a manner which does not discriminate between EU nationals.

The essence of the CJEU's preliminary ruling was clear from its reply to the referring court:

"The provisions of Article 1 in conjunction with Article 4 of ... Regulation ... 3577/92 ... must be interpreted as not precluding national legislation which establishes a system of prior authorisation for maritime cabotage services providing for the adoption of administrative decisions imposing compliance with certain timeslots for reasons relating, first, to the safety of ships and order in ports and, second, to public service obligations, provided that such a system is based on objective, non-discriminatory criteria which are known in advance, particularly in cases where more than one shipowner is interested in entering the same port at the same time. With respect to the administrative decisions imposing public service obligations, it is also necessary that a genuine public service need arising from the inadequacy of the regular transport services under conditions of free competition can be demonstrated. It is for the national court to determine whether in the main proceedings those conditions are met."

2000: *Commission v France*

7.278 On 13 July 2000, the CJEU ruled in *Commission v France*.[198] The case centred on a Commission allegation that France had failed to fulfil its obligations in regard to Regulation 3577/92 by maintaining unamended Article 257(1) of the French Customs Code of 11 May 1977 despite the adoption of Regulation 3577/92. Article 6 of the regulation provides:

"1. By way of derogation, the following maritime transport services carried out in the Mediterranean and along the coast of Spain, Portugal and France shall be temporarily exempted from the implementation of this Regulation:

  – cruise services, until 1 January 1995,
  – transport of strategic goods (oil, oil products and drinking water), until 1 January 1997,
  – services by ships smaller than 650 gt, until 1 January 1998,
  – regular passenger and ferry services, until 1 January 1999.

2. By way of derogation, island cabotage in the Mediterranean and cabotage with regard to the Canary, Azores and Madeira archipelagoes, Ceuta and Melilla, the French islands along the

---

198 Case C-160/99. Fifth Chamber composed of: Judges Edward (President of the Chamber), Sevón, Kapteyn (Rapporteur), Jann and Wathelet. AG Jacobs was the Advocate-General in the case.

Atlantic coast and the French overseas departments shall be temporarily exempted from the implementation of this Regulation until 1 January 1999."

7.279 Under Article 9 of the regulation, Member States are required, before adopting laws, regulations or administrative provisions in implementation of the regulation, to consult the Commission and to inform it of any measures thus adopted. The regulation entered into force on 1 January 1993. Article 257(1) of the Code provided that transport services carried out between the ports of metropolitan France are to be reserved to ships flying the French flag. However, the Minister responsible for the merchant navy may authorise a foreign ship to carry out a particular transport service. A footnote to Article 257 (the "Footnote") stated the following: "See also Council Regulation (EEC) No 3577/92 of 7 December 1992 applying the principle of freedom to provide services to maritime transport within Member States (maritime cabotage)". Article 258 of the Code provided as follows:

"1. Transport services carried out:

   (a) between the ports of the same French overseas department;
   (b) between the ports of the departments of Guadeloupe, French Guiana and Martinique shall also be reserved to ships flying the French flag.

2. The transportation of certain goods may, by order adopted by the Minister responsible for the merchant navy after obtaining an opinion from the Minister responsible for the budget, be reserved to French ships, where that transportation is provided:

   (a) between the ports of French overseas departments and the ports of metropolitan France;
   (b) between the ports of Réunion and the ports of other French overseas departments.

3. Derogations from the provisions of paragraphs (1) and (2) of this article may be permitted by decisions of the authority responsible for the local register of shipping."

7.280 Article 259(1) of the Code provided that, in exceptional circumstances temporarily interrupting shipping services reserved to vessels flying the French flag, the Government may, by decree adopted in cabinet presided over by the President of the Republic, suspend the application of Article 257 for as long as that interruption continues.

7.281 In 1994, the Commission reminded the French authorities of the obligation incumbent on them under Article 9 of the regulation. The Commission also asked to be notified of the legislation in force in France concerning maritime cabotage and of any new legislative or administrative measures adopted on or after the date of entry into force of the regulation. The French authorities replied that no new law, regulation or administrative measure had been adopted for the purposes of applying the regulation. The Commission, taking the view that Article 257(1) of the Code was contrary to Article 1 of the regulation, gave formal notice to France requiring it to bring that situation to an end. Ultimately, the Commission brought proceedings against France in the CJEU. The Commission argued that Article 257(1) of the Code is manifestly contrary to Article 1(1) of the regulation, in that it reserves the right to provide cabotage services (that is to say, transport services between the ports of metropolitan France) to ships flying the French flag. France did not deny that the article, as drafted, was not in conformity with the regulation; nor did it dispute that the draft amendment has not yet been passed. It stated, however, that it has taken two measures to ensure the temporary application of the Community rules pending adoption of the legislative amendments which are being prepared. The first of these concerns a circular setting out the contents of the regulation (Circular No 93-S-030 of 19 March 1993, published in Bulletin Officiel des Douanes (i.e. the Official Customs Notices) No 1139 of 19 March 1993 (the "Circular"), and the second was the Footnote.

7.282 The CJEU recalled settled law on the need to make it plain to everyone about the state of the law and decided the matter quite quickly:

> "22. According to settled case-law, if a provision of national law that is incompatible with a provision of Community law, even one directly applicable in the legal order of the Member States, is retained unchanged, this creates an ambiguous state of affairs by keeping the persons concerned in a state of uncertainty as to the possibility of relying on Community law; maintaining such a provision in force therefore amounts to a failure by the State in question to comply with its obligations under the Treaty (see, in particular, Case 74/86 *Commission v Germany* [1988] ECR 2139, paragraph 10).
> 23. In addition, as the Court has held on numerous occasions, the incompatibility of national legislation with Community provisions can be remedied for good only by means of binding national provisions having the same legal force as those which must be amended (see, in particular, Case 168/85 Commission v Italy [1986] ECR 2945, paragraph 13). Neither the circular nor the mere reference to the Regulation in the footnote can be regarded as constituting such provisions.
> 24. It follows from the foregoing that, by maintaining unamended Article 257(1) of the Code as regards Community shipowners covered by Article 1(1) of the Regulation, the French Republic has failed to fulfil its obligations under that regulation."

2010: *Commission v Malta*

7.283 On 28 October 2010, the CJEU delivered judgment in *Commission v Malta*.[199] In this case, the Commission made an application to the CJEU to declare that, by signing an exclusive public service contract with Gozo Channel Co. Ltd ("GCCL") on 16 April 2004 (days before Malta acceded to the EU), without having undertaken a prior call for tenders, Malta had failed to fulfil its obligations under Regulation 3577/92.

7.284 Article 2 of the Act concerning the conditions of accession of the 2004 Accession States (including Malta) and the adjustments to the Treaties on which the EU is founded (the "Act of Accession")[200] provided:

> "From the date of accession, the provisions of the original Treaties and the acts adopted by the institutions and the European Central Bank before accession shall be binding on the new Member States and shall apply in those States under the conditions laid down in those Treaties and in this Act."

7.285 During the negotiations for Malta's accession, on 26 October 2001, the EU adopted a common position[201] in relation to the chapter on transport policy. The common position stated:

---

199 Case C-508/08, [2010] ECR I-10589, ECLI:EU:C:2010:643. The court was composed of Judges Cunha Rodrigues (President) Arabadjiev, Lõhmus (Rapporteur), Ó Caoimh and Lindh. The Advocate-General was AG Sharpston.
200 OJ 2003 L236/33.
201 See Conference on accession to the EU – Malta – Doc. 20766/01 CONF-M 80/01.

"the EU notes that Malta intends to conclude explicit public service obligation contracts both with Sea Malta Co. Ltd and [with GCCL] of 5 years' duration each by 30 June 2002 and that upon termination of these contracts tendering procedures will apply in line with the relevant *acquis*".

In 2005, in response to a request for information to it from the Commission, Malta confirmed that the Maltese government had on 16 April 2004 concluded two six-year exclusive public service obligation contracts with GCCL and with Sea Malta Co. Ltd for the provision of maritime transport services between the islands of Malta and Gozo. The Commission therefore decided to initiate the procedure under Article 226 of the EC Treaty (now Article 258 of the TFEU). The Commission believed that the contracts, which had been concluded without a prior call for tenders, were not in compliance with EU law since, first, they had not been concluded by means of a non-discriminatory procedure and, second, it had not been demonstrated that they were either necessary or proportionate. The Commission was not satisfied by Malta's reply and the matter ultimately went before the CJEU.

7.286 The Commission argued that, first, it followed from the second subparagraph of Article 4(1) of Regulation 3577/92 that the conclusion of a public service maritime cabotage contract must be preceded by a tendering procedure conducted on a non-discriminatory and open basis at Community level, whereas the contract concluded on 16 April 2004 between the Maltese government and GCCL did not result from such a procedure. The Commission also argued that it was apparent from *Analir and Others*[202] that a public service contract complies with the requirements of Regulation 3577/92 only if a real public service need can be demonstrated. However, with regard to the contract concluded with GCCL, Malta did not demonstrate sufficiently either that there was such a need or that an exclusive contract was necessary and proportionate. In reply, Malta argued, as its main defence, that Regulation 3577/92 was not applicable to that contract, since it was concluded before Malta's accession to the EU on 1 May 2014. The Commission did not dispute that the regulation was not applicable to Malta on the date on which the contract at issue was signed, that is to say, on 16 April 2004. However, it contended that it was precisely from 1 May 2004 that, as regards that contract, the Member State was not in compliance with its obligations under the regulation. At the hearing, the Commission further stated that that non-compliance consisted in having maintained the contract in force after the date of accession of Malta to the EU.

7.287 Unfortunately, for the Commission, the pleadings did not reflect fully the case which it sought to make at the hearing (i.e. to include the breach post-accession) so the CJEU dismissed the matter summarily:

"16. In that regard, it should be borne in mind that it is clear from Article 38(1)(c) of the Rules of Procedure of the Court of Justice and from the case-law relating to that provision that an application must state the subject-matter of the proceedings and a summary of the pleas in law on which the application is based, and that that statement must be sufficiently clear and precise to enable the defendant to prepare his defence and the Court to rule on the application. It is therefore necessary for the essential points of law and of fact on which a case is based to be indicated coherently and intelligibly in the application itself and for the heads of claim to be set out unambiguously so that the Court does not rule *ultra petita* or indeed fail to rule on an objection (see Case C-412/04 *Commission v Italy* [2008] ECR I-619,

---

202 Case C-205/99 [2001] ECR I-1271, Case C-205/99 [2001] ECR I-1271, ECLI:EU:C:2001:107.

paragraph 103, and Case C-211/08 *Commission v Spain* [2010] ECR I-0000, paragraph 32 and case-law cited).

17. In the present case, it is quite clear both from the wording of the reasoned opinion and from the form of order sought in the Commission's application that the failure ... of Malta to fulfil obligations arising under Regulation ... 3577/92, alleged by the Commission, consists in having signed the contract at issue on 16 April 2004.

18. It follows that the contention that ... Malta was not in compliance with its obligations under that regulation as from 1 May 2004 does not correspond to the form of order sought in the application.

19. Consequently, after examining its merits, the Court cannot adjudicate on such a contention without ruling ultra petita.

20. As regards the subject-matter of the infringement as set out in the Commission's application, it must be observed that, pursuant to Article 2 of the Act of Accession, Regulation ... 3577/92 was applicable to the Republic of Malta, as the Commission acknowledges, only as from 1 May 2004, the date of the accession of that State to the European Union (see, by analogy, Case C-168/08 *Hadadi* [2009] ECR I-6871, paragraph 26).

21. In those circumstances, as the Advocate General stated at point 57 of her Opinion, the Commission's action could succeed only if Regulation ... 3577/92 nevertheless required Malta to comply with certain obligations before that date. In the context of the present case, such obligations would require, in particular, that the Member States refrain from concluding a public service contract in a manner inconsistent with Articles 1 and 4 of Regulation ... 3577/92 during the period before which that regulation was applicable to them.

22. It is, however, clear that the Commission in no way based the pleas put forward in support of its action on the possible existence of such obligations. On the contrary, as observed at paragraph 15 above, it stated, both in its reply and at the hearing, that it was from 1 May 2004, the date on which Regulation 3577/92 entered into force in respect of Malta because of its accession, that that Member State was not, in the Commission's view, in compliance with its obligations under that regulation.

23. In the light of the foregoing, and without there being any need to rule on the alternative pleas of the Republic of Malta in its defence, the Commission's action must be dismissed."

7.288 The case is somewhat unique and confined to circumstances where the impugned Member State engages in the challenged behaviour before accession. With respect, the CJEU could well (and probably should have) decided the matter otherwise. While there may be an argument that the Member State should not be challenged in respect of the behaviour prior to accession, as Malta had decided two weeks or so before accession on a course of action which would last for almost six years after accession, the CJEU might well have decided (e.g. on the basis of the solemn duties of Member States to comply with EU law and the principle of effectiveness) to condemned the conduct in so far as it related to the period after accession. While the CJEU was correct to recall that the Commission had, strictly speaking, not pleaded the matter in a way which would allow the CJEU to decide the matter fully, it was somewhat unfortunate that "form" triumphed over "substance".

2009: *Presidente del Consiglio dei Ministri v Regione Sardegna*

7.289 On 17 November 2009, the CJEU's Grand Chamber delivered a preliminary ruling in *Presidente del Consiglio dei Ministri v Regione Sardegna*.[203] The case related to

---

203 Case C-169/08 [2009] ECR I-10821, ECLI:EU:C:2009:709. The CJEU's Grand Chamber was composed of V Skouris, President Lenaerts, Bonichot, Lindh and Toader (Rapporteur), Timmermans, Rosas, Kūris, Juhász, Arestis, Borg Barthet, Ó Caoimh and Bay Larsen. The Advocate-General was AG J Kokott.

freedom to provide services and regional legislation establishing a tax on stopovers for tourist purposes by aircraft used for the private transport of persons, or by recreational craft, to be imposed only on operators whose tax domicile is outside the territory of that region. It was a reference to the CJEU for a preliminary ruling from the Italian Corte costituzionale. This case concerned the interpretation of, what are now, Articles 56 and 107 of the TFEU.

7.290 The reference was made in proceedings between the President of the Council of Ministers and the Region of Sardinia regarding the establishment by that region of a tax on stopovers for tourist purposes by aircraft used for the private transportation of persons, or by recreational craft, to be imposed only on operators whose tax domicile is outside the territory of that Region.

7.291 The CJEU recalled that Article 117 of the Italian Constitution provided that legislative power shall be exercised by the State and the Regions in accordance with the Constitution and within the limits set by Community law and international obligations. The CJEU then recalled the national legislation:

> "4. The first paragraph of Article 743 of the Sea and Air Navigation Code (Codice della navigazione) gives the following definition of aircraft:
>
>> '"Aircraft" means any machine intended for the transportation by air of persons or things.'
>
> 5. In Article 1(2) of the Recreational Sailing Code (Codice della nautica da diporto), introduced by Legislative Decree No 171 (Decreto legislativo n. 171) of 18 July 2005, recreational sailing is defined as follows:
>
>> 'For the purposes of this Code, recreational sailing means sailing in maritime and inland waters for sporting or leisure purposes and without a view to profit.'
>
> 6. Article 2(1) of the Recreational Sailing Code concerns the commercial use of recreational craft, which it defines as follows:
>
>> '1. Recreational craft are used for commercial purposes where:
>>
>>> (a) they are the subject of a contract of leasing or chartering;
>>> (b) they are used for professional training in recreational sailing;
>>> (c) they are used by diving and sub-aqua training centres as support craft for persons practising underwater diving for sports or leisure purposes...'."

7.292 The CJEU then reviewed the regional legislation:

> "7. Law No 4 of the Region of Sardinia of 11 May 2006 laying down miscellaneous provisions on revenue, reclassification of costs, social policy and development, as amended by Article 3(3) of Law No 2 of the Region of Sardinia of 29 May 2007 laying down provisions for the preparation of the annual and long-term budget of the Region – 2007 Finance Law ('Regional Law No 4/2006') contains an Article 4, entitled 'Regional tax on stopovers for tourist purposes by aircraft or recreational craft', which provides as follows:
>
>> '1. From 2006, a regional tax on stopovers for tourist purposes by aircraft or recreational craft shall be established.
>> 2. The pre-conditions for the tax shall be the following:
>>
>>> (a) stopovers in the period between 1 June and 30 September at airfields in the territory of the region by general aviation aircraft, as referred to in Article 743 et seq. of the Sea and Air Navigation Code, used for the private transport of persons;

(b) stopovers in the period between 1 June and 30 September in harbours, berths and mooring places situated in the territory of the region and at rigged moorings in territorial waters along the coasts of Sardinia by recreational craft, as referred to in Legislative Decree No 171 of 18 July 2005 (Recreational Sailing Code) or, in any event, by craft used for recreational purposes, of a length exceeding 14 metres, measured in accordance with the EN/ISO/DIS 8666 harmonised standards, as provided for in Article 3(b) of that legislative decree.

3. The persons liable for the tax shall be the natural or legal persons who operate the aircraft for the purposes of Article 874 et seq. of the Sea and Air Navigation Code, or who operate the recreational craft for the purposes of Article 265 et seq. of the Sea and Air Navigation Code, and whose tax domicile is outside the territory of the region.
4. The regional tax provided for in paragraph 2(a) shall be payable in respect of each stopover, and that provided for in paragraph 2(b) shall be payable annually.

...

6. The following shall be exempt from the tax:

    (a) vessels which make a stopover in order to take part in sporting regattas, rallies of vintage and monotype boats and in sailing events, including non-competitive sailing events, where the organisers have given the maritime authorities advance notification of the event; ARASE (Agenzia della Regione autonoma della Sardegna per le entrate; Revenue Office of the Autonomous Region of Sardinia) must be informed, before the berthing, that such notification has been given;
    (b) recreational craft which are moored throughout the year at harbour installations of the region;
    (c) technical stops, limited to the time necessary for those purposes.
    The procedure for certification of the grounds of the exemption shall be laid down by specific measure of ARASE.

7. The tax shall be paid:

    (a) in the case of aircraft referred to in paragraph 2(a), at the time of landing;
    (b) within 24 hours of the arrival of the recreational craft in harbours, berths and mooring places, or at rigged moorings, along the coasts of Sardinia;

    in accordance with procedures to be laid down by measure of ARASE."

7.293 The CJEU then considered the dispute in the main proceedings and the questions referred for a preliminary ruling. The CJEU recalled the two actions brought before the Corte costituzionale, the first in 2006 and the second in 2007, the President of the Council of Ministers raised questions concerning the constitutionality of laws in relation not only to Article 4 of Regional Law No 4/2006 but also to Articles 2 and 3 of that law and to Article 5 of Law No 2 of 29 May 2007, both in the original version and as amended. All those provisions establish regional taxes. With regard to Article 4 of Regional Law No 4/2006, the applicant in the main proceedings submitted in particular that the provision does not comply with the requirements of EU law, which are binding upon the legislature in Italy pursuant to the first paragraph of Article 117 of the Italian Constitution. In support of those actions, the applicant alleged (i) infringement of Articles 49 EC and 81 EC (now Articles 56 and 101 TFEU), read in conjunction with Articles 3(1)(g) EC and 10 EC (Article 10 EC is now Article 29 TFEU but Article 3 has been repealed as such), and (ii) infringement of Article 87 EC (now Article 107 TFEU). In a 2008 judgment, the Corte costituzionale, after joining the above two actions, ruled on the questions of constitutionality raised in the 2006 action and on some of the questions of that nature raised in the 2007 action. With regard, in particular, to Article 4 of Regional Law No 4/2006, which was the subject of the 2007 action, the Corte costituzionale declared inadmissible or unfounded the questions of constitutionality which had been raised in relation to constitutional provisions other than the first paragraph of Article 117. It therefore decided to disjoin the proceedings relating to that provision and to stay those proceedings until the date of delivery of the judgment of the CJEU on the reference for a preliminary ruling made in the order for reference. In addition, with regard to the alleged infringement of Articles 3(1)(g) EC, 10 EC and 81 EC, the Corte costituzionale considered it appropriate to reserve its right to rule subsequently. The Corte costituzionale decided to stay the proceedings and refer the following questions to the Court for a preliminary ruling:

> "1. Is Article 49 EC to be interpreted as precluding the application of a rule, such as that laid down in Article 4 of [Regional Law No 4/2006], under which the regional tax on stopovers for tourist purposes by aircraft is levied only on undertakings, operating aircraft which they use for the transport of persons in the course of 'general business aviation' activities, which have their tax domicile outside the territory of the Region of Sardinia?
> 2. Does Article 4 of [Regional Law No 4/2006], by providing for the imposition of the regional tax on stopovers for tourist purposes by aircraft only on undertakings, operating aircraft which they use for the transport of persons in the course of 'general business aviation' activities, which have their tax domicile outside the territory of the Region of Sardinia, constitute, within the meaning of Article 87 EC, State aid to undertakings carrying on the same activities which have their tax domicile in the Region of Sardinia?
> 3. Is Article 49 EC to be interpreted as precluding the application of a rule, such as that laid down in Article 4 of [Regional Law 4/2006], under which the regional tax on stopovers for tourist purposes by recreational craft is levied only on undertakings, operating recreational craft, which have their tax domicile outside the territory of the Region of Sardinia and whose commercial operations involve making such craft available to third parties?
> 4. Does Article 4 of [Regional Law No 4/2006], by providing for the imposition of the regional tax on stopovers for tourist purposes by recreational craft only on undertakings, operating recreational craft, which have their tax domicile outside the territory of the Region of Sardinia and whose commercial operations consist in making such craft available to third parties constitute, within the meaning of Article 87 EC, State aid to undertakings carrying on the same activities which have their tax domicile in the Region of Sardinia?"

7.294 The CJEU initially considered together the first and third questions, concerning Article 49 of the EC Treaty:

> "19. By its first and third questions, which should be examined together, the referring court asks, essentially, whether Article 49 EC must be interpreted as precluding tax legislation, adopted by a regional authority, such as Article 4 of Regional Law No 4/2006, which provides for the imposition of a regional tax in the event of stopovers for tourist purposes by aircraft used for the private transport of persons, or by recreational craft, where that tax is imposed only on undertakings which have their tax domicile outside the territory of the region.

Conditions for the application of Article 49 EC

> 20. In order to reply to such a question, it must first be determined whether Regional Law No 4/2006 falls within the scope of the freedom to provide services under Article 50 EC.

21. As is clear from the wording of Article 4 of Regional Law No 4/2006, the tax at issue in the main proceedings applies to stopovers for tourist purposes by general aviation aircraft used for the private transport of persons (Article 4(2)(a) of that law), or by recreational craft or craft used for recreational purposes to the extent that those craft exceed 14 m in length (Article 4(2)(b) of that law).

22. Accordingly, the regional tax on stopovers does not apply to civil transport undertakings which carry persons or goods. The referring court states that the tax applies inter alia to undertakings operating aircraft in order to carry out air transport operations free of charge for reasons connected with their business activities. With regard to recreational craft, the referring court adds that the tax applies inter alia to undertakings whose activity consists in making those craft available to third parties in return for remuneration.

23. In that regard, it should be borne in mind that, according to the case-law of the Court, the concept of 'services' within the meaning of Article 50 EC implies that they are ordinarily provided for remuneration and that the remuneration constitutes consideration for the service in question and is agreed upon between the provider and the recipient of the service (see Case 263/86 Humbel and Edel [1988] ECR 5365, paragraph 17; Case C-109/92 Wirth [1993] ECR I-6447, paragraph 15; and Case C-355/00 Freskot [2003] ECR I-5263, paragraphs 54 and 55).

24. In the present case, the regional tax on stopovers, as is apparent from the observations of the Region of Sardinia, applies to operators of means of transport which travel to the territory of the region and not to undertakings which carry out their activity in that region. However, as was stated by the Advocate General in point 34 of her Opinion, it cannot be inferred from the sole fact that the tax in question does not apply to the provision of transport services that the tax legislation at issue in the main proceedings has no connection at all with the freedom to provide services.

25. It follows from well-established case-law that, whilst the third paragraph of Article 50 EC refers only to the active provision of services – where the provider moves to the beneficiary of the services – that also includes the freedom of the persons for whom the services are intended, including tourists, to go to another Member State, where the provider is, in order to enjoy the services there (see, inter alia, Joined Cases 286/82 and 26/83 Luisi and Carbone [1984] ECR 377, paragraphs 10 and 16; Case C-76/05 Schwarz and Gootjes-Schwarz [2007] ECR I-6849, paragraph 36; and Case C-318/05 Commission v Germany [2007] ECR. I-6957, paragraph 65).

26. In the main proceedings, as the Advocate General stated in point 37 of her Opinion, persons operating a means of transport and the users of such transport receive a number of services on the territory of the Region of Sardinia, such as the services provided at the airports and ports. Consequently, the stopover is a necessary condition for receiving such services and the regional tax on stopovers has a certain link with their provision.

27. With regard to the regional tax on stopovers by recreational craft, it should in addition be pointed out that this also applies to the undertakings operating such recreational craft and, inter alia, to those whose commercial operations consist in making such craft available to third parties for remuneration. Thus, by enacting Regional Law No 4/2006, the Sardinian legislature established a direct tax on the provision of services within the meaning of Article 50 EC.

28. Finally, as was pointed out by the Commission of the European Communities, the services on which the regional tax on stopovers has an impact may have a cross-border character since, in the first place, that tax is likely to affect the ability of undertakings established in Sardinia to offer stopover services at the airports and ports to nationals of, or undertakings established in, another Member State and, in the second place, it affects the operations of outsider undertakings having their seat in a Member State other than the Italian Republic and operating recreational craft in Sardinia.

The existence of a restriction on the freedom to provide services

29. With regard to the question whether the legislation at issue in the main proceedings constitutes a restriction on the freedom to provide services, it should be borne in mind at the

outset that, in the field of freedom to provide services, a national tax measure restricting that freedom may constitute a prohibited measure, whether it was adopted by the State itself or by a local authority (see, inter alia, Joined Cases C-544/03 and C-545/03 Mobistar and Belgacom Mobile [2005] ECR I-7723, paragraph 28 and the case-law cited).

30. In the present case, it is common ground that the regional tax on stopovers is imposed on operators of aircraft or recreational craft having their tax domicile outside the territory of the region and that the chargeable event for tax purposes is the stopover of the aircraft or recreational craft in that territory. Even though, admittedly, that tax is applicable only in a particular part of a Member State, it applies to stopovers by the aircraft and recreational craft in question irrespective of whether they come from another region of Italy or from another Member State. In those circumstances, the regional character of the tax does not mean by definition that it cannot impinge on the freedom to provide services (see, by analogy, Case C-72/03 Carbonati Apuani [2004] ECR I-8027, paragraph 26).

31. The application of that tax legislation makes the services concerned more costly for the persons liable for that tax, who have their tax domicile outside the territory of the region and who are established in other Member States, than they are for operators established in that territory.

32. Such legislation introduces an additional cost for stopovers made by aircraft or boats operated by persons having their tax domicile outside the territory of the region and established in other Member States, and thus creates an advantage for some categories of undertaking established in that territory (see Case C-353/89 Commission v Netherlands [1991] ECR I-4069, paragraph 25; Case C-250/06 United Pan-Europe Communications Belgium and Others [2007] ECR I-11135, paragraph 37; and Case C-212/06 Government of the French Community and Walloon Government [2008] ECR I-1683, paragraph 50).

33. However, the Region of Sardinia states that, in view of the nature and objectives of the regional tax on stopovers, which was introduced for the protection of the environment, residents and non-residents are not in an objectively comparable situation and, accordingly, the fact that they are treated differently does not constitute a restriction on the freedom to provide services, according to the case-law of the Court and, in particular, the judgment in Case C-279/93 Schumacker [1995] ECR I-225. Whereas residents, by financing the activities of the Region of Sardinia through general taxation and, in particular, through income tax revenues, part of which fall within the regional budget, contribute to the resources to be used for conservation purposes, restoration and the protection of environmental assets, non-resident undertakings behave like environmental 'free riders', by using the resources without paying towards the costs of those activities.

34. In that regard, the Court has indeed accepted, in relation to direct taxation, that the situation of residents and the situation of non-residents in a given Member State are not generally comparable, since there are objective differences between them, both from the point of view of the source of the income and from the point of view of their ability to pay tax or the possibility of account being taken of their personal and family circumstances (see, inter alia, Schumacker, paragraphs 31 to 33, and Case C-527/06 Renneberg [2008] ECR I-7735, paragraph 59).

35. However, in order for the comparison of the situation of the taxpayers to be carried out, the specific characteristics of the relevant tax must be taken into account. Accordingly, a difference in treatment as between residents and non-residents may constitute a restriction on the freedom to provide services prohibited by Article 49 EC where there is no objective difference in the situation, with regard to the tax levy in question, which would justify different treatment between the various categories of taxpayer (see, to that effect, Renneberg, paragraph 60).

36. That is notably the case with the tax at issue in the main proceedings. As stated by the Commission, the obligation to pay that tax arises on account of stopovers made by aircraft used for the private transport of persons or by pleasure boats and not because of the financial situation of the taxpayers concerned.

37. It follows that, in terms of the consequences for the environment, all natural and legal persons who receive the services in question are – contrary to the contentions of the Region

of Sardinia – in an objectively comparable situation with regard to that tax, irrespective of the place where they reside or are established.

38. The fact that taxpayers in Sardinia contribute, through general taxation and, in particular, income tax, to the environmental protection activities undertaken by the Region of Sardinia, is irrelevant for the purposes of comparing the situation of residents with that of non-residents in relation to the regional tax on stopovers. As the Advocate General stated in point 87 of her Opinion, that tax is not of the same nature and does not pursue the same objectives as the other taxes paid by Sardinian taxpayers, which serve above all to fund the State budget in a general way and thereby to finance all regional activities.

39. It follows from the above that there is nothing in the documents before the Court to support a finding that residents and non-residents are not in an objectively comparable situation with regard to the regional tax on stopovers. The tax legislation at issue in the main proceedings therefore constitutes a restriction on the freedom to provide services in that it taxes only operators of aircraft used for the private transport of persons, or of pleasure boats, who have their tax domicile outside the territory of the region, without imposing the same tax on the operators established in that territory.

The possible justification of the legislation at issue in the main proceedings

– The justification related to the requirements of environmental protection and the protection of public health

40. The Region of Sardegna submits that, even admitting that the regional tax on stopovers constitutes a measure restricting the freedom to provide services, such a tax is justified on public interest grounds and, in particular, by environmental protection requirements which can be regarded as 'public health' grounds as expressly referred to in Article 46(1) EC.

41. In particular, justification for that tax is said to be found in a new regional policy for the protection of the environment and countryside of Sardinia. Under that policy, according to the Region of Sardinia, there are plans for a series of levies designed, first, to discourage squandering of the environmental and coastal landscape heritage and, secondly, to finance expensive measures to restore coastal areas. Such a tax can also be justified by the 'polluter pays' principle since, indirectly, it is imposed on the operators of the means of transport which are one of the sources of pollution.

42. In that regard, it should be borne in mind that, according to settled case-law, irrespective of the existence of a legitimate objective which serves overriding reasons relating to the public interest, a restriction on the fundamental freedoms guaranteed by the EC Treaty may be justified only if the relevant measure is appropriate to ensuring the attainment of the objective in question and does not go beyond what is necessary to attain that objective (see Case C-150/04 Commission v Denmark [2007] ECR I–1163, paragraph 46; Government of the French Community and Walloon Government, paragraph 55; and Case C-222/07 UTECA [2009] ECR I-0000, paragraph 25). Furthermore, national legislation is appropriate to ensuring attainment of the objective pursued only if it genuinely reflects a concern to attain it in a consistent and systematic manner (Case C-169/07 Hartlauer [2009] ECR I-0000, paragraph 55).

43. In the present case, it should be pointed out that, even if the reasons given by the Region of Sardinia could justify the establishment of the regional tax on stopovers, they cannot justify the way in which it is implemented and, in particular, the fact that operators whose tax domicile is outside the territory of the region – who are the only persons liable to pay that tax – are treated differently.

44. It is clear that those implementing rules, which entail a restriction on the freedom to provide services within the meaning of Article 49 EC, are not appropriate or necessary for the attainment of those general objectives. As the Advocate General stated in points 73 and 74 of her Opinion, even if it is accepted that private aircraft and recreational craft making stopovers in Sardinia constitute a source of pollution, that pollution is caused regardless of where those aircraft and boats come from and, in particular, it is not linked to the tax domicile of those operators. The aircraft and boats of residents and non-residents alike contribute to environmental damage.

45. Accordingly, the restriction on the freedom to provide services which is brought about by the tax legislation at issue in the main proceedings cannot be justified on grounds relating to environmental protection since the basis for applying the regional tax on stopovers introduced by that legislation is a distinction between persons which is unrelated to that environmental objective. Nor can such a restriction be justified on public health grounds, since the Region of Sardinia has not provided any evidence which would make it possible to hold that that legislation is intended to protect public health.

   – The justification related to cohesion of the tax system

46. In its observations, the Region of Sardinia, in order to justify the tax legislation at issue in the main proceedings, relies on the need to preserve the cohesion of its tax system. The regional tax on stopovers, imposed only on persons who have their tax domicile outside the territory of the region, is said to be justified by the fact that residents of the region pay other taxes which contribute to operations for the protection of the Sardinian environment.

47. In that regard, it should be borne in mind that the Court has acknowledged that the need to preserve the cohesion of a tax system may justify a restriction on the fundamental freedoms guaranteed by the Treaty, but has pointed out that such a justification requires a direct link between the tax advantage concerned and the offsetting of that advantage by a particular tax levy, with the direct nature of that link falling to be examined in the light of the objective pursued by the rules in question (see, inter alia, Case C-303/07 Aberdeen Property Fininvest Alpha [2009] ECR I-0000, paragraphs 71 and 72).

48. As was stated in paragraph 38 of the present judgment, the regional tax on stopovers does not pursue the same objectives as the taxes paid by taxpayers who are resident in Sardinia, which serve to fund the State budget in a general way and thereby to finance all the activities of the Region of Sardinia. The non-imposition of that tax on those residents cannot therefore be regarded as offsetting the other taxes imposed on them.

49. It follows from those considerations that the restriction on the freedom to provide services which is brought about by the tax legislation at issue in the main proceedings cannot be justified on grounds of the cohesion of the tax system of the Region of Sardinia.

50. In those circumstances, the answer to the first and third questions is that Article 49 EC must be interpreted as precluding tax legislation, adopted by a regional authority, such as that provided for under Article 4 of Regional Law No 4/2006, which establishes a regional tax on stopovers for tourist purposes by aircraft used for the private transport of persons, or by recreational craft, to be imposed only on undertakings whose tax domicile is outside the territory of the region."

7.295 The second and fourth questions related to Article 87 EC (now Article 107 of the TFEU) so they primarily related to State aid so it would be appropriate to be very brief about the case in this chapter on free movement of services. In essence, the CJEU stated:

"51. By its second and fourth questions, which should be examined together, the referring court asks whether Article [107 TFEU] must be interpreted as meaning that tax legislation, adopted by a regional authority, which establishes a regional tax on stopovers, such as that provided for under Article 4 of Regional Law No 4/2006, to be imposed only on operators whose tax domicile is outside the territory of the region, constitutes a State aid measure in favour of undertakings established in that territory.

52. It should be recalled at the outset that, according to the case-law of the Court, for a measure to be categorised as State aid within the meaning of the Treaty, each of the four cumulative conditions laid down in Article [107(1) TFEU] must be fulfilled. First, there must be an intervention by the State or through State resources; second, the intervention must be liable to affect trade between Member States; third, it must confer an advantage on the recipient; fourth, it must distort or threaten to distort competition (see, in particular, Case C-237/04 Enirisorse [2006] ECR I-2843, paragraphs 38 and 39 and the case-law cited).

53. In the present case, it is common ground that the tax at issue in the main proceedings satisfies the second and fourth criteria since it applies to services provided in connection with stopovers by aircraft and recreational craft, which concern intra-Community trade, and that

such a tax, by giving an economic advantage to operators established in Sardinia, as indicated in paragraph 32 of the present judgment, can distort competition.

54. The questions relating to the interpretation of Article [107 TFEU] thus concern the application of the two remaining criteria for categorising the regional tax on stopovers as State aid. The Region of Sardinia maintains that the tax cannot be regarded as State aid, both because it does not involve the use of State resources and because it is selective in nature. The Commission contends, in its written observations, that the tax satisfies all the criteria set out in Article [107 TFEU].

Use of State resources

55. According to the Region of Sardinia, the legislation at issue in the main proceedings does not involve any intervention using regional resources. There is no renunciation of regional revenue, since the resident undertakings already contribute to environmental expenditure through the revenue deriving from the taxes paid by them. The regional tax on stopovers increases that revenue by extending the obligation to pay towards protecting the environment to those who, as non-residents, do not contribute to that expenditure through general taxes.

56. In that regard, it should be noted that, according to settled case-law of the Court, the notion of aid can encompass not only positive benefits such as subsidies, loans or direct investment in the capital of enterprises, but also interventions which, in various forms, mitigate the charges which are normally included in the budget of an undertaking and which therefore, without being subsidies in the strict sense of the word, are of the same character and have the same effect (see Case C-156/98 Germany v Commission [2000] ECR I-6857, paragraph 25, and Joined Cases C-341/06 P and C-342/06 P Chronopost and La Poste v UFEX and Others [2008] ECR I-4777, paragraph 123 and the case-law cited).

57. As stated by the Commission, tax legislation such as that at issue in the main proceedings, which grants certain undertakings exclusion from the obligation to pay the tax in question, constitutes State aid, even if it does not involve the transfer of State resources, since it involves the renunciation by the authorities concerned of tax revenue which they would normally have received (Germany v Commission, paragraphs 26 to 28).

58. As a consequence, the fact that the provision made under the tax legislation at issue in the main proceedings is not the grant of a subsidy, but rather the exclusion from the obligation to pay the tax in question of operators of aircraft used for the private transport of persons, or of recreational craft, who have their tax domicile in the territory of the region, means that that exclusion from tax liability may be regarded as constituting State aid.

The selective nature of the tax legislation at issue in the main proceedings

59. According to the Region of Sardinia, the difference in treatment as between resident undertakings and non-resident undertakings does not constitute a selective advantage. The tax legislation at issue in the main proceedings is not selective from a geographic perspective because, in accordance with the interpretation of the Court in Case C-88/03 Portugal v Commission [2006] ECR I-7115, the framework for reference in which the 'general nature' of the measure should be assessed is that of the infra-State body, if it enjoys sufficient autonomy. That is so in the case in the main proceedings, since the Region of Sardinia has autonomous powers conferred on it by a statute having the authority of constitutional law which authorises it to establish its own taxes. In addition, in accordance with the more general principle of equal treatment in the area of taxation, that legislation taxes differently situations which are legally and factually distinct.

60. In that regard, it does indeed follow from the case-law relied upon by the defendant in the main proceedings that, with regard to a measure adopted not by the national legislature, but by an infra-State body, such a measure is not selective for the purposes of Article [107(1) TFEU] solely on the ground that it confers an advantage only in the part of the national territory in which the measure applies (see Portugal v Commission, paragraphs 53 and 57, and Joined Cases C-428/06 to C-434/06 UGT-Rioja and Others [2008] ECR I-6747, paragraphs 47 and 48).

61. However, it also follows from that case-law that, in order to determine whether a measure is selective, where it is adopted by an infra-State body which enjoys autonomy vis-à-vis the central government of the kind enjoyed by the Region of Sardinia, it is necessary to determine whether, with regard to the objective pursued by that measure, it constitutes an advantage for certain undertakings as compared with others which, within the legal framework in which that body exercises its competences, are in a comparable legal and factual situation (see Case C-143/99 Adria-Wien Pipeline and Wietersdorfer & Peggauer Zementwerke [2001] ECR I-8365, paragraph 41, and Portugal v Commission, paragraphs 56 and 58).

62. Thus it must therefore be established whether, having regard to the characteristics of the regional tax on stopovers, the undertakings having their tax domicile outside the territory of the region are, with reference to the legal framework in question, in a factual and legal situation comparable with that of undertakings which are established in that territory.

63. As is clear from paragraphs 36 and 37 of the present judgment, it must be held that, in the light of the nature and objectives of that tax, all the natural and legal persons who receive stopover services in Sardinia are, contrary to what is argued by the defendant in the main proceedings, in an objectively comparable situation, irrespective of their place of residence or the place where they are established. It follows that the measure cannot be regarded as general, since it does not apply to all operators of aircraft or pleasure boats which make a stopover in Sardinia.

…

66. In those circumstances, the answer to the second and fourth questions is that Article [107(1) TFEU] must be interpreted as meaning that tax legislation, adopted by a regional authority, which establishes a tax on stopovers, such as that at issue in the main proceedings, to be imposed only on natural and legal persons whose tax domicile is outside the territory of the region, constitutes a State aid measure in favour of undertakings established in that territory."

7.296 Ultimately, the CJEU ruled:

"1. Article [56 of the TFEU] must be interpreted as precluding tax legislation, adopted by a regional authority, such as that provided for under Article 4 of Law No 4 of the Region of Sardinia of 11 May 2006 (Miscellaneous provisions on revenue, reclassification of costs, social policy and development) as amended by Article 3(3) of Law No 2 of the Region of Sardinia of 29 May 2007 (Provisions for the preparation of the annual and long-term budget of the Region – 2007 Finance Law), which establishes a regional tax on stopovers for tourist purposes by aircraft used for the private transport of persons, or by recreational craft, to be imposed only on natural and legal persons whose tax domicile is outside the territory of the region.
2. Article [107(1) of the TFEU] must be interpreted as meaning that tax legislation, adopted by a regional authority, which establishes a tax on stopovers, such as that at issue in the main proceedings, to be imposed only on natural and legal persons whose tax domicile is outside the territory of the region, constitutes a State aid measure in favour of undertakings established in that territory."

1999: *Commission v Belgium*

7.297 On 14 September 1999, the CJEU gave judgment in *Commission v Belgium*.[204] The case involved an application by the Commission for a declaration that, by failing either to adjust the agreement with Zaire in such a way as to provide for fair, free and non-discriminatory access for EU nationals to the cargo-shares due to Belgium or to

---

204 Case C-170/98 [1999] ECR I-5493, ECLI:EU:C:1999:411. The Court was composed of Judges Jann (President of the Chamber) Edward (Rapporteur) Sevón. The Advocate-General was AG La Pergola.

denounce that agreement, Belgium has failed to fulfil its obligations under Regulation 4055/86. The CJEU recalled that Regulation 4055/86 was intended, first, to implement Regulation 954/79 of 15 May 1979 concerning the ratification by Member States of, or their accession to, the United Nations Convention on a Code of Conduct for Liner Conferences and, second, for Member States which had not yet ratified that convention, to implement the convention itself. The Code of Conduct was adopted on 6 April 1974. Its object, according to its first recital, is to improve the system of liner conferences. Zaire ratified it in 1974 and Belgium in 1988. The Code of Conduct was applied in EU law by Regulation 954/79. In order to implement certain specific aspects of the Code and to make it compatible with Community law, the Council adopted a number of regulations, including Regulation 4055/86. That regulation gives shipping lines rights relating to the provision of maritime services between Member States and between Member States and third countries.

7.298 In 1981, Belgium and Zaire signed an agreement on maritime transport under Article 1(1) of the agreement. The term "vessels of either Contracting Party" shall mean merchant vessels registered in the territory of that Party and flying its flag in accordance with its legislation. Article 3(3) of the agreement provided:

> "As regards maritime freight traffic of any kind between the two Parties, whatever the port of loading or unloading, the system to be applied by the Contracting Parties to vessels operated by their respective national shipping lines shall be based on the allocation formula 40/40/20, with respect to cargoes of freight and by volume."

Article 4 of the agreement provided: "Without prejudice to its international commitments, each Contracting Party shall have absolute disposal of its rights of traffic under the present Agreement." Article 18 of the agreement provides:

> "'This Agreement shall enter into force once the Contracting Parties have notified each other that the formalities required by their respective legislations have been completed. It shall remain in force for an indefinite period. However, it may be denounced at any time in writing by diplomatic channels, on six months' notice."

Ratification of the agreement was notified by Belgium to Zaire on 13 June 1983 and by Zaire to Belgium on 13 April 1987. The Commission considered that the cargo-sharing provisions in the agreement were contrary to the provisions of and obligations under Regulation 4055/86, as they reserved cargo transport between the parties to vessels flying the flag of one of the parties or operated by persons or lines with the nationality of one of the parties. So the Commission sent Belgium a letter of formal notice in 1991. In its reply Belgium stated that the agreement was an existing agreement, since it had been concluded before the date of entry into force of Regulation 4055/86 and had been applied de facto from its signature in 1981, so that it was not contrary to Article 5 of that regulation. The CJEU described the subsequent procedure in the following terms:

> "19. The Commission was not satisfied with the Belgian Government's reply and on 11 October 1993 sent it a reasoned opinion, stating that the Agreement was contrary to Article 5 of Regulation ... 4055/86 and that it reserved 40% of traffic to Belgian shipping lines to the exclusion of those of other Member States. The Commission further claimed that, being discriminatory, that exclusion was clearly prohibited by Article 1 of the regulation.
> 20. The Commission also stated that the Agreement was a new agreement because it had not entered into force until after 1 January 1987.

21. However, after a more detailed study of the case, and in view of the fact that the formalities required by Belgian legislation for the entry into force of the Agreement had been completed before Regulation ... 4055/86 entered into force, the Commission reached the conclusion that the Agreement could be regarded as an 'existing agreement' governed by Articles 3 and 4 of that regulation.
22. The Commission consequently, on 11 April 1996, sent ... Belgium a supplementary letter of formal notice. In that letter the Commission noted that despite the statements made by the Belgian Government on several occasions, in particular in its letter of 7 June 1991, it had no information to show that the adjustment of the Agreement had been accomplished. It therefore concluded that by failing either to adjust the Agreement to give all Community nationals, as defined in Article 1 of Regulation ... 4055/86, fair, free and non-discriminatory access to the cargo shares due to Belgium or to denounce the Agreement, as provided for by Article 18(2) thereof, ... Belgium had failed to fulfil its obligations under Articles 3 and 4 of Regulation ... 4055/86.
23. In its reply of 30 August 1996 the Belgian Government expressed its satisfaction that the Commission now considered that the Agreement came under Article 4 of Regulation ... 4055/86, and stated that it would take the necessary steps for its adjustment.
24. Following that reply, the Commission sent the Belgian Government a supplementary reasoned opinion on 23 June 1997.
25. The Belgian Government, in its reply of 10 September 1997, primarily contested the Commission's argument in its supplementary reasoned opinion that the period for adjustment of existing cargo-sharing arrangements, with respect to trades governed by the Code of Conduct, had expired on 30 May 1988. It submitted that the Commission had, after that date, favoured a pragmatic solution by recommending an exchange of letters cancelling the existing arrangements, and had even suspended the infringement procedure for a time.
26. Since it had not been notified that the Belgium-Zaire Agreement had in fact been adjusted, the Commission brought the present action.

The application

27. In the Commission's submission, it is clear from Article 1(1) of Regulation ... 4055/86 that the regulation applies the freedom to provide maritime transport services between Member States and between Member States and third countries to nationals of Member States who are established in a Member State other than that of the person for whom the services are intended. Articles 3 and 5 of the regulation lay down rules on the position as regards third countries; Article 3 applies to existing agreements and Article 5 to future agreements.
28. Since the Commission finds that Article 18 of the Agreement provides that the parties' intention is not to be bound until the formalities required by the irrespective legislations are completed, and those formalities were completed by ... Belgium with the enactment of the Law of 21 April 1983 approving the Agreement, which was notified to ... Zaire on 13 June 1983, before the entry into force of Regulation ... 4055/86, the Commission contends that the Agreement is an existing agreement subject to Articles 3 and 4 of that regulation.
29. The only exceptions to the application of the freedom to provide services made by Article 1(1) of Regulation ... 4055/86 are, with respect to unilateral restrictions, in Article 2, 'by way of derogation from Article 1', and, with respect to trades not governed by the Code of Conduct, in Article 4(1)(b), which allows an additional period for adjustment until 1 January 1993 at the latest.
30. No such period, on the other hand, is allowed to Member States for adjustment of cargo-sharing arrangements where trades are governed by the Code of Conduct, in accordance with Article 4(1)(a) of Regulation ... 4055/86.
31. In the Commission's submission, it follows that Member States which had already ratified the Code of Conduct at the date of entry into force of Regulation ... 4055/86 were obliged to adjust or phase out without delay the existing bilateral agreements, namely the cargo-sharing arrangements.

32. Since the Code of Conduct was ratified by ... Belgium in 1988, the Commission submits that ... Belgium should have adjusted the cargo-sharing arrangements on that date.
33. The Commission adds that even if the trade in question were to be treated as not being a trade governed by the Code of Conduct, under Article 4(1)(b) of Regulation ... 4055/86 the deadline for adjustment of the bilateral agreements concerned was 1 January 1993. In short, whether the trades are governed by Paragraph 1(a) or (b) of Regulation ... 4055/86, the period for adjustment of the cargo-sharing arrangements has long since expired.
34. The Commission stresses that it does not require denunciation of the Agreement, but only the adjustment or phasing out of the arrangements in it, in accordance with Article 3 of Regulation ... 4055/86 concerning 'existing' agreements. However, if that adjustment or phasing out was not accepted by the other party to the Agreement, the only available means of terminating the infringement would be to denounce the Agreement. In any event, the object of the present procedure is to ensure that the cargo-sharing arrangements are eliminated."

7.299 The CJEU ultimately held:

"38. It is common ground (...) that the Agreement is not a future agreement within the meaning of Article 5 of Regulation 4055/86, and is therefore an agreement to which Articles 3 and 4 of that regulation apply.
39. As regards determination of the date from which the Agreement should have been adjusted, Article 4(1) of Regulation 4055/86 distinguishes between trades governed by the Code of Conduct and trades not so governed. Only with respect to the latter does the regulation allow Member States a period expiring on 1 January 1993 for the adjustment prescribed. For trades governed by the Code of Conduct, no period is allowed for adjustment of an agreement.
40. On 30 March 1988 ... Belgium ratified the Code of Conduct. As the Advocate General has observed in point 10 of his Opinion, the fact that no period was allowed for adjustment of trades governed by the Code of Conduct means that the Agreement should have been adjusted immediately after ... Belgium ratified the Code.
41. The position of the Belgian Government is essentially that it does not contest the existence of the obligation to amend the provisions at issue, but submits that political developments in the Congo made it impossible to arrange negotiations. It undertakes to finalise the adjustment of the Agreement once the political situation in the Congo so permits.
42. The existence of a difficult political situation in a third State which is a contracting party, as in the present case, cannot justify a failure to fulfil obligations. If a Member State encounters difficulties which make it impossible to adjust an agreement, it must denounce the agreement.
43. Accordingly, by failing either to adjust the Belgium-Zaire Agreement in such a way as to provide for fair, free and non-discriminatory access by Community nationals to the cargo shares due to Belgium or to denounce that agreement, the Kingdom of Belgium has failed to fulfil its obligations under Regulation ... 4055/86, in particular Articles 3 and 4(1) thereof."

7.300 In essence, the CJEU declared that, by failing either to adjust the agreement with Zaire in such a way as to provide for fair, free and non-discriminatory access by EU nationals to the cargo-shares due to Belgium or to denounce that agreement, Belgium had failed to fulfil its obligations under Regulation 4055/86.

1999: *Commission v Belgium and Luxembourg*

7.301 On 14 September 1999, the CJEU gave judgment in *Commission v Belgium and Luxembourg*.[205] The case concerned the alleged failure by the two Member States to fulfil obligations by virtue of Regulation 4055/86. The Commission applied to the CJEU for declarations that, by concluding and maintaining in force the agreements containing cargo-sharing arrangements with the Togolese Republic and the Republic of Mali and by failing either to adjust the agreements with the Republic of Senegal and the Republic of Côte d'Ivoire in such a way as to provide for fair, free and non-discriminatory access by Community nationals to the cargo-shares due to Belgium and Luxembourg or to denounce those agreements, Belgium and Luxembourg had failed to fulfil their obligations under Regulation 4055/86, in particular Articles 3 and 4(1) thereof with respect to the Republic of Senegal and the Republic of Côte d'Ivoire and Article 5 thereof with respect to the Republic of Mali and the Togolese Republic. The CJEU agreed with the Commission's position and declared that,

> "by concluding and maintaining in force the agreements containing cargo-sharing arrangements with the Togolese Republic (C-171/98 and C-202/98) and the Republic of Mali (C-201/98 and C-202/98) and by failing either to adjust the agreements with the Republic of Senegal and the Republic of Côte d'Ivoire (C-201/98 and C-202/98) in such a way as to provide for fair, free and non-discriminatory access by Community nationals to the cargo shares due to Belgium and Luxembourg or to denounce those agreements, the Kingdom of Belgium (C-171/98 and C-201/98) and the Grand Duchy of Luxembourg (C-202/98) have failed to fulfil their obligations under Council Regulation (EEC) No 4055/86 of 22 December 1986 applying the principle of freedom to provide services to maritime transport between Member States and between Member States and third countries, in particular Articles 3 and 4(1) thereof with respect to the Republic of Senegal and the Republic of Côte d'Ivoire and Article 5 thereof with respect to the Republic of Mali and the Togolese Republic."

2000: *Commission v Portugal*

7.302 On 4 July 2000, the CJEU gave judgment in *Commission v Portugal*.[206] The case concerned an alleged failure by a Member State to fulfil its obligations in regard to Regulation 4055/86. The Commission applied to the CJEU for a declaration that, by failing to denounce or adjust the agreements concerning merchant shipping concluded with the Republic of Senegal, approved by Decree No 99/79 of 14 September 1979, with the Republic of Cape Verde, approved by Decree No 119/79 of 7 November 1979, with the Republic of Angola, approved by Decree No 71/79 of 18 July 1979, and with the Democratic Republic of São Tomé e Príncipe, approved by Decree No 123/79 of 13 November 1979, so as to provide for fair, free and non-discriminatory access by all Community nationals to the cargo-shares due to the Portuguese Republic, as provided for in Council Regulation 4055/86, Portugal had failed to fulfil its obligations under Articles 3 and 4(1)

---

205 Cases C-171/98, C-201/98 and C-202/98 [1999] ECR I-05517, ECLI:EU:C:1999:412. Case C-171198 and C-201/98 related to Belgium and Case C-202/98 related to Luxembourg. The Court was composed of Judges Jann (President of the Chamber), Edward (Rapporteur) and Sevón. The Advocate-General was AG La Pergola.

206 Case C-62/98 [2000] ECR I-5171, ECLI:EU:C:2000:358. The Court was composed of Judges Rodríguez Iglesias (President), Moitinho de Almeida, Edward (Rapporteur), Sevón, Schintgen, Gulmann, Puissochet, Hirsch, Jann, Ragnemalm and Wathelet. The Advocate-General was AG Mischo.

of that regulation. The CJEU agreed with the Commission's position. The CJEU therefore declared that, by failing to denounce or adjust the agreement on merchant shipping with the Republic of Angola so as to provide for fair, free and non-discriminatory access by all Community nationals to the cargo-shares due to the Portuguese Republic, as provided for in Regulation 4055, Portugal had failed to fulfil its obligations under Articles 3 and 4(1) of that regulation.

2000: *Commission v Portugal*

7.303 On 4 July 2000, the CJEU gave judgment in *Commission v Portugal*.[207] The case involved an application to the CJEU by the Commission for a declaration that Portugal had failed to fulfil its obligations under Articles 3 and 4(1) of Regulation 4055/86 by failing to denounce or adjust an agreement between Portugal and the Federal Republic of Yugoslavia. The Commission alleged that by not amending the agreement, there was a failure to provide for fair, free and non-discriminatory access by all EU nationals to the cargo-shares arising out of the agreement. The CJEU agreed:

> "38. It should be noted at the outset that the Commission and Portuguese Republic agree that the cargo-sharing clauses in the contested agreement call for adjustment in order to render the agreement compatible with Articles 3 and 4 of Regulation ... 4055/86.
>
> 39. In this case, the Portuguese Government has not succeeded in adjusting the contested agreement by recourse to diplomatic means within the time-limit laid down by Regulation ... 4055/86.
>
> 40. It must be borne in mind that the Court has already held that, in such circumstances, in so far as denunciation of such an agreement is possible under international law, it is incumbent on the Member State concerned to denounce it (see, to that effect, Case C-170/98 Commission v Belgium [1999] ECR I-5493, paragraph 42).
>
> 41. However, the Portuguese Government denies any failure to fulfil its obligations, essentially for four reasons.
>
> 42. First, it contends that, following the disintegration of the Federal Republic of Yugoslavia, the Commission should have amended its request to reflect the new circumstances.
>
> 43. As to that point, according to settled case-law (Case C-96/95 Commission v Germany [1997] ECR I-1653, paragraph 22), the purpose of the pre-litigation procedure is to give the Member State concerned an opportunity, on the one hand, to comply with its obligations under Community law and, on the other, to avail itself of its right to defend itself against the complaints made by the Commission.
>
> 44. In this case, the Portuguese Government has given no indication why it considers that the Commission's failure to amend its request following disintegration of the Federal Republic of Yugoslavia has affected either its ability to comply with its obligations under Community law or its rights of defence.
>
> 45. Second, the Portuguese Republic contends that the Commission's action is premature in view of the advanced stage reached in negotiations with the third countries concerned.
>
> 46. In that regard, it must be borne in mind that, given its role as guardian of the Treaty, it is for the Commission alone to decide whether it is appropriate to bring proceedings against a Member State for failure to fulfil its obligations (see Case C-431/92 Commission v Germany [1995] ECR I-2189, paragraph 22).
>
> 47. Third, the Portuguese Government submits that the complexity of the situation resulting from the disintegration of the Federal Republic of Yugoslavia justifies its position.

---

207 Case C-84/98 [2000] ECR I-5215, ECLI:EU:C:2000:359. The Court composed of Judges Rodríguez Iglesias (President), Moitinho de Almeida, Edward (Rapporteur), Sevón, Schintgen, Gulmann, Puissochet, Hirsch, Jann, Ragnemalm and Wathelet. The Advocate-General was AG Mischo.

48. As to that, the existence of a difficult political situation in a third State which is a contracting party, as in the present case, cannot justify a continuing failure on the part of a Member State to fulfil its obligations under the Treaty (see Commission v Belgium, cited above, paragraph 42).
49. Finally, the Portuguese Government contends, in essence, that, with regard to pre-Community conventions concluded between a Member State and a third country, although Article 234 of the Treaty imposes the obligation to take all appropriate steps to eliminate any incompatibility between a rule of the convention and a Community rule, that provision is not indifferent to the legal consequences and political costs flowing from that obligation. Cases where a convention must be denounced under Article 234 of the Treaty arise only exceptionally and in extreme circumstances. Such denunciation would involve a disproportionate disregard of the interests linked to its foreign policy as compared with the Community interest. Moreover, the Commission should have referred to that provision in the statement of the reasons for a request for a pre-Community convention to be adjusted or denounced.
50. It is therefore necessary to consider in what circumstances a Member State may maintain measures contrary to Community law in reliance upon a pre-Community convention concluded with a third country.
51. The first paragraph of Article 234 of the Treaty provides that the rights and obligations arising from agreements concluded before the entry into force of the Treaty between, on one hand, one or more Member States and, on the other, one or more third countries shall not be affected by the provisions of the Treaty. However, the second paragraph requires the Member States to take all appropriate steps to eliminate any incompatibilities between such an agreement and the EC Treaty.
52. Article 234 of the Treaty is of general scope and applies to any international agreement, irrespective of subject-matter, which is capable of affecting application of the Treaty (Case 812/79 Attorney General v Burgoa [1980] ECR 2787, paragraph 6, and Case C-158/91 Levy [1993] ECR I-4287, paragraph 11).
53. As is clear from Burgoa, cited above, the purpose of the first paragraph of Article 234 of the Treaty is to make it clear, in accordance with the principles of international law (see, in that connection, Article 30(4)(b) of the 1969 Vienna Convention on the Law of Treaties) that application of the EC Treaty is not to affect the duty of the Member State concerned to respect the rights of third countries under a prior agreement and to perform its obligations thereunder.
54. It follows that the Portuguese Republic must in all cases respect the rights which the Republic of Yugoslavia derives from the contested agreement.
55. However, the contested agreement contains a clause (Article 13) which expressly enables the contracting parties to denounce it, so that denunciation by the Portuguese Republic would not encroach upon the rights which the Republic of Yugoslavia derives from that agreement.
56. Consequently, the obligations to which the Portuguese Republic is subject by virtue of Articles 3 and 4 of Regulation ... 4055/86 are not affected by the principle laid down in the first paragraph of Article 234 of the Treaty.
57. As regards the Portuguese Government's argument that the obligation to have recourse to denunciation constitutes an exceptional obligation in the context of Article 234 of the Treaty, it is enough to note that, in this case, the obligation incumbent on the Portuguese Republic is based not on that provision of the Treaty but on the provisions of Regulation ... 4055/86.
58. Furthermore, although, in the context of Article 234 of the Treaty, the Member States have a choice as to the appropriate steps to be taken, they are nevertheless under an obligation to eliminate any incompatibilities existing between a pre-Community convention and the EC Treaty. If a Member State encounters difficulties which make adjustment of an agreement impossible, an obligation to denounce that agreement cannot therefore be excluded.
59. As regards the argument that such denunciation would involve a disproportionate disregard of foreign-policy interests of the Portuguese Republic as compared with the Community

interest, it must pointed out that the balance between the foreign-policy interests of a Member State and the Community interest is already incorporated in Article 234 of the Treaty, in that it allows a Member State not to apply a Community provision in order to respect the rights of third countries deriving from a prior agreement and to perform its obligations thereunder. That article also allows them to choose the appropriate means of rendering the agreement concerned compatible with Community law.

60. Finally, with regard to the absence of a legal basis as a result of the Commission's failure to refer to Article 234 of the Treaty, suffice it to note that in this case the Commission's request was based on Regulation ... 4055/86.

61. In those circumstances, it must be held that, by failing either to denounce or adjust the contested agreement so as to provide for fair, free and non-discriminatory access by all Community nationals to the cargo-shares due to the Portuguese Republic, as provided for in ... Regulation ... 4055/86, the Portuguese Republic has failed to fulfil its obligations under Articles 3 and 4(1) of that regulation."

The CJEU therefore declared

"that, by failing to denounce or adjust the agreement on merchant shipping with the Federal Republic of Yugoslavia so as to provide for fair, free and non-discriminatory access by all Community nationals to the cargo-shares due to the Portuguese Republic, as provided for in ... Regulation ... 4055/86, ... the Portuguese Republic failed to fulfil its obligations under Articles 3 and 4(1) of that regulation".

1998: *Commission v Belgium and Luxembourg*

7.304 On 11 June 1998, the CJEU delivered its judgment in *Commission v Belgium and Luxembourg*.[208] The case concerned a cargo-sharing arrangement. The case involved an application by the Commission for a declaration that, by introducing and maintaining in force cargo-sharing arrangements, in the agreement between the Belgo-Luxembourg Economic Union and Malaysia on maritime transport, which was approved by Belgium and Luxembourg and which entered into force after 1 January 1987, Belgium (C-176/97) and Luxembourg (C-177/97) had failed to fulfil their obligations under Article 5 of Regulation 4055/86 applying the principle of freedom to provide services to maritime transport between Member States and between Member States and third countries.[209] Under Article 31(1) of the convention of 25 July 1921 establishing the Belgo-Luxembourg Economic Union (hereinafter "the BLEU"), tariff and trade treaties and agreements as well as international payment agreements relating to foreign trade are to be common to both parties and are to be concluded by Belgium on behalf of the BLEU, subject to the right of the Luxembourg government to sign those treaties or agreements jointly with the Belgian government.

7.305 On 12 February 1985, the BLEU and Malaysia signed an agreement on maritime transport. The introduction to the agreement stated that the contracting parties were Belgium and Luxembourg. According to Article 1(1) of the agreement the term "vessels of either Contracting Party" shall mean merchant vessels flying the national flag of and registered in Malaysia or the Belgo-Luxembourg Economic Union respectively". Article

---

208 Joined Cases C-176/97 and C-177/97, the Court was composed of Judges Gulmann (President of the Chamber) Wathelet, Moitinhode Almeida, Edward (Rapporteur) L Sevón. The Advocate-General was AG La Pergola.
209 OJ 1986 L378, p. 1.

2(1) of the agreement provided: "Vessels of either Contracting Party may sail between the ports of the two countries which are open to foreign trade and engage in passenger and cargo services (hereinafter called the 'agreed services') between the two countries." Article 3 of the agreement provided: "Chartered vessels flying the flag of third countries but operated by national shipping companies of either Contracting Party, may also take part in the agreed services, unless otherwise notified by either Contracting Party." Article 16 of the agreement provided:

> "1. The Contracting Parties express their will to cooperate in the field of maritime transport in the spirit of the UN Code of Conduct for Liner Conferences.
> 2. The national shipping companies of the Contracting Parties may participate in the freight and volume of the seaborne trade between the Contracting Parties in accordance with the principles of equitable sharing and mutual benefit.
> 3. As regards seaborne freight traffic (liner traffic), both Parties shall have equal rights to participate in the traffic generated by the mutual foreign trade. Third country shipping lines shall have the right to acquire a significant part of this traffic in accordance with the principles of the UN Code of Conduct for Liner Conferences.
> 4. The control of cargo sharing for inward and outward traffic in the ports of both Parties shall be entrusted to their national shipping companies."

7.306 According to Article 21, the agreement was to enter into force on the date when the contracting parties had notified one another through diplomatic channels that their respective constitutional requirements had been complied with. On 15 July 1987 Belgium notified to the Malaysian authorities its law of 29 June 1987 approving the agreement. However, the Commission was unhappy about it and instituted proceedings in the CJEU to declare it incompatible with EU law.

7.307 The Commission argued to the CJEU that, since, under Articles 2, 3 and 16 of the agreement, only national shipping companies of the contracting parties could participate in the freight and volume of maritime trade between those States, ships operated by nationals of other Member States are excluded from that traffic. The Commission contended that agreement was therefore contrary to Article 5(1) of the regulation under which, save in exceptional circumstances, cargo-sharing arrangements in any future agreements with third countries are prohibited. The Commission added that the concept of "future agreement" in Article 5(1) covers agreements which did not bind Member States at the time when the regulation entered into force, that is to say, on 1 January 1987. The Belgian law approving the agreement was not notified to Malaysia until 15 July 1987. The Commission stated that, in this case, no request was sent to the Council on the basis of Articles 5(1) and 6 which would allow that institution to authorise such arrangements in "exceptional circumstances". The Commission argued that Luxembourg was also a party to the agreement since, pursuant to Article 31(1) of the convention, it was represented by Belgium when the agreement was concluded and approved. Belgium conceded that the agreement must be characterised as a future agreement within the meaning of Article 5(1) of the regulation and that its provisions must be amended to bring them into line with the provisions of the regulation on cargo-sharing arrangements. Not surprisingly, the CJEU first observed that, since the Belgian law approving the agreement was not notified to the Malaysian authorities until July 1987, the agreement, in accordance with Article 21 thereof, entered into force after 1 January 1987, the date on which the regulation entered into force. It therefore constitutes a "future agreement" within the meaning of Article 5(1) of the regulation. Then, the CJEU observed that, as the defendant governments themselves acknowledged, that agreement, which is binding on both Belgium and on Luxembourg, contains, in Articles 2, 3 and 16, cargo-sharing arrangements which, in the absence of an authorisation granted under Article 5(1) of the regulation, are contrary to that provision. The CJEU therefore ruled that it must

> "be declared that, by introducing and maintaining in force cargo-sharing arrangements, in the Agreement between the BLEU and Malaysia on maritime transport which was approved by ... Belgium both in its own name and on behalf of ... Luxembourg and which entered into force after 1 January 1987, ... Belgium and ... Luxembourg have failed to fulfil their obligations under Article 5 of the Regulation".

F. CONCLUSIONS

7.308 This chapter has charted the evolution of the law on the freedom to provide services in EU shipping law. It evolved from a period (before 1986) when the right was not explicitly or implicitly recognised to an intermediate stage (in 1986) when it was established for the purposes of international maritime transport services but cabotage (i.e. domestic) services were still capable of being restricted by coastal Member States. Ultimately, in 1992, the right to provide maritime transport services has been recognised for both international and cabotage traffic. Since then, there have been particular problems but these have been relatively small in the totality of the issues involved and, for the most part, the freedom to provide maritime services is now an established right in EU shipping law. The specific issues which have arisen, and are likely to arise in the future, include relic or remnant restrictions on the freedom, differential charging at ports, cargo-sharing arrangements and relations with third States.

CHAPTER 8

European Union law relating to employment in the shipping sector

A. INTRODUCTION

8.001 The purpose of this chapter is to provide an overview of selected aspects of the European Union ("EU") law relating to the employment of people in the shipping sector and, in particular, seafarers.[1] This chapter should be read in conjunction with the earlier chapter on the registration of ships[2] and other chapters in the book[3] because employment touches on various aspects of EU law. It is not proposed to set out the whole of the EU law relating to employment (which would justify a book in its own right) but to concentrate on certain aspects of EU law as they relate to employment in the shipping sector. In principle, the EU law relating to shore-based staff should be the same as on-board personnel but the EU has historically made a number of exceptions for seafarers to deny them some of the protections afforded to shore-based workers but those differences are being removed slowly as will be described in this chapter generally. It is also worth recalling that the employment of some workers in the sector – specifically, dockers – has proved very controversial with rioting in the streets in Brussels when the European Commission sought to change the rules on ports.[4]

8.002 In trying to contextualise the issue of employment in the maritime sector, it is useful to review the Athens Declaration of 7 May 2014 entitled *Mid-Term Review of the EU's Maritime Transport Policy until 2018 and Outlook to 2020* in which the EU's Transport Ministers stressed:

> "that competent seafarers with appropriate working conditions and employment rights are an essential prerequisite for global sea trade, and that the implementation of the ILO[5] Maritime Labour Convention 2006 (MLC) and of the IMO[6] International Convention on Standards of Training, Certification and Watchkeeping for Seafarers (STCW), as amended by the 2010 Manila amendments, is an important step to create a uniform and enforceable framework for the working and living conditions on board ships and the protection of the health, safety and standards of

---

1 Many of the EU's laws relating to employment law are set out at http://ec.europa.eu/employment_social/labour_law/index_en.htm. On EU employment law generally, see Barnard, *EU Employment* Law (4th ed., 2012). See also Mitroussi, "Employment of Seafarers in the EU Context: Challenges and Opportunities", (2008) Marine Policy, 32(6), p. 1043. On seafarers and the law generally, see Fitzpatrick and Anderson, *Seafarers' Rights* (2005).
2 See chap. 6.
3 E.g. chap. 15 on State aid.
4 See the discussion on various ports throughout the book touching on the employment of dockers and services in ports.
5 Ed., i.e. the International Labour Organization.
6 Ed., i.e. the International Maritime Organization.

competence of seafarers, thus substantially contributing to a more positive image of the maritime profession, thereby contributing to the recruitment of seafarers".

In the same Declaration, the Ministers went on to state:

"II. Human Resources, Seamanship and Maritime Know-how
[The Ministers...]
3. REAFFIRM the will to increase employment in the maritime sector as a whole and career mobility between on- and offshore jobs[7] to support the functioning of EU maritime clusters, to create a level playing-field by implementing the ILO Maritime Labour Convention 2006, to ensure fair treatment of seafarers including in the event of a maritime accident and to guarantee their welfare;
4. EMPHASIZE the importance of assessing living and working conditions in shipping as applied in the EU;
5. CALL for further concrete actions towards enhancing maritime know-how and improving the attractiveness of maritime careers for both men and women[8] with the active involvement of all relevant parties by encouraging links between education and industry to promote labour mobility and transferability of skills as well as the effective implementation of relevant international Conventions; in this context, REAFFIRM that the TTE[9] Council Conclusions of 2003 and 2005 'on improving the image of Community shipping and attracting young people to the seafaring profession' remain fully pertinent."

8.003 Seafarers have sometimes been the "poor relation" of EU employment law. They were deprived of some of the legal rights which had been conferred on shore-based workers. Ironically, a shore-based employee of a shipping company would have more rights than another employee of the same company who happens to be working on board a ship. The situation is typified by a ship's captain or chief engineer who "comes ashore" to be a superintendent or take up a managerial position in the head office and thereby acquires more rights as an employee. This difference in approach was because there was a belief that their circumstances were special. It is true that seafarers face particular or special challenges. Ironically, therefore, there ought to be *more*, not fewer, rights conferred on seafarers. There are welcome indications that this situation is being addressed as will be discussed below.

8.004 It is imperative that young people in the EU are encouraged to take up employment in the shipping sector otherwise there is a risk that the wealth of seafaring talent in the EU would disappear. Therefore a key part of the EU initiatives in this area has been to encourage young people and career-changers to become seafarers and to enter the shipping sector generally.

8.005 On 4 June 2015, Violeta Bulc, the European Commissioner for Transport launched the Social Agenda for Transport.[10] She recalled that 11 million people work in the EU transport sector generally with almost half of them working in road transport. She began by recalling the challenge of making transport an attractive sector for workers and recalled three related challenges: first, to ensure that it is a sector to which employees are

---

7 It is important to provide share-based job opportunities to seafarers who may not otherwise pursue a sea-based career if there are not shore-based opportunities for them in later years.

8 Ed., historically, there were few women working as seafarers (except in the area of catering and housekeeping on passenger vessels) but that has changed over time.

9 Ed., TFE is an abbreviation for the Transport, Telecommunications and Energy Council configuration ("TTE") of the Council.

10 Speech by Violeta Bulc, the European Commissioner for Transport spoke at "A Social Agenda for Transport – Brussels", Autoworld, 4 June 2015, http://europa.eu/rapid/press-release_SPEECH-15-5125_en.htm.

attracted; second, to offer transport workers the necessary qualifications and skills; and third, she said that the features of transport work are

> "specific and some are perceived negatively. Working times in the transport sector are often irregular and many transport mobile workers have to cope with long absences from home. Work autonomy in transport is relatively low. Problems caused by heavy physical work have been replaced by stress derived from time-pressures. Transport is also considered to include certain risks and sometimes to be a dangerous activity."

The fourth challenge

> "relates to technologies and innovation: The transport workforce also needs to adapt to be able to make the best possible use of the opportunities offered by technological innovation and the increased use of digital technologies. This trend affects all transport sectors. For instance, the driver's cabin of a high speed train becomes increasingly similar to an aircraft cockpit. Ships have also more and more sophisticated technology on board. We already know about driverless metros but driverless trucks may also soon become a reality."

She recalled that a third of transport workers are over 50 years old. Only 22% of workers in the transport sector are female and this figure is well below the figure for the overall economy, with 46% of women working in all the economic sectors.

8.006 Seafarers raise specific issues in the context of employment. They are often away from home for long periods. They are working for employers or companies which are not immediately obvious or even traceable easily. Inspection of employment standards on ships is an issue – especially when the vessels are at sea. Qualifications are issued in shipping by typically national (rather than international) authorities around the world and those authorities are of diverse quality and diligence. Seafarers are working in an environment which is often dangerous and where different languages are spoken. There are complicated tax and social security regimes. There is a tapestry of international conventions relating to the employment of seafarers. It is not easy to legislate in regard to the employment in the shipping sector but it is a necessary task because of the difficulties involved. Seafarers have the challenge of both working and living in the same confined location (i.e. the ship) which can raise various issues (e.g. sociological and psychological issues). Moreover, seafarers are often working and living in cramped conditions on a ship. They are often operating in a multicultural workplace. While there are substantial difficulties and differences involved, EU law (like other legal systems) must work towards ensuring adequate protection for seafarers. The Commission in its communication of 21 January 2009 entitled *Strategic goals and recommendations for the EU's maritime transport policy until 2018*[11] emphasised the importance of establishing an integrated legal framework in order to make the maritime sector more competitive but the EU has often chosen competitiveness over social protection.

8.007 There is a great deal of growing overlap between EU employment law as it relates to seafarers and EU maritime safety law but some differences remain. Poor employment conditions for seafarers could increase the incidence of incidents, injuries or even deaths. Therefore optimum employment conditions (e.g. adequate rest periods) are very important. Hence, there are measures considered in this chapter which would be equally at home in the later chapters on safety but they are addressed here for convenience as well.

---

11 http://eur-lex.europa.eu/legal-content/EN/TXT/HTML/?uri=CELEX:52009DC0008&from=EN.

B. THE PRINCIPAL PROVISIONS RELATING TO EMPLOYMENT IN THE TREATY ON THE FUNCTIONING OF THE EUROPEAN UNION

8.008 The Treaty on the Functioning of the European Union ("TFEU") has several provisions relating to employment and the free movement of workers. It is instructive to consider some examples. Title IV of the TFEU is entitled: "Free Movement of Persons, Services and Capital". Chapter 1 of the Title is entitled "Workers". It is useful to consider these general provisions before examining the detail.

8.009 Article 45 of the TFEU sets out the general rule on free movement of workers. It provides:

"1. Freedom of movement for workers shall be secured within the Union.
2. Such freedom of movement shall entail the abolition of any discrimination based on nationality between workers of the Member States as regards employment, remuneration and other conditions of work and employment.
3. It shall entail the right, subject to limitations justified on grounds of public policy, public security or public health:

   (a) to accept offers of employment actually made;
   (b) to move freely within the territory of Member States for this purpose;
   (c) to stay in a Member State for the purpose of employment in accordance with the provisions governing the employment of nationals of that State laid down by law, regulation or administrative action;
   (d) to remain in the territory of a Member State after having been employed in that State, subject to conditions which shall be embodied in regulations to be drawn up by the Commission.

4. The provisions of this Article shall not apply to employment in the public service."

This is the principal article which sets out the basic framework for the free movement of workers. The article enables EU citizens (and, in certain circumstances, their family members of whatever nationality in the world) to move freely around the EU and take up employment on the same basis as nationals of the host Member State. The regime does not extend to those in the public sector (e.g. the naval service) but it is a very wide ranging regime. It is worth noting that the regime relates to EU nationals. So, for example, a citizen of a State which is not (or no longer)[12] an EU Member State does not benefit from the regime. It should extend to EU employees even where their ships are sailing outside the EU where the shipowner is an EU one. ... It is also worth noting that the article deals with discrimination between EU nationals (e.g. between a Greek and French person) but not intra-country discrimination (e.g. between Spanish employees).

8.010 Article 46 of the TFEU provides:

"The European Parliament and the Council shall, acting in accordance with the ordinary legislative procedure[13] and after consulting the Economic and Social Committee, issue directives or make regulations setting out the measures required to bring about freedom of movement for workers, as defined in Article 45, in particular:

(a) by ensuring close cooperation between national employment services;
(b) by abolishing those administrative procedures and practices and those qualifying periods

---

12 The legislative landscape for the post-Brexit relationship between the UK and the EU has not been agreed at the time of writing so it is not possible to be precise about the position of UK nationals post-Brexit.
13 Ed., on the ordinary legislative procedure, see chap. 3.

in respect of eligibility for available employment, whether resulting from national legislation or from agreements previously concluded between Member States, the maintenance of which would form an obstacle to liberalisation of the movement of workers;

(c) by abolishing all such qualifying periods and other restrictions provided for either under national legislation or under agreements previously concluded between Member States as imposed on workers of other Member States conditions regarding the free choice of employment other than those imposed on workers of the State concerned;

(d) by setting up appropriate machinery to bring offers of employment into touch with applications for employment and to facilitate the achievement of a balance between supply and demand in the employment market in such a way as to avoid serious threats to the standard of living and level of employment in the various regions and industries."

This article provides for a detailed secondary legislative regime to be established to regulate the operation of the regime. So much of the detail and context of EU employment law are embodied in the secondary legislation rather than the primary legislation.

8.011 Article 47 of the TFEU states: "Member States shall, within the framework of a joint programme, encourage the exchange of young workers."

8.012 Article 48 of the TFEU states:

"The European Parliament and the Council shall, acting in accordance with the ordinary legislative procedure, adopt such measures in the field of social security as are necessary to provide freedom of movement for workers; to this end, they shall make arrangements to secure for employed and self-employed migrant workers and their dependants:

(a) aggregation, for the purpose of acquiring and retaining the right to benefit and of calculating the amount of benefit, of all periods taken into account under the laws of the several countries;
(b) payment of benefits to persons resident in the territories of Member States.

Where a member of the Council declares that a draft legislative act referred to in the first subparagraph would affect important aspects of its social security system, including its scope, cost or financial structure, or would affect the financial balance of that system, it may request that the matter be referred to the European Council. In that case, the ordinary legislative procedure shall be suspended. After discussion, the European Council shall, within four months of this suspension, either:

(a) refer the draft back to the Council, which shall terminate the suspension of the ordinary legislative procedure; or
(b) take no action or request the Commission to submit a new proposal; in that case, the act originally proposed shall be deemed not to have been adopted."

C. INTERNATIONAL LEGAL BACKGROUND ON THE EMPLOYMENT OF SEAFARERS

8.013 There are various international legal provisions which are also relevant in the context of employment in the shipping sector. Some of them are embodied in the United Nations Convention on the Law of the Sea ("UNCLOS III").[14] Part VII of UNCLOS III is entitled "High Seas". Section I of Part VII is entitled "General Provisions" which contains Articles 86 to 115. It is worth considering Articles 91(1), 92(1), 94(1) to (3) and 97(1) and (2) of that convention which provide, in particular:

---

14 Signed at Montego Bay on 10 December 1982, see www.un.org/depts/los/convention_agreements/convention_overview_convention.htm.

"Article 91
Nationality of Ships

1. Every State shall fix the conditions for the grant of its nationality to ships, for the registration of ships in its territory, and for the right to fly its flag. Ships have the nationality of the State whose flag they are entitled to fly. There must exist a genuine link between the State and the ship."

"Article 92
Status of Ships

1. Ships shall sail under the flag of one State only and, save in exceptional cases expressly provided for in international treaties or in this Convention, shall be subject to its exclusive jurisdiction on the high seas."

"Article 94
Duties of the flag State

1. Every State shall effectively exercise its jurisdiction and control in administrative, technical and social matters over ships flying its flag.
2. In particular every State shall:
...
   (b) assume jurisdiction under its internal law over each ship flying its flag and its master, officers and crew in respect of administrative, technical and social matters concerning the ship.
3. Every State shall take such measures for ships flying its flag as are necessary to ensure safety at sea."

"Article 97
Penal jurisdiction in relation to collision or in any other incident of navigation

1. In the event of a collision or any other incident of navigation concerning a ship on the high seas, involving the penal or disciplinary responsibility of the master or of any other person in the service of the ship, no penal or disciplinary proceedings may be instituted against such person except before the judicial or administrative authorities either of the flag State or of the State of which such person is a national.
2. In disciplinary matters, the State which has issued a master's certificate or a certificate of competence or licence shall alone be competent … to pronounce the withdrawal of such certificates, even if the holder is not a national of the State which issued them."

D. SOURCES OF EU LAW ON EMPLOYMENT IN THE SHIPPING SECTOR

8.014 There are various sources of EU law relating to employment in the sector. The primary source is EU treaty law (in particular, the TFEU) (which has just been considered in Part B) but there are also secondary laws (e.g. regulations, directives and decisions) which are considered in the remainder of the chapter. There is also jurisprudence developed by the Court of Justice of the European Union ("CJEU") and the Member State courts (some of the jurisprudence is considered either in this chapter or other chapters throughout the book).

8.015 Some of the secondary legislation prevented the application of EU employment law generally to seafarers. So a measure was adopted on 6 October 2015 (namely, Directive 2015/1794)[15] to extend more rights to seafarers. It is proposed to examine this directive first before considering other measures.

---

15 OJ L263/1, 8 October 2015. See http://data.consilium.europa.eu/doc/document/PE-33-2015-INIT/en/pdf and http://www.consilium.europa.eu/en/press/press-releases/2015/05/13-seafarers-labour-rights/.

E. DIRECTIVE 2015/1794: THE 2015 DIRECTIVE TO EXTEND CERTAIN RIGHTS TO SEAFARERS

Introduction

8.016 On 6 October 2015, the Council and the Parliament adopted Directive 2015/1794 to extend some more EU employment law rights to seafarers.[16] Directive 2015/1794 was adopted to amend Directives 2008/94,[17] 2009/38[18] and 2002/14[19] of the European Parliament and of the Council, and Council Directives 98/59[20] and 2001/23,[21] as regards seafarers. These five directives are considered below.[22]

8.017 The legal basis of Directive 2015/1794 was the TFEU generally and, in particular, Article 153(2)(b) in conjunction with Article 153(1)(b) and (e) of the TFEU. Article 151 of the TFEU enables the Parliament and Council to adopt various measures to support and complement the EU's activities in the area of employment law.

8.018 The Commission had proposed the directive on 18 November 2013.[23] The draft legislative act was sent to the Member State parliaments. The Economic and Social Committee ("EESC") gave its opinion.[24] Equally, the Committee of the Regions gave an opinion.[25] The directive was adopted in accordance with the ordinary legislative procedure.[26]

Background

8.019 The background to Directive 2015/1794 is that Directives 2008/94,[27] 2009/38,[28] and 2002/14[29] of the European Parliament and of the Council and Council Directives 98/59[30] and 2001/23,[31] either excluded certain seafarers from their scope or allowed

---

16 OJ L263/1, 8 October 2015.
17 OJ L283/36, 28 October 2008.
18 OJ L122/28, 16 May 2009.
19 OJ L80/29, 23 March 2002.
20 OJ L225/16, 12 August 1998.
21 OJ L82/16, 22 March 2001.
22 See para. 8.019.
23 IP/13/1094, 18 November 2013.
24 OJ C226/35 16 July 2014.
25 OJ C174/50, 7 June 2014.
26 Recital 1 of Dir. 2015/1794 recalls that under Art. 153 of the TFEU, the Parliament and the Council "may, in accordance with the ordinary legislative procedure, adopt, by means of directives, minimum requirements for gradual implementation aiming to improve the working conditions and the information and consultation of workers. Such directives must avoid imposing disproportionate costs, or administrative, financial and legal constraints in a way that would hold back the creation and development of small and medium-sized undertakings, which are the drivers of sustainable growth and jobs."
27 I.e. Dir. 2008/94 of the European Parliament and of the Council of 22 October 2008 on the protection of employees in the event of the insolvency of their employer (OJ L283/36, 28 October 2008).
28 I.e. Dir. 2009/38 of the European Parliament and of the Council of 6 May 2009 on the establishment of a European Works Council or a procedure in Community-scale undertakings and Community-scale groups of undertakings for the purposes of informing and consulting employees (OJ L122/28, 16 May 2009).
29 I.e. Dir. 2002/14 of the European Parliament and of the Council of 11 March 2002 establishing a general framework for informing and consulting employees in the European Community (OJ L80/29, 23 March 2002).
30 I.e. Dir. 98/59 of 20 July 1998 on the approximation of the laws of the Member States relating to collective redundancies (OJ L225/16, 12 August 1998).
31 I.e. Dir. 2001/23 of 12 March 2001 on the approximation of the laws of the Member States relating to the safeguarding of employees' rights in the event of transfers of undertakings, businesses or parts of undertakings or businesses (OJ L82/16, 22 March 2001).

Member States to exclude them. It is useful to present these five measures in tabular format to demonstrate their contents (see Table 8.1).

8.020 In essence, the 2013 proposal was designed to amend some existing directives: the Employer Insolvency Directive; the European Works Councils Directive; the Information and Consultation Directive; the Collective Redundancies Directive; and the Transfer of Undertakings Directive so as to give seafarers the same rights as their onshore colleagues.

2013: Proposal to extend certain EU employment rights to all seafarers

8.021 As a general principle, EU employment or labour law should apply to all workers in all economic sectors. However, there have been, at times, some exceptions for the likes of public officials, trainee doctors and seafarers. For example, this has meant that there has been the possibility under a number of employment directives that Member States are able to exclude seafarers from a right to, for example, information, consultation, participation in the company (e.g. works council-type arrangements) and transfer to the new owner on the sale of a business. This has meant that some seafarers are treated differently and less favourably within some Member States from other types of employees in those countries. It has also meant that seafarers in one Member State could be treated differently from seafarers in other Member States.

8.022 On 18 November 2013, the Commission proposed that seafarers would be brought automatically within the scope of five existing directives which confer various rights on shore-based employees and from which seafarers were excluded.[32] The proposal was designed to confer the same rights on seafarers as shore-based employees in the areas of collective redundancies, information, participation in European Works Councils and the transfer of undertakings.

8.023 The proposal was made by László Andor who was the then Commissioner for Employment, Social Affairs and Inclusion. His motivation is interesting. First, he said: "[o]ff-shore and on-shore workers should have equal rights, in particular when it comes to such a fundamental right as information and consultation". Second, he said that the "proposal would improve the living and working conditions of seafarers and so help to attract more young people to work in the maritime sector". This is important because there is a growing shortage of EU seafarers. He also indicated that it would also create equality in Europe's maritime sector, since all shipping and fisheries companies within the EU would have the same obligations.

8.024 The Commission stated that since the buying and selling of one or more vessels is very common in the maritime sector, some measures would also be introduced to ensure that EU shipping companies were not comparatively disadvantaged in these highly competitive markets. For example, under certain conditions, Member States could decide that the waiting period after the notification of planned collective redundancies to the competent public authorities would not apply in case of buying or selling a vessel.

---

32 IP/13/1094, 18 November 2013, http://europa.eu/rapid/press-release_IP-13-1094_en.htm. The proposal is contained in COM(2013) 798 final which is available at: http://ec.europa.eu/social/BlobServlet?docId=11129&langId=en.

Table 8.1 Key employment law directives in the shipping context

Directive	Subject matter of the directive	OJ reference
Directive 2008/94 of the European Parliament and of the Council of 22 October 2008	On the protection of employees in the event of the insolvency of their employer	OJ L283/36, 28 October 2008
Directive 2009/38 of the European Parliament and of the Council of 6 May 2009	On the establishment of a European Works Council or a procedure in Community-scale undertakings and Community-scale groups of undertakings for the purposes of informing and consulting employees	OJ L122/28, 16 May 2009
Directive 2002/14 of the European Parliament and of the Council of 11 March 2002	On establishing a general framework for informing and consulting employees in the European Community	OJ L80/29, 23 March 2002
Council Directive 98/59 of 20 July 1998	On the approximation of the laws of the Member States relating to collective redundancies	OJ L225/16, 12 August 1998
Council Directive 2001/23 of 12 March 2001	On the approximation of the laws of the Member States relating to the safeguarding of employees' rights in the event of transfers of undertakings, businesses or parts of undertakings or businesses	OJ L82/16, 22 March 2001

8.025 It is worth noting that the prospect of such a measure stretched back to 2007. The process which followed is outlined in the Commission's comments of 18 November 2013.[33] On 10 October 2007, the Commission had proposed, in a very welcome move, an integrated maritime policy for the EU.[34] In that context, on the same day, Commissioner Špidla (the then Commissioner for Employment, Social Affairs and Equal Opportunities) presented a review of labour law exemptions in the maritime sectors. The Commission invited seagoing workers to become involved in the new maritime policy.[35] This was an attempt to reassess the various exclusions of seafarers from the EU's social laws which had built up over time. The background was described well in the Commission press release in 2007:

> "Should the current exclusion of seafaring workers from certain EU social laws be eliminated, making them shipshape for a modern maritime sector? Is there a need for specific regulations for the seafaring profession within EU social legislation? What is the best way to improve health and safety on board sea vessels? These are all questions being put to workers' and employers' representatives today to reassess whether EU laws adequately protect seagoing workers.
>
> This first-phase consultation aims to strengthen the social dimension of maritime policy and to make the sector more attractive without undermining its competitiveness. It is a follow up to last year's Green Paper on the Future of Maritime Policy[36] and part of the new EU maritime package being adopted today.
>
> Commenting on the launch of the consultation, Vladimír Špidla, EU Commissioner for Employment, Social Affairs and Equal Opportunities said, 'Jobs in the maritime sector should be of the same standard as in other sectors: this includes working conditions and social protection. At the same time, the EU has to contribute to consolidating a global level playing field for the maritime sector. This is especially important if the latter wants to attract young, highly skilled professionals.'[37] He added, 'The views of workers and employers in the reassessment of any labour and social legislation are essential for any such discussions.'
>
> The 2006 Green Paper on the Future of Maritime Policy underlined the importance of a stable, simple and more consolidated regulatory framework for a competitive maritime economy. One of the issues raised in the consultation was the exclusion of maritime sectors from the scope of part of EU labour and social legislation and the need to reassess this situation in close cooperation with the social partners. The Commission's analysis presented today has been carried out against the background of the already extensive body of international conventions and standards. It reviews pertinent legislation, identifying exclusions or derogations affecting workers in maritime professions, problems raised by practical application and difficulties of interpretation of such legislation. These relate mainly to legislation on:
>
> - working conditions (for example the European Works Council Directive, Directive on Information and Consultation of Workers, [the directive on collective redundancies and the directive on the protection of employees in the case of insolvency]); and
> - health and safety at work (for example minimum health and safety requirements for the workplace, minimum health and safety requirements for medical treatment on board vessels).
>
> Today's Communication 'Reassessing the regulatory social framework for more and better seafaring jobs in the EU' invites the social partners to take a position on the Commission's analysis

---

33 2013/0390 (COD).
34 See IP/07/1463. See Carley, "EU: Commission Questions Exclusion of Maritime Workers from Employment Directives" (2007) IRS European Employment Review 406.
35 IP/07/1464.
36 Ed., COM(2006) 275 final, 7 June 2006.
37 Ed., the theory behind this statement is that young people would be discouraged from entering the maritime sector if the employment conditions were not attractive.

and to assess priority areas for action. They are being asked, in particular, to express their opinions on which 'exclusions' may need to be suppressed because they are not/no longer justified or which may need to be adapted. The social partners are also asked to provide input on what means of action would be appropriate in order to improve the social security protection of workers in seagoing professions and to improve health and safety on board, in particular on small fishing vessels.

The consultation with the social partners (under Article 138 of the Treaty)[38] will run for six weeks. If, after the consultation, the Commission considers Community action is advisable, it will consult the social partners on a proposal."

The Commission's 2007 communication and consultation was entitled *Reassessing the Regulatory Social Framework for More and Better Seafaring Jobs in the EU*.[39] In essence, the Commission argued that there should be greater inclusion of seafarers in the general employment regime.

Adoption of Directive 2015/1794

8.026 The proposal for what ultimately became Directive 2015/1794 was adopted by the Council of Ministers and the European Parliament. The Commission had stated that as

"there are differences between the 28 Member States in terms of the nature of their maritime sector and the extent they made use of the possibility to exclude seafarers, the proposal includes a transition period of 5 years for the Member States. The goal is to offer sufficient time to implement the proposal into the national legislation and practice."[40]

Entry into force of Directive 2015/1794

8.027 Under Article 9 of Directive 2015/1794, the directive entered into force on the day following that of its publication in the *Official Journal* (i.e. it entered into force on 9 October 2015).

Transposition of Directive 2015/1794

8.028 Under Article 8(1) of Directive 2015/94, Member States had to bring into force the laws, regulations and administrative provisions necessary to comply with the directive by 10 October 2017 and they had to inform the Commission immediately about such measures. When Member States adopted those measures, they had to contain a reference to the directive or be accompanied by such a reference on the occasion of their official publication. The method of making such a reference was to be laid down by Member States. Pursuant to Article 8(2) of Directive 2015/94, Member States had to communicate to the Commission the text of the main provisions of national law which they adopt in the field covered by the directive.

---

38 Ed., this is now, in essence, Art. 154 TFEU.
39 COM(2007) 591 final.
40 Press Release, IP/13/1094, 18 November 2013.

Background to Directive 2015/1794

8.029 The fourth to the sixth recitals to Directive 2015/1794[41] recall the background to the adoption of the directive:

> "(4) The existence of, and/or possibility of introducing, exclusions may prevent seafarers from fully enjoying their rights to fair and just working conditions and to information and consultation, or limit the full enjoyment of those rights. Insofar as the existence of, and/or possibility of introducing, exclusions is not justified on objective grounds and seafarers are not treated equally, provisions which allow such exclusions should be deleted.
> (5) The present legal situation, existing in part as a result of the specific nature of the seafaring profession, gives rise to unequal treatment of the same category of workers by different Member States, according to whether or not they apply the exclusions and optional exclusions allowed by the legislation in force. A significant number of the Member States have made no, or only limited, use of those optional exclusions.
> (6) In its Communication of 10 October 2007 entitled 'An Integrated Maritime Policy for the European Union', the Commission outlined that such a policy is based on the clear recognition that all matters relating to Europe's oceans and seas are interlinked, and that sea-related policies must develop in a joined-up way if they are to achieve the desired results. It also stressed the need for an increase in the number and quality of maritime jobs for citizens of the Union and the importance of improving working conditions on board, inter alia, through investment in research, education, training, health and safety."

8.030 Directive 2015/1794, the Council of Ministers and Parliament believed, is in line with previous policy initiatives,[42] changes in the sector[43] and international developments.[44] The directive is aimed at improving the conditions of seafarers.[45] There is, the

---

41 OJ L263/1, 8 October 2015.

42 The seventh recital to the directive states that the directive "is in line with the Europe 2020 Strategy and its employment objectives and with the strategy set out by the Commission in its communication of 23 November 2010 entitled 'An Agenda for new skills and jobs: A European contribution towards full employment'."

43 The tenth recital states that in "the framework of their social dialogue, the social partners in the maritime sector have reached a common understanding which is of major importance for this Directive. That common understanding strikes a good balance between the need to improve seafarers' working conditions and the need to take proper account of the sector's specific features." The eleventh recital provides that considering "the particular nature of the maritime sector and the particular working conditions of the workers affected by the exclusions deleted by this Directive, it is necessary to adapt some of the provisions of the Directives that are amended by this Directive to reflect the specificities of the sector concerned". The twelfth recital provides that having "regard to the technological developments of recent years, in particular as regards communications technology, the information and consultation requirements should be updated and applied in the most appropriate manner, including by using new technologies for remote communication and by enhancing the availability of the internet and ensuring its reasonable use on board, in order to improve the implementation of this Directive".

44 The fourteenth recital to the directive states that the "Maritime Labour Convention of 2006 of the International Labour Organization aims to achieve both decent working and living conditions for seafarers by providing for health and safety standards, fair terms of employment and professional training, and secure fair competition for ship owners through its global application as well as to guarantee an international level playing field with regard to some, but not all, employees' rights, regardless of nationality or vessel flag. That Convention, Council Directive 2009/13/EC and Directives 2009/16/EC and 2013/54/EU of the European Parliament and of the Council lay down seafarers' rights to decent working conditions in a wide range of areas, provide coherent rights and protection at work for seafarers, and contribute to a level playing field including within the Union" (footnotes omitted).

45 The eighteenth directive provides that the "Union should strive to improve working and living conditions on board ships, and to exploit the potential for innovation in order to make the maritime sector more attractive to Union seafarers, including young workers."

Council and Parliament believe, a need to respect human rights[46] and to take action at the EU, rather than the Member State, level.[47]

Changes brought about by Directive 2015/1794

8.031 Article 1 of Directive 2015/1794 amended Directive 2008/94 by replacing Article 1(3) of Directive 2008/94 by the following language: "[w]here such provision already applies in their national legislation, Member States may continue to exclude domestic servants employed by a natural person from the scope of this Directive".

8.032 Article 2 of Directive 2015/1794 amended Directive 2009/38 by deleting Article 1, paragraph 7 and adding the following subparagraphs to in Article 10(3):

> "A member of a special negotiating body or of a European Works Council, or such a member's alternate, who is a member of the crew of a seagoing vessel, shall be entitled to participate in a meeting of the special negotiating body or of the European Works Council, or in any other meeting under any procedures established pursuant to Article 6(3), where that member or alternate is not at sea or in a port in a country other than that in which the shipping company is domiciled, when the meeting takes place.
>
> Meetings shall, where practicable, be scheduled to facilitate the participation of members or alternates, who are members of the crews of seagoing vessels.
>
> In cases where a member of a special negotiating body or of a European Works Council, or such a member's alternate, who is a member of the crew of a seagoing vessel, is unable to attend a meeting, the possibility of using, where possible, new information and communication technologies shall be considered."

8.033 Article 3 of Directive 2015/1794 amended Directive 2002/14 by deleting Article 3(3) of that directive.

8.034 Article 4 of Directive 2015/1794 amended Directive 98/59 in a number of ways. Article 1(2), point (c) was deleted. Article 3(1) had the following subparagraph inserted after the second subparagraph: "[w]here the projected collective redundancy concerns members of the crew of a seagoing vessel, the employer shall notify the competent authority of the State of the flag which the vessel flies".

8.035 Article 5 amended Directive 2001/23. Article 1(3) of Directive 2001/23 was replaced by the following:

> "This Directive shall apply to a transfer of a seagoing vessel that is part of a transfer of an undertaking, business or part of an undertaking or business within the meaning of paragraphs 1 and 2, provided that the transferee is situated, or the transferred undertaking, business, or part of an undertaking or business remains, within the territorial scope of the Treaty.
>
> This Directive shall not apply where the object of the transfer consists exclusively of one or more seagoing vessels."

---

46 The thirteenth recital to the directive respects the fundamental rights and observes the principles recognised in the Charter of Fundamental Rights of the European Union, in particular the right to fair and just working conditions and to information and consultation within the undertaking. The directive should be implemented in accordance with those rights and principles.

47 The sixteenth recital to the directive provides that since "the objective of this Directive, namely to improve the working conditions of seafarers and their information and consultation, cannot be sufficiently achieved by the Member States but can rather, by reason of the scale and effects of the action, be better achieved at Union level, the Union may adopt measures, in accordance with the principle of subsidiarity as set out in Article 5 of the Treaty on European Union. In accordance with the principle of proportionality as set out in that Article, this Directive does not go beyond what is necessary in order to achieve that objective."

8.036 The level of protection for seafarers was addressed by Article 6. The article provided that the implementation of the directive "shall under no circumstances constitute grounds for a reduction in the general level of protection of persons covered by this directive, already afforded by the Member States in the fields covered by Directives [2008/94, 2009/38, 2002/14, 98/59 and 2001/23]".

Reporting by the Commission on the directive

8.037 The Commission, after consulting the Member States and the social partners at the EU level, must submit a report to the Parliament and Council on the implementation and application of Articles 4 and 5 by 10 October 2019.[48] It will be reviewed carefully but is likely to say that the change is working well but it will be interesting to see if every Member State implements it fully and on time.

F. DIRECTIVE 1999/63 CONCERNING THE AGREEMENT ON THE ORGANISATION OF WORKING TIME OF SEAFARERS CONCLUDED BY THE EUROPEAN COMMUNITY SHIPOWNERS' ASSOCIATION AND THE FEDERATION OF TRANSPORT WORKERS' UNIONS IN THE EUROPEAN UNION

Introduction

8.038 On 21 June 1999, the Council adopted Directive 1999/63 concerning the agreement on the organisation of working time of seafarers concluded by the European Community Shipowners' Association ("ECSA") and the Federation of Transport Workers' Unions in the European Union ("FST").[49] It has been amended by Council Directive 2009/13 of 16 February 2009.[50]

8.039 Under the then Article 139(2) of the then European Community ("EC") Treaty (post-Treaty of Amsterdam), "management and labour"[51] (i.e. the "social partners") may request jointly that agreements at the EU level be implemented by a Council decision on a proposal from the Commission. The Council had adopted Directive 93/104 of 23 November 1993 concerning certain aspects of the organisation of working time but sea transport[52] was one of the sectors of activity excluded from the scope of that directive.

8.040 There had also been various ILO conventions with regard to the organisation of working time, including in particular those relating to the hours of work of seafarers. So the European Commission, in accordance with Article 3(2) of the agreement on social policy, consulted both management and labour on the possible direction of EU action

---

48 Dir. 2015/1794, Art. 7.
49 OJ L167/33, 2 July 1999. Corrigendum: OJ L244, 16 June 1999, p. 64. The Commission said in Recital 14 of the directive that it had drafted its proposal for a directive, in accordance with its communication of 20 May 1998 on adapting and promoting the social dialogue at Community level.
50 OJ L124/30, 20 May 2009. The 2009 directive implements the agreement on Maritime Labour Convention, 2006, concluded on 19 May 2008 between the organisations representing management and labour in the maritime transport sector.
51 The term used in Recital 2 to the directive.
52 OJ L307/18, 13 December 1993.

with regard to the sectors and activities excluded from Directive 93/104[53] and, after that consultation, the Commission considered that EU action was desirable in that area and so consulted management and labour again at an EU level on the substance of the envisaged proposal in accordance with Article 3(3) of the agreement. The ECSA and the FST informed the Commission of their desire to enter into negotiations in accordance with Article 4 of the agreement on social policy. ECSA and FST concluded, on 30 September 1998, an agreement on the working time of seafarers. The agreement contained a joint request to the European Commission to implement the agreement by a Council decision on a proposal from the European Commission, in accordance with Article 4(2) of the agreement on social policy.

8.041 The Council, in a resolution of 6 December 1994 on "Certain Aspects for an EU Social Policy: A Contribution to Economic and Social Convergence in the Union"[54] asked management and labour to make use of the opportunities for concluding agreements, since they are close to social reality and to social problems.

8.042 The resultant agreement applies to seafarers on board every seagoing ship, whether publicly or privately owned, which is registered in the territory of any Member State and is ordinarily engaged in commercial maritime operations so it does not apply to, for example, naval vessels.

8.043 As a matter of law, the proper instrument for implementing the agreement is a directive because the latter binds the Member States as to the result to be achieved, while leaving national authorities the choice of form and methods. Interestingly, Recital 13 of the directive provides that with regard to terms used in the agreement which are not specifically defined in the directive, the directive leaves Member States free to define those terms in accordance with their national law and practice, as is the case for other social policy directives using similar terms, providing that those definitions respect the content of the agreement.

8.044 Article 1 of Directive 1999/63 provides that the directive's purpose is to put into effect the agreement on the organisation of working time of seafarers concluded on 30 September 1998 between the organisations representing management and labour in the maritime sector (i.e. the ECSA and FST) as set out in the annex to the directive.

8.045 Article 2 of Directive 1999/63 then sets out various minimum requirements. Article 2(1) provides that Member States may maintain or introduce more favourable provisions than those laid down in the directive. This means that the directive only sets minimum standards leaving open the possibility of more enhanced protection. Article 2(2) provides that the implementation of the directive must, under no circumstances, constitute sufficient grounds for justifying a reduction in the general level of protection of workers in the fields covered by the directive. This is without prejudice to the rights of Member States and/or management and labour to lay down, in the light of changing circumstances, different legislative, regulatory or contractual arrangements to those prevailing at the time of the adoption of the directive, provided always that the minimum requirements laid down in the directive are followed.

---

53 This is Dir. 93/104 of 23 November 1993 concerning certain aspects of the organisation of working times OJ L307/18, 13 December 1993.
54 OJ C368/6, 23 December 1994.

8.046 In terms of transposition of the directive into Member State law, Article 3(1) provides that Member States had to implement the directive by 30 June 2002, or to ensure that, by that date at the latest, management and labour had introduced the necessary measures by agreement, the Member States being required to take any necessary measure to enable them at any time to be in a position to guarantee the results imposed by the directive. The annex to the directive contained the agreement itself. It refers to the agreement on social policy annexed to the protocol on social policy attached to the then Treaty establishing the European Community.

Application of Directive 1999/63

8.047 Clause 1 of the agreement provides:

"1. The Agreement applies to seafarers on board every seagoing ship, whether publicly or privately owned, which is registered in the territory of any Member State and is ordinarily engaged in commercial maritime operations.
   For the purpose of this Agreement a ship that is on the register of two States is deemed to be registered in the territory of the State whose flag it flies.
2. In the event of doubt as to whether or not any ships are to be regarded as seagoing ships or engaged in commercial maritime operations for the purpose of the Agreement, the question shall be determined by the competent authority of the Member State. The organisations of shipowners and seafarers concerned should be consulted.
3. In the event of doubt as to whether any categories of persons are to be regarded as seafarers for the purpose of this Agreement, the question shall be determined by the competent authority in each Member State after consultation with the shipowners' and seafarers' organisations concerned with this question. In this context due account shall be taken of the Resolution of the 94th (Maritime) Session of the General Conference of the International Labour Organisation concerning information on occupational groups."

Definitions in Directive 1999/63

8.048 Clause 2 contains a number of definitions for the purpose of the agreement:

"(a) the term 'hours of work' means time during which a seafarer is required to do work on account of the ship;
(b) the term 'hours of rest' means time outside hours of work; this term does not include short breaks;
(c) the term 'seafarer' means any person who is employed or engaged or works in any capacity on board a ship to which this Agreement applies;
(d) the term 'shipowner' means the owner of the ship or another organisation or person, such as the manager, agent or bareboat charterer, who has assumed the responsibility for the operation of the ship from the owner and who, on assuming such responsibility, has agreed to take over the duties and responsibilities imposed on shipowners in accordance with this Agreement, regardless of whether any other organisation or persons fulfil certain of the duties or responsibilities on behalf of the shipowner."

The definition of "seafarer" is a useful one generally in the context of this chapter.

Working hours

8.049 The number of hours which seafarers have to work is often a vexed question because of the difficulty in policing working conditions. The agreement deals with it as follows:

"Clause 3
Within the limits set out in Clause 5, there shall be fixed either a maximum number of hours of work which shall not be exceeded in a given period of time, or a minimum number or hours of rest which shall be provided in a given period of time.

Clause 4
Without prejudice to Clause 5, the normal working hours' standard of seafarers is, in principle, based on an eight-hour day with one day of rest per week and rest on public holidays. Member States may have procedures to authorise or register a collective agreement which determines seafarers' normal working hours on a basis no less favourable than this standard.

Clause 5
1. The limits on hours of work or rest shall be either:

    (a) maximum hours of work which shall not exceed (i) fourteen hours in any 24 hour period; and (ii) 72 hours in any seven-day period;
    Or
    (b) minimum hours of rest which shall not be less than: (i) ten hours in any 24 hour period; and (ii) 77 hours in any seven-day period.

2. Hours of rest may be divided into no more than two periods, one of which shall be at least six hours in length and the interval between consecutive periods of rest shall not exceed 14 hours.
3. Musters, fire-fighting and lifeboat drills, and prescribed by national laws and regulations and by international instruments shall be conducted in a manner that minimises the disturbance of rest periods and does not induce fatigue.
4. In respect of situations when a seafarer is on call, such as when a machinery space is unattended, the seafarer shall have an adequate compensatory rest period if the normal period of rest is disturbed by call-outs to work.
5. With regard to paragraphs 3 and 4, where no collective agreement or arbitration award exists or if the competent authority determines that the provisions in the agreement or award are inadequate, it would be for the competent authority to determine such provisions to ensure that the seafarers concerned have sufficient rest.
6. With due regard for the general principles of the protection of the health and safety of workers, Member States may have national laws, regulations or a procedure for the competent authority to authorise or register collective agreements permitting exceptions to the limits set out in paragraphs 1 and 2. Such exceptions shall, as far as possible, follow the standards set out but may take account of more frequent or longer leave periods, or the granting of compensatory leave for watchkeeping seafarers or seafarers working on board ship on short voyages.
7. A table shall be posted, in an easily accessible place, with the shipboard working arrangements, which shall contain for every position at least:

    (a) the schedule of service at sea and service in port; and
    (b) the maximum hours of work or the minimum hours of rest required by the laws, regulations or collective agreements in force in the Member States.

8. The table referred to in paragraph 7 shall be established in a standardised format in the working language or languages of the ship and in English.

Clause 6
1. Night work of seafarers under the age of 18 shall be prohibited. For the purposes of this Clause, 'night' shall be defined in accordance with national law and practice. It shall cover a period of at least nine hours starting no later than midnight and ending no earlier than 5 a.m.
2. An exception to strict compliance with the night work restriction may be made by the competent authority when:

    (a) the effective training of the seafarers concerned, in accordance with established programmes and schedules, would be impaired; or
    (b) the specific nature of the duty or a recognised training programme requires that the seafarers covered by the exception perform duties at night and the authority determines, after consultation with the shipowners' and seafarers' organisations concerned, that the work will not be detrimental to their health or well-being.

3. The employment, engagement or work of seafarers under the age of 18 shall be prohibited where the work is likely to jeopardise their health or safety. The types of such work shall be determined by national laws or regulations or by the competent authority, after consultation with the shipowners' and seafarers' organisations concerned, in accordance with relevant international standards.

Clause 7
1. The master of a ship shall have the right to require a seafarer to perform any hours of work necessary for the immediate safety of the ship, persons on board or cargo, or for the purpose of giving assistance to other ships or persons in distress at sea.
2. In accordance with paragraph 1, the master may suspend the schedule of hours of work or hours of rest and require a seafarer to perform any hours of work necessary until the normal situation has been restored.
3. As soon as practicable after the normal situation has been restored, the master shall ensure that any seafarer who have performed work in a scheduled rest period are provided with an adequate period of rest.

Clause 8
1. Records of seafarers' daily hours of work or of their daily hours of rest shall be maintained to allow monitoring of compliance with the provisions set out in Clause 5. The seafarer shall receive a copy of the records pertaining to him or her which shall be endorsed by the master, or a person authorised by the master, and by the seafarer.
2. Procedures shall be determined for keeping such records on board, including the intervals at which the information shall be recorded. The format of the records of the seafarers' hours of work or of their hours of rest shall be established taking into account any available international guidelines. The format shall be established in the language provided by Clause 5, paragraph 8.
3. A copy of the relevant provisions of the national legislation pertaining to this Agreement and the relevant collective agreements shall be kept on board and be easily accessible to the crew.

Clause 9
The records referred to in Clause 8 shall be examined and endorsed at appropriate intervals, to monitor compliance with the provisions governing hours of work or hours of rest that give effect to this Agreement.

Clause 10
1. When determining, approving or revising manning levels, it is necessary to take into account the need to avoid or minimise, as far as practicable, excessive hours of work, to ensure sufficient rest and to limit fatigue.
2. If the records or other evidence indicate infringement of provisions governing hours of work or hours of rest, measures, including if necessary the revision of the manning of the ship, shall be taken so as to avoid future infringements.

3. All ships to which this Agreement applies shall be sufficiently, safely and efficiently manned, in accordance with the minimum safe manning document or an equivalent issued by the competent authority."

Age limits

8.050 Clause 11 of the agreement provides that no person under 16 years of age shall work on a ship.

Resources to ensure compliance

8.051 Clause 12 provides that shipowners must provide masters of vessels with the necessary resources for the purpose of compliance with obligations under the agreement, including those relating to the appropriate manning of the ship. The master must take all necessary steps to ensure that the requirements on seafarers' hours of work and rest arising from the agreement are complied with.

Fitness to work

8.052 Clause 13(1) provides that seafarers may not work on a ship unless they are certified as medically fit to perform their duties. Exemptions are permitted, by virtue of Clause 13(2) but only those permitted in the agreement. Under clause 13(3), the competent authority must require that, prior to beginning work on a ship, seafarers must hold a valid medical certificate attesting that they are medically fit to perform the duties they are to carry out at sea. To ensure that medical certificates genuinely reflect seafarers' state of health, Clause 13(4) in light of the duties they are to perform, the competent authority must, after consultation with the shipowners' and seafarers' organisations concerned, and giving due consideration to applicable international guidelines, prescribe the nature of the medical examination and certificate.

8.053 Clause 13(5) provides that the agreement is without prejudice to the International Convention on Standards of Training, Certification and Watchkeeping for Seafarers, 1978, as amended ("STCW Convention"). A medical certificate issued in accordance with the requirements of STCW Convention must be accepted by the competent authority, for the purposes of points 1 and 2 of Clause 13 of the agreement. A medical certificate meeting the substance of those requirements, in the case of seafarers not covered by STCW Convention must also be accepted. Under Clause 13(6), the medical certificate must be issued by a duly qualified medical practitioner or, in the case of a certificate solely concerning eyesight, by a person recognised by the competent authority as qualified to issue such a certificate. Practitioners must enjoy full professional independence in exercising their medical judgment in undertaking medical examination procedures.

8.054 Clause 13(7) provides that seafarers who have been refused a certificate or have had a limitation imposed on their ability to work, in particular with respect to time, field of work or trading area, must be given the opportunity to have a further examination by another independent medical practitioner or by an independent medical referee.

8.055 Clause 13 provides that each medical certificate must state in particular that: (a) the hearing and sight of the seafarer concerned, and the colour vision in the case of a seafarer to be employed in capacities where fitness for the work to be performed is liable to be affected by defective colour vision, are all satisfactory; and (b) the seafarer concerned is not suffering from any medical condition likely to be aggravated by service at sea or to render the seafarer unfit for such service or to endanger the health of other persons on board.

8.056 Clause 14 provides that the shipowners must provide information on watchkeepers and other night workers to the national competent authority if they so request.

8.057 Clause 15 provides that the seafarers must have safety and health protection appropriate to the nature of their work. Equivalent protection and prevention services or facilities with regard to the safety and health of seafarers working by day or by night shall be available.

8.058 Clause 16 provides that every seafarer must be entitled to paid annual leave. The annual leave with pay entitlement must be calculated on the basis of a minimum of 2.5 calendar days per month of employment and pro rata for incomplete months. The minimum period of paid annual leave may not be replaced by an allowance in lieu, except where the employment relationship is terminated.

G. DIRECTIVE 1999/95 OF THE EUROPEAN PARLIAMENT AND OF THE COUNCIL OF 13 DECEMBER 1999 CONCERNING THE ENFORCEMENT OF PROVISIONS IN RESPECT OF SEAFARERS' HOURS OF WORK ON BOARD SHIPS CALLING AT COMMUNITY PORTS

Introduction

8.059 On 13 December 1999, the Parliament and the Council adopted Directive 1999/95 concerning the enforcement of provisions in respect of seafarers' hours of work on board ships calling at EU ports.[55] Member States had to bring into force the measures necessary to comply with the directive no later than 30 June 2002.[56] It has not been amended since.

Background to Directive 1999/95

8.060 The recitals to the directive recall that EU "action in the field of social policy aims, *inter alia*, at improving the health and safety of workers in their working environment"[57] and EU "action in the field of maritime transport aims, *inter alia*, at improving shipboard living and working conditions of seafarers, safety at sea and the prevention of pollution caused by maritime accidents".[58]

8.061 The background to Directive 1999/95 is set out in Recitals 3 to 13:

"(3) During its eighty-fourth session of 8 to 22 October 1996 the [ILO] Conference (ILO) adopted ILO Convention No 180 concerning Seafarers' Hours of Work and the Manning of Ships, 1996 (hereinafter 'ILO Convention No 180' and the Protocol to the Merchant

---
55 OJ L14/29, 20 January 2000.
56 Dir. 1999/95, Art. 10.
57 Dir. 1999/95, Recital 1.
58 Dir. 1999/95, Recital 2.

Shipping (Minimum Standards) Convention, 1976 (hereinafter 'the Protocol to ILO Convention No 147');

(4) Council Directive 99/63/EC ... of 21 June 1999 concerning the Agreement on the organisation of working time of seafarers concluded by the European Community Shipowners' Association (ECSA) and the Federation of Transport Workers' Unions in the European Union (FST)[59] adopted under Article 139(2) of the Treaty, aims to put into effect the said Agreement concluded on 30 September 1998 (hereinafter the 'Agreement'); the content of the Agreement reflects certain provisions of ILO Convention No 180; the Agreement applies to seafarers on board every seagoing ship, whether publicly or privately owned, which is registered in the territory of any Member State and is ordinarily engaged in commercial maritime operations;

(5) The purpose of this Directive is to apply the provisions of Directive 1999/63 ... which reflect the provisions of ILO Convention No 180, to any ship calling at a Community port, irrespective of the flag it flies in order to identify and remedy any situation which is manifestly hazardous for the safety or health of seafarers; however, Directive 1999/63 ... includes requirements which are not to be found in ILO Convention No 180 and which should not therefore be enforced on board ships not flying the flag of a Member State;

(6) Directive 1999/63/EC applies to seafarers on board every seagoing ship registered in the territory of a Member State; Member States should monitor compliance with all the provisions of the said Directive by ships registered in their territory;

(7) In order to protect safety and to avoid distortions of competition, Member States should be allowed to verify compliance with the relevant provisions of Directive 1999/63/EC ... by all sea-going vessels calling at their ports, irrespective of the State in which they are registered;[60]

(8) In particular, ships flying the flag of a State which is not a party to ILO Convention No 180 or the Protocol to ILO Convention No 147 should not receive more favourable treatment than those flying the flag of a State which is a party to either the Convention or Protocol or to both of them;

(9) For the control of the effective enforcement of Directive 1999/63, ... it is necessary that Member States carry out inspections on board ships, notably after having received a complaint by the master, a crew member, or any person or organisation with a legitimate interest in the safe operation of the ship, shipboard living and working conditions or the prevention of pollution;

(10) For the purposes of this Directive Member States, on their own initiative, may designate, as appropriate, Port State Control inspectors to carry out inspections on board vessels calling at Community ports;

(11) Evidence that a ship does not comply with the requirements of Directive 1999/63 ... may be obtained after verification of the shipboard working arrangements and seafarers' records of hours of work or hours of rest, or when the inspector has a reasonable belief that seafarers are excessively fatigued;

(12) In order to rectify any conditions on board a ship which are clearly hazardous to safety or health, the competent authority of the Member State in whose port the ship has called may impose a prohibition on leaving the port until the deficiencies found have been rectified or the crew is sufficiently rested;

(13) Since Directive 1999/63/EC reflects the provisions of ILO Convention No 180, verification of compliance with the provisions of that Directive by ships registered in the territory of a third State can take place only when this Convention has entered into force."

These recitals demonstrate yet again the interaction between the EU and the ILO in this area.

---

[59] OJ L167, 2 July 1999, p. 37. Ed., see above in this chapter.

[60] Ed., Recitals 6 and 7 illustrate some of the illusion of Brexit – while Recital 6 would no longer apply to UK registered ships post-Brexit but as soon as such ships would visit EU ports then under Recital 7, they would be subject to the EU regime.

Purpose and scope of Directive 1999/95

8.062 The purpose and scope of the directive is set out in Article 1:

"1. The purpose of this Directive is to provide a mechanism for the verification and enforcement of compliance by ships calling at ports of Member States with Directive 1999/63 ... in order to improve maritime safety, working conditions and the health and safety of seafarers on board ships.
2. Member States shall take appropriate measures to ensure that ships which are not registered in their territory or not flying their flag comply with clauses 1 to 12 of the Agreement annexed to Directive 1999/63."

Application of Directive 1999/95

8.063 Article 11 of Directive 1999/95 provides that not only may Directive 1999/95 apply to EU ships but it may also apply to ships from non-Member States: the directive

"shall apply to ships not registered in the territory of, or not flying the flag of, a Member State only on the date of entry into force of ILO Convention No 180 and the date of entry into force of the Protocol to ILO Convention No 147".

Definitions of certain concepts in Directive 1999/95

8.064 Article 2 sets out a number of definitions for the purposes of Directive 1999/95:

"(a) 'ship' means any seagoing vessel, whether publicly or privately owned, which is ordinarily engaged in commercial maritime operations. Fishing vessels are not included in this definition,
(b) 'competent authority' means the authorities designated by the Member States to perform functions under this Directive,
(c) 'inspector' means a public-sector employee or other person, duly authorised by the competent authority of a Member State to inspect the working conditions on board, and responsible to that competent authority,
(d) 'complaint' means any information or report submitted by a member of the crew, a professional body, an association, a trade union or, generally, any person with an interest in the safety of the ship, including an interest in safety or health hazards to its crew".

Naval vessels are excluded. Pure research vessels which are not engaged in commercial maritime operations would be excluded. Leisure craft would also be excluded.

Preparation of reports

8.065 Article 3 of Directive 1999/95 provides that without prejudice to Article 1(2), if a Member State in whose port a ship calls voluntarily in the normal course of its business or for operational reasons receives a complaint which it does not consider manifestly unfounded or obtains evidence that the ship does not conform to the standards referred to in Directive 1999/63, it shall prepare a report addressed to the government of the country in which the ship is registered and, when an inspection carried out pursuant to Article 4 provides relevant evidence, the Member State shall take the measures necessary to ensure that any conditions on board which are clearly hazardous to the safety or the health of the crew are rectified. The identity of the person lodging the report or the complaint must not be revealed to the master or the owner of the ship concerned.

Inspection and more detailed inspection

8.066 Article 4 of Directive 1999/95 provides:

"1. When carrying out an inspection, in order to obtain evidence that a ship does not conform to the requirements of Directive 1999/63, ... the inspector shall determine whether:

- a table with the shipboard working arrangements has been established in the working language or languages of the ship and in English according to the model format reproduced in Annex I, or in an alternative equivalent format, and is posted on board in an easily accessible place;
- seafarers' records of hours of work or hours of rest have been established in the working language or languages of the ship and in English according to the model format reproduced in Annex II, or in an alternative equivalent format, and are kept on board and there is proof that the records have been endorsed by the competent authority of the State where the ship is registered.

2. If a complaint has been received or the inspector from his own observations on board believes that the seafarers may be unduly fatigued, the inspector shall conduct a more detailed inspection, pursuant to paragraph 1, to determine whether the working hours or rest periods recorded conform to the standards laid down in Directive 1999/63 ... and that they have been duly observed, taking into account other records relating to the operation of the ship."

Rectification of deficiencies

8.067 Article 5(1) of Directive 1999/95 provides that if the inspection or the more detailed inspection reveals that the ship does not conform to the requirements of Directive 1999/63 then the Member State must take the measures necessary to ensure that any conditions on board which are clearly hazardous to the safety or health of seafarers are rectified. Such measures may include a prohibition on leaving the port until deficiencies have been rectified or the seafarers have been sufficiently rested. Member States which fail to take such action would be liable for failure to comply with their obligations under EU law.

8.068 Article 5(2) of Directive 1999/95 states that if there is clear evidence that watchkeeping personnel for the first watch or subsequent relieving watches are unduly fatigued then the Member State must ensure that the ship shall not leave port until the deficiencies found have been rectified or the seafarers in question have been sufficiently rested. Member States which fail to take such action would be liable for failure to comply with their obligations under EU law.

Follow-up procedures

8.069 Article 6(1) of Directive 1999/95 provides that if a ship is prohibited from leaving the port pursuant to Article 5 then the competent authority of the Member State must inform the master, the owner or operator, the administration of the flag State or the State where the ship is registered or the relevant consul, or in the latter's absence the nearest diplomatic representative of the State, of the results of the inspections referred to in Article 4, of any decisions taken by the inspector and of corrective actions required, if necessary.

8.070 Article 6(2) of Directive 1999/95 provides that when carrying out an inspection under the directive, all possible efforts should be made to avoid a ship being unduly delayed. If a ship is unduly delayed, the owner or operator shall be entitled to compensation for any loss or damage suffered.[61] While the directive is silent on who pays the compensation, it is logical to assume that it is the Member State. In any instance of alleged undue delay, the burden of proof shall lie with the owner or operator of the ship.

Right of appeal

8.071 Pursuant to Article 7(1) of Directive 1999/95, the owner or the operator of the ship or his or her representative in the Member State has a right of appeal against a detention decision taken by the competent authority. An appeal shall not cause the detention to be suspended. Member States must establish and maintain appropriate procedures for this purpose in accordance with their national legislation.[62] The competent authority must properly inform the master of a ship referred to in Article 7(1) of the right of appeal.[63]

Administrative co-operation

8.072 Article 8 of Directive 1999/95 deals with so-called "administrative cooperation". It provides:

"1. Member States shall take the necessary steps to provide, in conditions compatible with those laid down in Article 14 of Directive 95/21/EC of 19 June 1995 concerning the enforcement, in respect of shipping using Community ports and sailing in the waters under the jurisdiction of the Member States, of international standards for ship safety, pollution prevention and shipboard living and working conditions (port State control),[64] for cooperation between their relevant authorities and the relevant competent authorities of other Member States to ensure the effective application of this Directive and shall notify the Commission of the provision made.
2. Information on the measures taken pursuant to Articles 4 and 5 shall be published in accordance with procedures such as those set out in the first paragraph of Article 15 of Directive 95/21."

"No more favourable" treatment clause

8.073 Article 9 of Directive 1999/95 provides that when inspecting a ship registered in the territory of or flying the flag of a State which has not signed ILO Convention No 180 or the Protocol to ILO Convention No 147, Member States must, once the convention and the protocol are in force, ensure that the treatment given to such ships and their crew is no more favourable than that given to a ship flying the flag of a State which is a party to either ILO Convention No 180 or the Protocol to ILO Convention No 147 or both of them.

---

61 Art. 6(2).
62 Art. 7(2).
63 Art. 7(3).
64 Ed., OJ L157/1, 7 July 1995. Directive as last amended by Dir. 98/42 (OJ L184, 27 June 1998, p. 40).

H. COUNCIL DECISION 2007/431 AUTHORISING MEMBER STATES TO RATIFY, IN THE INTERESTS OF THE EU, THE 2008 MARITIME LABOUR CONVENTION OF THE ILO

8.074 On 7 June 2007, the Council adopted the succinct Decision 2007/431 authorising Member States to ratify, in the interests of the EU, the 2006 Maritime Labour Convention of the ILO.[65] While the Commission had exclusive competence as regards the co-ordination of social security schemes, the EU could not stand in place of the Member States when a convention is ratified. The Council decision of 7 June 2007 allows the Member States to ratify the convention, which comprises aspects connected with co-ordination of social security schemes. The convention sought to bring about improvements aimed at promoting decent living and working conditions for seafarers and fairer competition conditions for operators and shipowners and it is therefore desirable that its provisions should be applied as soon as possible. The convention laid the foundations for an international maritime labour code by setting minimum labour standards. Recital 4 to the decision recalls that the EU "seeks to achieve the establishment of a level playing field in the maritime industry".

8.075 Article 19, paragraph eight of the ILO Constitution stated that

> "in no case, shall the adoption of any Convention or Recommendation by the Conference, or the ratification of any Convention by any Member, be deemed to affect any law, award, custom or agreement which ensures more favourable conditions to the workers concerned than those provided for in the Convention or Recommendation".

8.076 The sixth recital of Decision 2007/431 recalls that some provisions of the convention fell within the EU's exclusive competence as regards the co-ordination of social security schemes.

8.077 The seventh recital of Decision 2007/431 recalls that the EU may not ratify the convention, as only States may be parties thereto.

8.078 The eighth recital of Decision 2007/431 provides that the Council should authorise the Member States which are bound by the EU rules on the co-ordination of social security schemes to ratify the convention in the interests of the EU, under the conditions laid down in the decision.

8.079 Article 1 of Decision 2007/41 provides that Member States are authorised by the decision to ratify, for the parts falling under EU competence, the Maritime Labour Convention, 2006, of the ILO, adopted on 7 February 2006.

8.080 Article 2 of Decision 2007/431 provides that Member States "should" make efforts to take the necessary steps to deposit their instruments of ratification of the convention with the Director-General of the ILO as soon as possible, preferably before 31 December 2010.[66] The Council had to review the progress of the ratification before January 2010.

---

65 OJ 2007 L161/63. It is interesting to note that ratification was said to be in the interest of the EU rather than seafarers; saying it was in the interests of both would have been better.

66 Art. 2 says "should" and not "shall" thereby displaying a possible belief by the EU that it could not compel Member States to do so.

I. DIRECTIVE 2005/45 OF THE EUROPEAN PARLIAMENT AND OF THE COUNCIL OF 7 SEPTEMBER 2005 ON THE MUTUAL RECOGNITION OF SEAFARERS' CERTIFICATES ISSUED BY THE MEMBER STATES AND AMENDING DIRECTIVE 2001/25

Introduction

8.081 On 7 September 2005, the Parliament and the Council adopted Directive 2005/45 on the mutual recognition of seafarers' certificates issued by the Member States and amending Directive 2001/25.[67] Under Article 6 of the directive, the directive entered into force on the twentieth day following the publication in the *Official Journal*. The directive has three annexes. Annex I is entitled "Training Requirements of the STCW Convention referred to in Article 3". Annex I is also subdivided into seven chapters: general provisions; master and deck department; engine department; radio communication and radio personnel; special training and requirements for personnel on certain types of ships; emergency, occupational safety, medical care and survival functions; and alternative certification. Annex II is entitled "criteria for the recognition of Third countries[68] that have issued a certificate or under the authority of which was issued a certificate, referred is in Article 19(2)". Annex III set out in Part A amendments and in Part B the list of the time limits for transportation into national law (referred to in Article 32). The measure is more relevant to safety than employment, the seventh recital states that since the "Directive is aimed at facilitating the mutual recognition of certificates, it does not regulate the conditions concerning access to employment" – but is included here for convenience.

8.082 The legal basis of Directive 2005/45 was the Treaty establishing the European Community ("TEC") and, in particular, Article 80(2) of the TEC. This would now be the TFEU and Article 100(2) of the Treaty on the European Union ("TEU") respectively with the latter being the provision to enable secondary legislation on transport to be adopted.

8.083 The background to Directive 2005/45 is clear from the recitals:

"(1) In its conclusions of 5 June 2003 on improving the image of Community shipping and attracting young people to the seafaring profession, the Council highlighted the necessity of fostering the professional mobility of seafarers within the European Union, with particular emphasis on recognition procedures for seafarers' certificates of competency, while ensuring thorough compliance with the requirements of the International Maritime Organisation (IMO) Convention on Standards of Training, Certification and Watchkeeping for Seafarers, 1978 (the STCW Convention) in its up to date version."

It is interesting to see in the first recital the aim of attracting young people to the sector being highlighted.

"(2) Maritime transport is an intensively and rapidly developing sector of a particularly international character. Accordingly, in view of the increasing shortage of Community seafarers, the balance between supply and demand in personnel can be maintained more efficiently at the Community, rather than the national level. It is therefore essential that the common transport policy in the field of maritime transport be extended to facilitate the movement of seafarers within the Community."

---

67 OJ L255/160, 30 September 2005.
68 Ed., i.e. non-EU Member States.

The second recital therefore recognised the shortage of EU seafarers.

(3) As regards seafarers' qualifications, the Community has laid down minimum maritime education, training and certification requirements by way of Directive 2001/25 ... of the European Parliament and of the Council of 4 April 2001 on the minimum level of training of seafarers.[69] That Directive incorporates into Community law the international training, certification and watchkeeping standards laid down by the STCW Convention.

(4) Directive 2001/25 ... provides that seafarers must hold a certificate of competency issued and endorsed by the competent authority of a Member State in accordance with that Directive and entitling the lawful holder thereof to serve on a ship in the capacity and perform the functions involved at the level of responsibility specified therein.

(5) Under Directive 2001/25, ... mutual recognition among Member States of certificates held by seafarers, whether or not nationals of a Member State, is subject to Directives 89/48[70] ... and 92/51/EEC[71] setting up, respectively, a first and a second general system for the recognition of professional education and training. Those Directives do not provide for the automatic recognition of formal qualifications of seafarers, as seafarers may be subject to compensation measures.

(6) Each Member State should recognise any certificate and other evidence of formal qualifications issued by another Member State in accordance with Directive 2001/25 ... Therefore, each Member State should permit a seafarer having acquired his/her certificate of competency in another Member State, satisfying the requirements of that Directive, to take up or to pursue the maritime profession for which he/she is qualified, without any prerequisites other than those imposed on its own nationals."

This latter recital recognises and promotes the idea of mutual recognition of qualifications. The recital continues:

"(7) Since this Directive is aimed at facilitating the mutual recognition of certificates, it does not regulate the conditions concerning access to employment."

This seventh recital is important in that it categorises the measure more as a safety measure than an employment one but it is included in this chapter for completeness and convenience.

"(8) The STCW Convention specifies language requirements for seafarers. These requirements should be introduced into Community law to ensure effective communication on board ships and facilitate the free movement of seafarers within the Community.

(9) Today, the proliferation of certificates of competency of seafarers obtained by fraud poses a serious danger to safety at sea and the protection of the marine environment. In most cases, holders of fraudulent certificates of competency do not meet the minimum certification requirements of the STCW Convention. These seafarers could easily be involved in maritime accidents.

(10) Member States should therefore take and enforce specific measures to prevent and penalise fraudulent practices associated with certificates of competency as well as pursue their efforts within the IMO to achieve strict and enforceable agreements on the worldwide combating of such practices. The Committee on Safe Seas and the Prevention of Pollution from

---

69 Ed., OJ L136/17, 18 May 2001.

70 Ed., Council Dir. 89/48 of 21 December 1988 on a general system for the recognition of higher-education diplomas awarded on completion of professional education and training of at least three years' duration (OJ L19, 24 January 1989, p. 16). Directive as last amended by Dir. 2001/19 of the European Parliament and of the Council (OJ L206, 31 July 2001, p. 1).

71 Ed., Council Dir. 92/51 of 18 June 1992 on a second general system for the recognition of professional education and training to supplement Dir. 89/48 (OJ L209, 24 July 1992, p. 25). Directive as last amended by Comm. Dec. 2004/108 (OJ L32, 5 February 2004, p. 15).

Ships (COSS) is an appropriate forum for exchanging information, experience and best practices in this respect.
(11) Regulation ... 1406/2002,[72] established a European Maritime Safety Agency (the Agency), for the purpose of ensuring a high, uniform and effective level of maritime safety and prevention of pollution from ships. One of the tasks assigned to the Agency is to assist the Commission in the performance of any task assigned to it by Community legislation applicable to the training, certification and watchkeeping of ships' crews.
(12) The Agency should therefore assist the Commission in verifying that Member States comply with the requirements laid down in this Directive and Directive 2001/25.
(13) The mutual recognition among Member States of certificates held by seafarers, whether or not nationals of a Member State, should no longer be subject to Directives 89/48 ... and 92/51 ..., but should be governed by this Directive.
(14) Directive 2001/25 ... should therefore be amended accordingly.
(15) Since the objective of this Directive, namely the mutual recognition of the seafarers' certificates issued by the Member States, cannot be sufficiently achieved by the Member States and can therefore be better achieved at Community level, the Community may adopt measures in accordance with the principle of subsidiarity as set out in Article 5 of the Treaty. In accordance with the principle of proportionality, as set out in that Article, this Directive does not go beyond what is necessary in order to achieve that objective.
(16) In accordance with paragraph 34 of the Interinstitutional Agreement on better lawmaking,[73] Member States are encouraged to draw up, for themselves and in the interest of the Community, their own tables, which will, as far as possible, illustrate the correlation between this Directive and their transposition measures, and to make those tables public."

Scope of the directive

8.084 Article 1 deals with the scope of the directive: the directive applies to seafarers who are: (a) nationals of a Member State; and (b) non-nationals who hold a certificate issued by a Member State.

Definitions in the directive

8.085 Article 2 sets out various definitions for the purpose of the directive:

"Article 2(a) defines 'seafarer' as meaning a person who is trained and who is certificated by a Member State at least in accordance with the requirements laid down in Annex I to Directive 2001/25.
Article 2(b) defines the term 'certificate' as meaning a valid document within the meaning of Article 4 of Directive 2001/25.
Article 2(c) defines the phrase 'appropriate certificate' as meaning 'a certificate as defined in Article 1(27) of Directive 2001/25'.
Article 2(d) defines 'endorsement' as meaning a valid document issued by the competent authority of a Member State in accordance with Article 5(2) and (6) of Directive 2001/25.
Article 2(e) 'recognition' means the acceptance by the competent authorities of a host Member State of a certificate or appropriate certificate issued by another Member State;
Article 2(f) defines 'host Member State' as meaning 'any Member State in which a seafarer seeks recognition of his/her appropriate certificate(s) or other certificate(s)'.

---

72 Regulation (EC) No 1406/2002 of the European Parliament and of the Council of 27 June 2002 establishing a European Maritime Safety Agency (OJ L208, 5.8.2002, p. 1). Regulation as last amended by Regulation (EC) No 724/2004 (OJ L129, 29.4.2004, p. 1).
73 OJ C321, 31.

Article 2(g) provides that the phrase 'STCW Convention' as meaning the 'International Convention on Standards of Training, Certification and Watchkeeping for Seafarers, 1978, in its up-to-date version'.

Article 2(h) states that the term 'STCW Code' means the 'Seafarers' Training, Certification and Watchkeeping Code, as adopted by Resolution 2 of the 1995 STCW Conference of Parties, in its up-to-date version'.

Article 2(i) provides that phrase 'the Agency' means the European Maritime Safety Agency, established by Regulation 1406/2002."

8.086 Article 3 deals with recognition of certificates. It provides:

"1. Every Member State must recognise appropriate certificates or other certificates issued by another Member State in accordance with the requirements laid down in Directive 2001/25.
2. The recognition of appropriate certificates shall be limited to the capacities, functions and levels of competency prescribed therein and be accompanied by an endorsement attesting such recognition, however, the competent authorities of a host Member State may impose further limitations on capacities, functions and levels of competence relating to near-coastal voyages, as referred to in Article 7 of Directive 2001/25, or alternative certificates issued under Regulation VII/1 of Annex I to Directive 2001/25.
3. Member States must ensure the right to appeal against any refusal to endorse a valid certificate, or the absence of any response, in accordance with national legislation and procedures.
4. A host Member State must ensure that seafarers who present for recognition certificates for functions at the management level have an appropriate knowledge of the maritime legislation of that Member State relevant to the functions they are permitted to perform."

Operative provisions

8.087 Article 4 deals with amendments to Directive 2001/25. Directive 2001/25 was amended in that Article 4 was replaced by

"Article 4
Certificate
A certificate shall be any valid document, by whatever name it may be known, issued by or under the authority of the competent authority of a Member State in accordance with Article 5 and with the requirements laid down in Annex I."

8.088 A new article (i.e. Article 7a) was also inserted into Directive 2001/25 by virtue of Article 4(2) of Directive 2005/45.

"Article 7a
Prevention of fraud and other unlawful practices

1. Member States shall take and enforce the appropriate measures to prevent fraud and other unlawful practices involving the certification process or certificates issued and endorsed by their competent authorities, and shall provide for penalties that are effective, proportionate and dissuasive.
2. Member States shall designate the national authorities competent to detect and combat fraud and other unlawful practices and exchange information with the competent authorities of other Member States and of third countries concerning the certification of seafarers.
    Member States shall forthwith inform the other Member States and the Commission of the details of such competent national authorities.
    Member States shall also forthwith inform any third countries with which they have entered into an undertaking in accordance with Regulation I/10, paragraph 1.2 of the STCW Convention of the details of such competent national authorities.

3. At the request of a host Member State, the competent authorities of another Member State shall provide written confirmation or denial of the authenticity of seafarers' certificates, corresponding endorsements or any other documentary evidence of training issued in that other Member State."

8.089 The following Articles were inserted into Directive 2001/25 by Article 4(4) of Directive 2005/45

"Article 21a
Regular monitoring of compliance
Without prejudice to the powers of the Commission under Article 226 of the Treaty, the Commission, assisted by the European Maritime Safety Agency, established by Regulation (EC) No 1406/2002,[74] shall verify on a regular basis and at least every five years that Member States comply with the minimum requirements laid down by this Directive.

Article 21b
Compliance report
No later than 20 October 2010 the Commission shall submit to the European Parliament and the Council an evaluation report drawn up on the basis of the information obtained pursuant to Article 21a. In the report the Commission shall analyse the Member States' compliance with this Directive and, where necessary, make proposals for additional measures.

5. the following paragraph shall be inserted in Annex I, Chapter I:

'1a. Member States shall ensure that seafarers possess adequate language proficiency, as defined in Sections A-II/1, A-III/1, A-IV/2 and A-II/4 of the STCW Code so as to enable them to perform their specific duties on a vessel flying the flag of a host Member State.'"

8.090 Article 5 deals with the transportation of the directive into national law. Under Article 5(1), Member States had to bring into force the laws, regulations and administrative provisions necessary to comply with the directive by 20 October 2007. They had to forthwith inform the Commission thereof. When Member States adopted the measures, they had to contain a reference to the directive or be accompanied by such reference on the occasion of their official publication. The methods of making such reference must be laid down by Member States. Under Article 5(2), Member States had to communicate to the Commission the text of the provisions of national law which they adopt in the field covered by the directive.

J. DIRECTIVE 2008/106 OF THE EUROPEAN PARLIAMENT AND OF THE COUNCIL OF 19 NOVEMBER 2008 ON THE MINIMUM LEVEL OF TRAINING OF SEAFARERS

Introduction

8.091 On 19 November 2008, the Parliament and the Council adopted Directive 2008/106 on the minimum level of training of seafarers.[75] The legal basis of Directive 2008/106 was the TEC generally and, in particular, Article 80(2) or, now, TFEU and

---

74 Regulation (EC) No 1406/2002 of the European Parliament and of the Council of 27 June 2002 establishing a European Maritime Safety Agency (OJ L208, 5.8. 2002, p.1). Regulation as last amended by Regulation (EC) No 724/2004 (OJ L129, 29.4.2004, p.1).
75 OJ L323/33, 3 December 2008.

Article 100(2) respectively. The legislative history included a proposal from the Commission, an opinion of the EESC[76] and a consultation with the Committee of the Regions. Directive 2008/106 was amended by Directive 2012/35 of the European Parliament and of the Council.[77]

8.092 The background to Directive 2008/106 lies in Directive 2001/25 of 4 April 2001 on the minimum level of training of seafarers[78] which had been amended significantly on several occasions. So the new recast directive was adopted for the sake of clarity.[79]

8.093 The recitals to Directive 2008/106 recall:

> "(6) The mutual recognition of diplomas and certificates provided for under Directive 2005/36/EC does not always ensure a standardised level of training for all seafarers serving on board vessels flying the flag of a Member State. This is, however, vital from the viewpoint of maritime safety.
> (7) It is therefore essential to define a minimum level of training for seafarers in the Community. That level should be based on the standards of training already agreed at international level, namely the International Maritime Organisation (IMO) Convention on Standards of Training, Certification and Watchkeeping for Seafarers, 1978 (STCW Convention), as revised in 1995. All Member States are Parties to that Convention.
> (8) Member States may establish standards higher than the minimum standards laid down in the STCW Convention and this Directive.
> (9) The Regulations of the STCW Convention annexed to this Directive should be supplemented by the mandatory provisions contained in Part A of the Seafarers' Training, Certification and Watchkeeping Code (STCW Code). Part B of the STCW Code contains recommended guidance intended to assist Parties to the STCW Convention and those involved in implementing, applying or enforcing its measures to give the Convention full and complete effect in a uniform manner.
> (10) For the enhancement of maritime safety and pollution prevention at sea, provisions on minimum rest periods for watchkeeping personnel should be established in this Directive in accordance with the STCW Convention. Those provisions should be applied without prejudice to the provisions of Council Directive 1999/63/EC of 21 June 1999 concerning the Agreement on the organisation of working time of seafarers concluded by the European Community Shipowners' Association (ECSA) and the Federation of Transport Workers' Unions in the European Union (FST).[80]
> (11) Member States should take and enforce specific measures to prevent and penalise fraudulent practices associated with certificates of competency as well as pursue their efforts within the IMO to achieve strict and enforceable agreements on the worldwide combating of such practices."

The recitals then recall the importance of communications:

> "(12) In order to enhance maritime safety and prevent loss of human life and maritime pollution, communication among crew members on board ships sailing in Community waters should be improved.
> (13) Personnel on board passenger ships nominated to assist passengers in emergency situations should be able to communicate with the passengers.
> (14) Crews serving on board tankers carrying noxious or polluting cargo should be capable of coping effectively with accident prevention and emergency situations. It is paramount that

---

76 OJ L136/17, 18 May 2001.
77 OJ L343/78, 14 December 2012.
78 OJ L136/17, 18 May 2001.
79 Dir. 2008/106, Recital 1.
80 Ed., OJ L167/33, 2 July 1999.

a proper communication link between the master, officers and ratings is established, covering the requirements provided for in this Directive.

(15) It is essential to ensure that seafarers holding certificates issued by third countries and serving on board Community ships have a level of competence equivalent to that required by the STCW Convention. This Directive should lay down procedures and common criteria for the recognition by the Member States of certificates issued by third countries, based on the training and certification requirements as agreed in the framework of the STCW Convention.

(16) In the interests of safety at sea, Member States should recognise qualifications proving the required level of training only where these are issued by or on behalf of Parties to the STCW Convention which have been identified by the IMO Maritime Safety Committee (MSC) as having been shown to have given, and still to be giving, full effect to the standards set out in that Convention. To bridge the time gap until the MSC has been able to carry out such identification, a procedure for the preliminary recognition of certificates is needed.

(17) Where appropriate, maritime institutes, training programmes and courses should be inspected. Criteria for such inspection should therefore be established.

(18) The Commission should be assisted by a committee in carrying out the tasks related to the recognition of certificates issued by training institutes or administrations of third countries.

(19) The European Maritime Safety Agency established by Regulation ... 1406/2002 of the European Parliament and of the Council[81] should assist the Commission in verifying that Member States comply with the requirements laid down in this Directive.

(20) Member States, as port authorities, are required to enhance safety and prevention of pollution in Community waters through priority inspection of vessels flying the flag of a third country which has not ratified the STCW Convention, thereby ensuring no more favourable treatment to vessels flying the flag of a third country.

(21) It is appropriate to include in this Directive provisions on port State control, pending the amendment of Council Directive 95/21/EC[82] ... port State control of shipping in order to transfer to that Directive the provisions on port State control which are included in this Directive.

(22) It is necessary to provide for procedures for adapting this Directive to changes in international conventions and codes.

(23) The measures necessary for the implementation of this Directive should be adopted in accordance with Council Decision 1999/468/EC of 28 June 1999 laying down the procedures for the exercise of implementing powers conferred on the Commission.[83]

(24) In particular the Commission should be empowered to amend this Directive in order to apply, for the purposes of this Directive, subsequent amendments to certain international codes and any relevant amendment to Community legislation. Since those measures are of general scope and are designed to amend non-essential elements of this Directive, they must be adopted in accordance with the regulatory procedure with scrutiny provided for in Article 5a of Decision 1999/468/EC.

(25) The new elements introduced into this Directive only concern the committee procedures. They therefore do not need to be transposed by the Member States.

(26) This Directive should be without prejudice to the obligations of the Members States relating to the time limits for transposition into national law of the Directives set out in Annex III, Part B."

---

81 Ed., OJ 208/1, 5 August 2002.
82 Ed., OJ 157/1, 7 July 1995.
83 Ed., OJ 184/23, 17 July 1999.

Concepts in the directive

8.094 Article 1 sets out a number of basic definitions for the purposes of the directive.

8.095 The "master" means the person having command of a ship (i.e. the captain).[84]

8.096 The word "officer" means a member of the crew, other than the master, designated as such by national law or regulations or, in the absence of such designation, by collective agreement or custom.

8.097 The term "deck officer" means an officer qualified in accordance with the provisions of Chapter II of Annex I.[85]

8.098 The phrase "chief mate" means the officer next in rank to the master upon whom the command of the ship will fall in the event of the incapacity of the master.[86]

8.099 The phrase "engineer officer" means an officer qualified in accordance with the provisions of Chapter III of Annex I.

8.100 The title "chief engineer officer" means the senior engineer officer responsible for the mechanical propulsion and the operation and maintenance of the mechanical and electrical installations of the ship.

8.101 The phrase "second engineer officer" means the engineer officer next in rank to the chief engineer officer upon whom the responsibility for the mechanical propulsion and the operation and maintenance of the mechanical and electrical installations of the ship will fall in the event of the incapacity of the chief engineer officer.

8.102 The rank "assistant engineer officer" means a person under training to become an engineer officer and designated as such by national law or regulations.

8.103 The title "radio operator" means a person holding an appropriate certificate issued or recognised by the competent authorities under the provisions of the Radio Regulations.

8.104 The word "rating" means a member of the ship's crew other than the master or an officer.

8.105 The phrase "seagoing ship" means a ship other than those which navigate exclusively in inland waters or in waters within, or closely adjacent to, sheltered waters or areas where port regulations apply.

8.106 The phrase "ship flying the flag of a Member State" means a ship registered in and flying the flag of a Member State in accordance with its legislation; a ship not corresponding to this definition shall be regarded as a ship flying the flag of a third country.

8.107 The expression "near-coastal voyages" means voyages in the vicinity of a Member State as defined by that Member State.

8.108 The term "propulsion power" means the total maximum continuous rated output power in kilowatts of all of a ship's main propulsion machinery which appears on the ship's certificate of registry or other official document.

8.109 The phrase "oil-tanker" means a ship constructed and used for the carriage of petroleum and petroleum products in bulk.

8.110 The expression "chemical tanker" means a ship constructed or adapted and used for the carriage in bulk of any liquid product listed in Chapter 17 of the International Bulk Chemical Code, in its up-to-date version.

---

84 Dir. 2008/106, Art. 1(1).
85 Dir. 2008/106, Art. 1(3).
86 Dir. 2008/106, Art. 1(4).

8.111 The expression "liquefied-gas tanker" means a ship constructed or adapted and used for the carriage in bulk of any liquefied gas or other product listed in Chapter 19 of the International Gas Carrier Code, in its up-to-date version.

8.112 The phrase "Radio Regulations" means the revised radio regulations, adopted by the World Administrative Radio Conference for the Mobile Service in their up-to-date versions.

8.113 The phrase "passenger ship" means a seagoing ship which carries more than 12 passengers.

8.114 The phrase "fishing vessel" means a vessel used for catching fish or other living resources of the sea.

8.115 The term "STCW Convention" means the IMO Convention on Standards of Training, Certification and Watchkeeping for Seafarers, 1978, as it applies to the matters concerned taking into account the transitional provisions of Article VII and Regulation I/15 of the convention and including, where appropriate, the applicable provisions of the STCW Code, all being applied in their up-to-date versions.

8.116 The concept of "radio duties" includes, as appropriate, watchkeeping and technical maintenance and repairs conducted in accordance with the Radio Regulations, the International Convention for the Safety of Life at Sea, 1974 ("SOLAS 74") and, at the discretion of each Member State, the relevant recommendations of the IMO, in their up-to-date versions.

8.117 The concept of "ro-ro passenger ship" means a passenger ship with ro-ro cargo spaces or special-category spaces as defined in the SOLAS 74, in its up-to-date version.

8.118 The term "STCW Code" means the Seafarers' Training, Certification and Watchkeeping (STCW) Code as adopted by Resolution 2 of the 1995 STCW Conference of Parties, in its up-to-date version.

8.119 The word "function" means a group of tasks, duties and responsibilities, as specified in the STCW Code, necessary for ship operation, safety of life at sea or protection of the marine environment.

8.120 The word "company" means the owner of the ship or any other organisation or person such as the manager or the bareboat charterer who has assumed the responsibility for operation of the ship from the shipowner and who, on assuming such responsibility, has agreed to take over all the duties and responsibilities imposed on the company by the directive.

8.121 The phrase "seagoing service" means service on board a ship relevant to the issue or revalidation of a certificate of competency, certificate of proficiency or other qualification.

8.122 The word "approved" means approved by a Member State in accordance with the directive.

8.123 The phrase "third country" means any country which is not a Member State.

8.124 The word "month" means a calendar month or 30 days made up of periods of less than one month.

Scope of Directive 2008/106

8.125 Article 2 provides that the directive must apply to the seafarers mentioned in the directive serving on board seagoing ships flying the flag of a Member State with the exception of: (a) warships, naval auxiliaries or other ships owned or operated by a Member State and engaged only on government non-commercial service;[87] (b) fishing vessels; (c) pleasure yachts not engaged in trade; (d) wooden ships of primitive build.

Training and certification

8.126 Article 3(1) provides that Member States must take the measures necessary to ensure that seafarers serving on ships as referred to in Article 2 are trained as a minimum in accordance with the requirements of the STCW Convention, as laid down in Annex I to the directive, and hold certificates as defined in points (36) and (37) of Article 1, and for documentary evidence as defined in point 38 of Article 1. Article 3(2) provides that Member States must take the measures necessary to ensure that those crew members that must be certified in accordance with Regulation III/10.4 of the SOLAS 74 are trained and certificated in accordance with the directive.

Certificate

8.127 Article 4 was repealed by Directive 2012/35 of 21 November 2012. It had provided that a certificate must be any valid document, by whatever name it may be known, issued by or under the authority of the competent authority of a Member State in accordance with Article 5 and with the requirements laid down in Annex I.

Certificates and endorsements

8.128 Article 5 ("certificates of competency, certificates of proficiency and endorsements") provides that certificates of competency and certificates of proficiency are issued only to candidates who comply with the requirements of Article 5.[88] Certificates for masters, officers and radio operators must be endorsed by the Member State as prescribed in Article 5.[89] Certificates must be issued in accordance with Regulation I/2, paragraph 3, of the annex to the STCW Convention. Certificates of competency must be issued only by the Member States, following verification of the authenticity and validity of any necessary documentary evidence and in accordance with the provision laid down in Article 5 of the directive.[90] In respect of radio operators, Member States may: (a) include the additional knowledge required by the relevant regulations in the examination for the issue of a certificate complying with the Radio Regulations; or (b) issue a separate certificate indicating that the holder has the additional knowledge required by the relevant regulations.[91] At the discretion of a Member State, endorsements may be incorporated in the format of the certificates being issued as provided for in section A-I/2 of the STCW Code. If so incorporated then the form used shall be that set out in section A-I/2, paragraph 1. If issued otherwise, the form of endorsements used shall be that set out in paragraph 2 of

---

87 While the directive does not give an example, one example might be a purely scientific research ship which does not carry out commercial assignments.
88 Dir. 2008/106, Art. 5(1).
89 Dir. 2008/106, Art. 5(2).
90 Dir. 2008/106, Art. 5(3a).
91 Dir. 2008/106, Art. 5(4).

that section. A Member State which recognises a certificate under the procedure laid down in Article 19(2) must endorse that certificate to attest its recognition.[92] The form of the endorsement used shall be that set out in paragraph 3 of section A-I/2 of the STCW Code.[93] The endorsements referred to in paragraphs 5 and 6: (a) may be issued as separate documents; (b) shall each be assigned a unique number, other than endorsements attesting the issue of a certificate which may be assigned the same number as the certificate concerned, provided that that number is unique; and (c) shall each expire as soon as the certificate endorsed expires or is withdrawn, suspended or cancelled by the Member State or third country which issued them and, in any case, within five years of their date of issue.[94] The capacity in which the holder of a certificate is authorised to serve must be identified in the form of endorsement in terms identical to those used in the applicable safe-manning requirements of the Member State concerned.[95] A Member State may use a format different from the format laid down in section A-I/2 of the STCW Code, provided that, as a minimum, the required information is provided in Roman characters and Arabic figures, taking account of the variations permitted under section A-I/2.[96] Subject to Article 19(7) any certificate required by the directive must be kept available in its original form on board the ship on which the holder is serving.[97]

8.129 Article 6 ("training requirements") provides that the training required pursuant to Article 3 shall be in a form appropriate to the theoretical knowledge and practical skills required by Annex I, in particular the use of life saving and fire-fighting equipment, and approved by the competent authority or body designated by each Member State.

8.130 Article 7 ("principles governing near-coastal voyages") provides:

> "1. When defining near-coastal voyages Member States shall not impose training, experience or certification requirements on seafarers serving on board ships entitled to fly the flag of another Member State or another Party to the STCW Convention and engaged in such voyages in a manner resulting in more stringent requirements for such seafarers than for seafarers serving on board ships entitled to fly their own flag. In no case shall a Member State impose requirements in respect of seafarers serving on board ships flying the flag of another Member State or of another Party to the STCW Convention in excess of those of this Directive in respect of ships not engaged in near-coastal voyages.
>
> 1a. A Member State, for ships afforded the benefits of the near- coastal voyage provisions of the STCW Convention, which includes voyages off the coast of other Member States or of Parties to the STCW Convention within the limits of their near-coastal definition, shall enter into an undertaking with the Member States or Parties concerned specifying both the details of the trading areas involved and other relevant provisions.
>
> 2. With respect to ships entitled to fly the flag of a Member State regularly engaged in near-coastal voyages off the coast of another Member State or of another Party to the STCW Convention, the Member State the flag of which a ship is entitled to fly shall prescribe training, experience and certification requirements for seafarers serving on such ships at least equal to those of the Member State or the Party to the STCW Convention off the coast of which the ship is engaged, provided that they do not exceed the requirements of this Directive in respect of ships not engaged in near-coastal voyages. Seafarers serving on a ship which extends its voyage beyond what is defined as a near-coastal voyage by a Member

---

92 Dir. 2008/106, Art. 19(6).
93 Ibid.
94 Dir. 2008/106, Art. 5(7).
95 Dir. 2008/106, Art. 5(8).
96 Dir. 2008/106, Art. 5(9).
97 Dir. 2008/106, Art. 5(10).

State and enters waters not covered by that definition shall fulfil the appropriate requirements of this Directive.

3. A Member State may afford a ship which is entitled to fly its flag the benefits of the near-coastal voyage provisions of this Directive when it is regularly engaged off the coast of a non-Party to the STCW Convention on near-coastal voyages as defined by that Member State.

    3a. The certificates of competency of seafarers issued by a Member State or a Party to the STCW Convention for its defined near-coastal voyage limits may be accepted by other Member States for service in their defined near-coastal voyage limits, provided the Member States or Parties concerned enter into an undertaking specifying the details of the trading areas involved and other relevant conditions thereof.

    3b. Member States defining near-coastal voyages, in accordance with the requirements of this Article, shall:

        1. (a) meet the principles governing near-coastal voyages specified in Section A-I/3 of the STCW Code;
        2. (b) incorporate the near-coastal voyage limits in the endorsements issued pursuant to Article 5.

4. Upon deciding on the definition of near-coastal voyages and the conditions of education and training required thereof in accordance with the requirements of paragraphs 1, 2 and 3, Member States shall communicate to the Commission the details of the provisions they have adopted."

Prevention of fraud and other unlawful practices

8.131 Article 8 deals with prevention of fraud and other unlawful practices. It provides Member States shall take and enforce the appropriate measures to prevent fraud and other unlawful practices involving the certification process or certificates issued and endorsed by their competent authorities, and shall provide for penalties that are effective, proportionate and dissuasive.[98] Member States must designate the national authorities competent to detect and combat fraud and other unlawful practices and exchange information with the competent authorities of other Member States and of third countries concerning the certification of seafarers.[99] Member States must forthwith inform the other Member States and the Commission of the details of such competent national authorities.[100] Member States shall also forthwith inform any third countries with which they have entered into an undertaking in accordance with Regulation I/10, paragraph 1.2 of the STCW Convention of the details of such competent national authorities.[101] At the request of a host Member State, the competent authorities of another Member State must provide written confirmation or denial of the authenticity of seafarers' certificates, corresponding endorsements or any other documentary evidence of training issued in that other Member State.[102]

---

98 Dir. 2008/16, Art. 8(1).
99 Dir. 2008/16, Art. 8(2).
100 Ibid.
101 Ibid.
102 Dir. 2008/16, Art. 8(3).

Penalties or disciplinary measures

8.132 Article 9 of Directive 2008/16 addresses the issue of penalties or disciplinary measures. It provides:

"1. Member States shall establish processes and procedures for the impartial investigation of any reported incompetence, act or omission, that may pose a direct threat to safety of life or property at sea or to the marine environment, on the part of the holders of certificates of competency and certificates of proficiency or endorsements issued by that Member State in connection with their performance of duties relating to their certificates of competency and certificates of proficiency and for the withdrawal, suspension and cancellation of such certificates of competency and certificates of proficiency for such cause and for the prevention of fraud.
2. Member States shall take and enforce appropriate measures to prevent fraud and other unlawful practices involving certificates of competency and certificates of proficiency and endorsements issued.
3. Penalties or disciplinary measures shall be prescribed and enforced in cases in which:

   (a) a company or a master has engaged a person not holding a certificate as required by this Directive;
   (b) a master has allowed any function or service in any capacity which under this Directive must be performed by a person holding an appropriate certificate to be performed by a person not holding the required certificate, a valid dispensation or having the documentary proof required by Article 19(7); or
   (c) a person has obtained by fraud or forged documents an engagement to perform any function or serve in any capacity which under this Directive must be performed or fulfilled by a person holding a certificate or dispensation.

4. Member States within the jurisdiction of which any company which or any person who is believed on clear grounds to have been responsible for or to have knowledge of any apparent non-compliance with this Directive specified in paragraph 3, is located shall extend cooperation to any Member State or other Party to the STCW Convention which advises them of its intention to initiate proceedings under its jurisdiction."

Quality standards

8.133 Article 10 deals with quality standards. It provides that each Member State must ensure that: (a) all training, assessment of competence, certification, including medical certificates, endorsement and revalidation activities carried out by non-governmental agencies or entities under its authority are continuously monitored through a quality standards system to ensure the achievement of defined objectives, including those concerning the qualifications and experience of instructors and assessors in accordance with Section A-I/8 of the STCW code;[103] (b) where governmental agencies or entities perform such activities, there is a quality-standards system in accordance with Section A-I/8 of the STCW code; that (c) education and training objectives and related quality standards of competence to be achieved are clearly defined and that the levels of knowledge, understanding and skills appropriate to the examinations and assessments required under the STCW Convention are identified;[104] and (d) the fields of application of the quality

---

103 Dir. 2008/106, Art. 10(1)(a).
104 Dir. 2008/106, Art. 10(1)(c) the objectives and related quality standards referred to in this point may be specified separately for different courses and training programmes and shall cover the administration of the certification system. Art. 10(2) provides that the objectives and related quality standards referred to in point (c) may be specified separately for different courses and training programmes shall cover the administration of the certification system.

standards cover the administration of the certification systems, all training courses and programmes, examinations and assessments carried out by or under the authority of each Member State and the qualifications and experience required of instructors and assessors, having regard to the policies, systems, controls and internal quality-assurance reviews established to ensure achievement of the defined objectives.[105]

8.134 Member States must also ensure that independent evaluations of the knowledge, understanding, skills and competence acquisition and assessment activities, and of the administration of the certification system, are conducted at intervals of not more than five years by qualified persons who are not themselves involved in the activities concerned in order to verify that: (a) all internal management control and monitoring measures and follow-up actions comply with planned arrangements and documental procedures and are effective in ensuring that the defined objectives are achieved; (b) the results of each independent evaluation are documented and brought to the attention of those responsible for the area evaluated; (c) timely action is taken to correct deficiencies; and (d) all applicable provisions of the STCW Convention and Code, including amendments are covered by the quality standards system.[106] Member States may also include within this system the other applicable provisions of the directive.[107] Article 10(3) provides that a report relating to each evaluation conducted pursuant to Article 10(2) shall be communicated by the Member State concerned in Section A-l/7 of the STCW Code, within six months of the date of the evaluation.

Medical standards: issue and registration of certificates

8.135 Member States must establish standards of medical fitness for seafarers, particularly regarding eyesight and hearing.[108] Member States must ensure that certificates are issued only to candidates who comply with the requirements of Article 11.[109] Each candidate for certification must provide satisfactory proof: (a) of his or her identity; (b) that his or her age is not less than that prescribed in the regulations in Annex I relevant to the certificate applied for; (c) that he or she meets the standards of medical fitness, particularly regarding eyesight and hearing, established by the Member State and holds a valid document attesting to his or her medical fitness, issued by a duly qualified medical practitioner recognised by the competent authority of the Member State; (d) of having completed the seagoing service and any related compulsory training prescribed in the regulations in Annex I for the certificate applied for; and (e) that he or she meets the standards of competence prescribed in the regulations in Annex I for the capacities, functions and levels that are to be identified in the endorsement to the certificate.

8.136 Each Member State must undertake: (a) to maintain a register or registers of all certificates and endorsements for masters and officers and, as appropriate, ratings, which are issued, have expired or have been revalidated, suspended, cancelled or reported lost or destroyed and of dispensations issued; and (b) to make available information on the status of such certificates, endorsements and dispensations to other Member States or

---

105 Dir. 2008/106, Art. 10(1)(d).
106 Dir. 2008/106, Art. 10(2).
107 Dir. 2008/106, Art. 10(2)(d).
108 Dir. 2008/106, Art. 11(1).
109 Dir. 2008/106, Art. 11(2).

other Parties to the STCW Convention and companies which request verification of the authenticity and validity of certificates produced to them by seafarers seeking recognition of their certificates or employment on board ship.[110]

Revalidation of certificates

8.137 Article 12 deals with the revalidation of certificates.

8.138 Every master, officer and radio operator holding a certificate issued or recognised under any chapter of Annex I other than Chapter VI who is serving at sea or intends to return to sea after a period ashore must, in order to continue to qualify for seagoing service, be required at intervals not exceeding five years: (a) to meet the standards of medical fitness prescribed by Article 11; and (b) to establish continued professional competence in accordance with section A-I/11 of the STCW Code.[111]

8.139 Every master, officer and radio operator must, for continuing seagoing service on board ships for which special training requirements have been internationally agreed upon, successfully complete approved relevant training.[112]

8.140 Each Member State must compare the standards of competence which are required of candidates for certificates issued before 1 February 2002 with those specified for the appropriate certificate in Part A of the STCW Code, and shall determine the need to require the holders of such certificates to undergo appropriate refresher and updating training or assessment. Refresher and updating courses must be approved and include changes in relevant national and international regulations concerning the safety of life at sea and the protection of the marine environment and take account of any updating of the standard of competency concerned.[113]

8.141 Each Member State must, in consultation with those concerned, formulate or promote the formulation of a structure of refresher and updating courses as provided for in section A-I/11 of the STCW Code.[114]

8.142 For the purpose of updating the knowledge of masters, officers and radio operators, each Member State must ensure that the texts of recent changes in national and international regulations concerning the safety of life at sea and the protection of the marine environment are made available to ships entitled to fly its flag.[115]

Simulators

8.143 Article 13 deals with use of simulators. Under Article 13(1), the performance standards and other provisions set out in section A-I/12 of the STCW Code and such other requirements as are prescribed in Part A of the STCW Code for any certificate concerned shall be complied with in respect of: (a) all mandatory simulator-based training; (b) any assessment of competence required by Part A of the STCW Code which is carried

---

110 Dir. 2008/106, Art. 11(4).
111 Dir. 2008/106. Art. 12(1).
112 Dir. 2008/106, Art. 12(2).
113 Dir. 2008/106, Art. 12(3).
114 Dir. 2008/106, Art. 12(4).
115 Dir. 2008/106, Art, 12(5).

out by means of a simulator; and (c) any demonstration, by means of a simulator, of continued proficiency required by Part A of the STCW Code.

8.144 Member States shall, for the purpose of preventing drug and alcohol abuse, ensure that adequate measures are established in accordance with the provisions laid down in this article.

8.145 Member States shall take account of the danger posed by fatigue of seafarers, especially those whose duties involve the safe and secure operation of a ship.

8.146 All persons who are assigned duty as officer in charge of a watch or as a rating forming part of a watch, and those whose duties involve designated safety, prevention of pollution and security duties shall be provided with a rest period of not less than: (a) a minimum of 10 hours of rest in any 24-hour period; and (b) 77 hours in any seven-day period.

8.147 The hours of rest may be divided into no more than two periods, one of which shall be at least six hours in length, and the intervals between consecutive periods of rest shall not exceed 14 hours.

8.148 The requirements for rest periods laid down in paragraphs 4 and 5 need not be maintained in the case of an emergency or in other overriding operational conditions. Musters, firefighting and lifeboat drills, and drills prescribed by national laws and regulations and by international instruments, shall be conducted in a manner that minimises the disturbance of rest periods and does not induce fatigue.

8.149 Member States shall require that watch schedules be posted where they are easily accessible. The schedules shall be established in a standardised format in the working language or languages of the ship and in English.

8.150 When a seafarer is on call, such as when a machinery space is unattended, the seafarer shall have an adequate compensatory rest period if the normal period of rest is disturbed by call-outs to work.

8.151 Member States shall require that records of daily hours of rest of seafarers be maintained in a standardised format, in the working language or languages of the ship and in English, to allow monitoring and verification of compliance with this article. Seafarers shall receive a copy of the records pertaining to them, which shall be endorsed by the master, or by a person authorised by the master, and by the seafarers.

8.152 Notwithstanding the rules laid down in paragraphs 3 to 9, the master of a ship shall be entitled to require a seafarer to perform any hours of work necessary for the immediate safety of the ship, persons on board or cargo, or for the purpose of giving assistance to other ships or persons in distress at sea. Accordingly, the master may suspend the schedule of hours of rest and require a seafarer to perform any hours of work necessary until the normal situation has been restored. As soon as practicable after the normal situation has been restored, the master shall ensure that any seafarers who have performed work in a scheduled rest period are provided with an adequate period of rest.

8.153 With due regard for the general principles of the protection of the health and safety of workers and in line with Directive 1999/63 Member States may, by means of national laws, regulations or a procedure for the competent authority, authorise or register collective agreements permitting exceptions to the required hours of rest set out in point (b) of paragraph 4 and in paragraph 5 of this article provided that the rest period is no less than 70 hours in any seven-day period and respects the limits set out in paragraphs 12 and 13 of this article. Such exceptions shall, as far as possible, follow the standards set out but may take account of more frequent or longer leave periods, or the granting of compensatory leave for watchkeeping seafarers or seafarers working on board ships on short voyages. Exceptions shall, as far as possible, take into account the guidance regarding prevention of fatigue laid down in Section B-VIII/1 of the STCW Code. Exceptions to the minimum hours of rest provided for in point (a) of paragraph 4 of this article shall not be allowed.

8.154 Exceptions referred to in paragraph 11 to the weekly rest period provided for in point (b) of paragraph 4 shall not be allowed for more than two consecutive weeks. The intervals between two periods of exceptions on board shall not be less than twice the duration of the exception.

8.155 In the framework of possible exceptions to paragraph 5 referred to in paragraph 11, the minimum hours of rest in any 24-hour period provided for in point (a) of paragraph 4 may be divided into no more than three periods of rest, one of which shall be at least six hours in length and neither of the two other periods shall be less than one hour in length. The intervals between consecutive periods of rest shall not exceed 14 hours. Exceptions shall not extend beyond two 24-hour periods in any seven-day period.

8.156 Member States shall establish, for the purpose of preventing alcohol abuse, a limit of not greater than 0.05% blood alcohol level (BAC) or 0.25 mg/l alcohol in the breath or a quantity of alcohol leading to such alcohol concentration for masters, officers and other seafarers while performing designated safety, security and marine environmental duties.

Responsibilities of companies

8.157 Article 14(1) provides that in accordance with paragraphs 2 and 3 of the directive, Member States must hold companies responsible for the assignment of seafarers for service in their ships in accordance with Directive 2008/106, and must require every company to ensure that: (a) each seafarer assigned to any of its ships holds an appropriate certificate in accordance with the provisions of the directive and as established by the Member State; (b) its ships are manned in accordance with the applicable safe-manning requirements of the Member State; (c) documentation and data relevant to all seafarers employed on its ships are maintained and readily accessible, and include, without being limited to, documentation and data on their experience, training, medical fitness and competence in assigned duties; (d) on being assigned to any of its ships seafarers are familiarised with their specific duties and with all ship arrangements, installations, equipment, procedures and ship characteristics that are relevant to their routine or emergency duties; (e) the ship's complement can effectively coordinate their activities in an emergency situation and in performing functions vital to safety or to the prevention or mitigation of pollution; (f) seafarers assigned to any of its ships have received refresher and updating training as required by the STCW Convention; and (g) at all times on board its ships, there shall be effective oral communication in accordance with paragraph 3 and 4 of Chapter V of Regulation 14 of the SOLAS 74 as amended.[116]

8.158 Article 14(2) provides that companies, masters and crew members must each have responsibility for ensuring that the obligations set out in Article 14 are given full

---

[116] Virtue of Dir. 2012/35 OJ L343/78, 14 December 2012.

and complete effect and that such other measures as may be necessary are taken to ensure that each crew member can make a knowledgeable and informed contribution to the safe operation of the ship.

8.159 Article 14(3) provided that the company must provide written instructions to the master of each ship to which this directive applies, setting out the policies and the procedures to be followed to ensure that all seafarers who are newly employed on board the ship are given a reasonable opportunity to become familiar with the shipboard equipment, operating procedures and other arrangements needed for the proper performance of their duties, before being assigned to those duties. Such policies and procedures shall include: (a) the allocation of a reasonable period of time during which each newly employed seafarer will have an opportunity to become acquainted with: (i) the specific equipment the seafarer will be using or operating; and (ii) ship-specific watchkeeping, safety, environmental protection and emergency procedures and arrangements the seafarer needs to know to perform the assigned duties properly; and (b) the designation of a knowledgeable crew member who will be responsible for ensuring that each newly employed seafarer is given an opportunity to receive essential information in a language the seafarer understands.

8.160 Companies must ensure that masters, officers and other personnel, assigned specific duties and responsibilities on board their ro-ro passenger ships must have completed familiarisation training to attain the abilities that are appropriate to the capacity to be filled and duties and responsibilities to be taken up, taking into account the guidance given in Section B-1/14 of the STCW Code.

Fitness for duty

8.161 For the purpose of preventing fatigue (which is a serious illness on board ships), Member States must establish and enforce rest periods for watchkeeping personnel and require that watch systems are arranged in such a way that the efficiency of watchkeeping personnel is not impaired by fatigue and that duties are organised in such a way that the first watch at the start of a voyage and subsequent relieving watches are sufficiently rested and otherwise fit for duty.[117] All persons who are assigned duty as officer in charge of a watch or as a rating forming part of a watch must be allowed at least ten hours of rest in any 24-hour period. The hours of rest may be divided into no more than two periods, one of which shall be at least six hours long. Given the importance of fitness for duty and hours of work, it is useful to set out in Article 15 in full:

"For the purpose of preventing fatigue, Member States shall:

1. (a) establish and enforce rest periods for watchkeeping personnel and those whose duties involve designated safety, security and prevention of pollution duties in accordance with paragraphs 3 to 13;
   (b) require that watch systems are arranged in such a way that the efficiency of watchkeeping personnel is not impaired by fatigue, and that duties are organised in such a

---

117 Dir. 2008/106, Art. 15(1) notwithstanding paras 2 and 3, the minimum period of ten hours may be reduced to not less than six consecutive hours provided that no such reduction shall extend beyond two days and at least 70 hours of rest are provided each seven-day period. Member States must require that watch schedules be posted where they are easily accessible.

way that the first watch at the start of a voyage and subsequent relieving watches are sufficiently rested and otherwise fit for duty.

2. Member States shall, for the purpose of preventing drug and alcohol abuse, ensure that adequate measures are established in accordance with the provisions laid down in this Article.
3. Member States shall take account of the danger posed by fatigue of seafarers, especially those whose duties involve the safe and secure operation of a ship.
4. All persons who are assigned duty as officer in charge of a watch or as a rating forming part of a watch, and those whose duties involve designated safety, prevention of pollution and security duties shall be provided with a rest period of not less than:

   (a) a minimum of 10 hours of rest in any 24-hour period; and (b) 77 hours in any seven-day period.

5. The hours of rest may be divided into no more than two periods, one of which shall be at least six hours in length, and the intervals between consecutive periods of rest shall not exceed 14 hours.
6. The requirements for rest periods laid down in paragraphs 4 and 5 need not be maintained in the case of an emergency or in other over riding operational conditions. Musters, firefighting and lifeboat drills, and drills prescribed by national laws and regulations and by international instruments, shall be conducted in a manner that minimises the disturbance of rest periods and does not induce fatigue.
7. Member States shall require that watch schedules be posted where they are easily accessible. The schedules shall be established in a standardised format in the working language or languages of the ship and in English.
8. When a seafarer is on call, such as when a machinery space is unattended, the seafarer shall have an adequate compensatory rest period if the normal period of rest is disturbed by call-outs to work.
9. Member States shall require that records of daily hours of rest of seafarers be maintained in a standardised format, in the working language or languages of the ship and in English, to allow monitoring and verification of compliance with this Article. Seafarers shall receive a copy of the records pertaining to them, which shall be endorsed by the master, or by a person authorised by the master, and by the seafarers.
10. Notwithstanding the rules laid down in paragraphs 3 to 9, the master of a ship shall be entitled to require a seafarer to perform any hours of work necessary for the immediate safety of the ship, persons on board or cargo, or for the purpose of giving assistance to other ships or persons in distress at sea. Accordingly, the master may suspend the schedule of hours of rest and require a seafarer to perform any hours of work necessary until the normal situation has been restored. As soon as practicable after the normal situation has been restored, the master shall ensure that any seafarers who have performed work in a scheduled rest period are provided with an adequate period of rest.
11. With due regard for the general principles of the protection of the health and safety of workers and in line with Directive 1999/63/EC Member States may, by means of national laws, regulations or a procedure for the competent authority, authorise or register collective agreements permitting exceptions to the required hours of rest set out in point (b) of paragraph 4 and in paragraph 5 of this Article provided that the rest period is no less than 70 hours in any seven-day period and respects the limits set out in paragraphs 12 and 13 of this Article. Such exceptions shall, as far as possible, follow the standards set out but may take account of more frequent or longer leave periods, or the granting of compensatory leave for watchkeeping seafarers or seafarers working on board ships on short voyages. Exceptions shall, as far as possible, take into account the guidance regarding prevention of fatigue laid down in Section B-VIII/1 of the STCW Code. Exceptions to the minimum hours of rest provided for in point (a) of paragraph 4 of this Article shall not be allowed.
12. Exceptions referred to in paragraph 11 to the weekly rest period provided for in point (b) of paragraph 4 shall not be allowed for more than two consecutive weeks. The intervals

between two periods of exceptions on board shall not be less than twice the duration of the exception.
13. In the framework of possible exceptions to paragraph 5 referred to in paragraph 11, the minimum hours of rest in any 24-hour period provided for in point (a) of paragraph 4 may be divided into no more than three periods of rest, one of which shall be at least six hours in length and neither of the two other periods shall be less than one hour in length. The intervals between consecutive periods of rest shall not exceed 14 hours. Exceptions shall not extend beyond two 24-hour periods in any seven-day period.
14. Member States shall establish, for the purpose of preventing alcohol abuse, a limit of not greater than 0.05% blood alcohol level (BAC) or 0,25 mg/l alcohol in the breath or a quantity of alcohol leading to such alcohol concentration for masters, officers and other seafarers while performing designated safety, security and marine environmental duties."

Dispensation

8.162 In circumstances of exceptional necessity, competent authorities may, if in their opinion this does not cause danger to persons, property or the environment,[118] issue a dispensation permitting a specified seafarer to serve in a specified ship for a specified period not exceeding six months in a capacity, other than that of the radio operator, except as provided by the relevant Radio Regulations,[119] for which he or she does not hold the appropriate certificate, provided that the person to whom the dispensation is issued must be adequately qualified to fill the vacant post in a safe manner to the satisfaction of the competent authorities.[120] However, dispensations must not be granted to a master or chief engineer officer, except in circumstances of force majeure and then only for the shortest possible period.[121]

8.163 Any dispensation granted for a post must be granted only to a person properly certificated to fill the post immediately below.[122] Where certification of the post below is not required, a dispensation may be issued to a person whose qualification and experience are, in the opinion of the competent authorities, of a clear equivalence to the requirements for the post to be filled, provided that, if such a person holds no appropriate certificate, he or she must be required to pass a test accepted by the competent authorities as demonstrating that such a dispensation may safely be issued. In addition, the competent authorities shall ensure that the post in question is filled by the holder of an appropriate certificate as soon as possible.[123]

Responsibilities of Member States with regard to training and assessment

8.164 Article 17 ("responsibilities of Member States with regard to training and assessment") provides that Member States must designate the authorities or bodies which shall: (a) give the training referred to in Article 3 of the directive; (b) organise and/or supervise the examinations where required; (c) issue the certificates of competence

---

118 This is a significant test standard.
119 Art. 1 provides that the term "Radio Regulations" means "the radio regulations annexed to, or regarded as being annexed to, the International Telecommunication Convention, as amended".
120 Dir. 2008/106, Art. 16(1).
121 Ibid.
122 Dir. 2008/106, Art. 16(2).
123 Ibid.

referred to in Article 5 of the directive; and (d) grant the dispensations provided for in Article 16 of the directive. Member States must ensure, by virtue of Article 16(2), that: (a) all training and assessment of seafarers is: (i) structured in accordance with the written programmes, including such methods and media of delivery, procedures and course material as are necessary to achieve the prescribed standard of competence; and (ii) conducted, monitored, evaluated and supported by persons qualified in accordance with points (d), (e) and (f); (b) persons conducting in-service training or assessment on board ship do so only when such training or assessment will not adversely affect the normal operation of the ship and they can dedicate their time and attention to training or assessment; (c) instructors, supervisors and assessors are appropriately qualified for the particular types and levels of training or assessment of competence of seafarers either on board or ashore; (d) any person conducting in-service training of a seafarer, either on board or ashore, which is intended to be used in qualifying for certification under this directive: (i) has an appreciation of the training programme and an understanding of the specific training objectives for the particular type of training being conducted; (ii) is qualified in the task for which training is being conducted; and (iii) if conducting training using a simulator: has received appropriate guidance in instructional techniques involving the use of simulators, and has gained practical operational experience on the particular type of simulator being used; (e) any person responsible for the supervision of the in-service training of a seafarer intended to be used in qualifying for certification has a full understanding of the training programme and the specific objectives for each type of training being conducted; (f) any person conducting in-service assessment of the competence of a seafarer, either on board or ashore, which is intended to be used in qualifying for certification under this directive: (i) has an appropriate level of knowledge and understanding of the competence to be assessed; (ii) is qualified in the task for which the assessment is being made; (iii) has received appropriate guidance in assessment methods and practice; (iv) has gained practical assessment experience; and (v) if conducting assessment involving the use of simulators, has gained practical assessment experience on the particular type of simulator under the supervision and to the satisfaction of an experienced assessor; and (g) when a Member State recognises a course of training, a training institution or a qualification granted by a training institution, as part of its requirements for the issue of a certificate, the qualifications and experience of instructors and assessors are covered in the application of the quality standard provisions of Article 10; such qualification, experience and application of quality standards shall incorporate appropriate training in instructional techniques and training and assessment methods and practice and comply with all applicable requirements of points (d), (e) and (f).

On-board communication

8.165 Communications on board are critical – it is imperative that they are accurate and comprehensive because language difficulties can cause problems. Article 18 ("on-board communication") provides that Member States must ensure that: (a) without prejudice to points (b) and (d), there are at all times, on board all ships flying the flag of a Member State, means in place for effective oral communication relating to safety between all members of the ship's crew, particularly with regard to the correct and timely reception and understanding of messages and instructions; (b) on board all passenger ships flying the flag of a

Member State and on board all passenger ships starting and/or finishing a voyage in a Member State port, in order to ensure effective crew performance in safety matters, a working language is established and recorded in the ship's log-book; the company or the master, as appropriate, shall determine the appropriate working language; each seafarer shall be required to understand and, where appropriate, give orders and instructions and report back in that language; if the working language is not an official language of the Member State, all plans and lists that must be posted shall include translations into the working language; (c) on board passenger ships, personnel nominated on muster lists to assist passengers in emergency situations are readily identifiable and have communication skills that are sufficient for that purpose, taking into account an appropriate and adequate combination of any of the following factors: (i) the language or languages appropriate to the principal nationalities of passengers carried on a particular route; (ii) the likelihood that an ability to use elementary English vocabulary for basic instructions can provide a means of communicating with a passenger in need of assistance whether or not the passenger and crew member share a common language; (iii) the possible need to communicate during an emergency by some other means (e.g. by demonstration, hand signals or calling attention to the location of instructions, muster stations, life-saving devices or evacuation routes) when verbal communication is impractical; (iv) the extent to which complete safety instructions have been provided to passengers in their native language or languages; (v) the languages in which emergency announcements may be broadcast during an emergency or drill to convey critical guidance to passengers and to facilitate crew members in assisting passengers; (d) on board oil tankers, chemical tankers and liquefied gas tankers flying the flag of a Member State, the master, officers and rating are able to communicate with each other in a common working language(s); (e) there are adequate means for communication between the ship and the shore-based authorities; these communications shall be conducted in accordance with Chapter V, Regulation 14, paragraph 4, of the SOLAS 74; and (f) when carrying out port State control under Directive 95/21, Member States also check that ships flying the flag of a State other than a Member State comply with this article.

Recognition of certificates

8.166 Article 19 of the directive ("Regulation of Certificates of competency and certificates of proficiency") provides in paragraph 1 that seafarers who do not possess the certificates of competency issued by Member States and/or the certificates of proficiency issued by Member States to masters and officers in accordance with Regulations V/1–1 and V/1–2 of the STCW Convention, may be allowed to serve on ships flying the flag of a Member State, provided that a decision on the recognition of their certificates of competency and certificates of proficiency has been adopted through the procedure set out in paragraphs 2 to 6 of Article 19.

8.167 A Member State which intends to recognise, by endorsement, the certificates of competency and/or the certificates of proficiency referred to in Article 19(1) issued by a third country to a master, officer or radio operator, for service on ships flying its flag, must submit a request for recognition of that third country to the Commission, stating its reasons.[124] The Commission, assisted by the European Maritime Safety Agency

---

124 Dir. 2008/106, Art. 19(2).

("EMSA") and with the possible involvement of any Member State concerned, must collect the information referred to in Annex II and must carry out an assessment of the training and certification systems in the third country for which the request for recognition was submitted, in order to verify whether the country concerned meets all the requirements of the STCW Convention and whether the appropriate measures have been taken to prevent fraud involving certificates.[125]

8.168 The decision on the recognition of a third country must be taken by the Commission. These implementing acts must be adopted in accordance with the examination procedure referred to in Article 28(2) of the directive, within 18 months of the date of the request for the recognition.[126] The Member State submitting the request may decide to recognise the third country unilaterally until a decision is taken under Article 19(3) – this may be useful in the context of Brexit.

8.169 A Member State may decide, with respect to ships flying its flag, to endorse certificates issued by the third countries recognised by the Commission, account being taken of the provisions contained in Annex II, points (4) and (5).[127]

8.170 Recognitions of certificates issued by recognised third countries and published in the *Official Journal of the European Union*, C series, before 14 June 2005 remain valid.[128] These recognitions may be used by all Member States unless the Commission has subsequently withdrawn them pursuant to Article 20.[129] The Commission had to draw up and update a list of the third countries that have been recognised. The list had to be published in the *Official Journal of the European Union* (C series).[130]

8.171 Notwithstanding Article 5(6) of the directive, a Member State may, if circumstances require, allow a seafarer to serve in a capacity other than radio officer or radio operator, except as provided by the Radio Regulations, for a period not exceeding three months on board a ship flying its flag, while holding an appropriate and valid certificate issued and endorsed as required by a third country, but not yet endorsed for recognition by the Member State concerned so as to render it appropriate for service on board a ship flying its flag.[131] Documentary proof must be kept readily available that application for an endorsement has been submitted to the competent authorities.[132]

Non-compliance with the requirements of the STCW Convention

8.172 What happens if there is non-compliance with the requirements of the STCW Convention? Article 20 seeks to address that issue. Notwithstanding the criteria specified in Annex II of the directive.[133] Annex II is entitled "Criteria for the recognition of Third Countries that have issued a Certificate or under the Authority of which was issued. Certificate referred to in Article 19(2)" when a Member State considers that a recognised

---

125 Ibid.
126 Dir. 2008/106, Art. 19(3).
127 Dir. 2008/106, Art. 19(4).
128 Dir. 2008/106, Art. 19(5).
129 Ibid.
130 Dir. 2008/106, Art. 19(6).
131 Dir. 2008/106, Art 19(7).
132 Ibid.
133 Annex II is entitled "criteria for the Recognition of Third Countries that have issued a Certificate or under the Authority of which was issued. Certificate referred to in Article 19(2)."

third country no longer complies with the requirements of the STCW Convention, it must notify the Commission immediately, giving substantiated reasons therefor.[134] The Commission must without delay refer the matter to the Committee referred to in Article 28(1).[135]

8.173 Notwithstanding the criteria set out in Annex II, when the Commission considers that a recognised third country no longer complies with the requirements of the STCW Convention, it must notify the Member States immediately, giving substantiated reasons therefor. The Commission shall without delay refer the matter to the Committee referred to in Article 28(1).[136]

8.174 When a Member State intends to withdraw the endorsements of all certificates issued by a third country then it must without delay inform the Commission and the other Member States of its intention, giving substantiated reasons therefor.[137]

8.175 The Commission, assisted by the EMSA, must reassess the recognition of the third country concerned in order to verify whether that country failed to comply with the requirements of the STCW Convention.[138]

8.176 Where there are indications that a particular maritime training establishment then no longer complies with the requirements of the STCW Convention, the Commission must notify the country concerned that recognition of that country's certificates will be withdrawn in two months' time unless measures are taken to ensure compliance with all the requirements of the STCW Convention.[139]

8.177 The decision on the withdrawal of the recognition must be taken by the European Commission. Those implementing acts must be adopted in accordance with the examination procedure referred to in Article 28(2).[140] The Member States concerned must take appropriate measures to implement the decision.[141]

8.178 Endorsements attesting recognition of certificates, issued in accordance with Article 5(6) of the directive before the date on which the decision to withdraw recognition of the third country is taken, must remain valid.[142] Seafarers holding such endorsements may not claim an endorsement recognising a higher qualification, however, unless that upgrading is based solely on additional seagoing service experience.[143]

Article 27 deals with amendments and Article 27a addresses the exercise of the delegation. Under Article 27, the Commission is empowered to adopt delegated acts, in accordance with Article 27a, amending Annex V to the directive with respect to specific and relevant content and details of the information that needs to be reported by Member States provided that such acts are limited to taking into account the amendments to the STCW Convention and Code and respect the safeguards on data protection. Such delegated acts shall not change the provisions of anonymisation of data as required by Article 25a(3). Article 27a goes on to deal with the exercise of the delegation. Under Article 27a(1), the

---

134 Dir. 2008/106, Art. 20(1).
135 Ibid.
136 Ibid.
137 Dir. 2008/106, Art. 20(3).
138 Dir. 2008/106, Art. 20(4).
139 Dir. 2008/106, Art. 20(5).
140 Dir. 2008/106, Art. 20(6).
141 Ibid.
142 Dir. 2008/106, Art. 20(7).
143 Ibid.

power to adopt delegated acts is conferred on the Commission subject to the conditions laid down in Article 27a. Under Article 27a(2), the delegation of power referred to in Article 27 was conferred on the Commission for a period of five years from 3 January 2013. The Commission had to draw up a report in respect of the delegation of power not later than 4 April 2017. The delegation of power had to be tacitly extended for periods of an identical duration, unless the European Parliament or the Council opposed such extension not later than three months before the end of each period. Pursuant to Article 27a(3), the delegation of power referred to in Article 27 may be revoked at any time by the European Parliament or by the Council. A decision to revoke shall put an end to the delegation of the power specified in that decision. It shall take effect the day following the publication of the decision in the *Official Journal of the European Union* or at a later date specified therein. It shall not affect the validity of any delegated acts already in force. Under Article 27a(4), as soon as it adopts a delegated act, the Commission must notify it simultaneously to the European Parliament and to the Council. Under Article 27a(5), a delegated act adopted pursuant to Article 27 shall enter into force only if no objection has been expressed either by the European Parliament or the Council within a period of two months of notification of that act to the European Parliament and the Council or if, before the expiry of that period, the European Parliament and the Council have both informed the Commission that they will not object and that period shall be extended by two months at the initiative of the European Parliament or the Council.

Reassessment

8.179 The third countries that have been recognised under the procedure referred to in the first subparagraph of Article 19(3), including those referred to in Article 19(6), must be reassessed by the Commission, with the assistance of the EMSA, on a regular basis and at least every five years to verify that they fulfil the relevant criteria set out in Annex II and whether the appropriate measures have been taken to prevent fraud involving certificates.[144] The Commission must define the priority criteria for assessment of third countries on the basis of performance data provided by the port State control pursuant to Article 23, as well as the information relating to the reports of the independent evaluations communicated by third countries pursuant to section A-I/7 of the STCW Code.[145] The Commission must provide the Member States with a report on the results of the assessment.[146]

Port State control

8.180 There is an obvious connection between the directive and port State control. Article 22 deals with the issue of port State control. Article 22 should be read in conjunction with Article 23 which deals with port State control procedures. Article 22(1) provides that irrespective of the flag it flies each ship, with the exception of those types of ships excluded by Article 2, must, while in the ports of a Member State, be subject to port

---

144 Dir. 2008/106, Art. 21(1).
145 Dir. 2008/106, Art. 21(2).
146 Dir. 2008/106, Art. 21(3).

State control by officers duly authorised by that Member State to verify that all seafarers serving on board who are required to hold a certificate of competency and/or a certificate of proficiency and/or documentary evidence under the STCW Convention, hold a certificate of competency and/or a certificate of proficiency and/or documentary evidence under the STCW convention, hold such a certificate of competency or valid dispensation and/or certificate of proficiency and/or documentary evidence.[147] When exercising port State control under Directive 2008/106, Member States must ensure that all relevant provisions and procedures laid down in Directive 95/21 are applied.[148]

Port State control procedures

8.181 Article 23 of the directive deals with port State control procedures and should be read so as to understand fully Article 22. Without prejudice to Directive 95/21,[149] port State control pursuant to Article 22 shall be limited to the following: (a) verification that every seafarer serving on board who is required to hold a certificate of competency and/or a certificate of proficiency in accordance with the STCW Convention holds such a certificate of competency or valid dispensation and/or certificate of proficiency, or provides documentary proof that an application for an endorsement attesting recognition of a certificate of competency has been submitted to the authorities of the flag State; and (b) verification that the numbers and certificates of the seafarers serving on board are in accordance with the safe-manning requirements of the authorities of the flag State.

8.182 Article 23(2) provides that the ability of the ship's seafarers to maintain watch-keeping and security standards, as appropriate, as required by the STCW Convention must be assessed in accordance with Part A of the STCW Code if there are clear grounds for believing that such standards are not being maintained because any of the following has occurred: (a) the ship has been involved in a collision, grounding or stranding; (b) there has been a discharge of substances from the ship when under way, at anchor or at berth which is illegal under an international convention; (c) the ship has been manoeuvred in an erratic or unsafe manner whereby routing measures adopted by the IMO, or safe navigation practices and procedures have not been followed; (d) the ship is otherwise being operated in such a manner as to pose a danger to persons, property or the environment or compromise security; (e) a certificate has been fraudulently obtained or the holder of a certificate is not the person to whom that certificate was originally issued; and (f) the ship is flying the flag of a country which has not ratified the STCW Convention, or has a master, officer or rating holding a certificate issued by a third country which has not ratified the STCW Convention.

8.183 Notwithstanding verification of the certificate, assessment under Article 23(2) may require the seafarer to demonstrate the relevant competence at the place of duty.[150] Such a demonstration may include verification that operational requirements in respect of watchkeeping standards have been met and that there is a proper response to emergency situations within the seafarer's level of competence.

---

147 Dir. 2008/106, Art. 22(1).
148 Dir. 2008/106, Art. 22(2).
149 Dir. 95/21 OJ L157, 7 July 1995 but since repealed.
150 Dir. 2008/106, Art. 23(3).

8.184 The Committee's procedure is addressed by Article 28 of the directive. Under Article 28(1), the Commission shall be assisted by the Committee on Safe Seas and the Prevention of Pollution from Ships ("COSS") established by Regulation 2099/2002 of the European Parliament and of the Council.[151] That committee shall be a committee within the meaning of Regulation 182/2011 of the European Parliament and of the Council of 16 February 2011 laying down the rules and general principles concerning mechanisms for control by Member States of the Commission's exercise of implementing powers.[152] Under Article 28(2), where reference is made to Article 28(2), Article 5 of Regulation 182/2011 shall apply. Where the Committee delivers no opinion, the Commission shall not adopt the draft implementing act and the third subparagraph of Article 5(4) of Regulation 182/2011 shall apply.

Detention of vessels

8.185 Article 24 of the directive provides that without prejudice to Directive 95/21,[153] the following deficiencies, in so far as they have been determined by the officer carrying out the port State control that they pose a danger to persons, property or the environment, must be the only grounds under the directive on which a Member State may detain a ship: (a) failure of seafarers to hold certificates, to have appropriate certificates, to have valid dispensations or provide documentary proof that an application for an endorsement attesting recognition has been submitted to the authorities of the flag State; (b) failure to comply with the applicable safe-manning requirements of the flag State; (c) failure of navigational or engineering-watch arrangements to conform to the requirements specified for the ship by the flag State; (d) absence in a watch of a person qualified to operate equipment essential to safe navigation, safety radio communications or the prevention of marine pollution; (e) failure to provide proof of professional proficiency for the duties assigned to seafarers for the safety of the ship and the prevention of pollution; and (f) inability to provide for the first watch at the commencement of a voyage and for subsequent relieving watches persons who are sufficiently rested and otherwise fit for duty.

Regular monitoring of compliance

8.186 Without prejudice to the powers of the Commission, the Commission, assisted by the EMSA, must verify on a regular basis and at least every five years that Member States comply with the minimum requirements laid down by the directive.[154]

Information for statistical purposes

8.187 Article 25a of Directive 2008/106 deals with the issue of information for statistical purposes. Article 25a(1) provides that the Member States must communicate the information listed in Annex V of the directive to the Commission for the purposes of statistical analysis only and that such information may not be used for administrative, legal

---

151 OJ L324/1, 29 November 2002.
152 OJ L55/13, 28 February 2011.
153 OJ L157/1, 7 July 1995.
154 Dir. 2008/106, Art. 25.

or verification purposes, and is exclusively for use by Member States and the Commission in policy-making. Under Article 25a(2), that information must be made available by Member States to the Commission on a yearly basis and in electronic format and must include information registered until 31 December of the previous year. Equally, Member States must retain all property rights to the information in its raw data format and processed statistics drawn up on the basis of such information shall be made publicly available in accordance with the provisions on transparency and protection of information set out in Article 4 of Regulation 1406/2002. Under Article 25a(3), in order to ensure the protection of personal data, Member States must anonymise all personal information as indicated in Annex V by using software provided or accepted by the Commission before transmitting it to the Commission and the Commission must use this anonymised information only. Article 25a(4), Member States and the Commission must ensure that measures for collecting, submitting, storing, analysing and disseminating such information are designed in such a way that statistical analysis is made possible and, for these purposes, the Commission must adopt detailed measures regarding the technical requirements necessary to ensure the appropriate management of the statistical data. Those implementing acts shall be adopted in accordance with the examination procedure referred to in Article 28(2).

Reports

8.188 Article 26 deals with various reports. Not later than 14 December 2008, the Commission had to submit an evaluation report to the Parliament and the Council, based on a detailed analysis and evaluation of the provisions of the STCW Convention, the implementation thereof and new insights gained with regard to the correlation between safety and the level of training of ships' crews.[155] Not later than 20 October 2010 the Commission had to submit to the Parliament and the Council an evaluation report drawn up on the basis of the information obtained pursuant to Article 25.[156] In the report the Commission must analyse the Member States' compliance with the directive and, where necessary, make proposals for additional measures.[157]

Amendment and exercise of delegation

8.189 Article 27 deals with amendments and Article 27a addresses the exercise of the delegation. Under Article 27, the Commission is empowered to adopt delegated acts, in accordance with Article 27a, amending Annex V to the directive with respect to specific and relevant content and details of the information that needs to be reported by Member States provided that such acts are limited to taking into account the amendments to the STCW Convention and Code and respect the safeguards on data protection. Such delegated acts shall not change the provisions of anonymisation of data as required by Article 25a(3). Article 27a goes on to deal with the exercise of the delegation. Under Article 27a,[158] the power to adopt delegated acts is conferred on the Commission subject to the

---

155 Dir. 2008/106, Art. 26(1).
156 Dir. 2008/106, Art. 26(2).
157 Ibid.
158 Dir. 2008/106, Art. 27a(2).

conditions laid down in Article 27a. Under Article 27a(2), the delegation of power referred to in Article 27 was conferred on the Commission for a period of five years from 3 January 2013. The Commission had to draw up a report in respect of the delegation of power not later than 4 April 2017. The delegation of power had to be tacitly extended for periods of an identical duration, unless the European Parliament or the Council opposed such extension not later than three months before the end of each period. Pursuant to Article 27a(3), the delegation of power referred to in Article 27 may be revoked at any time by the European Parliament or by the Council. A decision to revoke shall put an end to the delegation of the power specified in that decision. It shall take effect the day following the publication of the decision in the *Official Journal of the European Union* or at a later date specified therein. It shall not affect the validity of any delegated acts already in force. Under Article 27a(4), as soon as it adopts a delegated act, the Commission must notify it simultaneously to the European Parliament and to the Council. Under Article 27a(5), a delegated act adopted pursuant to Article 27 shall enter into force only if no objection has been expressed either by the European Parliament or the Council within a period of two months of notification of that act to the European Parliament and the Council or if, before the expiry of that period, the European Parliament and the Council have both informed the Commission that they will not object and that period shall be extended by two months at the initiative of the European Parliament or the Council.

8.190 Article 30 deals with transitional provisions. Under the article, in respect of those seafarers who commenced approved seagoing service, an approved education and training programme or an approved training course before 1 July 2013, Member States may continue to issue, recognise and endorse, until 1 January 2017, certificates of competency in accordance with the requirements of this directive as they were before 3 January 2013. Until 1 January 2017, Member States were able to continue to renew and revalidate certificates of competency and endorsements in accordance with the requirements of this directive as they were before 3 January 2013.

8.191 Where pursuant to Article 12 a Member State reissues or extends the validity of certificates which it originally issued under the provisions which applied before 1 February 1997, the Member State may, at its discretion, replace tonnage limitations appearing on the original certificates as follows: (a) "200 gross registered tonnes" may be replaced by "500 gross tonnage"; and (b) "1600 gross registered tonnes" may be replaced by "3000 gross tonnage".

Penalties

8.192 Article 29 deals with penalties. Member States must lay down systems of penalties for breaching the national provisions adopted pursuant to Articles 3, 5, 7, 9 to 15, 17, 18, 19, 22, 23, 24, and Annex I, and must take all the measures necessary to ensure that they are implemented. The penalties provided for must be effective, proportionate and dissuasive.

Transitional provisions

8.193 The Committee's procedure is addressed by Article 28 of the directive. Under Article 28(1), the Commission shall be assisted by the COSS established by Regulation

2099/2002 of the European Parliament and of the Council.¹⁵⁹ That committee shall be a committee within the meaning of Regulation 182/2011 of the European Parliament and of the Council of 16 February 2011 laying down the rules and general principles concerning mechanisms for control by Member States of the Commission's exercise of implementing powers. Under Article 28(2), where reference is made to Article 28,¹⁶⁰ Article 5 of Regulation 182/2011 shall apply. Where the Committee delivers no opinion, the Commission shall not adopt the draft implementing act and the third subparagraph of Article 5(4) of Regulation 182/2011 shall apply.

Communication

8.194 Member States had to immediately communicate to the Commission the texts of all the provisions which they adopt in the field governed by the directive.[161] The Commission had to inform the other Member States of the provisions.[162]

Repeal

8.195 Directive 2001/25, as amended by the directives listed in Annex III, Part A, is repealed, without prejudice to the obligations of the Member States relating to the time limits for transposition into national law of the directives set out in Annex III, Part B. References to the repealed directive must be construed as references to the directive and shall be read in accordance with the correlation table in Annex IV.

K. EMPLOYEES AND THE PERFORMANCE OF PUBLIC DUTIES

Introduction

8.196 What if employees perform certain public functions and a Member State wishes to retain the exercise of those public functions to the Member State's own nationals or citizens? Article 45(4) of the TFEU provides an exception to the general regime for public service employees – it provides that Article 48 "shall not apply to employment in the public service". It is difficult to justify Member States reserving functions to their own nationals as opposed to nationals from other Member States unless there is a clear justification for the reservation (e.g. where citizenship matters) but the EU has been reluctant to interfere with the sovereignty of Member States in this regard. The CJEU considered the issue in cases such as *Colegio de Oficiales de la Marina Mercante Española v Administración del Estado*[163] and *Albert Anker, Klaas Ras, Albertus Snoek v Bundesrepublik Deutschland.*[164] It is useful to consider each of the cases separately.

---

159 OJ L324/1, 29 November 2002.
160 OJ L55/13, 28 February 2011.
161 Dir. 2008/106, Art. 31.
162 Dir. 2008/108, Art. 31.
163 Case C-405/01, [2003] ECR I-10391, ECLI:EU:C:2003:515.
164 Case C-47/02, [2003] ECR I-10447, ECLI:EU:C:2003:516. See Nesterowicz, "Sea Captains and Performance of Public Duties in European Law" [2004] LMCLQ 19.

The *Colegio de Oficiales de la Marina Mercante Española v Administración del Estado* case

Introduction

8.197 The issue of public functions meaning that free movement of workers was not absolute in the maritime context was considered in *Colegio de Oficiales de la Marina Mercante Española v Administración del Estado*.[165] This was a reference to the CJEU[166] on the basis of Article 267 of the TFEU by Spain's Tribunal Supremo for a preliminary ruling in the proceedings pending before that court between Colegio de Oficiales de la Marina Mercante Española (Spanish Merchant Navy Officers' Association (the "Association")) and Administración del Estado. The Asociación de Navieros Españoles (the "ANAVE") was an intervener. The case turned on the interpretation of Article 45 of the TFEU as well as Articles 1 and 4 of Regulation 1612/68 of 15 October 1968 on freedom of movement for workers within the Community[167] which is one of the key measures in this area.

8.198 The two questions were raised in the course of an action for annulment brought by the Association against a Spanish law entitled Real Decreto 2062/1999, por el que se regula el nivel mínimo de formación en profesiones marítimas (Royal Decree No 2062/1999 on the minimum level of training of seafarers) of 30 December 1999 (BOE of 21 January 2000, "Royal Decree No 2062/1999").

8.199 The case turned on the Spanish national legislation entitled Ley 27/1992, de Puertos del Estado y de la Marina Mercante (Law No 27/1992 on National Ports and the Merchant Navy), of 24 November 1992 (BOE, 25 November 1992, hereinafter "Law No 27/1992"), which provided in Article 77, entitled "Ships' Crews":

"1. The number of crew-members and their professional qualifications must be adequate to ensure at all times the safety of navigation and of the ship, having regard to its technical and operational characteristics, in accordance with conditions which shall be laid down by regulations.
2. The conditions as to the nationality of ships' crews shall also be determined by regulation, although, from the entry into force of this Law, citizens of Member States of the European Economic Community shall be eligible for employment as ships' crew, provided that such employment does not involve even on an occasional basis, the performance of public duties, which is reserved to Spanish citizens."

8.200 The CJEU stated that it was apparent from the fifteenth Additional Provision to Law No 27/1992 entitled "Special register of ships and shipowners", that the master and the chief mate of ships entered on the special register established by that provision must have Spanish nationality. That register concerned only ships of owners whose control centre for the operation of the ships was in the Canaries or, if it is situated elsewhere in Spain or abroad, who had in the Canaries a permanent establishment or representation enabling them to exercise the rights and to perform the obligations provided for by the Spanish legalisation. Only civilian vessels of not less than 100 tonnes, employed in

---

165 Case C-405/01, [2003] ECR I-10391, ECLI:EU:C:2003:515.
166 The court was composed of Rodríguez Iglesias (President), Puissochet, Wathelet (Rapporteur), Schintgen and Timmermans (Presidents of Chambers), Gulmann, Edward, La Pergola, Jann, Skouris, Macken, Colneric, von Bahr, Cunha Rodrigues and Rosas, Judges. The Advocate-General was AG Stix-Hackl.
167 OJ, English Special Edition 1968 (II), p. 475.

navigation for commercial purposes, excluding fishing vessels, may be entered on that register.

8.201 Article 8 of Royal Decree No 2062/1999 entitled "Specific rules on the recognition of professional qualifications of citizens of the European Union with diplomas issued by one of the Member States", provides:

> "1. The Directorate General of the Merchant Navy may directly recognise the professional diplomas or specialisation certificates of citizens of the European Union issued by one of those States, in accordance with the applicable national provisions.
> 2. Recognition of a professional diploma, authenticated by the issue of a Merchant Navy professional ticket, will be required for direct access to employment as a crew-member on board Spanish merchant ships, except for posts which involve or may involve the performance of public duties assigned by law to Spaniards, such as those of master, skipper or chief mate, which shall continue to be reserved for Spanish citizens.
> 3. Notwithstanding the provisions of the preceding paragraph, citizens of the European Union who hold a diploma issued by a Member State may have command of merchant ships of less than 100 gross register tonnes, which carry cargo or fewer than 100 passengers and operate exclusively between ports or points situated in areas where Spain has sovereignty, sovereign rights or jurisdiction, provided that the person concerned can prove that Spanish citizens have reciprocal rights in the State of which he is a national."

8.202 A critical issue was that several provisions of Spanish law conferred on masters of Spanish merchant navy ships public duties such as those relating to safety and public order, the notarising of documents and returns of births, marriages and deaths. In relation to safety and law-enforcement duties, Articles 110, 116(3)(f) and 127 of the Law No 27/1992 empowered masters, in exceptional circumstances, to take, in dangerous situations on board, all the public-order measures which they considered necessary for the safe progress of the vessel. Failure to comply with such measures and instructions was a serious offence. The master was responsible for recording infringements of that provision in the ship's log.

8.203 Under Article 610 of the Código de Comercio (Commercial Code), the master had the power, by virtue of the powers vested in his office, to impose penalties on board on those who disobeyed his orders or committed breaches of discipline. The offences and the measures taken must be recorded and the file transmitted to the competent authorities at the ship's first subsequent port of call.

8.204 Under Article 700 of the Commercial Code, all passengers had to comply with the master's orders in relation to the maintenance of order on board. In addition, in relation to the official certification or the registration of births, marriages and deaths, it was clear from Article 52 of the Código Civil (Civil Code) that the master may, in certain circumstances, solemnise marriages and, from Articles 722 and 729 of that code, that he had the power to receive wills and, if the testator dies on board, that he was responsible for ensuring the safekeeping of the will and its dispatch to the competent authorities.

8.205 In terms of the legal background, the CJEU recalled:

> "16. Pursuant to Article 19 of the Ley de Registro Civil (Law on the registration of births, marriages and deaths), the authorities and officials designated by the implementing regulation may register births, marriages and deaths occurring, in among other circumstances, on a sea voyage. The facts stated in such birth certificates have the same probative value as those recorded in entries in registers of births, marriages and deaths.

17. Under Article 71 of the Reglamento del Registro Civil (Regulations on the register of births, marriages and deaths), the document by virtue of which births, marriages and deaths are registered may be drawn up by the ship's master when those events occur during a sea voyage. Article 72 of those regulations provides that the master has the same rights and obligations as a registrar to certify births, deaths and stillbirths and to establish affiliation, as well as to issue burial permits.
18. In accordance with Article 705 of the Commercial Code, the master must draw up the death certificate if a person dies on board and he is empowered, after a period of 24 hours, to take the necessary steps in relation to the body.
19. Under Article 627 of the Commercial Code, the chief mate assumes the master's rights, obligations and responsibilities in the event of the incapacity of the master."

Factual background

8.206 The factual background was straightforward. The Officers' Association brought an action before the Tribunal Supremo for the annulment of certain provisions of the Royal Decree No 2062/1999. According to the Association, that decree, in particular Article 8(3), damaged the collective interests of the officers of the Spanish merchant navy and was contrary to Article 77 of Law No 27/1992 and to the fifteenth Additional Provision to that law in so far as it allowed nationals of other Member States to have command of certain Spanish vessels. The Tribunal Supremo, finding that masters and chief mates of merchant ships occasionally perform public order duties or duties which, in Spain, were usually entrusted to public officials, enquired whether the fact that a Member State reserved such employment for its nationals was compatible with Article 45 of the TFEU and the Court's case law.

8.207 According to that national court, if such a measure should be regarded as complying with EU law, Article 77(2) of Law No 27/1992, the fifteenth Additional Provision thereto and Article 8(2) of Royal Decree No 2062/1994, which reserve to Spanish nationals the posts of master and chief mate of merchant ships flying the Spanish flag, should be deemed lawful. The same would be true, a fortiori, of Article 8(3) of Royal Decree No 2062/1999, which gives nationals of other Member States access to the posts of master and chief mate on certain conditions and for certain vessels of the Spanish merchant navy.

8.208 The Tribunal Supremo observed, that an exception to the measure reserving the posts of master and chief mate to the nationals of the flag State such as that provided for by Article 8(3) of Royal Decree No 2062/1999 could be justified by the fact that masters and chief mates exercise only rarely their powers of official authority while they are posted on board small vessels engaged on near-coastal navigation. Moreover, if the Member States cannot maintain a measure reserving the posts of master and chief mate of ships flying their flag to their nationals and are required to offer the possibility for nationals of the other Member States to obtain access, in certain circumstances, to those posts, the Tribunal Supremo seeks to ascertain whether it is compatible with EU law to make that possibility subject to a condition of reciprocity, as laid down by Article 8(3) of the Royal Decree No 2062/1999. The Tribunal Supremo decided to stay the proceedings and refer the questions to the CJEU for a preliminary ruling.

8.209 The first question[168] to the CJEU asked whether Article 45(4) of the TFEU[169] is to be interpreted as meaning that it allows a Member State to reserve for its nationals the posts of master and chief mate of merchant ships flying its flag and whether, in that regard, account must be taken of the fact that, for certain types of shipping, the performance by the master or chief mate of public-service duties within the meaning of the treaty is limited and occasional. The Spanish, Danish, German, Greek, French and Italian governments[170] and the European Commission agreed that the posts of master and chief mate of merchant ships flying a Member State's flag may, in accordance with Article 45(4) of the TFEU, be reserved for nationals of that Member State in so far as those holding such a post may, by virtue of the domestic law of that State and several international instruments, such as the United Nations Convention on the Law of the Sea ("UNCLOS"), perform duties belonging to the "public service" within the meaning of that provision, as interpreted by the CJEU, concerning the maintenance of safety and the exercise of police powers, as well as public certification and the drawing-up of certificates of births, marriages and deaths.[171] Those governments supported their views by referring to the increased potential risks on the high seas and the fact that ships there are beyond the reach of the public authorities, which necessitates the presence on board of a representative of the State, with decision-making power, in the person of the master. The CJEU stated:

> "31. Case C-114/97 Commission v Spain [1998] ECR I-6717,[172] paragraph 33, and Case C-283/99 Commission v Italy [2001] ECR I-4363,[173] paragraph 25, from which it is clear that the concept of 'employment in the public service' does not encompass employment by a private natural or legal person, are not relevant, notwithstanding the fact that the master of a merchantman is employed by a private shipowner. According to the Danish, Greek, and French Governments and the Commission, what is important is that, even where there is no organic relationship with the administrative authorities, the master has powers conferred by public law for the purposes of the general interests of the State, which, as the German Government also submits, accords with the functional view of the public service underlying the Court's case-law.
>
> 32. However, the Spanish Government submits that reserving the posts of master and chief mate of ships flying the flag of a Member State for nationals of that State is compatible with Article [45(4) TFEU] only if the actual exercise of public duties is foreseeable and reasonable. That is the basis for Article 8(3) of Royal Decree No 2062/1999, which allows nationals of other Member States to have command of small and medium-sized Spanish ships the range of which is limited and which sail within Spanish territorial waters, so that acts in exercise of public law powers can easily be put off. Such is the case of vessels used mainly for leisure and tourism.
>
> 33. On the other hand, the Danish, Greek, French and Italian Governments and the Commission maintain that where the master of a vessel is entrusted by a Member State with powers

---

168 In specific terms, the first question stated: "1. Do Article 39 EC ... and Articles 1 and 4 of Council Regulation (EEC) No 1612/68 of 15 October 1968 on freedom of movement for workers within the Community permit a Member State to reserve the posts of master and chief mate of its merchant ships to its own nationals? If the reply is in the affirmative, may that reservation be formulated in absolute terms (for all types of merchant ships) or is it valid only in cases in which it is foreseeable and reasonable that it may be necessary for masters and chief mates on board actually to carry out certain public duties?"

169 Art. 45(4) of the TFEU provides: "The provisions of this Article shall not apply to employment in the public service."

170 The fact that so many Member States intervened demonstrates the sensitivity of the issue.

171 It is interesting to note that if the Member State allowed nationals of other States to perform such duties ashore then it would be difficult to see how the roles could be reserved to nationals on board ships.

172 Ed., ECLI:EU:C:1998:519.

173 Ed., ECLI:EU:C:2001:307.

under public law, the derogation provided for by Article [45(4) TFEU] may validly be invoked irrespective of the vessel's size, the number of passengers, its itinerary, its proximity to national territory or whether the master will actually perform the public duties in question, such as may be performed on vessels of any type at any time, whenever the situation on board so requires.

34. The Norwegian Government, after pointing out that, according to the Court's case-law, Article [45(4) TFEU], as an exception to the principle of freedom of movement of workers, must be strictly interpreted (see, among others, Case 152/73 Sotgiu [1974] ECR 153),[174] wonders whether the public duties traditionally devolved on ships' masters enable it to be stated that a master nowadays participates, directly or indirectly, in the exercise of powers conferred by public law. The Norwegian Government observes that, because of current technology, the need to make use of such authority is less than it formerly was, when ships were in general much longer at sea and when it was much more difficult to obtain instructions from national authorities. Moreover, more than half of the world's fleet is these days registered under flags of convenience and the fact that neither the master nor the crews of such vessels possess the nationality of the flag State does not, in general, cause any particular problem.

35. The Spanish, Greek, French and Italian Governments submit, in the alternative, that a Member State is entitled to reserve the posts of master and chief mate for its own nationals on the basis of Article [45(4) TFEU].

36. In that regard, the Commission contends that Article [45(4) TFEU] applies only to individuals whose personal conduct endangers public order or public safety. Furthermore, it is inappropriate to invoke it in order to exclude an entire profession from the application of the principle of freedom of movement for persons on the ground that its members are responsible for ensuring public order or safety on board (see, to that effect, Commission v Spain, cited above, paragraph 42). That view is borne out by Article 3(1) of Council Directive 64/221/EEC of 25 February 1964 on the co-ordination of special measures concerning the movement and residence of foreign nationals which are justified on grounds of public policy, public safety or public health (OJ, English Special Edition, Series I, 1963–1964, p. 117)."

8.210 The CJEU replied to the referring court in clear terms:

"37. It is appropriate to observe, at the outset, that Article [45(1) to (3) TFEU] lays down the principle of the free movement of workers and the abolition of all discrimination based on nationality between workers of the Member States. [Article 45(4) TFEU] provides, however, that the provisions of that article are not to apply to employment in the public service.

38. According to the Court's case-law, the concept of public service within the meaning of Article [45(4) TFEU] must be given uniform interpretation and application throughout the Community and cannot therefore be left entirely to the discretion of the Member States (see, in particular, Sotgiu, cited above, paragraph 5, and Case 149/79 Commission v Belgium [1980] ECR 3881,[175] paragraphs 12 and 18).

39. It covers posts which involve direct or indirect participation in the exercise of powers conferred by public law and duties designed to safeguard the general interests of the State or of other public authorities and thus presume on the part of those occupying them the existence of a special relationship of allegiance to the State and reciprocity of rights and duties which form the foundation of the bond of nationality (Commission v Belgium, cited above, paragraph 10, and Case C-290/94 Commission v Greece [1996] ECR I-3285,[176] paragraph 2).

40. On the other hand, the Article [45(4) TFEU] exception does not cover posts which, whilst coming under the State or other bodies governed by public law, still do not involve any

---

174 Ed., ECLI:EU:C:1974:13.
175 Ed., ECLI:EU:C:1980:297.
176 Ed., ECLI:EU:C:1996:265.

association with tasks belonging to the public service properly so called (Commission v Belgium, paragraph 11, and Commission v Greece, paragraph 2), nor, a fortiori, to employment by a private natural or legal person, whatever the duties of the employee (Commission v Spain, paragraph 33, and Commission v Italy, paragraph 25).

41. It is also clear from the Court's case-law that, as a derogation from the fundamental principle that workers in the Community should enjoy freedom of movement and not suffer discrimination, Article [45(4) TFEU] must be construed in such a way as to limit its scope to what is strictly necessary for safeguarding the interests which that provision allows the Member States to protect (see, in particular, Case 225/85 Commission v Italy [1987] ECR 2625,[177] paragraph 7).

42. In this case, Spanish law confers on masters and chief mates of merchant ships flying the Spanish flag, first, rights connected to the maintenance of safety and to the exercise of police powers, particularly in the case of danger on board, together with, in appropriate cases, powers of investigation, coercion and punishment, which go beyond the requirement merely to contribute to maintaining public safety by which any individual is bound, and, secondly, authority in respect of notarial matters and the registration of births, marriages and deaths, which cannot be explained solely by the requirements entailed in commanding the vessel. Such duties constitute participation in the exercise of rights under powers conferred by public law for the purposes of safeguarding the general interests of the flag State.

43. The fact that masters are employed by a private natural or legal person is not, as such, sufficient to exclude the application of Article [45(4) TFEU] since it is established that, in order to perform the public functions which are delegated to them, masters act as representatives of public authority, at the service of the general interests of the flag State.

44. However, recourse to the derogation from the freedom of movement for workers provided for by Article [45(4) TFEU] cannot be justified solely on the ground that rights under powers conferred by public law are granted by national law to holders of the posts in question. It is still necessary that such rights are in fact exercised on a regular basis by those holders and do not represent a very minor part of their activities. Indeed, as has been pointed out in paragraph 41 of this judgment, the scope of that derogation must be limited to what is strictly necessary for safeguarding the general interests of the Member State concerned, which cannot be imperilled if rights under powers conferred by public law are exercised only sporadically, even exceptionally, by nationals of other Member States.

45. It is clear from the statements of the referring court and the Spanish Government that the posts of master and chief mate in the Spanish merchant navy are posts in which exercise of the duty of representing the flag State is, in practice, only occasional.

46. Further, it should be noted that the United Nations Convention on the Law of the Sea does not require that a ship's master be a national of the flag State.

47. It remains to be considered whether the nationality condition to which access to the categories of employment in issue is subject may be justified on the basis of Article [45(3) TFEU].

48. In that regard, it is sufficient to recall that the right of Member States to restrict freedom of movement for persons on grounds of public policy, public security or public health is not intended to exclude economic sectors such as that of merchant shipping, or occupations, such as that of master or chief mate of merchantmen from the application of that principle as regards access to employment, but to allow Member States to refuse access to their territory or residence there to persons whose access or residence would in itself constitute a danger for public policy, public security or public health (see, as far as public health is concerned, Case 131/85 Gül [1986] ECR 1573,[178] paragraph 17, and as far as private security is concerned, Commission v Spain, paragraph 42).

49. Thus, a general exclusion from access to the posts of master and chief mate in the merchant navy cannot be justified on the grounds mentioned in Article [45(3) TFEU].

---

177 Ed., ECLI:EU:C:1987:284.
178 Ed., ECLI:EU:C:1986:200.

50. In view of the foregoing, the answer to the first question must be that Article [45(4) TFEU] is to be construed as allowing a Member State to reserve for its nationals the posts of master and chief mate of merchant ships flying its flag only if the rights under powers conferred by public law on masters and chief mates of such ships are actually exercised on a regular basis and do not represent a very minor part of their activities."

The second question

8.211 The second question to the CJEU asked, in essence, whether Article 45 of the TFEU must be interpreted as precluding a Member State making access by nationals of the other Member States to the posts of master and chief mate of merchant ships flying its flag such as those covered by Article 8(3) of the Royal Decree No 2062/1999 subject to a condition of reciprocity.

8.212 There were various observations made to the CJEU. Spain argued that the possibility of reserving the posts of master and chief mate of their merchant navy vessels for their nationals derives from a right conferred on the Member States by Article 45(4) of the TFEU, which they may exercise or restrict according to conditions laid down by their domestic legislation. France argued that, in so far as it excludes the employment which it refers to from the scope of the Treaty, Article 45(4) of the TFEU, constitutes a reservation of powers to the Member States and differs, in that regard, from the exceptions to the freedoms of movement provided for, in particular, by Articles 36, 45(3) and 52 of the TFEU. Moreover, France argued that contrary to what the Court has held in relation to recourse to the exceptions provided for by Article 36 of the TFEU, Member States cannot be required to justify the measures which they adopt in respect of such employment. A Member State should be free, France argued, to give access to certain such employment to nationals of certain Member States, on the conditions which it considers appropriate, such as on condition of reciprocity.[179] Norway also argued that, where a State allows workers from other Member States to occupy posts covered by Article 45(4) TFEU, no discrimination can be allowed with regard to such workers.

8.213 The Court's reply was crisp. The CJEU recalled[180] it was clear from the reply to the first question that the posts of master and chief mate in the merchant navy as referred to in Article 8(3) of Royal Decree No 2062/1999 cannot come within the scope of the exception provided for by Article 45(4) of the TFEU. Therefore, in accordance with Article 45(2)

---

179 The CJEU dismissed this line of argument: "54. Admittedly, the Court has held ... that once a Member State has admitted workers who are nationals of other Member States into its public service, Article 39(4) EC cannot justify discriminatory measures against them with regard to remuneration or other conditions of work. 55. However, the present case concerns the detailed rules themselves for access to employment in the public service, so that such case-law does not apply in the present case. Indeed, by confining themselves to laying down, for employment falling within the scope of Article [39(4) EC], an exception to the nationality condition for the nationals of only certain Member States with which, for example, there is reciprocity, the Spanish authorities have not abandoned the principle that such employment is reserved for Spanish nationals and have therefore not given general access to that employment. 56. The Commission maintains that the Member States may always decline to apply the exception laid down by Article [39(4) EC] for employment covered by that provision and give complete or partial access to such employment to the nationals of other Member States. However, where access is partial, it must be made subject to conditions which are objective and comply with Community law. 57. The requirement of reciprocity is incompatible with the principle of equal treatment (Case 1/72 *Frilli* [1972] ECR 457, [ECLI:EU:C:1972:56] paragraph 19, and Case 186/87 *Cowan* [1989] ECR 195 [ECLI:EU:C:1989:47], paragraph 20)."
180 In para. 59 of the judgment.

TFEU, any national of a Member State is entitled to access such posts free from any discrimination based on nationality. The CJEU also recalled[181] that it is evident from settled case law that implementation of the obligations imposed on Member States by the Treaty or secondary legislation cannot be made subject to a condition of reciprocity.[182] Therefore, the CJEU replied to the second question that Article 45 of the TFEU is to be construed as precluding a Member State making access by nationals of the other Member States to the posts of master and chief mate of merchant ships flying its flag, such as those covered by Article 8(3) of Royal Decree No 2062/1999, subject to a condition of reciprocity.

CJEU ruling to the Tribunal Supremo

8.214 The CJEU gave the following answers:

"1. Article [45(4) TFEU] is to be construed as allowing a Member State to reserve for its nationals the posts of master and chief mate of merchant ships flying its flag only if the rights under powers conferred by public law on masters and chief mates of such ships are actually exercised on a regular basis and do not represent a very minor part of their activities.
2. Article [45 of the TFEU] is to be construed as precluding a Member State making access by nationals of the other Member States to the posts of master and chief mate of merchant ships flying its flag, such as those covered by Article 8(3) of Royal Decree No 2062/1999 por el que se regula el nivel mínimo de formación en profesiones marítimas of 30 December 1999, subject to a condition of reciprocity."

Assessment

8.215 The preliminary ruling by the CJEU was a compromise between (a) the freedom of movement of employees and (b) the protection of the public policy exception. The CJEU does not want to interfere too much with the exception to be not just theoretical or possible but real.

The *Albert Anker, Klaas Ras, Albertus Snoek v Bundesrepublik Deutschland* case[183]

Introduction

8.216 On 30 September 2003, the CJEU ruled in the *Albert Anker, Klaas Ras, Albertus Snoek v Bundesrepublik Deutschland* case.[184] In general, the case concerned issues of free movement of workers and employment in the public service. In particular, it related to captains or masters of fishing vessels, the conferring on such persons of powers of public authority and the consequent reserving of these posts for nationals of the flag State. The case was a preliminary reference by the Schleswig-Holsteinisches Oberverwaltungsgericht in Germany on the interpretation of, what is now, Article 45(4) of the TFEU. In essence, the CJEU replied to the German court that

---

181 In para. 61 of the judgment.
182 E.g. Case C-163/99 *Portugal v Commission* [2001] ECR I-2613, ECLI:EU:C:2001:189, para. 22, and Case C-142/01 *Commission v Italy* [2002] ECR I-4541, ECLI:EU:C:2002:302, para. 7.
183 Case C-47/02. See Nesterowicz, "Sea Captains and Performance of Public Duties in European Law" [2004] LMCLQ 19. The Advocate-General was C Stix-Hackl.
184 Case C-47/02. See Nesterowicz, op. cit. at fn. 184 .

"Article [45(4) of the TFEU] must be construed as allowing a Member State to reserve for its nationals the post of master of vessels flying its flag and engaged in 'small-scale maritime shipping' ('Kleine Seeschifffahrt') only if the rights under powers conferred by public law granted to masters of such vessels are in fact exercised on a regular basis and do not represent a very minor part of their activities."

The case therefore recognised the rights of Member States to regulate certain matters (i.e. reserving certain posts to its own nationals) but only where there is a real need to do so. It was respectful of Member State sovereignty but intolerant of abuse of exception.

Essence of the dispute

8.217 The question arose in the course of proceedings between Messrs Anker, Ras and Snoek, who were Dutch nationals, and the Wasser- und Schiffahrtsdirektion Nord (i.e. Northern Authority for Waterways and Shipping) regarding access to employment as master of a fishing vessel flying the German flag.

Legal background

8.218 The CJEU began by considering the international perspective and examined Articles 91(1), 92(1), 94(1) to (3) and 97(1) and (2) of the UNCLOS. The court then turned to the Member State legislation. The CJEU recalled that paragraph 2(2) of the Schiffsbesetzungsverordnung (Ships' Crews Regulation) of 26 August 1998 (BGBl. I, p. 2577), as amended by the Verordnung of 29 October 2001 (BGBl. I, p. 2785), provided: "Irrespective of the gross registered tonnage, the master must be a German national within the meaning of the Grundgesetz [Basic Law] and hold a German certificate of competence." (It is notable that this was legislation from 2001 and not pre-European Economic Community ("EEC") legislation.) The CJEU then recalled:

"8. Certificates of competence obtained in another Member State or in [an EEA] Member State … by nationals of one of those States are recognised as equivalent to German certificates by virtue of Paragraph 21a(1) of the SchOffzAusbV, subject to compliance with the conditions laid down by Council Directive 89/48/EEC of 21 December 1988 on a general system for the recognition of higher-education diplomas awarded on completion of professional education and training of at least three years' duration (OJ 1989 L19, p. 16) or by Council Directive 92/51/EEC of 18 June 1992 on a second general system for the recognition of professional education and training to supplement Directive 89/48 (OJ 1992 L209, p. 25).[185] In particular, in relation to a position of command, Paragraph 21a(2) of the SchOffzAusbV requires proof that the person concerned has passed the aptitude test provided for by Article 4(1)(b) of Directive 89/48 or by Article 4(1)(b) of Directive 92/51. Under Paragraph 21c of the SchOffzAusbV, the Wasser- und Schiffahrtdirektion Nord is required, on application, to issue a certificate of validity of the qualifications recognised as equivalent in accordance with Paragraph 21a(1) of the SchOffzAusbV.

9. However, qualifications recognised as equivalent under Paragraph 21a of the SchOffzAusbV do not confer on persons who are not German nationals within the meaning of the Grundgesetz the right to command vessels flying the German flag. Paragraph 24 of the SchOffzAusbV provides as follows:

'The issue of certificates of competence to persons who are not German nationals within the meaning of the Grundgesetz but who fulfil the conditions for the grant of certificates

---

185 Ed, this case demonstrates that general EU law is also relevant to EU maritime employment law.

of competence (Paragraph 7) may be permitted. In that case, a certificate of seafaring competence shall not entitle the holder to command vessels sailing under the German flag. The certificate of competence shall bear an endorsement to that effect…'

10. In addition, under Paragraph 106 of the Seemannsgesetz (Law on Seafarers) of 26 July 1957 (BGBl. II, p. 713), as amended on several occasions, (hereinafter 'the SeemG'):

'1. The master shall be in command of all crew members (Paragraph 3) and of all other persons serving on board (Paragraph 7). Supreme authority shall be vested in him.
2. The master shall be responsible for the maintenance of order and safety on board and may take the measures necessary for that purpose under the following provisions and the legislation in force.
3. In case of direct danger to persons or the vessel, the master may enforce orders given to avert such danger, if need be by any necessary force, and temporary detention may be lawful. The fundamental rights under sentences 1 and 2 of Paragraph 2(2) and Paragraph 13(1) and (2) of the Grundgesetz may be curtailed. Where various means are available, those which involve the least prejudice to the persons concerned shall, as far as possible, be selected.
4. Physical force and temporary detention shall be lawful only where other means appear, from the outset, to be insufficient or have been shown to be so. Such measures shall be applied only so far as and to the extent that the performance of the master's duties under subparagraphs 2 and 3 requires them.
5. If the master is not in a position to exercise them himself, he may delegate his powers under subparagraphs 1 to 4 to the chief mate or chief engineer in the course of their duties. …'

11. Under Paragraph 115 of the SeemG, failure to obey the master's orders is punishable by criminal sanctions where such orders are given to combat dangers threatening persons, vessels or their cargo, to avoid disproportionate losses, to prevent serious disruption to the operation of the vessel, to comply with the provisions of public law on safety at sea and to maintain order and safety on board. The misuse of such power is itself punishable by criminal sanctions, under Paragraph 117, in conjunction with Paragraph 115(4), of the SeemG.
12. Several provisions of German law confer on masters of vessels flying the German flag duties in relation to the registration of births, marriages and deaths.
13. Thus, under Paragraph 45(1) of the Verordnung zur Ausführung des Personenstandsgesetzes (Regulation implementing the Law on personal status) of 12 August 1957 (BGBl. I, p. 1139), as last amended by the Verordnung of 17 December 2001 (BGBl. I, p. 3752, hereinafter 'the PersStdGAV'), the birth or death of a person on board a German vessel must be certified by a Registrar of births, marriages and deaths in the Registry of Berlin I. Under Paragraph 45(2), the birth or death must be notified to the master on the day after the event at the latest. If the person responsible for making the declaration terminates his passage prior to the expiry of that period, such notification must take place while that person is still on board the vessel in question. Under Paragraph 45(3), the master must draw up a formal report of the declaration of birth or death which he must then transmit to the first office for maritime registrations to which he can do so."

Factual background

8.219 The appellants were employed as seafarers on board fishing vessels flying the German flag and engaged in small-scale deep-sea fishing. They were holders of a "diploma voor Zeevisvaart SW V" (Netherlands Diploma in Seafaring on Fishing Vessels) which entitled them to command vessels of the category of those on which they were working.

8.220 The Wasser- und Schiffahrtsdirektion Nord granted Mr Ras authorisation to serve as chief mate or chief engineer on fishing vessels flying the German flag. Mr Ras then applied on the basis of Paragraph 21c of the SchOffzAusbV for a certificate of wider competence allowing him to serve also as master on fishing vessels flying the German flag. The Wasser- und Schiffahrtsdirektion Nord rejected that application.

8.221 Similar applications made by Messrs Anker and Snoek for authorisation to serve as master, chief mate or chief engineer on fishing vessels flying the German flag were also rejected by the Wasser- und Schiffahrtsdirektion Nord 1999 in so far as they related to the position of master. The Wasser- und Schiffahrtsdirektion Nord based its decision, in particular, on Paragraph 106(2) and (3) of the SeemG and on Paragraph 24, second sentence, of the SchOffzAusbV.

8.222 The actions brought against the Wasser- und Schiffahrtsdirektion Nord's rejections were dismissed, on the same grounds, by decisions of the Verwaltungsgericht (Administrative Court) of 14 November 2000. That court held that the position of ship's master involved the exercise of rights under powers conferred by public law for the purposes of, what is now, Article 45(4) of the TFEU.

8.223 Before the Oberverwaltungsgericht, the appellants in the main proceedings challenged the application, with regard to them, of Article 45(4) of the TFEU. The CJEU recalled that, as an exception to a freedom, Article 45(4) of the TFEU is to be construed strictly. They argued that the provision applies only where the post concerned presupposes a special relationship of allegiance to the State on the part of the person occupying it, which the bond of nationality seeks to safeguard. Such allegiance exists only if the post typically involves the exercise of rights under powers conferred by public law and if the holder is entrusted with responsibility for the general interests of the State. Those requirements are concurrent. The case of a master of a fishing vessel does not meet those requirements. Even if there are cases in which masters have made use of their rights under powers conferred by public law, these are of such secondary importance that they cannot in any event constitute the core of their activity.

The question referred

8.224 By its question, the referring court asked the CJEU, in essence, whether, what is now, Article 45(4) of the TFEU is to be interpreted as allowing a Member State to reserve for its nationals employment as the master of vessels which fly its flag and are engaged in "small-scale maritime shipping" ("Kleine Seeschifffahrt").

Ruling of the Court

8.225 The CJEU ruled:

"56. It is appropriate to observe, at the outset, that Article [45(1) to (3) TFEU] lays down the principle of the free movement of workers and the abolition of all discrimination based on nationality between workers of the Member States. Article [45(4) TFEU], however, provides that the provisions of that article are not to apply to employment in the public service.

57. The concept of public service within the meaning of Article [45(4) TFEU], must be given uniform interpretation and application throughout the EU and cannot therefore be left entirely to the discretion of the Member States.[186]
58. It covers posts which involve direct or indirect participation in the exercise of powers conferred by public law and duties designed to safeguard the general interests of the State or of other public authorities and thus presume on the part of those occupying them the existence of a special relationship of allegiance to the State and reciprocity of rights and duties which form the foundation of the bond of nationality...
59. On the other hand, the Article [45(4) TFEU], exception does not cover posts which, whilst coming under the State or other bodies governed by public law, still do not involve any association with tasks belonging to the public service properly so called nor, a fortiori, to employment by a private natural or legal person, whatever the duties of the employee.
60. It is also clear from the Court's case-law that, as a derogation from the fundamental principle that workers in the [EU] should enjoy freedom of movement and not suffer discrimination, Article [45(4) TFEU], must be construed in such a way as to limit its scope to what is strictly necessary for safeguarding the interests which that provision allows the Member States to protect...
61. In this case, German law confers on masters of fishing vessels flying the German flag rights connected to the maintenance of safety and to the exercise of police powers, particularly in the case of danger on board, together with, in appropriate cases, powers of investigation, coercion and punishment, which go beyond the requirement merely to contribute to maintaining public safety by which any individual is bound. Furthermore, certain auxiliary duties in respect of the registration of births, marriages and deaths, which cannot be explained solely by the requirements entailed in commanding the vessel, are conferred on the master, in particular that of receiving notification of a person's birth or death during a voyage, even if it is the responsibility of a registrar of births, marriages and deaths, on land, to issue the official certificates. While certain doubts may persist, in respect of those duties relating to the registration of births, marriages and deaths, as to whether they involve direct or indirect participation in the exercise of powers conferred by public law, doubts which it is the responsibility of the referring court to resolve, it is clear, on the other hand, that the duties connected to the maintenance of safety and to the exercise of police powers constitute participation in the exercise of rights under powers conferred by public law for the purposes of safeguarding the general interests of the flag State.
62. The fact that masters are employed by a private natural or legal person is not, as such, sufficient to exclude the application of Article [45(4) TFEU], since it is established that, in order to perform the public functions which are delegated to them, masters act as representatives of public authority in the service of the general interests of the flag State.
63. However, recourse to the derogation from the freedom of movement for workers provided for by Article [45(4) TFEU], cannot be justified solely on the ground that rights under powers conferred by public law are granted by national law to holders of the posts in question. It is also necessary that such rights are in fact exercised on a regular basis by those holders and do not represent a very minor part of their activities. Indeed, as has been pointed out in paragraph 60 of this judgment, the scope of that derogation must be limited to what is strictly necessary for safeguarding the general interests of the Member State concerned, which would not be imperilled if rights under powers conferred by public law were exercised only sporadically, indeed exceptionally, by nationals of other Member States.
64. It is clear from the statements of the referring Court that posts of master of small-scale deep-sea fishing vessels, which consist, essentially, in skippering small boats, with a small crew, and in participating directly in fishing and in the processing of the fish products, are posts in which the duty of representing the flag State is, in practice, insignificant.
65. ...the United Nations Convention on the Law of the Sea does not require that a ship's master be a national of the flag State.

---

[186] Ed., see, in particular, Case 152/73 *Sotgiu* [1974] ECR 153, ECLI:EU:C:1974:13, para. 5, and Case 149/79 *Commission v Belgium* [1980] ECR 3881, ECL1:EU:C:1982: 195, paras 12 and 18.

66. It remains to be considered whether the nationality condition to which access to the categories of employment in issue is subject may be justified on the basis of Article [45(4) TFEU].
67. In this regard, it is sufficient to recall that the right of Member States to restrict the free movement of persons on grounds of public policy, public security or public health is not intended to exclude economic sectors such as fishing or occupations, such as master of fishing vessels, from the application of that principle as regards access to employment, but to allow Member States to refuse access to their territory or residence there to persons whose access or residence would in itself constitute a danger for public policy, public security or public health (see, as far as public health is concerned, Case 131/85 Gül [1986] ECR 1573, paragraph 17, and, as far as private security is concerned, Commission v Spain, paragraph 42).
68. Thus, a general exclusion from access to the post of master of fishing vessels cannot be justified on the grounds mentioned in Article [45(4) TFEU].

8.226 The CJEU thus replied to the Schleswig-Holsteinisches Oberverwaltungsgericht that

"Article [45(4) TFEU], must be construed as allowing a Member State to reserve for its nationals the post of master of vessels flying its flag and engaged in 'small-scale maritime shipping' ('Kleine Seeschifffahrt') only if the rights under powers conferred by public law granted to masters of such vessels are in fact exercised on a regular basis and do not represent a very minor part of their activities."

It is reasonably clear that the CJEU was being respectful of the Member State's right to legislate for national exceptions to EU rights but only where there was a real, substantial and legitimate reason to do so.

L. COLLECTIVE ACTIONS AND SEAFARERS

The International Transport Workers' Federation, Finnish Seamen's Union v Viking Line ABP *case*

Introduction

8.227 On 11 December 2007, in the so-called *Viking* case[187] the Grand Chamber[188] of the CJEU[189] strengthened the principles of freedom of establishment and freedom to provide services vis-à-vis the rights of trade unions to take collective action. A key question for the CJEU was whether the "freedom of establishment" applied to collective action taken by a trade union to negotiate conditions of employment and workers' pay when it was notified of an employer's decision to reflag the vessel. The case is one of the most important in EU employment law generally and not just in EU maritime employment law. The *Viking* case was one of a quartet of cases decided over a six month period

---

187 The case was more fully entitled *International Transport Workers' Federation, Finnish Seamen's Union v Viking Line ABP, OÜ Viking Line Eesti.* It was numbered Case C-438/05. It is reported at [2007] ECR I-10779, ECLI:EU:C:2007:772. See Freedland and Prassi (eds), *Viking, Laval and Beyond* (2016).
188 The use of a Grand Chamber indicates the importance attached to the case by the CJEU.
189 Court composed of Judges Skouris (President), Jann, Rosas, Lenaerts, Lõhmus, Bay Larsen, Schintgen (Rapporteur), Silva de Lapuerta, Schiemann, Makarczyk, Kūris, Levits and Ó Caoimh. The Advocate-General was AG Poiares Maduro.

by the CJEU which were critical to the evolution of EU employment law: these were the *Viking*,[190] *Lavat*,[191] *Rüffert*[192] and *Commission v Luxembourg*[193] cases.

8.228 The facts of the *Viking* case were straightforward. It related to an action by the International Transport Federation ("ITF") against the collective bargaining agreement relating to Estonian seafarers working on board a ferry plying between Finland and Estonia. The result of the judgment was that the CJEU must respect the right of establishment while the right of collective action would also be confirmed provided the collective action was proportionate and it would be for a decision in each case whether it was proportionate.

8.229 The operative part of the judgment was straightforward and before examining the detail of the ruling, it is useful to bear it in mind given the complexity of the EU generally:

> "Article [49 TFEU] is to be interpreted as meaning that, in principle, collective action initiated by a trade union or a group of trade unions against a private undertaking in order to induce that undertaking to enter into a collective agreement, the terms of which are liable to deter it from exercising freedom of establishment, is not excluded from the scope of that article.
>
> Article [49 TFEU] is capable of conferring rights on a private undertaking which may be relied on against a trade union or an association of trade unions.
>
> Article [49 TFEU] is to be interpreted to the effect that collective action such as that at issue in the main proceedings, which seeks to induce a private undertaking whose registered office is in a given Member State to enter into a collective work agreement with a trade union established in that State and to apply the terms set out in that agreement to the employees of a subsidiary of that undertaking established in another Member State, constitutes a restriction within the meaning of that article.
>
> That restriction may, in principle, be justified by an overriding reason of public interest, such as the protection of workers, provided that it is established that the restriction is suitable for ensuring the attainment of the legitimate objective pursued and does not go beyond what is necessary to achieve that objective."

8.230 The case was a result of a preliminary reference from the Court of Appeal (Civil Division) in London. The reference sought a preliminary ruling concerning the interpretation of: (a) what is now Article 49 of the TFEU and (b) Regulation 4055/86 of 22 December 1986 applying the principle of freedom to provide services to maritime transport between Member States and between Member States and third countries.[194]

8.231 There had been a dispute before the English courts between, on the one hand, the ITF and the Finnish Seamen's Union (Suomen Merimies-Unioni ry (the "FSU") and, on the other hand, Viking Line ABP ("Viking") and its subsidiary OÜ Viking Line Eesti ("Viking Eesti"). Viking wanted to reflag one of its vessels from the Finnish flag to that of another Member State. The trade unions were involved in actual or threatened collective action to deter Viking from doing so. If there was such a dispute post-Brexit, it may well be that there would be no possibility of a preliminary reference to the CJEU from the English courts.

---

190 Case C-438/05, [2007] ECR I-10779, ECLI:EU:C:2007:772.
191 Case C-341/05, [2007] ECR I-11767, ECLI:EU:C:2007:809.
192 Case C-346/06, [2008] ECR I-1989, ECLI:EU:C:2008:189.
193 Case C-319/06, [2008] ECR I-4323, ECLI:EU:C:2008:350.
194 OJ 1986 L378/1, see chap. 7 generally.

Legal context

8.232 The CJEU begun by recalling the relevant EU law background. Article 1(1) of Regulation 4055/86 provides:

"Freedom to provide maritime transport services between Member States and between Member States and third countries shall apply in respect of nationals of Member States who are established in a Member State other than that of the person for whom the services are intended."

Article 1 of Regulation 4005/86 gave Viking the right to provide services. In terms of Finnish national law, the CJEU understood (from the reference) that, Article 13 of the Finnish Constitution, which confers on all individuals the freedom to form trade unions and freedom of association in order to safeguard other interests, has been interpreted as allowing trade unions to initiate collective action against companies in order to defend workers' interests. However, the right to strike was subject to certain limitations. Thus, according to Finland's Supreme Court, it may not be relied on, *inter alia*, where the strike is *contra bonos mores* or is prohibited under national law or under EU law.

The dispute

8.233 Viking was a Finnish ferry operator. It operated the vessel called the *Rosella* which, under the Finnish flag, plied the route between Tallinn (in Estonia) and Helsinki (in Finland). The FSU was a Finnish union of seafarers. The crew of the *Rosella* were members of the FSU. The FSU was affiliated to the ITF. The ITF grouped together 600 unions in 140 different States. One of the principal ITF policies was its "Flag of Convenience" ("FOC") policy. The primary objectives of this policy were, to establish a *genuine link* between the flag of the ship and the nationality of the owner and to protect and enhance the conditions of seafarers on FOC ships. ITF considers that a vessel is registered under a flag of convenience where the beneficial ownership and control of the vessel is found to lie in a State other than the State of the flag. In accordance with the ITF policy, only unions established in the State of beneficial ownership have the right to conclude collective agreements covering the vessel concerned. The FOC campaign is enforced by boycotts and other solidarity actions among workers.

8.234 So long as the vessel flew the Finnish flag, Viking was obliged under Finnish law and the terms of a collective bargaining agreement to pay the crew wages at Finnish levels. Estonian crew wages are lower than Finnish crew wages. The *Rosella* was running at a loss as a result of direct competition from Estonian vessels operating on the same route with lower wage costs. As an alternative to selling the vessel, Viking sought to reflag it by registering it in either Estonia or Norway, to be able to enter into a new collective agreement with a trade union established in one of those States. In accordance with Finnish law, Viking notified its plans to the FSU and to the crew of the *Rosella*. The FSU opposed the plans. The FSU sent an email to ITF which referred to the plan to reflag the *Rosella*. The email further stated that "the *Rosella* was beneficially owned in Finland and that FSU therefore kept the right to negotiate with Viking". FSU asked ITF to pass this information on to all affiliated unions and to request them not to enter into negotiations with Viking. The ITF then sent a circular (the "ITF circular") to its affiliates asking them to refrain from entering into negotiations with Viking or Viking Eesti. The affiliates were expected to follow this recommendation because of the principle of solidarity between trade unions and the sanctions which they could face if they failed to comply with that circular. The manning agreement for the *Rosella* expired and therefore the FSU was, as from that date, no longer under an obligation of industrial peace under Finnish law. Consequently, it gave notice of a strike requiring Viking, on the one hand, to increase the manning on the *Rosella* by eight and, on the other, to give up its plans to reflag the *Rosella*. Viking conceded the extra eight crew but refused to give up its plans to reflag. The FSU was still not prepared to accept the concession, however, it indicated that it would only accept such renewal on two conditions: first, that Viking, regardless of a possible change of the *Rosella*'s flag, undertook that it would continue to follow Finnish law, the collective bargaining agreement, the general agreement and the manning agreement on the *Rosella* and, second, that the possible change of flag would not lead to any laying-off of employees on any Finnish flag vessel belonging to Viking, or to changes to the terms and conditions of employment without the consent of the employees. In press statements, the FSU justified its position by the need to protect Finnish jobs.

8.235 Viking started legal proceedings before the employment tribunal in Finland for a declaration that, contrary to the view of the FSU, the manning agreement remained binding on the parties. On the basis of its view that the manning agreement was at an end, the FSU gave notice, in accordance with Finnish law on industrial dispute mediation, that it intended to commence strike action in relation to the *Rosella*. Viking learnt of the existence of the ITF circular. It brought proceedings before the Court of First Instance of Helsinki in Finland to restrain the planned strike action. A preparatory hearing date was set. According to the referring court, the FSU was fully aware of the fact that its principal demand, that in the event of reflagging, the crew should continue to be employed on the conditions laid down by Finnish law and the applicable collective agreement, would render reflagging pointless, since the whole purpose of such reflagging was to enable Viking to reduce its wage costs. Furthermore, a consequence of reflagging the *Rosella* to Estonia would be that Viking would, at least as regards the *Rosella*, no longer be able to claim State aid which the Finnish government granted to Finnish flag vessels. In the course of conciliation proceedings, Viking gave an undertaking, at an initial stage, that the reflagging would not involve any redundancies. Since FSU nevertheless refused to defer the strike, Viking put an end to the dispute accepting the trade union's demands and discontinuing judicial proceedings. Furthermore, it undertook not to commence reflagging prior to 28 February 2005. On 1 May 2004, Estonia became a member of the EU. Since the *Rosella* continued to run at a loss, Viking pursued its intention to reflag the vessel to Estonia. Because the ITF circular remained in force, on account of the fact that the ITF had never withdrawn it, the request to affiliated unions from the ITF in relation to the *Rosella* consequently remained in effect.

8.236 On 18 August 2004, Viking brought an action before the English High Court, requesting it to declare that the action taken by ITF and FSU was contrary to, what is now, Article 49 of the TFEU, to order the withdrawal of the ITF circular and to order FSU not to infringe the rights which Viking enjoys under EU law. The court granted the form of order sought by Viking, on the grounds that the actual and threatened collective action by the ITF and FSU imposed restrictions on freedom of establishment contrary to Article 49 of the TFEU and, in the alternative, constituted unlawful restrictions on freedom of movement for workers and freedom to provide services.

8.237 The CJEU described the background. Given the extensive questions asked, it is useful to cite the questions in full. It is useful to note that Article 43 of the EC Treaty is now Article 49 of the TFEU.

> "24. On 30 June 2005, ITF and FSU brought an appeal against that decision before the referring court. In support of their appeal they claimed, inter alia, that the right of trade unions to take collective action to preserve jobs is a fundamental right recognised by Title XI of the then EC Treaty and, in particular, Article 136 EC, the first paragraph of which provides that '[t]he Community and the Member States, having in mind fundamental social rights such as those set out in the European Social Charter signed at Turin on 18 October 1961 and in the 1989 Community Charter of the Fundamental Social Rights of Workers, shall have as their objectives the promotion of employment, improved living and working conditions, so as to make possible their harmonisation while the improvement is being maintained, proper social protection, dialogue between management and labour, the development of human resources with a view to lasting high employment and the combating of exclusion'.
>
> 25. It was argued that the reference to the European Social Charter and the Community Charter of the Fundamental Social Rights of Workers incorporated a reference to the right to strike recognised by those legal instruments. Consequently, the trade unions had the right to take collective action against an employer established in a Member State to seek to persuade him not to move part or all of his undertaking to another Member State.
>
> 26. The question therefore arises whether the Treaty intends to prohibit trade union action where it is aimed at preventing an employer from exercising his right of establishment for economic reasons. By analogy with the Court's rulings regarding Title VI of the Treaty (Case C-67/96 Albany [1999] ECR I-5751;[195] Joined Cases C-180/98 to C-184/98 Pavlov and Others [2000] ECR I-6451;[196] and Case C-222/98 Van der Woude [2000] ECR I-7111[197]), it is argued that Title III of the Treaty and the articles relating to free movement of persons and of services do not apply to 'genuine trade union activities'.
>
> 27. In those circumstances, since it considered that the outcome of the case before it depended on the interpretation of Community law, the Court of Appeal (England and Wales) (Civil Division) decided to stay proceedings and refer the following questions to the Court for a preliminary ruling:
>
> 'Scope of the free movement provisions
>
> (1) Where a trade union or association of trade unions takes collective action against a private undertaking so as to require that undertaking to enter into a collective bargaining agreement with a trade union in a particular Member State which has the effect of making it pointless for that undertaking to re-flag a vessel in another Member State, does that action fall outside the scope of Article 43 EC[198] and/or Regulation No 4055/86 by virtue of the EC's social policy including, inter alia, Title XI of the EC Treaty and, in particular, by analogy with the Court's reasoning in ... *Albany* (paragraphs 52 to 64)?
>
> Horizontal direct effect
>
> (2) Do Article [49 TFEU] and/or Regulation No 4055/86 have horizontal direct effect so as to confer rights on a private undertaking which may be relied on against another private party and, in particular, a trade union or association of trade unions in respect of collective action by that union or association of unions?

---

195 Ed., ECLI:EU:C:1999:430.
196 Ed., ECLI:EU:C:2000:428.
197 Ed., ECLI:EU:C:2000:475.
198 Ed., now Art. 49 of the TFEU.

Existence of restrictions on free movement

(3) Where a trade union or association of trade unions takes collective action against a private undertaking so as to require that undertaking to enter into a collective bargaining agreement with a trade union in a particular Member State, which has the effect of making it pointless for that undertaking to re-flag a vessel in another Member State, does that action constitute a restriction for the purposes of Article [49 TFEU] and/or Regulation No 4055/86?

(4) Is a policy of an association of trade unions which provides that vessels should be flagged in the registry of the country in which the beneficial ownership and control of the vessel is situated so that the trade unions in the country of beneficial ownership of a vessel have the right to conclude collective bargaining agreements in respect of that vessel, a directly discriminatory, indirectly discriminatory or non-discriminatory restriction under Article [49 TFEU] or Regulation No 4055/86?

(5) In determining whether collective action by a trade union or association of trade unions is a directly discriminatory, indirectly discriminatory or non-discriminatory restriction under Article [49 TFEU] or Regulation No 4055/86, is the subjective intention of the union taking the action relevant or must the national court determine the issue solely by reference to the objective effects of that action?

Establishment/services

(6) Where a parent company is established in Member State A and intends to undertake an act of establishment by reflagging a vessel to Member State B to be operated by an existing wholly owned subsidiary in Member State B which is subject to the direction and control of the parent company:

   (a) is threatened or actual collective action by a trade union or association of trade unions which would seek to render the above a pointless exercise capable of constituting a restriction on the parent company's right of establishment under Article [49 TFEU], and
   (b) after reflagging of the vessel, is the subsidiary entitled to rely on Regulation No 4055/86 in respect of the provision of services by it from Member State B to Member State A?

Justification
Direct discrimination

(7) If collective action by a trade union or association of trade unions is a directly discriminatory restriction under Article [49 TFEU] or Regulation No 4055/86, can it, in principle, be justified on the basis of the public policy exception set out in Article 46 EC[199] on the basis that:

   (a) the taking of collective action (including strike action) is a fundamental right protected by Community law; and/or
   (b) the protection of workers?

The policy of [ITF]: objective justification

(8) Does the application of a policy of an association of trade unions which provides that vessels should be flagged in the registry of the country in which the beneficial ownership and control of the vessel is situated so that the trade unions in the country of beneficial ownership of a vessel have the right to conclude collective bargaining agreements in respect of that vessel, strike a fair balance between the fundamental social right to take collective action and the freedom to establish and provide services, and is it objectively justified, appropriate, proportionate and in conformity with the principle of mutual recognition?

---

199 Ed., this is now, in substance, Art. 52 TFEU.

FSU's actions: objective justification

(9) Where:

- a parent company in Member State A owns a vessel flagged in Member State A and provides ferry services between Member State A and Member State B using that vessel;
- the parent company wishes to re-flag the vessel to Member State B to apply terms and conditions of employment which are lower than in Member State A;
- the parent company in Member State A wholly owns a subsidiary in Member State B and that subsidiary is subject to its direction and control;
  - it is intended that the subsidiary will operate the vessel once it has been re-flagged in Member State B with a crew recruited in Member State B covered by a collective bargaining agreement negotiated with an ITF affiliated trade union in Member State B;
- the vessel will remain beneficially owned by the parent company and be bareboat chartered to the subsidiary;
- the vessel will continue to provide ferry services between Member State A and Member State B on a daily basis;
- a trade union established in Member State A takes collective action so as to require the parent and/or subsidiary to enter into a collective bargaining agreement with it which will apply terms and conditions acceptable to the union in Member State A to the crew of the vessel even after reflagging and which has the effect of making it pointless for the parent to re-flag the vessel to Member State B,
  does that collective action strike a fair balance between the fundamental social right to take collective action and the freedom to establish and provide services and is it objectively justified, appropriate, proportionate and in conformity with the principle of mutual recognition?

(10) Would it make any difference to the answer to [Question] 9 if the parent company provided an undertaking to a court on behalf of itself and all the companies within the same group that they will not by reason of the reflagging terminate the employment of any person employed by them (which undertaking did not require the renewal of short term employment contracts or prevent the redeployment of any employee on equivalent terms and conditions)?'"

8.238 The CJEU made a number of preliminary observations. The CJEU recalled that

"it is solely for the national court before which a dispute has been brought, and which must assume responsibility for the subsequent judicial decision, to determine in the light of the particular circumstances of the case both the need for a preliminary ruling in order to enable it to deliver judgment and the relevance of the questions which it submits to the Court. However, the Court has regarded itself as not having jurisdiction to give a preliminary ruling on a question submitted by a national court where it is quite obvious, inter alia, that the interpretation of Community law sought by that court bears no relation to the actual facts of the main action or its purpose or where the problem is hypothetical."[200]

8.239 Interestingly, the CJEU rejected the request for interpretation of Regulation 4055/86 because it was hypothetical and the CJEU does not deal with hypothetical cases:

"29. In the present case, the reference for a preliminary ruling concerns the interpretation, first, of provisions of the Treaty on freedom of establishment, and secondly, of Regulation No 4055/86 applying the principle of freedom to provide services to maritime transport.

---

[200] Para. 28.

30. However, since the question on freedom to provide services can arise only after the reflagging of the Rosella envisaged by Viking, and since, on the date on which the questions were referred to the Court, the vessel had not yet been re-flagged, the reference for a preliminary ruling is hypothetical and thus inadmissible in so far as it relates to the interpretation of Regulation No 4055/86.
31. In those circumstances, the questions referred by the national court can be answered only in so far as they concern the interpretation of Article [49 TFEU]."

The first question

8.240 In the first question, the UK court asked whether Article 49 of the TFEU must be interpreted as meaning that collective action initiated by a trade union or a group of trade unions against an undertaking in order to induce that undertaking to enter into a collective agreement, the terms of which are liable to deter it from exercising freedom of establishment, falls outside the scope of that article. The CJEU opined:

"33. In this regard, it must be borne in mind that, according to settled case-law, Articles 39 EC,[201] 43 EC[202] and 49 EC[203] do not apply only to the actions of public authorities but extend also to rules of any other nature aimed at regulating in a collective manner gainful employment, self-employment and the provision of services.
34. Since working conditions in the different Member States are governed sometimes by provisions laid down by law or regulation and sometimes by collective agreements and other acts concluded or adopted by private persons, limiting application of the prohibitions laid down by these articles to acts of a public authority would risk creating inequality in its application.
35. In the present case, it must be stated, first, that the organisation of collective action by trade unions must be regarded as covered by the legal autonomy which those organisations, which are not public law entities, enjoy pursuant to the trade union rights accorded to them, inter alia, by national law.
36. Secondly, as FSU and ITF submit, collective action such as that at issue in the main proceedings, which may be the trade unions' last resort to ensure the success of their claim to regulate the work of Viking's employees collectively, must be considered to be inextricably linked to the collective agreement the conclusion of which FSU is seeking.
37. It follows that collective action such as that described in the first question referred by the national court falls, in principle, within the scope of Article [49 TFEU].
38. This view is not called into question by the various arguments put forward by FSU, ITF and certain Member States which submitted observations to the Court to support the position contrary to that set out in the previous paragraph.
39. First of all, the Danish Government submits that the right of association, the right to strike and the right to impose lock-outs fall outside the scope of the fundamental freedom laid down in Article [49 TFEU] since, in accordance with Article 137(5) EC,[204] as amended by the Treaty of Nice, the Community does not have competence to regulate those rights.
40. In that respect it is sufficient to point out that, even if, in the areas which fall outside the scope of the Community's competence, the Member States are still free, in principle, to lay down the conditions governing the existence and exercise of the rights in question, the fact remains that, when exercising that competence, the Member States must nevertheless comply with Community law.
41. Consequently, the fact that Article [153 of the TFEU]does not apply to the right to strike or to the right to impose lock-outs is not such as to exclude collective action such as that at issue in the main proceedings from the application of Article [49 of the TFEU].

---

201 Ed., Art. 49 TFEU.
202 Ed., Art. 49 TFEU.
203 Ed., Art. 56 TFEU which is similar to Art. 49 TEC.
204 Ed., Art. 153 TFEU draws on Art. 137 TEC.

42. Next, according to the observations of the Danish and Swedish Governments, the right to take collective action, including the right to strike, constitutes a fundamental right which, as such, falls outside the scope of Article [49 of the TFEU].

43. In that regard, it must be recalled that the right to take collective action, including the right to strike, is recognised both by various international instruments which the Member States have signed or cooperated in, such as the European Social Charter, signed at Turin on 18 October 1961 – to which, moreover, express reference is made in Article 136 EC[205] – and Convention No 87 concerning Freedom of Association and Protection of the Right to Organise, adopted on 9 July 1948 by the International Labour Organisation – and by instruments developed by those Member States at Community level or in the context of the European Union, such as the Community Charter of the Fundamental Social Rights of Workers adopted at the meeting of the European Council held in Strasbourg on 9 December 1989, which is also referred to in Article 136 EC, and the Charter of Fundamental Rights of the European Union proclaimed in Nice on 7 December 2000 (OJ 2000 C364, p. 1).

44. Although the right to take collective action, including the right to strike, must therefore be recognised as a fundamental right which forms an integral part of the general principles of Community law the observance of which the Court ensures, the exercise of that right may none the less be subject to certain restrictions. As is reaffirmed by Article 28 of the Charter of Fundamental Rights of the European Union, those rights are to be protected in accordance with Community law and national law and practices. In addition, as is apparent from paragraph 5 of this judgment, under Finnish law the right to strike may not be relied on, in particular, where the strike is contra bonos mores or is prohibited under national law or Community law.

45. In that regard, the Court has already held that the protection of fundamental rights is a legitimate interest which, in principle, justifies a restriction of the obligations imposed by Community law, even under a fundamental freedom guaranteed by the Treaty, such as the free movement of goods or freedom to provide services.

46. However, in Schmidberger and Omega,[206] the Court held that the exercise of the fundamental rights at issue, that is, freedom of expression and freedom of assembly and respect for human dignity, respectively, does not fall outside the scope of the provisions of the Treaty and considered that such exercise must be reconciled with the requirements relating to rights protected under the Treaty and in accordance with the principle of proportionality (see, to that effect, Schmidberger, paragraph 77, and Omega, paragraph 36).

47. It follows from the foregoing that the fundamental nature of the right to take collective action is not such as to render Article [49 of the TFEU] inapplicable to the collective action at issue in the main proceedings.

48. Finally, FSU and ITF submit that the Court's reasoning in Albany[207] must be applied by analogy to the case in the main proceedings, since certain restrictions on freedom of establishment and freedom to provide services are inherent in collective action taken in the context of collective negotiations.

49. In that regard, it should be noted that in paragraph 59 of Albany, having found that certain restrictions of competition are inherent in collective agreements between organisations representing employers and workers, the Court nevertheless held that the social policy objectives pursued by such agreements would be seriously undermined if management and labour were subject to Article [101 TFEU] when seeking jointly to adopt measures to improve conditions of work and employment.

50. The Court inferred from this, in paragraph 60 of Albany, that agreements concluded in the context of collective negotiations between management and labour in pursuit of such objectives must, by virtue of their nature and purpose, be regarded as falling outside the scope of Article [101(1) TFEU].

---

205 Ed., Art. 151 TFEU.
206 Ed., Case C-36/02 [2004] ECR I-9609, ECLI:EU:C:2004:614.
207 Ed., Case C-67/96 [1999] ECR I-5751, ECLI:EU:C:1999:430.

51. The Court must point out, however, that that reasoning cannot be applied in the context of the fundamental freedoms set out in Title III of the Treaty.
52. Contrary to the claims of FSU and ITF, it cannot be considered that it is inherent in the very exercise of trade union rights and the right to take collective action that those fundamental freedoms will be prejudiced to a certain degree.
53. Furthermore, the fact that an agreement or an activity are excluded from the scope of the provisions of the Treaty on competition does not mean that that agreement or activity also falls outside the scope of the Treaty provisions on the free movement of persons or services since those two sets of provisions are to be applied in different circumstances (see, to that effect, Case C-519/04 P Meca-Medina and Majcen v Commission [2006] ECR I-6991).[208]
54. Finally, the Court has held that the terms of collective agreements are not excluded from the scope of the Treaty provisions on freedom of movement for persons (Case C-15/96 Schöning-Kougebetopoulou [1998] ECR I-47;[209] Case C-35/97 Commission v France [1998] ECR I-5325;[210] and Case C-400/02 Merida [2004] ECR I-8471[211]).
55. In the light of the foregoing, the answer to the first question must be that Article [49 TFEU] is to be interpreted as meaning that, in principle, collective action initiated by a trade union or a group of trade unions against an undertaking in order to induce that undertaking to enter into a collective agreement, the terms of which are liable to deter it from exercising freedom of establishment, is not excluded from the scope of that article."

The second question

8.241 The second question was dealt with by the CJEU as follows:

"56. By that question, the referring court is asking in essence whether Article [49 TFEU] is such as to confer rights on a private undertaking which may be relied on against a trade union or an association of trade unions.
57. In order to answer that question, the Court would point out that it is clear from its case-law that the abolition, as between Member States, of obstacles to freedom of movement for persons and freedom to provide services would be compromised if the abolition of State barriers could be neutralised by obstacles resulting from the exercise, by associations or organisations not governed by public law, of their legal autonomy.
58. Moreover, the Court has ruled, first, that the fact that certain provisions of the Treaty are formally addressed to the Member States does not prevent rights from being conferred at the same time on any individual who has an interest in compliance with the obligations thus laid down, and, second, that the prohibition on prejudicing a fundamental freedom laid down in a provision of the Treaty that is mandatory in nature, applies in particular to all agreements intended to regulate paid labour collectively.
59. Such considerations must also apply to Article [49 TFEU] which lays down a fundamental freedom.
60. In the present case, it must be borne in mind that, as is apparent from paragraphs 35 and 36 of the present judgment, the collective action taken by FSU and ITF is aimed at the conclusion of an agreement which is meant to regulate the work of Viking's employees collectively, and, that those two trade unions are organisations which are not public law entities but exercise the legal autonomy conferred on them, inter alia, by national law.
61. It follows that Article [49 TFEU] must be interpreted as meaning that, in circumstances such as those in the main proceedings, it may be relied on by a private undertaking against a trade union or an association of trade unions.

---

208 Ed., ECLI:EU:C:2006:492.
209 Ed., ECLI:EU:C:1998:3.
210 Ed., ECLI:EU:C:1998:431.
211 Ed., ECLI:EU:C:200:737.

62. This interpretation is also supported by the case-law on the Treaty provisions on the free movement of goods, from which it is apparent that restrictions may be the result of actions by individuals or groups of such individuals rather than caused by the State.
63. The interpretation set out in paragraph 61 of the present judgment is also not called into question by the fact that the restriction at issue in the proceedings before the national court stems from the exercise of a right conferred by Finnish national law, such as, in this case, the right to take collective action, including the right to strike.
64. It must be added that, contrary to the claims, in particular, of ITF, it does not follow from the case-law of the Court referred to in paragraph 57 of the present judgment that that interpretation applies only to quasi-public organisations or to associations exercising a regulatory task and having quasi-legislative powers.
65. There is no indication in that case-law that could validly support the view that it applies only to associations or to organisations exercising a regulatory task or having quasi-legislative powers. Furthermore, it must be pointed out that, in exercising their autonomous power, pursuant to their trade union rights, to negotiate with employers or professional organisations the conditions of employment and pay of workers, trade unions participate in the drawing up of agreements seeking to regulate paid work collectively.
66. In the light of those considerations, the answer to the second question must be that Article [49 TFEU] is capable of conferring rights on a private undertaking which may be relied on against a trade union or an association of trade unions."

The remaining questions

8.242 The CJEU then considered the third to tenth questions as one. The CJEU said:

"By those questions, which can be examined together, the national court is essentially asking the Court of Justice whether collective action such as that at issue in the main proceedings constitutes a restriction within the meaning of Article [49 TFEU] and, if so, to what extent such a restriction may be justified."

8.243 The CJEU dealt with the existence and justification of restrictions:

"The existence of restrictions

68. The Court must first point out, as it has done on numerous occasions, that freedom of establishment constitutes one of the fundamental principles of the Community and that the provisions of the Treaty guaranteeing that freedom have been directly applicable since the end of the transitional period. Those provisions secure the right of establishment in another Member State not merely for Community nationals but also for the companies or firms referred to in Article [54 TFEU] (Case 81/87 Daily Mail and General Trust [1988] ECR 5483,[212] paragraph 15).
69. Furthermore, the Court has considered that, even though the provisions of the Treaty concerning freedom of establishment are directed mainly to ensuring that foreign nationals and companies are treated in the host Member State in the same way as nationals of that State, they also prohibit the Member State of origin from hindering the establishment in another Member State of one of its nationals or of a company incorporated under its legislation which also comes within the definition contained in Article [54 of the TFEU]. The rights guaranteed by Articles [49 TFEU to 54 TFEU] would be rendered meaningless if the Member State of origin could prohibit undertakings from leaving in order to establish themselves in another Member State (Daily Mail and General Trust, paragraph 16).
70. Secondly, according to the settled case-law of the Court, the definition of establishment within the meaning of those articles of the Treaty involves the actual pursuit of an economic activity through a fixed establishment in another Member State for an indefinite

---

[212] Ed., ECLI:EU:C:1998:456.

period and registration of a vessel cannot be separated from the exercise of the freedom of establishment where the vessel serves as a vehicle for the pursuit of an economic activity that includes fixed establishment in the State of registration (Case C-221/89 Factortame and Others [1991] ECR I-3905,[213] paragraphs 20 to 22).

71. The Court concluded from this that the conditions laid down for the registration of vessels must not form an obstacle to freedom of establishment within the meaning of Articles [49 TFEU to 54 TFEU] (Factortame and Others, paragraph 23).

72. In the present case, first, it cannot be disputed that collective action such as that envisaged by FSU has the effect of making less attractive, or even pointless, as the national court has pointed out, Viking's exercise of its right to freedom of establishment, inasmuch as such action prevents both Viking and its subsidiary, Viking Eesti, from enjoying the same treatment in the host Member State as other economic operators established in that State.

73. Secondly, collective action taken in order to implement ITF's policy of combating the use of flags of convenience, which seeks, primarily, as is apparent from ITF's observations, to prevent shipowners from registering their vessels in a State other than that of which the beneficial owners of those vessels are nationals, must be considered to be at least liable to restrict Viking's exercise of its right of freedom of establishment.

74. It follows that collective action such as that at issue in the main proceedings constitutes a restriction on freedom of establishment within the meaning of Article [49 TFEU].

Justification of the restrictions

75. It is apparent from the case-law of the Court that a restriction on freedom of establishment can be accepted only if it pursues a legitimate aim compatible with the Treaty and is justified by overriding reasons of public interest. But even if that were the case, it would still have to be suitable for securing the attainment of the objective pursued and must not go beyond what is necessary in order to attain it.

76. ITF, supported, in particular, by the German Government, Ireland and the Finnish Government, maintains that the restrictions at issue in the main proceedings are justified since they are necessary to ensure the protection of a fundamental right recognised under Community law and their objective is to protect the rights of workers, which constitutes an overriding reason of public interest.

77. In that regard, it must be observed that the right to take collective action for the protection of workers is a legitimate interest which, in principle, justifies a restriction of one of the fundamental freedoms guaranteed by the Treaty and that the protection of workers is one of the overriding reasons of public interest recognised by the Court.

78. It must be added that, according to Article 3(1)(c) and (j) EC, the activities of the Community are to include not only an 'internal market characterised by the abolition, as between Member States, of obstacles to the free movement of goods, persons, services and capital', but also 'a policy in the social sphere'. Article 2 EC states that the Community is to have as its task, inter alia, the promotion of 'a harmonious, balanced and sustainable development of economic activities' and 'a high level of employment and of social protection'.

79. Since the Community has thus not only an economic but also a social purpose, the rights under the provisions of the Treaty on the free movement of goods, persons, services and capital must be balanced against the objectives pursued by social policy, which include, as is clear from the first paragraph of Article 136 EC, inter alia, improved living and working conditions, so as to make possible their harmonisation while improvement is being maintained, proper social protection and dialogue between management and labour.

80. In the present case, it is for the national court to ascertain whether the objectives pursued by FSU and ITF by means of the collective action which they initiated concerned the protection of workers.

---

213 Ed., ECLI:EU:C:1991:320.

81. First, as regards the collective action taken by FSU, even if that action – aimed at protecting the jobs and conditions of employment of the members of that union liable to be adversely affected by the reflagging of the Rosella – could reasonably be considered to fall, at first sight, within the objective of protecting workers, such a view would no longer be tenable if it were established that the jobs or conditions of employment at issue were not jeopardised or under serious threat.

82. This would be the case, in particular, if it transpired that the undertaking referred to by the national court in its 10th question was, from a legal point of view, as binding as the terms of a collective agreement and if it was of such a nature as to provide a guarantee to the workers that the statutory provisions would be complied with and the terms of the collective agreement governing their working relationship maintained.

83. In so far as the exact legal scope to be attributed to an undertaking such as that referred to in the 10th question is not clear from the order for reference, it is for the national court to determine whether the jobs or conditions of employment of that trade union's members who are liable to be affected by the reflagging of the Rosella were jeopardised or under serious threat.

84. If, following that examination, the national court came to the conclusion that, in the case before it, the jobs or conditions of employment of the FSU's members liable to be adversely affected by the reflagging of the Rosella are in fact jeopardised or under serious threat, it would then have to ascertain whether the collective action initiated by FSU is suitable for ensuring the achievement of the objective pursued and does not go beyond what is necessary to attain that objective.

85. In that regard, it must be pointed out that, even if it is ultimately for the national court, which has sole jurisdiction to assess the facts and interpret the national legislation, to determine whether and to what extent such collective action meets those requirements, the Court of Justice, which is called on to provide answers of use to the national court, may provide guidance, based on the file in the main proceedings and on the written and oral observations which have been submitted to it, in order to enable the national court to give judgment in the particular case before it.

86. As regards the appropriateness of the action taken by FSU for attaining the objectives pursued in the case in the main proceedings, it should be borne in mind that it is common ground that collective action, like collective negotiations and collective agreements, may, in the particular circumstances of a case, be one of the main ways in which trade unions protect the interests of their members (European Court of Human Rights, Syndicat national de la police belge v Belgium, of 27 October 1975, Series A, No 19, and Wilson, National Union of Journalists and Others v United Kingdom of 2 July 2002, 2002-V, § 44).

87. As regards the question of whether or not the collective action at issue in the main proceedings goes beyond what is necessary to achieve the objective pursued, it is for the national court to examine, in particular, on the one hand, whether, under the national rules and collective agreement law applicable to that action, FSU did not have other means at its disposal which were less restrictive of freedom of establishment in order to bring to a successful conclusion the collective negotiations entered into with Viking, and, on the other, whether that trade union had exhausted those means before initiating such action.

88. Secondly, in relation to the collective action seeking to ensure the implementation of the policy in question pursued by ITF, it must be emphasised that, to the extent that that policy results in shipowners being prevented from registering their vessels in a State other than that of which the beneficial owners of those vessels are nationals, the restrictions on freedom of establishment resulting from such action cannot be objectively justified. Nevertheless, as the national court points out, the objective of that policy is also to protect and improve seafarers' terms and conditions of employment.

89. However, as is apparent from the file submitted to the Court, in the context of its policy of combating the use of flags of convenience, ITF is required, when asked by one of its members, to initiate solidarity action against the beneficial owner of a vessel which is registered in a State other than that of which that owner is a national, irrespective of whether or not that owner's exercise of its right of freedom of establishment is liable to have a harmful

effect on the work or conditions of employment of its employees. Therefore, as Viking argued during the hearing without being contradicted by ITF in that regard, the policy of reserving the right of collective negotiations to trade unions of the State of which the beneficial owner of a vessel is a national is also applicable where the vessel is registered in a State which guarantees workers a higher level of social protection than they would enjoy in the first State.

90. In the light of those considerations, the answer to the third to tenth questions must be that Article [49 TFEU] is to be interpreted to the effect that collective action such as that at issue in the main proceedings, which seeks to induce an undertaking whose registered office is in a given Member State to enter into a collective work agreement with a trade union established in that State and to apply the terms set out in that agreement to the employees of a subsidiary of that undertaking established in another Member State, constitutes a restriction within the meaning of that article. That restriction may, in principle, be justified by an overriding reason of public interest, such as the protection of workers, provided that it is established that the restriction is suitable for ensuring the attainment of the legitimate objective pursued and does not go beyond what is necessary to achieve that objective."

M. SEAFARERS REMAINING IN A MEMBER STATE AFTER BEING AT SEA

8.244 It is well known that EU citizens may move to other Member States to take up employment. However, what if employees retire or resign, may they still stay in the host Member State afterwards working there? EU law allows EU nationals to remain but what about a non-EU national? The CJEU has had to consider the issue but in the context of a non-EU national.

8.245 *Mehmet Sedef v Freie und Hansestadt Hamburg*[214] involved a preliminary ruling by the CJEU[215] in a case from the Bundesverwaltungsgericht in Germany. The case concerned the interpretation of Article 6(1)[216] and (2)[217] of Decision 1/80 of the Association Council of 19 September 1980 on the development of the Association. The Association Council was created by the agreement establishing an association between the then EEC and Turkey in 1963 and confirmed on behalf of the EU by Council Decision 64/732 of 23 December 1963[218] (the "Association Agreement").

---

214 Case C-230/03.
215 Timmermans, President of the Chamber along with Gulmann, Schintgen (Rapporteur), Arestis and Klučka, Judges.
216 Art. 6(1) provides: "[s]ubject to Article 7 on free access to employment for members of his family, a Turkish worker duly registered as belonging to the labour force of a Member State:

- shall be entitled in that Member State, after one year's legal employment, to the renewal of his permit to work for the same employer, if a job is available;
- shall be entitled in that Member State, after three years of legal employment and subject to the priority to be given to workers of Member States of the Community, to respond to another offer of employment, with an employer of his choice, made under normal conditions and registered with the employment services of that State, for the same occupation;
- shall enjoy free access in that Member State to any paid employment of his choice, after four years of legal employment."

217 Art. 6(2) provides: "Annual holidays and absences for reasons of maternity or an accident at work or short periods of sickness shall be treated as periods of legal employment. Periods of involuntary unemployment duly certified by the relevant authorities and long absences on account of sickness shall not be treated as periods of legal employment, but shall not affect rights acquired as the result of the preceding period of employment."
218 JO 1964 217, p. 3685.

8.246 The preliminary reference was made during proceedings between Sedef (a Turkish national) and Freie und Hansestadt Hamburg regarding the latter's decisions refusing to grant him an extension of his residence permit for Germany and ordering his removal from Germany. Sedef had been in Germany lawfully since 1977 although his wife and three children continued to reside in Turkey. Between 1977 and 1992, he was employed as a seaman on various ships flying the German flag and for that purpose obtained successive residence permits, granted for a limited period of time and restricted to employment in the merchant navy or, if necessary, to the grant of unemployment benefits, the last of those residence permits having ceased to be valid in 1993. No work permit was required for that paid employment. During the 15 years, the claimant actually worked for more than eight-and-a-half years in total, not counting interruptions in the periods of employment for reasons of sickness and involuntary unemployment duly certified by the relevant authorities.

8.247 Sedef's periods of employment had been interrupted 17 times, for periods of between one and 70 days amounting in total to around 13 months, for reasons other than an annual holiday, an absence due to sickness or a period of unemployment duly certified in Germany. The claimant described those breaks as periods of "unpaid holiday". According to him, during those breaks of unequal length between individual fixed-term contracts of employment in the merchant navy, he either remained in Germany, in the case of short breaks, to await the (sometimes delayed) arrival of a vessel on which he already had new employment, so that he considered it pointless to take steps to register himself as unemployed, or he used the longer breaks in excess of roughly three weeks to visit his family who remained in Turkey. According to the national court, breaks of that kind are typical of employment in maritime shipping. Following an accident at work which took place on a ship in 1979, Sedef had to undergo several operations which resulted in some long and some short periods of incapacity for work. Since 1993, Sedef had been pronounced unfit to work on ships on health grounds, although not wholly incapacitated from engaging in gainful employment. He was able to engage in employment on land as long as that does not demand physical effort which is too sustained.

8.248 In 1992, Sedef applied to be granted a residence permit which was not restricted to employment as a seaman, so as to be able to take paid employment on land. For that purpose he claimed, first, that he fulfilled the conditions laid down in the third indent of Article 6(1) of Decision 1/80 on account of the fact that he had been employed for more than four years on ships flying the German flag and, second, that his situation constituted a hardship case, as his state of health no longer allowed him to continue working as a seaman. He added that he had not been able to act on offers of employment on land which had been made to him as he did not hold the requisite residence permit. Both that application and his subsequent objection were rejected by Freie und Hansestadt Hamburg, which threatened him with removal if he had not left Germany within three weeks. Implementation of the decision to remove him was stayed.

8.249 In 1996, the Verwaltungsgericht Hamburg (Administrative Court, Hamburg) held Sedef's action to be well founded and ordered Freie and Hansestadt Hamburg to grant him the residence permit applied for.

8.250 The case progressed through the national courts and it eventually involved a preliminary reference to the CJEU. The German court made the following findings in the order for the preliminary reference to the CJEU.

"– Mr Sedef was engaged, for more than 15 years, in legal employment within the meaning of Article 6(1) through his work in the shipping industry of a Member State and he thus forms part of the duly-registered labour force of the host Member State for the purposes of that provision;
- he has several times been in such legal employment continuously with the same employer for more than one year, so that he fulfils the conditions of the first indent of that provision;
- the claimant is now unfit to work on ships on health grounds, but continues to be duly registered as belonging to the labour force in Germany, given that the accident which he suffered at work did not result in his becoming totally incapacitated for employment (see, to that effect, Case C-434/93 *Bozkurt* [1995] ECR I-1475, paragraphs 37 to 40) and that he is available to the employment services for the employment on land sought. The fact that he has not worked since 1993 is due, at least in part, to his lack of a residence permit and that cannot be held against him."

8.251 The CJEU said that, it was not certain that the breaks which Mr Sedef terms "unpaid holiday" had no effect on the entitlement he had already acquired under the first indent of Article 6(1) of Decision 1/80 and that those breaks did not also preclude the acquisition of entitlement under the third indent of the same paragraph. On the one hand, the CJEU had not yet given a specific ruling on such breaks. On the other hand, the Bundesverwaltungsgericht had until now held that the list of interruptions to employment specified in Article 6(2) of Decision 1/80 is exhaustive. The CJEU held that it was nevertheless doubtful whether that latter view could be maintained.

8.252 The German Court believed that if it were decided that the third indent of Article 6(1) did not in principle confer any entitlement on Mr Sedef since he cannot claim three years of uninterrupted employment with the same employer, it was still necessary to establish whether the fact that a change of employer before the expiry of three years was typical of the occupation of seaman must, by way of exception, be taken into consideration.

8.253 Ultimately, the Bundesverwaltungsgericht decided to stay the proceedings and to refer the following questions to the CJEU for a preliminary ruling:

"1. Are the third indent of Article 6(1) and Article 6(2) of Decision No 1/80 ... to be interpreted as meaning that a Turkish worker who has been legally employed by various employers in maritime shipping forming part of the duly-registered labour force of a Member State for more than 15 years since 1977 without a work permit being required and who has satisfied the requirements of the first indent of Article 6(1) of Decision No 1/80 during that time is entitled to a residence permit where – in addition to various breaks for reasons of illness and involuntary unemployment duly certified by the relevant authority – his employment in maritime shipping has undergone interruptions of between 1 and 70 days between individual employment relationships on 17 occasions (totalling approximately 13 months) and, by his own admission, the Turkish worker has spent the longer breaks with his family in Turkey without any involuntary unemployment then being certified? Does the answer depend on whether such interruptions are typical of the occupation concerned (in this case ... of maritime shipping)?
2. Is entitlement to a residence permit under the third indent of Article 6(1) of Decision No 1/80 conditional on the Turkish worker already satisfying the requirements of the second indent of Article 6(1) of Decision No 1/80? Does the answer depend on whether a change of employer before the expiry of three years is typical of the occupation concerned (in this case ... of maritime shipping)?"

8.254 Ultimately, the CJEU ruled that Article 6 of Decision 1/80 of 19 September 1980 on the development of the Association, adopted by the Association Council created by the agreement establishing an association between the EEC and Turkey, was to be interpreted as meaning that:

> "– enjoyment of the rights conferred on a Turkish worker by the third indent of paragraph 1 of that article presupposes in principle that the person concerned has already fulfilled the conditions set out in the second indent of that paragraph;
> – a Turkish worker who does not yet enjoy the right of free access to any paid employment of his choice under that third indent must be in legal employment without interruption in the host Member State unless he can rely on a legitimate reason of the type laid down in Article 6(2) to justify his temporary absence from the labour force;
> – Article 6(2) of Decision No 1/80 covers interruptions in periods of legal employment, such as those at issue in the main proceedings, and the relevant national authorities cannot, in this case, dispute the right of the Turkish worker concerned to reside in the host Member State."

N. STANDARDS FOR SEAFARERS: COUNCIL RECOMMENDATION 79/114 OF 21 DECEMBER 1978 ON THE RATIFICATION OF THE 1978 INTERNATIONAL CONVENTION ON STANDARDS OF TRAINING, CERTIFICATION AND WATCHKEEPING FOR SEAFARERS

8.255 On 21 December 1978, the Council adopted Recommendation 79/114 on the ratification of the 1978 International Convention on Standards of Training, Certification and Watchkeeping for Seafarers.

8.256 There were developments at the EU and international levels. At the EU level, there were two meetings. At its meeting on 7 and 8 April 1978 in Copenhagen, the European Council declared that the EU should make the prevention and combating of marine pollution, particularly from hydrocarbons, a major objective. At its meeting on 6 and 7 July 1978 in Bremen, the European Council deemed it necessary, taking into account the proposals of individual Member States and the Commission, to take further measures to increase the safety of maritime traffic. At the international level, an international convention on standards of training, certification and watchkeeping for seafarers was adopted in London in July 1978 – the STCW Convention.[219]

8.257 The Council believed that in the interests of shipping safety and the prevention of pollution, the convention should enter into force as soon as possible and the early ratification of the convention by the Member States would constitute a major contribution to the achievement of that objective.

8.258 The Council therefore recommended that the Member States sign the convention by 1 April 1979 and ratify it as soon as possible and not later than 31 December 1980. Moreover, Member States had to inform the Secretary-General of the Inter-Governmental Maritime Consultative Organization that they had signed and ratified the convention in accordance with the recommendation.

---

219 The IMO has stated (at www.imo.org/about/conventions/listofconventions/pages/international-convention-on-standards-of-training,-certification-and-watchkeeping-for-seafarers-(stcw).aspx): "The 1978 STCW Convention was the first to establish basic requirements on training, certification and watchkeeping for seafarers on an international level. Previously the standards of training, certification and watchkeeping of officers and ratings were established by individual governments, usually without reference to practices in other countries. As a result standards and procedures varied widely, even though shipping is the most international of all industries. The Convention prescribes minimum standards relating to training, certification and watchkeeping for seafarers which countries are obliged to meet or exceed."

O. COUNCIL DIRECTIVE 2009/13 OF 16 FEBRUARY 2009 IMPLEMENTING THE AGREEMENT CONCLUDED BY THE ECSA AND THE ETF ON THE MARITIME LABOUR CONVENTION, 2006, AND AMENDING DIRECTIVE 1999/63

Introduction

8.259 On 16 February 2009, Council Directive 2009/13 was adopted to implement the agreement concluded by the ECSA and the ETF on the Maritime Labour Convention, 2006, and amending Directive 1999/63.[220],[221]

8.260 It was based on the Treaty establishing the EC, and in particular Article 139(2) thereof.

Background

8.261 The background to the directive was described in the following terms:

"(1) Management and labour, hereinafter referred to as 'the social partners', may, in accordance with Article 139(2) of the Treaty, request jointly that agreements concluded by them at Community level be implemented by a Council decision on a proposal from the Commission.

(2) On 23 February 2006, the International Labour Organisation adopted the Maritime Labour Convention, 2006, desiring to create a single, coherent instrument embodying as far as possible all up-to-date standards of existing international maritime labour Conventions and Recommendations, as well as the fundamental principles to be found in other international labour conventions.

(3) The Commission has consulted management and labour, in accordance with Article 138(2) of the Treaty, on the advisability of developing the existing Community *acquis* by adapting, consolidating or supplementing it in view of the Maritime Labour Convention, 2006.

(4) On 29 September 2006 the European Community Shipowners' Associations (ECSA) and the European Transport Workers' Federation (ETF) informed the Commission of their wish to enter into negotiations in accordance with Article 138(4) of the Treaty.

(5) On 19 May 2008, the said organisations wishing to help create of a global level playing field throughout the maritime industry, concluded an Agreement on the Maritime Labour Convention, 2006, hereinafter referred to as 'the Agreement'. This Agreement and its Annex contain a joint request to the Commission to implement them by a Council decision on a proposal from the Commission, in accordance with Article 139(2) of the Treaty.

(6) The Agreement applies to seafarers on board ships registered in a Member State and/or flying flag of a Member State.

(7) The Agreement amends the European Agreement on the organisation of working time of seafarers concluded in Brussels on 30 September 1998 by the European Community Shipowners' Associations (ECSA) and the Federation of Transport Workers' Unions in the European Union (FST).

(8) For the purpose of Article 249 of the Treaty, the appropriate instrument for implementing the Agreement is a directive.

(9) The Agreement will enter into force simultaneously with the Maritime Labour Convention, 2006, and the social partners wish the national measures implementing this Directive to enter into force not earlier than on the date of entry into force of the said Convention.

(10) For any terms used in the Agreement and which are not specifically defined therein, this Directive leaves Member States free to define them in accordance with national law and practice, as is the case for other social policy Directives using similar terms, provided that those definitions respect the content of the Agreement.

---

220 OJ 2009 L124/30.
221 The agreement was set out in the annex to the directive.

(11) The Commission has drafted its proposal for a Directive, in accordance with its Communication of 20 May 1998 on adapting and promoting the social dialogue at Community level, taking into account the representative status of the signatory parties and the legality of each clause of the Agreement.

(12) The Member States may entrust management and labour, at their joint request, with the implementation of this Directive, as long as the Member States take all the necessary steps to ensure that they can at all times guarantee the results imposed by this Directive.

(13) The provisions of this Directive should apply without prejudice to any existing Community provisions being more specific and/or granting a higher level of protection to seafarers, and in particular those included in Community legislation.

(14) Compliance with the general principle of employer responsibility as provided for in Council Directive 89/391/EEC of 12 June 1989 on the introduction of measures to encourage improvements in the safety and health of workers at work,[222] and in particular in its Article 5(1) and (3), should be ensured.

(15) This Directive should not be used to justify a reduction in the general level of protection of workers in the fields covered by the Agreement annexed to it.

(16) This Directive and the Agreement lay down minimum standards. The Member States and/or the social partners should be able to maintain or introduce more favourable provisions.

(17) The Commission has informed the European Parliament and the European Economic and Social Committee, in accordance with its communication of 14 December 1993 concerning the application of the Agreement on Social Policy, by sending them the text of its proposal for a Directive containing the Agreement.

(18) This instrument complies with the fundamental rights and principles set out in the Charter of Fundamental Rights of the European Union and in particular with Article 31 thereof which provides that all workers have the right to healthy, safe and dignified working conditions, to a limit on their maximum working time and to weekly and daily rest periods and an annual period of paid leave.

(19) Since the objectives of this Directive cannot be sufficiently achieved by the Member States and can therefore, by reason of the scale or effects of the action, be better achieved at Community level, the Community may adopt measures, in accordance with the principle of subsidiarity as set out in Article 5 of the Treaty. In accordance with the principle of proportionality, as set out in that Article, this Directive does not go beyond what is necessary in order to achieve those objectives.

(20) In accordance with paragraph 34 of the Interinstitutional Agreement on better lawmaking,[223] Member States will be encouraged to draw up, for themselves and in the interest of the Community, their own tables which will, as far as possible, illustrate the correlation between this Directive and the transposition measures and to make them public.

(21) Council Directive 1999/63/EC of 21 June 1999 concerning the Agreement on the organisation of working time of seafarers concluded by the European Community Shipowners' Association (ECSA) and the Federation of Transport Workers' Unions in the European Union (FST)[224] containing the European Agreement on the organisation of working time of seafarers in its Annex should therefore be amended accordingly.

(22) The implementation of the Agreement contributes to achieving the objectives under Article 136 of the Treaty."

8.262 Article 1 provides that the directive implements the agreement on Maritime Labour Convention, 2006, concluded on 19 May 2008 between the organisations representing management and labour in the maritime transport sector (ECSA and ETF) as set out in the annex.

---

222 Ed., OJ L183/1, 29 June 1989.
223 Ed., OJ C321/1, 31 December 2003.
224 OJ L167/33, 2 July 1999.

8.263 Article 2 amends the annex to Council Directive 1999/63 as follows:

"1. in Clause 1, the following point 3 shall be added:

'3. In the event of doubt as to whether any categories of persons are to be regarded as seafarers for the purpose of this Agreement, the question shall be determined by the competent authority in each Member State after consultation with the shipowners' and seafarers' organisations concerned with this question. In this context due account shall be taken of the Resolution of the 94th (Maritime) Session of the General Conference of the International Labour Organisation concerning information on occupational groups.';

2. in Clause 2, points (c) and (d) shall be replaced by the following:

'(d) the term "shipowner" means the owner of the ship or another organisation or person, such as the manager, agent or bareboat charterer, who has assumed the responsibility for the operation of the ship from the owner and who, on assuming such responsibility, has agreed to take over the duties and responsibilities imposed on shipowners in accordance with this Agreement, regardless of whether any other organisation or persons fulfil certain of the duties or responsibilities on behalf of the shipowner.';

3. Clause 6 shall be replaced by the following:

'1. Night work of seafarers under the age of 18 shall be prohibited. For the purposes of this Clause, "night" shall be defined in accordance with national law and practice. It shall cover a period of at least nine hours starting no later than midnight and ending no earlier than 5 a.m.

2. An exception to strict compliance with the night work restriction may be made by the competent authority when:

   (a) the effective training of the seafarers concerned, in accordance with established programmes and schedules, would be impaired; or
   (b) the specific nature of the duty or a recognised training programme requires that the seafarers covered by the exception perform duties at night and the authority determines, after consultation with the shipowners' and seafarers' organisations concerned, that the work will not be detrimental to their health or well-being.

3. The employment, engagement or work of seafarers under the age of 18 shall be prohibited where the work is likely to jeopardise their health or safety. The types of such work shall be determined by national laws or regulations or by the competent authority, after consultation with the shipowners' and seafarers' organisations concerned, in accordance with relevant international standards.';

4. Clause 13 shall be replaced by the following:

'1. Seafarers shall not work on a ship unless they are certified as medically fit to perform their duties.

2. Exceptions can only be permitted as prescribed in this Agreement.

3. The competent authority shall require that, prior to beginning work on a ship, seafarers hold a valid medical certificate attesting that they are medically fit to perform the duties they are to carry out at sea.

4. In order to ensure that medical certificates genuinely reflect seafarers' state of health, in light of the duties they are to perform, the competent authority shall, after consultation with the shipowners' and seafarers' organisations concerned, and giving due consideration to applicable international guidelines, prescribe the nature of the medical examination and certificate.

5. This Agreement is without prejudice to the International Convention on Standards of Training, Certification and Watchkeeping for Seafarers, 1978, as amended (STCW). A medical certificate issued in accordance with the requirements of STCW shall be accepted by the competent authority, for the purpose of points 1 and 2 of this Clause. A medical certificate meeting the substance of those requirements, in the case of seafarers not covered by STCW, shall similarly be accepted.

6. The medical certificate shall be issued by a duly qualified medical practitioner or, in the case of a certificate solely concerning eyesight, by a person recognised by the competent authority as qualified to issue such a certificate. Practitioners must enjoy full professional independence in exercising their medical judgement in undertaking medical examination procedures.

7. Seafarers that have been refused a certificate or have had a limitation imposed on their ability to work, in particular with respect to time, field of work or trading area, shall be given the opportunity to have a further examination by another independent medical practitioner or by an independent medical referee.

8. Each medical certificate shall state in particular that:

    (a) the hearing and sight of the seafarer concerned, and the colour vision in the case of a seafarer to be employed in capacities where fitness for the work to be performed is liable to be affected by defective colour vision, are all satisfactory; and
    (b) the seafarer concerned is not suffering from any medical condition likely to be aggravated by service at sea or to render the seafarer unfit for such service or to endanger the health of other persons on board.

9. Unless a shorter period is required by reason of the specific duties to be performed by the seafarer concerned or is required under STCW:

    (a) a medical certificate shall be valid for a maximum period of two years unless the seafarer is under the age of 18, in which case the maximum period of validity shall be one year;
    (b) a certification of colour vision shall be valid for a maximum period of six years.

10. In urgent cases the competent authority may permit a seafarer to work without a valid medical certificate until the next port of call where the seafarer can obtain a medical certificate from a qualified medical practitioner, provided that:

    (a) the period of such permission does not exceed three months; and
    (b) the seafarer concerned is in possession of an expired medical certificate of recent date.

11. If the period of validity of a certificate expires in the course of a voyage, the certificate shall continue in force until the next port of call where the seafarer can obtain a medical certificate from a qualified medical practitioner, provided that the period shall not exceed three months.
12. The medical certificates for seafarers working on ships ordinarily engaged on international voyages must as a minimum be provided in English.
13. The nature of the health assessment to be made and the particulars to be included in the medical certificate shall be established after consultation with the shipowners' and seafarers' organisations concerned.

14. All seafarers shall have regular health assessments. Watchkeepers suffering from health problems certified by a medical practitioner as being due to the fact that they perform night work shall be transferred, wherever possible, to day work to which they are suited.
15. The health assessment referred to in points 13 and 14 shall be free and comply with medical confidentiality. Such health assessments may be conducted within the national health system.';

5. Clause 16 shall be replaced by the following:

'Every seafarer shall be entitled to paid annual leave. The annual leave with pay entitlement shall be calculated on the basis of a minimum of 2,5 calendar days per month of employment and pro rata for incomplete months. The minimum period of paid annual leave may not be replaced by an allowance in lieu, except where the employment relationship is terminated.'."

8.264 Article 3(1) provides that Member States may maintain or introduce more favourable provisions than those laid down in the directive.

Article 3(2) provides that the implementation of the directive shall under no circumstances constitute sufficient grounds for justifying a reduction in the general level of protection of workers in the fields covered by the directive. This shall be without prejudice to the rights of Member States and/or management and labour to lay down, in the light of changing circumstances, different legislative, regulatory or contractual arrangements to those prevailing at the time of the adoption of the directive, provided always that the minimum requirements laid down in the directive are complied with. Article 8(3) provides that the application and/or interpretation of the directive shall be without prejudice to any Community or national provision, custom or practice providing for more favourable conditions for the seafarers concerned. Article 3(4) provides that the provision of Standard A4.2 point 5(b) must not affect the principle of responsibility of the employer as provided for in Article 5 of Directive 89/391.

8.265 Article 4 provides that "Member States must determine what penalties are applicable when national provisions enacted pursuant to the Directive are infringed and the penalties must be effective, proportionate and dissuasive."

8.266 Article 5(1) provides that Member States must bring into force the laws, regulations and administrative provisions necessary to comply with the directive or shall ensure that management and labour have introduced the necessary measures by agreement, not later than 12 months after the date of entry into force of the directive. Article 5(2) provides that when Member States adopt provisions, they must contain a reference to the directive or shall be accompanied by such reference on the occasion of their official publication. The methods of making such reference shall be laid down by Member States. They must forthwith communicate to the Commission the text of those provisions. Article 5(3) provides that Member States must communicate to the Commission the text of the main provisions of national law which they adopt in the field covered by the directive.

8.267 Article 6 provides that the application of the principle of substantial equivalence mentioned in the preamble of the agreement is without prejudice to the obligations of the Member States emanating from the directive.

8.268 Article 7 provides that the directive must enter into force on the date of entry into force of the Maritime Labour Convention, 2006.

8.269 The agreement concluded by the ECSA and the ETF on the Maritime Labour Convention, 2006 reads as follows:

"AGREEMENT
concluded by
PREAMBLE
THE SIGNATORY PARTIES,

Whereas the ILO Maritime Labour Convention, 2006 (hereinafter referred to as the Convention) requires each Member to satisfy itself that the provisions of its laws and regulations respect, in the context of the Convention, the fundamental rights to freedom of association and the effective recognition of the right to collective bargaining, the elimination of all forms of forced or compulsory labour, the effective abolition of child labour and the elimination of discrimination in respect of employment and occupation;

Whereas the Convention provides that every seafarer has the rights to a safe and secure workplace that complies with safety standards, to fair terms of employment, to decent working and living conditions and to health protection, medical care, welfare measures and other forms of social protection;

Whereas the Convention requires Members to ensure, within the limits of its jurisdiction, that the seafarers' employment and social rights set out in the preceding paragraph of this preamble are fully implemented in accordance with the requirements of the Convention. Unless specified otherwise in the Convention, such implementation may be achieved through national laws or regulations, through applicable collective bargaining agreements or through other measures or in practice;

Whereas the signatory parties wish to draw particular attention to the 'Explanatory Note to the Regulations and Code of the Maritime Labour Convention', which sets out the format and structure of the Convention;

Having regard to the Treaty establishing the European Community (hereinafter referred to as the Treaty) and in particular Articles 137, 138 and 139 thereof;

Whereas Article 139(2) of the Treaty provides that agreements concluded at European level may be implemented at the joint request of the signatory parties by a Council Decision on a proposal from the Commission;

Whereas the signatory parties hereby make such a request;

Whereas the proper instrument for implementing the Agreement is a Directive, within the meaning of Article 249 of the Treaty, which binds Member States as to the result to be achieved, whilst leaving to national authorities the choice of form and methods; Article VI of the Convention permits Members of the ILO to implement measures that are to their satisfaction substantially equivalent to the Standards of the Convention which is aimed both at full achievement of the general objective and purpose of the Convention and at giving effect to the said provisions of the Convention; the implementation of the Agreement by a Directive and the principle of 'substantial equivalence' in the Convention are thus aimed at giving Member States the ability to implement the rights and principles in a manner provided by Article VI points 3 and 4 of the Convention,

HAVE AGREED THE FOLLOWING:
DEFINITIONS AND SCOPE OF APPLICATION

1. For the purpose of this Agreement and unless provided otherwise in particular provisions, the term:

    (a) 'competent authority' means the minister, government department or other authority designated by a Member State having power to issue and enforce regulations, orders or other instructions having the force of law in respect of the subject matter of the provision concerned;
    (b) 'gross tonnage' means the gross tonnage calculated in accordance with the tonnage measurement regulations contained in Annex I to the International

Convention on Tonnage Measurement of Ships, 1969, or any successor Convention; for ships covered by the tonnage measurement interim scheme adopted by the International Maritime Organisation, the gross tonnage is that which is included in the 'Remarks' column of the International Tonnage Certificate (1969);

(c) 'seafarer' means any person who is employed or engaged or works in any capacity on board a 'ship' to which this Agreement applies;

(d) 'seafarers employment' agreement includes both a contract of employment and articles of agreement;

(e) 'ship' means a ship other than one which navigates exclusively in inland waters or waters within, or closely adjacent to, sheltered waters or areas where port regulations apply;

(f) 'shipowner' means the owner of the ship or another organisation or person, such as the manager, agent or bareboat charterer, who has assumed the responsibility for the operation of the ship from the owner and who, on assuming such responsibility, has agreed to take over the duties and responsibilities imposed on shipowners in accordance with this Agreement, regardless of whether any other organisation or persons fulfil certain of the duties or responsibilities on behalf of the shipowner.

2. Except as expressly provided otherwise, this Agreement applies to all seafarers.

3. In the event of doubt as to whether any categories of persons are to be regarded as seafarers for the purpose of this Agreement, the question shall be determined by the competent authority in each Member State after consultation with the shipowners' and seafarers' organisations concerned with this question. In this context due account shall be taken of the Resolution of the 94th (Maritime) Session of the General Conference of the International Labour Organisation concerning information on occupational groups.

4. Except as expressly provided otherwise, this Agreement applies to all ships whether publicly or privately owned, ordinarily engaged in commercial activities, other than ships engaged in fishing or in similar pursuits and ships of traditional build such as dhows and junks. This Agreement does not apply to warships or naval auxiliaries.

5. In the event of doubt as to whether this Agreement applies to a ship or particular category of ships, the question shall be determined by the competent authority in each Member State after consultation with the shipowners' and seafarers' organisations concerned."

There are a number of provisions under various headings. These headings are called "titles". Title 1 is entitled "Minimum Requirements for Seafarers to Work on a Ship". Title 2 dealt with "Conditions of Engagement". Title 3 is entitled "Accommodation, Recreational Facilities, Food and Catering". Title 4 deals with "Health Protection, Medical Care and Welfare". Title 5 deals with "Compliance and Enforcement".

P. *COMMISSION V ITALY* ON AN ALLEGED FAILURE TO FULFIL OBLIGATIONS UNDER DIRECTIVE 1999/95

8.270 On 28 April 2005, the CJEU delivered its judgment in *Commission v Italy*.[225] This case related to a failure by Italy to fulfil its obligations under Directive 1999/95 (the

---

[225] Case C-410/03, ECLI:EU:C:2005, Fourth Chamber (Lenaerts (President of the Chamber), Colneric (Rapporteur) and Cunha Rodrigues (Judges) and Advocate-General Ruiz-Jarabo Colomer). The CJEU decided, after hearing the Advocate-General, to proceed to judgment without an opinion. On the case, see Chuah, "Implementation of the Directive Concerning the Enforcement of Provisions in Respect of Seafarers' Hours of Work" (2005) 11 JIML 376.

so-called "Enforcement Directive").[226] This directive concerned the enforcement of provisions in respect of seafarers' hours of work on board ships calling at EU ports. The objective of the directive is primarily to improve the shipboard living and working conditions of seafarers and safety at sea. The Commission alleged that Italy had failed to transpose the directive into national law within the prescribed period. Ultimately, the CJEU held: (a) by failing to adopt the laws, regulations and administrative provisions necessary to comply with Articles 3 to 7, 8(2) and 9 of Directive 1999/95, Italy had failed to fulfil its obligations under the directive; and (b) by failing to adopt the laws, regulations and administrative provisions necessary to comply with Articles 3 to 7, 8(2) and 9 of Directive 1999/95 concerning the enforcement of provisions in respect of seafarers' hours of work on board ships calling at Community ports, Italy had failed to fulfil its obligations under that directive.

8.271 Directive 1999/95 was aimed at giving practical effect to Council Directive 1999/63 of 21 June 1999 concerning the agreement on the organisation of working time of seafarers (i.e. the Seafarers' Working Time Directive). Directive 1999/63 concerned the agreement between the ECSA and the FST. The agreement mirrored the provisions of Convention No 180 of the International Labour Organization concerning seafarers' hours of work and the manning of ships which was adopted on 22 October 1996.

8.272 The CJEU held that a provision in a directive which concerns only relations between a Member State and the Commission or the other Member States need not, in principle, be transposed. However, each Member State to which a directive is addressed is obliged to adopt, within the framework of its national legal system, all the measures necessary to ensure that the directive is fully effective, in accordance with the objective it pursues. However, this was not so in the case of the first subparagraph of Article 3 of Directive 1999/95.[227] The CJEU therefore held that Italy had failed to comply with Articles 3–7, 8(2) and 9 of Directive 99/95. It is useful to examine the judgment in more depth.

8.273 The CJEU was of the view that Article 6(1) of Directive 1999/95 concerning the enforcement of provisions in respect of seafarers' hours of work on board ships calling at Community ports, to notify the administration of the flag State or the State in which a ship is registered or the Consul, or in his absence the nearest diplomatic representative of that State, is the corollary of that State's responsibilities under public international law.

8.274 The CJEU also believed that it is clear from Article 94(1) of the UNCLOS, which was approved by EU Decision 98/392 concerning the obligations of the flag State, that every State is effectively to exercise its jurisdiction and control in administrative, technical and social fields over ships flying its flag. In particular, pursuant to paragraphs 2(b) and 3(b) of Article 94(1), every State is to assume jurisdiction, under its internal law, over each ship flying its flag and its master, officers and crew in respect of administrative, technical and social matters concerning the ship, and every State is to take such measures for ships flying its flag as are necessary to ensure safety at sea, with regard, among other things, to the manning of ships, labour conditions and training of crews, taking account of

---

[226] OJ 2000 L14/29.
[227] The CJEU in paras 38–40 of the judgment held that the report addressed to the government of the country in which the ship is registered is intended to draw attention to a situation which is clearly hazardous to the safety or the health of the crew. It is intended immediately to eliminate that risk and does not concern only mere obligations to notify. To have full effect the rule therefore requires transposition.

the applicable international instruments. The CJEU also believed that it is also clear from Article 94(6) that, once advised of the fact that the proper control has not been exercised over a ship, the flag State is to undertake an investigation and, if appropriate, take any action necessary to remedy the situation. It follows that the notification required by Article 6(1) of Directive 1999/95 is intended directly to improve safety at sea in the case of a clearly hazardous situation. To have full effect that provision therefore requires express transposition into national law.

8.275 The CJEU then recalled Clause 4 of the agreement which provides:

"Without prejudice to Clause 5, the normal working hours' standard of seafarers is, in principle, based on an eight-hour day with one day of rest per week and rest on public holidays. Member States may have procedures to authorise or register a collective agreement which determines seafarers' normal working hours on a basis no less favourable than this standard."

Clause 5 of the agreement provides:

"1. The limits of hours of work or rest shall be either:

    (a) maximum hours of work which shall not exceed:

        (i) fourteen hours in any 24 hour period; and
        (ii) 72 hours in any seven-day period;

    or

    (b) minimum hours of rest which shall not be less than:

        (i) ten hours in any 24 hour period; and
        (ii) 72 hours in any seven-day period.

2. Hours of rest may be divided into no more than two periods, one of which shall be at least six hours in length and the interval between consecutive periods of rest shall not exceed 14 hours.

3. Musters, fire-fighting and lifeboat drills, and [drills] prescribed by national laws and regulations and by international instruments shall be conducted in a manner that minimises the disturbance of rest periods and does not induce fatigue.

4. In respect of situations when a seafarer is on call, such as when a machinery space is unattended, the seafarer shall have an adequate compensatory rest period if the normal period of rest is disturbed by call-outs to work.

5. With regard to paragraphs 3 and 4, where no collective agreement or arbitration award exists or if the competent authority determines that the provisions in the agreement or award are inadequate, it would be for the competent authority to determine such provisions to ensure that the seafarers concerned have sufficient rest.

6. With due regard for the general principles of the protection of the health and safety of workers, Member States may have national laws, regulations or a procedure for the competent authority to authorise or register collective agreements permitting exceptions to the limits set out in paragraphs 1 and 2. Such exceptions shall, as far as possible, follow the standards set out but may take account of more frequent or longer leave periods, or the granting of compensatory leave for watchkeeping seafarers, or seafarers working on board ship on short voyages.

7. A table shall be posted, in an easily accessible place, with the shipboard working arrangements, which shall contain for every position at least:

    (a) the schedule of service at sea and service in port; and
    (b) the maximum hours of work or the minimum hours of rest required by the laws, regulations or collective agreements in force in the Member States.

8. The table referred to in paragraph 7 shall be established in a standardised format in the working language or languages of the ship and in English."

8.276 The CJEU then recalled Clause 8 of the agreement which provided:

"1. Records of seafarers' daily hours of work or their daily hours of rest shall be maintained to allow monitoring of compliance with the provisions set out in Clause 5. The seafarer shall receive a copy of the records pertaining to him or her which shall be endorsed by the master, or a person authorised by the master, and by the seafarer.
2. Procedures shall be determined for keeping such records on board, including the intervals at which the information shall be recorded. The format of the records of the seafarers' hours of work or of their hours of rest shall be established taking into account any available international guidelines. The format shall be established in the language provided by Clause 5, paragraph 8.
3. A copy of the relevant provisions of the national legislation pertaining to this Agreement and the relevant collective agreements shall be kept on board and be easily accessible to the crew."

8.277 Clause 9 of the agreement provides: "The records referred to in Clause 8 shall be examined and endorsed at appropriate intervals, to monitor compliance with the provisions governing hours of work or hours of rest that give effect to this Agreement."

8.278 The fourth recital in the preamble to Directive 1999/95 states that the agreement applies to seafarers on board every seagoing ship, whether publicly or privately owned, which is registered in the territory of any Member State and is ordinarily engaged in commercial maritime operations. According to the fifth recital in the preamble to Directive 1999/95, its purpose is to apply the provisions of Directive 1999/63 which reflect the provisions of ILO Convention No 180 to any ship calling at a Community port, irrespective of the flag it flies, in order to identify and remedy any situation which is manifestly hazardous for the safety or health of seafarers.

8.279 Article 1 of Directive 1999/95 provides:

"1. The purpose of this Directive is to provide a mechanism for the verification and enforcement of compliance by ships calling at ports of Member States with Directive 1999/63/EC in order to improve maritime safety, working conditions and the health and safety of seafarers on board ships.
2. Member States shall take appropriate measures to ensure that ships which are not registered in their territory or not flying their flag comply with clauses 1 to 12 of the Agreement annexed to Directive 1999/63/EC."

8.280 Article 3 of Directive 1999/95, entitled "Preparation of reports", provides:

"Without prejudice to Article 1(2), if a Member State in whose port a ship calls voluntarily in the normal course of its business or for operational reasons receives a complaint which it does not consider manifestly unfounded or obtains evidence that the ship does not conform to the standards referred to in Directive 1999/63/EC, it shall prepare a report addressed to the government of the country in which the ship is registered and, when an inspection carried out pursuant to Article 4 provides relevant evidence, the Member State shall take the measures necessary to ensure that any conditions on board which are clearly hazardous to the safety or the health of the crew are rectified.

The identity of the person lodging the report or the complaint must not be revealed to the master or the owner of the ship concerned."

8.281 Article 4 of Directive 1999/95, entitled "Inspection and more detailed inspection", provides:

"1. When carrying out an inspection, in order to obtain evidence that a ship does not conform to the requirements of Directive 1999/63/EC, the inspector shall determine whether:

- a table with the shipboard working arrangements has been established in the working language or languages of the ship and in English according to the model format reproduced in Annex I, or in an alternative equivalent format, and is posted on board in an easily accessible place;
- seafarers' records of hours of work or hours of rest have been established in the working language or languages of the ship and in English according to the model format reproduced in Annex II, or in an alternative equivalent format, and are kept on board and there is proof that the records have been endorsed by the competent authority of the State where the ship is registered.

2. If a complaint has been received or the inspector from his own observations on board believes that the seafarers may be unduly fatigued, the inspector shall conduct a more detailed inspection, pursuant to paragraph 1, to determine whether the working hours or rest periods recorded conform to the standards laid down in Directive 1999/63/EC and that they have been duly observed, taking into account other records relating to the operation of the ship."

8.282 Article 5 of Directive 1999/95, entitled "The rectification of deficiencies", is worded as follows:

"1. If the inspection or the more detailed inspection reveals that the ship does not conform to the requirements of Directive 1999/63/EC, the Member State shall take the measures necessary to ensure that any conditions on board which are clearly hazardous to the safety or health of seafarers are rectified. Such measures may include a prohibition on leaving the port until deficiencies have been rectified or the seafarers have been sufficiently rested.
2. If there is clear evidence that watchkeeping personnel for the first watch or subsequent relieving watches are unduly fatigued, the Member State shall ensure that the ship shall not leave port until the deficiencies found have been rectified or the seafarers in question have been sufficiently rested."

8.283 Article 6 of Directive 1999/95, entitled "Follow-up procedures", states:

"1. In the event that a ship is prohibited from leaving the port pursuant to Article 5, the competent authority of the Member State shall inform the master, the owner or operator, the administration of the flag State or the State where the ship is registered or the Consul, or in his absence the nearest diplomatic representative of the State, of the results of the inspections referred to in Article 4, of any decisions taken by the inspector and of corrective actions required, if necessary.
2. When carrying out an inspection under this Directive, all possible efforts should be made to avoid a ship being unduly delayed. If a ship is unduly delayed, the owner or operator shall be entitled to compensation for any loss or damage suffered. In any instance of alleged undue delay, the burden of proof shall lie with the owner or operator of the ship."

8.284 Article 7 of the same directive, entitled "Right of appeal", provides:

"1. The owner or the operator of the ship or his representative in the Member State shall have a right of appeal against a detention decision taken by the competent authority. An appeal shall not cause the detention to be suspended.
2. Member States shall establish and maintain appropriate procedures for this purpose in accordance with their national legislation.
3. The competent authority shall properly inform the master of a ship referred to in paragraph 1 of the right of appeal."

8.285 Article 8 of that directive, entitled "Administrative cooperation", is worded as follows:

> "1. Member States shall take the necessary steps to provide, in conditions compatible with those laid down in Article 14 of Directive 95/21/EC of 19 June 1995 concerning the enforcement, in respect of shipping using Community ports and sailing in the waters under the jurisdiction of the Member States, of international standards for ship safety, pollution prevention and shipboard living and working conditions (port State control) (OJ 1995 L157, p. 1), for cooperation between their relevant authorities and the relevant competent authorities of other Member States to ensure the effective application of this Directive and shall notify the Commission of the provision made.
> 2. Information on the measures taken pursuant to Articles 4 and 5 shall be published in accordance with procedures such as those set out in the first paragraph of Article 15 of Directive 95/21/EC."

8.286 Article 9 of Directive 1999/95, entitled "'No more favourable' treatment clause", provides:

> "When inspecting a ship registered in the territory of or flying the flag of a State which has not signed ILO Convention No 180 or the Protocol to ILO Convention No 147, Member States shall, once the Convention and the Protocol are in force, ensure that the treatment given to such ships and their crew is no more favourable than that given to a ship flying the flag of a State which is a party to either ILO Convention No 180 or the Protocol to ILO Convention No 147 or both of them."

8.287 Article 10(1) of Directive 1999/95 provides that Member States are to bring into force the laws, regulations and administrative provisions necessary to comply therewith not later than 30 June 2002. Under Article 10(3), Member States are immediately to "notify the Commission of all provisions of domestic law which they adopted in the field governed by that directive. The Commission is to inform the other Member States thereof."

8.288 The national provisions were then reviewed. The Legislative Decree No 271 adapting the legislation on the health and safety of maritime workers on board national merchant fishing vessels to the requirements of Law No 485 of 31 December 1998 (Decreto legislativo N° 271, recante adeguamento della normativa sulla sicurezza e salute dei lavoratori marittimi a bordo delle navi mercantili da pesca nazionali, a norma della Legge 31 dicembre 1998, N° 485) of 27 July 1999 (GURI, General Supplement No 151 of 9 August 1999, hereinafter "the Legislative Decree"), applies, under Article 2 thereof, to maritime workers on board all new or existing merchant ships or vessels, involved in maritime navigation or fishing, as well as to temporarily laid-up merchant ships or vessels, to high-speed craft and to moving platforms.

8.289 Article 11(1), and (3) to (10) of the Legislative Decree provide:

> "1. 'Hours of work on board a ship' means time during which a maritime worker is required to carry out duties connected with its navigation. The following are included in the hours of work on board, in addition to the normal activities at sea and in port:
>
>   (a) musters for emergency drills for fire-fighting and abandoning ship, as well as all drills required by the safety regulations and by the London Convention for the Safety of Life at Sea referred to in Law No 313 of 23 May 1980, and its subsequent revisions, together called 'the Solas Conventions';
>   (b) activities required by the master connected with navigational safety, in case of danger to the crew or ship;

(c) training in respect of health and safety at work on board, concerning the duties performed;
(d) ordinary maintenance of the ship;
(e) activities required by the master in case of operations to assist other merchant or fishing vessels or for the rescue of persons.

...

3. Without prejudice to other provisions in the national collective agreements in the sector, the hours of work of maritime workers on board merchant ships and fishing vessels is fixed at eight hours per day, with one day of rest per week, in addition to public holidays.
4. The limits of the work or rest schedule on board ships shall be established as follows:

   (a) the maximum hours of work shall not exceed:

   1. 14 hours in any 24-hour period; and
   2. 72 hours in any seven-day period; or

   (b) the minimum hours of rest shall not be less than:

   1. 10 hours in any 24-hour period; and
   2. 77 hours in any seven-day period.

5. Hours of rest may not be divided into more than 2 separate periods, one of which shall be at least six consecutive hours in length and the interval between consecutive periods of rest shall not exceed 14 hours.
6. The activities referred to under subparagraphs 1(a) to (e) above shall be conducted in a manner that minimises the disturbance of rest periods and does not induce fatigue.
7. In respect of situations when a maritime worker is on call, he shall have an adequate compensatory rest period if the normal period of rest is disturbed by call-outs to work.
8. For ships used for short voyages and for particular categories of vessels used for port services, the collective agreement may derogate from the requirements of paragraphs 4 and 5, taking account of more frequent or longer rest periods or of the grant of compensatory rest to seafarers employed in the security service or seafarers who work on board.
9. On board all national merchant ships and fishing vessels, a table shall be posted, in an easily accessible place and in Italian and English containing the shipboard service arrangements, with for each rank or position:

   (a) the schedule of service at sea and the schedule of service in port;
   (b) the maximum hours of work and the minimum hours of rest prescribed by this decree or the collective agreements in force.

10. A copy of the Collective Agreement shall be kept on board, and shall be available to any worker on board and to the monitoring bodies."

8.290 Article 21(1) and (3) of the Legislative Decree provide:

"1. In order to check that the working environment continues to comply with the rules and each time that it is considered necessary, an occasional inspection shall be made on board the vessel as provided by Article 18(1)(c) by the competent maritime authority, either on its own initiative, or at the request of the competent local health authority (Azienda unità sanitaria locale), of trade union representatives, or of shipowners or seafarers. The inspection may also be requested directly by the workers through the representative responsible for the safety of the working environment referred to in Article 16.

...

3. Occasional inspections on board foreign merchant ships or vessels shall be carried out in accordance with the procedures mentioned in the Memorandum of Agreement on Inspection by the State of the port of docking."

8.291 The findings of the court are worth studying in full:

"Preliminary observations
As a preliminary point, it is appropriate to recall that whether a Member State has failed to fulfil its obligations must be determined by reference to the situation in that Member State at the end of the period laid down in the reasoned opinion (see, for example, Case C-71/99 *Commission v Germany* [2001] ECR I-5811,[228] paragraph 29, and Case C-110/00 *Commission v Austria* [2001] ECR I-7545,[229] paragraph 13). Therefore, Community Law No 306 of 31 October 2003 cannot be taken into consideration by the Court.

Since, in the grounds of its application, the Commission's only complaint against the Italian Government is that it had failed to show that measures satisfying the obligations imposed on the Member States by Articles 3 to 9 of Directive 1999/95 have been adopted, the action must be understood as referring only those provisions.

On Article 4 of Directive 1999/95
As the Court has consistently held, Member States must, in order to secure the full implementation of directives in law and not only in fact, establish a specific legal framework in the area in question (see Case C-360/87 *Commission v Italy* [1991] ECR I-791,[230] paragraph 13, and Case C-429/01 *Commission v France* [2003] ECR I-[4355],[231] paragraph 40).

Clearly the Legislative Decree does not satisfy that requirement in so far as Article 4 of Directive 1999/95 is concerned.

That provision requires specific inspections in order to obtain evidence that a ship does not conform to the requirements of Directive 1999/63. It states in detail the matters which the checks must cover and requires the carrying out, in the course of inspections described as 'detailed', particularly of cross-checks between, on the one hand, the register of hours of work and rest and, on the other hand, other registers relating to the operation of the ship concerned.

The Legislative Decree contains no such requirements.

Accordingly, the action must be held to be well founded in so far as it relates to Article 4 of Directive 1999/95.

On Article 3 of Directive 1999/95
The first paragraph of Article 3 of Directive 1999/95 imposes on the Member States a dual obligation. The first obligation consists, if a Member State receives a complaint or obtains evidence that a ship does not conform to the standards referred to in Directive 1999/63, in preparing a report addressed to the government of the country in which the ship is registered.

It is clear from the Court's case-law that a provision which concerns only relations between a Member State and the Commission or the other Members States need not, in principle, be transposed (see Case C-296/01 *Commission v France* [2003] ECR [I-13909],[232] paragraph 92, and Case C-429/01 *Commission v France*, cited above, paragraph 68).

It should be recalled that, according to equally settled case-law, each of the Member States to which a directive is addressed is obliged to adopt, within the framework of its national legal system, all the measures necessary to ensure that the directive is fully effective, in accordance with the objective it pursues (see, in particular, Case C-336/97 *Commission v Italy* [1999] ECR I-3771,[233] paragraph 19; Case C-97/00 *Commission v France* [2001] ECR I-2053,[234] paragraph 9; and Case C-478/99 *Commission v Sweden* [2002] ECR I-4147,[235] paragraph 15).

---

228 Ed., ECLI:EU:C:2001:433.
229 Ed., ECLI:EU:C:2001:538.
230 Ed., ECLI:EU:C:1991:86.
231 Ed., ECLI:EU:C:2003:643.
232 Ed., ECLI:EU:C:2003:626.
233 Ed., ECLI:EU:C:1999:272.
234 Ed., ECLI:EU:C:2001:149.
235 Ed., ECLI:EU:C:2002:281.

40. According to the second and seventh recitals in the preamble, the objective of Directive 1999/95 is primarily to improve the shipboard living and working conditions of seafarers and safety at sea. The report addressed to the government of the country in which the ship is registered is intended to draw attention to a situation which is clearly hazardous to the safety or the health of the crew. It is intended immediately to eliminate that risk and does not concern only mere obligations to notify. To have full effect the rule therefore requires transposition.
41. As a result, the Commission's action must be upheld in relation to that obligation.
42. As regards the second obligation under the first paragraph of Article 3 of Directive 1999/95, it requires the Member States to take the necessary remedial action when an inspection carried out pursuant to Article 4 provides evidence of non-compliance with the standards referred to in Directive 1999/63. Given that, as held in paragraph 36 of this judgment, Article 4 has not been transposed into Italian law, the Commission's action must also be held to be well founded in so far as it relates to that obligation.
43. The second paragraph of Article 3 of Directive 1999/95 provides that the identity of the person lodging the complaint must not be revealed to the master or the owner of the ship concerned.
44. None of the provisions of domestic law invoked by the Italian Government reproduces that prohibition.
45. As a result, the action is well founded in that regard.

On Article 5 of Directive 1999/95

46. That provision requires, particularly, that the measures for rectification of the deficiencies established may and, in certain conditions, must include, for the ship concerned, a prohibition on leaving the port until those deficiencies have been corrected.
47. It is not disputed that no such measures are set out in the provisions of domestic law invoked by the Italian Government.
48. Therefore, the action must be upheld in relation to Article 5 of Directive 1999/95.

On Article 6 of Directive 1999/95

49. Article 6(1) of Directive 1999/95 imposes on the competent authority of the Member State concerned a notification obligation if a ship is prohibited from leaving the port under Article 5 thereof.
50. The addressees of such notification are, first, the master, owner or operator of the ship and, secondly, the administration of the flag State or the State where the ship is registered or the Consul, or in his absence the nearest diplomatic representative of that State.
51. The domestic legislation invoked by the Italian Government contains no such notification obligation.
52. Admittedly, as pointed out in paragraph 38 of this judgment, a Member State need not, in principle, transpose provisions which concern only relations between the Member States.
53. It must be emphasised that, in this case, the obligation to notify the administration of the flag State or the State in which the ship is registered or the Consul, or in his absence the nearest diplomatic representative of that State, is the corollary of that State's responsibilities under public international law.

Indeed, it is clear from Article 94(1) of the United Nations Convention on the Law of the Sea, signed at Montego Bay on 10 December 1982, which entered into force on 16 November 1994 and was approved by Council Decision 98/392/EC of 23 March 1998 (OJ 1998 L179, p. 1), concerning the obligations of the flag State, that every State is effectively to exercise its jurisdiction and control in administrative, technical and social fields over ships flying its flag. In particular, pursuant to paragraphs 2(b) and 3(b) of that article, every State is to assume jurisdiction under its internal law over each ship flying its flag and its master, officers and crew in respect of administrative, technical and social matters concerning the ship, and every State is to take such measures for ships flying its flag as are necessary to ensure safety at sea, with regard, inter alia, to the manning of ships, labour conditions and training of crews, taking account of the applicable international instruments.

It is clear from Article 94(6) that, once advised of the fact that the proper control has not been exercised over a ship, the flag State is to undertake an investigation and, if appropriate, take any action necessary to remedy the situation.

It follows that the notification required by Article 6(1) of Directive 1999/95 is intended directly to improve safety at sea in the case of a clearly hazardous situation. To have full effect that provision therefore requires express transposition into national law.

As a result, the action must be upheld as regards Article 6(1) of Directive 1999/95.

As regards Article 6(2) of Directive 1999/95, it establishes rules relating to the protection of the financial interests of the persons concerned by inspections carried out under that directive. Such rules have no equivalent in the provisions of domestic law on which the Italian Government relies.

Consequently, the action must be upheld as regards Article 6(2) of Directive 1999/95.

On Article 7 of Directive 1999/95

As regards this complaint, it must be recalled that it is settled law that transposing a directive into national law does not necessarily require its provisions to be reproduced verbatim in a specific express legal rule; a general legal context may be sufficient, provided that it does effectively ensure the full application of the directive in a sufficiently clear and precise manner, in order that, where that directive seeks to create rights for individuals, those entitled to such rights are put in a position to ascertain the full extent of their rights and to invoke them, where appropriate, before the national courts (Case C-131/88 *Commission v Germany* [1991] ECR I-825,[236] paragraph 6, and Case C-49/00 *Commission v Italy* [2001] ECR I-8575,[237] paragraphs 21 and 22).

None of the domestic law provisions cited by the Italian Government relates to a right of appeal against a decision to detain a vessel taken by the competent national authority or the latter's obligation to inform the master of the ship concerned of that right.

Consequently, the Commission's action must be upheld in respect of Article 7 of Directive 1999/95.

On Article 8 of Directive 1999/95

63. Article 8(1) of that Directive concerns only relations between the Member States and relations between them and the Commission. As noted in paragraph 38 of this judgment, such provisions need not, in principle, be transposed.

    Nevertheless, given that the Member States are under an obligation to ensure full compliance with Community law, the Commission may show that compliance with the provision of a directive governing such relations requires the adoption of specific measures transposing that provision into the national legal order (see Case C-296/01 *Commission v France*, cited above, paragraph 92, and Case C-429/01 *Commission v France*, cited above, paragraph 68).

    Here, the Commission has not put forward any arguments to show that the Italian authorities have a practice which runs counter to the Member States' obligations under Article 8(1) of Directive 1999/95.

    As a result, the Commission's action must be rejected in that respect.

    On the other hand, it must be held to be well founded in so far as it concerns the obligation under Article 8(2) of Directive 1999/95 to publish, since the provisions relied upon by the Italian Government make no reference to such an obligation under national law.

On Article 9 of Directive 1999/95

The provisions of national law cited by the Italian Government do not contain any 'no more favourable' treatment clause within the meaning of Article 9 of Directive 1999/95.

Therefore, the action must be upheld as regards that provision.

Having regard to all the foregoing considerations, it is appropriate to declare that, by failing to adopt the laws, regulations and administrative provisions necessary to comply with Articles 3 to

---

236 Ed., ECLI:EU:C:1991:87.
237 Ed., ECLI:EU:C:2001:611.

7, 8(2) and 9 of Directive 1999/95, the Italian Republic has failed to fulfil its obligations under that directive, and to dismiss the remainder of the action. ...
  On those grounds, the Court (Fourth Chamber) hereby:
  Declares that, by failing to adopt the laws, regulations and administrative provisions necessary to comply with Articles 3 to 7, 8(2) and 9 of Directive 1999/95/EC of the European Parliament and of the Council of 13 December 1999 concerning the enforcement of provisions in respect of seafarers' hours of work on board ships calling at Community ports, the Italian Republic has failed to fulfil its obligations under that directive."

Q. MINIMUM LEVEL OF TRAINING OF SEAFARERS: DIRECTIVE 2008/106

8.292 On 19 November 2008, Directive 2008/106 was adopted by the European Parliament and the Council on the minimum level of training of seafarers.[238] This was amended by Directive 2012/35 of the European Parliament and of the Council of 21 November 2012 amending Directive 2008/106 on the minimum level of training of seafarers.[239]

R. THE *FIAMINGO* CASE

8.293 On 3 July 2014, the CJEU[240] delivered a preliminary ruling in *Maurizio Fiamingo, Leonardo Zappalà, Francesco Rotondo and Others v Rete Ferroviaria Italiana SpA*.[241] The case involved a request to the CJEU for a preliminary ruling from Italy's Corte suprema di cassazione. The case concerned the interpretation of Clauses 3 and 5 of the Framework Agreement on fixed-term work concluded on 18 March 1999 ("the Framework Agreement"), which is annexed to Council Directive 1999/70 of 28 June 1999 concerning the Framework Agreement on fixed-term work concluded by ETUC, UNICE and CEEP.[242,243] The proceedings involved a dispute between workers employed as seafarers and their employer, Rete Ferroviaria Italiana SpA ("RFI"), concerning the classification of contracts of employment between them.

8.294 Article 1 of Directive 1999/70 stated that the purpose of that directive is "to put into effect the framework agreement ... concluded ... between the general cross-industry organisations (ETUC, UNICE and CEEP) annexed hereto". The second to fourth paragraphs in the preamble to the Framework Agreement are worded as follows:

"The parties to this agreement recognise that contracts of an indefinite duration are, and will continue to be, the general form of employment relationship between employers and workers. They also recognise that fixed-term employment contracts respond, in certain circumstances, to the needs of both employers and workers.
  This agreement sets out the general principles and minimum requirements relating to fixed-term work, recognising that their detailed application needs to take account of the realities of specific national, sectoral and seasonal situations. It illustrates the willingness of the Social

---

[238] OJ 2008 L323/33.
[239] OJ 2012 L343/78.
[240] The Third Chamber was composed of Judges Ilešič (President of the Chamber), Fernlund, Ó Caoimh (Rapporteur), Toader and Jarašiūnas. The Advocate-General was AG Kokott but she did not give an opinion.
[241] Cases C-362/13, C-363/13 and C-407/13.
[242] ETUC is the European Trade Union Confederation, UNICE is the Union of Industrial and Employers' Confederations of Europe and CEEP is the European Centre of Employers and Enterprises.
[243] OJ 1999 L175/43.

Partners to establish a general framework for ensuring equal treatment for fixed-term workers by protecting them against discrimination and for using fixed-term employment contracts on a basis acceptable to employers and workers.

This agreement applies to fixed-term workers with the exception of those placed by a temporary work agency at the disposition of a user enterprise. It is the intention of the parties to consider the need for a similar agreement relating to temporary agency work."

8.295 Paragraphs 6 to 8 and 10 of the general considerations to the Framework Agreement stated:

"6. Whereas employment contracts of an indefinite duration are the general form of employment relationships and contribute to the quality of life of the workers concerned and improve performance;
7. Whereas the use of fixed-term employment contracts based on objective reasons is a way to prevent abuse;
8. Whereas fixed-term employment contracts are a feature of employment in certain sectors, occupations and activities which can suit both employers and workers;
…
10. Whereas this agreement refers back to Member States and social partners for the arrangements for the application of its general principles, minimum requirements and provisions, in order to take account of the situation in each Member State and the circumstances of particular sectors and occupations, including the activities of a seasonal nature."

8.296 Under Clause 1 of the Framework Agreement, entitled "Purpose":

"The purpose of this framework agreement is to:

(a) improve the quality of fixed-term work by ensuring the application of the principle of non-discrimination;
(b) establish a framework to prevent abuse arising from the use of successive fixed-term employment contracts or relationships."

8.297 Clause 2 of the Framework Agreement, entitled "Scope", provides:

"1. This agreement applies to fixed-term workers who have an employment contract or employment relationship as defined in law, collective agreements or practice in each Member State.
2. Member States after consultation with the social partners and/or the social partners may provide that this agreement does not apply to:

(a) initial vocational training relationships and apprenticeship schemes;
(b) employment contracts and relationships which have been concluded within the framework of a specific public or publicly-supported training, integration and vocational retraining programme."

8.298 Clause 3 of the Framework Agreement, entitled "Definitions", provides that for

"the purpose of this agreement the term 'fixed-term worker' means a person having an employment contract or relationship entered into directly between an employer and a worker where the end of the employment contract or relationship is determined by objective conditions such as reaching a specific date, completing a specific task, or the occurrence of a specific event."

8.299 Clause 5 of the Framework Agreement, entitled 'Measures to prevent abuse', provides:

"1. To prevent abuse arising from the use of successive fixed-term employment contracts or relationships, Member States, after consultation with social partners in accordance with national law, collective agreements or practice, and/or the social partners, shall, where there are no equivalent legal measures to prevent abuse, introduce in a manner which takes account of the needs of specific sectors and/or categories of workers, one or more of the following measures:

(a) objective reasons justifying the renewal of such contracts or relationships;
(b) the maximum total duration of successive fixed-term employment contracts or relationships;
(c) the number of renewals of such contracts or relationships.

2. Member States after consultation with the social partners and/or the social partners shall, where appropriate, determine under what conditions fixed-term employment contracts or relationships:

(a) shall be regarded as 'successive'
(b) shall be deemed to be contracts or relationships of indefinite duration."

8.300 Under the heading "Provisions on implementation", Clause 8(2) of the Framework Agreement states: "This Agreement shall be without prejudice to any more specific [European law] provisions, and in particular [European law] provisions concerning equal treatment or opportunities for men and women."

8.301 The case touched on Directive 2009/13. Article 1 of Council Directive 2009/13 of 16 February 2009 implementing the agreement concluded by the ECSA and the ETF on the Maritime Labour Convention, 2006, and amending Directive 1999/63[244] is worded as follows:

"This Directive implements the Agreement on [the] Maritime Labour Convention, 2006, concluded on 19 May 2008 between the organisations representing management and labour in the maritime transport sector (European Community Shipowners' Associations, ECSA and European Transport Workers' Federation, ETF) as set out in the Annex ['the agreement on the Maritime Labour Convention 2006']."

The part of that agreement entitled "Definitions and Scope of Application" provides:

"1. For the purpose of this Agreement and unless provided otherwise in particular provisions, the term:
...
(c) 'seafarer' means any person who is employed or engaged or works in any capacity on board a 'ship' to which this Agreement applies;
...
(e) 'ship' means a ship other than one which navigates exclusively in inland waters or waters within, or closely adjacent to, sheltered waters or areas where port regulations apply;
...
2. Except as expressly provided otherwise, this Agreement applies to all seafarers."

Within the part of the agreement entitled "The Regulations and the Standards", Title 2, which is headed "Conditions of Employment", contains, in particular, Regulation 2.1 concerning "Seafarers' employment agreements". Standard A2.1, paragraph 4, of Regulation 2.1 is worded as follows:

"Each Member State shall adopt laws and regulations specifying the matters that are to be included in all seafarers' employment agreements governed by its national law. Seafarers' employment agreements shall in all cases contain the following particulars:
...

---

244 OJ 2009 L124/30.

(c) the place where and date when the seafarers' employment agreement is entered into;

...

(g) the termination of the agreement and the conditions thereof, including:

  (i) if the agreement has been made for an indefinite period, the conditions entitling either party to terminate it, as well as the required notice period, which shall not be less for the shipowner than for the seafarer;
  (ii) if the agreement has been made for a definite period, the date fixed for its expiry; and
  (iii) if the agreement has been made for a voyage, the port of destination and the time which has to expire after arrival before the seafarer should be discharged."

Within the final part of the agreement, entitled "Final Provisions", the fourth paragraph provides the "Agreement shall be without prejudice to any more stringent and/or specific existing [European Union] legislation." In Italy, employment contracts for seafarers were governed by the rules of the Navigation Code, approved by Royal Decree No 327 of 30 March 1942 ("the Navigation Code"), which, pursuant to Article 1 thereof, takes precedence over the general rules of civil law applicable to employment contracts. Such contracts are therefore not subject to Legislative Decree No 368 of 6 September 2001 implementing Directive 1999/70 concerning the Framework Agreement on fixed-term work concluded by ETUC, UNICE and CEEP (decreto legislativo n. 368, Attuazione della direttiva 1999/70/CE relativa all'accordo quadro sul lavoro a tempo determinato concluso dall'UNICE, dal CEEP e dal CES) (GURI No 235 of 9 October 2001, p. 4). Article 325 of the Navigation Code provided:

"The employment contract may be concluded:

(a) for one or several given voyages;
(b) for a fixed term;
(c) for an indefinite duration.
...

For the purposes of the employment contract, the term 'voyage' means all the crossings made between the port of loading and the port of final destination, in addition to a possible crossing in ballast to return to the port of loading."

According to Article 326 of the Navigation Code:

"A fixed-term contract and a contract for several voyages may not be concluded for a period longer than one year; if they are concluded for a longer period they shall be considered to be contracts of indefinite duration.
 If, under a number of contracts for several voyages or a number of fixed-term contracts, or under a number of contracts of both types, the engaged seafarer is employed by the same shipowner continuously for a period longer than one year, the employment contract shall be governed by the rules concerning contracts of indefinite duration.
 For the purposes of the previous paragraph, the employment shall be considered to be continuous when the period between the ending of one contract and the conclusion of the subsequent contract is no more than [60] days."

Article 332 of the Navigation Code stated that the

"employment contract must indicate: ... (4) where the engagement is for voyages, the voyage or voyages to be made and the date on which the seafarer must begin work; where the engagement is for a fixed term, the starting point and duration of the contract".

Article 374 of the Navigation Code provided:

"The provisions of [Article] 326 ... may be derogated from by the norme corporative [special body of rules relating to a trade or profession]; they may not be derogated from in individual contracts, unless that derogation is to the advantage of the person employed. However, even under the norme corporative the period provided for in the first and second paragraphs of Article 326 may not be increased, nor may the period provided for in Article 326(3) be reduced."

8.302 The disputes in the main proceedings and the questions referred for a preliminary ruling:

"20. The appellants in the main proceedings are seamen enrolled in the register of seafarers. They were engaged by RFI under successive fixed-term contracts, concluded after 2001, to work on one or several voyages and for a maximum of 78 days, on board ferries making the crossing between Messina-Villa San Giovanni and Messina-Reggio Calabria (Italy). It is apparent from the orders for reference that under those contracts the appellants had worked for their employer for a period of less than one year and that a period of less than 60 days had elapsed between the end of one contract of employment and the conclusion of the subsequent contract.

21. Considering that their employment relationship had been unlawfully terminated following their disembarkation, the appellants in the main proceedings brought an action before the Tribunale di Messina (Court of Messina), seeking a declaration that their fixed-term employment contracts were void, the conversion of those contracts into employment contracts of indefinite duration, immediate re-engagement or reinstatement and compensation for loss suffered.

At first instance, the Tribunale di Messina upheld the claims of the appellants in the main proceedings in Case C-407/13 and dismissed the claims of the appellants in the main proceedings in Cases C-362/13 and C-363/13. On appeal, however, the Corte d'appello di Messina (Court of Appeal, Messina) dismissed the appellants' claims in their entirety.

The appellants in the main proceedings then brought an appeal before the Corte suprema di cassazione (Supreme Court of Cassation). They submitted that the Corte d'appello di Messina had wrongly held that the Framework Agreement was not applicable to seafarers and had wrongly considered that their fixed-term employment contracts were lawful even though those contracts did not indicate the termination date of the contracts but only their duration by the phrase 'a maximum of 78 days' and also failed to set out the objective reasons justifying the use of such contracts. According to the appellants, the use of fixed-term employment contracts was abusive because their use was explained not by the particular character of maritime work or the existence of objective reasons, but in order to remedy structural staff shortages.

As a result, the Corte suprema di cassazione considers that it is necessary to ask whether the Framework Agreement applies to employment relationships in the maritime sector. If it does, the arrangements for employment for a fixed term provided for by the Navigation Code might prove to be contrary to the Framework Agreement. Given that by Legislative Decree No 368 of 6 September 2001, implementing Directive 1999/70/EC concerning the Framework Agreement on fixed-term work concluded by ETUC, UNICE and CEEP, the Italian legislature fulfilled the obligation laid down in Clause 5 of that agreement to provide for measures designed to prevent abuse arising from the use of successive fixed-term employment contracts, it is possible that the provisions of that decree must equally be applied to employment relationships in the maritime sector.

The Corte suprema di cassazione decided to stay the proceedings and to refer the following questions to the Court of Justice for a preliminary ruling:

'(1) Are the clauses of the Framework Agreement ... applicable to maritime labour? In particular, does Clause 2(1) [of the Framework Agreement] also cover workers engaged for a fixed-term on ferries making daily sea crossings?

(2) Does the Framework Agreement, ... in particular Clause 3(1), preclude national legislation (Article 332 of the Navigation Code) that provides that the "duration" of the contract, rather than its "term", is to be indicated, and is it compatible with that directive to provide for the duration of the contract by indicating a terminating point that is definite as to its existence ("a maximum of 78 days") but indefinite as to when it occurs?

(3) Does the Framework Agreement, ... in particular Clause 3(1), preclude national legislation (Articles 325, 326 and 332 of the Navigation Code) in which the objective reasons for a fixed-term contract are expressed simply in terms of the voyage or voyages to be made, in essence equating the purpose of the contract (the services provided) with its cause (the reasons for concluding a fixed-term contract)?

(4) Does the Framework Agreement ... preclude national legislation (in the present case, the Navigation Code) which, in the event of the use of successive contracts (in a way that would amount to abuse for the purposes of Clause 5), excludes the conversion of those contracts into contracts of indefinite duration (the measure provided for in Article 326 of the Navigation Code only applies in situations in which the seafarer works continuously for more than one year and in situations in which the period between the ending of one contract and the conclusion of the subsequent contract is no more than 60 days)?'"

8.303 In response to the first question, the CJEU responded:

"40. In the light of the foregoing, the answer to the first question is that the Framework Agreement must be interpreted as meaning that it applies to workers, such as the appellants in the main proceedings, who are employed as seafarers under fixed-term employment contracts on board ferries making sea crossings between two ports situated in the same Member State."

8.304 In its second question, the referring court asked whether the provisions of the Framework Agreement, in particular Clause 3(1) must be interpreted as precluding national legislation which provided that fixed-term employment contracts have to indicate their duration, but not their termination date. The CJEU replied:

"44. ... Framework Agreement is not intended to harmonise all national rules relating to fixed-term employment contracts but simply aims, by determining general principles and minimum requirements, to establish a general framework for ensuring equal treatment for fixed-term workers by protecting them against discrimination and to prevent abuse arising from the use of successive fixed-term work agreements or contracts (see, in this regard, Del Cerro Alonso, EU:C:2007:509, paragraphs 26 and 36; Impact, C-268/06, EU:C:2008:223, paragraph 111; Huet, C-251/11, EU:C:2012:133, paragraph 41; and the order in Vino, C-20/10, EU:C:2010:677, paragraph 54).

45. The Framework Agreement does not contain any provision that lays down the formal particulars that must be included in fixed-term employment contracts.

46. In that regard, Clause 3(1) of the Framework Agreement, as both its heading and its wording clearly demonstrate, defines the concept of 'fixed-term worker' and, in that context, sets out the central characteristic of a fixed-term contract, namely the fact that the end of such a contract is determined 'by objective conditions such as reaching a specific date, completing a specific task, or the occurrence of a specific event'. However, that clause does not impose any obligation on Member States in respect of the rules of national law applicable to the conclusion of fixed-term employment contracts (see, to this effect, the order in Vino, EU:C:2010:677, paragraphs 60 to 62 and the case-law cited).

47. In any event, inasmuch as the present question must be understood as seeking to determine whether the Framework Agreement is applicable to workers whose employment contracts, such as those at issue in the main proceedings, indicate only their duration (by referring to a 'maximum of 78 days'), it suffices to state that such workers must be regarded as

'fixed-term workers' within the meaning of Clause 3(1) of the Framework Agreement, given that such a reference permits the end of those contracts to be determined objectively and that the Framework Agreement therefore applies to them.

48. In view of the foregoing, the answer to the second question is that the provisions of the Framework Agreement must be interpreted as meaning that they do not preclude national legislation, such as that at issue in the main proceedings, which provides that fixed-term employment contracts have to indicate their duration, but not their termination date."

8.305 By its third and fourth questions, the referring court asked, in substance, whether Clauses 3(1) and 5 of the Framework Agreement must be interpreted as precluding national legislation, which, on the one hand, considers that the mere indication of one or several voyages to be made constitutes objective justification for the fixed-term employment contract and, on the other hand, provides that fixed-term contracts are converted into employment contracts of indefinite duration only where the worker concerned has been employed continuously under such contracts by the same employer for a period longer than one year, the employment relationship being considered to be continuous when the time that elapses between the fixed-term employment contracts is less than or equal to 60 days. The CJEU replied:

"74. It follows from the foregoing that the answer to the third and fourth questions is that Clause 5 of the Framework Agreement must be interpreted as meaning that it does not preclude, in principle, national legislation, such as that at issue in the main proceedings, which provides for the conversion of fixed-term employment contracts into employment contracts of indefinite duration only in circumstances where the worker concerned has been employed continuously under such contracts by the same employer for a period longer than one year, the employment relationship being considered to be continuous where the fixed-term employment contracts are separated by time lapses of less than or equal to 60 days. It is, however, for the referring court to satisfy itself that the conditions of application and the effective implementation of that legislation result in a measure that is adequate to prevent and punish the misuse of successive fixed-term employment contracts or relationships."

S. THE *BAKKER* CASE

8.306 On 7 June 2012, the CJEU[245] delivered a preliminary ruling in *Bakker v Minister van Financiën*.[246] The case concerned social security rights for a worker holding Dutch nationality working, for an employer established in the Netherlands, on board dredgers flying the Dutch flag which operate outside the EU. It was a preliminary ruling resulting from a reference from the Dutch Hoge Raad der Nederlanden. The case concerned the interpretation of Title II of Regulation 1408/71 of 14 June 1971 on the application of social security schemes to employed persons, to self-employed persons and to members of their families moving within the Community.[247] The reference was made in proceedings between Mr Bakker and the Staatssecretaris van Financiën (State Secretary for Finance) concerning his compulsory affiliation to the Dutch social insurance scheme for 2004.

---

245 The Eighth Chamber.
246 Case C-106/11.
247 As amended and updated by Council Reg. (EC) No 118/97 of 2 December 1996 (OJ 1997 L28, p. 1), as amended by Council Reg. (EC) No 307/1999 of 8 February 1999 (OJ 1999 L38, p. 1) ("Regulation 1408/71").

8.307 In Article 1(a)(i) of Regulation 1408/71, the term "employed person" means any person who "is insured, compulsorily or on an optional continued basis, for one or more of the contingencies covered by the branches of a social security scheme for employed or self-employed persons or by a special scheme for civil servants". Article 2(1) provided that the "Regulation shall apply to employed or self-employed persons and to students who are or have been subject to the legislation of one or more Member States and who are nationals of one of the Member States". Article 13 of that regulation, which forms part of Title II thereof, entitled "Determination of the legislation applicable", provided:

> "1. Subject to Articles 14c and 14f, persons to whom this Regulation applies shall be subject to the legislation of a single Member State only. That legislation shall be determined in accordance with the provisions of this Title.
> 2. Subject to Articles 14 to 17:
> ...
>   (c) a person employed on board a vessel flying the flag of a Member State shall be subject to the legislation of the State."

8.308 Article 6 of the Netherlands' General Law on Old-Age Pensions (Algemene Ouderdomswet, Stb. 1956, No 281) provided:

> "1. Insured persons for the purpose of the present provisions are:
>   (a) residents, and
>   (b) non-residents subject to income tax in respect of salaried occupational activities carried out in the Netherlands, who have not yet reached the age of 65."

8.309 During 2004, Mr Bakker, who was Dutch, resided in Spain and was employed on board dredgers flying the Dutch flag for an undertaking established in the Netherlands. He carried out his activities mainly in the territorial seas of China and of the United Arab Emirates. The dredgers were recorded in the Dutch maritime shipping register. Mr Bakker challenged the assessment sent to him in respect of income tax and national insurance contributions for 2004 in the Netherlands. Following the dismissal by the Rechtbank te Breda (District Court, Breda) of the objection which he had raised against that assessment, Mr Bakker appealed to the Gerechtshof te 's-Hertogenbosch (Regional Court of Appeal, 's-Hertogenbosch), which confirmed the decision delivered at first instance.

8.310 The Gerechtshof te 's-Hertogenbosch took the view that, in respect of 2004, Mr Bakker could be regarded as affiliated to the Dutch social insurance scheme notwithstanding the fact that his activities were performed outside EU territory. That court based its assessment on the fact that Dutch social security legislation had been made applicable to Mr Bakker by Regulation 1408/71 and, more specifically, by Title II thereof. It found, in particular, that Mr Bakker worked on board seagoing vessels flying the Dutch flag, that is to say, the flag of a Member State within the meaning of Article 13(2)(c) of that regulation. The fact that those vessels were moored during dredging activities in territorial seas outside the EU was not conclusive, in the view of the Gerechtshof te 's-Hertogenbosch, since Article 13(2)(c) of Regulation 1408/71 does not lay down any restriction as to the type of vessel or the location of the activities.

8.311 Seised of an appeal on a point of law, the Hoge Raad der Nederlanden (Supreme Court of the Netherlands) held, however, that there are reasonable doubts as to the application of Title II of Regulation 1408/71 in the present case.

8.312 The Hoge Raad der Nederlanden decided to stay the proceedings and to refer the following questions to the Court of Justice for a preliminary ruling:

"1. Are the designation rules in Title II of Regulation ... No 1408/71 applicable in a case such as the present, where an employed person with Netherlands nationality residing in Spain is employed as a seafarer by an employer established in the Netherlands, and carries out his work on board dredgers which navigate outside the territory of the [EU] under the Netherlands flag, with the result that the legislation of the Netherlands is designated as the legislation applicable, so that consequently Netherlands national insurance contributions may be levied, whereas judging solely on the basis of the national legislation of the Netherlands he is not affiliated to the Netherlands social security scheme as a result of the fact that he does not reside in the Netherlands?
2. To what extent is it important in that regard that in the implementation of the Netherlands employed persons' insurance scheme a policy is followed by virtue of which seafarers in a case such as the present are considered by the implementing body to be insured persons on the basis of [EU] law?"

8.313 The CJEU summarised the first question as asking, in essence, whether Article 13(2)(c) of Regulation 1408/71 must be interpreted as precluding a legislative measure of a Member State from excluding from affiliation to the social security scheme of that Member State a person in the position of the applicant in the main proceedings, who holds that Member State's nationality but does not reside in it and is employed on board a dredger flying the flag of that Member State but operating outside EU territory. The Dutch government and the European Commission took the view that that question should be answered in the negative, Mr Bakker was of the opposite view. The CJEU began by recalling that Article 13(2)(c) of Regulation 1408/71 expressly provided that a person employed on board a vessel flying the flag of a Member State is to be subject to the legislation of the State. Thus, pursuant to that provision, a person in Mr Bakker's situation is, in principle, subject to Dutch social security legislation, in view of the professional activity which that person carries out on board a vessel flying the Dutch flag. However, Mr Bakker has put forward two arguments contesting the application of Article 13(2)(c) of Regulation 1408/71 to his situation. First, he argued that the dredgers on which he worked were not covered by the concept of "vessel" in Article 13(2)(c) of that regulation. The CJEU rejected that argument inasmuch as there is no condition laid down in that provision as to the type of "vessel" covered. Furthermore, it is apparent from the explanations provided by the national court that those dredgers held a certificate of registration and were recorded in the maritime shipping register of the Netherlands. Second, he argued that Article 13(2)(c) of Regulation 1408/71 does not apply to his situation in view of the fact that the dredgers in question operated principally in the territorial seas of China and of the United Arab Emirates. Under Article 2(1) of the UNCLOS, signed at Montego Bay (Jamaica) on 10 December 1982, which entered into force on 16 November 1994, was ratified by the Kingdom of the Netherlands on 28 June 1996 and was approved on behalf of the EC by Council Decision 98/392 of 23 March 1998 (OJ 1998 L179, p. 1), the sovereignty of a coastal State extends, beyond its land territory and internal waters, to an adjacent belt of sea, described as the territorial sea. Consequently, in Mr Bakker's submission, the professional activities carried out on board the dredgers in question come under the jurisdiction of the coastal States and not under that of the flag Member State, namely the Kingdom of the Netherlands.

8.314 The CJEU noted, in this regard, that it follows from the case law of the Court that the mere fact that a worker's activities are performed outside the territory of the EU is not sufficient to exclude the application of the EU rules on the free movement of workers, as long as the employment relationship retains a sufficiently close link with the territory of the EU. In a case such as that here at issue in the main proceedings, a link of that kind can be found in the fact, confirmed by the Hoge Raad, that Mr Bakker works on board a vessel registered in the Netherlands for an undertaking established in that Member State.

8.315 Furthermore, the CJEU went on to say that neither respect for the sovereignty of the coastal State nor the UNCLOS require that a worker in Mr Bakker's situation be deprived of the benefit of the social insurance provided for, in accordance with Regulation 1408/71, by the Member State whose flag the vessel flies, when that vessel is located in the territorial waters of a State other than that Member State.

8.316 The CJEU was clear that the sole purpose of Article 13(2)(c) of Regulation 1408/71 is to determine the national legislation applicable to persons employed on board a vessel flying the flag of a Member State. As such, the provision is not intended to lay down the conditions creating the right or the obligation to become affiliated to a social security scheme or to a particular branch under such a scheme. It was for the legislation of each Member State to lay down those conditions.

8.317 The CJEU thus decided that having regard to all of the foregoing, the answer to the first question is that Article 13(2)(c) of Regulation 1408/71 must be interpreted as precluding a legislative measure of a Member State from excluding, from affiliation to the social security scheme of that Member State, a person in the position of the applicant in the main proceedings, who holds that Member State's nationality but does not reside in it and is employed on board a dredger flying the flag of that Member State and operating outside the territory of the EU. Having regard to the answer given to the first question, it is not necessary to answer the second question.

T. THE *IRAKLIS HARALAMBIDIS V CALOGERO CASILLI* CASE

8.318 On 10 September 2014, the CJEU's Second Chamber gave judgment in *Iraklis Haralambidis v Calogero Casilli*.[248] The case concerned free movement of workers, Articles 45(1) and (4) of the TFEU, the concept of a worker, employment in the public service, the post of the president of a port authority and whether a nationality requirement was justified. The preliminary ruling was sent by the Italian Consiglio di Stato. The case concerned the interpretation of Articles 45, 49 and 51 of the TFEU, Directive 2006/123 of 12 December 2006 on services in the internal market,[249] and Articles 15 and 21(2) of the Charter of Fundamental Rights of the European Union ("the Charter"). The request was made in proceedings between Mr Haralambidis, a Greek national, and Mr Casilli concerning the appointment of Mr Haralambidis as President of the Autorità Portuale di Brindisi (the Port Authority of Brindisi).

---

248 Case C-270/13 ECLI:EU:C:2014:2185. The Court was composed of Judges Silva de Lapuerta (President of the Chamber), da Cruz Vilaça (Rapporteur), Arestis, Bonichot and Arabadjiev. The Advocate-General was AG Wahl.
249 OJ 2006 L376/36.

8.319 Article 51 of the Italian Constitution provided that "[t]he holding of public office or elected positions shall be open, on equal terms, to any citizen of either sex, in accordance with the conditions established by law" and that "[f]or the purposes of access to public offices and elected positions, Italians not belonging to the Republic may be deemed by law to be equivalent to citizens". The expression "Italians not belonging to the Republic" refers to citizens of Italian nationality residing abroad. Article 38(1) and (2) of Legislative Decree No 165 concerning general rules for the organisation of work in the public administration (decreto legislativo n.165, Norme generali sull'ordinamento del lavoro alle dipendenze delle amministrazioni pubbliche) of 30 March 2001 (Ordinary Supplement to GURI No 106 of 9 May 2001 ("Legislative Decree No 165/01") provides:

> "1. Citizens of [EU] Member States shall have access to posts in the public administration that do not involve the direct or indirect exercise of public powers, or do not relate to the protection of the national interest.
> 2. A decree of the President of the Council of Ministers ... shall determine the posts and functions for which access is restricted to Italian nationals, as well as the mandatory criteria governing the access to posts of the citizens referred to in paragraph 1."

8.320 Decree No 174 of the President of the Council of Ministers laying down the rules on access by citizens of EU Member States to posts within the public administration (Decreto del Presidente del Consiglio dei Ministri, Regolamento recante norme sull'accesso dei cittadini degli Stati membri dell'Unione europea ai posti di lavoro presso le amministrazioni pubbliche) of 7 February 1994 (GURI No 61 of 15 March 1994) sets out the posts and duties for which Italian nationality is required. That decree was adopted pursuant to the decree preceding Legislative Decree No 165/01, namely Legislative Decree No 29 of 3 February 1993 (GURI No 30 of 6 February 1993), where wording did not differ significantly from that of Legislative Decree No 165/01.

8.321 Article 1(1)(b) of Decree No 174 of 7 February 1994 provides:

> "The posts in the public administration to which access cannot be obtained without Italian citizenship include: ... (b) the highest administrative posts of the peripheral structures of the public administration, including autonomous administrations, of the non-economic public entities, of provinces and municipalities as well as regions, and of the Bank of Italy."

The Port Authority is a public body, created by Law No 84 concerning the recast of the rules on ports (Legge n. 84, Riordino della legislazione in materia portuale) of 28 January 1994 (Ordinary Supplement to GURI No 28 of 4 February 1994) ("Law No 84/94"). Article 6 of Law No 84/94 provides:

> "1. ... [A] Port Authority shall be established in the ports of ... Brindisi, ... entrusted with the following tasks:
>
>   (a) Direction, programming, coordination, promotion and control of port operations and other commercial and industrial activities in ports, with powers of regulation and order, including with respect to safety against risks of accidents related to such activities and health at work ...;
>   (b) Ordinary and extraordinary maintenance of common areas in the port area ...;
>   (c) Award and control of activities aimed at providing to port users, for remuneration, services of general interest which are not identical to individual port operations defined by decree of the Minister of Infrastructure and Transport, and which are not strictly connected with them.

2. The Port Authority is a legal person governed by public law and enjoys administrative autonomy, subject to the provisions of Article 12, as well as budgetary and financial autonomy, within the limits provided for by the present law. The provisions of Law No 70 of 20 March 1975, as amended subsequently, do not apply to it, nor do the provisions of Decree-Law No 29 of 3 February 1993, as amended and supplemented subsequently, except to the extent that that is expressly provided for in Article 23(2) of the present law.

The assets and financial management of the Port Authority are governed by an accounting regulation approved by the Minister of Transport and Navigation, in agreement with the Minister of the Treasury. The balance sheet of the Port Authorities is annexed to the estimate of expenditure and revenue of the Minister of Transport and Navigation for the financial year following that in which it was approved.

The financial statement of the Port Authority is subject to review by the Italian Court of Auditors."

Article 7 of Law No 84/94 states:

"2. The remuneration of the President ... is defrayed by the Port Authority and is determined by the Port Committee within the maximum limits established ... by decree of the Minister of Transport and Navigation...
3. The Minister of Transport and Navigation shall order by decree the removal from office of the President and the dissolution of the Port Committee where:

(a) after expiry of the period referred to in Article 9(3)(a), the three-year operational plan has not been approved within the following 30 days;
...
(c) the balance sheet is in deficit."

8.322 Article 8 of Law No 84/94 provided that the President must be appointed by decree of the Minister of Transport and Navigation, after obtaining the agreement of the region concerned, from a group of three highly qualified experts, whose competence is established in the fields of transport and port economics. The President represents the Port Authority and is appointed for a four-year term, which may be renewed only once. The President of the Port Authority had to: chair the Port Committee; submit to the Port Committee the three-year operational plan for adoption; submit to the Port Committee the port planning scheme for adoption; submit to the Port Committee the draft decisions on the budget estimate and the amendments thereto, the balance sheet and the remuneration of the General Secretariat, as well as the implementation of the contractual agreements for the staff of the technical and operational secretariat; propose to the Port Committee draft decisions on those concessions referred to in Article 6(5); ensure coordination of the activities carried out in the port by the various public administrations, as well as coordination and control of the activities subject to licensing and concession, and of port services; administer the State-owned maritime property in the area referred to in Article 6(7) on the basis of the applicable legislation, by exercising, after hearing the Port Committee, the functions defined in Articles 36 to 55 and 68 of the Navigation Code and the rules of implementation of those provisions; exercise the powers attributed to the Port Authority under Articles 16 and 18 and to award, after hearing the Port Committee, the authorisations and concessions provided for in those articles, when those have a duration not exceeding four years in duration, and determine the amount of the charges due; promote the establishment of a union for the port workers; ensure navigability in the port area for the purposes of excavation and maintenance works of the sea bed. In addition, he may organise, assuming the presidency thereof, an interdepartmental conference with the administrations concerned, to be concluded within a period of 60 days; in case of immediate necessity and urgency, he may adopt binding decisions; make proposals concerning the delimitation of free zones, after hearing the Maritime Authority and the local authorities concerned; and exercise any other powers which this law does not entrust to the other governance bodies of the Port Authority.

8.323 Under Article 12 of Law 84/94, entitled "Supervision of the Port Authority":

"1. The Port Authority is subject to the supervision of the Minister of Transport and Navigation.
2. The decisions of the President and of the Port Committee are subject to approval of the supervisory authority when they concern:

   (a) the approval of the estimated budget, possible amendments thereto and the balance sheet;
   (b) recruitment of the technical and operational staff secretariat."

8.324 Article 18 of Law 84/94, to which Article 8(3)(i) thereof refers, concerns the "concession of areas and docks" and provides that it is for the Port Authority to award such concessions to undertakings which are authorised to conduct operations and/or to supply port services. That article provides, moreover, that a concession, which is for the Port Authority to award, also concerns the execution and management of works connected with maritime and port activities, to be carried out in the port area.

8.325 It follows from the answer of the Italian government to the written questions of the Court that the President of a Port Authority is the administrative authority empowered to exercise the duties set out in Article 54 of the Navigation Code (Codice della Navigazione, approvato con R. D. 30 marzo 1942, n. 327, Parte aggiornata al l. 7 marzo 2001, n. 51), namely, the adoption of an administrative measure by which anyone who unlawfully occupies maritime areas located in a port area is ordered to restore them to their original status, with the option, in the event of non-execution, to carry out restoration ex officio, at the expense of the offender.

The dispute in the main proceedings and the questions referred for a preliminary ruling

8.326 In 2010, the date of expiry of the term of office of the President of the Port Authority of Brindisi, a procedure for the appointment of a new president was initiated by the Minister of Infrastructure and Transport. In that procedure, the Provincia di Brindisi (Province of Brindisi), the Comune di Brindisi (municipality of Brindisi) and the Camera di Commercio, Industria, Artigianato ed Agricoltura di Brindisi (Chamber of Commerce, Industry, Crafts and Agriculture of Brindisi) each nominated, in accordance with Article 8(1) of Law No 84/94, three experts in the fields of economics, transport and port economics, including Mr Haralambidis and Mr Casilli. By a 2011 decree, the Minister appointed Mr Haralambidis as President of the Port Authority of Brindisi. Mr Casilli brought an action before the Regional Administrative Court of Apulia for the annulment of that decree. In support of his action, Mr Casilli claimed that Mr Haralambidis could not be appointed president of that authority in so far as he did not possess Italian nationality.

8.327 In its order for reference, the Consiglio di Stato stated that, under Italian law, the issue of the legal classification of port authorities has been raised several times since they were created and that in the case law – including that of the Consiglio di Stato – they are classified as "public bodies" or "public economic entities". In that regard, the Consiglio di Stato states that it is necessary to determine the legal nature of the port authority in the case where a natural person who is not an Italian national is appointed as its president, since if that authority were recognised as having the status of public economic entity operating under private law, there would be no reason to oppose such an appointment. On the other hand, if that authority had the status of public body operating institutionally under public law, and having consequently, as a matter of law, the characteristics of a "public administration", that would not be the case. According to the Consiglio di Stato, it cannot be disputed that the powers of the President of a Port Authority, as provided for in Article 8(3) of Law No 84/94, are of a public nature. That court states that that president must ensure navigability in the port area, prepare the port planning scheme and draw up a three-year operational plan. Furthermore, the Consiglio di Stato states that the duties of the President of a Port Authority appear to resemble not an employment relationship with an administration, but the assignment of a mission entrusted by a governmental authority of the Italian State, limited in time and which must be performed in one's role as president of a legal (rather than natural) person which is treated under EU law as a body governed by public law.

8.328 The Consiglio di Stato decided to stay the proceedings and to refer the following questions to the Court for a preliminary ruling:

> "1. Given that the derogation laid down in Article 45(4) TFEU does not appear to apply to the present case (which concerns the appointment of a national of another Member State of the European Union as President of a Port Authority, a legal entity which can be classed as a body governed by public law) in that it relates to ... employment in the public service (which is not an issue ... in the present case) and given also that the fiduciary role of President of [the] Port Authority [of Brindisi] may nevertheless be regarded as an 'employment activity' in the broad sense, ... does the provision reserving that post exclusively to Italian nationals constitute discrimination on grounds of nationality prohibited by Article 45 TFEU?
> 2. Alternatively, may the holding of the office of President of an Italian Port Authority by a national of another Member State of the European Union be regarded as falling within the scope of the right of establishment laid down in Article 49 et seq. TFEU and, if so, does the prohibition laid down in national law on non-Italian nationals holding that office constitute discrimination on grounds of nationality, or would such a finding be precluded by Article 51 TFEU?
> 3. As a further alternative, in the event that the holding of the office of President of an Italian Port Authority by a national of another Member State of the European Union may be regarded as the provision of 'services' for the purposes of Directive 2006/123, is the exclusion of port services from the scope of that directive relevant in the present case and, if not, does the prohibition under national law in relation to the holding of that office constitute discrimination on grounds of nationality?
> 4. As a yet further alternative, ... in the event that the holding of the office of President of an Italian Port Authority by a national of another Member State of the European Union does not fall within the scope of any of the above provisions, may it nevertheless be regarded, more generally, in accordance with Article 15 of the Charter, ... as a prerogative coming under the right of Community citizens to 'work, to exercise the right of establishment and to provide services in any Member State', irrespective of the specific 'sectoral' provisions laid down in Article 45 and Article 49 et seq. TFEU, and in Directive 2006/123, ... and is the prohibition under national law in relation to the holding of that office accordingly inconsistent with the equally general prohibition of discrimination on grounds of nationality laid down in Article 21(2) of that Charter?"

8.329 The CJEU summarised the first question as asking, in essence, whether, on the assumption that Article 45(4) is applicable to a situation such as that at issue in the main proceedings, that provision must be interpreted as not authorising a Member State to reserve to its nationals the exercise of the duties of President of a Port Authority. The CJEU began by considering the concept of "worker" within the meaning of Article 45(1) of the TFEU. The referring court appeared to have doubts concerning the nature of the activity exercised by the President of a Port Authority. According to that court, that activity does not appear to resemble an employment relationship, for the purposes of Article 45. The CJEU recalled that the concept of "worker" for the purposes of Article 45 of TFEU has an autonomous meaning specific to EU law and must not be interpreted narrowly.[250]

8.330 Given the significance of the judgment – and the somewhat controversial outcome, it is useful to consider the main parts of the ruling in full:

"Consideration of the questions referred
The first question

25. By its first question, the referring court asks, in essence, whether, on the assumption that Article 45(4) is applicable to a situation such as that at issue in the main proceedings, that provision must be interpreted as not authorising a Member State to reserve to its nationals the exercise of the duties of President of a Port Authority.[251]

The concept of 'worker' within the meaning of Article 45(1) TFEU

26. First of all, it should be noted that it is apparent from the order for reference and, more specifically, the wording of the first question that the referring court has doubts concerning the nature of the activity exercised by the President of a Port Authority. According to that court, that activity does not appear to resemble an employment relationship, for the purposes of Article 45 TFEU.

27. In that regard, it should be noted that the concept of 'worker' for the purposes of Article 45 TFEU has an autonomous meaning specific to EU law and must not be interpreted narrowly (see, inter alia, judgment in Commission v Netherlands, C–542/09, EU:C:2012:346, paragraph 68).

28. Any person who pursues activities that are real and genuine, to the exclusion of activities on such a small scale as to be regarded as purely marginal and ancillary, must this be regarded as a 'worker' within the meaning of Article 45 TFEU. According to the case-law of the Court, the essential feature of an employment relationship is that for a certain period of time a person performs services for and under the direction of another person in return for which he receives remuneration (see judgments in Lawrie-Blum, 66/85, EU:C:1986:284, paragraph 17, and Petersen, C-544/11, EU:C:2013:124, paragraph 30).

29. It follows that subordination and the payment of remuneration are constituent elements of all employment relationships, in so far as the professional activity at issue is effective and genuine.

30. With regard to subordination, it follows from Law No 84/94 that the Minister has powers of management and supervision and, where appropriate, may sanction the President of a Port Authority.

31. The Minister appoints the president of such an authority for a term of four years renewable once (Article 8(1) and (2) of Law No 84/94) and may remove him if the three-year operational plan relating to management of the port is not approved and if the balance sheet is in

---

[250] C-542/09 *Commission v Netherlands* EU:C:2012:346, para. 68.
[251] Ed., this is, on reading, a controversial proposition because it means that there could be lawful discrimination against nationals of other Member States if the CJEU agreed that the job could be restricted to nationals of the State only.

deficit, that is to say, in the event of bad financial management (Article 7(3)(a) and (c) of Law No 84/94). It is apparent also from the Italian Government's answer to the written questions put by the Court that the termination of the mandate of the President of a Port Authority by the Minister 'may be ordered where there are found to be important irregularities concerning management, such as to compromise the proper functioning of the entity. Those powers may involve also termination of functions where the president fails to comply with the principles of good faith and mutual cooperation'.

32. Furthermore, the Minister exercises powers of supervision in so far as he approves the decisions of the President of a Port Authority relating, in particular, to the approval of the estimated budget, possible amendments thereto and the balance sheet, and to the establishment of the technical and operational staff secretariat (Article 12(2)(a) and (b) of Law No 84/94).

33. On the other hand, as the Advocate General stated in point 32 of his Opinion, the post of President of a Port Authority lacks the features which are typically associated with the functions of an independent service provider, namely, more leeway in terms of choice of the type of work and tasks to be executed, of the manner in which that work or those tasks are to be performed, and of the time and place of work, and more freedom in the recruitment of his own staff.

34. It follows that the duties of the President of a Port Authority are performed under the management and supervision of the Minister, and therefore in a relationship of subordination, within the meaning of the case-law cited in paragraph 28 above.

35. As regards the remuneration of the President of a Port Authority, it is apparent from the Italian Government's answer to the written questions put by the Court that it is established by a Ministerial Decree of 31 March 2003. Under that decree, that remuneration is calculated on the basis of the basic salary provided for the Directors-general of the Ministry. It is therefore set by reference to that of a senior official of the public administration.

36. The remuneration is paid to the President of a Port Authority in return for the fulfilment of the tasks assigned to him by law. It therefore has the predictability and regularity inherent in an employment relationship.

37. Finally, it should be noted that, as is apparent from the order for reference, in the main proceedings, the effective and genuine nature of the functions performed by the President of a Port Authority is not contested (see judgment in Lawrie-Blum, EU:C:1986:284, paragraph 21, last sentence).

38. In those circumstances, it should be found that, in situations such as those at issue in the main proceedings, the President of a Port Authority must be regarded as a worker within the meaning of Article 45(1) TFEU.

39. That finding cannot be invalidated by the assertion of the referring court that the appointment of the President of a Port Authority cannot amount to an employment relationship within the context of the 'civil service', but is the attribution of a 'trust mission' delegated by a government authority connected with the exercise of public tasks.

40. According to established case-law, the public law or private law nature of the legal relationship of the employer and employee is of no consequence in regard to the application of Article 45 TFEU (see judgments in Sotgiu, 152/73, EU:C:1974:13, paragraph 5, and Bettray, 344/87, EU:C:1989:226, paragraph 16).

41. Moreover, the Court has previously held, in the context of an examination of the link between a member of the board of directors of a capital company and that company, that board members who, in return for remuneration, provide services to the company which has appointed them and of which they are an integral part, who carry out their activities under the direction or control of another body of that company and who can, at any time, be removed from their duties, satisfy the criteria for being treated as workers within the meaning of the case-law of the Court (judgment in Danosa, C–232/09, EU:C:2010:674, paragraph 51).

The concept of 'employment in the public service' within the meaning of Article 45(4) TFEU

42. Article 45(1) to (3) TFEU lays down the fundamental principle of the freedom of movement for workers and the abolition of all discrimination based on nationality between

workers of the Member States. Article 45(4) TFEU provides however that the provisions of that article are not to apply to employment in the public service.

43. According to the Court's case-law, the concept of 'public service' within the meaning of Article 45(4) TFEU must be given uniform interpretation and application throughout the European Union and cannot therefore be left entirely to the discretion of the Member States (see, inter alia, judgments in Sotgiu, EU:C:1974:13, paragraph 5, and Colegio de Oficiales de la Marina Mercante Española, C–405/01, EU:C:2003:515, paragraph 38). Furthermore, that derogation must be construed in such a way as to limit its scope to what is strictly necessary for safeguarding the interests which it allows the Member States to protect (see judgment in Colegio de Oficiales de la Marina Mercante Española, C–405/01, EU:C:2003:515, paragraph 41).

44. In that regard, the Court has previously held that the concept of 'public service' within the meaning of Article 45(4) TFEU covers posts which involve direct or indirect participation in the exercise of powers conferred by public law and duties designed to safeguard the general interests of the State or of other public authorities and thus presume on the part of those occupying them the existence of a special relationship of allegiance to the State and reciprocity of rights and duties which form the foundation of the bond of nationality (see, inter alia, judgments in Commission v Greece, C–290/94, EU:C:1996:265, paragraph 2, and Colegio de Oficiales de la Marina Mercante Española, EU:C:2003:515, paragraph 39).

45. On the other hand, the exception provided for in Article 45(4) TFEU does not cover posts which, while coming under the State or other bodies governed by public law, still do not involve any association with tasks belonging to the public service properly so called (judgments in Commission v Greece, EU:C:1996:265, paragraph 2, and Colegio de Oficiales de la Marina Mercante Española, EU:C:2003:515, paragraph 40).

46. It is therefore necessary to determine whether the tasks attributed to the President of a Port Authority involve the exercise of powers of a public law and the safeguard of the general interests of the State such as to justify their being reserved to Italian citizens.

47. Article 8(3) of Law No 84/94 lists the tasks which are conferred on the President of a Port Authority.[252]

48. First of all, it should be noted that, beyond the Board of the Port Committee, the activities referred to in Article 8(3)(a) to (e) and (n) of that law are limited to duties of the President of a Port Authority to propose certain measures to the Port Committee connected with the ongoing management of the port.

49. Such activities cannot fall within the derogation provided for in Article 45(4) TFEU, particularly since the President of a Port Authority is not endowed with a decision-making power, which belongs to the Port Committee.

50. Likewise, the powers described in Article 8(3)(f) and (l) of Law No 84/94, in so far as they cover only powers of coordination and promotion of activities of other bodies, are not capable of coming within the exercise of powers of a public authority and duties designed to safeguard the general interests of the State.

51. It must be observed, in that regard, that it is not apparent from the case file submitted to the Court that the bodies whose activities are coordinated or promoted by the President of a Port Authority are themselves entrusted with duties in the public service, within the meaning of Article 45(4) TFEU.

52. Furthermore, under Article 8(3)(i) of Law No 84/94, read in conjunction with Article 18 of that law, the President of a Port Authority exercises the powers attributed to the Port Authority and awards authorisations and concessions of areas and docks to undertakings wishing to conduct operations or supply port services.

53. However, contrary to the submissions of the Spanish and Netherlands Governments, the award of those authorisations and concessions, in so far as they amount to management tasks which concern primarily economic considerations, can also not be regarded as coming within the scope of application of Article 45(4) TFEU.

---

[252] Ed., this demonstrates how such a restriction needed to be justified on the basis of an analysis of the law and facts.

54. Finally, in certain circumstances, the President of a Port Authority is empowered, in the exercise of his powers of injunction, to adopt binding decisions in order to safeguard the general interests of the State, in the present case the preservation of common assets.
55. Among those powers of injunction are, first, in the context of the administration of the maritime areas and property, the power to order a person who unlawfully occupies those areas, located within the port area, to restore them to their original status, with the option, in the event of non-execution of that injunction, to carry out the restoration ex officio at the expense of the offender (Article 8(3)(h) of Law No 84/94, read in conjunction with Article 54 of the Navigation Code).
56. Secondly, under Article 8(3)(m) of Law No 84/94, the President of a Port Authority ensures navigability of the port area and the carrying out of excavation and maintenance works of the sea bed. For that purpose, and in case of immediate necessity and urgency, the President has the power to adopt binding decisions.
57. In so far as those powers involve the exercise of powers of a public authority, they are capable of coming within the derogation to the freedom of movement for workers provided for in Article 45(4) TFEU.
58. However, recourse to that derogation cannot be justified on the sole ground that powers of a public authority are attributed under national law to the President of a Port Authority. It is also necessary that those powers be in fact exercised on a regular basis by that holder and do not constitute a minor part of his duties.
59. As noted in paragraph 43 above, that derogation must be construed in such a way as to limit its scope to what is strictly necessary for safeguarding the general interests of the Member State concerned, which cannot be imperilled if powers of a public authority are exercised only occasionally, or indeed exceptionally, by nationals of other Member States (see judgments in Colegio de Oficiales de la Marina Mercante Española, EU:C:2003:515, paragraph 44; Anker and Others, C–47/02, EU:C:2003:516, paragraph 63; and Commission v France, C–89/07, EU:C:2008:154, paragraph 14).
60. According to the information provided by the Italian Government, the powers of the President of a Port Authority are a marginal part of his duties, which are generally of a technical and financial management nature and which cannot be amended by the exercise of those powers. Furthermore, according to the Italian Government, those powers are intended to be exercised solely occasionally or in exceptional circumstances.
61. In those circumstances, a general exclusion of nationals of other Member States from access to the post of President of an Italian Port Authority constitutes discrimination on grounds of nationality prohibited by Article 45(1) to (3) TFEU.
62. Having regard to the foregoing, the answer to the first question is that, in circumstances such as those at issue in the main proceedings, Article 45(4) TFEU must be interpreted as not authorising a Member State to reserve to its nationals the exercise of the duties of President of a Port Authority.

The second to fourth questions

63. The second to fourth questions were asked in the alternative and on the assumption that Article 45 TFEU was not applicable to the main proceedings.
64. Given the answer to the first question, there is no need to answer the other questions."

8.331 It was a somewhat controversial outcome because many people would not ordinarily agree that the head of a port needed to be of the nationality of the Member State in which the port was located. It should be a judgment which will be construed narrowly in the future.

U. THE *JAN VOOGSGEERD V NAVIMER SA* CASE

8.332 On 15 December 2011, the CJEU delivered a preliminary ruling[253] in *Jan Voogsgeerd v Navimer SA*.[254] The case concerned the interpretation of Article 6 of the Rome Convention on the Law applicable to Contractual Obligations[255] and an employee carrying out his work in more than one Contracting State.

8.333 The reference was made in proceedings between Mr Voogsgeerd (a Dutch resident) and Navimer SA (a Luxembourg company) regarding a payment in lieu of notice to him for a breach of the employment contract which he had entered into with that undertaking.

8.334 Article 1(1) of the Rome Convention provides that the convention "is to apply to contractual obligations in any situation involving a choice between the laws of different countries". Article 3(1) provides that a

> "contract shall be governed by the law chosen by the parties. The choice must be expressed or demonstrated with reasonable certainty by the terms of the contract or the circumstances of the case. By their choice, the parties can select the law applicable to the whole or a part only of the contract."

Article 4(1) of that convention provided: "[t]o the extent that the law applicable to the contract has not been chosen in accordance with Article 3, the contract shall be governed by the law of the country with which it is most closely connected". Article 6 provided:

> "1. Notwithstanding the provisions of Article 3, in a contract of employment a choice of law made by the parties shall not have the result of depriving the employee of the protection afforded him by the mandatory rules of the law which would be applicable under paragraph 2 in the absence of choice.
> 2. Notwithstanding the provisions of Article 4, a contract of employment shall, in the absence of choice in accordance with Article 3, be governed:
>
>   (a) by the law of the country in which the employee habitually carries out his work in performance of the contract, even if he is temporarily employed in another country; or
>   (b) if the employee does not habitually carry out his work in any one country, by the law of the country in which the place of business through which he was engaged is situated;
>
> unless it appears from the circumstances as a whole that the contract is more closely connected with another country, in which case the contract shall be governed by the law of that country."

8.335 Article 80(2) of the Luxembourg Law of 9 November 1990 establishing a Luxembourg Public Maritime Register (Mémorial A 1990, p. 808), provided that the

> "wrongful termination of a seaman's contract of employment confers entitlement to damages and to the payment of interest. A dismissal which is contrary to law or is not based on genuine and serious grounds is wrongful and constitutes a socially and economically unacceptable measure. Legal proceedings for compensation in respect of the wrongful termination of a seaman's

---

253 The case involved a preliminary ruling from Belgium's Hof van Cassatie.
254 Case C-384/10 [2011] ECR I-13275, ECLI:EU:C:2011:842. The Fourth Chamber of the CJEU was composed of Judges Bonichot (President of the Chamber), Bay Larsen and Toader (Rapporteur). The Advocate-General was AG Trstenjak.
255 OJ 1980 L266/1.

contract of employment shall be brought before the court having jurisdiction in employment matters within three months of notification of dismissal or communication of the reasons, or else be time-barred. That period shall be validly interrupted where a written complaint is submitted to the employer by the seaman, his legal representative or his trade union."

Article 39 of the Belgian Law of 3 July 1978 on employment contracts (Belgisch Staasblad, 22 August 1978), stated:

> "In the case of a contract of indefinite duration, the party terminating the contract without urgent cause or without observing the period of notice laid down by Articles 59, 82, 83, 84 and 115 is required to pay the other party compensation equal to the current salary for the duration of the period of notice or for the period of notice remaining."

8.336 In 2001 at the headquarters of Naviglobe NV ("Naviglobe"), an undertaking established in Belgium, Mr Voogsgeerd entered into a contract of employment of indefinite duration with Navimer. The parties chose Luxembourgeois law to be the law applicable to that contract. Until April 2002, he served as chief engineer on ships belonging to Navimer and whose navigation area extended to the North Sea. In 2002, Naviglobe served a notice of dismissal on him. In 2003, he commenced proceedings against Naviglobe and Navimer before the Labour Court in Antwerp seeking an order that those undertakings, jointly and severally, make a payment in lieu of notice in accordance with the Belgian Law of 3 July 1978 on employment contracts, plus interest and costs.

8.337 Mr Voogsgeerd claimed that, based on Article 6(1) of the Rome Convention, the mandatory rules of Belgian employment law were applicable, irrespective of the choice made by the parties regarding the applicable law. In that respect, Mr Voogsgeerd claimed that he was bound, by his contract of employment, to the Belgian undertaking Naviglobe, and not to the Luxembourg undertaking Navimer, and that he had principally carried out his work in Belgium where he received instructions from Naviglobe and to which he returned after each voyage.

8.338 In support of his case, Mr Voogsgeerd argued in the main proceedings claims that the Belgian court hearing his case had infringed Articles 1, 3, 4 and 6 of the Rome Convention by finding that the evidence which he had put forward to establish the habitual carrying out of his work in Belgium under the authority of Naviglobe had no bearing on whether the provisions of the Rome Convention, and in particular Article 6(2)(b) of that convention, applied. The referring court observed that, insofar as that evidence is accurate, Naviglobe, which is established in Antwerp, could be regarded as being the business with which Mr Voogsgeerd is connected for his actual employment, for the purposes of Article 6(2)(b) of the Rome Convention. In those circumstances, the Hof van Cassatie decided to stay the proceedings and to refer the following questions to the CJEU for a preliminary ruling:

> "(1) Must the country in which the place of business is situated through which an employee was engaged, within the meaning of Article 6(2)(b) of the [Rome Convention], be taken to mean the country in which the place of business of the employer is situated through which, according to the contract of employment, the employee was engaged, or the country in which the place of business of the employer is situated with which the employee is connected for his actual employment, even though that employee does not habitually carry out his work in any one country?
> (2) Must the place to which an employee who does not habitually carry out his work in any one country is obliged to report and where he receives administrative briefings, as well as

instructions for the performance of his work, be deemed to be the place of actual employment within the meaning of the first question?
(3) Must the place of business with which the employee is connected for his actual employment within the meaning of the first question satisfy certain formal requirements such as, inter alia, the possession of legal personality, or does the existence of a de facto place of business suffice for that purpose?
(4) Can the place of business of another company, with which the corporate employer is connected, serve as the place of business within the meaning of the third question, even though the authority of the employer has not been transferred to that other company?"

8.339 The CJEU summarised the issues and said that by its questions, the referring court was asking, in essence, whether factors such as the place where the employee is actually employed, the place to which that employee is obliged to report and where he receives administrative briefings necessary for the performance of his work, and the de facto place of business of the employer affect the determination of the law applicable to the contract of employment under Article 6(2) of the Rome Convention. The CJEU recalled that Article 6 of the Rome Convention lays down special conflict of laws rules concerning individual employment contracts which derogate from the general rules contained in Articles 3 and 4 of the Rome Convention, concerning, respectively, the freedom of choice of the applicable law and the criteria for determining that law in the absence of such a choice. Thus, Article 6(1) of the Rome Convention provides that the choice made by the parties regarding the law applicable to the contract of employment cannot lead to the employee being deprived of the guarantees laid down by the mandatory provisions of the law which would be applicable to the contract in the absence of a choice. Article 6(2) sets out the linking factors of the employment contract on the basis of which the *lex contractus* must be determined in the absence of a choice by the parties.

8.340 Those factors are, first, that of the country in which the employee "habitually carries out his work" (Article 6(2)(a)) or, alternatively, if there is no such place, "the place of business through which he was engaged" (Article 6(2)(b)). Furthermore, according to the last sentence of Article 6(2), those two linking factors are not to apply where it appears from the circumstances as a whole that the contract of employment is more closely connected with another country, in which case the law of that other country is to apply.

8.341 In the case in the main proceedings, it is not disputed that the parties to the contract chose Luxembourg law as the *lex contractus*. However, irrespective of that choice, the question remains as to what is the law applicable to the contract, since the applicant in the main proceedings invokes the mandatory provisions of Belgian law as the basis of his right to a payment in lieu of notice. As is apparent from ... above, Mr Voogsgeerd claims that the court of appeal, which found, on the basis of Article 6(2)(b) of the Rome Convention, that Luxembourg law was applicable to the contract in issue, infringed several provisions of that convention and, in particular, Article 6 thereof. In that regard, Mr Voogsgeerd claims that, in the course of the carrying out of his work, he had no contact with Navimer, but that he was obliged to report for boarding at Antwerp with Naviglobe, which gave him instructions.

8.342 The CJEU ruled:

"On a proper construction of Article 6(2) of the Rome Convention, ... the national court seised of the case must first establish whether the employee, in the performance of his contract, habitually carries out his work in any one country, which is that in which or from which, in the light of all the aspects characterising that activity, the employee performs the main part of his duties to his employer...

If the national court should take the view that it cannot rule under Article 6(2)(a) of that convention on the action before it, Article 6(2)(b) of the Rome Convention must be interpreted as follows:

- 'the place of business through which the employee was engaged' must be understood as referring exclusively to the place of business which engaged the employee and not to that with which the employee is connected by his actual employment;
- the possession of legal personality does not constitute a requirement that must be met by the place of business of the employer within the meaning of that provision;
- the place of business of an undertaking other than that which is formally referred to as the employer, with which that undertaking has connections, may be classified as a 'place of business' within the meaning of Article 6(2)(b) of that convention if objective factors make it possible to establish that there exists a real situation different from that which appears from the terms of the contract, even though the authority of the employer has not been formally transferred to that other undertaking."

V. THE *RAAD VAN BESTUUR VAN DE SOCIALE VERZEKERINGSBANK V WIELAND AND ROTHWANGL* CASE

8.343 On 27 October 2016, the CJEU made an important preliminary ruling in *Raad van bestuur van de Sociale verzekeringsbank v Wieland and Rothwangl*.[256] The case concerned the entitlement of retired seafarers to old age benefit (i.e. a national security benefit). In particular, it related to the entitlement of former seafarers to pensions who are nationals of another country which became an EU Member State. The case turned on Articles 18 and 45 of the TFEU as well as Articles 3 and 94 of Regulation 1408/71 of 14 June 1971 on the application of social security schemes to employed persons, to self-employed persons and to members of their families moving within the Community, as amended and updated by Regulation 118/97 of 2 December 1996,[257] as amended by Regulation 647/2005 of 13 April 2005,[258] and Article 2(1) and (2) of Regulation 859/2003 of 14 May 2003 extending the provisions of Regulation 1408/71 and Regulation 574/72 to nationals of third countries who are not already covered by those provisions solely on the ground of their nationality.[259] The preliminary ruling was requested by the Higher Social Security Court in the Netherlands. The Dutch and Spanish governments as well as the European Commission intervened. The request was made in the context of two separate disputes between the Raad van bestuur van de Sociale verzekeringsbank (Board of the Social Insurance Bank, the "SVB"), on the one hand, and F Wieland and H Rothwangl, on the other hand, concerning the SVB's refusal to grant the latter two individuals an old-age pension.

---

256 Case C-465/14, ECLI:EU:C:2016:820, http://curia.europa.eu/juris/document/document.jsf;jsessionid=9ea7d2dc30d568c0d66831d74745b1eaa33c15e7f52f.e34KaxiLc3qMb40Rch0SaxyKaxr0?text=&docid=184897&pageIndex=0&doclang=en&mode=req&dir=&occ=first&part=1&cid=943131. The Court was composed of Judges Tizzano (vice-President of the Court acting as President of the First Chamber) Berger (Rapporteur), Borg Barthet, Rodin, and Biltgen. The Advocate-General, who gave an opinion, was AG Sharpston.
257 OJ 1997 L28/1.
258 OJ 2005 L117/1.
259 OJ 2003 L124/1.

8.344 Mr Wieland was born in Austria before that country joined the EU. He had Austrian citizenship by birth. Between 1962 and 1966, worked on ships owned by Holland-Amerika Lijn ("HAL") (a Dutch company operating ships between the Netherlands and the USA). In 1966, he moved to the USA and in 1969, he acquired American nationality and lost his Austrian nationality. In 2008, Mr Wieland asked the SVB to grant him an old-age pension from the date of his sixty-fifth birthday. The SVB rejected that request on the ground that during the period from his fifteenth to his sixty-fifth birthday, Mr Wieland was not insured under the AOW (Algemene Ouderdomswet).[260] He then informed the SVB that from a date in 2008, he was residing in Austria.

8.345 Mr Rothwangl was born in Austria and had Austrian nationality. For a few months between 1962 and 1963, he worked on vessels owned by HAL. In 2009, Mr Rothwangl asked the SVB to grant him an old-age pension. At that time, he resided in Austria, a country where, according to data from the SVB, he had lawful old-age insurance for a total period of 496 months from 1958 to 1998. Mr Rothwangl was entitled, with effect from 1 March 1998, to an Austrian occupational disability pension and, as of 1 September 1998, a Swiss invalidity pension. In addition, from 29 November 1998 to 1 December 2008, he was in receipt of a benefit. In 2009, the SVB refused to grant Mr Rothwangl the old-age pension sought on the ground that during the period from his fifteenth to his sixty-fifth birthday he had not been insured under the AOW.

8.346 Both Mr Wieland and Mr Rothwangl challenged the decisions of the SVB before the Rechtbank Amsterdam (District Court, Amsterdam, Netherlands), which ruled in their favour. The SVB appealed against that ruling to the referring court. In the order for preliminary reference to the CJEU, the Centrale Raad van Beroep (Higher Social Security Court, Netherlands) referred to the judgment of the European Court of Human Rights of 4 June 2002, *Wessels-Bergervoet v Netherlands*[261] in which that court held that the decision of the Dutch institution to pay a married woman, on the basis of the AOW, only a reduced pension had constituted a violation of Article 14 of the European Convention for the Protection of Human Rights and Fundamental Freedoms ("ECHR") read in conjunction with Article 1 of the Protocol to the ECHR. The referring court explained that, although the Dutch courts, in cases involving old-age pension rights of seafarers, applied the reasoning of the European Court of Human Rights in its judgment of *Wessels-Bergervoet v Netherlands*,[262] it nevertheless considered that the situation of Wieland and Rothwangl differed from those cases and that the difference in treatment based on nationality which the competent Netherlands authorities carried out in the main proceedings is justified under Article 14 of the ECHR. It asked whether Regulation 1408/71, read in conjunction with Regulation 859/2003 and with Articles 18 and 45 TFEU, could be relevant in those cases.

8.347 As regards Mr Rothwangl, the referred court considered that, due to his professional activities during the 1960s, he must now be regarded as a worker within the meaning not only of the TFEU but also of Regulation 1408/71. It also believed that the fact that the person concerned was not a national of a Member State between 1962 and 1963, during which time he was employed by HAL, did not preclude that regulation

---

260 General Law on old-age insurance, Stb. 1956, No 281, "AOW".
261 CE:ECHR:2002:0604JUD003446297.
262 CE:ECHR:2002:0604JUD003446297.

applying to professional activities carried out during this period, since Mr Rothwangl met the nationality requirement imposed by that regulation as a result of Austria's accession to this in 1995.

8.348 The referring court asked whether the period during which Rothwangl was employed as a seafarer by HAL should be regarded as a period of insurance within the meaning of Article 94(2) of Regulation 1408/71. It considered, in that regard, that account should be taken of Articles 18 and 45 TFEU and Article 3 of Regulation 1408/71.

8.349 With regard to Wieland, the referring court asked whether the answer to the question of the applicability of Regulation 1408/71 must be the same as that given in the case of Rothwangl, given that the free movement of workers did not apply to third-country nationals and that Wieland has no longer possessed, since 29 August 1969, Austrian nationality.

8.350 The Centrale Raad van Beroep (Higher Social Security Court) decided to stay proceedings and refer to the CJEU the following questions:

"(1) Must Article 3 and Article 94(1) and (2) of Regulation No 1408/71 be interpreted as meaning that a former seafarer who belonged to the crew of a vessel with a home port in a Member State, who had no place of residence on shore and who was not a national of a Member State cannot be denied (in part) an old-age pension, after the State of which that seafarer is a national acceded to the European Union or after Regulation No 1408/71 entered into force for that State, solely on the ground that that former seafarer was not a national of the (first-mentioned) Member State during the period of the (claimed) insurance cover?

(2) Must Articles 18 TFEU and 45 TFEU be interpreted as precluding a rule of a Member State under which a seafarer who belonged to the crew of a vessel with a home port in that Member State, who had no place of residence on shore and who is not a national of any Member State, was excluded from insurance cover for purposes of an old-age pension, whereas, under that rule, a seafarer who is a national of the Member State in which the vessel has its home port and who is otherwise in the same situation is deemed to be insured, if the State of which the first-named seafarer is a national has in the meanwhile, by the time of the determination of the pension, acceded to [a legal predecessor of] the European Union or Regulation No 1408/71 has in the meanwhile entered into force for that State?

(3) Must Questions 1 and 2 be answered in the same way in the case of a (former) seafarer who, at the time of his employment, was a national of a State which at a later date accedes to [a legal predecessor of] the European Union, but who, at the time of that accession or the entry into force of Regulation No 1408/71 for that State, and at the time of submitting his claim to entitlement to an old-age pension, was not a national of any Member State, but to whom Regulation No 1408/71 nevertheless applies pursuant to Article 1 of Regulation No 859/2003?"

8.351 The CJEU ruled:

"1. Article 94(1) and (2) of ... Regulation ... 1408/71 ... on the application of social security schemes to employed persons, to self-employed persons and to members of their families moving within the Community, in the version amended and updated by ... Regulation ... 118/97, ... as amended by Regulation ... 647/2005 ... must be interpreted as not precluding legislation of a Member State that does not take into account, when determining rights to old-age pension, an insurance period claimed to have been completed under its own legislation by a foreign worker when the State of which that worker is a national acceded to the European Union after the completion of that period.

2. Articles 18 and 45 TFEU must be interpreted as not precluding legislation of a Member State, such as that at issue in the main proceedings, under which a seafarer who, over a specified period, was part of the crew of a vessel which had its home port in the territory of

that Member State and who resided aboard that vessel, is excluded from benefiting from old-age insurance in respect of that period on the ground that he was not a national of a Member State during that period.
3. Article 2(1) and (2) of ... Regulation ... 859/2003 ... extending the provisions of Regulation ... 1408/71 and Regulation ... 574/72 to nationals of third countries who are not already covered by those provisions solely on the ground of their nationality, must be interpreted as not precluding legislation of a Member State which provides that a period of employment – completed pursuant to the legislation of that Member State by an employed worker who was not a national of a Member State during that period but who, when he requests the payment of an old-age pension, falls within the scope of Article 1 of that regulation – is not to be taken into consideration by that Member State for the determination of that worker's pension rights."

W. DIRECTIVE 2013/54 CONCERNING CERTAIN FLAG STATE RESPONSIBILITIES FOR COMPLIANCE WITH AND ENFORCEMENT OF THE MARITIME LABOUR CONVENTION, 2006

8.352 For completeness, it is proposed to mention that on 20 November 2013, the Parliament and the Council adopted Directive 2013/54 concerning certain flag State responsibilities for compliance with and enforcement of the Maritime Labour Convention, 2006.[263] The directive is addressed to the Member States.[264] The directive entered into force on the twentieth day following that of its publication in the *Official Journal of the European Union*. The legal basis of Directive 2013/54 is the TFEU generally and, in particular, Article 100(2) of the TFEU. Member States had to implement the directive by 31 March 2015.[265]

8.353 The background to the directive is clear from the recitals:

"(1) Union action in the field of maritime transport aims, inter alia, to improve the shipboard living and working conditions of seafarers, security and safety at sea and to prevent pollution caused by maritime accidents.
(2) The Union is aware of the fact that most accidents at sea are directly caused by human factors, especially fatigue.
(3) One of the main objectives of the maritime safety policy of the Union is to eradicate sub-standard shipping.
(4) On 23 February 2006, the International Labour Organisation (ILO), desiring to create a single, coherent and up-to-date instrument that also embodies the fundamental principles to be found in other international labour conventions, adopted the Maritime Labour Convention, 2006 (MLC 2006).
(5) According to Article VIII thereof, the MLC 2006 is to come into force 12 months after the date on which there have been registered ratifications by at least 30 Members of the ILO with a total share in the world gross tonnage of ships of 33%. This condition was fulfilled on 20 August 2012, and MLC 2006 therefore entered into force on 20 August 2013.
(6) Council Decision 2007/431/EC[266] authorised the Member States to ratify MLC 2006, and Member States are urged to do so as soon as possible.

---

263 OJ L329/1, 10 December 2013. The opinion of the EESC is available at OJ C299/153, 4 October 2012. The Commission issued a statement that it considered "that the title does not properly reflect the scope of the Directive".
264 Dir. 2013/54, Art. 9.
265 Art. 7(1).
266 Ed., Council Dec. 2007/431 of 7 June 2007 authorising Member States to ratify, in the interests of the European Community, the Maritime Labour Convention, 2006, of the International Labour Organisation (OJ L161, 22 June 2007, p. 63).

(7) MLC 2006 sets out minimum global standards to ensure the right of all seafarers to decent living and working conditions, irrespective of their nationality and irrespective of the flag of the ships on which they serve, and to establish a level playing field.

(8) Various parts of MLC 2006 have been introduced into different Union instruments both as regards flag State and port State obligations. The aim of this Directive is to introduce certain compliance and enforcement provisions, envisaged in Title 5 of MLC 2006, which relate to those parts of MLC 2006 in respect of which the required compliance and enforcement provisions have not yet been adopted. Those parts correspond to the elements set out in the Annex to Council Directive 2009/13.[267]

(9) Directive 2009/13/EC implements the Agreement concluded by the European Community Shipowners' Associations (ECSA) and the European Transport Workers' Federation (ETF) on the Maritime Labour Convention, 2006 ('the Agreement'), annexed thereto. This Directive is without prejudice to Directive 2009/13/EC and should therefore ensure compliance with more favourable provisions of Union law in conformity with that Directive.

(10) Although Directive 2009/21/EC of the European Parliament and of the Council[268] governs flag State responsibilities, incorporating the voluntary IMO Member States audit scheme into Union law, and introducing the certification of quality of national maritime authorities, a separate Directive covering the maritime labour standards would be more appropriate and would more clearly reflect the different purposes and procedures, without affecting Directive 2009/21/EC.

(11) Directive 2009/21/EC applies to IMO Conventions. In any event, Member States could develop, implement and maintain a quality management system for the operational parts of the flag State-related activities of their maritime administration falling within the scope of this Directive.

(12) Member States should ensure the effective discharge of their obligations as flag States with respect to the implementation, by ships flying their flag, of the relevant parts of MLC 2006. In establishing an effective system for monitoring mechanisms, including inspections, a Member State could, where appropriate, grant authorisation to public institutions, or to other organisations within the meaning of Regulation 5.1.2 of MLC 2006, under the conditions set out therein.

(13) According to Article 2(3)(c) of Regulation (EC) No 1406/2002 of the European Parliament and of the Council[269] the mandate of the European Maritime Safety Agency includes, as a core task, that the Agency should work with the Member States to provide, at the request of a Member State, appropriate information in order to support the monitoring of recognised organisations acting on behalf of that Member State, without prejudice to the rights and obligations of the flag State.

(14) Since the objectives of this Directive cannot be sufficiently achieved by the Member States but can rather, by reason of the scale and effects of the action, be better achieved at the level of the Union, the Union may adopt measures, in accordance with the principle of subsidiarity as set out in Article 5 of the Treaty on European Union. In accordance with the principle of proportionality, as set out in that Article, this Directive does not go beyond what is necessary in order to achieve those objectives.

(15) Under no circumstances should the application of this Directive lead to a reduction in the level of protection currently enjoyed by seafarers under Union law."

---

267 Ed., Council Dir. 2009/13 of 16 February 2009 implementing the Agreement concluded by the European Community Shipowners' Associations (ECSA) and the European Transport Workers' Federation (ETF) on the Maritime Labour Convention, 2006 and amending Dir. 1999/63 (OJ L124, 20 May 2009, p. 30).

268 Ed., Dir. 2009/21 of the European Parliament and of the Council of 23 April 2009 on compliance with flag State requirements (OJ L131, 28 May 2009, p. 132).

269 Regulation (EC) No 1406/2002 of the European Parliament and of the Council of 27 June 2002 establishing a European Maritime Safety Agency (OJ L208, 5 August 2002, p. 1).

8.354 Article 1 ("subject matter") provides that the directive

"lays down rules to ensure that Member States effectively discharge their obligations as flag States with respect to the implementation of the relevant parts of MLC 2006.[270] This Directive is without prejudice to Directives 2009/13/EC and 2009/21/EC, and to any higher standards for living and working conditions for seafarers set out therein."

8.355 Article 3 ("monitoring of compliance") provides that Member States must ensure that effective and appropriate enforcement and monitoring mechanisms, including inspections at the intervals provided for in Maritime Labour Convention 2006, are established in order to ensure that the living and working conditions of seafarers on ships flying their flag meet, and continue to meet, the requirements of the relevant parts of Maritime Labour Convention 2006.[271] Article 3(2) provides that with respect to ships of less than 200 gt not engaged in international voyages, Member States may, in consultation with the shipowners' and seafarers' organisations concerned, decide to adapt, pursuant to Article II, paragraph 6 of Maritime Labour Convention 2006, monitoring mechanisms, including inspections, to take account of the specific conditions relating to such ships. When fulfilling their obligations under Article 3, Member States may, where appropriate, authorise public institutions or other organisations, including those of another Member State, if the latter agrees, which they recognise as having sufficient capacity, competence and independence, to carry out inspections.[272] In all cases, a Member State shall remain fully responsible for the inspection of the living and working conditions of the seafarers concerned on ships that fly the flag of that Member State.[273] This provision is without prejudice to Directive 2009/15 of the European Parliament and of the Council.[274] Member States must establish clear objectives and standards covering the administration of their inspection systems, as well as adequate overall procedures for their assessment of the extent to which those objectives and standards are being attained.[275] A Member State must ensure that seafarers on board ships flying the flag of that Member State have access to a copy of the agreement. The access may be provided electronically.[276]

8.356 The issue of personnel in charge of compliance monitoring is addressed in Article 4. Member States shall ensure that personnel, including staff from institutions or other organisations ("recognised organisations" within the meaning of Maritime Labour Convention 2006), authorised to carry out inspections in accordance with Article 3(3) and in charge of verifying the proper implementation of the relevant parts of Maritime Labour Convention 2006, have the training, competence, terms of reference, full legal authority, status and independence necessary or desirable to enable them to carry out that verification and to ensure compliance with the relevant parts of Maritime Labour Convention

---

270 Ed., Art. 2 provides that for the purposes of the directive, the phrase "relevant parts of MLC 2006" means the parts of Maritime Labour Convention 2006 of which the content shall be considered as corresponding to the provisions in the annex to Dir. 2009/13.
271 Art. 3(1).
272 Art. 3(2).
273 Art. 3(3).
274 Dir. 2009/15 of the European Parliament and of the Council of 23 April 2009 on common rules and standards for ship inspection and survey organisations and for the relevant activities of maritime administrations (OJ L131, 28 May 2009, p. 47).
275 Art. 3(4).
276 Art. 3(5).

2006. In accordance with Maritime Labour Convention 2006, inspectors shall be empowered to take steps, as appropriate, to prohibit a ship from leaving port until necessary actions are taken.[277]

8.357 Article 5 deals with on-board complaint procedures, handling of complaints and corrective measures. Each Member State must ensure that, in its laws or regulations, appropriate on-board complaint procedures are in place. If a Member State receives a complaint which it does not consider manifestly unfounded or obtains evidence that a ship that flies its flag does not conform to the requirements of the relevant parts of Maritime Labour Convention 2006 or that there are serious deficiencies in its implementing measures, that Member State shall take the steps necessary to investigate the matter and ensure that action is taken to remedy any deficiencies found. Personnel dealing with or becoming aware of complaints shall treat as confidential the source of any grievance or complaint alleging a danger or deficiency in relation to seafarers' living and working conditions or a violation of laws and regulations and shall give no intimation to the shipowner, the shipowner's representative or the operator of the ship that an inspection was made as a consequence of such a grievance or complaint.

8.358 Article 6 deals with reports. The Commission must, in the context of its reports to be established in accordance with Article 9 of Directive 2009/21, include matters falling within the scope of the directive. No later than 31 December 2018, the Commission shall submit a report to the European Parliament and to the Council on the implementation and application of Regulation 5.3 of Maritime Labour Convention 2006 regarding labour-supplying responsibilities. If appropriate, the report may include proposals for measures to enhance living and working conditions in the maritime sector.

X. COUNCIL DIRECTIVE (EU) 2018/131 OF 23 JANUARY 2018 IMPLEMENTING THE AGREEMENT CONCLUDED BY THE ECSA AND THE ETF TO AMEND DIRECTIVE 2009/13 IN ACCORDANCE WITH THE AMENDMENTS OF 2014 TO THE MARITIME LABOUR CONVENTION, 2006, AS APPROVED BY THE INTERNATIONAL LABOUR CONFERENCE ON 11 JUNE 2014

8.359 On 23 January 2018, the Council adopted Directive 2018/131 implementing the agreement concluded by the ECSA and the ETF to amend Directive 2009/13 in accordance with the amendments of 2014 to the Maritime Labour Convention, 2006, as approved by the International Labour Conference on 11 June 2014.[278]

8.360 Article 1 of the directive implements the agreement concluded between the ECSA and the ETF on 5 December 2016 to amend Directive 2009/13 in accordance with the 2014 amendments to the Maritime Labour Convention.

8.361 Article 2 provides that in line with the social partners' agreement, the agreement concluded by the ECSA and the ETF on the Maritime Labour Convention, 2006, set out

---

277 Art. 4(1).
278 OJ L22/28, 26 January 2018, http://data.europa.eu/eli/dir/2018/131/oj.

in the annex to Directive 2009/13 is amended in accordance with the annex to the directive.

8.362 Article 3 provides that Member States must bring into force the laws, regulations and administrative provisions necessary to comply with the directive by 16 February 2020.

CHAPTER 9

Introduction to liner conferences: the concept of liner conferences and the United Nations code on liner conferences and the United Nations liner code

A. INTRODUCTION

9.001 The purpose of this chapter is to describe the background to liner conferences generally[1] and provide an overview of the United Nations' ("UN") treatment of liner conferences[2] so as to lay the groundwork for future chapters on how the European Union ("EU") deals, and has dealt, with liner conferences.

B. LINER CONFERENCES

9.002 Liner conferences are bodies or associations which consist of shipowners or operators who operate regular shipping services for the carriage of general cargo according to fixed schedules and rates (i.e. prices) on particular pre-determined routes.[3] The agreement on rates/prices is a key hallmark of a liner conference agreement.

9.003 Liner services are, in many ways, the opposite of tramp operations. Tramp services typically involve dry or liquid bulk cargo carried on bulk vessels or tankers and operate on routes in response to particular demand (i.e. unlike liner services, they are

---

1 See paras 9.002–9.012.
2 See paras 9.013–9.047.
3 On liner conferences, see Deakin and Seward, *Shipping Conferences: A Study of their Origins, Development and Economic Practices* (1973); Herman, *Shipping Conferences* (1983); Jansson and Shneerson, *Liner Shipping Economics* (1987); Juda, *The UNCTAD Liner Code: US Maritime Policy at a Crossroad* (1983); Liu, *Liner Conferences in Competition Law: A Comparative Analysis of European and Chinese Law* (2009); Lorenzon and Nazzini, *Shipping Pools and EC Competition Law* (2009); Marx, *International Shipping Cartels: A Study of Industrial Self-Regulation by Shipping Conferences* (1953); Ortiz Blanco, *Shipping Conferences under EC Antitrust Law* (2007); Pozdnakova, *Liner Shipping and EU Competition Law* (2008); Stewart, *Shipping Conferences* (1983); Stopford, *Maritime Economics* (1988); Sturmey, *Shipping Economics, Collected Papers* (1975); and Sturmey, *Workbook on the Application of the UN Liner Code* (1985). See also Bosies and Green, "The Liner Conference Convention: Launching an International Regulatory Regime" (1976) 6 L&P Int'l Bus 533; Devanney, Livanos and Ellsworth, "Competition or Rationalization in the Shipping Industry?" (1979) 10 JMLC 497; Faust, "The UN Convention on a Code of Conduct for Liner Conferences" 11 Discussion Papers of the UNCTAD Secretariat (1985); Gardner, "Steamship Conferences and the Shipping Act, 1916" (1960) 35 Tulane L Rev 129; Gardner, "EU Competition Policy and Liner Shipping Conferences" (1997) 31 J of Transport Economics and Policy 317; Kuyper, "The European Communities and the Code of Conduct for Liner Conferences" (1981) 12 Netherlands Yb of Intl L 73; Larsen and Vetterick, "The UNCTAD Code of Conduct for Liner Conferences: Reservations, Reactions and US Alternatives" (1981) 13 L&P In'tl Bus 223; Shah, "The Implementation of the UN Convention on a Code of Conduct for Liner Conferences" (1977) 9 JMLC 79; Vermote, "The Application of the United Nations Liner Code Within the European Communities" (1988) 23 ETL 571; and Walters, "Shipping Conferences: an Economic Analysis" (1972) 4 JMLC 93. See also Jansson and Shneerson, *Liner Shipping Economics* (1987) which doubted the economic rationale of liner conferences. See also the publications cited in footnotes 9–10.

irregular and not operating on the basis of schedules). The term "tramp services" was defined in the now repealed EU's Council Regulation 4056/86 as:

> "A group of two or more vessels – operating carriers which provide international liner services for the carriage of cargo on a particular route or routes within specified geographical limits and which has an agreement or arrangement, whatever its nature, within the framework of which they operate under uniform or common freight rates and any other agreed conditions with respect to the provision of liner services."[4]

Liner traffic has accounted for about 60% of world income from maritime activities.[5]

9.004 In 1974 the United Nations Conference on Trade and Development ("UNCTAD") adopted the United Nations Code of Conduct for Liner Conferences. The Code defines a liner conference as:

> "[a] group of two or more vessel-operating carriers which provides international liner services for the carriage of cargo on a particular route or routes within specified geographical limits and which has an agreement or arrangement, whatever its nature, within the framework of which they operate under uniform or common freight rates and any other agreed conditions with regard to the provision of liner services".

This definition was also used, word for word, in Article 1(3)(b) in the EU's Regulation 4056/86.[6] It is therefore clear that both the UNCTAD and the EU defined liner conferences in the same way.

9.005 Liner conferences invariably involve price-fixing and market-sharing arrangements which inevitably causes problems for competition agencies who oppose price-fixing and market sharing. It has been written that the liner conference is the:

> "most important regulating instrument created by the shipping companies to govern world line transport. Such conferences lay down for their members, in respect of certain transport regions and lines, binding provisions on freight rates, conditions of carriage and other details of sea transport. Since these conferences cannot be completely controlled by any single state, they are in a position to exercise considerable power."[7]

Liner conferences are normally classified as being either open or closed in terms of their membership.

Consortia v liner conference

9.006 The debate on the acceptability of liner conferences is a long-standing one which has occasionally raged rather savagely. The proponents of liner conferences argue that they help to co-ordinate efficiently various shipping services and allow a proper utilisation of resources as well as predictable services for consumers of such services (i.e. shipping). The opponents of liner conferences regard them as nothing more than anti-competitive cartels which manipulate markets to the prejudice of shippers and to the detriment of competition generally. Most EU Member States (with the exception of

---

4 Reg. 4056/86, Art. 1(3)(b).
5 Stoppard, *Maritime Economics* (2nd ed., 1997), p. 338.
6 OJ 1986 L378/4.
7 Parliament, *Report drawn up on behalf of the Committee on Regional Policy and Transport on Sea Transport Problems in the Community*, Doc, 305.74, para. 51.

Greece) have traditionally been somewhat non-committal, but they have favoured the closed conference system on occasion.[8]

9.007 Traditionally, the regulation of liner conferences was essentially a matter of national law. The English courts held that such conferences were not unlawful.[9] The United States legislated by way of the Shipping Act of 1916 to apply the rules of anti-trust or competition law to conferences involving trade between the US and other States.[10]

9.008 Unlike the US with its Shipping Acts of 1916 and 1984, EU Member States have been generally reluctant to legislate in this area. Such is their reluctance to legislate that some of them have positively encouraged shipowners and shippers to establish their own self-regulatory regimes. This self-regulatory approach was embodied in the 1964 Note of Understanding concluded between a number of European shippers and shipping companies. This Note was transformed in 1971 into the CENSA[11]-ESC[12] Code of Practice, which was ultimately unacceptable to developing States.

9.009 Many developing States have objected to the liner conference as an institution. The European Parliament's Committee on Economic and Monetary Affairs, in its *Interim Report on the Community Shipping Industry* in 1976, discussed the background to the Code in the following terms:

> "15. Especially since the 1960s and in respect of liners in particular, the South American countries, as well as certain Asian ones, have introduced flag discrimination measures discriminating in favour of ships flying their national flag, measures which usually reserve up to or beyond 50 per cent of incoming or outgoing cargo for these ships. Such measures have enabled the developing countries to achieve a high rate of growth in their world cargo fleet. Their share of total world shipping, however, fell from 7 to just over 6 per cent between 1970 and 1975, despite the declared aim of the United Nations Development Decade that it should rise to 10 per cent by 1980. Certain [EU] States, notably Germany and Italy, have taken some measures to counter this practice. The German Federal Government can restrict conditions of freight contracts and charters between residents of the Federal Republic of Germany and carriers which are residents of the countries which exclude German ships from free competition. Italy restricts the use of ships which discriminate against Italian flag ships; shipments on such vessels are subject to government authorisation."

9.010 Before progressing to review the background, it is useful to review the historical and commercial backgrounds to liner conferences.

9.011 In terms of the historical background, Dinger has commented:

> "The advent of the steamship from the 1850s onwards led to a number of changes in the shipping industry. Before, it had not been possible to offer a service based on a fixed schedule since the sailing times depended on the weather. Additionally, the volume of international trade and the transport capacity increased considerably. The reduced length of the Europe-Asia route resulting from the opening of the Suez canal in 1862 led to substantial excess capacity, and over-tonnage became one of the central problems. In order to combat the resulting cut throat competition, ship

---

8 Pozdnakova has commented in *Liner Shipping and EU Competition Law* (2008), p. 154: "Liner conferences are traditionally classified as being open or closed in terms of their membership. Closed liner conferences admit new members only if the existing members find it to be in their interests to accept a newcomer. By contrast, open conferences admit upon application any shipowner capable of satisfying minimum technical and financial standards of practice, it may be difficult to classify a particular conference as being 'open' or 'closed'."
9 E.g. *Mogul Steamship Co Ltd v McGregor, Gow & Co* [1892] AC 25.
10 See Gardner, "Steamship Conferences and the Shipping Act, 1916" (1960) 35 Tulane Law Review 129.
11 I.e. the Council of European and Japanese Shipowners' Associations.
12 I.e. the European Shippers' Councils.

owners began to enter into agreements regarding prices and other conditions of transport, called conferences. The first such conference concerned the United Kingdom – Calcutta, India route and started operation in 1875. The conference system soon spread throughout the world. At first, governments accepted its existence, based on arguments that are still prominent in current discussions. In England, the Royal Commission on Shipping Rings in 1909 referred to advantages such as rate stability and regularity of service. In the United States, the so-called Alexander Committee investigated the effects of shipping conferences in the light of the Sherman Act of 1890 and concluded that the advantages of the conference system significantly out-weighed the disadvantages. This led to the adoption of the Shipping Act of 1916 which allowed for conferences under government control (but nevertheless prohibited some specific practices, such as the use of fighting ships[13] and retaliatory measures against shippers using the services on non-conference carriers).

If the advent of the steamship caused a first revolution in maritime transport, a second revolution occurred with the invention of container shipping, starting in 1966 in the USA. Containerisation resulted in an enlargement of transport capacity and a speeding up of travel, due to the modern vessels used. It also created the possibility of door-to-door transport by way of intermodal or multimodal transport, that is a combination of sea and land transport offered by the same carrier. Further, the costs for stevedoring were reduced due to the possibility of mechanical loading and unloading. This was also faster, allowing the vessel to spend more time on sea generating profits. At the same time, containerisation made the purchase of new and expensive vessels necessary and carriers had to incur costs for the provision of containers. For the customer, the packaging costs were likely to be reduced; carriers regularly provided the containers free of charge. Goods transported in a container are also less susceptible to damage and pilferage. Containerisation led to structural changes in the maritime transport industry in the form of a new type of alliances, called consortia. Different from conferences, consortia do not focus primarily on price fixing. They are a form of co-operation with the aim of sharing the high costs involved in operating a modern container fleet (no longer affordable to the existing liner companies) while improving the quality of service. Consortia take such diverse forms as joint scheduling, slot and space exchanges, equipment pools, joint offices, joint terminal operations, cargo sharing, revenue sharing agreements and shared inland operations. Today, consortia are the most important form of cooperation in the field of maritime transport."[14]

9.012 In terms of the commercial background, Pozdnakova has observed that extensive

"links between competing undertakings [in the liner sector], relatively high concentrations,[15] transparency and high entry barriers are all characteristic of the liner shipping market. At the

---

13 Ed., This is a practice by which a conference accords its sailings to the sailing times of non-conference competitors. The conference ship offers a cheaper service, thereby undercutting the others' rate. This practice is continued until the non-conference competitor leaves the trade. Any losses that might be incurred by conference ships due to the very low rates are split between the members of the conference (but ultimately could be recouped when the competitor leaves); compare Joint Cases C-395/96 and C-396/96, *Compagnie maritime belge transports SA and others* [2000] ECR I-1365.

14 Dinger, "What Shall We do with the Drunken Sailor? EC Competition Law and Maritime Transport" BaslerSchriften zur europäischen Integration, 61, pp. 6–7 (some footnotes omitted). Dinger also commented: "[m]ore recently, yet another type of agreement emerged, called [a] talking agreement. This started in the 1980s when agreements began to include both conference and non-conference lines operating in the same trades. Talking agreements provide a forum within which conference and rivalling non-conference lines can co-ordinate their actions by acting together on such issues as capacity management, rates and various other charges and fees. This new type of agreement emerged because traditional conferences were not able to attract participation of the new independent lines which offered a service of comparable quality to that of liner conferences and which did not wish to give up their freedom. Talking agreements provided a broader and sufficiently flexible form of cooperation." (Footnotes omitted.)

15 Ed., i.e. there are relatively few competitors and those that do compete have relatively high market share so the market is concentrated in nature.

same time, they can encourage and facilitate anti-competitive coordination of tariff rates and other market policies by carriers, to the detriment of shippers and consumers. These structural characteristics can also enable carriers to obtain and exercise individual or collective market power vis-à-vis their competitors in order to eliminate or significantly restrict the remaining competition."[16]

9.013 Before proceeding further, it is also worth distinguishing between liner shipping, tramping and pooling:

(a) "Liner shipping" involves a shipping service where there is an advertised regular route and timetable for the operation of the ships. The rates charged to shippers are normally based on a tariff. The companies providing liner shipping services could organise themselves into a group called a "conference" (or "freight conference" or "shipping conferences") to offer a joint service. The conference members agree a set of prices (i.e. "tariffs"), terms and conditions of carriage, the number and type of ship which each member will contribute and the timetable for sailings. The conference usually has a secretariat (normally provided by one of the members) for the conference.
(b) "Tramping" is the opposite of liner shipping and involves a shipowner hoping to pick up voyage charters for its ship on the spot market. Feeder services involve services between smaller ports not on the main liner route and the nearest main port.
(c) "Pooling" involves a situation where an operator of a ship may form alliances or pools with other companies and share liner routes. In a pooled liner service, the cargo, having been booked by the ship operator, may actually be carried in one of the partners' ships. Each member of a pool may make its own bookings for its own ships, or it may pool the business, so that, for example, a container from Line X may be carried on a ship of either Line X or Line Y.

9.014 A consortia is defined by Article 2(1) of Commission Regulation 906/2009[17] as meaning

"an agreement or a set of agreements between two or more vessel operating carriers which provide international liner shipping services exclusively for the carriage of cargo relating to one or more trades, the object of which is to bring about cooperation in the joint operation of a maritime transport service, and which improves the service that would be offered individually by each of its members in the absence of the consortium, in order to rationalise their operations by means of technical, operational and/or commercial arrangements."

C. UNITED NATIONS CODE OF CONDUCT FOR LINER CONFERENCES

Introduction

9.015 It is clear that liner conferences have not just been of interest to national legal systems and the EU but also to the UN. The UNCTAD turned its attention to liner conferences in the 1970s and on 6 April 1974, the United Nations Convention on a Code of Conduct for Liner Conferences (the "UNCTAD Code" or "Code") was adopted after two

---

16 *Liner Shipping and EU Competition Law* (2008), p. 4.
17 OJ L256/31, 29 September 2009.

years of negotiations. The Code consists of a convention (containing seven chapters) with an annex (containing model rules of procedure for international mandatory conciliation) and three resolutions. The adoption of the convention was the most critical step in the development of the international law on liner conferences. It establishes certain norms relating to the conduct of liner conferences. It is a framework convention. There are many who see the Code as a compromise between the so-called North and the South economies (i.e. the developed and developing countries respectively). The UNCTAD was the product of the so-called New International Economic Order ("NIEO").

UNCTAD negotiations

9.016 The Code was prompted in part by the UK's Rochdale Committee on Shipping. However, the adoption of the Code involved several years of discussions and was inspired by several factors.

9.017 The discussions stretched back to the first meeting of UNCTAD (the so-called UNCTAD I meeting) in 1964 when it was decided that the "appropriate inter-governmental procedures, including any committee that might be deemed necessary, be established ... to study and report on economic aspects of shipping that might be referred to it".

9.018 At UNCTAD II in 1968, it was resolved that the

> "governments of Member States of UNCTAD should urge liner conferences and equivalent organisations, directly or through the shipowner members of them, to make provisions in their constitutions or working arrangements to the effect that they would discuss with shippers' councils or equivalent bodies questions pertaining to freight rates, conference practices, adequacy of shipping services and other matters of common interest within the consultation machinery of the country or group of countries concerned".

The Consultative Shipping Group drafted (after the 1968 UNCTAD II meeting) guidelines for the behaviour of liner conferences and these guidelines became known as the CENSA Code when adopted by the shipowners' association, the Council of European and Japanese National Shipowners' Association ("CENSA").

9.019 The UNCTAD III meeting in Santiago, Chile in 1972 called on the UN General Assembly to convene a conference on the subject. Resolution 66 of the Conference, which contained a draft code, called for the adoption of a Code as soon as possible; this resolution was supported by 74 votes to 19 with two abstentions. The negotiations commenced when the UN Conference of Plenipotentiaries met between 12 November 1973 and 15 December 1973, as well as between 11 March 1974 and 6 April 1974.

Objectives and principles of the UNCTAD Code

9.020 The Preamble to the convention provides that the parties to the convention agree to reflect in the Code the following three fundamental objectives and three basic principles:

> "(a) the objective to facilitate the orderly expansion of world sea-borne trade;
> (b) the objective to stimulate the development of regular and efficient liner services adequate to the requirement of the trade concerned;

(c) the objective to ensure a balance of interests between suppliers and users of liner shipping services;
(d) the principle that conference practices should not involve any discrimination against the shipowners, shippers or the foreign trade of any country;
(e) the principle that conferences hold meaningful consultations with shippers' organisations, shippers' representatives and shippers on matters of common interest, with, upon request, the participation of appropriate authorities;
(f) the principle that conferences should make available to interested parties pertinent information about their activities which are relevant to those parties and should publish meaningful information on their activities."

In effect, the 1974 Code meant that "[s]ince 1974, an antitrust exemption for liner conferences had been established at international level by the UNCTAD Convention on a Code of Conduct for Liner Conferences".[18]

9.021 It is probably true to say that the rules in the UNCTAD are very precise but that the rules in the EU's Regulation 4056/86 were, by contrast, somewhat general in nature.

Signature and entry into force of the Code

9.022 The convention was signed in Geneva on 6 April 1974. Some 83 States signed the convention. It entered into force on 6 October 1983 (in accordance with Article 49 of the convention) when the necessary number of ratifications (i.e. 24 States with a combined tonnage representing at least 25% of world tonnage) had been lodged for six months. Sixteen EU Member States have ratified the Code.[19]

Perspectives on the Code

9.023 The Code is a flexible (if not a loose) instrument. Despite this flexibility, the essence of the convention is the 40:40:20 formula, whereby the exporting and importing State's national lines have 40% each of the trade each with other States having the balance of 20%.

9.024 The Code has not achieved universal appeal. The US, Greece, Japan and Brazil all opposed it. However, for present purposes, the reaction of the EU is the most significant.

9.025 The European Parliament's Committee on Economic and Monetary Affairs, in its *Interim Report on the Community Shipping Industry*, stated in 1976 that:

"17. The trend towards flag discrimination was reinforced recently by the drafting of the United Nations Convention on a Code of Conduct for Liner Conferences. This Convention upholds as a basic principle that conference practices should not involve any discrimination against shipowners, shippers, or the foreign trade of any country. However, it also introduces the principle of cargo-sharing, on the basis of a 40–40–20 formula (i.e. 40 per cent each by the importing and exporting countries' ships, and 20 per cent by the ships of third countries).

---

18 Munari, "Liner Shipping and Antitrust after the Repeal of Regulation 4056/86" [2009] LMCLQ 42 at 42 (footnote omitted).

19 I.e. Belgium, Bulgaria, Czech Republic, Denmark, Finland, France, Germany, Italy, Malta, Netherlands, Portugal, Romania, Slovakia, Spain, Sweden and the UK. The Commission proposal to repeal Reg. 4056/86 (COM(2005) 651 final) refers (at para. 44) to 14 Member States but that was before the accession of Bulgaria and Romania.

Although the liner conferences (of which there are some 350 in the world, many with headquarters in Europe) involve only some 8 to 10 per cent of the total seaborne trade by volume, the principle involved is an important one, and one whose acceptance could seriously weaken the position of EEC shipping. Moreover, while accepting the desire of the developing countries to play a large part in world shipping as a legitimate one, one might well question whether the method proposed by the United Nations Convention was the best way of achieving this.

According to a study published on shipping in the Third World, developing countries could experience serious difficulties as a result of wide-scale cargo reservation schemes as they are applied to national flag fleets. Such policies, it is suggested, would not only result in a reduction of free competition but would often lead to a reduction in the frequency of services. The report stated that this would produce over-tonnaging which in turn would reduce the efficiency of vessel utilisation and result in increased shipping costs."

Application of the Code

9.026 The Code applies to liner conferences as defined in the Code.[20]

Provisions of the Code relating to relations between conference members

Introduction

9.027 Part One, Chapter II of the convention deals with relations among member lines (i.e. the shipping lines who are members of a conference).

Membership

9.028 Article 1 of the Code relates to membership and provides:

"1. Any national shipping line shall have the right to be a full member of a conference which serves the foreign trade of its country, subject to the criteria set out in Article 1, paragraph 2. Shipping lines which are not national lines in any trade of a conference shall have the right to become full members of that conference, subject to the criteria set out in Article 1, paragraphs 2 and 3, and to the provisions regarding the share of trade as set out in Article 2 as regards third-country shipping lines.
2. A shipping line applying for membership of a conference shall furnish evidence of its ability and intention."

Thus, there is a clear distinction between "national lines" and "non-national lines" with the former finding it easier to apply for membership of conferences.

Participation

9.029 Article 2 is the basis in the UNCTAD Code of the so-called "40:40:20" formula for cargo-sharing. The article provides:

"1. Any shipping line admitted to membership of a conference shall have sailing and loading rights in the trades covered by that conference.
2. When a conference operates a pool, all shipping lines members of the conference serving the trade covered by the pool shall have the right to participate in the pool for that trade.

---

20 See para. 9.004.

3. For the purpose of determining the share of trade which member lines shall have the right to acquire, the national shipping lines of each country, irrespective of the number of lines, shall be regarded as a single group of shipping lines for that country.
4. When determining a share of trade within a pool of individual member lines and/or groups of national shipping lines in accordance with Article 2, paragraph 2, the following principles regarding their right to participation in the trade carried by the conference shall be observed, unless otherwise mutually agreed:

   (a) The group of national shipping lines of each of the two countries the foreign trade between which is carried by the conference shall have equal rights to participate in the freight and volume of traffic generated by their mutual foreign trade and carried by the conference;
   (b) Third-country shipping lines, if any, shall have the right to acquire a significant part, such as 20 per cent, in the freight and volume of traffic by that trade.

5. If, for any one of the countries whose trade is carried by a conference, there are no national shipping lines participating in the carriage of that trade, the share of the trade to which national shipping lines of that country would be entitled under Article 2, paragraph 4 shall be distributed among the individual member lines participating in the trade in proportion to their respective share."

9.030 A third country shipping line is defined by Chapter I as being "a vessel-operating carrier in its operations between two countries of which it is not a national shipping line".

Decision-making

9.031 Article 3 of the Code deals with decision-making. Decisions relating to trade between two countries cannot be made without the consent of the national shipping lines of those two states. The article provides:

"The decision-making procedures embodied in a conference agreement shall be based on the equality of all the full member lines; these procedures shall ensure that the voting rules do not hinder the proper work of the conference and the service of the trade and shall define the matters on which decisions will be made by unanimity. However, a decision cannot be taken in respect of matters defined in a conference agreement relating to the trade between two countries without the consent of the national shipping lines of those two countries."

Sanctions

9.032 Article 4 deals with sanctions in the cases of withdrawals and expulsions of lines from liner conferences. The article provides:

"1. A shipping line member of a conference shall be entitled, subject to the provisions regarding withdrawal which are embodied in pool schemes and/or cargo-sharing arrangements, to secure its release, without penalty, from the terms of the conference agreement after giving three months' notice, unless the conference agreement provides for a different time period, although it shall be required to fulfil its obligations as a member of the conference up to the date of its release.
2. A conference may, upon notice to be specified in the conference agreement, suspend or expel a member for significant failure to abide by the terms and conditions of the conference agreement.

3. No expulsion or suspension shall become effective until a statement in writing of the reasons therefor has been given and until any dispute has been settled as provided in chapter VI.
4. Upon withdrawal or expulsion, the line concerned shall be required to pay its share of the outstanding financial obligations of the conference, up to the date of its withdrawal or expulsion. In cases of withdrawal, suspension or expulsion, the line shall not be relieved of its own financial obligations under the conference agreement or of any of its obligations towards shippers."

Self-policing

9.033 Article 5 deals with self-policing by conferences. The article provides:

"1. A conference shall adopt and keep up to date an illustrative list, which shall be as comprehensive as possible, of practices which are regarded as malpractices and/or breaches of the conference agreement and shall provide effective self-policing machinery to deal with them, with specific provisions requiring:

  (a) The fixing of penalties or a range of penalties for malpractices or breaches, to be commensurate with their seriousness;
  (b) The examination and impartial review of an adjudication of complaints, and/or decisions taken on complaints, against malpractices or breaches by a person or body unconnected with any of the shipping lines members of the conference or their affiliates, on request by the conference or any other party concerned;
  (c) The reporting, on request, on the action taken in connection with complaints against malpractices and/or breaches, and on a basis of anonymity for the parties concerned, to the appropriate authorities of the countries whose trade is served by the conference and of the countries whose shipping lines are members of the conference.

2. Shipping lines and conferences are entitled to the full co-operation of shippers and shippers' organisations in the endeavour to combat malpractices and breaches."

Conference agreements

9.034 Article 6 deals with the inspection conference agreements by the appropriate authorities. The article provides:

"All conference agreements, pooling, berthing and sailing rights agreements and amendments or other documents directly related to, and which affect, such agreements, shall be made available on request to the appropriate authorities of the countries whose trade is served by the conference and of the countries whose shipping lines are members of the conference."

Provisions of the Code relating to relations with shippers

Introduction

9.035 Chapter III of the Code deals with "Relations with Shippers".

Loyalty arrangements

9.036 Article 7 of the Code provides:

"1. The shipping lines members of a conference are entitled to institute and maintain loyalty arrangements with shippers, the form and terms of which are matters for consultation between conference and shippers' organisations or representatives of shippers. These loyalty arrangements shall provide safeguards making explicit the rights of shippers and conference

members. These arrangements shall be based on the contract system or any system which is also lawful.
2. Whatever loyalty arrangements are made, the freight rate applicable to loyal shippers shall be determined within a fixed range of percentages of the freight rate applicable to other shippers. Where a change in the differential causes an increase in the rates charged to shippers, the change can be implemented only after 150 days' notice to those shippers or according to regional practice and/or agreement. Disputes in connection with a change of the differential shall be settled as provided in the loyalty agreement.
3. The terms of loyalty arrangements shall provide safeguards making explicit the rights and obligations of shippers and of shipping lines members of the conference in accordance with the following provisions, inter alia:

   (a) The shipper shall be bound in respect of cargo whose shipment is controlled by him or his affiliated or subsidiary company or his forwarding agent in accordance with the contract of sale of the goods concerned, provided that the shipper shall not, by evasion, subterfuge, or intermediary, attempt to divert cargo in violation of his loyalty commitment;
   (b) Where there is a loyalty contract, the extent of actual or liquidated damages and/or penalty shall be specified in the contract. The member lines of the conference may, however, decide to assess lower liquidated damages or to waive the claim to liquidated damages. In any event, the liquidated damages under the contract to be paid to the shipper shall not exceed the freight charges on the particular shipment, computed at the rate provided under the contract;
   (c) The shipper shall be entitled to resume full loyalty status, subject to the fulfilment of conditions established by the conference which shall be specified in the loyalty arrangement;
   (d) The loyalty arrangement shall set out:

      (i) A list of cargo, which may include bulk cargo shipped without mark or count, which is specifically excluded from the scope of the loyalty arrangement;
      (ii) A definition of the circumstances in which cargo other than cargo covered by (i) above is considered to be excluded from the scope of the loyalty arrangement;
      (iii) The method of settlement of disputes arising under the loyalty arrangement;
      (iv) Provision for termination of the loyalty arrangement on request by either a shipper or a conference without penalty, after expiry of a stipulated period of notice, such notice to be given in writing; and
      (v) The terms for granting dispensation."

Thus, loyalty arrangements such as dual rate contracts and deferred rebates may exist.

Dispensation

9.037 Article 8 of the Code provides:

"1. Conferences shall provide, within the terms of the loyalty arrangements, that requests by shippers for dispensation shall be examined and a decision given quickly and, if requested, the reasons given in writing where dispensation is withheld. Should a conference fail to confirm, within a period specified in the loyalty arrangement, sufficient space to accommodate a shipper's cargo within a period also specified in the loyalty arrangement, the shipper shall have the right, without being penalised, to utilise any vessel for the cargo in question.
2. In ports where conference services are arranged subject to the availability of a specified minimum of cargo (i.e. on inducement), but either the shipping line does not call, despite due notice by shippers, or the shipping line does not reply within an agreed time to the notice

given by shippers, shippers shall automatically have the right, without prejudicing their loyalty status, to use any available vessel for the carriage of their cargo."

Availability of tariffs

9.038 Article 9 of the Code provides for the availability of tariffs and related conditions. In specific terms, the article provides:

"Tariffs, related conditions, regulations, and any amendments thereto shall be made available on request to shippers, shippers' organisations and other parties concerned at reasonable cost, and they shall be available for examination at offices of shipping lines and their agents. They shall spell out all conditions concerning the application of freight rates and the carriage of any cargo covered by them."

Annual reports

9.039 Article 10 of the Code relates to annual reports and provides:

"Conferences shall provide annually to shippers' organisations, or to representatives of shippers, reports on their activities designed to provide general information of interest to them, including relevant information about consultations held with shippers and shippers' organisations, action taken regarding complaints, changes in membership, and significant changes in service, tariffs and conditions of carriage. Such annual reports shall be submitted, on request, to the appropriate authorities of the countries whose trade is served by the conference concerned."

Consultation machinery

9.040 Article 11 of the Code establishes a machinery for consultation between the various interests involved in liner conferences. The article provides:

"1. There shall be consultations on matters of common interest between a conference, shippers' organisations, representatives of shippers and, where practicable, shippers, which may be designated for that purpose by the appropriate authority if it so desires. These consultations shall take place whenever requested by any of the above-mentioned parties. Appropriate authorities shall have the right, upon request, to participate fully in the consultations, but this does not mean that they play a decision-making role.

2. The following matters, inter alia, may be the subject of consultation:

   (a) Changes in general tariff conditions and related regulations;
   (b) Changes in the general level of tariff rates and rates for major commodities;
   (c) Promotional and/or special freight rates;
   (d) Imposition of, and related changes in, surcharges;
   (e) Loyalty arrangements, their establishment or changes in their form and general conditions;
   (f) Changes in the tariff classification of ports;
   (g) Procedure for the supply of necessary information by shippers concerning the expected volume and nature of their cargoes; and
   (h) Presentation of cargo for shipment and the requirement regarding notice of cargo availability.

3. To the extent that they fall within the scope of activity of a conference, the following matters may also be the subject of consultation:

   (a) Operation of cargo inspection services;
   (b) Changes in the pattern of services;

(c) Effects of the introduction of new technology in the carriage of cargo, in particular unitisation, with consequent reduction of conventional service or loss of direct services; and
(d) Adequacy and quality of shipping services, including the impact of pooling, berthing or sailing arrangements on the availability of shipping services and freight rates at which shipping services are provided; changes in the areas served and in the regularity of calls by conference vessels.

4. Consultations shall be held before final decisions are taken, unless otherwise provided in this Code. Advance notice shall be given of the intention to take decisions on matters referred to in Article 11, paragraphs 2 and 3. Where this is impossible, urgent decisions may be taken pending the holding of consultations.
5. Consultations shall begin without undue delay and in any event within a maximum period specified in the conference agreement, or in the absence of such a provision in the agreement, not later than 30 days after receipt of the proposal for consultations, unless different periods of time are provided in this Code.
6. When holding consultations, the parties shall use their best efforts to provide relevant information, to hold timely discussions and to clarify matters for the purpose of seeking solutions of the issues concerned. The parties involved shall take account of each other's views and problems and strive to reach agreement consistent with their commercial viability."

Provisions of the Code relating to freight rates

Introduction

9.041 Chapter IV of the Code deals with freight rates.

Criteria for freight rate determination

9.042 Article 12 of the Code provides:

"In arriving at a decision on questions of tariff policy in all cases mentioned in this Code, the following points shall, unless otherwise provided, be taken into account:

(a) Freight rates shall be fixed at as low a level as is feasible from the commercial point of view and shall permit a reasonable profit for shipowners;
(b) The cost of operations of conferences shall, as a rule, be evaluated for the round voyage of ships, with the outward and inward directions considered as a single whole. Where applicable, the outward and inward voyage should be considered separately. The freight rates should take into account among other factors, the nature of cargoes, the interrelation between weight and cargo measurement, as well as the value of cargoes;
(c) In fixing promotional freight and/or special freight rates for specific goods, the conditions of trade for these goods of the countries served by the conference particularly of developing and land-locked countries, shall be taken into account."

Conference tariffs and classification of tariff rates

9.043 Article 13 of the Code provides:

"1. Conference tariffs shall not unfairly differentiate between shippers similarly situated. Shipping lines members of a conference shall adhere strictly to the rates, rules and terms shown in the tariffs and other currently valid published documents of the conference and to any special arrangements permitted under this Code.
2. Conference tariffs should be drawn up simply and clearly, containing as few classes/categories as possible, depending on the commodity and, where appropriate, for each class/category; they should also indicate, wherever practicable, in order to facilitate statistical

compilation and analysis, the corresponding appropriate code number of the item in accordance with the Standard International Trade Classification, the Brussels Tariff Nomenclature or any other nomenclature that may be internationally adopted; the classification of commodities in the tariffs should, as far as practicable, be prepared in co-operation with shippers' organisations and other national and international organisations concerned."

General freight-rate increases

9.044 Article 14 of the Code provides:

"1. A conference shall give notice of not less than 150 days, or according to regional practice and/or agreement, to shippers' organisations or representatives of shippers and/or shippers and, where so required, to appropriate authorities of the countries whose trade is served by the conference, of its intention to effect a general increase in freight rates, an indication of its extent, the date of effect and the reasons supporting the proposed increase.
2. At the request of any of the parties prescribed for this purpose in this Code, to be made within an agreed period of time after the receipt of the notice, consultations shall commence, in accordance with the relevant provisions of this Code, within a stipulated period not exceeding 30 days or as previously agreed between the parties concerned; the consultations shall be held in respect of the basis and amounts of the proposed increase and the date from which it is to be given effect.
3. A conference, in an effort to expedite consultations, may or upon the request of any of the parties prescribed in this Code as entitled to participate in consultations on general freight-rate increases shall, where practicable, reasonably before the consultations, submit to the participating parties a report from independent accountants of repute, including, where the requesting parties accept it as one of the bases of consultations, an aggregated analysis of data regarding relevant costs and revenues which in the opinion of the conference necessitate an increase in freight rates.
4. If agreement is reached as a result of the consultations, the freight-rate increase shall take effect from the date indicated in the notice served in accordance with Article 14, paragraph 1, unless a later date is agreed upon between the parties concerned.
5. If no agreement is reached within 30 days of the giving of notice in accordance with Article 14, paragraph 1, and subject to procedures prescribed in this Code, the matter shall be submitted immediately to international mandatory conciliation, in accordance with Chapter VI. The recommendation of the conciliators, if accepted by the parties concerned, shall be binding upon them and shall be implemented, subject to the provisions of Article 14, paragraph 9, with effect from the date mentioned in the conciliators' recommendation.
6. Subject to the provisions of Article 14, paragraph 9, a general freight-rate increase may be implemented by a conference pending the conciliators' recommendation. When making their recommendation, the conciliators should take into account the extent of the above-mentioned increase made by the conference and the period for which it has been in force. In the event that the conference rejects the recommendation of the conciliators, shippers and/or shippers' organisations shall have the right to consider themselves not bound, after appropriate notice, by any arrangement or other contract with that conference which may prevent them from using non-conference shipping lines. Where a loyalty arrangement exists shippers and/or shippers' organisations shall give notice within a period of 30 days to the effect that they no longer consider themselves bound by that arrangement, which notice shall apply from the date mentioned therein, and a period of not less than 30 days and not more than 90 days shall be provided in the loyalty arrangement for this purpose.
7. A deferred rebate which is due to the shipper and which has already been accumulated by the conference shall not be withheld by, or forfeited to, the conference as a result of action by the shipper under Article 14, paragraph 6.
8. If the trade of a country carried by shipping lines members of a conference on a particular route consists largely of one or few basic commodities, any increase in the freight rate on

one or more of those commodities shall be treated as a general freight-rate increase, and the appropriate provisions of this Code shall apply.

9. Conferences should institute any general freight-rate increase effective in accordance with this Code for a period of a stated minimum duration, subject always to the rules regarding surcharges and regarding adjustment in freight rates consequent upon fluctuations in foreign exchange rates. The period over which a general freight-rate increase is to apply is an appropriate matter to be considered during consultations conducted in accordance with Article 14, paragraph 2, but unless otherwise agreed between the parties concerned during the consultations, the minimum period of time between the date when one general freight-rate increase becomes effective and the date of notice for the next general freight-rate increase given in accordance with Article 14, paragraph 1 shall not be less than 10 months."

This is a somewhat commercial approach to the issues involved.

Promotional freight rates

9.045 Promotional freight rates are dealt with by Article 15 of the Code. It provides:

"1. Promotional freight rates for non-traditional exports should be instituted by conferences.
2. All necessary and reasonable information justifying the need for a promotional freight rate shall be submitted to a conference by the shippers, shippers' organisations or representatives of shippers concerned.
3. Special procedures shall be instituted providing for a decision within 30 days from the date of receipt of that information, unless mutually agreed otherwise, on application for promotional freight rates. A clear distinction shall be made between these and general procedures for considering the possibility of reducing freight rates for other commodities or of exempting them from increases.
4. Information regarding the procedures for considering applications for promotional freight rates shall be made available by the conference to shippers and/or shippers' organisations and, on request, to the Governments and/or other appropriate authorities of the countries whose trade is served by the conference.
5. A promotional freight rate shall be established normally for a period of 12 months, unless otherwise mutually agreed between the parties concerned. Prior to the expiry of the period, the promotional freight rate shall be reviewed, on request by the shipper and/or shippers' organisation concerned, when it shall be a matter for the shipper and/or shippers' organisation, at the request of the conference, to show that the continuation of the rate is justified beyond the initial period.
6. When examining a request for a promotional freight rate, the conference may take into account that, while the rate should promote the export of the non-traditional product for which it is sought, it is not likely to create substantial competitive distortions in the export of a similar product from another country served by the conference.
7. Promotional freight rates are not excluded from the imposition of a surcharge or a currency adjustment factor in accordance with Articles 16 and 17.
8. Each shipping line member of a conference serving the relevant ports of a conference trade shall accept, and not unreasonably refuse, a fair share of cargo for which a promotional freight rate has been established by the conference."

Surcharges

9.046 Article 16 of the Code provides:

"1. Surcharges imposed by a conference to cover sudden or extraordinary increases in costs or losses of revenue shall be regarded as temporary. They shall be reduced in accordance with improvements in the situation or circumstances which they were imposed to meet and shall be cancelled, subject to Article 16, paragraph 6, as soon as the situation or circumstances which prompted their imposition cease to prevail. This shall be indicated at the moment of their imposition, together, as far as possible, with a description of the change in the situation or circumstances which will bring about their increase, reduction or cancellation.

2. Surcharges imposed on cargo moving to or from a particular port shall likewise be regarded as temporary and likewise shall be increased, reduced or cancelled, subject to Article 16, paragraph 6, when the situation in that port changes.

3. Before any surcharge is imposed, whether general or covering only a specific port, notice should be given and there shall be consultation, upon request, in accordance with the procedures of this Code, between the conference concerned and other parties directly affected by the surcharge and prescribed in this Code as entitled to participate in such consultations, save in those exceptional circumstances which warrant immediate imposition of the surcharge. In cases where a surcharge has been imposed without prior consultation, consultations, upon request, shall be held as soon as possible thereafter. Prior to such consultations, conferences shall furnish data which in their opinion justify the imposition of the surcharge.

4. Unless the parties agree otherwise, within a period of 15 days after the receipt of a notice given in accordance with Article 16, paragraph 3, if there is no agreement on the question of the surcharge between the parties concerned referred to in that Article, the relevant provisions for settlement of disputes provided in this Code shall prevail. Unless the parties concerned agree otherwise, the surcharge may, however, be imposed pending resolution of the dispute, if the dispute still remains unresolved at the end of a period of 30 days after the receipt of the above-mentioned notice.

5. In the event of a surcharge being imposed, in exceptional circumstances, without prior consultation as provided in Article 16, paragraph 3, if no agreement is reached through subsequent consultations, the relevant provisions for settlement of disputes provided in this Code shall prevail.

6. Financial loss incurred by the shipping lines members of a conference as a result of any delay on account of consultations and/or other proceedings for resolving disputes regarding imposition of surcharges in accordance with the provisions of this Code, as compared to the date from which the surcharge was to be imposed in terms of the notice given in accordance with Article 16, paragraph 3, may be compensated by an equivalent prolongation of the surcharge before its removal. Conversely, for any surcharge imposed by the conference and subsequently determined and agreed to be unjustified or excessive as a result of consultations or other procedures prescribed in this Code, the amounts so collected or the excess thereof as determined hereinabove, unless otherwise agreed, shall be refunded to the parties concerned, if claimed by them, within a period of 30 days of such claim."

Other substantive aspects of the Code

9.047 Currency changes are dealt with in Article 17 of the Code. Part One, Chapter V, deals with other provisions of the Code.

D. THE UNCTAD LINER CODE AND EU LAW

Introduction

9.048 The importance of the UN Liner Code for EU law is clear from the fact that the EU's last block exemption exempting price-fixing agreements relates to liner conferences. The third recital in Council Regulation 4056/86 provided that "the Regulation applying the rules of competition to maritime transport foreseen in the last recital of Council Regulation (EEC) 954/79 should take account of the adoption of the Code".

9.049 The background to UNCTAD has been described in the following terms:

"In 1966, US conferences seemed to be sailing on calm waters once more, although storm clouds in the shape of the UNCTAD Maritime Transport Committee were looming on the horizon.

Developing countries, being dissatisfied with the conference system, became more vocal in their desire to control conference activities and to participate actively in world maritime trade. The views of the developing countries were channelled through the Secretariat General and the Maritime Transport Committee of the United Nations Conference on Trade and Development (UNCTAD), set up in 1964. This simply increased the pressure towards greater formalisation of the relationship between conferences and their users and between conferences and the authorities of the countries whose ports they covered. The result was the codification and strengthening of the private rules of conduct governing relations between shipowners and shippers, in an attempt to counteract the clear trend in developing countries and in UNCTAD towards public control of liner conferences.

In July 1967, three years after the creation of UNCTAD, when the profound differences between developed and developing countries concerning maritime conferences had become clear, the British Government set up a Committee of Enquiry into Shipping, chaired by Viscount Rochdale, which became known as the Rochdale Committee. Although mainly concerned with the UK maritime industry, the Committee also had to take into account international aspects in order to make its recommendations. One of the matters which the Committee reviewed in its entirety, and on which it also made recommendations, was the question of maritime conferences. The Rochdale Committee concluded that 'on balance' it would not be in the public interest to prevent liner owners from forming associations by means of agreements to regulate or control maritime trade. However, it recommended that conference members operating from or to British ports should collectively adopt and publish a conference code of practice, as a precondition for continuing to enjoy their restrictive agreements. The details of that code were to be worked out by negotiation between representatives of the government, shipowners and shippers.

In order to avoid the chaos that would ensue if each government acted independently, the Committee took the view that the British Government, for reasons of national interest, should sponsor an international agreement on a Code of Conduct for liner conferences in general, especially those offering containerised transport services; the Committee thus advocated taking the initiative and requesting discussions between governments on this issue as soon as possible.

That recommendation of the Rochdale Committee, benefiting as it did from the similar mood within developing nations (and even developed nations), had far-reaching consequences for the activities of liner conference operations worldwide. Its reception both by governments and within the shipping circles of CSG [Consultative Shipping Group] countries, and within UNCTAD, was to bring about a fundamental change in the way in which conferences operated, since the Rochdale Report led directly to the CENSA Code, and indirectly to the UNCTAD Code of Conduct.

In order to give effect to the Rochdale Report recommendations, the United Kingdom, which had served as the CSG Secretariat since its inception, convened a meeting of the CSG in Tokyo in February 1971. The governments of the CSG asked their shipowners to prepare jointly a detailed code of practice to be presented to them for further consideration before 31 December 1971. The CSG 'Tokyo' recommendations placed much more emphasis on the idea of pure self-regulation, free of government intervention, than the Rochdale Committee. In any event, the point of the CSG's resolutions was perhaps not only to reinterpret the Rochdale Report in a less interventionist manner but also, in particular, to put the brakes on the developing countries' wish to use legislation to create a more formal instrument for controlling conferences with the aid of the UNCTAD Secretariat.

As requested by the CSG and in conjunction with the ESC, CENSA prepared a code of practice which was adopted in Genoa in October 1971 and submitted to and accepted by the CSG governments as satisfactory in November 1971.[21] This clear, even blatant, attempt by the CSG and its shipowners to restrain the developing countries, without even allowing them to participate (whether within UNCTAD or not) in the drawing up of the intended self-regulatory universal code of practice for conferences, was entirely unsuccessful. On the contrary, its effect was to speed up the process for the proposal and adoption in 1974 of an international convention on a Code of Conduct for liner conferences. Under the auspices of UNCTAD, this convention very

---

21 Ed., The Code of Practice for Conferences has been published jointly by CENSA and ESC, in London and The Hague, undated.

clearly reflected the views of developing countries concerning conferences. In addition, not only did it include aspects of a purely regulatory nature concerning conference practices but also, to the despair of the traditional maritime nations, it contained provisions designed to foster the development of the liner fleets of developing countries: the famous (and infamous) 40/40/20 rule for cargo sharing between national conference lines at both ends of a route, and cross-traders."[22]

9.050 It has been observed:

"The UNCTAD Code was the pretext and the catalyst for Community maritime transport policy, which until then had been non-existent. Given the need to reply in a united manner to the threat posed by the UNCTAD Code, the European Commission proposed and finally (after making many concessions) obtained Council Regulation 954/79, where the reservations that Member States should make to the Convention on the UNCTAD Code were agreed, in the event of their acceding to or ratifying it (something that certain countries, such as Greece, declared that they would never do).

Apart from serving to put into effect the until then non-existent Community maritime transport policy, the last recital to the Brussels Package (as Council Regulation 954/79 came to be known) contained a vitally important declaration regarding liner conferences:

'Whereas the stabilising role of conferences in ensuring reliable services to shippers is recognised, but it is nevertheless necessary to avoid possible breaches by conferences of the rules of competition laid down in the Treaty, whereas the Commission will accordingly forward to the Council a proposal for a regulation concerning the application of those rules to sea transport'.

This declaration made it clear that liner conferences would obtain a block exemption that was in line with the UNCTAD Code, but not necessarily one that was in line with an orthodox interpretation of the competition rules. In exchange for recovering the powers of investigation and sanction which the Commission had renounced in 1962 when proposing the adoption of Council Regulation 141/62, which prevented the application of Regulation 17/62 to the transport sector, the Commission had to adapt the competition rules to conferences rather than the other way round."[23]

9.051 Regulation 954/79 is the so-called "Brussels Package" which enables the Member States of the EU to accede to or ratify the UNCTAD Code. The relevant regulation, Regulation 954/79, provides that "the questions covered by the Code are of importance not only to the Member States but also to the Community, in particular from the shipping and trading point of view". By virtue of Regulation 954/79, the EU was authorising and inviting Member States to ratify the UNCTAD Code. The UNCTAD entered into force only in 1983 after it had been ratified by Germany and the Netherlands. Regulation 954/79 was repealed on 18 October 2008 by virtue of Regulation 1490/2007[24] which means, as Munari put it so well, "Member States will no longer have an '[EU] cover' allowing them to adhere to the UNCTAD Code of Conduct for Liner Conferences".[25]

9.052 There was no representation at the Conference from the Commission. The Member States of the EU were not united in their views on the UN Liner Code. This was unfortunate. The vote in April 1974 was a matrix of views.

---

22 Ortiz Blanco, "Personal Reflections on the Development of EC Maritime Competition Policy: Past and Future", EMLO Conference, Copenhagen, October 2008.
23 Ibid.
24 OJ L332/1, 18 December 2007.
25 (2009) LMCLQ 42 at 43.

9.053 The following Member States (at the time) voted in favour of the Code: Belgium, France and Germany. These three States were supportive of the Code from an early stage. France and Belgium could see cargo opportunities and so they voted along with the Group of 77 States,[26] the USSR and Spain. The following States voted against the Code: Denmark and United Kingdom. The following States abstained: Italy and the Netherlands. Both Italy and the Netherlands later acceded to the Code. Two States, namely Ireland and Luxembourg, did not attend the Conference. Meanwhile, the European Commission acted as an observer at the Conference because it would have been of limited relevance to them. The lack of unity may well have been fatal:

> "[i]t is extremely regrettable that the Member States of the Community were not able to adopt a joint position in due time, especially since if they had done so it might have been possible to influence the negotiations so that the end result would have been acceptable to all Member States".

Regulation 954/79 was the embodiment of the common position of the Member States. The Liner Code was finalised only two days after the CJEU adopted its judgment in *Commission v France (French Seafarers)*.[27] In that case, the CJEU confirmed that the Treaty applied to transport so that the Code could be in breach of EU law.

9.054 It has been written:

> "The Commission, fearing that the UNCTAD Code was not in line with [EU] competition law, first presented three proposals aiming to prevent Member States from becoming parties. This was followed by a common position. However, on the last day when the Convention containing the UNCTAD Code was open for signature, the governments of Belgium, France and Germany signed it, but stated that ratification could only take place if obligations arising from the Treaty of Rome[28] were not violated. A new Commission proposal then suggested that Member States may become parties to the Convention provided that the principle of free trade would prevail within the [EU] and in [relation] to all OECD [Organisation for Economic Co-operation and Development] countries. The measure passed by the Council to this effect in 1979 was Regulation 954/79. The Regulation provides for certain modifications of the rules under the UNCTAD code which the Member States have to respect (such as Art.3 on intra-[EU] cargo allocation). The Regulation is a compromise: on the one hand, the support of the UNCTAD code through [EU] legislation can be considered a concession to the developing countries, on the other hand the principles of [EU] competition law are protected."[29]

Compatibility of the Code with EU law: Regulation 954/79

9.055 Some elements of the Code were incompatible with EU law. In particular, the Code would violate against the EU law principles of non-discrimination on the basis of nationality, freedom of establishment in another Member State, freedom to provide services to persons in other Member States and the general rules on EU competition law. Regulation 954/79 was the mechanism adopted by the EU to deal with the incompatibility issue.

---

26 I.e. the developing States.
27 Case 167/73 [1974] ECR 359, ECLI:EU:C:1974:35.
28 Ed., i.e. what is now the TFEU.
29 Dinger, op. cit. at fn. 14, p. 10 (footnotes omitted).

Legislative history of Regulation 954/79

1974: Commission proposal

9.056 On 15 July 1974, the Commission published a communication entitled "Proposal for a decision of the Council concerning common action by the Member States in respect of the United Nations Convention on a Code of Conduct for Liner Conferences". This communication recalled that the general rules of the Treaty applied to sea transport (in the light of *Commission v France (French Seafarers)*)[30] and thus the Member States should take a common position on the UN Convention. In essence, the Commission believed that the Code could damage certain fundamental interests of the EU. The Commission proposed that the Member States should abstain from any measures connected with the signing and ratification of and the accession to the convention (Article 2 of the proposal) and that the Council should decide by 30 June 1975, on a proposal from the Commission, on a common procedure (Article 1 of the proposal).

1975: Commission proposal

9.057 The Commission followed up its 1974 communication with another entitled "Proposal concerning the opening of negotiations in respect of the United Nations Convention on a Code of Conduct for Liner Conferences". This document stated that there were specific incompatibilities between certain provisions of the Code and the then European Economic Community ("EEC") Treaty.

Code of Conduct: and the then existing EEC Treaty

9.058 Articles 1 and 2 of Chapter II of the Code reduced the effect of the European Community ("EC") competition rules and resulted in discrimination between Member State nationals by reason of their national base as well as shipping companies established in the Member States.

9.059 Belgium, France and Germany signed the UN Convention subject to ratification. The Commission protested and instituted proceedings against the States. Scarascia Mugnozza, the Vice-President of the Commission said, while answering a question in the European Parliament, on 13 October 1976:

> "The three Member States who have signed the Convention, subject to ratification, declare themselves bound to respect the obligations incumbent on them under the Treaty of Accession to the European Communities and are now ready to suspend ratification unless the Council of Ministers of the Community expressly authorises them to ratify. The Commission will not begin infringement proceedings before the Court of Justice. The Commission has had firm assurances that the three Member States will take active steps at Community level to formulate a common approach to the Code of Conduct. In the meantime, the Member States and the Commission reserve their position on the legal aspects of the problem."

9.060 Despite the incompatibility of some aspects of the Code with EU law, the EU decided in 1979 to allow Member States and the EU itself to become Contracting Parties to the Code. The EU's decision was embodied in Regulation 954/79. This is the so-called

---

30 Case 167/73 [1974] ECR 359, ECLI:EU:C:1974:35.

Brussels Package. The reason for this regulation is that the EU did not want to deprive those developing countries with which it has a special relationship, of the cargo-sharing arrangements involved in the Code.

Council

9.061 On 15 May 1979, the Council adopted Regulation 954/79. The political rationale for the regulation was the fact that the EU had a special relationship with a great number of developing countries and was keen to give them the benefit of the preferential treatment contained in the Code. Regulation 954/79 provided the legal means to make adhesion possible.

9.062 In essence, the EU decided that the 40:40:20 formula on cargo-sharing was inapplicable as far as the relations between EU Member States were concerned.

Contents of Regulation 954/79

9.063 Article 1 of Regulation 954/79 provides:

"1. When ratifying the United Nations Convention on a Code of Conduct for Liner Conferences, or when acceding thereto, Member States shall inform the Secretary-General of the United Nations in writing that such ratification or accession has taken place in accordance with this Regulation.
2. The instrument of ratification or accession shall be accompanied by the reservations set out in Annex I."

Existing conferences

9.064 Article 2 of Regulation 954/79 deals with existing conferences. It provides:

"1. In the case of an existing conference, each group of shipping lines of the same nationality which are members thereof shall determine by commercial negotiations with another shipping line of that nationality whether the latter may participate as a national shipping line in the said conference.
    If a new conference is created, the shipping lines of the same nationality shall determine by commercial negotiations which of them may participate as a national shipping line in the future conference.
2. Where the negotiations referred to in paragraph 1 fail to result in agreement, each Member State may, at the request of one of the lines concerned and after hearing all of them, take the necessary steps to settle the dispute.
3. Each Member State shall ensure that all vessel-operating shipping lines established on its territories under the Treaty establishing the European Economic Community are treated in the same way as lines which have their management head office on its territory and the effective control of which is exercised there."

Cargo allocation

9.065 Article 3 of Regulation 954/79 deals with cargo allocation. It provides:

"1. Where a liner conference operates a pool or a berthing, sailing and/or any other form of cargo allocation agreement in accordance with Article 2 of the Code of Conduct, the volume of cargo to which the group of national shipping lines of each Member State participating in that trade or the shipping lines of the Member States participating in that trade as third country shipping lines are entitled under the Code shall be redistributed, unless a decision is taken to the contrary by all the lines which are members of the Conference and parties to the present redistribution rules. This redistribution of cargo shares shall be carried out on the basis of a unanimous decision by those shipping lines which are members of the conference and participate in the redistribution, with a view to all these lines carrying a fair share of the conference trade.

2. The share finally allocated to each participant shall be determined by the application of commercial principles, taking account in particular of:

   (a) the volume of cargo carried by the conference and generated by the Member States whose trade is served by it;
   (b) past performance of the shipping lines in the trade covered by the pool;
   (c) the volume of cargo carried by the conference and shipped through the ports of the Member States;
   (d) the needs of the shippers whose cargoes are carried by the conference.

3. If no agreement is reached on the redistribution of cargoes referred to in paragraph 1, the matter shall, at the request of one of the parties, be referred to conciliation in accordance with the procedure set out in Annex II. Any dispute not settled by the conciliation procedure may, with the agreement of the parties, be referred to arbitration. In that event, the award of the arbitrator shall be binding.

4. At intervals to be laid down in advance, shares allocated in accordance with paragraphs 1, 2, and 3 shall be regularly reviewed, taking into account the criteria set out in paragraph 2 and in particular from the viewpoint of providing adequate and efficient services to shippers."

OECD Member States

9.066 Given the close links between the EU and the OECD, it is not surprising that the regulation dealt with the relationship. The relations with other Member States of the OECD are dealt with by Article 4 of the regulation. It provides:

"1. In a conference trade between a Member State of the Community and a State which is a party to the Code of Conduct and not an OECD country, a shipping line of another Member State of the OECD wishing to participate in the redistribution provided for in Article 3 of this Regulation may do so subject to reciprocity defined at governmental or ship-owners' level.

2. Without prejudice to paragraph 3 of this Article, Article 2 of the Code of Conduct shall not be applied in conference trades between Member States or, on a reciprocal basis, between such States and the other OECD countries which are parties to the Code.

3. Paragraph 2 of this Article shall not affect the opportunities for participation as third country shipping lines in such trades, in accordance with the principles reflected in Article 2 of the Code of Conduct, of the shipping lines of a developing country which are recognised as national shipping lines under the Code and which are:

   (a) already members of a conference serving these trades; or
   (b) admitted to such a conference under Article 1(3) of the Code.

4. Articles 3 and 14(9) of the Code of Conduct shall not be applied in conference trades between Member States or, on a reciprocal basis, between such States and other OECD countries which are parties to the code.

5. In conference trades between Member States and between these States and other OECD countries which are parties to the Code of Conduct, the shippers and shipowners of Member States shall not insist on applying the procedures for settling disputes provided for in Chapter VI of the Code in their mutual relationships or, on a reciprocal basis, in relation to shippers and ship-owners of other OECD countries where other procedures for settling disputes have

been agreed between them. They shall in particular take full advantage of the possibilities provided by Article 25(1) and (2) of the Code for resolving disputes by means of procedures other than those laid down in Chapter VI of the Code.
6. For the adoption of decisions relating to matters defined in the conference agreement concerning the trade of a Member State, other than those referred to in Article 3 of this Regulation, the national shipping lines of such State shall consult all the other Community lines which are members of the conference before giving or withholding their assent."

Decision-making procedures

9.067 Article 5 of the Code provides for decision-making procedures.

Reservations and interpretative reservations

9.068 Annex I to the regulation sets out the reservations and interpretative reservations which must be entered by the Member States when ratifying or acceding to the convention. These are:

"1. For the purposes of the Code of Conduct, the term 'national shipping line' may, in the case of a Member State of the Community, include any vessel-operating shipping line established on the territory of such Member State in accordance with the EEC Treaty.
2. (a) Without prejudice to paragraph (b) of this reservation, Article 2 of the Code of Conduct shall not be applied in conference trades between the Member States of the Community or, on a reciprocal basis, between such States and the other OECD countries which are parties to the Code.
   (b) Point (a) shall not affect the opportunities for participation as third country shipping lines in such trades, in accordance with the principles reflected in Article 2 of the Code, of the shipping lines of a developing country which are recognised as national shipping lines under the Code and which are:

   (i) already members of a conference serving these trades; or
   (ii) admitted to such a conference under Article 1(3) of the Code. Articles 3 and 14(9) of the Code of Conduct shall not be applied in conference trades between the Member States of the Community or, on a reciprocal basis, between such States and the other OECD countries which are parties to the Code

4. In trades to which Article 3 of the Code of Conduct applies, the last sentence of that Article is interpreted as meaning that:

   (a) the two groups of national shipping lines will co-ordinate their positions before voting on matters concerning the trade between their two countries;
   (b) this sentence applies solely to matters which the conference agreement identifies as requiring the assent of both groups of national shipping lines concerned, and not to all matters covered by the conference agreement."

9.069 The reservations were necessary because of the otherwise incompatible nature of the Code vis-à-vis the then EC Treaty.

E. REGULATION 1490/2007

9.070 Regulation 1490/2007[31] repealed Regulation 954/79 on 18 October 2008. This means that the Member States no longer have an "EU cover" allowing them to adhere to

---
31 OJ 2007 L332/1.

the UNCTAD Code of Conduct. As the Commission stated in its proposal[32] to repeal Regulation 4056/86:

> "45. If the liner conference block exemption is abolished the application of the Code becomes incompatible with the [EU] competition rules. This implies that the Member States that have ratified the Code of Conduct would have to denounce it.[33] It also implies that, for the sake of coherency, the Community legislator should repeal Regulation 954/79. The Commission will be tabling a proposal to that end.
> 46. Furthermore, national laws, regulations or administrative provisions implementing Regulation 954/79 will have to be adjusted. Two Member States may also have to revisit their international agreements with third countries that refer to the Code of Conduct or Regulation 4056/86.
> 47. As a consequence, the date of application of those provisions of Regulation (EC) No 4056/86 relating to the liner conference block exemption should be postponed for a period of two years. This concerns Articles 1(3) points (b) and (c), Articles 3 to 8 and 26.
> 48. The repeal of the liner conference block exemption would not have any implications for the international agreements entered into by the EU which contain a reference to Regulation 4056/86 and/or to the Code of Conduct. There are currently fourteen[34] such agreements ... Considering the way the provisions are phrased, the Commission holds the view that there is no need to modify these agreements if the Council decides to repeal Regulation 4056/86 because the texts do not impact on the ability of carriers to either party to the agreement to operate outside conferences."[35]

F. IMPLEMENTATION: RATIFICATION IN CERTAIN MEMBER STATES

Introduction

9.071 It is not the purpose of this book to review the implementation of the UN Code in each of the Member States and recourse should be had to the laws of each of those States for details on this point. However, some background information is provided by way of background.

The Netherlands

9.072 On 24 April 1981, the Commission adopted an opinion addressed to the Netherlands, regarding implementation of Regulation (EEC) No 954/79 of 15 May 1979 concerning the ratification by Member States of, or their accession to, the United Nations Convention on a Code of Conduct for Liner Conferences.[36] The opinion provided:

> "1. In a letter dated 30 May 1980 the Director-General for Shipping and Maritime Affairs of the Ministry of Transport and Waterways of the Netherlands submitted the following documents for the opinion of the Commission in accordance with Article 6 of Regulation (EEC) No 954/79[37]:

---

32 COM(2005) 651 final.
33 Ed., Art. 50 of the Code provides for denunciation to be notified in writing and to take effect at least one year later.
34 Ed., it is understood that this is now 16 since Bulgaria and Romania acceded after this proposal was made.
35 COM(2005) 651 final (footnote omitted).
36 OJ 1981 L129/68.
37 OJ 1979 L121/1.

- a Bill approving the United Nations Convention on a Code of Conduct for Liner Conferences,
- a Bill containing rules concerning the sea transport market (Sea Transport Act),
- an explanatory memorandum on each of these Bills.

2. Having examined these documents, the Commission is of the view that full account has been taken of the requirements of the said Regulation, subject to the need to modify Article 8 (2)(b) of the draft Sea Transport Act in order to take full account of the provisions for reciprocity referred to in Article 4 of the Regulation. The paragraph in question would read, as modified: "the definition of reciprocity referred to in Article 4".

3. The Government of the Netherlands has indicated its readiness to make this amendment and on this basis the Commission hereby delivers a favourable opinion on the proposed legislation."

Germany

9.073 On 17 December 1981, the Commission adopted an opinion addressed to the Federal Republic of Germany, regarding implementation of Regulation (EEC) No 954/79 of 15 May 1979 concerning the ratification by Member States of, or their accession to, the United Nations Convention on a Code of Conduct for Liner Conferences.[38] The opinion provided:

"1. In a letter dated 25 September 1981 the Federal Minister of Transport of the Federal Republic of Germany sent the following documents to the Commission for consultation purposes under Article 6 of the above Regulation:

(i) a draft Law concerning the United Nations Convention on a Code of Conduct for Liner Conferences, and
(ii) an Explanatory Memorandum.

2. Having examined these documents, the Commission considers that they meet all the obligations laid down in Regulation (EEC) No 954/79, provided that Article 1 of the draft Law concerning the Convention on the Code of Conduct is applied in such a way that full account is taken of Article 1 of Regulation (EEC) No 954/79.

3. As the Government of the Federal Republic of Germany indicates in the Explanatory Memorandum that it intends to do so, the Commission hereby delivers a favourable opinion on the draft Law submitted to it."

Denmark

9.074 On 22 February 1982, the Commission adopted an opinion addressed to Denmark, regarding implementation of Regulation (EEC) No 954/79 of 15 May 1979 concerning the ratification by Member States of, or their accession to, the United Nations Convention on a Code of Conduct for Liner Conferences.[39] The opinion provided:

"1. In a letter dated 16 November 1981, the Minister of Industry of Denmark submitted the following documents for the opinion of the Commission under Article 6 of the above Regulation:

(i) a draft act on liner conferences;
(ii) a draft order on liner conferences.

---

38 OJ 1982 L10/29.
39 OJ 1982 L65/28.

2. Having examined these documents, the Commission considers that they give rise to the following observations:

General form of the draft legislation

The order repeats (in fact it re-enacts) the directly applicable provisions already contained in the Council Regulation. In this connection it is relevant to note the remarks of the Court of Justice in Case 39/72, Commission v. Italy [1973] 1 ECR, 101, where the Court said in paragraphs 17 and 18 of the judgment:

'In substance the same decree, apart from some procedural provisions of a national character, confines itself to reproducing the provisions of the Community Regulations.

By following this procedure, the Italian Government has brought into doubt both the legal nature of the applicable provisions and the date of their coming into force.

According to the terms of Articles 189 and 191 of the Treaty, Regulations are, as such, directly applicable in all Member States and come into force solely by virtue of their publication in the Official Journal of the European Communities, as from the date specified in them, or in the absence thereof, as from the date provided in the Treaty.

Consequently, all methods of implementation are contrary to the Treaty, which would have the result of creating an obstacle to the direct effect of Community Regulations and of jeopardizing their simultaneous and uniform application in the whole of the Community.

Moreover, the implementing measures provided both by Law No 935 and by the decree of 22 March 1972 do not take into account the extension of the time allowed for slaughter by Regulation (EEC) No 580/70, so that Italian farmers have been misled as regards the extension of the time allowed for the slaughter of cows which have calved between 1 April and 30 May 1970.

The default of the Italian Republic has thus been established by reason not only of the delay in putting the system into effect but also of the manner of giving effect to it provided by the decree.'

In principle, therefore, the reproduction of a Community Regulation in national legislation is objectionable. In the present case, however, the intention of the Danish Government is merely to provide a comprehensive code of legislation which will be more intelligible to the reader than would be provisions scattered in several instruments (the relevant provisions of the code of conduct on liner conferences are also reproduced). In these circumstances the Danish draft legislation could be made acceptable, but only on the condition that it is made clearly apparent that the draft contains provisions reproduced from a Council Regulation and that they are identified. The relevant provisions could for example be printed in italics, the significance of which would be indicated by a footnote.

Act on liner conferences
Section 4
It would seem preferable to delete the reference to 'Danish Courts of Law'. It may happen for example that a Court other than Danish may be called upon to apply Danish law with reference to liner conferences.

Section 5
These provisions will be subject to those in the Convention on jurisdiction and enforcement of judgements in civil and commercial matters. Section 11
The Council Regulation applies generally to Denmark and this provision cannot be regarded as disapplying it.

Order
Article 4 (2)
A better view would seem to be that a contract term in a conference agreement etc. which is contrary to the Regulation or Code is void, not merely avoidable.

3. Subject to the abovementioned observations, the Commission hereby delivers a favourable opinion on the proposed legislation."

Belgium

9.075 On 16 March 1982, the Commission adopted an opinion addressed to Belgium, regarding implementation of Regulation (EEC) No 954/79 of 15 May 1979 concerning the ratification by Member States of, or their accession to, the United Nations Convention on a Code of Conduct for Liner Conferences.[40] The opinion provided:

> "1. By letter dated 22 December 1981, the Shipping and Inland Navigation Administration of the Ministry of Transport sent to the Commission the following documents, for consultation purposes, under Article 6 of the abovementioned Regulation: – a preliminary draft law concerning the ratification of the United Nations Convention on a Code of Conduct for Liner Conferences, and
>
>   – a draft explanatory memorandum on this preliminary draft law.
>
> 2. The following comments are called for in the light of examination of these documents:
>
> Preliminary draft
> Article 1 In order to comply with Article 1 of Regulation (EEC) No 954/79 of 15 May 1979, the following should be added to Article 1 of the preliminary draft:
>
> 'subject to the provisions of Regulation (EEC) No 954/79 of 15 May 1979'.
>
> Article 4
> This Article should include a statement that the term 'national shipping line' in the case of a Member State of the European Economic Community includes any shipping line established on the territory of such Member State in accordance with the EEC Treaty and which satisfies the recognition requirements.
>
>   In addition, it should be made clearer in the explanatory memorandum that these companies must be granted equal treatment.
>
> 3. The Commission therefore hereby expresses a favourable opinion on the preliminary draft law and explanatory memorandum communicated to it, subject to the above comments, and taking into account the fact that the principles set out in point 2 are mentioned in the explanatory memorandum."

United Kingdom

9.076 On 13 July 1982, the Commission adopted an opinion, Opinion 82/508, addressed to the UK, regarding implementation of Regulation (EEC) No 954/79 of 15 May 1979 concerning the ratification by Member States of, or their accession to, the United Nations Convention on a Code of Conduct for Liner Conferences.[41] The opinion provided:

> "1. Under cover of a letter dated 4 May 1982 the United Kingdom Department of Trade sent the Commission, for consultation, the following document pursuant to Article 6 of the above Regulation: a draft Bill, the Merchant Shipping (Liner Conferences) Bill 1982, concerning the ratification of the United Nations Convention on a Code of Conduct for Liner Conferences.
> 2. Examination of this document has satisfied the Commission that the draft Bill complies with the provisions of Council Regulation (EEC) No 954/79 on the basis that the Secretary of

---

40 OJ 1982 L99/39.
41 OJ 1982 L65/28.

State will exercise his powers under clauses 2 and 4 of the Bill in conformity with the relevant provisions of Regulation (EEC) No 954/79.
3. The Commission herewith delivers a favourable opinion on the draft Bill which it has received, subject to the above observation."

The UK implemented the Liner Code by means of the Merchant Shipping (Liner Conferences) Act 1982 (which entered into force on 23 July 1982) and other Member States such as, Denmark, France, Germany and the Netherlands have also implemented the Code.

France

9.077 On 28 February 1985, the Commission adopted an opinion, Opinion 85/185, addressed to France, regarding implementation of Regulation (EEC) No 954/79 of 15 May 1979 concerning the ratification by Member States of, or their accession to, the United Nations Convention on a Code of Conduct for Liner Conferences.[42] The opinion provided:

"1. In accordance with the consultation procedure referred to in Article 6 of Council Regulation (EEC) No 954/79 of 15 May 1979 concerning the ratification by Member States of, or their accession to, the United Nations Convention on a code of conduct for liner conference,[43] the French Permanent Representation to the European Communities, under a covering letter dated 21 November 1984, sent the Commission the following documents:

(a) a draft Law authorizing approval of the United Nations Convention on a code of conduct for liner conferences, together with an explanatory memorandum;

(b) a draft Law concerning the ratification of the United Nations Convention on a code of conduct for liner conferences, together with an explanatory memorandum.

These were discussed with the relevant Commission departments on 20 December 1984.
2. An examination of the documents calls for the following observations:

(a) draft Law referred to in 1 (a) above: no comments;
(b) draft Law referred to in 1 (b) above:

Article 1 of the draft Law should be applied in such a way as to take full account of Article 1 of Regulation (EEC) No 954/79, and in particular the reservations. As indicated in the explanatory memorandum, the French Government is prepared to do so.

Among the criteria for participating in commercial negotiations with a view to acceding to a given conference, Article 3 of the draft Law requires that companies must regularly and primarily use ships flying the French flag. According to information given by the French administration, French law permits foreigners to hold up to 100% of the registered capital of a company and therefore, particularly in view of the judgments of the Court of 4 April 1974 and 21 June 1974 in case No 167/73 and case No 2/74 respectively, this provision of the draft law does not run counter to the provisions concerning the right of establishment laid down in the Treaty.

Article 4 of the draft Law lays down criteria for conciliation proceedings between the parties concerned in the event of commercial negotiations breaking down.

The criteria include those provided for in the minutes of the Council meeting at which Regulation (EEC) No 954/79 was adopted.

---

42 OJ 1985 L71/18.
43 Ed., OJ 1979 L121/1.

Taking the criterion provided for in the first indent of Article 4 (recourse to chartering) in conjunction with the last indent of Article 3 (regularly and primarily using vessels flying the French flag) gives rise to the following comment: Whilst Article 3 permits recourse to chartering, the criterion laid down in the first indent of Article 4 give preference to shipowners. It would therefore seem that discrimination might occur in the following hypothetical case: A company based in another Member State could establish an agency or a branch in France but if it were regularly and primarily to make use of vessels flying the French flag it would have to use chartered ships only.

Under Article 3 the said agency or branch would then be able to participate in the commercial negotiations provided for in Article 2 (1) of Regulation (EEC) No 954/79. However, in the event of a dispute being brought before the administrative authorities, the said agency or branch would be penalized for the very fact of having used a chartered ship, because of the criterion laid down in the first indent of Article 4.

The representatives of the French Government have indicated that they will be able to amend the wording so as to eliminate the potential – unintended – discrimination against nationals of the Member States.

If such an amendment is made, the problem will be solved.

As far as Article 3 is concerned, it would be desirable for the French Government to amend Article 3 of its draft Law to the effect that, subject to reciprocity, shipping lines of other OECD member countries may be accepted as 'national lines'.

As regards the explanation of Article 3 in the explanatory memorandum, the Commission cannot agree with the French Government that the requirement to fly the national flag is consistent with the Code, even though one Article – Article 23 (2) – refers to the potential use of a flag. On the contrary, the text of the Code seems to be based rather on recognition of the possible need of developing countries to charter ships flying another flag (see the definition of a national line and Article 2 (11)).

3. Subject to the abovementioned conditions, the Commission therefore hereby issues a favourable opinion on the draft Law communicated by the French Government."

CHAPTER 10

An overview of European Union competition law generally and how it applies to the shipping sector generally

A. INTRODUCTION

10.001 This chapter contains: (a) an introduction to competition law;[1] and (b) an overview of Articles 101–106 of the Treaty on the Functioning of the European Union ("TFEU") which are the principal articles in the Treaty as it relates to competition.[2] The chapter lays the groundwork for later chapters which address some specific

---

1 United States' law uses the term "antitrust law" to describe that part of the area of law which EU lawyers call "competition law". EU competition law is wider than US antitrust law because EU competition law, unlike US antitrust law, includes areas such as State aid law (see Arts 107–109 of the TFEU) and controls on the behaviour of public authorities in the market place (see Art. 106 of the TFEU). This chapter does not examine State aid (see chap. 15), Merger Control (see chap. 16) or public procurement law (on EU public procurement law see Arrowsmith, *Law of Public and Utilities Procurement* (vol. 1, 2014 and vol. 2, 2018)).

2 Arts 101–106 TFEU were Arts 81–86 Treaty establishing the European Community ("TEC") before 1 December 2009 (when the Treaty of Lisbon entered into force), In the original European Economic Community ("EEC") Treaty, they were Arts 85–90 of the EEC Treaty until the amendment brought about by the Treaty of Amsterdam to the numbering in the Foundation Treaties when they became Arts 81–86 TEC.

On EU competition law generally, there is an enormous literature available including Rose and Bailey (eds), *Bellamy and Child: European Union Law of Competition* (7th ed., 2013); Clough and Randolph, *Shipping and EC Competition Law* (1991); Ezrachi, *EU Competition Law: An Analytical Guide to the Leading Cases* (2014); Freeman and Whish (eds), *Butterworths Competition Law* (looseleaf); Faull and Nikpay (eds), *The EC Law of Competition* (2nd ed., 2014); Furse *Competition Law of the EC and the UK* (7th ed., 2011); Gerber, *Law and Competition in Twentieth Century Europe* (1998); Jones and Smith, *EC Competition Law: Text, Cases and Materials* (5th ed., 2010); Korah, *An Introductory Guide to EC Competition Law and Practice* (9th ed., 2007); Power, *Competition Law and Practice* (2001); Slot and Johnston, *An Introduction to Competition Law* (1st English ed., 2006); Sokol, Cräne and Ezrachi, *Global Antitrust Compliance Handbook* (2014); Van Bael and Bellis, *Competition Law of the European Community* (5th ed., 2010); and Whish and Bailey, *Competition Law* (8th ed., 2015). See also the various journals on competition law and policy including *European Competition Law Review*, *European Competition Journal* and *World Competition*. For a sample of how EU competition law was applied to the transport sector in 2009, see Fruhling, Whiddington, Cassels and Decat, "The Application of European Competition Law in the Transport Sector" (2010) 1(2) JECL&P 144. See also Lista, "The Application of EC Competition Rules to the Maritime Sector", in Institute of Maritime Law, *Southampton on Shipping Law* (2008), chap. 12 and Ortiz Blanco, "Personal Reflections on the Development of EC Maritime Competition Policy: Past and Future" in Wareham and Power (eds), *Competition Law and Shipping: The EMLO Guide to EU Competition Law in the Shipping and Port Industries*, pp. 3–20. See also Dinger, "What Shall We Do with the Drunken Sailor? EC Competition Law and Maritime Transport" (BaslerSchriften zur europäischen Integration, No 61). On the economics of EU competition law see Bishop and Walker, *The Economics of EC Competition Law* (2010) and Neils, *Economics for Competition Lawyers* (2011). For an excellent summary of competition law, see Jones and Townley, "Competition Law", chap. 17 of Barnard and Peers (eds), *European Union Law* (2014).

aspects of European Union ("EU") competition law as they relate to the shipping sector.[3]

10.002 There are many practices in the shipping world which are prima facie anti-competitive. For example, shipbuilders could combine to exchange forecasts and swap competitively sensitive information as well as fix prices; governments could offer anti-competitive depreciation allowances, dredging subsidies, investment grants, training aid, cargo reservation schemes; ports could refuse unfairly to allow entry to their ports, discriminate in an anti-competitive manner between users, exchange information, favour unfairly their own operators or share markets with other ports; shipping companies/carriers could conclude contracts which are anti-competitive (e.g. because of particular clauses), combine together in anti-competitive cartels (e.g. arrangements to share markets/information and/or to fix prices) or abuse their individual or collective dominance (e.g. refusing unjustifiably to supply services or pricing in a predatory manner); and shippers could agree on the maximum freight rates they would pay. It would be logical therefore that there should be laws to address those problems. An example of such a case would be one where in the USA in January 2015, an executive of Japan-based Kawasaki Kisen Kaisha pleaded guilty, was sentenced to serve an 18-month prison term and pay a US$20,000 criminal fine for his involvement in a conspiracy to fix prices, allocate customers and rig bids of international ocean shipping services for roll-on, roll-off cargo.[4]

10.003 Despite the need for laws to address anti-competitive conduct, many (but not all)[5] competition laws are relatively recent and the introduction of some competition laws has been controversial. While over 120 jurisdictions worldwide[6] now have adopted competition laws, the vast majority have adopted them only in the last two decades.[7] These laws seek to control primarily anti-competitive arrangements (e.g. price-fixing, capacity sharing or market sharing arrangements), abuses of dominance (e.g. predatory pricing)[8] as well as anti-competitive mergers, acquisitions and joint ventures. EU law prohibits all these anti-competitive practices but also prohibits anti-competitive practices by Member

---

3 On shipping and EU competition law, see material cited in this chapter and throughout this book as well as Antapassis, Athanassiou and Røsæg (eds), *Competition and Regulation in Shipping and Shipping Related Industries* (2009); Clough and Randolph, op. cit. at fn. 2; Ortiz Blanco, *Shipping Conferences under EC Antitrust Law* (2007); Pozdnakova, *Liner Shipping and EU Competition Law* (2008); Spiteri, *The Application of EC Competition Law in the Maritime Transport Sector* (2012); Wareham and Power (eds), op. cit. at fn. 2; and Dinger, op. cit. at fn. 2. See also Eriksson, "EC Maritime Competition Law Reform: Opportunities and Options" (2005) 3 CLI 3; and Vanhamme, "EU Competition Law and International Maritime Transport: How to Create a Level Playing Field?" in Kannlnen, Korjus and Rosas (eds), *EU Competition Law in Context: Essays in Honour of Virpi Tiili* (2009), p. 73; as well as the literature cited in chaps 11–16.

4 See www.justice.gov/atr/public/press_releases/2015/311443.htm.

5 Competition laws date back to Roman times but modern competition laws owe their origin to the nineteenth century (e.g. Canada in 1889 and the US in 1890) as well as the last century (e.g. the EEC and the UK in the 1950s) however the real growth in, and spread of, competition laws occurred in the last three decades or so. See also Dabbah, *International Comparative Competition Law* (2010) and Sock-Young, "Competition Law and the International Transport Sectors" [2009] 5(2) Competition Law Review 193.

6 Including Australia, China, Japan, Russia, South Africa, Saudi Arabia, the UK and the USA as well as the EU and its Member States. See Holmes (ed.), *Competition Law and Practice: A Review of Major Jurisdictions* (2009).

7 Noonan, *Emerging Principles of International Competition Law* (2008). The International Competition Network's website has useful information on the growth of competition law worldwide: www.internationalcompetitionnetwork.org.

8 For an example of the application of the predatory pricing rules in ferry services, see the judgment of the Cour d'appel de Paris on 28 June 2005 in *Société Vedettes inter-îles Vendéennes v Régkes départementale des passages d'eau de la Vendée* no 2005/01605.

States such as anti-competitive interventions in the market and illegal State aid. In the context of shipping, competition laws prohibit generally such practices as market sharing arrangements, price-fixing agreements, anti-competitive exchanges of competitively sensitive information, capacity/management/ship sharing arrangements but prohibit always the abuse of dominance.

10.004 Competition laws are designed to promote rivalry between market participants, enhance consumer welfare, ensure optimal allocation of resources, stimulate innovation and to encourage merit of efficient operation of the market. A competitive market is characterised typically by productive efficiency,[9] allocative efficiency[10] and dynamic efficiency.[11] There ought to be lower prices and higher service standards in a competitive market than in an uncompetitive one. Competition law in the EU (unlike already integrated States) has the additional aim of integrating further the EU's internal market (i.e. creating or maintaining the internal market).[12] Competition law can also serve a political purpose by ensuring that private power does not trump the needs of society. Competition law is not about protecting competitors[13] but it is about protecting competition and the consumer. Ultimately, competition law is about enhancing consumer welfare. There has been some suggestion that the European Commission has used competition law to regulate maritime transport as a sector as well as address competition issues in the sector.[14] Competition law has also been used by parties to contracts to deny liability – for example, by arguing that a contract was void under EU competition law, the contract is therefore unenforceable against the defendant. Indeed, more generally, competition law can sometimes be used to avoid liabilities.[15]

10.005 The application of competition law in shipping matters is sometimes a highly charged political and emotive issue. Many shipping industry spokespersons denied for a long time that EU competition law should apply to the sector claiming, for example, that the sector was intensively competitive already, a capital intensive industry, a sector which needed predictability, a global industry or there was a greater need for predictability/service than price competition (e.g. liner conferences offered predictability). Nonetheless, EU competition law now applies, with full vigour, to the sector.

10.006 Competition law now typically controls arrangements and practices such as price-fixing (e.g. in a liner conference), market sharing, predatory pricing, capacity sharing (e.g. ship sharing), collusive tendering, distribution and other arrangements and

---

9 I.e. products are produced at the lowest cost possible and there is little or no wastage.

10 I.e. only those products for which there is demand are produced because resources are allocated efficiently and consumer preferences are met.

11 I.e. producers are forced by competition to innovate (i.e. be dynamic).

12 The fact that the objectives of EU competition law differ, in that respect at least, from other regimes demonstrates how different systems can have different aims. It also means that there can be different rules and different outcomes to the same cases internationally. The aims of a competition law regime in a single jurisdiction can also change over time.

13 Although this may be a side effect because it gives competitors a competitive market force in which to operate.

14 Vanhamme, op. cit. at fn. 3, p. 78, has written: "[o]ver the last decades, public authorities, especially the European Commission have discovered that ... competition law is a useful instrument ... in regulating maritime transport".

15 This may have been (but it is far from clear) an issue in *Ineos Vinyls Ltd v Huntsmen Petrochemicals (UK) Ltd* [2006] EWHC 1241; *Lauritzen Cool* [2004] EWHC 2607 and [2005] EWCA 579; and Case C-339/95 *SUNAG (no judgment)* – this latter case was settled before the Advocate-General gave an opinion or the CJEU gave a ruling.

practices which could distort competition. It covers unilateral behaviour (e.g. unilateral predatory pricing) as well as multilateral conduct (e.g. price-fixing between competitors). Equally, mergers, acquisitions, State aid and intervention by the State are all controlled by EU competition law. However, there is hardly any limit to the areas of commerce which might be regulated by competition law.

10.007 Anyone subject to the main rules of EU competition law (i.e. Articles 101 and 102 of the TFEU) is known as an "undertaking"[16] or an "association of undertakings". For undertakings to ignore EU competition law is perilous: for example, a business (such as a shipping company or a port company) may be fined up to 10% of its previous year's worldwide turnover under EU competition law.[17] Arrangements (e.g. contracts) breaching EU competition law are normally legally unenforceable in whole or in part at least before the Member State courts and tribunals (including arbitral tribunals). Non-Member State courts and tribunals could also decide not to enforce them but that is dependent on their law and policy. There may be actions for damages brought in Member State courts against any undertaking in breach of EU competition law.[18] There is also damage to the reputation of the undertaking which breaches competition law. It is possible that conduct which is in breach of EU law could also breach national laws (whether inside or outside the EU) (in particular, national competition law).[19] Some national laws (unlike EU law) impose personal criminal liability with the result that individuals may be imprisoned and/or fined.[20] Irrespective of the jurisdiction involved, competition investigations are a significant distraction for management and can be a worrying time for executives (e.g. some have faced dismissal, extradition, long trials, fines and, ultimately, prison).

10.008 Before examining the issues in depth, it is useful to consider a single case which puts many of the issues in context. This is the so-called *Marine Hose Cartel* case.[21] It had been alleged that various producers of marine hoses organised a clandestine cartel among themselves. Over time, it is alleged, they allocated contracts/tenders, fixed prices, fixed quotas, decided on sales conditions, divided markets geographically and also exchanged sensitive information on prices, volumes and tenders. One of the participants sought immunity from the European Commission and other competition authorities. As a

---

16 Member States are also subject to competition law but are usually not undertakings and typically fall outside the scope of Arts 101 and 102.

17 It is possible that some behaviour could also breach national competition laws while individuals who are not undertakings may be fined and/or imprisoned under some national competition laws. At present, EU competition law does not impose any penalty on individuals unless they constitute undertakings. Moreover, a breach of EU competition law is not regarded as a breach of criminal law although the consequences may be penal with fines running into the hundreds of millions of euro (and even over a billion euro on occasion).

18 See, in particular, Dir. 2014/104 on antitrust damages OJ L349/1, 5 December 2014. See also Commission, *White Paper on Damages Actions for Breach of the EU antitrust rules* (COM(2008) 165, 2 April 2008). See http://ec.europa.eu/competition/antitrust/actionsdamages/documents.html#link1.

19 E.g. the *Marine Hose Cartel*: on 28 January 2009, the European Commission imposed a total of €131,510,000 fines on five groups (i.e. Bridgestone, Dunlop Oil & Marine/Continental, Trelleborg, Parker ITR and Manuli) for breaching Art. 101 of the TFEU by participating in a cartel for marine hoses. However, there were also penalties at the national level in many jurisdictions around the world.

20 E.g. Ian Norris, a former Chief Executive of Morgan Crucible was sought by USA authorities for alleged anti-competitive behaviour in the USA and he was extradited to there from the UK in March 2010 after a battle in the UK courts for six years to prevent his extradition. Extradition of an individual would not usually apply in the case of a breach of EU competition law only.

21 EU Case COMP/39.406. Marine hoses are pipes or hoses used to load sweet or processed crude oil and other petroleum products from offshore facilities (e.g. buoys, floating production facilities, storage and offloading systems) on to vessels and to offload them back to offshore or onshore facilities (e.g. buoys or jetties).

result, that particular participant was not fined as it co-operated fully with the authorities and gave them information which they would probably not otherwise have obtained. Six months later, the Commission dawn raided[22] various business premises and a private home of one of the individuals involved (some evidence was found in the home which was not found in the offices raided). The Commission spent two years investigating the suspected cartel. Six participants (other than the one seeking immunity) were fined various amounts totalling €131 million. While the case relates to anti-competitive arrangements (i.e. Article 101 of the TFEU) and not abuse of dominance (i.e. Article 102 of the TFEU), the case demonstrates many of the issues often arising in both articles. While the cartel participant who reports the breach is rewarded by immunity from fines, the European Commission believes that it is useful to give the first informant immunity because otherwise the breach might never have come to light.

B. AN OVERVIEW OF EU COMPETITION LAW GENERALLY

Introduction

10.009 Before examining the detailed rules of EU competition law, it is useful to provide a more extensive overview of the subject.

10.010 In this context, competition is the rivalry which exists, or ought to exist, in a market. EU competition law is a means of achieving, among other aims, a fair, free and efficient internal market in the EU where businesses can thrive in a competitive environment free of undesirable anti-competitive arrangements and abuses of dominance, artificial barriers and unreasonable restraints.

10.011 The primary EU rules are contained in the TFEU. These rules control the behaviour of businesses or economic operators (i.e. "undertakings") and Member States. Article 101 of the TFEU prohibits generally (i.e. there could be some exceptions under Article 101(3)) anti-competitive arrangements between undertakings. Article 102 of the TFEU prohibits absolutely (i.e. there can be no exception) any abuse of dominance by any undertaking having a dominant position in the internal market or any substantial part of the internal market.[23] Articles 103–105 of the TFEU relate to the procedural dimension of EU competition law. Article 106 of the TFEU controls the intervention in the marketplace by a Member State where the State confers privileges or owns businesses. Articles 107–109 of the TFEU regulate the provision of State aid by Member States.

10.012 Articles 101 and 102 are interconnected and therefore should not be construed in isolation from each other. As the General Court stated in *Tetra Pak Rausing SA v Commission*,[24] "in the scheme for the protection of competition established by the Treaty the grant of exemption, [under Article 101(3) TFEU] cannot be such as to render inapplicable the prohibition set out in Article [102 TFEU]". In effect, this means that a breach of Article 102 means that the practice or arrangement is in breach of EU law and cannot therefore be exempted to operate lawfully under Article 101(3).

---

22 I.e. the Commission visited without warning or notice various premises to find evidence of a breach of competition law.
23 The term "internal market" is a synonym for the EU. It is the replacement term, formally under the Treaty of Lisbon, for the more traditional term "common market".
24 Case T-51/89 [1990] ECR II-309, ECLI:EU:1:1990:41, para. 25.

10.013 Apart from the primary rules (i.e. the TFEU rules), there are also various secondary sources of EU competition law. They are called "secondary" because they are secondary to the Treaty rules[25] but they are no less legally binding. These secondary sources include regulations, directives and decisions. Regulations tend to be used to set out procedural rules and block exemptions. Directives are used rarely in this area and have been used in regard to damages. Decisions addressed to individuals, undertakings and associations of undertakings are the instruments by which fines are imposed.

10.014 As well as these primary and secondary sources, there are also guidelines which are non-legally binding views.[26] In the area of EU shipping law, the Commission issued in 2008, "Guidelines on application of competition rules to maritime transport services"[27] but the Commission has chosen not to renew these guidelines.[28] It has also issued guidelines on issues such as horizontal agreements, vertical restraints, market definition and the fining policy of the Commission. These notices and guidelines are extremely informative and important.[29]

10.015 The Treaty rules relating to competition apply fully to the shipping sector and have always done so[30] but the procedural regulations did not apply until relatively recently. Now the general procedural regulation, Regulation 1/2003,[31] applies to the shipping sector.

Applicability of EU competition law

10.016 For all practical purposes, EU competition law applies to all economic sectors. Shipping was given special exemption for many years[32] and it is only since the adoption of Regulation 1419/2006[33] that EU competition law has applied in full to all shipping.[34] EU competition law has an international reach. Therefore, for example, the changes brought about by the adoption of Regulation 1419/2006[35] have international implications in that the repeal of the exemption in Regulation 4056/86 for liner conferences means that

---

25 Treaty rules as primary laws and prevail over the secondary rules.
26 See also Randolph, "Overview, Jurisdiction and Legal Status of Guidelines" in Wareham and Power (eds), op. cit. at fn. 2, pp. 21–34.
27 OJ 2008 C245/2. See IP/08/1063. See Lista, "Trick or Treat? Commission Guidelines on Maritime Transport Competition" (2008) 7 Shipping & Trade Law 1. See chap. 11 for a more detailed discussion of the Guidelines.
28 See chap. 11.
29 See the Commission's competition website. www.ec.europa.eu/competition/index_en.html. While they are not legally binding, the European Commission often relies on, and follows, them.
30 Case 167/73 *Commission v France (French Seafarers)* [1974] ECR 359, ECLI:EU:C:1974:35 where the CJEU stated at para. 32: "[while] under Article [100(2) TFEU], therefore, sea and air transport, so long as the Council has not decided otherwise, is excluded from the rules of the Title ... of the Treaty relating to the common transport policy, it remains, on the same basis as the other modes of transport, subject to the general rules of the Treaty." The CJEU went on to state in Cases 209–213/84 *Ministère Public v Lucas Asjes (Nouvelles Frontières)* [1986] ECR 1425, ECLI:EU:C:1986:188 the rules in the Treaty on competition, in particular Arts 101 to 106 of the TFEU are applicable to transport.
31 OJ L1/1, 4 January 2003.
32 E.g. by virtue of what is now Art. 100(2) TFEU and Reg. 4056/86 OJ 1986 L378/4. See chap.12.
33 OJ 2006 L269/1. See chap. 11.
34 It is worth stating that the full extent of the block exemption in Reg. 4056/86 was eroded somewhat by the Commission construing the block exemption narrowly and taking enforcement action in the shipping sector over time.
35 OJ 2006 L269/1.

it may be impractical to operate liner conferences elsewhere in the world where there is an effect on trade in the EU because EU competition law applies wherever there is an effect on trade in the EU even if the arrangement or practice occurs outside the EU. It is important to emphasise that EU competition law may apply to non-EU nationals and to events outside the EU where there is an effect on trade in the EU – this is due to the so-called "territoriality principle" (i.e. a State may legislate for whatever occurs within its territory) and the "effects principle" (a State may legislate for events outside its territory which have an effect inside the territory).[36] It is worth emphasising that an anti-competitive arrangement concluded in, for example, the USA or Russia is subject to EU competition law where there is an effect on trade in the EU.

10.017 The EU needs evidence before bringing cases alleging breaches of competition law. It secures evidence from, in particular, leniency/immunity applicants (in return for leniency), whistleblowers, public sources, studies and "dawn raids" in the EU. What about the EU collecting evidence about shipping companies (and others) outside the EU? This information may be supplied voluntarily by the party, or collected where the Member State and the recipient do not object, or might even be collected from within the EU even though the information may be located outside the EU but accessible from within the EU (e.g. by way of computer).[37] EU competition law may apply to cabotage services[38] where there is an effect on trade between Member States. Regulation 1/2003 (the EU competition procedural regulation)[39] applies to cabotage and also applies to tramp (i.e. non-liner) shipping services following the adoption of Regulation 1419/2006.[40]

10.018 Many undertakings in the shipping sector are used to escape the application of various laws by incorporating companies in various jurisdictions or flying flags of convenience. There is no escape from the possible application of EU competition law. The rules apply wherever there is an effect on trade between EU Member States irrespective of the nationality of the parties, the location of the arrangements, governing law or nationality/registration of the vessels involved.

Direct applicability of Articles 101 and 102 of the TFEU

10.019 Articles 101 and 102 of the TFEU are directly applicable in that they may be invoked before the courts of the Member States and may also be invoked in arbitration

---

36 See Joined Cases C-89/85, C-104/85, C-114/85, C-116/85, C-117/85 and C-125/85 to C-129/85 *Ahlström Osakeyhtiö and others v Commission* [1988] ECR 5193 (paras 12 and 13).

37 In regard to collecting information in the EU about matters outside the EU, Vanhamme, op. cit. at fn. 3, recalled, "in a case brought against the shipping group Ventouris, which is established in Panama, the Commission found evidence in the premises of a 'European Trust Agency', which was based in Athens and acted on behalf of Minoan Lines, a company linked to the same cartel as Ventouris. The [General Court] considered that such an exercise of inspection powers is legal (Case T-59/99, *Ventouris v Commission* [2003] ECR II-5257 [ECLI:EU:T:2003:334] paras 141–163)." There may be some residual doubts about obtaining information outside the EU from within the EU but the European Commission is unlikely to entertain such doubts except in exceptional circumstances; obviously, the legality of such an investigation is ultimately a matter for the CJEU rather than the Commission.

38 I.e. services between two ports in a single State.

39 OJ 2003 L1/1.

40 OJ 2006 L269/1. See an interesting article by Holmes and Davey, "Lines can still obtain some Legal Certainty to their Agreements despite New EU Competition Regime", Lloyd's List, 16 July 2003.

proceedings in those States. The Court of Justice of the European Union ("CJEU") confirmed this in *Belgische Radio en Televisie (BRT) v SABAM*.[41] The CJEU went on to confirm in *Guerin Automobiles v Commission*[42] that undertakings and individuals may be deemed to have rights afforded to them by these two articles. Article 101 is directly applicable in its entirety since the enactment of Regulation 1/2003[43] which means that a Member State court may see an otherwise anti-competitive arrangement (i.e. one breaching Article 101(1) of the TFEU) as valid by virtue of falling under Article 101(3) of the TFEU. Anyone aggrieved or injured by a breach of Articles 101 or 102 is able to sue in the Member State courts for damages;[44] indeed, aggrieved persons are positively encouraged by the European Commission to have recourse to private enforcement of EU competition law.

Market definition[45]

10.020 Competition does not exist in a vacuum. One needs to establish whether a particular arrangement or practice prevents, restricts or distorts competition in the context of the particular market at hand. Competition exists in the context of a market – the so-called "relevant market". Competition does not exist in a vacuum. Market definition is often (but not always)[46] an issue in merger control, anti-competitive arrangements, abuse of dominance, State aid and competition issues generally. This section introduces the issue of market definition – the analysis of it applies equally in the context of Articles 101 and 102. It is worth recalling that market definition is not an end in itself but is a tool to see the theatre (i.e. market) in which competition is occurring. It enables competition analysis to be undertaken in its correct market context.

10.021 The relevant market must always be defined where the definition of the market could influence the outcome of the proceedings.[47] For example, an operator in the market (i.e. an "undertaking") can be dominant if the market is defined narrowly but *not* dominant if the market is defined broadly so market definition is critical.[48] It is important to remember that market definition is often a difficult task and there is rarely absolute precision. It is also important to note that market definitions in one case or at one point in time do not necessarily apply in other cases or later (e.g. technology changes, new

---

41 Case 127/73 [1974] ECR 51, ECLI:EU:C:1974:25, para. 10.
42 Case C-282/95 P [1997] ECR I-1503, ECLI:EU:C:1997:159.
43 OJ 2003 L1/1.
44 Case C-295/04 *Manfredi v Lloyd Adriatico Assicurazioni SpA* [2006] ECR I-6619, ECLI:EU:C:1974:25 (paras 58–61).
45 See also Haegler, "Defining Relevant Markets in Liner Shipping: Why and How?" in Wareham and Power (eds), op. cit. at fn. 2, pp. 77–98. See, in particular, the Commission Notice on the Definition of the Relevant Market for the Purposes of Community Competition Law OJ 1997 C372/5.
46 It is sometimes possible to decide cases without defining the market with precision.
47 If there is no competition problem in a case then the market may not have to be defined precisely in an explicit way but even in cases where the market is not defined, there is always some general assumption about the way in which markets are defined even if the competition agency or court says that the arrangement or practice in hand does not cause a competition concern however the market is defined.
On market definition, see Coulter, "Market Definition in Shipping Markets", Lloyd's Maritime Academy, EU Competition Law in Shipping, London, 26 March 2009.
48 E.g. in *Irish Continental Group v Chambre de Commerce et Industries de Morlaix* [1995] 5 CMLR 177 the port (Roscoff) was dominant because the market was defined as Ireland-Brittany but it may not have been dominant if the geographical market was defined as Ireland-France.

facilities coming on stream elsewhere as well as changes in consumer behaviour and tastes can cause such changes in market definition over time).[49]

10.022 The relevant market[50] must be defined in terms of the product market,[51] the geographical market[52] and, occasionally, the temporal market.[53] The CJEU stated in *Hoffmann La Roche v Commission*:

> "[t]he concept of the relevant market in fact implies that there can be effective competition between the products which form part of it and this presupposes that there is a sufficient degree of interchangeability between all the products forming part of the same market insofar as a specific use of such product is concerned".[54]

The European Commission published in 1997 a "Notice on the Definition of the Relevant Market for the Purposes of Community Competition Law".[55] It provides some guidance on how to define markets for competition law purposes but so much turns on the specifics of each case. Defining the market is often of critical importance because it identifies the parameters in which competition exists or does not exist. An undertaking could be dominant in a narrow market definition but not dominant in a wider market definition. If the Commission defines the market incorrectly then the Commission's decision could be annulled by the General Court or, on appeal from the General Court, the CJEU. The Commission has also published "Guidelines on the Application of Article [101 of the TFEU] to Maritime Transport Services",[56] which will be considered in depth later,[57] but the Guidelines have not been renewed so it is unclear how useful they would be in market definition issues in the future. It is submitted that the Guidelines are generally persuasive rather than binding in themselves.

10.023 The "product market" examines the arena of rivalry in terms of where the particular product or service competes. What constitutes the product market is answered by a series of questions such as the characteristics of the product, what is the intended use of the product and what is the cross-elasticity of demand. One would examine, on the demand side, such factors as vessel type, vessel size, type of cargo, contract type, journey length, costs, price, technology and so on. The supply side would also be examined and that would include consideration of such factors as how easy can shipowners supply and switch vessels. The Small but Significant and Non-transitory Increase in Price ("SSNIP") test is used to decide whether products are substitutable or interchangeable and asks whether a 5% to 10% price increase in the price of one product would lead purchasers to switch to the other product. In the context of Article 102, the "market" is more relevant

---

49 Nonetheless, the approach taken in cases is often reflected in later cases.
50 It is proposed to examine the concepts of the product, temporal and geographical markets very briefly here and to consider them further below. The analysis in those paragraphs is set out in the context of Art. 102 of the TFEU but it is very much applicable in the context of Art. 101 of the TFEU as well as in the context of merger control and State aid (and vice versa).
51 The product market is the range of goods or services which compete with each other (e.g. stevedoring).
52 The geographical market is the arena or theatre in which competition occurs (e.g. the English Channel ferry ports).
53 The temporal market examines the time element of a market (e.g. summer cruising).
54 Case 85/76 [1979] ECR 461 ECLI:EU:C:1979:36, para. 28.
55 OJ 1997 C372/5.
56 OJ 2008 C245/2.
57 See chap.11.

than the size of the company.⁵⁸ Economists pay close attention to the SSNIP test. For example, a ferry service is extremely unlikely to be in the same product market as an oil tanker but is a ferry in the same market as short haul air or rail services and whether a small change in the price of ferry, air or train services would have any impact on the other services? For example, a ferry between Dover and Calais is more substitutable with the Eurotunnel train than the ferry would be with an oil tanker sailing the same route. Equally, the extent to which ro-ro (roll-on/roll-off) and lo-lo (lift-on/lift-off) services are substitutable would have to be decided on a case by case basis.

10.024 The "geographical market" considers the geographical or physical space dimension to the market (e.g. are ferry services between the UK and France substitutable with ferry services between the UK and the Netherlands or should the market be defined more narrowly (e.g. services between the UK and Brittany as opposed to services between the UK and France))? A particular route or bunch of routes can constitute a geographical market.⁵⁹ Typically, the longer the journey involves, the wider would be the geographical market.⁶⁰

10.025 The "temporal market" refers to any time dimension to the market in question – for example, ferry services or cruise services can involve a time or temporal dimension to the market in which they operate (e.g. summer cruising in the Arctic).

10.026 Lawyers tend to look at precedent in examining market definition issues. Precedent is helpful but not binding. For example, market conditions, technology and customer behaviour can change. The better approach is to have some regard to precedent but concentrate on the current market conditions which is the approach deployed by economists. However, it is done, market definition should be credible and realistic.

Undertaking⁶¹

Introduction

10.027 Article 101 of the TFEU relates to agreements, decisions or concerted practices entered into by "undertakings". It is thus essential to be able to define what is meant in this context by the term "undertaking". The definition of undertaking for the purposes of Article 101 is the same, for all practical purposes, for Article 102 as well as EU merger

---

58 A small undertaking could be dominant in a particular market while a large undertaking might not be dominant.

59 See e.g. Dec 92/262 *French-West African Shipowners' Committees* OJ 1992 L134/1; Dec 94/980 *Trans-Atlantic Agreement* OJ 1994 L376/1; and *Irish Continental Group v Chambre de Commerce et Industries de Morlaix* [1995] 5 CMLR 177.

60 E.g. cross-channel services between Britain and France would involve a narrow range of ports in both countries but the shipment of containers from Sweden to New Zealand could involve the potential use of a wide range of ports in Europe and Australasia.

61 See, in particular, Cases 209/78 *Von Landewyck v Commission* [1980] ECR 3125 at 3250, ECLI:EU:C:1980:248; Case C-41/90 *Höfner v Macratron* [1991] ECRI-1979 ECLI:EU:C:1991:161; and Case C-205/03 *FENIN v Commission* [2006] ECR I-6295. See, in particular, the following Commission decisions: *AOIP/Beyrard* OJ 1976 L6/8, [1976] 1 CMLR D14; *ARG/Unipart* OJ 1998 L45/34, [1988] 4 CMLR 513; *LdPE* OJ 1989 L74/21; *Polypropylene* OJ 1986 L230/1, [1988] 4 CMLR 347; *PVC* OJ 1989 L74/1; *RAI/UNITEL* OJ 1978 L157/39, [1978] 3 CMLR 306; *Reuter/BASF* OJ 1976 L254/40, [1976] 2 CMLR D44; *Welded Steel Mesh* OJ 1989 L260/1; *Zinc Producer Group* OJ 1984 L220/27, [1985] 2 CMLR 108; and *P&I Clubs* OJ 1985 L376/2, [1989] 4 CMLR 178. See also Odudu, "The Meaning of Undertaking within Article 81 EC" (2005) 7 CYELS 209.

control and State aid law. It is an absolute defence to an allegation of a breach of Article 101 or 102 if one is not an undertaking. One does not have to be an undertaking to invoke competition law[62] but one has to be an undertaking in order to be subject to most of the rules.

Definition

10.028 The TFEU does not define what is meant by the term "undertaking". This has not, however, given rise to many problems in the practical application of EU competition law. The EU institutions take a broad view of the concept. It is submitted that any entity, be it a natural or legal person, engaged in commercial or economic activities (whether or not for profit)[63] would constitute an undertaking for the purposes of EU competition law irrespective of whether it supplies goods or services (or both).[64] In the *Film Purchases by German Television Stations* case,[65] the Commission said that the "fundamental concept of undertaking in Article [101(1)] covers any activity directed at trade in goods or services irrespective of the legal form of the undertaking and regardless of whether or not it is intended to earn profits". The CJEU stated in *Federación Española de Empresas de Tecnología Sanitaria (FENIN) v Commission* that an undertaking is any entity engaged in an economic activity, regardless of its legal status and the way in which it is financed.[66] The navy of a State would generally not be an undertaking because it is generally not engaged in a commercial or economic activity.[67] In *Polypropylene*[68] the Commission said that the concept of an undertaking was not identical to the concept of legal personality for the purposes of fiscal or company law. A shipping company, a charterer, a port, a ship finance bank, a terminal operator or a ship management company would each typically be an undertaking. If a port is engaged in commercial or economic activities then it would be an undertaking.[69]

Consideration of whether particular entities are undertakings

Introduction

10.029 It may be helpful to enumerate some of the entities which have been held to be "undertakings" for the purposes of EU competition law. The following analysis assumes that the entities are engaged in economic activities.

---

62 E.g. to make a complaint to the European Commission or institute proceedings for damages.
63 Comm. Dec. 85/615 *P&I Clubs* OJ 1985 L376/2, [1989] 4 CMLR 178.
64 See e.g. Case 90/76 *Van Ameyde v UCI* [1977] ECR 1091, ECLI:EU:C:1977:101.
65 Comm. Dec. 89/536 OJ 1989 L284/36, [1990] 4 CMLR 841.
66 Case C-205/03P [2006] ECR I-.6925, ECLI:EU:C:2006: 453.
67 Of course, if a navy engaged in commercial or economic activities then it would be an undertaking in that specific context.
68 Comm. Dec. 86/398 OJ 1986 L230/1, [1988] 4 CMLR 347.
69 However, if the port were to engage in a non-economic or non-commercial activity (e.g., pollution control) then it would not be engaged in economic activities.

Companies

10.030 A commercial company is an undertaking.[70] Examples would include shipping companies, ship management companies, insurance companies, port companies[71] and crew supply companies.

Partnerships

10.031 A partnership is an undertaking: in *Re Italian Cast Glass*,[72] a firm which was established by four independent companies to supervise a quota-fixing agreement was held to constitute an undertaking. A partnership to own or manage a ship would be an undertaking or an association of undertakings; moreover, some or all of the partners would probably be undertakings in their own right.

State-owned corporations

10.032 State-owned corporations may be undertakings.[73]

Statutory bodies

10.033 A body or authority created by statute may constitute an undertaking[74] provided it is engaged in economic or commercial activities. A rule-making body as such would not constitute an undertaking unless it was really engaged in economic activities.[75] Equally, quasi-governmental bodies carrying on economic activities may fall within the framework of Articles 101 and 102.[76] Statutory port authorities would be undertakings in respect of their economic or commercial activities[77] but not in respect of the legislative activities.

Co-operatives

10.034 A co-operative is an undertaking.[78] A chamber of commerce carrying on an economic activity such as running a port would be subject to competition law.[79]

---

70 This includes trust companies: *Fides* OJ 1979 L57/33, [1979] 1 CMLR 650. A group of companies may constitute a single economic unit/undertaking: Cases 48, 49, 51–57 *ICI v Commission* [1972] ECR 619, and Case 170/83 *Hydrotherm v Compact* [1984] ECR 2999.

71 See Case C-179/90 *Merci convenzionali porto di Genova SpA v Siderurgica Gabrielli SpA* [1991] ECR 5889, ECLI:EU:C: 1991:464.

72 Comm. Dec. 80/1334 OJ 1980 L383/19, [1982] 4 CMLR 61. See also *Breeders' Rights: Roses* OJ 1985 L369/9. In respect of limited partnerships: Case 258/78 *Nungesser v Commission* [1982] ECR 2015, ECLI:EU:T:2000: 91.

73 See Case 155/73 *Italian State v Sacchi* [1974] ECR 409, ECLI:EU:C: 1974: 40 and Case 41/83 *Italy v Commission* [1985] ECR 873.

74 Even if it is not an undertaking, a State authority may still be subject, in certain circumstances, to EU competition law on State authorities (i.e., Art.106 of the TFEU) and State aid (i.e., Article 107 of the TFEU) even though it does not carry on economic activities.

75 See Case 123/83 *BNIC v Clair* [1985] ECR 391, ECLI:EU:C:1985:33 and Case 30/87 *Corrine Bodson v Pompes Funèbres* [1988] ECR 2479, ECLI:EU:C:1988.

76 Case 258/78 *Nungesser KG v Commission* [1982] ECR 2015.

77 See Case C-179/90 *Merci convenzionali porto di Genova SpA v Siderurgica Gabrielli SpA* [1991] ECR 5889, ECLI:EU:C:1991:464.

78 Case 61/80 *Co-operative Stremsel- en Kleurselfabriek v Commission* [1981] ECR 851, ECLI:EU:C:1981:75 and Comm. Dec. 86/596 *MELDOC* OJ 1986 L348/50.

79 *Irish Continental Group v Chambre de Commerce et Industries de Morlaix* [1995] 5 CMLR 177.

Trade associations

10.035 A trade association is an undertaking or, at least, an association of undertakings. Consequently, agreements between, and within, trade associations may fall within the scope of EU competition law.[80] This would include groups representing carriers, shippers and others but probably not a labour union (acting as a union).

Mutual societies and P&I clubs

10.036 A mutual insurance club, more specifically a protection and indemnity club (i.e. a P&I Club), has been regarded as an undertaking.[81]

Individuals

10.037 Individuals may constitute undertakings. Sole traders are obvious examples of undertakings.[82] Consultants are also possible undertakings.[83] In *AOIP v Beyrard*,[84] an individual was held to be an undertaking where a patent licence agreement had been concluded between him and a company. A self-employed ship's agent and a self-employed pilot would ordinarily constitute undertakings.

Controlling shareholder

10.038 A controlling shareholder was found to be an undertaking in *Vaessen v Morris*.[85]

Employees

10.039 An employee (such as a seafarer) acting as an employee would not be an undertaking.[86] A former employee who carries on an independent business in his or her own right would constitute an undertaking.[87] An employee who is a relatively small shareholder (e.g. by virtue of a share option scheme) would not be an undertaking.

Trade unions

10.040 A trade union is probably not an undertaking in so far as it does not carry on commercial activity. In so far as a trade union represents self-employed persons then it is an association of undertakings or if it engages in commercial activities then it is an undertaking. Irrespective of whether a trade union constitutes an undertaking, it would have the capacity to lodge a complaint under EU competition law,[88] thus a seafarer's union may not necessarily be an undertaking but could still have the *locus standi* under

---

80 See e.g. Case 71/74 *FRUBO v Commission* [1975] ECR 563 and Case 96/82 *IAZ International Belgium NV v Commission* [1983] ECR 3369, ECLI:EU:C:1983:310.
81 Comm. Dec. 85/615 *P and I Clubs* OJ 1985 L376/2. See Christodoulou, "Protection & Indemnity Clubs and Competition" in Antapassis, Athanassiou and Røsæg (eds), op. cit. at fn. 3, pp. 317–336.
82 See e.g. Case 258/78 *Nungesser v Commission* [1982] ECR 2015, ECLI:EU:C:1982:211.
83 See e.g. Comm. Dec. 76/743 *Reuter/BASF* OJ 1976 L254/40; Comm. Dec. 79/86 *Vaessen BV v Morris* OJ 1979 L19/32; Case 35/83 *BAT v Commission* [1985] ECR 363, ECLI:EU:C:1985:32; Case 42/84 *Remia BV and Verenigde Bedrijven Nutricia NV v Commission* [1985] ECR 2545; ECLI:EU:C:1985:327; Comm. Dec. 85/561 *Breeders' Rights: Roses* OJ 1985 L369/9.
84 Comm. Dec. 76/29 OJ 1976 L6/8.
85 OJ 1979 L19/32.
86 Cases 40/73 etc. *Suiker Unie v Commission* [1975] ECR 1663, ECLI:EU:C:1975:174, para. 539.
87 Comm. Dec. 76/743 *Reuter/BASF* OJ 1976 L254/40.
88 See *BP/Texaco*, Sixteenth Report on Competition Policy (1987), para. 43.

EU competition law to make a complaint to the Commission alleging breach of that body of law or, all other things being equal, to institute proceedings on the basis of EU law in a court.

Charities

10.041 In so far as a charity (such as one caring for the welfare of seafarers) does not carry on a commercial or economic activity then it should not be regarded as an undertaking for competition purposes. It is important to stress that the entity must carry on commercial activities but need not have a profit motive[89] or economic purpose in order to be an undertaking.[90]

Foreign trade organisations

10.042 Many socialist States have or had foreign trade organisations. These have been held to constitute undertakings notwithstanding that they have no separate existence from their States because they were engaged in commercial behaviour.[91]

Member States

10.043 Whether a Member State constitutes an undertaking is not always an easy issue to decide. It is submitted that, on the basis of *Corrine Bodson v Pompes Funèbres des Regions Libérees*[92] and the general principles of public international law on State immunity, a Member State could be an undertaking in so far as it was engaged in commercial activities which could be conducted by other non-State entities (e.g. owning and operating a ferry company) but not where it was engaged in non-commercial activities or State-only commercial activities (e.g. running a navy or engaged in regulation).

Public and local authorities

10.044 It has long been debated and disputed as to whether local authorities constitute undertakings. In *Corrine Bodson v Pompes Funèbres des Regions Libérées SA*,[93] the CJEU held that Article 101 of the TFEU (i.e. the general prohibition on anti-competitive arrangements) did not apply to licensing agreements between French municipalities acting in their capacity as public authorities and entities entrusted with the provision of a public service. It is submitted that where the authority is acting as a public authority exercising public official functions then it would not normally have the capacity to be an undertaking. However, a public authority engaging in, or investing in, commercial activities as a commercial operator would do, or operating in a commercial context, would be an undertaking.

---

89 *EEC v ANSEAU-NAVEWA* OJ 1982 L167/39; *Interpar v GVL mbH* OJ 1982 L370/49; and Comm. Dec. 85/615 *P and I Clubs* OJ 1985 L376/2.
90 Case 155/73 *Italian State v Sacchi* [1974] ECR 409, ECLI:EU:C:1974:40.
91 See Comm. Dec. 85/206 *Aluminium Products* OJ 1985 L92/1; and *Colombian Coffee* OJ 1982 L360/31. See also *Fourteenth Report on Competition Policy*, para. 57.
92 Case 30/87 [1988] ECR 2479, ECLI:EU:C:1988:225. See *Irish Aerospace (Belgium) NV v European Organisation for the Safety of Air Navigation* [1992] 1 Lloyd's Law Reports 383.
93 Case 30/87 [1988] ECR 2479, ECLI:EU:C:1988:225.

Connected entities generally

10.045 In some circumstances, the Commission and the courts will treat two or more entities as constituting one single undertaking. If the entities constitute one undertaking due to identical control or ownership (e.g. an agreement between a parent and a wholly owned subsidiary) then Article 101 does not (because it cannot) apply in relation to any agreement between them because there is only one undertaking involved but Article 102 could apply[94] assuming the other elements of Article 102 are satisfied.[95]

Parent and subsidiary[96]

10.046 An agreement may fall outside the scope of Article 101 where there is so close an economic relationship between all the parties that they constitute one economic entity (i.e. they amount to a single undertaking). This has been the approach used by the Commission in dealing with such agreements between parent companies and their wholly owned subsidiaries.[97] A parent company may be made liable for the wrongdoings of its subsidiaries. A parent company is liable for the activities of its subsidiaries and thus, in the case of a distribution agreement, a parent must ensure that competition further down the distribution chain is not anti-competitive.[98] A parent company outside the EU may be subject to EU competition law where its subsidiary affects trade in the EU. It can be quite uncomfortable for a chain of one-ship companies to be looked at in terms of economic substance (rather than legal formality) because in EU competition law such a chain may well be treated as one economic entity (i.e. one undertaking).[99] Economic reality triumphs over formality.

Principal and agent

10.047 If the relationship between a principal and agent is such that the agent does not have economic independence (at least in this regard) from the principal then (notwithstanding that they may be legally independent of one another), any agreement made between the principal and agent would almost always fall outside the scope of Article 101 of the TFEU.[100]

Branch offices

10.048 It has been held that a branch office does not usually in itself constitute a separate undertaking.[101]

---

94 This is because only one undertaking needs to be involved so as to breach Art. 102 TFEU.
95 Equally, the two parts could be one undertaking.
96 See *Johnson and Johnson* OJ 1980 L377/16.
97 See *Re Zinc Producers' Group* OJ 1984 L220/27; *Johnson and Johnson* OJ 1980 L377/16; Case 15/74 *Centrafarm v Sterling Drug* [1974] ECR 1147 at 1167, ECLI:EU:C:1974:114, para. 41; *Central Wine Buyers (South Leicester Ltd) v Moët et Chandon (London) Ltd* OJ 1982 L94/7; and Case 107/82 *AEG v Commission* [1983] ECR 315, ECLI:EU:C:1983:293.
98 *Johnson and Johnson* OJ 1980 L377/16, and Cases 100–103/80 *Musique Diffusion Francaise v Commission* [1983] ECR 1825, ECLI:EU:C:1983:158.
99 If a series of companies constitute one undertaking then Art. 101 of the TFEU cannot apply to arrangements between them because there is only one undertaking, but Art. 102 may apply where there is dominance and an abuse of that dominance. If a series of one-ship companies constituted one undertaking then any arrangement between "it" (i.e. the one undertaking) and another separate undertaking would trigger the application of Art. 101 of the TFEU.
100 See *Aluminium Imports from Eastern Europe* OJ 1985 L92/1 at 37 [1987] 3CMLR 813.
101 Comm. Dec. 82/174 *Fire Insurance* OJ 1982 L80/36, [1982] 2 CMLR 159.

Successive entities

10.049 If one entity succeeds another entity (e.g. one entity buys another and takes it over) so that the liabilities of the former entity are now attributed to the latter then the two entities may be treated as a single undertaking and thus Article 101 does not apply to new arrangements to them because there are not two or more undertakings party to the arrangement (unless there is another undertaking party to the arrangement). If a member of a cartel has been replaced by another then may the successor organisation be held liable for the "sins" of the earlier organisation? In *PVC*[102] the Commission held that the determining factor is whether there is a functional and economic continuity between the original infringer and the undertaking into which it was merged. The Commission went on to indicate that it is a matter for EU law to determine whether or not the new entity is responsible for the conduct of the old one – national law is not conclusive on the issue. It is interesting to note that the CJEU has held (in *Compagnie Royale Asturienne des Mines SA and Rheinzink GmbH v Commission*)[103] that "a change in the legal form and name of an undertaking does not create a new undertaking free of liability for the anti-competitive behaviour of its predecessor when, from an economic point of view, the two are identical".[104]

Foreign entities

10.050 The mere fact that the entity is incorporated or situated outside the EU is irrelevant from the perspective of whether it is or is not an undertaking.

C. AN OVERVIEW OF EU COMPETITION LAW GENERALLY

10.051 It is useful to present, in a short Table 10.1, the main sources of EU competition law.

While these rules normally operate in isolation of each other, the concepts involved in each are very similar and they can operate in combination.

Table 10.1

Issue or practice	EU law
Anti-competitive arrangements	Article 101 of the TFEU[1]
Abuse of dominance	Article 102 of the TFEU[2]
State authorities in the market	Article 106 of the TFEU[3]
State aid	Articles 107–109 of the TFEU
Merger control	Regulation 139/2004

Notes
1 This is reflected in Art. 53 of the European Economic Agreement ("EEA").
2 This is reflected in Art. 54 of the EEA.
3 This is reflected in Art. 57 of the EEA.

---

102 OJ 1989 L74/1, [1990] 4 CMLR 345, para. 42.
103 Cases 29, 30/83 [1984] ECR 1679, ECLI:EU:C:1984:130.
104 See Nicholson and Jetté, "Succession and Liability for Fines under EU Competition Law" in Wareham and Power (eds), op. cit. at fn. 2, pp. 303–320.

D. ARTICLE 101 OF THE TFEU: ANTI-COMPETITIVE ARRANGEMENTS

Introduction

10.052 Article 101 of the TFEU[105] deals with anti-competitive arrangements. Certain types of anti-competitive agreements between undertakings, decisions by associations of undertakings and concerted practices involving undertakings[106] which could affect trade between Member States and which have as their object *or* effect[107] the prevention, restriction or distortion of competition within the internal market[108] or any[109] part of the internal market are, in the light of Article 101(1), incompatible with the internal market and are thus void under Article 101(2) unless they are exempted under Article 101(3). In essence, Article 101 prohibits generally particular types of restrictive arrangements. It is designed to prevent anti-competitive arrangements between those engaged in economic or commercial activities. Article 101 deals with both horizontal and vertical arrangements and practices. The objective of Article 101, according to the Commission and the CJEU, is to promote consumer welfare.[110]

Text of Article 101 of the TFEU

10.053 Article 101 of the TFEU provides:

"1. The following shall be prohibited as incompatible with the internal market: all agreements between undertakings, decisions by associations of undertakings and concerted practices which may affect trade between Member States and which have as their object or effect the prevention, restriction or distortion of competition within the internal market, and in particular those which:

(a) directly or indirectly fix purchase or selling prices or any other trading conditions;
(b) limit or control production, markets, technical development, or investment;
(c) share markets or sources of supply;
(d) apply dissimilar conditions to equivalent transactions with other trading parties, thereby placing them at a competitive disadvantage;
(e) make the conclusion of contracts subject to the acceptance by other parties of supplementary obligations which, by their nature or according to commercial usage, have no connection with the subject of such contracts.

2. Any agreements or decisions prohibited pursuant to this Article shall be automatically void.
3. The provision of paragraph 1 may, however, be declared inapplicable in the case of:

 – any agreement or category of agreements between undertakings;
 – any decision or category of decisions by associations of undertakings;

---

105 On Art. 101, see Black, *Conceptual Foundations of Antitrust* (2005) and Odudu, *The Boundaries of EC Competition Law: The Scope of Article 81* (2006). See also Oliver, "Agreement: Concurrence of Wills, or Offer and Acceptance?" (2008) 4 European Competition Journal 103.

106 Note the concerted practice must involve undertaking.

107 It is important to note that object *or* effect suffices and there is no need for both to exist for a breach of Art. 101 to occur. It is equally important to note that the terms "object" and "effect" are not synonymous.

108 The term "internal market" is a synonym, in this context, for the EU.

109 Note for Art. 101 TFEU to apply, it is "any" part but for Art. 102 TFEU to apply. It must be a "substantial" part.

110 There may be a public policy dimension to Art. 101: see Townley, *Article 81 EC and Public Policy* (2009).

— any concerted practice or category of concerted practices; which contributes to improving the production or distribution of goods or to promoting technical or economic progress, while allowing consumers a fair share of the resulting benefit, and which does not:

   (a) impose on the undertakings concerned restrictions which are not indispensable to the attainment of these objectives;
   (b) afford such undertakings the possibility of eliminating competition in respect of a substantial part of the products in question."

Basic concepts in Article 101

Agreements, decisions and concerted practices

Introduction

10.054 Article 101(1) prohibits certain "agreements between undertakings, decisions by associations of undertakings and concerted practices". In this chapter, these three arrangements may be collectively referred to as "arrangements".

10.055 Article 101 only applies to arrangements involving two or more undertakings so an arrangement entirely within one undertaking would fall outside the scope of Article 101 (e.g. an agreement between a parent and a wholly owned subsidiary). It is imperative to determine what is meant in EU competition law, by the terms "agreement", "decision" and "concerted practice". The definition is a critical one because the Commission has interpreted the three terms widely but too wide an interpretation can prove (albeit in limited circumstances) to be the basis of a successful challenge to the Commission's finding in the General Court/CJEU. It is vital to remember that the three concepts overlap[111] and it is rare that a particular course of conduct constitutes only an agreement, a decision *or* a concerted practice.[112] It is also vital to remember that the list of examples of arrangements contained in Article 101(1) is not exhaustive.

10.056 The arrangement does not have to be legally enforceable to fall within the scope of Article 101;[113] if it had to be enforceable legally then undertakings intent on acting in an anti-competitive manner would only have to conclude "gentlemen's agreements" (i.e. non-legally binding agreements) and thereby circumvent EU competition law. The arrangement does not have to be in any particular form: for example, it may be an oral agreement.[114] It may even have to be inferred from the circumstances of the case.[115] There is no need for a restriction to constitute a legally binding agreement for Article 101 to apply – consensus is sufficient.[116] The economic effect is more important than the legal form.

---

111 See e.g. Comm. Dec. 78/670 *Fedetab* OJ 1978 L224/29 at 40, [1978] 3 CMLR 524.

112 See the comments of AG Reischl in Cases 209/78 etc. *Van Landewyck v Commission* [1980] ECR 3125 at 3310, ECLI:EU:C:1980:248.

113 See Cases 209/78 etc. *Van Landewyck v Commission* [1980] ECR 3125 ECLI:EU:C:1980:248. The full requirements of contract law do not have to be met (e.g. acceptance is not necessary: Comm. Dec. 87/13 *BVB/ABB* OJ 1987 L7/27).

114 Comm. Dec. 82/253 *National Panasonic* OJ 1982 L354/28. The rules of a market may be an agreement between participants in the market: Comm. Dec. *GAFTA Soya Bean Meal Futures Association Ltd* OJ 1987 L19/18.

115 See Case 28/77 *Tepea v Commission* [1978] ECR 1391 at 1412–1417, ECLI:EU:C:1978:133.

116 Comm. Dec. 99/271 *Greek Ferries Cartel* [1999] 5 CMLR 47.

Agreements between undertakings

10.057 An agreement between undertakings is a distinct concept from a concerted practice or a decision by an association of undertakings.[117] Nonetheless the "agreement" and the "concerted practice" are closely related. If a situation does not amount to an agreement then it may well amount to a concerted practice (or a decision by an association of undertakings).[118] Indeed, the Commission, in reaching its findings, has often said that the co-operation between the parties in a particular case amounts to an agreement or in any event if it is not an agreement, then it is a concerted practice.[119] It is thus submitted that for the purposes of EU competition law, there is no real importance in the distinction between: (a) an agreement between undertakings; (b) a decision by an association of undertakings; and (c) a concerted practice. The agreement may be made in writing, by conduct or oral.[120] The General Court stated in *Bayer AG*:

"[t]he existence of the subjective element that characterizes the very concept of the agreement, that is to say a concurrence of wills between economic operators on the implementation of a policy, pursuit of an objective, or the adoption of a given line of conduct on the market."[121]

There does not have to be any sanction for the non-enforcement of the "agreement".[122] The mental state of the participants (even where they are unwilling)[123] has been generally ignored by the Commission in its determination as to whether an arrangement existed[124] but the participants' unwillingness may be taken into account in assessing fines.[125] The Commission does not require direct proof that each participant has given its consent to the arrangement but will look at all the surrounding facts. Nor is there need for an agreement, notes of a meeting would suffice.[126]

10.058 The Commission stated in *Graphite Electrodes* that the "concept of agreement in Article [101(1)] of the TFEU would apply to the inchoate understandings and partial and conditional agreements in the bargaining process which led up to the definite agreement".[127] It is useful to survey examples of situations which have been held to amount to "agreements" for present purposes.

LEGALLY BINDING CONTRACTS

10.059 A legally enforceable contract is an agreement for present purposes.[128] Hence, an enforceable agreement between carriers or between a carrier and a shipper would be an agreement for the purposes of Article 101. This also means that a party to a contract could seek to escape liability by invoking Article 101 to prove that part or all of the contract was unenforceable and therefore the party ought not to be sued successfully for performance.

---

117 See Comm. Dec. 86/398 *Polypropylene* OJ 1986 L230/1, para. 86.
118 See AG Reischl in Case 209/78 *Van Landewyck v Commission* [1980] ECR 3125 at 3310, ECLI:EU:C:1980:248.
119 E.g. Comm. Dec. 76/29 *Re Floral* OJ 1980 L39/51.
120 Case 28/77 *Tepea v Commission* [1978] ECR 1391, ECLI:EU:C:1978:133.
121 Case T-41/96 *Bayer AG v Commission* [2000] ECR II-3383, ECLI:EU:T:2000:242, para. 173.
122 Comm. Dec. 86/398 *Polypropylene* OJ 1986 L230/1.
123 See Comm. Dec. 82/367 *Hasselblad* OJ 1982 L161/18, [1982] 2 CMLR 233.
124 Comm. Dec. 86/399 *Belgian Roofing Felt* OJ 1986 L232/15, on appeal Case 246/86 *Belasco v Commission*; *Polypropylene* [1989] ECR 2117, ECLI:EU:C:1989:301.
125 *Camera Care Ltd v Victor Hasselblad AB* OJ 1982 L161/18; *Wood Pulp* OJ [1985] L85/1, para. 131.
126 Comm. Dec. 2000/627 *FETTCSA*, Recitals 33–54.
127 OJ 2002 L100/1, para. 105.
128 Comm. Dec. 78/193 *Penney's Trade Mark* OJ 1978 L60/19.

COMPROMISE OF LITIGATION

10.060 A private compromise of litigation may constitute an agreement for the purposes where it satisfied the criteria of Article 101.[129]

UNENFORCEABLE AGREEMENT

10.061 "Gentlemen's agreements" have been held to be agreements.[130]

A SERIES OF COLLECTIVE AGREEMENTS

10.062 A number of collective agreements may constitute one agreement or arrangement for present purposes.[131]

CONSTITUTION OF A TRADE ASSOCIATION

10.063 The constitution of a trade association has been held to be an agreement.[132]

STANDARD CONDITIONS OF SALE

10.064 Standard conditions of sale are agreements.[133]

STANDARD FORM CONTRACTS

10.065 An agreement set out in a standard form contract has also been held to constitute an agreement.[134]

GUIDELINES

10.066 A set of guidelines issued by undertakings or associations of undertakings may constitute an agreement.[135]

SPENT AGREEMENTS

10.067 It has been held in a number of cases[136] that an agreement which has expired but its effects continue to be felt might be an agreement in circumstances where it has an effect on competition. A spent agreement would still give rise to liability for the period when it had the object or effect of preventing, restricting or distorting competition.

CONCLUSION

10.068 The breadth of meaning attached to the expression "agreement" is clear from the fact that "simple understandings" have been held to constitute agreements.[137] It appears that mere "contact" may be sufficient to arouse the suspicions of the Commission but may not be enough to constitute an agreement – it all depends on the nature and extent

---

129 *Re Penney's Trade Mark* OJ 1978 L60/19.
130 Case 41/69 *ACF Chemiefarma NV v Commission* [1970] ECR 661, ECLI:EU:C:1970:71.
131 Comm. Dec. *ENI/Montedison* OJ 1987 L354/28.
132 Comm. Dec. 84/191 *Nuovo CEGAM* OJ [1984] L99/29.
133 Case 30/78 *Distillers Company v Commission* [1980] ECR 2229, and Comm. Dec. 79/68 *Kawasaki Motors* OJ 1979 L16/9, [1979] 1 CMLR 448.
134 Comm. Dec. 79/68 *Kawasaki Motors (UK) Ltd* OJ 1979 L16/9, [1979] 1 CMLR 448.
135 See Comm. Dec. 89/95 *Uniform Eurocheques* OJ 1989 L36/16, [1989] 4 CMLR 907.
136 E.g. Cases 51/75 *EMI Records Ltd v CBS UK Ltd* [1976] ECR 811 at 848–849, ECLI:EU:C:1976:85.
137 *Re Stichting Sigarettenindustrie Agreements* OJ 1982 L232/1; and Comm. Dec. *National Panasonic* OJ 1982 L354/28.

of the contract. It is also clear that what appears to be a unilateral action may still amount to an agreement because of some tacit understanding on the part of a number of other undertakings.[138] Thus charterparties, cargo-sharing agreements, tacit understandings not to poach each other's customers, consortia agreements, liner conferences, understandings on the exchange rates for currencies or the level of surcharges would fall within the scope of "agreements".[139] The breadth of the term "concerted practice" means that "agreements" may easily be subsumed under the term "concerted practice".

Decisions by associations of undertakings

10.069 Article 101 of the TFEU also applies to certain decisions by associations of undertakings.[140] These associations are normally trade associations but may take any form of structure. They need not be profit-making. They may be associations of undertakings.[141] The decisions by associations of undertakings may well be agreements in themselves. It is useful, but only of limited use, to survey examples of situations which have been held to amount to "decisions" for present purposes. A constitution of a trade association is a decision of an association of undertakings.[142] A recommendation made by the association is a decision.[143] Even a non-binding recommendation may constitute a decision for these purposes.[144] A joint recommendation on pricing would be a decision by an association of undertaking. The association of undertakings does not have to possess legal personality of its own for its decisions to fall within the scope of Article 101.[145] If a trade association recommends to its members to engage in anti-competitive behaviour then not only will the members be liable but, because of this head of liability, the trade association itself will be liable.[146] It may be easier for the EU authorities to prove the existence of a decision by an association of undertakings than to prove individual agreements or a concerted practice: trade association officials are typically better at recording decisions than their members so trade association records often provide a better record of arrangements than might otherwise be the case. EU competition law does not prohibit the existence of associations of undertakings as such but is very cautious about decisions by associations of undertakings in these circumstances.

Concerted practices

10.070 Of the three types of measures regulated by Article 101 of the TFEU, the final one mentioned in Article 101(1) is a "concerted practice".[147] This is the most

---

138 Case 107/82 *AEG v Commission* [1983] ECR 3151 at pp. 3194–3195, ECLI:EU:C:1983:293. See also Comm. Dec. 82/506 *Stichting Sigarettenindustrie Agreements* OJ 1982 L232/1.
139 E.g. Comm. Dec. 97/84 *Ferry Operators – Currency Surcharges* OJ 1997 L26/23.
140 See *Publishers Association: Net Book Agreement*, OJ 1989 L22/12. The association need not have legal personality of its own: Comm. Dec. 89/96 *Emo* OJ 1979 L11/16. The TFEU does not define the concept of an "association of undertakings".
141 Comm. Dec. 82/349 *BPICA* OJ 1977 L299/18.
142 Comm. Dec. 80/917 *National Sulphuric Acid Association* OJ L260/24; Comm. Dec. 89/86 *Publishers' Association* OJ 1989 L22/12; Comm. Dec. 82/349 *BPICA* OJ 1977 L299/18; Comm. Dec. 70/333 *Re ASPA* OJ 1970 L148/9; and Comm. Dec. 2001/782 *Visa International* OJ 2001 L293/24, para. 53.
143 Case 8/72 *Vereeniging van Cementhandelaren v Commission* [1972] ECR 977, ECLI:EU:C:1972:84.
144 Case 96/82 etc. *IAZ International Belgium NV v Commission* [1983] ECR 3369, ECLI:EU:C:1983:310.
145 Comm. Dec. 69/90 *Cecimo* OJ 1969 L69/13.
146 Comm. Dec. 82/896 *AROW v BNIC* OJ 1982 L379/1.
147 See Korah, "Concerted Practices" (1973) 36 MLR 220.

controversial and complex of the three types of arrangement. It is also the most embracive of the three. Undertakings can operate in a parallel manner without there being a concerted practice – the undertakings can simply "read" or react to the market in an identical manner[148] – which is to be expected in an oligopolistic market with a homogeneous product. In *ICI v Commission (Dyestuffs)*[149] the CJEU described a "concerted practice" as "a form of co-ordination between undertakings which, without having reached the stage where an agreement properly so-called has been concluded, knowingly substitutes practical co-operation between them for the risks of competition". The CJEU developed this point in *Suiker Unie v Commission (Sugar Cartel)*[150] by saying that Article 101 prohibited strictly:

> "any direct or indirect contact between such operators, the object or effect whereof is either to influence the conduct on the market of an actual or potential competitor or to disclose to such a competitor the course of conduct which they themselves have decided to adopt or contemplate adopting on the market".

10.071 The Commission has held in some cases that a concerted practice does not require proof of a plan.[151] Proof is vital in bringing proceedings but it is rarely what might be termed "perfect proof". The undertakings could have destroyed or deleted emails, faxes, letters, text messages, records, other documentary evidence and even mobile phones and computers. The burden of proof rests on the EU authorities (in public proceedings) or private plaintiffs (in private proceedings) to prove a concerted practice. If there is insufficient evidence for the Commission to say that there was a concerted practice then the CJEU/General Court will be willing to set aside the Commission's decision.[152] The Commission has stated that the

> "importance of the concept of a concerted practice does not ... result so much from the distinction between it and an agreement as from the distinction between forms of collusion falling under Article [101(1)] and mere parallel behaviour with no element of concertation."[153]

A concerted practice involves, when compared with an agreement, more tacit than actual collusion. The party alleging the existence of a concerted practice therefore has some responsibility to demonstrate the existence of a concerted practice under Article 101 because otherwise the evidence could be quite flimsy. Mere parallel conduct would be insufficient to amount to an arrangement within the meaning of Article 101.

Agreements, decisions and concerted practices entered into outside the EU

10.072 Agreements, decisions and concerted practices entered into outside the EU may still fall within the scope of Article 101 where they have an effect on trade within the EU (a concept which is construed widely).[154] Otherwise, EU competition law would be

---

148 See Cases 29, [1985] 1 CMLR 688, 30/83 *Compagnie Royale Asturienne des Mines SA and Rheinzink GmbH v Commission* [1984] ECR 1679, and Comm. Dec. 89/93 *Italian Flat Glass* OJ 1989 L33/44.
149 Case 48/69 [1972] ECR 619, ECLI:EU:C:1972:70.
150 Cases 40/73 etc. [1975] ECR 1663, ECLI:EU:C:1975:174.
151 Comm. Dec. 86/398 *Polypropylene* OJ 1986 L230/1.
152 E.g. Cases 40/73 etc. *Suiker Unie v Commission* [1975] ECR 1663, ECLI:EU:C:1975:174; and Cases 29, 30/83 *Compagnie Royale Asturienne des Mines SA and Rheinzink GmbH v Commission* [1984] ECR 1679, ECLI:EU:C:1971:113.
153 *Polypropylene* OJ 1986 L230/1, para. 87.
154 Case 22/71 *Beguelin Import v GL Import Export* [1971] ECR 949, ECLI:EU:C:1971:113.

circumvented simply by concluding arrangements outside the EU (e.g. by holding meetings to fix prices outside the EU).

Participation in part of an arrangement

10.073 An undertaking is liable for the whole cartel if it participated in only some or part of the arrangement if "it is shown that it knows or must have known, that the collusion in which it participated ... was part of an overall plan [which] included all the constituent elements of the cartel".[155]

Object or effect of preventing, restricting or distorting competition

Introduction

10.074 Article 101 of the TFEU prohibits particular arrangements which have as their object or effect the prevention, restriction or distortion of competition. What is meant by "object" or "effect"? Moreover, what is meant by prevention, restriction or distortion of competition? In assessing this issue, regard should be had to the economic effect more than just the legal form or the arrangement. In *Société TecPnique Minière v Maschinenbau Ulm*[156] the CJEU held that the terms "object" or "effect" are to be read disjunctively. Thus, it is essential first to prove that the object of the arrangement was to prevent, restrict or distort competition and then, only if it was not clear that the *object* of an arrangement was to harm competition would it be necessary to consider whether it had the *effect* of doing so. Thus, where the *object* of the arrangement is to prevent, restrict or distort competition, there is no need to establish the *effect* on competition. Thus, an arrangement to fix prices, share markets or impose an export ban will be seen as being anti-competitive because it has the object of distorting competition even if it never succeeded in achieving that aim or effect. Either object *or* effect suffices for Article 101 to apply.

Object

10.075 In studying the "object" of the arrangement, one is not concerned with the subjective intention of the parties but must instead look at the "objective" intention of the arrangement – i.e. the purpose of the arrangement considered in the economic context in which it is to be applied (i.e. would such an agreement, seen objectively, have the aim or object of preventing, restricting or distorting competition?).[157]

Effect

10.076 If it is not clear that the "object" of the arrangement is anti-competitive then the *effect* of the arrangement must be considered. To do so, one must examine the arrangement in the context of its market:

---

155 Joined Cases T-305 etc/94 *NV Limburgse Vinyl Maatschappij v Commission* [1999] ECR II-931, ECLI:EU:C:1999:80, para. 773.
156 Case 56/65 [1966] ECR 235 at 249, ECLI:EU:C:1966:38. The whole legal and economic context must be examined.
157 Cases 29, 30/83 *Compagnie Royale Asturienne des Mines SA and Rheinzink GmbH v Commission* [1984] ECR 1679; ECLI:EU:C:1984:130. Cases 96/82 etc. *IAZ v Commission* [1983] ECR 3369, ECLI:EU:C:1983:310 and Case C-209/07 *Competition Authority v Beef Industry Development Society Ltd and Barry Brothers (Carrigmore) Meats Ltd* [2008] ECR I-8637, ECLI:EU:C:2008:467.

"it would be pointless to consider an agreement, decision or practice by reason of its effect if those effects were to be taken distinct from the market in which they are seen to operate, and could only be examined apart from the body of effects, whether convergent or not, surrounding their implementation. Thus in order to examine whether it is caught by Article [101(1)] an agreement cannot be examined in isolation from the above context, that is, from the factual or legal circumstances causing it to prevent, restrict or distort competition."[158]

Indeed, the comments of the CJEU in *Competition Authority v Beef Industry Development Society Ltd and Barry Brothers (Carrigmore) Meats Ltd*[159] are pertinent:

"to determine whether an agreement comes within the prohibition laid down in Article [101(1) TFEU], close regard must be paid to the wording of its provisions and to the objectives which it is intended to attain. In that regard, even supposing it to be established that the parties to an agreement acted without any subjective intention of restricting competition, but with the object of remedying the effects of a crisis in their sector, such considerations are irrelevant for the purposes of applying that provision. Indeed, an agreement may be regarded as having a restrictive object even if it does not have the restriction of competition as its sole aim but also pursues other legitimate objectives (*General Motors v Commission*,[160] paragraph 64 and the case-law cited). It is only in connection with Article [101(1) TFEU] that matters such as those relied upon by BIDS [Ed., i.e. the Beef Industry Development Society] may, if appropriate, be taken into consideration for the purposes of obtaining an exemption from the prohibition laid down in Article [101(1) TFEU]."

Preventing, restricting and distorting competition

10.077 It is legally irrelevant whether the arrangement prevents, restricts *and* distorts competition: it is sufficient that it does any *one* of the three. Distortion is in many ways the "catch-all" term.[161] Arrangements which involve price-fixing, market sharing and customer sharing would breach Article 101(1). Resale price maintenance (or "RPM") involves a supplier determining the particular or minimum price at which an independent intermediary resells the product. Maximum RPM is generally permitted in EU law and it means that there is a floor to the price at which the product may be resold. Minimum RPM is not permitted in EU competition law but it has been permitted in the United States at a federal level in recent years. The effect must be appreciable before Article 101 will apply.

10.078 In practice, certain arrangements are presumed to be anti-competitive – these include market sharing, bid rigging, price-fixing, absolute territorial protection and RPM. The anti-competitive effects should be demonstrated in all cases but it would be easier in those cases. In other cases, the anti-competitive effects would have to be assessed and determined.

---

158 Case 23/67 *Brasserie de Haecht v Wilkin* [1967] ECR 407, ECLI:EU:C:1967:54. Certain arrangements have a per se effect on competition (e.g. export bans). It is possible to look at the effects on third parties: Case 272/85 *Association nationale des travailleurs independants de la batellerie (Antib) v Commission* [1987] ECR 2201, ECLI:EU:C:1987:235.
159 Case C-209/07, [2008] ECR I-8637, ECLI:EU:C:2008:643, para. 21.
160 Ed., Case C-551/03P [2006] ECR I-3173, ECLI:EU:C:2006:229, para. 21.
161 See Comm. Dec. 87/69 *X/Open Group* OJ 1987 L35/36.

Effect on inter-State trade

Introduction

10.079 Only arrangements which, among other features, affect trade between Member States fall within the scope of Articles 101 and 102. The significance of this requirement (i.e. there must be an effect on inter-State trade) is critical. It constitutes the "boundary between the areas respectively covered by [EU] law and the law of the Member States".[162] If a particular arrangement is seen as having an effect on inter-State trade then the EU authorities have jurisdiction – the Member States may typically apply national competition law if their laws allow them to do so but the key point is that the EU institutions have jurisdiction once there is an effect on trade between Member States.[163] Thus, this criterion of an effect on trade between Member States is of critical importance in each case. A substantial part of the internal market must be affected for Article 102 to apply but this is not so in the case of Article 101 because Article 101 refers to affecting competition in any part of the internal market. In practice, shipping normally has an effect on trade between Member States even where only one EU port is involved alongside a non-EU port because shipping is ordinarily a cross-border activity (i.e. two EU ports are not required).[164] If an arrangement has an insignificant effect on inter-state trade then Articles 101 and 102 of the TFEU do not apply[165] but that would be very unusual in the context of international shipping activities affecting EU ports. The question of whether EU and/or Member State competition law applies is critical from the perspective of the penalties involved – for example, some Member State competition laws include penalties on individual executives. There may be an effect on trade between Member States notwithstanding that the arrangement or practice is confined to a single Member State (i.e. the Member State in which the port is located).

10.080 The CJEU laid down in several cases the test for deciding whether there is an effect on trade between Member States. The CJEU stated in *Volk v Etablissements J Vervaecke SPRL*:[166]

> "If an agreement is to be capable of affecting trade between Member States it must be possible to foresee with sufficient degree of probability on the basis of objective factors of law or of fact that the agreement in question may have an influence, direct or indirect, actual or potential, on the pattern of trade between Member States in such a way that it might hinder the attainment of the objectives of a single market between States."

Therefore, all that is required is a potential, and not necessarily an actual, effect.

10.081 Even though an effect on trade might *appear* to be confined to a single Member State, it may well be that there is an effect on trade between Member States.[167] For example, the refusal to grant facilities in a port can easily have an impact on trade

---

162 Case 22/78 *Hugin Kassaregister AB v Commission* [1979] ECR 1869 at 1899, ECLI:EU:C:1994:77.
163 It may happen that the substantive rule of the EU and the particular Member State in question are identical or near-identical so there is little difficulty for the court because the same rules are applicable either way but the penalties and procedure could well differ (cf. *Hendry v WPSCA* [2002] UKCLR 5).
164 In many ways, it should be presumed that there is an effect on trade in the vast majority of international shipping services if an EU port is involved in the case because that EU port is competing with other EU ports for trade to the non-EU port (e.g. in Africa).
165 Case 56/64 *Etablissements Consten Sarl v Commission* [1966] ECR 299, ECLI:EU:C:1975:1966:41.
166 Case 5/69 [1969] ECR 295, ECLI:EU:C:1969:35.
167 Case 8/72 *Vereniging Cementhandelaren (VCH) v Commission* [1972] ECR 677, ECLI:EU:C:1972:84.

between Member States where the services involved are cross-border even though the effect is apparently confined to a single Member State (e.g. the conduct relates to a port in a country).[168] For example, the EU has recognised an effect on trade between Member States even though the trade at issue is between an EU port and a third State (i.e. a non-Member-State).[169]

10.082 It is sufficient that even one provision in the arrangement has an effect on trade between Member States – the whole arrangement does not have to potentially affect trade between Member States.[170]

10.083 The safest starting point or presumption, so as to ensure compliance, is to assume that arrangements that restrict competition will fall within Article 101. It would be useful if there were a test by which one could determine whether or not a particular arrangement has an effect on inter-State trade. Sadly, there is no single universally acceptable and applicable test. There are, however, at least two which have developed: the *STM* test and the Structural test.

TEST 1: STM TEST

10.084 In *Société Technique Minière v Maschinenbau Ulm*[171] the CJEU stated that before Article 101 could apply

> "it must be possible to foresee with a sufficient degree of probability on the basis of a set of objective factors of law or of fact that the agreement in question may have an influence, direct or indirect, actual or potential, on the pattern of trade between Member States".

In practice, this means that the term "effect on inter State trade" is construed widely.

---

168 E.g. Comm. Dec. 94/19 *B&I Line plc v Sealink Harbours Ltd* OJ L15/8, 18 January 1994, [1992] 5 CMLR 255; Comm. Dec. 94/79 OJ L15/8, 18 January 1994, [1995] 4 CMLR 84; *Sea Containers Ltd v Stena Sealink Ports* OJ; Case IV/35.388 *Irish Continental Group v Chambre de Commerce et Industries de Morlaix* [1995] 5 CMLR 177; and *Euro-Port A/S v Denmark* [1994] 5 CMLR 457.

169 In a case concerning trade between France and third States (Comm. Dec. 92/262 *French West African Shipowners* OJ L134/1, 18 May 1992, the Commission found at Recital 43 that there was an effect on trade between Member States: "[t]he shipowners' agreements affect trade between Member States of the Community as follows: (i) the agreements are aimed at partitioning the trade between the [EU] and the eleven African States concerned: French shipping lines have privileged access to trade on the routes covered by the shipowners' committees in relation to the lines of other Member States or third countries. This mechanism has the effect of giving the former an undue competitive edge in world trade over all other lines, including the lines of other Member States; (ii) the application of the shipowners' agreements also has the effect of distorting competition between European shippers operating on African markets: French exporters are in an unfavourable position compared with their competitors sailing to the same destinations from other [EU] countries; French importers are equally at a disadvantage as regards both the supply of services and freight rates, (iii) the distortions described above can have repercussions on port activity in both Africa and Europe: the constraints imposed on French shippers by the restrictive practices of the committees discourage shippers in French ports from importing or exporting from the African countries concerned. French shippers that are dissatisfied with the quality of the services or freight rates offered by members of shipowners' committees are thus obliged: – either to operate from ports in the countries adjacent to France. Such 'deflections of trade' have the effect of favouring those ports in relation to French ports even if the 'deflections' are impeded by the fact that shippers are required to produce documents showing the provenance and destination of their goods, – or to give up trading with the African countries covered by the shipowners' committees, which has a depressive effect on the activity of French ports. This produces distortions in the competition between French and other [EU] ports for the transport of goods to or from West Africa."

170 Case 193/83 *Windsurfing International Inc v Commission* [1986] ECR 611, ECLI:EU:C:1986:75.

171 Case 56/65 [1966] ECR 235, ECLI:EU:C:1966:38.

TEST 2: STRUCTURAL TEST

10.085 This test examines the structure of the market. The CJEU has occasionally utilised this test (in such cases as *Commercial Solvents v Commission*,[172] *Greenwich Film Production v SACEM*[173] and *GVL v Commission*[174]) and the Commission (in such cases as *Re Vacuum Interrupters Ltd*[175] and *Polypropylene*[176]). An arrangement relating to trading outside the EU may still be subject to Article 101 where it has an effect on trade between the Member States.[177] In *Compagnie Royale Asturienne des Mines SA and Rheinzink GmbH v Commission*[178] an agreement between two undertakings in respect of exports to the Middle East was held to be subject to EU competition law because the agreement was ultimately a way of protecting the German market.

Agreements falling outside Article 101(1)

Introduction

10.086 Some arrangements fall outside Article 101(1). This section examines a selection of some such arrangements.

De minimis doctrine

10.087 An arrangement falls outside the scope of Article 101 where "it has only an insignificant effect on the market, taking into account the weak position which the persons concerned have on the market of the product in question".[179] Put another way, where the circumstances are such that the arrangement or practice could not distort competition (e.g. a trivial market share) then competition law would not apply.

10.088 The Commission has developed non-binding rules on *de minimis* arrangements but it is safer to begin by assuming that EU competition law applies. The Commission occasionally publishes "notices" which specify certain types of arrangements which are deemed not to infringe Article 101(1). There is a Commission *Notice on Agreements of Minor Importance*[180] on the subject of minor agreements. The *Co-operation Agreements Notice* outlines the types of co-operation agreements between independent firms which do not, according to the Commission, violate EU competition law. The Commission has also published a *Notice on Agreements between an Undertaking and a Sub-contractor*[181] which could both take an arrangement outside the scope of Article 101 in practical terms.

10.089 If an arrangement has an immaterial or minimal impact on competition then competition law does not seek to regulate it. This is an example of competition law taking a practical and realistic approach. EU competition law should only be concerned with those arrangements which have an appreciable effect on competition. The Commission

---

172 Cases 6, 7/73 [1974] ECR 223, ECLI:EU:C:1974:18.
173 Case 22/79 [1979] ECR 3275, ECLI:EU:C:1979:245.
174 Case 7/82 [1983] ECR 483, ECLI:EU:C:1983:52.
175 Comm. Dec. 77/160 OJ 1977 L48/32.
176 Comm. Dec. 86/398 OJ 1986 L230/1.
177 See *Re Franco-Japanese Ballbearings Agreement* OJ 1974 L343/19; *Re French and Taiwanese Mushroom Packers* OJ 1975 L29/26; *Aluminium Products* OJ 1985 L92/1; and *Siemens/Fanuc* OJ 1985 L376/29.
178 Cases 29–30/83 [1984] ECR 1679, ECLI:EU:C:1984:130.
179 Case 5/69 *Volk v Vervaecke* [1969] ECR 295, ECLI:EU:C:1969:35.
180 OJ 2001 C368/13.
181 OJ 1979 C1/2.

uses market share (as a proxy for market power) as a good indicator of appreciability. Under the Commission Notice of 22 December 2001,[182] arrangements involving parties with a combined market share of less than 10% (in the case of horizontal arrangements)[183] and 15% (in the case of vertical arrangements)[184] would be regarded as *de minimis*. The Commission believes that there is no appreciable effect on inter-State trade when the total market share and turnover of the parties are below certain thresholds.[185] The

---

182 OJ 2001 C368/13.
183 I.e. arrangements between undertakings at the same level of the economic chain (e.g. two shipping companies in an arrangement or two ports in an arrangement).
184 I.e. arrangements between undertakings at different levels of the economic chain (e.g. an arrangement between a shipping company and a port or between a manufacturer and a distributor).
185 Key elements of the text of the "Commission Notice on agreements of minor importance which do not appreciably restrict competition under Article 101(1) of the Treaty establishing the European Community" (OJ 2001 C368/07) are as follows: "1. Article [101](1) prohibits agreements between undertakings which may affect trade between Member States and which have as their object or effect the prevention, restriction or distortion of competition within the common market. The Court of Justice of the European [Union] has clarified that this provision is not applicable where the impact of the agreement on intra-Community trade or on competition is not appreciable. 2. In this notice the Commission quantifies, with the help of market share thresholds, what is not an appreciable restriction of competition under Article [101] of the TFEU. This negative definition of appreciability does not imply that agreements between undertakings which exceed the thresholds set out in this notice appreciably restrict competition. Such agreements may still have only a negligible effect on competition and may therefore not be prohibited by Article [101](1). 3. Agreements may in addition not fall under Article [101] (1) because they are not capable of appreciably affecting trade between Member States. This notice does not deal with this issue. It does not quantify what does not constitute an appreciable effect on trade. It is however acknowledged that agreements between small and medium-sized undertakings, as defined in the Annex to Commission Recommendation 96/280/EC(3), are rarely capable of appreciably affecting trade between Member States. Small and medium-sized undertakings are currently defined in that recommendation as undertakings which have fewer than 250 employees and have either an annual turnover not exceeding EUR 40 million or an annual balance-sheet total not exceeding EUR 27 million. 4. In cases covered by this notice the Commission will not institute proceedings either upon application or on its own initiative. Where undertakings assume in good faith that an agreement is covered by this notice, the Commission will not impose fines. Although not binding on them, this notice also intends to give guidance to the courts and authorities of the Member States in their application of Article [101]. 5. This notice also applies to decisions by associations of undertakings and to concerted practices. ... 7. The Commission holds the view that agreements between undertakings which affect trade between Member States do not appreciably restrict competition within the meaning of Article [101](1): (a) if the aggregate market share held by the parties to the agreement does not exceed 10% on any of the relevant markets affected by the agreement, where the agreement is made between undertakings which are actual or potential competitors on any of these markets (agreements between competitors); or (b) if the market share held by each of the parties to the agreement does not exceed 15% on any of the relevant markets affected by the agreement, where the agreement is made between undertakings which are not actual or potential competitors on any of these markets (agreements between non-competitors). In cases where it is difficult to classify the agreement as either an agreement between competitors or an agreement between non-competitors the 10% threshold is applicable. 8. Where in a relevant market competition is restricted by the cumulative effect of agreements for the sale of goods or services entered into by different suppliers or distributors (cumulative foreclosure effect of parallel networks of agreements having similar effects on the market), the market share thresholds under point 7 are reduced to 5%, both for agreements between competitors and for agreements between non-competitors. Individual suppliers or distributors with a market share not exceeding 5% are in general not considered to contribute significantly to a cumulative foreclosure effect. A cumulative foreclosure effect is unlikely to exist if less than 30% of the relevant market is covered by parallel (networks of) agreements having similar effects. 9. The Commission also holds the view that agreements are not restrictive of competition if the market shares do not exceed the thresholds of respectively 10%, 15% and 5% set out in point 7 and 8 during two successive calendar years by more than 2 percentage points. 10. In order to calculate the market share, it is necessary to determine the relevant market. This consists of the relevant product market and the relevant geographic market. When defining the relevant market, reference should be had to the notice on the definition of the relevant market for the purposes of Community competition law. The market shares are to be calculated on the basis of sales value data or, where appropriate, purchase value data. If value data are not available, estimates based on other reliable market information, including volume data, may be used. 11. Points 7, 8 and 9 do not apply to

General Court has referred to the "*de minimis*" rule and that the issue turns on appreciability.[186]

Agreements within a single economic unit

10.090 Article 101(1) does not apply to arrangements within a single economic unit. Thus, a parent and a wholly owned subsidiary may enter into an arrangement which would otherwise be void provided the subsidiary has no "economic independence" from the parent company notwithstanding that it may have a separate legal personality.[187] This is because it is not an agreement between two undertakings but rather an agreement within a single undertaking. In such circumstances, a full rigorous examination is made of the facts – for example, shareholdings, directors and actual influence – so as to determine economic independence or dependence.[188] In the case of a company having a majority shareholding in a company then it is presumed that the "parent" controls the subsidiary's business affairs.[189] An arrangement between a principal and an agent may fall outside Article 101 where the agent does not have economic independence from the principal (at least in this regard) notwithstanding that the parties may have separate legal personality. An arrangement between a contractor and a sub-contractor usually falls outside Article 101 because of the close economic connection between the parties.[190]

---

agreements containing any of the following hardcore restrictions: (1) as regards agreements between competitors as defined in point 7, restrictions which, directly or indirectly, in isolation or in combination with other factors under the control of the parties, have as their object: (a) the fixing of prices when selling the products to third parties; (b) the limitation of output or sales; (c) the allocation of markets or customers; (2) as regards agreements between non-competitors as defined in point 7, restrictions which, directly or indirectly, in isolation or in combination with other factors under the control of the parties, have as their object: (a) the restriction of the buyer's ability to determine its sale price, without prejudice to the possibility of the supplier imposing a maximum sale price or recommending a sale price, provided that they do not amount to a fixed or minimum sale price as a result of pressure from, or incentives offered by, any of the parties; (b) the restriction of the territory into which, or of the customers to whom, the buyer may sell the contract goods or services, except the following restrictions which are not hardcore: – the restriction of active sales into the exclusive territory or to an exclusive customer group reserved to the supplier or allocated by the supplier to another buyer, where such a restriction does not limit sales by the customers of the buyer,– the restriction of sales to end users by a buyer operating at the wholesale level of trade, – the restriction of sales to unauthorised distributors by the members of a selective distribution system, and – the restriction of the buyer's ability to sell components, supplied for the purposes of incorporation, to customers who would use them to manufacture the same type of goods as those produced by the supplier; (c) the restriction of active or passive sales to end users by members of a selective distribution system operating at the retail level of trade, without prejudice to the possibility of prohibiting a member of the system from operating out of an unauthorised place of establishment; (d) the restriction of cross-supplies between distributors within a selective distribution system, including between distributors operating at different levels of trade; (e) the restriction agreed between a supplier of components and a buyer who incorporates those components, which limits the supplier's ability to sell the components as spare parts to end users or to repairers or other service providers not entrusted by the buyer with the repair or servicing of its goods; (3) as regards agreements between competitors as defined in point 7, where the competitors operate, for the purposes of the agreement, at a different level of the production or distribution chain, any of the hardcore restrictions listed in paragraph (1) and (2) above. 12. (1) For the purposes of this notice, the terms 'undertaking', 'party to the agreement', 'distributor', 'supplier' and 'buyer' shall include their respective connected undertakings."

186 Case T-374/94 *European Night Services Ltd v Commission* [1998] ECR II-3141, ECLI:EU:C:1998:198.
187 Case 22/71 *Beguelin Import v GL Import Export* [1971] ECR 949, ECLI:EU:C:1971:113 and Case 15/74 *Centrafarm BV v Sterling Drug Inc* [1974] ECR 1147, ECLI:EU:C:1974:114.
188 See Case 107/82 *AEG Telefunken v Commission* [1983] ECR 3151, ECLI:EU:C:1983:293.
189 AG Warner in Cases 6,7/73 *Commercial Solvents v Commission* [1974] ECR 223, ECLI:EU:C:1974:18.
190 See the Commission's Notice on Agreements between an Undertaking and a Sub-Contractor OJ 1979 C1/2.

Objective necessity

10.091 Some arrangements have been held to be outside the scope of Article 101 because of the "objective necessity" principle. This means that some restrictions in contracts which have been held to be "objectively necessary" for the performance of those contracts are not within the scope of Article 101. Thus, reasonable restrictive covenants following on from the sale of a business have been held to be "objectively necessary" in certain circumstances and thus outside the scope of Article 101.[191] Restrictions in a licence on plant breeders' rights have been held to be essential, when viewed objectively, so as to allow the breeder to make full use of the seeds in question.[192] Provisions in a franchise agreement which protect, when viewed objectively, the franchisor's intellectual property rights would also be "objectively necessary".[193] This "commercial risk" exception is of limited value in practice and should only be relied upon after clear guidance has been given by the Commission and the CJEU. Where a particular arrangement contains provisions on exclusivity, those provisions could, in certain circumstances, be seen as falling outside Article 101 because of the risk accepted by the distributor, licensee or franchisee.[194]

Selective distribution system

10.092 Some selective distribution systems often fall outside the scope of Article 101 of the TFEU.[195]

Mergers

10.093 Some mergers might fall within the scope of Article 101 but the Commission has no power to deal with them because of Regulation 139/2004 (the Merger Control Regulation)[196] on the control of concentrations which disapplies the power of the Commission to apply Articles 101 and 102 of the TFEU to concentrations.[197] Thus a merger or concentrative joint venture between two or more shipping companies would not be subject to challenge by the Commission under Article 101 where it constituted a concentration which is regulated under the Merger Control Regulation.[198]

Transfer of assets

10.094 In *ENI/Montedison*[199] the Commission held that a swap of assets between two major undertakings in the thermoplastics industry which resulted in BPCL specialising in the production of polyethylene and ICI specialising in PVC was an agreement which distorted competition and was not simply a mere transfer of assets. In the end, an individual

---

191 Case 42/84 *Remia and Nutricia v Commission* [1985] ECR 2545, ECLI:EU:C:1985: 327.
192 Case 27/87 *Erauw-Jacquery v La Hesbignonne* [1988] ECR 1919, ECLI:EU:C:1988:183.
193 See Case 161/84 *Pronuptia v Schillgalis* [1986] ECR 353, ECLI:EU:C:1986:41.
194 Case 56/65 *STM v Maschinenbau* [1966] ECR 235, ECLI:EU:C:1966:38 and Case 258/78 *Nungesser v Commission* [1982] ECR 2015.
195 Leigh, "EEC Law and Selective Distribution: Recent Developments" [1986] ECLR 419.
196 OJ 2004 L24/1.
197 See chap. 16.
198 It is still possible (but very unusual) for a merger to be challenged on the basis of Art. 101 in an action before a Member State court because Reg. 139/2004 may not (as a regulation) disapply Art. 101 (i.e. a regulation may not disapply a provision of the Treaty).
199 OJ 1987 L5/13.

exemption under Article 101(3) was granted. In *Mecaniver-PPG*[200] the Commission held that a sale of shares amounted to a mere transfer of assets and was thus outside Article 101. Of course, the transfer of assets could have wider implications for competition and could thereby be caught by Article 101, Article 102 or Regulation 139/2004 so care should be taken with this exception.

State compulsion

10.095 If there is very strong evidence that the arrangement was solely[201] the result of compulsion by a State then it may be possible to argue that there was no arrangement[202] but that is a very difficult argue to sustain.[203]

Exemption

10.096 An arrangement which has been exempted under Article 101(3) cannot be struck down under Article 101(1).

Onus of proof

10.097 Who has the onus or burden of proof in contending that Article 101(1) applies? The onus is on the party alleging that the arrangement falls within the scope of Article 101(1) – typically, this would be the European Commission, the national competition authority or someone alleging in court or arbitration proceedings that the arrangement breaches Article 101(1).

Article 101(2): voidness[204]

Introduction

10.098 As a general principle, an arrangement which violates Article 101(1) is void by virtue of Article 101(2).[205] Thus, the arrangement will be unenforceable in proceedings in Member State courts because Article 101 has direct effect.[206]

Text of Article 101(2)

10.099 Article 101(2) provides: "Any agreements or decisions prohibited pursuant to this Article shall be automatically void." For the avoidance of doubt, Article 101(2) relates to agreements between undertakings, decisions by associations of undertakings and concerted practices.

---

200 OJ 1985 L35/54.
201 I.e. there was unwillingness by the parties to conclude the arrangement and it came about solely due to State compulsion.
202 Case 40/73 *Suiker Unie v Commission* [1975] ECR 166, ECLI:EU:C:1975:174.
203 E.g. the argument was rejected in Comm. Dec. 92/262 *French West African Shipowners' Committee* OJ 1992 L134/1, Recital 32; Comm. Dec. 93/8 *Cewal* OJ 1993 L34/20; and Case T-56/99 *Marlines v Commission* [2003] ECR I-5225, ECLI:EU:T:2003:333.
204 See Clough and Randolph, op. cit. at fn. 2, para. 3.2.3. See also Case 22/71 *Beguelin Import v G.L. Import-Export* [1971] ECR 949, ECLI:EU:C:1971:113.
205 The exception to this rule occurs where the arrangement is exempted under Art. 101(3).
206 Case 127/73 *BRT v Sabam (No.1)* [1974] ECR 51, ECLI:EU:C:1974:6.

Punishment element

10.100 An arrangement which violates Article 101(1) and not exempted under Article 101(3) is void under Article 101(2). This means that the parties may be open to fines and may not rely on that agreement, decision or concerted practice in any litigation or otherwise. Only those provisions of the arrangement which violate Article 101(1) are void provided the rest can be severed and still be operable.[207] Thus, the court or the arbitrator may, where possible, sever offending provisions and leave a viable rump in place.

Is this really a penalty at all?

10.101 If a number of undertakings conspire to distort competition (e.g. as in a cartel) then they may not want their "agreement" to be legally enforceable in court anyway – they are rarely going to petition a court so as to get the court's assistance in enforcing an anti-competitive agreement and thereby admit publicly to their cartel or other anti-competitive arrangements! However, the possible imposition of fines and the fact that the arrangement may not be lawfully operated are serious penalties in practice. Curiously, the real punishment of voidness is for those parties who intend to conclude a lawful arrangement but find that it is void rather than those who deliberately intend to behave anti-competitively and did not care about whether the arrangement is enforceable or not.

Article 101(3): exemption

Introduction

10.102 An arrangement which falls within the scope of Article 101(1) would be exempted by virtue of the provisions of Article 101(3) provided the conditions specified in Article 101(3) are satisfied. Such an exemption will not, however, be possible unless all the criteria set out in Article 101(3) are satisfied.[208] When all the conditions of Article 101(3) are satisfied then it is a *de jure* exemption (i.e. an exemption by operation of law and no application or authority need be made to avail of it).

Text of Article 101(3)

10.103 Article 101(3) sets out the criteria which arrangements must satisfy so as to be permitted under Article 101 even though they breach Article 101(1). These criteria use the economic efficiency and consumer benefit tests. Article 101(3) provides as follows:

"The provisions of paragraph 1 may, however, be declared inapplicable in the case of:

 – any agreement or category of agreements between undertakings;
 – any decision or category of decisions by associations of undertakings;
 – any concerted practice or category of concerted practices;

which contributes to improving the production or distribution of goods or to promoting technical or economic progress, while allowing consumers a fair share of the resulting benefit, and which does not:

---

207 Cases 56 and 58/64 *Établissements Consten SARL and Grundig-Verkaufs-GmbH v Commission* [1966] ECR 299, ECLI:EU:C:1966:41 and Case 56/65 *Société Technique Minière v Maschinenbau Ulm* [1966] ECR 235, ECLI:EU:C:1966:38. The question of severability is one of Member State law (Case 319/82 *Société de Vente de Ciments v Kerpen* [1983] ECR 4173, ECLI:EU:C:1983:374).
208 Equally, there must be no breach of Art. 102 of the TFEU either.

(a) impose on the undertakings concerned restrictions which are not indispensable to the attainment of these objectives;
(b) afford such undertakings the possibility of eliminating competition in respect of a substantial part of the products in question."

Position before, and after, 1 May 2004

Position prior to 1 May 2004

10.104 Before 1 May 2004, only the Commission could have granted an exemption – not even the CJEU/General Court or a Member State court or authority could have granted an exemption.[209] Exemptions could only have been granted either: (a) individually to an individual arrangement which had been specifically notified to the Commission; or (b) collectively to a type or species of arrangements (which had not been notified) but was being exempted en bloc (i.e. by category of arrangement). Article 101(3) sets out grounds or conditions for the granting of exemptions by the Commission. In fact, the Commission operated a very flexible regime and where it wanted to exempt a particular agreement and it would often do so without specifying the particular ground in Article 101(3). An exemption related (and still relates) only to Article 101(1) and not Article 102; Article 102 is applicable in any event provided the conditions for the application of Article 102 are satisfied. Before 1 May 2004, because the Commission was unable to issue formal legally binding decisions in very many cases because of the administrative difficulties involved, it issued so-called "comfort letters" in those cases where it had received a notification and believed that it would not take any enforcement action but was unable to adopt a formal decision.[210] These comfort letters were not legally binding in their own right but most lawyers treated them as if they were binding or would, at least, act to dissuade the Commission from taking action.

Position since 1 May 2004

10.105 On 1 May 2004, Regulation 1/2003[211] entered into force. It is now no longer possible to notify an arrangement to the Commission for the purposes of Article 101 of the TFEU so an individual exemption is no longer possible.[212] Instead, undertakings have to engage in self-assessment to see whether Article 101 applies – they first assess whether Article 101(1) applies and then if it does then they have to decide whether Article 101(3) applies.[213] Parties need to have the arrangements which breach Article 101(1) to fall within the scope of Article 101(3) otherwise the arrangements would be void under Article 101(2) and the arrangements could fit within the scope of Article 101(3) either by way of a block exemption or the terms of Article 101(3) are deemed to apply.

---

209 4056/86 (OJ 1986 L378/14) was an isolated instance of an entity other than the Commission (in that case the Council) granting an exemption. On Reg. 4056/86, see chap. 12.
210 Adopting formal decisions was relatively cumbersome.
211 The so-called "Modernisation Regulation" (i.e. Reg. 1/2003 OJ 2003 L1/1).
212 Notifications under the Merger Control Regulation (Reg. 139/2004) are still possible but they do not relate to Art. 101 arrangements. It is not possible to notify an arrangement or practice to see whether there is a breach of Art. 102 of the TFEU.
213 On self-assessment, see Wareham, "The Challenges of Self-Assessment" in Wareham and Power (eds), op. cit., at fn. 2, pp. 119–142.

Conditions for exemption under Article 101(3)

Contribution to improving the production or distribution of goods or promoting economic or technical progress

10.106 There must be a contribution to improving the production or distribution of goods or promoting economic or technical progress. This criterion is usually easily satisfied but is not enough on its own. There must a benefit which is objectively valuable to the EU as a whole. The advantages in the arrangement must outweigh the disadvantages.[214]

Fair share to the consumers

10.107 There must be a fair share of the benefit resulting from the arrangement reaching the consumer. In this situation, the "consumer" does not necessarily mean the private/personal consumer but instead means the user of the product or service. So, in this context, the term "consumer" could mean a business or a company (i.e. a consumer of goods or services) such as the shipper of goods.

No indispensable restrictions

10.108 There must be no indispensable restrictions. This does not mean however that there cannot be any restriction: for example, in research and development agreements, it may be indispensable for parent undertakings to agree to refrain from research in an area entrusted to a jointly owned subsidiary. However, it does mean that only indispensable restrictions are included. This elementary indispensability is often a difficult standard to reach in practice (i.e. proving that a restriction is indispensable). Many exemptions are not possible because this particular limb is not satisfied.

No substantial elimination of competition

10.109 An arrangement which *substantially* eliminates competition will not deserve an exemption. In *Re WANO Schwarzpulver GmbH*,[215] the Commission refused an exemption in respect of an agreement which would have sealed off the UK market to further infiltration from elsewhere in the EU.

Individual exemptions

10.110 It has been no longer possible to obtain an individual exemption since 1 May 2004. Before that date, under Article 9(1) of Regulation 17/62, the Commission had the exclusive power to grant individual exemptions from the sanction of voidness in Article 101(2) in respect of arrangements individually notified to the Commission and which fell within the scope of Article 101(3).[216] The Commission's decision on the issue of granting

---

214 Cases 56, 58/64 *Consten and Grundig v Commission* [1966] ECR 429, ECLI:EU:C:1966:41.
215 Comm. Dec. 78/921 OJ 1978 L322/26.
216 Reg. 17/62 did not apply to international maritime services because of Reg. 4056/86.

an individual exemption was subject to review by the General Court/CJEU. The Commission did not have enough staff to deal with all the possible applications for individual exemptions so the granting of individual exemptions was extremely rare relative to the number of notifications seeking exemption. The granting of *block* exemptions and the informal settlement of cases (through the use of "comfort letters" and occasional "discomfort letters") provided a partial but imperfect solution. Since 1 May 2004, parties to arrangements must "self-assess" whether their arrangements comply with Article 101(3).

Block exemptions

Introduction

10.111 The Commission may, under the powers conferred on it by the Council and on occasion, Parliament, issue block exemptions. These block exemptions are in the form of block exemption regulations (so-called "BERs"). Any arrangement falling within the scope of a block exemption is valid under Article 101 without specific further authorisation by the Commission. Individual arrangements should (where possible) be drafted in such a way as to benefit from a block exemption.[217] If a block exemption does not apply then the parties to the arrangement must make their own decision as to whether the arrangement complies with EU competition law. A block exemption normally (but not always) contains three types of clauses: white; black; and grey. White clauses are those provisions of an arrangement which are valid vis-à-vis the block exemption. Black clauses are those which, if included in the particular agreement, will remove the agreement from the benefit of the block exemption. Grey clauses are those which do not usually fall within Article 101 but are included in the block exemption for the purposes of certainty. So as to benefit from a block exemption, an arrangement must come within the generic type envisaged by the Commission when it issued the block exemption. This is the so-called issue of "characterisation".[218] A useful working definition of a block exemption was provided in a memorandum issued by the Commission at the time of its proposals in 2008 to amend the consortia block exemption regime:

"What is an EU block exemption?
A block exemption Regulation (BER) defines types of agreements which are compatible with EU competition rules provided that the agreements meet the conditions laid down in the Regulation. In the absence of a block exemption, companies must assess for themselves whether their agreements are compatible with the [TFEU]'s ban on restrictive business practices (Article [101]). A block exemption Regulation needs to be assessed at regular intervals, in order to determine whether the conditions which originally justified it, continue to exist."[219]

10.112 Block exemption regulations are reviewed regularly – the exception to this approach was Regulation 4056/86 which had no provision in it for regular review – so, for example, the block exemption regulation for consortia adopted in 1995 was amended

---

217 E.g. lawyers to shipping companies using consortia need to be particularly conversant with, for example, the consortia block exemption.
218 See e.g. Comm. Dec. 80/1334 *Italian Cast Glass* OJ 1980 L383/19.
219 MEMO/08/644.

in 2000,[220] 2005[221] and 2009.[222] Typically, there are changes in the block exemption regulation each time it is amended.

10.113 The interesting feature of Regulation 4056/86 in the shipping sector was that it was a Council block exemption rather than a Commission block exemption but virtually every other block exemption was, and is, a Commission instrument. It has been suggested from time to time that the Commission had been uncomfortable with the block exemption in Regulation 4056/86 because it was adopted by the Council and sought to limit its application accordingly but it is more likely that the Commission was uncomfortable with Regulation 4056/86 because it permitted practices (e.g. price-fixing) which the Commission has long since condemned.

Examples

10.114 Regulation 4056/86[223] was the block exemption for liner conferences. There are now block exemptions on matters as diverse as insurance, consortia,[224] specialisation as well as research and development.[225] While Regulation 4056/86 has been repealed, there are other block exemptions which may apply in specific circumstances such as those relating to consortia,[226] insurance, specialisation and so on so an advisor would be wise to consider the potential application of other block exemptions as well to a situation facing the advisor.

Arbitration

10.115 Article 101 is capable of being pleaded by individuals before Member State courts as it has direct effect. It is also capable of being pleaded in arbitration. Indeed, both courts and arbitrators must apply Article 101 where it applies.[227]

E. ARTICLE 102 OF THE TFEU: ABUSE OF DOMINANCE

Introduction

10.116 Article 102 of the TFEU prohibits the abuse of dominance[228] by any undertaking having a dominant position in the internal market or in any substantial part of the internal market. It therefore controls any abuse of market power or exclusionary or

---

220 Reg. 823/2000 OJ 2000 L100/24.
221 Reg. 611/2005 OJ 2005 L101/10.
222 Reg. 906/2009 OJ 2009 L256/31.
223 OJ 1986 L378/3.
224 Reg. 906/2009 on the application of Art. 101(3) of the Treaty to certain categories of agreements, decisions and concerted practices between liner shipping companies (consortia) OJ 2009 L256/31 but now extended: see chap. 14.
225 See www.ec.europa.eu/competition/index_en.html
226 See Reg. 906/2009 OJ 2009 L256/31.
227 Case C-126/97 *Eco-Swiss China Time Ltd v Benetton International NV* [1999] ECR I-3055, ECLI:EU:C:1999:269. See Nazzini, "International Arbitration and Public Enforcement of Competition Law" [2004] ECLR 153. The same applies with respect to Art. 102.
228 Dominance has an economic meaning or dimension which must be respected.

exploitative behaviour by dominant undertakings.[229] In essence, Article 102 provides that any *abuse* by one or more undertakings of a dominant position within the internal market or in a substantial part thereof is prohibited as being incompatible with the internal market in so far as it may affect trade between Member States. The article is designed to control the abusive exercise of monopoly as well as oligopolistic power and is complementary to Article 101.

10.117 Article 102 does not prevent the *existence* of dominance but it does prohibit the *abuse* of dominance by an undertaking of any size.[230] It is important to highlight that, unlike Article 101, Article 102 does not have an exemption procedure and thus a breach of Article 102 is incurable by way of exemption. It is interesting to recall that the first formal decision by the Commission in relation to what is now Article 102 was not taken until 1971 – 14 years after the signing of the Treaty; this was the *GEMA* decision.[231] Since 1971, Article 102 has been applied quite frequently and sometimes controversially.[232] Article 102 is as relevant to small undertakings as large ones: size is not the determinant but rather market power is the key.[233] Irrespective of the undertaking's absolute size, whenever an undertaking has a dominant position then it has a special responsibility not to abuse the dominance.

Text of Article 102

10.118 Article 102 of the TFEU provides:

"Any abuse by one or more undertakings of a dominant position within the internal market or in a substantial part of it shall be prohibited as incompatible with the internal market in so far as it may affect trade between Member States. Such abuse may, in particular, consist in:

(a) directly or indirectly imposing unfair purchase or selling prices or unfair trading conditions;
(b) limiting production, markets or technical development to the prejudice of consumers;
(c) applying dissimilar conditions to equivalent transactions with other trading parties, thereby placing them at a competitive disadvantage;
(d) making the conclusion of contracts subject to acceptance by the other parties of supplementary obligations which, by their nature or according to commercial usage, have no connection with the subject of such contracts."

---

229 On Art. 102 of the TFEU see O'Donoghue and Padilla, *The Law and Economics of Article 102 TFEU* (2013). See also Korah, "Interpretation and Application of Article 82 of the Treaty of Rome: Abuse of Dominant Position within the Common Market" [1978] 53 Notre Dame Lawyer 768; Temple Lang, "Monopolisation and the Definition of Abuse of a Dominant Position under Article 82 EEC Treaty" (1979) 16 CMLRev 345. See also Van Bael and Bellis, op. cit. at fn. 2, ch. 8. See also Communication from the Commission – Guidance on the Commission's enforcement priorities in applying Art. 82 of the EC Treaty to abusive exclusionary conduct by dominant undertakings OJ 2009 C45/7.

230 It is important to recall that an undertaking could be abusing its dominant position without necessarily having a monopoly or without it being a very large undertaking in terms of turnover. Dominance is not a factor of the absolute size of the undertaking but rather it is related to the relative market power held by the undertaking.

231 JO 1971 L134/15.

232 E.g. the *Microsoft* and *Intel* cases.

233 E.g. the cases have sometimes involved quite small undertakings. E.g. in a shipping context, the Chambre de Commerce et Industries in Morlaix in the *Roscoff* case: [1995] 5 CMLR 177.

Importance of economic evidence

10.119 Economic evidence is critical in all competition cases generally but it is particularly so in Article 102 cases[234] and therefore lawyers contemplating bringing proceedings under that provision are well advised to seek the opinions of economists at an early stage in the proceedings. This advice applies to all involved in all competition cases but particularly so in the case of abuse of dominance cases.

Interpretation of Article 102

10.120 The CJEU and the General Court have made clear in a number of cases that Article 102 must be interpreted by having regard to the spirit, general scheme and wording of the provision as well as to the general objectives of the TFEU itself.[235]

Economic rationale for Article 102

10.121 Korah has incisively set out the economic rationale for Article 102 in the following terms:

"[t]he objection to market power[236] expressed by economists is that a firm,[237] not sufficiently constrained by competitive pressures, may be able to operate inefficiently for long periods, or earn high profits, through charging higher prices than would be possible in more competitive conditions. The higher prices would reduce demand, so that some buyers, who would have been willing to pay the cost (including a normal profit on the funds employed) of an efficient operator, will be disappointed. The resources, that in terms of consumer demand might have been more usefully employed in making the monopolised product, would be devoted to less strongly desired uses. Classical economists objected to the discretion enjoyed by a monopolist. The emphasis of modern economics is even more general, and is focused upon the wide discretion enjoyed by firms with market power to pursue a variety of goals and to choose a range of productive means, unconstrained within wide limits by market pressures. In a more competitive market, each firm is limited by the value for money provided by other firms. In most markets many firms may enjoy some discretion over their production and marketing strategies, but this is not the general independence that enables high prices to be maintained over long periods."[238]

Check-list for the application of Article 102

10.122 Article 102 is somewhat curiously drafted. It would thus be useful to construct a check-list of the conditions which must be satisfied before Article 102 can be successfully applied:

---

234 E.g. on issues of market definition, dominance and abuse.
235 Case 6/72 *Europemballage Corpn and Continental Can Co Inc v Commission* [1973] ECR 215, ECLI:EU:C:1973:22; Joined Cases 6, 7/73 *Instituto Chemioterapico Italiano SpA and Commercial Solvents Corpn v Commission* [1974] ECR 223, ECLI:EU:C:1974:18; Case 27/76 *United Brands Co v Commission* [1978] ECR 207, ECLI:EU:C:1978:22; Case 85/76 *Hoffmann-La Roche and Co AG v Commission* [1979] ECR 461, ECLI:EU:C:1979:36; and Case 322/81 *Nederlandsche Banden-Industrie Michelin NV v Commission* [1983] ECR 3461, ECLI:EU:C:1983:313. On the interpretation generally of Art. 102 of the TFEU, see Korah, "Interpretation and Application of Article 82 of the Treaty of Rome: Abuse of Dominant Position within the Common Market" [1978] 53 Notre Dame Lawyer 768.
236 Ed., i.e. dominance in this context.
237 Ed., i.e. an undertaking.
238 Op. cit. at fn. 235, p. 109.

(1) is the entity involved an "undertaking"?;
(2) does the undertaking have a "dominant position"?;
(3) does the undertaking have a dominant position in "the internal market or a substantial part of it"?;
(4) is there an "abuse" of that dominant position?; and
(5) is it possible that the abuse may have an "effect on trade" between Member States?

Undertakings

10.123 Most of what was written above in relation to undertakings in the context of Article 101 is also relevant in the context of Article 102. Some points must, however, be made on the concept of an "undertaking" when used in the context of Article 102. First, an undertaking which has a "dominant position" conferred on it by law (e.g. by way of legislation creating a statutory monopoly) is still an undertaking and falls within the scope of Article 102.[239] Second, as a general rule, no Member State may confer an immunity from Article 102 on an undertaking by conferring on it certain legal privileges. This is based on the duties imposed on a Member State by virtue of EU law. The sole exception to this rule is in regard to the limited privileges which a Member State may confer on an undertaking by virtue of Article 106(2) of the TFEU. This sole exception is also a very limited one in that the Commission and the courts interpret the exception quite narrowly. Third, the dominant position may be held by one undertaking (i.e. a monopoly[240] or monopsony[241]) or it may be held by two or a relatively small number of undertakings (i.e. a duopoly or an oligopoly[242] or oligopsony[243]).

Concept of a dominant position or dominance and a further analysis of market definition

10.124 Article 102 applies to situations where there has been, or is, an abuse of a dominant position. Thus, it is critical to determine, among other things, what constitutes a dominant position. Dominance can only be determined in respect of a particular market – it is not an abstract concept. There is a wealth of judicial as well as academic[244] discussion on the concept and thus what is presented here is merely a précis of that discussion.

---

239 Case 311/84 *Centre Belge d'Etudes de Marche Tele-Marketing v CLT*; Case 26/75 *General Motors v Commission* [1975] ECR 1367, ECLI:EU:C:1975:150 and Case 41/83 *Italy v Commission* [1985] ECR 873, ECLI:EU:C:1985:120.
240 I.e. market with one seller.
241 I.e. market with one buyer.
242 I.e. market with few sellers.
243 I.e. market with few buyers.
244 See, among many others, Lovdahl Gormsen, *A Principled Approach to Abuse of Dominance in European Competition Law* (2010) and O'Donoghue and Padilla, op. cit. at fn. 229. See also Baden Fuller, "Article 82 EEC: Economic Analysis of the Existence of a Dominant Position" (1979) 4 ELRev 423; Gyselen and Kyriakis, "Article 82 EEC: The Monopoly Power Measurement Issue Revisited" (1986) 11 ELRev 134; and Korah, "Concept of a Dominant Position within the meaning of Article 82" (1980) 17 CMLRev 395.

There is no definition of dominance in the TFEU

10.125 The TFEU does not define the concept of "dominant position". Interestingly, Article 66(7) of the now expired European Coal and Steel Community ("ECSC") Treaty, which was the comparable provision for the purposes of the ECSC to Article 102 of the TFEU, included a definition. Article 66(7) of the ECSC Treaty provided:

> "If the High Authority [i.e. now the Commission] finds that public or private undertakings which, in law or in fact, hold or acquire in the market for one of the products within its jurisdiction a *dominant position shielding them against effective competition* in a substantial part of the common market[245] are using that position for purposes contrary to the objectives of this Treaty, it shall make to them such recommendations as may be appropriate to prevent the position from being so used. If these recommendations are not implemented satisfactorily within a reasonable time, the High Authority[246] shall, by decisions taken in consultation with the Government concerned, determine the prices and conditions of sale to be applied by the undertaking in question to draw up production or delivery programmes with which it must comply, subject to liability to the penalties provided for in Articles 58, 59 and 64 [of the ECSC Treaty]." (Emphasis added.)

So, in the context of the ECSC Treaty, dominance was seen as being shielded from effective competition. However, the European Economic Community ("EEC"), European Community ("EC"), EU and TFEU treaties have never sought to define dominance but the ECSC definition was an interesting starting point.

The definition used by the EU institutions

Introduction

10.126 The CJEU has in a number of cases[247] attempted[248] to determine what constitutes a dominant position and its view may be summarised by the words which it used in *Michelin v Commission* to define dominance as:

> "a position of economic strength enjoyed by an undertaking which enables it to hinder the maintenance of effective competition on the relevant market by allowing it to behave to an appreciable extent independently of its competitors and customers and ultimately of consumers".[249]

In essence, this means the power to act independently of competitors and consumers or to be able to effectively eliminate competition.

10.127 In *Continental Can*[250] the CJEU said:

> "[u]ndertakings are in a dominant position when they have the power to behave independently, which puts them in a position to act without taking into account their competitors, purchasers or suppliers. That is a position when, because of their share of the market, or of their share of the market combined with the availability of technical knowledge, raw materials or capital, they

---

245 Ed., the "common market" is now the "internal market".
246 Ed., the High Authority is now known as the Commission.
247 E.g. Case 27/76 *United Brands v Commission* [1978] ECR 207, ECLI:EU:C:1978:22; Case 85/76 *Hoffmann-La Roche v Commission* [1979] ECR 461, ECLI:EU:C:1979:36; Case 31/80 *L'Oreal NV v De Nieuwe AMCK PVBA* [1980] ECR 3775, ECLI:EU:C:1980:289; and Case 322/81 *Nederlandsche Banden-Industrie Michelin NV v Commission* [1983] ECR 3461, ECLI:EU:C:1983:313.
248 This is an ongoing process.
249 Case 322/81 [1983] ECR 3461, ECLI:EU:C:1983:313. See also Case 27/76 *United Brands v Commission* [1978] ECR 207, [1978] 1 CMLR 429.
250 Case 6/72 [1973] ECR 215, ECLI:EU:C:1973:22.

have the power to determine prices or to control production or distribution for a significant part of the products in question. This power does not necessarily have to derive from an absolute domination permitting the undertakings which hold it to eliminate all will on the part of their economic partners, but it is enough that they be strong enough as a whole to ensure to those undertakings an overall independence of behaviour, even if there are differences in intensity in their influence on the different partial markets."

10.128 The CJEU defined dominance in *United Brands v Commission* in the following terms:

"[t]he dominant position referred to in [Article 102] relates to a position of economic strength enjoyed by an undertaking which enables it to prevent effective competition being maintained on the relevant market by giving it the power to behave to an appreciable extent independently of its competitors, customers and ultimately of its competitors".[251]

10.129 Joint or collective dominance (rather than individual dominance) was defined in *Compagnie Maritime Belge Transports SA v Commission*: "[by] its nature and in light of its objectives, a liner conference ... can be characterised as a collective entity which presents itself as such on the market vis-à-vis both users and competitors".[252]

10.130 The General Court delivered in 2002 its judgement in *Airtours/First Choice*[253] where it set out a three-step procedure for a finding of collective dominance. According to the court, three criteria must be fulfilled:

(a) the existence of market transparency that each member of the oligopoly follows the same common policy;
(b) the existence of co-ordinated behaviour; and
(c) the guarantee that the current and prospective competitors could not overthrow the common policy implementation.

The Court stated in paragraph 61 of the judgment:

"A collective dominant position significantly impeding effective competition in the [internal] market or a substantial part of it may thus arise as the result of a concentration where, in view of the actual characteristics of the relevant market and of the alteration in its structure that the transaction would entail, the latter would make each member of the dominant oligopoly, as it becomes aware of common interests, consider it possible, economically rational, and hence preferable, to adopt on a lasting basis a common policy on the market with the aim of selling at above competitive prices, without having to enter into an agreement or resort to a concerted practice within the meaning of Article [101 TFEU] ... and without any actual or potential competitors, let alone customers or consumers, being able to react effectively."

10.131 Dominance is to be decided in each case. It is a question of fact. Market share is not in itself the sole determinant of the issue. Typically, undertakings which have over 40% of the market and have market shares considerably larger than other undertakings in that market could be regarded as being prima facie dominant but the test of dominance needs to be applied carefully (conversely, undertakings in a market share of less than 40% would rarely be seen as being dominant). What are the factors which the courts and the Commission/competition agencies take into account in determining the existence or non-existence of dominance? A non-exhaustive list of some of the attributes of dominance would, it is

---

251 Case 27/76 [1978] ECR 207, ECLI:EU:C:1978:22, para. 65.
252 Cases C-395/96 and C-396/96 P [2000] ECR I-1365, ECLI:EU:C:2000:132 (para.65).
253 Case T-342/99 *Airtours v Commission* [2002] ECR II-2585, ECLI:EU:T:2004:192.

submitted, include a high degree of vertical integration, a technological lead, significant intellectual property rights, a highly developed sales network and the absence of potential competition.[254] However, not all of these factors need to be present in any particular case. Regard must be had to the relevant product, geographical and temporal markets.

10.132 Reflecting the jurisprudence of the EU institutions, Temple Lang has written with characteristic perception:

> "a dominant position is economic power, due to lack of competition, of which the holder can take advantage to impede effective competition. An enterprise may have a dominant position, even if effective competition has not been eliminated. To determine whether a dominant position exists, all facts tending to prove or disprove the market power of the enterprise must be taken into account. The effect of a series of findings may be cumulative, especially if only one enterprise on the market enjoys all the competitive advantages considered. No single fact is necessarily decisive."[255]

Relevant product market

10.133 Dominance does not exist in the abstract or in a vacuum. It is necessary to determine the relevant product or services[256] market. The relevant product market is seen as comprising all those products and/or services which are regarded as interchangeable by the consumer, by reasons of the products' characteristics, prices and intended uses. Defining the market is often critical. The CJEU quashed the Commission's decision in the *Continental Can*[257] case because the Commission did not define properly the relevant product market. The Commission has now become more careful and, while a number of challenges have been brought on the basis of the Commission's determinations on "relevant product markets", the CJEU/General Court does not readily quash the Commission's determinations on this point.[258]

10.134 It is clear from the judgments that "interchangeability" is the essential element in the definition of the relevant product market: if goods or services can be interchanged then they are within the same product market. Thus, the CJEU said in *Continental Can v Commission* that it was necessary to look at those "characteristics of the products in question by virtue of which they are particularly apt to satisfy an inelastic need and are only to a limited extent interchangeable with other products".[259] The CJEU said in *United Brands v Commission*[260] that the issue of whether a product market existed turned on whether the product (in that case, bananas) can be "singled out by such special features distinguishing it from other fruits that it is only to a limited extent interchangeable with them and is only exposed to their competition in a way that is hardly perceptible". In determining

---

254 No distinction is made between services and goods in this context.
255 "Some Aspects of Abuse of Dominant Position in European Community Antitrust Law" (1979–1980) 3 Fordham Int'l LJ 1 at p. 4.
256 See Comm. Dec. 89/113 *Decca Navigator Systems* OJ 1989 L43/27.
257 Case 6/72 [1973] ECR 215, ECLI:EU:C:1973:22, para. 32.
258 Cases 6, 7/73 *ICI and Commercial Solvents v Commission* [1974] ECR 223, ECLI:EU:C:1974:18; Case 27/76 *United Brands v Commission* [1978] ECR 207, ECLI:EU:C:1978:22; and Case 322/81 *Nederlandsche Banden-Industrie Michelin v Commission* [1983] ECR 3461, ECLI:EU:C:1983:317.
259 Case 6/72 [1973] ECR 215, ECLI:EU:C:1973:22, para. 32. In Case 66/86 *Ahmed Saeed* [1989] ECR 803, ECLI:EU:C:1989:40, paras 39 and 40, the CJEU said (in relation to a scheduled flight and the issue of dominance): "the test to be employed is whether the scheduled flight on a particular route can be distinguished from the possible alternatives by virtue of specific characteristics as a result of which it is not interchangeable with those alternatives and is affected only to an insignificant degree by competition from them".
260 Case 27/76 [1978] ECR 207, ECLI:EU:C:1978:22.

interchangeability, regard must be had to, among other things, both demand-side and supply-side interchangeability where relevant and accurate evidence is available.[261] The emphasis is, however, on the demand-side interchangeability.

10.135 The physical characteristics of the goods involved in the market should be taken into account so as to test interchangeability. Thus, for example, in *United Brands v Commission*,[262] the CJEU took into account such physical characteristics of bananas (which were the goods in question in the case) as their taste, softness, consumption by the old and sick, seedlessness and handling quality.

10.136 It is also useful in determining the relevant product market, to establish what is the intended use to which the product may be put by the user. Thus, if a consumer requires a product for a particular purpose then that product will be within the same market only as products which satisfy the same purpose.[263] Thus, spare parts may form a separate market from the products for which they are needed or even some spare parts may be distinguishable from the machine itself.[264] So clearly, an oil tanker is not substitutable for a car ferry but the latter may be in three markets (at least): foot passengers; car passengers; and haulage freight. In determining the relevant product market, it is often useful to examine the structure of supply and demand on a market. Thus, in *Nederlandsche Banden-Industrie Michelin v Commission*[265] the CJEU found that the replacement tyre market was a distinct market from the new tyre market because replacement tyres were fitted in different circumstances from new tyres. Indeed raw material may constitute a separate product market from the finished product.[266]

10.137 Cross-elasticity of demand is high where an increase in the price of one product causes a significant switch by consumers to another product. Cross-elasticity is low where an increase in the price of one product will not cause a significant switch by consumers to another product. Thus, for example, if an increase in the price of one shipping service ("Service X") will probably cause an increase in the demand for other cheaper services ("Service Y" and "Service Z"). Thus, Services X, Y and Z are cross-elastic (i.e. cross-elasticity is high). On the other hand, an increase in the price of a shipping service ("Service X") will not cause consumers to switch from buying a more expensive newspaper ("Title A") to a cheaper one ("Title B"). Thus, there is no cross-elasticity of demand between Service X and Titles A and B. Products are not always interchangeable simply on the basis of price; an expensive luxury car may have the same essential physical characteristics as a cheap basic car, but the two would not necessarily be interchangeable at all.

10.138 The relevant product market may occasionally be neatly defined by means of legislation.[267] Thus, in *British Leyland v Commission*[268] the market (which was approval certificates for imported motor vehicles) was held in law by British Leyland in respect of British Leyland vehicles and no one else could interfere hence the market was easy to define and dominance easy to establish.

---

261 Case 6/72 *Continental Can v Commission* [1973] ECR 215, ECLI:EU:C:1973:22.
262 Case 27/76 [1978] ECR 207.
263 See Case 6/72 *Europemballage Corpn and Continental Can v Commission* [1973] ECR 215, ECLI:EU:C:1973:22 and Case 22/78 *Hugin v Commission* [1979] ECR 1869, ECLI:EU:C:1979:138.
264 Case 22/78 *Hugin v Commission* [1979] ECR 1869.
265 Case 322/81 [1983] ECR 3461, ECLI:EU:C:1983:313.
266 Cases 6, 7/73 *Commercial Solvents v Commission* [1974] ECR 223, ECLI:EU:C:1974:18.
267 E.g. a national or EU law may limit the use to which a product may be put by the user.
268 Case 226/84 [1986] ECR 3263, ECLI:EU:C:1986:421.

10.139 Occasionally, the Commission and the courts may have recourse to extrinsic evidence to define markets. This evidence may take the form of marketing plans or documents. Thus, for example, in *BBI/Boosey and Hawkes (Interim Measures)*[269] the Commission took into account internal documents in which Boosey and Hawkes identified a discrete or distinct market for *British* brass band musical instruments as opposed to brass musical instruments generally.

10.140 Supply-side substitutability should also be taken into account in some cases. This means that the market would be examined from the supplier's perspective.[270] This is, however, of limited relevance as far as most cases are concerned. In shipping cases, it will (as in all cases) depend on the facts but it may be a distinct market such as cruise liner services or ferry services or as broad as ro-ro/lo-lo where the circumstances permit. A shipping company with lo-lo ships would be in a different market from passenger cruising because it could not simply substitute its lo-lo ships for cruise liners but a lo-lo operator may overlap in a market with a ro-ro operator.

Relevant geographical market

10.141 The relevant geographical market must also be determined in Article 102 cases just as it is in Article 101 cases. There must be an area in which the goods or services are sold and in which the objective conditions of competition are the same for all competitors.[271] The geographical market in question must be either the internal market or a substantial part of the internal market if Article 102 is to apply. The market may be the whole of the EU,[272] but the market does not have to be geographically enormous: it could be, for example, two Member States (e.g. a route between the UK and Ireland) or even just a single State or even a single port.[273] Suffice it to say that if an undertaking operates on a localised basis then it may still possess power over that market.[274] The geographical market can sometimes be drawn easily. In *British Telecommunications*[275] the market was defined easily as it related to where particular telecommunications services were available. A particular ferry route may be the relevant geographical market.[276] In the ferry

---

269 OJ 1987 L286/36.
270 Case 6/72 *Continental Can v Commission* [1973] ECR 215, ECLI:EU:C:1973:22.
271 See Comm. Dec. 89/113 *Decca Navigator Systems* OJ 1989 L43/27. The CJEU described it in Case 27/76 *United Brands* [1978] ECR 207, ECLI:EU:C:1978:22 as "where the conditions of competition are sufficiently homogenous for the effect of economic power on the undertakings to be evaluated".
272 As in *Hilti* OJ 1988 L65/19.
273 See *B&I Line/Sealink Harbours Ltd* OJ L15/8, 18 January 1994, [1992] 5 CMLR 255; Comm. Dec. 94/19 *Sea Containers/Stena Sealink* OJ Case IV/35.388; and *Irish Continental Group plc/Chambre de Commerce et Industries de Morlaix* [1995] 5 CMLR 177.
274 See Commission, *Tenth Report on Competition Policy*, point 57.
275 Comm. Dec. 82/861 OJ 1982 L360/36, [1983] 1 CMLR 457 (upheld on appeal Case 41/83 *Italy v Commission* [1985] ECR 873, ECLI:EU:T:2000:91).
276 In answer to a written question in the European Parliament (Written Question 1377/83 at OJ 1984 C38/37), the Commission stated that the Harwich/Hook of Holland route was not a substantial part of the internal market but this view is open to serious doubt given subsequent cases. It is interesting to note that the Commission may be prepared to treat as a "substantial part" the market for the whole of a Member State's liner trade with certain non-EU states, which constitutes a substantial part of the trade between those States and the EU as a whole, because that State is the largest EU trading partner with the States concerned (e.g. the investigations into West and Central African trades referred to in the Commission's *Nineteenth Competition report*, para. 28) – for further details, see Clough and Randolph, op. cit. at fn. 2, para. 3.2.6.2, fn. 2.

cases, the geographical markets have been defined very narrowly.²⁷⁷ A particular route, sector or corridor may be the relevant geographical market where the route, sector or corridor exhibits all the characteristics of a specific market such as there is no substitutability or very limited substitutability with other routes, sectors or corridors. For example, in *Irish Continental Group/Chambre de Commerce et Industries de Morlaix*²⁷⁸ the relevant geographical market was Ireland to Brittany and not Ireland to France generally. In general, the Commission has adopted narrow geographical market definitions in passenger cases presumably because passengers generally tend to prefer shorter (rather than longer) sea crossings. While those cases were interim measure decisions (and therefore taken at some speed) and in an era when economic techniques were not deployed as rigorously as they are now, they appear to be broadly correct decisions.

Relevant temporal market

10.142 In determining the existence (or non-existence) of dominance, regard must be had to the temporal dimension of the market (as one does in regard to Article 101). An undertaking may, for example, be exposed to competition for parts of the year but entirely immune from it at other times of the year. This may be the case in such markets as fruit²⁷⁹ or heating oil.²⁸⁰ In the context of shipping, there may be certain seasonal trades and therefore this temporal dimension could be important (e.g. summer cruising) but, in practice, the temporal dimension rarely proves controversial.

Dominance/market power

Introduction

10.143 It is also necessary to determine whether or not the undertaking has sufficient market power as to be dominant. In *United Brands v Commission*,²⁸¹ the CJEU stated that dominance

> "relates to a position of economic strength enjoyed by an undertaking which enables it to prevent effective competition being maintained on the relevant market by affording it the power to behave to an appreciable extent independently of its competitors, customers and ultimately of its consumers".

Measuring market power

10.144 If a legal monopoly exists then the undertaking presumably has sufficient market power as to be regarded as dominant. It is clear from *Italy v Commission*²⁸² and

---

277 See *B&I Line/Sealink Harbours Ltd* OJ L15/8, 18 January 1994, [1992] 5 CMLR 255; Comm. Dec. 94/19 *Sea Containers/Stena Sealink* OJ Case IV/35.388; and *Irish Continental Group plc/Chambre de Commerce et Industries de Morlaix* [1995] 5 CMLR 177.
278 [1995] 1 CMLR 177.
279 Case 27/76 *United Brands v Commission* [1978] ECR 207, ECLI:EU:C:1978:22.
280 Comm. Dec. 77/327 *ABG* OJ 1977 L117/1.
281 Case 27/76 [1978] ECR 207, ECLI:EU:C:1978:22.
282 Case 41/83 [1985] ECR 873, ECLI:EU:T:2000:91.

Centre Belge d'Etudes de Marche Tele-Marketing v CLT[283] that notwithstanding that the undertaking has been granted a legal monopoly, it is still subject to Article 102, except in so far as it is in any way protected by Article 106(2) of the TFEU.

Market shares

10.145 Market share is an important (but not the sole) determinant of market power. As a simple rule, the larger the market share, the greater chance of dominance existing. A market share of 100% would almost inevitably constitute dominance.[284] A large market share is not in itself the sole determinant of dominance. An undertaking may have a large market share but may be selling its products at a highly marginal price. The CJEU said in *Hoffmann-La Roche v Commission*:

> "[f]urthermore although the importance of the market shares may vary from one market to another the view may legitimately be taken that very large shares are in themselves, and save in exceptional circumstances, evidence of the existence of a dominant position. An undertaking which has a very large market share and holds it for some time … is by virtue of that share in a position of strength."[285]

The Commission might well, however, place great reliance on market shares in a case where interim measures are sought and the Commission has to move quickly.[286] In such cases and in cases where the Commission and the courts are placing great emphasis on the market share, it is highly possible that a share of 40% to 45% or more would constitute dominance. There is a common view that market share of over 50% would be indicative usually of dominance.

Barriers to entry and/or barriers to expansion and/or barriers to exit

10.146 Market share is not the only determinant of dominance: it is necessary to look at other "barriers to entry". The Commission and the courts have interpreted the concept of a "barrier to entry" quite widely. If it is difficult to enter a market because of high barriers to entry and/or exit then incumbents could be dominant. The same applies to barriers to expansion or barriers to exit.

Economies of scale

10.147 The CJEU was willing in *United Brands v Commission*[287] to take into account "economies of scale" as a form of barrier to entry and thus as a factor in determining dominance. It is not just the courts who use the test. The Commission is also willing to take the economies of scale into account in determining the existence of dominance.[288]

---

283 Case 311/84 [1985] ECR 3261, ECLI:EU:C:1985:394.
284 See Comm. Dec. *GVL* OJ 1981 L370/49. However, if the 100% market share could disappear easily then the apparent dominance could be illusionary (e.g. in a market where the exclusive right to provide ferry services is tendered annually then the dominance could be more apparent than real).
285 Case 85/76 [1979] ECR 461, ECLI:EU:C:1979:36. See Case 27/76 *United Brands v Commission* [1978] ECR 207, ECLI:EU:C:1978:22, paras 65 and 66.
286 *ECS/AKZO* OJ 1983 L252/13.
287 Case 27/76 [1978] ECR 207, ECLI:EU:C:1978:22.
288 Comm. Dec. 89/22 *BPB Industries plc* OJ 1989 L10/50.

Evidence of the undertakings

10.148 The undertakings themselves could (externally and/or internally) express themselves to be dominant and such evidence can be useful but not determinative. In *BBI/ Boosey and Hawkes: Interim Measures*[289] the managers of Boosey and Hawkes wrote that its instruments were "automatically [the] first choice" of all the brass bands in Britain – such a statement would not be conclusive of dominance but it would be interesting and form part of the analysis.

Price movements

10.149 The fact that an undertaking was able to raise its prices unilaterally, with the market following suit and it did not care whether they did follow suit or not, could very well indicate dominance.[290]

Conduct

10.150 The conduct of the undertaking is relevant and admissible in determining whether or not it is in a dominant position in the market place.[291] This is somewhat circular: if it can act in a way which would amount to an abuse of dominance then it could well be dominant but it is not clear because a non-dominant undertaking could engage in below cost selling which would be an abuse of dominance if the undertaking were dominant but it is not an abuse of dominance if it were not dominant.

Overall strength and size of the undertaking(s)

10.151 Just because an undertaking is large does not mean that it is dominant, for example, small ports have been held to be dominant. Nonetheless, in *Hoffmann-La Roche v Commission*,[292] the Commission did take into account the size of the undertaking in question.

Legal provisions

10.152 National legal rules, such as intellectual property rights, can operate as barriers to entry and can be relevant in deciding whether dominance exists.[293]

Deep pocket

10.153 The existence of a relatively "deep pocket" on the part of an undertaking may, in practice, be regarded as evidence of dominance.[294]

---

289 Comm. Dec. 87/500 OJ 1987 L286/36, [1988] 4 CMLR 67, para. 18.
290 Comm. Dec. 88/518 *Napier Brown-British Sugar* OJ 1988 L284/41, para. 55.
291 See Case 27/76 *United Brands v Commission* [1978] ECR 207, ECLI:EU:C:1978:22, para. 122; Case 322/81 *Michelin v Commission* [1983] ECR 3461, ECLI:EU:C:1983:313 and Comm. Dec. 88/138 *Eurofix-Bauco v Hilti* OJ 1988 L65/19.
292 Case 85/76 [1979] ECR 461, ECLI:EU:C:1979:36.
293 Case 22/78 *Hugin v Commission* [1979] ECR 1869, ECLI:EU:C:1979:138.
294 Case 27/76 *United Brands v Commission* [1979] ECR 207, ECLI:EU:C:1978:22, para. 48.

Within the internal market or a substantial part of it

10.154 Having considered the element of "undertaking" and "dominant position", it is now appropriate to consider the concept of "within the internal market or a substantial part of it". If the dominant position is not in the whole or in a substantial part of the internal market then Article 102 cannot, by its own terms, apply. For example, dominance in Australia alone (i.e. entirely outside the EU) would be irrelevant to Article 102. However, the dominance could exist in a route or service between the EU and, say, Australia (so long as the EU was involved). The requirement to affect trade in the internal market or in a substantial part of it is a form of *de minimis* principle. If an undertaking (or undertakings) operates throughout the EU then there is little difficulty. If an undertaking (or undertakings) operates (or operate) in one Member State or in a part of a Member State then a number of points are worth remembering about the issue of "a substantial part of the internal market". First, each Member State is almost certainly "a substantial part of the internal market" for present purposes. Second, a part of a Member State may well constitute "a substantial part of the internal market" for present purposes.[295] In *Re European Sugar Cartel*, "Southern Germany" was held to constitute a "substantial part" of the internal market (presumably, it would be unreasonable to expect that a Member State would not constitute a substantial part of the internal market).[296] A port may constitute a substantial part of the internal market notwithstanding that it covers a small physical area because of the function which it serves (e.g. providing transport links to other parts of the internal market).[297] Third, there are no "fixed percentages". Indeed, in *BP v Commission*, the Advocate-General in the case (AG Warner) was of the opinion that the Dutch market for petrol – then 4.6% of the then EU total – constituted a substantial part of the internal market.[298]

Concept of "abuse of a dominant position"

10.155 Ultimately, Article 102 does not prohibit an undertaking from having or acquiring a dominant position as such; but it does prevent an undertaking *abusing* such a position. As the CJEU said in *Michelin v Commission*:[299]

> "A finding that an undertaking has a dominant position is not in itself a recrimination (*reproche*) but simply means that, irrespective of the reasons for which it has such a dominant position, the undertaking concerned has a special responsibility not to allow its conduct to impair genuine undistorted competition on the internal market."

This concept of a "special responsibility" is an extremely important concept in the law and practice relating to the abuse of dominance.

---

295 Case 40/73 *Suiker Unie v Commission* [1975] ECR 1663.
296 Comm. Dec. 73/109 OJ 1973 L140/17.
297 E.g. *B&I Line plc v Sealink Harbours Ltd*, ECLI:EU:C:1975:174; Comm. Dec. 94/19 *Sea Containers Ltd v Stena Sealink Ports*, Case IV/35.388; *Irish Continental Group PLC v Chambre de Commerce et Industries de Morlaix* [1995] 5 CMLR 177; and *Euro-Port A/S v Denmark* [1994] 5 CMLR 457, ECLI:EU:C:1975:174.
298 Case 77/77 [1978] ECR 1513.
299 Ibid.

Definition of abuse

10.156 Undertakings with a dominant position have a special responsibility not to weaken competition. Article 102 does not contain an exhaustive list of the "abuses" – the provision has in fact been applied to situations which are not set out expressly in the text. Nor does it define the concept of abuse. Juristically, the concept of abuse has been classified in different ways (e.g. exploitative and exclusionary abuses) but also into three branches: (a) anti-competitive abuses; (b) exploitative abuses; and (c) reprisal abuses. Temple Lang has offered the following view of the concept of abuse:

> "a dominant enterprise [can] act contrary to Article [102] for any of the following reasons: (1) if its behaviour takes advantage of economic power to obtain benefits or to impose burdens not obtainable or imposable in conditions of normal and reasonably effective competition, at the expense of the interests of customers or consumers (or, in the case or a dominant buyer, of suppliers). These are 'exploitative' abuses; (2) if its behaviour significantly restricts intra-brand or inter-brand competition, or alters the market in such a way that competition is likely to be significantly reduced, or increases or reinforces the dominant firm's economic power. However, normal and legitimate competition is lawful, even if it increases the market share or economic power of the dominant enterprise. These are 'anti-competitive' abuses; (3) if its behaviour is calculated to damage or seriously interfere with the business of another enterprise. If these abuses are to be regarded as a separate category, they can be called 'reprisal' abuses."[300]

10.157 Exploitation by an undertaking of its dominant position would normally constitute an abuse of its dominant position.[301] Article 102 also applies to anti-competitive behaviour. Such behaviour could be directed against new entrants or existing competitors. Thus, practices such as mergers which would be anti-competitive,[302] price discrimination,[303] requirements contracts and tie-ins,[304] export and import bans,[305] predatory pricing, delivered pricing, unjustified refusals to supply, loyalty arrangements whereby 100% loyalty contracts are imposed by dominant undertakings and disloyal shippers blacklisted would amount to an abuse of dominance and, unjustified refusals to supply[306] could be subject to the sanction of Article 102. The use of "fighting ships" by dominant undertakings would ordinarily be an abuse of dominance. The ships would involve: (a) ports of call and sailing times being deliberately altered to coincide with those of competitors – not so as to meet competition fairly but to do some damage to it; (b) freight rates being reduced not according to economic criteria but in order to be lower than competitors; and (c) losses suffered by the fighting ships are distributed between members of the conference or higher prices are imposed on other routes. Sometimes, an objective justification could convert what would have been an "abuse" of dominance into legitimate conduct but each case should be seen in its own right.

10.158 The significance of the concept of "abuse" is best seen in the context of "dominance" because the two concepts are so intertwined. Conduct which is "abusive" when practised by a dominant undertaking could well be perfectly lawful when practised by a

---

300 Op. cit. at fn. 255, pp. 363–364.
301 Comm. Dec. *British Telecommunications* OJ 1982 L360/36.
302 Cf. Case 6/72 *Europemballage Corpn and Continental Can Co. Inc. v Commission* [1973] ECR 215, ECLI:EU:C:1973:22.
303 See e.g. Comm. Dec. 82/861 *British Telecommunications* OJ [1982] L360/36.
304 Case 85/76 *Hoffmann-La Roche v Commission* [1979] ECR 461, ECLI:EU:C:1995:36.
305 Cf. Case 40/73 etc. *Suiker Unie v Commission* [1975] ECR 1663, ECLI:EU:C:1975:174.
306 Case 6/73 etc. *Commercial Solvents v Commission* [1974] ECR 223.

non-dominant undertaking. Such conduct is prohibited when practised by a dominant undertaking because of the negative impact of such conduct when practised by a dominant undertaking and there is the accompanying breach of the special responsibility by the dominant undertaking.

Effect on inter-State trade

10.159 It is submitted that the discussion above in relation to Article 101 relating to "effect on inter-State trade" is equally applicable to Article 102 and only one further point needs to be made in the present context. The CJEU stated in the course of its judgment in *Commercial Solvents v Commission*[307] that the requirement of having an effect on inter-State trade was satisfied where the conduct engaged in by the undertaking(s) resulted in an alteration of the structure of competition in the internal market. This is the so-called structural test. It has been applied by the Commission and the courts on a number of occasions – most notably, *United Brands v Commission*[308] and *London European-Sabena*.[309] It is submitted that it is the most suitable test for oligopolistic markets.

Example of Article 102 in practice: the Doctrine of Essential Facilities

10.160 The Doctrine of Essential Facilities is an important doctrine in competition law[310] and some of the most important cases in the EU on the doctrine have related to shipping.[311] It posits that an undertaking which owns or operates a facility or place (e.g. a port which is indispensable for others to compete) must provide access to that facility on reasonable terms where not to do so would be an abuse of dominance or anti-competitive. The doctrine could still be important but its utility seems limited by the *Oscar Bronner GmbH & Co. KG v Mediaprint Zeitungs-und Zeitschriftenverlag GmbH & Co. KG, Mediaprint Zeitungsvertriebsgesellschaft mbH & Co. KG and Mediaprint Anzeigengesellschaft mbH & Co KG*[312] case.

F. ENFORCEMENT OF ARTICLES 101–102 OF THE TFEU: COMPETITION PROCEDURE

Introduction

10.161 This book is about the substantive law of the EU as it relates to shipping and this chapter deals primarily with the substantive rules of EU competition law and must, by sheer limitation of size, touch only marginally on competition procedure. Thus, recourse should be had to the established works on EU procedural law for greater depth

---

307 Cases 6, 7/73 [1974] ECR 223, ECLI:EU:C:1974:18.
308 Case 27/76 [1978] ECR 207.
309 Comm. Dec. 88/589 OJ 1988 L317/47, para. 33.
310 See O'Donoghue and Padilla, op. cit. at fn. 229, *passim*. See also Temple Lang, "Defining Legitimate Competition: Companies' Duties to Supply Competitors and Access to Essential Facilities" in Hawk (ed.), 1994 Fordham Corp. L. Inst. (1995) 245.
311 See also Temple Lang and Snelders, "Essential Facilities in Maritime Transport" in Wareham and Power (eds), op. cit. at fn. 2, pp. 219–236.
312 Case C-7/97 [1998] ECR I-7791, ECLI:EU:C:1998:569.

and detail on the topic.³¹³ Nonetheless, this section is an introduction to the fascinating area of how EU competition law is enforced. Indeed, the substantive rules would be meaningless if there was not an adequate and effective enforcement regime to support the substantive rules.

10.162 Competition law could be enforced in various jurisdictions by different means: criminal sanctions; civil sanctions; and administrative sanctions such as so-called "evil fines". Each regime has to choose its own range of sanctions. The toughest sanctions are reserved for so-called hardcore cartels (e.g. involving market sharing and price-fixing).

10.163 All shipping companies, ports, liner conferences, consortia and other undertakings (however small) which operate within the EU or whole activities that could affect trade in the EU should contemplate setting up an internal competition compliance programme so as to ensure that their activities are compatible with EU competition law. Such a programme would minimise (but could not eliminate) the exposure to fines and breaches of competition law generally. Each undertaking should have someone (often called the "compliance officer") designated to deal with monitoring agreements and practices as well as organising responses to inquiries from competition authorities and dealing with dawn raids or other investigations.

Role of the Commission

10.164 Council Regulation 1/2003 is the primary³¹⁴ legislative basis for the Commission's actions in this area. It relates to the application and enforcement of Articles 101 and 102 of the TFEU. The Commission should administer the system of competition in a way which is above politics³¹⁵ and generally does so.

10.165 EU competition law is enforced both at an EU and a Member State level. In the past, enforcement was primarily at the EU level but the Member State courts and authorities are playing an increasingly important role in the enforcement of EU competition law. For example, before 1 May 2004 (when Regulation 1/2003³¹⁶ entered into force), only the European Commission could grant an exemption under Article 101(3) in respect of an agreement but now the Member State courts and national competition authorities ("NCAs")³¹⁷ have the ability to apply Article 101(3) of the TFEU (because this provision now has direct effect).

10.166 At the EU level, it is the Commission which enforces competition law on a day to day basis. In terms of public enforcement, EU competition law is primarily enforced by the Commission. In more specific terms, competition law is enforced by the Commission's Directorate-General for Competition ("DG Comp"). DG Comp is divided into

---

313 See Ortiz Blanco and others (eds), *EC Competition Procedure* (3rd ed., 2013) and Kerse and Khan, *Antitrust Procedure* (6th ed., 2012) as well as the books mentioned in fn. 2. See also Kreis, "Commission Procedures in Competition Proceedings: Recent Reforms in Practice and Law" in 1983 Fordham Corp. L. Inst. 145 (B. Hawk ed., 1984); and Kreis, "EEC Commission Investigation Procedures in Competition Cases" (1983) 17 Int'l Law 19.

314 Reg. 1/2003 is subject to the underlying Treaty regime. Reg. 1/2003 does not apply to concentrations within the meaning of Reg. 139/2004 (OJ 2004 L24/1).

315 See the editorial by Maitland-Walker entitled "The Unacceptable Face of Politics in Competition Cases" [1991] 1 ECLR 3.

316 OJ 2003 L1/1.

317 Under Art. 35 of Reg. 1/2003, Member States are required to designate NCAs.

Directorates. One of the directorates deals with services including maritime transport. The Commission deals with cases which have an EU-wide importance. The Council and the European Parliament are involved in the adoption of certain types of legislation but the Commission has considerable power delegated to it to adopt decisions to enforce EU competition law (e.g. to impose fines) or to adopt regulations (e.g. to set out the rules on which consortia agreements benefit from Article 101(3) of the TFEU). In practice, most of the work of the Commission in this area is undertaken by the Directorate General for Competition (DG Compiles) but the Directorate General for Mobility and Transport (DG MOVE) is also interested in these issues.[318] This public enforcement is supplemental in a small, but growing, way by private enforcement.

10.167 Appeals from the Commission's decisions are made to the General Court (formerly, the Court of First Instance) and from that Court to the CJEU. EU competition law may, as a general rule, be invoked before Member State courts and tribunals with the possibility of preliminary references being made to the CJEU from Member State courts under Article 267 of the TFEU.

Role of the Member State authorities and courts

10.168 The NCAs are part of the European Competition Network ("ECN").[319] The NCAs must co-operate with the Commission on the enforcement of EU competition law. These NCAs along with the Member State courts must ensure that Member State laws ensure that those undertakings or other parties injured by breaches of EU competition law have adequate remedies available to them.[320] The involvement of NCAs is part of a "modernisation" or "decentralisation" process.

10.169 Articles 101 and 102 of the TFEU are directly applicable in Member State law so they may be pleaded in Member State courts. The articles may also be invoked in arbitration proceedings. The national courts in the Member States therefore play a role in the enforcement of EU competition law. These courts may grant injunctions, award damages and order other remedies. Member State courts may decide whether or not an arrangement is compatible with EU competition law. A Member State court may award damages for breaches of EU competition law.

10.170 There is an element of internal competition compliance by undertakings themselves when they engage in "self-assessment" and when they operate competition compliance programmes. Self-assessment has always existed in EU competition law,[321] however, self-assessment became a real issue when the possibility of making individual notifications to the European Commission was abolished on 1 May 2004. Given that undertakings may no longer notify arrangements or practices to the Commission, there is

---

318 DG MOVE (formerly, in part, DG TREN) no longer deals with State aid in the transport sector since early 2010. State aid in transport is now dealt with by DG Comp.

319 See Basedow, "National Authorities in European Airline Competition Law" [1988] ECLR 342; and Bentil, "Common Market Anti-Trust Law and Restrictive Business Agreements or Practices prompted by National Regulatory Measures" [1988] ECLR 354.

320 Case C-453/99 *Courage v Crehan* [2001] ECR I-6297, ECLI:EU:C:2001:465.

321 Parties to arrangements and practices have always had to consider whether their arrangements and practices are valid as a matter of EU law.

a greater burden on undertakings to self-assess.³²² The abolition of notifications was significant but there was always a degree of self-assessment because parties (or at least their lawyers and economists) considered the compatibility (or lack of compatibility) of arrangements before notifying them to the European Commission and they had to devise the arguments for the notification as to why it was notifiable and could be exempted. Self-assessment should be undertaken by lawyers, in conjunction with economists and industry specialists, so as to ensure the maintenance of legal professional privilege.

10.171 There is a very high level of co-operation between the NCAs themselves as well as between the NCAs and the Commission in the enforcement of EU competition law.³²³

10.172 The courts in the Member States are able to apply Articles 101 and 102 of the TFEU. It is worth recalling that some anti-competitive practices and arrangements can be challenged before Member State courts by invoking not only under EU competition law rules but also invoking national laws such as those relating to tort or delict and unfair competition rules. If a Member State law would restrict competition in a way that prevents trade between Member States then Member State authorities empowered to apply Articles 101 and 102 are obliged to disapply such Member State laws given the primacy of EU law.³²⁴

10.173 Member State courts must provide adequate remedies where there is a breach of EU law including EU competition law. Member State courts must be able to consider whether a Member State law is in breach of EU law.³²⁵ The CJEU gave some guidance on these issues in such cases as *Manfredi*.³²⁶

10.174 It is worth noting the Member State courts and institutions may, as a general rule, apply EU and Member State competition laws.³²⁷ If EU and Member State competition law may apply in the same case then Member State competition law may be more onerous but must not undermine EU law.

Initiation of proceedings

10.175 Competition cases may be initiated in any one of four principal ways: a complaint by a third party to the Commission about the arrangements or activities of others; by the initiative of the Commission itself to investigate a particular case; by reason of an investigation by the Commission of a particular industrial sector; or by the institution of national court proceedings or a complaint to an NCA. On 26 November 1974, the Council adopted Regulation 2988/74 concerning limitation periods in proceedings and the enforcement of sanctions under the rules of the EEC relating to transport and

---

322 See Wareham, "The Challenges of Self-Assessment" in Wareham and Power (eds), op. cit. at fn. 2, *Competition law and shipping: the EMLO guide to EU competition law in the shipping and port industries* (2010), pp. 119–142.
323 See Brammer, *Co-operation between National Competition Agencies in the Enforcement of EC Competition Law* (2009).
324 Case C-198/01 *Consorzio Industries Fiammiferi (CIF) v AutoritàGarante della Concorrenza e del Mercato* [2003] ECR I-8055.
325 Case C-312/93 *Peterbroeck, Van Campenhout & Cie v Belgian State* [1995] ECR I-4599, ECLI:EU:C:1995:437.
326 Case C-294-298/04 *Manfredi v Lloyd Adriatico Assicurazioni SpA and others* [2006] ECR I-6619, ECLI:EU:C:2006:461.
327 The principal exception relates to the Merger Control Regulation.

competition[328] and advisors would find it useful to check whether proceedings are not time-barred and whether any sanctions are compatible with this regulation.

Complaints

10.176 A complaint may be made by any person to the Commission about the arrangements or activities of others. The complaint may be made by, for example, a Member State, a legal person or a human being. Any complainant other than a Member State must show that it has a legitimate interest – a precondition which is satisfied easily in practice. The complaint may be made in writing[329] or orally but written communications are the norm. Complaints have proved important in the port cases.[330]

Own-initiative investigations

10.177 The Commission has investigated many suspected breaches of competition law at its own initiative. It may have learned of developments by, for example, an investigation into another undertaking, seeing something reported in the media, being suspicious of activities or events or by monitoring developments generally.

Sectoral investigations or studies

10.178 The Commission has the power to investigate or study particular industrial sectors.[331] It has used this power on a number of occasions, most notably in the context of the brewing and pharmaceutical sectors.

Conduct of proceedings

Fact-finding

10.179 The Commission may establish the facts of a particular case either by requesting information from various quarters or conducting investigations.

Requests for information

10.180 The Commission has power to request information under Regulation 1/2003. The Commission may ask the addressee of the request to comply voluntarily with the request or may decide formally to compel the addressee to respond and fine the addressee for not responding.

---

328 OJ L319/1, 29 November 1974. It has since been amended (by Reg. 1/2003) and a consolidated version is available at: https://eur-lex.europa.eu/legal-content/AUTO/?uri=CELEX:01974R2988-20040501&qid=1522275030520&rid=1.
329 Form C has been provided by the Commission so as to facilitate complaints.
330 E.g. the *Holyhead, Rødby* and *Roscoff* cases referred to above.
331 See Reg. 1/2003, Art. 17.

Investigations/dawn raids

10.181 The Commission has the power to conduct investigations of premises (including ships) so as to gather information. Some of these investigations are unannounced and are often described dramatically as "dawn-raids". While conducting such an investigation, the Commission may ask questions and take copies or extracts from books or business records but the addressees of such questions have human rights (e.g. the right not to incriminate themselves). During such unannounced visits, officials rummage through documents, computer files and other records. The visits are often intrusive, invasive and disruptive but they often need to be so in order to be productive. They can last for several days. Once it is a lawful dawn raid, anyone refusing entry may be fined by the Commission.[332] The officials may examine and take copies of books and records as well as ask for explanations on the spot.

10.182 Businesses need to be prepared to respond to dawn raids. It is imperative that all businesses have one official and a number of deputies appointed in advance to deal with dawn raids should they arise. Ideally, the business should have a competition compliance programme and identified areas of exposure so as to eliminate any possible breach of competition law. Company staff (including receptionists, information technology personnel and public relations staff) should be briefed as to what to do (and not do) and who to call if officials arrive. External lawyers, preferably specialists in competition law, should be called immediately to attend to the premises and assist the business being dawn raided. Executives should be careful about answering questions: they should only answer what they know and not to engage in speculation or incriminate themselves. If documents or files are copied by the investigators then a second copy should be taken by the undertaking being investigated. Dawn raids have been used on the offices of, for example, ferry companies and liner conferences. For example, on 3 September 2003, the Commission announced that it had conducted "unannounced inspections" or "dawn raids" at the headquarters of a number of Nordic ferry operators in Denmark, Germany and Sweden as well as on cross-channel ferry operators. The Commission said that its purpose was to "ascertain whether there is evidence of suspected market sharing agreements and related illegal practices aimed at preventing access to the Nordic ferry market ... and to ferry services to and from the UK".[333] Conducting a dawn raid is not confirmation that there has been a breach of competition law – it is only, in its own right, a stage in the gathering of evidence and the case might or might not go further.

Burden of proof

10.183 Under Article 2 of Regulation 1/2003, the burden of proof under Article 101(1) is on the party alleging there has been an infringement. If the benefit of Article 101(3) is being claimed (i.e. that the arrangement is lawful by virtue of that provision) then the burden rests on the party alleging legality.

---

332 Comm. Dec. *Mewac* OJ 1983 L20/6.
333 Memo/03/167, 3 September 2003.

Standard of proof

10.184 The General Court has stated that typically there should be "convincing evidence" of an infringement before Articles 101(1), 102 and the Merger Control Regulation applies. Equally, the benefits alleged for Article 101(3) to apply must be real and quantified and not merely asserted.

Legal professional privilege

10.185 When undertakings are subject to dawn raids or being sued for alleged breaches of competition law, may they claim legal professional privilege over any legal advice which they received? In many jurisdictions, clients of lawyers do not have to disclose advice given to them by lawyers because of the principle of legal professional privilege – normally, the privilege may be waived if the client chooses to do so. It may be claimed in certain circumstances but it is not absolute because the Commission (and the General Court/CJEU) do not accept that in-house lawyers have professional privilege.[334]

Fines

10.186 Fines can be up to 10% of the undertaking's previous year's worldwide turnover. Fines for breaching EU competition law can be very severe. The *CEWAL* (the Central West Africa Conference) case involved fines totalling €10 million[335] on Comité Maritime Belge, Dafra-Lines, Deutsche Afrikabinien – Woermann Linie and Nedlloyd Lijnen but the fines were annulled on procedural grounds.[336] The *FETTSCA* (the Far East Trade Tariff Charges and Surcharges) case involved fines totalling €15 million across 15 lines in 2000 with the highest fine being €1,240,000 on PONL.[337] However, these fines were paltry compared to other fines which were imposed later on undertakings. In the case of *TACA*, fines totalling €272,980,000 were imposed on the members and while the fines were annulled on procedural grounds later, the scale of the fines indicates how serious this issue has become (for example, P&O Nedlloydd was fined €41,260,000 and AP Möller Maersk Line was fined €27,000,000).

10.187 Fines outside the shipping sector have been very high. Examples from cartel cases include fines of €479.6 million on Thyssenjrupp, €462 million on Hoffmann-La Roche, €396.5 million on Siemens, €272.2 million on ENI SpA and €249.6 million on Lafarge. There have been substantial fines in regard to the abuse of dominance including fines of over €1 billion on Intel and fines of €899 million and €499 million on Microsoft. Whether inside or outside the shipping sector, the fines can be damaging for the undertaking's reputation.

10.188 To minimise the possible exposure for undertakings, undertakings may seek leniency under the EU's leniency programme – this programme eliminates or reduces

---

334 Case C-550/07 P *Akzo Nobel Chemicals Ltd v Commission* [2010] ECR-8301. See Power, ECLI:EU:C:2010:512.
335 Comm. Dec. 2000/627 *FETTSCA* OJ 2000 L268/1.
336 Cases C-395/96P and C-396/96P *Compagnie Maritime Belge v Commission* [2000] ECR I-1365, [2000] 4 CMLR 1076.
337 Comm. Dec. 2000/627 *FETTSCA* OJ 2000 L268/1.

fines on undertakings who bring breaches to the Commission's attention or co-operate fully with the Commission.

10.189 There is no imprisonment for breaches of EU competition law. However, the conduct could give rise to penalties under other competition laws (e.g. Dutch, German, UK, US and other national competition laws). Some national regimes can punish executives by jail sentences and criminal fines.

Remedies

10.190 Plaintiffs may sue for remedies arising from breaches of competition law across the shipping sector generally. The block exemption for liner conferences has been abolished which means that claims can now be made in respect of any damage flowing from an anti-competitive liner conference. There could equally be claims in respect of tramp or cabotage services. Plaintiffs are able to obtain monetary damages from Member State courts but not from the Commission.[338] As mentioned above, the European Commission is encouraging plaintiffs who believe they have been injured by reason of breaches of EU competition law to sue for damages and other remedies in Member State courts[339] and has even instituted proceedings itself in the Belgian courts for alleged loss arising out of an alleged cartel in regard to the supply of lifts to Commission buildings following on from its own investigation of a cartel in these sectors.

Interim measures

10.191 Interim measures may be granted by the Commission pursuant to Article 8 of Regulation 1/2003 for breaches of Article 101 or 102 of the TFEU. Interim measures are like injunctions or interlocutory measures and are a useful way of responding quickly to competition breaches and they have been used in port cases quite effectively.

Termination of proceedings

10.192 The Commission may order the termination of breaches of competition law.[340] The Commission sends a statement of objections to the undertakings alleged to be in breach of EU competition law. It may decide to impose a fine on the undertakings. Fines may be up to 10% of the undertaking's previous year's worldwide turnover. Decisions of the Commission may be appealed to the CJEU (or, initially, to the General Court and then to the CJEU on points of law).

---

338 See Odudu and Edelman, "Compensatory Damages for Breach of Article 81" (2002) 27 ELRev 327.
339 See the Commission's White Paper on Damages COM (2008)165.
340 E.g. the *Holyhead* and *Roscoff* cases (see above).

Private enforcement: court actions by private parties to enforce EU competition law

10.193 An important,[341] though as yet relatively underused element of EU competition law enforcement is the action in court by private (as opposed to public) authorities.[342] In this context, plaintiffs who believe that they have suffered a loss because of an alleged breach of competition law would seek from the defendants who are alleged to have breached competition law any combination of damages, exemplary or punitive damages, injunctions, declarations and other remedies from Member State courts for breaches of EU competition law.[343] It is a "private" action in terms of both the plaintiffs and the defendants being private parties and not public authorities (or acting as public authorities).[344] The Member State's procedural rules apply but there must be equivalence and effectiveness which means that all Member States must provide a certain minimum level of protection and enforcement. The Member States apply their own rules relating to evidence, access to evidence, fault, causation, remoteness and limitations.

10.194 It is possible for plaintiffs to sue in Member State courts because Articles 101 and 102 of the TFEU are part of Member State law. Member State courts must apply EU competition law in full.[345] Anyone with sufficient standing, and not just the parties to an arrangement, may sue in respect of an arrangement and may invoke the notion of invalidity under Article 101(2) or Article 102; for example, a defendant in a contract enforcement action could defend successfully the action on the basis that the contract could not be enforced as to do so would be in breach of Article 101 or Article 102.

---

341 Former Competition Commissioner Kroes has said: "I am firmly of the view that private enforcement of competition law is an essential component of a truly effective and comprehensive anti-trust system" (Competition Day – Opening Session Vienna, 19 June 2006, Speech/06/382). See the Commission's White Paper on Private Enforcement – COM (2008)165. The Commission had proposed, but dropped, a directive on rules governing damages for competition law breaches. In 2011, it commenced a consultation on collective redress. There are various issues which need to be resolved before private litigation would be commonplace and they include the law in the EU or, at least, in the Member State in which the proceedings are being taken on issues such as passing-on of overcharges, disclosure of evidence, fault, limitation periods and so on. There have been some cases in regard to either EU or Member State competition law but not as many as some would have anticipated (e.g. the *Football Shirts* case in the UK and other cases such as *Carbon Graphites*, *Vitamins* and *Air Cargo*). Many of these cases have resulted in private settlements (e.g. the air passenger overcharging case). Some investors have sought to acquire litigation and then fund the litigation accordingly for a profit. The *Telefónica* case in Spain, which was brought by an Irish telephone directory company, did lead to an award of damages: in a judgment of 11 November 2005 (*Conduit v Telefonica*) (upheld by the Spanish Court of Appeal) €639,003 damages (plus the amount to be proved during the execution of the judgment) were awarded to Conduit following allegations that Telefonica had provided inaccurate and incomplete subscriber data in the directory enquiries telephone market, which caused the new entrant Conduit a competitive disadvantage and additional costs. The European Commission has recognised the importance of the mechanism of compensating parties: in *Nintendo*, the Commission reduced the fine in part because Nintendo paid substantial compensation to third parties (see "Commission Fines Nintendo and Seven of its European Distributors", *European Competition Policy Newsletter*, Spring 2003, p. 50).
342 See Randolph, "Private Actions for Damages in the Maritime Field", Lloyd's Maritime Academy, 26–27 April 2007. See Cases C-295/04-298/04 *Manfredi* [2006] ECR I-6619, ECLI:EU:C:2006:461; and C-453/99 *Courage Ltd v Crehan* [2001] ECR I-6297, ECLI:EU:C:2001:465.
343 The exact range of remedies would be dependent on what remedies are available from the Member State court in question but the Member State court must do enough to enforce EU competition law.
344 It is possible that a public authority might take a private action in respect of loss which the public authority incurred in the same way as a private party might do; e.g. the European Commission sued Otis in the Belgian courts alleging that the latter had overcharged it for lifts for some Commission buildings notwithstanding that the Commission (acting as a public authority) had also fined Otis.
345 Cases C-295/04-298/04 *Manfredi* [2006] EUR I-6619, ECLI:EU:C:2006:461.

10.195 It is important to be able to prove one's case in full by showing jurisdiction,[346] liability, breach, causation, damage, not being out of time (i.e. statute barred)[347] and so on. A finding by the European Commission of a breach of competition is important but not entirely decisive.[348] It is for each Member State to establish the procedural rules for damages actions but the rules for enforcement should be no less favourable than those governing similar domestic actions. Member State court judgments are sent to the Commission as part of the ECN regime. The entry into force of Directive 2014/104 on antitrust damages actions[349] on 27 December 2016 should make it easier for private plaintiffs to invoke EU competition law in Member States and seek damages – whether it will do so is still open to debate.

National competition law dimension

10.196 A breach of EU competition law could also constitute a breach of national competition law. There could be, for example, fines on the company or undertaking involved, fines and/or imprisonment on company executives, extradition of executives, damages claims from third parties and other national sanctions (e.g. disqualification from being a director of a company because an individual was involved in anti-competitive behaviour). In some Member States, actions for breaches of EU competition law have been categorised as actions for breach of statutory duty.[350] There may be a claim under Member State competition law as well as EU competition law; the two systems operate in parallel but if there is any conflict between Member State and EU competition law then the latter prevails.[351]

10.197 Private actions complement and supplement public enforcement. Therefore, the EU (and, in particular, the Commission) is encouraging private enforcement as much as possible because it helps the enforcement process. However, private litigation is not so simple because many issues are not yet resolved at either an EU or a Member State level so some novel issues have to be addressed and that is almost always expensive.[352] Over time, the position will become clearer and private enforcement will be more commonplace. It may well be that there would have to be public enforcement first to establish the breach and then there would be follow-on private enforcement given the fact that the breach has been established.[353]

---

346 E.g. the English courts will have jurisdiction if it can be demonstrated that the anti-competitive practice occurred in the UK (e.g. through the activities of a UK subsidiary). This is so notwithstanding that the main activities occurred outside the UK. See *Provimi Ltd v Aventis Animal Nutrition SA and Others* [2003] ELR 518.

347 The general rule is that the procedural restrictions which operate at the Member State level apply (e.g. six years in England and Wales unless there was fraud or concealment (which is perfectly possible with a cartel) in which case the period may be extended).

348 *Arkin v Borchard*, Colman J [2000] ELR 232. See also *Arkopharma v Ste Roche*, Tribual de Commerce de Nanterre of 11 May 2006.

349 OJ L349/1, 5 December 2014.

350 E.g. in *Garden Cottage Foods v Milk Marketing Board* [1984] AC 130.

351 Cases C-295/04-298/04 *Manfredi* [2006] ECR I-6619, ECLI:EU:C:2006:461.

352 See Holmes, "The Relevance of Competition Law in Shipping-related Private Actions" in Wareham and Power (eds), op. cit. at fn. 2, pp. 295–302.

353 There is evidence of this in the context of, for example, the air freight transport sector.

International dimension to competition enforcement

10.198 As shipping is such a global industry, it would be unfortunate if enforcement stopped at the borders of the EU or, at least, no account was taken by the EU of events outside the EU. The EU has therefore had to take account of the international dimension and has the power to find a breach of EU competition law where there is an act or practice outside the EU which has an effect inside the EU. The sanctions for breaching national competition law can be severe. In the US case of *Odfjell/State-Nielsen/JoTankers*(the so-called US Deep Sea Parcel Tanker Investigation), Odfjell Seachem accepted a fine in the USA of US$42.5 million while its President/CEO was fined US$250,000 and spent four months in prison while the Vice President was fined US$25,000 and spent three months in prison.

G. ARTICLE 106 OF THE TFEU

10.199 It is now appropriate to turn from the EU competition law rules which apply to undertakings generally and to examine very briefly how those rules apply to Member State authorities and to authorities entrusted with special or exclusive rights. Member States, because of their various powers, have an extraordinary ability to distort competition. Article 106 of the TFEU deals with the role of Member States and their role in the marketplace.

10.200 What is the role of Member States in the marketplace? This is a difficult question. Should Member States be treated like every other actor in the marketplace and be subjected to the competition rules in full? Or should the special role of Member States be recognised; for example, when they are providing public services?

10.201 Article 106 of the TFEU tries to address this issue.[354] It endeavours to consider how the competition rules in the Treaty (as well as other provisions of the Treaty) apply to: (a) State measures in respect of public undertakings; or (b) undertakings granted special or exclusive rights; or (c) undertakings entrusted with services of general economic interest.

10.202 Article 106 of the TFEU provides:

> "1. In the case of public undertakings and undertakings to which Member States grant special or exclusive rights, Member States shall neither enact nor maintain in force any measure contrary to the rules contained in the Treaties, in particular to those rules provided for in Article 18 and Articles 101 to 109.
> 2. Undertakings entrusted with the operation of services of general economic interest or having the character of a revenue-producing monopoly shall be subject to the rules contained in the Treaties, in particular to the rules on competition, in so far as the application of such rules does not obstruct the performance, in law or in fact, of the particular tasks assigned to them. The development of trade must not be affected to such an extent as would be contrary to the interests of the Union.
> 3. The Commission shall ensure the application of the provisions of this Article and shall, where necessary, address appropriate directives or decisions to Member States."

---

354 On Art. 106 of the TFEU, see e.g. Buendia Sierra, *Exclusive Rights and State Monopolies under EC Law* (2000).

10.203 It is important to recall that Article 345 of the TFEU provides that the Treaty "shall in no way prejudice the rules and Member States governing the system of property ownership" (i.e. it does not favour privatisation as some opponents of the EU claim). This means that EU law is neutral or agnostic as to whether property is owned publicly or privately but it does insist that where there is public ownership or an entity has been given special State privileges there is a regime in place to ensure fair competition.

10.204 It is useful to look at the architecture of Article 106. First, Article 106(1) is a prohibition which is addressed to Member States. Not all the entities which would be subject to it have to be publicly owned because it also relates to undertakings to which Member States grant special or exclusive rights irrespective of who owns those entities. Article 106(1) is, however, addressed to Member States in the sense that there is an obligation on Member States neither to enact nor to maintain in force any measure contrary to the TFEU rules, and the provisions of Article 18 as well as Articles 101–109 of the TFEU are merely illustrative because the obligation expands across the entirety of the Treaty. Second, Article 106(2) is somewhat different. It relates to undertakings entrusted with the operation of services of general economic interest (so-called "SGEI" services) or services having the character of a revenue-producing monopoly. Those types of services are subject to the rules of competition but this is only a general principle. Those entities with either SGEIs or revenue-producing monopolies are only subject to competition in so far as the application of the competition rules do not "obstruct the performance, in law or in fact, of the particular tasks assigned to them". This means that if an entity is, for example, engaged in an SGEI then the competition rules do not apply to them in so far as it relates to the SGEI activity. This is an important and quite broad escape hatch from the rules on competition. It is, therefore, imperative that the Commission as well as the courts limit the scope of this provision as much as possible. Third, Article 106(3) enables the Commission to adopt various measures (e.g. directives or decisions) to Member States where such measures are necessary to ensure the application of the provisions of Article 106. The leading case in this area is the *Altmark* judgment which has generated a great deal of commentary and analysis.[355]

10.205 Article 106 has proved to be important in the context of shipping. This has been most notable in the case of *Merci*[356] as well as *GT-Link A/S v De Danske Statsbanier*.[357] These cases are examined elsewhere in the book.[358]

H. SELECTED PRACTICES

10.206 There is no finite list of anti-competitive arrangements and practices. However, it would be useful to give some examples. Examples include market sharing, price-fixing and other practices which have the object or effect of preventing, restricting or distorting competition. In regard to pricing, two or more undertakings must not combine in any way which would have the object or effect of preventing, restricting or distorting competition. Such price-fixing arrangements could be horizontal (e.g. two carriers fixing the prices for

---

[355] Cases 280/00 *Altmark Trans GmbH v Nahverkehrs–gesellschaft* [2003] ECR I-7747, ECLI:EU:C:2003:415.
[356] Case C-179/90 [1991] ECR I-5889, ECLI:EU:C:1991:464.
[357] Case C-242/95 [1997] ECR I-4349, ECLI:EU:C:1997:376.
[358] See chap. 13.

a route) or vertical (e.g. a supplier fixing the price at which goods or services would be resold – a ferry company insisting that travel agents resell ferry tickets at a particular price). Where an undertaking at one level of the economic chain seeks to "maintain" or "determine" the price at which a product is resold then the process is known as "resale price maintenance" (or RPM) – EU competition law allows a supplier to recommend to a reseller the price at which the product is resold or to impose the maximum price at which the product is resold but a manufacturer may not set the minimum price at which the product is resold.[359] It is always worth recalling that competition law is a dynamic area which is always throwing up new challenges for all concerned because the theories and rules are not immutable.[360]

I. SELECTED CASE LAW

Introduction

10.207 It is useful to examine at this stage a very small selection of cases to illustrate how the rules apply in the context of shipping. These cases and others are dealt with elsewhere in this book so the cases selected here are just illustrative.

The *Ferry Operators–Currency Surcharges* case

10.208 The Commission adopted its decision in *Ferry Operators–Currency Surcharges* on 30 October 1996.[361] In essence, the Commission imposed fines totalling €645,000 on five ferry companies operating on the English Channel. The fines were in respect of a breach of Article 101. The companies had imposed a surcharge on freight shipments to compensate for the devaluation of the pound sterling vis-à-vis certain other European currencies in September 1992. The levies were identical and calculated in the same manner because they were the product of an agreement between the parties. The five companies involved were P&O, Stena Sealink, Brittany Ferries, Sea France and North Sea Ferries. Investigations were conducted by the Commission in April 1993 on the offices of four ferry operators. These investigations revealed documentary evidence

> "showing that a number of ferry operators had agreed the common imposition of a currency surcharge on freight following the devaluation of the pound sterling in September 1992. Five operators ... announced identical surcharges to be imposed on freight to be transported on United Kingdom-Continent routes, with a common introduction date and common method of calculation."[362]

The Commission defined the relevant market as:

> "the market for the provision of freight services by sea between the United Kingdom and France, Belgium and the Netherlands. It includes transport both to and from the United Kingdom.
> Geographically, this market includes all services between, on the one hand, ports on the east and south coasts of England, and on the other, ports in northern France, Belgium and The

---

359 By contrast, US federal antitrust law allows minimum RPM.
360 See Braakman, "Future Challenges for Legislators and Enforcers" in Wareham and Power (eds), op. cit. at fn. 2, pp. 321–326.
361 Comm. Dec. 97/84 OJ 1997 L26/23, [1994] CMLR 798.
362 It is notable that an undertaking could be fined without the need for a dawn raid.

Netherlands. It is possible to identify more narrowly delineated sectors within this market. In particular it can be broken down into three main sectors: short cross-Channel routes, western Channel routes and North Sea Routes. There is a significant competitive overlap between the western Channel and the short cross-Channel routes and the North Sea routes. This substitutability arises from the fact that the ports in question have good transport connections such that onward transportation to a variety of end destinations throughout the United Kingdom, or Continental Europe, respectively, is relatively easy and commonplace.

Transport of freight traffic between those ports could at the material time be effected only by means of ferry services, as the Channel Tunnel was not open at that time. The services in question were either roll-on, roll-off (ro-ro) or lift-on, lift-off (lo-lo). This includes, inter alia, driver-accompanied goods vehicles, unaccompanied trailers, containers, etc. The operators concerned by this Decision are all roll-on, roll-off ferry operators."

10.209 The ferry operators engaged in a concerted practice to impose simultaneously identical currency surcharges on all ro-ro freight charges. The surcharges were identical despite the companies each having different cost structures.[363] The Commission stated that unilateral surcharges were not an issue under Article 101 but collective surcharges were problematic:

> "the introduction of a currency surcharge is not, in itself, objected to by the Commission, as this was a commercial decision which each firm acting independently was entitled to take. However, the evidence clearly shows that almost all of the ferry operators in the relevant market contacted their competitors directly and discussed their intended response to the situation that had arisen."

The Commission found that there was a breach of Article 101:

> "55. Article [101(1) of the TFEU] prohibits as incompatible with the [Internal] Market all agreements between undertakings or concerted practices which may affect trade between Member States and which have as their object or effect the prevention, restriction or distortion of competition, and in particular those which directly or indirectly fix purchase or selling prices or any other trading conditions.
>
> 56. In order to establish the existence of a concerted practice, it is sufficient that the undertakings knowingly substitute practical cooperation for the risks of competition that might otherwise develop. A concerted practice requires direct or indirect contact between the competitors having the object or the effect of influencing their conduct on the market or of disclosing the conduct which they themselves have decided to adopt or contemplate adopting on the market. It is clear from the evidence that the parties engaged in direct discussions aimed at settling on a common course of conduct in relation to the introduction of currency surcharges. It is also clear that these discussions took place at senior levels between the parties, with the managing directors in particular being directly involved.
>
> 57. In light of the level of contact between the operators and the exchange of information between them in relation to the imposition of a surcharge, it is clear that the similarities between the surcharges imposed by several of them did not result from the transparency of the relevant market, as some of the operators have suggested. In particular, the information which was known to each of the parties to the infringement about the activities of the other parties, was known, not as a result of consultation with common customers, but instead as a result of direct exchanges of information between them.
>
> 58. In order for Article [101] to apply, it is necessary that the agreement or concerted practice between the parties has the object or effect of restricting competition. The clear object of the arrangement between the parties was to bring about the imposition of a common currency surcharge with effect from the same date. There can be no doubt that this arrangement amounted to a concerted practice, the object of which was to fix trading conditions by the parties thereto.

---

363 There could have been fines even if the surcharges were not absolutely identified.

59. The arrangements between the operators clearly falls within Article [101], notwithstanding the difficulties experienced by the operators in actually applying the surcharges announced to their customers. While it may be the case that the surcharges were not implemented in precisely the form which had been announced by the operators in mid-October 1992, the result of the operators' cooperation was nevertheless to influence the trading conditions in the relevant market."

10.210 The Commission thus found that the arrangement was a concerted practice with an effect on trade between Member States and it was therefore contrary to Article 101. The fines were imposed according to the extent of the involvement of the companies in the cartel and market share. The fines were moderate and commensurate with the limited success and application of the surcharges. P&O European Ferries was fined €400,000. Stena Line UK ("Stena Sealink") was fined €100,000. Sea France ("SNAT") was fined €60,000. Brittany Ferries was fined €60,000. North Sea Ferries was fined €25,000. Today, those fines would be much higher (probably in the millions of euro) not only because the undertakings' turnover would be higher in all probability but because the Commission imposes much higher fines now in relative terms.

The *P&O/Stena Line* case

10.211 On 13 March 1997, the Commission published a notice under Article 12(2) of Regulation 4056/86[364] concerning the proposed joint venture of P&O's and Stena's ferry operations on the Short French Sea and the Belgian Straits. P&O and Stena had notified the arrangement on 31 October 1996 to the Commission. The joint venture would have involved the pooling of some vessels and assets. The parties agreed not to compete with the joint venture. The Commission noted that the parties considered that

"the relevant market for tourist services is the carriage of passengers and vehicles across the Short French Sea which covers routes from (and including) Newhaven/Dieppe to Ramsgate/Dunkirk. The parties consider that the ... characteristics of the Short French Sea distinguish it as a market for tourist services from the adjoining maritime sectors."

The parties considered that the relevant freight services market included not only maritime freight services but also the English Channel Tunnel. The relevant geographical market was a broad Anglo/Continental market. The joint venture obtained a first, short exemption in January 1999.

10.212 On 26 January 1999, the Commission approved the joint venture between P&O and Stena Line for the operation of cross-Channel ferry services. The approval was however limited to three years (with retroactive effect to 10 March 1998) due to uncertainties as to the future developments in the market.[365]

10.213 On 22 December 2000, P&O Stena Line and its parents, P&O and Stena, applied for a renewed exemption under, what is now, Article 101(3) of the TFEU. The parties applied for exemption until 2020.

---

364 On Reg. 4056/86, see chap. 11.
365 See IP/99/56, OJ 1999 L163/61, [1999] S CMLR 682. See also the Commission's *Twenty-Fifth Report on Competition Policy* (1996), paras 84–87 and *Twenty-Seventh Report on Competition Policy* (1997), paras 81–84.

10.214 On 7 June 2001, the Commission announced that it did not oppose the continuation of the joint P&O Stena Line cross-Chanel ferry service.[366] The Commission thus granted the P&O Stena Line joint venture a six-year exemption to continue operating the cross-Channel ferry service for passengers and freight. The Commission's investigation did not reveal any valid market change which could justify forcing P&O and Stena to end their alliance. During the exemption period, which would expire on 7 March 2007, the Commission would closely follow any market developments in close contact with consumer organisations and national authorities. The Commission stated:

> "After a careful analysis and consultation of third parties, the Commission concluded to the absence of any material changes in the market that would justify denying a further, although limited, clearance.
>
> P&O Stena Line has had to face competition from both the Eurotunnel, Sea France, Hoverspeed and, more recently NorfolkLine. The investigation has revealed no evidence that P&O Stena Line and Eurotunnel, the main operators on the route, acted in parallel and the characteristics of the market are still such that the operators can be expected to continue to compete with each other rather than act in parallel fashion to raise prices.
>
> The Commission's review also established that customers benefit from cost savings and improvements to the service. Through the establishment of the joint venture, consumers have enjoyed the benefit of improved frequency of departure. The waiting time at the quay has been reduced through a continuous embarkation system. The costs savings from the joint service has also enabled P&O Stena Line to invest more in achieving a high quality standard in onboard services and other facilities.
>
> *Price increases*
> The Commission has studied comments from individual consumers and organisations regarding changes in pricing practices and generally higher prices.
>
> The investigation has, however, indicated that those price developments are not the result of the joint venture but rather reflect the market's adjustment to more normal market conditions for cross-Channel transport services, such as the end of duty free sales and the absorption of the new capacity created when Eurotunnel started its services in 1995. The market has also had to cope with considerably higher fuel prices in the last few years.
>
> Finally, another factor which also partly explains the price increases on cross-Channel services is the introduction by P&O Stena Line of a yield management system, whereby the ticket price is set according to demand, as is done in the airline sector. According to such a system, prices change daily and customers travelling in peak periods with little flexibility usually pay more.
>
> The Commission consulted the national competition authorities, including the UK Office of Fair Trading, on the P&O Stena Line's request for a new exemption.
>
> In any case and irrespective of the exemption, the Commission will continue to follow developments in cross-Channel transport services in close contact with consumer organisations and national authorities. The Commission has the possibility to change its position if it appears that the conditions for applying Article [101(3)] are no longer satisfied.
>
> After the parties requested new clearance in December 2000, the Commission on the 8th of March this year published in the Official Journal of the European Communities a summary of the parties' application for a renewal of the exemption of the joint venture and invited interested parties to submit comments.[367] Publication of the summary also triggered a 90-day period for the Commission to raise serious doubts if there was a need to continue the investigation.
>
> According to Regulation 4056/86, under which the deal was notified, if the Commission does not raise serious doubts within the 90-day period, an agreement is automatically exempted for six years. Since the Commission has not raised serious doubts the joint venture agreement is deemed exempt until 7 March 2007."[368]

---

366 IP/01/806. See also commission's *Thirty-First Report on Competition Policy* (2001), para. 160.
367 Ed., See IP/01/333.
368 IP/01/806, 7 June 2001.

10.215 On 8 August 2002, the Commission then cleared the de-merger of P&O Stena Line. The Commission summarised the decision in its press release as follows:

"Commission clears de-merger of cross-Channel ferry operator P&O Stena Line
The European Commission has approved a transaction by which P&O (UK) will acquire full control of P&O Stena Line, the cross-Channel ferry operator which currently is a joint venture between P&O and Stena Line UK Ltd. The analysis carried out by the Commission indicated that the change to sole control which constitutes a concentration within the meaning of the Merger Regulation – does not raise any competition concerns. The Commission however remains fully committed to closely follow cross-Channel market developments in contact with consumer organisations and national authorities.

The Peninsular and Oriental Steam Navigation Co (P&O) is a UK listed company involved, inter alia, in maritime shipping and port activities worldwide. In Europe, P&O, apart from its involvement in the P&O Stena Line joint venture, operates passenger and ferry services on the North Sea and the Western Channel. The P&O Stena Line joint venture is the leading ferry operator on the Dover-Calais route, formed in 1998 through a combination of P&O's and the Stena Line UK Ltd's interests on the 'Short Sea'. That term describes the routes across the Short French Sea (between Dover, Folkstone [sic], Ramsgate Newhaven and Calais, Dieppe, Boulogne and Dunkirk) and the Belgian Straits (Ramsgate and Ostend). P&O will acquire all the remaining shares in P&O Stena Line. The proposed concentration would therefore in effect be a de-merger of P&O's and Stena's interests in this area.

The Commission initially granted the creation of the P&O SL joint venture a three-year exemption under Article [101(3)] which was renewed in 2001 for a further six year period. In last year's investigation the Commission already stated clearly that it would continue to follow developments in cross-Channel transport services.

In the present case, the Commission concluded that the change in control of P&O Stena Line would not lead to the creation of a dominant position for the provision of freight and passenger services between the Continent and the United Kingdom, regardless of how the market was defined. The Commission also examined whether the possibility to control P&O Stena Line alone would give P&O additional advantages, which could enable it to force competitors out of the market and thereafter raise prices. However, the investigation showed that such a scenario is not likely considering the amount of actual or potential competition on the market and the low barriers to entry. Lastly, the Commission concluded that the market did not show the characteristics which would enable the operators (both the ferry operators and Eurotunnel) to act in parallel to raise prices rather than compete and that the fact that P&O will now be able to control P&O Stena Line alone would not change that structure.

The conclusion reached by the Commission in this specific transaction does however not affect its commitment to monitor market evolution in order to ensure that prices and trade conditions are in accordance with the European Competition rules.

Background
On 26 January 1999, the Commission approved the creation of the P&O Stena Line joint venture under Article [101(3)]. Due to uncertainties as to the future developments in the market, the approval was however limited to three years.[369] In December 2000, the parties applied for a renewal of the exemption until 2020. The application was made under Regulation 4056/86, under which the Commission has 90 days from publication of a summary of the application in the Official Journal of the European Communities to raise serious doubts if there is a need to continue the investigation. If no serious doubts are raised, the agreement is automatically exempted for six years from the date of such publication. The Commission concluded under that investigation that there had been no material changes in the market that would justify denying a further clearance

---

[369] http://europa.eu/rapid/start/cgi/guesten.ksh?p_action.gettxt=gt&doc=IP/99/56|0|AGED&lg=EN&display=" IP/99/56.

and did not raise serious doubts, with the effect that the P&O Stena Line joint venture was deemed exempted until 7 March 2007.[370]"

The *Greek Ferries* case

10.216 On 9 December 1998, the Commission imposed fines totalling €9.2 million on certain ferry operators in Greece for operating a price-fixing cartel in regard to ferry services between Greece and Italy.[371] The Commission found that Anex Lines, Kârâgeorgis Lines, Marlines SA, Minoan Lines and Strinzis Lines had fixed prices on ro-ro services between Ancona and Patras. The Commission also found that Adriatica di Navigazione SpA, Anek Lines, Kârâgeorgis Lines, Minoan Lines, Strinzis Lilnes and Ventrouns Group Enterprises SA had fixed fares for trucks on the Patras to Bari and Brindisi ferry route.[372]

10.217 Appeals were filed in February and March 1999 before the General Court by Marlines, Adriatica di Navigazione, Strinzis Lines and Minoan Lines. The General Court mainly upheld the Commission's decisions.[373]

10.218 The General Court's judgments were appealed to the CJEU by Strinzis Lines Shipping SA, Adriatica di Navigazione SpA, Marlines SA and Minoan Lines SA.[374] The appellants sought to have the General Court's judgment annulled or the fines reduced. They argued that the General Court had erred in finding that the Commission's investigation was legal and procedurally correct. The President of the CJEU issued orders on 15 September 2005 dismissing each of the appeals.

The *Bulk Liquids by Sea on Deep Sea Routes* case

10.219 On 11 April 2007, the Commission announced that it had sent a statement of objections to alleged participants in an alleged cartel in the market for the shipping of bulk liquids by sea on deep sea routes. The Commission alleged customer allocation, bid-rigging, price-fixing and the exchange of confidential information. The Commission based its concerns on dawn raids conducted in February 2003 and information subsequently supplied to the Commission under the Commission's 2002 Leniency Notice. Interestingly, on 8 May 2008, the Commission announced that it had closed its investigation. The Commission noted that, at the time of the alleged infringements, between 1998 and 2002, tramp vessel services were excluded from Regulation 4056/86 because they were non-regular and non-advertised shipping services. The Commission in its 2008 announcement stated that throughout the investigation,

> "significant efforts were made to clarify the type of maritime transport services offered by the parties. After careful consideration of the extensive replies to the Statement of Objections, the Commission concluded that there was a possibility that the services at stake were indeed tramp

---

370 http://europa.eu/rapid/start/cgi/guesten.ksh?p_action.gettxt=gt&doc=IP/01/806|0|AGED&lg=EN&display=" IP/01/806.
371 Dec. 1999/271 of 9 December 1998 relating to a proceeding pursuant to Art. 85 of the EC Treaty (IV/34.466 – Greek Ferries) (OJ 1999 L109, p. 24).
372 COMPIV/34.466 *Greek Ferries* OJ 1999 L109/24, [1999] 5 CMLR 47.
373 Cases T-56/99, T-61/99 and T-65/99 and T-66/99 [2003] ECR I-5225.
374 Cases C-110/04P, C-111/04P, C-112/04P and C-121/04.

vessel services. Therefore, the Commission has decided to close the case and informed the parties accordingly."[375]

Of course, the situation could not arise now because, as the Commission states:

"[a]s Regulation No 4056/86 was repealed in 2006 and the exemption for tramp services no longer exists, ... the issue of whether shipping services are tramp or not is irrelevant to assessing current infringements, as all shipping services are now subject to the general procedural rules for the Commission to apply the competition rules, laid down in Regulation 1/2003".

(Cabotage now comes within the scope of Regulation 1/2003.)[376] It is admirable that the Commission closed the case despite having investigated it because some agencies might have pursued matters after spending some resources on an investigation.

The *Ship Classification* case

10.220 On 29 and 30 January 2008, the Commission, accompanied by the relevant NCA officials, conducted unannounced inspections (i.e. "dawn-raids") at the premises of several providers of ship classification services[377] and associations of such service providers.[378] The European Free Trade Association ("EFTA") Surveillance Authority also conducted such a search with officials of the European Commission present at that search. The searches related to suspected breaches of what is now Article 101 of the TFEU.

10.221 The Commission was concerned about the ship classification market. The International Association of Classification Societies ("IACS") was the principal association of classification societies. During its investigation, the Commission came to the preliminary view that IACS may have reduced the level of competition in the ship classification market, mainly by preventing classification societies which were not already members of IACS from joining IACS, from participation in IACS' technical working groups (which develop IACS' technical resolutions that lay down requirements and interpretations to be incorporated into the classification rules and procedures of individual classification societies) and from access to technical background documents relating to IACS' technical resolutions. The Commission believed that, if true, such behaviour would have hindered the entry and/or expansion of classification societies, which were not members of IACS, in the ship classification market.

10.222 On 14 October 2009, the Commission announced that it had closed its investigation following the giving of legally binding commitments.[379] The Commission believes that it had brought about more competition in the ship classification market by making IACS' commitments legally binding.[380] The commitments had been market tested by the

---

375 Commission MEMO/08/297.
376 OJ 2003 L1/1.
377 As is well known, classification societies establish, apply and certify compliance with technical requirements relating to the design, construction, equipment, maintenance and survey of ships, which are laid down in their classification rules and procedures. More than 90% of the world's cargo carrying tonnage is covered by the classification rules and procedures set by the current ten members and one associate of IACS which are the largest classification societies in the world.
378 European Commission MEMO/08/65.
379 http://ec.europa.eu/competition/antitrust/cases/index/by_nr_78.html#i39_416. This demonstrates that not every case has to end in a fine.
380 IP/09/1513, 14 October 2009.

Commission during the summer of 2009.[381] The decision was based on Article 9(1) of Regulation 1/2003. The Commission did not conclude whether there had been or still was an infringement of the competition rules. However, if IACS were to breach its commitments then the Commission could impose a fine of up to 10% of IACS' total turnover without having to prove any violation of the competition rules. The IACS offered the following commitments: (a) to set up objective and transparent membership criteria and to apply them in a uniform and non-discriminatory manner. The commitments foresee detailed rules, including clear deadlines, for the different steps of the membership application, suspension and withdrawal procedure; (b) to ensure that classification societies which are not members of IACS will nonetheless be able to participate in IACS' technical working groups; (c) to put all current and future IACS resolutions and their related technical background documents into the public domain at the same time and in the same way as they are made available to IACS members; and (d) to set up an independent appeal board to settle possible disputes about access to, suspension or withdrawal of membership of IACS, participation in IACS' technical working groups and access to IACS' resolutions and to their technical background documents.

10.223 It was a positive outcome for the IACS in that there was no fine or an admission of wrongdoing (if there had been any wrongdoing at all). However, there is a risk that if there is any breach of the commitments then substantial fines may be imposed by the Commission without too much difficulty.[382]

The *GT-link* case

10.224 On 17 July 1997 the CJEU decided *GT-Link A/S v De Danske Statsboner (DSB)*.[383] It was a preliminary reference from a Danish court. The CJEU held:

"1. It is contrary to Article 95 of the EEC Treaty[384] for a Member State to impose a 40% import surcharge on a general duty levied on goods loaded, unloaded, or otherwise taken on board or landed within its ports or in the deep-water approach channels to its ports where goods are imported by ship from another Member State.
2. It is for the domestic legal order of each Member State to lay down the detailed procedural rules, including those relating to the burden of proof, governing actions for safeguarding rights which individuals derive from the direct effect of Article 102 of the (TFEU), provided that such rules are not less favourable than those governing similar domestic actions and do not render virtually impossible or excessively difficult the exercise of rights conferred by Community law.
3. Where a public undertaking which owns and operates a commercial port occupies a dominant position in a substantial part of the common market, it is contrary to Article [106]

---

381 On 10 June 2009, the Commission launched consultation for interested parties to give their views on the commitments proposed by IACS (see IP/09/898). The results of this market test have confirmed that the proposed commitments are appropriate and proportionate to remedy the concerns.
382 See Reg. 1/2003, Art. 9(1).
383 Case C-242/95, [1997] ECR I-4449, ECLI:EU:C:1997:376.
384 Ed., Art. 95 of the EEC Treaty provided: "A Member State shall not impose, directly or indirectly, on the products of other Member States any internal charges of any kind in excess of those applied directly or indirectly to like domestic products.
Furthermore, a Member State shall not impose on the products of other Member States any internal charges of such a nature as to afford indirect protection to other productions.
Member States shall, not later than at the beginning of the second stage, abolish or amend any provisions existing at the date of the entry into force of this Treaty which are contrary to the above rules."

(1) in conjunction with Article [102] of the [TFEU] for that undertaking to levy port duties of an unreasonable amount pursuant to regulations adopted by the Member State to which it is answerable or for it to exempt from payment of those duties its own ferry services and, reciprocally, some of its trading partners' ferry services, in so far as such exemptions entail the application of dissimilar conditions to equivalent services. It is for the national court to determine whether, having regard to the level of the duties and the economic value of the services supplied, the amount of duty is actually unfair. It is also for the national court to determine whether exempting its own ferry services, and reciprocally those of some of its trading partners, from payment of duties in fact amounts to the application of dissimilar conditions to equivalent services.

4. Article [106](2) of the Treaty does not permit a public undertaking which owns and operates a commercial port to levy for the use of port facilities duties which are contrary to Community law and which are not necessary to the performance of the particular task assigned to it.

5. Persons or undertakings on whom duties incompatible with Article [106](1) in conjunction with Article 86 of the Treaty have been imposed by a public undertaking which is responsible to a national ministry and whose budget is governed by the Budget Law are in principle entitled to repayment of the duty unduly paid."

CHAPTER 11

European Union competition law: the old regime relating to shipping – Regulation 4056/86

A. INTRODUCTION

11.001 For more than two decades, Council Regulation 4056/86 of 22 December 1986 was the centrepiece of the EU's competition regime relating to liner conferences.[1] The regulation had two striking features. First, it laid down detailed rules for the application[2] of what are now Articles 101[3] and 102[4] of the Treaty on the Functioning of the European Union ("TFEU") to some forms of international maritime transport. Second, and more substantially, it contained a block exemption for liner conferences from the effects of,

---

1 OJ 1986 L378/4. For the literature on Reg. 4056/86, see, among others, Clough and Randolph, *Shipping and EC Competition Law* (1991); Liu, *Liner Conferences in Competition Law: A Comparative Analysis of European and Chinese Law* (2009); Ortiz Blanco, *Shipping Conferences under EC Antitrust Law: Criticism of a Legal Paradox* (2008); Ortiz Blanco and Van Houtte, *EC Competition Law in the Transport Sector* (1996); Pozdnakova, *Liner Shipping and EU Competition Law* (2008); Spiteri, *The Application of EC Competition Law in the Maritime Transport Sector* (2012); and earlier editions of this book. See the literature cited through this chapter and see also Chuah, "Liner Conferences in the EU and the Proposed Review of EC Regulation 4056/86" [2005] LMCLQ 207; Greaves, *Transport Law of the European Community* (1991), chap. 11; Green, "Competition and Maritime Trade: A Critical View" (1988) 23 ETL 612; Kreis, "Maritime Transport and EEC Competition Rules" (1988) 23 ETL 562; Kreis, "European Community Competition Policy and International Shipping" [1989] 13 Fordham Int'l LJ 411; Rycken "European Antitrust Aspects of Maritime and Air Transport Law" [1987] ETL 483; Rabe and Schuette "EEC Competition Rules and Maritime Transport" [1988] LMCLQ 182; Ruttley, "International Shipping and EEC Competition Law" [1991] 1 ECLR 5; as well as Slot, in Slot and de Woude (eds), *Exploiting the Internal Market: Co-operation and Competition Towards* (1992).

For the background to Reg. 4056/86, see, among other sources, the Report of the Economic and Social Committee's ("EESC") Section for Transport and Communications on the Proposal for a Council Regulation (EEC) laying down Detailed Rules for the Application of Arts 85 and 86 of the Treaty to Maritime Transport (CES) 211/82 as well as the Interim Report drawn up on behalf of the Committee on Economic and Monetary Affairs on the proposal from the Commission of the European Communities to the Council for a Regulation laying down detailed rules for the application of Arts 85 and 86 of the Treaty to Maritime Transport (Rapporteur: Nyborg) (EP Doc.1-249/84/9). Arts 85 and 86 were the numbers described to what are now Arts 101 and 102 of the TFEU.

See also Athanassiou, *Aspects Juridiques de la Concurrence Maritime* (1996). See also Commission, *Towards Fair and Efficient Pricing in Transport* (COM(95)691, 20 December 1995). See Bonassies, "European Regulation 4056/86", International Colloquium, Antwerp 1994. See also Evans, "Competition Developments Affecting the Maritime Sector", European Maritime Law Organisation ("EMLO"), 14 October 2005.

On the definition of "maritime transport" or "maritime services" for present purposes, see para. 11.034.

See also Deakin, *Shipping Conferences* (1973) and Herman and Amos, *Shipping Conferences* (1984) on liner conferences generally.

2 It is important to note that what are now Arts 101 and 102 of the TFEU always applied to the maritime transport sector but there were no detailed rules applying the articles to the sector because Reg. 17/62 did not apply to the sector.

3 On Art. 101 of the TFEU, see chap. 10.

4 On Art. 102 of the TFEU, see chap. 10.

what is now, Article 101(1) of the TFEU[5] and, in particular, it exempted price-fixing in certain circumstances despite price-fixing being usually the most serious breach of competition law. It is therefore important to see Regulation 4056/86 as not just the "liner conference block exemption" but also the procedural regulation which enabled the European Union's ("EU") competition rules to be applied to certain aspects of the shipping sector until the repeal of the regulation with effect from 18 October 2008.[6] Some provisions of Regulation 4056/86 (such as those which provided that Article 101(1) did not apply to particular types of arrangement) could still be relevant today as a source of inspiration (though not legislation) even though the regulation itself has been repealed. By virtue of Regulation 4056/86, maritime transport was therefore insulated, in part, from the full effects of EU competition law.

11.002 The regulation was customised and dedicated to the international maritime transport sector. Regulation 4056/86 involved a unique exception to all the competition rules – a price-fixing[7] cartel in the form of a liner conference was exempted under EU competition law. However, it was more than just price-fixing which was exempted, it was also capacity regulation and market sharing. Liner conferences were therefore privileged arrangements unlike almost any other in EU competition law.[8]

11.003 Article 1(3)(b) of Regulation 4056/86 defined a liner conference, for the purposes of the regulation, as being:

> "a group of two or more vessel-operating carriers which provides international liner services for the carriage of cargo on a particular route or routes within specified geographical limits and which has an agreement or arrangement, whatever its nature, within the framework of which they operate under uniform or common freight rates and any other agreed conditions with respect to the provision of liner services".[9]

It is useful to dissect this definition to see its key ingredients – a liner conference was defined for the purposes of the regulation as being:

- a group of two or more vessel-operating carriers;
- which provides international liner services;
- for the carriage of cargo on a particular route or routes;
- within specified geographical limits;
- and which has an agreement or arrangement, whatever its nature;
- within the framework of which it operates under uniform or common freight rates; and
- any other agreed conditions with respect to the provision of liner services.

---

5 References in this chapter to Art. 101 TFEU are for convenience because during the life of Reg. 4056/86, the provision would have been numbered differently.

6 On the current new regime, see chap. 12.

7 I.e. the freight rates (i.e. prices) were being fixed by participants in a liner conference with immunity from the EU's competition rules on anti-competitive arrangements.

8 Dinger commented that "like a drunken sailor, something [was] seriously amiss with the way [EU] competition law [was] applied in this specific field" in "What Shall We Do with the Drunken Sailor? EC Competition Law and Maritime Transport" (BaslerSchriften zur europäischen Integration, No 61), p. 5.

9 Reg. 4056/86, Art. 1(3)(b). This definition is embodied in both Art. 1 of Reg. 4056/86 and the UN Convention on a Code of Conduct for Liner Conferences (which was adopted on 6 April 1974 and entered into force on 6 October 1983).

11.004 The Commission has described the background to liner conferences in the following terms:

> "Shipping companies have traditionally organised themselves since the nineteenth century as liner conferences whereby they would agree common or uniform freight rates in return for ensuring regular scheduled maritime transport services to shippers[10] and freight forwarders. Such liner conferences allow shipping companies to fix the price for transporting goods between the European Union and other countries, including the Far East and the United States.
>
> Liner shipping conferences have traditionally been granted some form of exemption or immunity from the competition rules in many jurisdictions. The European Union's Council of Ministers adopted a Liner Conference Block Exemption Regulation (4056/86) in 1986, which exempt[ed] price-fixing, capacity-regulation, under certain strict conditions and other agreements or consultations between liner shipping companies from the [TFEU] competition rules' ban on restrictive business practices.[11] The justification for the block exemption was the assumption that the rate-setting and other activities of liner conferences led to stable freight rates, which in turn assured shippers of reliable scheduled maritime transport services."[12]

11.005 The Commission, in contrast to the Council of Ministers which had adopted Regulation 4056/86, saw liner conferences as distorting competition because they restricted competition between members by, for example, fixing prices. In many ways, the benefits of Regulation 4056/86 were limited because the Commission construed the regulation narrowly and instead tried to apply the general principles of EU competition law to the liner shipping sector despite the existence of the regulation. The significance of the issue is clear from the fact that until the repeal of Regulation 4056/86 about two-thirds of the world's trade in terms of value and one-third in terms of volume was carried by liner conference traffic. Moreover, about 60% of the income globally from maritime activities was derived from liner activities.

11.006 Regulation 4056/86 ceased to have effect on 18 October 2008[13] so it is now of somewhat historical interest and therefore the regulation is described in this chapter in the past tense. The rules set out in the regulation were both substantive and procedural.[14] As mentioned above,[15] the regulation was quite unique: it "present[ed] many peculiar features for which one will look in vain in other Regulations which give effect to the principles of Articles [101] and [102]".[16] In part, this is attributable to the fact that it was a regulation adopted by the Council rather than the Commission (the regulation was adopted by the Council but the regulation was both largely distrusted and disliked by the Commission (and many of the latter's officials) to the point that the block exemption in the regulation was always construed narrowly or restrictively by the Commission) and also to the fact that maritime transport was outside the general rules on the application of competition law to the economy. The regulation applied to the international liner service

---

10 Ed., "shipper" means a person who sends or dispatches goods and is not, despite the use of the word "ship" the carrier.

11 Ed., the exemption was from what is now Art. 101 TFEU rather than Art. 102 TFEU. There was no exemption from the application of Art. 102 TFEU.

12 Commission Press Release IP/05/1408, 10 November 2005. The word "many" should have been inserted by the Commission at the start of this quotation because it was not the case that all shipping companies formed or joined conferences.

13 Following the entry into force of Reg. 1419/2006 OJ 2006 L269/1.

14 The substantive rules were set out, in particular, in Arts 1–9 of the regulation.

15 See paras 11.001–11.002.

16 Slot, op. cit. at fn. 1, p. 31.

sector and granted an open-ended block exemption for cargo liner conferences. It therefore required another regulation (i.e. Regulation 1419/2006)[17] to repeal Regulation 4056/86 and its block exemption. The regulation allowed certain liner conferences to fix prices and share markets in a manner which was alien to the usual position under Article 101 of the TFEU so its repeal was quite significant. Regulation 4056/86 applied to maritime transport services not only to, or from, Member States but also to or from one or more European Economic Area ("EEA") States[18] and any arrangement anywhere in the world which had an effect on trade in the EU so its repeal had wider implications.

11.007 It is worth observing that Regulation 4056/86 did not authorise every type of liner conference but its breadth was still too wide for its critics. The Council was willing in 1986 to tolerate an exemption for liner conferences because the Council believed that conferences had a stabilising effect on the market by giving regular and reliable services to shippers (i.e. persons sending goods). It was thought the Commission could tolerate such an exemption provided competition was not unduly restricted and there was competition from non-conference services, tramp vessels and even other transport modes. The Commission would not tolerate the continuance of Regulation 4056/86 so the Commission proposed its repeal and ultimately convinced the Council to repeal it.[19] The regulation was repealed because it was an anachronism under EU competition law and there was no evidence available to the Commission and the Council that liner conferences deserved an exemption because they delivered the claimed benefits. Ortiz Blanco concluded in his *Shipping Conferences under* EC *Competition Law*[20] that liner conferences did not merit a block exemption because the criteria in Article 101(3) of the TFEU were not capable of being satisfied by liner conferences. With the repeal of Regulation 4056/86, the current general EU competition regime, under Regulation 1/2003[21] became applicable to maritime transport generally including cabotage and international tramp services as well as liner conferences.

B. LEGISLATIVE HISTORY OF REGULATION 4056/86

Introduction

11.008 It is useful to trace the historical evolution of Regulation 4056/86. It will be recalled[22] that Regulation 17/62[23] gave operational effect to what are now Articles 101

---

17 OJ 2006 L269/1. See Press Release IP/06/1249 (25 September 2006) and MEMO/06/344 (25 September 2006). See chap. 12 on Reg. 1419/2006.
18 EEA Agreement, Annex VIII, point 50.
19 See chap. 12 for details of the repeal process.
20 2007.
21 OJ 2004 L1/1.
22 See chaps 5 and 10.
23 OJ Spec.Ed. 1959062, p. 87. This has now been repealed and replaced by Reg. 1/2003 OJ L1/1, 1 January 2004.

and 102 of the TFEU[24] but Regulation 141/62[25] disapplied Regulation 17/62 in relation to transport. The absence of a regulation applying Articles 101 and 102 of the TFEU to the transport sector could have led to confusion and difficulties – as the Commission said in an Information Memorandum (prior to the adoption of Regulation 4056/86):

> "Although the rules on competition, like all the general provisions of the Treaty apply to sea transport,[26] maritime and air transport are[27] the only branches of the economy for which detailed provisions applying those rules have not yet been laid down.
>
> Without provisions of this kind, the Commission does not possess the means to ensure effectively that shipping companies comply with Articles [101] and [102] of the [TFEU]. What is more, as these Articles are applicable directly by the authorities and courts of the Member States, there is a real risk that bodies of case law may evolve within the [EU] which will be inconsistent, if not contradictory."[28]

It is thus clear that the Commission lacked, in the absence of an appropriate regulation, the ability to apply Articles 101 and 102 of the TFEU.[29] The regulation gave the Commission such powers. Regulation 4056/86 also authorised liner conferences in a manner required by Regulation 954/79.

11.009 Regulation 4056/86 came relatively late in the development of the basic procedural rules of EU competition law. The procedural rules began in 1962 with the adoption of Regulation 17/62 (see footnote 21). Until 1986, air and sea transport were the only branches of the economy where there are currently no detailed provisions for implementing the competition rules. Regulation 17/62 had been in operation for almost a quarter of a century by the time Regulation 4056/86 was proposed. Nonetheless, what became Regulation 4056/86 was anticipated for many years. In the Preamble to Regulation 954/79 (adopted in 1979) concerning ratification or accession by Member States to the United Nations Code of Conduct on Liner Conferences,[30] it was proclaimed (in the last recital to the EU's Regulation 954/79)[31] that:

---

24 See para. 1 of *CMA CGM, Cho Yang Shipping Co. Ltd, Evergreen Marine Corp. Ltd, Hanjin Shipping Co. Ltd, Hapag-Lloyd Container Linie GmbH, Kawasaki Kisen Kaisha Ltd, Malaysia International Shipping Corporation Berhad, Mitsui OSK Lines Ltd, Neptune Orient Lines Ltd, Nippon Yusen Kaisha, Orient Overseas Container Line Ltd, P & O Nedlloyd Container Line Ltd, Senator Lines GmbH and Yangming Marine Transport Corp v Commission* which states: "Council Regulation No 17 of 6 February 1962 – First Regulation implementing Articles [81] and [82] of the Treaty (OJ, English Special Edition 1959–1962, p. 87) initially applied to all activities covered by the EEC Treaty. However, given that in the context of the common transport policy, and in view of the distinctive features of that sector, it proved necessary to lay down rules governing competition different from those laid down for other sectors of the economy, the Council adopted Regulation No 141/62 of 26 November 1962 exempting transport from the application of Council Regulation No 17 (OJ, English Special Edition 1959–1962, p. 291)."

25 OJ Spec. Ed. 1959–62, p. 291.

26 Ed., see Case 167/73 *Commission v France (French Seafarers' Case)* [1974] ECR 359, ECLI:EU:C:1974:35 and Cases 209–213/84 *Lucas Asjef and Others (Nouvelles Frontières)* [1996] ECR 1425, ECLI:EU:C:1974:35.

27 Ed., this position was altered in regard to maritime transport (as defined in Reg. 4056/86) by the adoption of Reg. 4056/86.

28 At the time of the adoption of Reg. 4056/86, the "Commission [had] no means of investigating directly cases of suspected infringements of Arts [101] and [102] in maritime transport" (Reg. 4056/86, Preamble, Recital 2).

29 Recitals 1–3 to Reg. 4056/86 set out the position clearly. See para. 11.017.

30 See chap. 9.

31 OJ 1979 L121/1,

"Whereas the stabilizing role of conferences in ensuring reliable services to shippers is recognized, but it is nevertheless necessary to avoid possible breaches by conferences of the rules of competition laid down in the Treaty; whereas the Commission will accordingly forward to the Council [of Ministers] a proposal for a Regulation concerning the application of those rules to sea transport."

It is therefore important to recall that while the Commission did not like the Council's block exemption, it was in existence for over 20 years.

11.010 Regulation 4056/86 had a long gestation: while the first proposal for the regulation was submitted by the Commission to the Council in 1981, the idea of such a proposal was raised at least as early as 1975.[32] The delay was due to the sharp political divisions, intensive negotiations and detailed studies conducted which had to be made before EU competition law could be applied by the Commission to this sector. During its passage from initiation to adoption, the proposal was amended formally at least four times. The eventual adoption of the regulation was an important event and cleared even further the path for eventual adoption of Regulations 3975/87[33] and 3976/87[34] on air transport. Its long gestation makes it clear that it was not a knee-jerk measure. It was however a controversial measure which did not enjoy too much support from the Commission – particularly in the later years of the regulation's life. Perhaps the shipowners who lobbied for the measure had been too successful in their efforts to the annoyance of Commission officials, many of whom believed that the block exemption went too far and should never have been adopted.

1981: Commission proposal

11.011 On 16 October 1981, a proposal for a regulation laying down detailed rules for the application of what are now Articles 101 and 102 of the TFEU to maritime transport was submitted by the Commission to the Council.[35] This was largely at the instigation of Commissioner Andriessen. The 1981 proposed regulation did not exempt, under, what is now Article 101(3) of the TFEU, arrangements in bulk transport because of a lack of adequate experience by the Commission in the field.

1983: EESC opinion

11.012 On 3 November 1981, the Council requested[36] the Economic and Social Committee ("EESC") to furnish an opinion on the Commission's proposal. On 27 January 1983, the EESC published its opinion.[37] This resulted from the Council's request and the EESC's Bureau deciding on 12 November 1981 to instruct the Section for Transport and Competition to draw up an opinion on the matter. The opinion, which was adopted by 89 votes to four with seven abstentions, approved the Commission's proposal subject to

---

32 See Commission, *Fifth Competition Report* (1975), at para. 15. See also the European Parliament's comments in EP Doc. 1-249 (see fn. 3), para. 2.
33 OJ 1987 L374/1.
34 OJ 1987 L374/9.
35 COM(81)423; OJ 1981 C282. See Commission Information Memo P-58, October 1981.
36 OJ 1981 C282/4.
37 Opinion on the Proposal for a Council Regulation laying down detailed rules for the application of Arts 85 and 86 of the Treaty to Maritime Transport, OJ 1983, C77/13 and OJ 1985 C344; CES 73/83.

some comments. The EESC contended that there should have been a dual basis of the regulation, namely, the then Articles 84(2) and 87 of the then European Economic Community ("EEC") Treaty.[38] It approved the exclusion of bulk transport from the scope of the regulation but noted the absence of a clear definition of bulk transport.[39] It also stated that the conditions attaching to the exemption were "vague and questionable".[40]

1984: European Parliament's report

11.013 On 12 November 1981, the Council requested, pursuant to the then Article 87 of the then EEC Treaty,[41] the Parliament to deliver an opinion on the proposal. The President of the Parliament referred the request to the Committee on Economic and Monetary Affairs, the Legal Affairs Committee as well as the Committee on Transport. On 11 May 1984, the Parliament's Committee on Economic and Monetary Affairs published an interim report[42] on the proposal. The body of the report stated that the Committee:

> "2. Welcomes the proposed Regulation on the application of the competition policy provisions laid down in the Treaty to maritime transport and stresses that the main aims of the regulation are compatible with the objectives of the UN Convention of 6 April 1979 on a Code of Conduct for Liner Conferences, which the Member States also accepted in the form of EEC Regulation 954/79 of 15 May 1979;[43]
> 3. Agrees in principle that there should be the greatest possible concordance between the UN Code and the Regulation with respect to the rules of competition laid down in the Treaty and stresses the need for the Regulation to take account of practical experience gained in the implementation of the Code;
> 4. The Committee on Economic and Monetary Affairs takes the view that, where compatible with the content of the proposed Regulation, the detailed provisions of Articles 4 and 5 [of the regulation] should be formulated to correspond closely to the following provisions in the Code:
>
>   – non-differentiation between shippers;
>   – formal consultation between shippers and conferences on matters of common interest;
>   – loyalty agreements, of which the form and content are the object of negotiation between the conference and shippers;
>   – access to clearly specified tariffs and similar conditions of transport etc. upon the request of any party concerned;
>   – services not covered by freight charged;
>
> 5. Therefore calls on the Commission to show the necessary flexibility when applying the Regulation and, where such is compatible with the principles of competition policy, to accept that the sector should regulate its own conduct;
> 6. Considers the Commission's proposed definition of bulk transport to be unclear and recommends that only cargo without mark or count or cargo for which the tariffs have been negotiated should be excluded from the scope of the Regulation;

---

38 Ibid., para. 1.1.3. The regulation, as finally adopted, included this provision. The then Art. 84 of the EEC Treaty related to transport while the then Art. 87 of the EEC Treaty related to competition. They would now be, for all intents and purposes, Arts 100(2) and 103 TFEU.

39 Ibid., para. 1.2.1.

40 Ibid., para. 1.3.6.

41 This is now Art. 103 TFEU.

42 Doc. 1-249/84/A, Rapporteur: Mr K Nyborg. The reports were published: OJ 1986 C172/178 and OJ 1986 C255/169.

43 OJ L121, 17.5.1979.

7. Agrees with the Commission that the question of access by outside shipping companies to conferences and the question of the internal organisation of conferences are covered by the general provisions of the Treaty and that there is therefore no need for an implementing Regulation in this connection; such matters can only be settled case by case;
8. Is aware of the international aspects of liner conferences and the fact that any regulation of these will necessarily come into conflict with the legal positions of those conference parties that are not Member States of the [EU]; therefore realizes that there is a risk of jurisdictional problems arising in this respect with third countries and wishes to avoid conflicts in this area."

11.014 The European Parliament ultimately passed two resolutions on the proposal: the "Resolution on the proposal from the European Commission to the EC Council for a Regulation laying down detailed rules for the application of Articles 85 and 86 of the Treaty to maritime transport"[44] and the "Resolution embodying the opinion of the European Parliament on Memorandum No. 3 from the European Commission to the EC Council and on the proposals *inter alia* for amendments to the Proposal for a Regulation laying down detailed rules for the application of Articles 85 and 86 of the Treaty to Maritime Transport".[45]

1985: Amended Commission proposal

11.015 A proposal for the regulation was ultimately contained in the Commission's communication of 14 March 1985 entitled "Progress Towards the Common Transport Policy – Maritime Transport".[46] This was an amended version of the 1981 proposal in the light of, among other things, the opinions of the Parliament as well as the EESC. In its Annual Report on Competition for 1985, the Commission identified the major issues deserving amendment:

"(i) redrafting certain definitions (conference, transport user, tramp vessel services) so as to be closer to the wording used by the UN Code of Conduct for Liner Conferences;
(ii) the requirements for application of the block exemption Regulation have been brought down to only one condition (*sine qua non*), namely the principle of non-discrimination. Requirements contained in the earlier version as conditions for application have now been converted into obligations, which while not barring coverage by the block exemption may nevertheless give rise to withdrawal of the benefit thereof;
(iii) adding an obligation on conferences to consult shippers and providing for loyalty agreements covering less than 100% of a shipper's cargo;
(iv) a clear and exhaustive definition of the special circumstances having effects incompatible with the conditions laid down in Article [101(3)] and justifying the withdrawal of the benefit of the block exemption; these are: acts of third states, acts of conferences and change of market conditions;
(v) the establishment of a differentiated regime for the efficient monitoring of the exempted conference agreements depending on the presence or elimination of outsider competition;
(vi) redrafting Article 8 which provides for the possibility of concluding agreements with third countries."

---

44 OJ 1989 C172/178. "Articles 85 and 86" are now Arts 101 and 102 of the TFEU.
45 OJ 1986 C255/12.
46 Doc. COM (85)90 Final. Dinger, op. cit. at fn. 8, p. 10, described the 1985 document as "the first attempt to develop an [EU] shipping policy in a systematic way".

1986: Commission amendment

11.016 The Commission published an amended proposal on 24 November 1986.[47] The amendment suggested changes to Articles 14 and 15 of the proposal. Article 14 related to liaison with the authorities of the Member States. Paragraphs 5 and 6 of the proposal had read:

> "5. Consultation shall take place at a joint meeting convened by the Commission; such meeting shall be held not later than fourteen days after dispatch of the notice convening it. This notice shall, in respect of each case to be examined, be accompanied by a summary of the case together with an indication of the most important documents, and a preliminary draft decision.
> 6. The Advisory Committee may deliver an opinion notwithstanding that some of its members or their alternates are not present. A report of the outcome of the consultative proceedings shall be annexed to the draft decision. It shall not be made public."

1986: Council adoption of Regulation 4056/86

11.017 Ultimately, in December 1986, the Council of Ministers, under the presidency of the UK, adopted Regulation 4056/86 as part of its package of four regulations on maritime transport (i.e. Regulations 4055/86, 4056/86, 4057/86 and 4058/86).[48] As will be discussed in the next chapter, Regulation 4056/86 ultimately was repealed by Regulation 1419/2006.[49] This present chapter is therefore largely devoted to considering what happened between 1986 and the adoption of Regulation 1419/2006.

11.018 Before analysing that interesting point, it is useful to reflect on two points. An examination of part of the recitals to the regulation is still instructive today:

> "[1] Whereas the rules of competition form part of the Treaty's general provisions which also apply to maritime transport;[50] whereas detailed rules for applying those provisions are set out in the Chapter of the [EEC] Treaty dealing with the rules on competition or are to be determined by the procedures laid down therein;
> [2] Whereas according to Council Regulation No. 141[/62], Council Regulation No. 17[/62] does not apply to transport; whereas Council Regulation (EEC) No. 1017/68 applies to inland transport only; whereas, consequently, the Commission has no means at present of investigating directly cases of suspected infringement of Articles 85[51] and 86[52] in maritime transport; whereas, moreover, the Commission lacks such powers of its own to take decisions or impose penalties as are necessary for it to bring to an end infringements established by it;
> [3] Whereas this situation necessitates the adoption of a Regulation applying the rules of competition to maritime transport; whereas Council Regulation (EEC) No. 954/79 of May 15, 1979, concerning the ratification by Member States of, or their accession to, the United Nations Convention on a Code of Conduct for Liner Conferences will then result in the application of the Code of Conduct to a considerable number of conferences serving the Community; whereas the Regulation applying the rules of competition to maritime transport foreseen in the last recital of Regulation (EEC) No. 954/79 should take account of the

---

47 OJ 1986 C324/6; COM(86) 676 final.
48 See chap. 5.
49 OJ 2006/L269/1.
50 Ed., see the judgment of the CJEU in Case 167/73 *Commission v France* (*French Seafarers' Case*) [1974] ECR 359, ECLI:EU:C:1974:35.
51 Ed., i.e. now Art. 101 of the TFEU.
52 Ed., i.e. now Art. 102 of the TFEU.

adoption of the Code; whereas, as far as conferences subject to the Code of Conduct are concerned, the Regulation should supplement the Code or make it more precise;

[4] Whereas it appears preferable to exclude tramp[53] vessel services from the scope of this Regulation, rates for these services being freely negotiated on a case-by-case basis in accordance with supply and demand conditions;

[5] Whereas this Regulation should take account of the necessity, on the one hand to provide for implementing rules that enable the Commission to ensure that competition is not unduly distorted within the [Internal] Market, and on the other hand to avoid excessive regulation of the sector."

In regard to Recital 3 of the regulation, which states that "as far as conferences subject to the Code of Conduct are concerned, the regulation should supplement the Code or make it more precise", the regulation did not say how the Code lacked precision.

11.019 Second, Recital 11 of the regulation stated:

"[w]hereas certain obligations should also be attached to the [liner conference] exemption ... in this respect, users must at all time be in a position to acquaint themselves with the rates and conditions of carriage applied by members of the conference, since in the case of inland transport organised by shippers, the latter continue to be subject to Regulation 1017/68".

Ruttley has made the following incisive observations on Recital 11.[54] He states that this

"clearly indicates that inland transport organised by shippers themselves ('merchant haulage') is regulated by the Inland Regulation, Regulation 1017/68; inland transport by carriers ('carrier haulage') is not covered; therefore surely carrier haulage is covered by Regulation 4056/86? This argument was at the centre of the long controversy whether liner conferences could have combined sea and inland tariffs ('multimodal tariffs') under the block exemption".[55]

He continued:

"[t]he Commission rejected the argument on the grounds that the reference to 'shippers' was a misprint – it should have said 'carriers' i.e., that inland transport supplied by carriers was subject to Regulation 1017/68 not 4056/86 [and] it would follow that inland transport by carriers could not be within the liner conference block exemption in Regulation 4056/86; [f]or six years (i.e., between 1981 and 1986), the EC Member States in the Council negotiated and debated on the basis of a 'misprint'; [and] no-one pointed out the 'misprint'; neither shippers, carriers, Community officials, Council delegates."[56]

C. ENTRY INTO FORCE OF REGULATION 4056/86

11.020 Regulation 4056/86 entered into force on 1 July 1987.[57] By virtue of Regulation 1419/2006, the ultimate cessation date for Regulation 4056/86 was set as 18 October 2008 because there had been a two year phasing out of the regulation from when Regulation 1419/2006 entered into force as a regulation.[58]

---

53 Ed., i.e. non-liner services.
54 At the EMLO conference in Brussels, on 13 October 2006.
55 Ibid.
56 Ibid.
57 Reg. 4056/86, Art. 27.
58 OJ 2006 L269/1, Art.1. There is an important difference between a regulation entering into force and when it has effect.

D. LEGAL BASES OF REGULATION 4056/86

11.021 Regulation 4056/86 was adopted on the bases of Articles 84(2) and 87 of the then EEC Treaty. The then Article 84(2) of the EEC Treaty provided that it was for the Council to decide whether, to what extent and by what procedure appropriate provisions may be laid down for sea and air transport. Prior to the Single European Act, Article 87 of the EEC Treaty provided that the adoption of regulations and directives to give effect to the principles set out in the then Articles 85 and 86 (now Articles 101 and 102 of the TFEU) required unanimity among Member States which was not always easy to obtain due to divergent approaches and interests of Member States.

11.022 The original proposal in 1981 for a regulation was to be adopted solely on the basis of the then Article 87.[59] The EESC[60] as well as the European Parliament[61] both objected to this approach. Clough and Randolph commented perceptively:

"The importance of the legal basis for the substantive content of Community legislation has been established in numerous cases by the European Court. This includes the difference in voting procedure between majority voting, required under [the then] Article 87 [of the EEC Treaty], and unanimity as required then under Article 84(2). However, in the present context of sea transport, set against the background of uncertainty as to whether the competition rules applied at all without EC Council action under [the then] Article 84(2) [of the EEC Treaty], the dual legal basis has more than procedural significance

The debate between the … Council and the … Commission over legal basis reflects an underlying difference over policy. Article 9 of the Regulation deals predominantly with what must be classified as transport policy, rather than competition policy. It therefore requires an appropriate legal basis which only could have been Article 84(2) [of the then EEC Treaty], in the absence of further progress with a common sea transport policy. However, it is not clear from the Regulation, or its legislative history, whether the … Council intended the liberal approach applied to closed liner conferences, with the emphasis on self-regulation under the UNCTAD Code, to reflect the triumph of transport policy over competition policy. The result, albeit short-lived, does.

In fact, despite its acceptance of the Brussels package and its endorsement of the UNCTAD Code [in 1979], the … Commission throughout the five years of its legislative history tried to introduce in the proposal provisions for preventing conferences from breaching the competition rules. In the end, the provisions falling into that category were brought much closer into line with the UNCTAD Code, as requested, for example, by the European Parliament.

It is understood that the … Commission eventually adopted the addition of Article 84(2) [of the then EEC treaty] to the legal basis on the ground that Article 9 of the Regulation is concerned with transport, as opposed to competition policy since it is concerned with international conflicts. Council Regulation (EEC) 4056/86 was adopted by the EC Council on the dual legal basis.

However, the inclusion of the transport policy legal basis, relating to sea and air transport in Article 84(2), is unusual. This is clear from the fact that the … Council regulations laying down the procedure for applying the competition rules and enabling the … Commission to adopt block exemption regulations for certain categories of agreements in the air transport sector were both adopted on the basis of Article 87 alone. The weight given to transport policy signified by the dual legal basis is unlikely to be repeated.

The … Commission has reinforced recently its opposition to repeating the liberal regime adopted in respect of liner conferences in Council Regulation (EEC) 4056/86, largely because of

---

59 See *Ninth Report on Competition Policy*, 1979, para. 15.
60 See Opinion on the Proposal for a Council Regulation laying down detailed rules for the Application of Arts 85 and 86 of the [EEC] Treaty to Maritime Transport, para.1.1, OJ 1987 C77/13.
61 Resolution of the European Parliament embodying the Opinion of the European Parliament on Memorandum No 3 from the EC Commission to the EC Council etc., para. 40, OJ C255/182, 13 October 1986.

transport policy considerations, in the case of other sea transport operations such as consortia and multi-modal arrangements."[62]

E. LEGAL EFFECT OF REGULATION 4056/86

11.023 Article 27 of Regulation 4056/86 provided that the regulation was binding in its entirety and directly applicable to all Member States. This is normal with all regulations. There was no need to have national legislation implementing the measure in Member State law given that the measure was a regulation. The regulation gave the Commission the means of implementing, in a practical but limited way, what are now Articles 101 and 102 of the TFEU in regard to certain aspects of maritime transport. It was limited because it did not relate to cabotage[63] or tramp[64] traffic.

F. INTERPRETATION OF REGULATION 4056/86

11.024 Regulation 4056/86 was wholly exceptional and was therefore always construed narrowly. Its exceptional nature was evident from the fact that it exempted price-fixing and market sharing which are ordinarily regarded as hard-core breaches of competition law. On 1 April 2003, Fabrizia Benini of the Directorate General for Competition ("DG COMP") spoke (in a personal capacity) at a seminar entitled "Seminar on EU Competition Law and Maritime Transport"[65] and stated that "it is constant Commission practice – and unlikely to change – to apply the provisions of the block exemption restrictively".

11.025 It is useful to note the following observations by the General Court in *Atlantic Container Line AB v Commission*[66] where it stated:

> "146. First, it should be recalled that, according to settled case-law, having regard to the general principle of the prohibition of agreements restricting competition in Article [101](1) of the TFEU], provisions derogating therefrom in an exempting regulation must, by their nature, be strictly interpreted (Compagnie maritime belge de transports [Case T-24/96 [1996] ECR II-01201, ECLI:EU:T:1996:139], paragraph 48; Case T-9/92 Peugeot v Commission [1993] ECR II-493 [ECLI:EU:T:1993:38], paragraph 37). This conclusion applies, a fortiori, to the provisions of Regulation No 4056/86 by virtue of its unlimited duration and the exceptional nature of the restrictions on competition authorised (horizontal agreement having as its object the fixing of prices). It follows that the block exemption provided for by Article 3 of Regulation No 4056/86 cannot be interpreted broadly and progressively so as to cover all the agreements which shipping companies deem it useful,

---

62 Op. cit. at fn. 1, para. 4.3.
63 Ortiz Blanco commented at the EMLO Conference in 2008: "the Regulation was based on the (as it turns out fallacious) premise that the exclusion from its scope of cabotage trades was of no great practical importance, since such restrictions on competition hardly ever came within the scope of the Community competition rules".
64 Ortiz Blanco commented at the EMLO Conference in 2008: "tramping represents about two-thirds in volume and three-quarters in tonnage miles of world maritime transport. In terms of transport capacity, the bulk carriers represented more than 70% of the world fleet in 1998. As a result, a significant part of international maritime transport was not caught by the Regulation. The fourth recital to the Regulation, which explained the reasons for excluding tramping from its scope alluded to it being unnecessary for the Community antitrust rules to apply given the competitive nature of that sector of the maritime industry. The unconvincing nature of this argument recalled the justification for excluding cabotage from the scope of the Regulation."
65 http://ec.europa.eu/competition/speeches/text/sp2003_008_en.pdf.
66 Case T-395/94 [2002] ECR II-875 ECLI:EU:T:2002:49.

or even necessary, to adopt in order to adapt to market conditions. The exemption can relate only to the types of agreement which the Council, when Regulation No 4056/86 was adopted, regarded, in the light of experience, as satisfying the conditions of Article [101](3) of the Treaty. Apart from the power enjoyed by the Council, if the need arose, to amend Regulation No 4056/86, the undertakings concerned also always have the option to apply for an individual exemption to offset any disadvantages of the limitations inherent in the block exemption.[67]

...

176. It must be stated that the applicants have not disputed any of these matters of fact which are indeed evident directly from the text of the TAA itself and that, in the light of those facts, the Commission rightly considered that the TAA was not a liner conference within the meaning of Article 1(3)(b) of Regulation No 4056/86 on the ground that that agreement provided a different tariff scheme for the two categories of members, and not uniform or common freight rates applicable by all the members.

...

177. It is clear from the foregoing, first, that the block exemption provided for in Article 3 of Regulation No 4056/86 can apply only to the liner conferences referred to in Article 1(3)(b) of that regulation and, second, that the TAA cannot be regarded as a liner conference within the meaning of that regulation."

11.026 Munari has also observed helpfully in this context:

"after an initial 'relaxed' implementation of the [EU] competition rules in liner shipping,[68] which was mainly justified by reasons of coexistence and co-operation with third countries in international maritime trade issues, the Commission (and also the [General Court]) made clear that the antitrust immunity enjoyed by liner conferences was not to be intended as an overall retreat of [EU] competition rules in the maritime sector...

It is particularly in their case law that the Commission and the [General Court] worked out a rigorous approach aimed at restricting as much as possible the block exemption established by Regulation 4056/86."[69]

11.027 The discrepancies which existed between the different language versions of the regulation caused difficulties for its interpretation.[70]

G. APPLICATION OF REGULATION 4056/86

Text of Article 1

11.028 Regulation 4056/86 was limited in its scope. Article 1 of the regulation provided:

"1. This Regulation lays down detailed rules for the application of Articles [101] and [102] of the Treaty to maritime transport services.
2. It shall apply only to international maritime transport services from or to one or more [EU] ports, other than tramp vessel services.
3. For the purposes of this Regulation:

---

67 Ed., this option to apply to the Commission for an individual exemption no longer exists since the abolition of individual exemptions since 1 May 2004 pursuant to the Adoption of Reg. 1/2003 (OJ 2004 21/1).
68 Ed., see the decisions in *Shipowners' Committees* [1992] OJ 1992 L134; *Cewal, Cowac, Ukwal* [1993] OJ L34.
69 "Liner Shipping and Antitrust after the Repeal of Regulation 4056/86" [2009] LMCLQ 42 at 46.
70 E.g. Case T-86/95 *Compagnie Generale Maritime and Others v Commission (FEFL)* [2002] ECR II-1011 (para. 243).

(a) 'tramp vessel services' means the transport of goods in bulk or in break-bulk in a vessel chartered wholly or partly to one or more shippers on the basis of a voyage or time charter or any other form of contract for non-regularly scheduled or non-advertised sailings where the freight rates are freely negotiated case by case in accordance with the conditions of supply and demand;

(b) 'liner conference' means a group of two or more vessel-operating carriers which provides international liner services for the carriage of cargo on a particular route or routes within specified geographical limits and which has an agreement or arrangement, whatever its nature, within the framework of which they operate under uniform or common freight rates and any other agreed conditions with respect to the provision of liner services;

(c) 'transport user' means an undertaking (e.g. shippers, consignees, forwarders, etc.) provided it has entered into, or demonstrates an intention to enter into, a contractual or other arrangement with a conference or shipping line for the shipment of goods, or any association of shippers."

11.029 Article 1 of the regulation differed from, and was more detailed than, Article 1 of the original proposal in 1981 which read simply:

"1. This regulation lays down detailed rules for the application of Articles [101] and [102] of the Treaty to maritime transport.
2. It shall apply only to international maritime transport operations other than bulk transports from or to one or more Community ports."

The Commission, in its Explanatory Memorandum[71] to that proposed draft of the regulation, wrote:

"In view of the jurisprudence of the Court[72] the regulation affects all sea transport services other than bulk which may affect trade between Member States. In principle it applies to all sea transport to or from a Community port, even if it concerns transport between the Community and a third country. Restrictive or abusive practices or lines between the Community and third countries may in fact affect trade between Member States by influencing the competitive position of the ports and the undertakings in their area of influence, even if potential, and by disturbing the usual flows of transport at Community level of both exports and imports."

Article 1, as adopted, was therefore much more detailed and precise than the relatively more vague original draft.

Effect of Article 1

11.030 Article 1 of the regulation (as adopted) provided, in the circumstances specified in the regulation, international liner conferences with an automatic open-ended group or block exemption subject to certain exceptions. In essence, it applied to liner services only and provided an exemption to certain liner cargo conferences within the meaning of the United Nations Convention on a Code of Conduct for Liner Conferences ("UNCTAD Code").

---

71 See COM(81)423 final.
72 *Cf.* considerations put forward by the [CJEU] in the following judgments: (1) Case 22/71 *Beguelin Import v SAGL Import-Export* [1971] ECR 949, at p. 959, [ECLI:EU:C:1971:113] paras 10 and 11; (2) Case 48/69 *Imperial Chemical Industries Ltd v Commission* [1972] ECR 619 [ECLI:EU:C:1972:70] at pp. 665–6; (3) Cases 6 and 7/73 *Commercial Solvents v Commission* [1974] ECR 223 [ECLI:EU:C:1974:18] at pp. 254–6; and (4) Case 36/74 *Walrave and Koch v Union Cycliste Internationale* [1974] ECR 1405, [ECLI:EU:C:1974:140] at p. 1421.

Transport services

11.031 The regulation applied only to certain types of maritime *transport* services.[73] Thus, it did not apply to any activity which was not a "transport" service, thus services which were ancillary or related to transport did not fall within the scope of the regulation.[74] Travel agency, shipping agency, ships' brokerage, container leasing or similar "ancillary" activities fell outside the scope of the regulation.

International transport services

11.032 The regulation applied only to certain types of *international* maritime transport services to or from one or more EU Member State ports, other than tramp vessel services.[75] Thus, the regulation did not apply to maritime transport within a Member State or, put another way, it did not apply to *cabotage* trade in a Member State. Nor did it apply to trade between ports in two different States where neither State was a Member State.[76] There was, of course, nothing stopping what are now Articles 101 and 102 (in themselves) from being applied to such a trade where there was an effect on trade between Member States but this would have proven difficult (but not impossible) in the absence of the rules found in Regulation 4056/86.[77] The regulation applied whenever the international journey began or ended in an EU port. The fourth recital to Regulation 4056/86 stated that it would be "preferable to exclude the tramp vessel services from the scope of this Regulation, [because] rates for these services [were] freely negotiated on a case-by-case basis in accordance with supply and demand conditions". As mentioned above, Ortiz Blanco has commented that:

> "the Regulation was based on the (as it turns out, fallacious) premise that the exclusion from its scope of cabotage trades was of no great practical importance, since such restrictions on competition hardly ever came within the scope of the Community competition rules."[78]

11.033 In regard to Article 1(2) of the regulation, Ortiz Blanco observed that:

> "Article 1(2) of the Regulation also excluded from its scope maritime transport between non-[EU] ports. The reasons that this type of transport were initially excluded from the scope of the maritime Regulation, both with respect to substantive and procedural matters, only appeared in the 1981 draft of Regulation 4056/86, which explained that it was unlikely that this type of transport would affect trade between [EU] Member States ... although such a presumption may appear reasonable – more so, in any event, than the similar presumption concerning cabotage or tramping – it cannot be categorically excluded that in certain circumstances restrictive agreements relating to maritime transport between third countries might appreciably affect intra-Community trade."[79]

---

73 Reg. 4056/86, Art. 1(2).
74 For a comparable situation in relation to ground-handling and reservation activities in the airline industry, see *Olympic Airways* OJ 1985 L46/51 and *London-European Airways–Sabena* OJ 1988 L317/47, respectively.
75 Reg. 4056/86, Art. 1(2).
76 This was too simplistic a view because arrangements outside the EU may affect trade in the EU where there is an effect on trade within the EU.
77 See Cases 89/85, 104/85, 114/85, 116/85 and 125-9/85 *Ahlstrom Osakeyhtio v Commission* [1988] ECR 5193, ECLI:EU:C:1988:447 (known as the *Wood Pulp* case).
78 EMLO conference, Copenhagen, 2008.
79 Ibid.

Maritime services

11.034 The regulation applied to *maritime* services. Unfortunately, the term "maritime services" was left undefined by the regulation. The Commission interpreted the term narrowly and saw it purely in the context of the sea-leg of a journey.[80] Thus, any other part of a multimodal journey fell outside Regulation 4056/86. Article 3 only related to cargo-carrying activities. Given the desire by the Commission to give a restrictive interpretation, this approach was sensible for the Commission but inconvenient for the industry.

Services other than tramp services

11.035 The regulation applied only to international maritime transport services from or to one or more EU ports *other than tramp vessel services*.[81] The non-application of the regulation to tramp services was at the insistence of Greece (a then new entrant to the EU and an important maritime nation in the EU and globally). For the purposes of the regulation, the term "tramp vessel services" was defined generously as meaning:

> "the transport of goods in bulk or in break-bulk in a vessel chartered wholly or partly to one or more shippers on the basis of a voyage or time charter or any other form of contract for non-regularly scheduled or non-advertised sailings where the freight rates are freely negotiated case by case in accordance with the conditions of supply and demand".[82]

Ruttley has criticised this definition and questioned whether it was a "dog's dinner".[83] He suggests that a simpler definition would be services with vessels operating as contract carriers on an infrequent or irregular schedule over varying routes determined largely by the cargo attached.

11.036 It is assumed by many (but not all) commentators that the bulk sector operated in a competitive environment in any case. The mere fact that Regulation 4056/86 did not apply to such services did not prejudice the fact that Articles 101 and 102 did apply to the sector. Nor did it prejudice the possibility that the Commission could have made a proposal for a regulation in this area. Nor again, did it prejudice the application of the regulation (i.e. Regulation 4056/86) where the trade is a tramp one but the freight rate has not been negotiated freely.

11.037 It was also assumed by some observers that tramp services were immune or outside the purview of EU competition law altogether because of Regulation 4056/86. This is not correct. What Regulation 4056/86 did was to prevent the Commission from applying, what are now, Articles 101 and 102 of the TFEU, to tramp vessel services under what was then the procedural regulation (i.e. Regulation 17/62). However, Regulation 4056/86 could not disapply a superior treaty article (i.e. either Article 101 or 102) and the Commission had an ongoing duty to ensure that competition law applied to the sector. So, the apparent exclusion was largely appearance rather than a reality.

---

80 See e.g. OJ 1990 C59/2, para. 1; OJ 1990 C130/3, para. 1; OJ 1990 C162/16, para. 20.
81 Reg. 4056/86, Art. 1(2).
82 Reg. 4056/86, Art. 1(3)(a). This was a controversial definition and one which resulted after considerable discussion.
83 EMLO conference, Brussels, 13 October 2006.

11.038 Ruttley enumerated five common types of maritime agreement which fell within the scope of Regulation 4056/86 but they required notification to the Commission[84] and exemption under Article 101(3) as they did not fall within the scope of the block exemptions provided by the regulation. The five types were:

"(1) joint venture agreements and other consortia agreements (for example, vessel pools),
(2) exclusive port utilisation agreements,
(3) management and shared route agreements,
(4) container 'slot charter' or slot exchange arrangements on vessels,
(5) agreements between liner conferences and independent shipping operators (the so-called 'outsider agreements')."[85]

11.039 The significance of classifying services as tramp services or not is clear from the Commission's investigation into alleged anti-competitive arrangements in the *Bulk Liquids by Sea* case before the repeal of Regulation 4056/86.[86] If the alleged activities (e.g. price fixing and customer collection) had occurred in the context of tramp services then the Commission did not have the power to act because Regulation 4056/86 did not apply to tramp services. If the event occurred today then the Commission could investigate it under Regulation 1/2003.

Transport users

11.040 The regulation only applied to certain agreements between transport users. In the context of the regulation, a "transport user" was an "undertaking" (e.g. shippers, consignees and forwarders) provided the arrangement entered into, or demonstrates an intention to enter into, a contractual or other arrangement with a conference or shipping line for the shipment of goods, or any association of shippers.[87] Who else was included? Bredima-Savopoulou and Tzoannos commented:

"[i]t is uncertain whether providers of ancillary services (insurers, classification societies, stevedores, shipping agents) are covered by the Regulation or whether they are subject to the ordinary rules of competition. Basically, the Regulation is of direct relevance only to shipowners and operators".[88]

Views differ on this point. It is submitted that such ancillary undertakings are engaged in activities which are ancillary to maritime transport and thus such agreements fell outside the scope of the block exemption contained in the regulation and so were subject to what is now Article 101(1) of the TFEU but may have been able to benefit from Article 101(3) but not by virtue of the block exemption in Regulation 4056/86. Thus, just as a ground handling agreement was outside the scope of the comparable regulation on air transport, thus a stevedoring agreement was outside the scope of Regulation 4056/86.

---

84 Notification was abolished in EU competition law generally on 1 May 2004 by virtue of Reg. 1/2003. See Holmes and Davey, "Is there any Legal Certainty Left for Shipping Lines and their Agreements?" (2003) 9 *JIML* 480 and Power, "Selected Developments in EU Shipping Law" (2003) 9 *JIML* 150 at 152.
85 Ruttley, op. cit., at fn. 1, p. 9.
86 See Memo/07/131 and Memo/08/297.
87 Reg. 4056/86, Art. 1(3)(c).
88 *The Common Shipping Policy* (1989), pp. 207–208, fn. 9.

Agreements between providers of ancillary services

11.041 As a general rule, the regulation provided no exemption for agreements between the providers of ancillary services such as shipping agents or for agreements between maritime transport service operators and the providers of ancillary services. The sole exception was contained in Article 2 of the regulation.

Passenger traffic

11.042 The transport of passengers fell within the scope of the regulation.[89] Passenger liner conferences were however not included in the definition of "liner conferences" for the purposes of Article 1(3)(b) of the regulation. International short sea services were also covered by the phrase "international maritime services".

Definition of a "liner conference"

11.043 Article 1(3)(b) of the regulation defined a "liner conference" as meaning

"a group of two or more vessel-operating carriers which provides international liner services for the carriage of cargo on a particular route or routes within specified geographical limits and which has an agreement or arrangement, whatever its nature, within the framework of which they operate under uniform or common freight rates and any other agreed conditions with respect to the provision of liner services".

Scope of Article 1

11.044 The somewhat ambiguous drafting of Article 1 meant that there was sufficient doubt that no categorical view can be expressed here as to who were the "beneficiaries" of the regulation. It also meant that the Commission had sufficient scope to restrict the application of the regulation because of the ambiguity.

Affecting trade between Member States

11.045 There was always a de facto and realistic presumption that liner conferences affect trade between Member States.[90]

H. TECHNICAL AGREEMENTS: ARTICLE 2 OF REGULATION 4056/86

Introduction

11.046 The seventh recital to Regulation 4056/86 provided that "certain types of technical agreements, decisions and concerted practices may be excluded from the prohibition on restrictive practices on the ground that they do not, as a general rule, restrict competition". Article 2 of the regulation related to certain types of agreements, decisions and

---

89 See the *Nineteenth Report on Competition Policy* (1989), para. 29.
90 E.g. Cases T-24/93, T-25/93 and T-28/93 *CEWAL I* [1996] ECR II-1201, ECLI:EU:T:1996:139, paras 202–203; and Case T-395/94 *Atlantic Container Liner AB and others v Commission ("TAA Case")* [2002] ECR II-875 ECLI:EU:T:2002:49, paras 71–74.

concerted practices[91] whose *sole* object and effect was to achieve technical improvements or co-operation by means of:

(a) the introduction of uniform application of standards or types in respect of vessels and other means of transport, equipment, supplies or fixed installations;
(b) the exchange or pooling for the purpose of operating transport services, of vessels, space on vessels or slots or other means of transport, staff, equipment or fixed installations;
(c) the organisation and execution of successive or supplementary maritime transport operations and the establishment or application of inclusive rates and conditions for such operations;
(d) the co-ordination of transport timetables for connecting routes;
(e) the consolidation of individual assignments; or
(f) the establishment or application of uniform rules concerning the structure and the conditions governing the application of transport tariffs.

An agreement with any other motive would not benefit from the exemption: the *sole* object and effect of the agreement must fall within the scope of Article 2 of the regulation. While Regulation 4056/86 has been repealed, a provision such as Article 2 could still be useful because it demonstrates what fell outside the scope of Article 101(1).

Text of Article 2

11.047 Article 2(1) of Regulation 4056/86 provided:

"1. The prohibition laid down in Article [101(1)] of the [TFEU] shall not apply to agreements, decisions and concerted practices whose sole object and[92] effect is to achieve technical improvements or co-operation by means of:

(a) the introduction of uniform application of standards or types in respect of vessels and other means of transport, equipment, supplies or fixed installations;
(b) the exchange or pooling for the purpose of operating transport services, of vessels, space on vessels or slots or other means of transport, staff, equipment or fixed installations;
(c) the organization and execution of successive or supplementary maritime transport operation and the establishment or application of inclusive rates and conditions for such operations;
(d) the co-ordination of transport timetables for connecting routes;
(e) the consolidation of individual assignments;
(f) the establishment or application of uniform rules concerning the structure and the conditions governing the application of transport tariffs.

2. The Commission shall, if necessary, submit to the Council proposals for the amendment of the list contained in paragraph 1."

11.048 The original proposal in 1981 was very similar to the provision which was finally adopted. The original provision read as follows:

---

91 On the concepts of agreements, decisions and concerted practices, see chap. 9.
92 Ed., note "object and effect" rather than the usual "object or effect" (as in Art. 101 of the TFEU).

"1. The prohibition laid down in Article [101(1)] of the Treaty shall not apply to agreements, decisions or concerted practices whose sole object and effect is to achieve technical improvements or co-operation by means of:

    (a) the introduction or uniform application of standards or types of vessels and other means of transport, equipment, supplies or fixed installation;
    (b) the exchange or pooling, for the purpose of operating transport services, of vessels and other modes of transport, staff, equipment or fixed installations;
    (c) the organisation and execution of successive or supplementary maritime transport operations and the establishment and application of inclusive rates and conditions for such operations;
    (d) the coordination of transport timetables for connecting routes;
    (e) the bulking of individual consignments;
    (f) the establishment or application of uniform rules concerning the structure and the conditions governing the application of transport on condition that such rules do not directly or indirectly fix rates and conditions of carriage;

2. The Commission shall, if necessary, submit to the Council proposals for the amendment of the list contained in paragraph 1 of this article."

11.049 The Commission commenting on this 1981 proposal said: "the list of exceptions hardly differs from that of Article 3 of Regulation (EEC) No 1017/68.[93] Account has been taken in particular of the fact this regulation only applies to one mode of transport."[94] This list (which may well be termed a "White List"[95] in that the arrangements did not breach Article 101(1) of the TFEU as such) was also quite similar to that contained in the comparable but later air transport measures. This list was not closed and other arrangements could obviously also fall outside Article 101(1). Article 2(2) of Regulation 4056/86 provided that the Commission had to, if necessary, submit to the Council proposals for the amendment of the list.

11.050 The Commission and the courts construed Article 2 narrowly. As the Commission wrote in its explanatory memorandum to the proposal to repeal Regulation 4056/86:

"19. Article 2 of Regulation (EEC) No 4056/86 states that the prohibition laid down in Article [101(1)] of the Treaty does not apply to agreements whose sole object and effect is to achieve technical improvements and co-operation, on the grounds that they do not restrict competition.
20. If an agreement restricts competition in the way provided by Article [101(1)], Article 2 will not apply. An evaluation of each single technical agreement even if listed in Article 2 is therefore necessary. Looking back on the application of this Article, this process has not been straightforward and has come at a cost to the industry. Carriers have often interpreted Article 2 broadly whilst the Commission and the [General Court] consider that agreements that are not purely technical but also involve some form of commercial co-operation will fall within the scope of Article [101(1)][96] and thus fall outside the scope of Article 2. Litigation has ensued."[97]

---

93 Ed., Reg. 1017/68 was the measure relating to competition in the road, rail and inland waterway sectors.
94 See COM(81)423 final, p. 5.
95 A White List is a collection of arrangements which benefit from the block exemptions.
96 Commission decisions in *FEFC* (OJ L378, 31.12.1994, p. 17 par 66) and *FETTCSA* (OJ L268, 20.10.2000, p. 1 par 146–147) with regard to provision for technical agreements in Article 3 of Regulation (EEC) No 1017/68 and Article 2(1) of Regulation (EEC) No 4056/86 respectively. For the General Court, see Case T-229/94 *Deutsche Bahn AG v Commission* [1997] ECR II-1689, [ed., ECLI:EU:T:1997:155] para 37 in relation to the similar exception for technical agreements provided for in Article 3 of Regulation (EEC) No 1017/68.
97 Proposal for a Council Regulation repealing Reg. (EEC) No 4056/86 laying down detailed rules for the application of Arts 85 and 86 to maritime transport, and amending Reg. (EC) No 1/2003 as regards the extension of its scope to include cabotage and international tramp services COM/2005/0651 final.

The introduction of uniform application of standards or types in respect of vessels and other means of transport, equipment, supplies or fixed installations

11.051 The introduction of uniform application of standards or types in respect of vessels and other means of transport, equipment, supplies or fixed installations is an inherently technical-type agreement which should ordinarily not distort competition.

The exchange or pooling for the purpose of operating transport services, of vessels, space on vessels or slots or other means of transport, staff, equipment or fixed installations

11.052 Where the *sole object and effect* of the arrangement must be the exchange or pooling for the purpose of operating transport services, of vessels, space on vessels or slots or other means of transport, staff, equipment or fixed installations then there would be no breach of Article 101(1).

The organisation and execution of successive or supplementary maritime transport operations and the establishment or application of inclusive rates and conditions for such operations

11.053 To fall within the scope of Article 2 of the regulation and therefore outside the scope of, what is now, Article 101(1) of the TFEU, sub-paragraph (c) of Article 2(1) of Regulation 4056/86 dealt with the organisation and execution of successive or supplementary maritime transport operations and the establishment or application of inclusive rates and conditions for such operations.

The co-ordination of transport timetables for connecting routes

11.054 To fall within the scope of Article 2 of the regulation and therefore outside the scope of Article 101(1) of the TFEU, the co-ordination of transport timetables for connecting routes was a purely technical matter and an agreement which aimed or effected solely the co-ordination of transport timetables for connecting routes would have benefited from Article 2 of the regulation.

The consolidation of individual assignments

11.055 To fall within the scope of Article 2 of the regulation and therefore outside the scope of Article 101(1) of the TFEU, the consolidation of individual assignments had to be a purely technical matter and any agreement which aimed at or effected solely the consolidation of individual assignments benefited from the automatic exemption contained in Article 2 of the regulation.

The establishment or application of uniform rules concerning the structure and the conditions governing the application of transport tariffs

11.056 To fall within the scope of Article 2 of the regulation and therefore outside the scope of Article 101(1) of the TFEU, an agreement had to be aimed at or affected only the establishment or application of uniform rules concerning the structure and the conditions governing the application of transport tariffs automatically benefited from the exemption contained in Article 2 of the regulation.

Amendment to Article 2

11.057 It is to be noted that the Council had the power to add to, delete from or amend the list of technical agreements upon a proposal from the Commission. However, the Council did not do so.

Assessment

11.058 The enumeration of technical agreements which fell outside the scope of Article 101 of the TFEU was helpful for everyone involved. It enabled shipping companies (and those advising them) to know what types of arrangement or practice fell outside the scope of Article 101(1) of the TFEU. While the regulation has been repealed, it is submitted that the principles involved are very probably still applicable and the arrangements still fall outside the scope of Article 101(1) of the TFEU. Nonetheless, it is important to remember that these arrangements fell outside the scope of Article 101 of the TFEU anyway and were not dependent on an exemption. So what Article 2 did was merely to clarify the situation. It is also worth recalling that the list of technical agreements falling outside the scope of Article 101(1) of the TFEU is limited anyway; for example, a price-fixing agreement or an agreement not to discount below published tariffs[98] would not be a technical agreement. Similarly, Article 102 of the TFEU would still apply in the event of there being an abuse of dominance. Interestingly, the Council believed that the provision on technical agreements was unnecessary and repealed it as part of Regulation 1419/2006[99] and did not replace it with any other provision.

I. BLOCK EXEMPTION FOR LINER CONFERENCES: ARTICLE 3 OF REGULATION 4056/86

Introduction

11.059 The famous or infamous block exemption which was contained in Article 3 of Regulation 4056/86 "provided the long aspired legal security as regards the application of the [TFEU's] competition rules to maritime transport".[100] It was the "main feature" of the regulation.[101] Articles 3 to 6 of the regulation represented a far-reaching conditional block

---

98 E.g. Comm. Dec. *FETTCSA*, OJ L268/1, 20 October 2000.
99 OJ 2006 L269/1, Recital 9 and Art. 1.
100 See e.g. Rabe, "Recent Developments in EEC Legislation Pertaining to Maritime Transport", IBA Strasbourg Conference 1989, at p. 12.
101 Ruttley, op. cit. at fn. 1, p. 10.

exemption for an unlimited time period for conferences and their agreements with users. It was unique in that it was a block exemption for a price-fixing arrangement. It was "exceptionally generous".[102] However, it was not an unlimited exemption. First, the exemption could have been withdrawn in certain circumstances. Second, it was not a complete exemption because conditions and obligations were attached to it. The block exemption[103] was only granted to certain types of liner conferences. However, Article 4 imposed a condition on this exemption and Article 5 imposed an obligation on the exemption. Ultimately, Regulation 4056/86 could be (and has been) repealed by the EU institutions. It was observed rather succinctly that in "short, there are two essential (or objectionable, as cargo interests would argue) objectives – price-fixing (and the rate discussions leading to it) and co-ordinated conditions of carriage".[104]

Liner conferences

11.060 It will be recalled that a "liner conference" was defined, for the purpose of the regulation, as being:

> "a group of two or more vessel-operating carriers which provides international liner services for the carriage of cargo on a particular route or routes within specified geographical limits and which has an agreement or arrangement, whatever its nature, within the framework of which they operate under uniform or common freight rates and any other agreed conditions with respect to the provision of liner services".[105]

Thus, consortia were not included because the liner conference involves an element of price-fixing. For the purposes of the regulation, liner conferences were bodies or associations which co-ordinated the operation of regular shipping services for the carriage of general cargo on set routes with fixed schedules and tariffs (i.e. prices). Such conferences standardised or harmonised the uniform freight rates, sailings and so on of the members of the conference. Liner conferences safeguarded their centralised system by means of a monopolistic structure operating on four levels:

(a) restricted membership;
(b) cargo sharing and pooling;
(c) loyalty arrangements; and
(d) agreements on a "common tariff" and "general conditions".[106]

Block exemption

11.061 Article 3 of Regulation 4056/86 exempted from Article 101(1) of the TFEU those liner conferences (as defined in Article 1(3)(b) of the regulation) when they had as

---

102 Evans, "Competition Developments Affecting the Maritime Sector", EMLO, 14 October 2005, London, p. 1, http://ec.europa.eu/competition/speeches/text/sp2005_018_en.pdf.
103 On the meaning of a block exemption, see chap. 9.
104 Chuah, op. cit. at fn. 1, p. 210.
105 Reg. 4056/86, Art. 1(3)(b).
106 See Report of the EESC's Section on Transport and Communications, op. cit. at fn. 37.

their objective the fixing of rates and conditions of carriage,[107] and, as the case may be, one or more of the following objectives: (a) the co-ordination of shipping timetables, sailing dates or dates of calls; (b) the determination of the frequency of sailings or calls; (c) the co-ordination or allocation of sailings or calls among members of the conference; (d) the regulation of the carrying capacity offered by each member; or (e) the allocation of cargo or revenue among members. This exemption was, however, subject to the condition imposed by Article 4 of the regulation.

It is worth highlighting the narrow scope and application of the block exemption. Arrangements which fell outside the scope of Article 3 did not benefit from the block exemption in the regulation. Its scope was narrow and it was construed narrowly.

11.062 Article 3 of the regulation provided:

"Agreements, decisions and concerted practices of all or part of the members of one or more liner conferences are hereby exempted from the prohibition in Article [101(1)] of the Treaty, subject to the condition imposed by Article 4 of this Regulation, when they have as their objective the fixing of rates and conditions of carriage, and, as the case may be, one or more of the following objectives:

(a) the co-ordination of shipping timetables, sailing dates or dates of calls;
(b) the determination of the frequency of sailings or calls;
(c) the co-ordination or allocation of sailings or calls among members of the conference;
(d) the regulation of the carrying capacity offered by each member;
(e) the allocation of cargo or revenue among members."

11.063 The original proposal had read:

"1. A liner conference means a group of vessel-operating carriers which provides liner services for the carriage of cargo or passengers on a particular route or routes within specified geographical limits and which jointly fixes freight rates and any other conditions for those services.
2. Agreements, decisions and concerted practices of all or part of the members of a conference or of several conferences are hereby exempted from the prohibition in Article [101(1)] of the Treaty, subject to the conditions imposed by Article 4 of this regulation, when they have one or more of the following objects:

   (a) the fixing of the above-mentioned rates and conditions of carriage and, as the case may be;
   (b) the co-ordination of shipping timetables, sailing dates or dates of calls;
   (c) the determination of the frequency of sailings or calls;
   (d) the co-ordination or allocation of sailings or calls among members of the conference;
   (e) the regulation of the carrying capacity offered by each member;
   (f) the allocation of cargo or revenue among members."

The extraordinary nature of the block exemption is clear from the fact that price-fixing is a hard-core breach of EU competition law.

---

107 This objective was necessary so as to benefit from the block exemption. If it was absent then it would have been necessary to seek an individual exemption if the agreement were to otherwise fall within the scope of Art. 101(1) of the TFEU. Individual exemptions were no longer possible after 1 May 2004 (because of the entry into force of Reg. 1/2003) so undertakings party to an arrangement would have to make a self-assessment as to whether Art. 101(3) of the TFEU applied.

11.064 The Commission in its Explanatory Memorandum to the original proposal[108] commented:

> "Article [101(3)] of the [TFEU] permits the exemption of a category of agreements from the prohibition set out in Article [101(1)]. It seems advisable to grant such an exemption by category to all conference agreements between shipowners. The conferences represent a considerable part of the transport committed to regular sea services throughout the world, and the fact that UNCTAD has devised a Code of Conduct for Liner Conferences implies in principle the recognition on a world-wide level of their beneficial role.
>
> The exemption concerns the fixing of prices and so-called rationalisation agreements.
>
> As far as prices are concerned, account must be taken of the fact that sea transport, more than any other mode of transport, is characterised by considerable fluctuations, both business and seasonal, in demand for cargo capacity. To this first cause of instability in the level of freight is added, as far as capacity is concerned, a cause which all modes of transportation have in common, that is the very considerable price variations resulting from marginal offers by shipowners wishing to avoid return voyages in ballast or to complete their cargoes.
>
> The instability of freight which would result from the total absence of market regulation would be unfavourable to carriers and users:
>
> – to the carriers who could not base themselves on any forecasts of profitability in order to run, maintain and renew their fleets and who could not give the users a reliable service at fixed prices;
> – to the users who could only count on transport under certain conditions, who would be submitted to excessive and unforeseeable variations in freight rates and who, in the longer term, would suffer from a gradual deterioration of the service offered because the fleet had not been modernised.
>
> Both the shipowners and the users try, through price agreements, to introduce some stability in ocean freights.
>
> Rationalization agreements are the logical consequence of price agreements. In order to avoid competition extending to offers of capacity available but also to ensure a proper service for difficult ports, the shipowners have concluded agreements concerning calls and capacity. The most elaborate agreements foresee a sharing of tonnage and even revenues, which assures a regular transport of the merchandise alongside even that which is the least remunerative."

11.065 The EESC had said that it looked favourably on the conferences but believed that the main priority was for any national shipping company which applied to be able to join the conference on the same conditions as existing members.[109] Recital 9 to the regulation provided some background to the issues generally:

> "Whereas provisions should be made for block exemption of liner conferences; whereas liner conferences have a stabilising effect, assuring shippers of reliable services; whereas they contribute generally to providing adequate efficient scheduled maritime transport services and give fair consideration to the interests of users; whereas such results cannot be obtained without the cooperation that shipping companies promote within conferences in relation to rates and where appropriate, availability of capacity or allocation of cargo for shipment, and income; whereas in most cases conferences continue to be subject to effective competition from both non-conference scheduled services and, in certain circumstances, from tramp services and from other modes of transport; whereas the mobility of fleets, which is a characteristic feature of the structure of availability in the shipping field, subjects conferences to constant competition which they are unable as a rule to eliminate as far as a substantial proportion of the shipping services in general is concerned."

---

108 See COM(81)423 final, pp. 6–7.
109 Op. cit. at fn. 37, para. 2.3.2.

11.066 Article 3 meant that activities other than maritime transport which were undertaken by shipowners were not subject to Regulation 4056/86. This meant, in turn, that shipowners' agreements to fix jointly the price of various other services did not benefit from the block exemption under Article 3 of Regulation 4056/86 because the regulation itself was inapplicable.

11.067 The Commission stated in *TAA*[110] in Recital 389 of the decision:

"In the Commission's view, price stability may constitute an objective within the scope of Article [101](3) of the Treaty for the following reasons:

- stability of rates for scheduled services enables shippers to know reasonably far in advance the cost of transporting their products and therefore their selling price on the market of destination, whatever the time, vessel or conference shipowner involved,
- stability of rates enables shipowners to forecast their income more accurately and thus makes it easier to organize regular, reliable, adequate and efficient services."

11.068 Ortiz Blanco has suggested that none of the four conditions for the application of Article 101(3) are satisfied by liner conferences. He described the block exemption as being "both atypical and striking, even shocking, that the most typical cartels in the world were approved to the extent that Regulation 4056/86 did so, and, moreover, using the European Community competition rules".[111] The debate is now over as the block exemption expired on 18 October 2008 by virtue of the entry into force of Regulation 1419/2006.[112]

The Article 4 condition attaching to the block exemption for liner conferences

11.069 Article 4 of the regulation provided a condition to be attached to the exemptions contained in Articles 3 and 6 of the regulation. Article 4 supplemented the UN Code on Liner Conferences. The effect of Article 4 was that differential rates and conditions were only permissible where they were economically justified. Article 4 of the regulation provided:

"The exemption provided for in Articles 3 and 6 shall be granted subject to the condition that the agreement, decision or concerted practice shall not, within the [internal] market, cause detriment to certain ports, transport users or carriers by applying for the carriage of the same goods and in the area covered by the agreement, decision or concerted practice, rates and conditions of carriage which differ according to the country of origin or destination or port of loading or discharge, unless such rates or conditions can be economically justified.

Any agreement or decision or, if it is severable, any part of such an agreement or decision not complying with this condition shall be void automatically under Article [101(2)] of the Treaty."

11.070 In its commentary to the provision as adopted, the Commission stated:

"A certain number of conditions are imposed on members of conferences. The general disposition of Article [95] of the [TFEU] which prohibits discrimination on the sole ground of country of origin or destination of the goods transported has been retained. Furthermore, the conditions imposed concerned fidelity agreements, by which the conferences try to secure for a certain

---

110 Comm. Dec. 94/980 of 19 October 1994 relating to a proceeding pursuant to Article 85 of the EC Treaty (IV/34.446 – *Trans-atlantic Agreement*) OJ 1994 L376/1, 31 December 1994.
111 Op. cit. at fn.1, preface, p. v.
112 See chap. 12.

period the custom of the shippers or forwarding agents, have as their object that the last mentioned:

(1) retain their freedom to choose their carriers and their ports;
(2) may release themselves from their commitment within a reasonable time period, and
(3) may not have imposed upon them clauses or types of agreements which would restrict their freedom too much.

Finally in order to avoid encroaching on an area regulated by Council Regulation (EEC) No. 1017/68 one condition protects the freedom of choice of the users so far as land legs are concerned."[113]

Obligations attaching to the exemption

Introduction

11.071 Article 5 of the regulation stated that in order to benefit from the exemption contained in Article 3 of the regulation, the particular liner conference must comply with obligations in five areas, namely: (a) consultations; (b) loyalty arrangements; (c) services not covered by the freight charges; (d) availability of tariffs; and (e) notification to the Commission of awards at arbitration and recommendations. Some of the obligations were taken from the UN Code of Conduct. Indeed, Article 5 was very similar to Article 11 of the Code of Conduct on Liner Conferences.

11.072 Article 5 of the regulation provided:

"The following obligations shall be attached to the exemption provided for in Article 3:

1. *Consultations*
There shall be consultations for the purpose of seeking solutions on general issues of principle between transport users on the one hand and conferences on the other concerning the rates, conditions and quality of scheduled maritime transport services.
   These consultations shall take place whenever requested by any of the abovementioned parties.

2. *Loyalty arrangements*
The shipping lines' members of a conference shall be entitled to institute and maintain loyalty arrangements with transport users, the form and terms of which shall be matters for consultation between the conference and transport users' organizations. These loyalty arrangements shall provide safeguards making explicit the rights of transport users and conference members. These arrangements shall be based on the contract system or any other system which is also lawful.
   Loyalty arrangements must comply with the following conditions:

   (a) Each conference shall offer transport users a system of immediate rebates or the choice between such a system and a system of deferred rebates:

   – under the system of immediate rebates each of the parties shall be entitled to terminate the loyalty arrangement at any time without penalty and subject to a period of notice of not more than six months; this period shall be reduced to three months when the conference rate is the subject of a dispute;
   – under the system of deferred rebates neither the loyalty period on the basis of which the rebate is calculated nor the subsequent loyalty period required before payment of the rebate may exceed six months; this period shall be reduced to three months where the conference rate is the subject of a dispute.

---

113 (1986), p. 7. Reg. 1017/68 was the regulation which enabled the Commission to apply competition law to the rail, road and inland waterway sectors.

(b) The conference shall, after consulting the transport users concerned, set out:

   (i) a list of cargo and any portion of cargo agreed with transport users which is specifically excluded from the scope of the loyalty arrangement; 100% loyalty arrangements may be offered but may not be unilaterally imposed;
   (ii) a list of circumstances in which transport users are released from their obligation of loyalty; these shall include:

   – circumstances in which consignments are dispatched from or to a port in the area covered by the conference but not advertised and where the request for a waiver can be justified, and
   – those in which waiting time at a port exceeds a period to be determined for each port and for each commodity or class of commodities following consultation of the transport users directly concerned with the proper servicing of the port.

The conference must, however, be informed in advance by the transport user, within a specified period, of his intention to dispatch the consignment from a port not advertised by the conference or to make use of a non-conference vessel at a port served by the conference as soon as he has been able to establish from the published schedule of sailings that the maximum waiting period will be exceeded.

3. Services not covered by the freight charges
Transport users shall be entitled to approach the undertakings of their choice in respect of inland transport operations and quayside services not covered by the freight charge or charges on which the shipping line and the transport user have agreed.

4. Availability of tariffs
Tariffs, related conditions, regulations and any amendments thereto shall be made available on request to transport users at reasonable cost, or they shall be available for examination at offices of shipping lines and their agents. They shall set out all the conditions concerning loading and discharge, the exact extent of the services covered by the freight charge in proportion to the sea transport and the land transport or by any other charge levied by the shipping line and customary practice in such matters.

5. Notification to the Commission of awards at arbitration and recommendations
Awards given at arbitration and recommendations made by conciliators that are accepted by the parties shall be notified forthwith to the Commission when they resolve disputes relating to the practices of conferences referred to in Article 4 and in points 2 and 3 above."

11.073 These five obligations were, according to Article 5 of the regulation, absolute in terms of their application.

Consultations

11.074 Consultations had to occur for the purpose of seeking solutions on general issues of principle between transport users on the one hand and liner conferences on the other concerning the rates, conditions and quality of scheduled maritime transport services.[114] These consultations were to take place whenever requested by the transport users or the conferences.[115]

---

114 Reg. 4056/86, Art. 5(1).
115 Ibid.

Loyalty arrangements

11.075 There was also an obligation in relation to loyalty arrangements. Article 5 of the regulation provided that the shipping lines' members of a conference were entitled to institute and maintain loyalty arrangements with transport users, the form and terms of which had to be matters for consultation between the conference and transport users' organisations. These loyalty arrangements had to provide safeguards which made explicit the rights of transport users and conference members. These arrangements were to be based on the contract system or on any other lawful system.

11.076 Article 5 of the regulation imposed a number of conditions on loyalty arrangements. First, each conference had to offer transport users a system of immediate rebates or the choice between such a system and a system of deferred rebates. Under the system of immediate rebates, each of the parties was entitled to terminate the loyalty arrangement at any time without penalty and subject to a period of notice of not more than six months; this period would have been reduced to three months when the conference rate was the subject of a dispute.[116] Immediate rebates are more in the nature of discounts. Under the system of deferred rebates, neither the loyalty period on the basis of which the rebate was calculated nor the subsequent loyalty period required before payment of the rebate could have exceeded six months; this period was again reduced to three months where the conference rate was the subject of a dispute.[117] Second, the conference had to set out, after consulting the transport users concerned, (i) a list of cargo and any portion of cargo agreed with transport users which was specifically excluded from the scope of the loyalty arrangement, 100% loyalty arrangements would be offered but may not be unilaterally imposed; and (ii) a list of circumstances in which transport users were released from their obligation of loyalty. These had to include circumstances in which consignments were dispatched from or to a port in the area covered by the conference but not advertised and where the request for a waiver could have been justified, and those in which waiting time at a port exceeded a period to be determined for each port and for each commodity or class of commodities following consultation of the transport users directly concerned with the proper servicing of the port.[118] In regard to these lists, the conference must, however, be informed in advance by the transport user, within a specified period, of its intention to dispatch the consignment from a port not advertised by the conference or to make use of a non-conference vessel at a port served by the conference as soon as it had been able to establish from the published schedule of sailings that the maximum waiting period will be exceeded.[119]

Services not covered by the freight charges

11.077 Transport users were entitled to approach the undertakings of their choice in respect of inland transport operations and quayside services not covered by the freight charge, and charges on which the shipping line and the transport user had agreed.[120] This

---

116 Reg. 4056/86, Art. 5(2).
117 Ibid.
118 Ibid.
119 Ibid.
120 Reg. 4056/86, Art. 5(3).

is provided that such services were not covered by the freight charges agreed between the shipping line and the transport user. The entitlement on the part of transport users was supplementary to the UNCTAD Code. Restrictive arrangements between liner companies offering passenger services were excluded from Article 3.

11.078 While tying clauses were exempt under Article 101(3) of the TFEU by virtue of Article 5(3) of Regulation 4056/86, they could be prohibited by, what is now, Article 102 of the TFEU where there was an abuse of dominance.[121]

Availability of tariffs

11.079 Article 5 of Regulation 4056/86 provided that tariffs, related conditions, regulations and any amendment of them had to be made available on request to transport users at reasonable cost, or they should have been available for examination at offices of shipping lines and their agents. They should have set out all the conditions concerning loading and discharge, and the exact extent of the services covered by the freight charge in proportion to the sea transport and the land transport or by any other charge levied by the shipping line and customary practice in such matters. Article 5(4) is comparable to Article 9 of the UNCTAD Code.

Notification to the European Commission of awards at arbitration and recommendations

11.080 Article 5 of Regulation 4056/86 provided that it was an obligation attaching to an exemption under Article 3 of that regulation that awards given at arbitration and recommendations made by conciliators that were accepted by the parties had to be notified immediately to the Commission when they resolved disputes relating to the practices of conferences such as discriminations, loyalty arrangements and services not covered by freight rates. This obligation no longer exists given that Article 5 is no longer in force but there is nothing to stop the awards and recommendations being sent to the Commission for information but it would be very difficult to see any practical value in doing so in the ordinary course of events.

Uniform or common freight rates

11.081 It has been observed that

"[t]he last part of Article 1(3)(b) of the Regulation implied that in order for conference members to qualify for the block exemption they had to 'operate under uniform or common freight rates and any other agreed conditions with respect to the provision of liner services' which means that the freight rates within tariffs must be non-discriminatory and unique for each product or class of products within the tariff. This method of fixing transport prices has been the tradition hallmark of Community liner conferences, which in turn is directly inspired by the United Nations Code of Conduct. In order to qualify for the block exemption under Article 3 of Regulation 4056/86, therefore, conferences had to fix the same freight rate for all their members without exception. This meant that the same freight rate applied within the conference: the rate could only vary

---

121 On the basis of Case T-51/89 *Tetra Pak Rausing SA v Commission* [1990] ECR II-309, ECLI:EU:T:1990:41.

according to the type of products, as established by the Code. It was not sufficient for a group of two or more shipowners to fix freight rates and therefore tariff structures that varied between one member and another, even when this took place within the same agreement. Freight rates had to be *common* and not just *established in common*. For this reason, agreement between shipowners to establish differential freight rates and agreements between conferences and independents with the same objectives did not comply with the definition of 'conference' contained in the Regulation and therefore could not take advantage of the block exemption contained in Article 3."[122]

J. BLOCK EXEMPTION FOR AGREEMENTS BETWEEN TRANSPORT USERS AND CONFERENCES CONCERNING THE USE OF SCHEDULED MARITIME TRANSPORT SERVICES

11.082 Article 6 of the regulation provided that agreements, decisions and concerted practices between transport users, on the one hand, and conferences, on the other, as well as agreements between transport users which may be necessary to that end, concerning the rates, conditions and quality of liner services were exempted under Article 6 of the regulation from the prohibition laid down in Article 101(1) of the TFEU as long as they were provided for in Article 5(1) and (2) of the regulation. It is clear that Article 6 was drafted in a way which was both vague and elusive. It is also clear that given its content, it was "of comparatively narrow scope".[123] Article 6 of the regulation provided:

> "Agreements, decisions and concerted practices between transport users, on the one hand, and conferences, on the other hand, and agreements between transport users which may be necessary to that end, concerning the rates, conditions and quality of liner services, as long as they are provided for in Articles 5(1) and (2) are hereby exempted from the prohibition laid down in Article [101(1)] of the Treaty."

A transport user was defined, for the purposes of the regulation, as being:

> "an undertaking (e.g. shippers, consignees, forwarders, etc.) provided it has entered into, or demonstrates an intention to enter into, a contractual or other arrangement with a conference or shipping line for the shipment of goods, or any association of shippers".[124]

K. MONITORING OF EXEMPTED AGREEMENTS

Introduction

11.083 Agreements or arrangements which benefited from an exemption under the regulation (i.e. exempted agreements) required monitoring given the exceptional nature of the exemption. Article 7 of the regulation provided for the monitoring of breaches of an obligation imposed under Article 5 of the regulation[125] and for effects which were incompatible with Article 101(3) of the TFEU.[126] Article 7 of the regulation provided:

---

122 Ortiz Blanco, "Personal Reflections on the Development of Maritime Competition Policy, Past and Future", EMLO Conference, 17 October 2008.
123 Ruttley, op. cit. at fn. 1, p. 13.
124 Reg. 4056/86, Art. 1(3)(c).
125 Reg. 4056/86, Art. 7(1).
126 Reg. 4056/86, Art. 7(2).

"1. Breach of an obligation

Where the persons concerned are in breach of an obligation which, pursuant to Article 5, attaches to the exemption provided for in Article 3, the Commission may, in order to put an end to such breach and under the conditions laid down in Section II:[127]

- address recommendations to the persons concerned;
- in the event of failure by such persons to observe those recommendations and depending upon the gravity of the breach concerned, adopt a decision that either prohibits them from carrying out or requires them to perform specific acts or, while withdrawing the benefit of the block exemption which they enjoyed, grants them an individual exemption according to Article 11(4) or withdraws the benefit of the block exemption which they enjoyed.

2. Effects incompatible with Article [101](3)

   (a) Where, owing to special circumstances as described below, agreements, decisions and concerted practices which qualify for the exemption provided for in Articles 3 and 6 have nevertheless effects which are incompatible with the conditions laid down in Article [101(3)] of the Treaty, the Commission, on receipt of a complaint or on its own initiative, under the conditions laid down in Section II,[128] shall take the measures described in (c) below. The severity of these measures must be in proportion to the gravity of the situation.

   (b) Special circumstances are, inter alia, created by:

      (i) acts of conferences or a change of market conditions in a given trade resulting in the absence or elimination of actual or potential competition such as restrictive practices whereby the trade is not available to competition; or

      (ii) acts of conference which may prevent technical or economic progress or user participation in the benefits;

      (iii) acts of third countries which:

- prevent the operation of outsiders in a trade,
- impose unfair tariffs on conference members,
- impose arrangements which otherwise impede technical or economic progress (cargo-sharing, limitations on types of vessels).[129]

   (c) (i) If actual or potential competition is absent or may be eliminated as a result of action by a third country, the Commission shall enter into consultations with the competent authorities of the third country concerned, followed if necessary by negotiations under directives to be given by the Council, in order to remedy the situation.

If the special circumstances result in the absence or elimination of actual or potential competition contrary to Article [101(3)(b)] of the Treaty the Commission shall withdraw the benefit of the block exemption. At the same time it shall rule on whether and, if so, under what additional conditions and obligations an individual exemption should be granted to the relevant conference agreement with a view, *inter alia*, to obtaining access to the market for non-conference lines;

      (ii) If, as a result of special circumstances as set out in (b), there are effects other than those referred to in (i) hereof, the Commission shall take one or more of the measures described in paragraph 1."

---

127 Ed., i.e. Section II of the regulation.
128 Ed., i.e. Section II of the regulation.
129 Ed., intervention in this scenario was more in the nature of a commercial policy instrument rather than in the nature of a competition law claim. See Commission, *Progress towards a Common Transport Policy: Maritime Policy* (COM(85) 90 final, point 63).

Commentary

11.084 Article 7 was critical to the whole regulation. If there was a breach of an obligation under Article 5 of the regulation then Article 7(1) of the regulation came into focus. It provided that where the persons concerned were in breach of an obligation which, pursuant to Article 5 of the regulation, attached to the exemption provided for in Article 3 of the regulation, then the Commission may have, in order to put an end to such breach and under the conditions laid down in Section II of the regulation, first, address recommendations to the persons concerned and, second, if there was a failure by those persons to observe those recommendations and depending on the gravity of the breach concerned, adopt a decision that either prohibits them from carrying out or requires them to perform specific acts or, while withdrawing the benefit of the block exemption which they enjoyed, grant them an individual exemption according to Article 11(4) of the regulation or withdraw the benefit of the block exemption altogether.[130] Article 7 meant that the Commission had the power to monitor exempted arrangements.[131] If the effects of the agreements, decisions or practices involved were incompatible with Article 101(3) of the TFEU then Article 7(2) of the regulation came into focus. It provided that where, owing to special circumstances,[132] agreements, decisions and concerted practices which qualify for the exemption provided for in Articles 3 and 6 have nevertheless effects which are incompatible with Article 101(3) of the TFEU, the Commission, on receipt of a complaint or on its own initiative, under the conditions laid down in Section II of the regulation, could have taken certain measures. Where actual or potential competition is absent or may be eliminated as a result of action by a third country, the Commission shall enter into consultations with the competent authorities of the third country concerned, followed, if necessary, by negotiations under directives to be given by the Council, in order to remedy the situation. The gravity of the measures must be in proportion to the gravity of the situation.[133] If the special circumstances resulted in the absence or elimination of actual or potential competition contrary to Article 101(3)(b) of the TFEU, the Commission had to withdraw the benefit of the block exemption. At the same time, it shall rule on whether and, if so, under what additional conditions and obligations an individual exemption would have been granted to the relevant conference agreement with a view, *inter alia*, to obtaining access to the market for non-conference lines.[134] If, as a result of one of the "special circumstances", there are effects other than these then the Commission had to take one or more of the measures mentioned in Article 7(1) of the regulation, namely, address recommendations to the persons concerned and, second, if there was a failure by those persons to observe those recommendations and depending on the gravity of the

---

130 Reg. 4056/86, Art. 7(1).
131 It will be recalled that only the Commission has the power to apply what is now Art. 101(3) of the TFEU until the entry into force of Reg. 1/2003 on 1 May 2004.
132 "Special circumstances" were defined by, in this context, as being created by (*inter alia*): (i) acts of conferences or a change of market conditions in a given trade resulting in the absence or elimination of actual or potential competition such as restrictive practices whereby the trade is not available to competition; or (ii) acts of conference which may prevent technical or economic progress or user participation in the benefits; or (iii) acts of third countries which prevent the operation of outsiders in a trade, impose unfair tariffs on conference members or impose arrangements which otherwise impede technical or economic progress (cargo-sharing, limitations on types of vessels).
133 Reg. 4056/86, Art. 7(2).
134 Reg. 4056/86, Art. 7(2)(c).

breach concerned, adopt a decision that either prohibited them from carrying out or required them to perform specific acts or, while withdrawing the benefit of the block exemption which they enjoyed, granted them an individual exemption according to Article 11(4) of the regulation or withdraw the benefit of the block exemption altogether.

L. ABUSE OF A DOMINANT POSITION: ARTICLE 102 OF THE TFEU

Introduction

11.085 Article 102 of the TFEU prohibits the abuse of a dominant position. Article 8(1) of the regulation provided that any abuse of a dominant position within the meaning of, what is now, Article 102 of the TFEU where maritime services (as defined by the regulation) were concerned would have been automatically prohibited, that is to say, there was no need for a prior decision to that effect. Nor would there be any exemption.[135] Where the Commission, either on its own initiative or at the request of a Member State, or of natural or legal persons claiming a legitimate interest, found that in any particular case the conduct of conferences benefiting from the exemption laid down in Article 3 of the regulation, nevertheless had effects which were incompatible with Article 102 of the TFEU, it had the power to withdraw the benefit of the block exemption and take, pursuant to Article 10 of the regulation, all appropriate measures for the purpose of bringing to an end infringements of Article 102 of the TFEU.[136] It has been written that:

> "The acts of a conference [could] not only offend Article [101] and the conditions laid down by Regulation 4056/86, but also Article [102] of the TFEU, as the Commission takes the view that the parties in a trade, which are members of a conference, may thereby be in a position of joint dominance. The relevant market in this context will be routes served by the conference and any interchangeable services on these routes, in accordance with Case 66/86 *Ahmed Saeed*.[137] This approach enables the Commission to impose fines directly, and not to bother about the escalating procedure, where they consider that the conference has committed an abuse. It is possible that the application of this approach by the Commission will be contested before the Court of Justice [of the European Union]."[138]

11.086 Article 8 of the regulation provided:

"Effects incompatible with Article [102] of the Treaty
1. The abuse of a dominant position within the meaning of Article [102] of the Treaty shall be prohibited, no prior decision to that effect being required.
2. Where the Commission, either on its own initiative or at the request of a Member State or of natural or legal persons claiming a legitimate interest, finds that in any particular case the conduct of conferences benefiting from the exemption laid down in Article 3 nevertheless has effects which are incompatible with Article [106] of the Treaty, it may withdraw the benefit of the block exemption and take, pursuant to Article 10, all appropriate measures for the purpose of bringing to an end infringements of Article [102] of the Treaty.
3. Before taking a decision under paragraph 2, the Commission may address to the conference concerned recommendations for termination of the infringement."

---

135 This is because, as a general principle, it would be impossible to allow an arrangement which breached Art. 102 TFEU to benefit from an exemption under Art. 101(3) TFEU.
136 Reg. 4056/86, Art. 8(2).
137 Ed., [1979] ECR 803, ECLI:EU:C:1989:140.
138 Close, in a paper entitled "Special Provision for Shipping in EEC Competition Law", addressed to the Norwegian Shipowners, Oslo, p. 13.

Commentary

11.087 Article 102 of the TFEU prohibits the abuse of a dominant position whether that dominance is individual or collective. Article 8(1) of the regulation provided that the abuse of a dominant position within the meaning of Article 102 of the TFEU would be prohibited and no prior decision to that effect was required. Thus, Article 102 of the TFEU applied to otherwise exempted conference agreements. Article 8(2) of the regulation went on to provide that where the Commission found that in any particular case the conduct of a conference benefiting from the exemption laid down in Article 3 of the regulation nevertheless has effects which are incompatible with Article 102 of the TFEU, it had the power to withdraw the benefit of the block exemption and take, pursuant to Article 10, all appropriate measures for the purpose of bringing to an end infringements of Article 102 of the TFEU. Before taking such a decision, the Commission had, however, to address to the conference the Commission's recommendations for the termination of the infringement.[139]

M. CONFLICTS OF NATIONAL LAWS

Text of Article 9 of the regulation

11.088 What if there was a conflict between the law of a third country (i.e. a non-EU Member State) and the regulation? Article 9 of the regulation provided:

"1. Where the application of this Regulation to certain restrictive practices or clauses is liable to enter into conflict with the provisions laid down by law, regulation or administrative action of certain third countries which would comprise important [EU] trading and shipping interests, the Commission shall, at the earliest opportunity, undertake with the competent authorities of the third countries concerned, consultations aimed at reconciling as far as possible the abovementioned interest with the respect of [EU] law. The Commission shall inform the Advisory Committee referred to in Article 15 of the outcome of these consultations.
2. Where agreements with third countries need to be negotiated, the Commission shall make recommendations to the Council, which shall authorize the Commission to open the necessary negotiations.
    The Commission shall conduct these negotiations in consultation with an Advisory Committee as referred to in Article 15 and within the framework of such directives as the Council may issue to it.
3. In exercising the powers conferred on it by this Article, the Council shall act in accordance with the decision-making procedure laid down in Article [100(2)] of the Treaty."

Commentary

11.089 Article 9 of the regulation dealt with conflicts of law or, put another way, conflicts with the laws of third states. It provided, in paragraph 1, that where the application of the regulation to certain restrictive practices or clauses was liable to create a conflict with the provisions laid down by law, regulation or administrative action of certain third countries (which would compromise important EU trading and shipping interests), the Commission had to, at the earliest opportunity, undertake with the competent authorities of the third countries concerned, consultations aimed at reconciling as far as possible these interests with the respect of EU law. The Commission was obliged under Article

---

139 Reg. 4056/86, Art. 8(3).

9(1) of the regulation to inform the Advisory Committee of the outcome of these consultations. If there was a need to conclude agreements with third countries,[140] then the Commission had to make recommendations[141] to the Council which in turn had to[142] authorise the Commission to open the necessary negotiations.[143] The Commission was obliged to conduct these negotiations in consultation with the Advisory Committee referred to in Article 15 of the regulation and within the framework of any directive which the Council may have made.[144] The Commission had contact on these matters with such foreign agencies as the US Federal Maritime Commission.

N. RULES OF PROCEDURE

Introduction

11.090 Section II of the regulation set out various rules of procedure.[145] The rules of procedure were similar to the procedural provisions in Regulation 17/62[146] implementing Articles 101 and 102 of the TFEU generally; Regulation 1017/68 relating to the rail, road and inland waterway transport; and Regulation 3975/87[147] in respect of air transport. All in all, however, what has emerged has been described as a "complicated and time-consuming procedure".[148] Some points deserve mention. First, the parties to an agreement were not obliged to notify their agreements, decisions or concerted practices to the Commission. Second, the rules of procedure did not provide for applications for negative clearances.[149] Third, the rules cast the Commission in the roles of investigator, prosecutor and judge.[150]

Complaints

Introduction and text of Article 10

11.091 An important feature of this type of situation was the possibility of complaints. Article 10 of the regulation provided:

"Acting on receipt of a complaint or on its own initiative, the Commission shall initiate procedures to terminate any infringement of the provisions of Articles [101(1)] or [102] of the Treaty or to enforce Article 7 of this Regulation.
    Complaints may be submitted by:

(a) Member States;
(b) Natural or legal persons who claim a legitimate interest."

---

140 I.e. non-EU Member States.
141 On the legal status of recommendations, see chap. 3.
142 In exercising this power, the Council would have acted in accordance with the decision-making procedure laid down in Art. 100(2) of the TFEU: see Reg. 4056/86, Art. 9(3).
143 Reg. 4056/86, Art. 9(2).
144 In exercising this power, the Council shall act in accordance with the decision-making procedure laid down in Art. 84(2) of the then EC Treaty: see Reg. 4056/86, Art. 9(3); Reg.4056/86, Art.9(2).
145 Art. 7 of Section I of Reg. 4056/86 also had procedural implications.
146 OJ 1962, 204; OJ 1959–62, 87.
147 OJ L374/1.
148 EESC (1983), op. cit. at fn. 37, para. 2.9.1.
149 Negative clearances were statements by the Commission that Art. 101(1) of the TFEU did not apply to the arrangement in question.
150 See the comments of the EESC (1983), op. cit. at fn. 37, para. 2.11.3.

Procedures on complaint or on the Commission's own initiative

11.092 Article 10 of the regulation provided that acting on receipt of a complaint or on its own initiative, the Commission would have had the power to initiate procedures to terminate any infringement of the provisions of Articles 101(1) or 102 of the TFEU or to enforce Article 7 of the regulation. The complaint had to be made in one of the official languages of the EU. There were no real restrictions on the content or form of the complaint.

Locus standi to submit a complaint

11.093 Article 10 of the regulation provided that complaints may have been submitted by: (a) Member States; and (b) natural or legal persons who claim a legitimate interest. Thus, the formal right of complaint accorded to Member State governments applied to other persons who had a "legitimate interest". The regulation did not define "legitimate interest"; thus it had to be decided on a case-by-case basis. In practice, it would be difficult to deny that a Member State making a complaint or that someone who was a competitor or customer would not have a legitimate interest.

Result of procedures on complaint or on the Commission's own initiative

Introduction

11.094 If the Commission found that there had been an infringement of Articles 101 and/or 102 of the TFEU then recourse had to be had to Article 11 of the regulation.

Text of Article 11

11.095 Article 11 of the regulation provided:

"Result of Procedures on Complaint or on the Commission's own Initiative
1. Where the Commission finds that there has been an infringement of Articles [101(1)] or [102] of the Treaty, it may by decision require the undertakings or associations of undertakings concerned to bring such infringement to an end.

    Without prejudice to the other provisions of this Regulation, the Commission may, before taking a decision under the preceding paragraph, address to the undertakings or associations of undertakings concerned, recommendations for termination of the infringement.
2. Paragraph 1 shall apply also to cases falling within Article 7 of this Regulation.
3. If the Commission, acting on a complaint received, concludes that on the evidence before it there are no grounds for intervention under Articles [101(1)] or [102] of the Treaty or Article 7 of this Regulation, in respect of any agreement, decision or practice, it shall issue a decision rejecting the complaint as unfounded.
4. If the Commission, whether acting on a complaint received or on its own initiative, concludes that an agreement, decision or concerted practice satisfies the provisions both of Article 101(1) and of Article 101(3) of the Treaty, it shall issue a decision applying Article 101(3). Such decision shall indicate the date from which it is to take effect. This date may be prior to that of the decision."

Commentary on Article 11

11.096 The result of the procedures on complaints or on the Commission's own initiative was dealt with by Article 11 of the regulation. If the Commission found that there had been an infringement of Articles 101(1) or 102 of the TFEU or Article 7 of the regulation,[151] then it had the power by way of a decision to require the undertakings or associations of undertakings concerned to bring such infringement to an end.[152] Without prejudice to the other provisions of the regulation, the Commission may, before taking a decision under the foregoing procedure, address to the undertakings or associations of undertakings concerned, recommendations for termination of the infringement.[153] If the Commission, acting on a complaint received, concludes that on the evidence before it there were no grounds for intervention under Articles 101(1) or 102 of the TFEU or Article 7 of the regulation, in respect of any agreement, decision or practice, then it had to issue a decision rejecting the complaint as unfounded.[154] If the Commission, whether acting on a complaint received or on its own initiative, concluded that an agreement, decision or concerted practice satisfied the provisions both of Article 101(1) and of Article 101(3) of the TFEU, it had to issue a decision applying Article 101(3). Such decision had to indicate the date from which it was to take effect. This date could have been before that of the decision.[155] The Commission was obliged to publish the decisions which it took pursuant to Article 11.[156] Such a publication had to state the names of the parties and the main content of the decision; it also had to have regard to the legitimate interests of the undertakings in the protection of their business secrets.[157]

Opposition procedure

Introduction

11.097 Article 12 of the regulation provided for an opposition procedure for any agreement, decision or concerted practice which did not qualify for the block exemption under Article 3 of the regulation. This opposition procedure facilitated (to some extent) the granting of an individual exemption. Parties to an arrangement (i.e. agreement between undertakings, decision by an association of undertakings or concerted practice involving undertakings) had the ability to apply formally for, under Article 12, an exemption under Article 101(3) of the TFEU for the arrangement. Interestingly, Article 12 of the regulation did not contemplate an application for a negative clearance.

Text of Article 12

11.098 Article 12 of the regulation provided:

"*Application of Article [101(3)) – Objections*

---

151 Reg. 4056/86, Art. 11(2).
152 Reg. 4056/86, Art. 11(1), sub-paragraph 1.
153 Reg. 4056/86, Art. 11(1), sub-para. 2.
154 Reg. 4056/86, Art. 11(3).
155 Reg. 4056/86, Art. 11(4).
156 Reg. 4056/86, Art. 25(1).
157 Reg. 4056/86, Art. 25(2).

1. Undertakings and associations of undertakings which seek application of Article [101(3) of the TFEU] in respect of agreements, decisions and concerted practices falling within the scope of Article [101(1)] to which they are parties shall submit applications to the Commission.
2. If the Commission judges such an application admissible and is in possession of all the available evidence, and no action under Article 10 has been taken against the agreement, decision or concerted practice in question, then it shall publish as soon as possible in the Official Journal of the European Communities a summary of the application and invite all interested third parties and the Member States to submit their comments to the Commission within 30 days. Such publications shall have regard to the legitimate interest of undertakings in the protection of their business secrets.
3. Unless the Commission notifies applicants, within 90 days from the date of such publication in the Official Journal of the European Communities, that there are serious doubts as to the applicability of Article [101(3) of the TFEU], the agreement, decision or concerted practice concerned shall be deemed to be exempt, insofar as it conforms with the description given in the application, from the prohibition for the time already elapsed and for a maximum of six years from the date of publication in the Official Journal of the European Communities.

    If the Commission finds, after expiry of the 90-day time limit, but before expiry of the 6 year period, that the conditions for applying Article [101(3) of the TFEU] are not satisfied, it shall issue a decision declaring that the prohibition in Article [101(1) of the TFEU] is applicable. Such decision may be retroactive where the parties concerned have given inaccurate information or where they abuse the exemption from the provisions of Article [101(1) of the TFEU].
4. The Commission may notify applicants as referred to in the first subparagraph of paragraph 3 and shall do so if requested by a Member State within 45 days of the forwarding to the Member State of the application in accordance with Article 15(2). This request must be justified on the basis of considerations relating to the competition rules of the Treaty.

    If it finds that the conditions of Article [101(1)] and of Article [101(3)] are satisfied, the Commission shall issue a decision applying Article [101(3)]. The decision shall indicate the date from which it is to take effect. This date may be prior to the date of the application."

Commentary

11.099 If undertakings or associations of undertakings sought application of Article 101(3) of the TFEU[158] in respect of agreements, decisions and concerted practices falling within the scope of Article 101(1) of the TFEU to which they were parties then such undertakings or associations of undertakings had, before 1 May 2004, to submit applications to the Commission.[159] Notification was made using the so-called "MAR form". If the Commission judged such an application to be admissible and it was in possession of all the available evidence, and no action under Article 10 of the regulation had been taken against the agreement, decision or concerted practice in question, then it had to publish as soon as possible in the *Official Journal of the European Communities* a summary of the application and invite all interested parties and the Member States to submit their comments to the Commission within 30 days.[160] The regulation provided for commercial confidentiality because it stated that such publications had to have regard to the legitimate interest of undertakings in the protection of their business secrets.[161] There was then a

---

158 I.e. seek an individual exemption.
159 Reg. 4056/86, Art. 12(1).
160 Reg. 4056/86, Art. 12(2).
161 Ibid.

default-type mechanism. Unless the Commission notified applicants, within 90 days from the date of the publication in the *Official Journal*, that there were serious doubts as to the applicability of Article 101(3) of the TFEU,[162] then the agreements, decisions or concerted practices concerned had to be deemed to be exempt, in so far as it conformed with the description given in the application, from the prohibition for the time already elapsed and for a maximum of six years from the date of publication in the *Official Journal*.[163] That was not however the end of the matter. If the Commission found, after the expiry of the 90-day time limit but before the expiry of the six-year one, that the conditions for applying Article 101(3) of the TFEU were not satisfied, it had to issue a decision declaring that the prohibition in Article 101(1) of the TFEU was applicable. Such decision could have been retroactive where the parties concerned had given inaccurate information or where they abused the exemption from the provisions of Article 101(1) of the TFEU.[164] The Commission could notify applicants and had to do so, if requested by a Member State within 45 days of the forwarding to the Member State of the application in accordance with Article 15(2) of the regulation.[165] This request had to be justified on the basis of considerations relating to the competition rules of the Treaty.[166] If the Commission found that the conditions of Articles 101(1) of the TFEU and 101(3) of the TFEU were satisfied, the Commission had to issue a decision applying Article 101(3) of the TFEU. Such a decision had to indicate the date from which it was to take effect[167] which could have been prior to the date of the application.[168] If the Commission issued a decision applying Article 101(3) of the TFEU (i.e. an exemption) and such a decision was taken on the basis of either Article 11(4) or the second paragraph of Article 12(4), then the decision had to indicate the period for which it was to be valid.[169] Such a period would normally be not less than six years.[170] The exemption could not have been absolute and thus conditions and obligations could have been attached to it.[171]

11.100 The exemption was able to be renewed if the conditions for applying Article 101(3) of the TFEU continued to be satisfied.[172] Conversely, the Commission could revoke or amend the exemption or prohibit some specified act on the part of the parties.[173] The Commission had the ability to exercise such powers in four specified circumstances: (a) where there had been a change in any of the facts which were basic to the making of the decision; (b) where the parties committed a breach of any obligation attached to the decision;[174] (c) where the decision was based on incorrect information or was induced by deceit;[175] or (d) where the parties abused the exemption from the provisions of Article

---

162 I.e. the exemption provision in Art. 101 of the TFEU.
163 Reg. 4056/86, Art. 12(3).
164 Reg. 4056/86, Art. 12(3).
165 Reg. 4056/86, Art. 12(4).
166 Ibid.
167 Ibid.
168 Ibid.
169 Reg. 4056/86, Art. 13(1).
170 See ibid.
171 Ibid.
172 Reg. 4056/86, Art. 13(2).
173 See Reg. 4056/86, Art. 13(3).
174 In this case, the Exemption may be revoked with retrospective effect: Reg. 4056/86, Art. 13(2).
175 In this case, the Exemption may be revoked with retrospective effect: Reg. 4056/86, Art. 13(2).

101(1) of the TFEU granted to them by the decision.[176] The Commission was obliged to publish the decisions which it took pursuant to Article 12(3), second paragraph and 12(4).[177] Such publication had to state the names of the parties and the main content of the decision; it also had to have regard to the legitimate interests of the undertakings in the protection of their business secrets.[178] Rabe has commented:

> "A recurrent topic that has been given a lot of public attention is the possibility under Article 12 of the Regulation of granting exemptions with regard to agreements between conferences and non-conference shipping lines, so-called outsiders. Here an individual decision is necessary since the liner conference block exemption – Article 3 of the Regulation – does not apply. An example are the agreements between the liner conferences serving the US-Europe North Atlantic routes and several major non-conference competitors. These 'tolerated outsider agreements', generally referred to under the common denotation EUROCORDE, were the object of formal complaints by Shippers' Councils. The Commission under Article 10 of the Regulation opened formal proceedings and this triggered applications by the conferences and one outsider for individual exemptions under Article 12 of the Regulation.
>
> A matter of growing concern in the recent past have been the cases where conferences acquired a dominating market position. It has been argued that such a situation has notably developed with regard to the North Atlantic conference. Under such circumstances it is obvious that special attention has to be paid to the question whether the present arrangement adequately secures and implements the Treaty's regime of competition law. The increasing exclusion on non-conference trade definitely affects not just the competitiveness of the [EU] merchant fleet but has also serious repercussions as regards the competiveness of the Community's exports and imports and thus its foreign trade generally.
>
> The Commission has also directed its attention towards the closed-trade practices of some countries. In these cases national legislative or administrative instruments regulate the access to cargo. An example are the central freight offices used in the West Africa trade. The Commission regards these practices as incompatible with the competition rules."[179]

11.101 The Commission received various notifications of joint operating agreements between ferry companies including: (a) SNCF/Sealink (on the France/UK route); (b) SMZ/Sealink (on the Netherlands/UK route); and (c) Sealink/B&I (Ireland/UK route). These notifications are discussed below.

Duration and revocation of individual exemptions

Introduction

11.102 Article 13 of the regulation dealt with the duration and revocation of individual exemptions granted under Articles 11(4) or 12(4) of the regulation.

Text of Article 13

11.103 Article 13 of the regulation provided:

> "*Duration and Revocation of Decisions Applying Article [101(3)]*
> 1. Any decision applying Article 101(3) taken under Article 11(4) or under the second subparagraph of Article 12(4) shall indicate the period for which it is to be valid; normally such

---
176 In this case, the Exemption may be revoked with retrospective effect: Reg. 4056/86, Art. 13(2).
177 Reg. 4056/86, Art. 25(1).
178 Reg. 4056/86, Art. 25(2).
179 Rabe, op. cit. at fn. 102, pp. 2, 12–13.

period shall not be less than six years. Conditions and obligations may be attached to the decision.
2. The decision may be renewed if the conditions for applying Article 101(3) continues to be satisfied.
3. The Commission may revoke or amend its decision or prohibit specified acts by the parties:

(a) where there has been a change in any of the facts which were basic to the making of the decision;
(b) where the parties commit a breach of any obligation attached to the decision;
(c) where the decision is based on incorrect information or was induced by deceit; or
(d) where the parties abuse the exemption from the provisions of Article 101(2) granted to them by the decision.

In cases falling within (b), (c) or (d), the decision may be revoked with retroactive effect."

Renewal and revocation of the exemption

11.104 Article 13(2) of the regulation made clear that the decision could be renewed if the conditions for applying Article 101(3) of the TFEU continued to be satisfied. The Commission could revoke its decision in any one of four situations: (a) where there had been a change in any of the facts which were basic to the making of the decision; (b) where the parties committed a breach of any obligation attached to the decision; (c) where the decision was based on incorrect information or was induced by deceit; or (d) where the parties abused the exemption from the provisions of Article 101(2) of the TFEU granted to them by the decision. In the case of the last three situations, the decision to revoke the decision could be retrospective.

Amendment of the exemption

11.105 The Commission could have amended its decision in any one of four situations: (a) where there had been a change in any of the facts which were basic to the making of the decision; (b) where the parties committed a breach of any obligation attached to the decision; (c) where the decision was based on incorrect information or was induced by deceit; or (d) where the parties abused the exemption from the provisions of Article 101(2) of the TFEU granted to them by the decision. It would appear from the drafting of Article 13(3) of the regulation that the decision could not have been amended with retrospective effect.

Prohibition of specified acts by the parties

11.106 The Commission could prohibit specified acts by the parties in any one of four situations: (a) where there had been a change in any of the facts which were basic to the making of the decision; (b) where the parties committed a breach of any obligation attached to the decision; (c) where the decision was based on incorrect information or was induced by deceit; or (d) where the parties abused the exemption from the provisions of Article 101(2) of the TFEU granted to them by the decision. It would appear from the drafting of Article 13(3) of the regulation that a prohibition of specified acts by the parties could not be imposed with retrospective effect.

Publication of the decision

11.107 The Commission was obliged to publish the decisions which it took pursuant to Article 13(3) of the regulation.[180] Such publication had to state the names of the parties and the main content of the decision; it also had to have regard to the legitimate interests of the undertakings in the protection of their business secrets.[181]

Powers of the Commission

11.108 Article 14 of the regulation provided:

"Powers
Subject to review of its decision by the Court of Justice, the Commission shall have sole power:

– to impose obligations pursuant to Article 7
– to issue decisions pursuant to Article [101(3)].

The authorities of the Member States shall retain the power to decide whether any case falls within the provisions of Article 101(1) or Article 102, until such time as the Commission has initiated a procedure with a view to formulating a decision in the case in question or has sent notification as provided for in the first subparagraph of Article 12(3)."

Commentary

11.109 The Commission had, by virtue of Article 14 of the regulation, the sole power: (a) to impose obligations pursuant to Article 7 of the regulation; and (b) to issue decisions pursuant to Article 101(3) of the TFEU. The authorities of the Member States retained the power to decide whether any case fell within the provisions of Articles 101(1) or 102 of the TFEU, until such time as the Commission had initiated a procedure with a view to formulating a decision in the case in question or had sent notification as provided for in the first sub-paragraph of Article 12(3) of the regulation. The Commission's powers were however subject to review by the Court of Justice of the European Union ("CJEU").[182] Articles 101 and 102 of the TFEU were (and remain) directly applicable in the legal systems of the Member States and thus proceedings may be instituted in the national courts on the bases of Articles 101 and 102 of the TFEU. It is worth remembering that the national courts did not have the power to grant exemptions under Article 101(3) of the TFEU until the entry into force on 1 May 2004 of Regulation 1/2003.[183]

Liaison with the authorities of the Member States

Introduction

11.110 Article 15 of the regulation dealt with the possibility of the Commission liaising with the authorities of the Member States of the EU. Article 15 of the regulation provided:

---

180 Reg. 4056/86, Art. 25(1).
181 Reg. 4056/86, Art. 25(2).
182 Reg. 4056/86, Art. 14.
183 OJ L1/1, 1 January 2004.

"Liaison with the Authorities of the Member States
1. The Commission shall carry out the procedures provided for in this Regulation in close and constant liaison with the competent authorities of the Member States; these authorities shall have the right to express their views on such procedures.
2. The Commission shall immediately forward to the competent authorities of the Member States copies of the complaints and applications, and of the most important documents sent to it or which it sends out in the course of such procedures.
3. An Advisory Committee on agreements and dominant positions in maritime transport shall be consulted prior to the taking of any decision following upon a procedure under Article 10 or of any decision issued under Article 10 or of any decision issued under the second sub-paragraph of Article 12(3), or under the second subparagraph of paragraph 4 of the same Article. The Advisory Committee shall also be consulted prior to the adoption of the implementing provisions provided for in Article 26.
4. The Advisory Committee shall be composed of officials competent in the sphere of maritime transport and agreements and dominant positions. Each Member State shall nominate two officials to represent it, each of whom may be replaced, in the event of his being prevented from attending, by another official.
5. Consultation shall take place at a joint meeting convened by the Commission; such meeting shall be held not earlier than fourteen days after dispatch of the notice convening it. This notice shall, in respect of each case to be examined, be accompanied by a summary of the case together with an indication of the most important documents, and a preliminary draft decision.
6. The Advisory Committee may deliver an opinion notwithstanding that some of its members or their alternates are not present. A report of the outcome of the consultative proceedings shall be annexed to the draft decision. It shall not be made public."

Commentary

11.111 Article 15(1) of the regulation provided that the Commission had to carry out the procedures provided for in the regulation in close and constant liaison with the competent authorities of the Member States; such authorities having the right to express their views on such procedures. The Commission was obliged immediately to forward to the competent authorities of the Member States copies of the complaints and applications, and of the most important documents sent to it or which it sends out in the course of such procedures.[184] Article 15 provided for an Advisory Committee on Agreements and Dominant Positions in Maritime Transport. The Committee was the equivalent for the maritime transport sector of the Advisory Committee on Restrictive Practices which dealt with most other industrial sectors. The Maritime Transport Committee was composed of officials competent in the sphere of maritime transport and agreements and dominant positions.[185] Each Member State had to nominate two officials to represent it, each of whom could be replaced, in the event of his being prevented from attending, by another official.[186] The Committee was to be consulted prior to the taking of any decision following upon a procedure under Article 10 of the regulation, or of any decision issued under the second sub-paragraph of Article 12(3) of the regulation, or under the second sub-paragraph of Article 12(4).[187] The Committee was also to be consulted prior to the

---

184 Reg. 4056/86, Art. 15(2).
185 Reg. 4056/86, Art. 15(4).
186 Reg. 4056/86, Art. 15(4). A similar committee was established for the air transport sector by Art. 8 of Reg. 3975/87 (OJ L374/1).
187 Reg. 4056/86, Art. 15(3).

adoption of the implementing provisions provided for in Article 26 of the regulation. Consultation had to take place at a joint meeting convened by the Commission with such a meeting being held not earlier than 14 days after the dispatch of the notice convening it.[188] The Committee had the ability to deliver an opinion notwithstanding that some of its members or their alternates were not there.[189] Interestingly, the report of the outcome of the consultative proceedings was annexed to the draft decision but it was not made public.[190] The national authorities were given exceptionally wide powers under the regulation and it is submitted that the role of the national authorities was minimised in coming years because of the danger of confidential information being circulated to national authorities which could have had alternative (commercial) agendas.

Commission requests for information

Introduction

11.112 So as to carry out its functions under the regulation, the Commission needed to be able to obtain all necessary information. Article 16 of the regulation provided for this eventuality. Article 16 of the regulation provided:

> "*Requests for Information*
> 1. In carrying out the duties assigned to it by this Regulation, the Commission may obtain all the necessary information from the Governments and competent authorities of the Member States and from undertakings and associations of undertakings.
> 2. When asking a request for information to an undertaking or association of undertakings, the Commission shall at the same time forward a copy of the request to the competent authority of the Member State in whose territory the seat of the undertaking or association of undertakings is situated.
> 3. In its request, the Commission shall state the legal basis and the purpose of the request, and also the penalties provided for in Article 19(1)(b) for supplying incorrect information.
> 4. The owners of the undertakings or their representatives and, in the case of legal persons, companies or firms, or of associations having no legal personality, the person authorized to represent them by law or by their constitution, shall be bound to supply the information requested.
> 5. Where an undertaking or association of undertakings does not supply the information requested within the time limit fixed by the Commission, or supplies incomplete information, the Commission shall by decision require the information to be supplied. The decision shall specify what information is required, fix an appropriate time limit within which it is to be supplied and indicate the penalties provided for in Article 19(1)(b) and Article 20(1)(c) and the right to have the decision reviewed by the Court of Justice.
> 6. The Commission shall at the same time forward a copy of its decision to the competent authority of the Member State in whose territory the seat of the undertaking or association of undertakings is situated."

---

188 Reg. 4056/86, Art. 15(5). Such notice must, in respect of each case to be examined, be accompanied by a summary of the case together with an indication of the most important documents and a preliminary draft decision: Reg. 4056/86, Art. 15(5).
189 Reg. 4056/86, Art. 15(6).
190 Ibid.

Commentary

11.113 The Commission had various powers to obtain all the necessary information which it required for the purpose of carrying out the duties assigned to it under the regulation.[191] In its request, the Commission was obliged to state the legal basis and the purpose of the request as well as the penalties provided for in Article 19(1)(b) for supplying incorrect information.[192] The owners of the undertakings or their representatives and, in the case of legal persons, companies or firms, or of associations having no legal personality, the person authorised to represent them by law or by their constitution, was bound to supply the information requested.[193] If an undertaking or association of undertakings did not supply the information requested within the time limit fixed by the Commission, or supply incomplete information, the Commission had the power, by decision, to require the information to be supplied.[194] Such a decision had to specify what information was required, fix an appropriate time limit within which it was to be supplied and indicate the penalties provided for in Article 19(1)(b) and Article 20(1)(c) of the regulation as well as the right to have the decision reviewed by the CJEU.[195] The Commission was obliged under Article 16(6) of the regulation to forward a copy of the decision to the competent authority of the Member State in whose territory the seat of the undertaking or association of undertakings was situated.[196] When sending a request for information to an undertaking or association of undertakings, the Commission was obliged to simultaneously forward a copy of the request to the competent authority of the Member State in whose territory the seat of the undertaking was situated.[197]

Investigations

Introduction

11.114 To request information under Article 16 of the regulation may have proven insufficient or even injudicious because it may have "tipped-off" a guilty party of Commission action. Article 18 of the regulation therefore provided:

"*Investigating Powers of the Commission*
1. In carrying out the duties assigned to it by this Regulation, the Commission may undertake all necessary investigations into undertakings and associations of undertakings.
    To this end the officials authorized by the Commission are empowered:

    (a) to examine the books and other business records;
    (b) to take copies of or extracts from the books and business records;
    (c) to ask for oral explanations on the spot;
    (d) to enter any premises, land and vehicles of undertakings.

2. The officials of the Commission authorized for the purpose of these investigations shall exercise their powers upon production of an authorization in writing specifying the subject

---

191 See Reg. 4056/86, Art. 16.
192 Reg. 4056/86, Art. 16(3).
193 Reg. 4056/86, Art. 16(4).
194 Reg. 4056/86, Art. 16(5).
195 Ibid.
196 Reg. 4056/86, Art. 16(6).
197 Ibid.

matter and purpose of the investigation and the penalties provided for in Article 19(1)(c) in cases where production of the required books or other business records is incomplete. In good time before the investigation, the Commission shall inform the competent authority of the Member State in whose territory the same is to be made of the investigation and of the identity of the authorized officials.

3. Undertakings and associations of undertakings are obliged to submit to investigations ordered by a decision of the Commission. The decision shall specify the subject matter and purpose of the investigation, appoint the date on which it is to begin and indicate the penalties provided for in Article 19(1)(c) and Article 20(1)(d) and the right to have the decision reviewed by the Court of Justice.

4. The Commission shall take decisions referred to in paragraph 3 after consultation with the competent authority of the Member State in whose territory the investigation is to be made.

5. Officials of the competent authority of the Member State in whose territory the investigation is to be made, may at the request of such authority or of the Commission, assist the officials of the Commission in carrying out their duties.

6. Where an undertaking opposes an investigation ordered pursuant to this Article, the Member State concerned shall afford the necessary assistance to the officials authorized by the Commission to enable them to make their investigation. To this end, Member States shall take the necessary measures, after consulting the Commission, before 1 January 1989."

Commentary

11.115 The powers of investigation of the Commission are extensive: Article 18(1) of the regulation provided that in carrying out the duties assigned to it by the regulation, the Commission could undertake all necessary investigations into undertakings and associations of undertakings.[198] To this end, the officials authorised by the Commission were empowered: (a) to examine the books and other business records; (b) to take copies of or extracts from the books and business records; (c) to ask for oral explanations on the spot; and (d) to enter any premises, land and vehicles of undertakings.[199] The officials of the Commission authorised for the purpose of these investigations exercised their powers upon production of an authorisation in writing specifying the subject matter and purpose of the investigation and the penalties provided for in Article 19(1)(c) of the regulation in cases where production of the required books or other business records was incomplete.[200] Article 18(2) of the regulation provided that, in good time before the investigation, the Commission had to inform the competent authority of the Member State in whose territory the same was to be made of the investigation and of the identity of the authorised officials.[201] Undertakings and associations of undertakings were obliged to submit to investigations ordered by a decision of the Commission.[202] The Commission could not take such a decision until it had consulted with the competent authority of the Member State in whose territory the investigation was to be made.[203] The decision, when it was made, had to specify the subject matter and purpose of the investigation, appoint the date on which it is to begin and indicate the penalties (provided for in Article 19(1)(c) and

---

198 Reg. 4056/86, Art. 18(1).
199 Ibid. For details of a raid, see "EEC sends Lawyers into UKWAL Offices", Lloyd's List, 24 July 1989, p. 1.
200 Reg. 4056/86, Art. 18(2).
201 Ibid.
202 Reg. 4056/86, Art. 18(3).
203 Reg. 4056/86, Art. 18(4).

Article 20(1)(d) of the regulation) and the right to have the decision reviewed by the Court of Justice.[204] If an undertaking opposed an investigation ordered under Article 18 of the regulation then the Member State concerned was obliged to afford the necessary assistance to the officials authorised by the Commission to enable them to make their investigation.[205]

Investigations by authorities of the Member States

11.116 The Commission has the power to request the competent authorities of Member States to undertake the investigations which the Commission considers to be necessary under Article 18(1) of the regulation or which the Commission has ordered by a decision pursuant to Article 18(3) of the regulation.[206] The officials of the competent authorities of the Member States responsible for conducting the investigations are entitled to exercise their powers upon production of an authorisation in writing issued by the competent authority of the Member State in whose territory the investigation is to be made.[207] Such an authorisation must specify the subject matter and the purpose of the investigation.[208] The officials of the competent authority in the Member States may be assisted by Commission officials, at the request of either the Commission or the competent authorities of the Member State involved.[209] Article 17 of the regulation provided:

> "*Investigations by the authorities of the Member States*
> 1. At the request of the Commission, the competent authorities of the Member States shall undertake the investigations which the Commission considers to be necessary under Article 18(1), or which it has ordered by decision pursuant to Article 18(3). The officials of the competent authorities of the Member States responsible for conducting these investigations shall exercise their power upon production of an authorisation in writing issued by the competent authority of the Member State in whose territory the investigation is to be made. Such authorisation shall specify the subject matter and purpose of the investigation.
> 2. If so requested by the Commission or by the competent authority of the Member State in whose territory the investigation is to be made, the Commission officials may assist the officials of such authority in carrying out their duties."

Secrecy of information gathered

11.117 Information acquired as a result of the application of Articles 17 and 18 of the regulation could only be used for the purpose of the relevant request or investigation: it could not be used for any other purpose.[210] Without prejudice to the provisions of Articles 23 and 25 of the regulation, the Commission and the competent authorities of the Member States, their officials and other servants were prohibited from disclosing information acquired by them as a result of the application of the regulation and of the kind covered

---

204 Reg. 4056/86, Art. 18(3).
205 Reg. 4056/86, Art. 18(6). To this end, the Member States were obliged to take the necessary measures, after consulting with the Commission, before 1 January 1989.
206 Reg. 4056/86, Art. 17(1).
207 Ibid.
208 Ibid.
209 Reg. 4056/86, Art. 17(2).
210 Reg. 4056/86, Art. 24(1).

by the obligation of professional secrecy.[211] It was however possible that general information or surveys which did not contain information relating to particular undertakings or associations of undertakings may be published.[212]

Fines and periodic penalty payments

Fines

11.118 Article 19 of the regulation provided:

"*Fines*
1. The Commission may by decision impose on undertakings or associations of undertakings fines of from 100 to 5000 ECU where, intentionally or negligently:

    (a) they supply incorrect or misleading information, either in a communication pursuant to Article 5(5) or in an application pursuant to Article 12; or
    (b) they supply incorrect information in response to a request made pursuant to Article 16(3) or (5), or do not supply information within the time limit fixed by a decision taken under Article 16(5); or
    (c) they produce the required books or other business records in incomplete form during investigations under Article 17 or Article 18, or refuse to submit to an investigation ordered by decision issued in implementation of Article 18(3).

2. The Commission may by decision impose on undertakings or associations of undertakings fines of from 1000 to one million ECU, or a sum in excess thereof but not exceeding 10% of the turnover in the preceding business year of each of the undertakings participating in the infringement, where either intentionally or negligently:

    (a) they infringe Article [101(1)] of the Treaty, or do not comply with an obligation imposed under Article 7 of this Regulation;
    (b) they commit a breach of any obligation imposed pursuant to Article 5 or to Article 13(1).

    In fixing the amount of the fine, regard shall be had both to the gravity and to the duration of the infringement.
3. Article 15(3) and (4) shall apply.
4. Decisions taken pursuant to paragraphs 1 and 2 shall not be of criminal law nature.

    The fines provided for in paragraph 2(a) shall not be imposed in respect of acts taking place after notification to the Commission and before its Decision in application of Article [101(3)] of the Treaty, provided they fall within the limits of the activity described in the notification.

    However, this provision shall not have effect where the Commission has informed the undertakings concerned that after preliminary examination it is of the opinion that Article [101(1)] of the Treaty applies and that application of Article [101(3)] is not justified."

11.119 It is worth recalling that the fine which can be imposed is up to 10% of the worldwide (i.e. not just the EU) turnover during the previous year. The CJEU had a jurisdiction under Article 261 of the TFEU to review fines and penalties which have been imposed.

11.120 *Procedural wrongdoings.* The Commission had power under Article 19 of the regulation to impose fines on undertakings or associations of undertakings. The fines

---

211 Reg. 4056/86, Art. 24(2).
212 Reg. 4056/86, Art. 24(3).

ranged from €100 to €5,000.²¹³ The Commission could impose a fine where, intentionally or negligently, the undertaking or association of undertakings: (a) supply incorrect or misleading information, either in a communication pursuant to Article 5(5) of the regulation or in an application pursuant to Article 12 of the regulation;²¹⁴ or (b) supply incorrect information in response to a request made pursuant to Article 16(3) or (5) of the regulation, or did not supply information within the time limit fixed by a decision taken under Article 16(5) of the regulation; or (c) produce the required books or other business records in incomplete form during investigations under Articles 17 or 18 of the regulation, or refuse to submit to an investigation ordered by decision issued in implementation of Article 18(3) of the regulation. It was important to stress that a decision taken pursuant to Article 19(1) was not of a criminal nature.²¹⁵

11.121 *Substantive wrongdoings.* The Commission has power to impose, by way of a decision, on undertakings or associations of undertakings fines of from €1,000 to €1 million, or a sum in excess thereof, but not exceeding 10% of the turnover of the preceding business year of each of the undertakings participating in the infringement, where either intentionally or negligently: (a) they infringe Article 101(1) TFEU, or did not comply with an obligation imposed under Article 7 of the regulation;²¹⁶ or (b) they committed a breach of any obligation imposed pursuant to Article 5 or to Article 13(1) of the regulation.²¹⁷

11.122 In fixing the amount of the fine, the Commission had to have regard to both the gravity and to the duration of the infringement.²¹⁸ It was important to stress that a decision taken pursuant to Article 19(2) was not of a criminal nature.²¹⁹ In regard to fines generally, Article 15(3) and (4) of the regulation applied.²²⁰

Periodic penalty payments

11.123 Article 20 of Regulation 4056/86 provided:

"*Periodic Penalty Payments*
1. The Commission may by decision impose on undertakings or associations of undertakings periodic penalty payments of from 50 to 1000 ECU per day, calculated from the date appointed by the decision, in order to compel them:

   (a) to put an end to an infringement of Article [101(1)] or Article 102 of the Treaty the termination of which it has ordered pursuant to Article 11, or to comply with an obligation imposed pursuant to Article 7;
   (b) to refrain from any act prohibited under Article 13(3);
   (c) to supply complete and correct information which it has requested by decision taken pursuant to Article 16(5);

---

213 The ECU in this context is the ECU adopted in drawing up the budget of the Community in accordance with Arts 207 and 209 of the EC Treaty (Reg. 4056/86, Art. 22).
214 Reg. 4056/86, Art. 19(1)(a).
215 Reg. 4056/86, Art. 19(4).
216 In the case of these fines, they shall not be imposed in respect of acts taking place after notification to the Commission and before its decision in application of, what is now, Art. 101(3) of the TFEU, provided they fall within the limits of the activity described in the notification: Reg. 4056/86, Art. 19(4).
217 Reg. 4056/86, Art. 19(2).
218 Reg. 4056/86, Art. 19(2).
219 Reg. 4056/86, Art. 19(4).
220 Reg. 4056/86, Art. 19(3).

(d) to submit to an investigation which it has ordered by decision taken pursuant to Article 18(3).

2. Where the undertakings or associations if undertakings have satisfied the obligation which it was the purpose of the periodic penalty payment to enforce, the Commission may fix the total amount of the periodic penalty payment at a lower figure than that which would arise under the original decision.
3. Article 15(3) and (4) shall apply."

11.124 The Commission had the power to impose periodic penalty payments in addition to fines.[221] Article 20(1) of the regulation provided that the Commission may by decision impose on undertakings or associations of undertakings periodic penalty payments of from €50 to 1,000 per day. The amount was calculated from the date appointed by the decision.[222] The purposes for the periodic penalty payments were as follows: (a) to put an end to an infringement of Article 101(1) or Article 102 of the TFEU, the termination of which the Commission has ordered pursuant to Article 11 of the regulation, or to comply with an obligation imposed pursuant to Article 7 of the regulation;[223] (b) to refrain from any act prohibited under Article 13(3) of the regulation[224]; (c) to supply complete and correct information which it had requested by decision taken pursuant to Article 16(5) of the regulation;[225] or (d) to submit to an investigation which it had ordered by decision taken pursuant to Article 18(3) of the regulation.[226] If the undertakings or association of undertakings has satisfied the obligations which it was the purpose of the periodic penalty payment to enforce then the Commission may fix the total amount of the periodic penalty payment at a lower figure than that which would arise under the original decision.[227] Again like fines, Article 15(3) and (4) of the regulation applied to periodic penalty payments.[228]

Hearings of the parties and others

Introduction

11.125 In a number of specified situations, the Commission was obliged under the terms of the regulation to give a hearing to the parties involved. Article 23 of the regulation provided:

"*Hearing of the Parties and of Third Persons*
1. Before taking decisions as provided for in Articles 11, 12(3) second sub-paragraph, and 12(4), 13(3), 19 and 20 the Commission shall give the undertakings concerned the opportunity of being heard on the matters to which the Commission has taken objection.
2. If the Commission or the competent authorities of the Member States consider it necessary, they may also hear other natural or legal persons. Applications to be heard on the part of such persons where they show a sufficient interest shall be granted.

---

221 Reg. 4056/86, Art. 20.
222 Reg. 4056/86, Art. 20(1).
223 Reg. 4056/86, Art. 20(1)(a).
224 Ibid..
225 Reg. 4056/86, Art. 20(1)(c).
226 Reg. 4056/86, Art. 20(1)(d).
227 Reg. 4056/86, Art. 20(2).
228 Reg. 4056/86, Art. 20(3).

3. Where the Commission intends to give negative clearance pursuant to Article [101(3)] of the Treaty, it shall publish a summary of the relevant agreement, decision or concerted practice and invite all interested third parties to submit their observations within a time limit which it shall fix being not less than one month. Publication shall have regard to the legitimate interest of the undertakings in the protection of their business secrets."

Commentary

11.126 Article 23(1) of the regulation provided that before taking decisions as provided for in Articles 11, 12(3) second paragraph, and 12(4), 13(3), 19 and 20 of the regulation, the Commission had to give the undertaking or association of undertakings concerned the opportunity of being heard on the matters to which the Commission had taken objection. If the Commission or the competent authorities of the Member States considered it necessary then they could also hear other natural or legal persons.[229] The Commission could also entertain other persons and applications where such persons applied to be heard and demonstrated a sufficient interest in the case.[230] If the Commission intended to give a negative clearance pursuant to Article 101(3) of the TFEU, it had to publish a summary of the relevant agreement, decision or concerted practice and invite all interested third parties to submit their observations within a time limit which it shall fix, but such a time limit had to be not less than one month.[231] Such a publication had to have regard to the legitimate interests of the undertakings in the protection of their business interests.[232]

Review by the Court of Justice of the fines and periodical penalty payments

Introduction

11.127 Article 21 of the regulation provided that the CJEU may review fines and periodical penalty payments. Article 21 of the regulation provided:

"*Review by the Court of Justice*
The Court of Justice shall have unlimited jurisdiction within the meaning of Article [261 of the TFEU] to review decisions whereby the Commission has fixed a fine or periodical penalty payment; it may cancel, reduce or increase the fine or periodic penalty payment imposed."

Commentary

11.128 Article 21 of the regulation explicitly stated that the Court of Justice had unlimited jurisdiction within the meaning of Article 172 of the EC Treaty[233] to review decisions whereby the Commission had fixed a fine or periodical penalty payment and may cancel, reduce or increase the fine or penalty payment imposed.

---

229 Reg. 4056/86, Art. 23(2).
230 Ibid.
231 Reg. 4056/86, Art. 23(3).
232 Reg. 4056/86, Art. 23(3).
233 Art. 172 EC would now be, broadly, Art. 261 TFEU.

Publication of decisions

11.129 The Commission was obliged to publish the decisions which it took pursuant to Articles 11, 12(3) second paragraph, 12(4) and 13(3) of the regulation.[234] Such publication had to state the names of the parties and the main content of the decision; it also had to have regard to the legitimate interests of the undertakings in the protection of their business secrets.[235]

Implementing provisions

11.130 Article 26 of the regulation provided that the Commission had to have power to adopt implementing provisions concerning the scope of the obligations of communication pursuant to Article 5(5); the form, content and other details of complaints pursuant to Article 10; applications pursuant to Article 12; and the hearings provided for in Article 23(1) and (2) of the regulation.[236] Regulation 4260/88 was the resultant measure. This latter regulation entered into force on 1 January 1989.

O. PROCEDURE: COMMISSION REGULATION 4260/88

Introduction

11.131 Commission Regulation 4260/88 of 16 December 1988 dealt with the communications, complaints, applications and hearings provided for in Council Regulation 4056/86.[237] It will be referred to in this section as Regulation 4260/88. Regulation 4260/88 was the procedural companion to Regulation 4056/86. It also provided for the use of Form MAR which was the equivalent of Form A/B. Section I of Regulation 4260/88 dealt with notifications, complaints and applications.

Legal basis and background

11.132 Regulation 4260/88 was adopted by the Commission and not the Council of Ministers. Article 26 of Regulation 4056/86 provided that the Commission

> "shall have power to adopt implementing provisions concerning the scope of the obligation of communication pursuant to Article 5(5), the form, content and other details of complaints pursuant to Article 10, applications pursuant to Article 12 and the hearings provided for in Article 23(1) and (2)".

Notifications

11.133 Article 1 of Regulation 4260/88 provided:

"*Notifications*

1. Awards at arbitration and recommendations by conciliators accepted by the parties shall be notified to the Commission when they concern the settlement of disputes relating to the practices of conferences referred to in Articles 4 and 5(2) and (3) of Regulation No. 4056/86.

---

234 Reg. 4056/86, Art. 25(1).
235 Reg. 4056/86, Art. 25(2).
236 Reg. 4056/86, Art. 26.
237 OJ 1988 L376/1. On procedure generally in this area, see Clough and Randolph, op. cit. at fn. 1, chap. 5.

2. The obligation of notification applies to any party to the dispute resolved by the award or recommendation.
3. Notifications shall be submitted forthwith by registered letter with an acknowledgment of receipt or shall be delivered by hand against receipt. They shall be written in one of the official languages of the Community.

   Supporting documents shall be either originals or copies. Copies must be certified as true copies of the original. They shall be submitted in their original language. Where the original language is not one of the official languages of the Community, a translation in one of the official languages shall be attached.
4. When representatives of undertakings, of associations of undertakings, or of natural or legal persons sign such notifications, they shall produce written proof that they are authorized to act."

The background to this provision is set out in Recital 2 to Regulation 4260/1988:

"whereas the obligation of communication to the Commission of awards at arbitration and recommendations by conciliators provided for in Article 5(5) of [Regulation 4056/86] concerns the settlement of disputes relating to the practices of conferences referred to in Article 4 and 5(2) and (3) of that Regulation; whereas it seems appropriate to make the procedure for this notification as simple as possible; whereas it is appropriate, therefore, to provide for notifications to be made in writing, attaching the documents containing the text of the awards and recommendations concerned".

Complaints

11.134 Regulation 4260/88 laid down a procedure for submitting complaints under Regulation 4056/86. This procedure was set out in Article 2 of Regulation 4260/88. Article 2 of Regulation 4260/88 provided:

"*Complaints*

1. Complaints pursuant to Article 10 of Regulation No. 4056/86 shall be submitted in writing in one of the official languages of the Community, their form, content and other details being left to the discretion of complainants.
2. Complaints may be submitted by:

   (a) Member States
   (b) natural or legal persons who claim a legitimate interest.
3. When representatives of undertakings, of associations of undertakings, or of natural or legal persons sign such complaints, they shall produce written proof that they are authorized to act."

Recital 3 to Regulation 4260/1988 recalled that

"complaints pursuant to Article 10 of Regulation 4056/86 may make it easier for the Commission to take action for infringements of Articles 101 and 102 of the TFEU in the field of maritime transport; whereas it would consequently seem appropriate to make the procedure for submitting complaints as simple as possible; whereas it is appropriate, therefore, to provide for complaints to be submitted in one written copy, the form, content and details being left to the discretion of the complainants".

Applications for exemptions

11.135 Regulation 4260/88 laid down a procedure for submitting applications for exemptions of the competition rules. This procedure was laid down in Article 4 of Regulation 4260/88. Article 4 provided:

"Submission of Applications

1. Applications pursuant to Article 12 of Regulation 4056/86 shall be submitted on Form MAR shown in Annex I.[238]
2. Several participating undertakings may submit an application on a single form.
3. Applications shall contain the information requested in the form.
4. Fourteen copies of each application and of the supporting documents shall be submitted to the Commission.
5. The supporting documents shall be either originals or copies. Copies must be certified as true copies of the original.
6. Applications shall be in one of the official languages of the Community. Supporting documents shall be submitted in their original language. Where the original language is not one of the official languages, a translation in one of the official languages shall be attached.
7. The date of submission of an application shall be the date on which it is received by the Commission. Where, however, the application is sent by registered post, it shall be deemed to have been received on the date shown on the postmark of the place of posting.
8. Where an application submitted pursuant to Article 12 of Regulation No. 4056/86 falls outside the scope of that Regulation, the Commission shall without delay inform the applicant that it intends to examine the application under the provisions of such other Regulation as is applicable to the case; however, the date of submission of the application shall be the date resulting from paragraph 7. The Commission shall inform the applicant of its reasons and fix a period for him to submit any comments in writing before it conducts its appraisal pursuant to the provisions of that other Regulation."

Hearings

11.136 Section II of Regulation 4260/88 laid down the procedure to be followed for hearings when companies have the opportunity to express their views regarding the objections raised against them. Article 5 of Regulation 4260/88 provided: "Before consulting the Advisory Committee on Agreements and Dominant Positions in the field of Maritime Transport the Commission shall hold a hearing pursuant to Article 23(1) of Regulation 4056/86."

Article 6 of Regulation 4260/88 provided:

"1. The Commission shall inform undertakings and associations of undertakings in writing of the objections raised against them. The communication shall be addressed to each of them or to a joint agent appointed by them.
2. The Commission may inform the parties by giving notice in the Official Journal of the European Communities, if from the circumstances of the case this appears appropriate, in particular where notice is to be given to a number of undertakings but no joint agent has been appointed. The notice shall have regard to the legitimate interest of the undertakings in the protection of their business secrets.
3. A fine or a periodic penalty payment may be imposed on an undertaking or association of undertakings only if the objections were notified in the manner provided for in paragraph 1.
4. The Commission shall, when giving notice of objections, fix a period within which the undertakings and associations of undertakings may inform the Commission of their views."

---

238 I.e. Annex I of Reg. 4260/88.

Communicating awards and recommendations to the Commission

11.137 The regulation set out an obligation to communicate to the Commission arbitration awards and recommendations by conciliators.

P. CASE LAW RELATING TO REGULATION 4056/86 AND SELECTED COMPETITION CASES IN THE SHIPPING SECTOR

11.138 There was an enormous amount of litigation concerning the application of Regulation 4056/86.[239] This case law involved decisional practice before the European Commission (which was generally antagonistic towards the block exemption which it saw as a block exemption for price-fixing agreements) and then appeals to the General Court and the CJEU. There were some fascinating points in this litigation which have been largely addressed by previous editions of this book and other works on the subject. In the interests of space, however, it is not proposed to review this case law because it is now largely of historical significance only but there are aspects of it which are still relevant and they have been identified elsewhere in this edition.[240]

Q. REFORM OF REGULATION 4056/86

11.139 In 2003, the Commission commenced a regulatory review of the justification for block exemption for liner conferences. The Commission was always opposed to the block exemption so it is not surprising that the result of the review process was that the Commission proposed the abolition of the block exemption. There was extensive consultation with industry, shippers, carriers and consumers. On 25 September 2006, the Council agreed to adopt Regulation 1419/2006 to repeal the block exemption on liner conferences. Conferences were given a transitional period of two years until 18 October 2008 to adapt to the new situation. Therefore, between 1987 and 18 October 2008, liner conferences had been free to fix prices and regulate capacity under the conditions laid down in Regulation 4056/86 but that changed. Now, any violation of competition law by a liner conference is punishable. Norway followed the EU model and amended Regulation 964/1992 so since 18 October 2008, the liner block exemption has been repealed and Norwegian competition law applies with full force. The reform of Regulation 4056/86 and the new regime is considered in chapter 12.

---

239 See, in particular, Antapassis and Athanassiou, *Competition and Regulation in Shipping and Shipping Related Industries* (2009); Clough and Randolph, op. cit. at fn. 1; Dinger, *The Future of Liner Conferences in Europe: A Critical Analysis of Agreements in Liner Shipping Under Current European Competition Law* (2004); Hongyan Liu, *Liner Conferences in Competition Law: A Comparative Analysis of European and Chinese Law* (2010); Ortiz Blanco, op. cit. at fn. 1; Pozdnakova, op. cit. at fn. 1; Spiteri, op. cit. at fn. 1. See also previous editions of this book and previous editions of the main works on EU competition law.

240 It would have been interesting to include the review of the case law which had been drafted but it would have lengthened this chapter five-fold and would have been of historical significance only.

R. ASSESSMENT

11.140 It has been written that the

"purpose of this Regulation as set forth in the preambular paragraphs is to steer a middle course between two evils: undue distortion of competition within the internal market by a complete laissez-faire attitude and excessive regulation of the sector. Adoption of the competition rules originates in the misgivings expressed by developing countries in the 1970s about the functioning of the conference system."[241]

The same authors have commented that

"the Regulation attempts to steer a middle course between conflicting interests of liner conferences and shippers. The result of this Regulation is group exemption to liner conferences couched in the widest possible terms, i.e., a very generous treatment of liner conferences unprecedented in other fields of competition law of the Community."[242]

11.141 Helmut Kreis, the former Deputy Head of the Administrative Unit for Transport and Tourism in the Directorate General IV (or the Directorate General for Competition which is now also known as DG COMP), writing personally in 1989 stated that the regulation is a way by which the EU accepted the self-regulatory system enshrined in the UNCTAD Code.[243] He has also written that the regulation is "important because it provides for a fairly liberal regime, increases legal security, and clarifies the relationship between liner conferences and transport users".[244]

11.142 Regulation 4056/86 did not provide a complete competition regime in relation to shipping. Towage probably fell outside its scope. The same may be said of salvage and offshore supply services. Many tramp services fell outside its scope. Similarly, many non-scheduled services did as well. It was also controversial and somewhat unique because it exempted (by way of a Council (and not a Commission)) regulation certain behaviour and, moreover, that behaviour was price-fixing which was the very arrangement which ordinarily would never be exempted. Reform was inevitable but repeal was the result.

---

241 Bredima-Savopoulou and Tzoannos, op. cit. at fn. 88, p. 180, footnote omitted.
242 Ibid., p. 181.
243 (1989–90) 13 Fordham Int'l LJ 411, at p. 418.
244 Ibid., p. 418. Clough and Randolph, op. cit. at fn. 1, have commented that the regulation seeks to reconcile the EC's transport policy commitment to the UNCTAD Code and to the scheduled liner cartel, enshrined in the 1979 Brussels package, with the EEC competition rules (p. 151).

CHAPTER 12

European Union competition law: the new regime relating to shipping – Regulation 1419/2006

A. INTRODUCTION

12.001 Regulation 1419/2006 has established a new European Union ("EU") competition regime for the shipping sector.[1] This is a dramatic change for the sector[2] because it had for many years benefited from the protective regime embodied in Regulation 4056/86[3] which exempted the sector from the full rigours of EU competition law enforcement by the European Commission.[4] The scope of Regulation 4056/86 meant that, in

---

1 OJ 2006 L269/1, http://eur-lex.europa.eu/LexUriServ/LexUriServ.do?uri=OJ:L:2006:269:0001:0003:EN:PDF.

See MEMO/07/131, 11 April 2007. See Antapassis, Athanassiou and Rosæg (eds), *Competition and Regulation in Shipping and Shipping Related Industries* (2009); Ortiz Blanco, *Shipping Conferences under EC Antitrust Law* (2007); Pozdnakova, *Liner Shipping and EU Competition Law* (2008); Spiteri, *The Application of EC Competition Law in the Maritime Transport Sector* (2012); and Wareham and Power (eds), *Competition Law and Shipping: The EMLO Guide to EU Competition Law in the Shipping and Port Industries* (2010).

See also Benini and Bermig, "Milestones in Maritime Transport: EU ends Exemption" (2007) *Competition Policy Newsletter*, Spring, p. 20; Chuah, "Liner Conferences in the EU and the Proposed Review of EC Regulation 4056/86" [2005] LMCLQ 207; Munari, "Liner Shipping and Antitrust after the Repeal of Regulation 4056/86" [2009] LMCLQ 42; Munari, "Liner Shipping, Antitrust and the Repeal of Regulation 4056/86: A New Era of Global Maritime Confrontation" in Antapassis, Athanassiou and Røsæg, op. cit., p. 7; and Stamatiou and Neocleous, "The New Era of EC Competition Law in the Shipping Industry" [2009] ICCLR 1. See also Evans, "Competition Developments Affecting the Maritime Sector", European Maritime Law Organisation ("EMLO"), 14 October 2005. There are also many other relevant sources cited throughout this chapter and others throughout the book. See also Lista, "The Application of the EU Competition Rules to the Marine Sector" in Baatz (ed.), *Maritime Law* (2014), chap. 13.

2 The preface to Antapassis, Athanassiou and Rosæg (eds), op. cit. at fn. 1, states at p. ix: "few pieces of legislation have shaken the [shipping] industry as much as the recent extension of the general European competition legislation to the maritime sector". A tangible example would be the fact that the Far Eastern Freight Conference ("FEFC") ceased trading because of the repeal of the block exemption for liner conferences in Reg. 4056/86 by virtue of Reg. 1419/2006. The FEFC represented about 70% of the Europe–Asia trade and had operated since 1879. It comprised in 2008 companies such as ANL, CMA, CGM, Egyptian International Shipping, HHM, Maersk, MOL, NYK, Safmârine, ZIM, APL, CSAV, Hapag-Lloyd, KLine, MISC, MSG, OOCL and Yang Ming. The global implications were clear from the fact that Mitsui OSK Lines (MOL) resigned from the Transpacific Stabilization Agreement (TSA) and the Canada Transpacific Stabilization Agreement (CTSA) because of the change in EU law and the fact that it was extremely difficult to align its entire organisation with regional differences.

3 I.e. Reg. 4056/86 OJ 1986 L378/4. Munari described the regime under Reg. 4056/86 as "extravagant" in his article entitled "Liner Shipping and Antitrust after the Repeal of Regulation 4056/86" op. cit. at fn. 1, p. 48. See chap. 11.

4 Indeed, the dramatic nature of the legislative change in 2008 was compounded by the decline in the fortunes of the world economy which occurred at almost the same time (i.e. October 2008 when the new EU regime entered fully into effect and the financial markets froze following the collapse of Lehman Brothers). These two changes (i.e. the legislative change and the financial collapse) had a dramatic impact on shipping – either would have been significant on its own. These changes could lead to mergers and an increased focus on alternative solutions (including the inevitable switch towards consortia and slot chartering).

terms of Commission enforcement, what are now, Articles 101 and 102 of the TFEU applied before October 2008 only to liner shipping; this meant that, for example, tramp shipping and cabotage were not subject to European Commission enforcement.[5] Regulation 4056/86 had enabled the Commission to apply what are now Articles 101 and 102 of the TFEU directly to maritime transport in certain but limited circumstances[6] but it also contained a controversial block exemption[7] for liner conferences. Since 18 October 2006, all maritime services[8] are subject to the European Commission's competition jurisdiction by virtue of Regulation 1419/2006[9] and the repeal of the pre-existing regime embodied in Regulation 4056/86. However, a two-year transition period was allowed for liner conferences which met the conditions of Regulation 4056/86 at the time of the entry into force of Regulation 1419/2006 (i.e. 18 October 2006). Therefore, since 18 October 2008,[10] the liner conference[11] block exemption in Regulation 4056/86 no longer exists and Regulation 1419/2006[12] is the relevant regulation along with Regulation 1/2003.[13] This means that EU competition law applies to the maritime transport sector in full so that the European Commission may now apply EU competition law to the shipping sector in its entirety.[14] It also means that the liner conferences operating in the context of the EU could no longer do so.[15] The radical nature of the change is clear from the fact that liner conferences had operated for over 130 years and were brought to an end, as far as the EU is concerned at least, by this new regime. The repeal of Regulation 4056/86 was the lifting of the EU competition kimono on the sector. Now, the general EU competition law

---

5 As Munari recalls (op. cit. at fn. 1, p. 42, footnote omitted), before the new regime, "tramp shipping and cabotage were exempted from the legal regime established to implement [Arts 101 and 102 of the TFEU]; by virtue of this exemption, [EU] antitrust rules could be applied to these sectors only with the 'provisional instruments' set forth by the [TFEU, Art. 104], i.e., through a set of delegation of powers to national antitrust authorities. In fact, no case can be recalled regarding the application of this provision in any of these sectors." It will be recalled that Arts 101 and 102 of the TFEU applied to the sector in its entirety but the Commission lacked the enforcement mechanism to apply the rules to the entire sector. See fn. 14.

6 See chap. 11 generally.

7 The block exemption only related to Art. 101(1) of the TFEU and did not provide any exemption from Art. 102 of the TFEU. See chap. 11 on the block exemption in Reg. 4056/86.

8 The bulk sector which was excluded under Reg. 4056/86 from the full application of EU competition law became subject to the EU competition regime by virtue of Reg. 1419/2006.

9 OJ 2006 L269/1.

10 I.e. two years from the entry into force of Reg. 1409/2006.

11 It will be recalled that a "liner conference" is, essentially, an agreement whereby ocean carriers conduct a trade on a particular route and agree to do so on common terms and conditions (e.g. rates, services and schedules). They carry cargo (usually in containers) on a particular pre-advertised and pre-scheduled route and do so on common agreed terms and conditions (see chap. 10). Unlike a consortia agreement, participants in a liner conference also agree on price.

12 OJ 2006 L269/1.

13 OJ 2003 L1/1.

14 EU competition law was (and is still) always applicable to the sector but it was not always easy for the Commission to apply competition law to the sector. As the Commission observed in the Explanatory Memorandum to the proposal to repeal Reg. 4056/86: "12. Cabotage and international tramp vessel services are currently the only remaining sectors that are excluded from the [EU] competition implementing rules. [Citing Art. 32(a) and (b) of Reg. 1/2003.] The lack of effective enforcement powers for these sectors is an anomaly from a regulatory point of view. 13. The proposal to bring these services under the common competition implementing rules does not involve a substantive change for the industry as the substantive competition rules, set out in Articles [101 and 102] of the [TFEU], already apply."

15 The European Economic and Social Committee ("EESC") believed in 2007 that there were around 150 liner conferences operating worldwide and that some 28 of them were operating along routes connecting EU Member States (see EESC Opinion (OJ 2007 C256/12)). Liner conferences outside the EU with no impact on trade in the EU could continue to operate as a matter of EU law.

regime (including Regulation 1/2003)[16] applies to the shipping sector in its entirety (including cabotage and tramp services where there is an effect on trade between EU Member States. While the full rigours of EU competition law applied to the sector since 18 September 2006, there was the two-year transition period and also a set of guidelines[17] which were specific to the sector and applicable until 26 September 2013 but those guidelines are now no longer in force[18] so even the sector specific guidelines have been removed so the general competition rules apply fully to the sector.

B. DEBATE ON THE OLD REGIME: REGULATION 4056/86

12.002 The Commission, shippers and some others were long concerned about the block exemption for liner conferences in Regulation 4056/86. The Commission tried to limit the scope of the block exemption in Regulation 4056/86 as much as it could in terms of how it construed and applied the block exemption and it was quite forceful in that approach.[19] However, there was a limit to what it could achieve by that means. Ultimately, any unease would only be removed by the repeal of the block exemption in particular and the regulation generally. The Commission conducted various rounds of public consultations, held a public hearing and published several documents including a white paper. Eventually, the Commission proposed, and the relevant other EU institutions agreed, that Regulation 4056/86 be repealed. It is useful to review this process and while there is a certain amount of repetition in the information, it is interesting to see how the reform process evolved.

---

16 OJ 2003 L1/1.

17 On the guidelines see OJ C245/2, 26 September 2008. The guidelines dealt with the issues of market definition, information exchange between competitors and how the horizontal cooperation rules would apply between tramp shipping operators in shipping pools.

18 Although the Guidelines have been withdrawn, the Guidelines are still of some inspiration as to what the law might be but the Guidelines are in no way binding.

19 There were many in the liner sector who believed that the Commission was opposed to liner conferences in an unreasonable way. The Commission has rejected those claims. In a very lucid article in Lloyd's List on 18 September 2003, Janet Porter, under the heading "EC defends treatment of lines" wrote: "the European Commission has hit back at suggestions that it 'loathes' the liner shipping industry. In a robust response, Brussels describes the allegations as 'both unfair and unfounded'. Amelia Torres, spokeswoman for competition commissioner Mario Monti, points out in a letter to Lloyd's List that liner shipping has benefitted from very generous exemptions from European Union competition rules which enable carriers to fix prices and regulate capacity. Furthermore, the Commission last year approved a revised version of the controversial Trans-Atlantic Conference Agreement, despite opposition from shippers. 'The Commission therefore has no negative bias towards the liner shipping sector', Ms Torres writes. At the same time, Brussels 'has a duty' to investigate customer grievances, the letter continues. 'Cartel investigations are one of the core activities of the competition authorities'. But if those investigated, such as the ferry companies recently raided by EU inspectors, have not broken the law, 'they have nothing to fear'. The re-statement of EU competition policy comes as the Commission reviews the rules pertaining to liner shipping, with replies to a questionnaire now being studied. Shippers from around the world, who have finished a three-day meeting in France, renewed their calls for an end to the traditional conference system. The Tripartite Shippers' Group 'believes that the primary function and roles of conferences and discussion agreements have far outlived their original purpose'. In today's marketplace, 'collective pricing for services have been eliminated in every other industry except liner shipping', shippers said in a joint statement. The Brussels review should 'bring about reforms which recognise that pricing should be individually set, based on a carrier's individual costs calculated with a fair return on investment and reasonable profit', the European Shippers' Council, the National Industrial Transportation League, and a number of Asian shipper organisations, urged at the end of their meeting." See Benini, "Milestones in Maritime Transport: EU Ends Exemptions" (2007) *European Commission Competition Policy Newsletter* 20.

12.003 Having long been concerned about Regulation 4056/86,[20] on 27 March 2003, the Commission launched a review of the liner conference block exemption in Regulation 4056/86. It was interesting that, unlike other block exemptions, Regulation 4056/86 had contained no review clause so the Commission had to initiate the review (i.e. there was no automatic review). The review was justified on several grounds. There had been changes in the way in which liner conferences operated.[21] In essence, the nature of the block exemption in Regulation 4056/86 was unique because it exempted price-fixing, was open-ended in time and was never reviewed according to a pre-determined timetable (unlike other block exemptions).[22] There had been the growth of containerisation, alliances and consortia since the block exemption was adopted in 1986.[23] Consortia benefited from their own block exemptions which had been adopted after the adoption of Regulation 4056/86.[24] There had been a significant report from the Organisation for Economic Co-operation and Development ("OECD") in 2002 on liner conferences which called into question whether liner conferences should be exempted at all.[25] The adoption of Regulation 1/2003 highlighted the unique position of liner conferences and maritime transport when compared to the rest of the economy. The Lisbon Agenda (a plan to stimulate the economy of the EU) was regarded by the Commission as another reason for reforming and repealing the regime.[26] It was not surprising that the ultimate result of the review was the proposal to repeal the block exemption given the Commission's antipathy towards the Council's block exemption. Before analysing the debate on whether Regulation 4056/86 ought to be retained or how it might be changed, it is useful to go back to 2002.

12.004 In 2002, the OECD's Secretariat published a report on liner conferences.[27] The OECD concluded in its report:

> "[many parties] have portrayed the liner shipping sector as 'unique' and therefore requiring special treatment under competition law. This is true insofar as any industry is unique and certainly there are convincing reasons to allow carriers to co-ordinate certain operational aspects linked to the provision of ocean shipping services. However, it is more difficult to perceive in which manner liner shipping is more 'unique' than any other industries, or why it should be

---

20 E.g. this concern by the Commission was manifested through its restrictive construction of the block exemption and the concerns which it had articulated over time and applied in the Commission's case law (see chap. 11 generally).

21 The theory had been that liner conferences had a stabilising effect on the industry with their regular and reliable services for shippers. The notion was that conferences could be tolerated where competition was still present through non-conference services, tramp services and other forms of transport (although the latter was unusual) (see Reg. 4056/86, Recital 8). However, various parties no longer believed in the theory.

22 On 1 April 2003, Fabrizia Benini of the Directorate General for Competition ("DG COMP") spoke (in a personal capacity) at a seminar in London entitled "Seminar on EU Competition Law and Maritime Transport" and said in the context of Reg. 4056/86 not having a review mechanism: "[t]his in itself [leaving aside the other unique features of Reg. 4056/86] would be sufficient justification to undertake a review because it is standard Commission practice to ensure that legislation is regularly updated to take account of changes in market conditions", http://ec.europa.eu/competition/speeches/text/sp2003_008_en.pdf.

23 Consortia differ from liner conferences in that consortia do not involve price-fixing. On consortia, see chap. 14.

24 Consortia benefited from a block exemption adopted in 2000 (Reg. 823/2000) which has since been updated and amended: see chap. 14.

25 This was extremely important in the development of the Commission's thinking on the need to repeal the block exemption but was more a corroboration rather than a stimulation. See the OECD's *Final Report on Competition Policy in Liner Shipping* (DSTI/DOT (2002) 2 (16 April 2002)). See para. 12.04.

26 It is difficult to see how the Lisbon Agenda would have been a reason to repeal the block exemption in its own right but it was part of the rationale according to the Commission.

27 DSTI/DOT(2002) 2 (16 April 2002) (or, in this chapter, the "OECD Report").

treated more favourably or even differently from other transport providers with respect to price-fixing and rate discussions. The cost structure of the industry is not significantly different from that of other transport industries and returns in liner shipping are similar to those of other scheduled transport providers. While it is true that ships cost considerably more than, say, a new lorry or locomotive, each ship can also earn significantly more revenue. Seasonal and directional trade imbalances are not unique to the liner sector and must be faced by most transport service providers – in some cases these imbalances pose much more of a problem since some vehicles are not as standardised as container ships. In the end, liner shipping is about as 'different' from other like industries as, for example, trucking is from freight air services or freight air is from rail freight – with the exception that price-fixing is allowed in liner shipping and nearly universally dis-allowed in these other industries."[28]

The OECD then went on to recommend that:

"Member countries,[29] when reviewing the application of competition policy in the liner shipping sector, seriously consider removing anti-trust exemptions for price fixing and rate discussions. Exemptions for other operational arrangements may be retained so long as these do not result in excessive market power."[30]

Munari has summarised skilfully and succinctly the OECD's further recommendations:

"it was suggested that [OECD] Member States adopt rules on competition in liner shipping based on the following principles:

(a) *freedom to negotiate*: shippers and carriers should always have the option of freely negotiating rates, surcharges and other terms of carriage on an individual and confidential basis;
(b) *freedom to protect contracts*: carriers and shippers should always be able contractually to protect key terms of negotiated service contracts, including information regarding rates, and this confidentiality should be given maximum protection; [and]
(c) *freedom to co-ordinate operations*: carriers should be able to pursue operational and/or capacity agreements with other carriers as long as these do not confer undue market power to the parties involved."[31],[32]

In regard to the OECD Report, it has also been commented:

"Another incentive for the review process [of Regulation 4056/86] was the publication in April 2002 of a report on competition policy in liner shipping by the Secretariat of the OECD. The report casts doubt on the validity of the assumption that collective rate setting by members of a liner conference is an indispensable pre-requisite for reliable liner shipping services and invites [OECD] Member countries to review antitrust exemptions for price fixing. But it also recognises that carriers have legitimate operational needs that may require co-operation with other competing carriers. As long as these and other operational arrangements do not result in excessive market power, the OECD recommends that they be eligible for exemption.

In response to the work carried out by the OECD, the Commission's services, in agreement with the [EU] Member States, decided to revisit the way in which the EU's own competition rules are applied to the maritime sector. Importantly, the current review process does not cover the consortium block exemption – Regulation 823/2000[33] – which, subject to certain conditions,

---

28 OECD Report, § 187, p. 75.
29 Ed., all EU Member States are members of the OECD. The reference in the quote to "Member Countries" refers to OECD state members.
30 OECD Report, § 201, p. 78.
31 OECD Report, §§ 206, 208, 212, pp. 79–80.
32 Munari, "Liner Shipping and Antitrust after the Repeal of Regulation 4056/86" op. cit. at fn. 1, p. 48.
33 Ed., this has since been replaced, see chap. 14.

allows shipping lines to jointly operate liner services and thus achieve through a rationalisation of the services potentially important economies of scale."[34]

There is no doubt that the 2002 OECD Report was a significant factor in the impetus to reform and, ultimately, repeal Regulation 4056/86.[35] The OECD became an international and external ally upon which the Commission could rely. As the Commission was intent on resisting and perhaps repealing Regulation 4056/86 long before the 2002 OECD Report, the OECD document was, in some ways, a convenience for the Commission which the Commission welcomed.

12.005 As mentioned above,[36] the Commission's review process commenced with the publication of a consultation paper on 27 March 2003. The Commission issued an interesting press release on the same day:

"Commission starts consultation on application of competition rules to maritime transport
The European Commission is seeking comments from governments and the industries concerned regarding the application of the European Union competition rules to maritime transport. Shipping companies which are part of liner conferences currently benefit from antitrust immunity granted more than 15 years ago by the EU Council of Ministers. The Commission wants to ascertain whether this immunity, which allows companies to fix prices and limit supply, still produces the benefits expected and continues to be justified.

'Most of the world's trade is carried out by sea. It is, therefore, high time to examine whether the exceptionally generous antitrust immunity, which benefits shipping companies when they operate in liner conferences, is in line with today's market conditions. Most significantly, the Commission will want to see whether the Liner Conference Regulation[37] results in reliable and efficient scheduled shipping services that meet the requirements of transport users, as was the legislator's initial aim', Competition Commissioner Mario Monti said.

Interested parties are invited to submit their views before 3 June 2003 on the Consultation Paper issued today by the Commission.

Liner conferences are groupings of shipping companies, which provide regular international transport services for cargo most significantly on routes between Europe, on the one hand, and North America and the Far East, on the other hand.

Origin of the exemption
In 1986, [the] European Union Council of Ministers agreed a regulation which exempts price-fixing, capacity-sharing and other agreements or consultations between liner shipping companies from EU competition rules (Articles [101 and 102]). The justification for the Liner Conference Block Exemption Regulation 4056/86 was the assumption that the rate-setting and other activities of liner conferences lead to stable freight rates, which in turn assured shippers of reliable scheduled maritime transport services.

The review does not concern the Consortium Block Exemption Regulation 823/2000, which allows shipping lines to engage in operational co-operation (vessel-sharing, co-ordination of routes and schedules) but not to fix prices. The latter extended an exemption granted in 1995 until 2005 after it was found to be working well by both shipping lines and transport users.

---

34 Fabrizia Benini of the DG COMP spoke (in a personal capacity) on 1 April 2003 at the "Seminar on EU Competition Law and Maritime Transport" in London, http://ec.europa.eu/competition/speeches/text/sp2003_008_en.pdf.

35 Joos Stragier, the then Head of Transport Unit in DG COMP in the European Commission said (in a personal capacity) at the Tenth Annual European Maritime Law Organisation conference on 18 June 2004: "[t]he Commission's review process has in particular been inspired by the OECD Secretariat Report, that was published in April 2002 and that has put into question the maintenance of the block exemption for liner shipping conferences".

36 Para. 12.03.

37 Ed., i.e. Reg. 4056/86.

The Liner Conference Regulation has never been reviewed despite the fact that it was adopted more than 15 years ago and that it is customary for the Commission to carry out periodic reviews into block [exemption] Regulations which exempt certain categories of agreements from the general prohibition of restrictive practices and agreements. This is because Council Regulation 4056/86 unlike almost all other such exemptions remains in force for an unlimited period. The Commission will closely associate the Member States to this review exercise as only they can revoke or modify this Regulation.[38]

Other jurisdictions revise policy
Three developments have also led support for a review. First of all, the modernisation of the general Regulation which lays down the rules and procedures to implement Arts. [101 and 102]. Regulation 1/2003, which replaces Regulation 17/62, will come into force in May 2004 and now that the procedural review has been completed it seems appropriate to consider whether the substantive rules can also be modernised and simplified.

Secondly, in recent years the Union's major trading partners have also conducted reviews of their own liner shipping exemptions. The United States, for example, in 1998 adopted the Ocean Shipping Reform Act amending the US Shipping Act.

In a report of April 2002, the Organisation for Economic Co-operation and Development cast doubts on the general wisdom that collective rate setting was an indispensable pre-requisite for reliable liner shipping services and invited its Member countries to review the way in which competition rules were applied to the sector.

Thirdly, the growing trend towards container transport has also led to a re-organisation of the sector into consortia or alliances as the shipping companies tend to share out the costs of bigger vessels and to organise services differently.

Three-pronged approach
The Consultation Paper published by the Commission today identifies the issues that require examination in the light of current market conditions. For this purpose, it formulates a list of questions that go to the heart of the justification for the block exemption. It also invites comments on the need to simplify and modernise the Regulation in other substantive respects.

At this stage, therefore, the Commission does not put forward any firm policy options, nor does it carry out an in-depth market analysis.

The input gathered will enable the Commission to put forward, in a second stage, a series of policy options either in a Green or White Paper and to follow that up with legislative proposals, if considered necessary."[39]

12.006 On 1 April 2003, Fabrizia Benini of, what is now the Directorate General for Competition ("DG COMP") spoke (in a personal capacity) at the "Seminar on EU Competition Law and Maritime Transport".[40] She made the following interesting observations about the Commission's consultative paper:

"The Commission has recognised that stability of rates for scheduled services may be beneficial because it allows shippers to know in advance the costs of transporting their goods and enables shipowners to forecast their income and better organise regular reliable and efficient services.[41]

The Consultation Paper therefore does not cast doubt on the objectives in themselves, but does ask whether an exemption for, among other things, horizontal price-fixing is a necessary and proportionate way of achieving those objectives, and whether the assumed benefits still outweigh the obvious disadvantages.

---

38 Ed., this is because only the Council of Ministers could revoke Reg. 4056/86 which had been adopted by the Council of Ministers (in which Member States are represented).
39 IP/03/445.
40 http://ec.europa.eu/competition/speeches/text/sp2003_008_en.pdf.
41 Ed., Comm. Dec. IV/34.446 *TAA*, OJ L376/1, 31 December 1994, Recital 389 where the Commission stated that price stability may constitute an objective within the scope of Art. 101(3).

In particular the main questions the Commission seeks to address are:

- the extent to which conferences contribute to the stability of prices;
- the extent to which price fixing is necessary to ensure that scheduled services are maintained over time;
- whether the present arrangements result in efficient, adequate maritime transport services; and finally
- whether there are other less restrictive ways to achieve the above mentioned objectives."

She also stated:

"The Commission's services embark on this review process without any preconceived idea of what the end product should be. The Consultation Paper does not make any policy choice but rather it seeks to involve both sides of the industry in a review of the rules in the light of current market conditions so as to determine whether the serious restrictions on competition authorised more than fifteen years ago – when the block exemption entered into force – continue to be justified and continue to deliver the intended results. In addition, we are very aware that shipping is a global industry that has to operate efficiently under overlapping jurisdictions and throughout this process therefore we shall be keeping our main trading partners updated of developments."

She went on to observe:

"The decision to undertake a review of the main maritime regulation was prompted by different, concurring factors. First there is the fact that the block exemption for liner conferences is in many ways exceptional, not only because it grants exemption for a hardcore restriction of competition [i.e. price-fixing] but also because unlike almost all other block exemptions it is not time-limited and has never been reviewed. This in itself would be sufficient justification to undertake a review because it is standard Commission practice to ensure that legislation is regularly updated to take account of changes in market conditions.

Another incentive for the review process was the publication in April 2002 of a report on competition policy in liner shipping by the Secretariat of the OECD. The report casts doubt on the validity of the assumption that collective rate setting by members of a liner conference is an indispensable pre-requisite for reliable liner shipping services and invites Member countries to review antitrust exemptions for price fixing. But it also recognises that carriers have legitimate operational needs that may require co-operation with other competing carriers. As long as these and other operational arrangements do not result in excessive market power, the OECD recommends that they be eligible for exemption.

In response to the work carried out by the OECD, the Commission's services, in agreement with the [EU] Member States, decided to revisit the way in which the EU's own competition rules are applied to the maritime sector. Importantly, the current review process does not cover the consortium block exemption. Regulation 823/200 which, subject to certain conditions, allows shipping lines to jointly operate liner services and thus achieve through a rationalisation of the services potentially important economies of scale."

12.007 The Commission set 3 June 2003 as the deadline for responses to the consultation paper. DG COMP commissioned a group of economists from Erasmus University in Rotterdam to assist DG COMP to process the responses. DG COMP published on its website the replies to the consultation paper and the final Erasmus report. There were 36 responses to the consultation paper with these responses being from governments, industry and third parties.

12.008 On 4 December 2003, a public hearing was held on the issue by DG COMP. It was designed to enable parties to expand on written submissions and to debate the issues.

12.009 On 22 April 2004, Lowri Evans of the DG COMP spoke (in a personal capacity) at Containerisation International's Seventh Annual Liner Shipping Conference in

London.⁴² The paper was a stocktaking exercise and a very comprehensive overview of the options facing the Commission. Her starting point was that liner shipping was, or ought to be, subject to competition law just like any other industry. The paper also described a three-phase approach: fact-finding; Commission paper or papers; and legislative proposals being tabled. She recalled that Regulation 4056/86 was the only block exemption to exempt price-fixing. (It will also be recalled that not only did it exempt price-fixing but also allowed a regulation of supply,⁴³ was unlimited in time, did not contemplate any review and was not based on the experience of the Commission having to deal with cases before the regulation was adopted.) The paper also recalled the conditions for the application of Article 101(3) of the TFEU, and how price stability is not a sufficient rationale for an exemption. She stated that the "core question" was whether there was a "need for price fixing and supply regulation by liner conferences in the present market circumstances?" Citing the General Court's approach in *TAA*, she stated: "stability cannot be more important than competition".⁴⁴ Having considered the conditions necessary for the application of Article 101(3) of the TFEU, she concluded by outlining the three options for the Commission: maintain;⁴⁵ amend;⁴⁶ or repeal⁴⁷ Regulation 4056/86.

12.010 On 28 May 2004, the Commission held an informal Advisory Committee meeting with the competition and transport experts of the Member States to discuss DG COMP's working document on the process up to that point.

12.011 In June 2004, the Commission published a discussion document which was a review of the maritime transport block exemption.

12.012 On 18 June 2004, Joos Stragier (a Commission official speaking in a personal capacity) addressed the European Maritime Law Organisation's ("EMLO") annual conference.⁴⁸ He stated:

"Regulation [4056/86] had a dual function. First, it enabled the Commission to apply Articles [101 and 102 of the TFEU] directly to the maritime transport sector (procedural part). Secondly, it provides for a block exemption for liner conferences (substantive part). The first function has become redundant with the entering into force of Regulation 1/2003, that provides for competition enforcement rules for basically all sectors, including the maritime transport sector (with some exceptions). The substantive part of the ... Regulation however has not been changed until today. After the procedural changes, a logical next step is to review whether there is, in the current market circumstances, still a justification for the remaining substantive specific competition provisions in the transport sector...

The review is particularly important given that ... Regulation [4056/86] since its adoption 18 years ago has never been reviewed before, while the liner shipping market has changed. In particular, the role of independent operators on most routes has become more important, in addition operational forms of co-operation such as consortia and alliances have increased and furthermore

---

42 http://ec.europa.eu/competition/speeches/text/sp2004_003_en.pdf.
43 The rationale according to the framers of Reg. 4056/86 was that liner conferences bring stability to the system (Reg. 4056/86, Recital 8).
44 Case T-395/94 *Atlantic Container Line and others v Commission* [2002] ECR II-875, ECLI:EU:T:2002:49, paras 261–262.
45 Supporters of this argument contended, according to Lowri Evans, that liner shipping remained special and there were no market changes that necessitated removal of the block exemption and there were no viable alternatives.
46 She mentioned that only a few concrete proposals had been made in this regard.
47 She recalled that supporters of the repeal option argued that Reg. 4056/86 no longer complied with EU competition policy and the industry would be better served by competition.
48 http://ec.europa.eu/competition/speeches/text/sp2004_006_en.pdf.

there has been a substantial growth of long term contracting, such as individual service contracts...

The argument has been made that the liner shipping industry, because of its specific features [i.e. high fixed costs, high investment risks, inelastic demand and supply, asymmetries in demand etc.] would be inherently unstable and that this would require special treatment under [EU] competition law.

It is stating the obvious if I say that the Maritime Regulation deviates notably from the orthodoxy of European competition law. The explanation is historical. ... Regulation [4056/86] codified generalised practices of liner conferences since 1875. It is time to review the situation and look forward. No convincing arguments have been advanced to maintain the *status quo*. Resistance to substantial change is completely in line of expectation. But we should not be afraid to be the first to propose such change if we have strong arguments."

12.013 On 6 August 2004, the European Liner Affairs Association ("ELAA") which represented major carriers in the liner conference sector made a proposal to the Commission. While shippers (i.e. the transport customers or users) believed that the consortia block exemption was sufficient and there was no need for a special regime for liner conferences, the ELAA argued that there was a need for an exchange of information systems which would potentially cover the whole liner shipping market. The Commission commented later that for

> "such a system to be acceptable it must respect the Court case law and the Commission practice on exchanges of information between competitors. Some elements of the ELAA proposal appear to be in line with these requirements. However, others are problematic notably because they do not differ in effect from what conferences do today. Accepting the proposal as such would remove all the pro-competitive effects of the abolition of the conference system."[49]

12.014 On 13 October 2004, the Commission published a White Paper on the subject.[50] It stated that there was no conclusive economic evidence to support the continuation of the block exemption for liner conferences or, put another way, there was no justification in terms of competition policy, for the retention of the block exemption. The Commission therefore proposed the repeal of the block exemption in Regulation 4056/86 and, indeed, Regulation 4056/86 in its entirety. The Commission's thinking was in line with its long-standing view but it was also corroborated by the OECD's 2002 report.[51] As Vanheule commented:

> "The White Paper's trend points to the repealing [of Regulation 4056/86]: the Commission, largely inspired by a 2002 OECD report, believes that there is no evidence that the assumptions on which [the] block exemption was based 18 years ago are still valid in the present market conditions. In other words, the Commission is no longer of the opinion that liner conferences bring stability, and by so doing provide consumers with reliable services."[52]

The Commission tentatively proposed, at that stage, that Regulation 4056/86 be abolished and that other forms of co-operation between shipping companies be permitted but without the price-fixing (or "rate-setting" or "tariff-setting") element which was embodied in Regulation 4056/86. The Commission concluded that there was no justification for continuing the block exemption for liner conferences. If Regulation 4056/86 had been a

---

49 COM(2004) 675 final.
50 COM(2004) 675 final.
51 See para. 12.004.
52 "EU Maritime – Update: October 2004–January 2005" [2005] ETL 3 at 3.

Commission regulation then it would have been repealed much earlier by the Commission itself but it was saved by being a Council of Ministers regulation and therefore more difficult for the Commission to see removed from the body of EU law.

12.015 On 10 November 2005, the Commission published a study by experts[53] on the impact of repealing Regulation 4056/86. The study demonstrated that the repeal of the block exemption would not damage the competitiveness of European liner shipping firms and would result in lower transport costs for shippers. More specifically, the study found that repealing the exemption was likely to lead to a decrease in transport prices (i.e. freight rates) and would either have no impact or a positive impact on the competitiveness of European liner shipping undertakings. The study also suggested that the repeal of the exemption would see an improvement in service reliability on deep sea and short sea trades, either no change or an improvement in service quality, no negative impact (or even a possible impact) on EU ports, employment and trade while there would be no negative impact on developing countries.

12.016 The study also recommended that an alternative information exchange system, which had been proposed by the ELAA[54] should not be accepted in its then current form because it could facilitate collusion between shipping companies to the detriment of consumers. The consultants characterised the proposal as an "invitation to collude" between the liner shipping carriers.

12.017 The Commission believed that circumstances had changed since the enactment of Regulation 4056/86. As Lowri Evans of the European Commission had said (in a personal capacity) in 2005:

> "[t]he Commission is bound to ensure that the rules in place reflect today's market conditions. The last nineteen years have seen considerable changes in the liner market. There is a continuing trend towards full containerisation and an increase in co-operative arrangements between shipping lines in the form of consortia and global alliances. We have seen average growth rates of world container trade close to 8% during the last 10 years.
>
> The sector is important for the economy as a whole. Scheduled services in container transport account for about 40% of the EU's external trade by sea in value terms. Today, conferences are allowed to fix prices on all major shipping routes, and these prices are generally assumed to act as a benchmark for the prices actually applied in the market.
>
> In addition to the benchmark effect of the conference tariff, an average of 30% of the price of transport is made up of charges and surcharges jointly fixed by lines participating in conferences. The same levels of charges are very often applied by non-conference carriers.
>
> In overall terms for the European economy, this means that 18% of imports and 21% of EU exports are affected by carriers' ability to jointly fix prices in the liner conference block exemption.
>
> The legislation setting out how Articles [101 and 102] apply to international maritime transport cannot continue to be anchored in the market scenario of the 19th Century.[55] The review is necessary because the block exemption has no end date and it will remain in force until positive action is taken…
>
> The rules may have been in standstill, but the market has not…
>
> … there has been a series of mergers in the liner sector in the past six months. The consolidation process is positive because the liner shipping industry still has a low concentration rate – at

---

53 The consultants were Global Insight (an international consultancy firm), the Berlin University of Technology and the Institute for Shipping Economics and Logistics in Bremen.
54 The ELAA represented more than 70% of the global liner shipping industry.
55 Ed., this is an allusion to the approach of the English courts to the tolerance of liner conferences.

the level of individual lines – and a greater rationalisation should help the European industry to compete more efficiently on the global market...

The changes in market conditions and the modernisation of the competition rules of procedure were the two main driving forces behind the decision to review Regulation 4056/86.[56]

... After three years of reviewing this sector, our view is that the structure of the liner market is only as unique as that of any other transport sector. And price fixing is unheard of elsewhere.

... Conferences today agree voluntarily on formulae for certain surcharges and ancillary charges, in particular currency and bunker adjustment factors (CAFs[57] and BAFs[58]) and terminal handling charges.

The same level of charges, or adjustment factors, is often applied by non-conference members.

It is far from clear that the joint fixing of terminal handling charges falls within the scope of the conference block exemption regulation. It is very clear that the joint fixing of charges and surcharges by lines that are not members of a conference do not. It will be difficult to advance a case that such price-fixing is compatible with the competition rules.

... Shippers ... are adamant that the conference system is a relic of the past and that to meet the challenges of a global market place, carriers must embrace competition fully. They consider the block exemption regulation sufficient to guarantee a sustainable and reliable supply of shipping services, and are pressing for the abolition of the conference system."[59]

12.018 As mentioned above, the ELAA represented major carriers in the liner conference sector. It made various submissions and arguments to the Commission. It submitted to the Commission that the block exemption should be replaced by an information exchange system. The Commission believed that the ELAA's information exchange system would undo the benefits which it said would be derived from the repeal of the block exemption in Regulation 4056/86 for liner conferences.[60]

12.019 The European Shippers Council ("ESC"), representing customers, believed that a liner conference block exemption was unnecessary and that the consortia block exemption (which did not involve price-fixing) was adequate.

12.020 On 20 September 2005, the Committee of the Regions adopted an opinion[61] welcoming the European Commission's White Paper on liner shipping of 13 October 2004 but also made certain observations including calling on the Commission to produce more evidence, conduct an impact analysis to retain the provision for purely technical agreements and to address the conflict of laws issues.

12.021 On 14 December 2005, the Commission published formal legislative proposals to repeal Regulation 4056/86.[62] The Commission adopted a proposal to: (a) repeal Regulation 4056/86; and (b) bring tramp vessel services and cabotage within the general competition law regime. The proposal was the culmination of at least three years of review by the Commission. The Commission believed that repealing

---

56 Ed., the Commission was opposed to Reg. 4056/86 long before the modernisation process commenced.
57 Ed., CAF is the Currency Adjustment Factor.
58 Ed., BAF is Bunker Adjustment Factor.
59 Speech entitled "Competition Developments Affecting the Maritime Sector", EMLO, 14 October 2005.
60 The ELAA has since ceased to exist. The ELAA had been created in response to the banning of the FEFC by the EU. In 2010, it declared its job done and its surviving functions will be assumed by the World Shipping Council ("WSC") from 1 July 2010. The ELAA members took the view that there was unlikely to be any new regulatory issues for the industry before the renewal of the EU's Guidelines in 2013. Regulatory issues would now be handled by the Brussels office of the Washington-based WSC, the main international body representing global general cargo and container shipping but WSC's responsibilities were not extended to the ELAA database.
61 Committee of the Regions 485/2004, 13 April 2004.
62 See COM(2005) 651 final, Commission IP/05/1586 and MEMO/05/480.

"the exemption will benefit EU exporters by lowering transport prices whilst maintaining reliable services. This will enhance the competitiveness of EU industry, furthering the Lisbon Strategy. The Commission proposal would also bring maritime tramp and cabotage services under the scope of the competition implementing rules (Regulation 1/2003), giving the Commission jurisdiction to apply the competition rules in the sector."[63]

The Commission wrote:

"Liner shipping, the provision of regular, scheduled maritime freight transport, has been organised in the form of cartels – called liner conferences – since the 1870s. These bring together most or all lines operating container services on a particular route. Defenders of conferences claim that the liner shipping market is unique, requiring special competition law treatment. However, in the 20 years that the block exemption has been in force, the market has changed considerably.

Liner shipping is an important part of the EU economy – 40% by value of EU external trade by sea is transported by liner carriers – about 18% of all imports and 21% of all exports transported by land, sea or air. But liner conferences do not deliver the benefits for which the block exemption was established and the Commission's impact assessment shows that lower transport prices are likely to result from the block exemption's repeal. The impact on the shipping industry itself is also expected to be positive: service quality and innovation are likely to improve.

To allow shipping lines time to adapt to a competitive market and to give Member States time to review their international obligations, the Commission proposes that the repeal of the block exemption should take effect only two years after adoption by the Council of the decision to do so.

The Commission and the liner shipping industry have discussed whether a replacement of the conference system is necessary. If the current block exemption is repealed, the Commission is minded to issue appropriate guidelines on how to apply competition rules to all forms of co-operation in the maritime transport sector, including information exchange. This would help smooth the transition to a more competitive environment.

The guidelines which should be brought forward by the end of 2007, would treat issues such as an independent data warehouse, the creation of a trade association and of trade fora, the publication of a price index and common formulae for charges and surcharges. The guidelines will explain how the competition rules apply to the liner sector in general, including timely and regular exchange and publication of capacity utilisation information. As an interim step, the Commission will publish an issues paper on liner shipping in September 2006.

The Commission's proposal also covers tramp and cabotage services. Tramp services are the non-regular, maritime transport of non-containerised bulk cargo, and include economically important services such as the transport of oil, agricultural and chemical products. Cabotage services are maritime transport services between ports of a single Member State. The proposal to bring these services under Council Regulation 1/2003, the common competition implementing rules, does not involve a change to the applicable law as EU competition rules already apply to the sectors. It rather establishes equality of treatment between these sectors of the economy and all others to which the implementing rules already apply.

Any guidelines would also cover the application of EU competition rules to tramp services. The Commission has already started discussions with industry to better identify concerns and will be tendering a study on the characteristics of the tramp shipping market."[64]

12.022 The Commission was clearly convinced of the economic benefits of the reform – as it said in another context:

"the repeal of the conference block exemption and that of Articles 2 and 9 is the best available option to lower transport costs whilst maintaining reliability of services on all trades; enhancing the competitiveness of European industry, in particular transport users without endangering that

---

63 IP/05/1586, 13 December 2005.
64 IP/05/1586, 13 December 2005.

of European carriers and meeting the objectives of the Lisbon agenda for the simplest and most cost effective legislative option".[65]

12.023 The Commission published a series of "frequently asked questions" about the proposed repeal of Regulation 4056/86.[66] It recognised that it was "exceptional for a block exemption Regulation to be incorporated in a Council Regulation as is the case of the liner conference block exemption. It is also exceptional for such an exemption to be open-ended in terms of duration."[67] The Commission noted that "liner conferences do not engage in operational co-operation and do not provide joint liner shipping services. It is up to the individual lines, consortia or alliances to offer such services."[68]

12.024 The Commission considered the possibility that there could be different regimes around the world with different views as to whether liner conferences should be tolerated:

> "The Commission is particularly aware of the international dimension of this dossier and of the fact that up to now conferences have been tolerated worldwide. That is why it has taken the initiative to establish close and frequent contacts with our major international partners (US, Canada, Australia, Japan). The outcome of those contacts is positive. We intend to keep up these bilateral contacts throughout discussions in Council.
>
> If the EU were to repeal the present EU liner conference block exemption regulation this would mean that carriers (EU and non-EU) that are presently part of conferences operating on trades to and from the EU would have to stop their conference activities on those trades (namely price fixing and capacity regulation). Nothing would stop them from continuing being part of price fixing conferences on non-EU trade routes. To give a concrete example, an EU carrier like Maersk, member of the Trans-Atlantic conference Agreement (TACA), could no longer be involved in price fixing and capacity regulation on the North Atlantic-EU and EU-North Atlantic trades, but could still do so on the US-Pacific trades. The same applies to non-EU carriers.
>
> This is a logical consequence of the fact that there is not an identical competition regime in force world-wide. In fact, already today there are differences in what liner shipping companies are allowed to do in different jurisdictions. For example, today US law allows carriers to fix prices jointly on inland transport, while EU law does not.
>
> A conflict of law does not arise. This would only be the case if one jurisdiction were to require carriers to participate in conferences, whereas another were to prohibit it. This is not the case today."[69]

Some of the Commission's questions and answers are instructive, so it is useful to examine the various questions.

12.025 The first question posed by the Commission was: "[t]he liner shipping industry is asking for a new regime to replace the conference block exemption. What will the Commission do about that?"

The Commission responded to its own question in the following terms:

> "Industry is divided on the need for a substantive alternative to Regulation 4056/86. The European Liner Affairs Association (ELAA), a carrier association representing roughly 80% of world capacity has proposed that the conference block exemption should be replaced with an exchange of information system. Details of the proposal and of the Commission's assessment of it under

---

65 COM(2005) 651 final, para. 1.10.1.
66 MEMO/05/480, 14 December 2005.
67 MEMO/05/480, 13 December 2005.
68 MEMO/05/480, 13 December 2005.
69 MEMO/05/480, 13 December 2005.

the EU competition rules are available at: http://ec.europa.eu/competition/antitrust/legislation/maritime/

The European Shippers Association (ESC) representing over 100,000 exporting companies, and generating around 90% of the EU's international maritime traffic, considers that a replacement regime is not necessary because carriers are already allowed to co-operate extensively under the consortia block exemption Regulation (prolonged and amended in April 2005 – see IP/05/477). This co-operation results in the provision of reliable liner services by groups of shipping lines in consortia and alliances. The European business organisation UNICE and consumer associations back this position.

To be acceptable, any new system for information exchange must respect the competition rules. Some elements of the current ELAA proposal appear to be in line with these requirements. However, others are problematic notably because they do not differ in effect from what conferences do today. Accepting the ELAA proposal as it is today would remove all the pro-competitive effects of the abolition of the conference system.

The Commission remains committed to continuing the dialogue with the ELAA with a view to assisting it in developing an alternative system compliant with EU competition rules. It has acknowledged that exchanges of information leading to greater market transparency may contribute to the improvement in the way liner services are provided, in the interest of carriers, transport users and the public in general.

Discussions will be focusing on the details of the various elements of the ELAA proposal. Thereafter, the Commission intends to issue guidelines on the application of the competition rules apply to liner and tramp shipping. The guidelines would treat issues such as an independent data warehouse, the creation of a trade association and of trade fora, the publication of a price index and common formulae for charges and surcharges. The guidelines would explain how the competition rules apply to the liner sector in general, including exchange and publication of capacity utilisation information. As an interim step, the Commission will publish an issues paper on liner shipping in September 2006."

12.026 The Commission then asked: "[w]hat is the impact of the proposal on small liner shipping carriers and on small short sea trades?" The Commission responded:

"The European Community Shipowners' Associations (ECSA) and the European Parliament have drawn the Commission's attention to the needs of specific services, particularly short sea services and services to smaller trades. Since such trades generally do not require a large number of vessels to be serviced, relatively small carriers might be able to operate side by side with large carriers on these trades. ECSA and the European Parliament, therefore, questioned whether these relatively small carriers would be more affected by a repeal than large ones.

The Commission is not aware of any liner shipping carrier that would fall with the scope of the Commission Recommendation concerning the definition of small and medium sized enterprises.[70]

After significant research, the Commission did not find that relatively small EU carriers would be adversely affected by a repeal of the conference block exemption. To the contrary, liberalisation creates a market environment that allows for quicker growth than a regulated environment, in particular for small companies. It creates more new services and new niche markets which especially small companies are able to quickly enter. These market niches usually allow for rapid growth. Hence, small innovative companies are able to grow much quicker in a competitive environment – see for example the rapid growth of Ryanair that started as a small company with a new innovative business model in the recently deregulated aviation market. The success of small carriers depends on their ability to adapt to a competitive environment and not on their actual size."

---

[70] Commission Recommendation 2003/361/EC of 6 May 2003 concerning the definition of micro, small and medium-sized enterprises, OJ L124, 20 May 2003.

12.027 The Commission then asked: "[w]hat are the economic effects of the repeal of the block exemption?" Its reply was:

"The Commission has concluded that a repeal of the block exemption will bring about substantial benefits to EU industry and consumers, in particular in the areas of transport prices, reliability of liner shipping services, competitiveness of the EU liner shipping industry and small EU liner carriers. The repeal of the block exemption would therefore also positively contribute to the Lisbon objectives.

The Commission's main findings of the potential economic impact of repealing the conference block exemption are:

- transport prices for liner shipping services will decline
- service reliability on deep sea and short sea trades is expected to improve
- service quality will either be unaffected or will improve
- there will be either a positive impact or no impact on the competitiveness of EU liner shipping firms
- small liner shipping carriers will not experience particular problems and
- no negative impact or even a positive impact on EU ports, employment, trade and/or developing countries.

The Commission's conclusions take account of three independent studies undertaken to establish the impact of the repeal of the block exemption. The latest study (see IP/05/1408) is the combined work of Global Insight, an international consultancy with significant experience in liner shipping, the Berlin University of Technology and the Institute of Shipping Economics and Logistics in Bremen."

12.028 The next question raised by the Commission was: "[d]oes the proposal have an impact on the maritime consortia block exemption Regulation?" Its reply was reassuring:

"The Commission's proposal does not concern the maritime consortia Block Exemption Regulation 823/2000. This Regulation allows shipping lines to engage in operational co-operation (vessel-sharing, co-ordination of routes and schedules) but not to fix prices. This Regulation has recently been reviewed and extended until 2010 after it was found to be working well by both shipping lines and transport users (IP/05/477). This exemption is of particular significance in terms of volume of trade. For example, the majority of cargo transported between the EU and US is transported by shipping lines in consortia and alliances using individual service contracts instead of conference tariff prices."

12.029 The Commission then raised the issue of guidance by asking: "[w]ill the Commission be issuing guidance to the tramp sector?" and responded:

"Tramp services are the non-regular, maritime transport of bulk cargo that is not containerised, and include a range of economically important services such as the transport of oil, agricultural and chemical products. In the consultation process various submissions emphasised the need to provide guidance to the tramp sector on the application of the [EU] competition rules. For that purpose the Commission is engaged in discussions with tramp operators so as better to understand the issues at stake. It is also in the process of tendering for a study on the sector in early 2006.

Although any guidance can be formally issued only after the Commission has been empowered by Regulation 1/2003, the Commission is currently exploring with industry whether it is necessary and appropriate to provide informal guidance before the changes to Regulation 1/2003 are made. Ultimately, the Commission intends to issue guidelines on the application of the competition rules to the maritime sector, including tramp services."

12.030 The Commission then turned its attention to the tramp sector and asked: "[w]hat is the impact of the proposal on international tramp vessel services?" Its reply was:

"The competition rules of the [TFEU] already apply to these sectors. The impact of the proposal should therefore not be substantive. It is rather a question of including these sectors within the generally applicable procedural framework laid down by Council Regulation 1/2003.

Doing so will have advantages for industry in terms of clarity. At present, both industry and competition authorities, have to devote considerable resources to assessing whether a service fulfils all of the criteria set out in Regulation 4056/86[71] before determining what action could be taken and by which authority."

12.031 The Commission placed its proposal in the context of trying to enhance the competitiveness of European industry in light of the Lisbon Agenda.[72] The Commission recalled that approximately 40% of the external trade of the then 25 Member States was represented by scheduled services in container transport services which meant that 18% of the imports and 21% of exports were affected by the "carriers' ability to fix prices jointly under the liner conference block exemption".[73] The Commission also recalled the changes in the marketplace since the adoption of the block exemption in 1986:

"4. The liner shipping market has changed considerably since Regulation 4056/86 was adopted. The continuing trend towards containerisation has led to an increase in the number and size of fully-cellular container vessels and to an emphasis on global route networks. This has contributed to the popularity of consortia and alliances as a means of sharing costs. The growth in importance of these operational arrangements has been accompanied by a decline in the significance of conferences. The latter trend has been particularly marked on the trades between the EU and the United States, largely as a consequence of pro-competitive Commission decisions applying Articles [101 and 102 of the TFEU] and changes in US legislation, which have promoted individual service contracts at the expense of carriage under the conference tariff.

5. Transport users (shippers and freight forwarders) seek customer-focused relationships with carriers, reciprocal performance related compensation and integrated logistic solutions. They have systematically questioned the conference system which they consider does not deliver adequate, efficient and reliable services suited to their needs. They call for the abolition of conferences.

6. Other jurisdictions and international organisations have also questioned the benefits of maintaining the conference system. In April 2002 the OECD published a report[74] calling for [OECD] member countries to remove antitrust exemption for common pricing and rate discussions but to retain the exemptions from other operational agreements between liner carriers. Australia has also been carrying a review of the sector and has recently reached similar conclusions.[75]

7. Against this background the Commission launched a review of Regulation 4056/86 to determine whether reliable scheduled maritime services could be achieved by less restrictive means than horizontal price fixing and capacity regulation. A Consultation Paper issued in March 2003 was followed by a public hearing in December 2003 and the adoption of a White Paper in October 2004. Numerous submissions were received from all stakeholders. The European Parliament,[76] the Economic and Social Committee[77] and the Committee of the

---

71 The transport of goods in bulk or in break-bulk in a vessel charted (wholly or partly) to one or more shippers on the basis of a voyage or a time charter on any other form of contract for non-regularly scheduled or non-advertised sailings where freight rates are freely negotiated case by case in accordance with the conditions of supply and demand.
72 Explanatory Memorandum to the Proposal, para. 1 (COM(2005) 651 final).
73 Explanatory Memorandum to the Proposal, para. 3 (COM(2005) 651 final).
74 DSTI/DOT (2002) 2, 16.4.2002.
75 Review of Part X of the Trade Practices Act 1974: International Liner Cargo shipping, Productivity. Commission Inquiry report released by the Government on 23 February 2005.
76 Own initiative report of the Committee for Transport and Tourism, ... 11 October 2005.
77 TEN/208 – CESE 1650/2004 – 16 December 2004.

Regions[78] issued opinions. Three meetings with Member State competition and transport experts were held. The Commission contracted three studies from independent consultants to look into the issues arising from a repeal of the conference block exemption. All documents are published in DG COMP website[79]."[80]

12.032 The Commission also recalled the changes which would occur in regard to cabotage and tramp services:

"1.5.1. General remarks
12. Cabotage and international tramp vessel services are currently the only remaining sectors that are excluded from the [EU] competition implementing rules.[81] The lack of effective enforcement powers for these sectors is an anomaly from a regulatory point of view.
13. The proposal to bring these services under the common competition implementing rules does not involve a substantive change for the industry as the substantive competition rules, set out in Articles [101 and 102] of the Treaty, already apply.

1.5.2. Cabotage
14. Regulation 4056/86 does not explain why cabotage is excluded from its scope. The only indirect reference is to be found in recital 6 which states that the Regulation's objective is to avoid excessive regulation of the sector, implying that in a majority of cases cabotage services would not affect intra-Community trade. However, this does not justify why these services should from the outset be excluded from the scope of Regulation 1/2003.

1.5.3. Tramp
15. Non-regular maritime transport services of bulk and break-bulk today cover a wide range of highly diversified services of significant economic importance of which most have a clear European dimension. The fourth recital of Regulation 4056/86 suggests that the exclusion is due to these services operating on a free and competitive market. This however is presumed to be the case for all de-regulated services, without it being deemed necessary to exclude such services from the implementing regulations.
16. Including these services within the scope of the implementing Regulation will increase legal certainty. Under Regulation 4056/86, industry as well as the competition authorities have to devote considerable resources into assessing whether a service fulfils all of the five criteria set out in Article 1(3)(a) of the Regulation[82] before determining what action could be taken and by whom."

12.033 It was clear that the Commission was opposed to the retention of the block exemption – as the Commission wrote in its explanatory memorandum:

"22. The block exemption is both highly generous and unique. It is generous because it permits liner conferences to engage in activities that would normally constitute a hard core restriction of competition (collective price fixing and capacity regulation) and which are unlikely to fulfil the conditions of Article [101(3)].[83] It is unique because it is contained in a Council Regulation[84] which was adopted even though the Commission had not gained any

---

78 CdR 485/2004, 13 April 2004.
79 http://europa.eu.int/comm/competition/antitrust/legislation/maritime/.
80 Explanatory Memorandum to the Proposal (COM(2005) 651 final).
81 Article 32(a) and (b) of Regulation 1/2003.
82 The transport of goods in bulk or in break-bulk in a vessel charted (wholly or partly) to one or more shippers on the basis of a voyage or a time charter on any other form of contract for non-regularly scheduled or non-advertised sailings where freight rates are freely negotiated case by case in accordance with the conditions of supply and demand.
83 See Commission notice on Guidelines on the application of Article 81 (3) of the Treaty, OJ C101, 27.4.2004, p.27, paragraph 46.
84 The Council usually empowers the Commission to adopt Block Exemption Regulations. Of the fifteen block exemptions currently in force only one besides Regulation 4056/86 is adopted by the Council (Regulation 1017/68). These are the only two block exemption regulations that do not have an expiry date or review clause.

experience in granting individual exemptions in the sector. Furthermore, it contains no market share thresholds and is unlimited in time.

23. The adoption of this exceptionally generous block exemption regulation can only be explained in its historical and political context. It was the result of the discussions that sought to reconcile the contradictory requirements of the UNCTAD Code of Conduct for Liner Conferences,[85] to which some Member States had acceded, and the [EC, now the Treaty].

24. The industry has sought to apply the provisions of the block exemption broadly and extensively so as to cover all activities the carriers deemed useful or necessary to adapt to changing market conditions. This has led to a series of Commission decisions and subsequently litigation whereby the Court confirmed that the block exemption – despite its exceptional nature – cannot derogate from the Treaty competition provisions and must be given strict interpretation.[86]

25. The justification for the liner conference block exemption in essence assumes that conferences bring stability, assuring exporters of reliable services which cannot be achieved by less restrictive means.

26. After a thorough review process the Commission has concluded that liner shipping is not unique as its cost structure does not differ substantially from that of other industries. There is therefore no evidence that the industry needs to be protected from competition.

27. In present day market circumstances, the four cumulative conditions of Article [101(3)] of the Treaty needed to justify an exemption for liner conference price fixing and capacity regulation are not fulfilled.

28. To fulfil the first condition of Article [101(3)] of the Treaty, it must be established that concrete economic benefits flow from the price fixing and capacity regulation by conferences. A direct causal link between the alleged stability and the provision of reliable shipping services must be established.

29. Carriers consider the reliability of service as the main benefit that derives from conferences. However, in today's market, conferences are not able to enforce the conference tariff and do not manage the capacity that is made available on the market. The majority of cargo is carried under confidential individual agreements between carriers and transport users rather than under the conference tariff. The proportion of contract cargo is very high ranging from 90% and above in the Transatlantic trade to 75% in the Europe to Australian trade. The same occurs in the Europe to Far East trades. Thus, under the current market circumstances, price stability and the reliability of services are brought about by individual service contracts.

30. The second condition of Article [101(3)] of the Treaty requires that, if liner conferences were to achieve economic benefits, a fair share of these benefits should be passed on to consumers. Yet transport users (shippers and freight forwarders) fail to see any benefits of price fixing by conferences and call for their abolition. Although the conference tariff is no longer enforced it may in some instances act as a benchmark for the setting of individual contracts. [Moreover conferences are still setting surcharges and the same level of charges or adjustment factors are often applied by non-conference members.] These charges and surcharges account for on average 30% of the price of transport.

31. Under the third condition of Article [101(3)] of the Treaty, the test is basically whether there are less restrictive alternatives than conference price fixing which would assure reliable liner services to the benefit of consumers.

32. Today, scheduled liner services are provided in several ways. Independent carriers operate outside conferences on all main trades to and from Europe. Co-operation arrangements

---

85 http://www.admiraltylawguide.com/conven/liner1974.html.
86 Judgment of the Court of First Instance of 28.2.2002 in Case T-395/94 *Atlantic Container Line and others v Commission* [2002] ECR II-875, paragraph 146.

between liner shipping lines not involving price fixing, such as consortia and alliances,[87] have increased and have important shares of the market in all major trades. Under certain conditions, consortia are block exempted from the prohibition set out in Article [101] of the Treaty by Commission Regulation (EC) No 823/200 of 19 April 2000[88] on account of the rationalisation they bring to the activities of member companies and the economies of scale they allow in the operation of vessels and port facilities. Moreover, confidential individual service contracts between individual carriers and individual shippers account for the majority of cargo transported. The restrictions permitted under Regulation 4056/86 (price fixing and capacity regulation) are therefore not indispensable for the provision of reliable shipping services."[89]

12.034 The Commission Staff Working Document was also published on 14 December 2005.[90] It set out in detail the Commission's thinking. It canvassed the "no action",[91] "repeal option"[92] and the "replace option".[93] It concluded that the "repeal option" was the

> "superior option in social and economic aspects. It also positively contributes to the Lisbon [Agenda] objectives. With respect to the four areas [of] transport of prices, reliability of services, competitiveness of EU liner shipping and small EU carriers, which are of particular importance to the review process, the 'Repeal option' would bring about substantial benefits to industry and consumers."[94]

12.035 On 27 April 2006, a Director at DG COMP, Lowri Evans, spoke at the Eighth Global Shipping Conference about the future framework for liner shipping. She stated that the "regulatory regime put in place in the 1980's [principally, in this context, Regulation 4056/86] is out of synch with market requirements today". She was adamant that the findings of the review of Regulation 4056/86 demonstrated that the criteria under, what is now, Article 101(3) of the TFEU, were not satisfied in the case of liner conferences:

> "Looking at today's market conditions, the Commission found that the liner conference block exemption does not fulfil the four cumulative conditions of Article [101(3) of the TFEU] which are necessary for it to continue.
>
> The first condition requires that concrete benefits resulting from price fixing and capacity regulation are identified. The review process showed that there is no direct causal link between price fixing by conferences, and reliable liner services. Conferences are not able to enforce the conference tariff, nor do they manage the capacity that is available in the market. However, the conference tariff still acts as a benchmark, and this impacts on the negotiations of individual contracts. There is not really free price negotiation if there's a fixed starting point.
>
> What specially surprised the Commission was to find the extent to which carriers are not competing for the totality of the price of freight.

---

87 Council Regulation (EEC) No 479/92, based on Article 87 [now 83 of the TFEU] of the Treaty empowered the Commission to apply Article 81(3) [now 101(3) of the TFEU] of the Treaty to liner shipping companies grouped in consortia and providing a joint service (OJ 1992 L55/3).

88 OJ L100, 20.4.2000, p.24 as amended by Commission Regulation (EC) No 463/2004 of 12 March 2004, OJ L77, 13.3.2004 and by Commission Regulation 611/2005, OJ L101, 21.4.2005, p. 10.

89 COM(2005) 651 final.

90 SEC(2005) 1641.

91 I.e. keep Reg. 4056/86, convert it into a Commission block exemption for five years and have a subsequent review (as with other block exemption regulations).

92 I.e. repeal Reg. 4056/86, not replace with any specific measure and thereby bring the sector into the confines of the general rules on competition law.

93 The third option "would be to repeal the present block exemption, but also to establish an alternative regime that allows other forms of cooperation between carriers operating liner services to and from the EU, ... in addition to current forms of co-operation for which there exists a legal framework (e.g., consortia, alliances or mergers)" (p. 4 of the Staff Working Paper).

94 Para. 180.

Charges and ancillary charges account for, on average, 30% of the price of transport being fixed jointly. This percentage can be much higher on certain trades. There is no price competition between conference members, and also non-conference members, for this part of the price. It is questionable whether this practice is lawful even under the very generous liner conference block exemption today.

And as to the passing on of economic benefits to consumers – the second condition – transport users have opposed the conference system which they do not consider to deliver adequate services.

The third condition is indispensability, so [the question needs to be asked] whether price fixing and capacity regulation is indispensable for the provision of reliable services. We note that today reliable scheduled liner services are provided in several ways.

The fourth condition requires liner conferences not to eliminate competition on a substantial part of the market. Given the extent of the relationships between the carriers in conferences, consortia, alliances and vessel sharing agreements, determining the extent to which a conference is subject to outside competition is a complex analysis that must be carried out on a case by case basis. We note however that whether in a conference or not, all carriers operating on the same trade tend to apply the same charges and surcharges."

She also discussed what options were available to shipping companies in the absence of the liner conference block exemption:

"Let me summarise what carriers are already allowed to do under EU law, conferences apart.

The consortia block exemption regulation allows for extensive cooperation arrangements between liner shipping lines to provide regular joint services that result in benefits for shippers. The extent of the possible co-operation ranges from the pooling of vessels to the joint use of port terminals and the setting up of cargo or revenue pools. Temporary capacity adjustments are also allowed. The consortia regulation has been reviewed every 5 years since 1995 and found to be working well to the satisfaction of both carriers and shippers.

As for information exchanges, these require a case by case analysis. In general they are not restrictive of competition. Today's networked economy shows a greater need and indeed a greater ease for information to be exchanged. A number of safeguards however are necessary. The Commission focuses its analysis on (i) the characteristics of the information exchange itself and (ii) the structural characteristics of the market on which the exchange takes place.

In addition, carriers, just like any other industry, are allowed to set up trade associations. The collection, examination and dissemination of non-commercially sensitive data are not the only roles of trade associations. Usually trade associations are also usefully involved in market promotion and they lobby authorities on behalf of their members. All these activities are lawful."

12.036 In June 2006, the Parliament adopted a report supporting the Commission's proposal on the basis that the Commission would put guidelines in place on the types of co-operation which would be permitted. The Guidelines would eventually be adopted by the Commission. The Commission sought the guidelines so as to ensure clarity.

12.037 While it was not published in the *Official Journal* until 16 December 2006, the European Economic and Social Committee's ("EESC")[95] opinion was interesting. The EESC noted the rationale for the repeal of the block exemption but reserved its opinion on whether the benefits of the repeal identified by the Commission (e.g. lower rates) would be sustainable. The EESC also recommended that the Commission take the human resources and safety aspects into account as well as the pure competition considerations. The EESC also noted that any consolidation which might occur in the industry following the reform should not lead to a lessening of competition in the relevant markets. The

---

95 On the EESC, see chap. 3.

EESC was concerned about the legal vacuum which might emerge from the repeal of Regulation 4056/86.

12.038 The torrent of suggestions from the Commission for not just reform but repeal meant that the Council would ultimately repeal Regulation 4056/86. On 25 September 2006, the Council (in particular, the Competitiveness Council) adopted Regulation 1419/2006 to repeal Regulation 4056/86.[96] This regulation repealed Regulation 4056/86. The regulation was aimed at

> "repealing Regulation (EEC) No. 4056/86 laying down detailed rules for the application of, [what are now, Articles 101 and 102 of the TFEU] to maritime transport, and amending Regulation (EC) No. 1/2003 as regards the extension of its scope to include cabotage and international tramp services".[97]

There was to be a two-year transition period[98] until 18 October 2008; this would allow existing operators to continue operating and enable them to transition to the new regime. The Council also amended Regulation 1/2003 to extend its scope to cover tramp shipping[99] and cabotage.[100],[101] Tramp and cabotage services were excluded from the competition rules before the adoption of Regulation 1419/2006. The competition rules could be applied to them but competence lay with the Member States rather than the Commission. As Lowri Evans of the European Commission had said (in a personal capacity) in 2005:

> "tramp and cabotage ... are currently excluded from the competition enforcement rules.
> It is hard to advance any justification for the fact that these sectors are the only ones to which Regulation 1/2003 does not apply. The rules of substance set out in the Treaty in Articles [101 and 102] already apply to cabotage and tramp vessel services. The debate is only about whether the general procedural rules should also apply. The tramp industry has asked for the Commission to provide guidance on how competition rules would apply to their sector, in particular in relation to agreements such as pools that are common practice in this and other industries."[102]

12.039 It is useful to consider the new regulation in depth. It is worth noting that the process leading to the adoption of Regulation 1419/2006 and the accompanying Guidelines was extraordinarily thorough – as Olivier Guersent, the Acting Director for Transport, Post and other Services at DG COMP stated at the EMLO meeting in Copenhagen on 24 October 2008:

> "I would say that the review process – the repeal of the liner block exemption and the Guidelines – was indeed the most thorough and the most dialogue oriented that I have ever seen in DG COMP. I should also note that the [European Liner Affairs Association ("ELAA")] is on record as expressing its gratitude to DG COMP for the thoroughness of the review process. According to the ELAA, the Guidelines are 'fit for purpose' and will be an important help post-conference."

To bolster his observation, it is noteworthy that the ELAA stated in its comments on the draft guidelines that it "commends the Commission for its effort to understand the needs

---

96 OJ 2006 L269/1. Commission Press Release IP/06/1249 and MEMO/06/344.
97 Title of Reg. 1419/2006.
98 This transition period has also been seen by some as a moratorium or an amnesty.
99 I.e. non-regular maritime transport of non-containerised bulk cargo.
100 I.e. cabotage is the transport of goods or passengers between ports in the same State without any call being made at the port of another State..
101 Tramp and cabotage shipping were already covered by Arts 101 and 102 but the Commission could now apply the normal procedural rules for the enforcement of the TFEU provisions on competition.
102 Speech entitled "Competition Developments Affecting the Maritime Sector", EMLO, 14 October 2005.

of the liner shipping industry and to find solutions for effective information exchanges within the boundaries of competition law".[103]

12.040 Munari has made some interesting observations about the change in the circumstances from the time before the adoption of the 1979 Brussels Regulation (Regulation 954/79)[104] to the adoption of Regulation 1419/2006:

"The political and economic changes in modern maritime liner transportation: from NIEO[105] to liberalized container trades
The antitrust immunity enjoyed for so many decades by liner shipowners had, substantially, two main grounds. First, historically it served the need to guarantee an equitable participation in liner trades for liner shipping companies belonging to less developed countries: this was the main rationale for the UN Code of Conduct, which was rooted in the principles elaborated at the time of the so-called New International Economic Order (NIEO). More precisely, within any given liner conference, the restrictions of competition among shipowners, coupled with the rigid allocation of liner cargo percentages according to the nationality of the same shipowners (the 40:40:20 formula, where 20% of trade was reserved to cross-traders) permitted national shipping lines to ply for trade even if less efficient than other carriers operating on the same routes.

Secondly, the success story of liner conferences had its basis in economic theory. It was argued and accepted that liner conferences were necessary to secure stability of trade.

This belief was established among economic (and legal) scholars since the early years of the US antitrust doctrine, and had become almost a dogma – at least on the eastern side of the Atlantic Ocean – even before the origins of the EC antitrust policy, let alone the EC maritime competition policy. This dogma established that liner shipping companies must not be subject to cartel prohibitions, since price competition would have undermined the stability of maritime trades. Therefore, liner conferences were instrumental to the needs of international commerce, whereas competition in shipping would have jeopardized its growth and even existence.

As a matter of fact, every now and then this economic tenet encountered some (weak) criticism, albeit not sufficient to reverse it. Hence, scholars had to wait until the second half of the 1980s for a seminal study persuasively casting doubt on the correctness of those predominant economic theories opposing the application of competition rules to liner shipping.

Remarkably, in the same years international liner shipping underwent two further massive changes: on the one hand, the definitive replacement of older traditional liner shipping methods by container shipping, on the other hand, the modified patterns of international trade developing from the collapse of the socialist bloc and the economic models based on state-planned economics.

From the first viewpoint, the advent of containerization in liner shipping brought about a substantial concentration in the market, through a Mergers and Acquisitions (M&A) process that started some 20 years ago, which led to the acquisition of many 'national shipping lines' by larger undertakings operating worldwide, and is still under way. From the second one, liberalization in international trade affected also liner shipping companies and their claim to carry a portion of their 'national trade'; more generally, it fostered an historical and political contest which was quite different from that in which the UNCTAD Code of Conduct and had been devised and, thereafter, adopted.

Meanwhile, containerization in liner shipping had brought about new forms of co-operation among shipowners (the so called consortia agreements), and at the same time had also modified patterns of trade between countries, through the creation of transhipment port and a 'hub and spoke' organizational model for liner shipping not dissimilar to the airborne transportation.

While these processes are long and still continuing, one cannot seriously deny that the present picture is totally different from that in which liner conferences, [and] the UN Code of Conduct Regulation 4056/86 flourished. Yet, in this completely changed world, the liner conference

---

103 ELAA Comment on EC Commission Draft Guidelines, p. 1.
104 OJ 1979 L1 21/1.
105 Ed., i.e. the New International Economic Order.

model persisted, and in some trades even improved, especially because of the opportunity it gave – and still gives – for discussing rates and tariffs among liner shipping companies."[106]

12.041 A very interesting perspective was offered by Fotis Karamitsos who was the Director, Maritime Transport in the old Directorate General for Transport and Energy ("DG TREN") – demonstrating that the view within the European Commission was not uniformly enthusiastic about repealing the block exemption – when he wrote:

> "In my years in [the DG TREN] I have witnessed the 'harvest phase' of competition-related measures: approval by the Commission of several tonnage taxes, the review of the Guidelines on State aid to maritime transport, re-flagging towards Europe. Since I have been actively involved in taking care of competitiveness. I took part in the review of Regulation 4056/86 with lots of worries. For quite a long time I had no sympathy for the idea that shipping conferences would be abolished in Europe. My worry was – and to a certain extent is – that part of our efforts towards the success of maritime Europe could be jeopardized by a bold innovation which would put Europe at the forefront of competition law worldwide, but in a disadvantageous position vis-à-vis its counterparts.
>
> No doubt, from a legal perspective the block exemption of which shipping lines availed themselves for so many years was quite odd. It was actually so odd that it had become obsolete in practice, at least as far as price-fixing was concerned. There were however some advantages, in terms of continuity and homogeneity across the maritime world.
>
> Anyway, this is now history. The Commission proposed the abolition of the block exemption and the Council enthusiastically approved it. Let us look forward."[107]

C. ADOPTION OF THE NEW REGIME: REGULATION 1419/2006

12.042 With the debate over, it is now time to turn to the adoption of the new regime. On 25 September 2006, Regulation 1419/2006[108] was adopted by the Council with the support of the European Parliament.[109] Regulation 1419/2006 repealed Regulation 4056/86. The legal basis generally of Regulation 1419/2006 was the then EC Treaty (now the TFEU) and, in particular, Article 83 (now Article 103 of the TFEU). The combined effect of Regulations 1419/2006 and 1/2003 is that maritime transport is subject to EU competition law like almost every other sector of the economy.

12.043 The Commission very much welcomed the new measure[110] and issued a detailed press release which is worth studying in full:

> *"Competition: Commission welcomes Council agreement to end exemption for liner shipping conferences*
> The European Commission has welcomed the unanimous adoption, at the 25th September [2006] Competitiveness Council, of the Commission's proposal to repeal the exemption from the ... Treaty's ban on restrictive business practices (Article [101]) for liner conferences on routes to and from the EU. The current block exemption, established by Council Regulation 4056/86 allows carriers to fix prices and regulate capacity jointly. The repeal will enter into effect in October 2008. To ensure that the new regime fosters competitive markets, the Commission will issue Guidelines on the application of the competition rules to maritime transport before the end of the transitional period. The Council also empowered the Commission to apply ... Treaty

---

106 [2009] LMCLQ at 44–45.
107 Karamitsos, "EC Law and Maritime Transport: Preliminary Remarks" in Antapassis, Athanassiou and Røsæg (eds), op. cit. at fn. 1, p. 2. As always, such remarks are personal and do not bind the Commission.
108 OJ 2006 L269/1.
109 Approval required a qualified majority.
110 See IP/06/1249, 25 September 2006.

competition rules to cabotage and tramp shipping, by extending the scope of the competition implementing rules (Regulation 1/2003).

Commissioner Charlie McCreevy, who handled the proposal,[111] said 'I am delighted the Council has adopted this proposal less than a year after we presented it. The European shipping industry will benefit from the more competitive market that will result from the repeal of the block exemption and the EU economy as a whole stands to benefit from lower transport prices and more competitive exports.'

Liner shipping (i.e. the provision of regular, scheduled maritime freight transport, chiefly by container) has been organised in the form of cartels – called liner conferences – since the 1870s. Liner shipping is an important part of the EU economy as 40% by value of EU external trade by sea is transported by liner carriers. Liner conferences are agreements between liner shipping companies on prices and other conditions of carriage: as such they reduce competition between members of those conferences, and lead to higher prices for users.

The Commission's proposal to repeal the block exemption for liner conferences was the result of a three year in-depth investigation by the Commission during which extensive consultations with carriers and transport users (shippers and freight forwarders) took place. Carriers recognise that price fixing is no longer necessary in today's market conditions and the shippers expect the reform to trigger a new era of customer-focused relations with carriers.

The abolition of the exemption for liner conferences will affect EU and non-EU carriers operating on routes both to and from Europe. The market distorting effects of price fixing will be corrected, and lower prices for sea containers are likely to result.

In order to ease the transition to a fully competitive regime, the Commission will, in line with a recommendation by the European Parliament, issue Guidelines on the application of the competition rules to maritime transport services, in consultation with all stakeholders.

The Guidelines will be issued before the end of the transitional period of two years for existing liner shipping conferences in 2008. With a view to collecting stakeholders' comments, the Commission will shortly publish a staff paper on the market impact of the industry's proposal for a new information exchange system.

The Council also extended the scope of Regulation 1/2003. This does not involve a change to the applicable law as EU competition rules already apply to cabotage and tramp shipping. It rather establishes that the Commission can enforce the competition rules in these sectors, in addition to national competition authorities and courts.

In the liner shipping sector, as in others sectors, competition rules are not applied in the same way worldwide. Noting that liner conferences will continue to be tolerated in other jurisdictions, the Commission will take appropriate initiatives to advance the removal of price fixing liner conferences and thus promote further competitive reform of the liner shipping sector."[112]

12.044 Commissioner McCreevy said that the "European shipping industry is strong and has everything to gain from a competitive market. Customers are clamouring for business in this industry to be conducted as it is in all other sectors."[113] The Commission also issued a memorandum of frequently asked questions and it is worth studying:

"Competition: repeal of block exemption for liner shipping conferences – frequently asked questions

The Competitiveness Council has agreed on 25th September 2006 to repeal Regulation 4056/86 putting an end to the possibility for liner carriers to meet in conferences, fix prices and regulate capacities as of October 2008.

The process of reviewing the exemption from [the then EC Treaty] competition rules for liner shipping conferences, as laid down in Council Regulation 4056/86, was launched in March 2003 with the publication of a Consultation Paper (see IP/03/445). A White Paper was published in October 2004 (see IP/04/1213). The Commission adopted a legislative proposal on 14 December

---

111 Ed. given Commissioner Kroes' previous involvement with shipping, she recused herself.
112 IP/06/1249, Brussels, 25 September 2006.
113 IP/05/1586.

2005 (see IP/05/1586 and MEMO/05/480). The European Parliament issued a report in July 2006. All relevant documents are available at: http://ec.europa.eu/competition/antitrust/legislation/maritime/

The Competitiveness Council has also amended Regulation 1/2003 – the general regulation setting out the procedural rules needed to implement Articles [101 and 102 of the TFEU] – extending its scope to include cabotage and tramp shipping.

What happens next?
Existing liner conferences will be able to continue operating on routes to and from Europe until October 2008. After that date, conference activities and in particular price fixing and capacity regulation will no longer be permitted.

Before the end of the two-year transitional period, the Commission will publish Guidelines on the application of the competition rules to maritime transport services. Their purpose is to explain how competition rules apply to maritime transport services in general and in particular to the liner and tramp sectors.

As an interim step in the preparation of the Guidelines, the Commission will shortly publish a staff 'issues paper'. It will set out, with a view to collecting stakeholders' comments, a preliminary assessment of the issues relating to information exchanges raised by the industry's revised proposal concerning the impact of information exchange in the liner market.

What process will be followed for the adoption of the Commission Guidelines?
Guidelines are prepared in consultation with stakeholders. The Commission has been discussing with the liner and tramp shipping industries how best to issue appropriate guidance on how competition law should apply to the sector, once Regulation 4056/86 would be abolished. This dialogue has resulted in a number of submissions from the shipping industry, which are all available on the Commission website.

The Guidelines will be drafted and adopted by the Commission. Preparatory work towards the finalisation of the draft will be carried out in the European Competition Network (ECN)[114] working party for maritime transport. The working party is made up of representatives of Member States' competition authorities, of transport ministries and other relevant government authorities.

The Commission will adopt draft Guidelines, which will be published to allow all interested parties to make submissions. The consultation period will last one month from the date of publication.

Member States' views will then be sought in the Advisory Committee.[115] In response to the consultation process, the Commission may revisit its text. The Commission will then adopt the final text of the Guidelines and publish it in the Official Journal.

Further to the repeal of the Regulation 4056/86 will other legislation be changed?
Yes. It may be necessary to repeal Council Regulation (EEC) No 954/79[116] concerning the conditions under which Member States may accede to the UN Convention on a Code of Conduct for Liner Conferences.

As conferences will be abolished on trade to/from ports of the European Union in 2008, Regulation No. 954/79 will have to be revisited. The European Parliament has also requested the Commission to examine this question. A proposal from the Commission will be forthcoming shortly.

---

114 Ed., the European Competition Network ("ECN") was set up by Regulation 1/2003 amongst other things to ensure consistency of application of competition rules following modernisation. The subgroup on maritime transport will be made up of members of national competition authorities and transport representatives. The ECN is chaired by DG COMP and has solely a consultative role. In the case of the repeal of Reg. 4056/86 it serves to assure Member States that their concerns are heard in the process leading to the drafting of the Guidelines.
115 In accordance to paragraph 64 of the European Competition Network Notice.
116 Ed., OJ 1979 L121/1.

What is a Block Exemption Regulation?
Article [101(1) of the TFEU] prohibits agreements which affect trade between Member States and which have as their object or effect the prevention, restriction or distortion of competition within the [internal] market. Under Article [101(3) of the TFEU] a restrictive agreement may be exempted from the prohibition of Article [101(1) of the TFEU] if the positive effects brought about by the agreement outweigh its negative effects and a fair share of these benefits is passed on to consumers.

For certain sectors, the Council has empowered the Commission to exempt whole categories of agreements by means of adopting Regulations, the so called 'block exemption' Regulations. This creates a safe harbour for the agreements covered by the regulation, which are all deemed compatible with the competition rules on condition that they respect the rules laid down in the Regulations. Before granting a block exemption, the Commission needs to be absolutely certain that the agreements covered are compatible with the competition rules. Moreover, Commission block exemption Regulations are always limited in time so that the Commission can regularly check if market developments have not altered the compatibility conditions.

It is exceptional for a block exemption Regulation to be incorporated in a Council Regulation as is the case of the liner conference block exemption. It is also exceptional for such an exemption to be open-ended in terms of duration as was Regulation 4056/86.

What are liner conferences?
Shipping companies have organised themselves since the nineteenth century in the form of liner conferences to fix prices and regulate capacity. Liner conferences are most prevalent on routes between Europe, on the one hand, and North America and the Far East, on the other hand. They are associations of ship-owners operating on the same route, served by a secretariat. The block exemption contained in Council Regulation 4056/86 allows them to set common freight rates, to take joint decisions on the limitation of supply and to coordinate timetables. The exemption was granted on the assumption that it was necessary to ensure the provision of reliable services.

Liner conferences do not engage in operational co-operation and do not provide joint liner shipping services. It is up to the individual lines, consortia or alliances to offer such services.

Liner conferences are tolerated in other jurisdictions. Do other jurisdictions have to change their regime?
The decision to end the exemption from the competition rules means that as of October 2008 all EU and non EU carriers which currently take part in conferences operating on trades to and from the EU will have to end their conference activities, that is price fixing and capacity regulation, on those trades. Nothing would prevent them from taking part in price fixing conferences on non-EU trade routes. To give a concrete example, an EU carrier like Maersk Line, member of the Trans-Atlantic Conference Agreement (TACA), can no longer be involved in price fixing and capacity regulation on the North Atlantic-EU and EU-North Atlantic trades as of October 2008, but could still do so on the US-Pacific trades. The same applies to non-EU carriers.

This is a logical consequence of the fact that different competition regimes are in force worldwide. In fact, already today there are differences in what liner shipping companies are allowed to do in different jurisdictions. For example, today US law allows carriers to fix prices jointly on inland transport, while EU law does not.

A conflict of law does not arise. This would only be the case if one jurisdiction were to require carriers to participate in conferences, whereas another were to prohibit it. This is not the case today.

As liner conferences will continue to be tolerated in other jurisdictions, the Commission will take all appropriate initiatives to advance the removal of price fixing liner conferences that exist elsewhere in the world and thus promote further competitive reform of the liner shipping sector. That is why it has taken the initiative to establish close and frequent contacts with our major international partners (e.g. US, Canada, Australia, Japan, China, Singapore).

The liner shipping industry is asking for a new regime to replace the conference block exemption. What will the Commission do about that?
Industry is divided on the need for a substantive alternative to Regulation 4056/86. The European Liner Affairs Association (ELAA), a carrier association representing roughly 90% of world capacity has proposed that the conference block exemption should be replaced by an information exchange system. Details of their proposal of June 2006 are available at: http://ec.europa.eu/competition/antitrust/legislation/maritime/

The European Shippers Association (ESC) representing over 100,000 exporting companies, and generating around 90% of the EU's international maritime traffic, considers that a replacement regime is not necessary because carriers are already allowed to co-operate extensively under the consortia block exemption Regulation (prolonged and amended in April 2005 – see IP/05/477). This co-operation results in the provision of reliable liner services by groups of shipping lines in consortia and alliances. The European business organisation UNICE, the European freight forwarders' association CLECAT and consumer associations back this position.

To be acceptable, any new system for information exchange must respect the competition rules. Some elements of the current ELAA proposal appear to be in line with these requirements. However, others are problematic, notably because their effects would be alike to those of the current conferences. Accepting the revised ELAA proposal in its current form would annihilate the pro-competitive effects of the abolition of the conference system. As explained above, DG COMP is about to launch a consultative 'issues paper' on the impact of the proposal on the liner shipping market.

What is the impact of the repeal on small liner shipping carriers and on small short sea trades?
The European Community Shipowners' Associations (ECSA) and the European Parliament have drawn the Commission's attention to the needs of specific services, particularly short sea services and services to smaller trades. Since such trades generally do not require a large number of vessels to be serviced, relatively small carriers might be able to operate side by side with large carriers on these trades. ECSA and the European Parliament, therefore, questioned whether these relatively small carriers would be more affected by a repeal than large ones.

The Commission is not aware of any liner shipping carrier that would fall within the scope of the Commission Recommendation concerning the definition of small and medium sized enterprises.[117]

After extensive research, the Commission did not find that relatively small EU carriers would be adversely affected by a repeal of the conference block exemption. To the contrary, liberalisation creates a market environment that allows for quicker growth than a regulated environment, in particular for small companies. It creates more new services and new niche markets which especially small companies are able to enter quickly. These market niches usually allow for rapid growth. Hence, small innovative companies are able to grow much quicker in a competitive environment. The success of small carriers depends on their ability to adapt to a competitive environment and not on their actual size.

What are the economic effects of the repeal of the block exemption?
The Commission has concluded that a repeal of the block exemption will bring about substantial benefits to EU industry and consumers, in particular as regards transport prices, reliability of liner shipping services, competitiveness of the EU liner shipping industry and small EU liner carriers. The repeal of the block exemption will therefore also contribute to the Lisbon objectives.

The Commission's main findings of the potential economic impact of repealing the conference block exemption are:

- transport prices for liner shipping services will decline
- service reliability on deep sea and short sea trades is expected to improve

---

117 Commission Recommendation 2003/361/EC of 6 May 2003 concerning the definition of micro, small and medium-sized enterprises, OJ L124, 20 May 2003.

- service quality will either be unaffected or will improve
- there will be either a positive impact or no impact on the competitiveness of EU liner shipping firms
- small liner shipping carriers will not experience particular problems and
- no negative impact or even a positive impact on EU ports, employment, trade and/or developing countries.

The Commission's conclusions take account of three independent studies undertaken to establish the impact of the repeal of the block exemption. The latest study (see IP/05/1408) is the combined work of Global Insight, an international consultancy with significant experience in liner shipping, the Berlin University of Technology and the Institute of Shipping Economics and Logistics in Bremen.

Does the repeal have an impact on the maritime consortia block exemption Regulation?
No. Liner carriers will continue to be allowed to offer joint services. Block Exemption Regulation 823/2000 on maritime consortia allows shipping lines to engage in operational co-operation (vessel-sharing, co-ordination of routes and schedules) but not to fix prices. In 2005, this Regulation was reviewed and extended until 2010 after it was found to be working well by both shipping lines and transport users (see IP/05/477). This exemption is of particular significance in terms of volume of trade. For example, the majority of cargo between the EU and the US is transported by shipping lines in consortia and alliances using individual service contracts instead of conference tariff prices.

Will the Commission be issuing guidance to the tramp sector?
Yes. The forthcoming Guidelines on the application of competition rules to maritime transport services will cover tramp shipping. Tramp services concern the non-regular, maritime transport of bulk cargo that is not containerised, and include a range of economically important services such as the transport of oil, agricultural and chemical products. Preparatory work is already underway and the Commission engaged in discussions with tramp operators so as to better understand the issues at stake. It also has contracted an external study on the sector, to be finalised by the end of the year.

What is the impact of the repeal on international tramp vessel services?
The impact on international tramp vessel services should not be substantial because [TFEU] competition rules (Articles [101 and 102 of the TFEU]) already apply to cabotage and tramp shipping. It is rather a question of including these sectors within the generally applicable procedural framework laid down by Council Regulation 1/2003 and so enable the Commission, in addition to national authorities and courts, to apply these rules to cabotage and tramp shipping.

This will have advantages for industry in terms of clarity. At present, both industry and competition authorities, have to devote considerable resources to assessing whether a service fulfils all of the criteria set out in Regulation 4056/86[118] before determining what action could be taken and by which authority."

12.045 Competition Commissioner, Neelie Kroes, stated later:

"Given the importance of maritime transport of goods to so many areas of the European economy, I have to make sure that the sector is operating as competitively as possible, keeping prices down and quality of service high. By providing guidance to maritime operators on EU competition rules, these Guidelines mark a significant step towards better enforcement in the maritime sector."[119]

---

118 The transport of goods in bulk or in break-bulk in a vessel charted (wholly or partly) to one or more shippers on the basis of a voyage or a time charter on any other form of contract for non-regularly scheduled or non-advertised sailings where freight rates are freely negotiated case by case in accordance with the conditions of supply and demand.
119 http://europa.eu/rapid/press-release_IP-08-1063_en.htm?locale=en.

D. EFFECT OF THE NEW REGIME: REGULATION 1419/2006

12.046 The adoption of Regulation 1419/2006 means that the maritime sector is now subject to the same substantive and procedural rules of EU competition law as most areas of the economy: the special regime has disappeared. Put another way, the adoption of Regulation 1419/2006 had four principal effects.

12.047 First, Regulation 1419/2006 repealed Regulation 4056/86.

12.048 Second, Regulation 1/2003 sets out the general rules of procedure for competition generally across all sectors. Regulation 17/62[120] had given the Commission the power to enforce competition law in the economy generally but Regulation 141/62 removed the power to do so in the case of the transport sector. Regulation 4056/86 gave the Commission the power to enforce Articles 101 and 102 in regard to international maritime transport services to or from one or more EU ports since 1987. Regulation 1/2003 repealed the special perceived rules with effect from 1 May 2004. Since then, maritime transport has been subject to the general EU competitive law regime. Regulation 1/2003 gives the Commission wide and vigorous powers: the Commission may investigate alleged breaches, conduct sectoral enquiries, conduct dawn raids, request information, send statements of objection and ultimately impose massive fines of up to 10% of worldwide turnover. Article 32 of Regulation 1/2003 had provided, until the entry into force of Regulation 1419/2006, that Regulation 1/2003 did not apply to: (a) international tramp vessel services as defined in Article 1(3)(a) of Regulation 4056/86; and (b) any maritime transport service which took place exclusively between ports in one and the same Member State (i.e. cabotage) (presumably because there was no effect on trade between Member States). Article 32 of Regulation 1/2003 was repealed by virtue of Regulation 1419/2006. Regulation 1419/2006 amended Regulation 1/2003 to extend the latter to cover tramp shipping[121] and cabotage[122] so that the Commission may apply its normal procedural enforcement rules to those two sectors. Obviously, Articles 101 and 102 of the TFEU apply to both of those sectors (where the conditions for the application of those articles apply) but the Commission lacked the power to apply its normal procedural rules.

12.049 Third, the shipping industry generally (including the tramp and cabotage services), and not just the liner shipping sector, has been rendered, by Regulation 1419/2006, subject to the application by the Commission of Articles 101 and 102 of the TFEU as well as Regulation 1/2003 on the implementation of Articles 101 and 102 of the TFEU. Under the old regime, the Commission had enforcement powers only over the liner industry. This was because the Commission had not been granted jurisdiction under Regulation 17/62 or Regulation 1/2003 (as originally adopted) but Regulation 1419/2006 changed the regime.

12.050 Fourth, given that liner conferences operate globally and even though the changes in Regulation 1419/2006 are confined to the EU, the effect of the regulation had global effects. As Olivier Guersent, the then Acting Director for Transport, Post and other Services at DG COMP stated at the EMLO meeting in Copenhagen on 24 October 2008:

---

120 JO 1962 L13/2004.
121 I.e. the non-regular maritime transport of goods (normally non-containerised bulk cargo) on the basis of individually negotiated terms.
122 I.e. the maritime transport of goods or passengers between two ports in the one State.

"I note with satisfaction that several liner conferences started winding down their activities a few months before the deadline. I also noticed the press coverage of conferences ceasing their activities on 17 October. So, from the point of view of the Commission – and hopefully from the point of view of the lines, conferences are already a thing of the past."

12.051 While individual exemptions are no longer possible since the entry into force of Regulation 1/2003[123] and Regulation 4056/86 has been repealed, there are other block exemptions which may apply in specific circumstances such as those relating to consortia, insurance, specialisation and so on, so an advisor would be wise to consider the potential application of other block exemptions as well.

12.052 At a practical level, the implications were that conferences could not be continued, conference-agreed business plans were no longer lawful, conference-agreed surcharges and ancillary charges were no longer permitted, conference-agreed freight rates were prohibited and the exchange of current individual market share, volume and price data were prohibited. However, much could continue including the very existence of a trade association (including meetings provided there was no exchange of competitively sensitive data or other anti-competitive activity), individual pricing, individual charges, the exchange of historical data (that is to say, information which is not competitively sensitive), the use of an aggregated price index by trade as well as publication of demand and supply forecasts (but only the basis of publicly available sources and, in the case of demand forecasts, from aggregated data only).

E. THE TRANSITIONAL PERIOD FOR THE NEW REGIME: REGULATION 1419/2006 AND PROCEDURAL DIMENSION OF REGULATION 1419/2006

12.053 There is clearly a new EU competition regime relating to shipping since 18 October 2006 when Regulation 1419/2006 entered into force. However, the ending of the block exemption in Regulation 4056/86 for the liner conference sector was a very dramatic change. A transitional period of two years was therefore embodied in Regulation 1419/2006. Liner conferences, whether EU[124] or non-EU, could continue operating to and from the EU until 18 October 2008 but since then it would be illegal to operate any arrangement or practice being in breach of Article 101 of the TFEU. It would be irrelevant that the arrangement or practice would have been legal elsewhere in the world.

12.054 So as to assist with the dramatic change that had to be planned for during the transition, the Commission adopted guidelines on the application of Article 101 of the TFEU to maritime transport services. Guidelines in relation to Article 101 were important because there are so many arrangements and other forms of co-operation in the shipping sector. This need for guidance was all the greater given the abolition of the block exemption. There was a need for guidance in particular in relation to pooling arrangements for tramp shipping operators and information exchange arrangements for everyone.

12.055 It is useful to outline the evolution of the procedural regime including the current position. The Commission was given, by Regulation 17/62,[125] the power to enforce, what are now, Articles 101 and 102 of the TFEU. However, the adoption of

---

123 Fn. 9.
124 Or affecting trade in the EU.
125 JO 1962 13/204.

Regulation 141/62 meant that the Commission could not apply the Competition rules to the transport sector. Regulation 4056/86[126] gave the Commission the power to apply Articles 101 to 102 of the TFEU to international maritime transport services to or from EU ports with effect from 1987. Regulation 17/62 was repealed, and replaced, by Regulation 1/2003.[127] This latter regulation entered into force on 1 May 2004. The Competition regime was not applied completely. Regulation 4056/86 did not give the Commission the power to enforce the competition rules in the context of cabotage or international tramp services.[128] These two exceptions were continued by Article 32 of Regulation 1/2003 until 18 October 2006 when Article 2 of Regulation 1419/2006 entered into force. The Commission may now apply Articles 101 and 102 of the TFEU to the maritime sector.

F. AN INTRODUCTION TO THE COMMISSION'S GUIDELINES ON MARITIME SERVICES

Introduction

12.056 The Commission's "Guidelines on the Application of Article 81 of the EC Treaty to Maritime Transport Services"[129] were very helpful.[130] (Article 81 of the EC Treaty is now Article 101 of the TFEU.) The Commission adopted in 2008 Guidelines on the application of competition law to maritime transport services.[131] The final version of the Guidelines were published in July 2008 on the Commission's website and ultimately published in the *Official Journal* on 26 September 2008.[132] They were a very welcome statement of the law on this area – particularly, as there was so much change brought about by the repeal of Regulation 4056/86. They were the result of five years of work including ten months of consultation on the published draft.[133] While the Guidelines could not provide absolute legal certainty – and no guidelines can do so – they were nonetheless useful and the result of a thorough process. Such sector-specific guidelines were unusual because more guidelines are issued for the entire economy. They covered both the liner and tramp sectors. The maritime sector, which became subject to the general competition

---

126 OJ 1986 L378/4.
127 OJ 2003 L1/1.
128 Recital 12 of Reg. 14/9/2006 described these exclusions as a "regulatory anomaly".
129 OJ 2008 C245/2. Art. 81 of the EC Treaty is now Art. 101 of the TFEU. The term "common market" has been amended to "internal market".
130 OJ 2008 C245/2. See also article at (2007) 217 EU Focus 8 on the draft guidelines. See also Camesasca and Schmidt, "EC Commission's Post-Conference Maritime Transport Guidelines: True Guidance to Navigate through Antitrust Compliance" [2009] 30(3) ECLR 143; Guersent, "The Guidelines on Maritime Transport Services", EMLO, Copenhagen, 24 October 2008. Holmes, "Maritime Transport: A Look at the New Commission Guidelines", *Competition Law Insight*, 21 October 2008, p. 9; and Lista, "Trick or Treat? Commission Guidelines on Maritime Transport Competition" (2008) 7 Shipping & Trade Law 1; and The EFTA Surveillance Authority issued a Notice which contained comparable guidelines. See Randolph, "The European Commission's Draft Guidelines: A Promising Starting-Point or a Missed Opportunity?" (2008) 7(1) Shipping & Transport International 11.
131 OJ 2008 C245/2. On the Guidelines, see Guersent, op. cit. at fn 132.
132 OJ 2008 C245/2.
133 The final version was not too different from the draft but the debate was nonetheless welcome. Some typographical errors had been removed, the somewhat general language in parts of the draft was tightened, the commentary in regard to trade associations was made more specific while the ambiguity and generality of EU competition law was emphasised more in the final version. The substantive changes related principally to the provisions on pools and efficiency.

regime on 18 October 2008, was fortunate to have sector specific guidelines and such a thorough process of consultation – nonetheless, no set of guidelines (including this set) could be perfect. They were focused on shipping pools. They were not a sop or advantage to the sector, instead they outlined the Commission's intention to apply the competition regime to the sector. However, in 2013, the Commission decided not to renew the Guidelines when they expired in 2013.

Adoption process

12.057 There was strong lobbying by the sector to have such Guidelines. The Commission was very prudent and deliberate in the way in which it adopted the Guidelines. It did not simply adopt Guidelines without consulting. It went through a number of steps. On 29 September 2006, the Commission published an issues paper (or staff paper) on the potential impact of information exchanges between liner carriers on the market for liner shipping.[134] The Commission was concerned that exchanges of information could lead in practice to a co-ordination of prices and other trading conditions between liner carriers. Stakeholders were invited to submit their comments. The paper was a step in the preparation of Guidelines. On 13 September 2007, the Commission published draft Guidelines.[135] On 1 July 2008, the Commission adopted the final Guidelines.[136] There was little difference between the ultimate Guidelines and the draft ones. These Guidelines do not answer all the questions[137] which could be answered but it would be impossible to provide answers to all of these anyway. The Guidelines were ultimately the product of more than five years of consultation between the Commission (principally, DG COMP), the Member States, the European Parliament, the lines (represented primarily by the ELAA and the shippers (represented primarily by the ESC).

Purpose of the Guidelines

12.058 Paragraph 1 of the Guidelines states that the

"Guidelines set out the principles that the Commission of the European Communities will follow when defining markets and assessing cooperation agreements in those maritime transport services directly affected by the changes brought about by Council Regulation (EC) No 1419/2006 of 25 September 2006, i.e. liner shipping services, cabotage and international tramp services."[138]

12.059 The Guidelines continue in paragraph 2 by stating that they

"are intended to help undertakings and associations of undertakings operating those services, mainly if operated to and/or from a port or ports in the European Union, to assess whether their

---

134 See http://ec.europa.eu/competition/antitrust/legislation/maritime/issues_paper_shipping.pdf. By way of background, see IP/06/1283.
135 OJ 2007 C215/3.
136 See Commission Press Release IP/08/1063 and MEMO/08/460.
137 Randolph commented at the EMLO Conference on 17 October 2008: "the Commission missed several opportunities to clarify important legal uncertainties in various areas impacting on the shipping industry. It also makes clear that to an extent, the Commission could do little else given the fact that it is the case law of the [General Court] and the Court of Justice which must be determinative in the long run of those present legal uncertainties. All the Commission can do is suggest what its position might be on certain key points."
138 Footnote omitted.

agreements are compatible with Article [101 of the TFEU]. The Guidelines do not apply to other sectors."[139]

12.060 The Guidelines serve as a warning to the shipping sector that the Commission is intent on enforcing competition law. However, they are also a clear help from the Commission to the industry because the Commission deliberately sought to assist the sector by giving guidance on issues which were not so well covered either by case law, block exemptions or other guidance[140] – in that respect, the shipping industry has benefited from guidance which other sectors have not received.[141]

12.061 The Guidelines also gave guidance in an area of law which was (and is still) notoriously unclear, namely, information exchange. The Guidelines gave guidance on market definition and the assessment of co-operation agreements in the maritime sector. The Guidelines gave some guidance in the aftermath of the repeal of Regulation 4056/86. The Guidelines also gave some guidance on co-operation between tramp operators in pools.

Duration of the Guidelines

12.062 Paragraph 8 of the Guidelines states that the "Commission will apply these Guidelines for a period of five years." However, it is unclear as to when the five-year period commenced. It is assumed that it is their date of publication but not much may turn on when they end in any event. It is interesting to note that the draft gave the impression that the Guidelines would last for an *initial* period of five years but the final version conveys the impression that the Guidelines would last for five years only as a way of transitioning the sector to the new environment – it would appear that, from the outset, the Commission did not believe that the Guidelines would be renewed. In May 2012, the Commission opened a consultation on whether there was still a need for the Guidelines. The Commission said that its provisional view was that the Guidelines should lapse. The consultation closed on 27 July 2012. Despite the fact that they were not continued, they are nonetheless of some value as a possible source of inspiration. On 19 February 2013, the Commission announced that it had decided not to continue or renew the Guidelines.[142] The Guidelines therefore expired on 26 September 2013. The Commission believed that the Guidelines were unnecessary as they had fulfilled their role at ensuring a smooth transition and the more up to date 2010 Horizontal Guidelines were more useful. The Commission also dislikes sector specific guidance.

Place and status of the Guidelines in EU competition law generally

12.063 What is the legal standing or status of the Guidelines? Olivier Guersent, the then Acting Director for Transport, Post and other Services at DG COMP stated at the EMLO meeting in Copenhagen on 24 October 2008:

---

139 They would nonetheless be helpful for other sectors.
140 E.g. the Art. 101(3) guidelines OJ 2004 C101/97.
141 E.g. virtually every other sector of the economy had to grapple with self-assessment on 1 May 2004 when Reg. 1/2003 entered into force.
142 IP/13/122.

"the Commission is not prepared to make broad, absolute pronouncements. *This is because guidelines are binding on the Commission.* So, generally speaking, by adopting guidelines, the Commission effectively restricts its own margin of discretion in future cases. As the Court has said, guidelines are rules from which the Commission may not depart in an individual case without giving adequate reasons." (Emphasis added.)

12.064 It is unusual for the Commission to adopt measures which are dedicated to specific sectors' circumstances. The Maritime Guidelines are very specific to the sector but they should also be read in the context of, in particular: (a) the Guidelines on the Applicability of Article 101 to Horizontal Co-operation Agreements;[143] (b) the Guidelines on the Application of Article 101(3);[144] (c) the Guidelines on the Effect of Trade Concept;[145] and (d) the Guidelines on the Definition of the Relevant Market.[146] The Maritime Guidelines do not address the issue of consortia as they are already covered by the block exemption on consortia. While the Guidelines address Article 101, there are some elements which could apply equally to Article 102 (e.g. market definition issues) but would do so by analogy.

12.065 The Commission recognises the limitations of the Guidelines; paragraph 7 of the Guidelines states:

"[t]hese Guidelines are without prejudice to the interpretation of Article [101] of the Treaty which may be given by the Court of Justice [of the European Union] or the [General Court]. The principles in the Guidelines are to be applied in the light of the circumstances specific to each case."

However, they may have greater legal effect than would be apparent; as Randolph has commented incisively:

"It might have been thought ... that the Guidelines were indicative and no more. However, in *Dansk Rorindustri*,[147] the Court of Justice made the following comments in relation to the guidelines on leniency in competition investigations:

'The Court has already held, in a judgment concerning internal measures adopted by the administration, that although those measures may not be regarded as rules of law which the administration is always bound to observe, they nevertheless form rules of practice from which the administration may not depart in an individual case without giving reasons that are compatible with the principle of equal treatment. Such measures therefore constitute a general act and the officials and other staff concerned may invoke their illegality in support of an action against the individual measures taken on the basis of the measures...' (paragraph 209)

'That case-law applies *a fortiori* to rules of conduct designed to produce external effects, as is the case of the Guidelines, which are aimed at traders.' (paragraph 210)

'In adopting such rules of conduct and announcing by publishing them that they will henceforth apply to the cases to which they relate, the institution in question imposes a limit on the exercise of its discretion and cannot depart from those rules under pain of being found, where appropriate, to be in breach of the general principles of law, such as equal treatment or the protection of legitimate expectations. It cannot therefore be precluded that, on certain conditions

---

143 OJ 2011 C11/1.
144 OJ 2004 C101/97.
145 OJ 2004 C101/81.
146 OJ 1997 C327/5.
147 Joined Cases C-189/02P, C-202/02P, C-205/02P–C-208/02P and C-213/02 *Dansk Rorindustri and others v Commission* [2005] ECR I-5425, ECLI:EU:C:2005:408.

and depending on their content, such rules of conduct, which are of general application, may produce legal effects.' (paragraph 211)

Accordingly, despite their nomenclature, it cannot be excluded that the Guidelines could produce legally-binding effects."[148]

It is submitted that the Guidelines did produce some legal effects and cannot be departed from easily or lightly or without explanation. They will be taken into account by those involved in shipping in the self-assessment which they must undertake given that the Commission championed the abolition of notification of arrangements under Articles 101 and 102 of the TFEU. The Guidelines can have some relevance worldwide provided there is an effect on trade in the EU.

Limitations

12.066 According to paragraph 1 of the Guidelines, the Guidelines set out the "principles" that the Commission "will follow" when defining markets and assessing co-operation agreements in those maritime transport services directly affected by the changes brought about by Regulation 1419/2006, that is to say, liner shipping services, cabotage and international tramp services. So, they are only a statement of "principles" but, in reality, nothing more could be expected from such a document. The Guidelines deal only with the application of Article 101 of the TFEU.

Non-renewal

12.067 The Guidelines were not renewed in 2013 when they expired. The significance of non-renewal is that the Commission is now treating the maritime sector as being no different from any other sector and not requiring specific guidance. The Commission had announced its preliminary view on 4 May 2012 that the Guidelines should not be renewed but invited submissions by 27 July 2012 by way of a Commission Staff Working Document entitled *The Future of the Commission Guidelines on the Application of Article 101 TFEU to Maritime Transport Services*.[149] Ultimately, the Commission decided not to change its mind and the Guidelines have not been renewed. The Commission believed that the Guidelines had become unnecessary given the two-year transition period and the five years which had passed since the entry into force of Regulation 1419/2006. Moreover, the Commission generally dislikes sector specific guidance and thought more modern general guidance would be better. There was a view in some quarters that the

---

148 EMLO Conference, 17 October 2008, and published in Wareham and Power (eds), op. cit. at fn. 1, chap. 2 (with modification).
149 See http://ec.europa.eu/competition/consultations/2012_maritime_guidelines/guidelines_working_document_en.pdf.

Guidelines added little or nothing to the knowledge of how competition law would apply to the maritime sector.[150]

12.068 While the liner sector had the benefit or burden of the application of competition law since the entry into force of Regulation 4056/86, the tramp sector had no such experience because the Commission had not applied Article 101 to the sector as such. So, the main focus of the Guidelines was the tramp sector and then shipping pools within the sector. In terms of product market definition, it points out as being relevant such factors as vessel size, vessel type, special features of vessels and the type of cargo carried on vessels. In terms of geographical market definition, the Guidelines made it clear that the market might not be the world but rather much narrower having regard to loading and discharging ports and the Guidelines recommended single directional markets as the norm. The Guidelines also made it clear that in terms of calculating annual market shares, one should look at data such as the number of voyages, the parties' volume or value share in the overall transport of a specific cargo between port pairs or ranges, the parties' share in the market for time charter contracts and the parties' capacity shares in the relevant fleet by vessel type and size.

12.069 The Guidelines saw standard pools as having "joint production features" which means that they are permissible under the Horizontal Guidelines because joint selling is seen as indispensable for joint production.

G. MARKET DEFINITION

Introduction

12.070 The definition of the market is often critical in competition law; decisions can often be overturned by an appellate court because the market was defined incorrectly by the decision-making institution. The Commission has published its Guidelines on the Definition of the Relevant Market[151] and those guidelines remain relevant to the issue of market definition in the maritime sector as well. However, the Maritime Guidelines are also pivotal in this case. There can then be specific market definitions in the context of specific sectors or specialisms (e.g. ro-ro, passenger ferry services,[152] reefer,[153] LNG etc.). It is important to recall that market definition is case-specific; definitions found in one case can be interesting in later cases but they are not conclusive or definitive because circumstances can change over time. That said, there is often a consistency of approach and, in many ways, the Commission's approach to market definition in the Maritime Guidelines is unsurprising as it is based on the Commission's precedents and decision-making generally.

---

150 E.g. the position on market definition (a) was already well established in the Commission's 1997 Market Definition Notice and the decisional practice of both the Commission and the CJEU and (b) depends on an empirical analysis of each case. Equally, some believed that the issues relating to pools were governed by the general principles of EU competition law anyway (e.g. whether Art. 101(1) applied and, if it did, whether Art. 101(3) then applied to counteract the breach of Art. 101(1)). Critics might have accepted that the Guidelines added some colour to the debate on information exchange in 2008, the law has become somewhat (though not entirely) clearer since and therefore the Guidelines would add little.
151 OJ 1997 C327/5.
152 The *Wallenius/Wilhelmsen/Hyundai* and *CMLA/CGM/Delmas* cases.
153 See *NYK/Lauritzen Cool/Laucool* and *APMM/PONL* cases.

Liner shipping

12.071 In terms of the product market, containerised liner shipping services have been identified as the relevant market for liner shipping in several decisions and judgments. It is not possible to easily substitute other modes of transport for such services; for example, it would be too expensive (and sometimes impossible) to send large cargo items by aircraft and sometimes land transport is simply not an option (e.g. Europe to New Zealand). It is possible that the market would be narrower such as where perishable goods are involved. As a general principle, bulk and containerised freight are not substitutable. In terms of the geographical market, the particular geographical area where the services are marketed and operated would be the relevant geographical market. The Northern European ports have been seen as in a separate market from the Mediterranean ports in liner traffic.[154]

Tramp shipping

12.072 Article 101 of the TFEU had not been capable of being applied to tramp shipping by the European Commission (because the Commission lacked the procedural machinery) therefore there was no precedent on which to rely. As Karamitsos who was the Director, Maritime Transport in the old DG TREN stated:

> "the full application of competition rules to tramp [shipping] ... is entirely new. We all know that competition rules applied to tramp [shipping] in the past. But the absence of precedents due to the inapplicability of the general procedural rules could make the application quite difficult, especially at the level of national jurisdictions. Let us hope that we will have 'good precedents' in this respect, and no 'victims', who set precedents, so to say."[155]

12.073 The Guidelines therefore play an important role in giving guidance on this issue. However, the Guidelines are relatively brief on tramp shipping. This level of brevity was due in part to the lack of specific precedents.

12.074 In terms of demand-side substitutability, several criteria would be relevant. First, the type of contract (e.g. time charter, voyage charter and contract of affreightment) would be relevant. Second, the type of vessel would be relevant.

12.075 In terms of supply-side substitutability, the physical and technical conditions of the cargo and the substitutability of the vessels types (including volume and size) would be relevant.

12.076 The definition of the relevant market for tramp shipping services is somewhat unclear. At paragraph 21 of its Guidelines, the Commission states that undertakings may consider the following elements in their assessment inasmuch as they are relevant to the tramp shipping services they provide:

> "*Elements to take into account when determining the relevant product market from the demand side (demand substitution)*
> 22. The 'main terms' of an individual transport request are a starting point for defining relevant service markets in tramp shipping since they generally identify the essential

---

154 See *TACA* as discussed later in this chapter. In this case, the Commission found that based on the range of ports for liner shipping purposes, Northern Europe and the Mediterranean were separate markets.

155 Karamitsos, op. cit. at fn. 109, p. 3.

elements[156] of the transport requirement at issue. Depending on the transport users' specific needs, they will be made up of negotiable and non-negotiable elements. Once identified, a negotiable element of the main terms, for example the vessel type or size, may indicate, for instance, that the relevant market with respect to this specific element is wider than laid down in the initial transport requirement.

23. The nature of the service in tramp shipping may differ and there is a variety of transport contracts. It may be necessary, therefore, to ascertain whether the demand side considers the services provided under time charter contracts, voyage charter contracts and contracts of affreightment to be substitutable. Should this be the case they may belong to the same relevant market.

24. Vessel types are usually subdivided into a number of standard industrial sizes.[157] Due to considerable economies of scale, a service with a significant mismatch between cargo volume and vessel size may not be able to offer a competitive freight rate. Therefore, the substitutability of different vessel sizes needs to be assessed case by case so as to ascertain whether each vessel size constitutes a separate relevant market.

Elements to take into account when determining the relevant product market from the supply-side (supply substitution)

25. The physical and technical conditions of the cargo to be carried and the vessel type provide the first indications as to the relevant market from the supply side.[158] If vessels can be adjusted to transport a particular cargo at negligible cost and in a short time-frame,[159] different tramp shipping service providers are able to compete for the transport of this cargo. In such circumstances, the relevant market from the supply side will comprise more than one type of vessel.

26. However, there are a number of vessel types that are technically adapted and/or specially built to provide specialised transport services. Although specialised vessels may also carry other types of cargo, they may be at a competitive disadvantage. The ability of specialised service providers to compete for the transport of other cargo may, therefore, be limited.

27. In tramp shipping, port calls are made in response to individual demand. Mobility of vessels may however be limited by terminal and draught restrictions or environmental standards for particular vessel types in certain ports or regions.

Additional considerations to take into account when determining the relevant product market

28. The existence of chains of substitution between vessel sizes in tramp shipping should also be considered. In certain tramp shipping markets, vessel sizes at the extreme of the market are not directly substitutable. Chain substitution effects may nevertheless constrain pricing at the extremes and lead to their inclusion in a broader market definition.

29. In certain tramp shipping markets, consideration must be given to whether vessels can be considered as captive capacity and should not be taken into account when assessing the relevant market on a case by case basis.

---

156 For voyage charter for instance the essential elements of a transport requirement are the cargo to be carried, the cargo volume, the loading and discharging ports, the laydays or the ultimate date by which the cargo has to arrive and technical details regarding the vessel required.

157 It appears to be the industry's perception that vessel sizes constitute separate markets. The trade press and the Baltic Exchange publish price indexes for each standard vessel size. Consultants' reports divide the market on the basis of vessel sizes.

158 For example, liquid bulk cargo cannot be carried on dry bulk vessels or reefer cargo cannot be transported on car carriers. Many oil tankers are able to carry dirty and clean petroleum products. However, a tanker cannot immediately carry clean products after having transported dirty products.

159 Switching a dry bulk vessel from the transport of coal to grain might require only a one-day cleaning process that might be done during a ballast voyage. In other tramp shipping markets this cleaning period may be longer.

30. Additional factors such as the reliability of the service provider, security, safety and regulatory requirements may influence supply and demand-side substitutability, for example the double hull requirement for tankers in Community waters.[160]

Geographic dimension
31. Transport requirements usually contain geographic elements such as the loading and discharging ports or regions. These ports provide the first orientation for the definition of the relevant geographic market from the demand-side, without prejudice to the final definition of the relevant geographic market.
32. Certain geographic markets may be defined on a directional basis or may occur only temporarily for instance when climatic conditions or harvest periods periodically affect the demand for transport of particular cargos. In this context, repositioning of vessels, ballast voyages and trade imbalances should be considered for the delineation of relevant geographic markets."

12.077 Following the adoption of Regulation 1419/2006, the liner sector was given a two-year transition period to adapt to the new regime. The tramp sector was not given a transition regime. The Commission believed that the "impact [of the change] should not be substantial because [TFEU] competition rules already apply to cabotage and tramp shipping". However, the Commission has had limited experience of dealing with tramp services as its attention had been focused on liner shipping. This means that those involved in tramp shipping have to conduct a self-assessment to see whether their arrangements or practices are in breach of competition law. The parties need to define the market,[161] consider whether there is an effect on trade[162] and decide whether there is a significant effect on competition. Typically, in fragmented markets with many small owners, there is little or no competition problem. However, there can be difficulties arising in self-assessment because statistics and market information can be difficult to find. It is necessary to determine whether customers have countervailing buyer power. The geographical market can be difficult to define on occasion.

12.078 There can also be a horizontal and a vertical dimension to the market defined. The horizontal dimension would involve the competitors in a particular market (i.e. all competing at the same level). The vertical dimension would involve, for example, a shipping company buying a port through which it was operating (i.e. an upstream acquisition).

12.079 Once the market has been defined then the market shares for liner shipping should be assessed taking into account volume and/or capacity data.

12.080 Once the market has been defined then the market shares for tramp shipping should be assessed by reference to the number of voyages, volume or value share of the specific cargo, share in the market time charter contracts or share by reference to the vessel type and size.

---

160 Regulation (EC) No 417/2002 of the European Parliament and of the Council of 18 February 2002 on the accelerated phasing-in of double hull or equivalent design requirements for single hull oil tankers and repealing Council Regulation (EC) No 2978/94 (OJ L64, 7.3.2002).
161 See Notice on definition of relevant market (OJ C372/5, 9 December 1997).
162 See Guidelines on the Effect on Trade Concept (OJ C101/81, 27 April 2004).

Technical agreements

12.081 Article 2 of Regulation 4056/86 declared that certain technical agreements fell outside the scope of Article 101 of the Treaty in certain specific circumstances. Article 2 of Regulation 4056/86 has been repealed by Regulation 1419/2006. It is useful to recall the Commission's comments on why Article 2 was being repealed:

> "21. The argument has been put forward that, in spite of its declaratory nature, Article 2 should be maintained because it might provide guidance notably in the context of modernisation, when undertakings have to assess for themselves whether their agreements are caught by Article [101(1)] of the Treaty. The case law of the Commission and the Court is clear on the very limited scope of the provision which merely intends to confirm that agreements which are not restrictive of competition in the first place do not fall under Article [101(1)] of the Treaty and as such are not prohibited.[163] Article 2 therefore does not add legal security. It should also be recalled that, for similar reasons, the Council in 2004 repealed a similar provision on technical agreements in the air transport sector."[164],[165]

12.082 The Guidelines, which followed on from the repeal of Regulation 4056/86, consider the competition law implications of so-called "technical agreements". Paragraph 37 of the Guidelines state:

> "Technical agreements
> 37. Certain types of technical agreements may not fall under the prohibition set out in Article [101] of the Treaty on the ground that they do not restrict competition. This is the case, for instance, of horizontal agreements the sole object and effect of which is to implement technical improvements or to achieve technical cooperation. Agreements relating to the implementation of environmental standards can also be considered to fall into this category. Agreements between competitors relating to price, capacity, or other parameters of competition will, in principle, not fall into this category."[166]

This is a narrow construction of the law but a correct one. The "sole object and effect" of the arrangement must be technical and only technical.

H. INFORMATION EXCHANGE

Introduction

12.083 This part of the chapter examines EU competition law as it relates to the sharing of information between competitors in the shipping sector in the new regime.[167] This topic involves the analysis of such questions as: what is "information exchange"?; what information may be exchanged lawfully?; what information may not be exchanged

---

163 See in this regard also the Commission Notice on horizontal guidelines (OJ C3 of 06.01.2001 p. 2), para 24.
164 See Council Reg. 411/2004 of 26 February 2004 (OJ L68 of 6 March 2004, p. 1).
165 COM (2005) 651.
166 Comm. Dec. 2000/627 of 16 May 2000 (Case IV/34.018 – *Far East Trade Tariff Charges and Surcharges Agreement (FETTCSA)*) (OJ L268, 20 October 2000, p. 1), para. 153. Judgment of the Court of First Instance of 21 October 1997 in Case T-229/94, *Deutsche Bahn AG v Commission* [1997] ECR II-1689, para. 37.
167 See Bourne, "Information Exchange", Lloyd's Maritime Academy, EU Competition Law in Shipping, London, 26 March 2009; Power, "The EU Law on Sharing Information between Competitors", Lloyd's Maritime Academy, EU Competition Law in Shipping, London, 26 March 2009; and Power, "What You Can and Can't Do Sharing Information and Communicating with Others", Lloyd's Maritime Academy, EU Competition Law in Shipping, London, 26 March 2009.

lawfully?; what about prices, forecasts and trading patterns?; what are the guidelines on information exchange?; and what is the CJEU, the General Court and the Commission saying about the law on information exchange?

What is information exchange?

12.084 Information exchange is, at its simplest, the communication of fact, fiction or opinion between different parties. It is noteworthy that the law on information exchange applies even when mere opinions are exchanged or even when deliberately misleading information is exchanged; it is not just the exchange of hard or accurate data or facts which trigger the application of the rules.

12.085 The Commission has defined an "information exchange system" in the Commission's "Guidelines on the Application of Article 81 of the EC Treaty to Maritime Transport Services" as entailing

> "an arrangement on the basis of which undertakings exchange information amongst themselves or supply it to a common agency responsible for centralizing, compiling and processing it before returning it to the participants in the form and at the frequency agreed".

Therefore it is not just "direct" information exchange between competitors which is subject to the rules, it is also "indirect" information exchange which occurs through the medium of, for example, trade associations, publications and market research agencies which can be subject to scrutiny.

12.086 It is useful to consider the issue of information exchange in its own right. Obviously, the exchange of information can form part of a wider anti-competitive arrangement (e.g. a cartel)[168] but this section of this chapter considers the issue of pure information exchange in its own right. This chapter also considers information exchange between undertakings rather than information exchange between competition authorities which is an entirely different topic.

12.087 The topic of information exchange is described in some jurisdictions as the "dissemination of information among competitors" or "data dissemination". The exact label does not matter in the legal analysis.

Nature of the law on information exchange

12.088 The law on information exchange is one of the most difficult and opaque areas of all of competition law. It is difficult to discern the law because each case turns on its own facts. The rules are also vague and information exchange often arises in the context of other issues (e.g. cartels). As paragraph 45 of the Guidelines states: "the actual or potential effects of an information exchange must be considered on a case-by-case basis as the results of the assessment depend on a combination of factors, each specific to an individual case". It is opaque because the rules, laid down either in case law or in the

---

168 E.g. if competitors hear that others are able to charge a higher price then prices would tend to drift upwards towards the "norm". The converse is less likely to occur because competitors would lose profit without the competitive incentive to do so. Irrespective of price, if detailed information is exchanged then market participants can see each other's positions and strategies with the result that they can adjust their behaviour accordingly.

policy statements of the EU institutions have been, by necessity, vague. Despite the twin challenge of difficulty and opaqueness, it is necessary to set out the law on the area as clearly as possible, recognising that there are shortcomings involved.

12.089 The law on this area is neither precise nor indeed extensive. In terms of the extent of the case law, there are relatively few cases on information exchange in EU competition law – a phenomenon which is reflected in US antitrust law as well. The development of the case law is entirely dependent on cases coming before either the Member State institutions or the EU institutions. There is case law from the CJEU and the General Court but it is somewhat general in nature. Those cases which are decided are highly fact-specific and somewhat sporadic so it is difficult to have a comprehensive understanding of the law on this area.

Topicality of the issue of information exchange

12.090 Information exchange is always topical. It is of great practical importance to businesses including those businesses in the shipping sector. This is because all businesses across all economic sectors share information to a greater or lesser extent with each other. Such exchanges occur through media or channels such as trade associations, employees, meetings between managers and other forms of interaction whether formal or informal and whether regular or sporadic. These exchanges often occur through necessity (e.g. two businesses co-operating on a particular project) or in the context of planning for acquisitions (e.g. due diligence of the target business) or joint ventures.

12.091 Despite the subject being always topical, the issue of information exchange is particularly topical at the moment in the shipping world given the abolition of the block exemption for liner conferences in Regulation 4056/86 and the call by some interested parties for an information exchange system to be put in place. The European Commission has responded to these calls by adopting on 1 July 2008, the Guidelines on various issues including the topic of information exchange. The Guidelines are a welcome addition to the knowledge on the area. They helped to consolidate or codify the Commission's thinking on this area but they were also limited in many respects because they did not – nor could they – answer all the questions which arise in practice or provide a finite set of precise tools with which to examine each possible situation. Section 3.2 of the Guidelines (i.e. paragraphs 38–59 inclusive) deal with the issue of information exchange. In particular, those paragraphs deal with information exchanges between competitors in liner shipping.

Situations where information exchange is an issue

12.092 It is useful to examine the situations in which the issue arises. Some examples help demonstrate where the issue arises and the legal problems which could flow.

12.093 The issue of information exchange is closely connected with the topic of trade associations because such associations are often the fora for the exchange of information between undertakings who are members of these associations. Indeed, officials of trade associations often encourage and facilitate the exchange of information between competitors through the use of surveys among members and then distributing the results (whether aggregated or disaggregated) among members.

12.094 Information exchange is also an issue of considerable practical importance in the context of mergers and acquisitions. Purchasers and sellers invariably exchange information; sometimes this exchange is necessary (e.g. for the purchaser to know what it is buying) and sometimes it is unnecessary but it nonetheless occurs (e.g. parties exchange information out of curiosity). Some participants in mergers and acquisitions do not give enough attention to the dangers of illegal exchanges of information in the context of these negotiations and the fact that such exchanges may be illegal in certain circumstances.

12.095 The importance of the topic of information exchange has grown significantly since the development of the internet and so-called "Business to Business" ("B2B") sites. Internet or email exchanges make the exchange of information so much easier by, for example, facilitating the collection, dissemination, storage, retrieval and interrogation of large amounts of information. The easy availability and exchange of information means that many businesses now have information on their systems of which many managers can be entirely unaware. The use of electronic communication also means that there is also a very reliable evidence chain demonstrating the exchange of information because the exchange is now so easy to prove.

12.096 Information exchange between undertakings (including exchanges among competitors) is also an issue in litigation. For example, if a number of competitors are suing or being sued then there may need to be some form of information exchange so as to allow them to litigate effectively. This raises the issue of so-called "joint defence agreements" or "joint plaintiff agreements". Typically, competitively sensitive information might be shared between the lawyers and other advisors (e.g. economists) in litigation but the competitively sensitive information would not be shared among the competing undertakings themselves.

Types of information exchange

12.097 Before analysing the law, it is also useful to classify, and distinguish between, different types of information exchange for the purposes of describing and discussing the phenomenon. However, from a legal perspective, the distinctions are of little significance because what matters most is whether there is the object or effect of preventing, restricting or distorting competition.

12.098 *Formal or informal exchanges.* Exchanges are organised on either a formal basis (such as the structured exchange of information within the confines of a trade association (e.g. a survey)) or on an informal basis (such as the ad hoc exchange of information between individual employees in different companies who meet (e.g. socially or at a conference) and exchange information about their employers' activities). Examples of formal exchanges would involve the exchange of information at meetings of trade associations or through surveys conducted by trade associations.

12.099 *Direct or indirect exchanges.* The exchange of information can be either direct (as in an exchange of information between competitors in a trade association) or indirect (as in the case of benchmarking through an intermediary). It is essentially irrelevant from a legal perspective whether the exchange is direct or indirect provided there is: (a) an anti-competitive arrangement; or (b) an abuse of dominance. An indirect exchange could be organised because of a desire to "cover tracks" but that would not assist or help in escaping liability where there is an anti-competitive arrangement or abuse of dominance.

A difficult issue arises where information is passed through an intermediary such as where a supplier passes information between retailers (e.g. a supplier tells retailer X that retailer Y will increase its retail price or, in the shipping context, a freight forwarder is told by carrier X that it will raise rates and the forwarder tells Carrier Y).

12.100 *Once-off or sustained exchanges.* Exchanges can be either once-off or sustained over time. Once-off exchanges occur when, for example, executives meet by chance at, for example, a trade show, a sports event or a social gathering. Sustained exchanges could occur, for example, where information is systematically exchanged on a regular basis such as in a trade association or industry forum.

12.101 *General or specific exchanges.* Exchanges of information can be part of either a wider arrangement or a specific arrangement in its own right. The Commission has written that

> "[t]he exchange of information may be a facilitating mechanism for the implementation of an anti-competitive practice, such as monitoring compliance with a cartel. Where an exchange of information is ancillary to an anti-competitive practice its assessment must be carried out in combination with an assessment of that practice."[169]

In this regard, managers in the shipping sector charged with competition compliance should be suspicious of colleagues possessing ongoing specific information about competitors which could have come from competitors.

12.102 *Merger-related exchanges and non-merger-related exchanges.* Some exchanges occur in the context of mergers. First, there is often an exchange of information during the negotiation of a merger or acquisition: the buyer needs to understand what it is buying and the seller is keen to advertise its asset to increase its price. Second, exchanges can occur in due diligence as well as the negotiation of representations and warranties. Third, it could occur when acquirers "jump the gun" and exchange information improperly (i.e. as if the business had lawfully become one). Gun-jumping can occur for various reasons including the enthusiasm of the merger parties, the desire or need to achieve efficiencies quickly, the need not to lose competitive advantage as well as frustration over the length of competition review by regulators.

12.103 The Guidelines deal with exchanges which are ancillary to anti-competitive behaviour and exchanges which are illegal in their own right. The Commission drew the following distinction in its Guidelines:

> "42. The exchange of information may be a facilitating mechanism for the implementation of an anti-competitive practice, such as monitoring compliance with a cartel; where an exchange of information is ancillary to such an anti-competitive practice its assessment must be carried out in combination with an assessment of that practice ..."[170]
>
> 43. However, an exchange of information, in its own right, might constitute an infringement of Article [101] of the [TFEU] by reason of its effect.[171] This situation arises when the information exchange reduces or removes the degree of uncertainty as to the operation of the market in question with the result that competition between undertakings is restricted. Every economic operator must determine autonomously the policy which it intends to pursue on the market. The [CJEU] further considered that undertakings are, therefore,

---

169 Guidelines on the application of Art. 81 of the EC Treaty to maritime transport services, OJ C245/2, 26 September 2008.
170 Ed., i.e. if it is ancillary to a cartel then it should be analysed in the context of the cartel.
171 Ed., it is notable that the Guidelines refer only to "effect" and not "object".

precluded from direct or indirect contacts with other operators which influence the conduct of a competitor or reveal their own (intended) conduct if the object or effect of those contacts is to restrict competition, i.e. to give rise to conditions of competition which do not correspond to the normal conditions of the market in question, taking into account the nature of the products or the services provided, the size and number of the undertakings and the volume of the market. By contrast, in the wood pulp market, the [CJEU] has found that unilateral quarterly price announcements made independently by producers to users constitute in themselves market behaviour which does not lessen each undertaking's uncertainty as to the future attitude of its competitors and hence, in the absence of any preliminary concerted practice between producers, do not constitute in themselves an infringement of Article [101(1)] of the Treaty."

12.104 In passing, it is notable that the comment by the Commission that the exchange of information constitutes a breach of Article 101 of the TFEU where it reduces or removes the degree of uncertainty as to the operation of the market in question with the result that competition between undertakings is restricted is central to the entire analysis. One might put it another way and say that the exchange of information which removes the element of "surprise" or uncertainty is more likely to be a breach of competition law. It is appreciated that this is somewhat circular because the definition requires that the exchange breaches competition law.

Competition law has to strike the right balance

12.105 The Commission has written that

"[i]t is common practice in many industries for aggregate statistics and general market information to be gathered, exchanged and published. This published market information is a good means to increase market transparency and customer knowledge, and thus may produce efficiencies. However, the exchange of commercially sensitive and individualised market data can, under certain circumstances, breach Article [101] of the Treaty."[172]

12.106 As the Commission identified, at paragraph 44 of the Guidelines, the dilemma which is caused by information exchange:

"The case law of the [EU] Courts provides some general guidance in examining the likely effects of an information exchange. The Court has found that where there is a truly competitive market, transparency is likely to lead to intensification of competition between suppliers. However, on a highly concentrated oligopolistic market, on which competition is already greatly reduced, exchanges of precise information on individual sales at short intervals between the main competitors, to the exclusion of other suppliers and of consumers, are likely to impair substantially the competition that exists between suppliers. In such circumstances, the sharing, on a regular and frequent basis, of information concerning the operation of the market has the effect of periodically revealing to all competitors the market positions and strategies of the various individual competitors. The Court has also found that an information exchange system may constitute a breach of the competition rules even when the market is not highly concentrated but there is a reduction of the undertakings' decision-making autonomy resulting from pressure during subsequent discussions with competitors."

12.107 The more concentrated the market then the more likely that exchanges would amount to an illegal exchange.

---

172 Maritime Guidelines, para.39.

12.108 While there are clear competition law concerns or dangers associated with information exchanges, it would be entirely wrong for competition law to prohibit all interaction between businesses because to do so would be to stifle commerce. Equally, it would be wrong to permit, without question, all exchanges because there are some exchanges which cause serious competition law problems. So competition law has to strike the balance between these two extremes.

12.109 In terms of striking that balance, it is useful to see the benefits of information exchange so it would be wrong to assume that all information exchange is problematical. The Commission recognises that it can be sometimes beneficial to have transparency in the market and competitors can adapt to the behaviour of others so as to "meet competition".

12.110 So, if there are benefits, what concerns could there be with information exchange? Unfortunately, there are real concerns. Competition law is concerned with the information exchange between undertakings which could distort competition rather than the disclosure of information as such. For example, it is anti-competitive for undertakings to exchange confidential pricing information privately between themselves but it is not anti-competitive for undertakings to submit such information to governmental or EU authorities or to publish it to the world.

12.111 A competitive market is one where rivals surprise each other with their actions; if there is such an exchange of information privately then the element of surprise has been removed from the market then it could well become an anti-competitive market. Competition law is concerned about the exchange of information in even the most informal of situations – such as the exchange of rates of commission by shipping brokers at a dinner party!

12.112 Competition law is concerned with the exchange of competitively sensitive information between competitors because the normal rivalry or competition which ought to exist between them is eliminated or potentially eliminated. As the Commission has recognised, an exchange of information may even have in itself the object of restricting competition.

12.113 Competition law is not concerned with the exchange of information as such but rather its actual or potential impact on competition. The difficulty is trying to distinguish between the pro-competitive exchange of information and the anti-competitive exchange of information. The distinction can be a fine one. It can also be difficult to draw the distinction. The legality of the exchange is not determined by the nature of the information because the same information could be either legitimate or illegitimate depending on the circumstances.

What are the EU rules, as set out in the guidelines, on information exchange?

Is there an anti-competitive arrangement or abuse of dominance?

12.114 EU competition law is not concerned with the exchange of information as such but it is most certainly concerned where the exchange is: (a) part of an anti-competitive arrangement among undertakings contrary to Article 101 of the TFEU; and/or (b) an abuse of dominance by an undertaking having a dominant position contrary to Article 102 of the TFEU. If the exchange of information has the object or effect of assisting in the implementation of an anti-competitive practice or abuse of dominance then such an exchange will be legal under EU competition law. How then does one analyse the situation? It is useful to ask a series of questions.

What is the structure of the market?

12.115 In reviewing information exchange arrangements, the Commission states that certain features should be assessed including the structural features of the market (e.g. the levels of concentration and the structure of supply and demand). The Guidelines are succinct on the issue of the structure of the market:

> "47. The level of concentration and the structure of supply and demand on a given market are key issues in considering whether an exchange falls within the scope of Article [101(1)] of the Treaty.
> 48. The level of concentration is particularly relevant since, on highly concentrated oligopolistic markets, restrictive effects are more likely to occur and are more likely to be sustainable than in less concentrated markets. Greater transparency in a concentrated market may strengthen the interdependence of firms and reduce the intensity of competition.
> 49. The structure of supply and demand is also important, notably the number of competing operators and the symmetry and stability of their market shares and the existence of any structural links between competitors. The Commission may also analyse other factors such as the homogeneity of services and the overall transparency in the market."

12.116 If the market is concentrated then an information exchange is more likely to strengthen the interdependence of undertakings in that market and the agreement is therefore more likely to breach Article 101.

What is the nature of the information being exchanged?

12.117 In reviewing the legality of an information exchange arrangement, the Commission states that certain features should be assessed including the nature of the information exchanged.

Exchange of commercially sensitive data

12.118 The exchange of commercially sensitive unpublished information would potentially raise competition difficulties. Examples of this type of information would include data relating to issues such as price, cost, capacity, plans, production, research and so on. Paragraph 50 of the Guidelines states that the

> "exchange of commercially sensitive data relating to the parameters of competition, such as price, capacity or costs, between competitors, is more likely to be caught by Article [101](1) of the Treaty than other exchanges of information. The commercial sensitivity of information should be assessed taking into account the criteria set out [in the Guidelines]."

Exchange of public and unpublished information

12.119 The exchange of already published or publicly available information usually causes no difficulty under Article 101. This is because the exchange does not reduce the level of uncertainty in the market. If there is an exchange which reduces the level of uncertainty in the market then that would be more likely to infringe Article 101 of the TFEU because it reduces the rivalry or level of competition between the undertakings involved in the exchange. Paragraph 51 of the Guidelines states that the

> "exchange of information already in the public domain does not in principle constitute an infringement of Article [101(1)] of the [TFEU]. However, it is important to establish the level of transparency of the market and whether the exchange enhances information by making it more accessible and/or combines publicly available information with other information. The resulting information may become commercially sensitive and its exchange potentially restrictive of competition."

12.120 There can still be a breach of Article 101 where the information is false, inaccurate or even misleading. The information does not have to be precise for there to be a breach of Article 101.

12.121 Examples of the type of competitively sensitive information which could cause competition difficulties when exchanged include information on: costs; details of bids or tenders; discount history; pricing; stock levels; future plans; and advertising and marketing plans.

Aggregated and disaggregated data

12.122 The exchange of individualised (as opposed to aggregate) information is more likely to be in breach of Article 101 than the exchange of aggregate information provided the information is not capable of being easily disaggregated (e.g. the market shares of a small number of competitors or a market where the shares of individual competitors would be easily discernible). Paragraph 52 of the Guidelines states:

> "Information may be individual or aggregated. Individual data relates to a designated or identifiable undertaking. Aggregate data combines the data from a sufficient number of independent undertakings so that the recognition of individual data is impossible. The exchange of individual information between competitors is more likely to be caught by Article [101(1)] of the Treaty than the exchange of aggregated information which, in principle, does not fall within Article [101(1)] of the Treaty. The Commission will pay particular attention to the level of aggregation. It should be such that the information cannot be disaggregated so as to allow undertakings directly or indirectly to identify the competitive strategies of their competitors."

12.123 What is the position of aggregate and disaggregated data in the context of liner conferences? Paragraph 53 of the Guidelines states:

> "However, in liner shipping caution should be used when assessing exchanges of capacity forecasts even in aggregate form, especially when they take place in concentrated markets. In liner markets, capacity data is the key parameter to coordinate competitive conduct and it has a direct effect on prices. Exchanges of aggregated capacity forecasts indicating in which trades capacity will be deployed may be anticompetitive to the extent that they may lead to the adoption of a common policy by several or all carriers and result in the provision of services at above competitive prices. Additionally, there is a risk of disaggregation of the data as it can be combined with individual announcements by liner carriers. This would enable undertakings to identify the market positions and strategies of competitors."

Age of the data

12.124 The exchange of historical information is generally not regarded as breaching Article 101. The difficulty is in deciding what is "historical". A rule of thumb is that information which is more than a year old is generally seen as historical but the accuracy of this approach depends entirely on the industry and the circumstances involved. In slower moving markets, the exchange of older information is more troubling than it would be in fast moving markets. The exchange of "future information" is particularly problematical. So, information about future price or production changes could be easily problematical in the context of Article 101.

12.125 Paragraph 54 of the Guidelines states:

"The age of the data and the period to which it relates are also important factors. Data can be historic, recent or future. Exchange of historic information is generally not regarded as falling within Article [101(1)] of the Treaty because it cannot have any real impact on the undertakings' future behaviour. In past cases, the Commission has considered information which was more than one year old as historic whereas information less than one year old has been viewed as recent. The historic or recent nature of the information should be assessed with some flexibility taking into account the extent to which data becomes obsolete in the relevant market. The time when the data becomes historic is likely to be shorter if the data is aggregated rather than individual. Exchanges of recent data on volume and capacity are similarly unlikely to be restrictive of competition if the data is aggregated to an appropriate level such that individual shippers' or carriers' transactions cannot be identified either directly or indirectly. Future data relates to an undertaking's view of how the market will develop or to the strategy it intends to follow in that market. The exchange of future data is particularly likely to be problematic, especially when it relates to prices or output. It may reveal the commercial strategy an undertaking intends to adopt in the market. In so doing, it may appreciably reduce rivalry between the parties to the exchange and is thus potentially restrictive of competition."[173]

---

173 It is interesting to read the comment by Professor Haralambides on the draft of this paragraph:

"Draft Guidelines on the Application of Article 81 of the Treaty to the Maritime Sector: A comment on the suggested amendments by the ELAA.

In the context of its response to the European Commission's Draft Guidelines, ELAA has asked me to comment on its suggestion to rephrase the 4th sentence of Paragraph 53 as follows: '...The historic or recent nature of the information should be assessed with some flexibility taking into account the fact that liner shipping data becomes obsolete relatively quickly...'. As I understand, ELAA also suggests that the Commission insert an illustrative example of how data (at various levels of aggregation) becomes historic. I see the merit of both suggestions, believing that – besides economically to the point – they can be constructive, and thus appropriate, in terms of helping industry participants understand better the meaning of 'historic' data in the context of EC competition law. This, in my view, is the best way of avoiding possible future disputes.

The Commission starts from the correct premise that 'recent' volume data, when sufficiently aggregated, is not restrictive of competition, and that the more aggregated information is, the faster it becomes 'historic' and thus can be released without infringement of Article [101] of the Treaty.

As a result of its nature – consumed as soon as it is produced – the shipping service is 'perishable' and volume/capacity data which, incidentally, are much less sensitive than 'price' data, become 'historic' much sooner than those of other goods or services. In this context, the ELAA position that disaggregated six-month-old data can be released without an effect on competition stands to reason. By that time, such data has lost its commercially sensitive value but can still be used for more efficient – individually and competitively – adjustment of shipping supply to demand developments.

The period of data release could as a matter of fact be shorter, say four months, as long as individual carriers are not identified. Obviously, no data should be exchanged that allows the identification of shipper information.

Liner carriers in principle deal with three broad categories of customers: Spot market customers; freight forwarders; and direct accounts. None of the pricing negotiations with such customers can be affected by

Frequency of the exchanges

12.126 If information is exchanged frequently then it is more likely that there would be a difficulty under Article 101. If the information is exchanged on several occasions and there is only a relatively short gap between the exchanges then that is more likely to raise an issue because the uncertainty or unpredictability which would otherwise exist has been removed or reduced. Paragraph 55 of the Guidelines states:

> "[t]he frequency of the exchange should also be considered. The more frequently the data is exchanged, the more swiftly competitors can react. This facilitates retaliation and ultimately lowers the incentives to initiate competitive actions on the market. So-called hidden competition could be restricted."

Manner of the exchange

12.127 The manner of the exchange can be important. As the Guidelines state in paragraph 56 of the Guidelines:

> "How data is released should also be looked into to assess the effect(s) it may have on the market(s). The more the information is shared with customers, the less likely it is to be problematic. Conversely, if market transparency is improved for the benefit of suppliers only, it may deprive customers of the possibility of getting the advantage of increased 'hidden competition'."

---

the envisaged information exchange in any way other than by making both shipper and carrier better informed of the actual market situation. The effect on competition, in other words, will be, actually, a more efficient market.

In the case of spot customers and freight forwarders, information becomes historic much sooner, apparently, with relevant time periods ranging from two weeks to two months respectively; i.e. much sooner than the expected data release periods.

For direct accounts, the situation is different and one could construe the argument in theory that information exchange is to be used either as a collusive benchmark or as a means of detecting deviation from a collusive scheme; neither argument, however, is plausible in the realities of liner shipping.

Contracts with direct accounts are bilaterally and independently negotiated on a yearly basis by means of competitive tendering. In such a context, it is hard to envisage adherence to a collusive benchmark, even if one were able to realistically assume the existence of collusive practices following the demise of conferences.

The use by carriers of six-month-old volume/capacity data to detect deviation from a collusive practice is also a far cry and an implausible assumption. Even if this was possible, in the absence of a policing mechanism, deviation would go unpunished and it would only be a matter of time before other carriers could adjust their prices downwards too. Tendering ensures this.

To my view, therefore, the proposed exchange of information can in no way influence pricing decisions or sustain collusive practices. Its value is in the ability of carriers to better adjust medium to long-term supply to demand developments, thus avoiding socially wasteful overinvestment which, in view of the structure of liner shipping, is a great and latent threat to the industry.

As I have repeatedly argued in the literature, ... including the Erasmus Report, prepared for the European Commission, liner shipping is a high fixed – low marginal cost industry prone to destructive competition. In the absence of national industrial polices, conferences had in the past provided a low cost self-regulatory mechanism ensuring sustainability in the long run. As with all systems, there were admittedly shortcomings that have led to the demise of the conference system.

The current system of 'timely' information exchange, and the ensuing better capacity planning, appears, indeed, to be a much better one, as this leads to transparency and economic and technical efficiency similar to this achieved through alliances, if not better: Here, carriers are able to adjust capacity individually (on the basis of information available to them) and not collectively.

The Commission prudently accepts the foundation of this efficiencies argument. Indeed, overcapacity will have to be paid for by the consumer itself at some point in time."

A great deal therefore turns on to whom the information is released. If the information is released to customers then it is less likely that there would be a competition issue. If information is released to suppliers only then it is more likely that there would be a competition issue. It is clear that there is no defence or immunity to be derived from the information being exchanged through an agency or other third party.

Price indexes

12.128 If a price index is exchanged then it would be unlikely to breach Article 101 where the information was sufficiently aggregated that there could be no distortion of competition to the exchange. However, if the uncertainty which would ordinarily surround future conduct was to be reduced by reason of the index then the dissemination of such an index would ordinarily breach Article 101. Paragraphs 57–58 of the Guidelines deal with the issue in some depth:

> "57. In liner shipping, price indexes are used to show average price movements for the transport of a sea container. A price index based on appropriately aggregated price data is unlikely to infringe Article [101(1)] of the Treaty, provided that the level of aggregation is such that the information cannot be disaggregated so as to allow undertakings directly or indirectly to identify the competitive strategies of their competitors. If a price index reduces or removes the degree of uncertainty as to the operation of the market with the result that competition between undertakings is restricted, it would violate Article [101(1)] of the Treaty. In assessing the likely effect of such a price index on a given relevant market, account should be given to the level of aggregation of the data and its historical or recent nature and the frequency at which the index is published. In general it is important to assess all individual elements of any information exchange scheme together, in order to take account of potential interactions, for example between exchange of capacity and volume data on the one hand and of a price index on the other.
>
> 58. An exchange of information between carriers that restricts competition may nonetheless create efficiencies, such as better planning of investments and more efficient use of capacity. Such efficiencies will have to be substantiated and passed on to customers and weighed against the anti-competitive effects of the information exchange in the framework of Article [101(3)] of the Treaty. In this context, it is important to note that one of the conditions of Article [101(3)] is that consumers should receive a fair share of the benefits generated by the restrictive agreement. If all four cumulative conditions set out in Article [101(3)] are fulfilled, the prohibition of Article [101(1)] does not apply."

12.129 What would be the change in the level of competition in the absence of the information exchange? In considering the competitive impact of the information exchange, it is necessary to consider the actual or potential effects of the information exchange compared to the competitive situation that would result in the absence of the information exchange agreement. To fall within the scope of Article 101(1) of the TFEU, the exchange must have an appreciable adverse impact on the parameters of competition.

Exchange of information in the context of liner conferences

12.130 The ELAA submitted to the Commission a paper on suggesting that the block exemption be replaced by an information exchange system. The ESC believed that such a system was unnecessary because sufficient co-operation was possible under the consortia block exemption. The Commission considered some aspects of the ELAA's proposals problematical under competition law.

12.131 The Guidelines deal specifically with the issue of information exchange in the context of liner conferences:

> "53. ... in liner shipping caution should be used when assessing exchanges of capacity forecasts even in aggregate form, especially when they take place in concentrated markets. In liner markets, capacity data is the key parameter to coordinate competitive conduct and it has a direct effect on prices. Exchanges of aggregated capacity forecasts indicating in which trades capacity will be deployed may be anticompetitive to the extent that they may lead to the adoption of a common policy by several or all carriers and result in the provision of services at above competitive prices. Additionally, there is a risk of disaggregation of the data as it can be combined with individual announcements by liner carriers. This would enable undertakings to identify the market positions and strategies of competitors.
>
> 54. The age of the data and the period to which it relates are also important factors. Data can be historic, recent or future. Exchange of historic information is generally not regarded as falling within Article [101(1)] of the Treaty because it cannot have any real impact on the undertakings' future behaviour. In past cases, the Commission has considered information which was more than one year old as historic whereas information less than one year old has been viewed as recent. The historic or recent nature of the information should be assessed with some flexibility taking into account the extent to which data becomes obsolete in the relevant market. The time when the data becomes historic is likely to be shorter if the data is aggregated rather than individual. Exchanges of recent data on volume and capacity are similarly unlikely to be restrictive of competition if the data is aggregated to an appropriate level such that individual shippers' or carriers' transactions cannot be identified either directly or indirectly. Future data relates to an undertaking's view of how the market will develop or to the strategy it intends to follow in that market. The exchange of future data is particularly likely to be problematic, especially when it relates to prices or output. It may reveal the commercial strategy an undertaking intends to adopt in the market. In so doing, it may appreciably reduce rivalry between the parties to the exchange and is thus potentially restrictive of competition."

12.132 The position of trade associations is also dealt with in paragraph 59 of the Guidelines:

> "In liner shipping, as in any other sector, discussions and exchanges of information can take place in a trade association provided the association is not used as (a) a forum for cartel meetings; (b) a structure that issues anti-competitive decisions or recommendations to its members; or (c) a means of exchanging information that reduces or removes the degree of uncertainty as to the operation of the market with the result that competition between undertakings is restricted while not fulfilling the Article [101(3)] conditions. This should be distinguished from the discussions that are legitimately conducted within trade associations, for example on technical and environmental standards."

Holmes has observed:

> "It is curious that it is only under the liner section that the Commission points out that an exchange of information 'may even have in itself the object of restricting competition'. Perhaps this is based on [the] container/liner market being more concentrated than the tramp market. Or perhaps it is just that the Commission is being more sensitive to liner information exchange, given the long period of time that liner shipping has been allowed to exchange substantial information which would be unacceptable in other sectors. Perhaps because of the unusual situation of lines having to produce their own new tariffs at around the same time, concerns over signalling are a particular issue for carriers. The Guidelines offer comfort in drawing attention to the fact that unilateral price announcements, made independently by producers in the wood pulp

market, did not breach Article [101](1). Guidance on information exchange and aggregation stresses that capacity data is a key parameter to co-ordinate competitive conduct, so, along with price, it is very sensitive requiring the data to be both historical and aggregated. The new trade body, ELAA (European Liner Affairs Association), has been set up by the container industry offering information services such as demand and supply forecasting, based closely on the allowed exchange as set out in the detail in the Guidelines."[174]

Exchange of information in the context of liner consortia

12.133 The Commission makes plain in paragraph 40 of its Guidelines that

"the liner shipping sector, exchanges of information between shipping lines taking part in liner consortia which would otherwise fall under Article [101(1)] of the Treaty are permitted to the extent that they are ancillary to the joint operation of liner transport services and the other forms of cooperation covered by the block exemption and Regulation (EC) No. 823/2000."

The Guidelines explicitly state at paragraph 40 that they do not deal with these information exchanges in the context of liner consortia.

Concluding remarks and observations

12.134 The Commission recognises in its Guidelines that it is "common practice in many industries for aggregate statistics and general market information to be gathered, exchanged and published". However, notwithstanding that it may be a common practice, EU competition law does not permit it simply because it is a common practice.

12.135 The exchange of information is recognised as a good means to increase market transparency and customer knowledge, and thus may produce efficiencies. Notwithstanding this apparent and benign view of the exchange of information, EU competition law is very suspicious of the exchange of information and, therefore, the guidelines state that the exchange of commercially sensitive and individualised market data can, under certain circumstances, breach Article 101 of the TFEU.

12.136 May the guidelines be relied upon or used by those outside the liner conference arena? The Guidelines may certainly be used by undertakings outside the liner shipping sector but they probably cannot be relied upon by such "outsiders".

12.137 How much use are the Guidelines to assisting undertakings in regard to the exchange of information? The guidelines are useful in that, before those Guidelines, one had to piece together the law on the area from the various cases and these guidelines are "intended to assist the providers of liner shipping services in assessing when such exchanges breach the competition rules". However, the challenge will lie in their application over time and in circumstances not contemplated by the Guidelines.

12.138 Paragraph 51 outlines the type of information which may be exchanged which would not ordinarily cause competition difficulties. The paragraph states:

"The exchange of information already in the public domain does not in principle constitute an infringement of Article [101(1)] of the Treaty.[175] However, it is important to establish the level of transparency of the market and whether the exchange enhances information by making it more

---

174 "Maritime Transport: A Look at the New Commission Guidelines", *Competition Law Insight*, 21 October 2008.
175 TACA judgment, cited above in footnote 20, paragraph 1154.

accessible and/or combines publicly available information with other information. The resulting information may become commercially sensitive and its exchange potentially restrictive of competition."

This paragraph restates the law in that the exchange of publicly available information should not cause difficulties in certain circumstances. It is not enough to state that the information is in the public domain, there must be more conditions satisfied. Put another way, the exchange of publicly available information must not be the means by which an anti-competitive arrangement is brought about.

12.139 What if the information exchanged is aggregated? Paragraph 52 of the Guidelines states:

"Information may be individual or aggregated. Individual data relates to a designated or identifiable undertaking. Aggregate data combines the data from a sufficient number of independent undertakings so that the recognition of individual data is impossible. The exchange of individual information between competitors is more likely to be caught by Article [101](1) of the Treaty[176] than the exchange of aggregated information which, in principle, does not fall within Article [101](1) of the Treaty. The Commission will pay particular attention to the level of aggregation. It should be such that the information cannot be disaggregated so as to allow undertakings directly or indirectly to identify the competitive strategies of their competitors."

12.140 Paragraph 55 is very succinct:

"The frequency of the exchange should also be considered. The more frequently the data is exchanged, the more swiftly competitors can react. This facilitates retaliation and ultimately lowers the incentives to initiate competitive actions on the market. So-called hidden competition could be restricted."

12.141 How data is released should also be looked into to assess the effect(s) it may have on the market(s). The more the information is shared with customers, the less likely it is to be problematic. Conversely, if market transparency is improved for the benefit of suppliers only, it may deprive customers of the possibility of getting the advantage of increased "hidden competition".

12.142 Paragraph 57 states:

"In liner shipping, price indexes are used to show average price movements for the transport of a sea container. A price index based on appropriately aggregated price data is unlikely to infringe Article [101(1)] of the Treaty, provided that the level of aggregation is such that the information cannot be disaggregated so as to allow undertakings directly or indirectly to identify the competitive strategies of their competitors. If a price index reduces or removes the degree of uncertainty as to the operation of the market with the result that competition between undertakings is restricted, it would violate Article [101(1)] of the Treaty. In assessing the likely effect of such a price index on a given relevant market, account should be given to the level of aggregation of the data and its historical or recent nature and the frequency at which the index is published. In general it is important to assess all individual elements of any information exchange scheme together, in order to take account of potential interactions, for example between exchange of capacity and volume data on the one hand and of a price index on the other."

This is a somewhat pure view of competition law.

---

176 Commission Decision 78/252/EEC of 23 December 1977 in Case IV/29.176 – *Vegetable Parchment* (OJ L70, 13.3.1978, p. 54).

I. SHIPPING POOLS

12.143 What is the position, in terms of competition law, of pools in this new regime?[177] Pools are horizontal, rather than vertical, arrangements (i.e. they involve relationships between actual or potential competitors in the economic chain) and are therefore more likely to raise competition issues than vertical arrangements. Nonetheless, despite being arrangements between competitors, pools are not unlawful as such but where they breach Article 101(1) of the TFEU then they must meet the criteria set out in Article 101(3) of the TFEU otherwise the arrangements would be void under Article 101(2) of the TFEU and the undertakings involved exposed to the penalties under EU competition law. In certain circumstances, there could also be a breach of Article 102 of the TFEU provided the circumstances for that provision's application are met. Helpfully, the Maritime Guidelines give some guidance on the issue of the application of Article 101. The Commission's Guidelines were more favourable to pools than many may have suspected.

12.144 Before examining the competition law aspects, it is useful to examine briefly the commercial background to shipping pools. There are various types of pools and therefore each case should be assessed on its own merits. A standard pool involves a number of vessels being brought together under a single administration with joint selling. The pools are responsible for various aspects of shipping including chartering, scheduling, operating, bunkering, marketing, demurrage and risk management aspects of the operations. Typically, similar ships are included in each pool. The shipping service is typically provided by the individual shipowners and their crews. Proponents of pooling would argue that the pools "market" is a very efficient, transparent and competitive one and that it is a bidding market with the shipowners being price takers. They would claim that there are efficiencies to be gained from the way in which pools operate with improved ballast, fewer days in port or lying idle, increased safety standards, greater fuel efficiency, increased utilisation, reduced costs and, indeed, the sharing of costs generally. Moreover, pools enable shipowners to bid for contracts of affreightment which individually they could not service (that is to say, the combined offering of several shipowners in the pool "opens doors" which would not otherwise be open).

12.145 The Commission's Horizontal Co-operation Guidelines would also be relevant in the case of some pools. However, if a pool is a full-function joint venture operating on a lasting basis then the creation of the pool would be reviewable under the Merger Control Regulation.[178] However, the position of pools is not always so clear cut. Some pools may fall outside the scope of Article 101 altogether – for example, where they have no appreciable or actual effect on trade between Member

---

177 See Majumdar, "An Economist's Perspective on Self Assessment for Shipping Pools", Lloyd's Maritime Academy, EU Competition Law in Shipping, London, 26 March 2009; and Wareham, "Tramp Shipping and Pooling Agreements", Lloyd's Maritime Academy, EU Competition Law in Shipping, London, 26 March 2009.
178 Being reviewable under the Merger Control Regulation has the attraction of legal certainty and predictability in that the agreement is notified to the Commission and if approved then the parties do not have to rely on self-assessment.

States.¹⁷⁹ A pool whose impact on competition would be *de minimis* would also fall outside the scope of Article 101. The final version of the Guidelines omits a sentence which was contained in the draft guidelines that pools involving competing companies that are not able to provide the services covered by the pool agreement separately are unlikely to breach Article 101(1) but the principle is probably correct in that arrangements between non-competitors typically do not raise competition concerns. Ultimately, each pool has to be examined on its own individual merits. If pool members are not actual or potential competitors then there is very unlikely to be any competition issue. If pool members have very small market shares (i.e. little market power) then it is unlikely that there would be serious competition issues unless the parties engaged in the more egregious competition law breaches such as price-fixing or market sharing. If there is a pool which involves a breach of Article 101(1) then one would seek to examine the possible application of Article 101(3) of the TFEU to the arrangement to see whether the arrangement could be permitted.

12.146 Some types of pools definitely fall within the scope of Article 101(1). These are pools where the competitors have the object or effect of restricting competition by means of price-fixing by joint selling. In terms of determining whether there is a breach of Article 101, each case has to be assessed on its merits to see if there is an arrangement between undertakings which has the object or effect of preventing, restricting or distorting competition. One has to self-assess each of the elements:

(a) Is the agreement capable of being classified as a pooling agreement?
(b) Are the participants undertakings?
(c) If there is no object to prevent, restrict or distort competition then the effect must be examined and that requires a market assessment of the effects. The market must be assessed in terms of the product, geographical and temporal dimensions.
(d) If there is no object to prevent, restrict or distort competition and one is examining the effects of the arrangement then there would have to be an appreciable effect on competition.[180]
(e) If there is a possible breach of Article 101(1) of the TFEU then would the criteria set out in Article 101(3) of the TFEU apply to exempt it?[181]

As mentioned, each case (i.e. each pool) must be examined on its own merits and context.[182] The "centre of gravity" test is applied[183] which means that the centre of gravity

---

179 The Commission has stated in its *De Minimis* Notice that arrangements involving competitors where the combined market share is less than 10% do not typically raise concerns under Art. 101(1) of the TFEU: "7. The Commission holds the view that agreements between undertakings which affect trade between Member States do not appreciably restrict competition within the meaning of Article [101(1)]: (a) if the aggregate market share held by the parties to the agreement does not exceed 10 % on any of the relevant markets affected by the agreement, where the agreement is made between undertakings which are actual or potential competitors on any of these markets (agreements between competitors)" (Commission Notice on agreements of minor importance which do not appreciably restrict competition under Article [101(1)] of the [TFEU] (*de minimis*) (OJ 2001C 368/07)). This principle does not always apply (e.g. where there is price-fixing) (see para.11 of the Commission Notice).
180 Case 374/94 *European Night Services* [1998] ECR II-3141 and Case T-112/99 *Metropole TV* [2001] ECR II-2458.
181 If the criteria under Art. 101(3) of the TFEU will not help then it may be necessary to amend some of the terms of the agreement but that may not be enough to escape the sanction of Art. 101(1).
182 Maritime Guidelines, para. 62.
183 Maritime Guidelines, para. 62.

of each pool must be assessed to see if there is a breach of Article 101(1) – this involves assessing the legal structure and economic context of the pool. The nature of the agreement should be examined to consider the structure of the pool, the authority of the pool manager and the contract profile. One should consider the market definition,[184] the level of market shares,[185] the level of market concentration,[186] barriers to entry, barriers to exit, countervailing buyer power, whether parties are members of several pools, whether there are non-compete clauses, lock-in periods and their duration, notice periods to exit, market trends, the type and level of information exchanged and any other relevant factor.

12.147 The consortia and specialisation block exemptions tend to be of little use in the present context because of the nature of pools but they could be in certain circumstances.

12.148 Joint selling is a key feature of shipping pools. There is also an element of joint production. Joint selling, being a variation of joint commercialisation, is deemed to be prohibited by Article 101(1) except in the framework of a joint production venture.

12.149 Holmes has commented on pools in the context of the Guidelines:

"On the tramp side, shipping pools are the main focus [of the Guidelines]. The Guidelines cover how to define the market by product (the ship and the cargo carried), and geographically.

With regard to product, the following are relevant: vessel size; vessel type; special features of the vessel, such as the requirement for double hulls; and the cargo carried.

As regards the geographic dimension, many tramp owners view the world as their markets, but the Guidelines make clear that a more refined market analysis is necessary. Looking at loading and discharge ports, as well as single directional markets, is recommended.

Other suggested data to look at when calculating annual market shares are: (1) the number of voyages; (2) the parties' volume or value share in the overall transport of a specific cargo (between port pairs or port ranges); (3) the parties' share in the market for time charter contracts; and (4) the parties' capacity shares in the relevant fleet (by vessel type and size).

This is interesting and in contrast to the consortia block exemption (823/2000, as amended), which provides that international liner companies should calculate market share by 'reference to the volume of goods carried (freight tonnes or 20 foot equivalent units)' (see article 6 of Regulation 823/2000, as amended by 611/2008)."[187]

---

184 This is often critical because so much flows from it. The main purpose of market definition is to identify in a systematic way the competitive constraints faced by an undertaking (Maritime Guidelines, para. 16).

185 Market shares can be interesting but rarely conclusive in their own right: a high market share may indicate a lack of competition but it is not conclusive because it could be transient. However, the Maritime Guidelines state at para. 70: "if the pool has a low market share, it is unlikely to produce restrictive effects".

186 This is typically done by undertaking a so-called Herfindahl-Hirschman Index ("HHI") analysis which involves measuring the market shares of the parties in percentage terms, squaring each of the results (e.g. a 3% market share becomes "9"), adding the square numbers and then establishing the level of concentration by reference to the total score. The USA's Department of Justice has stated: "'HHI' means the Herfindahl-Hirschman Index, a commonly accepted measure of market concentration. It is calculated by squaring the market share of each firm competing in the market and then summing the resulting numbers. For example, for a market consisting of four firms with shares of thirty, thirty, twenty and twenty percent, the HHI is 2600 (302+302+202+202=2600). The HHI takes into account the relative size and distribution of the firms in a market and approaches zero when a market consists of a large number of firms of relatively equal size. The HHI increases both as the number of firms in the market decreases and as the disparity in size between those firms increases. Markets in which the HHI is between 1000 and 1800 points are considered to be moderately concentrated, and those in which the HHI is in excess of 1800 points are considered to be concentrated. Transactions that increase the HHI by more than 100 points in concentrated markets presumptively raise antitrust concerns under the Horizontal Merger Guidelines issued by the U.S. Department of Justice and the Federal Trade Commission" (www.justice.gov/atr/public/testimony/hhi.htm).

187 *Competition Law Insight*, 21 October 2008, p. 10.

12.150 The Guidelines gave some guidance in regard to pools. The Guidelines generally gave the impression that the Commission was more disposed towards smaller pools than larger ones. The Guidelines took the view that tramp pools can be pro-competitive where, if the criteria laid down in Article 101(3) of the TFEU can be met, they lead to efficiency gains in terms of better utilisation and economies of scale (e.g. efficiency by reducing the number of empty/ballast voyages, enable contracts to be bid for by a combination of operators who could not bid individually because they were too small and spreading the vessels geographically. This guidance in the Guidelines was criticised by some as being too vague and limited. However, there is another side to the argument – as Olivier Guersent, the then Acting Director for Transport, Post and other Services at DG COMP stated at the EMLO meeting in Copenhagen on 24 October 2008:

> "Turning to the alleged lack of detail in the section dealing with tramp pools, there are also several reasons for the relative brevity of that section in the Guidelines. First, guidelines usually build on the Commission's accumulated experience in a particular sector or with a particular issue. Since the Commission has almost no practical experience in this sector, there is no case-law to describe and interpret. As many of you know, the tramp sector only came within the scope of the Commission's full investigation and enforcement powers in 2006. Therefore, the section on pools is necessarily shorter.
>
> Second, we believe that many questions regarding tramp shipping pools are not novel. This does not mean that the replies are easy. But clearly the issues at stake have been considered previously and there is guidance issued by the Commission that is of direct relevance to assess these agreements. I refer in particular to the Horizontal Guidelines and to the Guidelines on Article [101(3)]. The Maritime Guidelines do not replace and do not deviate from these other guidelines.
>
> Third, the 'categorisation' of a pool agreement as 'joint production' or 'joint selling' is highly case-specific, and therefore there was no reason to elaborate more on this in the Guidelines. As you know, the centre of gravity test determines whether a particular agreement is closer to joint production or closer to joint selling. This centre of gravity analysis will depend in particular on the degree of integration that is brought about by the agreement.
>
> Fourth, it may be that in the future the Commission will acquire experience from actual cases, which will also provide more guidance to the industry. But I want to assure you that the Commission is not going to go after pool agreements for its own sake. There is no ideological bias against pools. We are not making threats. All we do is to apply the competition rules that already apply to all other sectors. We understand from our market investigation and from the comments received during the consultation that
>
> - many pools bring together non-competitors;
> - many pools are small;
> - and pools often bring benefits to their customers.
>
> I also want to remind you that the Commission will be open to the possibility of finding countervailing efficiencies under Article [101(3)]. It is possible that a pool agreement with joint selling will be redeemed by its efficiencies. Of course it is up to the pool members to show the Commission that the pool produces economies of scale and scope that are passed on to customers in the form of lower prices than would otherwise be the case.
>
> One recurrent comment from the industry on this point is that the Guidelines should contain more guidance on Article [101(3)]. The final version of the Guidelines expanded a bit on Article [101(3)] compared to the draft version of September 2007. But it is a fact that that section is still fairly short. The Commission's view was simply that a more detailed notice is already devoted to that question, which therefore did not deserve any specific treatment.
>
> Finally, I also want to warn the industry that in an antitrust assessment, non-compete clauses, lock-in periods and exit clauses may well attract a particular interest from competition enforcement authorities. For example, it may be that a pool member feels that he could operate his

vessels more efficiently outside the pool. Pool members constantly benchmark their earnings via the pool versus their potential earnings on their own. So let's say a member wants to leave the pool or he wants a more limited non-compete clause. Between competitors, an unduly restrictive exit clause or non-compete clause may be anti-competitive. For example, in the consortia block exemption, it is stated that the members must be able to leave the consortium without penalty and with a maximum six-month notice period. The same reasoning could be applied by analogy to tramp pools, with some possible adjustments."

12.151 The difficulty then arises in respect of pools which may fall within the scope of Article 101(1). If the object of the pool agreement is not anti-competitive then its effects should be examined. A pool agreement which appreciably reduces rivalry between the parties in any way, or between the parties and third parties, may be prohibited by Article 101(1). The Guidelines state:

"67. If the pool does not have as its object a restriction of competition, an analysis of its effects in the market concerned is necessary. An agreement is caught by Article [101(1)] of the Treaty when it is likely to have an appreciable adverse impact on the parameters of competition on the market such as prices, costs, service differentiation, service quality, and innovation. Agreements can have this effect by appreciably reducing rivalry between the parties to the agreement or between them and third parties.

68. Some tramp shipping pools do not involve joint selling but nevertheless entail some degree of coordination on the parameters of competition (e.g. joint scheduling or joint purchasing). Such cases are only subject to Article [101(1)] of the Treaty if the parties to the agreement have some degree of market power.

69. The pool's ability to cause appreciable negative market effects depends on the economic context, taking into account the parties' combined market power and the nature of the agreement together with other structural factors in the relevant market. It must also be considered whether the pool agreement affects the behaviour of the parties in neighbouring markets closely related to the market directly affected by the cooperation. This may be the case for example where the pool's market is that for the transport of forest products in specialised box shaped vessels (market A) and the pool's members also operate ships in the dry bulk market (market B).

70. Concerning the structural factors in the relevant market, if the pool has a low market share, it is unlikely to produce restrictive effects. Market concentration, the position and number of competitors, the stability of market shares over time, multi-membership in pools, market entry barriers and the likelihood of entry, market transparency, countervailing buying power of transport users and the nature of the services (for example, homogenous versus differentiated services) should be taken into account as additional factors in assessing the impact of a given pool on the relevant market.

71. With regard to the nature of the agreement, consideration should be given to clauses affecting the pool or its members' competitive behaviour in the market such as clauses prohibiting members from being active in the same market outside the pool (non-compete clauses), lock-in periods and notice periods (exit clauses) and exchanges of commercially sensitive information. Any links between pools, whether in terms of management or members as well as cost and revenue sharing should also be considered.

3.3.4. Applicability of Article [101(3)] of the Treaty

72. Where pools are caught by Article [101(1)] of the Treaty, the undertakings involved need to ensure that they fulfil the four cumulative conditions of Article [101(3)]. Article [101(3)] does not exclude a priori certain types of agreements from its scope. As a matter of principle all restrictive agreements that fulfil the four conditions of Article [101(3)] are covered by the exception rule. This analysis incorporates a sliding scale. The greater the restriction of competition found under Article [101(1)], the greater the efficiencies and the pass-on to consumers must be.

73. It is up to the undertakings involved to demonstrate that the pool improves the transport services or promotes technical or economic progress in the form of efficiency gains. The efficiencies generated cannot be cost savings that are an inherent part of the reduction of competition but must result from the integration of economic activities.

74. Efficiency gains of pools may for instance result from obtaining better utilisation rates and economies of scale. Tramp shipping pools typically jointly plan vessel movements in order to spread their fleets geographically. Spreading vessels may reduce the number of ballast voyages which may increase the overall capacity utilisation of the pool and eventually lead to economies of scale.

75. Consumers must receive a fair share of the efficiencies generated. Under Article [101(3)] of the Treaty, it is the beneficial effects on all consumers in the relevant market that must be taken into consideration, not the effect on each individual consumer. The pass-on of benefits must at least compensate consumers for any actual or potential negative impact caused to them by the restriction of competition under Article [101(1)]. To assess the likelihood of a pass-on the structure of tramp shipping markets and the elasticity of demand should also be considered in this context.

76. A pool must not impose restrictions that are not indispensable to the attainment of the efficiencies. In this respect it is necessary to examine whether the parties could have achieved the efficiencies on their own. In making this assessment it is relevant to consider, inter alia, what is the minimum efficient scale to provide various types of services in tramp shipping. In addition, each restrictive clause contained in a pool agreement must be reasonably necessary to attain the claimed efficiencies. Restrictive clauses may be justified for a longer period or the whole life of the pool or for a transitional period only.

77. Lastly, the pool must not afford the parties the possibility of eliminating competition in respect of a substantial part of the services in question."[188]

It is possible that an arrangement may be covered by the consortia block exemption so regard should be had to that block exemption as well.

J. SELF-ASSESSMENT

12.152 One of the hallmarks of the new regime is "self-assessment". Ironically, the wealth of cases built up in the area of liner shipping means that undertakings have to make their own evaluation of whether their arrangements or practices comply with competition law.

K. EFFECT ON TRADE BETWEEN MEMBER STATES

12.153 Before EU competition law may apply, there must be an appreciable effect on trade between Member States. The topic is considered in chapter 9. The Commission and the courts have opined on this topic on several occasions. The Commission has indeed issued guidelines on the subject.[189] However, the Guidelines go one step further by looking at the effect on trade between Member States in the very specific context of shipping. The Guidelines provide:

"2.2. Effect on trade between Member States
13. Article [101] of the Treaty applies to all agreements which may appreciably affect trade between Member States. In order for there to be an effect on trade it must be possible to

---

188 Footnotes omitted.
189 Commission Guidelines on the Effect on Trade concept contained in Arts 101 and 102 of the Treaty, OJ 2004 C101/81.

foresee with a sufficient degree of probability on the basis of a set of objective factors of law or fact that the agreement or conduct may have an influence, direct or indirect, actual or potential, on the pattern of trade between Member States.[190] The Commission has issued guidance on how it will apply the concept of affectation of trade in its Guidelines on the effect of trade concept contained in Articles [101] and [102] of the Treaty.[191]

14. Transport services offered by liner shipping and tramp operators are often international in nature linking Community ports with third countries and/or involving exports and imports between two or more Member States (i.e. intra Community trade[192]). In most cases they are likely to affect trade between Member States inter alia on account of the impact they have on the markets for the provision of transport and intermediary services.[193]

15. Effect on trade between Member States is of particular relevance to maritime cabotage services since it determines the scope of application of Article [101] of the Treaty and its interaction with national competition law under Article 3 of Regulation (EC) No 1/2003 on the implementation of the rules on competition laid down in Articles [101 and 102] of the Treaty. The extent to which such services may affect trade between Member States must be evaluated on a case by case basis.[194]"

12.154 The Commission therefore believes, and it is not too surprising, that because of their international nature, shipping services are likely to affect trade between Member States.

12.155 It is of note that paragraph 13 of the Guidelines is interesting because of the use of the word "appreciably" before "affect trade". This is no different from what is the current state of law but it is important because it shows that the Commission will not be likely to target non-appreciable effects of competition therefore small pools would not be often or easily targeted.

L. LINER SHIPPING IN THE NEW REGIME

Introduction

12.156 EU competition law applies in full to liner shipping. On liner shipping and the new regime, regard should be had to this entire chapter as well these few remarks.

12.157 The Guidelines described, in paragraph 10, the concept of liner shipping:

---

190 Case 42/84, *Remia BV and Others v Commission* [1985] ECR 2545, paragraph 22. Case 319/82, *Ciments et Bétons de l'Est v Kerpen & Kerpen* [1983] ECR 4173, paragraph 9.
191 OJ C101/81, 27.4.2004.
192 The fact that the service is to/from a non-EU port does not in itself preclude that trade between Member States is affected. A careful analysis of the effects on customers and other operators within the Community that rely on the services needs to be carried out to determine whether they fall under Community jurisdiction. See Guidelines on the effect on trade concept contained in Articles 81 and 82 of the Treaty, cited above in [previous] footnote.
193 Commission Decision 93/82/EEC of 23 December 1992 (Cases IV/32.448 and IV/32.450, CEWAL) (OJ L34, 10.2.1993, p. 1), paragraph 90, confirmed by the Court of First Instance in Joined Cases T-24/93 to T-26/93 and T-28/93, *Compagnie Maritime Belge and Others v Commission* [1996] ECR II-1201, paragraph 205. TAA decision, cited above in footnote 10, paragraphs 288–296, confirmed by the Judgment of the Court of First Instance of 28 February 2002, in Case T-395/94, *Atlantic Container Line and Others v Commission* (hereinafter the TAA judgment), paragraphs 72–74; Commission Decision 1999/243/EC of 16 September 1998 (Case IV/35.134 – Trans-Atlantic Conference Agreement) (hereinafter the TACA decision) (OJ L95, 9.4.1999, p. 1), paragraphs 386–396; Commission Decision 2003/68/EC of 14 November 2002 (Case COMP/37.396 – Revised TACA) (hereinafter the Revised TACA decision) (OJ L26, 31.1.2003, p. 53), paragraph 73.
194 For guidance on the application of the effect on trade, see the Commission Guidelines cited above in footnote [192].

"Liner shipping involves the transport of cargo, chiefly by container, on a regular basis to ports of a particular geographic route, generally known as a trade. Other general characteristics of liner shipping are that timetables and sailing dates are advertised in advance and services are available to any transport user."

Market definition

Introduction

12.158 The Guidelines gave some guidance on the issue of market definition in liner shipping. The guidance was welcome but contained little that was new because it encapsulates the case law in the area.

Product market definition

12.159 The Guidelines dealt with the issue of product market definition in the context of liner shipping in the following manner:

"18. Containerised liner shipping services have been identified as the relevant product market for liner shipping in several Commission decisions and Court judgments.[195] Those decisions and judgments related to maritime transport in deep sea trades. Other modes of transport have not been included in the same service market even though in some cases these services may be, to a marginal extent, interchangeable. This was because only an insufficient proportion of the goods carried by container can easily be switched to other modes of transport, such as air transport services.[196]

19. It may be appropriate under certain circumstances to define a narrower product market limited to a particular type of product transported by sea. For example, the transport of perishable goods could be limited to reefer containers or include transport in conventional reefer vessels. While it is possible in exceptional circumstances for some substitution to take place between break bulk and container transport,[197] there appears to be no lasting change over from container towards bulk. For the vast majority of categories of goods and users of containerised goods, break bulk does not offer a reasonable alternative to containerised liner shipping.[198] Once cargo becomes regularly containerised it is unlikely ever to be transported again as non-containerised cargo.[199] To date containerised liner shipping is therefore mainly subject to one way substitutability.[200]"

12.160 While the guidelines have not been renewed, it is submitted that the observations remain valid. Holmes observed helpfully:

---

195 Commission Decision 1999/485/EC of 30 April 1999 (Case IV/34.250 – Europe Asia Trades Agreement) (OJ L193, 26.7.1999, p. 23); TAA decision, cited above in footnote 10, and the TACA decision, cited above in footnote 15, paragraphs 60–84. The market definition in the TACA decision was confirmed by the Court of First Instance in its Judgment in Joined Cases T-191/98, T-212/98 to T-214/98, *Atlantic Container Line AB and Others v Commission* [2003] ECR II-3275 (hereinafter the TACA judgment), paragraphs 781–883.

196 Paragraph 62 of the TACA decision, cited above in footnote 15 and paragraphs 783–789 of the TACA judgment, cited above in [the previous] footnote...

197 Ed., *TACA* decision, para. 1.

198 Ed., *TAA* judgment, para. 273 and *TACA* judgment, para. 809.

199 Ed., *TAA* judgment, para. 281. Comm. Dec. of 29 July 2005 in Case COMP/M.3829 – *MAERSK/PONL*, para. 13.

200 Ed., *TACA* decision, paras 62–75; *TACA* judgment, para. 795 and Comm. Dec. in *MAERSK/PONL*, paras 13 and 112–117.

"[f]rom the early days of non-opposition exemption for consortia, the Commission has made it clear that, in its view, cargo, once containerised, rarely switches back to non-containerised cargo and, on that basis, containers are generally viewed as a separate market. In this regard, however, the Commission has been more flexible (by contrast, North Europe and Mediterranean markets have been effectively set in stone) and has accepted some substitution, especially in relation to less mature markets."[201]

Geographic market definition

12.161 The Guidelines provided in paragraph 20:

"The relevant geographic market consists of the area where the services are marketed, generally a range of ports at each end of the service, determined by ports' overlapping catchment areas. As far as the European end of the service is concerned, to date the geographical market in liner cases has been identified as a range of ports in Northern Europe or in the Mediterranean. As liner shipping services from the Mediterranean are only marginally substitutable for those from Northern European ports, these have been identified as separate markets."[202]

While the Guidelines have not been renewed, the principles remain valid.

12.162 Holmes commented that the *TACA*

"decision ... concluded that Europe has two separate markets based on the range of ports for liner shipping purposes: Northern Europe and the Mediterranean. That case concerned the North Atlantic, but this market definition has been applied to all liner routes from Europe reviewed by the Commission."[203]

M. TRAMP SHIPPING IN THE NEW REGIME

Introduction

12.163 Tramp shipping is covered by the new regime. Regard should be had to the entire chapter as well as these few remarks.

12.164 Following the entry into force of Regulation 1419/2006, tramp shipping became part of the EC's general competition regime (i.e. Regulation 1/2003). In terms of tramp shipping, the Guidelines give particular guidance on the issue of pools.

Market definition

Introduction

12.165 While previous cases and decisions are not binding precedent, they are helpful. Before Regulation 4056/86, there was obviously no precedent in regard to tramp services so market definition in this area has to be devised from first principles. The Guidelines were therefore helpful in this context.

---

201 Op. cit. at fn. 132, p. 9 at 9.
202 Ed. *TACA* decision, paras 76–83 and revised *TACA* decision, para. 39.
203 Op. cit. at fn. 132, p. 9 at 9.

Product market definition

12.166 In defining the product market, several criteria are relevant including vessel size, vessel type, vessel features and the cargo carried.

12.167 In terms of vessel features, the availability of double hull would be relevant in terms of defining tankers.

12.168 A different approach is taken to calculating annual market shares in this context than with consortia. Under the consortia block exemption,[204] one calculates market share by "reference to the volume of goods carried (freight tonnes or 20 foot equivalent units)".[205] In the context of tramp shipping, one would examine the number of voyages, the parties' volume and value share in the overall cargo; the parties' share in the market for time charter contracts; and the parties' capacity shares in the relevant market (by vessel type and size).

Geographic market definition

12.169 While, in theory, the world is the geographic market, the Guidelines urge a narrower approach. One should consider the loading and discharging ports. Single directional markets may be appropriate.

Pools between undertakings who are not actual or potential competitors

12.170 Paragraph 64 of the Guidelines states:

"64. Pool agreements do not fall under the prohibition of Article [101](1) of the Treaty if the participants to the pool are not actual or potential competitors. This would be the case, for instance, when two or more ship-owners set up a shipping pool for the purpose of tendering for and performing contracts of affreightment for which as individual operators they could not bid successfully or which they could not carry out on their own. This conclusion is not invalidated in cases where such pools occasionally carry other cargo representing a small part of the overall volume."

This is a helpful provision but it is likely to be of relevance to only very small operators.

Pools of minor importance in competition terms

12.171 Paragraph 65 of the Guidelines states: "Pools whose activity does not influence the relevant parameters of competition because they are of minor importance and/or do not appreciably affect trade between Member States,[206] are not caught by Article [101(1)] of the Treaty."

12.172 This may give more comfort than one should take. It is certainly comforting for those pools which have only a non-appreciable effect on trade between EU Member States. Such pools would be those with low market shares and occasional visits to EU ports and therefore should not raise an issue anyway. It is possible that pools with more

---

204 Reg. 823/2000.
205 Reg. 823/2000 (as amended by Reg. 611/2005), Art. 6.
206 Commission Notice on agreements of minor importance which do not appreciably restrict competition under Article 81(1) of the Treaty (OJ C368, 22.12.2001, p. 13) and Guidelines on the effect on trade concept.

activities in the EU than merely occasional ones may be able to benefit from the comfort provided by paragraph 65.

Pools between competitors limited to joint selling

12.173 From the comfort of paragraph 65, it is useful to review paragraph 66 of the Guidelines which goes on to state: "66. Pool agreements between competitors limited to joint selling have as a rule the object and effect of coordinating the pricing policy of these competitors."[207]

12.174 This gives some concern for pools which involve joint selling. However, it is clear that they should undertake self-assessment. There is no obvious appreciability test in this paragraph so every such pool should undertake self-assessment but not everyone will be in breach of Article 101(1).

Full function joint ventures

12.175 The Guidelines state in paragraph 63:

"Pools that fall within the scope of Council Regulation (EC) No 139/2004[208] because they are created as a joint venture performing on a lasting basis all the functions of an autonomous economic entity (so called full-function joint ventures, see Article 3(4) of Regulation (EC) No 139/2004) are not directly affected by the changes brought about by Regulation (EC) No 1419/2006 and are not dealt with in these Guidelines. Guidance on full-functionality can be found, inter alia, in the Commission Consolidated Jurisdictional Notice under Regulation (EC) No 139/2004 on the control of concentrations between undertakings.[209] Insofar as such pools have as their object or effect the coordination of the competitive behaviour of their parents, the coordination shall be appraised in accordance with the criteria of Article [101(1) and (3)] of the [TFEU] with a view to establishing whether or not the operation is compatible with the [internal] market."[210]

12.176 The Guidelines do not define the concept of "lasting basis" or "autonomous" in the context of pools in the shipping sector.

12.177 It has been observed:

"Good news for pools is the fact that standard pools are viewed by the Commission as having 'joint production features'. Under Commission Regulation 2658/2000/EC covering specialisation agreements, as also referred to in the horizontal guidelines, joint selling is viewed as indispensable for joint production, and is therefore allowed, subject to a 20% market share threshold.

The Guidelines were out in draft [in 2008]. Following consultation with the shipping industry, the final guidelines contain an important improvement from the pools perspective in that they now make clear that a pool which is predominantly [Contract of Affreightment] oriented, brought together to tender for contracts which an individual operator could not do alone, can also accept spot cargo without 'invalidating' a positive self-assessment."[211]

---

207 Guidelines on Horizontal Cooperation Agreements, C245/2, 26 September 2008, Section 5. The activities of an independent ship-broker when "fixing a vessel" do not fall under this category.
208 Council Regulation (EC) No 139/2004 on the control of concentrations between undertakings (the EC Merger Regulation) (OJ L24, 29.1.2004, p. 1).
209 OJ C95, 16.4.2008, p. 1.
210 Article 2(4) of Council Regulation (EC) No 139/2004.
211 Holmes, op. cit. at fn. 132, p. 9 at 10.

12.178 It has also been written that:

"Restrictive clauses that will have to be assessed in pool arrangements include: non-compete clauses; lock-in periods; notice periods (exit clauses); and information exchange. While these are flagged up [in the Guidelines] as competition issues, no answers are given.

So, for example, if you delete a non-compete clause in a pool arrangement, this may make the arrangement less restrictive. But how do you deal with calculating market share when members are in several pools in the same market? And what do you do about 'information spillage', especially as the Guidelines point out that 'an exchange of information may even have in itself the object of restricting competition' (see paragraph 42)? The same applies to managers of pools in overlapping markets."[212]

12.179 The Commission's Maritime Guidelines continue:

"3.3. Pool agreements in tramp shipping
60. The most recurrent form of horizontal cooperation in the tramp shipping sector is the shipping pool. There is no universal model for a pool. Some features do, however, appear to be common to most pools in the different market segments as set out below.
61. A standard shipping pool brings together a number of similar vessels[213] under different ownership and operated under a single administration. A pool manager is normally responsible for the commercial management (for example, joint marketing[214], negotiation of freight rates and centralization of incomes and voyage costs[215]) and the commercial operation (planning vessel movements and instructing vessels, nominating agents in ports, keeping customers updated, issuing freight invoices, ordering bunkers, collecting the vessels' earnings and distributing them under a pre-arranged weighting system etc.). The pool manager often acts under the supervision of a general executive committee representing the vessel owners. The technical operation of vessels is usually the responsibility of each owner (safety, crew, repairs, maintenance etc.). Although they market their services jointly, the pool members often perform the services individually."

The Commission may, by virtue of this paragraph, be more open to hearing arguments that the parties were involved in joint production.

"62. It follows from this description that the key feature of standard shipping pools is joint selling, coupled with features of joint production. The guidance on both joint selling, as a variant of a joint commercialisation agreement, and joint production in the Commission Guidelines on the applicability of Article [101] of the Treaty to horizontal cooperation agreements ... is therefore relevant. Given the variation in pools' characteristics, each pool must be analysed on a case-by-case basis to determine, by reference to its centre of gravity ..., whether it is caught by Article [101(1)] and, in the affirmative, if it fulfils the four cumulative conditions of Article [101(3)]."

N. CABOTAGE UNDER THE NEW REGIME

12.180 The new regime applies to cabotage so regard should be had to the entire chapter. The Guidelines do not apply to cabotage. Nonetheless, the same principles should apply to both cabotage and international services. The Guidelines state:

---

212 Holmes, op. cit. at fn. 132, p. 9 at 10.
213 This results in the pool being able to attract large contracts of affreightment, combine various contracts of affreightment and reduce the number of ballast legs by careful fleet planning.
214 For example, the pool's vessels are marketed as one commercial unit offering transport solutions regardless of which ship performs the actual voyage.
215 For example, the pool's income is collected by the central administration and revenue is distributed to the participants based on a complex weighting system.

"3. Regulation (EC) No 1419/2006 extended the scope of Council Regulation (EC) No 1/2003 of 16 December 2002 on the implementation of the rules on competition laid down in Articles 81 and 82 of the Treaty[216] and Commission Regulation (EC) No 773/2004 of 7 April 2004 relating to the conduct of proceedings by the Commission pursuant to Articles 81 and 82 of the Treaty[217] to include cabotage and tramp vessel services. Consequently, as of 18 October 2006, all maritime transport services sectors are subject to the generally applicable procedural framework.

4. Regulation (EC) No 1419/2006 also repealed Council Regulation (EEC) No 4056/86 of 22 December 1986 on the application of Articles 85 and 86 (now 81 and 82) of the Treaty to maritime transport[218] containing the liner conference block exemption which allowed shipping lines meeting in liner conferences to fix rates and other conditions of carriage, as the conference system no longer fulfils the criteria of Article 81(3) of the Treaty. The repeal of the block exemption takes effect as of 18 October 2008. Thereafter, liner carriers operating services to and/or from one or more ports in the European Union must cease all liner conference activity contrary to Article 81 of the Treaty. This is the case regardless of whether other jurisdictions allow, explicitly or tacitly, rate fixing by liner conferences or discussion agreements. Moreover, conference members should ensure that any agreement taken under the conference system complies with Article 81 as of 18 October 2008.

5. These Guidelines complement the guidance already issued by the Commission in other notices. As maritime transport services are characterised by extensive cooperation agreements between competing carriers, the Guidelines on the applicability of Article 81 of the Treaty to horizontal cooperation agreements[219] (the Guidelines on Horizontal Cooperation) and the Guidelines on the application of Article 81(3) of the Treaty ... are particularly relevant.

6. Horizontal cooperation agreements in liner shipping regarding the provision of joint services are covered by Commission Regulation (EC) No 823/2000 of 19 April 2000 on the application of Article 81(3) of the Treaty to certain categories of agreements, decisions and concerted practices between liner shipping companies (consortia) .... It sets out the conditions, pursuant to Article 81(3) of the Treaty, under which the prohibition in Article 81(1) of the Treaty does not apply to agreements between two or more vessel operating carriers (consortia). It will be reviewed following the changes introduced by Regulation (EC) No 1419/2006 ....

2. MARITIME TRANSPORT SERVICES

2.1. Scope

9. Liner shipping services, cabotage and tramp services are the maritime transport sectors directly affected by the changes brought about by Regulation (EC) No 1419/2006

...

11. Article 1(3)(a) of Regulation (EEC) No 4056/86 defined tramp vessel services as the transport of goods in bulk or in break bulk in a vessel chartered wholly or partly to one or more shippers on the basis of a voyage or time charter or any other form of contract for non-regularly scheduled or non-advertised sailings where the freight rates are freely negotiated case by case in accordance with the conditions of supply and demand. It is mostly the unscheduled transport of one single commodity which fills a vessel.[220]

---

216 Ed., OJ L1/1, 4 January 2003.
217 Ed., OJ L123/18, 27 April 2004.
218 Ed., OJ L378/4, 31 December 1986.
219 Ed., OJ C3/2, 6 January 2001.
220 The Commission has identified a series of characteristics specific to specialised transport which render it distinct from liner services and tramp vessel services. They involve the provision of regular services for a particular cargo type. The service is usually provided on the basis of contracts of affreightment using specialised vessels technically adapted and/or built to transport specific cargo. Commission Decision 94/980/EC of 19 October 1994 in Case IV/34.446 – *Trans-Atlantic Agreement* (OJ L376, 31.12.1994, p. 1) (hereinafter the TAA decision), paragraphs 47–49.

> 12. Cabotage involves the provision of maritime transport services including tramp and liner shipping, linking two or more ports in the same Member State.[221] Although these Guidelines do not specifically address cabotage services they nevertheless apply to these services insofar as they are provided either as liner or tramp shipping services.
>
> 2.3. The relevant market
> 16. In order to assess the effects on competition of an agreement for the purposes of Article 81 of the Treaty, it is necessary to define the relevant product and geographic market(s). The main purpose of market definition is to identify in a systematic way the competitive constraints faced by an undertaking. Guidance on this issue can be found in the Commission Notice on the definition of the relevant market for the purposes of Community competition law. ... This guidance is also relevant to market definition as regards maritime transport services.
> 17. The relevant product market comprises all those products and/or services which are regarded as interchangeable or substitutable by the consumer, by reason of the products' characteristics, their prices and their intended use. The relevant geographic market comprises the area in which the undertakings concerned are involved in the supply and demand of products or services, in which the conditions of competition are sufficiently homogeneous and which can be distinguished from neighbouring areas because the conditions of competition are appreciably different in those areas. ... A carrier (or carriers) cannot have a significant impact on the prevailing conditions of the market if customers are in a position to switch easily to other service providers."[222]

12.181 It will be recalled that cabotage (i.e. domestic services between two ports in the same Member State) and tramp vessel services were excluded from the normal means of applying and enforcing EC competition law which caused practical and real difficulties. Regulation 1419/2006 therefore addressed the issue in the recitals:

> "12. Cabotage and international tramp vessel services have been excluded from the rules implementing Articles 81 and 82 of the Treaty originally laid down in Regulation (EEC) No. 4056/86 and subsequently in Regulation (EC) No. 1/2003. They are currently the only remaining sectors to be excluded from the Community competition implementing rules. The lack of effective enforcement powers for these sectors is an anomaly from a regulatory point of view.
> 13. The exclusion of tramp vessel services from Regulation (EC) No. 1/2003 was based on the fact that rates for these services are freely negotiated on a case by case basis in accordance with supply and demand conditions. However, such market conditions are present in other sectors and the substantive provisions of Articles 81 and 82 already apply to these services. No convincing reason has been brought forward to maintain the current exclusion of these services from the rules implementing Articles 81 and 82 of the Treaty. Similarly, although cabotage services often have no effect on intra Community trade, this does not mean that they should be excluded from the scope of Regulation (EC) No. 1/2003 from the outset.
> 14. As the mechanisms enshrined in Regulation (EC) No. 1/2003 are appropriate for applying the competition rules to all sectors, the scope of that Regulation should be amended so as to include cabotage and tramp vessel services.
> 15. Regulation (EC) No. 1/2003 should therefore be amended accordingly."

---

221 Article 1 of Council Regulation (EEC) No 3577/92 of 7 December 1992 applying the principle of freedom to provide services to maritime transport within Member States (maritime cabotage) (OJ L364, 12.12.1992, p. 7).

222 Some footnotes omitted.

O. COMPLIANCE WITH THE NEW REGIME

12.182 In terms of compliance with the new regime,[223] those undertakings involved in maritime transport (and their advisors) have to bear in mind several different factors.

12.183 First, they must bear in mind the general EU competition law regime. Second, the new specific regime in Regulation 1419/2006 has to be taken into account along with the Guidelines. But what types of issues are likely to arise in practice?

12.184 Unilateral behaviour by a shipping company will not usually raise any issue under Article 101 of the TFEU but may raise an issue under Article 102 of the TFEU where the undertaking is dominant. Agreements involving a shipping company will not raise an issue under Article 101 of the TFEU where the arrangements are purely in-house (e.g. an agreement between a parent company and a wholly owned subsidiary). An agreement between a principal and an agent (i.e. a genuine agent under EU competition law)[224] would be unlikely to raise any competition law issue under Article 101(1) but Article 101(1) would apply to: (a) arrangements involving non-genuine agents and (b) arrangements concluded by the agent on behalf of the principal where the arrangement itself was in breach of Article 101(1) so, for example, if an agent enters into a price-fixing agreement with the principal's competitors then that is caught by Article 101(1).[225]

12.185 Pricing is the most obvious competition law issue. Pricing must be done unilaterally so as to avoid a problem under Article 101 of the TFEU. This means that while naturally a price may be agreed between a buyer and a seller of a service (e.g. a shipper and a carrier), there must not be any understanding (however loose) between different undertakings (e.g. different carriers agreeing the price below which they would each not provide a service). There is almost no end to potential breaches of competition law in terms of pricing but it is useful to consider some examples. First, there ought not to be horizontal price-fixing among competitors.[226] For example, if carriers were to agree (however informally or loosely) between themselves that about price (or any element of price including surcharges,[227] discounts,[228] exchange rates[229] and so on) then such an arrangement would breach competition law. Second, there ought not to be any hub and spoke practices whereby competitors (e.g. carriers) are colluding but are doing so by virtue of an intermediary such as a freight forwarder. It does not matter if the price-fixing among competitors covers all of the services or just part of the services.[230] Third, there must be no activity now which was once permitted under Regulation 4056/86 therefore "new habits" have to be learned – there can be no joint setting of tariff freight rates and no joint setting of surcharges or other comparable charges. Instead, there has to be unilateral pricing decisions which will not be as easy or as comfortable as price-setting in the old regime. It is important to have a full understanding of one's costs and revenue streams. Fourth, while "price leadership" is a common phenomenon in many industries,

---

223 See Rees, "Competition Law Compliance in a World without the Liner Conference Block Exemption", London, 27 March 2009.
224 See Commission's Guidelines on Vertical Agreements.
225 *Greek Ferries*. An agent does not need the principal's permission to participate in a cartel (that is irrelevant).
226 E.g. *Greek Ferries* and *Far Eastern Freight Conference*.
227 E.g. fuel surcharges/bunker adjustment factors and terminal handling charges.
228 E.g. understandings on the level of discounts or even agreements not to discount at all.
229 E.g. currency adjustment factors. E.g. *Ferry Operators* case.
230 E.g. *Greek Ferries* and *Far Eastern Freight Conference*.

there must be no understanding (however loose) among competitors that they will follow the pricing decisions of one particular competitor (the "leader"). Fifth, there must not be signalling to competitors about pricing or future intentions. The signalling must not be direct (e.g. between competitors) or indirect (e.g. by way of freight forwarders receiving information about one carrier and then passing it on to other carriers).[231]

12.186 The exchange of information is an obvious competition law issue. There must be no illegal exchange of information among competitors or, indeed, among any undertakings where the exchange would have the object or effect of preventing, restricting or distorting competition. Each case has to be assessed on its merits but the key question is whether the element of surprise is removed and whether the exchange would reduce or remove the degree of market uncertainty faced by competitors such that the normal risks of competition would be removed. The most likely negative effect occurs where the exchange is between competitors. The exchange cannot be either direct or indirect.[232] It is worth recalling that competition law has regard to the entirety of the undertaking so information which comes into an undertaking through a subsidiary (e.g. a logistics subsidiary) is ordinarily regarded as information for the whole organisation therefore care should be taken with how the undertaking as a whole exchanges information and, if needed, "Chinese Walls" may have to be put in place to ensure that there is no illegal or improper exchange of information. There is no difficulty with lawful exchanges of information but it is often difficult to discern between the two. The safest course is to have no discussions with competitors on pricing (whether rates or surcharges) or market intelligence issues. Any exchange of information which influences the conduct of a competitor or reveals their future conduct is usually problematical. On market intelligence, there is no difficulty with using publicly available sources (e.g. newspapers, magazines and industry publications). A good practice is for undertakings to "tag" interesting information which they receive from legitimate sources (i.e. state on it where the information came from) so as to ensure that if there were a dawn raid or investigation, it would be possible to demonstrate that the information was obtained lawfully. There are specific regimes where some exchange of information is possible – for example, under the consortia block exemption – but such exchanges usually have to be ancillary and necessary.[233] If there is a proposed exchange of information then one may have to engage in self-assessment to determine whether it is possible to exempt the practice. The assessment has to be on a case by case basis and taking into account the general competition rules as well as the specific guidelines for the maritime transport sector.[234] It is possible for the exchange to be exemptible under Article 101(3) of the TFEU but a careful examination is needed. As stated above, each case has to be assessed on its merits but the key question is whether the element of surprise is removed and whether the exchange would reduce or remove the degree of market uncertainty faced by competitors such that the normal risks of competition would be removed. It is important to review the *market structure* and the

---

231 Obviously, a carrier needs to give information to a freight forwarder but a carrier should not use a freight forwarder as a means of passing information on to other carriers. Ideally, one should state explicitly that the information (e.g. pricing) must not be shared with other carriers.
232 Indirect exchanges occur when, for example, third parties (e.g. suppliers) carry information between competitors (e.g. customers) or information is exchanged through the medium of trade associations.
233 E.g. some exchanges have been permitted under the consortia block exemption.
234 On the guidelines, see above.

participants in the exchange: how concentrated is the market and how transparent is information in the sector? Then it is important to examine the *type of information* being exchanged: is the information commercially sensitive, is the information related to individual businesses or is it aggregated to such an extent that it is anonymous, the age of the information,[235] the frequency of exchange,[236] and could the exchange of this information distort competition? The safest course, but always the most practical, is to determine one's conduct unilaterally.

12.187 Market control or manipulation is also a potential issue. It is possible that either competitors or combinations of market participants could decide to manipulate the market in various ways. It would be useful to consider a number of examples of such practices. First, there ought not to be arrangements relating to limiting capacity (e.g. deliberately mothballing[237] a certain amount of capacity on routes so as to reduce supply and thereby increase price). It could be as simple as carriers agreeing not to fill 20% of their capacity on each ship because that would thereby reduce capacity and drive up price. Equally, if carriers were to agree to slow their ships by a particular amount then that would also increase price. Carriers must make decisions to introduce, suspend[238] or withdraw tonnage on a unilateral basis. This might be disguised as capacity management but it would, in reality, be a way of manipulating supply, and hence price, to the market. The sharing of vessels is something which ought to be undertaken after consideration of the legal issues involved – would the sharing have an anti-competitive effect (e.g. strengthening of market power leading to a reduction in competition). There can be slot sharing, slot charter or slot swap agreements in the context of the consortia block exemption.

12.188 Abuse of dominance is also a potential problem. The dominance being abused could be either individual dominance or collective dominance. The use of "fighting ships" has been highlighted in the past.

12.189 There is a need to be vigilant in all relationships and interactions with third parties and not just in those interactions with competitors.

12.190 Internal compliance is critical. It is also an ongoing process and there is a need for continuous vigilance. It is important for undertakings to be aware of any possibility that they are dominant whether in one or more markets because that would influence the type of behaviour in which they may engage. The burden of compliance has increased since the abolition of the possibility of individual notifications under Articles 101 and 102 of the TFEU with the adoption of Regulation 1/2003.

12.191 Document creation, management and destruction are important functions that need to be performed carefully. Documents should be destroyed in a carefully monitored and managed way otherwise there could be negative implications drawn from the destruction of some documents.

---

235 E.g. is it historical (in which case there would be unlikely to be a competition law issue) or is it very current (in which case there could well be a competition law issue)?

236 The more frequent the exchange of information, the more complete a picture that competitors get of the market and the better and quicker they are able to respond. Unfortunately, armed with this information about their competitors, undertakings could compete less vigorously than they would if they did not know where their competitors were going to go.

237 Also referred to as "parking in the desert".

238 E.g. decisions to dry dock vessels must be unilateral.

12.192 All those involved in the shipping sector need to ensure that they are ready to deal with dawn raids and other possible investigations by the European Commission or other national competition agencies.

P. THE *BULK LIQUID SHIPPING* CASE

12.193 The Commission commenced but has now closed an investigation into a possible bulk liquid shipping cartel. On 11 April 2007, the Commission announced that it had sent a statement of objections to a number of undertakings regarding their alleged role in cartel arrangements for shipping liquids in bulk on deep sea routes.[239] The Commission considered that it had evidence that the undertakings had been involved in customer allocation, bid-rigging, price-fixing and the exchange of confidential information. On 8 May 2008, the Commission announced that it has closed its investigation into a possible breach of Article 81(1) by undertakings active in the market for the shipping of bulk liquids by sea.[240] The Commission was satisfied that the companies were offering tramp vessel services which, at the time of the alleged infringement, were excluded from the procedural rules which enabled the Commission to enforce Articles 81. The companies had argued that they had been providing tramp vessel services and as at the time of the alleged infringements, 1998 to 2002, tramp vessel services were excluded from Regulation 4056/86, the Commission was not able to apply the normal procedural rules for enforcement of the Treaty provisions in this sector. The Commission closed the file stating that, after careful consideration of the extensive replies to its statement of objections, it has concluded that there was a possibility that the services at issue were indeed tramp vessel services. Therefore, the Commission has decided to close the case.

Q. THE *IACS: INTERNATIONAL ASSOCIATION OF CLASSIFICATION SOCIETIES* CASE

12.194 On 14 December 2009, the Commission adopted a decision relating to a proceeding under Article 101 of the TFEU and Article 53 of the European Economic Area ("EEA") Agreement relating to ship classification.[241] Commitments were offered by the International Association of Classification Societies ("IACS") to remove barriers to non-IACS members accessing the ship classification market. The IACS made commitments which were rendered binding.

12.195 The Commission carried out unannounced inspections in the ship classification market in January 2008.[242] In the course of its investigation, the Commission came to the preliminary view that IACS could have reduced the level of competition in the ship classification market, principally by preventing classification societies which are not already

---

239 MEMO/07/131, 11 April 2007.
240 MEMO/08/297, 8 May 2008.
241 Comm. Dec. COMP/39.416. See Filliptsch and Schafer, "More 'Cartel' Investigations could Follow" (2009–2010) 23(10) MRI 16. The Commission stated (IP/09/1513) that "[c]lassification societies establish, apply and certify compliance with technical requirements relating to the design, construction, equipment, maintenance and survey of ships, which are laid down in their classification rules and procedures. More than 90% of the world's cargo carrying tonnage is covered by the classification rules and procedures set by the current ten members and one associate of IACS which are the largest classification societies in the world".
242 See MEMO/08/65. See also (2009) EU Focus, No 264, p. 7.

members of IACS from joining IACS, from participation in IACS' technical working groups (which develop IACS' technical resolutions that lay down requirements and interpretations to be incorporated into the classification rules and procedures of individual classification societies) and from access to technical background documents relating to IACS' technical resolutions.

12.196 The Commission had concerns that IACS may have infringed Article 101 of the TFEU and Article 53 of the EEA Agreement. The Commission's concerns were that IACS might have prevented classification societies, which are not members of IACS, from joining IACS,[243] from participating in IACS' technical working groups and from access to technical background documents. Such behaviour would have hindered the entry and development of classification societies, which were not members of IACS, in the ship classification market. The IACS proposed a series of commitments, including the establishment of qualitative membership criteria and guidance for their application, the possibility for non-IACS classification societies to participate in IACS' working groups and full access to IACS' technical resolutions and related background documents. The commitments were market tested by the Commission this summer.[244] The decision was based on Article 9(1) of Regulation 1/2003. It ended the Commission's investigation but did not conclude whether there has been or still is an infringement of the antitrust rules. If IACS were to breach its commitments then the Commission may impose a fine of up to 10% of IACS' total turnover without having to prove any violation of the Treaty's and the agreement's competition rules. Competition Commissioner Neelie Kroes commented:

> "This decision opens up the ship classification market to the benefit of both classification societies which are not members of IACS and customers of ship classification services. This paves the way for more competition in this market, which should generate lower prices, more customer choice and improved quality of service."

12.197 The IACS offered the following commitments: (a) to set up objective and transparent membership criteria and to apply them in a uniform and non-discriminatory manner. The commitments foresee detailed rules, including clear deadlines, for the different steps of the membership application, suspension and withdrawal procedure; (b) to ensure that classification societies which are not members of IACS will nonetheless be able to participate in IACS' technical working groups; (c) to put all current and future IACS resolutions and their related technical background documents into the public domain at the same time and in the same way as they are made available to IACS members; and (d) to set up an independent appeal board to settle possible disputes about access to, suspension or withdrawal of membership of IACS, participation in IACS' technical working groups and access to IACS' resolutions and to their technical background documents.

12.198 On 10 June 2009, the Commission launched a consultation for interested parties to give their views on the commitments proposed by IACS.[245] The results of this

---

243 It was believed that more than 90% of the world's cargo carrying tonnage was covered by the classification rules and procedures established by the ten members and one associate member of the IACS which was the largest classification society in the world.
244 See IP/09/898.
245 See IP/09/898.

market test confirmed that the proposed commitments were appropriate and proportionate to remedy the concerns and the case was closed.

R. THE *BALTIC MAX FEEDER* CASE

12.199 On 15 January 2010, the Commission announced that it had opened a formal investigation into the "Baltic Max Feeder" scheme for European feeder vessel owners.[246] The Commission was investigating a possible breach of Article 101 of the TFEU. The Commission was concerned that the scheme, by European shipowners collectively agreeing to cover the costs of removing feeder vessels from service, may be aimed at reducing capacity and therefore at pushing up charter rates for such vessels. Typically, feeder vessels collect shipping containers from different ports and transport them to central container terminals where they are loaded on to bigger vessels.

12.200 The Commission described the background to the case:

"The Commission's investigation concerns the 'Baltic Max Feeder' scheme, whereby European owners of feeder vessels plan to collectively cover the costs of taking vessels out of service, also known as 'laying vessels up'. The Commission will in particular examine whether this has the explicit aim of reducing the available capacity of feeder vessels in Europe, which in turn could increase the rates of chartering feeder vessels.

Feeder vessels are smaller container ships for short-sea transport and are in general the first and last link in the maritime transport chain. They transport or 'feed' containers arriving at or departing from central container terminal ports (such as Hamburg or Rotterdam) served by large deep-sea container vessels, to smaller ports in the region. Feeder vessel operators either own the vessels they operate or charter them from the vessel owners.

The 'Baltic Max Feeder' scheme has been elaborated and promoted by Anchor Steuerberatungsgesellschaft mbH, a German tax advisor, as a response to the current overcapacity of feeder container vessels, which has brought charter rates down."[247]

12.201 On 26 March 2010, the Commission closed the investigation.[248] The Commission stated it had

"closed an investigation into a potential breach of European Union competition rules in the planned 'Baltic Max Feeder' scheme for 'feeder' vessel owners since the scheme was abandoned. The Commission opened an investigation in January this year (see IP/10/21) into the 'Baltic Max Feeder' scheme whereby European 'feeder' vessel owners agreed to jointly cover the costs of removing vessels from service. Feeder vessels are small container ships for short-sea transport and are in general the first and last link in the maritime transport chain. They transport or 'feed' containers arriving at, or departing from, central container terminal ports (such as Hamburg or Rotterdam) served by large deep-sea container vessels, to smaller ports in the region. Feeder vessel operators own the vessels they operate or charter them from the vessel owners. The investigation aimed to establish whether the scheme's purpose was to reduce capacity and, therefore, push up charter rates for such vessels. If confirmed this would likely have been tantamount to a breach of Art 101 of the Treaty, which bans agreements restrictive of competition. In response to the opening of proceedings by the Commission, Anchor Steuerberatungsgesellschaft mbH, the company at the origin of the scheme, informed the Commission in February that the planned scheme had been abandoned. Under these circumstances, the Commission considered that there were no reasons to further investigate and decided to close the case."

---

246 IP/10/21.
247 IP/10/21.
248 IP/10/374.

S. THE *CONTAINER LINER SHIPPING* CASE

12.202 On 17 May 2011, the Commission confirmed unannounced inspections in the container liner shipping sector.[249] The Commission confirmed that on the 17 May 2011, Commission officials undertook unannounced inspections at the premises of companies active in the container liner shipping in several Member States.[250] The Commission said it had reason to believe that the companies concerned may have violated Articles 101 and 102 of the TFEU.

12.203 On 21 November 2013, the Commission initiated proceedings in the case.[251] It was initiated as Case AT.39850 – Container Shipping. The Commission said it intended

> "to investigate the practice of the companies involved to make regular public announcements of price increase intentions through press releases on their websites and in the specialised trade press. These announcements are made several times a year and contain the amount of increase and the date of implementation, which is generally similar for all announcing companies."

The Commission had

> "concerns that this practice may allow the companies to signal future price intentions to each other and may harm competition and customers on the market for container shipping transport services on routes to and from Europe. The Commission will now investigate whether this behaviour amounts to a concerted practice in breach of Article 101 [of the TFEU] and of Article 53 of the European Economic Area (EEA) Agreement."

It is notable that the claim about a possible breach of Article 102 was abandoned. On 22 November 2013, the Commission published a press release on the case:

> "The European Commission has opened formal antitrust proceedings against several container liner shipping companies to investigate whether they engaged in concerted practices, in breach of EU antitrust rules. Container liner shipping is the transport of containers by ship at a fixed time schedule on a specific route between a range of ports at one end (e.g. Shanghai – Hong Kong – Singapore) and another range of ports at the other end (e.g., Rotterdam – Hamburg – Southampton). Opening of proceedings does not prejudge the outcome of the investigation.
>
> Since 2009, these companies have been making regular public announcements of price increase intentions through press releases on their websites and in the specialised trade press. These announcements are made several times a year and contain the amount of increase and the date of implementation, which is generally similar for all announcing companies. The announcements are usually made by the companies successively a few weeks before the announced implementation date.
>
> The Commission has concerns that this practice may allow the companies to signal future price intentions to each other and may harm competition and customers by raising prices on the market for container liner shipping transport services on routes to and from Europe. The Commission will now investigate whether this behaviour amounts to a concerted practice in breach of Article 101 of the Treaty on the Functioning of the European Union (TFEU) and of Article 53 of the European Economic Area (EEA) Agreement.
>
> Background
> Article 101 TFEU prohibits anticompetitive agreements and concerted practices.
>
> Article 11(6) of the Antitrust Regulation provides that the initiation of proceedings by the Commission relieves the competition authorities of the Member States of their competence to

---

249 MEMO/11/307, http://europa.eu/rapid/press-release_MEMO-11-307_en.htm?locale=en.
250 http://europa.eu/rapid/pressReleasesAction.do?reference=MEMO/11/307&format=HTML&aged=1&language=EN&guiLanguage=en.
251 http://ec.europa.eu/competition/antitrust/cases/dec_docs/39850/39850_2081_6.pdf.

also apply EU competition rules to the practices concerned. Article 16(1) further provides that national courts must avoid giving decisions, which would conflict with a decision contemplated by the Commission in proceedings that it has initiated.

The Commission has informed the container liner shipping companies concerned and the competition authorities of the Member States that it has opened proceedings in this case.

There is no legal deadline for bringing an antitrust investigation to an end. The duration of an investigation depends on a number of factors, including the complexity of the case, the cooperation of the undertakings with the Commission and the exercise of the rights of defence."

On 16 February 2016, the Commission published the commitments which were offered by the following companies: ZIM, UASC, OOCL, NYK, MSC, MOL, Maersk, HMM, Hapag Lloyd, Hanjin, Hamburg Süd, Evergreen, CSCL, COSCO and CMA CGM. Also on 16 February 2016, the Commission published a Market Test Notice pursuant to Article 27(4) of Regulation 1/2003 entitled "Communication of the Commission published pursuant to Article 27(4) of Council Regulation (EC) No 1/2003 in Case AT.39850 – Container Shipping". In specific terms, the notice stated;

"Communication of the Commission published pursuant to Article 27(4) of Council Regulation (EC) No 1/2003 in Case AT.39850 – Container Shipping
(2016/C 60/04)
1. Introduction

(1) According to Article 9 of Council Regulation (EC) No 1/2003 of 16 December 2002 on the implementation of the rules on competition laid down in Articles 81 and 82 of the Treaty,[252] the Commission may decide – in cases where it intends to adopt a decision requiring that an infringement is brought to an end and the parties concerned offer commitments to meet the concerns expressed to them by the Commission in its preliminary assessment – to make those commitments binding on the undertakings. Such a decision may be adopted for a specified period and shall conclude that there are no longer grounds for action by the Commission without concluding whether or not there has been or still is an infringement.

(2) According to Article 27(4) of the same Regulation, the Commission shall publish a concise summary of the case and the main content of the commitments. Interested parties may submit their observations within the time limit fixed by the Commission.

2. Summary of the case

(3) On 21 November 2013 and 13 November 2015, the Commission initiated proceedings against the following container shipping companies (hereinafter 'the parties') who have now offered the Commission commitments in order to meet its competition concerns:

1. China Shipping (China)
2. CMA CGM (France)
3. COSCO (China)
4. Evergreen (Taiwan)
5. Hamburg Süd (Germany)
6. Hanjin (South Korea)
7. Hapag Lloyd (Germany)

---

[252] Ed., OJ L1/1, 4 January 2003. With effect from 1 December 2009, Arts 81 and 82 of the EC Treaty have become Arts 101 and, respectively, 102 of the Treaty on the Functioning of the European Union ("TFEU"). The two sets of provisions are in substance identical. For the purposes of this notice, references to Arts 101 and 102 of the TFEU should be understood as references to Arts 81 and 82 of the EC Treaty when applicable.

8. HMM (South Korea)
9. Maersk (Denmark)
10. MOL (Japan)
11. MSC (Switzerland)
12. NYK (Japan)
13. OOCL (Hong Kong)
14. UASC (UAE)
15. ZIM (Israel)

(4) The parties to these proceedings have regularly announced their intended (future) increases of prices for containerized shipping services by sea, at least on routes from Far East Asia to Northern Europe and the Mediterranean (westbound), on their websites, via the press, or in other ways. These announcements indicate the amount of the increase in US-Dollars per transported container unit (twenty-foot equivalent unit, 'TEU'), the affected trade route and the date of implementation. Such announcements are widely known in the industry as 'General Rate Increase Announcements' or 'GRI Announcements'. They generally concern sizable rate increases of several hundred US-Dollars per TEU.

(5) GRI Announcements are made typically 3 to 5 weeks before their intended implementation date, and during that time some or all parties announce similar intended rate increases for the same or similar routes and the same or similar implementation date. Announced GRIs have sometimes been postponed or modified by some parties, possibly aligning them with the GRIs announced by other parties.

(6) In the preliminary assessment, the Commission expressed the concern that GRI Announcements may be of very little value for customers; stating only the amount of an intended increase may not inform customers of the new full price they will be asked to pay in the future. In addition, the Commission has concerns that GRI Announcements may have only limited committal value and thus, customers may not be able to rely on them for their purchasing decisions.

(7) In the preliminary assessment, the Commission expressed the concern that this practice may allow the parties to explore each other's pricing intentions and to coordinate their behaviour. The Commission is concerned that the practice may enable the parties to 'test', without incurring the risk of losing customers, whether they can reasonably implement a price increase and thereby may reduce strategic uncertainty for the parties and diminish the incentives to compete. The Commission is concerned that this conduct may amount to a concerted practice in violation of Article 101 TFEU and Article 53 of the EEA Agreement.

3. Main content of the offered commitments

(8) The parties do not agree that they have engaged in the practice described above nor do they agree with the legal analysis in the Commission's preliminary assessment. The parties have nevertheless offered commitments pursuant to Article 9 of Regulation (EC) No 1/2003 to meet the Commission's competition concerns in relation to the abovementioned practice. The parties have emphasised that this should not be interpreted as an acknowledgement that they have infringed the EU competition rules, or as an admission of liability.

(9) The commitments are briefly described below and published in full in English on the website of the Directorate-General for Competition at: http://ec.europa.eu/competition/index_en.html

(10) The parties offer to stop publishing and communicating GRI announcements, i.e. changes to prices expressed solely as the amount or percentage of the change.

(11) The parties will not be obliged to publish or communicate (hereinafter referred to as 'announce') their prices, but should they choose to do so, the announcements must

enable purchasers to understand and rely on them. For that purpose the parties offer that price announcements will contain at least the following information:

(a) the amount of the base rate, bunker charges ('BAF'), security charges, terminal handling charges ('THC') and peak season charges ('PSS', or similar charges);
(b) which other charges may apply;
(c) the services to which they apply;
(d) the period to which they relate (which can be either expressed as a fixed period or open ended, in which case prices are valid until further notice).

Announcements will not be made more than 31 days before implementation day.

(12) The parties shall be bound by their price announcements during their validity period as maximum prices, but will be free to offer lower prices.
(13) In order to facilitate the conduct of business, the parties include two exceptions to the commitments in situations that would be unlikely to give rise to the Commission's competition concerns. The commitments will not apply to:

(a) communications with purchasers who on that date have a rate agreement in force on the route to which the communication refers;
(b) communications during bilateral negotiations or communications tailored to the needs of identified purchasers.

The parties shall however remain bound by the maximum prices set out in relevant price announcements that are applicable to the same services and customers referred to in the communications, under the conditions set out in the commitments.

(14) The commitments will apply for 3 years to all routes to and from the EEA.
(15) The commitments will not prevent the parties from complying with requirements based on laws or regulations of other jurisdictions.

4. Invitation to make comments

(16) Subject to market testing, the Commission intends to adopt a decision under Article 9(1) of Regulation No 1/2003 declaring binding the commitments summarised above and published on the Internet, on the website of the Directorate-General for Competition.
(17) In accordance with Article 27(4) of Regulation 1/2003, the Commission invites interested third parties to submit their observations on the proposed commitments. These observations must reach the Commission not later than one month following the date of this publication. Interested third parties are also asked to submit a non-confidential version of their comments, in which any information they claim to be business secrets and other confidential information should be deleted and replaced as required by a non-confidential summary or by the words 'business secrets' or 'confidential'.
(18) Answers and comments should preferably be reasoned and should set out the relevant facts. If you identify a problem with any part of the proposed commitments, the Commission would also invite you to suggest a possible solution.
(19) Observations can be sent to the Commission under reference AT.39850 — Container Shipping, either by email (COMP-GREFFE-ANTITRUST@ec.europa.eu), by fax (+32 22950128) or by post, to the following address:

European Commission
Directorate-General for Competition
Antitrust Registry
1049 Bruxelles/Brussel
BELGIQUE/BELGIË"

On 7 July 2016, the Commission published a press release indicating that it had accepted commitments by the container companies.[253] The press release read:

"Antitrust: Commission accepts commitments by container liner shipping companies on price transparency

Brussels, 7 July 2016
The European Commission has adopted a decision that renders legally binding the commitments offered by fourteen container liner shipping companies. The commitments aim to increase price transparency for customers and to reduce the likelihood of coordinating prices.

The commitments address the Commission's concerns that the companies' practice of publishing their intentions on future price increases may have harmed competition and customers. This practice may have raised prices on the market for container liner shipping services on routes to and from Europe, in breach of EU antitrust rules.

Commissioner in charge of competition policy, Margrethe Vestager, said: 'Container shipping accounts for the vast majority of the non-bulk freight carried by sea to and from Europe. Competitive shipping services are therefore essential for European companies and for the EU's economy as a whole. The commitments offered by 14 carriers will make prices for these services more transparent and increase competition'.

Container liner shipping is the transport of containers by ship according to a fixed time schedule on a specific route between a range of ports at one end (e.g. Shanghai – Hong Kong – Singapore) and another range of ports at the other end (e.g. Rotterdam – Hamburg – Southampton). More than half of EU imports and exports are carried by sea, of which around 40% is shipped in containers.

The General Rate Increases announcements
Fourteen container liner shipping companies ('carriers') have regularly announced their intended future increases of freight prices on their websites, via the press, or in other ways. The carriers are CMA CGM (France), COSCO (China), Evergreen (Taiwan), Hamburg Süd (Germany), Hanjin (South Korea), Hapag Lloyd (Germany), HMM (South Korea), Maersk (Denmark), MOL (Japan), MSC (Switzerland), NYK (Japan), OOCL (Hong Kong), UASC (UAE) and ZIM (Israel).

These price announcements, known as General Rate Increases or GRI announcements, do not indicate the fixed final price for the service concerned, but only the amount of the increase in US Dollars per transported container unit (twenty-foot equivalent unit, 'TEU'), the affected trade route and the planned date of implementation. They generally concern sizable increases of several hundred US Dollars per TEU.

General Rate Increase announcements are made typically three to five weeks before their intended implementation date, and during that time some or all of the other carriers announce similar intended rate increases for the same or similar route and same or similar implementation dates. Carriers are not bound by the announced increases and some carriers have indeed postponed or modified announced general rate increases, possibly aligning them with those announced by other carriers.

The Commission's competition concerns
The Commission had concerns that General Rate Increase announcements do not provide full information on new prices to customers but merely allow carriers to be aware of each other's pricing intentions and may make it possible for them to coordinate their behaviour.

Announcing future price increases may signal the intended market conduct of carriers and by reducing the level of uncertainty about their pricing behaviour, decrease their incentives to compete against each other. Because the announcements provide only partial information to customers, and may not be binding on the carriers, customers may not be able to rely on them and therefore carriers may be able to adjust prices without the risk of losing customers.

---
[253] IP/16/2446, http://europa.eu/rapid/press-release_IP-16-2446_en.htm.

This practice may lead to higher prices for container liner shipping services and harm competition and customers, in breach of EU and European Economic Area (EEA) competition rules' ban on concerted practices between companies (Article 101 of the Treaty on the Functioning of the European Union (TFEU) and Article 53 of the EEA Agreement).

The carriers' commitments
In order to address the Commission's concerns, the carriers offered the following commitments:

the carriers will stop publishing and communicating General Rate Increase announcements, i.e. changes to prices expressed solely as an amount or percentage of the change in order for any future price announcements to be useful for customers, the carriers will announce figures that include at least the five main elements of the total price (base rate, bunker charges, security charges, terminal handling charges and peak season charges if applicable)
price announcements will be binding on the carriers as maximum prices for the announced period of validity (but carriers will remain free to offer prices below these ceilings)
price announcements will not be made more than 31 days before their entry into force, which corresponds to the period when customers usually start booking in significant volumes (typically, customers plan their shipments between 4 weeks and 1 week before they need to move their consignments) and the commitments will not apply to:

a) communications with purchasers who already have an existing rate agreement in force on the route to which the communication refers
b) communications during bilateral negotiations or communications tailored to the needs of specific identified purchasers.

After carrying out a market test of the commitments, the Commission is satisfied that they address its concerns. They will increase price transparency for customers and reduce the likelihood of concerted price signaling by binding the carriers to the prices announced.

The Commission has therefore made the commitments legally binding on the carriers for a period of three years starting from 7 December 2016.

Background
Article 101 of the Treaty on the Functioning of the European Union (TFEU) and Article 53 of the EEA Agreement prohibit agreements and concerted practices which may affect trade and prevent or restrict competition.

The Commission opened formal antitrust proceedings on its own initiative to investigate the practice of publishing General Rate Increase announcements in November 2013. The Commission invited comments from interested parties on the commitments offered by the carriers in February 2016. After the market test China Shipping was restructured and it exited the container liner shipping business. It was therefore not necessary for it to offer commitments.

Article 9 of the EU's Antitrust Regulation (Regulation 1/2003) allows the Commission to conclude an antitrust investigation by making commitments offered by a company legally binding. Such a decision does not conclude that there is an infringement of the EU antitrust rules but legally binds the companies concerned to respect the commitments offered. If a company breaks such commitments, the Commission can impose a fine of up to 10% of the company's worldwide turnover, without having to find an infringement of the EU antitrust rules. A policy brief on commitment decisions under Article 9 is available here.

More information, including the full non-confidential version of the decision and commitments, will be made available on the Commission's competition website in the public case register under case number 39850, once any confidentiality issues have been resolved."

T. THE *MARITIME CAR CARRIERS* CASE

12.204 On 7 September 2012, the European Commission confirmed

"that on 6 September 2012 Commission officials carried out unannounced inspections at the premises of several providers of maritime transport services for cars and construction and agricultural rolling machinery. Inspections took place in several Member States in coordination with the US and Japanese Competition Authorities. The Commission has reasons to believe that the companies concerned may have violated Article 101 of the TFEU, which prohibits cartels and restrictive business practices."

It explained that unannounced inspections are

"a preliminary step in investigations into suspected cartels. The fact that the European Commission carries out such inspections does not mean that the companies are guilty of anti-competitive behaviour; nor does it prejudge the outcome of the investigation itself. The European Commission respects the rights of defence, in particular the right of companies to be heard in antitrust proceedings."

U. OUTLOOK

12.205 The fact that the Commission may now apply the EU competition rules to the entire shipping sector (including tramp and cabotage) means that the industry has to be very careful to comply with competition law. Market participants have to be scrupulous to avoid price-fixing, exchanging competitively sensitive information, allocating customers, dividing up markets or other possible breaches of competition law. The maritime sector is now as subject to all areas of competition law as any other sector so it will be fascinating to see how the rules of EU competition law will be applied to the sector.

CHAPTER 13

European Union competition law: ports

A. INTRODUCTION

Scope of the chapter

13.001 This chapter examines the application of European Union ("EU")[1] competition law to ports.[2] It builds on chapter 10 which contains an overview of EU competition law generally and focuses on how these general competition law rules have been, and could be, applied to ports.[3]

---

1 The chapter confines its analysis to EU competition law but it should be recalled that national competition law (e.g. national case law) can also be relevant (e.g. the UK's case law relating to the *SvitzerWijsmuller/ Adstream* merger has a great deal of interesting analysis on competition in ports and market definition in the context of towage services in a port: www.competition-commission.org.uk/inquiries/ref2006/adsteam/pdf/ notice_of_acceptance_of_final_undertakings.pdf, as well as studies by the Irish and Portuguese competition agencies on competition in ports. It is possible, in a world of growing "modernisation"/"decentralisation" of EU competition law that Member State competition law could become even more important. However, as there is usually a cross-border element to port competition cases (with the limited exception of purely cabotage services), EU competition law will remain important.

2 See the EU's submission to the Organisation for Economic Co-operation and Development's ("OECD") Directorate for Financial and Enterprise Affairs' Competition Committee on competition in ports entitled "Competition Concerns in Ports and Port Services" DAF/COMP/WP2/WD(2011)40 and dated 27 June 2011.

On EU competition law and ports, see Lindström-Rossi, "The Application of EC Competition Rules to the Port Sector" in Antapassis, Athanassiou and Røsæg (eds), *Competition and Regulation in Shipping and Shipping Related Industries* (2009), p. 139. More generally, see Chlomoudis and Pallis, *European Port Policy: Towards a Long-Term Strategy* (2002). See also Pallis, "Towards a Common Ports Policy? EU-Proposals and the Industry's Perceptions" (1997) 24 *Maritime Policy and Management* 365. See also Giles, "Ports, Vertical Issues and Finding Solutions", Lloyd's Maritime Academy, "EU Competition Law in Shipping", 27 March 2009; Power, "European Union Seaports Law: The General Principles of European Union Law" in Van Hooydonk (ed.), *European Seaports Law* (2003), p. 17; Power, "Aspects of EC Maritime Policy: A Lawyer's Reaction" [1996] ETL 179; Power, "European Union Law and Sea-Ports", Academy of European Law, Trier and Institute of the Law of the Sea and of Maritime Law Hamburg, Hamburg, 19 June 2001; Power, "European Union Ports Law", British Tugowners' Association, Glasgow, 27 April 2001; Power, "EU Ports Law: The Latest Developments and a Primer for Everyone Involved", United Kingdom Harbourmasters' Association, London, 26 September 2001; Power, "European Union Ports Law", Keynote Address to European Commission/ DG Enlargement Seaport Policy Conference, Gdansk, Poland, 17 October 2002; Power, "EC Competition Law Affecting Ports", European Ports' Forum Workshop, Rotterdam, 21 May 2003; Power, "An Overview of EC Competition Law as it relates to the Shipping and Port Sectors", European Maritime Law Organisation ("EMLO") Conference, Gdansk, Poland, 8 May 2006; Power, "European Union Legal Aspects of Ports", Irish Ports Association, Galway, 29 September 2006; Power, "European Union State Aid Law and Ports", EMLO, Eugenides Foundation, Athens, 18 April 2008; Power, "State Aid and Ports: General Principles and a Comparative Perspective", EMLO, 15th Annual Conference, London, 23–24 October 2009; Power, "The Applicability of General EU Transport and European Law to the Port Sector", University of Antwerp, 7 December 2000; and Power, "The European Union's Proposed Directive on Port Services", London, United Kingdom Harbour Masters' Association, 21 March 2001.

3 Obviously, this chapter relates to seaports, but many of the principles relating to airports and other transport facilities could also be relevant to seaports as well.

Relevance of competition law to ports

13.002 Competition law has become a lively issue for ports in recent years. This is, in part, because the way in which many ports perform their operations has changed in recent years – for example, there has been an increased incidence of privatisation, deregulation and/or liberalisation.[4] There has been a move towards more efficient work practices in ports. Port users are demanding more competition, lower prices, more flexible work practices and the ability to self-supply some services.[5] There has also been the development of so-called public–private partnerships in some ports whereby there is an interplay between the State/public and commercial private sectors. EU law is neutral in terms of the ownership of property (i.e. EU law does not prefer public or private ownership)[6] so competition law applies irrespective of whether the port or the port infrastructure is owned publicly or privately.

13.003 Many of the competition law issues arising in ports relate to the issues of cargo handling, pricing, discrimination, conditions of operation and access to ports.[7] In regard to cargo handling, for example, some port users have wanted to be able to load or discharge cargo themselves without having to use the port's staff or the port's preferred suppliers of workers. In regard to access to ports, some cases have involved ferry operators seeking access to ports, better facilities or more attractive pricing within ports. There could be illegal market partitioning in ports.

13.004 Competition in ports can be made more difficult by virtue of high barriers to entry, high level of supply-side concentration, high capacity utilisation rate of port infrastructures and the consequent risk of bottlenecks, vertical integration of certain port operators and the absence of countervailing buyer power among some users of port infrastructures. The presence of such factors does not mean that there would always be an anti-competitive issue but they are indicators to be monitored.

Competition law applies to ports

13.005 The principles of EU competition law have been applied to ports by the EU in cases relating to, for example, Holyhead, Genoa, Rødby and Roscoff.[8] This is, in relative terms, one of the boom areas of EU shipping law but there have not been many reported cases in recent years.[9] These cases have involved a consideration of each of the

---

4 This liberalisation process is designed to enable other service providers (i.e. providers other than the port itself) to enter the port, increase competition and provide a choice for the users of the port.

5 E.g. self-handling which enables operators of ships to load and discharge cargo without the need to use the port's staff.

6 TFEU, Art. 345.

7 In the EU report sent to the OECD (see fn. 2), the EU stated: "2. [t]he pattern of activity within ports is very complex. Certain activities pertain to typical public authority tasks (e.g. traffic control). Other activities are economic in nature, for example the provision of access to port infrastructure and services (essentially cargo handling and technical-nautical services, such as pilotage, towage and mooring) which are increasingly provided by private undertakings. There is wide diversity as to the ownership, organisation and financing of ports in Europe with an increasing number of private sector participation in the provision of port services. Nevertheless, and as opposed to maritime transport services, port services have not yet been liberalised in the European Union. Two legislative proposals (in 2003 and 2006) on market access to port services drafted by the Commission were rejected by the European Parliament."

8 These and other cases are examined in the remainder of the chapter.

9 It is clear that the principles developed in the earlier cases have been applied in later unreported cases without the need to institute proceedings or make complaints.

competition provisions of the Treaty on the Functioning of the European Union ("TFEU") but also a combination of Articles (e.g. Article 102 of the TFEU coupled with Article 106 of the TFEU). Indeed, Articles 102 and 106 have been particularly significant but Article 101 is no less relevant even if there are very few cases in the public domain relating to Article 101. These cases will be examined individually later in the chapter.

13.006 Before considering the specific application of competition law to ports, it is useful to consider the background to ports generally. It is trite but true that ports are an indispensable part of the shipping chain. This is no different in the case of the ports in the EU. Joe Borg, the former Commissioner for Fisheries and Maritime Affairs, stated:

> "European maritime regions are connected to other regions and continents by world maritime traffic. The strategic importance of Europe's 1,200 ports is constantly increasing: around 90% of the EU's foreign trade and 40% of its internal trade is carried out by sea. This explains why the European Union is making considerable efforts to develop seaports. For the period 2000–2006, the total amount of aid flowing to seaports from different instruments such as the cohesion fund, the European Regional Development Fund, or ERDF, and the Financial Instrument for Fisheries Guidance, the FIFG, amounted to 3.6 billion euros."[10]

He also spoke of the functions of ports in the following terms:

> "[p]orts ... play a central role in our economy. Although ports may originally have been built to simply load and unload ships, they have grown to become crucial industry and service hubs in a worldwide logistics chain. In turn, port cities have become prime locations for the siting of industrial activities, for tourism and residential areas. Far from being dedicated to solely one activity, they have now become truly multi-functional...
>
> The multi-functional role of ports and port cities means that ports' policy cannot be based on the transport considerations alone. A broader perspective is a must. This needs to include environmental and regional development issues, as well as the relationship between the port and its host city, for example. In much the same way that ports deal with a multi-faceted reality so too does the maritime sector at large."[11]

The Commission has written:

> "80% of world trade is carried by sea whilst short-sea shipping carries 40% of intra-European freight. With more than 400 million sea passengers passing through European ports each year, maritime transport has ... a direct impact on the quality of life of citizens, both as tourists and inhabitants of islands and peripheral regions."[12]

The EU's 1,200 ports handle around 40% of the tonne-kilometres carried in intra-EU trade and provide more than half a million jobs. Apart from the economic, transport, employment, social, cultural and other dimensions, ports also have an environmental dimension because greater use of ports means a reduced use of roads and this reduces damage to the environment.

13.007 If there is a lack of competition at the port level – for example, if there are higher prices than there ought to be (e.g. due to price-fixing) or there is no competition in terms of the supply of services and therefore the cost of using the port is higher than it

---

10 Borg, "Redefining Europe's Borders: Bringing the Sea to the Forefront", 11 May 2007, Speech/07/304. The "ERDF" refers to the European Regional Development Fund. The FIFG refers to the Financial Instrument for Fisheries Guidance.

11 Borg, op. cit. at fn. 10.

12 Commission, *Communication from the Commission to the European Parliament, the Council, the European Economic and Social Committee and the Committee of the Regions – Strategic Goals and Recommendations for the EU's Maritime Transport Policy until 2018* (COM(2009) 0008 final).

ought to be – then that increased price cascades down the supply chain such that consumers down the economic chain pay more for the goods which have passed through ports and could get supplies later or not at all. Equally, because ports play an important cross-roads role between different transport modes,[13] any increased prices or anti-competitive behaviour imports can have a contagion effect across different modes and across the economy generally.

13.008 There is an enormous diversity between EU ports in terms of their ownership, structure, financing, regulation and so on. For example, some ports are owned publicly (e.g. by the State or regional authorities) or privately (e.g. by companies whose shares are listed on stock exchanges). Some ports are structured and operated as landlord ports (leaving aspects of the operation of the port to others) while some ports are operated by the port owners. All of this diversity is challenging for the EU but EU law is neutral on the choice between public and private ownership.[14] The EU competition rules can thus be applied to ports whether public or private provided such ports are "undertakings" for the purposes of competition law. While many ports are publicly owned, there is a growing number of private ports. In the case of publicly owned ports, there is a risk that the role of the port in assisting the local economy and other public interest goals can distort the normal forces of competition in the market so competition law needs to address this issue and it does so primarily through the rules on (a) State aid as well as (b) State authorities as well as the general competition law rules.

13.009 Competition law can be an issue for ports in different ways: the port as gatekeeper of facilities; the port as infrastructure owner; the port as a competitor with other ports; the port as owner of the facilities; and the allocator of resources and facilities within the port. As just mentioned, sometimes ports act simply as a landlord and let others perform the services. At other times, the port operates the port services itself. In that respect, competition is a multidimensional issue for ports.

13.010 Competition in ports is somewhat complicated by the fact that the issues are often about the use or cost of infrastructure – this is all the more complicated where the infrastructure could not be supplemented, replicated or contracted easily. It is often impossible to increase or decrease supply (i.e. capacity) at ports very easily or quickly (as capacity often cannot be added easily or quickly). It is often easier for a carrier to add "tonnage" (i.e. a new ship) than for a port to add capacity within the port (e.g. facilities) so this can prove to be a challenge. There is often the allegation that port operators could be charging monopoly profits because of their dominance in the port and the difficulties facing others (and indeed the port itself) to expand capacity and the facilities.

13.011 Pricing by ports is often a little more complicated than in many other sectors. There is usually a fixed supply of equipment and services such that expansion is quite difficult to achieve in the short term. Charges are usually one of two types: (a) charges often known as concession fees or licence fees paid by the providers of port services in the port (e.g. stevedore or terminal operator) in return for the use of infrastructure; and (b) charges known as port dues paid by vessels (e.g. shipowner) calling at the port to use the port

---

13 See the comment of Lindström-Rossi, op. cit. at fn. 2, p. 139 on the connection between ports and other modes of transport.
14 TFEU, Art. 345.

itself. The person who sets the charges can vary from case to case – for example, sometimes it is the port and sometimes it is a local or central authority.

13.012 There are several trends and situations which accentuate the need for competition law intervention in ports. First, there are increasing levels of vertical integration whereby ports are owned by carriers with the same owner operating the port and operating *in* the port in competition with others. Second, there are increasing levels of consolidation in the port sector. Third, towage, wharfage, pilotage and other issues have become more involved over the years with more than one supplier actually or wanting to supply services. Fourth, there is ongoing provision of State aid to ports and while there has always been State aid, the EU rules are relatively recent in terms of their effect and being well-known in the context of ports.[15]

Absence of specific competition law rules in the context of ports

13.013 There is no sector-specific EU competition legislation relating to ports. This means that Articles 101–109 of the TFEU apply in full to competition in ports. It means that the principles used in regard to airports, intellectual property rights and other sectors of the economy can be, and need to be, applied to ports in addition to the jurisprudence which has developed in regard to ports.

Examples of need to comply with competition law

13.014 Ports must ensure that they comply with competition law because they would suffer if they do not comply (e.g. fines). It is useful to take two examples.

13.015 Ports have to be careful that they do not enter into arrangements[16] which have the object or effect of preventing, restricting or distorting competition in the internal market or any part of the internal market because such arrangements would be prohibited under Article 101(1) of the TFEU and void under Article 101(2) of the TFEU unless the arrangements could be capable of falling within the scope of Article 101(3) of the TFEU.

13.016 It is easy to allege that a port is in a dominant position for the purposes of Article 102 of the TFEU because every port has some unique feature which could suggest dominance but it is necessary to define the correct market in which the port is operating to determine whether the port is dominant and where there is an abuse of dominance. However, it will be recalled from chapter 11 generally, that being in a dominant position does not constitute a breach of Article 102. Instead, it would have to be demonstrated that the port or other undertaking had a dominant position and, moreover, abused that dominance. It is possible, in the very specific circumstances of a case, that even a small port could have a dominant position.[17]

---

15 On State aid law, see, in particular, chap. 15.
16 I.e. agreements between undertakings, decisions by associations of undertakings and concerted practices involving undertakings.
17 This is often case with ferry ports (e.g. see the Holyhead, Roscoff and Rødby cases mentioned later in this chapter).

Competition law rules relevant to ports

13.017 In so far as the EU, and the European Commission in particular, want to liberalise (or make more competitive) ports and services within ports then it can use the competition provisions as part of its toolbox or armoury. (Despite the perception in some quarters, the EU does not want to privatise ports.) The most pertinent provisions, to date, have been Article 102 of the TFEU and Articles 106 of the TFEU but Articles 101 and 107–109 of the TFEU are also relevant. Article 106 is particularly relevant where there is a Member State-imposed obstacle to competition because it is addressed to Member States and can be used in combination with another provision of the treaty (most often, in this context, Article 102 of the TFEU).

13.018 It will be recalled that Article 106(1) of the TFEU prohibits Member States, in the case of public undertakings and undertakings to which they grant special or exclusive rights, from enacting or maintaining measures contrary to the rules of the TFEU and, in particular, the competition rules of the TFEU. However, Article 106(2) of the TFEU deals with undertakings entrusted with the operation of services of general economic interest (so-called SGEIs) which are the subject of the competition rules in the TFEU but only in so far as the application of those rules does not obstruct the performance, in law or in fact, of the particular tasks assigned to those undertakings. The CJEU has stated that cargo handling services in a port are typically not services of general economic interest[18] but are commercial activities and therefore subject to the competition rules. The CJEU said that, on the other hand, so-called technical/nautical services (e.g. pilotage, towage and mooring in ports) may well fall within the definition of an SGEI provided certain conditions are satisfied.[19]

13.019 The Essential Facilities Doctrine has been important in the case of ports. The Doctrine posits that the owner of a facility (e.g. port infrastructure) which has a dominant position in a market could be abusing its dominance contrary to Article 102 of the TFEU where it refuses unjustifiably access to the facility to actual or potential competitors on non-discriminatory terms. The doctrine covers facilities other than purely physical ones such as intellectual property rights.[20] The European Commission has been more ambitious about applying the doctrine[21] than the European Courts.[22] The Doctrine is part of the wider law relating to refusal to supply as an abuse of dominance. While the Doctrine remains useful and could well be used in appropriate port cases, it is not proving as useful as it appeared it would do following the early European Commission cases.

---

18 Case C-179/90 *Merci Convenzionali Porto di Genova SpA v Siderurgica Gabrielli SpA* [1991] ECR I-5889, ECLI:EU:C:1991:464.

19 E.g. in Case C-266/96 *Corsica Ferries France SA v Gruppo Antichi Ormeggiatori del porto di Genova Coop. arl, Gruppo Ormeggiatori del Golfo di La Spezia Coop. arl and Ministero dei Trasporti e della Navigazione* [1998] ECR I-3949, ECLI:EU:C:1998:306 (*Corsica Ferries III*) the Court of Justice of the European Union ("CJEU") held that mooring services were SGEIs. The European Commission stated in a non-paper entitled *Services of general economic interest and state aid* (12 November 2002) at para. 16: "[the CJEU] considered that the loading, unloading, transshipment, storage and general movement of goods or material of any kind within a port are not necessarily of a general economic interest exhibiting special characteristics as compared with the general economic interest of other economic activities".

20 E.g. Cases C-241/91 P and C-242/91 P *Magill* [1995] ECR 743, ECLI:EU:C:1995:98.

21 E.g. *Holyhead I: Sealink/B&I* Case IV/34.174, OJ 1994 L15/8, [1992] 5 CMLR 255, and *Holyhead II: Sea Containers/Sealink* Case IV/34.689, OJ L15/8, 18 January 1994.

22 E.g. Case C-7/97 *Bronner v Mediaprint and Others* [1998] ECR I-7791, ECLI:EU:C:1998:569 and Case T-374/94 *European Night Services* [1998] ECR II-3141, ECLI:EU:T:1998:198.

Application of competition law to undertakings: ports as undertakings

13.020 It will be recalled that competition law essentially only applies to the behaviour of "undertakings". Thus, for example, Articles 101, 102 and 106 of the TFEU apply only to control "undertakings". A port is very likely to be an undertaking where it is engaged in economic activities[23] but it is not an undertaking in respect of all of its activities. For example, if a port is engaged in non-economic or non-commercial activities (e.g. regulatory and environmental clean-up activities) then the EU competition law rules do not apply to the port in that particular context.

13.021 It will be recalled that undertakings are those entities engaged in economic activities. The CJEU had to consider in *Diego Calì*[24] whether anti-pollution surveillance in an oil port constituted an economic activity to which the EU competition rules apply even though the activity in question had been entrusted to a private entity by public authorities and the users were charged a fee to finance the activity. The CJEU held that the port was not an undertaking in that context:

"16. As regards the possible application of the competition rules of the [TFEU], a distinction must be drawn between a situation where the State acts in the exercise of official authority and that where it carries on economic activities of an industrial or commercial nature by offering goods or services on the market (Case 118/85 Commission v Italy [1987] ECR 2599, paragraph 7).25

17. In that connection, it is of no importance that the State is acting directly through a body forming part of the State administration or by way of a body on which it has conferred special or exclusive rights (Case 118/85 Commission v Italy, cited above, paragraph 8).

18. In order to make the distinction between the two situations referred to in paragraph 16 above, it is necessary to consider the nature of the activities carried on by the public undertaking or body on which the State has conferred special or exclusive rights (Case 118/85 Commission v Italy, cited above, paragraph 7).

19. On this point, it is clear from the order for reference26 and the wording of the first question that the main proceedings concern the payment to be made by Calì for anti-pollution surveillance exercised by SEPG in relation to the loading and unloading of acetone products transported by Calì in the oil port of Genoa.

20. Furthermore, it is common ground that the dispute in the main proceedings does not concern the invoicing of any action by SEPG necessitated by pollution actually produced during loading or unloading operations.

21. Article 1 of Order No 32 of the President of CAP27 referred to above expressly distinguishes, moreover, between surveillance intended to prevent pollution and intervention in a case where pollution has occurred and it provides (Article 1(b)(2)) that those responsible for the pollution are to bear the costs arising from any action deemed necessary or advisable.

---

23 See, for example, the cases in this chapter relating to Holyhead, Roscoff and Rødby.
24 Case C-343/95 *Diego Calì & Figli Srl v Servizi ecologici porto di Genova SpA* [1997] ECR I-1547, ECLI:EU:C:1997:160.
25 Ed., ECLI:EU:C:1987:283.
26 Ed., the order for reference is the document sent to the CJEU by the Member State court making the reference.
27 Ed., the judgment states at para. 3: "[a]t the material time, the port of Genoa was managed by the Consorzio Autonomo del Porto (hereinafter 'CAP'), which was replaced in 1994 by the Autorità Portuale (Port Authority). The CAP was a public body upon which both the administrative and economic functions relating to the management of the port had been conferred by legislation."

22. The anti-pollution surveillance for which SEPG was responsible in the oil port of Genoa is a task in the public interest which forms part of the essential functions of the State as regards protection of the environment in maritime areas.
23. Such surveillance is connected by its nature, its aim and the rules to which it is subject with the exercise of powers relating to the protection of the environment which are typically those of a public authority. It is not of an economic nature justifying the application of the Treaty rules on competition (Case C-364/92 SAT Fluggesellschaft v Eurocontrol [1994] ECR I-43,28 paragraph 30).
24. The levying of a charge by SEPG for preventive anti-pollution surveillance is an integral part of its surveillance activity in the maritime area of the port and cannot affect the legal status of that activity (Case C-364/92 SAT Fluggesellschaft v Eurocontrol, cited above, paragraph 28). Moreover, as stated in paragraph 8 of this judgment, the tariffs applied by SEPG have been approved by the public authorities.
25. In the light of the foregoing considerations, the answer to Question 1 must be that Article [106 of the TFEU] is to be interpreted as not being applicable to anti-pollution surveillance with which a body governed by private law has been entrusted by the public authorities in an oil port of a Member State, even where port users must pay dues to finance that activity."

13.022 The Court of Justice of the European Union ("CJEU") had to consider a similar (but not identical) issue in *Jean Claude Becu Annie Verweire, NV Smeg & NV Adia Interim*.[29] This case related to Belgian legislation which reserved dock work in port areas to recognised dock workers. The conditions relating to the work were governed by collective agreement which were concluded on the basis of the Belgian law. The CJEU held that the recognised dock workers performed the work for, and under, the direction of each of various undertakings in the port and as a result of this they were to be regarded as "workers" and would not be regarded as "undertakings" for the purposes of EU competition law. The CJEU stated:

"Article [106(1) of the TFEU], read in conjunction with the first paragraph of Article [18 of the TFEU] and Articles [101 and 102 of the TFEU], must be interpreted as meaning that it does not confer on individuals the right to oppose the application of legislation of a Member State which requires them to have recourse, for the performance of dock work, exclusively to recognised dockers such as those referred to in the Belgian Law of 8 June 1972 organising dock work, and to pay those dockers remuneration far in excess of the wages of their own employees or the wages which they pay to other workers."

Application of the EU competition rules to ports generally

13.023 All of the rules of EU competition law apply to ports. So it is a matter of applying the concepts and rules of EU competition law generally in the context of ports. Market definition is a very significant issue in port cases.[30] In practice, the cases relate more often to abuse of dominance rather than anti-competitive arrangements – for example, the Essential Facilities Doctrine (normally part of the law on abuse of dominance) has been

---

28 Ed., ECLI:EU:C:1994:7.
29 Case C-22/98 *Jean Claude Becu, Annie Verweire, NV Smeg and NV Adia Interim* [1999] ECR I-05665, ECLI:EU:C:1999:419.
30 E.g. in *Irish Continental Group v Chambre de Commerce et Industries de Morlaix* [1995] 5 CMLR 177, the outcome of the case could have been different had the geographical market been the wider Ireland–France market rather than the narrower Ireland–Brittany market – the Commission held that the latter market definition was the relevant one.

particularly important in the case of ports and is discussed below. Concentration control is also relevant in the context of the sale and purchase of ports as well as joint ventures involving ports. As many ports in the EU are State-owned, the rules on State authorities are also relevant. Indeed, whether the ports are publicly or privately owned, the State aid rules are very pertinent where Member States provide assistance to ports or port users. Specific competition thinking such as those relating to issues such as information exchange, price-fixing, discriminatory pricing, privatisation, and so on can be very important for ports.

B. OBTAINING ACCESS TO PORTS

Introduction

13.024 The threshold or preliminary issue in regard to the application of competition law to ports is that of "access to ports". Without access, all other issues (e.g. pricing and discrimination) would be entirely theoretical. Competition law has been used by some shipping companies so as to obtain access to ports. In part, it was necessary to use competition law because there is no general EU legislation enabling users of port infrastructure to have the right to access port facilities.[31]

Anti-competitive arrangements

13.025 If two undertakings (e.g. a port and an operator in the port) agreed to deliberately keep out an actual or potential operator/user of the port in the EU then one would presume that such an agreement or concerted practice would have the object or effect of preventing, restricting or distorting competition in the internal market or any part of the internal market and thereby be in breach of Article 101 of the TFEU. This would be a rare situation and would arise in the case of, for example, a collective boycott of a potential user. If, for example, ports shared with other ports information on credit histories or records of port users then whatever may be the competition law issue associated with the information exchange, it would ordinarily be a breach of Article 101 for the ports to agree collectively not to supply services to a user until that user had paid all of them in full.

Abuse of dominance

13.026 If a port is in a dominant position and it refuses to allow a putative user access to the port then the refusal could, in certain circumstances, amount to an abuse of dominance. This is based, in certain cases, on the Doctrine of Essential Facilities. The case law – and the right to access – covers not only *existing* customers but also *new* customers. Any unjustified refusal to supply by a dominant undertaking could well be in breach of Article 102 of the TFEU.

---

31 Unlike, for example, the air transport sector where one can access slots at EU airports by virtue of EU legislation.

Roscoff: **Irish Continental Group v CCI Morlaix**

13.027 It is useful to consider just one example of a case relating to obtaining access to a port.[32] *Irish Continental Group v CCI Morlaix*[33] is a leading EU case on access to ports. In essence, the case involved the granting of interim measures to Irish Continental Group ("ICG")[34] which had sought access to the port of Roscoff in Brittany in France which was operated by the Chambre de Commerce et d'Industrie de Morlaix ("CCI") but was refused access by the CCI. ICG complained to the Commission and sought interim measures which the Commission then granted on the basis of the abuse of dominance by the CCI.

13.028 It is useful to consider the case in more depth. ICG was (and is) an Irish-based ferry operator. In November 1994, ICG applied to the CCI to seek access from May 1995 to the port of Roscoff with a view to operating a service between Ireland (in particular, using the ports of Cork and Rosslare) and Roscoff in France. According to ICG, following negotiations between ICG and the CCI, the parties agreed in principle on 16 December 1994 on the terms of access to the port. ICG said that sailing schedules and certain technical matters were agreed and sailings would commence on 27 May 1995. In December 1994, ICG advertised the service and took a significant number of bookings (i.e. many thousands of passengers booked). In January 1995, CCI indicated its wish to ICG to suspend the arrangement. ICG wanted to continue with the arrangement. Subsequent negotiations proved fruitless. ICG believed that there was an agreement between the parties. CCI denied that there was an agreement. In February 1995, ICG complained to the Commission that it was being denied access to the port of Roscoff when ICG could not change CCI's mind on the issue. A hearing was held before the Commission in March 1995. Ultimately the Commission made a decision on 16 May 1995 ordering interim measures. The Commission found that there was a prima facie case that the CCI had abused its dominance as the operator of the port. The geographical market was found to be the Ireland–Brittany market and not the broader Ireland–France market. The Commission saw the market as Ireland to Brittany rather than Ireland to France because the route to Brittany was much shorter (almost 50% shorter). Roscoff was the only port at the time capable of providing adequate port facilities in Brittany for services between Brittany and Ireland.[35] The Commission held that Roscoff represented a substantial part of the internal market in regard to the Irish–Brittany ferry route and that the port authority's refusal to allow access was an abuse of dominance. The abuse of dominance involved an unjustified refusal to supply services. The Commission found that serious and irreparable harm would be caused to the applicant (i.e. ICG) had it been denied access to the port. The Commission ordered CCI to grant ICG access to the port of Roscoff by 10 June 1995 (or at such other time as the parties may agree). The interim measures would endure until the end of the summer season for that year pending a final decision. As the parties subsequently agreed on a five-year contract beginning from 14 June 1995, ICG withdrew its

---

[32] This case involved a new applicant seeking access.
[33] [1995] 5 CMLR 177. The decision was not published in the *Official Journal*. See Commission, *Competition Policy Newsletter* (Summer 1995) 1(5), p. 12.
[34] Incidentally, ICG bought B&I Line which featured in the *Holyhead I* case (discussed below) so unusually the same corporate group has benefited from the award of interim measures in two port cases.
[35] Another port (i.e. St. Malo) in Brittany which had a ferry ramp was unsuitable navigationally for the ferry intended to be used by ICG.

complaint and there was no final decision. Commenting in its annual report on competition policy, the Commission stated:

> "Interim measures are not justified merely to allow a new entrant to enter a market. In this case the Commission considered that [ICG] had been led to believe that it could begin operations, and that CCI Morlaix was largely responsible for the situation which developed as a result."[36]

This comment is interesting because it implies that new entrants could not benefit from the regime unless they could demonstrate some fault on the part of the undertaking refusing entry. In that way, the case was partly about fault or some form of estoppel.

C. OBTAINING ACCESS TO SERVICES IN PORTS

Introduction

13.029 It is interesting to turn from the concept of obtaining *access* to the port as such to the concept of obtaining *access to services* in ports (i.e. once access has been obtained).

13.030 Users of a port require various services in a port. Examples of such services include pilotage, towage, mooring, cargo handling, wharfage, medical services, environmental services, bunkers, water, electricity and so on.

13.031 There are certain situations where access to some transport facilities (e.g. airports)[37] is regulated by legislation. However, seaports currently have no such legislation. The proposal to adopt a directive on access to the port services market was rejected twice (in both 2003 and 2006).[38] In 2013, a regulation was proposed but has not, at the time of writing, been adopted. In the absence of a measure, the general principles of EU law (including EU competition law) apply. A distinction, but an imperfect one, is sometimes drawn between measures such as the failed directives being aimed at opening competition *for* the market and EU competition law at being aimed at opening or promoting competition *in* the market. EU competition law has forced competition in various contexts, most notably, in a series of cases relating to Italian ports.

Genoa: **Merci Convenzionali Porto di Genova SpA v Siderurgica Gabrielli SpA**

13.032 *Merci Convenzionali Porto di Genova SpA v Siderurgica Gabrielli SpA*[39] is an important case on the application of competition law to ports. The case involved a preliminary ruling by the CJEU in a reference from the Tribunale di Genova under Article 267 of the TFEU. This was an important case because it raises issues of port inefficiency as being an abuse of dominance.

---

36 Commission, *Report on Competition Policy (for 1995)*, p. 121.
37 E.g. Council Dir. 96/67 of 15 October 1996 on access to the groundhandling market at Community airports (OJ 1996 L272/36).
38 Lindström-Rossi has stated (op. cit. at fn. 2,, p. 139 at 143), that one of "the main objections to the proposed directive related to self-handling, i.e., the ability to use ship-crew rather than the established dock workers for cargo-handling, which was strongly opposed by the trade unions. At present, ports therefore remain the only part of transport which has not been liberalised through EU legislation."
39 Case C-179/90, [1991] ECR I-5889, ECLI:EU:C:1991:464.

13.033 A number of dock companies in Italy had a monopoly in the provision of port stevedoring services.[40] Under the Italian law at the time, the employees of such companies had to be of Italian nationality.[41] The port of Genoa was managed by the Conzorzio Autonomo del Porto which was a public body. This body granted exclusive management rights in the port to two wholly owned subsidiaries. One company handled container traffic. The other company, Merci Convenzionali Porto di Genova SpA ("Merci"), handled other goods. These two companies employed administrative personnel only because the two companies were obliged, as just mentioned, under the Italian Navigation Code to employ the services of Italian dockers in the port. These dockers were organised into a single company which had a monopoly for the loading and discharging of cargo in the port. This meant that there was a monopoly at the levels of both management (i.e. Merci) and dockers.

13.034 This monopoly was questioned before the Italian courts following industrial and commercial disputes. The facts of the case were straightforward. Siderurgica Gabrielli of Padua imported a shipment of steel from Hamburg. The ship on which the steel was carried had the necessary equipment to discharge the cargo itself. However, the ship was obliged by Italian law to use the services of Merci when in the port of Genoa. Meanwhile, Merci was obliged under the Italian Navigation Code to assign the work to the company of dockers operating in the port of Genoa and these dockers had to be Italian nationals.[42] These dockers were on strike. The cargo was unloaded three months late. Siderurgica instituted proceedings in an Italian court for damages. The Italian court referred the matter to the CJEU by way of a preliminary reference under Article 267 of the TFEU.

13.035 The questions posed were:

"(1) In the present state of [EU] law, where goods from a Member State of the [EU] are imported by sea into the territory of another Member State, does Article [106] of the [TFEU], together with the prohibitions contained in Articles [18 of the TEU as well 36, 101 and 102 of the TFEU], confer on persons subject to [EU] law rights which the Member States must respect, where a dock-work undertaking and/or company formed solely of national dock workers enjoys the exclusive right to carry out at compulsory standard rates the loading and unloading of goods in national ports, even when it is possible to perform those operations with the equipment and crew of the vessel?

(2) Does a dock-work undertaking and/or company formed solely of national dock workers, which enjoys the exclusive right to carry out at compulsory standard rates the loading and unloading of goods in national ports constitute, for the purposes of Article [106(2) of the TFEU], an undertaking entrusted with the operation of services of general economic interest and liable to be obstructed in the performance by the workforce of the particular tasks assigned to it by the application of Article [86(1) of the TFEU or the prohibitions under Articles 36, 101 and 102 of the TFEU]?"[43]

---

40 Italy's Codice della Navigazione, Art. 110.
41 The European Court of Justice ("ECJ") stated (at para. 3) that "in Italy the loading, unloading, tranship-ment, storage and general movement of goods or material of any kind within the port are reserved, under Section 110 of the Codice della Navigazione (Navigation Code), to dock-work companies whose workers, who are also members of these companies, must, under Section 152 and 156 of the Regolamento per la Navigazione Marittima (Regulation on Maritime Navigation), be of Italian nationality. Any failure to respect the exclusive rights vested in the dock-work companies results in the imposition of the penalties laid down by Section 1172 of the Codice dalla Navigazione."
42 Regolamento Navigazione Marittima, Arts 152 and 156.
43 It is notable that the first question referred to intra-EU trade but the same conclusions would probably apply in regard to imports from outside the EU because the cargo would be traded in the internal market.

13.036 The Advocate-General, Walter Van Gerven, delivered a very interesting opinion. A number of points about the opinion deserve comment. First, the Advocate-General believed that the port of Genoa is a substantial part of the internal market because of: (i) the extent of the activity at the port of Genoa; (ii) the fact that Genoa is one of the most important ports in the EU; (iii) the fact that Genoa is the most important port in Italy; and (iv) users frequently do not have a choice about using the port of Genoa because of that port's infrastructure. Second, according to the Advocate-General, the imposition by Merci of *unrequested* services on a port user could constitute an abuse within the meaning of Article 106(2)(a) because there was evidence that the service could be provided at a lower cost but, as it was impossible to determine the exact price, there was no definitive evidence of abuse. Third, there could be an abuse contrary to Article 102(2)(b) where a dominant undertaking refused to have recourse to modern technology so as to cause loss to customers.

13.037 In its judgment, the CJEU reiterated that an undertaking which has a legal monopoly in a substantial part of the internal market could be regarded as being in a dominant position within the meaning of Article 102. The Court defined the relevant market as the market of managing and organising port operations on behalf of third parties where these related to ordinary and conventional freight. The Court held that the port of Genoa is a substantial part of the internal market because of the volume of traffic and its international significance.

13.038 The CJEU held that Article 106(1) of the TFEU,[44] when seen in conjunction with Articles 30,[45] 45[46] and 102[47] of that Treaty, precludes rules of a Member State which confer on an undertaking established in that State the exclusive right to organise dock work and requires it for that purpose to have recourse to a dock-work company whose workforce is to be composed exclusively of nationals of that Member State.

13.039 The CJEU also examined Article 18 of the TFEU (on non-discrimination on the ground of nationality) and held that the provision applies independently only to situations governed by EU law in regard to which the Treaty lays down no specific prohibition on discrimination.

13.040 The Court noted that a dock-work undertaking enjoying the exclusive right to organise dock work for third parties, as well as a dock-work company having the exclusive right to perform dock work must be regarded as an undertaking to which the exclusive rights have been granted by the State within the meaning of Article 106(1) of the TFEU.[48] The Court also noted that an undertaking has a statutory monopoly over a substantial part of the internal market may be regarded as having a dominant position within the meaning of Article 102 of the TFEU.[49] The Court went on to state that

---

44 The CJEU saw no reason for Art. 106(2) of the TFEU to apply because the two companies involved were not given exclusive rights for reasons of "general economic interest".
45 Art. 30 embodies the principle of free movement of goods.
46 Art. 45 embodies the principle of free movement of workers.
47 Art. 102 prohibits the abuse of dominance by an undertaking having a dominant position in the internal market or in a substantial part of the internal market.
48 Art. 90(1) of the Treaty provides: "In the case of public undertakings and undertakings to which Member States grant special or exclusive rights, Member States shall neither enact nor maintain in force any measure contrary to the rules contained in this Treaty, in particular those rules provided for in Article 6 and Articles 85 to 94."
49 See Case C-41/90 *Hofner and Elser v Mactrotron* [1991] ECR I-1979, ECLI:EU:C:1991:161 and Case C-260/89 *ERT v DEP* [1991] ECR I-2925, ECLI:EU:C:1991:254.

"[a]s regards the definition of the market in question, it may be seen from the order for reference that it is that of the organization on behalf of third persons of dock work relating to ordinary freight in the Port of Genoa and the performance of such work. Regard being had in particular to the volume of traffic in that port and its importance in relation to maritime import and export operations as a whole in the Member State concerned, that market may be regarded as constituting a substantial part of the [internal] market."[50]

13.041 The Court stated that the "simple fact of creating a dominant position by granting exclusive rights within the meaning of Article [106](1) of the [TFEU] is not as such incompatible with Article [102]".[51] The Court had on occasion, in various cases, said that a Member State is in breach of the prohibitions contained in Articles 102 and 106(1) of the Treaty if the undertaking in question, merely by exercising the exclusive rights granted to it, cannot avoid abusing its dominant position[52] or when such rights are liable to create a situation in which that undertaking is induced to commit such abuses.[53] The Court stated:

"18. According to subparagraphs (a), (b) and (c) of the second paragraph of Article [102] of the Treaty, such abuse may in particular consist in imposing on the persons requiring the services in question unfair purchase prices or other unfair trading conditions, in limiting technical development, to the prejudice of consumers, or in the application of dissimilar conditions to equivalent transactions with other trading parties.

19. In that respect it appears from the circumstances described by the national court and discussed before the Court of Justice that the undertakings enjoying exclusive rights in accordance with the procedures laid down by the national rules in question are, as a result, induced either to demand payment for services which have not been requested, to charge disproportionate prices, to refuse to have recourse to modern technology, which involves an increase in the cost of the operations and a prolongation of the time required for their performance,54 or to grant price reductions to certain consumers and at the same time to offset such reductions by an increase in the charges to other consumers.

20. In those circumstances it must be held that a Member State creates a situation contrary to Article [102] of the Treaty where it adopts rules of such a kind as those at issue before the national court, which are capable of affecting trade between Member States as in the case of the main proceedings, regard being had to the factors,55 relating to the importance of traffic in the Port of Genoa."

13.042 On Article 30 of the TFEU, the Court stated that

"it is sufficient to recall that a national measure which has the effect of facilitating the abuse of a dominant position capable of affecting trade between Member States will generally be incompatible with that article, which prohibits quantitative restrictions on imports and all measures having equivalent effect[56] in so far as such a measure has the effect of making more difficult and hence of impeding imports of goods from other Member States."[57]

---

50 Judgment, para. 15.
51 Judgment, para. 16.
52 See Case C-41/90 *Hofner*, para. 29.
53 Case C-260/89 *ERT v DEP* [1991] ECR I-2925, ECLI:EU:C:1991:254, para. 37.
54 Ed., This element of a port taking longer to provide a service could be of enormous practical significance.
55 Ed., these factors are set out in para. 15 of the judgment. Para. 15 of the judgment provides: "[a]s regards the definition of the market in question, it may be seen from the order for reference that it is that of the organization on behalf of third persons of dock work relating to ordinary freight in the Port of Genoa and the performance of such work. Regard being had in particular to the volume of traffic in that port and its importance in relation to maritime import and export operations as a whole in the Member State concerned, that market may be regarded as constituting a substantial part of the [internal] market."
56 Ed., Case 13/77 *GB-INNO-BM v ATAB* [1977] ECR 2115, ECLI:EU:C:1977:185, para. 35.
57 Para. 21.

The fact was that the unloading of the cargo could have been done more cheaply by the ship's crew so that the compulsory recourse to the services of the "two undertakings enjoying exclusive rights involved extra expense and was therefore capable, by reason of its effect on the prices of the goods, of affecting imports."[58]

13.043 The Court thus answered the first question in the following terms:

"Article [106](1) of the ... Treaty, in conjunction with Articles 30, [45] and [102] of the Treaty, precludes rules of a Member State which confer on an undertaking established in that State the exclusive right to organize dock work and require it for that purpose to have recourse to a dock-work company formed exclusively of national workers; Articles 30, [43] and [102] of the Treaty, in conjunction with Article [106], give rise to rights for individuals which the national courts must protect."

13.044 The second question asked whether

"a dock-work undertaking and/or company formed solely of national dock workers, which enjoys the exclusive right to carry out at compulsory standard rates the loading and unloading of goods in national ports constitute, for the purposes of Article [106](2) of the ... Treaty, an undertaking entrusted with the operation of services of general economic interest and liable to be obstructed in the performance by the workforce of the particular tasks assigned to it by the application of Article [106](1) or the prohibitions under Articles [18 of the TEU and Articles, 30, [101] and [102] of the TFEU]?"

The Court summarised this question as

"whether Article [106](2) of the Treaty must be interpreted as meaning that a dock-work undertaking and/or company in the situation described in the first question must be regarded as being entrusted with the operation of services of general economic interest within the meaning of that provision."[59]

The Court stated:

"26. For the purpose of answering that question it should be borne in mind that in order that the derogation to the application of the rules of the Treaty set out in Article [106](2) thereof may take effect, it is not sufficient for the undertaking in question merely to have been entrusted by the public authorities with the operation of a service of a general economic interest, but it must be shown in addition that the application of the rules of the Treaty obstructs the performance of the particular tasks assigned to the undertaking and that the interests of the Community are not affected.60

27. In that respect it must be held that it does not appear either from the documents supplied by the national court or from the observations submitted to the Court of Justice that dock work is of a general economic interest exhibiting special characteristics as compared with the general economic interest of other economic activities or, even if it were, that the application of the rules of the Treaty, in particular those relating to competition and freedom of movement, would be such as to obstruct the performance of such a task.

28. The answer to the second question should therefore be that Article [106](2) of the Treaty must be interpreted as meaning that a dock-work undertaking and/or company in the position described in the first question may not be regarded, on the basis only of the factors set out in that description, as being entrusted with the operation of services of general economic interest within the meaning of that provision."

---

58 Judgment, para. 22.
59 Judgment, para. 25.
60 *Cf.* see the judgments in Case 311/84 *CEBM v Compagnie Luxembourgeoise* [1985] ECR 3261, para. 17 and in Case C-41/90 *Hofner*, para. 24.

13.045 The Court held therefore:

"(1) Article [106(1)] of the [TFEU], in conjunction with Articles [30], [48] and [102] of the Treaty, precludes rules of a Member State which confer on an undertaking established in that State the exclusive right to organize dock work and require it for that purpose to have recourse to a dock-work company formed exclusively of national workers;
(2) Articles [30], [48] and [102] of the [TFEU], in conjunction with Article [106], give rise to rights for individuals which the national courts must protect;
(3) Article [106](2) of the [TFEU] must be interpreted as meaning that a dock-work undertaking and/or company in the position described in the first question may not be regarded, on the basis only of the factors set out in that description, as being entrusted with the operation of services of general economic interest within the meaning of that provision."

13.046 After the *Merci* decision, the regime in Italy was to be reformed by the abolition of the monopoly. Nonetheless, the dock-work companies retained the exclusive rights under Italian law to provide temporary labour to other cargo-handling companies and that was the subject matter of the *Silvano Raso* case which is discussed below.[61]

Holyhead I: **B&I Line v Sealink Harbours Ltd**

13.047 Another striking example of competition law being applied to ports and the access to services is the *B&I Line plc v Sealink Harbours Ltd and Sealink Stena Ltd* case in regard to the port of Holyhead in Wales.[62] It is sometimes known as *Holyhead I* as there was a second case also relating to Holyhead.[63] This case is best seen in the light of the "Essential Facilities" doctrine which is well-developed in the US and posits that the holder of an essential facility may not abuse its privilege in its dealings with competitors by denying access to infrastructure which is an absolute requirement for the putative user in order to compete in the market.

13.048 In broad terms, the facts were straightforward. Sealink owned, by means of a subsidiary company, the port facilities at Holyhead. Sealink, by means of another group company, operated a ferry service from Holyhead to Dun Laoghaire (which is in Dublin Bay in Ireland). A competitor, B&I Line, operated a ferry service from Holyhead to Dublin. Stena, as ferry operator, changed its timetable in a way which prejudiced B&I's operations. B&I complained to the Commission.

13.049 In its decision, the Commission laid down the principles that:

"41. [a] dominant undertaking which both owns or controls and itself uses an essential facility, i.e. a facility or infrastructure without access to which competitors cannot provide services to their customers, and which refuses its competitors access to that facility or grants access to competitors only on terms less favourable than those which it gives its own services, thereby placing the competitors at a competitive disadvantage, infringes Article [102], if the other conditions of that Article are met. A company in a dominant position may not discriminate in favour of its own activities in a related market (Case C-260/89, Elliniki Radiophonia,[64] paras. [37]–[38]). The owner of an essential facility which uses its power in one market in order to strengthen its position in another related market, in particular, by

---

61 See 13.058.
62 Case IV/34.174, OJ 1994 L15/8, [1992] 5 CMLR 255. See Maltby, *"Restrictions as Port Operators: Sealink/B&I—Holyhead"* [1993] 5 ECLR 223.
63 On the second case, see the discussion below.
64 Ed., Case C-260/89 [1991] ECR I-02925, ECLI:EU:C:1991:254.

granting its competitor access to that related market on less favourable terms than those of its own services, infringes Article [102] where a competitive disadvantage is imposed upon its competitor without objective justification...

42. The owner of the essential facility, which also uses the essential facility, may not impose a competitive disadvantage on its competitor, also a user of the essential facility, by altering its own schedule to the detriment of the competitor's service, where, as in this case, the construction or the features of the facility are such that it is not possible to alter one competitor's service in the way chosen without harming the other's. Specifically, where, as in this case, the competitor is already subject to a certain level of disruption from the dominant undertaking's activities, there is a duty [on] the dominant undertaking not to take any action which will result in further disruption. That is so even if the latter's actions make, or are primarily intended to make its operations more efficient.65 Subject to any objective elements outside its control, such an undertaking is under a duty not to impose a competitive disadvantage upon its competitor in the use of the shared facility without objective justification."

This is not an isolated case but it is an important one in setting the precedent that a port operator may not abuse its dominance in related markets. It is also not about obtaining access to the port (a threshold issue) but deals with the circumstances of access to those facilities and access is not in doubt.

13.050 The views of the European Commission are worth studying in some depth. First, the European Commission wrote that a port (even a small one as in this case) may be a substantial part of the internal market:

"it is important to stress that a port, an airport or any other facility, even if it is not itself a substantial part of the [internal] market, may be considered as such in so far as reasonable access to the facility is indispensable for the exploitation of a transport route which is substantial for the purposes of the application of Article [102] of the [TFEU]. The Commission recalls that, in the case of *British Midland/Aer Lingus*, it was the route that was taken into account and not solely Heathrow Airport."[66]

It is therefore clear that even a small geographical area may be a substantial part of the internal market because of the function which the area performs. Second, the European Commission expressed important views on "essential facilities": it

"considered that a company which both owns and uses an essential facility – in this case a port – should not grant its competitors access on terms less favourable than those which it gives its own services. This consequence of Article [102 of the TFEU] is of essential importance in the context of deregulation, which regularly raises the problem of market access for new entrants."[67]

The Commission had thus found that the port was an essential facility and that the provision of access by the port owner was an abuse of dominance since it was "on less favourable terms than those of its own services". Third, from a competition law perspective, it is interesting to see how the European Commission took such a narrow definition of the market. This is despite the fact that the undertakings involved see themselves as competing on a bundle of routes rather than on individual routes. Finally, so much of the Commission's thinking centred on the promotion of efficiency.

---

65 Ed., this sentence ("[t]hat is so even if the latter's actions make, or are primarily intended to make its operations more efficient") is very significant because the increase in efficiency is not a defence to all breaches of competition law.
66 *Twenty Second Report on Competition Policy 1992*, point 219.
67 Ibid., point 219.

Holyhead II: **Sea Containers v Stena Sealink**

13.051 The port of Holyhead was also at the centre of a second case, *Sea Containers v Stena Sealink – Interim Measures*, when on 21 December 1993, the European Commission adopted Decision 94/19 relating to a proceeding pursuant to what is now Article 102 of the TFEU.[68]

13.052 The case involved three parties. The first party was Sea Containers Limited which was a Bermudan company which was engaged in the sale and leasing of specialised forms of marine cargo containers as well as the ownership and operation of ports and harbours. A subsidiary, Sea Containers Ferries Limited, operated passenger, car and freight ferry services. The second party was Stena Sealink Line whose principal activity, in this context, was the business of operating ferry services between the United Kingdom and Ireland as well as between the United Kingdom and France. It had been part of the Stena Line AB group of companies since 1990. The third party was Stena Sealink Ports ("SSP")[69] which owned the port of Holyhead in Wales. The shares in SSP were held by Stena Sealink Limited and Stena Sealink (Holdings) Limited. The second and third parties can be referred to as Stena or Sealink because they were effectively one economic unit, had the same officers and, as the Commission recorded, employees even confused them.

13.053 On 15 April 1993, Sea Containers Limited applied under Article 3 of Regulation 17/62 to the Commission requesting interim measures because of an alleged infringement of, what is now, Article 102 of the TFEU by SSP and Stena Sealink Line. The complaint requested the Commission to take interim measures to:

"(a) prohibit Sealink from developing the port of Holyhead in a way which would have the effect of reducing the current capacity of the port;[70]
(b) require Sealink to enter into an agreement with Sea Containers which would allow Sea Containers to operate a fast ferry service, through the central corridor, between Holyhead (in Wales) and Dun Laoghaire (in Ireland) commencing in May 1994."

13.054 The grounds of the complaint were that SSP had abused its dominant position as the owner and operator of the port of Holyhead, contrary to, what is now, Article 102 of the TFEU, by failing to allow Sea Containers access on a reasonable basis to an essential facility or infrastructure, and had relied on its exclusive right to protect its commercial interests as a ferry operator, without objective justification.[71] Sea Containers argued that Stena Sealink Line had a dominant position in the market for the provision of passenger and car-ferry services on the "central corridor" route between Britain and Ireland as well as benefiting from any protection it afforded with regard to new operators seeking to enter the market. Sea Containers argued that Sealink had not adequately separated its role as port operator from its role as ferry operator.

13.055 On 16 July 1993, the Commission decided to open proceedings in the case. On 21 December 1993, the Commission adopted its decision after consulting the Advisory Committee on Restrictive Practices and Dominant Positions as well as giving SSP and Stena Sealink Line an opportunity to make known their views.

---

68 Case IV/34.689, OJ L15/8, 18.1.94.
69 It was known as Sealink Harbours Limited prior to 16 November 1992: para. 4 of the decision.
70 Ed., this is an important issue because it shows that the complainant believed that it could stop a dominant undertaking from developing its own property.
71 Dec. 94/19, Art. 9.

13.056 In its 21 December 1993 decision, the Commission identified the relevant market as the market for the provision of port services for passenger and vehicle ferries, over the "central corridor route" between Britain and Ireland.[72] The Commission had defined three corridors: the northern, central and southern corridors. It is interesting to observe how the Commission chose between the three alternatives:

"[t]he substitutability of the three corridors across the Irish sea for any traveller depends on the traveller's point of origin and his or her intended destination for the journey in question. The northern and southern corridors, which service routes between Scotland and Northern Ireland and South Wales and Ireland respectively, cannot be considered viable alternatives for the central corridor for the majority of leisure users, with or without cars. Almost one third of Ireland's population resides in the Greater Dublin area and Holyhead is easily reached by inhabitants of Birmingham, Manchester and Liverpool. The Irish ports on the northern and southern corridors are far from Dublin which is the single most important destination on the Irish side. The roads from Dublin to all the rest of Ireland are faster, and the public transport more satisfactory, than the roads or public transport from Larne, Belfast or Rosslare."[73]

13.057 Ultimately, as the underlying factual situation had changed, there were no interim measures granted but the principles were consistent with the earlier *B&I Line/ Sealink: Holyhead* case but this was a case which conferred a right to have access to the port and not just better access or operational conditions.[74]

Silvano Raso

13.058 The CJEU judgment in *Silvano Raso*[75] decided that although merely creating a dominant position by granting exclusive rights within the meaning of Article 106(1) of the TFEU is not in itself incompatible with Article 102 of the TFEU, a Member State is in breach of the prohibitions contained in those two provisions if the undertaking in question, merely by *exercising* the exclusive rights granted to it, is led to *abuse* its dominant position or when such rights are liable to create a situation in which that undertaking is led to commit such abuses. This would arise where a national law does not merely grant a dock-work company the exclusive right to supply temporary labour to terminal concessionaires and to other undertakings authorised to operate in the port but also enables it to compete with them on the market in dock services. That is because merely *exercising* its monopoly will enable it to distort in its favour the equal conditions of competition between the various operators on the market in dock-work services and it is led to abuse its monopoly by imposing on its competitors in the dock-work market unduly high costs for the supply of labour or by supplying them with labour less suited to the work to be done.

---

72 Dec. 94/19, para. 12. The Commission had earlier (at para. 11) identified the sea routes for passenger and car ferries then operated between Britain and Ireland as: (a) the "northern corridor" between the port of Stranraer in Scotland and Belfast and Larne in Northern Ireland; (b) the "central corridor" between Holyhead in Wales, and Dublin and Dun Laoghaire in Ireland; and (c) the "southern corridor" between the ports of Swansea, Pembroke and Fishguard in Wales, and Cork and Rosslare in Ireland.
73 Para. 13. The analysis is sound but succinct by modern standards.
74 Comm. Dec. 94/19 OJ 1994 L15/8, [1995] 4 CMLR 84.
75 Case C-163/96 *Silvano Raso* [1998] ECR I-553, ECLI:EU:C:1998:54. The CJEU was composed of the following judges (as the CJEU's then Fifth Chamber): Gulmann (President of the Chamber); Wathelet (Rapporteur); Moitinho de Almeida; Jann; and Sevón. Advocate-General was AG Fennelly.

13.059 The case arose from a preliminary reference to the CJEU under Article 267 of the TFEU by the Pretura Circondariale in La Spezia in Italy. The questions arose during criminal proceedings against Raso and ten other persons, the legal representatives of La Spezia Container Terminal SRL ("LSCT"), the concessionaire for a terminal within the port of La Spezia, and four other undertakings authorised to carry out dock work there. They were accused of having unlawfully used and supplied labour in breach of Article 1(1) of Italy's Law No 1369 of 23 October 1960 (the "1960 Law"). Between 1990 and 1994, LSCT contracted out for labour to be supplied by the co-operative associations Duveco and Il Sole 5 Terre as well as the companies Sincor and Bonifiche Impiantistica e Manutenzioni Generali Di Moise Pietro. Although the four undertakings were authorised to do dock work they were not former dock-work companies. The criminal proceedings were brought before the Pretora Circondariale, for the unlawful supply of labour.

13.060 Before the CJEU's judgment in *Merci Convenzionali Porto di Genova*,[76] Italian seaports were administered by public port authorities. Under Article 110 of the Codice della Navigazione (i.e. the Italian Shipping Code (the "Code")), dock workers were formed into companies or groups ("dock-work companies") having their own legal personality, to whom all dock work was reserved. This monopoly was reinforced by Article 1172 of the Code, which prescribed penalties for any person who used for dock work any labour which was not affiliated to a dock-work company. Article 111 of the Code empowered the relevant port authorities to grant concessions for "the carrying on of port operations for third parties". The undertakings granted such concessions were, as a rule, private undertakings which organised the provision of services, including dock work, for users of Italian ports. In order to do so, they were obliged to use labour supplied by the dock-work companies. The scale of fees and other rules governing the services performed by the dock-work companies were fixed by the port authorities, in accordance with Article 112 of the Code and Article 203 of the Regolamento per la Navigazione Marittima (i.e. the relevant Italian Maritime Shipping Regulation).

13.061 In the *Merci Convenzionali*[77] judgment, the CJEU had held that Article 106(1) of the TFEU, in conjunction with Articles 30, 48 and 102 of the TFEU, precluded rules of a Member State which required an undertaking established in that State, to which the exclusive right to organise dock work had been granted, to have recourse for that purpose to a dock-work company formed exclusively of national workers in the circumstances of the case.

13.062 As a result of the *Merci Convenzionali* judgment, Italy adopted legislation in the form of decree laws which were applied, by virtue of successive renewals, until the entry into force of Law No 84/94 of 28 January 1994 amending the legislation applicable in respect of ports (Gazzetta Ufficiale della Repubblica Italiana No 21 of 4 February 1994, the "1994 Law"), which in effect codified the rules contained in certain emergency decrees. The new rules essentially restricted the monopoly of the former dock-work companies to the supply of temporary labour.

13.063 Article 18(1) of Law No 84/94 provided that, for the purposes of carrying out dock work, concessions may be granted in State-owned areas and wharves in the port

---

76 Case C-179/90 [1991] ECR I-5889, ECLI:EU:C:1991:464.
77 Case C-179/90 *Merci convenzionali porto di Genova SpA v Siderurgica Gabrielli SpA.* [1991] ECR I-05889, ECLI:EU:C:1991:464.

area, with the exception of State-owned property used by public authorities for the discharge of functions relating to maritime and port activities.

13.064 Article 18(2) provided that the duration of the concession, the supervisory and inspection powers of the authorities in issuing concessions, the terms of renewal of the concession and the concession of facilities to a new concessionaire were to be governed by a decree of the Minister for Transport and Shipping in conjunction with the Minister for Finance (i.e. there was official investment by Italy). Article 18(3) of the 1994 Law laid down the criteria to be observed by the port or maritime authorities in issuing concessions in order to reserve operational zones within the port area for dock work to be carried on by other undertakings not enjoying concessions, and adapts the rules concerning the concession of port zones and wharves to the EU law. The CJEU recalled that other undertakings which did not have a concession, therefore, may have only carried out dock work, defined in Article 16(1) of Law No 84/94 as loading, unloading, transhipment, storage and movement in general of goods and other materials carried out in the port area. The same article provided that authorised undertakings were to be entered in a special register (paragraph 3) and undertakings to whom a concession had been granted in accordance with Article 18 were likewise authorised for that purpose for a period equal to that of the concession (paragraph 6). The maximum number of authorisations was determined by the operating requirements of the port and of traffic, but ensuring maximum competition in the sector (paragraph 7).

13.065 The CJEU then recalled that contrary to what was the case before it in *Silvano Raso*, authorised undertakings, including concessionaires, may by virtue of Article 27 of the 1994 Law use their own employees to physically execute dock work. They did not therefore need to have had recourse to the dock-work companies in normal circumstances. However, Article 17(1) of the 1994 Law provided that where the employees of the authorised undertakings, including the concessionaires, and the staff employed under the "temporary mobility" conditions within the meaning of Article 23(3) of the 1994 Law were not sufficient to meet operating requirements, the undertakings may ask the companies or co-operatives referred to in Article 21(1)(b) of the Law to provide the staff necessary to provide services comprising only labour.

13.066 Article 21(1)(b) of the 1994 Law concerned the former dock-work companies. It required them to reconstitute themselves by 18 March 1995 into either of two forms of enterprise, namely:

> "(a) a company or a cooperative of the kind provided for in Titles V and VI of Book 5 of the Civil Code, to carry out port operations under competitive conditions;
> (b) a company or a cooperative of the kind provided for in Titles V and VI of Book 5 of the Civil Code, to supply services, including, by way of derogation from Article 1 of Law No 1369 of 23 October 1960, services comprising only labour, until 31 December 1995."

13.067 By virtue of those provisions, the CJEU recalled that the 1994 Law therefore introduced a derogation from the general prohibition on supplying labour laid down by the 1960 Law in favour of the reconstituted former dock-work companies. Article 1(1) and (2) of the 1960 Law made it a criminal offence for an undertaking to contract for the provision of services comprising only of labour by having recourse to a workforce engaged and paid for by the contractor or its intermediary whatever the nature of the work or service concerned. Any form of contract or subcontract, including those for the execution of works or services, whereby the contractee uses capital, machinery and equipment supplied by the contractor is to be regarded as a contract for the provision of services comprising only labour. Undertakings were likewise prohibited from entrusting to intermediaries work to be carried out on a piece-work basis by providers of services engaged and paid by such an intermediary. The purpose of the rules was to protect workers against exploitation and undermining of their rights resulting from the fact that the person technically described as their employer is not their real employer, in fact, but merely an intermediary.

13.068 The CJEU said that it appeared from the observations submitted to the CJEU by the referring court, and in particular the replies given by the Italian government to questions posed at the hearing, that both forms of reconstituted company under Article 21(1)(b) of the 1994 Law was able to perform dock work in competition with undertakings which held authorisations under Article 16(3) thereof. Consequently, a company such as that operating at the Port of La Spezia, which had been reconstituted pursuant to Article 21(1)(b), may have both competed, in the supply of services to port users, with authorised undertakings and the holders of terminal concessions and simultaneously enjoyed an exclusive right regarding the provision of temporary labour for those undertakings. (Again, like the Holyhead cases, the duality of roles can be problematic.) This was inherently unfair. LSCT was the concessionaire of a terminal within the Port of La Spezia, described by the national court as the leading Mediterranean container port. LSCT handled about 70% of the container traffic of the port. Its clients were shippers and shipping lines of the various Member States.

13.069 In terms of the compatibility with EU law of the monopoly exercised by the reconstituted former company as regards the supply of temporary labour, the national court referred three questions to the CJEU:

"1. Does Article [59] of the [TFEU] preclude Italian legislation which prohibits an undertaking holding a port terminal concession from having recourse to work done by other undertakings – not set up by former port companies and groups – comprising the supply of services of the kind provided for users, including those belonging to other Member States, with the further implication that, as a result of the Italian legislation, the terminal operator itself is required to make available the whole range of services that might be required by users in the port terminal, giving rise to the risk of hampering access to the market for the provision of individual services by undertakings authorised to operate in the port other than those referred to by Article 21(1)(b) of Law No 84/94?

2. Does Article [106] of the [TFEU], in conjunction with Article [102], preclude national legislation which (by reason of its effects on the market, namely, first, the fact that it prevents undertakings other than the terminal operator – not set up by former port companies and groups – from providing services within the confines of the port for would-be users; secondly, the fact that the terminal operator is obliged to provide all port operations and services required at the terminal; and, thirdly, the fact that it is impossible for users to entrust certain services to undertakings of their own choice other than the terminal operator) gives rise to arrangements in the market whereby users may have contractual relationships only with the terminal operator for the whole range of services which they need when visiting a port in which the terminal operator or operators hold a dominant position in the market within the Article [102] of the Treaty?

3. Do Articles [59] and [106] of the [TFEU], in conjunction with Article [102], in any event preclude national legislation which only allows an undertaking operating in a port to provide to other undertakings operating in the port, and in particular terminal operators, services limited to the mere supply of labour?"

13.070 The CJEU interpreted the questions, in particular the third one, as asking whether EU law precluded a national provision whereby the right to supply temporary labour to other undertakings operating in the port in which it is established is reserved to a dock-work company, having regard to the fact that that company is also authorised to carry out dock work.

13.071 The CJEU begun by remarking that an undertaking with a monopoly in the supply of labour to other undertakings authorised to carry out dock work is an undertaking which has been granted exclusive rights by the State within the meaning of Article 106(1) of the Treaty.[78]

13.072 The CJEU also recalled that Article 106 provides that in the case of such undertakings with dominant positions, Member States must neither enact nor maintain in force any measure contrary to the rules contained in the TFEU, in particular those relating to competition. The CJEU also said that it was settled law that an undertaking having a statutory monopoly in a substantial part of the internal market may be regarded as having a dominant position within the meaning of Article 102 of the TFEU.[79]

13.073 On the definition of the market in question, the CJEU said that it appeared from the order for reference that it was that of the organisation on behalf of third persons of dock work relating to container freight in La Spezia. Having regard to the volume of traffic in that port, which is regarded as the leading Mediterranean port for container traffic, and its importance in intra-EU trade, that market may be regarded as constituting a substantial part of the internal market.[80]

13.074 The CJEU said that it should be recalled that although merely creating a dominant position by granting exclusive rights within the meaning of Article 106(1) of the TFEU is not in itself incompatible with Article 102, a Member State is in breach of the prohibitions contained in those two provisions if the undertaking in question, *merely by exercising the exclusive rights granted to it, is led to abuse its dominant position or when such rights are liable to create a situation in which that undertaking is led to commit such abuses.*[81]

13.075 In view of that finding, the CJEU stated that it was clear that in so far as the scheme laid down by the 1994 Law did not only grant the former dock-work company (as reconstituted) the exclusive right to supply temporary labour to terminal concessionaires and to other undertakings authorised to operate in the port but also enabled it to compete with them on the market in dock services, such former dock-work company (as reconstituted) would have a conflict of interest. The CJEU continued:

> "29. That is because merely exercising its monopoly will enable it to distort in its favour the equal conditions of competition between the various operators on the market in dock-work services (Case C-260/89 ERT v DRP [1991] ECR I-2925, [ECLI:EU:C:1991:254], paragraph 37, and Case C-18/88 GB-Inno-BM [1991] ECR I-5941, ECLI:EU:C: paragraph 25)."

---

[78] The CJEU cited Case C-179/90 *Merci Convenzionali*, [1991] ECR I-5889, ECLI:EU:C:1991:464, para. 9.

[79] Case C-41/90 *Höfner and Elser v Macrotron* [1991] ECR I-1979, ECLI:EU:C:1991:161, para. 28; Case C-260/89 *ERT v DRP* [1991] ECR I-2925, ECLI:EU:C:1991:254, para. 31; and Case C-179/90 *Merci Convenzionali* [1991] ECR I-5889, ECLI:EU:C:1991:464, para. 14.

[80] The CJEU referred to para. 15 of Case 179/90 *Merci Convenzionali* [1991] ECR I-5889, ECLI:EU:C:1991:464.

[81] Case C-41/90, para. 29; Case C-260/89 *ERT v DRP* [1991] ECR I-2925, ECLI:EU:C:1991:254, para. 37; Case C-179/90, [1991] ECR I-05889, ECLI:EU:C:1991:464, para. 17, and Case C-323/93 *Centre d'Insémination de la Crespelle* [1994] ECR I-5077, ECLI:EU:C:1994:368, para. 18.

30. The result is that the company in question is led to abuse its monopoly by imposing on its competitors in the dock-work market unduly82 high costs for the supply of labour or by supplying them with labour less suited to the work to be done.
31. In those circumstances a legal framework such as that which results from the 1994 Law must be regarded as being in itself contrary to Article [106](1) in conjunction with Article [102] of the [TFEU]. In that regard, it is therefore immaterial that the national court did not identify any particular case of abuse by the reconstituted former dock-work company (Case C-18/88, paragraphs 23 and 24).83
32. In the light of those considerations the reply to the third question must be that Articles [102] and [106] of the [TFEU] must be interpreted as precluding a national provision which reserves to a dock-work company the right to supply temporary labour to other undertakings operating in the port in which it is established, when that company is itself authorised to carry out dock work.
33. In the light of the reply given to the third question in so far as it relates to Articles [102] and [106] of the [TFEU], there is no need to answer that question in so far as it relates to Article [59] of the TFEU or to answer the other questions referred by the national court."

The CJEU therefore ruled that Articles 102 and 106 of the TFEU must be interpreted as precluding a national provision which reserves to a dock-work company the right to supply temporary labour to other undertakings operating in the port in which it is established, when that company is itself authorised to carry out dock work. Commenting on the *Silvano Raso* case, it has been observed:

> "[In the case the CJEU] recalled that while the mere creation of a dominant position by granting exclusive rights within the meaning of [Article 106(1) of the TFEU] is not in itself incompatible with [Article 102 of the TFEU], a Member State is in breach of the prohibitions contained in these two provisions if the undertaking in question, merely by exercising the exclusive rights granted to it, is led to abuse its dominant position or when such rights are liable to create a situation in which that undertaking is led to commit such abuses. In this case there was a conflict of interest for the former dockwork companies in that while they were competing with the other cargo-handling companies for the provision of cargo-handling services, the former dockwork companies had an exclusive right to provide temporary labour."[84]

13.076 While the rules of competition law are primarily aimed at enhancing/maximising consumer welfare, there is an element of competition law which seems to be about ensuring fairness and avoiding conflict of interests.

Coe Clerici Logistics SpA v Commission

13.077 On 17 June 2003, the General Court decided *Coe Clerici Logistics SpA v Commission*.[85] The case involved an application for annulment of the Commission's letter of 20 December 1999 refusing to act on the applicant's complaint based on, what are now, Articles 102 and 106 of the TFEU.

13.078 The background to the case was straightforward. As a result of the judgment of the CJEU in *Merci Convenzionali Porto di Genova v Siderurgica Gabrielli*,[86] Italy

---

82 Ed., note the word "unduly" which means that some due or reasonable costs could be possible.
83 Ed., this is fascinating because no finding of abuse was needed.
84 Lindström-Rossi, op. cit. at fn. 2, p. 139 at 145.
85 Case T-52/00, ECLI:EU:T:2003:168. The General Court's Fifth Chamber decided the matter and it was composed of Judges Cooke (President of the Chamber), García-Valdecasas and Lindh.
86 Case C-179/90 [1991] ECR I-5889, ECLI:EU:C:1991:464.

adopted Law No 84/94 of 28 January 1994 amending the legislation applicable in respect of ports (GURI No 21 of 4 February 1994; hereinafter "Law No 84/94") and Decree No 585 of the Ministry of Transport and Shipping of 31 March 1995 concerning the regulation referred to in Article 16 of Law No 84/94 (GURI No 47 of 26 February 1996; hereinafter "Decree No 585/95"), which reformed the legal framework applicable to the Italian port sector. As part of that reform, the activity of the former dock-work companies, which became port authorities under Law No 84/94, was confined to managing the ports and they are now prohibited from supplying, directly or indirectly, dock-work services, which are defined in Article 16(1) of Law No 84/94 as the loading, unloading, transhipment, storage and general movement of goods or material of any kind, performed on the site of the port.

13.079 The Court reviewed the Italian legislative background:

"3. Those port authorities have legal personality under public law and are responsible, inter alia, for granting quay concessions to dock businesses.
4. In that regard, Article 18(1) of Law No 84/94 provides that concessions over State-owned areas and quays included on the port site may be given for the performance of dock work, with the exception of State-owned buildings used by public administrative authorities for the performance of tasks connected with shipping and port activities. Article 18(2) of Law No 84/94 lays down, in addition, the criteria to be complied with by port authorities so as to ensure that, when concessions are granted, operational areas on the port site are reserved for the performance of dock work by non-concession-holding businesses.
5. Decree No 585/95 provides that the port authority may, by way of derogation from the concessions granted, authorise self-handling operations, that is to say, the possibility for a ship to carry out dock work using its own crew, such authorisation derogating from concessions granted. Under Article 8 of that decree, the port authority may grant authorisation to maritime carriers and shipping undertakings to carry out dock work at the time of arrival or departure of ships having the appropriate mechanical equipment and crew.
6. Circular No 33 of 15 February 1996, issued by the Directorate-General for Maritime and Dock Labour of the Italian Ministry of Transport and Shipping, clarifies the scope of Article 8 of Decree No 585/95 by defining the conditions for carrying out self-handling. It provides that self-handling operations may take place on quays and in areas held under concessions only when there is no, or insufficient, utilisable space allocated for public use and that it is for the port authority to regulate the carrying out of such operations in general and, more specifically, in each instrument of concession, in agreement with the concession holder.
7. With regard to the Port of Ancona, the Autorità Portuale di Ancona (Port Authority of Ancona) granted concessions to three undertakings: Ancona Merci (quays Nos 1, 2, 4, 15, 23 and 25), Silos Granari della Sicilia (quay No 20) and Sai (quay No 21).
8. On 20 March 1998, the president of the Autorità Portuale di Ancona adopted Bye-Law No 6/98 governing the carrying out of self-handling operations in the Port of Ancona. Article 5a, which governs the circumstances in which quays held under concessions may be made available for self-handling operations when the public quays are already allocated or insufficient, was inserted in Bye-Law No 6/98 by Bye-Law No 21/99 of 8 September 1999.
9. Article 5a provides that the Autorità Portuale di Ancona is to request one or more concession-holders to make available quays which they have not planned to use during the period which is the subject of a request for self-handling operations where it is found that there are no or insufficient quays already allocated or still to be allocated for public use. In that regard, loading or unloading operations only are to be authorised without the use of a storage area held under concession. Authorisation to carry out such operations is to be granted in accordance with the detailed rules laid down in Article 3 of Bye-Law No 6/98, specifying which quays are available after obtaining from the concession-holder a declaration of availability, an indication of the berthing quay and agreements on the practical arrangements. In addition, although the concession-holder is obliged not to hinder

availability of the quays during the period for which authorisation is granted, he may, at any time, have the self-handling operations suspended if he wishes to make use of mechanical equipment installed on one of his quays. Finally, self-handling operators are to pay to concession-holders a fee in return for the use of the quay. Where the concession-holder considers that he is unable to satisfy the requirements of the Autorità Portuale di Ancona, the latter may, at any time, check whether the quays are unavailable."

13.080 The Court then recalled the facts and reached conclusions:

"10. The applicant, Coe Clerici Logistics SpA, operates in the bulk dry raw materials shipping sector. Among other things, it transports coal for ENEL SpA, the electricity generating undertaking which is also responsible for the distribution of electricity in Italy. ENEL has a storage depot for its goods in the Port of Ancona. That depot is linked, by a fixed system of conveyors and hoppers also belonging to ENEL, to quay No 25 in the Port of Ancona, over which the company Ancona Merci has been given a concession.
11. The applicant claims that, in order to adapt itself to that fixed system of conveyors and hoppers belonging to ENEL, it fitted its ships, including the Capo Noli, with special equipment.
12. According to the applicant, quay No 25 is the only one suitable for its coal unloading operations for ENEL, it being:

　　– the only quay equipped with a crane with which goods can be unloaded;
　　– the only quay with sufficient depth;
　　– the only quay directly linked to ENEL's depot by means of a fixed system of conveyors and hoppers.

13. In August 1996, the applicant applied to the Autorità Portuale di Ancona for authorisation to carry out self-handling on quay No 25.
14. By a document dated 13 February 1998, the applicant formally called upon the Autorità Portuale di Ancona to express a view on the grant of that authorisation.
15. By letter of 17 February 1998, the president of the Autorità Portuale di Ancona justified the delay in replying by stating that grant of an authorisation required the prior consent of Ancona Merci under Article 9 of its concession.
16. Article 9 of Ancona Merci's concession provides that it is to allow the operators referred to in Article 8 of Decree No 585/95 to work on the quays of which it is the concession-holder if it is found that there are no or insufficient quays or areas intended for public use. That authorisation to carry out self-handling operations on the quays held under concession must be granted in accordance with the terms and conditions laid down by the regulations in force and by the specific regulations to be adopted by the Autorità Portuale di Ancona, in agreement with the concession-holder, in accordance with Ministerial Circular No 33 of 15 February 1996.
17. In its letter of 17 February 1998, the Autorità Portuale di Ancona also stated that a draft regulation had been submitted to Ancona Merci for examination.
18. By letter of 13 March 1998, the Autorità Portuale di Ancona informed the applicant that the rules governing self-handling on quays held under concession were to be reviewed by an ad hoc committee and that it had the option of carrying out self-handling operations on the public quays and areas of the Port of Ancona.
19. Since it considered that the provisions adopted by the Autorità Portuale di Ancona interfered with the exercise of its right of self-handling by according Ancona Merci exclusive rights to carry on its business on the quays over which concessions had been granted, the applicant, on 30 March 1999, complained to the Commission of infringement of Articles [102 and 106 TFEU]. The applicant's complaint also alleged the grant of State aid to the Port of Ancona.
20. In that complaint, the applicant referred, inter alia, to Article 5a of Bye-Law No 6/98, which restricted its right to self-handle on quays held under concession, and primarily on quay No 25. In conclusion, the applicant asked the Commission to find that:

'The port authority, in the exercise of its exclusive regulatory power, is preventing the free exercise of the right of self-handling by the [the applicant] by allowing Ancona Merci de facto to act with the benefit of exclusive rights on quays held under concession, thus engaging in conduct contrary to Articles [102 and 106 TFEU].'

21. By letter of 26 April 1999, the Secretariat-General of the Commission acknowledged receipt of its complaint.
22. By letter of 10 August 1999, the Directorate-General for Transport (DG VII) of the Commission informed the applicant that it intended to investigate the aspects of the complaint relating to State aid and that the Directorate-General for Competition (DG IV) was competent to investigate the aspects relating to infringement of Articles [102 and 106 TFEU].
23. By letter of 20 December 1999 ('the contested act'), the Commission informed the applicant that it was going to take no action on its complaint.
24. In that document, the Commission explains, by way of introduction, that it 'covers only aspects relating to the alleged infringement of Articles [102 and 106 TFEU]'. It then asserts that the investigation undertaken by the Commission revealed certain discrepancies compared with what was stated in the complaint, namely:

   – quay No 22 seems to be a public quay;
   – quays Nos 20 (given under concession to Silos Granari della Sicilia) and 22 (public) seem to be of a depth and length suitable for berthing the applicant's ship;
   – the need to use the cranes on quay No 25 is not clearly established since the complaint is based on the refusal to allow the applicant to work with its own crane using its own resources. The Commission therefore considers that the only factor which can justify the usefulness to the applicant of quay No 25 is the presence on that landing stage of the fixed system of conveyors and hoppers.

25. In the contested act, the Commission argues that the presence of that fixed system of conveyors and hoppers is not, however, sufficient to justify the classification of quay No 25 as an essential facility. It states that the conditions laid down by the Court of Justice in Case C-7/97 Bronner v Mediaprint and Others [1998] ECR I-7791 for establishing an abuse of a dominant position are not satisfied in this case. The applicant had continued to carry out its operations for ENEL for two years despite the refusal which it had received and also had alternative solutions available to it for unloading its customer's coal.
26. In the contested act, the Commission concludes by stating that it is unable to take any action on the complaint. Moreover, since the complaint concerns breach of the competition rules by a Member State, it does not confer on the complainant 'standing' under Council Regulation No 17 of 6 February 1962, First Regulation implementing Articles [81] and [82] of the Treaty (OJ, English Special Edition, 1959–1962, p. 87), as amended and supplemented by Regulation No 59 (OJ, English Special Edition 1959–1962, p. 249), Regulation No 118/63/EEC of 5 November 1963 (OJ, English Special Edition 1963–1964, p. 55) and Regulation (EEC) No 2822/71 of 20 December 1971 (OJ, English Special Edition 1971 (III), p. 1035) and under Commission Regulation No 2842/98 of 22 December 1998 on the hearing of parties in certain proceedings under Articles [101] and [102] of the [TFEU] (OJ 1998 L354, p. 18). That standing is granted only to complainants who allege breach of the rules on competition by undertakings.
27. By letter of 5 January 2000, the applicant requested the Commission to make clear whether the contested act was in the nature of a decision. The applicant reiterated its request by letter of 9 February 2000.
28. The Commission did not reply in writing to those letters."

The applicant brought an action before the General Court to annul the contested act. The Commission raised an objection of admissibility but that is not relevant for present purposes. The applicant put forward a number of substantive legal arguments:

"56. The applicant puts forward a number of pleas in law in support of its action. They are grouped together around two issues relating, in essence, on the one hand, to the refusal to grant it the procedural rights provided for by Regulation No 2842/98 and, on the other hand, to the rejection by the Commission of the classification of quay No 25 as an 'essential facility'.

– The refusal to apply Regulation No 2842/98 in favour of the applicant

57. The applicant alleges that the Commission infringed its right to a fair hearing by not disclosing to it the observations submitted by the parties involved in the administrative procedure. The applicant therefore submits that the Commission infringed Articles 6 to 8 of Regulation No 2842/98.
58. It also maintains that, apart from the fact that the regulation should have been applied to it even in the case of an infringement of Articles [102 and 106 TFEU], at least one of the parties against which its complaint is directed being an undertaking, the Commission's decision not to apply Regulation No 2842/98 in its favour is attributable to the Commission's disregard for the fact that it alleged, in its complaint, an infringement by Ancona Merci of Article [102 TFEU].
59. In that regard, Ancona Merci abused its dominant position by making the carrying out of self-handling on quay No 25 subject to conditions and by charging excessive prices for the provision of cargo unloading services.
60. The applicant further claims that the Commission committed an abuse of process by adopting the contested act, first, without complying with the 'timetable for the procedure concerning infringements of Article [102 TFEU]', as described in the judgment in Case T-127/98 UPS Europe v Commission [1999] ECR II-2633 and, second, on the basis of a partial investigation and in breach of the obligations laid down in Article 6 of Regulation No 2842/98.
61. The Commission contends, in essence, that the applicant's complaint was based solely on infringement of Article [102 TFEU] in conjunction with Article [106 TFEU] by the Autorità Portuale di Ancona and not on a separate infringement by Ancona Merci of Article [102 TFEU]. In that context, the applicant's arguments relating to the application of Regulation No 2842/98 are irrelevant.

– The refusal to classify quay No 25 as an 'essential facility'

62. The applicant asserts that the Commission stated, in the contested act, that there had been no abuse of a dominant position by Ancona Merci because quay No 25 did not constitute an essential facility within the meaning of the Bronner judgment, cited above.
63. However, the Commission failed to take into account certain facts when adopting the contested act. Those are, first, the circumstance that quays Nos 20 and 22 of the Port of Ancona are designed exclusively for unloading grain, a type of cargo incompatible with coal. Second, the length and depth of those quays preclude their use as alternatives to quay No 25 because they do not have a fixed system of conveyors and hoppers similar to those of quay No 25 and do not permit the handling of cargo under environmentally compatible and economically viable conditions.
64. Moreover, the alternative envisaged by the Commission for the applicant to carry out its dock work on a self-handling basis, whereby it would conclude commercial agreements with Ancona Merci, fails to take account of the fact that ENEL alone is entitled to conclude such agreements.
65. The applicant submits, moreover, that it had no choice but to have ENEL's coal unloaded by Ancona Merci onto quay No 25 using the fixed system of conveyors and hoppers, although the prices charged by Ancona Merci are considerably higher than its own. The Commission should therefore have found that Ancona Merci is refusing access for third parties to the essential infrastructure constituted by quay No 25 in order to offer services at higher costs, thereby committing an abuse of a dominant position.

66. In that regard, the applicant submits that the Commission misinterpreted the concept of 'essential facility' and refers to the judgment in Bronner. In order to conclude that there has been a refusal of right of access to an essential facility, it is necessary that there be a structure substantially equivalent in its results, that it be effectively usable without causing excessive economic disadvantage, and that there be no obstacles of a technical, regulatory or economic nature such as to render duplication of the facility impossible or exceptionally difficult.

67. However, in this case there is no practicable substitute for the use of quay No 25 in view of the financial costs which the applicant has already borne in order to fit its ship, the Capo Noli, with an automatic unloading system compatible with ENEL's facility on quay No 25, or which it is currently bearing in order to unload the coal onto other quays and ensure its transport by lorry to ENEL's depot. The environmental impact of this latter solution also precludes its being regarded as a satisfactory alternative.

68. Quay No 25 must therefore be classified as an essential facility and the Commission's decision not to act on the complaint – without having carried out a proper investigation and, therefore, without having given an adequate 'statement of reasons' – benefits an undertaking that is abusing its dominant position by preventing cargo unloading operations from being carried out on the basis of advanced technologies and at controlled costs and by performing them itself at higher costs.

69. The Commission challenges the admissibility of the applicant's argument that it did not adequately examine the complaint alleging abuse of a dominant position by Ancona Merci and did not investigate excessive prices charged by it. It also disputes the validity of the other arguments relied on in support of this group of pleas."

The Court then made the following findings:

"70. The parties disagree, first, on the question whether the contested act constitutes in part a rejection of the applicant's complaint as regards an independent infringement of Article [102 of the TFEU] by Ancona Merci. Secondly, the parties disagree on whether the applicant is entitled to bring an action for annulment of the contested act to the extent that the Commission decided not to take any action on the applicant's complaint in so far [as] it relates to infringement of Article [102 TFEU] in conjunction with Article [106 TFEU] by the Autorità Portuale di Ancona.

71. With regard to the first of those questions, it must first be observed that, although the Commission did not express a view on an alleged independent infringement of Article [102 TFEU], such a failure to do so cannot be held unlawful in the context of a review of legality under Article [263 TFEU]. Consequently, the applicant may not plead a manifest error of assessment in the application of Article [102 TFEU] and an associated failure to investigate, or claim the benefit of Regulation No 2842/98, unless the rejection of its complaint relates separately to Article [102 TFEU].

72. In that regard, the contested act states that the refusal of the applicant's request to unload coal on a self-handling basis onto quay No 25 of the Port of Ancona constitutes, in the applicant's view, 'an infringement of Article [106 TFEU] in conjunction with Article [102 TFEU]'.

73. The contested act then states that the Commission's investigation enabled it to establish certain factual discrepancies in relation to the claims in the applicant's complaint and that quay No 25 of the Port of Ancona is not an 'essential facility' within the meaning of the Bronner judgment.

74. In the conclusion of the contested act, the Commission states that:

'In the light of the above, we find no need to act on the [applicant's] complaint. Moreover, [the Commission] wishes ... to point out that since the [complaint] concerns an alleged infringement of the Treaty rules on competition by a Member State, it does not confer on [the applicant] the "standing" which follows from Council Regulation No 17 and Commission Regulation No 2842/98. That "standing" is recognised only in relation to an applicant who pleads breach of those rules by undertakings.'

75. It is therefore clear from the wording of the contested act that the Commission, having taken the view that the complaint did not relate to an alleged infringement by Ancona Merci of Article [102 TFEU], did not express any view on conduct which might be contrary to that article.

76. Moreover, it must be pointed out that the Commission's interpretation of the complaint as relating only to infringement of Article [102 TFEU] in conjunction with Article [106 TFEU] by the Autorità Portuale di Ancona was already apparent from the letters which the Commission sent to the applicant during the administrative procedure.

77. Thus, it is clear from the letter of 26 April 1999 sent to the applicant, acknowledging receipt of the complaint, that the Commission had interpreted the complaint as relating only to the conduct of the public authority concerned.

78. Contrary to what is maintained by the applicant, the same may be inferred from the letter sent to it by the Commission on 10 August 1999, which states, in particular, as follows:

> '… according to this complaint, the Port Authority has allegedly infringed Article [102 TFEU] and Article [106 TFEU] by using its exclusive regulatory power to obstruct the carrying out by Coe Clerici Logistics SpA of self-handling operations…'

79. At that stage of the administrative procedure and in the light of those letters, it was open to the applicant, if it disagreed as to the scope of the complaint, to draw the Commission's attention to the fact that it also intended to allege in that complaint, in addition to infringement of Article [102 TFEU] in conjunction with Article [106 TFEU] by the Autorità Portuale di Ancona, an independent infringement of Article [102 TFEU] EC by Ancona Merci.

80. In any event, if, on reading the contested act, the applicant considered that the Commission had failed to give a decision on an alleged infringement of Article [102 TFEU] by Ancona Merci, the onus was then on it to request the Commission to express a view on that aspect of the complaint and, if necessary, to bring an action under … Article [265 TFEU] for a declaration by the [EU] judicature that the Commission had failed to act.

81. Consequently, since the Commission did not make any assessment of the alleged independent infringement by Ancona Merci of Article [102 TFEU], the action, in so far as it relies on that article on its own, is devoid of purpose. It follows that there is no need to rule on an error of assessment by the Commission in relation to Article [102 TFEU] on its own, on a failure to investigate that aspect, on infringement of the applicant's procedural rights under Regulation No 2842/98 or on an abuse of process.

82. With regard to the second of those questions, the admissibility of the action must be examined in so far as it relates to the Commission's decision not to act on the applicant's complaint of infringement of Article [102 TFEU] in conjunction with Article [106 TFEU].

83. It is clear from the applicant's complaint and from its written submissions, as clarified at the hearing, that it disputes the compatibility with Community law of Article 5a of Bye-Law No 6/98 of the Autorità Portuale di Ancona (see paragraph 9 above) in so far as it makes access by the applicant to quay No 25, the concession held by Ancona Merci, subject to conditions, thereby permitting a restriction on the applicant's freedom to exercise the right of self-handling. The Autorità Portuale di Ancona thereby acted contrary to Articles [102 and 106 TFEU].

84. The applicant's complaint constitutes, in that regard, a request made to the Commission to use the powers which it has under Article [106(3) TFEU]. In that context, the contested act constitutes a refusal by the Commission to address a decision or directive to Member States pursuant to Article [106(3) TFEU].

85. It is settled case-law that Article [106(3) TFEU] requires the Commission to ensure that Member States comply with their obligations as regards the undertakings referred to in Article [106(1) TFEU] and expressly empowers it to take action, where necessary, for that purpose by way of directives or decisions. The Commission is empowered to determine

that a given State measure is incompatible with the rules of the Treaty and to indicate what measures the State to which a decision is addressed must adopt in order to comply with its obligations under [EU] law (Bundesverband der Bilanzbuchhalter v Commission, cited above, paragraph 23).

86. As is apparent from Article [106(3) TFEU] and from Article [106 TFEU] as a whole, the supervisory power which the Commission enjoys vis-à-vis Member States responsible for infringing the rules of the Treaty, in particular those relating to competition, necessarily implies the exercise of a wide discretion by the Commission as regards, in particular, the action which it considers necessary to be taken (Bundesverband der Bilanzbuchhalter v Commission, paragraph 27, and Vlaamse Televisie Maatschappij v Commission, paragraph 75).

87. Consequently, the exercise of the Commission's power to assess the compatibility of State measures with the Treaty rules, which is conferred by Article [106(3) TFEU], is not coupled with an obligation on the part of the Commission to take action (order in Bilanzbuchhalter v Commission, paragraph 31, and judgments in Ladbroke v Commission, paragraphs 36 to 38, and Koelman v Commission, paragraph 71).

88. It follows that legal or natural persons who request the Commission to take action under Article [106(3) TFEU] do not, in principle, have the right to bring an action against a Commission decision not to use the powers which it has under that article (order in Bilanzbuchhalter v Commission, paragraph 31, and judgment in Koelman v Commission, paragraph 71).

89. However, it has been held that it cannot be ruled out that an individual may find himself in an exceptional situation conferring on him standing to bring proceedings against a refusal by the Commission to adopt a decision in the context of its supervisory functions under Article [106(1) and (3) TFEU] (Bundesverband der Bilanzbuchhalter v Commission, paragraph 25, and, with regard to an action for failure to act, see, to that effect, TF1 v Commission, paragraphs 51 and 57).

90. However, in this case, the applicant has not pleaded any exceptional circumstance which would enable its action against the Commission's refusal to act to be regarded as admissible. The only circumstance cited by the applicant, namely that it competes with Ancona Merci, could not, even if proved, constitute an exceptional situation such as to confer on the applicant standing to bring proceedings against the Commission's refusal to act in regard to the measures adopted by the Autorità Portuale di Ancona in order to regulate the grant of authorisations to maritime carriers to carry out self-handling on quays held under concessions.

91. Consequently, the applicant is not entitled to bring an action for annulment of the contested act in so far as the Commission decides in it not to use the powers conferred on it by Article [106(3) TFEU].

92. However, at the hearing, the applicant claimed that its action, in so far as it relates to infringement by the Autorità Portuale di Ancona of Articles [102 and 106 TFEU], should be declared admissible pursuant to the principle established in max.mobil v Commission. The Commission contends that the principle in question, under which an individual is entitled to bring an action for annulment against its decision not to use the powers conferred on it by Article [106(3) TFEU], constituted a reversal of precedent and that the judgment of the [General] Court ... in question was the subject of an appeal now pending before the Court of Justice.

93. In that regard, if the contested act, in so far as it concerns infringement of Article [102 TFEU] in conjunction with Article [106 TFEU], must be classified as a decision rejecting a complaint as referred to in max.mobil v Commission, the applicant should, as complainant and addressee of that decision, be regarded as entitled to bring the present action (max.mobil v Commission, paragraph 73).

94. In such a case, it has been held that, in view of the broad discretion enjoyed by the Commission in the application of Article [106(3) TFEU], the review carried out by the [General] Court ... must be limited to verification of the Commission's fulfilment of its duty to undertake a diligent and impartial examination of the complaint alleging infringement of Article

[106(1) TFEU] (see, to that effect, max.mobil v Commission, paragraphs 58 and 73, and order of 27 May 2002 in Case T-18/01 Goldstein v Commission [2002], not published in the ECR, paragraph 35).

95. In the present case, the applicant alleges that the Commission adopted the contested act without taking into consideration certain facts or on the basis of incorrect facts. At the hearing, the applicant asserted that this shows that the Commission did not undertake a diligent and impartial examination of the complaint.

96. However, it cannot be held that the Commission failed in this case in its duty to undertake a diligent and impartial examination of the applicant's complaint.

97. It is apparent from the contested act that the Commission identified the central objection among the arguments set forth in the complaint of infringement by the Autorità Portuale di Ancona of Articles [102 and 106 TFEU] by taking into consideration the main relevant matters relied on by the applicant in that complaint. That is clear from the fact that the Commission indicated, in the contested act, that the investigation which it had carried out had enabled it to establish certain discrepancies in relation to the facts which the applicant had set out in its complaint.

98. Those facts were relied on by the applicant in order to demonstrate that there is no alternative to the use of quay No 25 in order to unload, by self-handling, the coal which it transports on behalf of ENEL. The applicant infers from this that the quay in question therefore constitutes an 'essential facility' within the meaning of the Bronner judgment, which lays down the conditions under which access to a facility must be regarded as essential to the exercise by the undertaking in question of its activity.

99. In that regard, the reasoning followed by the Commission in the contested act seeks to show that, as the facts alleged by the applicant in support of its argument are unproven, quay No 25 cannot be classified as an essential facility. The Commission therefore concludes, as it maintained at the hearing, that application of the regulations adopted by the Autorità Portuale di Ancona, and more specifically of Article 5a of Bye-Law No 6/98, cannot have had the effect of impeding access by the applicant to an essential facility. Consequently, without expressing a view on liability for the conduct in question, the Commission considered that it did not have to use the powers conferred on it by Article [106(3) TFEU] against the Autorità Portuale di Ancona.

100. It is important to note that in its action the applicant has either not disputed the correctness of the facts as stated by the Commission in the contested act, offered supporting evidence which does not establish the truth of its allegations, or merely relied on matters which it had not mentioned in its complaint.

101. Thus, with regard to quay No 22, the applicant did not dispute the Commission's assertion in the contested act that it is a public quay. As to the applicant's allegation that quays Nos 20 and 22 are intended exclusively for loading and unloading grain and not coal, it is important to note that that factual situation is not apparent from the triennial operational plan annexed by the applicant to its application, which merely indicates that those quays are suitable for handling cereals.

102. Furthermore, the applicant did not dispute the Commission's assertion in the contested act, and confirmed by the Autorità Portuale di Ancona at the hearing, that those quays are deep enough and long enough to allow the applicant's ship, the Capo Noli, to berth.

103. As regards the complaint alleging failure by the Commission to consider the argument that the contract which the applicant has concluded with ENEL prevents it from concluding, with quay concession-holders, commercial agreements relating to the performance of its dock work, the Court notes that there is no clause in that contract, which is annexed to the application, to substantiate that argument, as indeed the applicant acknowledged at the hearing. It must be pointed out in that regard that none of the clauses in that contract relates to the conditions for unloading coal for ENEL.

104. The applicant also challenges the Commission's interpretation of the concept of 'essential facility' and submits that quay No 25 of the Port of Ancona must be classified as such under the principle in *Bronner*. However, it is sufficient in that regard to observe that that

argument cannot be a matter for review by the Community judicature of the Commission's compliance with its duty to examine the complaint diligently and impartially.

105. It follows that the present action, in so far as it seeks the annulment of a Commission decision not to initiate the procedure under Article [106 TFEU], must be dismissed as inadmissible and, in any event, as unfounded in law.

106. It follows from all the foregoing that the application must be dismissed in its entirety."

D. INFORMATION EXCHANGE IN THE CONTEXT OF PORTS

13.081 The exchange of information in relation to port activities is an issue which has not arisen often in EU competition case law but it is a real issue in practice. The exchange could relate to the exchange of information between, for example, (a) ports, (b) users in a port and even (c) a port and a user in a port.[87]

13.082 Are there competition law risks where two or more operators in a port seek to have discussions on an issue such as scheduling or how overcrowding could be managed? An example might be a ferry port where all the operators would like to arrive and leave at a similar time because of the needs of markets, the preferences of passengers or freight drivers, tides, train timetables or whatever. Another example might be a popular and congested cruise port with limited berths and where all the cruise lines seek to arrive early in the morning and leave in the evening with little or no demand for overnight slots.

13.083 The guiding principle should be that competitors should not co-ordinate activities or conduct. It is the rivalry which exists between them which is the hallmark of competition and the reason why markets would work efficiently. However, a complete ban on communications would be both undesirable and unworkable. EU competition law has been somewhat tolerant of dialogue between shipping companies on issues such as timetables. The consortia block exemption permits it in certain circumstances. The expired Regulation 4056/86 also contemplated the exchange of information in certain limited circumstances. It would be important that the object and purpose of the exchange is purely technical or operational in nature and would have neither the object nor effect of preventing, restricting or distorting competition.

13.084 If there is to be exchange of information between competitors then a manager or intermediary might be a useful model but even then, there should be no anti-competitive information exchanged. The "messenger model" prevents direct exchange of information but the messenger must ensure that the exchanges/information flows which do occur are limited to what is necessary and not involving the anti-competitive exchange of information. The discussions and the information should be available publicly so as to ensure no distortion of competition.

13.085 Irrespective of how the discussions take place, the discussions should be limited to what is essential for the co-ordination of timetables but not go any further. This is because if there is a breach of Article 101(1) then Article 101(3) will only exempt that which is indispensable. It is better to avoid a breach of Article 101 in the first place.

---

87 Recourse should be had to specialists' works on EU competition law to understand further the EU competition law on information exchange.

E. PRICING IN PORTS

13.086 EU competition law is concerned with many aspects of pricing. It is concerned with pricing in the context of both anti-competitive arrangements and abuse of dominance.

13.087 The *Helsingborg* cases[88] are interesting examples of how competition law applies to charging in ports. In 1997, Scandlines Sverige and Sundbusserne complained to the European Commission alleging that Helsingborg (in southwest Sweden) was infringing Article 102 of the TFEU. The complainants alleged that there were excessive and discriminatory charges being imposed for services provided to ferry operators. In specific terms, three complaints were made. First, the prices actually charged to ferry operators were *excessive* because they were unfair in themselves when compared to the costs of providing the services. In this case, the term "cost" meant, according to the complainants, the cost and a reasonable profit. The complainants alleged that the price was excessive when compared to the costs imposed on non-ferry operators and in a comparable port (Elsinore in Denmark being the comparator port). Second, the complainants alleged that the prices charged to ferry operators were *discriminatory* when compared to those charged to certain cargo operators and this put the ferry operators at a comparative disadvantage. Third, the complainants alleged that the port charges were excessive and discriminatory because they were not cost-based and pricing was not *transparent*. In deciding the complaints, the Commission followed the CJEU's approach in *United Brands*[89] on the issue of excessive pricing. It therefore assessed the costs actually incurred by the port and compared them with the prices actually charged to ferry operators. The Commission then tried to determine whether the difference was excessive. In regard to the unfair price allegation, the Commission sought to determine whether the prices were unfair when compared to the prices charged to other users, whether the prices where unfair vis-à-vis other ports and whether the charges were unfair in themselves. The Commission found the complaints were unfounded and therefore rejected them. Nonetheless, the Commission made some comments on the issues involved and those comments are useful to recall. In trying to determine whether the prices were excessive, the Commission stated that only the costs related to ferry operations could be taken into account.[90] This meant that prices for other services should be ignored. The Commission's approach in regard to deciding whether the prices were unfair was reviewed by Forrester, MacLennan and Komnios in the following terms:

> "The Commission ... assessed whether the prices charged by the port to the ferry operators were unfair, expressing regret from the outset that the Courts and its own decisional practice provided little guidance on how to determine when a price was to be considered unfair in itself.[91] The complainants claimed that the assessment should be made by calculating the economic value of the product or service provided, following a cost-plus approach. According to this method, the economic value would equal the costs incurred in providing the service or product, plus a reasonable profit which would be a percentage of the production costs. Any prices exceeding the economic value thus determined should be deemed unfair.[92]

---

88 Decisions: COMP/36.358 *Scandlines Sverige AB/Port of Helsingborg* and CMOP/36.570 *Sundbusserne/Port of Helsingborg*. See the comments of Forrester, MacLennan and Komnios in (2005) 24 YEL 584.
89 Case 29/76 *United Brands v Commission* [1978] ECR 207.
90 *Scandlines Sverige* decision, paras 137–138.
91 Para.158 of the *Scandlines Sverige* decision.
92 Ed., Case 27/76 *United Brands Company and United Brands Continentaal BV v Commission* [1978] ECR 207, para. 219.

The Commission conceded that the legitimacy of a price could also be assessed by using a cost-plus framework examining the respective relations between the production costs, the price (or the profit margin) and the economic value of the service. However, in addition to the cost-plus approach, certain other criteria should be taken into account. Firstly, the costs should be calculated taking into account the cost of capital as well as production costs. Secondly, it was of the utmost importance to take into account non-cost related factors such as demand, which increased a product's economic value because customers valued it highly and were therefore willing to pay more for it. This sort of case is likely to arise again and will always be very difficult to predict."[93]

Port charges

13.088 On 17 May 1994 the CJEU delivered its opinion in *Corsica Ferries Italia Srl v Corpo dei Piloti del Porto di Genova*.[94] The CJEU held that EU law precluded the application of different tariffs for identical piloting services based on whether the undertaking providing the shipping services between two Member States flies the flag of that State and is consequently authorised for maritime cabotage. Under Italian law, the failure to use the piloting service in the port of Genoa would be a criminal offence. Italian-flagged vessels paid a lower tariff. Corsica Ferries was an Italian company operating a liner service between Genoa and various Corsican ports using two ferries flying the Panamanian flag and could not therefore benefit from the reduced tariff. The CJEU noted that the Treaty prohibited discrimination and that piloting services were services provided for consideration to the shipping undertakings by the Italian authorities. The CJEU believed that differences in tariffs would affect those undertakings as providers of maritime transport services in so far as they have an effect on the cost of the services and placed them at a disadvantage with other operators who benefited from the preferential rate. The CJEU expressed the view that Article 1(1) of Regulation 4055/86 prohibited a Member State from applying different tariffs for identical piloting services, depending on whether or not an undertaking operates a vessel entitled to operate cabotage services. The CJEU also advised that a Member State court infringes Article 106(1) when coupled with Article 102 of the TFEU if, by approving the tariffs adopted by the undertaking, the State induces the undertaking to abuse its dominant position by applying dissimilar conditions to equivalent transactions with its trading partners within the meaning of Article 106(c) of the TFEU.

General pricing issues

13.089 The general competition law rules apply to pricing issues in ports. Examples of pricing issues which arise in ports include excessive pricing, discriminatory pricing and price-fixing. It is beyond the scope of this book to deal with the issue of pricing in depth and recourse should be had to general competition law books.

---

93 (2005) 24 YEL 584 at 585–586.
94 Case C-18/93, 17 May 1994, [1994] ECR I-1783.

Rødby

13.090 On 21 December 1993 the Commission adopted Decision 94/119 in regard to a refusal to grant access to facilities in the port of Rødby in Denmark.[95] The Commission's *Twenty-Second Report on Competition Policy* summarised the case (at point 522):

> "Following a complaint lodged by a private shipping line concerning the refusal by the Danish Government to grant it access to Rodbyhavn to operate a regular ferry service between that port and the German port of Puttgarden, the Commission sent a letter of formal notice to that Government on the basis of Article [106(3) of the TFEU].
>
> In the Commission's opinion, the effect of this refusal is to protect the monopoly enjoyed by Danish (DSB) and German (DB) railways, which jointly operate a ferry link on this route. Such a refusal would be incompatible with Article [106(1)], read in conjunction with Article [102] of the Treaty."

It is useful to examine the decision in more depth. Having given the Danish authorities and the undertaking DSB the opportunity to make known their views on the objections raised by the Commission with regard to Denmark's refusal to allow "Euro-Port A/S", a subsidiary of the Swedish group "Stena Rederi AB" (Stena)[96] either to build a new terminal in the immediate vicinity of the port of Rødby or to have access to the existing terminal at this port with a view to operating a ferry service between Rødby and Puttgarden. In 1990, the Danish Transport Minister refused to allow "Euro-Port A/S" to build a private commercial port in the immediate vicinity of the port of Rødby. Also in 1990, the same Minister rejected the request by "Euro-Port A/S" to operate from the public port of Rødby. DSB was a public undertaking with the status of a department of the Transport Ministry and a budget provided for in the Finance Law. It held the exclusive right to organise rail traffic in Denmark. It was also the owner of the port of Rødby and was responsible for its management. Utilisation of the port terminals, however, required the authorisation of the Minister, acting on a proposal from DSB. DSB operated ferry services between Denmark and neighbouring countries but did not hold any exclusive rights to such services. The Rødby–Puttgarden route was operated jointly by DSB and DB (Deutsche Bundesbahn), a German public undertaking. Their co-operation extended, among other things, to joint ticket sales, joint fixing of timetables and rates, and the granting of identical discounts. There were no other companies providing ferry services on the sea route in question. Scheduled ferry services between Rødby and Puttgarden essentially linked the ports on the east coast of Denmark (island of Zealand) and the west coast of Sweden with Germany and the rest of Western Europe. The Commission considered whether air transport was substituted with ferry transport but found it was not. Air transport was a far more costly option that was available only to a small number of passengers without cars and was capable of carrying only a small proportion of the freight (light goods with high added value) – air transport was thus interchangeable with transport by ferry only to a limited extent. The Commission then considered whether container traffic was substitutable. Another way of transporting goods was by container carrier (notably between Sweden and Germany). However, the Commission found that this solution,

---

95 OJ 1994 L55/52.
96 "Stena Rederi AB" ("Stena") was a Swedish shipping group which specialised in ferry services and wished to operate between Denmark and Germany through two subsidiaries: (a) Europort A/S, a Danish company; and (b) Scan-Port GmbH, a German company.

chiefly used between Goeteborg and Hamburg-Bremen, was suitable only for goods that can be packed in containers. In addition, North Sea routes (in particular between Goeteborg and Hamburg-Bremen, to the west of Denmark) were much longer, and this increased the transit times for goods. Lastly, container transport would require special inland logistical infrastructure to transport the goods to the port of departure and then from the port of arrival to their final destination. This was not a convenient means of transport for shippers, who preferred to load a lorry providing a door-to-door service. It should also be noted that the other maritime links between eastern Denmark and Germany are not straightforward alternatives to the Rødby–Puttgarden link owing to: (a) their geographical location – Rødby and Puttgarden have better motorway links, whereas Rostock and Warnemuende, situated in the former German Democratic Republic ("GDR") some 120 km east of Luebeck, are not directly connected by motorway to the western German motorway network and are, therefore, better situated to the transport of passengers or goods to or from Berlin and the territories of the former GDR (whereas Puttgarden, near Hamburg, offers easy access to western Germany and, from there, to western and southern Europe); and (b) the duration of the crossings – one hour from Rødby to Puttgarden (as the crow flies), two hours from Gedser to Warnemuende, three-and-a-half hours from Gedser to Rostock.

Around 70.8% of travellers and 87.9% of lorries crossing by sea between Denmark and Germany use the Rødby–Puttgarden route (for 1991 traffic). Similarly, the Rødby–Puttgarden route cannot easily be substituted by the other passenger sea routes between Sweden and Germany. In view of the excellent motorway connections between Rødby and Helsingoer, which is only 15 minutes by boat from the Swedish port of Helsingborg, the direct link between Germany and Sweden, Travemuende–Trelleborg, in 1991 only accounted for 1,102,463 passengers and 159,484 cars, while the Rødby–Puttgarden route accounted for 8,024,654 passengers and 1,209,065 cars during the same period. This indicates that passengers prefer the Puttgarden-Helsingborg route, regarded as more direct and faster (the Travemuende–Trelleborg crossing between Sweden and Germany takes from seven to nine hours). Similarly, while the Goeteborg–Frederikshavn crossing meets some of the traffic demand on the route between Sweden, on the one hand, and Denmark and the rest of Western Europe, on the other, it still has drawbacks compared with the Rødby–Puttgarden route due to the duration of the crossing (three-and-a-quarter hours instead of one hour) and poorer motorway connections. Finally, the route across the Great Belt (between the islands of Zealand and Fyn to Jutland) involves a sea crossing of the same duration of Rødby–Puttgarden but adds 165 km to the distance to be travelled on land between Copenhagen and Hamburg. This alternative route is thus not as advantageous as the main Helsingoer–Copenhagen–Rødby–Puttgarden route. It is true that, once the proposed fixed link across the Great Belt between Zealand and Fyn is built, it will be easier to divert some of the traffic between Sweden and Copenhagen, on the one hand, and Germany, on the other hand, through Jutland. However the fixed link is not yet in service (the rail link is to open in 1995, the motorway link in 1998) and a charge will in any event be made for the Great Belt link, as for the sea crossings. Accordingly, the Commission considers that the Rødby–Puttgarden crossing is an important link and cannot easily be substituted by the other existing forms of transport and routes between Denmark and Sweden, on the one hand, and Germany, on the other. The Commission recalled that Article 106(1) of the TFEU provides that Member States must neither enact nor maintain in force any measure contrary to the rules of the Treaty in the case of public undertakings and undertakings granted special or exclusive rights. DSB was a public undertaking within the meaning of Article 106(1) of the TFEU. The two refusals by the Danish Transport Minister were State measures within the meaning of Article 106(1). The Commission then turned to examine Article 102 of the TFEU. It began by examining the relevant market. The Commission found:

> "(7) The relevant market is the market for the organization of port services in Denmark for ferry services operating on the Rødby-Puttgarden route (passengers and vehicles).
>
> As the Court of Justice has stated, the organization on behalf of a third party of port operations in a single port can constitute a relevant market within the meaning of Article 86 (Porto di Genova judgment of 10 December 1991, Case C179/90, paragraph 15).
>
> This is due to the fact that operators wishing to provide a transport service on a given sea route must have access to the port facilities located at both ends of the crossing in order to attain their objective.
>
> In the case in question, there is no real alternative with the same advantages as those offered by the port of Rødby for sea transport between eastern Denmark, on the one hand, and Germany and the rest of western Europe, on the other...
>
> (8) Rødby handles over 70.8% of passengers and 87.9% of lorries travelling by sea between Denmark and Germany. In 1991 8,024,654 passengers and 207,255 lorries transited through Rødby, representing a turnover of DM 320 million. The port of Rødby thus constitutes a substantial part of the common market.
>
> (9) In addition, the maritime transport services between Rødby and Puttgarden constitute a neighbouring but separate market which may be affected by the behaviour of an undertaking on the market for the organization of port services.
>
> As emerges from the particulars given [above], the Rødby-Puttgarden route has specific characteristics as a result of which it is not a straightforward alternative to the other transport routes and faces only limited competition from them."

The Commission then considered whether there was a dominant position. The Commission recalled that according to the case law of the CJEU, an undertaking with a legal monopoly of supply of certain services may hold a dominant position within the meaning of Article 102 of the TFEU and cited the *Télémarketing* case.[97] The Commission continued:

> "DSB is a public undertaking which, by virtue of the exclusive right granted by the State in its capacity as port authority, holds a dominant position in Denmark on the market for the organization of port operations with regard to the transport of passengers and vehicles by ferry between Rødby and Puttgarden. This is a dominant position which is relevant in considering the compatibility with the Treaty of the state measures referred to in this decision.
>
> DSB also operates, in conjunction with DB, as a carrier on the Rødby-Puttgarden route. The Court of First Instance recently found that the links between the members of a liner conference (within the meaning of Council Regulation (EEC) No 4056/86 laying down detailed rules for the application of Articles [101 and 102] of the Treaty to maritime transport) may be such that the positions of the member undertakings must be considered jointly in order to determine the existence of an abuse of dominant position within the meaning of Article [102] of the [TFEU]...
>
> The links established by DSB and DB in order to operate the Rødby-Puttgarden route ... are similar to those between members of a conference (fixing of common rates, coordination of timetables, joint marketing).
>
> Consequently, the position of DB and DSB on the route in question must be assessed jointly.

---

97 Case C-311/84 [1985] 3261, ECLI:EU:C:1985:394.

DB and DSB are the only ferry companies operating between Rødby and Puttgarden and therefore hold a joint dominant position on that route. This dominant position on the market for transport services is protected by state measures related to the market for the organization of port operations on which the dominant position referred to in point 10 is exercised."

The Commission then had to consider whether there was an abuse of dominant position:

"(12) The refusal to allow 'Euro-Port A/S', a subsidiary of the Swedish group 'Stena Rederi AB' (Stena) to operate from Rødby has the effect of eliminating a potential competitor on the Rødby-Puttgarden route and hence of strengthening the joint dominant position of DSB and DB on that route.

According to the case law of the Court, an abuse within the meaning of Article 86 is committed in cases where, without any objective necessity, an undertaking holding a dominant position on a particular market reserves to itself an ancillary activity which might be carried out by another undertaking as part of its activities on a neighbouring but separate market, with the possibility of eliminating all competition from such undertaking (Case 311/84 *CBEM v. CLT and IPB* [1985] ECR 3261, paragraph 27).

Thus an undertaking that owns or manages and uses itself an essential facility, i.e. a facility or infrastructure without which its competitors are unable to offer their services to customers, and refuses to grant them access to such facility is abusing its dominant position.

Consequently, an undertaking that owns or manages an essential port facility from which it provides a maritime transport service may not, without objective justification, refuse to grant a shipowner wishing to operate on the same maritime route access to that facility without infringing Article [102].

(13) According to the case-law of the Court (judgment of 13 December 1991 in Case C-18/88, paragraphs 20 and 21), Article [106(1)] prohibits Member States from placing, by law, regulation or administrative provision, public undertakings and undertakings to which they grant exclusive rights in a position in which those undertakings could not place themselves by their own conduct without infringing Article [102]. The Court added that, where the extension of the dominant position of a public undertaking or an undertaking to which the State has granted exclusive rights resulted from a State measure, such a measure constituted an infringement of Article [106], read in conjunction with Article [102] of the Treaty. This principle was confirmed in the judgment of 17 November 1992 in Cases C-271, 281 and 289/90 (paragraph 36).

Thus, for the reasons given above, any firm in the same position as DSB which refused to grant another shipping operator access to the port it controlled would be abusing a dominant position. Where, as in the present case, a Member State has refused such access and has strengthened the effects of the refusal by also refusing to authorize the construction of a new port, it constitutes a State measure in breach of Article [106], read in conjunction with Article [102].

(14) The reasons given by the Danish Transport Ministry for rejecting both requests of 'Euro-Port A/S', a subsidiary of the Swedish group 'Stena Rederi AB' (Stena) are the following:

- the plan of 'Euro-Port A/S', a subsidiary of the Swedish group 'Stena Rederi AB' (Stena), to build a new terminal is not acceptable as that undertaking has allegedly 'not established that there is an unsatisfied demand for a ferry service' and it is 'most unlikely that such a demand would arise' (letter of 9 May 1990 referred to in paragraph 1),
- 'Euro-Port A/S', a subsidiary of the Swedish group 'Stena Rederi AB' (Stena) could not operate from the existing port facilities as this would have the effect of preventing the companies already operating in the port from expanding their activities.

This line of reasoning was set out in the letter dated 8 August 1990 from the Danish Transport Minister, by the summer of 1991, DSB and DB had increased the number of daily sailings between Rødby and Puttgarden from 98 to 112.

The Commission concludes from the foregoing that:

- there was indeed an unsatisfied demand for ferry services in May 1990 since one year later DSB and DB had expanded their services,
- the increase in the activities of DB and DSB in 1991 confirms that the port of Rødby was not saturated.

(15) The Commission also considers that there is no evidence that the existing facilities at Rødby would today be saturated or that, subject to alterations which Stena has informed the Commission it is prepared to finance, existing port capacity is unable to cope with an increase in trade.

The Commission also notes that the Swedish group 'Stena Rederi AB' (Stena) has acquired land adjacent to the port facilities of Rødby which is perfectly suitable for development as a terminal by Stena.

It therefore concludes that there are no technical constraints preventing the Stena group from sailing between Rødby and Puttgarden.

(16) In their letter of 22 February 1993 which constitutes the reply to the letter of formal notice sent by the Commission on 24 November 1992, the Danish authorities rejected the latter's request, stressing that their refusals were justified under Community law. They stated that it would be impossible to allow Stena access to the existing facilities, giving technical reasons and referring for the first time, without any further details, to obligations incumbent upon DB and DSB in the general interest.

This would appear to indicate that, in the view of the Danish authorities, the technical feasibility of access to the port is not a problem or is not the only problem and that they also have a duty to protect the public undertaking DSB from a competitor on the market for ferry services.

Nor can the Commission share the view of the Danish authorities that the alleged saturation of the existing port facilities would make pointless any attempt to introduce competition since this could not in any event lead to an increase in the number of sailings between Rødby and Puttgarden.

Even on a saturated market, an improvement in the quality of products or services offered or a reduction in prices as a result of competition is a definite advantage for consumers; this could also lead to an increase in demand which, in the present case, could be met by expanding the port.

It is clear from the foregoing that the statement by the Danish authorities that they would be prepared to re-examine the request to build a new port made by the Stena subsidiary in 1989 and rejected in 1990 does not constitute a firm commitment either to approve the request or to allow the Stena subsidiaries access to the existing port. Refusing to acknowledge that they have any obligation under Community law, the Danish authorities are prepared only to review the case without stating whether or when the Stena subsidiaries will be granted the right to operate on the route in question on comparable terms to those offered to operators already present on the market. This position, which in any case further defers recognition of the legitimate rights of the Stena subsidiaries, does not constitute a satisfactory reply to the letter of formal notice sent by the Commission to the Danish Government.

Effects on trade between Member States

(17) The double refusal referred to in this decision has the effect of preventing the entry of new operators on the market for ferry services between Denmark and Germany. Therefore it has an appreciable effect on trade between Member States, taking account of the volume of traffic on the Rødby-Puttgarden route (see paragraphs 5 and 8 above).

Article [106]

...(18) The Commission considers that the application of the competition rules in the present case does not impede the particular task entrusted to the public undertaking DSB namely to organize rail services and manage the port facilities at Rødby. Therefore the exception provided for in Article [106](2) does not apply.

The Commission is not aware that DSB has been entrusted with particular tasks other than that referred to above. If (as the letter of 22 February 1993 from the Danish authorities appears to indicate) DSB is indeed subject to a 'transport obligation' the Commission points out that neither their nature nor scope has been specified by the Danish authorities. Consequently, the exception provided for in Article [106](2) does not justify maintaining the monopoly held by DB and DSB on the Rødby-Puttgarden route."

Ultimately, the Commission concluded that the measures constituted infringements of Article 106(1) of the TFEU in conjunction with Article 102. In its decision, Article 1 provided that the

"refusal of the Danish Government to allow 'Euro-Port A/S', a subsidiary of the Swedish group 'Stena Rederi AB' (Stena) to build a new port in the immediate vicinity of the port of Rødby ... or to operate from the existing port facilities at Rødby ... is incompatible with Article [106(1) of the TFEU], read in conjunction with Article [102 of the TFEU]."

Article 2 provided that the

"Danish Government shall bring to an end the infringement referred to in Article 1 of this decision and shall inform the Commission within two months of the date of notification of this decision of the measures it has taken to bring to an end its prohibition on Euro-Port and Scan-Port either to build a new port in the vicinity of the public port of Rødby or to operate from the existing port facilities."

Article 3 noted that the decision was addressed to Denmark.

Port of Kristiansand and Fjord Line

13.091 The EU's competition rules (in particular, Articles 101 and 102 of the TFEU) are mirrored in the European Economic Area Agreement's ("EEA") competition regime (in particular, Articles 53 and 54 of the EEA). Therefore some of the issues relating to ports in EU competition law can also arise in the context of EEA competition law. In November 2008, Fjord Line (a ferry operator) complained to the European Free Trade Association ("EFTA") Surveillance Authority (the EEA equivalent of the EU's Directorate General for Competition) that the company was being blocked from using the port of Kirstiansand. The port had required that ferry operators wishing to use the port had to operate a year-round service. Fjord Line contended that this requirement effectively excluded it particularly as it used catamaran craft which could not be relied upon in rough winter weather and they did not carry cargo so winter services would have been loss-making. The case ultimately got resolved because the Coastal Administration and the Ministry for Fisheries and Coastal Affairs overturned the conditions set down by the port. On 21 December 2009, the EFTA Surveillance Authority published a press release announcing that it was closing its investigation into the Port of Kristiansand after Fjord Line had been granted access to the port:

"The Authority closes its investigation against Port of Kristiansand after Fjord Line is granted access to the Port
On 16 December 2009, the Authority decided to close its case relating to the exclusion of Fjord Line from the Port of Kristiansand. The Port refused to grant Fjord Line access in 2009 on the grounds that Fjord Line did not provide year-round transport for passengers and cargo. The

closure of the Authority's investigation follows a decision by the Norwegian authorities obliging the Port to grant Fjord Line access in the future.

The Authority received a complaint from Fjord Line in November 2008 alleging infringement of the EEA competition rules. At that time, the Port of Kristiansand had decided that all ferry operators were required to provide year-round services for passengers and cargo in order to be allowed to operate out of the harbour. Fjord Line used a high speed catamaran on its route from Kristiansand to Northern Jutland, and claimed that it was not able to meet that requirement: the catamaran does not carry cargo and is unsuitable in the winter months since it cannot sail in rough sea.

In parallel with the investigation by the Authority, Fjord Line also lodged a complaint with the Norwegian Coastal Administration, alleging that the Port's requirements were contrary to Norwegian harbour legislation. On 8 May 2009, the Coastal Administration found in favour of Fjord Line, and access to the harbour was granted.

Against that background, the Authority considers that there are no longer sufficient grounds for pursuing the case."[98]

Fjord Line had earlier issued an interesting press release:

"Fjord Line is backed by ESA (06.11.09)
The 'EFTA' Surveillance Authority (ESA) – the authority responsible for overseeing the enforcement of the EEA-agreement in the 'EFTA'-countries – gives Fjord Line full support in the shipping company's legal battle against the exclusion of Fjord Line from The Port of Kristiansand. ESA is content that national authorities have given Fjord Line its due rights of access to the port's facilities, and has closed the case regarding breach of competition legislation against Kristiansand Port Authority.

Fjord Line has been given permission to operate a summer service in 2010 using the vessel Fjord Line Express, and ESA states that The Kristiansand Port Authority is barred from excluding Fjord Line in the future. The statement from ESA however also makes clear that a full investigation into breach of competition legislation may be reopened should The Kristiansand Port Authority again attempt to exclude Fjord Line.

In November of 2008 Fjord Line launched a complaint against The Kristiansand Port Authority before ESA, claiming that the exclusion from the port was in breach of the competition rules of the EEA-agreement. The port authority demanded that any ferry operator wishing to use The Port of Kristiansand should offer a year-round service for both passengers and cargo. These conditions served only to exclude Fjord Line, as the company operates the service with a high-speed passenger vessel, unable to carry cargo and operate on the Skagerrak during the winter.

In May of 2009 The Norwegian Costal Administration (NCA) overturned the decision by The Kristiansand Port Authority that demanded a year-round service, and ordered the port authority to reconsider the matter. The port authority unsuccessfully appealed to The Ministry for Fisheries and Coastal Affairs to have the decision by The NCA overturned, and later gave Fjord Line permission to use the port's facilities for the upcoming summer of 2009. Having received the permission at such a late date, Fjord Line was unable to offer any services in 2009, but will offer a passenger service between Kristiansand and Hirtshals next summer. As a result of the exclusion from the port in 2009 Fjord Line has launched a simultaneous lawsuit against The Kristiansand Port Authority in order to get compensation for the losses incurred as a result of the exclusion. ESA also states that the investigation into possible breaches by the port authority of the freedom to provide maritime services within the EEA-area continues.

– In its letter to Fjord Line, ESA goes a long way towards agreeing with Fjord Line in our fight against the exclusion from The Port of Kristiansand, says CEO of Fjord Line, Ingvald Fardal. – ESA points out that the decision to close the case regarding breach of competition legislation is a direct consequence of the port authority's acceptance of the decision to suspend the demand for a year-round service. However, ESA also points out that a full

---

98 PR(09)101.

investigation into the matter will be launched should the port authority decide to reinstate any such peculiar conditions for use of the port's facilities. For us, this is satisfying. Our objective has never been for ESA to impose fines on The Kristiansand Port Authority, but to see the end of a regime that has served to give one operator a monopoly on ferry services between Kristiansand and Denmark.

Fardal further points out that the letter from ESA provides several legal assessments that will be employed by Fjord Line in the pending legal case against The Kristiansand Port Authority. He further states that the reasons given by spokespersons for the port authority supporting the claim for a year-round service, among them the need for a return on capital, the risk that Color Line would cease its year-round service and the desire to have a year-round alternative to Color Line, have all been declared irrelevant when considering a possible breach of competition legislation. This includes ESA's strong refutation of the claim that competition legislation was not applicable as the port authority was not itself operating a ferry service.

– We are very pleased that we have obtained permission to operate from Kristiansand during the summer of 2010, and that ESA in a letter 15 pages long provides a framework that will render it impossible for The Port of Kristiansand to attempt to exclude Fjord Line in the future."

Harbour agreements in Sandefjord (Norway) and Strømstad (Sweden): Color Line

13.092 The EFTA Surveillance Authority submitted a statement of objections to Color Line (a ferry operator). Competitors complained that Color Line's harbour agreements infringed competition rules by securing long term exclusive access to harbour facilities with the result that these agreements prevented others from accessing the ports. On 18 December 2009, the EFTA Surveillance Authority issued a press release confirming that it had sent a Statement of Objections to Color Line:

"Preliminary findings of the Authority suggest that Color Line has acted in breach of EEA competition rules
The Authority can confirm that on 16 December 2009 it sent a Statement of Objections to O.N. Sunde AS, Color Group ASA, Color Line AS and Color Line Transport AS ('Color Line'). The Statement of Objections sets out the Authority's preliminary view that Color Line has infringed Articles 53 and 54 of the EEA Agreement through long-term exclusive agreements in Sandefjord and Strömstad which have prevented other ferry companies from obtaining access to harbour facilities.
Following a complaint, the Authority has carried out an extensive market investigation. On the basis of that investigation, the Statement of Objections sets out the Authority's preliminary view that the harbour agreements have restricted competition on passenger ferry routes between ports on the Norwegian coast between Sandefjord and Langesund and ports on the Swedish coast in the Municipality of Strömstad. Pursuant to those agreements, Color Line has secured long-term exclusive access to harbour facilities in Sandefjord and in Strömstad. That has enabled it to prevent potential competitors from obtaining access to the relevant market, in breach of Articles 53 and 54 of the EEA Agreement.
Color Line has two months to reply to the Statement of Objections, and will then have the right to be heard in an oral hearing. If the preliminary views expressed in the Statement of Objections are confirmed, the Authority may require Color Line to cease the conduct restrictive of competition and may impose a fine.

Background
A Statement of Objections is a formal step in antitrust investigations in which the Authority informs the parties concerned in writing of the objections raised against them. The addressees of a Statement of Objections can reply in writing to the Statement of Objections, setting out all facts

known to them which are relevant to their defence against the objections raised by the Authority. They may also request an oral hearing to present their comments on the case. The Authority may then take a decision on whether the conduct addressed in the Statement of Objections is compatible or not with the antitrust rules in the EEA Agreement. Sending a Statement of Objections does not prejudge the final outcome of the procedure."[99]

13.093 The matter has not been resolved at the time of completion of this manuscript.

F. NEGOTIATIONS RELATING TO PORTS

13.094 *Humber Oil Terminal Trustees Limited v Associated British Ports*[100] is a judgment of the English High Court.[101] In essence, the claimant sought to renew its leases of docking facilities which it leased from the landlord defendant. The defendant resisted the request for renewal saying it intended to operate its own business. The claimant alleged that the defendant was abusing its dominant position to demand excessive rents. The defendant sought to strike out that part of the claim. The court held that the allegation of abuse of dominant position failed. It was not the case that a proposal, made in the course of negotiations, of a rent or price which is excessive can – without more – constitute the imposition of an unfair rent or price for the purposes of Article 102 of the TFEU or its UK domestic equivalent. Furthermore the claimant had failed to particularise the allegation. The related parts of the claim were therefore struck out by the court.

13.095 The facts were straightforward. Associated British Ports ("ABP") was, as the successor in title to the British Transport Docks Board, the freehold owner and operator of the Port of Immingham on the south bank of the river Humber. One of the facilities of the port was the Immingham Oil Terminal ("IOT"). This was constructed in the 1960s to serve two inland refineries called the Lindsey Oil Refinery and the Humber Oil Refinery, later owned by Total UK Ltd ("Total") and ConocoPhillips Ltd ("Conoco") respectively. It consisted of a jetty with a number of berths, an onshore oil depot, other land used for associated purposes and substantial pipe and oil storage works. Since June 1966 the IOT had been operated by Associated Petroleum Terminals (Immingham) Ltd ("APT"), a joint venture company owned and controlled by Total and Conoco. In 1970 the predecessor in title of ABP, by two separate leases, which were later supplemented by two further leases, demised the land on which the IOT is situated to Humber Oil Terminals Trustee Ltd ("HOTT"), another joint venture company of Total and Conoco, for a term of 40 years expiring on 31 December 2009 or 1 January 2010. There are four material features of those leases: (1) possession was granted to HOTT thereby excluding others from using the terminal, (2) the rent was set by reference to the historic cost of construction, (3) there was no provision for any open market rent review during the term and (4) HOTT was relieved of any obligation to pay ships or goods dues during the term. In 1995 negotiations between ABP and HOTT commenced in which HOTT sought extended leases of IOT. No agreement was reached. HOTT alleges that the failure of the negotiations was due, at least in part, to the fact that ABP sought payment of excessive rent. The negotiations recommenced in 2005 and after February 2008 were conducted on a without

---

99 PR(09)98.
100 [2011] EWHC 352 (Ch).
101 England and Wales High Court (Chancery Division), [2011] EWHC 352 (Ch) (24 February 2011), www.bailii.org/ew/cases/EWHC/Ch/2011/352.htm.

prejudice basis. In July 2008 ABP indicated to HOTT that its preferred course was to take operational control of IOT so that it might be made available to third parties as well as HOTT. In 2009 ABP served on HOTT the notices required by section 25 of the Landlord and Tenant Act 1954 to terminate each of the four leases and indicating, as required by section 25(6), that ABP would oppose the grant of a new tenancy to HOTT. Proceedings for the grant of new tenancies were commenced by HOTT against ABP in the Great Grimsby County Court on 21 December 2009. In its defences served on 15 January 2010 ABP asserted, in reliance on section 30(l)(g), that:

> "[t]he Defendant intends to occupy the premises (and all associated land holdings presently leased to the Defendant) for the purposes of a business to be run by it for the import and export of oil products with a view to (a) ensuring continuity of supply to Total and Conoco (and their respective refineries) and (b) exploring and implementing the supply of oil and other products which are deemed appropriate over or through the premises, to other third parties".

In summary, the tenant contended that ABP was abusing its dominant position in the provision of deep-water facilities in the Port of Immingham in five specified respects, namely: (1) demanding, in the course of negotiations, abusively high prices for the provision of those facilities by way of (a) rent under the new leases, and (b) port access charges; (2) now seeking from the court orders for abusively high rents under the new leases; (3) relying on a statutory provision relating to landlord and tenant law as a means to force the tenant to accept abusively high rents and port charges; (4) being unable to operate the facility independently from and as efficiently or effectively as the other party if the defence succeeds; and (5) using its rights as a landowner to acquire the business and equipment on site at an undervalue. The competition law claims did not succeed.

G. PORTS AND STATE AID

13.096 There have been several cases relating to the application of EU State aid law to ports. The topic is considered in chapter 15.

CHAPTER 14

European Union competition law: consortia

A. INTRODUCTION

14.001 Consortia were defined in 1990 by the European Commission as: "coalitions of several independent shipping lines seeking some form of co-operation in order to maintain profitability through rationalisation in the widest sense and to spread the expense of investment in container operations".[1]

14.002 Writing in 2008, the Commission stated:

"[a] consortium is a grouping of shipping lines which co-operate to provide joint maritime cargo transport services. Such agreements usually allow shipping lines to rationalise their activities and achieve economies of scale. If consortia are faced with sufficient competition, the users of the services provided by consortia usually benefit from improvements in productivity and service quality."[2]

14.003 Again writing in 2008, the Commission stated: "[a] consortium is an operational co-operation between two or more liner shipping[3] carriers with a view to providing a joint service on a trade. Such cooperation cannot cover pricing or output restrictions."[4]

14.004 The combination of these three statements gives a very good insight into this very important feature of modern shipping life. Consortia normally involve such conditions as joint fleet operations, joint terminal contracts or operations, joint offices, joint equipment pools, the pooling of cargoes or revenues, joint marketing, joint documentation but *not*, and this is critical, joint price-fixing.[5] In essence, in consortia, shipping lines enter into operational co-operation arrangements for the purpose of providing a joint service but they may not engage in price-fixing.

---

1 Communication by the Commission, *Report on the Possibility of a Group Exemption for Consortia Agreements in Liner Shipping*, COM(90)260 final (referred to in this chapter as the "1990 Communication"), para. 3.2. On consortia, see Athanassiou, "The New Liner Shipping Regulation" [2010] 1 JECL&P 129; Chuah, "A Snapshot of Some Recent EU Legal Developments" [2009] 15(4) JIML 358; Green, "Consortia and Multi-Modal Transport", Second EEC Shipping Law Conference, Antwerp, 7–8 February 1991; Mylonas-Widdall, "Consortia Regulation Draft Approved", Lloyd's List, 20 December 1991, p. 4; Prisker, "Commission Adopts New Block Exemption Regulation for Liner Shipping Consortia", European Competition Newsletter, No 1, 2010, p. 8; Randolph, "The New Consortia Block Exemption and its Impact on the Shipping Industry" (2009), *Shipping & Transport International*, 7(.4), p. 18; Randolph, "Consortia Legislation", Lloyd's Maritime Academy, EU Competition Law in Shipping, London, 26 March 2009; Ruttley, "The Consortia Regulation", IBC Conference, 2 March 1997; Stamatiou, "European Union: Competition – Shipping" [2010] 21 ICCLR N48; and Williams, "Adoption of Regulation 823/2000 Renewing the Block Exemption for Liner Shipping Consortia", *European Commission Competition Newsletter*, No 3, October 2000, p. 44.
2 IP/08/1566, 22 October 2008.
3 Ed., the Commission defined liner shipping in the same memorandum (MEMO/08/644) as involving "the transport of cargo, chiefly by container, on a regular basis to ports on a particular geographic route, generally known as a 'trade'. Timetables and sailing dates are advertised in advance and the services are available to any transport user."
4 MEMO/08/644. The qualifications about pricing and output are critical points of difference between consortia and liner conferences.
5 Communication, op. cit. at fn. 1, para. 3.2.

14.005 Associations or arrangements involving shipowners usually fall into two categories: liner conferences and consortia. Consortia do not involve price-fixing while liner conferences involve price-fixing. Athanassiou has commented:

> "[liner conferences] are rate-fixing agreements representing hardcore cartels from the competition law point of view whereas [consortia] respond to rationalization needs resulting from the containerization of liner trades. Despite the difference in objectives, the functioning of these associations has in practice been interlinked in various ways. First, consortia have frequently been operating under the umbrella of liner conferences, thus introducing a second-level restriction which had to be taken into account by the legislation. Second, consortia not related to conferences operated in a highly cartelized environment – a factor which could not be ignored."[6]

14.006 It has been commented that

> "[l]iner consortia emerged in response to the increased capital requirements of shipowners seeking to purchase and maintain the large cost-effective vessels required by the introduction of containerisation in the international transport sector. They involve the carrying out of activities in common by independent shipping lines in order to rationalise operations or costs. They are distinguishable from liner conferences which, inter alia, pursue the objective of coordinating tariffs. Regulation 246/2009628 empowers the Commission to issue a block exemption in respect of such consortia and the current block exemption is Regulation 906/2009."[7]

14.007 As the principal difference between a consortium and a liner conference is that a consortium does not involve pricing or output restrictions, it is not surprising that the Commission (particularly, the Directorate General for Competition ("DG COMP")) favoured co-operation within consortia as opposed to co-operation within liner conferences. It has been commented by de Broca, Riga and Suboès:

> "[m]aritime consortia are fundamentally different from maritime conferences. Conferences were equivalent to a cartel; an industry forum to discuss and agree on prices and capacity on given trades. Conversely, the purpose of a consortium is to bring about cooperation between carriers in the joint operation of a maritime transport service. This obviously explains the different assessment in antitrust terms."[8]

14.008 The purposes of consortia vary – examples of the Statement of Purposes in various consortia agreements surveyed by the Commission include:

> "the purpose of the Agreement is to establish a joint service/consortium capable of securing the economies and advantages of modern shipping technology through co-ordinated management of roll-on/roll-off, container or similar modern vessels, and all related activities"

or

> "to enable the parties to operate a service as defined in the agreement in the most economical and efficient way; to promote and maximize the trade and the movement of cargoes between the points and ports referred to"

or

> "the purpose of this Agreement is to authorize the parties to continue their joint service in the trades covered by this Agreement."[9]

---

6 Op. cit. at fn. 1, p. 130.
7 Rose and Bailey (eds), *Bellamy and Child: European Union Law of Competition* (7th ed., 2013), para. 12.181 (footnote omitted).
8 Faull, Nikpay and Taylor (eds), *Faull & Nikpay: The EU Law of Competition* (3rd ed., 2014), para. 15.151.
9 Communication, op. cit. at fn. 1, para. 3.2.

14.009 It has been commented[10] that it is possible to identify certain common categories of consortia, in particular, consortia which involve:

- joint scheduling;
- slot and space exchanges;
- equipment pools;
- joint offices;
- joint terminal operations;
- cargo sharing;
- revenue sharing arrangements;[11]
- joint sales and joint use of bills of lading;
- price fixing; and
- shared inland operations (e.g. joint consolidation and haulage).[12]

14.010 There is a wide variety of consortia agreements. The third recital to Regulation 906/2009[13] stated:

"[c]onsortium agreements vary significantly ranging from those that are highly integrated, requiring a high level of investment for example due to the purchase or charter by their members of vessels specifically for the purpose of setting up the consortium and the setting up of joint operations centres, to flexible slot exchange agreements. For the purposes of this Regulation a consortium agreement consists of one or a set of separate but interrelated agreements between liner shipping companies under which the parties operate the joint service. The legal form of the arrangements is less important than the underlying economic reality that the parties provide a joint service."

14.011 It was estimated by the European Commission that there were about 57 consortia operating worldwide as of June 1990.[14] At least 40 of these 57 operated in European Union ("EU") liner trades.[15] There has been a heavy presence of European shipping companies in consortia. There was also an overlap between carriers being members of both consortia and conferences.

14.012 Consortia aim at rationalising shipping operations so that the members of consortia can benefit from the economies of scale. They are primarily based on multimodal transport. There are co-operation agreements including the joint lease of containers and container chassis. They also involve joint marketing such as a uniform bill of lading and common electronic databases and computerised tracking of shipped goods.

14.013 When Regulation 4056/86 was adopted, the Council asked the Commission whether there was a possibility for granting a block exemption for consortia. It was four years later, in 1990, when the Commission published its proposal.[16]

---

10 Green, op. cit. at fn. 1, pp. 5–6.
11 This revenue sharing should not involve any form of price co-ordination.
12 Green, op. cit. at fn. 1, pp. 5–6.
13 This is the current block exemption for consortia as its duration was extended until 25 April 2022 by Comm. Reg. 697/2010 OJ L184/3, 25 June 2014.
14 Communication, op. cit. at fn. 1, para. 3.2.
15 Communication, op. cit. at fn. 1, para. 3.2.
16 COM90(260) final.

14.014 The Commission in its 1990 communication on consortia[17] – which accompanied the Commission's proposal for a block exemption for consortia – identified the background to the development of consortia:

> "2.1 The Commission is aware of present and prospective developments and organisational changes in world shipping and the implications which these may have for the [EU's] shipping and competition policies. Competition in the liner shipping industry has created the need for companies to be efficient in order to compete on the world market. The shipping industry is a capital intensive one, with a high proportion of fixed to variable costs. Ships therefore need to be as fully utilised as possible if the capital costs are to be covered. Individual enterprises acting alone without having strong financial resources are in a vulnerable position if heavy overcapacity shows itself on their particular trade routes.
>
> 2.2 The development of container services has increased pressures for co-operation and rationalisation, especially on the longer deep sea trade routes. Because of the large amounts of cargo which can be handled daily from a containership, operators have been able to use bigger ships without increasing, and indeed even reducing, port time. However, since the amount of cargo available remains much the same, fewer of the larger ships are needed to serve a particular trade. [EU] shipowners have difficulty to operate with container ships of the size needed to obtain the available economies of scale and thus minimise costs, whilst maintaining a satisfactory frequency of service.
>
> 2.3 Other related pressures towards closer association between operators on containerised trade routes were that:
>
> – the establishment of a container service necessitated an initial capital investment greater than that required to replace tonnage on conventional services. Individual lines therefore hesitated to make this investment on their own account;
> – container ships were less free to transfer from one trade to another because many were designed for a particular trade route; in addition many ports did not have the equipment and infrastructure to handle container ships (a problem which still exists in some developing countries).
>
> 2.4 These pressures for co-operation led individual shipping lines to enter into joint fleet operations usually described as consortia."

14.015 A number of observations flow from this statement. First, in essence, consortia are usually ways of reducing costs and enhancing efficiency.[18] Second, consortia cover ship sharing "chiefly by container". Third, the pressures for co-operation have led individual shipping lines to enter into joint fleet operations (i.e. consortia).

14.016 Consortia did not fall within the scope of Council Regulation 4056/86 (i.e. the block exemption for liner conferences) because they did not involve price-fixing and were of a different nature. Therefore, a special regime had to be found for consortia if there were to be a block exemption.

14.017 The current position is that there is no block exemption for liner conferences (following the repeal of Regulation 4056/86)[19] but there is a block exemption regulation for consortia (or as they might be termed, liner shipping consortia) (i.e. Regulation 906/2009[20] as extended by Regulation 697/2014[21]). It allows shipping lines to enter into consortia arrangements for the purpose of providing a joint service – in other words, it

---

17 Op. cit. at fn. 1.
18 Green, op. cit. at fn. 1, p. 2.
19 See chaps 11 and 12.
20 OJ 2009 L79/1.
21 OJ L184/3, 25 June 2014.

permits for the purposes of Article 101(3) of the Treaty on the Functioning of the European Union ("TFEU") – those consortia arrangements which would otherwise breach Article 101(1) of the TFEU provided the arrangement meets with certain conditions (i.e. the conditions laid down in the block exemption regulation). The current block exemption regulation, "Regulation (EC) No 906/2009 of 28 September 2009 on the application of Article 81(3) of the Treaty to certain categories of agreements, decisions and concerted practices between liner shipping companies (consortia)",[22] applied initially from 26 April 2010 until 25 April 2015[23] but it was then extended by Regulation 691/2014 until 25 April 2020.[24] It is the successor to a series of block exemptions adopted in 1995,[25] 2000[26] and 2005.[27] The consortia regime is perceived by the European Commission as working well. However, in recent times, the European Commission believed that circumstances had changed since the enactment of Regulation 4056/86. Lowri Evans of the European Commission's DG COMP said (in a personal capacity) in 2005:

> "[the Consortia block exemption is] another generous block exemption. Since 1995, the Commission has accepted that co-operation amongst liner shipping companies for the provision of a joint service improves the quality of the service that would be offered by the lines individually.
> This consortia block exemption (Regulation 823/2000) was recently found to be working well and extended until 2010. This means that – apart from price fixing – carriers are able to enter into very extensive co-operation provided that it results in a joint service. Consortia and global alliances have flourished in the past years, often servicing 40–50% of the entire market.
> So, if conferences are abolished,[28] co-operation between liner shipping companies will continue to take place in consortia and alliances. The concentration ratio would then diminish significantly in major East West trades, less so in North South trades where conferences and consortia members are often the same.
> As the reliability of services is [a] function of the competitive situation in the trade, it appears unlikely that it will be affected by the removal of the conference system. Service innovation and service quality are only spurred by competition."[29]

14.018 The Commission stated in its *Guidelines on the application of Article 81 of the EC Treaty to maritime transport services*:[30]

> "6. Horizontal cooperation agreements in liner shipping regarding the provision of joint services are covered by Commission Regulation (EC) No 823/2000 of 19 April 2000 on the application of Article 81(3) of the Treaty to certain categories of agreements, decisions and concerted practices between liner shipping companies (consortia). ... It sets out the conditions, pursuant to Article 81(3) of the Treaty, under which the prohibition in Article 81(1) of the Treaty does not apply to agreements between two or more vessel operating carriers (consortia). It will be reviewed following the changes introduced by Regulation (EC) No 1419/2006."[31]

---

22 OJ 2009 L256/31.
23 Reg. 906/2009, Art. 7.
24 OJ L184/3, 25 June 2014.
25 Reg. 870/95 OJ 1995 L89/7.
26 Reg. 823/2000 OJ 2000 L100/24.
27 Reg. 611/2005 OJ 2005 L101/10.
28 Ed., ultimately, they were abolished: see chap. 11.
29 Speech, "Competition Developments Affecting the Maritime Sector", European Maritime Law Organisation, 14 October 2005.
30 OJ 2008 C245/2. Obviously, Art. 81 of the EC Treaty is now Art. 101 of the TFEU. The Guidelines were not renewed.
31 *Guidelines on the application of Article 81 of the EC Treaty to maritime transport services* OJ 2008 C245/2, para. 6.

14.019 The European Commission believes that consortia benefit shippers for various reasons. Consortia rationalise costs. They provide better multimodal services. They allow efficient tracking systems. There are efficiency gains because of the cross-chartering of space on other vessels and pooling vessels.

14.020 The background has been described by de Broca, Riga and Suboès in the following terms:

> "15.152 In 1986, when Regulation 4056/86 was adopted, the Commission undertook to report within a year whether such a block exemption would be appropriate. The report was delayed until 1990 since the Commission was unable to gather the necessary information from the industry.... However, it concluded that a block exemption was justified for consortia and proposed the adoption of an enabling Council Regulation which was subsequently adopted in 1992 (Regulation 479/92).... Article 2 of Regulation 479/92 provides for a maximum duration of the block exemption for five years. The Commission adopted the first block exemption in 1995 (Regulation 870/95) and, since it then found that the conditions for exemption were still valid, the Commission has until now renewed the exemption three times. Regulation 823/2000 initially expired in April 2005, but was extended for a further five years until April 2010 by Regulation 611/2005. The latter Regulation included some substantive amendments of a relatively limited nature. Indeed, at the time, the Commission considered that pending the more fundamental review of the block exemption on maritime conferences, leading to its repeal, it was not appropriate to carry out an extensive review of the consortia block exemption.
>
> 15.153 Regulation 906/2009 (the Consortia Regulation) was adopted in 2009, granting an exemption from 26 April 2010 until 25 April 2015. It resulted from a rather extensive investigation. In summer 2007, the Commission launched a comprehensive market investigation and sent questionnaires to all major shipping lines as well as to transport users (shippers and freight forwarders). The market investigation aimed at: (a) collecting information on (p. 1818) consortia agreements; (b) assessing the implementation of the exemption in practice; and (c) analysing the extent to which transport users benefit from the cooperation between shipping lines in consortia. Information was received from a number of the carriers operating in consortia to and from Europe and from transport users and their respective representative organizations. In accordance with the enabling Regulation, the Commission published a draft Regulation for consultation in October 2008. The Commission received 19 submissions from carriers and transport users as well as from some Member States.
>
> 15.154 As a result of this process, the Commission adopted a substantially amended Regulation: compared to earlier versions, it was shortened and simplified and half the articles had been repealed."[32]

14.021 The objectives of the most recent review were described in the following terms:

> "15.155 The review process that led to the adoption of Regulation 906/2009 pursued three main objectives.
>
> 15.156 First, the Commission intended to update the Consortia Regulation in light of the new regulatory framework. To that end, Regulation 906/2009 had to reflect the end of the liner conference block exemption Regulation, ... therefore every explicit or implicit reference to liner conferences and to the practices allowed under a price-fixing conference system have been removed. Similarly, following the full application of Regulation 1/2003 to the maritime sector, some provisions had become redundant and had to be repealed.

---

32 Faull, Nikpay and Taylor (eds), op. cit. at fn. 8, paras 15.152–15.154 (footnotes omitted).

15.157 Secondly, the Commission wanted to ensure greater convergence between Regulation 906/2009 and other horizontal block exemption Regulations, such as the block exemption Regulations on specialization agreements, on research and development agreements, or on technology transfer agreements. For instance, in line with the approach in other horizontal block exemption Regulations, a new article on hardcore restrictions (Art 4 of the Consortia Regulation) provides that the most severe antitrust infringements, such as price or capacity fixing and customer or market allocation, will take away the benefit of the block exemption. The aim of bringing the market share threshold closer to the thresholds applied in other block exemption Regulations for horizontal cooperation is described in more detail later and is also a step in this direction.

15.158 Thirdly, the Commission aimed at reflecting possible market changes. In the periodical reviews, the Commission has to ensure that the scope of the block exemption Regulation and the conditions under which undertakings may benefit from it still reflect the current market environment and practice."[33]

14.022 While there is now a block exemption relating to consortia[34] and it obviously concerns only consortia, it is possible that some of the principles embodied in the exemption would be useful for lawyers advising on other activities and practices as well. Indeed, it is possible for a consortia agreement which does not fall within the scope of the block exemption to be still lawful under Article 101 either because there is no breach of Article 101(1) or the criteria set out in Article 101(3) are satisfied following a self-assessment. It is important therefore to recall that the block exemption for consortia is not a strait-jacket into which all consortia must fit otherwise there could be consortia which either do not breach Article 101(1) at all or benefit from Article 101(3).

B. JURIDICAL NATURE OF CONSORTIA

Introduction

14.023 The juridical nature of consortia is a matter of critical concern. Were they subject to Regulation 4056/86?[35] Are they concentrations and thus subject to the Merger Control Regulation? The thinking on aspects of this issue has not yet crystallised but it is useful to consider briefly the juridical character of the consortia block exemption.

Merger control regulation

14.024 The Commission has concluded, based on its review of the consortia agreements submitted to it, that they do not constitute mergers or concentrations because of: (a) the provisions relating to termination with different periods of notice; and (b) there is

---

33 Faull, Nikpay and Taylor (eds), op. cit. at fn. 8, paras 15.155–15.158 (footnotes omitted).
34 It will be recalled that the block exemption regulation sets out the conditions that liner shipping companies have to fulfil if they want to benefit automatically from an exemption from the prohibition set out in Art. 101 TFEU in relation to consortia. By benefiting from the block exemption then they have no doubt that their arrangements (i.e. their operational and technical co-operation agreements to provide joint liner services) are compliant with Art. 101 TFEU. If the arrangement does not comply with the block exemption then they have to undertake a self-assessment to see if the arrangement complies with Art. 101 TFEU but they may no longer notify the arrangement to the European Commission for an individual exemption which means that the more secure method of ensuring compliance is to fall within the block exemption.
35 On Reg. 4056/86, see chap. 12.

no evidence of a transfer of assets or activities to the consortium.[36] It is submitted that such a view is reasonable in the circumstances. Consortia are merely vehicles (of limited duration) used by various shipping companies (who still remain largely independent of each other) so as to exploit particular market opportunities and that various companies may be a member of more than one consortium. The partners do not completely and irreversibly transfer all of their assets into the consortium. If they did, and the consortium fell within the scope of the EU's merger control regulation (i.e. Regulation 139/2004) (the so-called "Merger Control Regulation"),[37] then they would fall outside the scope of the consortia block exemption regulation because of what was Article 22(2) of Regulation 4064/89[38] or, now, the comparable provision of Regulation 139/2004.[39]

Regulation 4056/86

14.025 It is useful, for historical purposes, to analyse consortia agreements to see if they could fit within the scope of Regulation 4056/86 (i.e. the now repealed block exemption on liner conferences). The Commission concluded that consortia are not normally[40] pure technical agreements and thus they fell outside the scope of the exemption in Article 2 of Regulation 4056/86.[41] This is in direct contradiction to the views of the Committee of European Community Shipowners ("CAACE") and Committee on European and Japanese National Shipowners' Associations ("CENSA"). The Commission reasoned thus:

> "The information available suggests that there are few if any consortia agreements whose sole object and effect are to achieve technical improvements or co-operation in the sense of Article 2 of Regulation No. 4056/86.
>
> All but two of the 23 agreements[42] examined contain arrangements not only on joint fleet and terminal operations but also on pooling and/or conference rights, pricing, marketing or inland operations. One of the two exceptions concerns a Slot Charter Agreement containing arrangements on joint schedule and space/slot exchange and arrangements on capacity restrictions for one of the parties regarding certain European ports. The other case concerns an agreement containing arrangements on joint fleet and terminal operations. However, it also provides for cost sharing arrangements for ships, administration and equipment. In addition it provides that conference trading rights may only be exercised by agreement of the consortium policy committee and that the parties, without having joint marketing, 'may combine their interests'.
>
> In all these cases the consortium's sole object and effect are not purely technical.[43]
>
> There are, according to CAACE's descriptive list,[44] some other consortia agreements limited to arrangements on joint fleet and terminal operations. However, these agreements cannot be

---

36 Communication, op. cit. at fn. 1, para. 5.1.
37 See OJ L184/3, 25 June 2014.
38 Statement for entry into the Council minutes entitled "Commission Statement re Article 3(2), first indent of the Merger Control Regulation," Doc. No 10958/89 RC 51 at p. 4, 19 December 1989. It is possible that a particular consortium may be a concentration within the meaning of Regulation 4064/89 and thus the question must be individually examined.
39 I.e. Council Regulation (EC) No 139/2004 of 20 January 2004 on the control of concentrations between undertakings OJ 2004 L24/1.
40 It would be possible but unlikely that a consortium agreement would be a technical agreement within the meaning of Art. 2 of Reg. 4056/86.
41 See chap. 12 , on Reg. 4056/86.
42 Ed., the agreements were examined by the Commission in its study for its communication.
43 Ed., on the significance of technical agreements, see Art. 2 of Reg. 4056/86 (see chap. 12 on Art. 2 of Reg. 4056/86).
44 Ed., this was a list of consortia agreements submitted by the CAACE to the Commission.

regarded as purely technical since for instance one agreement also contains, *inter alia*, the parties' agreement to avoid unreasonable or unfair sales and marketing competition amongst themselves through a common freight policy. Such agreements restrict competition and cannot be considered as having exclusively technical objects and effects. Finally, the parties to consortia agreements regulate the use of their vessel capacities in given trade routes and are actual or potential competitors.

For all these reasons consortia cannot, other than perhaps in very exceptional cases, be considered as falling within the scope of Article 2 of Council Regulation 4056/86."[45]

14.026 It is equally necessary to consider whether consortia fell within the scope of the liner conferences block exemption within Regulation 4056/86. In the words of the Commission:

"conferences are arrangements which exist essentially to ensure that their members charge the same rates of freight. Some conferences also agree members' participation in a particular trade (which is defined either as sailing rights, i.e., the right to berth x number of sailings per annum from one area to another or as percentage shares in the trade) or even 'pool' either earnings or liftings (freight grt) or both: the intention generally being to equate 'share' with earnings and liftings."[46]

14.027 The Commission is clear that consortia were not covered by the conference block exemption in Regulation 4056/86:

"Consortia are pursuing different objectives and are different in organisation [from consortia]. The size of container ships (say 3 to 6 conventional ships = 1 container ship) means that most single shipping companies are no longer capable of providing, on their own, a satisfactory liner service to shippers. To be viable, a shipping service must perform a frequent, say weekly, service to its customers. Rationalisation of schedules is, therefore, a *sine qua non* of liner shipping with each participating line being allocated slots for each sailing. This is not the role of conferences. Shipowners agree that consortia are different from conferences.

Consortia agreements restrict or eliminate competition between the parties in some or all of the following areas:

- the provision and use of capacity and transport facilities;
- timings and sailings;
- marketing;
- inland operations;
- their policies as conference members; and
- price competition (which is eliminated either by conference membership, or by arrangements in the consortium agreements which are to that extent equivalent to a conference agreement, or by some combination of the two).

A considerable number of consortia agreements thus contain restrictive arrangements which go beyond the scope of Article 3 of Council Regulation No. 4056/86 and would therefore not be covered by the block exemption for conferences, even if they could be considered as conference agreements...

Consortia are increasingly concerned with combined sea/land door-to-door transport. Multilateral agreements on combined sea/land transport are not covered by the conference block exemption, which applies only to the maritime sector.[47]

5.4 It follows that consortia agreements which restrict competition and affect trade between Member States must, if they are not to be considered null and void in accordance with

---

45 Communication, para. 5.2.
46 Communication, para. 5.3.
47 Ed., communication, para. 5.3.

Article [101(2)] of the Treaty, be covered either by an individual or by a block exemption. In view of the number of consortia agreements and the need for shipowners to retain the flexibility necessary to change their agreements in response to changing competitive circumstances, it is desirable for administrative reasons to give a group exemption as far as possible. Accordingly, the Commission has examined the scope for granting such a group exemption."

14.028 It is clear therefore that consortia are neither concentrations nor conferences. It is also clear that consortia are *sui generis* in nature.

C. COMMERCIAL VIEW ON CONSORTIA

14.029 The views of the shipping industry on consortia are mixed. The Commission summarises these views in the following terms:

"4.1 CAACE and CENSA have argued, in various submissions to the Commission,[48] that [EU] shipping lines need to participate in consortia in order 'not to be put at a disadvantage compared with their competitors, the single entity, multi-trade giants'.[49] In their view consortia are either excepted, as technical agreements, under Article 2 of Regulation No. 4056/86,[50] or are covered by the block exemption in Article 3 of the same regulation.[51] For cases not so covered there should be a group exemption. These views were not shared by the Union of Greek Shipowners who argued that the Commission should only grant individual exemptions, where appropriate.

4.2 The British Shippers' Council has informed the Commission that, in its view, consortia are covered neither by Article 2[52] nor by Article 3 of Regulation No. 4056/86[53] and that a new block exemption would be inappropriate. Individual exemptions should be granted only with special conditions and obligations. The European Shippers' Council hold similar views, arguing that consortia should apply for individual exemption and that conditions and obligations, including an obligation to meaningful consultations with shippers, should be attached."[54]

14.030 The Commission has rehearsed the merits of consortia agreements in some of the recitals to Regulation 906/2009 (as extended by Regulation 697/2014)[55] (i.e. the current block exemption regulation for consortia). The fifth recital records the generally positive nature of consortia:

"Consortia, as defined in this Regulation, generally help to improve the productivity and quality of available liner shipping services by reason of the rationalisation they bring to the activities of member companies and through the economies of scale they allow in the operation of vessels and utilisation of port facilities. They also help to promote technical and economic progress by facilitating and encouraging greater utilisation of containers and more efficient use of vessel capacity. For the purpose of establishing and running a joint service, an essential feature inherent in consortia is the ability to make capacity adjustments in response to fluctuations in supply and demand. By contrast, unjustified limitation of capacity and sales as well as the joint fixing of freight rates or market and customer allocation are unlikely to bring any efficiency. Therefore, the exemption provided for in this Regulation should not apply to consortium agreements that involve such activities, irrespective of the market power of the parties."

---

48 Ed., in connection with the communication mentioned in fn. 1.
49 Ed., in particular, those large shipping companies from South-East Asia.
50 Ed., see chap. 12.
51 Ed., see chap. 12.
52 Ed., see chap. 12.
53 Ed., see chap. 12.
54 Communication, op. cit. at fn. 1.
55 OJ L184/1, 25 June 2014, Art. 1.

14.031 It will be noted that the Commission is being somewhat tentative in that it recognises that consortia "generally" help to improve the productivity and quality of available liner services but do not always do so. The Commission also places great emphasis on the rationalisation, efficiency and utilisation benefits which flow from consortia agreements. It is generally accepted that consortia agreements achieve these aims of rationalisation and efficiency thereby improving the productivity and quality of the services provided. However, those benefits will only flow to shippers if there is sufficient competition in the market.

14.032 The sixth and seventh recitals of Regulation 906/2009 go on to state:

> "6. A fair share of the benefits resulting from the efficiencies should be passed on to transport users. Users of the shipping services provided by consortia may benefit from the improvements in productivity which consortia can bring about. Those benefits may also take the form of an improvement in the frequency of sailings and port calls, or an improvement in scheduling as well as better quality and personalised services through the use of more modern vessels and other equipment, including port facilities.
> 7. Users can benefit effectively from consortia only if there is sufficient competition in the relevant markets in which the consortia operate. This condition should be regarded as being met when a consortium remains below a given market share threshold and can therefore be presumed to be subject to effective actual or potential competition from carriers that are not members of that consortium. In order to assess the relevant market, account should be taken not only of direct trade between the ports served by a consortium but also of any competition from other liner services sailing from ports which may be substituted for those served by the consortium and, where appropriate, of other modes of transport."

D. 1990 COMMUNICATION ON CONSORTIA

Introduction

14.033 On 18 June 1990, the Commission sent a communication[56] to the Council of Ministers which contained a report on the possibility of a group exemption[57] for consortia agreements in liner shipping[58] as well as a proposal for a "Council Regulation on the application of Article 85(3) of the EEC Treaty[59] to certain categories of agreements, decisions and concerted practices between shipping companies".

Background to the communication on consortia

14.034 When the Council of Ministers adopted Regulation 4056/86[60] as part of the December 1986 Package of Measures, the Commission undertook to report to the Council of Ministers within one year on whether it was appropriate to provide for block exemptions for consortia and to make proposals where necessary.[61] This followed the Council of Ministers' statement when it adopted Regulation 4056/86:

---

56 COM(90)260 final, 18 June 1990.
57 A group exemption is a block licence under Art. 101(3) for certain types of arrangements under Art. 101(1).
58 On liner shipping, see chap. 11.
59 Ed., Art. 85(3) of the Treaty was the exemption provision for Art. 85(1). These provisions are now Arts 101(1) and 101(3) of the TFEU.
60 On Reg. 4056/86 generally, see chap. 12.
61 Council Doc. No 11584/86 MAR 84 of 19 December 1986, Annex III.

"The Council of Ministers invites the Commission to study the situation regarding competition in the sectors of passenger shipping, tramp shipping, joint ventures, consortia and agreements between transport users to consider whether it is necessary to submit new proposals. The Council notes, however, that where the object and effect of joint ventures and consortia is either to achieve technical improvements or co-operation as provided for in Article 2 of the Regulation or where close-knit consortia only cover minor market shares, the prohibition laid down in Article [101(1)] of the Treaty does not apply to them."[62]

14.035 While the Commission made an interim report in 1988, it was unable to make such a final report[63] to the Council of Ministers in the light of the fact that "despite its repeated efforts to complete its work within one year because the industry did not make available to it a sufficient number of consortia agreements to constitute a satisfactory basis for analysis".[64] Ultimately, it was able to make its proposal in 1990.

E. THE NEED FOR A BLOCK EXEMPTION

14.036 Having discounted the possibility that consortia would be either technical agreements[65] or conferences[66] and thus outside any block exemption, the Commission decided that it was necessary to specifically exempt consortia agreements. The Commission decided against a policy of granting individual exemptions as and when agreements were notified because of the "number of consortia agreements and the need for shipowners to retain the flexibility necessary to change their agreements in response to changing economic circumstances, it is desirable for administrative reasons to give a group exemption as far as possible".[67] It is fortunate that it took this approach because ultimately, individual exemptions were no longer possible after 1 May 2004 when Regulation 1/2003[68] entered into force.

14.037 The European Commission justified the exemption on the basis that the EU's shipping industry:

"needs to attain the necessary economies of scale to compete on the world liner conference market. Consortia can help to provide the necessary means for improving the productivity of liner shipping services and promoting technical and economic progress by facilitating and encouraging the use of containers.

Users of the shipping services offered by consortia obtain several important advantages. First, they are ensured regular sailings at prices which do not depend on which ships are used for their containers. Second, economies of scale in the use of ships and on-shore facilities are achieved. Third, since consortia tend to bring about higher levels of capacity utilisation, costs are reduced for this reason also. Fourth, consortia increase the quality of shipping services by using more modern ships and equipment as well as port facilities. Last, but not least, through provision of joint inland services they are responding to many shippers' requirements for efficient door-to-door transport.

Thus, users can obtain a share of the benefits resulting from the improvement in productivity and service. However, any group exemption must give a sufficient guarantee that consortia are able to realise their advantages to the fullest extent and that users get a fair share of the resulting rationalisation and reduction in costs.

---

62 Ibid.
63 See Doc. No 4130/MAR 3, 11 January 1988 and Doc. No 10048/88 MAR 38 of 13 December 1988.
64 COM(90)260 final, para. 1.2.
65 And thus within Art. 2 of Reg. 4056/86.
66 I.e. liner conferences.
67 Communication, para. 5.4.
68 OJ 2003 L1/1.

In order, therefore, to ensure that all the requirements of Article [101(3)] are met it would be necessary, *inter alia*, to attach to the block exemption certain conditions and/or obligations to ensure that a fair share of the benefits would be passed on to shippers and that competition in respect of a substantial part of the trades in question was not eliminated."[69]

14.038 The Commission continued its defence of the need for a separate block exemption and not simply amendments to the various regulations in issue at that time (i.e. Regulations 17/62,[70] 1017/68[71] and 4056/86[72]) by saying that such an "independent, self-contained regulation" was necessary because of: (a) the great variety of different consortia arrangements operating under different circumstances; (b) the impossibility of drafting a block exemption for joint ventures (and consortia are after all, a specialised form of joint venture); and (c) the fact that many consortia deal with multi-modal transport operations which fall partly within the scope of Regulation 4056/86[73] and partly under Regulation 1017/68[74] and, in so far as containers are concerned, partly under Regulation 17/62.[75,76] Some consortia agreements might, theoretically at least, fall within the scope of Regulation 4056/86 but clearly not all such agreements. It is more realistic to imagine that a separate block exemption is needed because consortia agreements often involve transport other than international sea transport and thus would not fall within the scope of Regulation 4056/86. It is also submitted that given the ever-changing composition of most consortia, it would be very difficult to have a situation where virtually every change in membership might require separate applications for individual exemptions.

F. ADOPTION OF CONSORTIA BLOCK EXEMPTION REGIMES OVER TIME

14.039 The current block exemption is not the first block exemption.

14.040 A block exemption regime was adopted in 1995. This was Regulation 870/95. Regulation 870/95 was extended in 2000 by way of Regulation 823/2000[77] which was adopted on 19 April 2000 to prolong for five years the block exemption for liner joint ventures/consortia embodied in Regulation 870/95[78] (which expired on 25 April 2000). The Commission was very favourably disposed towards consortia (as opposed to liner conferences) and in its annual competition report for 2000, the Commission stated that its

> "favourable view of consortia is due to the advantages of this form of cooperation. In general, by rationalising the activities of the member companies and achieving economies of scale, consortia help improve both the productivity and the quality of liner transport services offered to transport users."[79]

However, the most important change relates to thresholds; as the Commission records in its annual competition report for 2000:

---

69 Communication, para. 6.1.
70 I.e. the general implementing regulation for competition generally.
71 I.e. the implementing regulation for road, rail and inland waterway.
72 I.e. the implementing regulation for maritime transport.
73 In respect of the maritime transport aspect.
74 In respect of the inland waterway, road or railway aspects.
75 In respect of any aspect not covered by Regs 1017/68 or 4056/86.
76 Communication, para. 6.2.
77 OJ L100/24, 20 April 2000. See IP/00/404, 25 April 2000.
78 OJ L89/7, 21 April 1995.
79 Para.193.

"The most important change that Regulation (EC) No 823/2000 makes to the block exemption as compared with Regulation (EC) No 870/95 is in referring to market share thresholds instead of trade share thresholds (i.e. the share of trade held by the consortium between the pairs of ports that it actually serves). Market share is the usual indication of market power used in competition legislation. The trade share criterion was adopted in the previous regulation because shipping companies had considered that market shares would be difficult to calculate; experience had however shown that shipping companies were able to provide market shares."

The background to the 2000 block exemption was described in the following terms:

"Consortia concerned by the possible block exemption are concerted practices between freight carriers on regular international lines from and to Community ports. The exemptions concern solely 'operational agreements' of consortia, i.e. common fixing of travel timetables, the exchange of slots on vessels, the pooling of port installations ... It is important to stress that maritime conferences price agreements are not covered but are managed by Reg.EEC/4056/86 on [c]onferences.

From the proposal, it appears that the *procedures* for benefitting from an exemption remain the same. However, emphasis is not limited to interpretation clarification and some major amendments to the *conditions* deserve further explanations.

Obviously, the four conditions of Article [101(3)] must still be fulfilled and the three different exemption procedures still remain. In short, a consortium with a maximum 30% market share benefits from an automatic exemption, while a consortium with a share between a 30 and 50% threshold may benefit from simplified opposition procedure. Third, those whose market share is above 50% must ask the Commission for an individual exemption.

The major amendment is to be found in the market share criteria which has supplemented the trade share one. In so doing, the Commission had enlarged the so-called "relevant market" that was to be taken into consideration, while assessing any distortion of competition on a specific market.

The trade share test was actually not suitable because it excluded substitutable ports and equally included a port not substitutable with the other ports served. Reference was made to ports actually served by the consortium to the exclusion of third range ports to which it could call after having sailed to its regular ports of call (substitutable criteria).

Moreover, the 'direct trade' approach did not consider transhipment of cargo between ports within the same range, in the framework of a consortium's regular feeder service."[80]

14.041 The amendments introduced in Regulation 823/2000 helped to clarify matters and embodied the approach taken by the Commission in its interpretation of Regulation 870/95 (i.e. the first block exemption on consortia). The block exemption would explicitly state that it would apply to consortia operating on more than one trade[81] and that the market share thresholds are required to be met in respect of each market on which the consortium operates.[82]

14.042 On 25 April 2005, the Commission decided that the block exemption for liner conferences embodied in Regulation 823/2000 was to be extended until 25 April 2010. The 2005 block exemption for consortia (Regulation 611/2005) involved relatively minor changes. The exemption covered liner conference consortia with a market share less than 30%. If the consortia operated outside the liner conference regime then the threshold was 35%. Under the original regulation, a consortium with a market share above those ceilings but below 50% may have still benefited from the block exemption if the agreement had been notified to the Commission and the Commission did not object to it within six

---

80 Vanheule, "Current EU News on Maritime Law" [2000] ETL 3 at 3–4.
81 Art. 1(1).
82 Arts 6 and 7.

months. However, on 12 March 2004, this was amended by Regulation 463/2004 because of the modernisation regulation (Regulation 1/2003) because the possibility of making notifications to the Commission was abolished by Regulation 1/2003. The 2005 block exemption (i.e. Regulation 611/2005) involved relatively minor changes to the pre-existing Regulation 823/2000. The change included the right for a consortia member to withdraw without financial penalty from a consortia agreement after a period of 12 months' notice rather than six months' notice. The possibility of effective price competition within the consortium has also been extended by taking into account the various individual contracts. The block exemption for consortia adopted in 2005 was due to expire on 25 April 2010 hence the need for a new block exemption. This new block exemption was Regulation 906/2009[83] which extended the regime until 2020.

G. BACKGROUND TO THE CURRENT CONSORTIA BLOCK EXEMPTION REGIME

14.043 The block exemption for consortia adopted in 2005, Regulation 61/2005, was due to expire on 25 April 2010 and there was therefore a need to have a new regulation to take effect on 26 April 2010. The repeal of Regulation 4056/86 also meant that the consortia block exemption needed to be amended.

14.044 The current regime involves: (a) a Council regulation – Regulation 246/2009 which empowers the Commission to adopt a block exemption regulation for consortia; and (b) a Commission regulation, based on Regulation 246/2009, to provide for that block exemption and this Commission regulation is Regulation 906/2009 (as extended by Commission Regulation 697/2014).[84]

14.045 Before adopting Regulation 906/2009, the European Commission published[85] a draft regulation for consultation and has published a technical paper for discussion and information. The proposed block exemption regulation clarified the definition of a consortium, revised the list of activities exempted by the consortia block exemption regulation, reduced the market share threshold from 35% to 30% and clarified how the market share figure was to be calculated. The Commission also invited comments on provisions such as the duty to consult with shippers and the exit clauses for consortium members.

14.046 The Commission made the following helpful observations in 2008:

"Why does the consortia block exemption need to be reviewed?
In view of the expiry of the current block exemption Regulation on 25th April 2010, the revision process has two main objectives: First, to take account of the repeal of the liner conference block exemption Council Regulation 4056/86 (to which the consortia block exemption refers) and, secondly to ensure a greater convergence of the new Regulation and other block exemption Regulations for horizontal cooperation currently in force whilst taking into account current market practices in the liner industry."[86]

14.047 As mentioned above, the European Commission has described the process leading up to the proposed changes in the following terms:

---

83 OJ 2009 256/31.
84 OJ L184/3, 25 June 2014.
85 On 21 October 2008, the European Commission published the draft of the new block exemption regulation.
86 MEMO/08/644.

"[t]he review process of the Regulation was launched in 2007 with a market investigation on the basis of questionnaires sent to carriers and shippers. After consulting Member States, the Commission is now publishing a preliminary draft of the Regulation for public comments. Interested parties can submit their comments until 21st November 2008. The Commission will then again consult the Member States in 2009. The adoption of the final Regulation is planned for the second half of 2009. This will allow the sector sufficient time to adjust to the new Regulation, which should enter into force on 26 April 2010 for a further five-year duration."[87]

14.048 The Commission explained why it was proposed to aggregate market shares in the draft regulation in the following terms:

"[l]iner shipping carriers are often members of several consortia. In addition, carriers often offer services, both individually and within a consortium. These practices may alter the competitive behaviour of the market participants (for example, by way of information spill-over among members of several consortia on the same relevant market). The assessment of the market position of a given consortium should therefore be based on market reality, taking into account whether the consortium is subject to effective (external) competition. As a consequence the interlinked activities must be taken into account when calculating the consortium's relevant market share for the application of the block exemption.

A block exemption regulation can only exempt clear-cut situations which can be assumed with sufficient certainty to satisfy the conditions of Article [101 (3) of the TFEU], allowing to derogate from the ... Treaty's general ban on agreements between undertakings where such agreements foster productivity and innovation, provided that they pass on a fair share of the benefit to consumers, are proportionate and do not eliminate competition on the market. All other agreements need to be assessed on a case-by-case basis."[88]

H. COUNCIL REGULATIONS TO ENABLE THE COMMISSION TO ADOPT BLOCK EXEMPTIONS

14.049 Before the Commission may adopt a block exemption, it must be given the power to do so. The current Commission block exemption for consortia (Commission Regulation 246/2009)[89] is based on Council Regulation 246/2009.[90]

14.050 On 25 February 1992, the Council adopted Regulation 479/92 on the application of the then Article 85(3) (now Article 101(3)) of the Treaty to certain categories of agreements, decisions and concerted practices between liner shipping companies (consortia).[91] It was amended several times.[92] Ultimately, the Council adopted Regulation 246/2009[93] to codify Regulation 479/92 and its amendments "in the interests of clarity and rationality".[94] The current Council regime to enable the Commission a block exemption in regard to consortia is therefore Regulation 246/2009. It entered into force on 26 April 2010.[95]

---

87 MEMO/08/644.
88 MEMO/08/644.
89 OJ 2009 L79/1.
90 OJ 2009 L79/1.
91 OJ 1992 L55/3. The consortia block exemption (Reg. 870/95) was adopted on the basis of Reg. 479/92. Regulation 870/95 has since been repeated.
92 E.g. Reg. 823/2000, OJ L100/24, 20 April 2000..
93 See Athanassiou, op. cit. at fn. 1, p. 129; Fruhling, Whiddington, Cassels and Decat, "The Application of European Competition Law in the Transport Sector" (2010) 1(2) JECL&P 144; Pozdnakova, "New Liner Consortia Block Exemption: A Legislative Commentary" [2010] 31(10) ECLR 415; Prisker, op. cit. at fn. 1, p. 1; and Randolph, op. cit. at fn. 1, p. 18.
94 Reg. 246/2009, Recital 1.
95 Art. 8 provided that the regulation entered into force on the twentieth day following that of its publication in the *Official Journal of the European Union*.

14.051 The Council recognised the value in consortia agreements in Recitals 4–10 of Regulation 246/2009:

"(4) Liner shipping is a capital intensive industry. Containerisation has increased pressures for cooperation and rationalisation. The [EU] shipping industry should attain the necessary economies of scale in order to compete successfully on the world liner shipping market.

(5) Joint-service agreements between liner shipping companies with the aim of rationalising their operations by means of technical, operational and/or commercial arrangements (described in shipping circles as consortia) can help to provide the necessary means for improving the productivity of liner shipping services and promoting technical and economic progress.

(6) Maritime transport is important for the development of the [EU's] trade and the consortia agreements may play a role in this respect, taking account of the special features of international liner shipping. The legalisation of these agreements is a measure which can make a positive contribution to improving the competitiveness of shipping in the [EU].

(7) Users of the shipping services offered by consortia can obtain a share of the benefits resulting from the improvements in productivity and service, by means of, *inter alia*, regularity, cost reductions derived from higher levels of capacity utilisation, and better service quality stemming from improved vessels and equipment.

(8) The Commission should be enabled to declare by way of Regulation that the provisions of Article [101(1)] of the Treaty do not apply to certain categories of consortia agreements, decisions and concerted practices, in order to make it easier for undertakings to cooperate in ways which are economically desirable and without adverse effect from the point of view of competition policy. The Commission, in close and constant liaison with the competent authorities of the Member States, should be able to define precisely the scope of these exemptions and the conditions attached to them.

(9) Consortia in liner shipping are a specialised and complex type of joint venture. There is a great variety of different consortia agreements operating in different circumstances. The scope, parties, activities or terms of consortia are frequently altered. The Commission should therefore be given the responsibility of defining from time to time the consortia to which a group exemption should apply.

(10) In order to ensure that all the conditions of Article [101(3)] of the Treaty are met, conditions should be attached to group exemptions to ensure in particular that a fair share of the benefits will be passed on to shippers and that competition is not eliminated."

Conferral by the Council of the power on the commission to adopt a block exemption

14.052 Article 1 of Council Regulation 246/2009 conferred the power on the Commission to adopt a block exemption regulation but within limitations:

"1. The Commission may by Regulation and in accordance with Article [101(3)] of the Treaty, declare that Article [101(1)] of the Treaty shall not apply to certain categories of agreements between undertakings, decisions of associations of undertakings and concerted practices that have as an object to promote or establish cooperation in the joint operation of maritime transport services between liner shipping companies, for the purpose of rationalising their operations by means of technical, operational or commercial arrangements with the exception of price fixing (consortia).

2. Such Regulation adopted pursuant to paragraph 1 of this article shall define the categories of agreements, decisions and concerted practices to which it applies and shall specify the conditions and obligations under which, pursuant to Article [101(3)] of the Treaty, they shall be considered exempted from the application of Article [101(1)] of the Treaty."

14.053 Recital 1 to Commission Regulation 906/2009 (the current block exemption) states:

"Regulation ... 246/2009 empowers the Commission to apply Article [101(3)] of the Treaty by regulation to certain categories of agreements, decisions and concerted practices between shipping companies relating to the joint operation of liner shipping services (consortia), which, through the cooperation they bring about between the shipping companies that are parties thereto, are liable to restrict competition within the common market and to affect trade between Member States and may therefore be caught by the prohibition contained in Article [101(1)] of the Treaty."

Duration and amendment of the block exemption regulation

14.054 Article 2 of Regulation 246/2009 provides:

"1. The Regulation adopted pursuant to Article 1 shall apply for a period of five years, calculated as from the date of its entry into force.
2. The Regulation adopted pursuant to Article 1 may be repealed or amended where circumstances have changed with respect to any of the facts which were basic to its adoption."

Five years would be a common duration for block exemption regulations so it was not surprising.

Potential retroactive effect of the block exemption regulation

14.055 Article 3 of Council Regulation 246/2009 provides for potential retroactive effect back to the date of entry into force of the block exemption regulation:

"The Regulation adopted pursuant to Article 1 may include a provision stating that it applies with retroactive effect to agreements, decisions and concerted practices which were in existence at the date of entry into force of such Regulation, provided they comply with the conditions established in that Regulation."

14.056 Article 4 of Council Regulation 246/2009 goes on to provide:

"The Regulation adopted pursuant to Article 1 may stipulate that the prohibition contained in Article [101(1)] of the Treaty shall not apply, for such a period as fixed by that Regulation, to agreements, decisions and concerted practices already in existence at 1 January 1995, to which Article [101(1)] applies by virtue of the accession of Austria, Finland and Sweden and which do not satisfy the conditions of Article [101(3)]. However, this Article shall not apply to agreements, decisions and concerted practices which, as at 1 January 1995, already fell under Article 53(1) of the EEA Agreement."

Public consultation on the draft block exemption regulation

14.057 Article 5 of Council Regulation 246/2009 provides that there must be public consultation on the draft block exemption regulation:

"Before adopting the Regulation referred to in Article 1, the Commission shall publish a draft thereof to enable all the persons and organisations concerned to submit their comments within such reasonable time limit as the Commission shall fix, but in no case less than one month."

The Commission did publish the draft block exemption regulation[96] and invited comments. Indeed, the Commission recorded in 2008:

"What were the previous steps and what are the next steps of the review?
The review process of the Regulation was launched in 2007 with a market investigation on the basis of questionnaires sent to carriers and shippers. After consulting Member States, the Commission is now publishing a preliminary draft of the Regulation for public comments. Interested parties can submit their comments until 21st November 2008. The Commission will then again consult the Member States in 2009. The adoption of the final Regulation is planned for the second half of 2009. This will allow the sector sufficient time to adjust to the new Regulation, which should enter into force on 26 April 2010 for a further five-year duration."[97]

Consultation with the Advisory Committee on restrictive practices and dominant positions on the draft block exemption regulation

14.058 Article 6 of Regulation 246/2009 provides that there must be consultation with the Advisory Committee on Restrictive Practices and Dominant Positions on the draft block exemption regulation:

"Before publishing the draft Regulation and before adopting the Regulation pursuant to Article 1, the Commission shall consult the Advisory Committee on Restrictive Practices and Dominant Positions referred to in Article 14 of Council Regulation (EC) No 1/2003 of 16 December 2002 on the implementation of the rules on competition laid down in Articles 81 and 82 of the Treaty."

I. CURRENT BLOCK EXEMPTION: COMMISSION REGULATION 906/2009 (AS AMENDED)

Introduction

14.059 On 28 September 2009, the Commission adopted Regulation 906/2009 on the application of, what was then, Article 81(3) of the EC Treaty[98] to certain categories of agreements, decisions and concerted practices between liner shipping companies (consortia)[99] and Commission Regulation 906/2009 was extended for five years until 25 April 2020. This is the last remaining block exemption in the maritime transport sector. The essence of the consortia block exemption is that there is a block exemption for shipping consortia as they relate to international liner shipping consortia to or from one or more EU ports for the carriage of cargo provided that the combined market share of the participants does not exceed 30% and the agreement does not involve so-called "hard-core" restrictions such as price-fixing, limitation or capacity or sales and the allocation of business (i.e. markets or customers). The block exemption thereby allows co-ordination of timetables for sailing, cross-chartering of space or slots, pooling of vessels, pooling of port installations, use of joint operation offices and the provision of containers. There is even possible allowance for capacity adjustments in response to changes in supply and

---

96 OJ 2008 C266/1.
97 MEMO/08/644.
98 Art. 81(3) of the EC Treaty is now Art. 101(3) of the TFEU.
99 OJ 2009 L256/31. See Prisker (2010), Competition Policy Newsletter, Spring, p. 8 and Randolph, op. cit. at fn. 1, p. 18. On the consolidated version, see http://eur-lex.europa.eu/legal-content/EN/TXT/HTML/?uri=CELEX:02009R0906-20150425&qid=1438981945106&from=EN.

demand as well as the joint operation/use of port terminals. Regulation 697/2014 is a very simple regulation in that it extended the block exemption regulation until 25 April 2020 and provided that the regulation would enter into force on 26 June 2014.

Legislative basis for the commission block exemption regulation

14.060 The Commission was enabled to adopt Regulation 906/2009 because the Council adopted Regulation 246/2009 on 26 February 2009 on the application of, what was then, Article 81(3) of the EC Treaty[100] to certain categories of agreements, decisions and concerted practices between liner shipping companies (consortia).[101] The Council was acting on the basis of the Treaty generally and what was Article 83 of the then EC Treaty (now Article 103 of the TFEU). As the Commission Regulation 906/2009 (i.e. the block exemption) recites in the first recital:

> "Regulation ... 246/2009 empowers the Commission to apply Article [103](3) of the Treaty by regulation to certain categories of agreements, decisions and concerted practices between shipping companies relating to the joint operation of liner shipping services (consortia), which, through the cooperation they bring about between the shipping companies that are parties thereto, are liable to restrict competition within the common market and to affect trade between Member States and may therefore be caught by the prohibition contained in Article [101](1) of the Treaty."

Regulation 479/92[102] had been used to enable the Commission to adopt block exemptions for consortia but Regulation 479/92 (as amended) was repealed by Article 7 of Regulation 246/2009.

Duration of the block exemption regulation

14.061 In accordance with Article 7 of Regulation 906/2009, the regulation entered into force on 26 April 2010 and will apply until 25 April 2015. This means that there is a block exemption from Article 101(3) (but not Article 102) where the consortia agreements fall within the scope of the block exemption.

Structure of the block exemption regulation

14.062 The short regulation is divided into chapters which are, in turn, sub-divided into articles. Chapter I (containing Articles 1 and 2) deals with "Scope and Definitions". Chapter II (containing Articles 3 and 4) contains a number of exemptions. Chapter III (containing Articles 5–6) sets out the conditions for exemption. Chapter IV is the "final provisions".

Legislative and commercial background to the block exemption regulation

14.063 Regulation 906/2009 was needed because the pre-existing block exemption regime was due to expire on 25 April 2010 and if the Commission was to continue having

---

100 Now Art. 101(3) of the TFEU.
101 OJ 2009 L79/1.
102 OJ L55/3, 29 February 1992.

a block exemption for consortia then it would have to adopt a new regulation. It was not simply a matter of extending the pre-existing regime because there had been both legislative and commercial changes.

14.064 In terms of legislative change, the major change had been the abolition of the block exemption for liner conferences in Regulation 4056/86. As Athanassiou commented:

"[Liner conferences] are rate-fixing agreements representing hardcore cartels from the competition law point of view whereas [consortia] respond to rationalization needs resulting from the containerization of liner trades. Despite the difference in objectives, the functioning of these associations has in practice been interlinked in various ways. First, consortia have frequently been operating under the umbrella of liner conferences, thus introducing a second-level restriction which had to be taken into account by the legislation. Second, consortia not related to conferences operated in a highly cartelized environment – a factor which could not be ignored.

Taking this into account, Regulation 1419/2006[103] marked the end of the antitrust immunity historically granted to liner conferences – an immunity which had been granted under Regulation 4056/86.

Simultaneously, Regulation 1419/2006 underlined the conviction that the liner sector is not unique and does not, therefore, require special treatment under competition law.

That shift is confirmed with the adoption of the new consortium [block exemption regulation, i.e. Regulation 906/2009], which completes the reform by aligning the treatment of the maritime sector with the standards applied in other areas of economic activity."[104]

Another legislative change was the entry into force and operation of Regulation 1/2003[105] – the so-called "Modernisation Regulation" – which altered the way in which EU competition law is enforced. In particular, the abolition by Regulation 1/2003 of the individual notification procedure meant that parties to a consortium agreement which fell outside the scope of the block exemption would not be able to individually notify the agreement to the European Commission and would have to engage in self-assessment.

14.065 There were also commercial changes to be taken into account. Athanassiou commented:

"The new economic environment constituted an additional element to be taken into account. Within the current trend of maritime liberalisation, consortia are the main form of cooperation restricting competition while producing recognisable pro-competitive effects. The market investigation carried out by the European Commission revealed that consortia indeed form the common vehicle of cooperation on the main trade routes, encompassing various forms (vessel sharing, swaps and slot-charters) and covering various categories of traffic – in addition to the container one. It has also been revealed that the firms involved often have cross-participation (on one and the same trade or on different ones) and that several carriers were offering services on an individual basis (external competition)."[106,107]

The new block exemption follows the approach of modern EU competition law as it applies to co-operative or horizontal agreements between competitors in the economy generally. It replaced Regulation 823/2000 as amended by Commission Regulations 463/2004 and 611/2005.

---

103 OJ 2006 L269/01.
104 Op. cit. at fn. 1, p. 130.
105 OJ 2003 L1/1.
106 Ed., Commission, *Technical Paper on the Revision of Regulation 823/2000*, p. 9 ff.
107 Op. cit. at fn. 1, p. 130.

European Commission perspective on the background to the 2009 changes to the consortia agreement

14.066 When the European Commission commenced its consultation process on 22 October 2008 relating to what became the current block exemption, the then Competition Commissioner, Neelie Kroes, said: "It is time to adjust the block exemption for liner shipping consortia to current market practices in the liner industry and to current antitrust law."[108]

14.067 The second recital to Regulation 906/2009 states:

"The Commission has made use of its power by adopting Commission Regulation (EC) No 823/2000 of 19 April 2000 on the application of Article [101(3)] of the Treaty to certain categories of agreements, decisions and concerted practices between liner shipping companies (consortia),[109] which will expire on 25 April 2010. On the basis of the Commission's experience to date it can be concluded that the justifications for a block exemption for liner consortia are still valid. However, certain changes are necessary in order to remove references to Council Regulation (EEC) No 4056/86 of 22 December 1986 laying down detailed rules for the application of Articles [101] and [102] of the Treaty to maritime transport[110] ... which allowed liner shipping lines to fix prices and capacity, but has now been repealed. Modifications are also necessary to ensure a greater convergence with other block exemption regulations for horizontal cooperation in force whilst taking into account current market practices in the liner industry."

14.068 Olivier Guersent, the Acting Director for Transport, Post and other Services at DG COMP described the background to the changes when he spoke at the European Maritime Law Organisation ("EMLO") meeting in Copenhagen on 24 October 2008:

"The proposed changes are put forward in the light of three main objectives:

1. First, we take account of the repeal of the liner conference block exemption regulation. This first objective relates to all provisions in the current text that reflect the price fixing element previously allowed by the repealed liner conferences block exemption regulation.[111] These provisions made of course only sense when consortia could operate within price fixing conferences. There is a legal obligation for the Commission to bring the current text in conformity with existing law and we have therefore engaged ourselves in a 'cleaning' procedure to delete or adapt the provisions in question. This 'cleaning' exercise concerned also more generally the recitals of the regulation.
2. Second, we want to ensure a greater convergence between the consortia block exemption regulation and other horizontal block exemption regulations, such as the block exemption regulation on specialisation agreements, on research and development agreements or on technology transfer.
   It is the aim of the Commission to have consistent rules in the horizontal legislation as well as in the sector specific legislation such as the consortia block exemption regulation. Although maritime transport still benefits from a preferential sectoral treatment compared to other industry sectors, it is the general policy of the Commission to move towards applying the same rules in the transport sector than in all other sectors.
3. And last but not least with some of the proposed amendments we want to take into account current market practices in liner shipping. Markets change and evolve constantly and therefore block exemption regulations have to be reviewed periodically. It has to be ensured that the scope of the regulation and the conditions under which undertakings may benefit from the block exemption still reflect the current market practice."

---

108 IP/08/1566.
109 OJ L100, 20.4.2000, p. 24.
110 OJ L378, 31.12.1986, p. 4.
111 Ed., i.e. Reg. 4056/86.

Changes in the new consortia block exemption regime

14.069 The second recital to Commission Regulation 906/2009 records:

"On the basis of the Commission's experience to date it can be concluded that the justifications for a block exemption for liner consortia are still valid. However, certain changes are necessary in order to remove references to Council Regulation (EEC) No 4056/86 of 22 December 1986 laying down detailed rules for the application of Articles [101] and [102] of the Treaty to maritime transport[112] which allowed liner shipping lines to fix prices and capacity, but has now been repealed. Modifications are also necessary to ensure a greater convergence with other block exemption regulations for horizontal cooperation in force whilst taking into account current market practices in the liner industry."

14.070 It has been observed:

"The *content* of the exempted activities has been modified mainly to reflect the repeal of conference antitrust immunity. Some of the currently accepted practices linked to the functioning of the liner conference system are deleted. This is the case for the cargo, revenue, and net revenue pools which inevitably imply the transparency of prices between members (art.3(2)(d) Reg.823/2000), the joint exercise of voting rights held by the consortium in the conference which becomes meaningless (art.3(2)(e) Reg.823/2000) and the joint marketing structure and the issue of a joint bill of lading (art.3(2)(f) Reg.823/2000). Despite its commercially sensitive nature, the latter can be justified if it is ancillary to the provision of the joint service and does not involve price-fixing (art.3(4) Reg.906/2009). Special reference has to be made to the 'capacity adjustments' which constitute an essential feature of the rationalising impact of the consortia (Recital 5 Reg.906/2009). The word 'temporary' used by the current block exemption is replaced by reference to the purpose for which the adjustment is carried out 'fluctuations in supply and demand' (new art 3(para.2)). It is clear that the exemption does not cover reductions and other forms of non-utilization of existing capacity aimed at increasing prices."[113]

The consultation obligation has been repealed. When it proposed the block exemption, the Commission stated:

"What are the main changes proposed?
The major changes in the draft are a clarification of the definition of a consortium, a revision of the activities exempted by the Regulation, a decrease of the market share threshold from 35% to 30% and clarifications on how to calculate this market share threshold. Other provisions such as the obligation to consult with shippers and the exit-clauses for consortium members have not been revised at this stage, but views on these issues are welcome during the public consultation. A technical paper explaining the proposed changes to the Regulation in detail has been published on the website of DG Competition http://ec.europa.eu/comm/competition/antitrust/legislation/maritime/technical_paper.pdf."[114]

Overall perspective on the block exemption regulation

14.071 It is generally believed that the new regime is more streamlined and better than the previous regimes. The definition of "consortia" is much wider because it covers all forms of liner shipping and not just those services which are "chiefly by container" as had been the case under Regulation 823/2000. There is a clearer list of the hardcore

---

112 Ed. OJ 1986 L378/4.
113 Athanassiou, op. cit. at fn. 1, p. 131.
114 MEMO/08/644.

restrictions. The lock-in period has been increased. There has been some clarification of the exempted capacity decisions.[115]

Scope and application of the block exemption regulation

14.072 Article 1 is very simple. It states that the "Regulation shall apply to consortia only in so far as they provide international liner shipping services from or to one or more Community[116] ports." This means that it does not apply to cabotage services. There must be a "Community" port (or now, more accurately a "Union" port (since the entry into force of the Treaty of Lisbon on 1 December 2009 which changed references from "Community" to "Union")) involved but there need only be one EU port involved so the regulation applies to services involving third States as well.

Concept of consortium or consortia agreement

14.073 Article 2(1) of Regulation 906/2009 defines a "consortium" as meaning:

> "an agreement or a set of interrelated agreements between two or more vessel-operating carriers which provide international liner shipping services exclusively for the carriage of cargo relating to one or more trades, the object of which is to bring about cooperation in the joint operation of a maritime transport service, and which improves the service that would be offered individually by each of its members in the absence of the consortium, in order to rationalise their operations by means of technical, operational and/or commercial arrangements."

14.074 One can parse this definition further in certain respects.

14.075 First, the term "liner shipping" is defined by Article 2(2) of Regulation 906/2009 as meaning

> "the transport of goods on a regular basis on a particular route or routes between ports and in accordance with timetables and sailing dates advertised in advance and available, even on an occasional basis, to any transport user against payment."

14.076 Second, the term "transport user" is defined by Article 2(3) of the regulation as meaning "any undertaking (such as shipper, consignee or forwarder) which has entered into, or intends to enter into, a contractual agreement with a consortium member for the shipment of goods". Consortia are no longer restricted to services operating chiefly by container but includes all cargo on a ship (i.e. the regulation refers to "carriage of cargo"). This means that the regime is no longer confined to containerised traffic. However, the use of the word "cargo" does mean that the block exemption does not apply to the carriage of passengers. Equally, the use of the phrase "liner services" excludes tramp services.[117] Some difficulties might arise in respect of more specialised services which lie between liner and non-regular services – the prevailing view is that such services will be covered by the block exemption if they fall within the category of liner shipping (i.e. regularity and occasional advertising etc.) – it may well be that the service is not a liner service in the pure sense but if one self-assesses the situation and finds that the service

---

115 The "capacity adjustments in response to fluctuations in supply and demand".
116 Ed., i.e. EU ports.
117 Arrangements between undertakings providing tramp services would have to be reviewed under Arts 101 and 102 of the TFEU. This would involve self-assessment.

does prevent, restrict or distort competition then the provisions of Article 101(3) apply in any event.[118]

14.077 Article 2(2) then defines the term "liner shipping" as meaning

"the transport of goods on a regular basis on a particular route or routes between ports and in accordance with timetables and sailing dates advertised in advance and available, even on an occasional basis, to any transport user against payment."

This is an uncontroversial definition.

14.078 Article 2(3) goes on to define the term "transport user" as meaning "any undertaking (such as shipper, consignee or forwarder) which has entered into, or intends to enter into, a contractual agreement with a consortium member for the shipment of goods". Again, it is an uncontroversial but also quite a wide definition.

14.079 Article 2(4) defines the term "commencement of the service" as meaning "the date on which the first vessel sails on the service".

Exempted agreements

14.080 Article 3 (entitled "Exempted agreements") sets out the arrangements which are exempted under Regulation 906/2009:

"Pursuant to Article [101](3) of the Treaty and subject to the conditions laid down in this Regulation, it is hereby declared that Article [101](1) of the Treaty shall not apply to the following activities of a consortium:

1. the joint operation of liner shipping services including any of the following activities:

    (a) the coordination and/or joint fixing of sailing timetables and the determination of ports of call;
    (b) the exchange, sale or cross-chartering of space or slots on vessels;
    (c) the pooling of vessels and/or port installations;
    (d) the use of one or more joint operations offices;
    (e) the provision of containers, chassis and other equipment and/or the rental, leasing or purchase contracts for such equipment;

2. capacity adjustments in response to fluctuations in supply and demand;
3. the joint operation or use of port terminals and related services (such as lighterage or stevedoring services);
4. any other activity ancillary to those referred to in points 1, 2 and 3 which is necessary for their implementation, such as:

    (a) the use of a computerised data exchange system;
    (b) an obligation on members of a consortium to use in the relevant market or markets vessels allocated to the consortium and to refrain from chartering space on vessels belonging to third parties;

---

118 Athanassiou has commented that the new definition of consortium "will not prevent difficulties arising in the assessment, under the criteria used in the definition, of new forms of transport, lying at the frontier between liner and non-regular services, as in the case of specialized shipping. The latter (known also as 'neo-bulk' or 'industrial' or 'semi-liner') covers the transport of different products, refrigerated cargo, forest products, motor vehicles, chemicals, etc. Such services will be covered only if they are consistent with the 'liner definition' provided for in art.2(2) – a definition which requires regularity and the existence of a prior advertisement, even on an occasional basis, for the form of transport to be covered", in op. cit. at fn. 1, p 131.

(c) an obligation on members of a consortium not to assign or charter space to other vessel-operating carriers in the relevant market or markets except with the prior consent of the other members of the consortium."

The scope of the exempted activities and arrangements has changed from the pre-existing regime. Consortia are no longer restricted to services operating chiefly by container but include all cargo on a ship. This means that the regime is no longer confined to containerised traffic. The essence of Article 3 is that provided that no hardcore restrictions exist (i.e. direct or indirect price fixing, the allocation of markets or customers, or the limitation of capacity or sales expressly prohibited in Article 3(2)), and the conditions stipulated are satisfied, then the block exemption applies. As an exemption, the block exemption regulation should be given a restrictive construction.

Hardcore restrictions which render Regulation 906/2009 inapplicable

14.081 Article 4 enumerates the three "hardcore restrictions" which if any[119] one of them is present, the block exemption in the regulation does not apply:

"The exemption provided for in Article 3 shall not apply to a consortium which, directly or indirectly, in isolation or in combination with other factors under the control of the parties, has as its object:

1. the fixing of prices when selling liner shipping services to third parties;
2. the limitation of capacity or sales except for the capacity adjustments referred to in Article 3(2);
3. the allocation of markets or customers."

14.082 Article 4 reflects the thinking in the eighth recital to the regulation:

"This Regulation should not exempt agreements containing restrictions of competition which are not indispensable to the attainment of the objectives justifying the grant of the exemption. To that end, severely anti-competitive restraints (hardcore restrictions) relating to the fixing of prices charged to third parties, the limitation of capacity or sales and the allocation of markets or customers should be excluded from the benefit of this Regulation. Other than the activities which are expressly exempted by this Regulation, only ancillary activities which are directly related to the operation of the consortium, necessary for its implementation and proportionate to it should be covered by this Regulation."

14.083 Article 4 contains new hardcore restrictions: first, the one on price-fixing (because of the repeal of Regulation 4056/86) and the allocation of markets or customers (simply for uniformity with other block exemption regulations because it is already prohibited under Article 101(1) of the TFEU).[120] The output restriction was already prohibited under Article 4 of Regulation 823/2000.

14.084 Article 4 is to be construed broadly; if it could be easily circumvented then it would be meaningless. The breadth of the language used (e.g. "directly or indirectly, in isolation or in combination with other factors") demonstrates that it is to be construed broadly and not technically.

---

119 The regulation does not make it explicitly clear that the block exemption does not apply if even one of these restrictions is present but it would be a nonsensical construction of the regulation that one was entitled to, for example, price-fix or limit markets but still benefit from the block exemption because one had not allocated markets or customers.
120 Technical Paper, op. cit. at fn. 108, p.19.

Market share restrictions which potentially render Regulation 906/2009 inapplicable

14.085 Article 5 of Regulation 906/2009 sets out the conditions relating to market share. It provides:

> "1. In order for a consortium to qualify for the exemption provided for in Article 3, the combined market share of the consortium members in the relevant market upon which the consortium operates shall not exceed 30% calculated by reference to the total volume of goods carried in freight tonnes or 20-foot equivalent units.
> 2. For the purpose of establishing the market share of a consortium member the total volumes of goods carried by it in the relevant market shall be taken into account irrespective of whether those volumes are carried:
>
>   (a) within the consortium in question;
>   (b) within another consortium to which the member is a party; or
>   (c) outside a consortium on the member's own or on third party vessels.
>
> 3. The exemption provided for in Article 3 shall continue to apply if the market share referred to in paragraph 1 of this Article is exceeded during any period of two consecutive calendar years by not more than one tenth.
> 4. Where one of the limits specified in paragraphs 1 and 3 of this Article is exceeded, the exemption provided for in Article 3 shall continue to apply for a period of six months following the end of the calendar year during which it was exceeded. That period shall be extended to 12 months if the excess is due to the withdrawal from the market of a carrier which is not a member of the consortium."

14.086 The background to this provision is clear from the ninth and tenth recitals to the regulation:

> "9. The market share threshold and the other conditions set out in this Regulation, as well as the exclusion of certain conduct from its benefit, should normally ensure that the agreements to which the block exemption applies do not give the companies concerned the possibility of eliminating competition in a substantial part of the relevant market in question.
> 10. For the assessment of whether a consortium fulfils the market share condition, the overall market shares of the consortium members should be added up. The market share of each member should take into account the overall volumes it carries within and outside the consortium. In the latter case account should be taken of all volumes carried by a member within another consortium or in relation to any service provided individually by the member, be it on its own vessels or on third party vessels pursuant to contractual arrangements such as slot charters."

14.087 The figure of 30% in Regulation 906/2009 was a reduction from the 35% under the previous regime for consortia operating outside a liner conference and 30% for those operating within a conference; now, it is a uniform 30%. If an agreement involves parties with market shares above 30% then they must engage in self-assessment to see whether Article 101(1) of the TFEU applies and, if it does, whether Article 101(3) applies. This reduction is more in keeping with the way in which EU competition law is moving.[121] Olivier Guersent, the then Acting Director for Transport, Post and other Services at DG COMP described the background to the changes when he spoke (in a personal capacity) at the EMLO meeting in Copenhagen on 24 October 2008:

---

121 However, just because the figure of 30% in the case of consortia is in line with the figure used for other areas such as washing powder in the vertical agreements regime is no justification for moving from 35% to 30%. It is often pleasing to the eye to have uniformity but there should be some justification for the uniformity.

"We propose to reduce the market share threshold necessary to benefit from the block exemption from 35% to 30%. This modification would be a first step towards bringing the consortia block exemption regulation into line with market share thresholds currently in force in other horizontal block exemption regulations. At the same time we consider this threshold to be necessary to guarantee that only consortia subject to effective external competition can benefit from the block exemption.

As the general threshold in the block exemption regulations for horizontal cooperation is 20% (or 25% for R&D), the maritime transport will still benefit from a preferential sectoral treatment with a threshold of 30% compared to other industry sectors. And not only the higher market share threshold is a preferential treatment but also the fact, that the 15 consortia block exemption regulation is one of the very few remaining sectoral block exemption regulations.

What is the practical implication of a lower threshold? Even if a consortium is above the 30% threshold, this will not automatically mean that such consortium is illegal. The members of the consortium will then – just like any other undertaking – need to self assess if their cooperation restricts competition and if so, satisfies the conditions of Article [101](3) of the Treaty."

14.088 In regard to aggregation of market shares, commenting on the draft regulation, Levitt observed:

"First, it creates a level of uncertainty which is inappropriate in block exemption legislation. In particular, when lines are considering *ex ante* whether to form, or join, a consortium and are assessing whether the consortium would benefit from the block exemption, the aggregation rule would require them to take into account such an indeterminate number of factors that the block exemption would be rendered effectively impossible to apply. If the Commission has legitimate concerns about the potential impact on competition between consortia linked by common membership, it should address this concern in the manner adopted in all other block exemption – namely, by way of *ex post* assessment and withdrawal.

Secondly, the practical assessment of the rule would require lines to disclose information which is likely to be confidential – such as the existence of agreements between lines and the market shares that they represent. Indeed, if the aggregation rule were to require the market shares of second order arrangements to be included, the risk of not being able to identify the relevant agreements or obtain the relevant information would be all but insurmountable. That is to say, in a consortium between lines A, B and C, line A may have an arrangement with line X which needs to be taken into account. In these circumstances, A can be expected to identify its own arrangement with X and to know the volumes covered by it. But if, as a condition for the block exemption of the consortium between A, B and C, the aggregation rule also requires that arrangements between X, Y and Z be taken into account – this would raise the profound practical difficulties referred to above.

[In regard to the scope of the aggregation rule, the] uncertainty in the application of the aggregation rule is exacerbated by the uncertainty surroundings its scope. In particular, the Commission should confirm that slot swap arrangements and simple slot charter arrangements between consortia and individual carriers (or between individual carriers) do not constitute a sufficient link to require the aggregation of market shares under this provision. These are mechanisms that allow full and efficient use of capacity on the basis of very little information sharing and no joint operations or services.

The exclusion of such arrangements from the aggregation rule is supported by the definition of "consortium", which is drafted to cover agreements for the provision of true "joint operations" between services. It is also supported by the explanations and examples given in the Commission's Technical Paper at paragraphs 75 to 79. At paragraph 78 in particular the Commission provides a list of activities which may represent forms of coordinated commercial policy, including capacity allocation, marketing activities, sailing schedules or port calls. None of these activities occurs in the case of slot swaps or slot charters. The Technical Paper at paragraph 39, however, appears to suggest that reciprocal slot charters may in themselves constitute a consortium, creating some ambiguity in the guidance.

It is a reasonable proposition that only arrangements which envisage the integration of services should require the aggregation of market shares under the block exemption. However, the Commission should give explicit guidance on these two types of arrangement (slot swaps and simple slot charters) to ensure certainty and clarity."[122]

14.089 At the EMLO meeting in Copenhagen on 24 October 2008, Oliver Guersent (the then Acting Director for Transport, Post and other Services at DG COMP) discussed, in a personal capacity, the possible changes to the consortia regime:

"the so-called aggregation rule
In order to assess the scope of the block-exemption, the draft regulation proposes to aggregate the market shares under certain circumstances. The criteria for aggregating the market shares concern mainly two situations:

- First, the parallel activity. In this situation the carrier provides services both individually and within a consortium on the same relevant market.
- And secondly, the interlinked activity. In this scenario the carrier is a party to various agreements on the same relevant market and thereby interlinks these agreements.

These criteria have always been taken into account in the assessment of whether the consortium members are subject to effective external competition and are therefore not new as such. In view of the proposal to delete the current Article 5 (which stipulates effective competition as a basic condition for the grant of exemption) it seems necessary to spell out this safeguard and integrate it into the market share condition.

Moreover, we have seen that many carriers are linked with each other by agreements and that there is a whole network of agreements on some of the trades. This fact cannot be ignored, as a block exemption regulation can only give exemption to clear-cut situations. The calculation of the market shares has therefore to be based on market reality, taking into account these interlinked agreements.

This aggregation rule has been the focus of most of the informal comments received so far. And I can understand why. Because of this rule, a number of consortia would not be block exempted. But I think it is worth reminding the very purpose of a BER. A BER provides legal certainty that some forms of agreements in certain market conditions are unproblematic in competition law terms. Such legal certainty can only be provided in situations where it is safe to assume that no competition problem will arise. Some commentators have referred to routes where interlinked liners represent 80% of the trade. Well, to those commentators, I can only indicate that the Commission is precisely not ready to give a *blanc-seing*[123] in such situations. I am not saying that there is for sure a competition problem in such a case. I am simply saying that it is not impossible that there is a competition problem. The Commission cannot a priori exempt such situations from the application of Article [101]."

Consortia agreements falling outside the scope of the block exemption

14.090 Block exemptions are, by necessity, somewhat limited because they cannot provide for every possible eventuality. So what happens if an arrangement falls outside the scope of the block exemption? The fourth recital to Regulation 906/2009 provides that it is not fatal:

"The benefit of the block exemption should be limited to those agreements for which it can be assumed with a sufficient degree of certainty that they satisfy the conditions of Article [101](3)

---

122 In Wareham and Power (eds), *Competition Law and Shipping: The EMLO Guide to EU Competition Law in the Shipping and Port Industries* (2010), pp. 47–48.
123 Ed., i.e. a blank cheque.

of the Treaty. However, there is no presumption that consortia which do not benefit from this Regulation fall within the scope of Article [101](1) of the Treaty or, if they do, that they do not satisfy the conditions of Article [101](3) of the Treaty. When conducting a self-assessment of the compatibility of their agreement with Article [101] of the Treaty, parties to such consortia may consider the specific features of markets with small volumes carried or situations where the market share threshold is exceeded as a result of the presence in the consortium of a small carrier without important resources and whose increment to the overall market share of the consortium is only insignificant."

This means that there is no presumption that consortia agreements falling outside the scope of Regulation 906/2009 automatically fall within the scope of Article 101(1) TFEU or do not benefit from Article 101(3) TFEU.

Relationship with Article 102 of the TFEU

14.091 Recital 14 of the regulation makes it plain that it is without prejudice to the application of Article 102 of the TFEU which means that an abuse of dominance contrary to Article 102 is not condoned or exempted by virtue of the regulation. Therefore an abuse of dominance (whether individual or collective) would be prohibited notwithstanding the apparent application of the block exemption to immunise the arrangement from the effects of Article 101(1).

Withdrawal from a consortium agreement

14.092 Article 6 of Regulation 906/2009 provides for withdrawal from a consortium agreement:

"In order to qualify for the exemption provided for in Article 3, the consortium must give members the right to withdraw without financial or other penalty such as, in particular, an obligation to cease all transport activity in the relevant market or markets in question, whether or not coupled with the condition that such activity may be resumed after a certain period has elapsed. That right shall be subject to a maximum period of notice of six months. The consortium may, however, stipulate that such notice can only be given after an initial period of a maximum of 24 months starting from the date of entry into force of the agreement or, if later, from the commencement of the service.

In the case of a highly integrated consortium the maximum period of notice may be extended to 12 months and the consortium may stipulate that such notice can only be given after an initial period of a maximum of 36 months starting from the date of entry into force of the agreement or, if later, from the commencement of the service."

The philosophy behind Article 6 is clear from Recital 11 to the regulation which provides:

"In addition, the benefit of the block exemption should be subject to the right of each consortium member to withdraw from the consortium provided that it gives reasonable notice. However, provision should be made for a longer notice period and a longer initial lock-in period in the case of highly integrated consortia in order to take account of the higher investments undertaken to set them up and the more extensive reorganisation entailed in the event of a member leaving."

Withdrawal of the block exemption by the European Commission

14.093 Recital 12 of Regulation 906/2009 provides:

"In particular cases in which the agreements falling under this Regulation nevertheless have effects incompatible with Article [101](3) of the Treaty, the Commission may withdraw the benefit of the block exemption, on the basis of Council Regulation (EC) No 1/2003 of 16 December 2002 on the implementation of the rules on competition laid down in Articles [101] and [102] of the Treaty. In that respect, the negative effects that may derive from the existence of links between the consortium and/or its members and other consortia and/or liner carriers on the same relevant market are of particular importance."

Withdrawal of the block exemption by a Member State competition authority

14.094 Recital 13 of Regulation 906/2009 provides:

"where agreements have effects which are incompatible with Article [101](3) of the Treaty in the territory of a Member State, or in a part thereof, which has all the characteristics of a distinct geographic market, the competition authority of that Member State may withdraw the benefit of the block exemption in respect of that territory pursuant to Regulation (EC) No 1/2003."

Arrangements falling outside the scope of the block exemption

14.095 If an arrangement falls outside the scope of the block exemption then it does not mean that it is automatically illegal. The parties to the agreement would have to do their own self-assessment to see whether the arrangement complies with Articles 101 and 102 of the TFEU.

Consultation

14.096 The Commission commenced an informal consultation in 2013 about the future of the block exemption. This was two years ahead of the expiry of Regulation 906/2009. While the Commission is moving away from sectoral block exemptions, there is some value in retaining the consortia block exemption because it gives specific guidance on maritime issues. The then existing block exemption was due to expire on 25 April 2015. In June 2014, the EU decided to extend the block exemption for five years.

J. 2018 CONSULTATION

14.097 The current Regulation 906/2009[124] is due to expire on 25 April 2020. On 7 May 2018, the Commission published a "roadmap" on the evaluation of the liner shipping consortia block exemption (i.e. Regulation 906/2009).[125] The Commission's purpose in conducting the consultation is to evaluate the block exemption and to consider whether, in view of the general policy of harmonising competition rules, and the developments in the liner shipping industry in recent years, the block exemption is still relevant and delivering on its objectives. The process could mean that the block exemption will lapse, be

---

[124] OJ 2009 L256/31.
[125] OJ 2009 L256/31.

extended on the same terms or be extended but with modifications. The Commission aims to publish a consultation in Q3 of 2018, followed by an evaluation Staff Working Document in Q4 of 2018.

K. CONCLUSIONS

14.098 The consortia regime has worked well and has the support of the European Commission. The regime has fared well and the members of consortia have benefited from the evolving block exemption regulation regime which has adapted well to evolving circumstances.

CHAPTER 15

European Union state aid law: shipping and ports

A. INTRODUCTION

15.001 This chapter considers the application of European Union ("EU") State aid law[1] to shipping[2] and ports[3] while chapter 22 considers state aid in the context of shipbuilding.

15.002 The law on this area is complex and complicated because it represents interference by the EU with Member State sovereignty, discretion, policy choices; involves the enactment of relatively new law; and, very often, involves the interplay of State aid, public procurement, tax law and the law relating to State authorities. This chapter does not seek to consider the whole of the law of State aid (which is an enormous topic in its own right and the subject of entire books)[4] but rather concentrates on the law of State aid in the maritime context.

15.003 While many jurisdictions around the world have competition law regimes dealing with topics such as cartels, abuse of dominance and merger control, the EU is virtually unique in having a body of rules *controlling* and *supervising* State aid provided by its Member States; in effect, the Member States have established a system whereby the European Commission may determine whether Member States may spend their own national resources (e.g. money).[5] While many States around the world have rules controlling the provision of unfair funding or financial support by *foreign* governments (so-called dumping laws), the EU is different in that it controls the provision of aid by its own States by means of its own State aid law.

15.004 State aid law is part of EU competition law. The primary rules on State aid are set out in Articles 107–109 of the Treaty on the Functioning of the European Union ("TFEU"). They are supplemented by regulations, decisions, guidelines/notices and case law. The Commission's notices/communications are extremely important in the area of State aid and are tantamount to quasi-legislation in that the Commission adopts these notices and then follows them very often as if they were legislation.

---

1 On EU State aid law generally, see Bacon, *European Union Law of State Aid* (2017); Hancher, Ottevanger and Slot, *EU State Aids* (5th ed., 2016); Hofman and Micheau (eds), *State Aid Law of the European Union* (2016); Quigley, *European State Aid Law and Policy* (2015); as well as Werner and Verouden (eds), *EU State Aid Control: Law and Economics* (2016). See also Ortiz Blanco and Van Houtte (eds), *EU Regulation and Competition Law in the Transport Sector* (2nd ed., 2017), paras 14.44–14.74.
2 On EU State aid law and shipping, see, in particular, Bacon, op. cit. at fn. 1, paras 12.83–12.114; Quigley, op. cit. at fn. 1, pp., 456–459; and Woll and Meaney in Werner and Verouden, op. cit. at fn. 1, chap. 17 and, in particular, pp. 625–638.
3 On EU State aid law and ports, see below.
4 See fn. 1.
5 This was very obvious during the Financial Crisis where the USA was providing State aid to its banks without too much difficulty but the EU Member States had to obtain the prior approval, usually subject to conditions, from the European Commission.

15.005 The purpose of EU State aid law is to ensure that competition is not distorted by controlling the intervention by EU (and, indeed, European Economic Area ("EEA")) Member States; if the aid was not controlled then State aid could distort competition in the internal market in a very material and damaging manner. This is clear when one recalls that the average Member State has multiples of the economic power of even the largest global corporations not only because of their economic resources but their legislative ones too.

15.006 EU State aid law is a balancing act: there is a general prohibition of State aid in Article 107(1) of the TFEU followed by some exceptions which are either exceptions to the prohibition which are permitted automatically under Article 107(2) (i.e. the aid is automatically authorised) or authorised in certain circumstances under Article 107(3) (i.e. the aid is authorised on a case by case basis or on the basis that it falls within a particular category). So, it is not that there is an absolute prohibition on State aid (that would be both undesirable and unworkable) but rather there are choices made in different circumstances.

15.007 EU State aid law and policy is evolutionary. For example, the rules on State aid have been updated recently as part of the EU's so-called State Aid Modernisation ("SAM") programme.[6] The law on this area is certainly not static. Instead, it has begun to examine new sectors (e.g. aviation, energy and maritime transport). It could be said that the rules are being devised over time[7] but that would be slightly misleading; in reality, the basic rules are set out in Articles 107–109 of the TFEU (and those rules remain largely (though not entirely))[8] unchanged since the first provisions in the EEC Treaty (i.e. Articles 87–89 of the EEC Treaty) but what has changed is how they are applied and the relevant policy and jurisprudence involved.

15.008 It is useful to highlight, by way of an introduction to the chapter, a selection of issues which potentially involve the State aid so as to contextualise the chapter. Member States could give aid to build ships, repair ships, modernise or extend vessels, make vessels more environmentally friendly (e.g. by subsidising scrubbing) or safer, build or expand ports, construct infrastructure, employ seafarers, train seafarers, reduce tax bills for shipowners and seafarers, subsidise financing costs, transfer cargo or passengers from one mode of transport to another and so on. Some of these interventions raise State aid law issues and the interventions should be prohibited or curbed to some extent while other interventions are desirable. State aid law seeks to draw a distinction between the two types of interventions. State aid can also be used by competitors to complain about competitors; such complaints (which are usually self-serving) must nonetheless be taken seriously because competitors are often the only ones aware of the issues on the ground.

15.009 The administration of the State aid rules lies largely in the hands of the Commission subject to appeal to the General Court and, in turn, to the Court of Justice of the European Union ("CJEU"). The Commission was chosen (as opposed to the Council or the Parliament) because the Commission is meant to be more detached and independent than other institutions – the political nature of the Commission should not however be

---

6 See http://ec.europa.eu/competition/state_aid/modernisation/index_en.html.
7 A cynic might say "on the hoof" or a more polite and accurate view would be that they are evolving over time as circumstances unfold and cases are presented to the EU institutions (particularly, the Commission).
8 The changes which have occurred are not material for present purposes (e.g. relating to culture and the former German Democratic Republic).

underestimated and some of the decisions (particularly in the area of State aid) have been political in nature and in motivation – there is almost always a legal basis to what has been decided but the underlying motivation can be political. The structure of the regime is that Member States must often notify to the Commission proposed aid so as to allow the Commission to decide on whether the aid should be permitted and the aid must not be granted until the Commission approves it. This gives the Commission the power to prevent measures which could distort competition but it also gives the Commission the power and discretion to decide policy. Given the fact that the General Court and the CJEU gives, in appeals to those courts from Commission decisions, considerable leeway to the Commission in its decision-making, there is a great deal of power lying with the Commission in this area. In essence, the rules are primarily enforced by the European Commission.

15.010 It is worth highlighting that the primary relationship in State aid law lies between the Commission (as adjudicator) and the Member State providing what might be aid. The recipient or beneficiaries of the aid are somewhat distant from the relationship; they can be (and increasingly are) involved in the process but they are like children in a custody battle between the parents. It is not possible for a recipient/beneficiary to notify the aid to the Commission (they may of course inform the Commission of the aid but that may annoy the Member State involved) but only the Member State involved in providing the aid may notify it. Of course, anyone (including entities outside the EU) may complain to the Commission about alleged State aid. Indeed, the centrality of the Commission is clear from the fact that it is largely the only institution which may authorise State aid and even the Member State courts may not do so (but they may find that State aid exists).

15.011 Unlike competition law where the undertaking breaching the competition law rules is usually fined and the fine is paid to the Commission by the errant undertaking or association of undertakings, the position is more complicated with State aid. If a Member State gives illegal State aid then it is not a fine which is paid but rather the Commission usually orders the Member State to recover the illegal State aid (usually with interest) from the beneficiary. This means that the beneficiary loses out but, ironically, the Member State recovers the aid which it paid out so it could well be seen as being on an "even bet" in that if the aid turns out to be illegal then it gets it back but it also could have the benefit of the aided project succeeding.

15.012 The fact that the EU's State aid rules involve a policy choice is clear from the fact that in the maritime sector, the Commission allows Member States to provide tax breaks for ship-owning and ship management companies as well as seafarers so as to allow them to compete with third States and to retain tonnage in the EU. It is therefore clear that the EU is making a choice to protect the EU and its Member States rather than taking a pure "let the world market decide" approach. This is, unlike many other areas of EU State aid and competition law, an example of the EU using State aid law as a form of protectionism. The EU is not however making a choice which would involve supporting the EU shipping sector at any price – instead, it is seeking only to support efficient, new, environmentally friendly and safe shipping but, it has to be said, EU-based, managed and linked shipping.

15.013 While the EU has done a great deal for shipping over the years, the decline in tonnage, numbers of ships and employment have been significant. Member State accession has helped with the likes of Greece and Malta as well as Cyprus which brought its prowess in ship management to the EU. However, problems remained relating to issues such as fiscal/tax rules and social arrangements which meant that EU-registered vessels were more expensive than vessels which were flying flags of convenience or other low-cost regimes. In some ways, the EU adopted an approach of "if you can't beat them, join them to some extent" by relaxing the EU State aid regime to some extent. It did so first in 1989, then in 1997 and most recently in 2004 with State aid guidelines which were accommodating to investment in the sector. The EU did so in a way which is quite clever because it insisted that the management, ownership and operation of the vessels remain within the EU. Equally, the EU will not support measures which encourage or tolerate overcapacity or anti-competitive activity but would support a lean, efficient and modern EU shipping industry.

B. CONCEPT OF STATE AID

15.014 Before examining the rules in detail, it is useful to consider the concept of State aid. There is no finite list of aids or precise definition of an aid so care is needed. State aid may take many forms. The concept of State aid includes direct subsidies, guarantees, tax breaks, tax measures, financial guarantees, preferential commercial terms and so on. The Commission has issued a notice on the concept of an aid[9] so as to give guidance on what the Commission regards as constituting a State aid. It summarises the Commission's decisional practice and the CJEU's jurisprudence. The notice is helpful in giving guidance on the Commission's views but the notice is always subject to the views of the CJEU (including the General Court).

15.015 A "State aid" is usually seen to involve:

(a) intervention by a Member State or through Member State resources (i.e. there is a *use of Member State resources*);[10]
(b) providing the beneficiary with an advantage (i.e. there is an *advantage*);[11]
(c) an advantage provided on a selective basis which means that it is not available to others in comparable situations (i.e. there is *selectivity*);[12]
(d) a distortion of competition;[13]
(e) an effect on trade between EU Member States.[14]

15.016 The CJEU used in *Belgium v Commission* (the *TSE* case) a formulation which it has used in many cases:

"31. For the purposes of the present appeal, it should be borne in mind that, for a national measure to be categorised as State aid within the meaning of Article 107(1) TFEU, there must, first, be an intervention by the State or through State resources; second, the intervention must be liable to affect trade between Member States; third, it must confer a selective advantage on the recipient and, fourth, it must distort or threaten to distort competition."[15]

---

9 Commission Notice on the Notion of Aid OJ 2016 C262/1.
10 Aid by a non-Member State might be subject to the EU's dumping rules but not its State aid rules.
11 A burden would not be an aid but a mixed benefit/burden would be an aid in so far as it confers an advantage.
12 Selectivity is critical; a general or universal measure is not an aid. In practice, it is often quite difficult to discern what is selective and what is not.
13 This criterion is usually quite easy to find in practice.
14 This criterion is usually quite easy to find in practice.
15 Case C-270/15 P, ECLI:EU:C:2016:489.

C. SOURCES OF EU STATE AID LAW

Introduction

15.017 The primary source of EU State aid law is always the TFEU. Articles 107–109 of the TFEU deal with State aid.[16] Every other source of EU State aid law (e.g. decisions in particular cases) must be compatible with the TFEU generally and, in particular, Articles 107–109 of that treaty.

Treaty provisions

Introduction

15.018 The primary rules are contained in Articles 107 to 109 of the Treaty on the TFEU.

Article 107 of the TFEU

15.019 Article 107 sets out the general rule of EU State aid law. The Article generally prohibits State aid and only allows aid in limited circumstances where the aid is justified by reasons of general economic development. It is useful to parse the three paragraphs of Article 107 separately.

15.020 First, Article 107(1) provides that

> "[s]ave as otherwise provided in the Treaties, any aid granted by a Member State or through State resources in any form whatsoever which distorts or threatens to distort competition by favouring certain undertakings or the production of certain goods shall, in so far as it affects trade between Member States, be incompatible with the internal market".

This paragraph provides a definition of aid but also provides for an exemption or exception mechanism.

15.021 Second, Article 107(2) sets out three categories of State aid which are *automatically* compatible with the internal market and do not need to be approved by the EU:

> "(a) aid having a social character, granted to individual consumers, provided that such aid is granted without discrimination related to the origin of the products concerned;
> (b) aid to make good the damage caused by natural disasters or exceptional occurrences; [and]
> (c) aid granted to the economy of certain areas of the Federal Republic of Germany affected by the division of Germany, in so far as such aid is required in order to compensate for the economic disadvantages caused by that division. Five years after the entry into force of the Treaty of Lisbon, the Council, acting on a proposal from the Commission, may adopt a decision repealing this point."

This paragraph provides for three categories of aid to be automatically exempted by virtue of the TFEU itself. No further action is needed even though the Member State in question would be wise to alert the Commission that it is relying on the provision.

---

16 Art. 93 of the TFEU is relevant to State aid but only in the context of land transport. It could theoretically be extended to maritime transport but it is unlikely because it would require the Commission to make a proposal (along with the Council and Parliament agreeing to adopt that proposal) but the Commission is unlikely to make such a proposal because it would involve the Commission losing power and influence over the area.

15.022 Third, Article 107(3) describes various categories of aid which *require approval* (i.e. they are not automatically compatible with the internal market but require approval). Article 107(3) provides that the

> "following may be considered to be compatible with the internal market:
>
> (a) aid to promote the economic development of areas where the standard of living is abnormally low or where there is serious underemployment, and of the regions referred to in Article 349, in view of their structural, economic and social situation;
> (b) aid to promote the execution of an important project of common European interest or to remedy a serious disturbance in the economy of a Member State;
> (c) aid to facilitate the development of certain economic activities or of certain economic areas, where such aid does not adversely affect trading conditions to an extent contrary to the common interest;
> (d) aid to promote culture and heritage conservation where such aid does not affect trading conditions and competition in the Union to an extent that is contrary to the common interest; [and]
> (e) such other categories of aid as may be specified by decision of the Council on a proposal from the Commission."

These are the categories of aid which *may* be permitted. The list is somewhat flexible as was demonstrated by the fact that the banking crisis commencing in 2007 involved the Commission approving State aid to Member States under the heading "to remedy a serious disturbance in the economy of a Member State" even though there is nothing explicit addressing that sector in that provision.

Article 108 of the TFEU

15.023 Article 108 of the TFEU deals with some of the procedural aspects of EU State aid law. It provides:

> "1. The Commission shall, in cooperation with Member States, keep under constant review all systems of aid existing in those States. It shall propose to the latter any appropriate measures required by the progressive development or by the functioning of the internal market.
> 2. If, after giving notice to the parties concerned to submit their comments, the Commission finds that aid granted by a State or through State resources is not compatible with the internal market having regard to Article 107, or that such aid is being misused, it shall decide that the State concerned shall abolish or alter such aid within a period of time to be determined by the Commission.
>
> If the State concerned does not comply with this decision within the prescribed time, the Commission or any other interested State may, in derogation from the provisions of Articles 258 and 259, refer the matter to the Court of Justice of the European Union direct.
>
> On application by a Member State, the Council may, acting unanimously, decide that aid which that State is granting or intends to grant shall be considered to be compatible with the internal market, in derogation from the provisions of Article 107 or from the regulations provided for in Article 109, if such a decision is justified by exceptional circumstances. If, as regards the aid in question, the Commission has already initiated the procedure provided for in the first subparagraph of this paragraph, the fact that the State concerned has made its application to the Council shall have the effect of suspending that procedure until the Council has made its attitude known.
>
> If, however, the Council has not made its attitude known within three months of the said application being made, the Commission shall give its decision on the case.

3. The Commission shall be informed, in sufficient time to enable it to submit its comments, of any plans to grant or alter aid. If it considers that any such plan is not compatible with the internal market having regard to Article 107, it shall without delay initiate the procedure provided for in paragraph 2. The Member State concerned shall not put its proposed measures into effect until this procedure has resulted in a final decision.
4. The Commission may adopt regulations relating to the categories of State aid that the Council has, pursuant to Article 109, determined may be exempted from the procedure provided for by paragraph 3 of this Article."

This provision highlights the monitoring and adjudication roles of the Commission in this area.

Article 109 of the TFEU

15.024 Article 109 of the TFEU is also procedural in nature. It enables for regulations to be adopted. It provides:

"The Council, on a proposal from the Commission and after consulting the European Parliament, may make any appropriate regulations for the application of Articles 107 and 108 and may in particular determine the conditions in which Article 108(3) shall apply and the categories of aid exempted from this procedure."

15.025 These regulations have proven important in terms of developing so-called block exemption regulations ("BERs") to enable certain types of State aid to be automatically approved where they meet the criteria in the relevant BER.[17]

Article 106

15.026 Article 106 of the TFEU is also relevant. It provides:

"1. In the case of public undertakings and undertakings to which Member States grant special or exclusive rights, Member States shall neither enact nor maintain in force any measure contrary to the rules contained in the Treaties, in particular to those rules provided for in Article 18 and Articles 101 to 109.
2. Undertakings entrusted with the operation of services of general economic interest or having the character of a revenue-producing monopoly shall be subject to the rules contained in the Treaties, in particular to the rules on competition, in so far as the application of such rules does not obstruct the performance, in law or in fact, of the particular tasks assigned to them. The development of trade must not be affected to such an extent as would be contrary to the interests of the Union.
3. The Commission shall ensure the application of the provisions of this Article and shall, where necessary, address appropriate directives or decisions to Member States."

15.027 Article 106 is a compromise provision. It begins in the first paragraph with the notion that the competition and State aid rules apply to public sector undertakings but the

---

17 See http://ec.europa.eu/competition/state_aid/legislation/block.html. There is a general block exemption – Commission Reg. 651/2014 of 17 June 2014 declaring certain categories of aid compatible with the internal market in application of Arts 107 and 108 of the Treaty (OJ L187/1, 26 June 2014) as well as Commission Reg. 2017/1084 of 14 June 2017 amending Reg. (EU) No 651/2014 as regards aid for port and airport infrastructure, notification thresholds for aid for culture and heritage conservation and for aid for sport and multifunctional recreational infrastructures, and regional operating aid schemes for outermost regions and amending Reg. (EU) No 702/2014 as regards the calculation of eligible costs which has relevance for ports (OJ L156/1, 20 June 2017).

second paragraph then goes on to provide an exception for such undertakings. If the exception under Article 106(2) is to apply then the exception must be both necessary and proportionate and there must be no distortion of trade. In the context of Article 106, the leading case is the so-called *Altmark* case.[18] The *Altmark* jurisprudence is not easy to understand but the essence of it is that services of general economic interest would fall outside the scope of the State aid rules (and neither notification nor authorisation is therefore needed) where:

(a) the undertaking providing the service has been entrusted with clearly defined public service obligations in advance;
(b) the parameters of funding have been set out transparently, objectively and in advance;
(c) the compensation given to the undertaking for providing the service must not exceed "costs plus reasonable profit" (i.e. there is no overcompensation for the task); and
(d) the level of compensation must be established by way of either (i) a tender or (ii) a bench-marking exercise with a typical well-run enterprise.

Public service contracts must not normally run longer than six years. In practice, these guidelines are not easy to apply but they can be important in the context of ports because occasionally Member States could then provide assistance to a port to operate a particular service and the assistance could be classified as not being State aid thereby obviating the need to comply with the rules.

Commission communications

15.028 The Commission has four communications on State aid in the maritime sector:

(a) Commission Communication C(2004)43 – Community guidelines on State aid to maritime transport;[19]
(b) Communication from the Commission providing guidance on State aid complementary to Community funding for the launching of the motorways of the sea;[20]
(c) Communication from the Commission providing guidance on State aid to ship-management companies;[21] and
(d) Communication from the Commission – Updating the Annex to Commission Communication C(2004) 43 – Community guidelines on State aid to maritime transport.[22]

15.029 Communications are not sources of law. Nor are they legislative instruments. Instead, they are statements of the law and policy as viewed by the Commission. They are opinions of law and policy expressed by the Commission. But they are not law. However, the Commission often treat them as a rulebook which the Commission must follow but, in reality, they are a rule book written by the Commission itself for its own purposes. They are always subject to the interpretation of the CJEU (including the General Court).

---

18 Case C-280/00 *Altmark Trans GmbH* [2003] ECR I-7747, ECLI:EU:C:2003:415.
19 OJ C013/3, 17 January 2004.
20 OJ C317/10, 12 December 2008.
21 OJ C132, 11 June 2009, p. 6.
22 OJ C120/10, 13 April 2017.

Decisions and judgments

15.030 There are Commission decisions and Court judgments in the area but they are often quite specific (e.g. factually and temporally) so the concentration in this chapter is on the legislation and policy.

D. STATE AID AND THE MARITIME SECTOR GENERALLY

15.031 While State aid law is generally aimed at ensuring competition, it is clear that State aid law in the area of maritime transport has some additional dimensions. The rules are aimed at not only controlling State aid but also promoting the use of EU Member State flags, the increased employment of EU Member State seafarers and, ultimately, the promotion of the EU maritime transport sector.[23]

15.032 In this context, it is proposed to examine:

(a) the 2004 Community Guidelines on State Aid to Maritime Transport;
(b) the 2008 communication from the Commission providing guidance on State aid complementary to Community funding for the launching of the motorways of the sea;
(c) the 2009 communication from the Commission providing guidance on State aid to ship management companies;
(d) State aid and ports: generally and under the General Block Exemption Regulation.

E. EUROPEAN COMMISSION GUIDELINES ON STATE AID IN MARITIME TRANSPORT

Introduction

15.033 In 1997, the Commission issued the first set of guidelines on State aid to maritime transport.[24] They were welcome because they gave some sector-specific guidance and insight into the Commission's thinking on the subject of State aid in this sector. They were adopted so as to counter, at least in part, the decline in the fortunes of EU shipping. They have now been replaced by the "2003" or "2004"[25] Guidelines it is these guidelines – the current ones – which are the subject to this analysis.

2003/2004 Guidelines

Introduction

15.034 In October 2003, the Commission issued revised guidelines on State aid to maritime transport.[26] The guidelines applied from 17 January 2004 hence they are sometimes known as the 2004 Maritime State Aid Guidelines despite being issued in 2003.

---

23 See Community Guidelines on State Aid to Maritime Transport OJ 2004 C13/3, s. 2.2.
24 OJ 1997 C205/5. See earlier editions of this work for information.
25 The guidelines were revised in 2003 but applied from 2004 hence the two years are sometimes used to refer to the same guidelines.
26 OJ 2004 C13/3, 17 January 2004; the Guidelines are also referred to as Commission communication C(2004) 43 which is published at the same place.

15.035 The Maritime Transport State Aid Guidelines set out the conditions under which State aid is compatible with EU law (i.e. compatible with the internal market). Some of the chapters in the Guidelines are very short (e.g. a single sentence) but it is an important starting point for those seeking guidance. If a package of aid is contemplated and it does not fall within the scope of the Guidelines then that does not mean that the aid cannot be authorised (because the Commission may do so) but rather it requires individual notification. It would be prudent to cite, where possible, the principles and provisions of the Guideline in supporting the case for the approval of aid falling outside the scope of the Guidelines.

Purposes or objectives of the Guidelines

15.036 The primary purpose is to give guidance on when State aid is compatible with EU law. However, there are a number of other purposes or effects. The Guidelines help to: protect the EU maritime sector; preserve employment in the EU; retain know how in the sector in the EU; develop the sector in the EU; protect the environment; and promote maritime safety. They are not a simple purist State aid/competition-focused analysis but rather a sector-focused measure.

Analysis of the Guidelines

15.037 It is useful to review and comment on the text of the Guidelines.

Part 1 of the Guidelines: "Introduction"

15.038 The first part of the Guidelines ("Introduction") reads:

> "The White Paper "European transport policy for 2010: time to decide"[27] stresses the vital importance of maritime transport services for the Community economy. 90% of all trade between the Community and the rest of the world is transported by sea. Short sea shipping accounts for 69% of the volume of goods transported between the Member States (this percentage is 41% if domestic transport is included). Community maritime transport and its related activities remains one of the most important in the world."

These figures were correct at the time and while they change over time (depending on the mix of Member States (e.g. the accession of land locked Member States means that the proportions will fall)), the figures certainly demonstrate the need for State aid guidance in this area.

> "The shipping companies of the Member States still manage about a third of the world fleet today. The accession of Cyprus and Malta[28] in 2004 will increase still further the Union's share of shipping, as the shipping registers of these two countries currently account for about 10% of world tonnage."

---

27 Ed., similar statements have been made in other EU publications and instruments over time. The proportion rose with the accession of States such as Cyprus, Denmark, Greece, Ireland, Malta and the UK but would fall again if the UK leaves. The level of maritime trade among the original six Member States was much lower as they were all linked together by land routes.

28 The sixth and the fifth world registers of ships in terms of tonnage respectively (vessels of more than 300 gt. Source: ISL 2001).

This is another reason why guidance is needed – not only for the trade carried *within* the EU but because of the tonnage owned and controlled from within the EU. The Guidelines continue: "Since the 1970s the European fleet has been faced with competition from vessels registered in third countries which do not take much care to observe social and safety rules in force at international level." This comment related to, primarily, some South-East Asian states as well as the former Communist states. The Guidelines continue:

> "The lack of competitiveness of Community-flagged vessels was recognised at the end of the 1980s[29] and, in the absence of harmonised European measures, several Member States adopted different arrangements for aiding maritime transport. The strategies adopted and the budgets allocated to support measures differ from one Member State to the other in reflection of the attitude of those States to public aid or the importance they attach to the maritime sector."

This type of individualist approach would not be helpful to the development of an overall EU strategy and regime. The Guidelines continue: "In addition, to encourage the re-registering of vessels, Member States have relaxed rules concerning crews, notably through the creation of second registers." This meant that the "flagging out" which had occurred to the flags of convenience and the emerging second registers had to be reversed. The Guidelines continue:

> "Second registers comprise, firstly, 'offshore registers' belonging to territories which have a greater or lesser autonomy in relation to the Member State, and secondly, 'international registers', attached directly to the State which created them.
>
> In spite of the efforts made, a large part of the Community fleet continues to be registered under the flags of third countries. This is because the registers of third countries which apply open registration policies – some of which are called 'flags of convenience' – have continued and are still continuing to enjoy a significant competitive edge over the registers of Member States.

Aid to the shipping industry since 1989[30]
In the light of the differences between the aid systems adopted by Member States faced with more intense competition from non-Community flagged vessels, in 1989 the Commission defined its first guidelines on this subject to ensure a certain convergence between the actions of the Member States. This method nevertheless proved to be ineffective and the decline of Community fleets continued. The guidelines were accordingly reviewed, leading to a 1997 communication defining new Guidelines on State aid to maritime transport.[31]

The major development in recent years concerning support measures from the Member States for maritime transport is the widespread extension in Europe of flat rate tonnage taxation systems ('tonnage tax').[32] Tonnage tax entered into force very early in Greece and was progressively extended to the Netherlands (1996), to Norway (1996), to Germany (1999), to the United Kingdom (2000), to Denmark, to Spain and to Finland (2002) and to Ireland (2002). Belgium and France also decided to adopt it in 2002, while the Italian Government is envisaging this possibility.

---

29 Ed., particularly, towards the end of the 1980s with the adoption of the so-called Positive Measures package in 1989.

30 Ed., 1989 was the year in which the Positive Measures package was proposed and is a natural starting point for this review.

31 Community guidelines on State aid to maritime transport (97/C 205/05) (OJ C205, 5.7.1997, p. 5).

32 Ed., this involves the shipowner paying tax not on the basis of the profit earned but rather by reference to the tonnage which it operates. It is therefore a flat tax and is blind to the level of profits. The Commission regards it as a form of State aid. The use of tonnage tax regimes by Member States indicates that the Member States were acting somewhat unilaterally and independently so as to protect their own industries.

Results of measures proposed by Member States and approved by the Commission compared with the general objectives of the 1997 revised Guidelines

(a) Trends of the Community-flagged fleet (competitiveness of the fleet)
According to the replies provided by the Member States mid-2002 to the Commission's questionnaire and to the most recent statistical data,[33] Member States which have introduced aid measures, particularly in the form of tax relief, have obtained re-registration under the national flag of a significant volume of tonnage in all the registers taken together. In percentage terms, the fleet as entered in the registers of the Member States increased as follows: the number of vessels by 0,4% on average per year, tonnage by 1,5% and container ships by 12,4%. Even if, in the case of the first registers, the number of units entered declined practically everywhere in the period 1989 to 2001, these figures can be viewed as a reversal of the trend, observed up to 1997, of abandoning Community flags.

During the same period, however, the share of Member State registers in total world tonnage fell slightly. While world shipping increased, the growth of the Community-managed fleet registered under third-country flags was faster than that of the fleet registered under the flags of the Member States.

(b) Employment trends
According to the most recent estimates, the number of seafarers on board Community-flagged vessels fell from 188000 in 1996 to approximately 180000 in 2001.[34] The total number of Community nationals employed on board vessels flying Community flags is currently about 120000, a figure which is 40% lower than that of 1985, while the number of nationals of third countries employed on board Community vessels has gone up from 29000 in 1983 to approximately 60000 today. When assessing the drop in the total number of seafarers, the following factors must be taken into account:

- first, productivity per vessel has continued to increase. Accordingly, a smaller crew makes it possible to transport an equal if not higher volume than that carried in the past,
- secondly, the Community-flagged fleet was renewed in the period 1997 to 2001. The average age of vessels went down from 22,9 years to 17,2 years.[35] 35% of the fleet in service on 1 January 2001 had been built in the period 1996 to 2000. New vessels, of more advanced technology, need better trained but smaller crews.

Notable differences between the Member States in the employment rate of Community seafarers are nevertheless apparent. However, nothing in these figures indicates a reversal of the trend whereby the Community-flagged fleet depends more and more on third-country seafarers. This trend was pointed out by the Commission in 2001 in its Communication on the training and recruitment of seafarers.[36]

(c) Contribution to economic activity as a whole
Maritime industries are inextricably linked with maritime transport. This association is a strong argument in favour of positive measures whose aim is to maintain a fleet dependent on Community shipping. Since maritime transport is one of the links in the chain of transport in general and in the chain of the maritime industries in particular, measures seeking to maintain the competitiveness of the European fleet also have repercussions on

---

33 ISL, Shipping Statistics 2001.
34 Total combined number of Community and non-Community seafarers.
35 Ed., this was a sizeable drop in the average age.
36 Communication from the Commission on the training and recruitment of seafarers of 6 April 2001, COM(2001) 188 final.

investments on land in maritime-related industries[37] and on the contribution of maritime transport to the economy of the Community as a whole and to jobs in general.

The significance of shipping and the whole maritime cluster varies considerably with the countries under consideration. However, the importance of the European maritime cluster and its direct economic impact can be clearly illustrated by the following figures: 1,550 million direct employees, a turnover of EUR 160 billion in 1997 (about 2% of GDP in the Community).[38] Data on Denmark (3% of the GDP generated by the maritime cluster), Greece (2,3%) and the Netherlands (2%) can be taken as a valid example.

In this context, therefore, it is not insignificant to note that the fleet managed by European operators based in the Community has stayed at a level of around 34% of world tonnage, while the latter increased by 10% during the period. Given the mobility of the maritime industry and the facilities offered by third countries, one may conclude that support measures for maritime transport may contribute to avoiding widespread displacement of allied industries.

To sum up, it can be affirmed that, where measures in line with the 1997 Guidelines have been adopted, the structural decline of the Community registers and the Community's fleet has been halted and the objectives set by the Commission have been attained, at least in part.

The share of open registers in world tonnage continued, however, to increase during the period, rising from 43% in 1996 to 54% in 2001, and nothing indicates any significant reversal of the trend whereby the fleet had, and is continuing to have, increasing recourse to seafarers from third countries. The campaign undertaken in recent years must be pursued but it must be better targeted. Measures to promote Community seafarers must in particular be the subject of more active monitoring.

The results of the measures taken by the Member States and authorised by the Commission will have to be systematically analysed.

As a consequence, and even though as a matter of principle operating aid should be exceptional, temporary, and degressive, the Commission estimates that State aid to the European shipping industry is still justified and that the approach followed by the 1997 Guidelines was correct. This communication is therefore based on the same basic approach."

This was a useful background discussion and description of what steps needed to be taken.

Part 2 of the Guidelines: "Scope and General Objectives of the Revised State Aid Guidelines"

15.039 The second part of the Guidelines is entitled "Scope and General Objectives of the Revised State Aid Guidelines". It sets out the aims to be achieved. It provides:

"2. SCOPE AND GENERAL OBJECTIVES OF THE REVISED STATE AID GUIDELINES
This communication – replacing the 1997 Guidelines – aims at setting the parameters within which State aid to maritime transport will be approved, pursuant to Community State aid rules and procedures, by the Commission under Article [107](3)(c) and/or Article [106](2) of the [TFEU].

---

37 These activities include port services, logistics, the construction, repair, maintenance, inspection and classification of vessels, ship management and brokerage, banking activities and international financial services, insurance, advice and professional services.
38 Study undertaken by the European Commission, DG Enterprise (published in the Europa internet site).

Aid schemes should not be conducted at the expense of other Member States' economies[39] and must be shown not to risk distortion of competition between Member States to an extent contrary to the common interest. State aid must always be restricted to what is necessary to achieve its purpose and be granted in a transparent manner. The cumulative effect of all aid granted by State authorities (including national, regional and local levels) must always be taken into account.

These Guidelines are applicable to "maritime transport" activities as defined in Regulation (EEC) No 4055/86[40] and in Regulation (EEC) No 3577/92,[41] that is to say, to the 'transport of goods and persons by sea'. They also, in specific parts, relate to towage and dredging.

2.1. Scope of revised State aid guidelines
These Guidelines cover any aid granted by Member States or through State resources in favour of maritime transport. This includes any financial advantage, conferred in any form whatsoever, funded by public authorities (whether at national, regional, provincial, departmental or local level). For these purposes, 'public authorities' may include public undertakings and State-controlled banks. Arrangements whereby the State guarantees loans or other funding by commercial banks may also fall within the definition of aid. The Guidelines draw no distinction between types of beneficiary in terms of their legal structure (whether companies, partnerships or individuals), nor between public or private ownership, and any reference to companies shall be taken to include all other types of legal entity."

The foregoing is in line with general EU State aid law principles. The Guidelines continue:

"These guidelines do not cover aid to shipbuilding (within the meaning of Council Regulation (EC) No 1540/98[42] or any subsequent instrument).[43] Investments in infrastructure are not normally considered to involve State aid within the meaning of Article [107](1) of the Treaty if the State provides free and equal access to the infrastructure for the benefit of all operators concerned. However, the Commission may examine such investments if they could directly or indirectly benefit particular shipowners. Finally, the Commission has established the principle that no State aid is involved where public authorities contribute to a company on a basis that would be acceptable to a private investor operating under normal market-economy conditions."

This latter sentence relates to the so-called "market economy operator" or "market economy investor" principle. In essence, if a Member State can demonstrate that it is acting solely as a private market operator would act then it is not providing State aid. The Guidelines continue:

"2.2. General objectives of revised State aid guidelines
The Commission has stressed that increased transparency of State aid is necessary so that not only national authorities in the broad sense but also companies and individuals are aware of their rights and obligations. These Guidelines are intended to contribute to this and to clarify what State aid schemes may be introduced in order to support the Community maritime interest, with the aim of:

– improving a safe, efficient, secure and environment friendly maritime transport,
– encouraging the flagging or re-flagging to Member States' registers,

---

39 Ed., this is the principle that problems should not be transferred from one Member State to another Member State by reason of the aid being provided.
40 Council Regulation (EEC) No 4055/86 of 22 December 1986 applying the principle of freedom to provide services to maritime transport between Member States and between Member States and third countries (OJ L378, 31.12.1986, p. 1). Ed., see chap. 7 of this book.
41 Council Regulation (EEC) No 3577/92 of 7 December 1992 applying the principle of freedom to provide services to maritime transport within Member States (maritime cabotage) (OJ L364, 12.12.1992, p. 7). Ed., see chap. 7 of this book.
42 OJ L202, 18.7.1998, p. 1.
43 Ed., the EU shipbuilding regime ended in 2013. See chap. 22 of this book.

- contributing to the consolidation of the maritime cluster established in the Member States while maintaining an overall competitive fleet on world markets,
- maintaining and improving maritime know-how and protecting and promoting employment for European seafarers, and
- contributing to the promotion of new services in the field of short sea shipping following the White Paper on Community transport policy.

State aid may generally be granted only in respect of ships entered in Member States' registers. In certain exceptional cases, however, aid may be granted in respect of ships entered in registers under point (3) of the Annex, provided that:

- they comply with the international standards and Community law, including those relating to security, safety, environmental performance and on-board working conditions,
- they are operated from the Community,
- their shipowner is established in the Community and the Member State concerned demonstrates that the register contributes directly to the objectives mentioned above.

Additionally, flag-neutral aid measures may be approved in certain exceptional cases where a benefit to the Community is clearly demonstrated."

Part 3 of the Guidelines: "Fiscal and Social Measures to Improve Competiveness"

15.040 The third part of the Guidelines is entitled "Fiscal and Social Measures to Improve Competiveness". While there has been a recent spotlight shown on State aid and tax in the light of the tax rulings cases,[44] it is interesting to see how the Commission was thinking about State aid and tax in the maritime sector many years earlier. It provides:

"3. FISCAL AND SOCIAL MEASURES TO IMPROVE COMPETITIVENESS
3.1. Fiscal treatment of shipowning companies
Many third countries have developed significant shipping registers, sometimes supported by an efficient international services infrastructure, attracting shipowners through a fiscal climate which is considerably milder than within Member States. The low-tax environment has resulted in there being an incentive for companies not only to flag out their vessels but also to consider corporate relocation. It should be emphasised that there are no effective international rules at present to curb such tax competition and few administrative, legal or technical barriers to moving a ship's registration from a Member State's register. In this context, the creation of conditions allowing fairer competition with flags of convenience seems the best way forward.

The question of fiscal competition between Member States should be addressed. At this stage, there is no evidence of schemes distorting competition in trade between Member States to an extent contrary to the common interest. In fact, there appears to be an increasing degree of convergence in Member States' approaches to shipping aid. Flagging out between Member States is a rare phenomenon. Fiscal competition is mainly an issue between Member States on the one hand and third countries on the other, since the cost savings available to shipowners through third country registers are considerable in comparison to the options available within the Community.

For this reason, many Member States have taken special measures to improve the fiscal climate for shipowning companies, including, for instance, accelerated depreciation on investment in ships or the right to reserve profits made on the sale of ships for a number of years on a tax-free basis, provided that these profits are reinvested in ships.

These tax relief measures which apply in a special way to shipping are considered to be State aid. Equally, the system of replacing the normal corporate tax system by a tonnage tax is a State

---

44 See http://ec.europa.eu/competition/state_aid/tax_rulings/index_en.html for various.

aid. 'Tonnage tax' means that the shipowner pays an amount of tax linked directly to the tonnage operated. The tonnage tax will be payable irrespective of the company's actual profits or losses.

Such measures have been shown to safeguard high quality employment in the on-shore maritime sector, such as management directly related to shipping and also in associated activities (insurance, brokerage and finance). In view of the importance of such activities to the economy of the Community and in support of the objectives stated earlier, these types of fiscal incentive can generally be endorsed. Further, safeguarding quality employment and stimulating a competitive shipping industry established in a Member State through fiscal incentives, taken together with other initiatives on training and enhancement of safety, will facilitate the development of Community shipping in the global market.

The Commission is aware that the income of shipowners today is often obtained from the operation of ships under different flags – for instance, when making use of chartered vessels under foreign flags or by making use of partner vessels within alliances. It is also recognised that the incentive for expatriation of management and ancillary activities would continue if the shipowner obtained a significant financial benefit from maintaining different establishments and accounting separately for Community flag earnings and other earnings. This would be the case, for example, if the non-Community flag earnings were liable either to the full rate of corporate taxation in a Member State or to a low rate of tax overseas if overseas management could be demonstrated.

The objective of State aid within the common maritime transport policy is to promote the competitiveness of the Community fleets in the global shipping market. Consequently, tax relief schemes should, as a rule, require a link with a Community flag. However, they may also, exceptionally, be approved where they apply to the entire fleet operated by a shipowner established within a Member State's territory liable to corporate tax, provided that it is demonstrated that the strategic and commercial management of all ships concerned is actually carried out from within the territory and that this activity contributes substantially to economic activity and employment within the Community. The evidence furnished by the Member State concerned to demonstrate this economic link should include details of vessels owned and operated under Community registers, Community nationals employed on ships and in land-based activities and investments in fixed assets. It must be stressed that the aid must be necessary to promote the repatriation of the strategic and commercial management of all ships concerned in the Community and, in addition, that the beneficiaries of the schemes must be liable to corporate tax in the Community. In addition, the Commission would request any available evidence to show that all vessels operated by companies benefiting from these measures comply with the relevant international and Community safety standards, including those relating to onboard working conditions.

As was argued in the above paragraph, it should not be forgotten that, as a matter of principle, tax relief schemes require a link with the flag of one of the Member States. Before aid is exceptionally granted (or confirmed) to fleets which also comprise vessels flying other flags, Member States should ensure that beneficiary companies commit themselves to increasing or at least maintaining under the flag of one of the Member States the share of tonnage that they will be operating under such flags when this Communication becomes applicable. Whenever a company controls ship operating companies within the meaning of the Seventh Council Directive 83/349/EEC[45] (Article 1), the abovementioned tonnage share requirement will have to apply to the parent company and subsidiary companies taken together on a consolidated basis. Should a company (or group) fail to respect that requirement, the relevant Member State should not grant further tax relief with respect to additional non-Community flagged vessels operated by that company, unless the Community-flagged share of the global tonnage eligible for tax relief in that Member State has not decreased on average during the reporting period referred to in the next paragraph. The Member State must inform the Commission of the application of the derogation. The Community-tonnage share requirement set out in this paragraph does not apply to undertakings operating at least 60% of their tonnage under a Community flag.

---

45 OJ L193, 18.7.1983, p. 1.

In all cases, where fiscal schemes have been approved on the above exceptional basis and in order to allow the Member State concerned to prepare, every three years, the report required under Chapter 12 ('Final Remarks'), recipients must provide the Member State concerned with proof that all the conditions for the derogation from the flag link have been fulfilled during the period. Furthermore, evidence must be provided that, in the case of the beneficiary fleet, the tonnage share requirement laid down in the previous paragraph has been observed and that each vessel of that fleet complies with the relevant international and Community standards, including those relating to security, safety, environmental performance and on-board working conditions. Should recipients fail to provide such evidence, they will not be allowed to continue to benefit from the tax scheme.

It is also of interest to stipulate that whereas Community-based shipping companies are the natural recipients of the above tax schemes, certain ship management companies established in the Community may also qualify under the same provisions. Ship management companies are entities providing different kind of services to shipowners, such as technical survey, crew recruiting and training, crew management, and vessel operation. In some cases ship managers are assigned both technical and crewing management of vessels. In this case they act as classic 'shipowners' as far as transport operations are concerned. Moreover, as in the case of the shipping industry, this sector is experiencing strong and increasing competition at an international level. For these reasons, it seems appropriate to extend the possibility of tax relief to that category of ship managers.

Ship management companies may qualify for aid only in respect of vessels for which they have been assigned the entire crew and technical management. In particular, in order to be eligible, ship managers have to assume from the owner the full responsibility for the vessel's operation, as well as take over from the owner all the duties and responsibilities imposed by the ISM Code.[46] Should ship managers also provide other specialised services, even related to vessel operation, separate accounting for such activities, which do not qualify for the tax relief schemes, should be ensured. The requirement regarding Member States' flag share described above also applies to ship management companies.[47]

These guidelines apply only to maritime transport. The Commission can accept that the towing at sea of other vessels, oil platforms, etc. falls under that definition."

15.041 The Guidelines continue to deal with towage:

"The Commission has, however, become aware that in certain cases Member States allow tugboats which are designed for work at sea to benefit from aid even though they are not active at sea, or rarely so. Thus it is useful to state in these guidelines which line the Commission has taken and will take on this point.

'Towage' is covered by the scope of the Guidelines only if more than 50% of the towage activity effectively carried out by a tug during a given year constitutes 'maritime transport'. Waiting time may be proportionally assimilated to that part of total activity effectively carried out by a tug which constitutes 'maritime transport'. It should be emphasised that towage activities which are carried out inter alia in ports, or which consist in assisting a self-propelled vessel to reach port do not constitute 'maritime transport' for the purposes of this communication. No derogation from the flag link is possible in the case of towage.

Similarly in the case of dredging, the experience gained during the recent years suggests that some points should be made."

This last paragraph neatly demonstrates how State aid law and policy is an evolutionary phenomenon.

---

46 "ISM Code", International Management Code for the Safe Operation of Ships and for Pollution Prevention, adopted by the International Maritime Organization (IMO) by resolution A.741(18).

47 The Commission will examine the effects of these provisions on ship management after three years of implementation of this communication.

15.042 The Guidelines continue to deal with dredging:

" 'Dredging' activities are, in principle, not eligible for aid to maritime transport. However, fiscal arrangements for companies (such as tonnage tax) may be applied to those dredgers whose activity consists in 'maritime transport' – that is, the transport at deep sea of extracted materials – for more than 50% of their annual operational time and only in respect of such transport activities. Eligible dredgers are only those registered in a Member State (no derogation from the flag link is possible). In such cases, separate accounting for maritime transport activities is required.[48]

Finally, the method of assessing tonnage tax systems notified up to now has consisted of the following steps: a virtual profit for shipowners has been calculated by applying a notional profit rate to their tonnage; national corporate tax has been applied to the amount so determined. The resulting amount is the 'tonnage tax' to be paid.

The notional profit rates provided for by Member States have been homogeneous up to now. However, since corporate tax rates may vary significantly across the Community, the tonnage taxes to be paid for the same tonnage might be very uneven in the different Member States. In order to keep the present equitable balance, the Commission will only approve schemes giving rise to a tax-load for the same tonnage fairly in line with the schemes already approved.

In all cases, the benefits of schemes must facilitate the development of the shipping sector and employment in the Community interest. Consequently, the fiscal advantages mentioned above must be restricted to shipping activities; hence, in cases where a shipowning company is also engaged in other commercial activities, transparent accounting will be required in order to prevent 'spill-over' into non-shipping activities. This approach would help Community shipping to be competitive, with tax liabilities comparable to levels applying elsewhere in the world, but would preserve a Member State's normal tax levels for other activities and personal remuneration of shareholders and directors."

15.043 A critical issue for State aid is any subsidisation or aiding of employment costs. Seafarers are a significant cost and the temptation for shipowners is to employ the cheapest crew possible. The cheapest crew members are rarely European so there is a need to facilitate the employment of European seafarers. The Commission continues:

"3.2. Labour-related costs
As was mentioned earlier, maritime transport is a sector experiencing fierce international competition. Support measures for the maritime sector should, therefore, aim primarily at reducing fiscal and other costs and burdens borne by Community shipowners and Community seafarers towards levels in line with world norms. They should directly stimulate the development of the sector and employment, rather than provide general financial assistance.

In keeping with these objectives, the following action on employment costs should be allowed for Community shipping:

- reduced rates of contributions for the social protection of Community seafarers employed on board ships registered in a Member State,
- reduced rates of income tax for Community seafarers on board ships registered in a Member State.

For the purposes of this point, 'Community seafarers' is defined as:

- Community/EEA citizens, in the case of seafarers working on board vessels (including ro-ro ferries[49]) providing scheduled passenger services between ports of the Community,

---

48 The ships used by these operators also extract or dredge materials which they carry afterwards. Extraction or dredging as such do not qualify for State aid to maritime transport.
49 See Article 2, point (a), of Council Directive 1999/35/EC of 29 April 1999 on a system of mandatory surveys for the safe operation of regular ro-ro ferry and high-speed passenger craft services (OJ L138, 1.6.1999, p. 1).

– all seafarers liable to taxation and/or social security contributions in a Member State, in all other cases.

The previous 1997 Guidelines allowed such reductions for all seafarers working on board vessels registered in a Member State and subject to tax and or social security contributions in a Member State. However, since then it has become clear that pressure by international competition on European shipowners is very strong in the case of international freight transport, while it is lighter in the case of intra-Community scheduled passenger transport. Boosting the competitiveness of European shipping industry is therefore a prior objective of aid in the former case. Preventing Member States from granting tax relief to all seafarers in this case would have very negative effects on the competitiveness of European shipowners, which could be encouraged to flag-out. At the same time it has been noticed that employment of European citizens is significant, in percentage terms and in numbers, in intra-Community scheduled passenger transport. Protection of employment in the Community is therefore a priority for aid in this case. For internal fiscal reasons some Member States prefer not to apply reduced rates as mentioned above, but instead may reimburse shipowners – partially or wholly – for the costs arising from these levies. Such an approach may generally be considered equivalent to the reduced-rate system as described above, provided that there is a clear link to these levies, no element of overcompensation, and that the system is transparent and not open to abuse.

For the maritime part of towage and dredging activities (maritime transport of materials), aid in favour of the employment of Community seafarers may be granted by analogy to the rules contained in this point, but only if the aid relates to Community seafarers working on board seagoing, self-propelled tugs and dredgers, registered in a Member State, carrying out maritime transport at sea for at least 50% of their operational time.[50]

Finally, it should be recalled that aid to employment is covered by the block exemption provided for by Commission Regulation (EC) No 2204/2002 of 12 December 2002 on the application of Articles [107 and 108 of the TFEU] to State aid for employment,[51] which also applies to maritime transport."

Part 4 of the Guidelines: "Crew Relief"

15.044 The fourth (and very short) part is entitled simply "Crew Relief". It reads:

"4. CREW RELIEF
Aid for crew relief tends to reduce the costs of employing Community seafarers, especially those on ships operating in distant waters. Aid, which is subject to the ceiling (as set out in Chapter 11), may, therefore, be granted in the form of payment or reimbursement of the costs of repatriation of Community seafarers working on board ships entered in Member States' registers."

This chapter[52] is important in terms of easing the financial burden on shipping companies in the EU who have to repatriate EU seafarers working on ships registered on a Member State registry. It is a protectionist measure because it only relates to reducing the costs of repatriating EU seafarers working on board ships entered in Member States' registries so it does not cover costs in other circumstances (e.g. repatriating a non-EU seafarer who is living in the EU and employed on board a vessel registered in an EU Member State).

---

50 Thus dredging activities carried out, inter alia, mainly in ports will not qualify for aid in favour of employment of Community seafarers.
51 OJ L337, 13.12.2002, p. 3.
52 Ortiz Blanco, Aliende Rodriguez, Vandenbussche and Rusche in Ortiz Blanco and Van Houtte (eds), op. cit. at fn. 1, para. 14.67.

Part 5 of the Guidelines: "Investment Aid"

15.045 The fifth part of the Guidelines is entitled "Investment Aid". It states:

"5. INVESTMENT AID
Subsidies for fleet renewal are not common in other transport modes such as road haulage and aviation. Since they tend to distort competition, the Commission has been reluctant to approve such schemes, except where they form part of a structural reform leading to reductions in overall fleet capacity.

Investment must comply with Regulation (EC) No 1540/98 or any other Community legislation that may replace it.

Within the framework of these guidelines, other investment aid may, however, be permitted, in line with the Community safe seas policy, in certain restricted circumstances to improve equipment on board vessels entered in a Member State's registers or to promote the use of safe and clean ships. Thus aid may be permitted which provides incentives to upgrade Community-registered ships to standards which exceed the mandatory safety and environmental standards laid down in international conventions and anticipating agreed higher standards, thereby enhancing safety and environmental controls. Such aid must comply with the applicable Community provisions on shipbuilding.

Since shipping is essentially very mobile, regional aid for maritime companies in disadvantaged regions, which often take the form of investment aid to companies investing in the regions, may only be permitted where it is clear that the benefits will accrue to the region over a reasonable time period. This would, for example, be the case of investment related to the construction of dedicated warehouses or to the purchase of fixed transhipment equipment. Investment aid for maritime companies in disadvantaged regions may then only be permitted where it also complies with the regional aid rules (see Chapter 6)."

Part 6 of the Guidelines: "Regional Aid on the Basis of Article 107(3)(a) and (c)"

15.046 The sixth part contains a single sentence. It provides:

"6. REGIONAL AID ON THE BASIS OF ARTICLE 87(3)(a) AND (c)
In the context of regional aid schemes, the Commission will apply the general rules set out in its communications or other provisions on national regional aid or future amendments thereto."

Part 7 of the Guidelines: "Training"

15.047 The seventh part provides:

"7. TRAINING
It should be recalled, firstly, that aid to training is covered by the block exemption provided for by Commission Regulation (EC) No 68/2001 of 12 January 2001 on the application of Articles 87 and 88 of the EC Treaty to training aid,[53] which also applies to maritime transport.

Moreover, many training schemes followed by seafarers and supported by the State are not considered to be State aid because they are of a general nature (whether vocational or academic). These are, therefore, not subject to notification and examination by the Commission.

If a scheme is to be regarded as including State aid, notification is, however, required. This may be the case if, for example, a particular scheme is specifically related to on-board training and the benefit of State financial support is received by the training organisation, the cadet, seafarer or shipowner. The Commission takes a favourable attitude towards aid, granted on a non-discriminatory basis, to training carried out on board ships registered in a Member State.

---

[53] OJ L10, 13.1.2001, p. 20.

Exceptionally, training on board other vessels may be supported where justified by objective criteria, such as the lack of available places on vessels in a Member State's register.

Where financial contributions are paid for on-board training, the trainee may not, in principle, be an active member of the crew but must be supernumerary. This provision is to ensure that net wage subsidies cannot be paid for seafarers occupied in normal crewing activities.

Similarly, to safeguard and develop maritime expertise in the Community and the competitive edge of the Community maritime industries, further extensive research and development efforts are necessary, with a focus on quality, productivity, safety and environmental protection. For such projects, State support may also be authorised within the limits set by the Treaty.

Aid aimed at enhancing and updating Community officers' skills may be allowed during their whole career. The aid may consist of a contribution to the cost of the training and/or compensation for the wage paid to the officer during the training period. The schemes must, however, be designed in a way which prevents the aid for training from being directly or indirectly diverted into a subsidy to officers' wages.

Aid aimed at professional retraining of high-sea fishermen willing to work as seafarers may also be allowed."

Part 8 of the Guidelines: "Restructuring Aid"

15.048 Part 8 of the Guidelines provides:

"8. RESTRUCTURING AID
Although the Community guidelines on restructuring and rescuing firms in difficulty[54] apply to transport only to the extent that the specific nature of the sector is taken into account, the Commission will apply those guidelines or any other Community instrument replacing them in considering restructuring aid for maritime companies."

This chapter provides that for restricting aid purposes, the general rules in the rescue and restructuring guidelines apply in the maritime transport sector.

Part 9 of the Guidelines: "Public Service Obligations and Contracts"

15.049 Part 9 of the Guidelines provides:

"9. PUBLIC SERVICE OBLIGATIONS AND CONTRACTS
In the field of maritime cabotage, public service obligations (PSOs) may be imposed or public service contracts (PSCs) may be concluded for the services indicated in Article 4 of Regulation (EEC) No 3577/92. For those services, PSOs and PSCs as well as their compensation must fulfil the conditions of that provision and the Treaty rules and procedures governing State aid, as interpreted by the Court of Justice.

The Commission accepts that if an international transport service is necessary to meet imperative public transport needs, PSOs may be imposed or PSCs may be concluded, provided that any compensation is subject to the above-mentioned Treaty rules and procedures.

The duration of public service contracts should be limited to a reasonable and not overlong period, normally in the order of six years, since contracts for significantly longer periods could entail the danger of creating a (private) monopoly."

---

54 OJ C288, 9.10.1999, p. 2.

Part 10 of the Guidelines: "Aid to Short Sea Shipping"

15.050 Part 10 embodies the Commission's commitment to aid to short sea shipping:

"10. AID TO SHORT SEA SHIPPING
There is no legal definition of 'Short Sea Shipping'. However, the communication from the Commission on the development of Short Sea Shipping in Europe of 29 June 1999[55] has provided a working definition of Short Sea Shipping, to be understood as 'the movement of cargo and passenger by sea between ports situated in geographical Europe or between those ports and ports situated in non European countries having a coastline on the enclosed seas bordering Europe'.[56] In this communication the Commission underscored the role of this transport mode to promote sustainable and safe mobility, to strengthen cohesion within the Community and to improve transport efficiency as part of an intermodal approach. The Commission also recognises that the promotion of short-sea shipping must be carried out at all levels, whether Community, national or regional.

Since aid to Short Sea Shipping aims to improve the intermodal chain and to decongest roads in the Member States, the definition of Short Sea Shipping such as provided by the 1999 communication should, for the purposes of this communication, be restricted to transport between ports in the territory of the Member States.

The Commission recognises that launching short-sea shipping services may be accompanied by substantial financial difficulties which the Member States may wish to attenuate in order to ensure the promotion of such services.

When such is the case, the Commission will be able to approve aid of this kind, on condition that it is intended for shipowners within the meaning of Article 1 of Regulation (EEC) No 4055/86 in respect of ships flying the flag of one of the Member States. Aid of this kind will have to be notified and to fulfil the following conditions:

- the aid must not exceed three years in duration and its purpose must be to finance a shipping service connecting ports situated in the territory of the Member States,
- the service must be of such a kind as to permit transport (of cargo essentially) by road to be carried out wholly or partly by sea, without diverting maritime transport in a way which is contrary to the common interest,
- the aid must be directed at implementing a detailed project with a pre-established environmental impact, concerning a new route or the upgrading of services on an existing one, associating several shipowners if necessary, with no more than one project financed per line and with no renewal, extension or repetition of the project in question,
- the purpose of the aid must be to cover, either up to 30% of the operational costs of the service in question,[57] or to finance the purchase of trans-shipment equipment to supply the planned service, up to a level of 10% in such investment,
- the aid to implement a project must be granted on the basis of transparent criteria applied in a non-discriminatory way to shipowners established in the Community. The aid should normally be granted for a project selected by the authorities of the Member State through a tender procedure in compliance with applicable Community rules,
- the service which is the subject of the project must be of a kind to be commercially viable after the period in which it is eligible for public funding,
- such aid must not be cumulated with public service compensation (obligations or contracts)."

---

55 Communication from the Commission to the European Parliament, the Council, the Economic and Social Committee and the Committee of Regions, "The development of Short Sea Shipping in Europe: a dynamic alternative in a sustainable transport chain – Second two-yearly report", COM(1999) 317 final.

56 Communication, p. 2.

57 In case of Community financing or eligibility under different aid schemes, the ceiling of 30% applies to the combined total of aid/financial support. It should be noticed that the aid intensity is the same as that provided for modal shift actions within the Marco Polo Community initiative: cf. Article 5(2) of Regulation (EC) No 1382/2003 (OJ L196, 2.8.2003, p. 1).

15.051 The Commission laying down rules such as 10% and 30% is a clear indication that the Commission is essentially legislating through the means of communications.

Part 11 of the Guidelines: "Ceiling"

15.052 Part 11 deals with the imposition of a ceiling on State aid. It provides:

"11. CEILING
As was explained above, certain Member States support their maritime sectors through tax reduction whilst other Member States prefer to make direct payments – for instance, by providing reimbursement of seafarers' income tax. In view of the current lack of harmonisation between the fiscal systems of the Member States, it is felt that the two alternatives should remain possible. Obviously, those two approaches may, in some instances, be combined. However, this risks causing a cumulation of aid to levels which are disproportionate to the objectives of the Community common interest and could lead to a subsidy race between Member States.

A reduction to zero of taxation and social charges for seafarers and a reduction of corporate taxation of shipping activities such as is described in point 3.1 (penultimate paragraph) is the maximum level of aid which may be permitted. To avoid distortion of competition, other systems of aid may not provide any greater benefit than this. Moreover, although each aid scheme notified by a Member State will be examined on its own merits, it is considered that the total amount of aid granted under Chapters 3 to 6 should not exceed the total amount of taxes and social contributions collected from shipping activities and seafarers."

Part 12 of the Guidelines: "Final Remarks"

15.053 Part 12 provides the so-called "final remarks" (which are not final remarks because the communication continues):

"12. FINAL REMARKS
The Commission will continue to monitor regularly and closely the market conditions for shipping. Should the latter change, and should consequently the need for State aid be reduced or overcome, the Commission will take the necessary measures in good time.

All new proposals for measures notified to the Commission must include a calendar indicating, for the next six years, the expected quantified effects for each objective of point 2.2. In particular, the expected macro-economic return on the corresponding maritime cluster, together with an estimation of the number of jobs saved or created, is to be presented in such proposals.

For all the aid schemes – whether existing or new – falling within the scope of this Communication, Member States are to communicate to the Commission an assessment of their effects during their sixth year of implementation.

When aid has been approved and granted to a beneficiary, under the derogation from the flag link referred to in point 3.1, the relevant Member State must report to the Commission every three years starting from the date when the grant was granted. In its report, the Member State will quantify the effects produced and compare the results with the expected effects. The reporting requirements set out in this communication will enter into force upon its publication.

Furthermore, should it prove necessary, for example following a justified complaint, the Member State concerned must provide the Commission with evidence that the assistance granted to the respective beneficiary under an agreed scheme has been limited to the strict definition therein and has also produced the effects expected."

Part 13 of the Guidelines: "Appropriate Measures"

15.054 Part 13 provides:

"13. APPROPRIATE MEASURES
These guidelines will apply from the date of their publication in the Official Journal of the European Union. In accordance with Article 88(1) of the Treaty, the Commission proposes that Member States amend their existing aid schemes relating to State aid covered by these guidelines so as to comply with them by 30 June 2005 at the latest. Member States are invited to confirm that they accept these proposals for appropriate measures in writing by 30 June 2004 at the latest.

Should a Member State fail to confirm its acceptance in writing by that date, the Commission will apply Article 19(2) of Regulation (EC) No 659/1999 and, if necessary, initiate the proceedings referred to in that provision.

These guidelines will be reviewed within seven years of their date of application."

Annex

15.055 The annex to the communication (entitled "Definition of Member States' Registers") defines the Member States' registries within the meaning of the communication: this is important as it clarified which registers are within the scope of the communications.

" 'Member States' registers' should be understood as meaning registers governed by the law of a Member State applying to their territories forming part of the European Community.

1. All the first registers of Member States are Member States' registers.
2. In addition, the following registers, located in Member States and subject to their laws, are Member States' registers:

    - the Danish International Register of Shipping (DIS),
    - the German International Shipping Register (ISR),
    - the Italian International Shipping Register,
    - the Madeira International Ship Register (MAR),
    - the Canary Islands register.

3. Other registers are not considered to be Member States' registers even if they serve in practice as a first alternative for shipowners based in that Member State. This is because they are located in and subject to the law of territories where the Treaty does not, in whole or in substantial part, apply. Hence, the following registers are not Member States' registers:

    - the Kerguelen register (the Treaty does not apply to this territory),
    - the Dutch Antilles' register (this territory is associated with the Community; and only Part IV of the Treaty applies to it; it is responsible for its own fiscal regime),
    - the registers of:
    - Isle of Man (only specific parts of the Treaty apply to the Isle – see Article 299(6)(c) of the Treaty; the Isle of Man parliament has sole right to legislate on fiscal matters),
    - Bermuda and Cayman (they are part of the territories associated to the Community, and only Part IV of the Treaty applies to them; they enjoy a fiscal autonomy).

4. In the case of Gibraltar, the Treaty applies fully and the Gibraltar register is, for the purposes of these Guidelines, considered to be a Member State's register."

2017: Update to the 2004 communication

15.056 In 2017, the European Commission updated the annex to the 2004 communication. The 2017 updating communication was published on 13 April 2017 and applied from that date. It is quite short:

"INTRODUCTION
The Maritime Transport Guidelines[58] (the 'Guidelines') provide criteria for the compatibility of State aid to maritime transport with the internal market, under Article 107(3)(c) and Article 106(2) of the Treaty on the Functioning of the European Union.

In particular, the Guidelines list a number of specific objectives in the Union maritime interest, including 'the flagging or re-flagging to Member States' registers'.

The flagging or re-flagging of eligible ships is thus connected with registration in Member States' ship registers.

The Guidelines make a distinction, for the purposes of Union State aid law, between different categories of ship registers created by Member States, namely 'first registers' and 'second registers'. For the purposes of the Guidelines, second registers comprise, firstly, 'offshore registers' belonging to territories which have a greater or lesser autonomy in relation to the Member State, and secondly, 'international registers', attached directly to the State which created them (sixth paragraph of point 1 of the Guidelines).

The Annex to the Guidelines defines the term 'Member States' registers'. According to that definition, in order to qualify as Member States' registers, ship registers must be 'governed by the law of a Member State applying to their territories forming part of the European Community [Union]' (first sentence of the Annex to the Guidelines).

On the basis of that definition, points 1 to 4 of the Annex spell out which registers are considered to be Member States' registers, and which are not.

Point 2 of the Annex provides an exhaustive list of second registers, located in Member States and subject to their laws, which are considered to be Member States' registers.

The current version of the Annex, and thus the exhaustive list in point 2 thereof, was adopted at the same time as the Guidelines, which have been applied since 17 January 2004. Since then, it has not been updated.

The Commission is aware that Member States may create new ship registers or alter or abolish existing ones. For instance, France created its 'Registre International Français' in 2005. Therefore, the exhaustive list of second registers that qualify as Member States' registers in point 2 of the Annex to the Guidelines is liable to change over time. In order to keep pace with the situation in all register-keeping Member States, the list would have to be regularly updated.

For those reasons, the character of the list in point 2 of the Annex should be changed from exhaustive to non-exhaustive, while maintaining the definition in the first sentence of the Annex, on the basis of which second registers can qualify as Member States' registers.

The change will ensure both the necessary flexibility in the implementation of the Guidelines with respect to second registers of Member States and legal certainty regarding the treatment of second registers of Member States that were created after the adoption of the Guidelines and thus would otherwise not fall under any of the points of the Annex. Overall, the change will achieve the State aid control objectives of the Guidelines with a minimum of administrative burden, in full respect of the Treaties.

In the light of the foregoing, point 2 of the Annex to the Guidelines should be updated and is to be read as follows:

'2. In addition, registers located in Member States and subject to their laws, are Member States' registers, if they are located in and subject to the law of territories where the Treaty applies. For example, at the time these Guidelines were adopted, the following registers were considered to fall under this category:

---

58 Commission communication "Community guidelines on State aid to maritime transport" (OJ C13, 17.1.2004, p. 3).

- the Danish International Register of Shipping (DIS),
- the German International Shipping Register (ISR),
- the Italian International Shipping Register,
- the Madeira International Ship Register (MAR),
- the Canary Islands register.'

This update will apply from the date of its publication in the Official Journal of the European Union."

F. EU STATE AID LAW AND THE MOTORWAYS OF THE SEAS

15.057 In 2008, the Commission adopted a communication on State aid in the context of the Motorways of the Seas. The communication is entitled: "Communication from the Commission providing guidance on State aid complementary to Community funding for the launching of the motorways of the sea".[59] This is, in many ways, aimed at improving the environmental performance of the freight transport system.

15.058 The motorways Commission begins with a short single paragraph introduction:

"INTRODUCTION
1. The White Paper 'European transport policy for 2010: time to decide' of 2001[60] introduced the concept of 'motorways of the sea' as high quality transport services based on short sea shipping. Motorways of the sea are composed of infrastructure, facilities and services spanning at least two Member States. The motorways of the sea aim to shift significant shares of freight transport from road to sea. Their successful implementation will help achieving two main objectives of the European transport policy, that is, reduction of congestion on the roads and a reduced environmental impact of freight transport. The mid-term review of the White Paper[61] points to the increasing problem of road congestion, costing the Community about 1% of GDP, and to the threat of greenhouse gasses emissions from transport with respect to Kyoto targets and reconfirms the importance of the motorways of the sea."

15.059 The communication then moves to a section entitled: "Complementary State Aid for Marco Polo II 'Motorways of the Sea' Projects":

"COMPLEMENTARY STATE AID FOR MARCO POLO II 'MOTORWAYS OF THE SEA' PROJECTS

2. Chapter 10 of the Community Guidelines on State aid to maritime transport[62] allow, under certain conditions, for start-up aid to new or improved short sea shipping services with a maximum duration of three years and a maximum intensity of 30% of operational cost and 10% of investments costs.
3. The second 'Marco Polo' programme (further referred to as Marco Polo II) established by Regulation (EC) No 1692/2006 of the European Parliament and of the Council of 24 October 2006 establishing the second 'Marco Polo' programme for the granting of Community financial assistance to improve the environmental performance of the freight transport system (Marco Polo II) and repealing Regulation (EC) No 1382/2003[63] is one of the two Community funding instruments directly and explicitly supporting the motorways of

---

59 OJ 2008 C317/08.
60 COM(2001) 370.
61 COM(2006) 314 final: Communication from the Commission to the Council and the European Parliament "Keep Europe moving – Sustainable mobility for our continent – Mid-term review of the European Commission's 2001 Transport White Paper".
62 Commission communication C(2004) 43 (OJ C13, 17.1.2004, p. 3).
63 OJ L328, 24.11.2006, p. 1.

the sea, as one out of the five actions that are supported for avoiding traffic or shifting traffic away from road. Marco Polo II provides support mainly to the services part of the motorways of the sea. That support is attributed through yearly calls for proposals directed to the industry players. The allocated financial support is constrained by the grants available under the Marco Polo programme. Funding to the motorways of the sea can also be provided through the Regional Policy.

4. Under Article 5(1)(b) of Regulation (EC) No 1692/2006, in the framework of Marco Polo II programme 'Motorways of the Sea Actions' are, under certain conditions, eligible to Community financial assistance with a maximum intensity of 35% of the total cost for establishing and operating the transport service and a maximum duration of 60 months, as fixed by Annex I, points 1(a) and 2(a) of column B.

5. Article 7 of Regulation (EC) No 1692/2006 reads: Community financial assistance for the actions covered by the Programme shall not prevent those actions from being granted State aid at national, regional or local level, insofar as such aid is compatible with the State-aid arrangements laid down in the Treaty and within the cumulative limits established for each type of action set out in Annex I.

6. According to Article 7 of Regulation (EC) No 1692/2006, therefore, Member States' authorities may complement Community financing by allocating their own financial resources to projects selected according to the criteria and procedures laid down in that Regulation, within the ceilings set out in the Regulation. The objective of Article 7 of Regulation (EC) No 1692/2006 is to make it possible for undertakings interested in a project to count on a predetermined amount of public funding irrespective of its origin. As a matter of fact, it may be the case that the Community financial resources allocated by the Regulation (EC) No 1692/2006 are not sufficient to provide all the selected projects with the maximum possible support. Actually, if a large number of valid projects are presented in a given year, some projects may be granted limited amounts of Community funding. While the fact of having a large number of selected projects would be a sign of success for Marco Polo II, this success would be jeopardised if the involved undertakings were to withdraw their submission or were discouraged from future submissions because of the lack of public funding, necessary for the start-up of the relevant services. Moreover, fixing a predetermined amount of public funding that can be relied on is essential for potential bidders.

7. Against this background, the Commission has noticed that amongst stakeholders and Member States' authorities there are doubts about the possibility for the latter to grant complementary State aid to Marco Polo II projects going beyond what is allowed for short sea shipping under Chapter 10 of the Community Guidelines on State aid to maritime transport. Actually, the eligibility conditions for schemes under the Guidelines on State aid to maritime transport are slightly different from those of Marco Polo II. The Guidelines provide for a maximum intensity of 30% of operational costs (35% of the total expenditure in Marco Polo II) and a maximum duration of three years (in comparison to five years under Marco Polo II). Such differences have probably confused potential bidders for motorways of the sea actions.

8. For the above reasons, the Commission considers that maximum duration and intensity of State aid and Community funding for projects which have been selected under the Regulation should be the same. Therefore, on the basis of Article 87(3)(c) of the Treaty, in the absence of Community funding, or to the extent not covered by Community funding, the Commission will authorise State aid to the start-up of Marco Polo II 'Motorways of the Sea' projects with a maximum intensity of 35% of operational costs and a maximum duration of five years.[64] The same will apply to projects selected under Marco Polo II but for which funding is finally provided through the European Regional Development Fund (ERDF) ... or the Cohesion Fund.[65]

---

64 It should be noticed that the clause contained in Annex I(2)(b) of the Marco Polo II Regulation (about the limits to funding based on freight actually shifted from road) applies to Community funding, but not to complementary State aid addressed in the present communication.
65 Regulation (EC) No 1084/2006 of 11 July 2006 (OJ L210, 31.7.2006, p. 79).

9. Start-up aid to operational costs may not exceed the above-mentioned duration and intensity, irrespective of the source of funding. Aid can not be cumulated with public service compensation. The Commission also recalls that the same eligible costs cannot benefit from two Community financial instruments.
10. Member States will have to notify to the Commission State aid that they intend to grant on the basis of the present communication to projects selected under Regulation (EC) No 1692/2006."

15.060 The third part is entitled: "Complementary State Aid for Ten-T 'Motorways of the Sea' Projects":

"COMPLEMENTARY STATE AID FOR TEN-T 'MOTORWAYS OF THE SEA' PROJECTS
11. Article 12a of Decision No 1692/96/EC of the European Parliament and of the Council of 23 July 1996 on Community guidelines for the development of the trans-European transport network ... provides for the setting up of 'Motorways of the Sea' concentrating flows of freight on sea-based logistical routes in such a way as to improve existing maritime links or to establish new viable regular and frequent maritime links for the transport of goods between Member States so as to reduce road congestion and/or to improve access to peripheral and islands regions and State. The trans-European network of motorways of the sea must consist of facilities and infrastructure concerning at least two ports in two different Member States.
12. The Community guidelines for the development of the trans-European transport network concern Community support for the development of infrastructure, including in the case of the motorways of the sea. However, second indent of Article 12a(5) of Decision No 1692/96/EC, includes a possibility of granting Community support for start-up aid to a project, without prejudice to Articles 87 and 88 of the Treaty. This support may be granted to the extent it is deemed necessary for the financial viability of the project. In fact, the case may arise that the proposing consortium of ports and operators incurs start-up losses within the launching period of the motorways of the sea services.
13. Start-up support under the Community guidelines for the development of the trans-European transport network is limited to 'duly justified capital costs', to be understood as investment support. This may include the depreciation of ships allocated to the service.[66] Under the Community guidelines for the development of the trans-European transport network, start-up support is limited to two years with a maximum intensity of 30%.
14. In the framework of TEN-T projects, financial resources may be provided by Member States to the extent that Community funding is not available. In the case of start-up aid to shipping services, however, the second indent of Article 12a(5) of Decision No 1692/96/EC makes a reference to the provisions on State aid of the Treaty. Therefore, Member States may provide complementary aid to the extent that Community funding is not available, but they have to respect the rules on State aid while doing so. Since in the matter of aid to short sea shipping, guidance on the application of State aid rules has been provided by Chapter 10 of the Guidelines on State aid to maritime transport, the latter applies to complementary State aid. The Community Guidelines on State aid to maritime transport, however, allow for aid to investment with a maximum intensity of 10% during three years. As a result, if a motorway of the sea project is selected as a TEN-T project, but it is not granted the maximum Community support to investment, i.e. 30% during two years, it may happen that public support will not achieve the maximum possible amount, if national State aid may not go beyond the 10% over three years authorised by the Community Guidelines on State aid to maritime transport. Furthermore, the difference in the maximum duration of the two schemes (two years under Decision No 1692/96/EC and three years under the Community Guidelines on State aid to maritime transport) is capable of generating uncertainty and confusion. For the sake of clarity and in order to allow for a pre-determined public

---

66 Vade mecum of 28 February 2005 issued in conjunction with the call for proposals for the TEN-T 2005; paragraph 4.3 (Start-up aid related to capital costs).

support to undertakings taking part in a motorway of the sea TEN-T project, the maximum intensity and duration of complementary State aid to be provided by Member States should be the same as the maximum intensity and duration of Community funding.

15. For the above reasons, on the basis of Article [107](3)(c) of the Treaty, in the absence of Community funding for start-up aid or for the part not covered by Community funding, the Commission will authorise State aid to investment with a maximum intensity of 30% and a maximum duration of two years to projects corresponding to Article 12a of Decision 1692/96/EC and selected in accordance with the procedure laid down in Regulation (EC) No 680/2007 of the European Parliament and of the Council of 20 June 2007 laying down general rules for the granting of Community financial aid in the field of the trans-European transport and energy networks.[67] The same will apply where the Member States decide to fund the project through the European regional development Fund or the Cohesion Fund.

16. Start-up aid to investment may not exceed the duration and intensity referred to in this point, irrespective of the source of funding. It can not be cumulated with public service compensation. Also for this case, the Commission recalls that the same eligible costs cannot benefit from two Community financial instruments.

17. Member States will have to notify to the Commission State aid that they intend to grant on the basis of the present communication to projects selected under Regulation (EC) No 680/2007."

15.061 The last part of the communication deals with the application of the communication:

"APPLICATION
18. The Commission will apply the guidance provided for in this communication from the day following that of its publication in the Official Journal."

G. EU STATE AID LAW AND SHIP MANAGEMENT COMPANIES

15.062 The Commission has issued a communication on aid to technical and crew ship managers.[68] It is entitled "Communication from the Commission providing guidance on State aid to ship management companies".[69] The communication extends the eligibility for State aid to ship management companies in certain circumstances.

15.063 The scope of the communication is set out in chapter 1:

"1. SCOPE
This Communication deals with the eligibility of crew and technical managers of ships for the reduction of corporate tax or the application of the tonnage tax under Section 3.1 of Commission Communication C(2004) 43 – Community guidelines on State aid to maritime transport[70] ('the Guidelines'). It does not deal with State aid to commercial managers of ships. This Communication applies to crew and technical management irrespectively of whether they are individually provided or jointly provided to the same ship."

15.064 The communication contains some introductory remarks in chapter 2:

"2. INTRODUCTION
2.1. General context
The Guidelines provide for the possibility that ship management companies qualify for the tonnage tax or other tax arrangements for shipping companies (Section 3.1). However, eligibility

---
67 OJ L162, 22.6.2007, p. 1.
68 OJ 2009 C132/6.
69 OJ 2009 C132/06.
70 CJ C13/3, 17.1.2004.

is limited to the joint provision of both technical and crew management for a same vessel ('full management'), while those activities are not eligible to the tonnage tax or other tax arrangements when provided individually.

The Guidelines stipulate that the Commission will examine the effects of the Guidelines on ship management after three years.[71] This Communication sets out the results of that fresh assessment and draws conclusions on the eligibility of ship management companies for State aid.

2.2. Ship management

Ship management companies are entities providing different services to shipowners, such as technical survey, crew recruiting and training, crew management and vessel operation. There are three main categories of ship management services: crew management, technical management and commercial management.

Crew management consists, in particular, in dealing with all the matters relating to crew, such as selecting and engaging suitably qualified seafarers, issuing payrolls, ensuring the appropriateness of the manning level of ships, checking the certifications of seafarers, providing for seafarers' accident and disability insurance coverage, taking care of travel and visa arrangements, handling medical claims, assessing the performance of the seafarers and, in some cases, training them. Crew management represents by far the largest part of the ship management industry worldwide.

Technical management consists in ensuring the seaworthiness of the vessel and its full compliance with technical, safety and security requirements. In particular, the technical manager is responsible for making decisions on the repair and maintenance of a ship. Technical management represents a significant part of the ship management industry, although much smaller than crew management.

Commercial management consists in promoting and ensuring the sale of ships' capacity, by means of chartering the ships, taking bookings for cargo or passengers, ensuring marketing and appointing agents. Commercial management represents a very small part of the ship management industry. To date the Commission does not have complete information about commercial management at its disposal. Commercial management is therefore not addressed by this Communication.

Like any maritime activity, ship management is a global business by nature. In the absence of international law regulating third party ship management, the standards in this field have been settled within the framework of private law agreements.[72]

In the Community, ship management is mainly carried out in Cyprus. There are, however, ship management companies in the United Kingdom, Germany, Denmark, Belgium and the Netherlands. Outside the Community, ship management companies are mainly established in Hong Kong, Singapore, India, United Arab Emirates and the USA.

2.3. Review of the eligibility conditions for ship management companies

Since the publication of the Guidelines in January 2004, several maritime countries have entered the Community, amongst them Cyprus, which features the largest ship management industry in the world.

The accession of Cyprus and its preliminary work for complying with the Guidelines, as well as a study realised by a consortium for the administration of that Member State,[73] allowed for a more complete understanding of this activity and of its evolution. More awareness has been acquired in particular in respect of the link between technical and crew management on the one hand, and shipping on the other, as well as the possibility that crew and/or technical managers can help achieving the objectives of the Guidelines."

---

71 Ed., OJ C13/J, 17 January 2004, fn. 3.

72 An example is the "BIMCO's Standard Ship Management Agreement SHIPMAN 98" which is frequently used in relations between ship management companies and shipowners.

73 Study on Ship Management in Cyprus and in the European Union of 31 May 2008, carried out for the Cypriot government by a consortium under the direction of the Vienna University of Economics and Business Administration.

15.065 The communication examines in chapter 3 how to assess the eligibility of ship management companies:

"3. ASSESSMENT OF ELIGIBILITY OF SHIP MANAGEMENT COMPANIES
Unlike other maritime-related services, ship management is a standard core-activity of maritime carriers, normally provided in-house. Ship management is one of the most characteristic activities of ship operators. Nowadays, however, it is outsourced to third-party ship management companies in some cases. It is because of this link between ship management and shipping that third-party ship management companies are professional operators with the same background as shipowners, although segmented according to their specialisation, operating in their same business environment. Shipowners are the only customers of ship management companies.

Against this background the Commission considers that outsourcing of ship management should not be fiscally penalised with respect to in-house ship management, provided that the ship management companies meet the same requirements as are applicable to shipowners and that the provision of the aid to the former contributes to the achievement of the objectives of the Guidelines in the same way as the provision of aid to shipowners.

In particular the Commission considers that, precisely because of their specialisation and the nature of their core-business, ship management companies may substantially contribute to the achievement of the objectives of the Guidelines, in particular the achievement of an 'efficient, secure and environment friendly maritime transport' and of the 'consolidation of the maritime cluster established in the Member States'.[74]"

15.066 The fourth part of the communication deals with the extension to ship management companies of eligibility to State aid:

"4. EXTENSION TO SHIP MANAGEMENT COMPANIES OF ELIGIBILITY TO STATE AID
On the basis of what has been explained in Section 3 above, the Commission will authorise under Article [107](3)(c) of the Treaty establishing the European Community, tax relief for ship management companies, as referred to in Section 3.1 of the Guidelines, with respect to joint or separate crew and technical management of ships, provided that the conditions set out in Sections 5 and 6 of this Communication are fulfilled."

15.067 The fifth part of the communication deals with the conditions for eligibility applicable to both technical and crew managers:

"5. CONDITIONS FOR ELIGIBILITY APPLICABLE TO BOTH TECHNICAL AND CREW MANAGERS
In order to qualify for aid ship management companies should present a clear link with the Community and its economy, in line with Section 3.1 of the Guidelines. Moreover, they should contribute to the objectives of the Guidelines, such as those laid down in Section 2.2 of the Guidelines. Technical and crew managers are eligible to State aid, provided that the ships they manage comply with all the requirements set out in Sections 5.1 to 5.4 of this Communication. Eligible activities must be entirely carried out from the territory of the Community.

5.1. Contribution to the economy and employment within the Community
The economic link with the Community is proven by the fact that ship management is carried out in the territory of one or more Member States and that mainly Community nationals are employed in land-based activities or on ships.

5.2. Economic link between the managed ships and the Community
Ship management companies may benefit from State aid with respect to ships entirely managed from the territory of the Community, irrespective of whether management is provided in-house or whether it is partially or totally outsourced to one or more ship management companies.

---

74 Section 2.2 of the Guidelines.

However, since ship management companies do not have full control of their customers, the above requirement is deemed to be fulfilled if at least two thirds of the tonnage of the managed ships is managed from the territory of the Community. Tonnage in excess of that percentage which is not entirely managed from the Community is not eligible.[75]

5.3. Compliance with international and Community standards
Ship management companies are eligible if all the ships and crews they manage comply with international standards and Community law requirements are fulfilled, in particular those relating to security, safety, training and certification of seafarers, environmental performance and on-board working conditions.

5.4. Flag-share requirement (flag link)
The flag-share requirement, as laid down in the eighth paragraph of Section 3.1 of the Guidelines applies to ship management companies. The share of Community flags to be considered as the benchmark is that of the day on which this Communication is published in the Official Journal of the European Union. For new companies the benchmark is to be calculated one year after the date on which they started activity."

15.068 The sixth part sets out the additional requirements for crew managers:

"6. ADDITIONAL REQUIREMENTS FOR CREW MANAGERS
6.1. Training of seafarers
Crew managers are eligible for State aid as long as all seafarers working onboard managed ships are educated, trained and hold a certificate of competency in accordance with the Convention of the International Maritime Organisation on Standards of Training, Certification and Watchkeeping for Seafarers, 1978, as amended (STCW), and have successfully completed training for personal safety on board ship. Moreover, crew managers are eligible if they fulfil the STCW and Community law requirements regarding responsibilities of companies.

6.2. Social conditions
In order to be eligible for State aid, crew managers must ensure that on all managed ships the provisions of the Maritime Labour Convention, 2006, of the International Labour Organisation ('MLC'),[76] are fully implemented by the seafarer's employer, be it the shipowner or the ship management companies. The ship management companies must ensure, in particular, that the provisions of the MLC concerning the seafarer's employment agreement,[77] ship's loss or foundering[78] medical care,[79] shipowner's liability including payment of wages in case of accident or sickness,[80] and repatriation[81] are properly applied.

Crew managers must also ensure that the international standards regarding hours of work and hours of rest provided for by the MLC are fully complied with.

Finally, in order to be eligible, crew managers must also provide financial security to assure compensation in the event of the death or long-term disability of seafarers due to an occupational injury, illness or hazard."

---

75 Regulation (EC) No 1080/2006 of 5 July 2006 (OJ L210, 31.7.2006, p. 1).
76 It should be recalled that the European social partners adopted an agreement taking up the relevant part of the Maritime Labour Convention 2006 which has been integrated into Community law by Council Directive 2009/13/EC of 16 February 2009 implementing the Agreement concluded by the European Community Shipowners' Associations (ECSA) and the European Transport Workers' Federation (ETF) on the Maritime Labour Convention, 2006, and amending Directive 1999/63/EC (OJ L124, 20.5.2009, p. 30).
77 Regulation 2.1 and Standard A2.1 (Seafarers' employment agreement) of Title 2 of MLC.
78 Ibid. Regulation 2.6 and Standard A2.6 (Seafarer compensation for the ship's loss or foundering) of Title 2.
79 Ibid. Regulation 4.1 and Standard A4.1 (Medical care on board ship and ashore Shipownrs' [sic] liability); Regulation 4.3 and A4.3 (Health and safety protection and accident prevention); Regulation 4.4 (Access to shore-based welfare facilities) of Title 4.
80 Ibid. Regulation 4.2 and Standard A4.2 (Shipowners' liability) of Title 4.
81 Ibid. Regulation 2.5 and Standard A2.5 (Repatriation) of Title 2.

15.069 Chapter 7 deals with the calculation of tax:

"7. CALCULATION OF TAX

Also in the case of ship management companies the Commission will apply the principle contained in the Guidelines, according to which, in order to avoid distortion, it will only authorise schemes giving rise to a homogeneous tax-load across the Member States for the same activity or the same tonnage. This means that total exemption or equivalent schemes will not be authorised.[82]

The tax base to be used for ship management companies can obviously not be the same as that applied to shipowners since, with respect to a given ship, the turnover of the ship management companies is much lower than that of the shipowner. According to the study mentioned in Section 2.3, as well as to notifications received in the past, the tax-base to be applied to ship management companies should be approximately 25% (in terms or tonnage or notional profit) of that which would apply to the shipowner for the same ship or tonnage. The Commission, therefore, requires that a percentage of no less than 25% is applied under ship management tonnage tax schemes.[83]

If ship management companies engage in activities which are not eligible for State aid under the present Communication, they must keep separate accounts for those activities.

In case ship management companies subcontract part of their activity to third parties, the latter are not eligible to State aid."

15.070 Chapter 8 of the communication provides:

"8. APPLICATION AND REVIEW

The Commission will apply the guidance provided for in this Communication from the day following that of its publication in the Official Journal of the European Union.

State aid to ship management companies will be included in the general revision of the Guidelines such as foreseen in Section 13 of the latter."

H. STATE AID AND PORTS: GENERALLY AND UNDER THE GENERAL BLOCK EXEMPTION

Introduction

15.071 State aid rules apply to ports but not every form of assistance to a port (or port user) is State aid. For example, a breakwater or other purely safety/navigational aid would not usually be subject to the State aid rules. It is proposed to consider the position of State aid and ports generally and then consider the General Block Exemption Regulation (i.e. Commission Regulation (EU) 2017/1084 of 14 June 2017 amending Regulation (EU) 651/2014 as regards aid for port and airport infrastructure, notification thresholds for aid for culture and heritage conservation and for aid for sport and multifunctional recreational infrastructures, and regional operating aid schemes for outermost regions and amending Regulation (EU) 702/2014 as regards the calculation of eligible costs)[84] which has a specific relevance for ports. It is also worth bearing in mind the previous comments above including those relating to the motorways of the seas as well as the Commission's guidelines for the development of the trans-European transport network.

---

82 The Commission takes this opportunity within the present Communication to emphasise that the mechanism used to calculate the tax to be paid by both ship management companies and shipowners is irrelevant as such; in particular, it is irrelevant whether or not a system based on notional profit is applied.
83 The shipowner, if eligible, remains liable for the whole tonnage tax.
84 OJ L156/1, 20.6.2017.

15.072 It is worth recalling that there is an enormous value in permitting some State aid for ports given their centrality to the EU project as a whole (e.g. the free movement of goods and people) as well as to the success of the EU, Member State and local economies and societies.

15.073 EU law and policy has to be mindful of the role and function of individual ports – in an island economy, for example, ports are much more critically important than a port in a continental landmass of several countries and multiple ports. Similarly, ports can be either transhipment or gateway ports with the former operating in a much larger market and subject to competition from a greater range of ports while the latter type of port may be more sheltered from competition but are critically important for the locality and hinterland.

15.074 There is a certain topicality to the issue of State aid and ports. For example, port operators are beginning to complain about alleged State aid in other ports (e.g. ABP complaining about alleged State aid for the Liverpool Cruise Terminal); ships are getting bigger (particularly, container vessels and cruise liners) hence requiring new and bigger facilities; some of the facilities in the EU's 1,200 commercial seaports simply need upgrading (e.g. breakwaters in Great Yarmouth); the Commission has become much more active in regard to ports and State aid; the Commission extended the General Block Exemption Regulation for State aid (the "GBER") to ports and thereby to bring greater certainty and impose less administration to the sector.

15.075 At a practical level, advisors to ports have to be very careful. When a deal is too good to be true, then it probably is too good! There are many examples of State aid issues in practice: the provision of land in a port at less than market value; the provision of facilities or services in a port at less than market value; the writing off of fees or payments in a port when a "market economy operator" would not have done so; the provision of favourable but discriminatory tax breaks (e.g. reliefs or rates) for port activities; the provision of investment by State bodies on terms which a market economy operator would not have invested; and the construction of port infrastructure which is supposedly open to all but is really destined for one operator or a select number of operators.

I. STATE AID AND PORTS GENERALLY

Introduction

15.076 While there is a growing awareness among seaports and port users about the application of the European Community's rules on State[85] aid to ports,[86] it is clear that this is territory which has neither been fully explored nor entirely understood by ports,

---

[85] In this context, the term "State" means a Member State of the EU. The State aid rules only apply to EU Member States.

[86] See e.g. cases such as *Great Yarmouth Outer Harbour* N 503/2005, IP/05/1671 (21 December 2005); *Flemish Ports* N520/2003, IP/04/1267 (20 October 2004); and *Rotterdam* IP/07/555 (24 April 2007) which all indicate that Member States are aware of State aid issues in ports.

users and, indeed, regulators.[87] This is despite the fact that ports have been receiving State aid to some extent probably since the establishment of the State itself.

15.077 This lack of awareness among ports and those advising ports is, in some ways, forgivable because even some of the EU institutions have called for clarity. For example, the European Parliament issued an interesting statement on 4 September 2008 (reflecting an earlier press release on 25 June 2008) on the very subject of State aid and ports:

"Guidelines urgently needed on state aid to ports, says European Parliament
Transport
The European Parliament is urging the European Commission to adopt guidelines on state aid to ports by the end of this year. In an own-initiative report on European ports policy adopted by MEPs, the House urges the Commission to identify possible distortions of competition and to clarify in the state aid guidelines what types of aid to port authorities should be treated as state aid. MEPs also look at ways to upgrade the port system to meet the EU's future transport needs.

The own-initiative report adopted with 572 votes in favour, 12 against and 10 abstentions on the Commission communication on European Ports Policy, points out that the EU port sector is expanding fast and that the maritime sector is particularly affected by globalisation. It highlights the need to take account of major changes in international traffic resulting from technological and economic progress, the widening of the Panama Canal and the increase and size of capacity of vessels.

Links to port hinterland
Members also stress that maritime and river transport should not be isolated from land and air transport. Given that links to a port's hinterland are of great importance to its commercial success, one aim of the 2010 mid-term review of the trans-European network should be to integrate maritime and river transport with land transport via European ports, they say.

Customs controls
Parliament also recommends that Community-cleared goods should be exempt from customs controls in short-sea shipping in the Community. It advocates creating separate port zones for intra-community and international traffic, simplifying internal transport, and standardising and identifying special containers. It calls on the Commission and the sector to encourage shipping companies to reduce the number of empty containers transported, so as to reduce environmental impact, whilst at the same time taking account of the specific needs of clients.

Social dialogue in the port sector
The House urges that a social dialogue be established on port-related subjects, including worker's rights, concessions and the 1979 International Labour Organisation Convention on the occupational safety and health of dock workers. It also stresses the importance of protecting and ensuring the highest possible standard of training for port workers.

---

87 The Commission recognised this need when it said succinctly in October 2007: "[g]uidelines on State Aid to ports and more transparency of port accounts are needed" (Commission Staff Working Document, Accompanying Document to Communication on a European Ports Policy Full Impact Assessment, COM(2007) 616 final, SEC(2007) 1340). It is worth stressing that guidelines are always useful but rarely (if ever) comprehensive or specific enough to anticipate every situation and eventuality.

Scanning US-bound cargo
Finally, MEPs urge the Commission to pursue its efforts to win a reform of the US regulation requiring that 100% of US-bound cargo be scanned. It urges the Commission to evaluate the potential cost of this measure to business."[88]

15.078 This press release from the European Parliament demonstrates the much wider context in which State aid and ports interact. It is not simply an issue of grants, subsidies, capital investments and write-offs.

15.079 It is useful to consider the application of these rules to ports by concentrating on three issues: (a) highlighting the relevance of the State aid rules or, put another way, why ports and shipping companies need to know (and, on occasion, worry) about these rules; (b) outlining what are the State aid rules; and (c) considering some practical issues in the application of the rules in the context of ports.[89] It is worth recalling that State aid inevitably means a "conflict of interests between the recipient economic agents and their competitors in other Member States".[90] State aid law and policy is therefore seeking to strike a balance between these tensions.[91]

Relevance of state aid rules for ports

15.080 There is no doubt that States around the world support ports financially to a greater or lesser extent. Indeed, there are aspects of port investment which require State investment either because of the scale of the investment[92] or because the investment would not be commercially viable. Ports might well argue that States do not support them enough but there is clearly a significant level of support. The question therefore arises as to whether such support or assistance is aid and then whether it is legal or illegal aid.

15.081 Why should ports and shipping companies be concerned about the EU's State aid rules? In many ways, there is no difference between the concerns of ports and shipping companies so it is easier to group the concerns together. The main concern is that if

---

88 It is interesting that the debate on State aid and ports has shifted over time between having "guidelines" and having a "framework on infrastructure charging". The port organisations have favoured guidelines. At one point, the Commission had declared that it would issue guidelines on State aid and ports: see Commission, *The Development of Short Sea Shipping in Europe: Prospects and challenges* (COM (95) 317), 1995, p. 36. The distinction between guidelines and a framework has been described by FEPORT (FEPORT represents the interests of large variety of terminal operators and stevedoring companies performing operations and carrying out activities over 400 terminals in the seaports of the EU) and ESPO (ESPO represents the port authorities, port associations and port administrations of the seaports of 23 Member States of the EU and Norway at EU political level. ESPO also has observer members in Iceland, Ukraine and Israel) in the following terms: "a framework is different from State Aid guidelines since it focuses on cost recovery of (infrastructure) investments (charging) whereas guidelines indicate where public financial support is allowed under art. [87] of the EC Treaty (financing)." FEPORT and ESPO continue by saying that there "are also legal and procedural differences between a framework and guidelines. A charging framework would have to take the form of a Council Directive whereas the development of guidelines would be the sole responsibility of the Commission. State aid guidelines would therefore be able to offer a pragmatic solution to the achievement of a level playing field much more quickly than a charging framework."

89 This chapter does not examine related issues such as regional aid but instead concentrates on State aid in the context of ports.

90 Commission, First Report on Competition Policy (1971), para. 133.

91 See Evans and Martin, "Socially Acceptable Distortion of Competition: Community Policy on State Aid" (1991) 16 ELRev 79.

92 Port activities can be enormously expensive: e.g. in the case of the 2007 Rotterdam State aid case, the investments notified to the Commission amounted to €2.8 billion (Rotterdam IP/07/555 (24 April 2007)).

illegal State aid is provided to either: (a) a port; or (b) a shipping company using a port then the port or the shipping company may be legally compelled to repay the aid element to the Member State. This is a serious issue because not only could the recipient be unable to repay the aid but it may be called upon to do so with interest and at a very inconvenient time. It is also a concern for those who buy ports or shipping companies because they may find that the business which they have just bought has been the beneficiary of illegal State aid and the entity must therefore repay this aid. This is a form of "black hole" which can be hugely problematical for a purchaser of such a business. There is a growing willingness on the part of shipping companies and ports to consider complaints about alleged State aid in ports and this phenomenon is likely to grow rather than retreat.

15.082 State aid can be an issue at various levels within a port. For example, there may be State aid issues with aid being provided (directly or indirectly): (a) to the port itself by the State; (b) to the user of a port; or (c) a service provider in a port.

15.083 State aid could arise in the context of the provision, expansion and financing of port infrastructure. For example, a port may be unable or unwilling (more likely the former) to fund investment in a new facility and turns to the Member State for assistance. Such assistance, if provided, could constitute illegal State aid.

15.084 The issue can also arise in the case of the sale or purchase of land and buildings. For example, if a Member State were to provide land to a port at significantly less than market value then the "gap" could well constitute State aid.[93]

15.085 It may be useful to draw a distinction between various types of infrastructure in ports – it can be classified in different ways. First, there is general infrastructure and specific infrastructure: the former is open to everyone while the latter is open to specific entities. The latter (i.e. specific infrastructure) is more likely to cause State aid concerns. Second, there is so-called access infrastructure and port infrastructure with the former involving the underlying infrastructure that ports need (e.g. breakwaters and locks) while the latter involve operational facilities for port users exploiting the commercial features of the port (e.g. yards and warehouses). Third, there is user specific infrastructure which would include port superstructure, yards and works to enable construction to occur. Finally, there can be expenditure leading to fixed or movable assets (e.g. buildings and cranes respectively).

15.086 State aid is not just an issue for ports in the context of infrastructure, it is also relevant in the context of services such as towage, warehousing and so on.

15.087 More broadly, given the constructive and deconstructive roles of State aid, the issue is one of critical concern for the development of port policy generally.[94] Some development may be impossible without State aid. If port development is to be undertaken in a competitive and co-ordinated manner then the position on State aid must be clear and the rules implemented fairly and consistently.

---

93 E.g. a port needs extra land to expand (e.g. a new terminal for new or expanded operations or to convert land into a marshalling yard for storage of containers for a particular shipping company) and this land is then provided by the State (e.g. through a local council) at a reduced cost (or even for free) to the port company. (The other conditions of State aid (discussed below) must be satisfied for it to constitute State aid.)

94 On evolving EC port policy, see Commission Staff Working Document: Accompanying document to Communication on a European Ports Policy Full Impact Assessment (COM(2007) 616 final) (SEC(2007) 1340).

15.088 A non-exhaustive list[95] of examples of such transfers from Member State resources include: subsidies;[96] grants; tax/fiscal rebates and reliefs; rent holidays and reductions where the State is the landlord or providing the financial intervention; debt write-offs where the State is the lender or funding the write-off; interest rate subsidies where the State is the lender or funding the subsidy; provision of services by the Member State at preferential or discounted rates; subsidised services or goods; rescue aid; guarantees which would not be commercially justified; capital injection;[97] sale or provision by the State of land and buildings at less than market value; and purchase by the State of land and buildings at more than market value.

15.089 It will be recalled that Article 107(1) of the TFEU refers to the aid being "in any form whatsoever" and this is an elastic concept. A recent example from the port sector illustrates the point very clearly. The Port of Tallinn Ltd decided to invest €116 million in a harbour extension in the port of Muuga which would consist of new infrastructure. The Commission reviewed the matter[98] and decided that the investment was not State aid because, in the Commission's words:

> "[s]ince this investment is financed by Port of Tallinn, which will own and operate the new infrastructure, through its own revenues or through resources found by this company on the markets without State intervention, the Commission has come to the conclusion that this investment does not involve any transfer of State resources and hence any State aid to Port of Tallinn Ltd."[99]

Therefore, the investment simply fell outside the scope of the State aid rules because State resources were not being transferred to the recipient. It is possible that money does not have to be transferred because the mere fact that a company has a credit line made available to it may be sufficient for State aid to exist.[100] This is why guarantees, without drawdown, raise State aid issues.

15.090 To constitute State aid, the recipient must be engaged in economic activities in the context of the assistance provided. In this context, an undertaking is any entity engaged in economic or commercial activities. It usually causes little difficulty in the port sector as most ports involve economic or commercial activities (whether or not they are profitable). One should assume that a port is an undertaking with the exception of, for example, naval ports. However, it is possible that a port might not be an undertaking in respect of a particular function (i.e. engaged in a non-commercial/non-economic one) in a particular context and therefore it is possible that some forms of assistance may be outside the scope of the State aid rules where the port is operating in the context of the assistance as a non-undertaking. The 2007 State aid case involving the Port of Rotterdam is instructive in this regard; the Commission stated:

---

95 The absence of a definition in the EC Treaty means that there is no finite or definite list of what is meant by the term "State aid". See Quigley, "The Notion of a State Aid in the EEC" (1988) 13 ELRev 242.

96 While subsidies are aids; see Case 30/59 *De Gezamenlijke Steenkolenmijnes in Limburg v High Authority* [1961] ECR 1 of 19 and Case C-387/92 *Banco de Crédito Industrial SA (now Banco Exterior de España SA) v Ayuntamiento de Valencia* [1994] ECR I-877.

97 Case 84/92 *Germany v Commission* [1984] ECR 1451 and Cases 296 and 318/82 *Netherlands and Leeuwarder Papierwarenfabriek v Commission* [1985] ECR 809.

98 Commission Press Release IP/07/152, 7 February 2007.

99 Ibid.

100 *France Telecom*, 2 August 2004.

"[t]he Dutch State will contribute to the construction of infrastructures that cannot be commercially exploited (the construction of a sea wall, the prolongation and widening of the existing maritime access route and the creation of infrastructure bundles such as rail tracks, roads, piping and conduit). This State contribution does not concern investments in port facilities which may generate revenues for the Port Authority (e.g. charging commercial fees for the use of facilities, receiving rent for new terminals, etc.) ... Therefore, the Commission has concluded that this measure does not constitute State aid."[101]

This case tends to indicate that charging "commercial fees" (and not just fees) is a relevant criterion. Similarly, in *Flemish Ports*,[102] the Commission held that the financing for construction and maintenance works in maritime access routes to Antwerp, Bruges-Zeebrugge and Ostend as well as for sealocks and internal access routes was not State aid because ensuring access was not an economic activity liable to distort competition; instead, the Commission saw it as a public task in the general interest.

15.091 In order to be State aid, the assistance must favour certain undertakings or the production of certain goods or services.[103] In other words, there must be an element of *selectivity* with the recipients being favoured over others in a comparable context. By contrast, a measure of general application is not selective and therefore not State aid. For example, a universal reduction in corporate tax rates by 5% would be a measure of general application (and not State aid) but a reduction for seaport companies only or port companies established in a particular region of a State would be selective and could therefore be a State aid where all the other conditions are satisfied. The aid must favour certain undertakings or the production of goods or services. This means that if the benefit is available to all then it is not selective and therefore not State aid. However, if there is selectivity then one of the conditions for State aid is satisfied. There is no State aid being provided to end users where the facility or infrastructure is provided to all on a non-discriminatory basis. That is to say, if all users are benefiting then there is no difficulty under State aid law. Conversely, if infrastructure is built or developed for the benefit of one particular shipowner or user of the port then that is user specific infrastructure and the element of selectivity is satisfied.

15.092 If assistance is to constitute State aid then it must distort or threaten to distort competition. In practice, this criterion is easily satisfied as it is in the context of Articles 101 and 102 of the TFEU.

15.093 As has been stated above, the State aid rules are designed to prevent Member States misusing their enormous power and financial muscle in the marketplace. So, if a Member State acts in the same way that a market economy investor (i.e. a private commercial operator) would do then, it follows logically, that what the Member State does should not be seen as State aid. This welcome and realistic view finds expression in the so-called "Market Economy Investor Principle" ("MEIP"). This principle posits that the behaviour of the Member State must be compared with that of the hypothetical private (or market economy) investor. It is a test which is easy to describe but sometimes difficult to apply in practice. If the benefit is not one which would be provided by a market economy investor then it is State aid. The test can be modified depending on the circumstances

---

101 Rotterdam IP/07/555, 24 April 2007.
102 IP/04/1267, 20 October 2004.
103 See Commission Notice on the Application of the State Aid Rules to Direct Taxation OJ 1998 C384/3. See also *R v Customs & Excise ex parte Lunn Poly* [1999] 1 CMLR 1337.

such that one may have to have regard to the private supplier (in the case of goods or services being supplied) or the private creditor (in the case of credit or guarantees being supplied). A very good example of a Member State acting as a private investor would be that of the Dutch State in terms of its increased investment in the port of Rotterdam[104] so as to assist in the further development of the port: the Commission stated in its 2007 decision:

> "[a]s for the purchase of new shares, the Dutch State is paying a market price for them and would like to share in the income generated by the port of Rotterdam. The Commission has found that the decision is motivated and guided by the prospects of profitability. Thus the Dutch State acts like a private investor and therefore, the purchase of shares cannot be considered as a State aid either."[105]

15.094 It is also useful before continuing to examine the application of State aid to ports to recall the *Altmark* criteria set out above. Having set out the general rules, it is useful to consider some of the exceptions. If a port is an undertaking then clearly Article 107 applies. However, Article 106 may also apply to ports. If a port is a public authority and not a commercial undertaking for the purposes involved then there is no State aid involved. If the assistance involved is below the financial levels set out in the *de minimis* rules then the assistance would not constitute State aid but the *de minimis* rules are such that such investments would not be commercially significant because they would be of such a small scale. It is widely assumed that if the assistance is the result of a tender procedure then the assistance would not constitute State aid but this general principle requires careful scrutiny in practice. The *Altmark* principles, which are to be read in the context of Article 106 have been considered above.

Some practical issues in the application of the state aid rules in the context of ports

Introduction

15.095 Having considered the "bones" in terms of the rules, it is useful to now put "flesh" on those bones by applying the legal rules identified above to seaports and the type of situations which can cause difficulties for ports and those who use them. Before examining some specific issues, it is worth recalling that the EU is keen to promote the EU maritime sector and recognises that the EU maritime sector faces strong competition from the rest of the world with ports being part of that competitive equation.[106] As the Commission recalled in 2001,[107] when referring to the Commission's 1997 Green Paper

---

104 The investment would be in the Port of Rotterdam Authority (i.e. Havenbedrijf Rotterdam) which is a company under private law of which the municipality of Rotterdam is currently a 100% shareholder (according to the Commission's press release on the case).
105 Rotterdam IP/07/555, 24 April 2007.
106 The Commission's communication, "Community Guidelines on State Aid to Maritime Transport" (2004/C 13/03) puts the issue into context: "[the Commission's] White Paper 'European transport policy for 2010: time to decide' stresses the vital importance of maritime transport services for the Community economy. 90% of all trade between the Community and the rest of the world is transported by sea. Short sea shipping accounts for 69% of the volume of goods transported between the Member States (this percentage is 41% if domestic transport is included). Community maritime transport and its related activities remains one of the most important in the world."
107 Commission staff working document on public financing and charging practices in the Community sea port sector, SEC(2001) 234, p. 3.

on Seaports and Maritime Infrastructure,[108] "[t]he efficient functioning of ports as part of the door-to-door intermodal chain is an essential pre-requisite to stimulate the development of maritime transport, in particular as a sustainable alternative to land transport". There is often a distinction which can be made between port *infrastructure* and port *superstructure*. Infrastructure can be general or user-specific. Superstructure relates to items such as mobile assets and operational services.

Market definition

15.096 While it is usually not a difficult issue in the context of State aid and ports, it is worth considering very briefly the issue of market definition. It is an integral and essential part of understanding whether the assistance breaches the State aid rules. It will be recalled that there must be an effect on competition before the assistance is illegal, this means that the "theatre of competition" in which the assistance is to operate must be examined. For example, aid within the port of Marseilles is probably not going to affect competition in Gothenburg but there are circumstances where it could and therefore that analysis is needed.

Is a port an "undertaking" under Article 107?

15.097 In general, ports are undertakings. Ports, when engaged in economic activities, are undertakings so that element of the several tests for the application of Article 107 is met. However, when seaports are acting as "public authorities" (i.e. not engaged in economic activities) then they are not undertakings and the State aid rules do not apply. The difficulty is in striking the right balance and delineating between the two (i.e. the port as *undertaking* and the port as *public authority*). Seaports are probably not undertakings when they are engaged in public-type functions such as police, pollution, customs, safety, security and other similar matters but they are certainly undertakings when they are engaged in profit-making activities. In some ways, the test is whether they are acting in a commercial capacity or a regulatory one.

15.098 The *Rotterdam* port case illustrates the point well when one contrasts the Netherlands engaging in a public service type activity (i.e. building non-profit-making activities but staying away from profit-making activities and leaving that to the commercial port company:

"[the] Dutch State will contribute to the construction of infrastructures that cannot be commercially exploited (the construction of a sea wall, the prolongation and widening of the existing maritime access route and the creation of infrastructure bundles such as rail tracks, roads, piping and conduit). This State contribution does not concern investments in port facilities which may generate revenues for the Port Authority (e.g. charging commercial fees for the use of facilities, receiving rent for new terminals, etc.). ... Therefore, the Commission has concluded that this measure does not constitute State aid."[109]

---

108 COM (1997) 678 Final, 10 December 1997.
109 Rotterdam IP/07/555, 24 April 2007.

By confining itself to the non-profit-making activities (which might still be commercial – a seawall is not built for decorative purposes!), the Member State avoids State aid issues arising.

15.099 On 10 July 2007, the Commission announced that it decided to approve a local real estate tax exemption, worth €520,000 to benefit Polish port management entities for their non-commercial activities (in particular, the construction, extension, maintenance and upgrading of infrastructure ensuring access to the port and the publicly accessible port infrastructure).[110] The Commission believed that the non-commercially exploitable parts of the Polish ports' activities that would benefit from the measure were not liable to distort competition. Therefore, the State aid rules are largely irrelevant in the non-commercial space in which a port operates. The difficulty however remains in trying to establish what is or is not commercial.

Sale of land to ports and the purchase of land for ports

15.100 The Commission has published a communication on State aid elements in sale of land and buildings by public authorities.[111] While not written for the port sector specifically, it is relevant whenever there is a transfer of land or facilities whether at a port or not.

15.101 Ports need to be careful where they receive from the State any land or building at less than fair market value or they are paid more than fair market value for land or buildings which they sell or lease to the State. The 2007 State aid case involving Rotterdam is instructive in this regard; the Commission stated: "the Port Authority is going to pay a market price for the lease of the grounds on which the port will be extended. Therefore, the Commission has concluded that this measure does not constitute State aid."[112]

15.102 Shipping companies which use ports also need to ensure that property is changing hands at fair market value otherwise they may suffer by having to repay aid at a later stage.

15.103 There is no State aid where there is either: (a) open or unconditional bidding procedure; or (b) an independent valuation to establish the price and there is no greater variation than 5%.

15.104 Shipping companies have to be careful when they are being offered port offices because the provision of offices (however small) at ports can, in some cases, require review under the State aid rules.[113]

Construction of infrastructure which would be open to all equally

15.105 The financing of infrastructural work which is open to all potential users on equal and non-discriminatory terms does not involve State aid. Therefore, investment in open roads and railroads to ports, open infrastructure as well as open facilities does not usually constitute State aid. Put another way, State aid is not an issue if infrastructure is

---

110 IP/07/1049, 10 July 2007.
111 OJ 1997 C209.
112 Rotterdam IP/07/555, 24 April 2007.
113 E.g. the provision of, *inter alia,* offices at Charleroi Airport to an airline operating there required State aid review and analysis.

constructed and is open to all on a non-restricted basis. Equally, it is not an issue if the infrastructure is made available at a price which is the result of a fair and free tender or competition. Tenders should be well publicised, open and bidding must be unconditional.

Construction of infrastructure which would be user-specific/selective

15.106 If infrastructure was constructed using what would otherwise be State aid then it would be illegal State aid where the infrastructure was constructed for a specific user because there would be the element of selectivity. For example, if a particular type of port facility (e.g. a facility to store grain or paper) was constructed for a particular shipping company then, assuming all the other conditions were satisfied, that would constitute State aid. There are areas which have not yet been considered fully such as where a facility has an existing operator and it is being expanded for the benefit of the existing user but others would be allowed to use the facility subject to the grandfather rights of the pre-existing user. In that scenario, it is the grandfather rights which could constitute the element of selectivity but, on the other hand, it would seem harsh to prevent expansion; perhaps, the solution to this conundrum is to use the MEIP as the test on whether the investment is State aid or not.

Construction of facilities with significant state funding

15.107 It is useful to keep the amount of State funding as low as possible as a proportion of the total cost.[114] The higher the proportion then the more likely it is to be more of an issue under State aid law. This is another context where the MEIP is helpful.

Construction of facilities which would be available on a priority basis for one operator

15.108 This is where it is difficult to be precise in the absence of other factors. However, it is possible (but not inevitable) that priority use may constitute sufficient selectivity for that element of the requirements of State aid to be satisfied. Each case will turn on its own facts. So, for example, if a new ferry port ramp or linkspan was built for use by a long-established and heavy user of the port which would take "grandfather" rights then it may not be such an issue if the same facility was open to others to use throughout the rest of the day.

What if security measures at a port are paid for by the state?

15.109 The Commission announced on 3 August 2006 that it believes that the financing of maritime security measures imposed by law is generally not State aid.[115] The challenge is to ensure that the financial assistance does not go beyond the security measures because otherwise the surplus would be aid.

---

114 Freight Facilities Grant *N649/2001* and *Flemish Ports*, op. cit. at fn. 86.
115 Commission Report, COM(2006) 431 final and Commission IP/06/1086.

Mergers and acquisitions

15.110 Anyone involved in a merger or acquisition of a port ought to check the State aid dimensions. First, one should check whether the port has been in receipt of State aid, whether it was notified and, if not, whether it should be now notified. Second, one should check whether there is any State aid element to the transaction itself such as where the purchase price has been reduced by an inducement or payment of some sort.

Operation of a "public service" between ports

15.111 Ports sometimes fund or have a service to and from their ports which is not commercially viable but which needs to be subsidised in some way because there is a value to having such service. This type of issue falls outside the scope of this chapter but there are situations where aid can be provided lawfully by virtue of Article 106(2) but the circumstances are limited.[116]

What if a Member State never notifies the European Commission of the aid?

15.112 A practical problem for ports, port users as well as financiers, vendors and buyers of ports (and indeed their counterparts across the economy) is where a Member State provides assistance which may or may not be State aid but which the Member State in question chooses not to notify the Commission about. This puts the recipient in a perilous position. It cannot have the aid authorised because only Member States may notify it. It cannot realistically contact the Commission about it and thereby cause difficulties for its relationship with the Member State.[117] It is the child in the custody battle between the Commission and the Member States with neither parent talking to each other. There is therefore merit in providing a double lock or safety valve in enabling recipients to notify aid. While the proposal would enhance the efficacy of the system quite considerably, it is difficult to see Member States agreeing to a change in the Treaty which could expose their wrongdoing by failing to notify.

What are the principles which can be discerned from the Commission's analysis of port cases?

15.113 There are fewer seaport cases than airport cases but the principles may be transferable at least in part. The cases are very diverse. For example in regard to Klaipėda in Lithuania, the Commission authorised State aid totalling €49.2 million in respect of the construction of the passenger and cargo ferries terminal but there had been eight requests for information from the Commission and the process took 22 months. In regard to Katakolo in Greece, the Commission approved aid for an infrastructure project but it took only six months, the aid level was €11,190,240 with five requests for information. The project

---

116 See Comm. Dec. of 28 November 2005 on the application of Art. 86(2) of the EC Treaty to State aid in the form of public service compensation granted to certain undertakings entrusted with the operation of services of general economic interest (2005/842) OJ L312/7, 29 November 2005, pp. 67–73.

117 It should be noted however that the European Court of Justice ("ECJ") has said that recipients must, in some circumstances, act as a diligent recipient and contact the Commission in similar circumstances.

was to enhance the docking facilities for cruise vessels and to improve safety at the port and enable new generational longer vessels to be accommodated. In regard to the threshold question of is there State aid? Recital 34 in the Port of Katakolo case is instructive:

> "in order to conclude on whether state aid is present, it must therefore be assessed whether the cumulative criteria listed in Article 107(1) TFEU (i.e. transfer of State resources, selective advantage, potential distortion of competition and effect on intra-EU trade) are met for each of the measures identified"

and the Commission found that there was State aid being provided. By contrast, the Commission held in the *Great Yarmouth Outer Harbour* case that the financing of parts of the development of the outer harbour did not involve State aid because the works did not involve State aid – as Recital 23 of the decision stated:

> "As far as maritime infrastructure is concerned, the practice and policy of the Commission has been to consider that public investments in maritime access routes (breakwaters, locks, navigable channels, dredging, etc.), and other maritime infrastructure that benefit the maritime community as a whole do not normally give rise to issues of state aid concern."

15.114 A number of principles flow from the infrastructure port cases. In practice, one must establish: (a) the involvement of an undertaking;[118] (b) whether the infrastructure is general or project-specific – activities that fall under State responsibility in the exercise of its powers as a public authority are not of an economic nature and do not fall within the scope of the State aid rules; and (c) whether Member State resources are involved and whether the resources deployed could be imputed to the Member State. The aid must flow from a Member State. If it flows entirely from a private source then it is not State aid. If it flowed from a third country then it is not State aid. But what if it flows, indirectly, from EU funds? The Commission stated very succinctly in the *Katakolo Port* case:

> "(44) ... this project shall be financed partly though public resources, up to the total amount of EUR 11,190,240. The [European Regional Development Fund ("ERDF")] resources that shall be made available for co-financing this project are placed at the disposal of the Greek authorities, and in particular the relevant Managing Authority. Therefore, they amount to State resources.
> (45) As regards imputability to the State of the public financing, ... it is noted that the Greek authorities enjoy a high degree of control in the selection at national level of the projects of this nature to be financed. The notified funding for this project was directly chosen by, and is therefore imputable to the Greek State."

A similar statement was made in the Port of Bahía de Cadiz case.

Conclusions

15.115 The law on this area is still developing and is not entirely clear in so far as it has developed. Ports and users of ports need to be more careful and more aware of the rules than they have been up to now. While some schemes and investments are being

---

[118] This criterion is satisfied easily in this context. As the CJEU has stated in various cases such as *Hofner and Elsner*, *Poucet* and *Pistre v AGF*, whenever an entity is engaged in an economic activity then it is an undertaking regardless of how it is financed. The General Court expanded on the point in Leipzig-Halle where it stated that the construction of an infrastructure which will be exploited commercially amounts to an economic activity. This is all the more so in the case of commercial ports.

notified, one cannot help but believe that they are in the minority. One anticipates that the growing number of complaints in the port sector should lead to greater clarification of the rules. The Treaty rules on State aid are expressly succinct and almost simple but this means that there is a certain vagueness about them and a lack of precision for those who have to apply them and comply with them. The Commission could assist the port community by regularly updating its vade mecum and providing guidelines. The establishment of useful guidelines is always difficult because of various factors including the different ways in which ports are financed, the divergence of approaches to port financing in Member States caused by the variety of port management models, the fact that the Commission can be hindered in its later freedom of action if it adopts guidelines, as well as the differences in accounting procedures and financing methods. In any event, the views of the Commission are, with respect, the views of the institution charged with administering the rules and one may find that like all comparable agencies, they do not always get the rules right according to the judicial review and political reform which are always possible. The vagueness of the law means that the GBER is very welcome.

J. GENERAL BLOCK EXEMPTION REGULATION

15.116 On 24 May 2017, the Commission adopted Commission Regulation (EU) 2017/1084 of 14 June 2017 amending Regulation (EU) 651/2014 as regards aid for port and airport infrastructure, notification thresholds for aid for culture and heritage conservation and for aid for sport and multifunctional recreational infrastructures, and regional operating aid schemes for outermost regions and amending Regulation (EU) 702/2014 as regards the calculation of eligible costs which simplified the rules for investment in, among other causes, ports and the outermost regions of the EU.[119] The net effect was that Commission approval, under the State aid rules, was no longer necessary for investments within the scope of the amending measure thereby facilitating investment.

15.117 Many investment projects do not cause problems from a State aid perspective (e.g. because there is no State aid or any State aid does not distort competition) so it was sensible to give a blanket authorisation for many investments without the need to bother the Commission.

15.118 A key part of the 2017 GBER amendment related to ports and was justified because the Commission had taken more than 30 State aid decisions on ports giving the Commission an insight on how such investments could be reviewed and permitted. The 2017 GBER helps reduce administrative burden and complication for businesses such as ports.

15.119 In case of ports, the 2017 GBER now exempts investments by Member States of up to €150 million in seaports and up to €50 million in inland ports. This includes dredging costs that certain ports need to incur to keep the waterway deep enough for ships to dock. For ports these costs are non-negotiable because of their geography, regardless of how efficient and competitive the ports are in practice.

15.120 The GBER contains many definitions and some of those relate to ports:

---

119 OJ L156/1, 20 June 2017.

"Definitions for Aid for ports

(154) 'port' means an area of land and water made up of such infrastructure and equipment, so as to permit the reception of waterborne vessels, their loading and unloading, the storage of goods, the receipt and delivery of those goods and the embarkation and disembarkation of passengers, crew and other persons and any other infrastructure necessary for transport operators in the port;
(155) 'maritime port' means a port for, principally, the reception of sea-going vessels;
(156) 'inland port' means a port other than a maritime port, for the reception of inland waterway vessels;
(157) 'port infrastructure' means infrastructure and facilities for the provision of transport related port services, for example berths used for the mooring of ships, quay walls, jetties and floating pontoon ramps in tidal areas, internal basins, backfills and land reclamation, alternative fuel infrastructure and infrastructure for the collection of ship-generated waste and cargo residues;
(158) 'port superstructure' means surface arrangements (such as for storage), fixed equipment (such as warehouses and terminal buildings) as well as mobile equipment (such as cranes) located in a port for the provision of transport related port services;
(159) 'access infrastructure' means any type of infrastructure necessary to ensure access and entry from land or sea and river by users to a port, or in a port, such as roads, rail tracks, channels and locks;
(160) 'dredging' means the removal of sediments from the bottom of the waterway access to a port, or in a port;
(161) 'alternative fuel infrastructure' means a fixed, mobile or offshore port infrastructure allowing a port to supply vessels with energy sources such as electricity, hydrogen, biofuels as defined in point (i) of Article 2 of Directive 2009/28/EC, synthetic and paraffinic fuels, natural gas, including biomethane, in gaseous form (compressed natural gas (CNG)) and liquefied form (liquefied natural gas (LNG)), and liquefied petroleum gas (LPG) which serve, at least partly, as a substitute for fossil oil sources in the energy supply to transport and which have the potential to contribute to its decarbonisation and enhance the environmental performance of the transport sector;
(162) 'vessels' mean floating structures, whether self-propelled or not, with one or more surface displacement hulls;
(163) 'sea-going vessels' mean vessels other than those which navigate solely or mainly in inland waterways or in waters within, or closely adjacent to, sheltered waters;
(164) 'inland waterway vessels' mean vessels intended solely or mainly for navigation on inland waterways or in waters within, or closely adjacent to, sheltered waters;
(165) 'infrastructure for the collection of ship-generated waste and cargo residues' means fixed, floating or mobile port facilities capable of receiving ship-generated waste or cargo residues as defined in Directive 2000/59/EC of the European Parliament and of the Council."

15.121 The detail is set out in Section 15 ("Aid for ports") in the GBER:

"*Aid for ports*
Article 56b
Aid for maritime ports
1. Aid for maritime ports shall be compatible with the internal market within the meaning of Article 107(3) of the Treaty and shall be exempted from the notification requirement of Article 108(3) of the Treaty, provided that the conditions laid down in this Article and in Chapter I are fulfilled.
2. The eligible costs shall be the costs, including planning costs, of:

   (a) investments for the construction, replacement or upgrade of port infrastructures;
   (b) investments for the construction, replacement or upgrade of access infrastructure;
   (c) dredging.

3. Costs relating to non-transport related activities, including industrial production facilities active in a port, offices or shops, as well as for port superstructures shall not be eligible costs.
4. The aid amount shall not exceed the difference between the eligible costs and the operating profit of the investment or dredging. The operating profit shall be deducted from the eligible costs ex ante, on the basis of reasonable projections, or through a claw-back mechanism.
5. The aid intensity per investment referred to in point (a) of paragraph 2 shall not exceed:

   (a) 100% of the eligible costs where total eligible costs of the project are up to EUR 20 million;
   (b) 80% of the eligible costs where total eligible costs of the project are above EUR 20 million and up to EUR 50 million;
   (c) 60% of the eligible costs where total eligible costs of the project are above EUR 50 million and up to the amount laid down in point (ee) of Article 4(1).

   The aid intensity shall not exceed 100% of the eligible costs determined in point (b) of paragraph 2 and point (c) of paragraph 2 up to the amount laid down in point (ee) of Article 4(1).
6. The aid intensities laid down in points (b) and (c) of the first subparagraph of paragraph 5 may be increased by 10 percentage points for investments located in assisted areas fulfilling the conditions of point (a) of Article 107(3) of the Treaty and by 5 percentage points for investments located in assisted areas fulfilling the conditions of point (c) of Article 107(3) of the Treaty.
7. Any concession or other entrustment to a third party to construct, upgrade, operate or rent aided port infrastructure shall be assigned on a competitive, transparent, non-discriminatory and unconditional basis.
8. The aided port infrastructure shall be made available to interested users on an equal and non-discriminatory basis on market terms.
9. For aid not exceeding EUR 5 million, the maximum amount of aid may be set at 80% of eligible costs, as an alternative to application of the method referred to in paragraphs 4, 5 and 6.

Article 56c
Aid for inland ports
1. Aid for inland ports shall be compatible with the internal market within the meaning of Article 107(3) of the Treaty and shall be exempted from the notification requirement of Article 108(3) of the Treaty, provided that the conditions laid down in this Article and in Chapter I are fulfilled.
2. The eligible costs shall be the costs, including planning costs, of:

   (a) investments for the construction, replacement or upgrade of port infrastructures;
   (b) investments for the construction, replacement or upgrade of access infrastructure;
   (c) dredging.

3. Costs relating to non-transport related activities, including industrial production facilities active in a port, offices or shops, as well as for port superstructures shall not be eligible costs.
4. The aid amount shall not exceed the difference between the eligible costs and the operating profit of the investment or dredging. The operating profit shall be deducted from the eligible costs ex ante, on the basis of reasonable projections, or through a claw-back mechanism.
5. The maximum aid intensity shall not exceed 100% of the eligible costs up to the amount laid down in point (ff) of Article 4(1).
6. Any concession or other entrustment to a third party to construct, upgrade, operate or rent aided port infrastructure shall be assigned on a competitive, transparent, non-discriminatory and unconditional basis.
7. The aided port infrastructure shall be made available to interested users on an equal and non-discriminatory basis on market terms.

8. For aid not exceeding EUR 2 million, the maximum amount of aid may be set at 80% of eligible costs, as an alternative to application of the method referred to in paragraphs 4 and 5."

K. TONNAGE TAX

15.122 In 2017, when the Commission approved the Maltese Tonnage Tax Scheme, Competition Commissioner Margrethe Vestager said

"tonnage tax systems are meant to promote the competitiveness of the EU shipping industry in a global market without unduly distorting competition. ... Moreover, by encouraging the registration of ships in the EU, the scheme will enable the European shipping industry to keep up its high social and environmental standards."[120]

The Commission's tonnage tax regime is designed to "encourage ship registration in Europe".[121]

15.123 There have been a number of cases where the Commission has approved tonnage tax regimes. They are very comparable (e.g. in 2016, the Commission approved the Swedish tonnage tax scheme[122] and in 2017, the Commission approved the Lithuanian tonnage tax scheme[123]) so it is proposed to take one sample decision as an illustrative example. The example relates to the tonnage tax scheme and other State measures in favour of shipping companies in Malta. On 19 December 2017, the Commission approved under the State aid rules, but subject to commitments, Malta's tonnage tax scheme and other State measures in favour of shipping companies in Malta.[124] The scheme will last for a period of ten years. It is worth noting that the Commission's in-depth investigation took five years. The commitments were designed to, in the words of the Commission's press release, "ensure a level playing field between Maltese and other European shipping companies, and will encourage ship registration in Europe".[125] The in-depth investigation found various features of the original scheme (e.g. tax exemptions applied to Maltese residents and the broad scope of the scheme extending to vessels not carrying out maritime transport activities) would have breached EU State aid law. So as to secure Commission approval, Malta made various commitments. Malta committed to introduce a number of changes to its scheme to: (a) prevent any discrimination between shipping companies; (b) avoid undue competition distortions; (c) restrict the scope of the scheme to maritime transport; and (d) to remove those tax exemptions for shareholders which constitute State aid. Under the scheme, a shipping company is taxed on the basis of ship net tonnage (i.e. based on its volume) rather than the actual profits of the company. The tonnage taxation is applied to a shipping company's: (a) core revenues from shipping activities, such as cargo and passenger transport; (b) certain ancillary revenues that are closely connected to shipping activities (which are, however, capped at a maximum of 50% of a ship's operating revenues); and (c) revenues from towage and dredging subject to certain conditions. For a shipping company that wants to benefit from the Maltese scheme, a significant part of its fleet must fly the flag of an EEA Member State. Moreover, any new entrant to the

---

120 IP/17/2181.
121 IP/17/2181.
122 SA.43642.
123 SA.45764, http://ec.europa.eu/competition/elojade/isef/case_details.cfm?proc_code=3_SA_45764.
124 SA.33829, IP/17/5361.
125 IP/17/2181.

scheme must have at least 25% of its fleet subject to tonnage tax with an EEA flag. The Commission believed that the amended scheme was aimed at addressing global competition and would "provide the right incentives to maintain maritime jobs within the EU, whilst preserving competition within the EU Single Market".[126] The Commission recalled the background:

> "To address the risk of flagging out and relocating of shipping companies to low-tax countries outside of the EU, the Commission's 2004 Guidelines on State aid to maritime transport allow Member States to adopt measures that improve the fiscal climate for shipping companies. One of the most important measures is tonnage tax, whereby shipping companies can apply to be taxed based on a notional profit or the tonnage they operate, instead of being taxed under the normal corporate tax system. Only companies that are active in maritime transport are eligible for such measures under the Maritime Guidelines. Shareholders in shipping companies are excluded from preferential tax treatment.
>
> Since 2004, the Commission's decision-making practice under the Maritime Guidelines has further clarified the eligible transport activities and compatibility conditions to ensure that the main objectives of the Maritime Guidelines are met. The Commission has to ensure that there are no spill-over of the favourable tax treatment of shipping companies into other sectors unrelated to maritime transport and there is no discrimination of other EEA State registries and flags."[127]

L. SHIPPING SECTOR

15.124 On 6 November 2017, the European Commission approved, under the EU's State aid rules,[128] various Belgian tax measures designed to assist the maritime transport sector.[129] In essence, the Commission approved, under the EU State aid rules, the prolongation until the end of 2022 of various Belgian support measures for maritime transport including measures to encourage shipping companies to register their ships in the EU and to ensure higher social, environmental and safety standards. As part of the approval process, Belgium committed to a number of changes to its scheme to prevent any discrimination between shipping companies and registries of different EEA States and to avoid undue competition distortions. This was because the European Commission (as guardian of the EU treaties) must ensure that there is no discrimination between nationals of the EU/EEA. Under the approved Belgian scheme, a shipping company is taxed on the basis of ship tonnage (i.e. based on size of shipping fleet) rather than the actual profits of the company – this is the so-called "tonnage tax" concept which is now used by several States. In particular, tonnage taxation will be applied to a shipping company's

- core revenues from shipping activities, such as cargo and passenger transport;
- certain ancillary revenues that are closely connected to shipping activities (which are now capped at a maximum of 50% of a ship's operating revenues); and
- revenues from towage and dredging as well as onshore ship management activities, subject to certain conditions.

---

126 IP/17/2181.
127 IP/17/5361.
128 These rules are principally contained in Arts 107–109 of the TFEU as supplemented by various measures adopted (principally) by the European Commission and as construed by the CJEU.
129 Case number SA.41330. See the European Commission's Press Release IP/17/4382, http://europa.eu/rapid/press-release_IP-17-4382_en.htm. The Commission's decision has *not yet been* published but will be published in due course and will be worth careful analysis.

The Belgian scheme requires that if a shipping company wants to benefit from the scheme, a significant part of its fleet flies the flag of an EU or EEA State (and not just Belgium). In this regard, Belgium has committed to extend the benefit of tonnage tax to all eligible ships that fly an EEA flag. This will prevent any discrimination between shipping companies and registries of different EEA States and preserve internal market rules on freedom of establishment.

In its press release, the Commission stated that it had assessed the amended measures under EU State aid rules, in particular its 2004 Guidelines on State aid to Maritime Transport.[130] The Commission concluded that the Belgian scheme is in line with EU State aid rules, because it will provide incentives to maintain maritime jobs within the EU, while preserving competition within the EU's Single Market. More specifically, it will encourage shipping companies to register their ships in Europe and thus commit to high social, environmental and safety standards.

This decision prolongs the earlier European Commission decision to approve the Belgian tax measures in favour of maritime transport until 31 December 2012 in State aid case C20/2003.[131] It also follows a line of recent decisions including the Swedish tonnage tax scheme (Case SA.43642),[132] a German scheme for the reduction of social contributions for seafarers (Case SA.45258)[133] and the Lithuanian tonnage tax scheme (Case SA.45764).[134]

In general, the European Commission has been favourably disposed towards Member States' State aid schemes which help promote the maritime sector in the EU/EEA provided such schemes operate on a non-discriminatory basis.

M. SEAFARERS

15.125 It is not proposed to repeat the commentary of earlier sections as they relate to seafarers; suffice it to say, that regard should be had to the earlier sections generally as they relate to seafarers. This section will comment on a few specific developments in regard to State aid and seafarers.

15.126 In November 2016, the Commission approved the German scheme for the reduction of social contributions for seafarers.[135] It is worth recalling three paragraphs:

"(13) The aid is granted in the form of a non-repayable grant for the reduction of social security contributions and is determined per vessel on the basis of the seafarers who are covered by the scope of the present scheme. The grant is the sum of the employer's mandatory contributions to the German social security system.

(14) The aid will cover a maximum of 50% of the social contributions, corresponding to the employer's liability for payment of those contributions. The aid may exceptionally cover 100% of the contributions regarding accident insurance, as the employer is liable to

---

130 The 2004 Guidelines were entitled the "Community Guidelines on State Aid to Maritime Transport" (see OJ C13/3, 17 January 2004 and http://eur-lex.europa.eu/legal-content/EN/ALL/?uri=CELEX:52004XC0117(01)). The 2004 Guidelines were recently updated (see OJ C120/10, 13 April 2017 and http://eur-lex.europa.eu/legal-content/EN/TXT/?uri=uriserv:OJ.C_.2017.120.01.0010.01.ENG&toc=OJ:C:2017:120:TOC).
131 See OJ L150/1, 10 June 2005.
132 See http://ec.europa.eu/competition/state_aid/cases/261398/261398_1830463_166_2.pdf.
133 See http://ec.europa.eu/competition/state_aid/cases/264071/264071_1847335_61_2.pdf.
134 See http://ec.europa.eu/competition/state_aid/cases/264914/264914_1905495_72_2.pdf.
135 SA.45258, http://ec.europa.eu/competition/elojade/isef/case_details.cfm?proc_code=3_SA_45258.

contribute 100% to the seafarer's accident insurance. Shipping companies do not receive other support for these costs.

(15) The estimated overall budget amounts to EUR 264 million."

15.127 The Commission had also approved the prolongation of the tax exemption regimes for seafarers in Belgium.[136] The Commission had also approved the prolongation of the tax exemption regimes for seafarers in Sweden.[137]

N. CONCLUSION

15.128 The EU has been pragmatic, rather than dogmatic, about giving State aid support to the shipping sector. It has supported measures and initiatives which would boost European-based shipping. It has also given assistance on a social basis[138] or on a sectoral basis.[139] It has tried to move traffic from the road to the sea. It has required real links to the EU so as to support EU industry. While more needs to be done, there is no doubt but the EU's initiatives and work in this area have helped stem the decline of (at least in part), and stimulate innovation in (at least in part), the EU shipping sector. Ultimately, the EU has balanced competition and protectionism and while giving a nod to the latter, it has largely upheld the former.

---

136 Decision of 14 September 2015 in case SA.38336, Prolongation of the exemption from social security contributions for seafarers in the sectors of maritime transport and dredging, C:2015:403:1.

137 Decision of 24 March 2014 in case SA.38240, Shipping Aid, C:2014:348:18.

138 E.g. a block exemption for social aid for maritime transport for residents of remote regions has been provided by Comm. Reg. 651/2014 of 17 June 2014 declaring certain categories of aid compatible with the internal market in application of Arts 107 and 108 of the Treaty, OJ 2014 L187/1, Art. 51.

139 See *Danish Cable Laying vessels* OJ 2009 L119/23.

CHAPTER 16

European Union merger control: shipping, ports and shipbuilding

A. INTRODUCTION

16.001 The European Union ("EU") needs to be able to control, on competition grounds, the merger or acquisition[1] of businesses[2] in all sectors of the economy including the shipping, port and shipbuilding sectors. The EU has therefore adopted the Merger Control Regulation (often abbreviated as "MCR", "EUMR" or "ECMR"), which is Council Regulation 139/2004 of 20 January 2004,[3] so as to enable the European Commission[4] to adjudicate on whether or not such transactions (i.e. "concentrations") should be: (a) prohibited (i.e. not permitted to proceed at all);[5] (b) allowed to proceed conditionally;[6] or (c) permitted unconditionally.[7] Of the three options, the unconditional approval is the

---

1 Mergers or acquisitions are normally known in EU competition law as "concentrations".

2 Businesses are known in EU competition law as "undertakings" (see chap. 10). The same concept of "undertaking" applies in the present context (of concentrations) as in the context of Arts 101 and 102 of the Treaty on the Functioning of the European Union ("TFEU").

3 OJ 2004 L24/1, http://eur-lex.europa.eu/legal-content/EN/TXT/?uri=uriserv:OJ.L_.2004.024.01.0001.01. ENG. The full title of the Regulation is "Council Regulation (EC) No. 139/2004 of 20 January 2004 on the control of concentrations between undertakings (the EC Merger Regulation)". The legal basis of Reg. 139/2004 was the EC Treaty generally and, in particular, Arts 83 and 308 of that Treaty. Its legal basis would now be the TFEU generally and, in particular, Arts 103 and 352 of the TFEU.

4 It is generally thought to be better for the Commission, rather than the more political Council, to decide on such matters. However, the role of politics in some decisions by the Commission should not be entirely dismissed or underestimated (see, for example, Maitland Walker, "The Unacceptable Face of Politics in Competition Cases" [1991] ECLR 3). Instead of using the Commission, it would be theoretically possible to just use the Court of Justice of the European Union ("CJEU") to also adjudicate on concentrations at the first phase (as opposed to on appeal from Commission decisions as currently happens) but the courts would not be well suited to the task (e.g. given the speed required, administrative effort involved in reviewing notifications etc. in concentration control) unless the Commission were to be obliged to go to the General Court to prohibit a transaction (analogous to the model in the USA) but, for now, it is the Commission which decides whether to permit or prohibit a transaction (subject to limited judicial review by the CJEU). Consideration should be given to an independent competition adjudication body but there is little appetite in EU circles for such a body to be created.

5 This has not yet occurred in the maritime sector.

6 E.g. a concentration might be allowed to proceed on condition that the purchaser disposes of some businesses (e.g. overlapping subsidiaries) (see Hoeg, *European Merger Remedies* (2014) generally on remedies used in this context).

7 On the MCR generally, see Broberg, *The European Commission's Jurisdiction to Scrutinise Mergers* (3rd ed., 2006); Cook and Kerse, *EC Merger Control* (2009); Drauz and Jones (eds), *EU Competition Law* (2006), vol. 2; Lindsay and Berridge, *The EC Merger Regulation: Substantive Issues* (3rd ed., 2009); and Lowe and Marquis (eds), *European Competition Law Annual 2010: Merger Control in European and Global Perspective* (2013). See also Korah, *An Introductory Guide to EC Competition Law and Practice* (9th ed., 2007), chap. 12; Van Bael and Bellis, *Competition Law of the European Community* (5th ed., 2010), chap. 7; and Whish and Bailey, *Competition Law* (7th ed., 2012), chap. 21. See Tupper, "Merger Regulation: Possibilities and Pitfalls", Lloyd's Maritime Academy, EU Competition Law in Shipping, London, 26 March 2009. There is a wealth of material published on the MCR and this is just a sample of what is available.

most common outcome. This chapter considers the MCR as it relates to shipping, ports and shipbuilding.[8] The chapter begins with an overview of the MCR and then analyses its application to the three sectors.[9]

16.002 In some ways, it would be possible to control concentrations by using Articles 101[10] and 102[11] of the Treaty on the Functioning of the European Union ("TFEU") but it would be very unsatisfactory[12] to apply these provisions to concentrations because those general provisions in the TFEU were not designed to deal with concentrations. For example, in the case of Article 101 of the TFEU,[13] there would now (after the "modernisation" of EU competition law)[14] be no notification process for clearance by reference to Articles 101 and 102 of the TFEU so merging parties would have to make their own assessment as to whether the transaction could proceed and, if an exemption were relevant to the concentration then what would happen if the conditions for the exemption were no longer satisfied?[15] Similarly, in regard to Article 102 of the TFEU, that Article controls only those concentrations which involve the abuse of an existing dominant position so there could be other problematical concentrations which would *not* involve an abuse of *existing* dominance and therefore could not be controlled by EU law if it had to rely on Article 102 alone. Therefore, a specific concentration control measure was required. Despite the long[16] resistance of some Member States, eventually the EU adopted

---

8 This chapter confines its analysis to EU cases but it should be recalled that Member State case law can also be relevant (e.g. the UK's case law relating to the *SvitzerWijsmuller/Adstream* merger has a great deal of interesting analysis on competition in ports and market definition in the context of towage services in a port (see www.competition-commission.org.uk/inquiries/ref2006/adsteam/pdf/notice_of_acceptance_of_final_undertakings.pdf)).

9 While there are other books which deal with issues in mergers and acquisitions such as due diligence, taxation and drafting agreements, this chapter looks solely at the merger control dimension (i.e. the competition dimension).

10 Art. 101 of the TFEU relates to anti-competitive arrangements. On Art. 101 generally, see chap. 10 and in the context of concentrations, see Cases 142 and 156/84 *BAT and Reynolds v Commission* [1987] ECR 4487, ECLI:EU:C:1987:490.

11 Art. 102 of the TFEU relates to abuse of dominance. On Art. 102 generally, see chap. 10 and in the context of concentrations, see Case 6/72 *Continental Can v Commission* [1973] ECR 215, ECLI:EU:C:1973:22.

12 See Recital 7 of Reg. 139/2004 which recalls that "Articles [101] and [102], while applicable, according to the case law of the Court of Justice, to certain concentrations, are not sufficient to control all operations which may prove to be incompatible with the system of undistorted competition, envisaged in the Treaty." See Banks, "Mergers and Partial Mergers under EEC Law" in Hawk (ed.), [1987] Fordham Corporate Law Institute, chap. 17; Korah, reply to Banks, "Mergers and Partial Mergers under EEC Law" in Hawk (ed.), [1987] Fordham Corporate Law Institute, chap. 19; and Venit, "The 'Merger' Control Regulation: Europe Comes of Age or Caliban's Dinner" (1990) 27 CMLRev 7.

13 E.g. if a merger were void under Art. 101 of the TFEU then which elements of it would be void? How could exemptions operate? How long would the exemptions last for? What if the conditions for the exemption were not fulfilled or stop being fulfilled after the concentration was consummated?

14 See chap. 10.

15 E.g. would the concentration have to be unwound if the criteria under Art. 101(3) of the TFEU became no longer satisfied and the elements of the merged business handed back to the original owners? Hostile takeovers would be virtually impossible because bidders would argue that Art. 101(1) did not apply or, even if it did apply then Art. 101(3) applied but targets who did not welcome the bid would argue that the proposed transaction would be void under Art. 101(2) with the result that disputes would probably be mired in the courts with the result that commerce could not proceed.

16 The proposal for a regulation was made in the early 1970s but was not adopted until 1989 when the first merger control regulation (i.e. Reg. 4064/89 OJ 1998 395/1 with a corrected version published at OJ 1990 L257/13) was adopted. Interestingly, while the original merger control regulation (i.e. Reg. 4064/89) had a long gestation of over 17 years, once the concept was accepted, there was an amendment relatively quickly (i.e. in 1997 with Reg. 1310/97 OJ 1997 L180/7) and the regime was amended in its entirety relatively quickly with Reg. 139/2004 being adopted in 2004 (on the Commission's proposal, see OJ 2003 C20/4).

a regulation to deal with the competition law aspects of concentrations.[17] This was Regulation 4064/89[18] which was subsequently amended by Regulation 1310/97.[19] However, since 1 May 2004,[20] the EU has operated under Regulation 139/2004 which repealed[21] and replaced Regulations 4064/89[22] and 1310/97.[23] Despite the doubts and difficulties involved in adopting a regime, there are few today who would advocate the repeal of the MCR and thereby a reversion to different tests and timetables in different Member States.

16.003 In operating Regulation 139/2004, the Commission *appears* to take a generally positive view towards concentrations because the vast majority of transactions notified to the Commission are approved unconditionally by the Commission but there is no presumption in the regulation either in favour of, or against, a proposed concentration.

16.004 Transactions falling within the scope of the MCR have an important role to play in the EU and internal market project:[24] concentrations help to ensure consolidation of industry and they often result in the achievement of efficiencies which might not be otherwise possible.[25]

16.005 Regulation 139/2004 is only concerned with transactions which are cross-border in nature and does not deal with transactions which are largely (or entirely) domestic in nature (i.e. largely within the confines of a single Member State) so the regulation seeks to control only those concentrations with, what is described in the text of the regulation, a "Community dimension". However since the abolition of the European "Community" and its replacement by the European "Union", this term is now "Union dimension" but the text in the MCR still refers to the "Community dimension".[26]

16.006 One of the principal advantages of Regulation 139/2004 is that it provides a "one-stop shop" for concentration control within the EU (and, indeed, the whole of the

---

17 Unlike today, many Member States did not have national merger control laws until the 1970s to 1980s and even the 1990s in some cases.

18 OJ 1989 L395/1. Corrected version in OJ 1990 L257/13. Reg. 4064/89 was amended by Reg. 1310/97 (OJ 1997 L180/1 with a corrected version in OJ 1998 L40/17). Reg. 4064/89 was ultimately replaced by Reg. 139/2004.

19 OJ 1997 L180/1 with a corrected version in OJ 1998 L40/17.

20 Reg. 139/2004, Art. 26 provides that Reg. 139/2004 entered into force on 1 May 2004.

21 Reg. 139/2004, Art. 25.

22 OJ 1989 L395/1. Corrected version in OJ 1990 L257/13. Reg. 4064/89 was amended by Reg. 1310/97 (OJ 1997 L180/1 with a corrected version in OJ 1998 L40/17). Reg. 4064/89 was ultimately replaced by Reg. 139/2004.

23 OJ 1997 L180/1 with a corrected version in OJ 1998 L40/17.

24 In this context, it is useful to review Recitals 3–5 of Reg. 139/2004: "(3) The completion of the internal market and of economic and monetary union, the enlargement of the European Union and the lowering of international barriers to trade and investment will continue to result in major corporate reorganisations, particularly in the form of concentrations. (4) Such reorganisations are to be welcomed to the extent that they are in line with the requirements of dynamic competition and capable of increasing the competitiveness of European industry, improving the conditions of growth and raising the standard of living in the Community. (5) However, it should be ensured that the process of reorganisation does not result in lasting damage to competition; Community law must therefore include provisions governing those concentrations which may significantly impede effective competition in the internal market or in a substantial part of it." Recital 6 addresses the limited scope of Reg. 139/2004: "In accordance with the principles of subsidiarity and of proportionality as set out in ... the TFEU, this Regulation does not go beyond what is necessary in order to achieve the objective of ensuring that competition in the common market is not distorted, in accordance with the principle of an open market economy with free competition."

25 E.g. the theory that incumbent management often perform well because they believe that if they do not do so then their company could be acquired and they would be out of a job.

26 The terms "Community dimension" and "Union dimension" are used interchangeably in this chapter.

European Economic Area ("EEA")) for a particular type and size of transaction.[27] If a transaction falls within the scope of the MCR then it does not have to be notified to, and approved by, Member State competition authorities; notification to, and approval by, the European Commission suffices. This avoids as many as 32 notifications (i.e. notifications to each of the 28 EU Member States and three EEA Member States and, possibly, the Commission itself if it still received notifications) (as it did before 1 May 2004) which would otherwise have to occur. This one-stop shop under the MCR is not always guaranteed[28] but it is a useful way of expediting transactions and making their approval as efficient as possible within the EEA – obviously, merger notifications would still have to be made in various other jurisdictions around the world (e.g. Canada, China and the USA) but the MCR's one-stop shop reduces the number of notifications within the EU and EEA.

16.007 The now expired European Coal and Steel Community Treaty (the "ECSC" Treaty or Treaty of Paris) had a provision relating to merger or concentration control[29] but the European Economic Community ("EEC") (later the European Community ("EC")) Treaty and now the TFEU had (and still has) no comparable provision to the ECSC provision. Consolidation and concentration in the coal and steel sectors were recognised as being real issues in the early 1950s hence a provision was inserted in the ECSC Treaty[30] but concentration in other sectors of the economy (e.g. in shipping or shipbuilding as well as in other sectors generally) was not such a pressing issue at that time and many Member States did not adopt national legislation on merger control until the 1970s, 1980s or later. As mentioned above, Articles 101 and 102 of the TFEU could be used to control concentrations but they are neither ideal nor efficient instruments of concentration control because there are no time limits, no certainty and no practical mechanisms to allow for conditions to be imposed so Regulation 139/2004 instead provides the mechanism to deal with these (and other) issues.

16.008 Staying with these introductory remarks on the EU's merger control regime, it is useful to touch briefly on the economic, as opposed to the legal, dimension to concentrations. First, in the last few years, the economic dimension to concentrations has become more pronounced in concentration control analysis. This means that concentration control is now less formalistic and more intent on determining the real economic effects of a proposed transaction on competition internationally. However, the review of transactions is not entirely confined to economic analysis. Second, tests such as "consumer welfare", "substantially lessening competition" and "significant impediment of effective competition" (this latter test is the one used in Regulation 139/2004) have been uppermost in the mind of competition agencies worldwide. Such agencies are usually oblivious to issues

---

27 Recital 6 of Reg. 139/2004 provides: "[a] specific legal instrument is ... necessary to permit effective control of all concentrations in terms of their effect on the structure of competition in the Community and to be the only instrument applicable to such concentrations". Recital 8 provides that the "provisions [of] this Regulation should apply to significant structural changes, the impact of which on the market goes beyond the national borders of any one Member State. Such concentrations should, as a general rule, be reviewed exclusively at Community level, in applications of a 'one-stop shop' system and in compliance with the principle of subsidiarity."
28 E.g. parts of, or indeed all, transactions may be remitted back to Member States for review under Art. 9 of Reg. 139/2004.
29 Art. 66 of the ECSC Treaty.
30 I.e. Art. 66 of the ECSC Treaty.

such as the impact of a transaction on levels of employment, regional development and conditions of employment.[31] Third, how the market is defined (i.e. the issue of "market definition")[32] is often key to merger control. There are circumstances where a competition authority (e.g. the Commission in the case of Regulation 139/2004) does not have to define the market in a particular case because no matter how the market is defined, there is no competition concern. On the other hand, there are cases where the definition of the market is of crucial importance to the point of whether the proposed concentration would be permitted, prohibited or permitted only on certain conditions. Much can depend on how the market is defined (e.g. in a "narrow" market, the transaction could be prohibited but if the market were defined more broadly, the transaction could be permitted because there would be adequate alternative competition even after the concentration). Finally, competition law is not concerned with the very fact that a concentration will lead to one competitor fewer (if it were concerned simply about maintaining the number of competitors then there could be no concentrations at all) but is more concerned with the level or intensity of actual or potential competition which remains in the market post-transaction.[33] Competition agencies are interested to see how likely entry would be into the market post-transaction (i.e. "potential competition") as well as actual competition: if entry by others was likely, timely and substantial then the transaction is less likely to be anti-competitive because the merged entity could not raise its prices significantly or behave anti-competitively (e.g. raise prices or upgrade service beyond what the market would otherwise bear) because it could not exploit its position as alternative competitors would enter the market or incumbents would expand operations to counter such anti-competitive behaviour.

16.009 There is a connection between arrangements and concentrations (within the meaning of Regulation 139/2004). Concentrations can provide an attractive alternative to shipping companies who want legal certainty by virtue of having a more permanent arrangement[34] approved under Regulation 139/2004 rather than having a less permanent structure which would involve having to do self-assessment with the risk that changing competitive conditions may mean that a less permanent arrangement may be compatible or not compatible with competition law at different times. It may be that undertakings would prefer, instead of having a loose arrangement which may or may not be lawful, to have a concentration[35] (i.e. a more permanent arrangement) which would be approved by the Commission and would be in permanent form.[36] Any arrangement which constitutes a concentration and is approved under the EU concentration regime cannot be prohibited by the Commission (within the meaning of Regulation 139/2004) under the EU prohibitions on anti-competitive arrangements or abuse of dominance.[37]

---

31 I.e. competition agencies typically (and this includes the Commission acting under the MCR) would not prohibit a transaction merely because it would lead to substantial job losses.

32 E.g. in a merger of container shipping companies is the market for (a) ro-ro; or (b) lo-lo or (c) ro-ro and (d) lo-lo combined? (See chap. 10).

33 Concentration control is therefore said to be a forward-looking analysis even though it takes into account evidence of past behaviour but as an indicator of the future.

34 E.g. merger, acquisition or full function joint venture.

35 E.g. mergers, acquisitions or certain forms of joint ventures.

36 By contrast, arrangements which are not concentrations may not be notified to, or approved by, the Commission so there is always some level of uncertainty surrounding the status of the arrangement.

37 This is because the Commission does not have the power to apply Arts 101 or 102 of the TFEU where Reg. 139/2004 applies.

16.010 After these introductory remarks, the chapter commences with an overview of the type of transactions which are subject to the EU's merger control regime and it does this by examining the concept of concentrations (in part B), the concept of a concentration with a "Union Dimension" (in part C), the process of notification (in part D), an examination of how the Commission assesses a proposed concentration (in part E), remedies to deal with any anti-competitive concentration so as to permit it to proceed (in part F), the issue of market definition (in part G) and the role of the Member States in the process (in part H), ancillary restrictions (in part I), minority stakes (in part J), the rules of the Courts of Justice of the European Union (in part K), the MCR in the shipping sector (in part L) and the MCR in the shipbuilding section (in part M). In the interests of space, it is not possible to deal with every case.

B. CONCEPT OF CONCENTRATIONS

16.011 Regulation 139/2004 applies to "concentrations".[38] There are three types of transaction which amount to "concentrations" and are therefore potentially covered by Regulation 139/2004: (a) mergers; (b) acquisitions; and (c) certain types of joint ventures.

16.012 Article 3 of Regulation 139/2004 defines what is, and what is not, a concentration with some precision.

16.013 Article 3(1) of Regulation 139/2004 states that a

> "concentration shall be deemed to arise where a change of control on a lasting basis results from: (a) the merger of two or more previously independent undertakings or parts of undertakings, or (b) the acquisition, by one or more persons already controlling at least one undertaking, or by one or more undertakings, whether by purchase of securities or assets, by contract or by any other means, of direct or indirect control of the whole or parts of one or more other undertakings".

Exercising decisive influence is a critical feature.

16.014 The element of "control" is critical to the concept of concentration and Article 3(2) provides that control

> "shall be constituted by rights, contracts or any other means which, either separately or in combination and having regard to the considerations of fact or law involved, confer the possibility of exercising decisive influence on an undertaking, in particular by: (a) ownership or the right to use all or part of the assets of an undertaking; (b) rights or contracts which confer decisive influence on the composition, voting or decisions of the organs of an undertaking".

16.015 This element of control in Article 1(2) then begs the question as to when control is acquired. So Article 3(3) provides that control

> "is acquired by persons or undertakings which: (a) are holders of the rights or entitled to rights under the contracts concerned; or (b) while not being holders of such rights or entitled to rights under such contracts, have the power to exercise the rights deriving therefrom".

---

38 Recital 20 of Reg. 139/2004 provides that it "is expedient to define the concept of concentration in such a manner as to cover operations bringing about a lasting change in the control of the undertakings concerned and therefore in the structure of the market. It is therefore appropriate to include, within the scope of this Regulation, all joint ventures performing on a lasting basis all the functions of an autonomous economic entity. It is moreover appropriate to treat as a single concentration transactions that are closely connected in that they are linked by condition or take the form of a series of transactions in securities taking place within a reasonably short period of time."

Therefore there has to be an element of real control or influence over the undertaking in question.

16.016 The creation of a joint venture can constitute a concentration for the purposes of Regulation 139/2004 but only where the "creation of a joint venture performing on a lasting basis all the functions of an autonomous economic entity shall constitute a concentration within the meaning of paragraph 1(b)" of Article 3 of Regulation 139/2004.[39] Therefore to be a concentration, the joint venture must have some lasting or near permanent dimension. A concentration would therefore be more permanent than a consortia agreement.

16.017 There are circumstances where control is acquired over an undertaking but it would be inappropriate to categorise it as a concentration for merger control purposes and render the transaction subject to a complicated process under the regulation. Examples would be where, for example, (a) banks are investing temporarily in corporate stock with a view to reselling the stock, or (b) insolvency practitioners acquire control of an undertaking. Therefore Article 3(5) of Regulation 139/2004 provides a list of exceptions to the concept of a concentration (i.e. situations where control may be acquired but it does not amount to a concentration) and therefore the MCR does not apply and no notification to the Commission is required to constitute a concentration.[40]

16.018 It is clear that there must be a change of control on a lasting basis for a concentration to occur[41] but the concept of "control" is not always easy to define because it is a somewhat nebulous concept. It is constituted by rights, contracts or any other means which, either separately or in combination and having regard to the considerations of fact or law involved, confer the possibility of exercising decisive influence on an undertaking. "Control" could be achieved by, in particular: (a) ownership or the right to use all or part of the assets of an undertaking; or (b) rights or contracts which confer decisive influence on the composition, voting or decisions of the organs of an undertaking.

16.019 A concentration could be a merger of two or more previously independent undertakings or parts of undertakings. It could also be the acquisition, by one or more

---

39 Art. 3(1)(b) provides: "the acquisition, by one or more persons already controlling at least one undertaking, or by one or more undertakings, whether by purchase of securities or assets, by contract or by any other means, of direct or indirect control of the whole or parts of one or more other undertakings" is deemed to be a concentration.

40 Art. 3(5) of Reg. 139/2004 provides: "[a] concentration shall not be deemed to arise where: (a) credit institutions or other financial institutions or insurance companies, the normal activities of which include transactions and dealing in securities for their own account or for the account of others, hold on a temporary basis securities which they have acquired in an undertaking with a view to reselling them, provided that they do not exercise voting rights in respect of those securities with a view to determining the competitive behaviour of that undertaking or provided that they exercise such voting rights only with a view to preparing the disposal of all or part of that undertaking or of its assets or the disposal of those securities and that any such disposal takes place within one year of the date of acquisition; that period may be extended by the Commission on request where such institutions or companies can show that the disposal was not reasonably possible within the period set; (b) control is acquired by an office-holder according to the law of a Member State relating to liquidation, winding up, insolvency, cessation of payments, compositions or analogous proceedings; (c) the operations referred to in paragraph 1(b) are carried out by the financial holding companies referred to in Article 5(3) of Fourth Council Directive 78/660/EEC of 25 July 1978 based on Article 54(3)(g) of the Treaty on the annual accounts of certain types of companies provided however that the voting rights in respect of the holding are exercised, in particular in relation to the appointment of members of the management and supervisory bodies of the undertakings in which they have holdings, only to maintain the full value of those investments and not to determine directly or indirectly the competitive conduct of those undertakings."

41 Reg. 139/2004, Art. 3(1).

persons already controlling at least one undertaking, or by one or more undertakings, whether by purchase of securities or assets, by contract or by any other means, of direct or indirect control of the whole or parts of one or more other undertakings.

16.020 What level of stake must be acquired before there is a concentration? The acquisition of the entire target (whether in terms of shares or assets) would be a concentration. The acquisition of a stake of more than 50% would be a concentration. The acquisition of a minority stake is more complicated and will depend on how widely the target's ownership is dispersed and whether the acquirer of the stake has veto rights (e.g. over the appointment of management, business plans and budgets – in other words, whether "control" is being acquired)[42] – this is an area of EU competition law which is in gestation.

16.021 A concentration agreement may be governed by a non-EU legal system and still be subject to Regulation 139/2004 so, for example, a merger under Japanese law of two Japanese shipping companies could be subject to the regulation where the requisite level of turnover[43] is generated in the EU (i.e. it is a concentration with a Union or Community Dimension). Equally, the vast majority of the turnover could be generated outside the EU but the regulation still applies provided the requisite minimum turnover occurs in the EU.[44] The governing law, the place of signature, the place of performance or domicile of the undertakings involved would be irrelevant – otherwise the regime could be easily circumvented.

16.022 Substance will always triumph over form in this context. In particular, economic reality will win out over legal form. So the law will not be concerned with the niceties of company law and would treat the acquisition of a group of one-ship companies as a single transaction even though legally they may be regarded as separate transactions.

C. CONCENTRATIONS WITH A UNION DIMENSION

16.023 It would be absurd if every "concentration" affecting trade in the entire EU had to be notified to the Commission irrespective of how small or insignificant the transaction was financially or economically. Otherwise, the purchase of one ship by the owner of another ship could potentially have to be notified to the Commission. Therefore the MCR covers only concentrations with a "Community dimension". A set of turnover-based tests have been adopted to decide which concentrations have a Community dimension. Recital 9 of Regulation 139/2004 provides that the "scope of application of this Regulation should be defined according to the geographical area of activity of the undertakings concerned and be limited by quantitative thresholds in order to cover those concentrations which have a Community dimension". The use of quantitative rather than qualitative criteria means that parties to a concentration have some certainty whether the MCR applies

---

42 See Ezrachi and Gilo, "EC Competition Law and the Regulation of Passive Investments Among Competitors" (2006) 26 Oxford Journal of Legal Studies 327. A stake as high as 29% might not, in the specific circumstances of a case amount to a concentration: see Case T-411/07 *Aer Lingus v Commission* [2010] ECR-II 3691, ECLI:EU:T:2010:281 but it could be where the shares are widely dispersed.

43 The requisite level of turnover is the one set down in the MCR.

44 Recital 10 of Reg. 139/2004 provides that a "concentration with a Community dimension should be deemed to exist where the aggregate turnover of the undertakings concerned exceeds given thresholds: that is the case irrespective of whether or not the undertakings effecting the concentration have their seat or their principal fields of activity in the Community, provided they have substantial operations there".

or not; if a shipping company had a particular turnover in its previous financial year then that is easily determinable while, for example, a market share test, an asset value test or some vague assessment of market power would be more difficult to determine with precision.

16.024 There are two tests in Regulation 139/2004 to determine whether there is a Union dimension. Either test suffices for the regulation to apply so it is necessary to consider the two tests for present purposes but only one test needs to be satisfied in practice for the MCR to apply. The first test was included in the original merger control regulation in 1989 while the second was added later – to extend the scope of the MCR regime largely because businesses wanted the one-stop facility of the MCR in more transactions than simply those possible under the first test.[45]

16.025 The first test in Regulation 139/2004[46] provides that a concentration has the requisite dimension where:

(a) the combined aggregate worldwide turnover of all the undertakings concerned is more than €5,000 million; and
(b) the aggregate Union-wide turnover of each of at least two of the undertakings concerned is more than €250 million,

unless each of the undertakings concerned achieves more than two-thirds of its aggregate Union-wide turnover within one and the same Member State.

16.026 The second alternative test in Regulation 139/2004[47] provides that where the first test does not apply then a concentration has the requisite dimension where:

(a) the combined aggregate worldwide turnover of all the undertakings concerned is more than €2,500 million;
(b) in each of at least three Member States, the combined aggregate turnover of all the undertakings concerned is more than €100 million;
(c) in each of at least three Member States included for the purpose of point (b), the aggregate turnover of each of at least two of the undertakings concerned is more than €25 million; and
(d) the aggregate EU-wide turnover of each of at least two of the undertakings concerned is more than €100 million,

unless each of the undertakings concerned achieves more than two-thirds of its aggregate Community-wide turnover within one and the same Member State. The second test covers undertakings which do not have a huge global turnover but have turnover in three or more Member States.

16.027 A key concept in this context is that of "turnover". It is defined, to some extent, in Article 5 of Regulation 139/2004. While some of the rules in Article 5 deal with banks and insurance undertakings which are of little direct relevance to concentrations in the shipping sector, there are some key rules in the Article:

---

45 The second test extended the number of transactions covered by the regulation and meant that more cases could be notified to the Commission under the one-stop shop approach of the MCR which meant that there had to be fewer multiple notifications to the Member State authorities.
46 Reg. 139/2004, Art. 1(2).
47 Reg. 139/2004, Art. 1(3).

"Article 5
Calculation of turnover
1. Aggregate turnover within the meaning of this Regulation shall comprise the amounts derived by the undertakings concerned in the preceding financial year from the sale of products and the provision of services falling within the undertakings' ordinary activities after deduction of sales rebates and of value added tax and other taxes directly related to turnover. The aggregate turnover of an undertaking concerned shall not include the sale of products or the provision of services between any of the undertakings referred to in paragraph 4.

Turnover, in the Community or in a Member State, shall comprise products sold and services provided to undertakings or consumers, in the Community or in that Member State as the case may be.

2. By way of derogation from paragraph 1, where the concentration consists of the acquisition of parts, whether or not constituted as legal entities, of one or more undertakings, only the turnover relating to the parts which are the subject of the concentration shall be taken into account with regard to the seller or sellers.

However, two or more transactions within the meaning of the first subparagraph which take place within a two-year period between the same persons or undertakings shall be treated as one and the same concentration arising on the date of the last transaction.

3. ...

4. Without prejudice to paragraph 2, the aggregate turnover of an undertaking concerned within the meaning of this Regulation shall be calculated by adding together the respective turnovers of the following:

   (a) the undertaking concerned;
   (b) those undertakings in which the undertaking concerned, directly or indirectly:

      (i) owns more than half the capital or business assets, or
      (ii) has the power to exercise more than half the voting rights, or
      (iii) has the power to appoint more than half the members of the supervisory board, the administrative board or bodies legally representing the undertakings, or
      (iv) has the right to manage the undertakings' affairs;

   (c) those undertakings which have in the undertaking concerned the rights or powers listed in (b);
   (d) those undertakings in which an undertaking as referred to in (c) has the rights or powers listed in (b);
   (e) those undertakings in which two or more undertakings as referred to in (a) to (d) jointly have the rights or powers listed in (b).

5. Where undertakings concerned by the concentration jointly have the rights or powers listed in paragraph 4(b), in calculating the aggregate turnover of the undertakings concerned for the purposes of this Regulation:

   (a) no account shall be taken of the turnover resulting from the sale of products or the provision of services between the joint undertaking and each of the undertakings concerned or any other undertaking connected with any one of them, as set out in paragraph 4(b) to (e);
   (b) account shall be taken of the turnover resulting from the sale of products and the provision of services between the joint undertaking and any third undertakings. This turnover shall be apportioned equally amongst the undertakings concerned."

16.028 It is worth making a number of observations on Article 5 of the regulation. First, turnover is a quantifiable figure which is capable of being defined precisely unlike, for example, market shares which are not always capable of being defined precisely. Second, it is the *preceding* financial year which matters and then it is in respect of the undertaking's "ordinary activities". Third, turnover in the EU and Member States is calculated by reference to products sold and services provided to undertakings in the EU or Member States. Fourth, there is an anti-avoidance provision that transactions within a two-year period are aggregated. Finally, it is not always easy to determine the geographical location of turnover. The MCR does not address the issue and so an analysis has to be undertaken in each case. So, for example, if a French shipper made a contract governed by Dutch Law with a Spanish agent to take goods by ship from Germany to France then where does the turnover lie? The answer turns on the specific facts of each case. However, it would be assumed that the geographical location of freight or a passenger fare would be divided equally between the country of departure and the country of arrival.[48]

16.029 The Commission's Consolidated Jurisdictional Notice ("CCJN")[49] covers a wide range of issues of jurisdiction relevant for establishing the Commission's competence under the MCR including issues relating to jurisdiction, notification and analysis. It is useful for anyone considering the possible application of the MCR to study the CCJN carefully.

D. NOTIFICATION

16.030 Unlike EU competition law generally, parties do not have to rely entirely on a "self-assessment" regime in the area of concentration control. Transactions must be notified to the Commission for them to be reviewed by the Commission and a decision issued by the Commission unless the parties withdraw the notification. Parties to a proposed concentration may not simply rely on their own assessment of whether the transaction is compatible with EU law or not. The Commission has the power to prohibit transactions proceeding or to impose conditions on how they may proceed.

16.031 The notification process can be arduous and voluminous; it should not be underestimated; it is not uncommon for the Commission to reject a notification because it is incomplete and the parties then have to submit the full notification (e.g. *Blohm+Voss/Lisnave*).[50] It is highly unusual for there to be no pre-notification dialogue with the Commission. Instead, there would be extensive pre-notification discussions with the Commission. Such pre-notification discussions would address such issues as the type of information which the Commission would require to be included in the notification as well as such information as the Commission would "waive" as unnecessary. The Commission would also identify areas of concern which it may have about the possible transaction. The pre-notification discussions can often stretch for several weeks or even months. Notifying parties sometimes take comfort from the Commission's disposition during these pre-notification discussions but nothing has been decided at that stage.

---

48 By analogy, see the Commission Decision in Case No COMP/M.4439 *Ryanair/Aer Lingus* in regard to airline tickets: "30 ... it is concluded that, of the possible alternative methodologies for geographic allocation of turnover in respect of transactions for which the location of the customer at the time of purchase cannot be identified and cannot affect the conditions of such purchase, in particular the 50/50 methodology, as well as the methodology based on place of departure with splitting the two one-way flights of a round trip tickets bought at the same time, seem to be the most appropriate". It is submitted that the analogy would be equally relevant in the case of shipping.
49 OJ 2008 C95/1.
50 Case IV/M.1004.

16.032 In terms of timing, concentrations with a Community or Union dimension (as defined in Regulation 139/2004)[51] must be notified to the Commission (a) prior to their implementation and (b) following the conclusion of the agreement, the announcement of the public bid or the acquisition of a controlling interest.[52] However, an agreement is not always a pre-requisite to notification because Article 4(1) of the regulation also provides that notification may also be made where the undertakings concerned demonstrate to the Commission a good faith intention to conclude an agreement or, in the case of a public bid, where they have publicly announced an intention to make such a bid, provided that the intended agreement or bid would result in a concentration with a Community dimension.

16.033 The allocation of responsibility for the notification depends on the circumstances. Article 4(2) of the regulation provides that a concentration which consists of a merger within the meaning of Article 3(1)(a) of the regulation or in the acquisition of joint control within the meaning of Article 3(1)(b) the regulation shall be notified jointly by the parties to the merger or by those acquiring joint control as the case may be. In all other cases, the notification shall be effected by the person or undertaking acquiring control of the whole or parts of one or more undertakings.

16.034 The notification is normally made by way of the so-called "Form CO".[53] This is not a short or simple form to be completed but is a rubric or framework for supplying information to the Commission. The outline form is available on the Commission's website[54] but the completed notification in any case is not published or released to the public by the Commission although some of the information in it will appear in the Commission's decision and press release on the case (subject to business secrets). The Form CO is divided into 11 sections:

Section 1:   Description of the Concentration;
Section 2:   Information about the Parties;
Section 3:   Details of the Concentration;
Section 4:   Ownership and Control;
Section 5:   Supporting Documentation;
Section 6:   Market Definitions;
Section 7:   Information on Affected Markets;
Section 8:   General Conditions in Affected Market;
Section 9:   Overall Market Context and Efficiencies;
Section 10: Cooperative Effects of a Joint Venture; and
Section 11: Declaration.

Much of the information contained in the notification would be confidential and its release would be very sensitive so there are special safeguards in place to deal with this

---

51 See Parts B and C.
52 Reg. 139/2004, Art. 4(1).
53 OJ 2004 L133/9. There are other forms which are used in specific circumstances. There is a short Form CO which can be used in less difficult cases. Form RS is used for Reasoned Submissions and specifies the information that requesting parties should provide when making a reasoned submission for a pre-notification referral under Art. 4(4) or (5) of Reg. 139/2004.
54 See Reg. 802/2004 implementing Reg. 139/2004 (the so-called "Implementing Regulation") which contains the various forms (i.e. Form CO, Short Form CO and Form RS) OJ 2004 L133/1 as amended by Reg. 1033/2008 OJ 2008 L279/3.

situation.⁵⁵ No fee is paid to the Commission for the notification process. Article 4 of Regulation 139/2004 addresses the issue of notification but much of the detail on notifications is contained in Regulation 802/2004.⁵⁶

16.035 If there is a valid notification then a short notice about it is published in the EU's *Official Journal*.⁵⁷ Third parties are invited, in the notice, to comment. These invitations come not only through a notice in the *Official Journal* but also in terms of individual invitations to comment addressed to various parties such as competitors, customers and suppliers. These interveners may be complainants/opponents, supporters or neutral on the proposed transactions.

16.036 Article 4 of Regulation 139/2004 addresses the issue of whether a case should be considered by the Member State competition authorities (instead of by the Commission). It is worthwhile reciting the article in full. The article states:

"Prior notification of concentrations and pre-notification referral at the request of the notifying parties
1. Concentrations with a Community dimension defined in this Regulation shall be notified to the Commission prior to their implementation and following the conclusion of the agreement, the announcement of the public bid, or the acquisition of a controlling interest.

    Notification may also be made where the undertakings concerned demonstrate to the Commission a good faith intention to conclude an agreement or, in the case of a public bid, where they have publicly announced an intention to make such a bid, provided that the intended agreement or bid would result in a concentration with a Community dimension.

    For the purposes of this Regulation, the term 'notified concentration' shall also cover intended concentrations notified pursuant to the second subparagraph. For the purposes of paragraphs 4 and 5 of this Article, the term 'concentration' includes intended concentrations within the meaning of the second subparagraph.
2. A concentration which consists of a merger within the meaning of Article 3(1)(a) or in the acquisition of joint control within the meaning of Article 3(1)(b) shall be notified jointly by the parties to the merger or by those acquiring joint control as the case may be. In all other cases, the notification shall be effected by the person or undertaking acquiring control of the whole or parts of one or more undertakings.
3. Where the Commission finds that a notified concentration falls within the scope of this Regulation, it shall publish the fact of the notification, at the same time indicating the names of the undertakings concerned, their country of origin, the nature of the concentration and the economic sectors involved. The Commission shall take account of the legitimate interest of undertakings in the protection of their business secrets.
4. Prior to the notification of a concentration within the meaning of paragraph 1, the persons or undertakings referred to in paragraph 2 may inform the Commission, by means of a reasoned

---

55 Art. 17 of Reg. 139/2004 provides: "Professional secrecy. 1. Information acquired [by the Commission] as a result of the application of this Regulation shall be used only for the purposes of the relevant request, investigation or hearing. 2. Without prejudice to Article 4(3), Articles 18 and 20, the Commission and the competent authorities of the Member States, their officials and other servants and other persons working under the supervision of these authorities as well as officials and civil servants of other authorities of the Member States shall not disclose information they have acquired through the application of this Regulation of the kind covered by the obligation of professional secrecy. 3. Paragraphs 1 and 2 shall not prevent publication of general information or of surveys which do not contain information relating to particular undertakings or associations of undertakings."

56 OJ L133/1, 30 April 2004.

57 Reg. 139/2004, Art. 4(3) provides: "Where the Commission finds that a notified concentration falls within the scope of this Regulation, it shall publish the fact of the notification, at the same time indicating the names of the undertakings concerned, their country of origin, the nature of the concentration and the economic sectors involved. The Commission shall take account of the legitimate interest of undertakings in the protection of their business secrets."

submission, that the concentration may significantly affect competition in a market within a Member State which presents all the characteristics of a distinct market and should therefore be examined, in whole or in part, by that Member State.

The Commission shall transmit this submission to all Member States without delay. The Member State referred to in the reasoned submission shall, within 15 working days of receiving the submission, express its agreement or disagreement as regards the request to refer the case. Where that Member State takes no such decision within this period, it shall be deemed to have agreed.

Unless that Member State disagrees, the Commission, where it considers that such a distinct market exists, and that competition in that market may be significantly affected by the concentration, may decide to refer the whole or part of the case to the competent authorities of that Member State with a view to the application of that State's national competition law.

The decision whether or not to refer the case in accordance with the third subparagraph shall be taken within 25 working days starting from the receipt of the reasoned submission by the Commission. The Commission shall inform the other Member States and the persons or undertakings concerned of its decision. If the Commission does not take a decision within this period, it shall be deemed to have adopted a decision to refer the case in accordance with the submission made by the persons or undertakings concerned.

If the Commission decides, or is deemed to have decided, pursuant to the third and fourth subparagraphs, to refer the whole of the case, no notification shall be made pursuant to paragraph 1 and national competition law shall apply. Article 9(6) to (9) shall apply mutatis mutandis.

5. With regard to a concentration as defined in Article 3 which does not have a Community dimension within the meaning of Article 1 and which is capable of being reviewed under the national competition laws of at least three Member States, the persons or undertakings referred to in paragraph 2 may, before any notification to the competent authorities, inform the Commission by means of a reasoned submission that the concentration should be examined by the Commission.

The Commission shall transmit this submission to all Member States without delay.

Any Member State competent to examine the concentration under its national competition law may, within 15 working days of receiving the reasoned submission, express its disagreement as regards the request to refer the case.

Where at least one such Member State has expressed its disagreement in accordance with the third subparagraph within the period of 15 working days, the case shall not be referred. The Commission shall, without delay, inform all Member States and the persons or undertakings concerned of any such expression of disagreement.

Where no Member State has expressed its disagreement in accordance with the third subparagraph within the period of 15 working days, the concentration shall be deemed to have a Community dimension and shall be notified to the Commission in accordance with paragraphs 1 and 2. In such situations, no Member State shall apply its national competition law to the concentration."

E. HOW DOES THE COMMISSION ASSESS A PROPOSED CONCENTRATION? THE TEST FOR APPROVAL (OR OTHERWISE) OF A PROPOSED CONCENTRATION

16.037 Having received the notification, how would the Commission assess the proposed transaction? Article 2 of Regulation 139/2004 sets out the basis on which the Commission must assess whether or not to approve the transaction. Article 2(1) of Regulation 139/2004 provides:

> "Concentrations within the scope of this Regulation shall be appraised in accordance with the objectives of this Regulation and the following provisions with a view to establishing whether or not they are compatible with the common market.

In making this appraisal, the Commission shall take into account:

(a) the need to maintain and develop effective competition within the common market in view of, among other things, the structure of all the markets concerned and the actual or potential competition from undertakings located either within or outwith the Community;
(b) the market position of the undertakings concerned and their economic and financial power, the alternatives available to suppliers and users, their access to supplies or markets, any legal or other barriers to entry, supply and demand trends for the relevant goods and services, the interests of the intermediate and ultimate consumers, and the development of technical and economic progress provided that it is to consumers' advantage and does not form an obstacle to competition."

16.038 The test for considering concentrations is whether the proposed concentration would amount to a "significant impediment to effective competition" ("SIEC"). This is a different test from the one in the earlier merger central regulation (i.e. Regulation 4064/89).[58] So, a concentration which would not significantly impede effective competition in the internal market or in a substantial part of it, in particular as a result of the creation or strengthening of a dominant position, is declared to be compatible with the internal market.[59] However, a concentration which would significantly impede effective competition, in the common[60] market or in a substantial part of it, in particular as a result of the creation or strengthening of a dominant position, must be declared incompatible with the internal market.[61]

16.039 To the extent that the creation of a joint venture has as its object or effect the co-ordination of the competitive behaviour of undertakings that remain independent then such co-ordination is appraised in accordance with the criteria of Article 101(1) and (3) of the TFEU, with a view to establishing whether or not the operation is compatible with the internal market, rather than the SIEC test under Regulation 139/2004.[62] In making this appraisal, the Commission must take into account in particular: (a) whether two or more parent companies retain, to a significant extent, activities in the same market as the joint venture or in a market which is downstream or upstream from that of the joint venture or in a neighbouring market closely related to this market; and (b) whether the co-ordination which is the direct consequence of the creation of the joint venture affords the undertakings concerned the possibility of eliminating competition in respect of a substantial part of the products or services in question.[63]

16.040 Article 6 of Regulation 139/2004 addresses how the Commission examines the notification and initiates proceedings. The Commission must examine the notification as soon as it is received.[64] If the Commission concludes that the proposed concentration

---

58 Art. 2(3) of Reg. 4064/89 provided that "[a] concentration which creates or strengthens a dominant position as a result of which effective competition would be significantly impeded in the common market or in a substantial part of it shall be declared incompatible with the common market". The new test covers situations where a dominant position is created.
59 Reg. 139/2004, Art. 2(1).
60 The Treaty of Lisbon changed the term "common market" to "internal market" but the regulation has not been amended.
61 Reg. 139/2004, Art. 2(3).
62 Reg. 139/2004, Art. 2(4).
63 Reg. 139/2004, Art. 2(5).
64 Reg. 139/2004, Art. 6(1). In practice, as part of the pre-notification process, the Commission has already commenced reviewing matters before the notification is received formally. The Commission can also informally control the timing of the notification by indicating, during the pre-notification phase, when it wants the notification to be filed.

notified does not fall within the scope of the regulation then the Commission must record that finding by means of a decision[65] which would then be capable of judicial review. If the Commission finds that the notified concentration, although falling within the scope of the regulation, does not raise serious doubts as to its compatibility with the internal market, then the Commission must decide not to oppose it and must declare that it is compatible with the internal market.[66] A decision declaring a concentration compatible must be deemed to cover restrictions directly related and necessary to the implementation of the concentration.[67] As a general principle, without prejudice to Article 6, paragraph 2, where the Commission finds that the concentration notified falls within the scope of the regulation and raises serious doubts as to its compatibility with the internal market, the Commission must decide to initiate proceedings.[68] Without prejudice to Article 9 of the regulation, such proceedings must be closed by means of a decision as provided for in Article 8(1) to (4), unless the undertakings concerned have demonstrated to the satisfaction of the Commission that they have abandoned the concentration.[69]

16.041 The Commission may revoke the decision it took pursuant to Article 6(1)(a) or (b) where either: (i) the decision is based on incorrect information for which one of the undertakings is responsible or where it has been obtained by deceit; or (ii) the undertakings concerned commit a breach of an obligation attached to the decision.

16.042 May the parties complete or perfect the proposed transaction while the Commission is considering the notification? If a transaction is notifiable to the Commission then it is generally not permissible to complete the transaction unless and until the Commission approves it. Article 7 of the regulation provides:

"Suspension of concentrations
1. A concentration with a Community dimension as defined in Article 1, or which is to be examined by the Commission pursuant to Article 4(5), shall not be implemented either before its notification or until it has been declared compatible with the common market pursuant to a decision under Articles 6(1)(b), 8(1) or 8(2), or on the basis of a presumption according to Article 10(6).
2. Paragraph 1 shall not prevent the implementation of a public bid or of a series of transactions in securities including those convertible into other securities admitted to trading on a market such as a stock exchange, by which control within the meaning of Article 3 is acquired from various sellers, provided that:

   (a) the concentration is notified to the Commission pursuant to Article 4 without delay; and
   (b) the acquirer does not exercise the voting rights attached to the securities in question or does so only to maintain the full value of its investments based on a derogation granted by the Commission under paragraph 3.

3. The Commission may, on request, grant a derogation from the obligations imposed in paragraphs 1 or 2. The request to grant a derogation must be reasoned. In deciding on the request, the Commission shall take into account inter alia the effects of the suspension on one or more undertakings concerned by the concentration or on a third party and the threat to competition posed by the concentration. Such a derogation may be made subject to conditions

---

65 Reg. 139/2004, Art. 6(1)(a).
66 Reg. 139/2004, Art. 6(1)(b).
67 Ibid.
68 Reg. 139/2004, Art. 6(1)(c).
69 Ibid.

and obligations in order to ensure conditions of effective competition. A derogation may be applied for and granted at any time, be it before notification or after the transaction.

4. The validity of any transaction carried out in contravention of paragraph 1 shall be dependent on a decision pursuant to Article 6(1)(b) or Article 8(1), (2) or (3) or on a presumption pursuant to Article 10(6).

This Article shall, however, have no effect on the validity of transactions in securities including those convertible into other securities admitted to trading on a market such as a stock exchange, unless the buyer and seller knew or ought to have known that the transaction was carried out in contravention of paragraph 1."

F. REMEDIES

16.043 What if a proposed concentration would significantly impede effective competition but the proposed transaction could be allowed provided some remedies or commitments are made? Article 6(2) of Regulation 139/2004 provides that:

"[w]here the Commission finds that, following modification by the undertakings[70] concerned, a notified concentration no longer raises serious doubts within the meaning of [Article 6] paragraph 1(c), it shall declare the concentration compatible with the common market pursuant to [Article 6] paragraph 1(b)."

For example, two shipping companies might be allowed by the Commission to merge if they divested themselves of some ships or port facilities so as to allow others to compete with the merged entity. The Commission has published a "notice on remedies acceptable under Council Regulation (EC) No 139/2004 and under Commission Regulation (EC) No 802/2004".[71] On balance, the Commission prefer so-called "structural" rather than "behavioural" remedies (e.g. disposal of subsidiaries rather than conduct-related commitments which need to be verified on an ongoing basis). As will be seen in the case law below, remedies have included leaving consortia and liner conferences (to avoid interconnections between various market participants) and could involve, for example, disposing of ships or port facilities.

G. MARKET DEFINITION

16.044 As mentioned above, market definition is a key feature of concentration control. Notifying parties tend to argue for wide markets while complainants or interveners argue for narrow markets. Typically, competition agencies tend to examine whether there would be an issue on the basis of narrowest conceivable market and if there is no issue in that context then agencies tend to approve transactions. Very often, competition agencies such as the Commission might simply decide not to define the market precisely in a particular case having established that the proposed concentration does not significantly impede effective competition (i.e. SIEC) irrespective of how the market is defined; in other words, the market definition is left open. The concepts of product and geographical market definitions have been defined earlier.[72]

---

70 Ed., i.e. the parties. The term "undertaking" is sometimes taken to mean a "promise" or "commitment".
71 OJ 2008 C267/1.
72 See chap. 9.

H. ROLE OF THE MEMBER STATES IN THE PROCESS

16.045 While the Commission provides a one-stop shop and is the sole decision-making body in the process, Member States still play a role. In essence, they do so in three ways. First, some concentrations which lack an EU dimension may be referred to the Commission by the Member States (i.e. the transaction could be adjudicated upon by the Commission and not the Member States).[73] Second, concentrations which have a Community dimension and would, in the ordinary course, be reviewed by the Commission, may be referred for decision by the Commission to the Member States for decision in the circumstances outlined in Article 9 of the regulation.[74] Third, whenever the Commission is considering a proposed transaction, the Member States are involved in the process both formally (through the Advisory Committee on Concentrations) and informally.[75] The possibility of referral to, or from, the Commission seeks to strike an interesting balance – as Recital 11 of Regulation 139/2004 states:

> "[t]he rules governing the referral of concentrations from the Commission to Member States and from Member States to the Commission should operate as an effective corrective mechanism in the light of the principle of subsidiarity; these rules protect the competition interests of the Member States in an adequate manner and take due account of legal certainty and the 'one-stop shop' principle."

16.046 Recital 14 of Regulation 139/2004 gives an insight into the way in which the Commission and Member States co-operate. It provides:

> "The Commission and the competent authorities of the Member States should together form a network of public authorities, applying their respective competences in close cooperation, using efficient arrangements for information-sharing and consultation, with a view to ensuring that a case is dealt with by the most appropriate authority, in the light of the principle of subsidiarity and with a view to ensuring that multiple notifications of a given concentration are avoided to the greatest extent possible. Referrals of concentrations from the Commission to Member States and from Member States to the Commission should be made in an efficient manner avoiding, to the greatest extent possible, situations where a concentration is subject to a referral both before and after its notification."

In practice, the Commission has the ultimate power in the relationship (between the Commission and the Member States) rather than the Member States but there is more co-operation than might otherwise be suspected.

16.047 Recital 16 of Regulation 139/2004 deals with how undertakings may request referrals to, or from, the Commission:

> "The undertakings concerned should be granted the possibility of requesting referrals to or from the Commission before a concentration is notified so as to further improve the efficiency of the system for the control of concentrations within the Community. In such situations, the Commission and national competition authorities should decide within short, clearly defined time limits whether a referral to or from the Commission ought to be made, thereby ensuring the efficiency of the system. Upon request by the undertakings concerned, the Commission should be able to refer to a Member State a concentration with a Community dimension which may significantly affect competition in a market within that Member State presenting all the characteristics of a

---

73 Reg. 139/2004, Art. 22.
74 Reg. 139/2004, Art. 9.
75 Recital 13 of Reg. 139/2004 provides that the "Commission should act in close and constant liaison with the competent authorities of the Member States from which it obtains comments and information."

distinct market; the undertakings concerned should not, however, be required to demonstrate that the effects of the concentration would be detrimental to competition. A concentration should not be referred from the Commission to a Member State which has expressed its disagreement to such a referral. Before notification to national authorities, the undertakings concerned should also be able to request that a concentration without a Community dimension which is capable of being reviewed under the national competition laws of at least three Member States be referred to the Commission. Such requests for pre-notification referrals to the Commission would be particularly pertinent in situations where the concentration would affect competition beyond the territory of one Member State. Where a concentration capable of being reviewed under the competition laws of three or more Member States is referred to the Commission prior to any national notification, and no Member State competent to review the case expresses its disagreement, the Commission should acquire exclusive competence to review the concentration and such a concentration should be deemed to have a Community dimension. Such pre-notification referrals from Member States to the Commission should not, however, be made where at least one Member State competent to review the case has expressed its disagreement with such a referral."

16.048 As mentioned above, there are some transactions which do not fall within the scope of Regulation 139/2004 but which Member States should be able to refer to the Commission for review.[76] Again as mentioned above, there are situations where, as a matter of formality, a proposed transaction falls within the jurisdiction of the Commission but should, in reality, be considered by Member State competition authorities. Article 9 of Regulation 139/2004 provides that the Commission may refer a proposed transaction to a Member State.[77]

16.049 The Member States are not permitted to apply their national legislation on competition to concentrations with a Community dimension unless Regulation 139/2004 provides for it.[78] Article 21 of Regulation 139/2004 (in part) provides:

"3. No Member State shall apply its national legislation on competition to any concentration that has a Community dimension.
   The first subparagraph shall be without prejudice to any Member State's power to carry out any enquiries necessary for the application of Articles 4(4), 9(2) or after referral, pursuant to Article 9(3), first subparagraph, indent (b), or Article 9(5), to take the measures strictly necessary for the application of Article 9(8).

---

76 Recital 15 of Reg. 139/2004 provides: "A Member State should be able to refer to the Commission a concentration which does not have a Community dimension but which affects trade between Member States and threatens to significantly affect competition within its territory. Other Member States which are also competent to review the concentration should be able to join the request. In such a situation, in order to ensure the efficiency and predictability of the system, national time limits should be suspended until a decision has been reached as to the referral of the case. The Commission should have the power to examine and deal with a concentration on behalf of a requesting Member State or requesting Member States."

77 I.e. the proposed transaction is a "concentration" with a "Community dimension" within the meaning of Reg. 139/2004. Recital 15 to Reg. 139/2004 provides that the "Commission should be able to refer to a Member State notified concentrations with a Community dimension which threaten significantly to affect competition in a market within that Member State presenting all the characteristics of a distinct market. Where the concentration affects competition on such a market, which does not constitute a substantial part of the common market, the Commission should be obliged, upon request, to refer the whole or part of the case to the Member State concerned."

78 Reg. 139/2004, Recital 18. The recital provides: "The relevant powers of national authorities should be limited to cases where, failing intervention by the Commission, effective competition is likely to be significantly impeded within the territory of a Member State and where the competition interests of that Member State cannot be sufficiently protected otherwise by this Regulation. The Member States concerned must act promptly in such cases; this Regulation cannot, because of the diversity of national law, fix a single time limit for the adoption of final decisions under national law."

4. Notwithstanding paragraphs 2 and 3, Member States may take appropriate measures to protect legitimate interests other than those taken into consideration by this Regulation and compatible with the general principles and other provisions of Community law.

Public security, plurality of the media and prudential rules shall be regarded as legitimate interests within the meaning of the first subparagraph.

Any other public interest must be communicated to the Commission by the Member State concerned and shall be recognised by the Commission after an assessment of its compatibility with the general principles and other provisions of Community law before the measures referred to above may be taken. The Commission shall inform the Member State concerned of its decision within 25 working days of that communication."

16.050 The exclusive application of Regulation 139/2004 to concentrations with a Community dimension is without prejudice to Article 346 of the TFEU, and does not prevent the Member States from taking appropriate measures to protect "legitimate interests" other than those pursued by the regulation, provided that such measures are compatible with the general principles and other provisions of EU law.[79]

I. ANCILLARY RESTRICTIONS

16.051 Many concentrations include restrictions which are ancillary to the transaction itself. Examples include non-compete restrictions on vendors re-entering the market for a period of time after the concentration. In practice, this rarely raises serious issues provided the restrictions are reasonable. Recital 21 of the MCR provides that this

"Regulation should also apply where the undertakings concerned accept restrictions directly related to, and necessary for, the implementation of the concentration. Commission decisions declaring concentrations compatible with the common market in application of this Regulation should automatically cover such restrictions, without the Commission having to assess such restrictions in individual cases. At the request of the undertakings concerned, however, the Commission should, in cases presenting novel or unresolved questions giving rise to genuine uncertainty, expressly assess whether or not any restriction is directly related to, and necessary for, the implementation of the concentration. A case presents a novel or unresolved question giving rise to genuine uncertainty if the question is not covered by the relevant Commission notice in force or a published Commission decision."

J. MINORITY STAKES

16.052 What if an undertaking acquires a minority stake in another undertaking? While it is possible that such stakes could give rise to anti-competitive effects,[80] each case has to be evaluated on its own merits. The stake would, at least, have to give some element of control within the scope of the regulation. The Commission has consulted on, and considered, whether the MCR regime would be reformed to address the control of the acquisition of minority stakes and it is too early to say whether there will be significant change.[81]

---

79 Reg. 139/2004, Recital 19.
80 See Ezrachi and Gilo, op. cit. at fn. 42.
81 http://ec.europa.eu/competition/consultations/2014_merger_control/index_en.html.

K. ROLE OF THE CJEU

16.053 The Commission is given exclusive competence to apply the regulation but this is subject to review by the CJEU.[82] Article 16 of Regulation 139/2004 provides that the Court of Justice has unlimited jurisdiction within the meaning of Article 261 of the TFEU to review decisions whereby the Commission has fixed a fine or periodic penalty payments; it may cancel, reduce or increase the fine or periodic penalty payment imposed. In practice, this means that decisions by the Commission under the regulation are appealed in the first instance to the General Court and then, where appropriate, appealed to the CJEU. The CJEU has generally upheld the Commission's decisions in this area but has also, somewhat spectacularly, annulled a number of Commission decisions highlighting, in particular, the need for more sophisticated economic analysis in its decision-making.

L. THE MCR IN THE SHIPPING SECTOR

Introduction

16.054 The regulation may apply to concentrations involving undertakings in the shipping, port and shipbuilding sectors. The Commission has cleared transactions in those sectors either unconditionally or subject to conditions. It is useful to review the cases which have arisen so far. This review covers most of the cases from the shipping, shipbuilding and ports sectors.

16.055 There was a flurry of activity in 2005 with various transactions in the container liner shipping sector.[83] It has been commented by three Commission officials writing in the Commission's *Competition Policy Newsletter*:

> "[p]rior to these acquisitions the container liner shipping industry was considered to be non-concentrated at the individual carrier level. Even after the acquisition of PONL, Maersk's worldwide capacity share remains below 20%. However, for the merger analysis the position of the parties on the relevant market is crucial ... containerised liner shipping does not constitute a worldwide market but has to be assessed on the basis of single trades, defined by the range of ports which are served at both ends of the service. Further, the co-operation of liner shipping companies in conferences, consortia and alliances has to be taken into account when analysing the competitive constraints on each trade."[84]

There was also some increase in activity due to the need for increased scale and efficiency (e.g. among cruise and container companies) as well as the need to deal with the repeal of the block exemption on liner conferences as well as the economic crisis.

16.056 It is proposed to examine some (indeed, most) of the concentrations involving the shipping sector but not all because some of them were so-called "simplified procedure" cases which means that they raised no issue at all and the published decisions therefore tell us relatively little. Some of the cases were also very fact specific so the analysis will concentrate on the more useful cases.

---

82 Reg. 139/2004, Recital 17.
83 See Benini, Gadas and Miersch, "Consolidation in Container Liner Shipping: Merger Control Aspects", Competition Policy Newsletter, Spring 2006, p. 84.
84 Ibid., p. 84. The comment that the market is not worldwide is correct but may come as a surprise to some in the sector. It is not enough that ships are similar or even identical on a worldwide basis, what matters is the level of competition, pre- and post-concentration, in a particular market.

1998: *DFO/Scandlines*

16.057 On 29 January 1998, the Commission approved a concentration whereby: (a) Deutsche Bahn AG ("DB") and (b) the Danish Ministry of Transport ("DMT") would acquire joint control of Scandlines AG ("SAG").[85] The latter was a newly created company constituting a joint venture, into which DB and DMT would transfer their respective entire shareholdings in their subsidiaries Deutsche Fährgesellschaft Ostsee mbh ("DFO") and Scandlines A/S ("SAS").

16.058 DB provided rail transport services for passenger and freight in Germany, ferry and related activities in the Baltic region. DMT provided rail transport services for passenger and freight in Denmark, ferry and related activities in the Baltic region and operation of the Great Belt and the Øresund fixed links. DFO provided ferry and related services in the Baltic region. SAS also provided ferry and related services in the Baltic region.

16.059 In terms of the transaction, all the shares in SAG would be owned in equal proportions by DB and DMT, and their voting rights were in proportion to their shareholdings. Decisions required a majority. Each shareholder would appoint two of the four directors who comprised the Management Board. The Management Board's operations would be overseen by a Supervisory Board, comprising two members nominated by each of DB and DMT, plus two employee representatives. Initially, the Chairman of the Supervisory Board would be appointed by DB, and the Deputy Chairman by DMT; thereafter the Supervisory Board would make its own appointments. The Chief Executive Officer would be initially appointed by DB and DMT, but thereafter would be appointed by the Supervisory Board from the Management Board. SAG would take over the entire ferry operations of the two parents. The effect was thus to bring those operations, previously under the sole control of each party, under joint control. Accordingly, the Commission found that the notified operation had a Community dimension because of the parties' turnovers and it constituted a concentration for the purposes of the MCR.

16.060 In terms of the competitive assessment, the Commission found that the operations would bring together a total of 21 Baltic sea ferry services operated by the parties individually (12 routes by SAS, one by DFO), operated together (one route) or operated jointly with third parties (SAS five routes, DFO two routes). The routes varied considerably in importance, from "through routes" linking north Germany to Denmark and/or Sweden (e.g. Rødby–Puttgarden, Rostock–Gedser and Sassnitz–Trelleborg) and carrying road and rail traffic, both freight and passenger, to minor local routes between islands carrying foot passengers only. The parties considered it necessary to merge their operations in order to rationalise them and so maintain profitability in the face of developments which they believe would have significant effects on the sector. The first development was the creation of fixed links (tunnels and bridges) across the Great Belt (linking the Danish islands of Fyn, already linked to the mainland, and Sjaelland – the island on which Copenhagen is located), and across the Øresund (between Sjaelland and the Swedish mainland near Malmo which would enable road and rail traffic to make an uninterrupted land journey between northern continental Europe and Scandinavia. The Great Belt link was already operational for rail traffic and would open for road traffic later that year; the

---

85 Case IV/M.1045.

Øresund link was due to open in 2000. The parties expected that this development would have a significant adverse effect on the volumes of traffic of all kinds using their services on "through" routes, and also on certain local ones (a number of which they plan to close once the links are operational). DMT was the owner of the Great Belt link and co-owner (with the Swedish government) of the Øresund link. However, the parties considered that neither DMT nor the national governments would have any interest in operating the fixed links in any way which would benefit the operations of SAG. The second development of concern to the parties was the then planned abolition of duty-free concessions for intra-Community travel (which eventually transpired); this would, they suggested, further affect the profitability of many routes, since they rely heavily on income from such sales to help reduce ticket prices.

16.061 In terms of the relevant product markets, the parties identified four possible relevant product markets: for freight, passengers, duty-free sales and tourist excursions (all in the Baltic region). However, it was not necessary to further delineate relevant product markets because, in all alternative market definitions considered – notably, for individual routes, for freight or for passenger transport – effective competition would not be significantly impeded in the EEA or any substantial part of that area. There was no overlap on individual routes, and market shares and/or overlaps on other bases were small.

16.062 The parties' interest in excursions was small (it accounted for a small share of their total turnover) and competition was, and was expected to remain, very intense as the business was highly price-sensitive and there were a large number of actual and potential operators. Accordingly and in the absence of any indication having been found during the Commission's examination that the proposed transaction would have had significant adverse effects on competition in these areas, they were not considered further by the Commission.

16.063 The parties' interests also included port facilities. The operation of port services had been identified (quite rightly) in a Commission decision of 1993 concerning the provision of port services at the port of Rødby[86] as a separate market. SAS owned the ports of Gedser and Rødby. DB owned the land-based facilities at the port of Puttgarden, where DFO owned the ferry terminal. However the proposed transaction would not have any significant impact in this area according to the Commission. Its only effect was to bring under the same control the port facilities at Puttgarden with those of Rødby, and in practice these facilities would have already been operated in close conjunction with each other, since DFO and SAS have for some time operated their Rødby–Puttgarden ferry service as a joint venture – this was a significant finding and an alternative construction was that two parts which were connected would come under common control thereby preventing further competitors.

16.064 In terms of the *geographic* dimension, the notifying parties argued that the relevant geographic market was the market for international transportation over land, sea or air, between Scandinavia, on the one hand, and Continental Europe. However, the Commission said that it was not necessary to further delineate relevant geographic markets because, on all alternative geographic market definitions considered, the merger would not significantly impede effective competition in the EEA or any substantial part of that area.

---

86 OJ 1994 L55/52.

16.065 The Commission found that the parties did not operate competing services on any route. The absence of an overlap is significant. The merger's principal impact on competition was therefore limited to the loss of DFO and SAS as potential competitors on any individual route or groups of routes which would be substitutes for each other. As regards possible inter-route competition (i.e. competition between routes) on the through-routes, the port of Rødby decision found that the Rødby–Puttgarden service could not easily be substituted by other ferry links between Denmark and Sweden and Germany, some of which were operated by third parties. That decision observed in particular that there was no motorway link from western Germany to Rostock and Warnemunde, by contrast with Puttgarden, which was in any case nearer to Hamburg (through which most traffic between Western Europe and Scandinavia must pass). It also observed that the crossing-time was notably longer via Rostock, and that traffic flows were much lower on the easterly routes than on the more westerly route. Finally it added that use of the fixed links (which were at that time planned but not built) would still require the payment of a toll. The Commission was able to approve the present transaction unconditionally because:

> "12. The parties argued that improvements in third parties' services on the other routes, both as to time and frequency, plus the opening of the Great Belt for rail traffic, meant that for many customers there was now a number of viable alternatives to the Rødby-Puttgarden route, and that with the completion of the links these alternatives would appeal to an even larger proportion of customers than they do at present. They pointed to a reduction across the board in volumes of traffic on the Rødby-Puttgarden route between 1991 and 1996, and a significant growth in traffic on certain of the more easterly routes. As regards the fixed link tolls, the parties argued that proposals for the Great Belt would result in prices well below those currently charged for the ferry crossing (30–50% lower). Pricing for the Øresund link had yet to be decided; but the parties expected that prices will be pitched at a level that, in combination with the Great Belt link and the improved ferry services on the other routes, would have a negative effect on their traffic volumes, and thus on profitability.
> 13. It is difficult to assess precisely the impact of all these present and future developments on the extent to which inter-route competition exists (or will do so) and will be affected by the merger. However, if inter-route competition is a reality on any of the ferry routes affected by the merger, then it is most likely to arise between Rødby-Puttgarden and Gedser-Rostock, since these are the closest geographically. If these routes are indeed in competition with each other (and it should be noted that unlike Rødby-Puttgarden, Gedser-Rostock carries no rail traffic) then the merger's main effect would be to remove DFO as a potential entrant to Gedser-Rostock. This possibility, and its effect, are considered further below.
> 14. As regards the extent to which the fixed links should be considered as substitutes for the Germany-Scandinavia ferries generally, this too is unclear as the links are not yet fully operational. Moreover, as already described, the parties (and the relevant national governments) have some interest in them, although, according to the parties, the national governments have no interest in operating them in such a way as to benefit the parties' ferry operations. There is also the difficulty of assessing customers' preferences in terms of time and cost. For example, to reach Copenhagen from Hamburg via the Great Belt link will involve an additional road journey of about 150km by comparison with the route via the Rødby-Puttgarden ferry. But in terms of total journey time, allowing for the one-hour ferry crossing, the difference between the routes is likely to be small – less than an hour for road traffic. As for the costs of the alternative methods, there will be some additional fuel involved in using the Great Belt link, however on the parties' information the toll will be significantly less than the ferry fare, so on that basis the road route should be cheaper overall, and in some instances (eg at peak times, when ferry fares are highest) substantially so. Some professional drivers may however not be able to use the fixed links as an

alternative to the ferry, in view of their need to comply with statutory limits on the number of hours they spend at the wheel. Whether they will be sufficiently numerous to allow the parties to price-discriminate (which would probably involve raising prices for all truck-drivers, since the parties could not readily identify those who were likely to be affected by the limitation) is unclear, but does not appear likely. If the fixed links are substitutes for the ferries, then the creation or reinforcement of dominance as a result of the merger is much less likely; but even if they are not, the merger's primary effect is on potential rather than actual competition, and on the basis of the assessment below, that effect is not likely to be significant. Market definition can therefore be left open.

15. The merger creates no direct overlaps between the parties in terms of individual routes. The shares and/or overlaps in terms of individual types of traffic are small. The parties do not compete directly with each other over any individual route, so the merger will not lead to any increased market share in any product category on that basis. On a wider basis, their combined shares of all international freight (excluding air freight, and also rail freight, which they no longer carry except on one route operated by DFO with third parties) between Scandinavia and Northern Continental Europe are estimated by the parties at [deleted as business secret, under 25%], the bulk of this accounted for by a single route – the jointly operated Rødby-Puttgarden crossing. So far as can be established, there are no significant categories of freight in which the merger will create or enhance large market shares. As regards passengers, they estimate their current combined share of all passenger traffic between Northern Continental Europe and Scandinavia (excluding rail) at [deleted as business secret, 30–50%]. Moreover the increment arising from the merger is minimal ([deleted as business secret], derived from the addition of the Sassnitz-Trelleborg route, operated jointly by DFO and SAB of Sweden) and one of the main SAS routes concerned (Halsskov – Knudshoved, responsible for [deleted as business secret, 10–20%]) will close next year as it parallels the crossing made by the Great Belt link. All three passenger train routes (Rødby-Puttgarden, Sassnitz-Trelleborg and Rostock-Trelleborg) are already operated by DFO jointly with either SAS, in the case of Rødby-Puttgarden, or SAB. Consequently, since these arrangements (which include joint control of prices and timings) are expected to continue, the merger will not lead to any increment in the parties' share of this category. Moreover the parties expect their shares in all categories to fall significantly (by at least [deleted as business secret – substantial]) following completion of the fixed links."

The Commission then considered the impact of the proposed transaction on competition:

"16. If inter-route competition exists at all, the merger's impact on it should be slight. The only potentially significant routes, from this point of view, appear to be the two adjacent Germany-Denmark routes, Rødby-Puttgarden (already jointly operated) and Gedser-Rostock, where the merger will have the effect of removing DFO as a potential competitor. However DFO does not appear to have been a likely entrant in any case; a few years ago it withdrew from a partnership with SAS on the route. [deleted as business secret] and its total traffic is much less than on Rødby-Puttgarden (currently about [deleted as business secret] in terms of freight and [deleted as business secret] in terms of passengers). Since the fixed links seem likely to have some effect on the volumes of passengers and freight on these routes, even if they are not true substitutes (ie they do not constrain prices for the incumbents) they should nonetheless make entry on the ferry routes less attractive, and thereby further reduce the impact of the loss of DFO as a potential competitor to SAS on Gedser-Rostock, either in combination with Rødby-Puttgarden or (if there is no inter-route competition) alone."

The Commission obtained some comfort from their market investigation:[87]

---

[87] A market investigation involves the Commission considering the competition implications of the proposed transaction with various stakeholders (e.g. customers, competitors, consumers, potential new entrants and so on). The Commission does not usually discuss its likely decision with them (although it may eventually inquire of their views on potential remedies) as well as elicit information from them as to their views on the proposed concentration.

"17. This analysis, and the approach to market definition, was broadly borne out by the Commission's enquiries of customers, competitors and other interested parties. The majority of respondents were generally unconcerned by the merger, and considered that the fixed links would probably improve the competitive situation for Germany-Scandinavia traffic of all kinds, though their views varied as to the extent to which this would be the case. Some ferry operators expressed concerns, however. These concerns were broadly of two kinds: that the merged entity would have excessive financial power, enabling it to cross-subsidise operations and make long-term investments that would result in competitors being driven from the market; and that the merger would allow the parties to abuse their position as owners of the ports of, respectively, Rødby and (land-side facilities only) Puttgarden by denying access, at all, or on reasonable terms, to potential entrants – of whom there currently appear to be at least two.

18. The first concern does not appear to be justified. Both parties, individually, already have considerable financial strength, deriving in part from government involvement. It is unclear whether and if so to what extent the merger will lead to a strengthening of the merged entity's financial position. But increased financial strength is not of itself anti-competitive. The merger does not reduce competition significantly on an intra-route or inter-route basis, limiting the scope for improved profits, and no evidence has been found to suggest that a predatory pricing strategy by the merged entity would be rational or effective.

19. The second concern is, in effect, that barriers to entry on the relevant route will be increased as a result of the merger. The 1993 decision already referred to[88] found, among other things, that DSB and DB (the predecessors of the parties to the present merger) had a dominant position on the route concerned (which they operated jointly) and that DSB was dominant in the provision of port services at Rødby. As discussed above, however, the merger does not materially affect competition in regard to port services and so does not create or strengthen a dominant position in them. Applications for entry at the two ports by operators wishing to offer a competing service on Rødby-Puttgarden have been the subject of, or are currently under, consideration by the relevant national authorities in Denmark and Germany."

The Commission cleared the transaction unconditionally.

1998: *GE Capital/GE SeaCo*

16.066 On 28 April 1998, the Commission approved unconditionally the proposed transaction whereby General Electric Capital Corporation ("GE Capital") of the USA and Sea Containers Ltd ("Sea Containers") acquired joint control of a new joint venture company GE SeaCo SRL ("GE SeaCo").[89]

16.067 GE Capital was a subsidiary of the General Electric Company. GE Capital was a diversified financial services company, providing equipment management, specialised financing, speciality insurance and a variety of consumer services, such as car leasing, home mortgages, and credit cards. One of GE Capital's businesses was marine container operating leasing, which it conducted solely through its subsidiary Genstar Container Corporation ("Genstar").

16.068 Sea Containers was engaged in three main business activities: marine container operating leasing; ferry, rail and port operations; and leisure industry activities. Furthermore, Sea Containers also manufactured containers, and operated storage depots and

---

88 Ed., OJ 1994 L55/52.
89 M.1020.

servicing operations for repairing, servicing and storing marine containers for itself and third parties.

16.069 The transaction was a concentrative joint venture between GE Capital and Sea Containers and would be accomplished by the creation of a new joint venture entity ("GE SeaCo"). The entirety of the marine container operating leasing business of each of the parties was being contributed to the joint venture and the parent companies would effectively withdraw from the marine container operating lease business. In particular, the operation would result in the parties' marine container operating leasing infrastructure being combined in GE SeaCo by the transfer into the latter of the office premises and equipment, including the computerised tracking systems, contracts, containers, human resources and related business assets.

16.070 The Commission found that joint control was being acquired. This was because the annual budget of GE SeaCo had to be approved by the board and no significant transaction could be undertaken by GE SeaCo or any of its subsidiaries without the approval of the Board of Managers. A detailed list of significant transactions covered by these provisions was annexed to the Omnibus Agreement between the parties and included items such as: (a) any incurrence of indebtedness for borrowed money at any time outstanding in excess of US$100,000 per occurrence; (b) any adoption of, or material amendment to, the annual capital and operating budgets; (c) any adoption of or revision of any policy with respect to customer credit, risk management, financial accounting, public relations or business ethics and integrity; (d) any commencement or participation in any business other than the shipping container business, or making any investment in, loan to, or guarantee of the obligations of, any other person, or creating any subsidiary of GE SeaCo; and (e) any acquisition or establishment of manufacturing, depot or repair facilities other than as approved in the annual budget. GE Capital and Sea Containers would each appoint half of the eight person Board of Managers, and there would be no casting vote. Furthermore, the Board could only decide by majority. Therefore, one party would always be able to block any significant transaction. Consequently, GE SeaCo would be jointly controlled by GE Capital and Sea Containers.

16.071 The Commission found that the proposed transaction amounted to an autonomous full function joint venture on a lasting basis. GE SeaCo would be a full market participant competing with other marine container operating leasing companies. It would have its own staff and other resources, which would make it a full function joint venture, which was able to operate on a lasting basis. GE SeaCo would initially operate a fleet of approximately 1,165,000 teu (i.e. twenty foot equivalent unit containers). It would own only a small fraction of these containers. Most of its containers would be leased from the parent companies. GE SeaCo would itself purchase new containers. It was, therefore, foreseen that the proportion of containers owned by GE SeaCo would increase over time as the containers leased from the parent companies were being phased out and new ones were acquired directly by GE SeaCo. GE Capital did not own any depot or repair facility for containers. Instead GE Capital contracted with third parties. Sea Containers operated a number of depots and repair facilities for containers. Sea Containers did not service both its own as well as third party containers. However, the number of facilities was not sufficient to meet the needs of Sea Containers. As was customary in the industry, the company, therefore, also contracted with a number of third parties for the supply of these services. Sea Containers would continue to operate a number of depots and repair facilities, which would service GE SeaCo as well as third parties. GE SeaCo would be supplied these services at rates customary to third parties. Furthermore, GE SeaCo would also have to contract with third parties for these services. The fact that GE SeaCo would purchase a part of its needs for storage and repair facilities from Sea Containers, therefore, did not affect the full function nature of the joint venture.

16.072 The Commission was satisfied that the GE SeaCo would be an autonomous full function joint venture established on a lasting basis and therefore constituted a concentration within the meaning of the MCR. The transaction also had a Community dimension and therefore the MCR applied.

16.073 In terms of the relevant *product* markets, the Commission recalled that marine containers were built to precise international standards, which allowed standardised handling and transportation of containers. Containers were basically available as 20 and 40 foot units. For purposes of analysis, the marine container industry used as a standard of measurement a teu ("twenty foot equivalent unit"), which represented the length and width of a standard 20-foot long container. The principal categories of containers were: (a) dry freight standard; (b) dry freight specials; (c) refrigerated containers (reefers); and (d) tanks. The standard container was the dry freight standard category. It was estimated that this category accounted for about 87% of all containers in the global container fleet, whereas the three other categories consisted of more specialised containers, which accounted for the balance. Dry freight special containers were thus characterised by having for example different loading doors. Reefers were used to transport perishable goods, and tanks to transport liquids. The Commission's interviews of competitors and customers (as part of the market investigation) indicated that the above four categories of containers could be separate relevant product markets. However, it was not necessary to finally decide this question for the purpose of the case, since the operation would not create or strengthen a dominant position[90] on even the narrowest possible product market definition.

16.074 In terms of the relevant *geographic* markets, the parties argued that the geographic market for marine container operating leasing was global. The customers and competitors interviewed by the Commission agreed. The Commission recalled that

> "containers are moving around globally without any barriers, leasing rates are quoted in [US dollars], and basically reflects the length of the lease. Furthermore, several customers and competitors in particular emphasised that the marine container operating leasing business required a global presence of a company. The scope of the relevant geographic market is, therefore, global."[91]

The Commission observed that Transamerica was the market leader in all categories. After the transaction, GE SeaCo would become the market leader in reefers, but on the basis of the total market, Transamerica and GE SeaCo would be the largest operators of a comparable size with some 20% each of the overall market. The Commission went on to find:

> "19. Important competitors exist to the parties and Transamerica in all categories with the exception of dry freight special containers. In this category GE SeaCo and Transamerica will have a share of more than 60% of the market following the operation. In principle such

---

90 This was tested under Reg. 4064/89 which was the original MCR.
91 Para. 16.

a market concentration, in the absence of other sizeable competitors, could give rise to a duopolistically dominant position. However, in the present industry this is not the case, since important operators exist in the other container categories. These companies are strong and credible potential competitors, who could relatively easily create an important container capacity for the dry freight special containers. Consequently the operation will not lead to the creation or strengthening of a dominant position."

16.075 The Commission also has to deal with the issue of ancillary restraints because the parties had agreed to a non-competition agreement. It provided that GE Capital and Sea Containers were precluded from entering the business areas of the joint venture as long as they owned 20% of the class A securities of GE SeaCo and for a period of two years thereafter. The non-compete agreement reflected the lasting withdrawal of the parents from the markets of the joint venture, and was, therefore, covered by the Commission's decision as long as the joint venture existed. As far as the extension of the non-compete clause to the two years following a possible termination of the joint venture is concerned, the Commission observed that the extension related to a possible future operation, which was not part of the notified transaction and therefore the two year extension of the non-compete clause was not covered by the decision. The Commission decided not to oppose the notified operation and declared it compatible with the internal market.

1999: *Maersk/Safmarine*

16.076 On 7 May 1999, the Commission approved unconditionally the acquisition by Maersk A/S ("Maersk") of sole control of Safmarine Container Lines N.V. ("SCL").[92]

16.077 SCL was the liner business of Safmarine, which was part of the South African group Safren Ltd. SCL was mainly active on North–South trades. SCL had an extensive network of agents and it operated a fleet of more than 50 owned and chartered liner vessels with a total capacity of 56,000 teu. SCL also operated a wide range of container equipment and it had a road haulage business providing support to the shipping lines. SCL was also active in inland waterways vessel operations in Europe and was involved in warehousing.

16.078 Maersk was a holding company owning a number of Maersk Line container shipping agencies around the world. Maersk was a member of the A.P. Møller Group.

16.079 The transaction involved Maersk buying the Safmarine liner business through the purchase of the SCL shares and liner assets. The acquisition also included certain landside activities, such as trucking, barging and warehousing.

16.080 The Commission found that the relevant product sector involved was liner shipping, where Maersk was one of the world's largest players. The markets affected by the transaction were on the North–South trades.[93]

16.081 The Commission recalled that in

---

92 M.1474.
93 The North–South trades operated between the three major industrial areas of North America, Western Europe and Asia, and economies in the southern hemisphere. In contrast, the East–West trades circled the globe in the northern hemisphere linking the three major industrial areas.

"previous cases in the maritime transport field[94] the Commission has defined the relevant market as a service supplied between a range of ports on either the Northern European or the Mediterranean coast and a range of ports in another continent or region; the service between two ranges of ports is called a 'trade'. Consequently, attention must be paid to both the definition of this service and to its geographic aspects."[95]

16.082 In terms of relevant *product* markets, the Commission recalled that the parties argued that the definition of the relevant product market was containerised liner shipping services.[96] This was in line with the product market definition

"given by the Commission in *P&O/Nedlloyd*. In that decision, the Commission did not include break-bulk transport (i.e. non-containerised transport) in the definition of the relevant product market because it found that there was no lasting substitution from container towards break-bulk in the vast majority of cases. In the present case the parties argue that on the Europe/Southern Africa trades the Commission should take into account non-containerised refrigerated transport ('reefer transport'). According to the parties, in the North-South trades there would be considerable substitutability between containerised and reefer transport, in particular for perishable goods. Therefore, the parties argue that on these trades reefer transport should be included in the relevant market definition."

The Commission also stated that its

"enquires indicate that even though there are a number of commodities which are carried only by container, in several cases there is some substitutability between container and non-containerised reefer transport services. In the present case, however, it is unnecessary to determine whether the relevant product market definition should include also reefer transport since even on the basis of the narrower market definition the transaction does not create or strengthen a dominant position."

16.083 In terms of the *geographic* aspects of the service, the Commission recalled that: "[in] previous cases the Commission has found that transport to and from Northern Europe constitutes a distinct service market from transport to and from the Mediterranean".[97] The Commission found that in the case, the trades which would be affected by the transaction were: (a) Northern Europe/Southern Africa; (b) Mediterranean/Southern Africa; (c) Northern Europe/West Africa; (d) Mediterranean/West Africa; (e) Northern Europe/East Africa; and (f) Northern Europe/Middle East. Third parties agreed in general that these trades constituted distinct relevant markets. Ultimately, the Commission stated that it was not necessary in the case to define the market precisely, as the transaction would not create or strengthen a dominant position on either market definition to/from Red Sea/East Africa. So, it found that the relevant markets for the present case comprised the provision of the service by shipping companies between ports in either Northern Europe or the Mediterranean and ports in each of the non-European areas, as mentioned above.

16.084 The Commission's competitive assessment was very interesting. It stated:

---

94 See e.g. IV/M.831 *P&O/Nedlloyd*; Commission Decision of 16 September 1998 (IV/35.134 – *Trans-Atlantic Conference* Agreement), OJ L95, 9.4.1999, p. 1.

95 Para. 8.

96 Containerised liner shipping services involve the carriage of goods by container, that is to say in boxes of standard shape and size (usually 20 feet or 40 feet long) on ships specially equipped for the purpose, see Comm. Dec. of 19 October 1994 (IV/34.446 – Trans-Atlantic Agreement), OJ L376, 31 December 1994, p. 1, at paras 39 to 41.

97 Para. 11.

"15. Conferences and consortia are contractual arrangements between shipping lines that play an important role in the organisation of the liner shipping industry and restrict competition between their members. Liner conferences are defined as ''a group of two or more vessel-operating carriers which provides international services for the carriage of cargo on a particular route or routes within specified geographical limits and which has an agreement or an arrangement, whatever its nature, within the framework of which they operate under uniform or common freight rates and any other agreed conditions with respect to the provision of liner services'.[98],[99] Liner conferences have the effect of limiting competition amongst their members in respect of pricing, timetabling, frequency of service, ports called at, carrying capacity, and allocation of cargo and revenue.

16. Consortium agreements are 'agreements between two or more vessel operating carriers which provide international liner shipping services exclusively for the carriage of cargo, chiefly by container, relating to a particular trade in order to rationalize their operations by means of technical, operational and/or commercial arrangements, with the exception of price fixing'.[100] Consortium agreements may limit competition amongst the members of consortia by, for example, capacity planning, the operation of joint sailing timetables and determination of ports of call, and joint marketing structure.

17. Not every carrier operating on a particular trade is a member of a conference or consortium. On some trades important carriers operate outside conferences and consortia.

18. In P&O/Nedlloyd, the Commission considered to what extent the parties' membership in different consortia and conferences had to be taken into account in the assessment of the operation. The Commission concluded that the structural link resulting from the merger must also be seen in relation to the contractual links with the co-members of the consortia and conferences. The Commission concluded further in that decision that after the operation the parties would be contractually linked to other shipping lines with which they consequently would not be in full competition. The Commission therefore investigated whether the operation would strengthen the cohesion within an existing conference or consortium which would create dominance or whether the transaction would reinforce already existing dominance.

19. In the present case there are two trades on which the membership of the parties in the relevant conferences/consortia must be taken into account for the assessment of the transaction: the Northern Europe/South Africa trade and the Northern Europe/Middle East trade."

16.085 The Commission then undertook a competitive assessment of the affected markets:

"20. Based on the information provided by the parties, they would, following the transaction become market leaders in four trades: Northern Europe/West Africa, Mediterranean/West Africa, Northern Europe/East Africa and Northern Europe/Middle East. The Northern Europe/South Africa trade is also relevant for the analysis, since in that trade both parties belong to a shipping conference and to consortia. On the remaining Mediterranean/Southern Africa trade the market position of the parties is such that the transaction is unlikely to lead to any reduction of competition.

21. Based on their own market share information, the parties would have [25–35%] of the Mediterranean/West Africa trade. However, there are, according to the parties, a number of other operators on this trade, such as Messina ([15–25%]), Grimaldi ([10–20%]), Delmas and MSC ([5–15% each]). Competitors have in general allocated a larger share of the trade to Messina and Delmas. On the basis of the foregoing, the parties' market share is not considered to be indicative of a dominant position.

---

98 Council Regulation (EEC) No 4056/86, OJ L378 of 31 December 1986.
99 Ed., this decision pre-dated the abolition of the EU block exemption for liner conferences.
100 Council Regulation (EC) No 870/95, OJ L89 of 21 April 1995. Ed., the absence of price-fixing was the distinguishing feature between liner conferences and consortia agreements.

22. On the Northern Europe/East Africa trade, where the parties would also have [25–35%] of the trade, the situation is more balanced as the parties would face strong competition in particular from MSC ([25–35%]) and West European Container Line ([15–25%]). Other operators on this trade include Delmas ([5–15%]) and P&O ([5–15%]). It is to be noted that some third parties have estimated the parties' combined market share to be considerably lower, slightly above [5–15%]. Therefore, given the existence of competing operators, the parties' market share is not considered to be likely to raise competition concerns.

23. On the Northern Europe/West Africa trade the parties have estimated their combined market share as [25–35%]. Delmas would have [15–25%] of the trade, OT Africa Line [10–20%] and Grimaldi [0–10%]. Some competitors have provided market share estimates according to which Delmas would actually have some [25–35%] of the trade. Customers have indicated that there is sufficient competition on the trade. Based on the foregoing, the parties' market share is not considered to be indicative of a dominant position.

Northern Europe/Middle East.

24. The parties belong to IPBCC (the India Pakistan Bangladesh Ceylon Conference), the main conference on the Northern Europe/Middle East trade, which has collectively [55–65%] of the market. In addition, Maersk operates on that trade in a joint service with Sea Land (the Maersk/Sea Land Alliance). SCL operates on the trade as a member of EPIC (the European Pakistan Indian Consortium)...

25. It can be seen from above that the parties' combined market share would be [10–20%]. P&O/Nedlloyd would have [5–15%] of the trade and UASC and CMA [5–15%] each. It should be noted that there are also a number of different alliances active on the trade, most importantly Grand Alliance, New World Alliance, United Alliance and SCI/ZIM/Ying Ming Alliance. The market position of the parties themselves does not give rise to any competition concerns.

26. Nor would the operation strengthen the market position of IPBCC. Third parties have not raised any concerns about the transaction on this trade in general nor have they voiced concerns over the possible links being created between EPIC and Maersk/Sea Land Alliance. Customers in particular have indicated that there are a sufficient number of strong competitors operating on the trade; indeed, there are also other conferences operating on this trade. It is also to be noted that it is easy for the carriers already operating Europe – Far East services to enter the market by way of transhipment. Therefore, on the basis of the foregoing, it is concluded that the operation is unlikely to lead to any competition concerns.

Northern Europe/South Africa.

27. As mentioned above, the parties contend that Northern Europe/South Africa traffic should include also the reefer trade. The parties have therefore provided market share figures both excluding and including the reefer trade on the Northern Europe – South Africa trade, as given below.

28. With regard to the Northern Europe/South Africa trade, the relevant consortium for the analysis in the present case is SAECS (which operates currently under name 'SAECS III') and the relevant conference is ESAC (Europe Southern Africa Conference). SAECS operates within ESAC. SCL is a member of both ESAC and SAECS. Maersk is not a member of either of these.

29. ... the combined market share of the parties would be [20–35%], depending on whether the reefer trade is included or not. The largest single competitor would be MSC, which operates outside conferences and consortia. MSC would have [20–35%] of the market. Reefers would represent up to [25–35%] of the market. Given these figures alone, it is unlikely that the operation would give rise to any competition concerns.

30. The parties have indicated that Maersk will 'most probably' join SAECS. Several third parties have drawn the Commission's attention to the fact that since entering the market in 1998, Maersk has built up a market share of approximately [5–15%], much of which has been at the expense of SAECS whose utilisation rate has declined. Several third parties have indicated that, in case Maersk were to join SAECS, this would merely restore

SAECS's competitive position before Maersk's entry. Third parties have pointed out that the combined share of the new entity within SAECS would be larger than the one held by SCL alone. Replies to the Commission's enquiries show, however, that customers and competitors consider the impact on the trade to be a limited one. Customers have confirmed competitive conditions on the trade and have also suggested that the impact of the conferences/consortia has decreased during the past few years due to severe competition on the trade."

16.086 The Commission therefore decided not to oppose the notified operation and to declare it compatible with the common market and with the EEA Agreement.

1999: *Maersk/Sea-Land*

16.087 On 6 October 1999, the Commission approved a transaction whereby the A.P. Møller Group would acquire the international container liner business of Sea-Land Service Inc. ("Sea-Land").[101] Maersk would also acquire certain of Sea-Land's related activities, including terminals, vessels and containers. The transaction consisted in the acquisition by the A.P. Møller Group of control of the international container liner business and related services of Sea-Land Service Inc. ("Sea-Land"), by purchase of shares and assets.

16.088 The Commission considered the relevant service markets. The first market was described as "containerised liner shipping services". The Commission recalled that the relevant market was for containerised liner shipping between a range of ports in either Northern Europe or the Mediterranean and a range of ports on another continent or in another region with a service between two ranges of ports being called a "trade". The decision recalled that the notifying party identified the market for containerised liner shipping services as the service market primarily affected by the operation and this was consistent with the service market definition adopted by the Commission in cases such as *P&O/Royal Nedlloyd*,[102] *Maersk/Safmarine*[103] and *TACA*.[104] The second market concerned sea transport services relating to intra-Europe shipping. The decision recalled that the parties were also active on a number of short-sea container shipping routes within Europe (i.e. "intra-Europe shipping"). The services concerned consist of shipping containers from one European port to another, either as "direct hinterland traffic" (traffic to or from a particular hinterland that is connected to the port of origin or the destination) or as "feeder traffic" (transhipping containers from and to deep-sea ports). The notifying party argued that the relevant market included other forms of transport, in particular road transport. In the present case, it is not necessary to determine whether the relevant product market includes other forms of transport. The Commission's investigation had shown that even on the basis of a narrower market definition consisting of containerised liner shipping services on a particular route or bundle of routes, the notified operation would not create or strengthen a dominant position. The third service market was that of terminal services. A.P. Møller also acquired certain landside activities operated by Sea-Land, in particular, terminals. These terminals were partly used for captive purposes and partly provided

---

101 M.1651, 6 October 1999.
102 Case IV/M.831.
103 Case IV/M.1474.
104 Case IV.35.134.

services to other container lines, i.e. loading and unloading, storing, etc. (also referred to as stevedoring services). Services for container ships were different from services for ships carrying, for example, liquid bulk cargo, essentially because a different infrastructure ("superstructure") was required. The Commission said that the market for stevedoring services could be further sub-divided according to the size of the vessels which require handling, i.e. deep-sea vessels (operating between continents, more than 3,000 teu) or short-sea vessels (operating on shorter distances), given that different berthing and land-side equipment facilities were needed. However, the Commission's investigation had shown that even on the basis of this narrower market definition, the notified operation would not create or strengthen a dominant position.

2001: *HBG/Ballast NEDAM/Baggeren JV*

16.089 On 3 August 2001, the Commission approved a joint venture between Dutch companies Hollandse Beton Groep N.V. and Ballast Nedam N.V. in the dredging sector.[105] The parent companies would each remain separately active in their principal activities of building and construction while transferring their dredging activities to a joint venture, called Ballast HAM Baggeren N.V. The Commission stated that in line with its previous decision in *Boskalis/HBG* (approved in 2000[106] but not consummated), the markets considered by the Commission were the market for large dredging projects, which has an international or at least EEA-wide scope, and the Dutch market for small dredging projects, which has a national scope. The Commission recognised that while the transaction would create a larger player in the markets for large and small dredging projects, it would not lead to a dominant position in any of the markets because, the Commission found, on both markets, a number of strong competitors were present and the markets would remain competitive. Therefore, the operation did not raise competitive concerns in either market and the Commission decided to clear the transaction.

2002: *Vopak/Van der Sluijs*

16.090 On 25 February 2002, the Commission approved the deal whereby the Vopak Group and Van der Sluijs would acquire joint control of the Interstream joint venture which would be active in inland mineral oil tanker transport.[107] Both of these Dutch companies would transfer their inland tanker broker and barging activities on the German and Swiss Rhine and in the Benelux countries to the Interstream joint venture. This joint venture would mainly transport mineral oil products for the large oil companies in the Amsterdam–Rotterdam–Antwerp area and on the Rhine river. The Commission approved the transaction on the basis that there were several sizeable competitors and a large number of smaller shipping companies who offered transport in the area. Therefore the Commission was not so concerned with the fact that the joint venture would be the largest operator in the market. The Commission found that the combined market share of the joint venture would be less than 15%. The Commission also found that the transaction

---

105 M.2503. See also IP/01/1187.
106 See IP/00/710.
107 M.2597, 25 February 2002.

would not have any significant competitive impact on the parents' positions in other markets such as the storage of petroleum products, inland oil tankerage in other waters and inland tankerage and storage of petroleum products, inland oil tankerage in other waters and inland tankerage and storage of other products such as chemicals, vegetable oils, liquefied gases and ocean tanker shipping.

2002: *Wallenius Lines/Wilhelmsen/Hyundai*

16.091 On 29 November 2002, the Commission cleared the acquisition by Wallenius (of Sweden) and Wilhelmsen (of Norway) of Hyundai Merchant Marine's deep-sea car carrier business.[108] Wallenius and Wilhelmsen provided their car carrier services through a 50/50 joint venture called Wallenius Wilhelmsen Lines ("WWL"). Korean company Hyundai Merchant Marine ("HMM") was a member of the Hyundai Group and provided dedicated car carrier services to the Hyundai Motor Company ("HMC") and its subsidiary KIA, as well as services to other manufacturers. Although HMC and KIA had been recently separated from the Hyundai Group, these companies were still heavily dependent on the dedicated shipping services provided by the HMM car carrier division. Under the notified transaction, Wallenius and Wilhelmsen would acquire HMM's car carrier business, which would be renamed Ro-Ro Korea. Besides the car carrier vessels of HMM, the main assets to be acquired were the car carriage contracts between the latter on the one hand and HMC and KIA on the other. The Commission had assessed the transaction on the basis of a product market consisting of the deep-sea transportation of vehicles other than in liner shipping (i.e. scheduled services).

16.092 The Commission's clearance was however subject to commitments. During the notification process, the Commission became concerned that the deal might significantly reduce competition and lead to higher prices for the transport of cars between Europe and the Near East. In specific terms, the Commission found that the concentration, as originally notified, led to competition concerns on two trade routes, namely the Northern Europe–Near East and the Mediterranean–Near East trades respectively. Wallenius' and Wilhelmsen's joint venture WWL operated on these routes through the WALLNYK conference, together with one of their main competitors, Nippon Yusen Kaisha ("NYK"). The addition of the HMM car carrier business would have substantially increased the market power of this conference. But Wallenius and Wilhelmsen offered to withdraw from the WALLNYK shipping conference with NYK, one of their main competitors, and that action would fully remove these concerns. They agreed that they would not enter into any similar agreement with any competing carrier on the routes in question without the prior consent of the Commission. The termination of the agreement and the fact that NYK would become an independent competing supplier of car carriage services on the relevant trades re-established the competitive situation prevailing prior to the proposed merger on the Mediterranean–Near East trade and substantially would, the Commission believed, reduce the impact of the merger on the Northern Europe–Near East trade.

---

108 See also IP/02/1780.

2003: *Van Oord/BHD/Bagger Holding JV*

16.093 On 11 December 2003, the Commission cleared the dredging joint venture between the BAM and Van Oord groups.[109] The dredging activities of Dutch company Koninklijke BAM Groep would merge with Van Oord Groep N.V., a joint venture between MerweOord and NPM. The merger would create the world leader for the removal of sand and other materials from sea and river beds, but it would still face sufficient competition. The joint venture in the dredging sector would be called Bagger Holding. BAM would contribute its Ballast HAM Dredging B.V. to the joint operation while MerweOord and NPM would bring their jointly owned Van Oord Groep N.V. BAM would remain active in its principal activities of building and construction. The Commission was satisfied that the number of remaining big players and the presence of other well-equipped worldwide players would mean that sufficient competitive pressure would remain. There would still be three sizeable competitors and many small competitors remaining. In any event, in both large and small markets, contract awards are based on open tendering, and very often by public procurement.

16.094 It is useful to pause for a moment and consider the way in which the Commission analysed the markets. The Commission recalled that the dredging markets had already been defined in previous merger cases.[110] The parties followed these definitions in their notifications. The Commission recognised that there were two relevant product markets for dredging projects in Europe with each requiring different types of contractors and dredging equipment without supply-side substitutability.[111] A distinction was therefore made between large international projects and small national projects on the basis of the value of the projects. The Commission believed that although

> "the dividing line between both markets is subject to a dynamic appreciation based on market variables, such as availability of the right equipment, distance between the project site and equipment, time between projects, 'hunger for work' and the occupancy rate of the equipment, it can be determined at a project value of approximately €5 million."[112]

The small dredging projects are normally national in scope because they require a relatively small financial and operational size and because it would be uneconomical to move the smaller scale equipment used over long distances. In the case of small contracts, a local operational presence and local knowledge can be very important (or, according to the Commission, "essential").[113]

2008: *DP World/Conti 7/Rickmers/DP World Breakbulk*

16.095 On 18 November 2008, the Commission approved a proposed joint venture for breakbulk[114] terminal services between DP World, Conti 7 and Rickmers at Antwerp

---

109 M.3311 *Van Oord/BHD/Bagger Holding JV*.
110 Case Nos COMP/M.2503 – *HBG/Ballast Nedam/Baggeren JV* of 3 August 2001 and COMP/M.1877 – *Boskalis/BHG* of 4 July 2000. The latter concentration was not executed because of certain issues that arose between the Parties after the Commission had cleared the transaction. It is worth noting however that decisions on market definition are of limited precedent value.
111 Decision, para. 9.
112 Decision, para. 10.
113 Decision, para. 11.
114 Breakbulk is cargo not suitable for either bulk or container transportation but often packed on pallets.

port.[115] The Commission cleared the creation of a joint venture between DP World of Dubai and the shipping companies Conti 7 of Belgium and Rickmers of Germany. The joint venture, called DP World Breakbulk, would take over DP World's former activities in breakbulk terminal services at Antwerp. The Commission concluded that the transaction would not significantly impede effective competition in the EEA or in any substantial part of it. DP World, previously P&O Ports Europe, belonged to Dubai World which was owned by the Emirate of Dubai. DP World was active in discharging and loading vessels and related activities, such as the handling of trucks, rail, barges, warehousing, container repair and container storage. DP World intended to transfer its terminal breakbulk services at the port of Antwerp to the joint venture. Conti 7 belonged to the Conti group, which provided maritime transportation services worldwide. Rickmers owned and managed ships and co-owned a breakbulk terminal at the German port of Hamburg. The joint venture, DP World Breakbulk, would carry out breakbulk terminal services at Antwerp. The Commission found that the proposed transaction would not lead to increased market shares in breakbulk terminal services at Antwerp, as the activity of DP World would be brought into the joint venture and neither Conti 7 nor Rickmers were active there. In a wider geographic market, the transaction would bring about only minor additions in market shares, due to Rickmers' activities at Hamburg. The Commission therefore concluded that the transaction would not lead to competition concerns on the basis of horizontal or vertical relationships between the parties' activities.

2008: *DPWL/ZIM/Contarsa*

16.096 On 27 June 2008, the Commission approved a notification of a proposed concentration by which DP World Ltd and ZIM Integrated Shipping Services would acquire joint control over Contarsa Sociedad de Estiba, SA by way of purchase of shares.[116] The business activities of the undertakings concerned were: (a) for DP World Ltd: global marine terminal operator; (b) for ZIM: global transportation (container liner shipping services) and logistics services, operation of container terminals; and (c) for Contarsa: provision of stevedoring services in the Port of Tarragona. The transaction was dealt with under the simplified procedure and did not result in a SIEC.

2008: *APMM/Swift Tankers Pool*

16.097 On 11 November 2008, the Commission approved unconditionally a proposed concentration, following a referral of the transaction to the Commission pursuant to Article 4(5) Regulation 139/2004, by which A.P. Møller-Maersk ("APMM") would acquire control of Teekay's participation in the Swift Tankers pool by way of purchase of shares and assets. There was no SIEC. The business activities of the undertakings concerned were: (a) for APMM: shipping, container terminal services, inland transportation, logistics, harbour towage, tankers, oil and gas exploration and production, and supermarkets; and (b) for Swift: transport of bulk liquid products. It was a transaction which was cleared under the simplified procedure.

---

115 M.5093.
116 M.5163.

2009: *APMM/Broström*

16.098 This concentration involved A.P. Møller-Maersk, ("APMM") of Denmark[117] acquiring sole control of Broström of Sweden.[118],[119] This was the first Commission decision in the area of concentrations in the tramp shipping sector.[120] The Commission cleared the concentration on 14 January 2009 having been notified of it on 2 December 2008 so it was dealt with expeditiously. The concentration lacked a Union dimension (i.e. the turnovers of the parties did not reach the turnover thresholds set out in Article 1 of Regulation 139/2004; nonetheless, by way of a reasoned submission, the parties informed the Commission that the concentration was capable of being reviewed under the national competition laws of at least three EU Member States and one EEA State[121] so it was then capable of being notified to the Commission (and none of the EU/EEA Member States concerned disagreed with the case being referred to the Commission)) so the transaction was deemed to have a Union dimension pursuant to Article 4(5) of Regulation 139/2004 and the Commission had sole competence to take a decision by virtue of Article 57(2)(a) of the EEA Agreement.

16.099 The Commission recalled that according to its own (then extant) Maritime Guidelines,[122] the elements to be taken into account in market definition in the tramp sector examining the vessel types, cargo types, vessel sizes and contract types. This meant that the Commission had to undertake a considerable amount of market testing to gather information and form its views.[123]

16.100 In terms of product market definition and vessels, the Commission included, in this case, liquid bulk vessels (including product tankers and chemical tankers) equipped with tanks, pumps and other loading equipment designed for "clean" and "dirty" petroleum products, chemicals and vegetable oils. However, the Commission excluded container ships (as they could not carry liquid bulk products), dry bulk vessels (as they could not carry liquid bulk products) and tankers which were not double hulled.[124] The Commission also had to consider the size of vessels. In terms of market definition and cargo type, the Commission had to consider whether vessels carrying clean and vessels carrying

---

117 Para. 2 of the decision recalls: "2. The APMM group is an international conglomerate based and listed in Copenhagen. Although it is mainly known for its shipping business (Maersk Line and Maersk Tankers), the APMM group has a wide range of activities, including container terminal services, inland transportation, logistics, harbour towage, oil and gas exploration and production, and retail. APMM is active in 130 countries around the world."

118 Para. 3 of the decision recalls: "3. Broström, which is based in Gothenburg, Sweden, and listed on the Stockholm stock exchange, provides maritime transportation services by product tankers. Broström's customers consist primarily of oil companies. Other significant customer groups include brokers of oil cargoes and industrial users of oil products. Broström's activities also include maritime logistics (e.g. combined transport and storage solutions) and ownership, technical operation and crewing for most of its vessels."

119 COMP/M.5346.

120 The Commission in Recital 9 of the decision stated: "9. The tramp shipping sector relates generally to the transport of a single commodity which fills a single ship. Unlike in the liner sector, tramp shipping markets are unscheduled, in the sense that vessels do not sail on advertised, pre-determined routes on particular days. When they are not laden, idle/empty tramp vessels bid for business in their area or move to a loadport in order to pick up cargo or move to a more promising area ('repositioning' or 'ballasting')." (Footnote omitted.)

121 Namely Bulgaria, Cyprus, Estonia, Germany, Greece, Latvia, Slovakia and the UK, as well as one EEA state, namely Norway.

122 See chap. 10.

123 Decision, para. 11.

124 Reg. 417/2002 on the accelerated phasing-in of double hull or equivalent design requirements for single hull oil tankers meant that the market should be defined as excluding single hull vessels.

dirty petroleum products were in the same market. The Commission also considered the type of contract[125] which was involved and ultimately found that there was no distinction based on the contract type. Interestingly, the Commission also considered whether legislation could influence the definition of the market:

> "14. Furthermore, the double-hull requirement under Regulation no. 417/20028 is taken into account when defining the vessel type to be included in the relevant market (Maritime Guidelines, paragraph 30). Indeed, tankers entering EU waters must comply with Regulation no. 417/2002. Therefore, in accordance with that regulation, only vessels meeting the double-hull requirement and non-double-hull vessels delivered after 1982 are taken into account for present purposes."

16.101 In terms of the *product market*, the Commission was able to leave the product market definition open because no matter how the market was defined, no issue would arise about a SIEC.

16.102 In terms of the *geographical market*, the Commission analysed various possible market definitions (e.g. worldwide, west of Suez, east of Suez, Europe as opposed to other areas and European Atlantic coast as opposed to Mediterranean Sea/Black Sea). Ultimately, the Commission did not have to reach any decision on the market definition because the transaction would be permitted irrespective of how the market was defined. The Commission was able to consider the proposed concentration on different market definitions across the type of cargo carried by the vessels, the size of the vessels and the geographical regions of operation. The Commission concluded:

> "39. In any event, the exact geographic market definition can be left open in the present case, as there are no competition concerns on any possible market definition.
> 40. Therefore, the relevant geographic market may be worldwide or based on the distinction between the area lying 'west of Suez' and the area lying 'east of Suez', which is widely used in the industry, or on further geographic subdivisions ('Europe', defined as the European Atlantic Coast from Russia to Gibraltar, the Mediterranean Sea and the Black Sea; or the 'European Atlantic Coast' on one side and the 'Mediterranean Sea/Black Sea' on the other side)."

16.103 In terms of the product and geographical markets, the Commission concluded:

> "41. In conclusion, the present transaction has to be assessed on the basis of several possible market definitions, namely the dirty petroleum products market; clean products, including easychems; and dirty and clean petroleum products as well as easychems; for (a) the worldwide market, (b) the area West of Suez, (c) Europe, (d) the European Atlantic Coast (EAC) and (e) the Mediterranean Sea/Black Sea area; and broken down by DWT range ((i) 10,000–60,000 DWTs; (ii) 10,000–25,000 DWTs and (iii) 25,000–60,000 DWTs)."

16.104 The Commission found that the market was a bidding one so the market shares were less relevant than the number of bidders for each contract. It also found that the customers (typically, major oil companies) were in a strong position to negotiate price. The Commission also noted that there was overcapacity in the industry which would drive down price or at least keep price competitive.

16.105 The Commission found that there were several horizontally affected markets in the 10,000–60,000 dwt (deadweight tons) range but there were no vertically affected markets or conglomerate issues.

---

125 E.g. voyage charters, time charters, contracts of affreightment and consecutive voyage charters.

16.106 The Commission recalled that in previous merger decisions in the liner sector,[126] the Commission assessed the competitive situation on the basis of teu capacity (and not on the basis of actual liftings or number of vessels). However, when it came to this case in the tramp sector, no Commission precedent existed in the tramp sector. The Commission recalled that the Maritime Guidelines stated, at paragraph 29, "[i]n certain tramp shipping markets, consideration must be given to whether vessels can be considered as captive capacity and should not be taken into account when assessing the relevant market on a case by case basis". However, the Commission believed that:

> "44. ... in the present case, it is not necessary to examine this issue further because this concentration does not raise competition concerns even in the worst case scenario, i.e., if the captive fleet is excluded from the relevant market.
>
> 45. This method can be regarded as sufficiently accurate because (a) APMM and Broström's vessels are distributed along the range from 10,000 to 60,000 DWTs; (b) vessels are often not loaded to 100% capacity, and vessels that have different DWT capacities compete with each other to some extent; and (c) in bidding markets, vessel numbers matter more than actual liftings. In the present case, the competitive situation is therefore assessed on the basis of the number of vessels."

16.107 The Commission also had to consider the issue of pools:

> "47. Pools are essentially joint selling or joint production agreements whereby shipowners agree to bring their vessels together under a single commercial manager, which is usually one of the pool members.
>
> 48. The Handytankers pool brings together product tankers in the 30,000–40,000 DWT range belonging to five shipowners including APMM. APMM also acts as pool manager, which means that it sets the prices for all vessels in the pool. APMM is therefore both a pool member and in charge of the joint selling. On this basis, the notifying party proposes that all Handytankers vessels should be aggregated to APMM's fleet, and, therefore, market share.
>
> 49. In view of the fact that the members of the Handytankers pool effectively present themselves on the market as one company and engage in joint selling through APMM, for the purpose of the present case, all Handytankers vessels are aggregated with APMM's fleet in the competitive analysis below."[127]

16.108 In reaching its conclusions on the horizontal issues (there being no vertical issues), the Commission recalled that the parties' activities overlap in the 10,000–60,000 dwt range. On the various markets, APMM and Broström would strengthen their leading position, with the merged entity's largest competitor having less than 8% market share. However, for the reasons detailed below and since no significant concerns had been raised by market participants in the course of the market investigation, it was considered that the operation did not significantly impede effective competition on any of the identified markets. The relevant markets could be characterised as bidding markets with a relatively fragmented supply side. As confirmed by the market investigation, charterers often contacted several brokers and had a choice between several vessels. Moreover, the markets at issue were not capacity constrained; on the contrary, many respondents to the market investigation expected a certain degree of overcapacity in the market in the future as a result of the current order book of vessels and lower demand for oil products.

---

126 Case COMP/M.3829 – *Maersk/PONL*, case COMP/M.3863 – *TUI/CP Ships* and case COMP/M.3973 – *CMA CGM/Delmas*.
127 Footnotes omitted.

Moreover, output levels could not easily be scaled back in the relevant markets, as vessels have a long lifespan and the market was fragmented. By contrast, the demand side was relatively concentrated, with large oil traders, oil majors, chemical companies and food producers making up the bulk of the demand. The expected overcapacity was expected to further improve the bargaining power of these customers. The Commission found that several companies had recently entered the market and one more company was expected to enter the market, according to the notifying party. APMM also claimed that new entry was possible with one or two vessels. The market investigation indicated that one vessel was enough to enter the Voyage Charter and Time Charter segments,[128] but that a new entrant would need six or seven vessels to become a credible COA operator. In practice, recent entrants had entered the market with six to eight vessels. The market investigation also showed that customers regularly multisource and switch suppliers. Although some respondents to the market investigation cited vessel financing, quality crewing and vetting approvals as possible entry barriers, these barriers applied equally to established firms and newcomers. Moreover, capital costs to enter the market or to operate more vessels were not very high – it was possible to charter a vessel from a non-operating owner. It was also possible to buy a second-hand vessel. Accordingly, the Fearnleys report explained that "the tanker market has very low barriers to entry. [...] The second hand market for both dirty and clean tankers is highly liquid, and there are a number of transactions taking place every year." The Commission found that it was not difficult for a new entrant or an established player to build scale in the market by chartering in some tonnage, buying new or second-hand vessels, or forming/joining pools that were in compliance with Article 101 of the TFEU. Thus the merged entity did not enjoy a unique competitive advantage due to its size. It should also be borne in mind that scale allowed for better fleet deployment and better fleet utilisation, to the benefit of operators, customers and the environment. Third, while APMM and Broström competed on the market, the market investigation clearly indicated that they were not each other's closest competitors.

16.109 The Commission cleared the transaction unconditionally because it concluded:

"59. Finally, as the merger would in all likelihood not cause a significant reduction in the number of vessels in the relevant markets, and since charterers often have a choice of several vessels in addition to the parties' vessels (according to the market investigation, customers regularly multisource and switch suppliers), it would be very difficult for the merged entity to raise prices. Even if the merged entity attempted to raise prices in a particular region, vessels could move in from another region. While vessels may not be ready to move to a neighbouring region in the event of a small increase in price, they would be more inclined to move to a neighbouring region in the event of a larger price increase and compete away the profits. ... Further competitive constraints result from the fact that clean and dirty petroleum vessels as well as different vessel sizes are at least to a certain extent substitutable to each other."

---

128 The Commission had recalled that there are, generally speaking, four contract types in the tanker business: voyage charters ("VCs"), time charters ("TCs"), contracts of affreightment ("COAs"), and consecutive voyage charters ("CVs"). VCs are also known as the "spot" market. TCs, COAs and CVs are also known as "contract" shipping.

2008: *Hutchison/Evergreen*

16.110 On 17 December 2008, the Commission approved unconditionally the acquisition of joint control over Taranto Container Terminal SpA of Italy by Hutchison Whampoa Limited Group and Evergreen Group.[129] The Commission concluded that the operation would not result in a SIEC in the EEA or in any substantial part of it. Hutchison Group provided deep-sea container stevedoring services with operations worldwide. It was also active in retail and manufacturing, telecommunications and internet infrastructure, real estate and hotels and the supply of energy and infrastructure projects. Evergreen Group was a conglomerate of shipping, transportation and associated service companies controlled by Dr Chang Yung-Fa and his family. Taranto Container Terminal operated a container terminal in Taranto, Italy. The Commission found that the horizontal overlaps brought about by the transaction in the provision of deep-sea stevedoring services in the Mediterranean market were limited and would not lead to any competition concerns.

2005: *NYK Reefers/Lauritzen*

16.111 On 19 August 2005, the Commission approved, under the MCR, a joint venture between NYK Reefers and Lauritzen.[130] The case involved the proposed creation of a joint venture, LauritzenCool (or LauCool), between NYK Reefers and Lauritzen. LauCool, had been a full subsidiary of Lauritzen, operating and managing bulk refrigerated vessels used for the transport by sea of perishable goods. The Commission found that although NYK Reefers was also active in the transport by sea of perishable goods, the transaction would not result in a SIEC. NYK Reefers belonged to the Japanese NYK Group, which had interests in international liner and bulk shipping, as well as global logistics. NYK Reefers was an owner and operator of a fleet of bulk refrigerated ("reefer") vessels used for the transport of fruit and other perishable produce by sea. Lauritzen was a Danish shipping group which was engaged in the transport of a variety of products. Its subsidiary LauCool was part of the Lauritzen Reefer division and specialised in commercial and operational management of bulk reefer vessels. LauCool did not own any reefer vessel capacity, but chartered in the capacity it needs at arm's length from independent owners of reefer vessels and from Lauritzen.

16.112 The transaction consisted of the acquisition by NYK Reefers of 50% of the shares in LauCool from Lauritzen. Simultaneously, NYK Reefers would transfer its business of commercial and operational management of the trades operated by NYK Reefers to LauCool joint venture. On the basis of operated capacity, the joint venture became the second largest bulk reefer vessel operator worldwide.

16.113 The Commission's examination of the proposed transaction demonstrated that the proposed concentration did not raise competition concerns either on a worldwide basis or on the basis of geographical corridors from individual regions to the EU.[131] Even though LauCool would be the leading bulk reefer operator on a number of these corridors,

---

129 M.5398.
130 COMP/M.379. See IP/05/1059, 22 August 2005.
131 The Commission stated at para. 28 of the decision: "The exact market definition can be left open as the concentration does not lead to competition concerns even under the narrowest plausible market definition of specialised bulk reefer transport services (with a possible separate market for the transport of bananas) in geographic corridors from each exporting region to Northern Europe and the Mediterranean respectively."

it would continue to face strong competition both from other bulk reefer operators and from operators of refrigerated container vessels.[132]

2005: *Maersk/PONL*[133]

16.114 AP Møller ("Maersk") bid for the Dutch-UK Royal P&O Nedlloyd ("PONL"). Maersk had been the leading global container company. PONL was the fourth largest carrier in the world. The Commission found that serious doubts existed regarding the compatibility of the proposed concentration because of the co-ordinated effects of the transaction. The conference member had to leave various conferences[134] and consortia[135] so as to permit the transaction to be approved. The Commission concluded that it was foreseeable that the concentration would produce non-co-ordinated effects (i.e. unilateral effects) in the refrigerated container transport market between Europe and South Africa. The Commission applied a narrower market definition than would be the norm.

16.115 On 29 July 2005, the Commission approved the planned acquisition of PONL by Maersk but subject to conditions.[136] The clearance was conditional on the divestiture of PONL's business on the trade between Europe and South Africa and the withdrawal of PONL from several conferences and consortia. In light of those commitments, the Commission concluded that the proposed transaction would not significantly impede effective competition. The transaction was handled with the Commission by the Internal Market Commissioner (Charlie McCreevy) rather than the Competition Commissioner (Neelie Kroes) because of a possible conflict of interests. Commission McCreevy stated on the transaction being approved:

> "[m]ost of the world's trade is carried by sea. When the number one carrier reinforces its market position by buying its third largest competitor, we must ensure that shippers and end-consumers

---

132 E.g. para. 41 of the decision recalled: "As regards a possible separate relevant market for the transportation of bananas in bulk reefer vessels, the only overlap between the parties' activities on the basis of 2004 figures would be in the Central America to Northern Europe corridor. Nevertheless, their combined market share even in this narrow market does not exceed 15% and there are significant competitors active in this segment such as Seatrade, Chiquita, Del Monte, Dole and Fyffes. Furthermore, as of the beginning of this year NYK has lost all its banana contracts in this geographical corridor."

133 M.3829, 29 July 2005.

134 Para. 176 of the decision provides that: "Maersk commits to withdraw PONL from the following liner shipping conferences at the earliest date permitted after acquisition of control of PONL:
- Australia/New Zealand to Europe Liner Association (ANZELA) • Europe to Australia and New Zealand Conference (EANZC)
- Europe East Africa Conference (EEAC)
- European/South Pacific & Magellan Fright Conference (ESPMC)
- North Europe/Djibouti Conference (NE/DC)
- New Caribbean Service Rate Agreement (NCS)
- Association of the West India Trans-Atlantic Steam Ship Lines (WITASS)."

135 Para. 177 of the decision provides: "Maersk commits to withdraw PONL from the following liner shipping consortia at the earliest date permitted after acquisition of control of PONL:
- Eurosal/NCS Consortium (Eurosal)
- Grand Alliance.
- New ANZ Consortium (NANZC).
- Slot Charter Agreement between PONL and MSC on Europe – East Africa Trade (SCA MSC).
- Vessel Sharing Agreement between PONL and Hamburg Süd on the Europe – East Coast South America Trade (VSA Hamburg Süd)."

136 See IP/05/1026, 29 July 2005. The decision was a long 66-page document.

do not lose out. Following our investigation and the remedies offered we are satisfied this would not be the case."

16.116 The merger created the world's then largest shipping company, deploying over 800 container vessels and created a worldwide turnover of roughly €28 billion. AP Møller owned the shipping container lines Maersk and Safmarine and was also active in container terminal services, harbour towage, tankers, logistics, oil and gas exploration, air transport, shipbuilding and supermarkets. PONL was mainly a container liner shipping company, also involved in container terminal services, logistics and air transport.

16.117 The parties' activities overlapped mainly in the container shipping business and to a lesser extent in the terminal services business.

16.118 The Commission's extended market investigation focused on the shipping trade lanes to and from Europe to determine whether the parties' market shares and the links created by their participation in various conferences and consortia with their competitors would result in anti-competitive effects whereby markets could be shared and prices increased to the detriment of shippers and final consumers.

16.119 The Commission found that the merger created links between Maersk and the conferences and consortia to which only PONL was a member. Where their combined market shares gave rise to competition concerns, the Commission made its approval of the transaction conditional on the withdrawal of PONL from these conferences and consortia so as to sever the ties that linked them.

16.120 Another area of concern was trade between Europe and Southern Africa, especially the transport of refrigerated goods in reefer containers where the parties' market share was higher than 50%. Maersk offered to divest PONL's business dealing with the transport of cargo from South Africa to Europe.

16.121 The Commission's conditions were imposed to remove concerns relating to potential co-ordination between the merged entity and its competitors arising from their mutual membership of liner conferences and consortia.

2005: *TUI/CP Ships*[137]

16.122 TUI (a German logistics and tourism company) owned Hapag-Lloyd (a shipping company) ("HL"). It sought to acquire sole control of CP Ships of Canada. CP Ships was mainly a container shipping company with some activities in container terminal services. The transaction would create the fifth largest company in the world in terms of capacity at that time. HL was a member of two conferences in the Europe–North America trade. As a result of the proposed merger and the continued membership of the conferences, there would be a link created between the leading participants. The notified operation was a concentration with a Union dimension so the MCR applied. On 22 October 2005, the Commission cleared the proposed transaction but subject to conditions. In essence, the merged entity would have to withdraw from the two conferences that operated on the Europe–North American trade.[138] It was an important decision on the application of the MCR to the shipping sector.

---

137 M.3863, 12 October 2005.
138 M.3863.

16.123 In terms of the relevant product market, the Commission considered four possible markets: (a) containerised liner shipping; (b) container terminal services; (c) in-land transportation of containerised goods; and (d) freight forwarding.

16.124 The Commission saw containerised liner shipping as involving:

> "7. ... the provision of regular, scheduled services for the carriage of cargo by container. It can be distinguished from non-liner shipping (charter, tramp, specialised transport) because of the regularity and frequency of the service. In addition, the use of containerised transportation separates it from other non-containerised transport such as bulk vessel. Previous merger decisions have defined the market for containerised liner shipping services on one or more trades.[139] A possible narrower product market is that for the transport of refrigerated goods, which could be limited to reefer (refrigerated) containers only or could include transport in conventional reefer (refrigerated) vessels.[140]
>
> 8. In line with the recent Maersk/PONL decision, on trades with a share of reefer containers in relation to all containerised cargo below 10% in both directions, transport in reefer containers is not assessed separately, but as part of the overall market for container liner shipping services. On imbalanced trades with high shares of transport in reefer containers in relation to all containerised cargo in one direction and relatively low shares in the other direction, the market position of the parties on a possible market for the transport of reefer containers only will be taken into consideration.
>
> 9. The geographical dimension of containerised liner shipping services consists of single trades, defined by the range of ports which are served at both ends of the service. Each trade has specific characteristics depending on the volumes shipped, the types of cargo transported, the ports served and the length of the journey from the point of origin to the point of destination. Considering that in liner shipping supply has to be provided by a sufficient number of vessels to generate a scheduled service, these characteristics influence the level of barriers to entry that may be present on the trade. Relevant trades are those from Northern Europe to other non European areas[141] and back and from the Mediterranean to other non European areas and back.[142]
>
> 10. The parties put forward that the two directions of a trade should not be distinguished and that for certain trades Northern European and Mediterranean ports should be part of the same market. However, the market conditions on the two directions of a trade can be different, in particular in the case of trade imbalances or different characteristics of the products shipped.[143] In these instances, a distinction between the two directions of a trade is justified.
>
> 11. As regards substitution between Northern European and Mediterranean ports, the possibility of inland transport and transhipment between Northern Europe and the Mediterranean does not seem to lead to substitution to a considerable extent. For the trades to and from North America, this is confirmed by decisions of the Commission[144] and not disputed by the parties. For the other trades it is not necessary to conclude on a precise definition of the geographic dimension because the competition analysis will not significantly differ under both alternative market definitions."

16.125 Staying with the product market definition, the Commission also considered container terminal services. The Commission recalled that previous merger decisions had

---

139 M.831 – *P&O/Royal Nedlloyd*; M.1651 – *Maersk/Sealand*; M.3576 – *ECT/PONL/Euromax*; M.3829 – *Maersk/PONL*.
140 M.3829 – *Maersk/PONL*.
141 Such as North America, Far East, Indian Subcontinent, Middle East, East Africa, South Africa, West Africa, Caribbean/Central America, East Coast South America, West Coast South America and Australia/New Zealand.
142 See M.3829 – *Maersk/PONL*.
143 E.g. mainly technical products in one direction and food in the other direction.
144 See in particular the decision in the antitrust case COMP/37.396 – Revised TACA.

defined the market for stevedoring services for deep-sea container ships, broken down by traffic flows to hinterland traffic (=direct deep-sea) and transhipment traffic (=relay/feeder).[145] As HL was only active in Hamburg, the relevant geographical dimension of stevedoring services was in its broadest scope Northern Europe (for transhipment traffic) and in its narrowest possible scope the catchment area of the ports in the range Hamburg–Antwerp (for hinterland traffic).

16.126 In terms of the "in-land transportation of containerised goods", the Commission recalled that in the past, it had indicated that various means of transport probably constituted separate product markets and that geographically the market may be national or even wider.[146] It was therefore not necessary to conclude on a precise definition of the relevant market in this case as the transaction did not lead to competition concerns under any alternative market definition.

16.127 In regard to freight forwarding, in which both parties were active, the Commission recalled that in previous cases, this was defined as the organisation of transportation of items (possibly including ancillary activities such as customs clearance, warehousing, ground services etc.), on behalf of customers according to their needs.[147] The Commission in the past considered subdividing the market into domestic and cross-border freight forwarding; land, air and sea freight forwarding; and express and standard freight forwarding.[148] The geographic scope of the markets was either national or wider. In this case, however, it was not necessary to define the market precisely, because under any possible market definition no competition concerns arose.

16.128 Having defined (or not so much defined, as identified) markets, the Commission then turned to the competitive assessment of the proposed transaction.

16.129 In regard to containerised liner shipping, the Commission recalled that HL was, according to the parties, the thirteenth largest global carrier with a share of capacity of less than 10% while CP Ships was the sixteenth with a share of again less than 10%. The then recently created entity Maersk/PONL was the largest global carrier with a worldwide share of capacity of between 10 and 20%. The second and third placed carriers each had shares of less than 10%. The merged entity would become the fourth largest global carrier with a combined capacity share of less than 10%. On some EU trades, the combined market shares of the parties are above 15% – the affected markets were therefore the trades relating to North Europe–North America, Mediterranean–North America, North Europe–Caribbean and Central America, North Europe–Australia/New Zealand as well as Mediterranean–Australia/New Zealand.

16.130 HL and CP Ships were members of various liner conferences, consortia and alliances. The Commission recalled that these three arrangements restricted competition between their members. Then the Commission observed:

> "21. The combined market position of the members of conferences and consortia can be substantial. Carriers are often members of a conference and of one or more consortia on the same trade. This enables them to cumulate the benefits of the Conference Block Exemption Regulation (price fixing) and of the Consortia Block Exemption Regulation (operational arrangements for the provision of a joint service). In line with previous merger decisions,

---

145 JV.55 – *Hutchison/RCPM/ECT* and JV.56 – *Hutchison/ECT*; M.3576 – *ECT/PONL/Euromax*.
146 M.2905 – *Deutsche Bahn/Stinnes*.
147 See e.g. case M.1794 – *Deutsche Post/Air Express International*.
148 M.1794 – *Deutsche Post/Air Express International*.

the parties' membership in conferences and consortia is taken into account in the assessment of the consequences of the operation on the affected markets.[149] Therefore, market shares of the merged entity and those of relevant conferences and consortia are considered. The market share of a conference or a consortium is the aggregated market share of their members, calculated on the basis of the members' volume which is carried under the conference or consortium agreement. However, in order to assess the risk of coordination between the members of a conference or a consortium and to evaluate the strength of the carriers interlinked due to their conference or consortium membership, it is appropriate to take into account the total volume transported by the conference or consortium members in the relevant trade.[150]

22. Depending on the parties' membership, the proposed transaction will have different effects on conferences and consortia. The following alternatives may occur:

In cases where the parties are currently in the same conference or consortium and the merged entity maintains the membership, the concentration would not change the total market share of the conference or consortium. Depending on the structure of the conference or consortium, however, this could lead to a strengthening of the internal cohesion and eventually lead to the merged entity controlling the conference.

In some instances HL is in a conference or consortium, but not CP Ships, even though it is active on the same trade. If HL maintains its membership, CP Ships can be expected to be integrated into the conference or consortium. The market share of the conference or consortium will rise. Even without such integration, CP Ships' volume is no longer independently competing with the conference or consortium. If only CP Ships is in a conference or consortium, the merger would create a link between HL and the conference and/or the consortium. This link would enable HL to take part in the exchange of information within the conference and/or the consortium. HL could use the commercially sensitive information exchanged therein to adapt over time its conduct on the market, thus increasing the risk of market sharing or lessening of competition between itself and the other members of the conference or the consortium. Even without integrating itself into the conference or the consortium, HL would no longer be an independent competitor because it controls a member of the conference or the consortium.

23. The effects of the proposed transaction will be assessed for each affected market. The assessment is generally based on the information provided by the parties. In some cases the market investigation has shown a discrepancy between the market shares indicated by the parties and the figures provided by third parties. Where relevant, this is signalled."

16.131 The case is quite complex but very fact-specific. For present purposes, it is sufficient to have regard to the Commission's press release:

"Mergers: Commission clears the planned acquisition of CP Ships by TUI, subject to conditions:

The European Commission has cleared under the EU Merger Regulation the proposed acquisition of the Canadian shipping company CP Ships by the German company TUI, which owns the shipping company Hapag-Lloyd. The Commission's clearance is conditional upon the withdrawal of Hapag-Lloyd from two liner shipping conferences that operate between Europe and North America. In light of the commitment to withdraw from these conferences, the Commission has concluded that the transaction will not significantly impede effective competition in the European Economic Area (EEA) or any part of it.

Competition Commissioner Neelie Kroes said: 'The clearance of this merger paves the way to the creation of a leading European player in the industry. The remedies ensure that the merger does not lead to anticompetitive coordination between shipping lines on the important trade lanes between Europe and North America.'

---

149 M.831 – PO/Royal Nedlloyd; M.1651 – Maersk/Sealand; M.3829 – Maersk/PONL.
150 See M.3829 – Maersk/PONL, par. 130 ff.

Both CP Ships and Hapag-Lloyd are mainly active in container liner shipping. Through the merger they will become the world's fourth largest operator and a leading competitor on some shipping trade lanes.

The Commission's extended market investigation focused on the trade lanes to and from Europe to determine whether the parties' market shares and the links created by their participation in various conferences and consortia with their competitors would result in anti-competitive effects whereby markets could be shared and prices increased to the detriment of shippers and final consumers.

Under the European Union's competition rules applicable to shipping, liner conferences (groupings of shipping companies engaged in regular scheduled services) benefit from antitrust immunity granted nearly 20 years ago. Shipping lines grouped in consortia also benefit from an antitrust exemption. After a two year investigation, in October 2004 the European Commission issued a White Paper concluding that the exemption for liner conferences should be abolished because it no longer results in efficient and reliable services that meet shippers' requirements (see IP/04/1213). A proposal from the Commission is due before the end of the year.

In the shipping trade lanes between Europe and North America, Hapag-Lloyd is a member of two conferences. As a result of the merger and continued membership of the conferences, a link would be created between the leading players on the shipping trade lanes. The Commission considered that the combined market shares of the conference members gave rise to competition concerns and the Commission has therefore made its approval of the merger conditional on the withdrawal of Hapag-Lloyd from these two conferences."[151]

The case is an important one. It is one of the most sophisticated in terms of analysis of merger control in shipping. While the decision is not a precedent in the same way that a court judgment might be, because it is so fact-specific, it is nonetheless well reasoned and should be regarded as an important decision for the future.

2006: *Costa Crociere/Royal Caribbean/Marinvest/RCT*

16.132 On 4 May 2006, the Commission approved a concentration whereby Costa Crociere SpA (of Italy) (controlled by Carnival of the US, Royal Caribbean Cruises of Liberia and Marinvest of Italy) would acquire joint control of Rome Cruise Terminal Srl (of Italy) by way of a purchase of shares in a newly created company constituting a joint venture.[152] The port was in the port of Civitavecchia which is north of Rome. The Commission found that the simplified procedure applied and therefore the transaction was found to be compatible with Regulation 139/2004 so it was approved unconditionally.

2005: *Svitzer/Wilhelmsen Offshore/JV*

16.133 On 28 October 2005, the Commission approved under the simplified procedure a joint venture between Svitzer and Wilhelmsen Offshore.[153] The business activities of the undertakings concerned were: (a) for Svitzer: towage services, emergency response and rescue services and provision of crew boat services; (b) for Wilhelmsen: crew boat services and chartering of vessels for special transportation, as well as marine services; and (c) for the joint venture: crew boat activities which are located in South-East Asia and the Middle East. It was approved under the simplified procedure and raised no issues.

---

151 IP/05/1265, 12 October 2005.
152 M.3947.
153 M.3947.

2005: *CMA CGM/Delmas*[154]

16.134 CMA CGM, the French shipping company, acquired Delmas, another French shipping company. Delmas was a relatively small company but it was important in the Mediterranean and Africa. The merged entity became the third largest company worldwide.

16.135 The Commission found that serious doubts existed regarding the compatibility of the proposed concentration because of co-ordinated effects of the transaction. The conference member had to leave the conference so as to permit the transaction to be approved. The Commission stated in its press release:

> "Mergers: Commission clears the planned acquisition of Delmas by CMA CGM
> The European Commission has cleared under the EU Merger Regulation the proposed acquisition of the shipping company Delmas by the global French shipping company CMA CGM. The Commission considers that although both companies are active on some routes between Africa and Europe, the increased market share will not be sufficient to significantly impede effective competition in the European Economic Area (EEA) or any part of it.
> CMA CGM is a global shipping company primarily active in the containerised liner shipping sector. The company also operates Roll on – Roll off (Ro-Ro) shipping services which provide regular transport for cars and trucks and also container terminal services.
> Delmas is a subsidiary of the French Bolloré group and is active in shipping in the trade routes to and from Africa. Through its subsidiary Sudcargos, it is also active in Ro-Ro shipping mainly between the Mediterranean and Maghreb countries.
> The Commission looked at whether the parties' market shares and the links created by their participation in various conferences and consortia with their competitors would result in anti-competitive effects whereby markets could be shared and prices increased to the detriment of shippers and final consumers.
> Liner conferences (groupings of shipping companies engaged in regular scheduled services) benefit from a block exemption from the EC Treaty's competition rules under a Regulation (4056/86) adopted by the EU's Council of Ministers nearly twenty years ago. Shipping lines grouped in consortia also benefit from a similar block exemption (see IP/05/477). After a two year investigation, in October 2004 the European Commission issued a White Paper concluding that the exemption for liner conferences should be abolished because it no longer results in efficient and reliable services that meet shippers' requirements (see IP/04/1213). A proposal from the Commission is due before the end of the year (see also IP/05/1408).
> The Commission found that although the transaction would result in an increase of the market share of the parties on some trade routes between Africa and Europe in the market for container shipping services and Ro-Ro services, this would not be sufficient to impede effective competition. Further, the transaction would not have the result of appreciably strengthening conferences or consortia to which the parties are members."[155]

2006: *Veolia – BCP/SNCM*

16.136 On 29 May 2006, the Commission approved the acquisition of joint control of Société Nationale Maritime Corse Méditerranée ("SNCM") by Veolia Transport and Butler Capital Partners ("BCP") (an investment fund management company).[156] SNCM, which until the acquisition was controlled by the French State, was mainly active in the transport of passengers and freight between mainland France (operating out of the ports

---

154 M.3973, 1 December 2005.
155 IP/05/1522, 1 December 2005.
156 IP/06/692.

of Marseille, Nice and Toulon) and Corsica, Algeria, Tunisia and, occasionally, Sardinia. SNCM was party to a public service delegation agreement with the Corsican regional authorities on sea transport between the mainland and Corsica. The principal business of Veolia Transport was the operation of passenger transport services on behalf of local, regional and national authorities. It ran mainly road and rail networks, offering sea transport services as a sideline. Veolia Transport was a subsidiary of Veolia Environment, which groups together, besides the transport division, water treatment, energy services and waste management businesses. BCP managed various investment funds. The Commission found that the transaction would not bring about any change in the competitive situation, whether in the market for passenger sea transport services or in that for freight sea transport services (more commonly known as ferry activities). BCP was not at all active in these markets and while Veolia Transport, which is active only in passenger sea transport services it did not do business in the same geographic area as SNCM.

2006: *RREEF/Peel Port Holdings/Peel Ports*

16.137 On 11 December 2006, the Commission approved, using the simplified procedure, a proposed concentration by which the fund RREEF Pan-European Infrastructure Fund LP ("RREEF"), which was ultimately managed by Deutsche Bank and Peel Ports Holdings (Guernsey) Limited (belonging to the Peel group of companies) would acquire joint control over Peel Ports Holdings (Cl) Ltd ("Peel Ports"), by way of purchase of shares. Before the transaction, Peel Ports was solely controlled by Peel Ports Holdings. Peel Ports operated and maintained port facilities in the UK and Ireland including the provision of terminal services. It was therefore a move from sole control to joint control but the transaction was not a SIEC.

2007: *Allianz/3i/Scandlines*

16.138 On 21 August 2007, the Commission approved unconditionally, using the simplified procedure, a proposed concentration by which ACP Vermögensverwaltung GmbH & Co. KG Nr. 4c ("ACP"), an entity ultimately controlled by the Allianz Group ("Allianz") and 3i Group plc and investment funds managed by 3i Investments plc and 3i Gestion S.A. would acquire joint control of Scandlines AG by way of purchase of shares. The business activities of the undertakings concerned were: (a) Allianz: insurance services, banking and asset management; (b) 3i: private equity investor; and (c) Scandlines: ferry transport services for passengers and freight in the Baltic Area. This meant that there was no overlap and therefore there was no SIEC.

2007: *WWL/EUKOR/ARMACUP/AGENCIE*

16.139 On 10 May 2007, the Commission approved a proposed concentration by which the undertakings Wallenius Wilhelmsen Logistics AS ("WWL") and EUKOR Car Carries Inc. ("EUKOR"), both jointly controlled by Walleniusrederierna AB (Sweden) and Wilh. Wilhelmsen ASA, and Oxford Trust ("Oxford", New Zealand) would acquire joint control, together with Raffles Foundation Trust, of the undertakings Armacup Maritime Services Ltd ("Armacup") and Agencie Maritime Holdings Ltd ("Agencie") by way of a purchase of shares. The business activities of the parties did not overlap in any way which would give rise to a SIEC: (a) for WWL: providing sea transportation for roll-on/roll-off ("ro-ro") cargo, operating sea terminals and inland processing/logistic centres; (b) for EUKOR: providing sea transportation for ro-ro cargo, providing logistic services to the automotive industry; (c) for Armacup: general agent for Agencie; and (d) for Agencie: operating regular ro-ro services from Korea and Japan to Fiji and New Zealand.

2007: *PSA/IPH*

16.140 On 31 October 2007, the Commission approved a proposed concentration by which the undertaking PSA Europe Pte Ltd, an affiliate of PSA International Pte Ltd ("PSA") which is ultimately controlled by the Singapore Ministry of Finance via a holding company, Temasek Holdings Pte Ltd ("Temasek") and the undertaking IPH (Jersey) Limited, a newly formed company owned by affiliated funds Global Infrastructure Partners which is ultimately jointly controlled by General Electric Company ("GE", USA), Credit Suisse Group ("CSG", Switzerland) and Global Infrastructure Management Participation LLC would acquire joint control in a newly created company constituting a joint venture. It was not clear from the decision as to the activities of the joint venture but it was not one which would result in a SIEC so it was dealt with under the simplified procedure.

2007: *China Shipbuilding Industry Corporation/Wärtsilä/Mitsubishi Heavy Industries*

16.141 On 24 April 2007, the Commission decided under Article 6(1)(b) of Regulation 139/2004 to approve the joint venture between: (a) China Shipbuilding Industry Corporation ("China Shipbuilding"); (b) Wärtsilä; and (c) Mitsubishi Heavy Industries ("MHI"). The joint venture would manufacture large low-speed marine engines in China (in particular, two stroke low-speed marine diesel engines). China Shipbuilding's ownership in the joint venture would be 50%, Wärtsilä's 27% and MHI's 23%.[157] China Shipbuilding built ships and was active in marine equipment engineering, designing and manufacturing. Wärtsilä was a Finnish ship power supplier and global service network operator. Mitsubishi was a Japanese heavy machinery manufacturer. The Commission was able to deal with the case under the simplified procedure.

2007: *Peter Döhle Schiffahrts-KG/GE Transportation Finance Inc*

16.142 On 8 June 2007, the Commission decided under Article 6(1)(b) of Regulation 139/2004 to approve, under the simplified procedure, the acquisition of joint control of a newly created company GDM Shipping GmbH & Co KG ("GDM").[158] This was a joint venture between Peter Döhle Schiffahrts-KG ("PD") and GE Transportation Finance Inc ("GETF"). PD was a German company that owned and operated vessels and related services for the shipping sector. GETF was a financial services company which was part of

---

157 COMP/M.4286.
158 COMP/M.4648.

the US' General Electric Group. GDM would operate container vessels and related services.

2008: *Eurogate/AP Moller-Maersk Joint Venture*

16.143 Under the MCR, the Commission authorised a joint venture between EURO-GATE and AP Møller-Maersk ("APMM") for the operation of a container terminal in Wilhelmshaven in Germany.[159] APMM would acquire a 30% share in EUROGATE Container Terminal Wilhelmshaven GmbH & Co. KG and EUROGATE Container Terminal Wilhelmshaven Beteiligungsgesellschaft mbH (together the JadeWeserPort Container Terminal operating companies), both solely controlled by EUROGATE GmbH & Co. KGaA, KG ("EUROGATE"). EUROGATE (the parent) was mainly active in the provision of stevedoring services at ports, through the operation of container terminals in Europe (Bremerhaven, Hamburg and Genoa). APMM was an international group with activities in container shipping, container terminal services (in Europe in Aarhus, Algeciras, Bremerhaven, Dunkirk, Le Havre, Rotterdam and Zeebrugge), harbour towage, operation of tankers, inland transportation, logistics, oil and gas exploration and production, retail and air transport. EUROGATE held a concession to operate the JadeWeserPort Container Terminal in the port of Wilhelmshaven. APMM was not a party to the concession agreement but would assume, under the joint venture, joint liability for the future obligations of EUROGATE. Although APMM would acquire only a 30% controlling share in the JadeWeserPort Container Terminal, up to 49% of the Terminal's capacity would be dedicated to Maersk Line and/or its affiliates (together "APMT"). The Commission found that the parties' activities overlapped in the provision of stevedoring services in deep sea container terminals. However, in all possible product and geographic markets, the parties would jointly control, through the JadeWeserPort Container Terminal, less than 15% of either the available total operational or the total non-captive capacity. Even if APMM were to control fully all of the terminals in which it had a controlling interest/stake, under all possible product and geographic market definitions, its market shares would remain below 30%, and competitors would be present.

16.144 The Commission also scrutinised the vertical link between APMM's activities in the provision of stevedoring services in container terminals and APMT's container shipping activities. Despite APMT enjoying high market shares in a number of deep sea container trades to and from Northern Europe, the total volumes concerned were rather low compared to the total volume on the trades to and from Northern Europe on the one hand and of the area's container handling capacities on the other. The Commission found that there were strong internationally active competitors present for these trades. Consequently, the Commission concluded that no competition concerns would arise in the container terminal service market.

16.145 The Commission also considered possible co-ordinated effects in the market for the provision of stevedoring services in container terminals between EUROGATE and APMM. The Commission found that the low market share of the JadeWeserPort Container Terminal itself and the fact that there were no indications that such co-ordination

---

159 M.5066. See http://ec.europa.eu/comm/competition/mergers/cases/index/m101.html#m_5066. See also IP/08/89, 6 June 2008.

had taken place up to date as a result of the EUROGATE and APMM joint venture in the Bremerhafen terminal, meant that the proposed transaction would not be likely to trigger co-ordinated effects.

2009: *COSTA/MSC/MPCT*

16.146 On 6 February 2009, the Commission approved the proposed concentration by which (a) Costa of Italy (controlled by Carnival of the US) and MSC (controlled by the Mediterranean Shipping Company) would acquire joint control of (b) Marseille Provence Cruise Terminal SAS ("MPCT").[160] Costa and MSC operated cruise ships. MPCT managed the cruise terminal covered by the concession awarded by Port Autonome de Marseille. The Commission found that the simplified procedure applied and therefore the transaction was found to be compatible with Regulation 139/2004 so it was approved unconditionally.

2009: *BPH/Euroports Holding*

16.147 On 20 August 2009, the Commission announced that it has decided under Article 6(1)(b) of Regulation 139/2004 to approve the acquisition of sole control of Benelux Port Holding S.a.r.l. of Luxembourg by Euroports Holding S.a.r.l., also of Luxembourg.[161] Both parties operate ports, handle cargo and provide related services. The transaction was examined under the simplified merger procedure.

2011: *Acquisition of Douala International Terminal JV by APMM and Bollore*

16.148 On 5 August 2011, the Commission announced that it had approved under Article 6(1)(b) of Regulation 139/2004 the acquisition of joint control of Douala International Terminal JV ("DIT") by AP Møller-Maersk A/S ("APMM") and Bolloré S.A.[162] Both, the Danish company APMM and the French company Bolloré, as well as DIT were active in the provision of port terminal (stevedoring) services to deep-sea vessels. However, DIT was only active in Cameroon and had no foreseen activities in the EEA. The transaction was therefore examined under the simplified merger review procedure and approved easily.

2011: *Acquisition by Socimac and Bollore of Joint Control of Societe d'exploitation du Terminal de Vridi*

16.149 On 12 December 2011, the Commission decided under Article 6(1)(b) of the MCR to approve the acquisition by Socimac (a wholly owned subsidiary of AP Møller-Maersk) and Bolloré of joint control over Société d'exploitation du Terminal de Vridi, by way of purchase of shares.[163] AP Møller-Maersk was a Dutch company active in containerised liner shipping, terminal services, inland transportation, logistics, harbour towage,

---

160 M.5423.
161 COMP/M.5881.
162 COMP/M.6200.
163 COMP/M.6328.

tankers, oil and gas exploration and production, retail, and air transport. Bolloré was a French company that was active in transportation and logistic services, the manufacture of plastic films, ticket machine terminals, batteries and electric vehicles, fuel distribution, communication and media including advertising, and commercialisation of plantations. Société d'exploitation du Terminal de Vridi, of the Ivory Coast, developed, managed and operated a container terminal within the Port Autonome d'Abidjan and provided services to its common users. It was a simplified procedure case.

2011: *Arcelormittal/Atic Services*

16.150 On December 2011, the Commission approved the proposed acquisition of ATIC Services Group of France by ArcelorMittal Netherlands BV.[164] Although ATIC had significant market shares in certain EU areas for seaport terminal services for imports of iron ore and coal, key inputs for steel production, the Commission concluded that ArcelorMittal would have neither the ability nor the incentive to prevent its steel competitors from importing iron ore and coal to an extent that would affect competition in the EU. Some of the largest seaport terminals affected by the transaction were jointly controlled by ATIC and operated at arm's length, independently of their shareholders (EMO-EKOM in Rotterdam and OBA in Amsterdam). The Commission's assessment, therefore, focused on the vertical integration of ATIC's activities with those of ArcelorMittal. The investigation showed that ArcelorMittal was unlikely to exert decisive influence on decisions relating to individual customers of these terminals. The market investigation also confirmed that large steel producers tend to have their own captive terminals in the region or use terminals outside the relevant geographic areas. There were some alternative terminals for smaller steel competitors currently using ATIC's terminals. The Commission took into consideration that terminal handling costs amount for only a small proportion of the overall steel production costs, and the existence of some spare capacity at the relevant ATIC terminals as well as at competing terminals. The Commission therefore concluded that the transaction would not significantly impede effective competition in the EEA or any substantial part of it.

2011: *Teekay/Marubeni/Maersk LNG*

16.151 On 12 December 2011, using the simplified procedure, the Commission approved unconditionally the transaction whereby Teekay LNG Partners (through its wholly owned subsidiary Teekay LNG Operating) and Japan's Marubeni Corporation would acquire indirect joint control over Maersk LNG A/S (Denmark), by way of a purchase of shares.

2013: *FSI/Merit/Yildirim/CMA CGM*

16.152 The Commission cleared the acquisition of joint control over CMA CGM, a French company active in the sector of maritime shipping services, by the French Fonds Stratégique d'Investissement ("FSI"), the Turkish joint stock company Merit Corporation

---

164 http://ec.europa.eu/competition/elojade/isef/case_details.cfm?proc_code=2_M_6376.

and the Lebanese holding company Yildirim Holding. FSI was controlled by the French public group Caisse des dépôts et consignations ("CDC") which in parallel indirectly co-controlled SNCM. Both CMA CGM and SNCM provided short-sea ro-ro shipping services on the Marseilles–Tunis and Marseilles–Algiers/Mostaganem/Oran lanes. The Commission's investigation found that the transaction would not raise competition concerns due to SNCM's limited market position and the presence of several credible competitors. The operation was examined under the normal merger review procedure.

2013: *NORDIC Capital/Unicorn*

16.153 The Commission cleared the acquisition of Unicorn by Nordic Capital VIII Limited, one of the four active general partners to the Nordic Capital private equity funds.[165] The Nordic Capital funds invested in large and medium-sized companies, predominantly in Europe. Unicorn was a Danish company active, through its subsidiary Unifeeder, in maritime transportation services for containerised goods mainly in Northern Europe. The operation was examined under the simplified merger review procedure.

2014: *CSAV/HGV/Kühne Maritime/HAPAG-LLOYD AG*

16.154 On 11 September 2014, the Commission approved, but subject to conditions, the merger between Hapag Lloyd ("HL") and Compañia Sud Americana de Vapores S.A. ("CSAV") in the container liner shipping sector.[166] The Commission cleared the proposed merger between HL (the German shipping company with worldwide activities) and Chile's CSAV. The clearance was conditional upon the withdrawal of CSAV from two consortia on the trade between Northern Europe and the Caribbean and South America's west coast, where the merged entity would have faced insufficient competitive constraint to avoid a risk of price rises. The commitments offered by the two companies addressed the Commission's concerns. The merger would create the fourth largest container liner shipping company worldwide, after Maersk, MSC and CMA CGM. The activities of HL and CSAV overlapped in the container liner shipping business and have limited vertical links. As with many other carriers, the two companies offered container liner shipping services mainly through co-operation agreements with other shipping companies known as "consortia". The Commission examined the effects of the merger on competition in the market for container liner shipping services on 12 trade routes connecting Europe with the Americas, Asia and the Middle East. Consortia members decide on capacity setting, scheduling and the list of ports of call, which are all important parameters of competition. The Commission found that the merger, as initially notified, would have created new links between previously unconnected consortia. The Commission had concerns that these new links would have resulted in anti-competitive effects on two trade routes: the route between Northern Europe and the Caribbean, and the route between Northern Europe and South America's west coast. On these routes, the merged entity, through the consortia that the two companies belong to, may have influenced capacity and therefore prices to the detriment of shippers and consumers. In order to address these concerns the

---

165 http://ec.europa.eu/competition/mergers/cases/decisions/m6926_20130604_20310_3102865_EN.pdf.
166 http://ec.europa.eu/competition/mergers/cases/decisions/m7268_20140911_20212_3869708_EN.pdf.

companies offered to terminate the two consortia in which CSAV currently participated on these two trade routes – i.e. the Euroandes consortium and the Ecuador Express consortium, both with MSC. This would eliminate the additional links between previously unrelated consortia that the merger would have created on the two routes. In view of the remedies proposed, the Commission concluded that the proposed transaction, as modified, would not raise competition concerns anymore. This decision was conditional upon full compliance with the commitments. As regards the vertical links created by the transaction between the market for container liner shipping services and the market for (i) container terminal services, (ii) inland transportation services, (iii) freight forwarding services and (iv) harbour towage services, the Commission found no competition concerns because of the limited market share of the parties in the upstream and downstream markets. HL was an international container liner shipping company. Through a joint venture with a subsidiary of HGV, HL AG also offered port terminal services in Hamburg-Altenwerder. HL AG's main shareholders include HGV, Kühne Maritime and TUI AG ("TUI"), a company active in the travel sector. CSAV provided container liner shipping services and had limited activities in the freight forwarding and inland transportation sector. CSAV was controlled by Quiñenco S.A. (Chile), a Chilean company which provided, among others, terminal, stevedoring, towage and other associated services through its subsidiary SM SAAM S.A. On the route between Northern Europe and the Caribbean, HL was currently a member of the Eurosal consortium with HSDG and CMA CGM; CSAV was a member of the Euroandes consortium with MSC. On the route between Northern Europe and South America's west coast, HL was currently a member of the Eurosal consortium with HSDG and CMA CGM; CSAV was a member of the Euroandes consortium and the Ecuador Express consortium, both with MSC. Consortia are operational agreements between shipping companies for the provision of a joint service. The members of a consortium jointly agree on the capacity that will be offered by the service, on its schedule and ports of call. Generally, each party provides vessels for operating the joint service and in exchange receives a number of container slots across all vessels in the service, based on the total vessel capacity contributed. The allocation of container slots is usually pre-determined and shipping companies are not compensated if the slots attributed to them are not used. The costs for the operation of the service are generally borne by the vessel providers individually, so that there is in principle no cost sharing between the members of a consortium. A trustee had to be appointed.[167]

2015: *Acquisition of ODPR by CMA CGM*

16.155 On 29 June 2015, the Commission approved the acquisition of the shares in Germany's Oldenburg-Portugiesische Dampfschiffs-Rhederei ("OPDR") by France's CMA CGM.[168] CMA CGM was the world's third largest container shipping company. The seller was Bernhard Schulte GmbH & Co. KG. Both OPDR and CMA CGM (through its subsidiary MacAndrews) were active in intra-European short-sea container shipping, including port-to-port as well as door-to-door activities. The acquisition of OPDR by CMA CGM was designed to develop the position of the CMA CGM Group in the

---
167 http://ec.europa.eu/competition/mergers/cases/additional_data/m7268_1459_3.pdf.
168 M.7523 *CMA CGM/OPDR*.

short-sea shipping sector in the Iberian Peninsula and more generally in Europe. It would also enable the expansion of the CMA CGM Group's presence in North Africa, and its entry on the Canary Islands market. The Commission concluded that the transaction would raise no competition concerns because of: first, the low switching costs for customers, who could also use alternative means of transport, such as road or rail; second, the low barriers to entry or expansion for new or existing competitors – they could simply add new ships or new ports of call in the intra-EEA short-sea shipping market; and, third, the low overall size of the affected markets. The transaction was examined under the ordinary merger review procedure.

2016: *Triton/KKR/EM*

16.156 On 6 January 2016, the Commission approved the acquisition of joint control over a newly created joint venture by Embarcadero Maritime LLC ("EM") of the Marshall Islands, ultimately controlled by KKR & Co L.P. of the US and Nordic Tankers A/S ("NT") of Denmark, ultimately controlled by Triton Managers III Limited and TTF III Limited of Jersey.[169] KKR is a global investment firm. EM operates a fleet of container, chemical, product and LPG vessels. Triton is a group of independent European private equity funds and companies dedicated to investing in medium-sized businesses in Northern Europe. NT is a fully integrated shipping company active in the transport of specialised liquid products in bulks. Through the joint venture, EM and NT would combine some of their stainless steel chemical tankers business in Europe, with focus on North-Western Europe and the Baltic region. The Commission concluded that the proposed acquisition would raise no competition concerns given the moderate market positions in the tramp shipping sector resulting from the transaction. It was a simplified procedure case.

2016: *CMA CGM/Bollore/Kribi JV*

16.157 On 12 April 2016, the Commission approved the acquisition of joint control over a new container terminal to be built in the deep sea port of Kribi, in Cameroon, by CMA CGM S.A. and Bolloré S.A.[170] During the construction phase of the new terminal, CMA CGM and Bolloré would operate a smaller, existing but currently idle container terminal in that harbour. CMA CGM provides container liner shipping and port terminal management services. Bolloré is active in the areas of transportation and logistics, communication and media, and energy solutions. The Commission concluded that the proposed transaction would raise no competition concerns since the new terminal would increase the port's capacity for offering container terminal services, making them more competitive. The existing but currently idle container terminal would be taken over by a new entrant once the construction of the new terminal was completed. It was examined under the simplified procedure.

---

169 M.7760.
170 M.7853.

2016: *CMA CGM/NOL*

16.158 In an interesting and more involved decision than usual in regard to maritime transport and the MCR, the Commission approved on 29 April 2016, subject to conditions, a merger in the container liner shipping sector between CMA CGM and Neptune Oriental Lines ("NOL").[171] In essence, the case involved the proposed acquisition of NOL of Singapore by rival CMA CGM, a French shipping company with worldwide activities. The clearance was given but conditional on NOL leaving the G6 liner shipping alliance. The Commission found that the transaction would lead to the combination of two competitors in the container liner shipping business. As it said in its press release:

> "[l]ike many other carriers, CMA CGM and NOL offer their services on many trade routes mainly through cooperation agreements with other shipping companies known as 'consortia'. Consortia with the same members operating across several trade routes are often grouped into alliances. CMA CGM is a founding member of the Ocean Three Alliance ('O3') whereas NOL is currently a member of the G6 Alliance. The Commission examined the effects of the merger on competition for container liner shipping services on seventeen trade routes connecting Europe with the Americas, the Middle East, the Indian Subcontinent, the Far East as well as Australasia & Oceania. Consortia members decide on capacity setting, scheduling and the list of ports of call, which are all important parameters of competition. The Commission found that the merger, as initially notified, would have created new links between previously unconnected consortia in the O3 and G6 alliances. The Commission had concerns that these potential new links would have resulted in anti-competitive effects on two trade routes: (i) between Northern Europe and North America, and (ii) between Northern Europe and the Middle East. On these routes, competition from liner shippers who have no connection with the merged entity or its alliance partners would have been insufficient. As a result, the transaction could have enabled the merged entity, through the consortia that the two companies belong to, to influence capacity and therefore prices to the detriment of shippers and consumers for a very large part of those markets. The transaction would also create limited vertical links, arising from CGM CMA's activity in container terminal services, which may be required by container liner shipping companies. However, the Commission found no competition concerns in this area because of the companies' limited market share in most upstream markets and the small increment brought about by the transaction on the downstream markets."

It therefore would only permit the transaction with commitments. Again, the press release stated that in order to address the Commission's concerns,

---

171 M.7908. The 49-page decision is available at: http://ec.europa.eu/competition/mergers/cases/decisions/m7908_1366_3.pdf. The Commission's press release described the companies and products in the following terms: "The CMA CGM Group is the world's third largest container liner shipping company and is active worldwide with a fleet of 470 vessels that serves 450 commercial ports. CMA CGM operates 170 shipping lines on the main commercial trade routes. CMA CGM is a member of the O3 Alliance, with UASC and CSCL. NOL is Southeast Asia's largest container shipping company and has a fleet of 94 vessels. It operates through its brand American President Lines ('APL') at ports in over 50 countries worldwide. APL provides six weekly services to/from the EEA (operating 12 ships), with direct port calls in 9 countries. NOL is currently a member of the G6 Alliance, together with Hapag Lloyd, Hyundai Merchant Lines, Orient Overseas Container Line, Nippon Yusen Kaisha and Mitsui O.S.K. Lines. Consortia are operational agreements between shipping companies for the provision of a joint service. The members of a consortium jointly agree on the capacity that will be offered by the service, on its schedule and ports of call. Generally, each party provides vessels for operating the joint service and in exchange receives a number of container slots across all vessels in the service, based on the total vessel capacity contributed. The allocation of container slots is usually pre-determined and shipping companies are not compensated if the slots attributed to them are not used. The costs for the operation of the service are generally borne by the vessel providers individually, so that there is in principle no cost sharing between the members of a consortium."

"the companies offered to make the transaction contingent upon the removal of the link that would have been created between CMA CGM's O3 Alliance and NOL's G6 Alliance. Although CMA CGM had previously stated publicly that it intended to remove NOL from the G6 alliance, the formal commitment to do so was necessary to remove the risk of anti-competitive effects on the two trade routes described above. Although NOL will continue to operate for G6 until 31 March 2017 to guarantee an orderly exit, the commitments foresee that a trustee will ensure that no anti-competitive information is shared between the alliance and the merged entity during that remaining period. This will eliminate the potential additional links between previously unrelated consortia that the merger would have created on the two routes. In view of the remedies proposed, the Commission concluded that the proposed transaction, as modified, would no longer raise competition concerns. The decision is conditional upon full compliance with the commitments."

As the transaction was notified to the Commission on 8 March 2016 and decided on 29 April 2016 but with commitments, this would appear to be a case where the parties planned well and engaged thoroughly on the remedies which were needed.

2016: *Royal Caribbean Holdings de España, S.L. of Spain by Royal Caribbean Cruises LTD of the US and Springwater Capital LLC of Switzerland*

16.159 On 20 July 2016, the Commission approved the acquisition of joint control over Royal Caribbean Holdings de España, S.L. of Spain by Royal Caribbean Cruises LTD ("RCL") of the US and Springwater Capital LLC of Switzerland.[172] Royal Caribbean Holdings supplied ocean cruises in Spain, France and Portugal under the brands "Pullmantur" and "Croisières de France". The company was controlled by RCL. RCL was a global cruise vacation company. Springwater was a private equity firm which uses the brand "Wamos Air" for the provision of air passenger transport services. The Commission concluded that the proposed acquisition would raise no competition concerns, because of its limited impact on the market structure. The transaction was examined under the simplified procedure.

2017: *CK Hutchison/TMA HOLDING/TMA Logistics*

16.160 In a simplified procedure, the Commission approved the CK Hutchison/TMA Holding/TMA Logistics proposed concentration.[173] HPN was a subsidiary of Hutchison Port Holdings ("HPH") Limited – owned by CK Hutchison Holding Limited – and operated ports and deep-sea container terminals. In Europe, the HPH Group provided stevedoring services in ports in Belgium, Germany, Poland, Spain, Sweden, the Netherlands and the United Kingdom. TMA Holding was involved in stevedoring services (mainly at an inland container terminal in Harlingen, the Netherlands), freight forwarding services and contract logistics services. TMA Logistics provided logistics solutions for land, sea and air transport, stevedoring (containers and bulk goods), cargo transhipment, project cargoes, storage and customs handling, including the provision of stevedoring services for containers at container terminals in Velsen and Amsterdam, and ro-ro stevedoring

---

172 M.8069. The decision is available at: http://ec.europa.eu/competition/mergers/cases/decisions/m8069_93_3.pdf.
173 M.8654. The decision is available at: http://ec.europa.eu/competition/mergers/cases/decisions/m8654_121_3.pdf.

services in Velsen (all in the Netherlands). The proposed transaction involved HPN and TMA Holding acquiring TMA Logistics.

2018: *PSA/TIL/PPIT*

16.161 On 6 February 2018, the Commission approved, under the simplified procedure, the proposed concentration pursuant to Article 4 of the MCR by which the undertakings PSA International Pte. Ltd. (Singapore) and Terminal Investment Limited SARL (Switzerland), jointly controlled by MSC Mediterranean Shipping Company Holding S.A. (Switzerland), Global Infrastructure Management (United States) and Global Infrastructure Partners (United States) acquired within the meaning of Article 3(1)(b) and 3(4) of the MCR joint control over the whole of the undertaking PSA Panama International Terminal S.A. (Panama), controlled by PSA International Pte Ltd, by way of purchase of shares.[174] PSA International Pte Ltd was involved in stevedoring services at ports, with a particular focus on terminal services for containerised liner ships. Terminal Investment Limited SARL was involved in investment, development and management of container terminals. PSA Panama International Terminal SA was involved in operating a container terminal in the Port of Rodman, Panama. The Commission was convinced that the proposed transaction would not significantly impede effective competition.

2018: *Acquisition of Maersk Product Tankers by APMH Invest and Mitsui*

16.162 On 16 March 2018, the Commission approved the acquisition of joint control of Maersk Product Tankers A/S of Denmark by APMH Invest A/S of Denmark and Mitsui & Co., Ltd. of Japan.[175] Maersk Product Tankers A/S was active in the maritime tramp vessel sector for the transport of liquid bulk products, specifically refined oil products and certain chemicals. APMH Invest A/S was a holding company with interests in banking, infrastructure and financial investments in fixed income and securities. Mitsui & Co., Ltd was pursuing business that ranged from product sales, worldwide logistics and financing through to the development of major infrastructure and other projects. The Commission concluded that the proposed acquisition would raise no competition concerns because of the limited impact it would have on the market. The transaction was examined under the simplified merger review procedure.

M. THE MCR IN THE SHIPBUILDING SECTOR

Introduction

16.163 The ECMR also applies to concentrations involving shipyards. There have been various notifications of proposed concentrations but many have related either to yacht/boat building or naval vessels so they are of limited relevance for present purposes.

---

174 M.8695. The decision is available at: http://eur-lex.europa.eu/legal-content/EN/TXT/HTML/?uri=OJ:C:2018:053:FULL&from=EN.

175 M.8697.

1999: *UPM-Kymmene/STORA ENSO/Metsallito/JV*

16.164 On 3 December 1999, the Commission approved in the uncontroversial UPM-Kymmene/STORA ENSO/Metsallito joint venture.[176]

1998: *Blohm+Voss/Lisnave*

16.165 On 18 June 1998, the Commission approved a notification[177] of a proposed operation by which Germany's Thyssen Weften and Portugal's Navivessel would acquire joint control of Portugal's Lisnave-Estaleiros Navais.[178] While Thyssen Weften would have a minority stake in the joint venture, it would have sufficient control or influence over the running of the joint venture that it would hold joint control. The proposed joint venture would be active in the fields of ship repairing and conversion of offshore units. In terms of the product market, the Commission found that the proposed joint venture would be active in repairing ships and in conversion of cargo vessels and offshore units. The Commission found that the market definition could be left open and there was no need to decide whether ship repairing and conversion belonged to one and the same product market or both activities constituted separate relevant product markets as "in neither alternative the concentration would not lead to the creation or strengthening of a dominant position".[179] The Commission believed that it could also leave open the definition of the geographical market in this case.[180] The Commission was mindful of the fact that the undertakings involved would have relatively small combined market shares post-concentration and that they would face several important competitors within Europe and from around the world. The Commission found that the proposed concentration would not create or strengthen a dominant position as a result of which effective competition would be significantly impeded in the common market or in a substantial part of it so the transaction was approved unconditionally.

1999: *Preussag/Babcock/Celsius*

16.166 On 9 November 1999, the Commission received a notification[181] whereby the Swedish state-owned defence company Celsius would acquire joint control, together with Preussag Aktiengesellschaft, over Howaldswerke-Deutsche Werft ("HDW"), a subsidiary of Preussag active in the fields of conventionally powered submarines and large defence naval vessels. As part of the same operation, HDW would acquire 100% of Kockrums AB (Celsius' subsidiary active in the fields of conventionally powered submarines and small defence naval vessels). The case involved a long discussion of the various possible markets including different types of submarine and different types of warship. The Commission approved the transaction because of the absence of any ability to create or

---

176 M.1744.
177 It was originally declared incomplete.
178 Case IV/M.1004.
179 Para. 14.
180 The parties argued that the market was global because ships or offshore units could be moved to where the customer wanted them to be located from yards all over the world.
181 It was originally declared incomplete.

strengthen a dominant position.¹⁸² The Commission was influenced by the fact that the parties could not, post-merger, successfully engage in selective actions aimed at other competitors or, more generally, derive market power from the market shares.

2000: *Aker Maritime/Kvaerner (Withdrawn)*

16.167 In July 2000, Aker Maritime had entered into several agreements effectively giving it 26.7% of the voting rights in Kvaerner. Aker notified the acquisition of the controlling stake in Kvaerner to the Commission for regulatory clearance on 23 October 2000. Aker Maritime and Kvaerner both had significant activities in the oil and gas sector as well as in shipbuilding. On 7 December 2000, the Commission opened an in-depth investigation. The Commission's initial investigation showed that the notified transaction would have its main impact on the markets for Engineering, Procurement, Construction and Installation ("EPCI") contracts for oil and gas platforms. It would also have raised competition concerns on the market for the modification and maintenance of existing platforms. The combined Aker Maritime/Kvaerner would have had a high combined market share in both markets particularly on the Norwegian continental shelf of the North Sea. On 11 December 2000, Aker informed the Commission that it would take a number of measures so that the notified transaction would no longer constitute a concentration. On 12 December 2000, Aker Maritime withdrew the notification of its proposed takeover of Kvaerner.¹⁸³ Aker Maritime informed the Commission that it had agreed to limit its stake in Kvaerner and took a number of measures so the notified transaction would no longer constitute a concentration. This means that Aker Maritime would not acquire control over Kvaerner and that its notification had been withdrawn. Aker Maritime would irrevocably cancel its option agreements as regards 8.9% of the Kvaerner shares, thereby limiting to 17.8% the number of shares that it would acquire. The financial institutions that held the option shares would sell these within a pre-defined period, during which Aker Maritime would not vote the 17.8% holding. Therefore Aker Maritime would not acquire control over Kvaerner. In view of the structure of the notified transaction, the Commission therefore considered this to be sufficient for Aker Maritime's withdrawal of the notified takeover and would not take any further action. The Commission would not take any further action with regard to the transaction.

2005: *Rabobank/IHC*

16.168 On 14 February 2005, the Commission approved, under the simplified procedure, the acquisition by Rabo Participaties II BV (controlled by Rabobank Group) of the whole of IHC Caland NV (both undertakings being from the Netherlands). The acquirers were financial services/private equity operators. IHC was involved in shipbuilding. The Commission found that the simplified procedure applied and therefore the transaction was found to be compatible with Regulation 139/2004 so it was approved unconditionally.

---

182 M.1709.
183 M.2117. IP/00/1445, 12 December 2000.

2005: *ThyssenKrupp AG/Hellenic Shipyards*

16.169 On 10 November 2005, the Commission approved, under the simplified procedure, the proposed acquisition by ThyssenKrupp AG ("TK") of the whole of Hellenic Shipyards SA of Greece. TK produced steel, capital goods including civil shipbuilding as well as maintenance and repairs of ships. Hellenic Shipyards was involved in ship building and repair as well as production of industrial construction. The Commission found that the simplified procedure applied and therefore the transaction was found to be compatible with Regulation 139/2004 so it was approved unconditionally.

2006: *Aker Yards ASA/Chartiers de l'Atlantique*

16.170 On 27 March 2006, the Commission approved, under Article 6(1)(b) of Regulation 139/2004, the acquisition by Aker Yards ASA of Chartiers de l'Atlantique.[184] Aker was an international shipbuilding group. It operated 13 yards in Brazil, Finland, Germany, Norway and Romania. It concentrated on sophisticated commercial vessels (including cruise liners and ferries). The target also concentrated on high value commercial vessels (including cruise liners and ferries) as well as naval vessels. The Commission believed that the overlap related to large cruise ships over 30,000 gt. Nonetheless, the Commission found that the market was global (but with main supplies being European based). The transaction transformed Aker into the second largest builder of cruise ships worldwide. The parties submitted that the

> "relevant product market should be defined as commercial shipbuilding in general. They claim that (i) on the supply-side there is a significant substitutability between the various types of commercial vessels and that (ii) on the demand side there are a number of large integrated ship owners which operate a variety of commercial vessels."[185]

The Commission recalled that it had

> "left open as to whether all commercial vessels belong to one relevant product market. However, in e.g., Case No COMP/M.2772 – *HDW/Ferrostaal/Hellenic Shipyard*,[186] the Commission indicated that the market for commercial shipbuilding could be divided into several separate product markets according to the main groups of ships such as oil tankers, bulk carriers, container ships, product and chemical carriers, LNG tankers, LPG tankers, roll-on roll-off vessels, ferries, cruise ships, offshore/specialised vessels etc. The market investigation in the current case also supported such a segmentation of the market."[187]

The Commission found that there was no competition concern because there would still be strong competition from existing competitors and there would still be strong competition from the buyer side (i.e. a single customer represented an important part of the overall turnover in the market). In respect of ferries, where there was also an overlap, the market was highly competitive.

---

184 Case COMP/M.4104. See also IP/06/385.
185 Para. 8.
186 Commission decision of 25/04/2002.
187 Para. 9.

2006: *Thyssemkrupp/EADS/Atlas*

16.171 The Commission approved the acquisition of the German naval electronics supplier Atlas Elektronik GmbH by ThyssenKrupp Technologies AG ("TKT") and EADS Deutschland.[188] The Commission found that the proposed transaction, leading to a vertical integration of a formerly independent supplier of TKT, would not significantly impede effective competition in the EEA or any substantial part of it. Atlas was a supplier of naval and civil electronics, producing for example so-called "Combat Management Systems" (systems for the integration of incoming signals), sonar systems, torpedoes and mine systems for submarines and naval vessels, as well as maritime safety and hydrography systems for civilian applications. As TKT is a leading naval shipyard and a major customer of Atlas, the Commission examined whether the vertical integration of Atlas might create a risk of cutting off other suppliers of naval electronics or other shipbuilders from the markets. Its investigation, however, showed that even before the proposed takeover, Atlas sold the majority of its products to TKT. The change brought about by the proposed takeover would, therefore, remain limited. Furthermore, the Commission found that even after the transaction a sufficient number of shipyards would be available as customers for the remaining suppliers of naval electronics to guarantee their further existence. The investigation finally confirmed, according to the Commission, that other shipyards would not be deprived of access to naval electronics after the proposed takeover. In fact, many shipyards are already procuring naval electronics in-house. Even for those shipyards which are not vertically integrated, a sufficient number of competitors supplying naval electronics to third parties would remain available.

2006: *Candover/Ferretti*

16.172 On 20 December 2006, in a simplified procedure, the Commission approved a concentration whereby Candover Partners (a private equity investor) would acquire Ferretti SpA (a designer, producer and seller of luxury motor boats).[189] The Commission found that the simplified procedure applied and therefore the transaction was found to be compatible with Regulation 139/2004 so it was approved unconditionally.

2007: *Thales/DCN*

16.173 On 20 March 2007, the Commission approved Thales' participation in DCN.[190] This involved the proposed acquisition of joint control by Thales (a French defence equipment supplier and naval prime contractor), together with France, of the French military shipyard DCN. The Commission found that the transaction would not significantly impede effective competition in the EEA or any substantial part of it and so approved it. The Commission summarised its analysis in the following terms:

"Thales S.A. is a supplier of military and civil electronics and equipment, producing for example so-called 'Combat Management Systems', 'Command and information systems (CIS)', sonars, torpedoes and other systems for naval, aeronautical and terrestrial applications. Thales is also

---

188 M.4160. See also IP/06/599.
189 M.4492.
190 M.4191. See also IP/07/349.

active as a prime contractor for naval vessels. DCN is a military shipyard building, repairing, refitting and decommissioning naval vessels and submarines. As a result of the transaction, Thales would acquire joint control of DCN, which until now has been wholly owned by the French State. The transaction concerns exclusively markets for military goods.

The Commission examined the overlaps between the parties' activities in the sector (frigates, combat management systems for surface naval vessels, command and information systems), but concluded that they would not give rise to competition concerns. Thales and DCN already cooperate on many of the concerned markets via their joint venture company Armaris. Therefore, the competitive impact of the planned transaction would be limited. In addition, a number of effective competitors would continue to operate in the markets concerned after the proposed transaction.

As DCN is a leading naval shipyard and an important customer of Thales, the Commission also looked carefully at whether the vertical integration of Thales might create a risk of cutting off other suppliers of naval equipment or other shipbuilders from the markets. The market investigation, however, revealed that already before the merger, Thales sold the majority of its products to DCN. The change brought about by the merger would, therefore, remain limited. Furthermore, even after the transaction a sufficient number of shipyards would be available as customers for the remaining suppliers of naval equipment to guarantee their further existence.

The investigation finally confirmed that other shipyards would not be deprived of access to naval equipment after the merger. Even for those shipyards which are not vertically integrated, a sufficient number of competitors supplying naval equipment to third parties would remain available. The Commission further took into account the strong bargaining position of Defence Ministries, who are the clients in this sector, and are able to influence the sub-contracting process of the prime contractor for equipment.

In addition to the merger agreement, the parties concluded an 'Agreement on Industrial and Commercial Cooperation' shaping their future cooperation. The Commission's decision is without prejudice to an analysis of any aspect of this agreement, which would not be directly related and necessary to the operation, under [EU] ... anti-trust law (Articles [101 and 102 of the TFEU])."[191]

2007: *Bain Capital/Bavaria Yachtbau*

16.174 On 31 July 2007, under the simplified procedure, the Commission approved a transaction whereby Bain Capital (of the US) acquired Bavaria Yachtbau by way of a purchase of shares.[192] The acquirer was a private equity investment firm. The target was a manufacturer of boats and yachts. The Commission found that the simplified procedure applied and therefore the transaction was found to be compatible with Regulation 139/2004 so it was approved unconditionally.

2007: *BAE Systems/VT/JV*

16.175 On 17 October 2007, the Commission approved the creation of a joint venture between BAE Systems and VT Group. The joint venture would operate in naval surface shipbuilding and related support services. The Commission found that the joint venture would not significantly impede effective competition in the EU. The Commission approved the transaction and summarised its 15-page decision in the following terms:

---

191 IP/07/349.
192 M.4783.

"The proposed joint venture would bring together the two remaining UK companies having the capability of designing and building naval surface ships. In addition, the parties would integrate their existing joint venture, Fleet Support Limited (FSL), which is active in naval surface ship support, into the new joint venture.

The Commission's investigation showed that there has been little if any competition between BAE and VT for the design and building of naval surface ships in the UK in the past ten years, as each company has focussed on different classes of ships. As a result, the proposed joint venture would not bring about any significant change in this respect. This is also true for markets in the rest of the EEA as BAE and VT have never bid against each other for the design and build of a naval surface ship in the past decade.

BAE and VT are already active in the markets of naval support through their joint venture FSL, which will be integrated into the new joint venture. The Commission therefore concluded that the change brought about by the proposed transaction would also be limited. The Commission's investigation confirmed that existing arrangements between the UK Ministry of Defence and market participants in naval support would not be affected by the creation of the joint venture.

The Commission also examined the potential impact of the joint venture both upstream and downstream as regards naval systems and weapons in the UK given BAE's strong position in these markets. The Commission's investigation confirmed that the position of the UK Ministry of Defence as the sole customer in the UK gave it the ability to influence the sub-contracting process for naval systems and weapons in such a way that BAE's competitors would still have access to the joint venture as a customer."[193]

2007: *Carlyle/Zodiac Marine*

16.176 On 18 September 2007, the Commission approved the acquisition of Zodiac Marine by Carlyle. Zodiac Marine was active worldwide in six business areas: above-ground swimming pools; swimming pool care products; inflatable recreational boats and rafts; inflatable military and professional boats; inflatable safety equipment; and waste water collection and treatment for the marine industry. Carlyle was a global private equity firm and controlled, *inter alia*, Jandy Pool Products, Inc. (Jandy), a US based company active in pool and spa products, mainly in the US. The Commission found that the proposed transaction showed that the horizontal overlaps between the activities of Zodiac Marine and Carlyle were very limited as Jandy has limited sales in Europe. The Commission's examination also showed that, for the products concerned, in particular salt water chlorinators and pool heating equipment, the combined entity would continue to face effective competition from other suppliers active in the sector. It was not so much a case about shipbuilding as about the building of boats.

2008: *Aker Yards/STX*

16.177 On 5 May 2008, the Commission approved the acquisition of a controlling shareholding in the Norwegian shipbuilder Aker Yards by STX of South Korea.[194] After an in-depth investigation, launched in December 2007,[195] the Commission concluded that effective competition on the shipbuilding markets would not be significantly impeded as a result of the proposed transaction. Aker Yards was active in the construction of cruise

---

193 IP/07/1541.
194 M.4956. IP/08/682. http://ec.europa.eu/comm/competition/mergers/cases/index/m99.html#m_4956.
195 IP/07/1979.

ships and ferries and also built merchant vessels and offshore vessels. It was one of the three main players on the global market for the construction of cruise ships, together with Fincantieri in Italy and Meyer Werft in Germany. STX was a Korean shipbuilder mostly active in building various types of cargo vessels, such as container ships or gas tankers. Until now, STX had not built cruise ships or ferries. The Commission summarised its decision in the following terms:

16.178

"The Commission's in-depth investigation of the proposed transaction dispelled the initial doubts. The Commission found that by itself STX was still far from close to becoming an effective competitive constraint on the existing cruise ship construction market. The in-depth investigation also showed that STX was not the only possible market entrant and that post-merger a number of other Far-East shipbuilders would be as equally well placed as STX to enter the market.

The Commission found that, regardless of whether any of the financial instruments granted to STX in the past were subsidies, the current financial position of STX would not give the merged entity a dominant position.

In addition, the Commission found no evidence indicating that STX was likely to receive subsidies in the future which could significantly strengthen its financial position and enable it to impede competition in the markets concerned.

In particular, the Commission found that even if the type of future hypothetical subsidies identified by the third party (subsidised loans and guarantees) were granted, the advantage would not be such as to enable the merged entity to acquire a dominant position on the cruise ship market. This is because:

(i) the current financial position of STX would not give the merged entity a dominant position;
(ii) Aker Yards is also not currently dominant, as it competes with the market leader Fincantieri and Meyer Werft;
(iii) there are a number of structural features of the market such as buyer power of a few large customers, that would make very unlikely any attempts by STX to monopolise the cruise ship construction market based on the alleged subsidised pricing in the current market structure.

The Commission therefore concluded that competition on the market for cruise ships would not be reduced as a result of the transaction. The Commission also analysed the ferries market, where similar concerns were raised, and came to the same conclusion.

The in-depth investigation also confirmed that there are no competition concerns arising from minor overlaps of the merging companies' activities in the area of certain types of cargo ships or from the vertical integration of STX into engine production or shipping services."[196]

2017: *WÄRTSILÄ/CSSC/JV*

16.179 On 30 June 2017, the Commission cleared, by way of the simplified procedure, a transaction whereby Wärtsilä Technology Oy Ab (of Finland) and CSSC Electronics Technology (of China) would acquire joint control of the undertaking CSSC Wärtsilä Electrical & Automation (Shanghai) Co Limited by way of a purchase of shares in a newly created company constituting a joint venture.[197] The joint venture would be involved in the supply of marine electrical, automation and navigation systems in China. Wärtsilä was involved in the supply of complete lifecycle power solutions for the marine

---

196 IP/08/682.
197 M.8439, http://ec.europa.eu/competition/mergers/cases/decisions/m8439_85_3.pdf and press release: MEX/17/1878.

and energy markets. CSSC was involved in shipbuilding and production of marine-related equipment as well as non-marine related activities as well.[198]

N. CONCLUSIONS

16.180 There is no doubt that there will be many more interesting concentrations in the shipping and shipbuilding sectors. The ones to date have been relatively straightforward but given further consolidation in the sector, there is no doubt but that they will become more involved and complex. There has been no prohibition in the maritime transport sector in the same way as there has been in some other sectors. That is not to say that the cases have been always easy. Many cases are beset with practical issues and difficulties. These difficulties include uncertainty over market definition, the availability (or, more accurately, non-availability) of data, the clashes of the commercial and regulatory timetables, costs including those of economists and advisors as well as the attitude of competition authorities. Nonetheless, it is a system which is working well.

---

198 See the Commission Notice on a Simplified Procedure for the Treatment of Certain Concentrations under Council Regulation 139/2004 (OJ C366/5, 14.12.2013).

CHAPTER 17

Regulation 4057/86: dumping of shipping services and the unfair pricing of shipping services

A. INTRODUCTION

17.001 "Dumping" occurs when a product or service from one country is introduced on to another country's market at less than the normal value of that product or service. This practice has serious consequences for the economy in which the goods or services are dumped because it undermines unfairly industry in that second economy.[1] Dumping can be a temporary phenomenon but the consequences can be long lasting. The European Union ("EU") has fallen victim to dumping in sectors such as photocopiers, textiles, footwear and, most importantly for present purposes, shipping services.[2] There is no doubt that the dumping by some non-EU shipowners particularly, the former USSR, of their freight rates on the EU markets had a detrimental effect on EU shipowners.[3] The former USSR was able to "dump" shipping services because it had a desire for hard currency,[4] a large shipping fleet and a cost base lower than western shipowners because it did not fact the same expenses (e.g. insurance and lower wage costs). The EU responded to such dumping by adopting Council Regulation 4057/86,[5] which was the first EU anti-dumping

---

1 It can also have negative consequences for the economy from which the goods or services have been exported but the adverse consequences are more pronounced in the second economy because its indigenous industry could be damaged or even destroyed by the dumping.

2 On EU dumping law, generally, see Andersen, *EU Dumping Determinations and WTO Law* (2009); Giannakopoulos, *A Concise Guide to the EU Anti-Dumping/Anti-Subsidies Procedures* (2006); Van Bael and Bellis, *Anti-Dumping and other Trade Protection Laws of the EEC* (4th ed., 2004); Vermulst and Waer, *EC Anti-dumping Law and Practice* (1996); and Vermulst, *EU Anti-Dumping Law & Practice* (2004).

3 On Soviet merchant shipping services being dumped in the EU, see Berstrand, "Soviet Merchant Shipping", *Marine Policy*, March 1990, p. 112.

4 E.g. pounds sterling, French francs, German marks etc. at the time.

5 OJ 1986 L378/14. See Bellis, Vermulst and Musquar, "The New EEC Regulation on Unfair Pricing Practices in Maritime Transport: A Forerunner of the Extension of Unfair Trade Concepts to Services?" (1988) 22 Journal of World Trade 47; Bentley and Ronanye, "Anti-Dumping Extended to Shipping Prices" (1987) 12 ELR 212; Elsner, "Unfair Pricing Practices in Maritime Transport" (1988) ETL 590; Hutchings, "Unfair Pricing Practices: Procedure", at "The EEC and Shipping", Institute of Maritime Law, Conference, London, 11 November 1988; Randolph, "Dumping: Unfair Pricing Practices of Non-EEC Lines" at "The EEC and Shipping", Institute of Maritime Law, Conference, London, 11 November 1988; Smith, "The EEC's Unfair Pricing Practices Regulation: New Wave of Competition or Protectionism in Community Shipping?" (1988) Fordham Int'l L J 883; and Steenbergen, "Unfair Pricing Practices in Maritime Transport" at EEC Shipping Law Conference, 4–5 February 1988. See also Aspinwall, *Moveable Feast* (1995), pp. 122–124; Lovett, *United States Shipping Policies and the World Market* (1996), pp. 145–147; Bredima-Savopoulou and Tzoannos, *The Common Shipping Policy* (1989), p. 192; as well as Clough and Randolph, *Shipping and Competition Law* (1991), p. 64.

measure to deal with services.[6] The purpose of Regulation 4057/86 is to provide a remedy against:

> "unfair pricing practices by certain third country[7] shipowners engaged in international cargo liner shipping, which causes serious disruption of the freight pattern on a particular route to, from or within the [EU] and cause or threaten to cause major injury to [EU] shipowners operating on that route and to [EU] interests."[8]

It is therefore a limited measure in that it relates only to international cargo liner shipping and to behaviour by non-EU State shipowners (i.e. "third country" shipowners). However, it was also a unilateral protectionist measure which the EU would say was justified given the issues involved but nonetheless it was protectionist of EU interests. It favoured shipowners but not consumers.[9] It has been commented:

> "Regulation 4057 came about because of a desire to promote collective competitiveness: it put new tools into the hands of the [EU], to be used at the discretion of the Council, and was a response to external pressures from Soviet-bloc fleets that (at least since the 1970s) had been poaching cargoes on lucrative runs at below market prices in order to gain hard currency. It was not the subject of dispute between member states, who were in favour of it, nor between members and the Commission. Rather, it was seen as a necessary response to challenge from third countries, and represented an implicit trade-off for shipowners, who were required to open their national markets under regulation [4055/86].[10]
>
> Yet consumers were adamantly opposed to it, and the debate over the details was between shipowners and consumers; the outcome clearly favoured the former. The reasons for this are largely the same as for [Regulation 4056/86]. First, carriers, as 'concentrated winners,' were able to lobby more effectively than consumers, who were 'dispersed losers'. Consumers did not have [Directorate General for Competition ("DG COMP")] to bat for them on this measure. Carriers, transport ministers, and [Directorate General for Transport] formed a European version of the iron triangle in which it was assumed that the interests of consumers would not be harmed as much as carriers would benefit. In any case, there was legitimate concern about the impact of third country practices."[11]

B. COUNCIL REGULATION 4057/86

Introduction

17.002 Many non-EU shipping companies (especially Eastern European (while they were socialist and communist in the years leading up to the adoption of Regulation 4057/86) and South-East Asian ones)) were engaging in unfair practices to the detriment of their EU counterparts. Non-EU shipping companies were engaged in various unfair practices consisting of, among other things, cheap or even below-cost freight rates brought about by subsidies from their governments. EU shipping companies suffered as a consequence of this dumping. There was, according to some market participants, a need

---

6 Anti-dumping measures in the EU and General Agreement on Tariffs and Trade ("GATT") have traditionally dealt only with goods.
7 Ed., in EU law terms, the term "third country" means non-EU Member States.
8 Reg. 4057/86, Art. 1.
9 Reg. 4057/87 was primarily of benefit to shipowners (the only dissenting shipowning community was the Union of Greek Shipowners because it was worried about the possibilities of retaliation in cross-trades).
10 Ed., i.e. the EU was simultaneously proclaiming the virtue of opening markets in Reg. 4055/86 and being protectionist in Reg. 4057/86 which were both adopted on the same day.
11 Aspinwall, op. cit. at fn. 5, p. 164.

for some EU-driven legislation to deal with the issue because there was need for a collective and co-ordinated response to the problem.

17.003 On 23 December 1976, the European Parliament's Committee on Economic and Monetary Affairs published its Interim Report on the Community Shipping Industry.[12] The report, written at a time when Eastern European countries were largely State-trading economies and EU carriers were in an economic recession, stated:

> "26. Most countries with a merchant fleet accord it certain subsidies, either direct or through favourable fiscal provisions. The Third World, especially the Arab countries, is rapidly developing its own State fleets. The policies followed by the State-trading countries are of particular concern here, as certain elements making up a significant part of [EU] shipping costs, such as insurance, are not included as a shipping cost by lines in State-trading countries, with the results that these latter can naturally charge lower rates. Between 1963 and 1974, the [then] USSR and other Eastern European countries increased their share of world tonnage from 5.2% to 7.6%, while the share of the OECD countries fell from 75.7% to 60%.[13] The gross tonnage of the fleets of State-trading countries has increased by about 400% in 15 years.[14]
>
> 27. Because of their different system of calculating costs, and the fact that their personnel receive a different system of remuneration which results in lower wages costs than those for [EU] fleets, the fleets of State-trading [i.e. communist] countries have been able to offer freight rates between 10 and 50% lower than those offered by [EU] shipping; this is, in effect, a practice of dumping.
>
> 28. Concern has been expressed in several quarters over the expansion of Soviet and Eastern European shipping fleets. The 'World Trade Review and Outlook' (published by the shipbrokers, Lambert Brothers Shipping) suggests that undercutting of freight rates by the Russians, aided by the East Europeans and some sympathetic developing countries, is making Western liner services insolvent and ripe for State subsidies or public ownership. With nearly 10 million grt already afloat, Russia has the world's largest general cargo liner fleet, nearly a third of which is competing for scarce cargoes at cut rates against western shipping in western ports.[15]
>
> As an example of problems faced, the percentage of the United Kingdom's seaborne exports to the Soviet Union by value, carried in Russian ships in 1975, was 78% and in British ships 18%. The corresponding figures for the United Kingdom's imports from the Soviet Union were 74% and 10% respectively.[16]
>
> The Soviet merchant fleet, according to the General Council of British Shipping, now ranks sixth in the world, and the Soviet Union has the largest conventional cargo liner fleet in the world – 6.9 million gross registered grt in 1974 (the UK has 6.4 million). Moreover, the Eastern bloc could account for up to 20 per cent of all liner tonnage on order.[17]
>
> 29. The most obvious practices used by Eastern bloc countries, in particular the Soviet Union, to divert cargoes to their own shipping, fell under four main headings:
>
>> (a) a strict enforcement of f.o.b. purchase/c.i.f. sale contract terms in their direct trades with no flexibility, resulting in a near total monopoly of cargo movements;
>> (b) a systematic policy of undercutting in their cross-trading activities by charging freight rates which were uneconomic, certainly in Western terms;
>> (c) inter-governmental (either bilateral or multilateral) agreements reserving part or all of the cargo moving in the trade;

---

12 Doc. 479/76, Rapporteur: Mr J L Prescott.
13 Information from Lloyd's Register of Shipping.
14 COM(76)341 final.
15 *The Times*, London, 25 March 1976.
16 *The Times*, London, 27 April 1976.
17 General Council of British Shipping, "Red Ensign versus Red Flag—a Critical Choice".

(d) the establishment of so-called joint shipping agencies in foreign countries without reciprocity; Western shipping companies were not afforded the same possibility to run their business in Eastern bloc countries with the same freedom.[18]

30. Shipping interests have called for Western governments to consider concerted action against uncommercial Eastern bloc practices, and for shippers to bear in mind that the immediate attractions of using Soviet cut rates will only be short-term and there would be a big longer-term price to be paid. Estimates of the significance of the threat from Comecon[19] shipping vary considerably, however; the arguments are complex, and the facts are in some dispute. A study published in February 1976 by Seatrade Publications entitled 'Soviet Shipping' suggests, however, that the expansion of the Russian fleet in the next five years may not be as dramatic as supposed by certain European and American shipping sources. This study makes the following important points:

   1. 'A Confidential study from the Committee on European and Japanese National Shipowners' Associations (CENSA) has offered to accept government involvement in their affairs in return for curbs on the "uncommercial practices" of socialist shipping lines'.
   2. Soviet shipping minister Timofei Guzhenko stated that the socialist share of world shipping was not expanding since over 80% of world orders for dry cargo ships were being placed by capitalist countries, with socialist countries accounting for only 3% and this was declining.
   3. CENSA also accuses Comecon fleets of slashing freight rates on cross trades, and of costing practices which relieve shipping lines of the capital costs of building ships, as well as the cost of insurance. The Russians deny that their companies receive any such government subsidies.
   4. 'The US and other western lines can easily outgun the Soviets and other East bloc carriers in both ship capacity and service, but when trade slumps the inoffensive Soviet tonnage becomes a bigger threat.'
   5. 'The USSR's modest $200m. trade surplus with the West in 1974, has plummeted to a staggering $5.5 billion deficit in 1975 ... the Comecon bloc as a whole is in hock to the West to the tune of $12bn.'
   6. Soviet shipping has had to cross trade to stay viable, because the USSR's annual tonnage of maritime exports greatly exceeds imports, and cross-trading therefore helps to utilise capacity. In addition, the seasonality of many Soviet sea routes, which are blocked by ice in winter, releases ships elsewhere."

17.004 The EU responded with Regulation 4057/86 on unfair pricing practices in maritime transport.[20] This is in part a procedural measure and is a hybrid of anti-dumping as well as countervailing duty legislation.[21] It attempts to deal with some of the unfair practices by non-EU undertakings[22] (especially State-owned undertakings) in the shipping sector by establishing procedures for those acting on behalf of EU shipping companies who consider themselves injured or threatened by unfair pricing practices to lodge a complaint to the Commission. It only applies to the cargo liner shipping sector, that is to say, services operating on regular routes at regular intervals and operating according to

---

18 Press release on a speech by Mr W. R. Russell, retiring Chairman of the Council of European and Japanese National Shipowners' Associations (CENSA) in London on 11 December 1975.
19 Ed., Comecon was the international organisation for Central and Eastern European countries when they were Soviet/State-trading states.
20 OJ 1986/L378/14.
21 Bellis, Vermulst and Musquar, op. cit. at fn. 5, p. 60.
22 In this context, the term "shipowner" includes shipping companies which charter-in tonnage for the purposes of providing a liner service.

published schedules. Thus, it does not apply to tramp or bulk operations.[23] In essence, the regulation attempts to protect EU shipping lines from certain unfair pricing practices operated by non-EU shipping lines. The regulation allows for duties to be imposed on freight rates charged by non-EU shipping operators where the rate charged on a route to, from or within the EU is unfair. The regulation also allows for undertakings (i.e. commitments) to be accepted from non-EU shipping lines where rates are revised upwards. In summary, the regulation comes into play when six circumstances are satisfied, namely, where the pricing practice:

(a) is "unfair";
(b) causes serious disruption of the freight pattern on a particular route to, from or within the EU;
(c) is in the international cargo liner shipping sector;
(d) perpetrated by a non-EU ship operator engaged in international liner services;
(e) constitutes a "major injury" to EU ship operators; and
(f) it is in the interests of the EU to act to counteract the practice.

Regulation 4057/86 is closely modelled on the EU's anti-dumping legislation generally, thus in many instances reference to the general EU law relating to dumping will be of assistance in interpreting the regulation.[24] It is important for shipping companies to ensure that their practices do not fall foul of Regulation 4057/86, or else their services may be subject to redressive duties.

The regulation only applies to liner shipping.

Legal basis

17.005 Article 84(2) of the then European Economic Community ("EEC") Treaty[25] provided the legal basis for Regulation 4057/86.[26] Regulation 4057/86 is similar, in many ways, to Regulation 2176/84 which was the basic regulation in EU law laying down the anti-dumping and subsidy law. It is somewhat open to question as to whether the correct legal basis has been used for the regulation. The basis which is being explicitly referred to is Article 100(2) of the Treaty on the Function of the European Union ("TFEU"). This provision is in the Title of the Treaty relating to transport. However, the measure in question, Regulation 4057/86, is very much concerned with the external commercial policy of the EU rather than the transport policy of the EU. While nothing may turn on the precise legal basis, it is possible that at some stage someone affected by a redressive measure under the regulation (or otherwise affected by the regulation) might seek to rely on this and seek the annulment of the regulation. It is not yet clear however whether such a claim would succeed.

---

23 It would have been difficult to apply the regulation to such services because they are based on freely negotiated rates which differ from case to case.
24 See Elsner, op. cit. at fn. 5.
25 Now, with amendment, Art. 100(2) of the TFEU.
26 Reg. 4057/86, Preamble.

Commercial background

17.006 The Preamble to the regulation states that there was reason

"to believe, *inter alia*, on the basis of the information system set up by Council Decision 78/774,[27] that the competitive participation of [EU] shipowners in international liner shipping is adversely affected by certain unfair practices of shipping lines of third countries"[28]

with those unfair practices consisting of "continuous charging of freight rates for the transport of selected commodities which are lower than the lowest freight rates charged for the same commodities by established and representative shipowners"[29] with those pricing practices being made possible "by non-commercial advantages granted by a State which is not a member of the [EU]".[30] This evidence was the result of the monitoring system established under Decision 77/774.[31]

Legal history

17.007 As is normal, Regulation 4057/86 started life as a draft submitted by the Commission to the Council. It was contained in the 1985 *Communication on Progress Towards a Common Transport Policy*.[32] The Economic and Social Committee[33] and the European Parliament[34] then delivered their opinions. The regulation is similar in many ways to Regulation 2423/88,[35] the Anti-Dumping and Anti-Subsidy Regulation.

Entry into force

17.008 Regulation 4057/86 entered into force on 1 July 1987.[36] Being a regulation, it did not need implementing legislation in each Member State.

Purpose

17.009 Article 1 of Regulation 4057/86 provides:

"This Regulation lays down the procedure to be followed in order to respond to unfair pricing practices by certain third country shipowners engaged in international cargo liner shipping, which causes serious disruption of the freight pattern on a particular route to, from or within the Community and cause or threaten to cause major injury to Community shipowners operating on that route or to Community interests."

---

27 Ed., OJ 1978 L258/35.
28 Reg. 4057/86, Preamble, Recital 1.
29 Reg. 4057/86, Preamble, Recital 3.
30 Reg. 4057/86, Preamble, Recital 4.
31 OJ 1978 L238/35.
32 COM(85)90 final.
33 OJ 1985 C344/31.
34 OJ 1986 C255/169.
35 OJ 1988/L209/1.
36 Reg. 4057/86, Art. 18.

The regulation allows the EU to respond to such unfair practices by being able to take redressive action against the unfair pricing practices.[37] It is important to study each of the elements in Article 1 to ensure the correct application of the regulation.

Application of the regulation

17.010 It is clear from Regulation 4057/86 itself that it applies only to international cargo liner shipping. The regulation applies to nationals of the EU who are based outside the EU as well as those EU nationals based within the EU. As Recital 3 of the Preamble to the regulation provides:

> "the structure of the Community shipping industry is such as to make it appropriate that the provisions of this Regulation should also apply to nationals of Member States established outside the Community or cargo shipping companies established outside the Community and controlled by nationals of Member States, if their ships are registered in a Member State in accordance with its legislation."

The twelfth recital to the regulation made plain that the regulation may not be abused so as to obviate or avoid the application of Regulation 4056/86.[38] In the light of the definition given in Regulation 4057/86 for "Community Shipowners" and the general thrust of the regulation, only shipowners can be beneficiaries under the regulation. There is a minimum of four issues to be determined before the regulation may be applied: (a) the third country shipowner (engaged in international cargo liner shipping) has enjoyed "non-commercial advantages" (which constitute unfair pricing practices); (b) the "normal freight rate" must be determined; (c) the rates actually charged by the third country shipowner must be established; and (d) a comparison must be drawn between the "normal freight rate" and the freight rate actually charged by the third country shipowner with the "dumped" rate causing serious disruption of the freight pattern on a particular route to, from or within the EU.

Concepts

Concept of dumping

17.011 Dumping occurs where a product or service of one country is introduced into the commerce of another country at less than the normal value of the product or service. In the context of this regulation, it occurs where there are, among other conditions, charges which are lower than normal freight rates.

Concept of an unfair pricing practice

17.012 There are no internationally agreed rules as to what constitutes an unfair price in the maritime transport field.[39] However, Article 3(b) of Regulation 4057/86 defines "unfair pricing practices", for the purposes of the regulation, as the:

> "continuous charging on a particular shipping route to, from or within the Community of freight rates for selected or all commodities which are lower than the normal freight rates charged

---

37 Reg. 4057/86, Preamble, Recital 5.
38 On Reg. 4056/86, see chap. 11.
39 Reg. 4057/86, Preamble, Recital 6.

during a period of at least six months, when such lower freight rates are made possible by the fact that the shipowner concerned enjoys non-commercial advantages which are granted by a State which is not a member of the Community."

Thus, lower freight rates may only be challenged where they result from "non-commercial advantages". The Commission had originally proposed that state-ownership, state control, cargo reservation and non-adherence to certain International Maritime Organization ("IMO") and International Labour Organization ("ILO") Conventions were advantages giving rise to possible unfair price competition. The specifics were omitted from the final version. This meant that the Commission has a wide discretion on what constitutes an unfair pricing practice. The definition of an unfair pricing practice has a number of elements which must be carefully analysed. Third Country shipowners excludes nationals of Member States established outside the EU or cargo shipping companies established outside the EU but controlled by nationals when their ships are registered in an EU Member State.

Concept of non-commercial advantage

17.013 Regulation 4057/86 as adopted,[40] does not define or give examples of "non-commercial advantages". This is unhelpful for anyone concerned with the regulation but is understandable given the difficulties associated with defining such a nebulous and unpredictable concept. As a consequence of this lack of a definition, the EU institutions have reserved to themselves considerable flexibility[41] in their approach to the application of this regulation – the institutions must however be careful in exercising this discretion lest in their attempts to ensure an open shipping policy, they themselves do not prove to be too protectionist.[42] The Commission had in its draft proposal to the Council provided that the EU could adopt defensive measures against shipowners which enjoyed the advantages of being: (a) owned or controlled directly or indirectly by any non-EU Member State; (b) more favourably placed than EU shipowners as to the access to cargo in ocean trades through national legislation; and/or (c) the operators of ships flying the flag of countries which have not ratified and do not implement the international conventions of the IMO and ILO.[43] The Council did not, however, adopt the Commission's approach because:

> "this approach would appear to have been both too narrow and too wide: too narrow, because it would have only allowed three distinct situations to fall under the terms of non-commercial advantage, and too wide, because it would have introduced an unnecessary automatism in that, e.g. any State-owned third country shipowner would have fulfilled this condition."[44]

17.014 Despite the absence of a definition, it is nonetheless necessary to give some examples of the concept. In broad terms, subsidies, grants, aids, soft loans, moratoria on

---

40 The original proposal included some examples of non-commercial advantages.
41 Bellis, Vermulst and Musquar, op. cit. at fn. 5, describe this as "a deliberate oversight" which enables "the Community authorities to use the Regulation as a 'catch-all' weapon against any form of government subsidies".
42 See the comments of UNICE in 1135 Agence Europe, *Business Brief*, p. 4.
43 One presumes that the Commission was specifically referring to those conventions dealing with seafarers' wages and conditions.
44 Elsner, op. cit. at fn. 5, p. 594.

debts,[45] and unfair tax breaks[46] as well as cargo reservation schemes[47] could potentially constitute non-commercial advantages. Similarly, the non-adherence to or non-enforcement by a non-EU State of basic international standards on such matters as safety, crewing and so on may constitute an unfair advantage for that State's shipping companies. It might well be deduced that a "non-commercial advantage" is a benefit which does not arise from the normal activity of the marketplace but is instead a result of the interference by governmental or other forces so as to distort the workings of the normal shipping market. The term "third country shipowners" excludes nationals of Member States established outside the EU or cargo shipping companies established outside the EU but controlled by national Member States when those ships are registered in an EU Member State.

17.015 There are two tests for establishing the normal freight rate. The first is the so-called third party test. The second analyses the actual costs of the service. Regrettably, the choice of tests, which will always prove critical,[48] will lead to confusion and perhaps conflicting results. It is an important strategic decision in each case as to which test will be used. The "normal freight rate" is determined (for the purposes of Regulation 4057/86) by taking into account:

(a) the comparable rate actually charged in the ordinary course of shipping business for the like service on the same or a comparable route by established and representative companies not enjoying non-commercial advantages which are granted by a State which is not a member of the EU; or
(b) otherwise the constructed rate which is determined by taking the costs of comparable companies not enjoying the non-commercial advantages which are granted by a State which is not a member of the EU, plus a reasonable margin of profit. This cost shall be computed on the basis of all costs incurred in the ordinary course of shipping business, both fixed and variable, plus a reasonable amount for overhead expenses.

This first test is the comparable rate actually[49] charged in the ordinary course of the shipping business for a similar service on the same or a similar route by established and representative shipping companies which do not enjoy the non-commercial advantages outlined in the regulation. There will be a great deal of dispute over whether or not the shipping companies chosen are established at all or comparable to the company being investigated. Similarly, disputes will arise over the comparability of the service or routes involved. Parties who have their rates challenged under this regulation would be advised to establish differences between their own company, service as well as route and those offered by the Commission as being comparable. The second test is based on the costs of service. If there is no comparable service offered in the ordinary course of the shipping business (for the purposes of the first test), then the Commission will have to construct the normal freight rate. The Commission will construct the normal freight rate by taking

---

45 See *Hyundai*, in para. 17.017.
46 Ibid..
47 Ibid.
48 In *Hyundai*, ibid. the company sought to be compared to Jebsen but the final figures were determined by comparison with Eagle Container Line plus a profit margin of 3%.
49 I.e. actually and not constructively charged.

into account the costs of comparable companies[50] not enjoying the non-commercial advantages covered by the regulation and a reasonable profit margin.[51] These costs are to be computed on the basis of all costs incurred in the ordinary course of the shipping business – both fixed and variable plus a reasonable amount for overhead business. It has been commented that these tests focus on the prices or costs of what could be termed the "surrogate company" which may even be the complainant company itself.[52] The Preamble to the regulation provides:

> "in order to determine the existence of unfair pricing practices, provision should ... be made for an appropriate method of calculation [and] when calculating the 'normal freight rate' account should be taken of the comparable rate actually charged by established and representative companies operating within or outside conferences or otherwise of a constructed rate based on the costs of comparable companies plus a reasonable margin of profit."[53]

It is interesting to note that much (but not all) of the regulation is similar to Regulation 2176/84 on dumping generally.

Concept of "serious disruption of a freight pattern"
17.016 Once again, Regulation 4057/86 does not define a key concept. The notion of a "serious disruption of a freight pattern" is again a nebulous one. It is probable that some of the causes of injury to EU shipowners would also amount to a serious disruption of a freight pattern. The disruption may arise in regard to services from, to or within the EU.

Concept of "injury to community ship operators"
17.017 The existence of injury is necessary for the imposition of redressive duties. In determining the existence of injury, the examination by the EU institutions shall cover two principal factors, namely the freight rates offered by EU ship operators' competitors on the route in question, in particular in order to determine whether they have been significantly lower than the normal freight rate offered by EU ship operators,[54] and the level of service offered by all the companies concerned. The EU institutions must examine whether the rates offered by the non-EU ship operators are "significantly lower than the normal freight rate" offered by EU shipowners. Comparisons would be made with the freight rates of EU shipowners and, for example, in the *Hyundai* case,[55] the Commission alleged that Hyundai was undercutting the prices charged by EU companies by between 17% and 43%. The effect of the price cutting and the level of service on EU ship operators may be gauged by taking into account trends in a number of economic indicators such as:

- sailings,
- utilisation of capacity,
- cargo bookings,

---

50 Parties who have their rates challenged by the Commission should seriously consider challenging the companies proposed by the Commission and contend that they are not, in fact, comparable at all.
51 The Commission is likely to have considerable discretion as to what constitutes a reasonable profit margin in this context.
52 Bellis, Vermulst and Musquar, op. cit. at fn. 5, p. 50.
53 Reg. 4057/86, Preamble, Recital 5.
54 On the definition of Community shipowner, see para. 13.019.
55 See below.

- market share,
- freight rates (that is depression of freight rates or prevention of freight rate increases which would normally have occurred),
- profits,[56]
- return of capital,
- investment[57] and
- employment.

If a threat of injury is alleged, the Commission may also examine whether it is clearly foreseeable that a particular situation is likely to develop into actual injury. In this regard, account may also be taken of factors such as:

(a) the increase in tonnage deployed on the shipping route where the competition with the EU shipowners is taking place;
(b) the capacity which is already available or is to become available in the foreseeable future in the country of the foreign shipowners and the extent to which the tonnage resulting from that capacity is likely to be used on the shipping route referred to above in (a).[58]

The application of the regulation is difficult to predict because of the absence of any specific indicators as to what is a "major" injury and what is not. This undefined line could prove to be the basis of many challenges by companies alleged to be engaged in unfair practices.

Concept of "Community interest"

17.018 The fundamental concept "Community interest" is, like many other fundamental concepts in Regulation 4057/86, left undefined. However, Article 12 gives some guidance. It provides that "[i]n deciding on the redressive duties, the Council shall also take due account of the external trade policy considerations as well as port interests and the shipping policy considerations of the Member States concerned".

Concept of third country shipowner

17.019 A third country shipowner[59] is a cargo liner shipping company other than an EU or Community shipowner.[60] According to Regulation 4057/86, an EU shipowner is:

"(a) a cargo shipping company established under the [TFEU] in a Member State of the [EU]; or
(b) a national of a Member State established outside the [EU] provided the company's ships are registered in an [EU] Member State in accordance with that State's legislation; or
(c) a cargo shipping company established outside the [EU] and controlled by nationals of Member States provided the company's ships are registered in an [EU] Member State in accordance with that State's legislation."[61]

---

56 Ibid.
57 Ibid.
58 Reg. 4057/86, Art. 4(2).
59 This term includes those companies which charter in tonnage so as to provide a cargo liner shipping service.
60 Reg. 4057/86, Art. 3(a).
61 Reg. 4057/86, Art. 3(d).

The breadth of drafting used in this provision means that there will be considerable flexibility. What of ships registered in Kerugulen?[62] Are they registered in France? It is submitted that the ambiguity of the provision will only be resolved on a case-by-case basis and the EU institutions will decide on the basis of the type of EU interest being undermined by the practice.

Role of EU institutions under the regulation

The Commission

17.020 The Directorate General for Mobility and Transport ("DG MOVE") has responsibility for administering the regulation. It receives the complaints, conducts the investigations, calculates the duties, accepts any undertakings or terminates proceedings. DG COMP normally deals with competition matters, but because of the special problems associated with dumping in shipping, it is DG MOVE which deals with Regulation 4057/86. It is well to remember that the Commission does not have the power to impose duties.

The Council of Ministers

17.021 It is only the Council[63] which has the legal power to impose a duty. The Commission does not have the power to impose duties.

The Court of Justice of the European Union

17.022 A party affected by a decision of the Council to impose duties may appeal to the Court of Justice of the European Union ("CJEU"). For example, Hyundai appealed to the court.

Complaints

Complaint procedure

17.023 It was necessary to establish under the regulation procedures "for those acting on behalf of the [EU] shipping industry who consider themselves injured or threatened by unfair pricing practices to lodge a complaint".[64]

Who may lodge a complaint?

17.024 Any natural or legal person, or any association not having legal personality, acting on behalf of the EU shipping industry who considers themselves injured or threatened by unfair pricing practices may lodge a written complaint.[65] This includes seafarers.

---

62 I.e. part of the French Antarctic.
63 On the Council of Ministers, see para. 3.021.
64 Reg. 4057/86, Preamble, Recital.
65 Reg. 4057/86, Art. 5(1). In the light of the *BP/TGWU* (16th Report on Competition Policy) and *Scottish Steel Campaign/British Steel* (1991), trade unions may have *locus standi* to complain but they have not been given the express right to do so.

If, in the absence of any complaint, a Member State is in possession of sufficient evidence both of unfair pricing practices[66] and of injury resulting therefrom for EU shipowners[67] then that Member State is obliged immediately to communicate such evidence to the Commission.[68] This complaint mechanism affords EU shipping companies to complain to the Commission and therefore initiate action on particular unfair pricing practices by some non-EU shipping companies. Conversely, non-EU shipping companies need to monitor their activities carefully so that they do not violate the rules contained in Regulation 4057/86 and thereby fall victim of a complaint under that regulation. Seafarers' unions are not given an express right under the regulation to lodge a complaint despite the support for such a right from the Parliament and the Transport Commissioner. Nonetheless, it is submitted that such trade unions have the power to file a complaint. In part, this right is based on the terms of Article 5(1) but also the fact that the minutes of the Council of Ministers indicates that the Commission considered that "both sides of the industry, shipowners and seafarers" have standing.[69]

Form of complaint

17.025 Regulation 4057/86 provides that the complaint must be made in writing.[70] The regulation does not however lay down any other formalities for the complaint. There is no particular form to be used, as is the case with many other areas of competition law.

Contents of the complaint

17.026 The complaint should contain sufficient evidence of the existence of the unfair pricing practice and injury resulting therefrom.[71] This "sufficient evidence" must demonstrate the existence of the unfair pricing practice and the resulting injury. Such evidence would include details of the routes, cargoes, rates charged or likely to be charged by the EU and non-EU companies, operators, the non-commercial advantages, effects on EU shipping and the resulting injuries. While it would be better to approach the Commission with "sufficient evidence" at the beginning, it may well be the case that prima facie evidence will suffice so as to encourage the Commission to begin investigations. If it becomes apparent after consultation that the complaint does not provide sufficient evidence to justify initiating an investigation then the complainant is so informed by the Commission.[72] In most situations, it would be wiser to have preliminary discussions/consultations with the Commission before lodging the complaint.

---

66 As defined in para. 13.012.
67 See para. 13.017.
68 Reg. 4057/86, Art. 5(6).
69 See Council Regulation Applying the Principle of Freedom to Provide Services to Maritime Transport between Member States and between Member States and Third Countries – Statement of the Council of Ministers, 11584/86, Brussels, 15 December 1986, p. 9.
70 Reg. 4057/86, Art. 5(1).
71 Reg. 4057/86, Art. 5(2).
72 Reg. 4057/86, Art. 5(5).

EU SHIPPING LAW

To whom is the complaint made?

17.027 The complaint may be made to the Commission[73] and the Commission then sends each Member State a copy of the complaint received.[74] Equally, the complaint may be made to a Member State of the EU and that State shall then forward it to the Commission.[75]

Confidentiality of the complaint

17.028 The complainant may request the Commission to keep certain parts of its complaint confidential. If the Commission is satisfied that parts of its complaint should be kept confidential then it will ask the complainant to prepare a "confidential complaint" (copies of which will only be circulated to the Commission and the Member States) and a "non-confidential complaint" which will be circulated generally.

Withdrawal of the complaint

17.029 A complaint may be withdrawn.[76] If it is withdrawn then proceedings may be terminated *unless* such termination would not be in the interest of the EU.[77]

Consultation

17.030 Provision is made in Article 6 of the regulation for consultations. Such consultations are a preliminary step before the initiation of proceedings.[78] Article 6(4) provides that consultation shall in particular cover: (a) the existence of unfair pricing practices and the amount thereof; (b) the existence and extent of injury; (c) the causal link between the unfair pricing practices and injury; and (d) the measures which, in the circumstances, are appropriate to prevent or remedy the injury caused by unfair pricing practices and the ways and means for putting such measures into effect. Such consultations shall be held immediately on request by a Member State or on the initiative of the Commission.[79] Any consultations provided for in the regulation must take place within an Advisory Committee.[80] The Advisory Committee consists of representatives of each Member State with a representative of the Commission acting as Chairman.[81] The Committee may either meet or conduct its business in writing. If it meets then it meets when convened by its Chairman[82] who shall provide the Member States, as promptly as possible, with all relevant information.[83] Where necessary, consultation may be in writing only and in such case the Commission shall notify the Member States and shall specify a period within which they

---

73 Reg. 4057/86, Art. 5(3).
74 Ibid.
75 Ibid.
76 Reg. 4057/86, Art. 5(4).
77 Ibid.
78 See Reg. 4057/86, Art. 7(1).
79 Reg. 4057/86, Art. 6(1).
80 Ibid.
81 Ibid.
82 Reg. 4057/86, Art. 5(2).
83 Reg. 4057/86, Art. 6(2).

shall be entitled to express their opinions or to request an oral consultation.[84] The Commission is not bound to accept the views of the Advisory Committee, but it is unlikely that a unanimous view of the Committee will be ignored by the Commission because the views of the Committee may be tantamount to the views of the Member States and those views will probably surface again at the Council.

Initiation and investigation

Initiation

17.031 Consultation[85] is a pre-requisite before initiation and investigation. It is only where, after consultation, it is apparent that there is sufficient evidence to justify initiating a proceeding that the Commission may do so.[86] If it is apparent that there is sufficient evidence to justify initiating a proceeding then the Commission must immediately do three things, namely:

(a) announce the initiation of a proceeding in the *Official Journal of the European Communities*. This notice will invite interested third parties to comment on the investigation;[87,88]
(b) advise the shipowners, shippers and freight forwarders known to the Commission to be concerned and the complainants; and
(c) commence the investigation at EU level, acting in co-operation with the Member States.[89]

In practical terms, the Commission may decide to postpone the initiation of an investigation until it has sufficient staff to deal with the case. The length of an investigation depends on the circumstances of the case, but it would normally take months, rather than weeks, and could take several months or even years.

Contents of the investigation

17.032 The investigation must cover both unfair pricing practices and injury resulting therefrom and shall be carried out in accordance with Article 5 of the regulation which lays down some basic rules. The first of these rules is that an investigation of unfair pricing practices should normally cover a period of not less than six months immediately prior to the initiation of the proceedings.[90] In the *Hyundai* case, it was ten months. Where appropriate, the Commission shall seek all the information it deems necessary and attempt to check this information with the shipowners, agents, shippers, freight forwarders,

---

84 Reg. 4057/86, Art. 6(3).
85 On consultation, see para. 13.030.
86 Reg. 4057/86, Art. 7(1).
87 On the confidentiality of information supplied, see para. 13.028.
88 Reg. 4057/86, Art. 7(1)(a).
89 Reg. 4057/86, Art. 7(1)(a) provides that the announcement in the *Official Journal of the European Communities* must, first, indicate the foreign shipowner concerned and its country of origin, second, give a summary of the information received, third, provide that all relevant information should be communicated to the Commission and, finally, state the period within which interested parties may make known their views in writing and may apply to be heard orally by the Commission.
90 Reg. 4057/86, Art. 5(1)(c).

conferences, associations and other organisations, provided that the undertakings or organisations concerned give their consent.[91]

Where necessary the Commission shall, after consultation, carry out investigations in third countries (i.e. non-EU States), provided that the firms concerned give their consent and the government of the country in question has been officially notified and raises no objection and the Commission shall be assisted by officials of those Member States which so request.[92] The Commission may enlist the help of EU Member States by requesting them to supply information, to carry out all necessary checks and inspections (particularly among shippers, freight forwarders, EU shipowners and their agents) and to carry out investigations in third countries, provided the firms concerned give their consent and the government of the country in question has been officially notified and raises no objection.[93] Member States are obliged to take whatever steps are necessary in order to give effect to requests from the Commission, including sending to the Commission the information requested, together with the results of all inspections, checks or investigations carried out.

Invitation to the allegedly guilty party to make their case

17.033 The Commission will send pro forma questionnaires to the ship operators who are allegedly violating Regulation 4057/86. The time period within which the recipients will have to reply is five weeks from the date of the notification of the investigation in the *Official Journal*, but this may be extended or waived.

Co-operation

17.034 The Commission does not have the legal power to compel the parties to co-operate with the investigation or supply any information requested by the Commission. It requests co-operation. The Commission would normally carry out on-the-spot verifications at the premises of the informants on the accuracy of the information supplied.

A party whose co-operation is sought by the Commission should carefully consider whether or not it should co-operate. It is almost invariably wiser to co-operate because the Commission might well decide the matter "on the basis of the information available to it" and thereby not take into account the views of parties who did not co-operate.

Confidentiality of information supplied

17.035 An informant may request the Commission to keep certain parts of its information confidential. If the Commission is satisfied that all or part of the information should be kept confidential then it will do so.

---

91 Reg. 4057/86, Art. 5(2)(a).
92 Reg. 4057/86, Art. 5(2)(b).
93 Reg. 4057/86, Art. 5(3)(a).

Conclusion of the first stages of investigation

17.036 After concluding the first stages of investigation, the Commission would be expected to discuss in broad terms its findings with the parties involved. This preliminary-type discussion is often useful (in other areas of EU dumping law) to clarify any misconceptions and allow the parties to make representations to the Commission on any matter of interest.

Formal rights of the parties

17.037 The parties have three particular rights. They have a right to:

(a) inspect non-confidential information made available by other parties to the Commission;
(b) a hearing with the Commission;
(c) request a "confrontation meeting" attended by the complainants and the allegedly guilty.

A "confrontation meeting" is a meeting attended by the complainants and the allegedly guilty shipping companies. The meeting would be presided over by a Commission official. There is no obligation on the "other side" (i.e. the party who did not request the meeting) to attend such a meeting.

Outcome of the Commission's investigations

Introduction

17.038 There are three possible outcomes from the Commission's investigations, namely:

(a) the investigation is terminated without any action being taken; or
(b) the investigation is terminated after the acceptance of an undertaking; or
(c) "redressive duties" are imposed.

No action

17.039 The proceedings are terminated if the Commission, after consultation, determines that protective measures are unnecessary and no Member State objects within the Advisory Committee.[94] If a Member State does object then the Commission must submit to the Council of Ministers a report on the results of the consultation along with a proposal that the proceedings be terminated.[95] The proceedings will be terminated unless the Council, acting by way of a qualified majority, decides otherwise.[96]

---

94 Reg. 4057/86, Art. 9(1).
95 Reg. 4057/86, Art. 9(1).
96 Ibid.

Undertakings

Introduction

17.040 The complaint may be "settled" by the non-EU shipowner giving an acceptable written undertaking to the Commission.[97] It may be an undertaking to raise the freight rate or withdraw from the service altogether. In this context "undertaking" means a commitment or promise and not its more usual meaning in EU competition law. Undertakings given in dumping cases are not normally published. The acceptance or rejection of the undertaking is a matter of discretion for the Commission. The acceptance of an undertaking means that a redressive duty would not normally be imposed per se. The breach or withdrawal of the undertaking would, however, mean that such a duty could be imposed and imposed with retrospective effect. If the Commission accepts an undertaking but nonetheless continues with its investigation and finds that there was no breach then the undertaking would lapse.

Duration of undertakings

17.041 An undertaking lapses five years after it was confirmed by the Commission or last amended. It may however continue: where an interested party shows that the expiration would lead to injury or threat of injury then the Commission must conduct a review and the undertakings will remain in force pending the outcome of this review.

Review of undertakings

17.042 The Commission may carry out a review at any time either on its own initiative or at the request of an EU Member State. Any interested party may ask the Commission to review the undertaking provided that at least one year has elapsed since its confirmation.

Redressive duties

17.043 Article 2 of the regulation provides that in response to the unfair pricing practices prohibited by the regulation which cause major injury, redressive duties may be applied by the EU.[98] For example, in the *Hyundai* case, a duty of €450 was imposed for each 20 ft container.[99] These duties may be imposed where it has been shown on investigation by the Commission that: (a) there is an unfair pricing practice; (b) such practice has caused injury to the Community shipowner; and (c) it is in the interest of the EU to impose duties. The Council must also take into account, when deciding whether to impose redressive duties, "the external trade policy considerations as well as the port interests

---

97 Reg. 4057/86, Art. 10(1).
98 Reg. 4057/86 does not confer the power to impose provisional duties.
99 Seong Deog Yi and Chong Ju Choi comment ("The Community's Unfair Pricing Practices in the Maritime Transport Sector" (1991) ELR 279 at 279 that Reg. 4057/86 "received many criticisms from countries outside the [EU] on account of its tendency towards protectionism. In fact, in the light of the economic situations surrounding the *Hyundai* case, the pricing practice of the Hyundai Company may not be considered unfair in terms of the Regulation. But it appears that the Commission decided to impose redressive duties based on the Regulation without examining all relevant economic factors. This case seems to show a tip of the [EU's] tendency towards protectionism in the area of trade in services."

and the shipping policy considerations of the Member States concerned".[100] A threat of major injury may only give rise to an examination.[101]

Power to impose redressive duties

17.044 Redressive duties may only be imposed by the Council following on from a recommendation of the Commission.

Calculation of the redressive duties

17.045 The redressive duty to be imposed must not exceed the difference between the freight rate charged by the non-EU ship operator and the "normal freight rate" established by the Commission's investigation. The duty imposed may be related to units of cargo, value of the products or whatever. For example, in *Hyundai* the duty was a fixed amount for each type of container. There is undoubtedly considerable flexibility in the way in which it may be calculated.

Imposition of redressive duties

17.046 The redressive duties are imposed by way of a Council's regulation. The regulation must state the reasons for the regulation, the amount and type of duty, the commodities concerned and the country of origin of the non-EU ship operators. The duties may be imposed on non-EU shipowners only. The duties are applicable to the transport of the particular commodities when they are loaded[102] or unloaded at any EU port.

Collection of redressive duties

17.047 The collection of redressive duties imposed under a regulation of the Council is the task of the customs authorities in the Member States.

Duration of the redressive duties

17.048 An undertaking lapses five years after it was confirmed by the Commission or last amended.[103] It may however continue. Where an interested party shows that the expiration would lead to injury or threat of injury then the Commission must conduct a review and the duties will remain in force pending the outcome of this review.

---

100 Reg. 4057/86, Art. 12. This provision is somewhat unclear. Guidance might be had from the amendment proposed by the Parliament on this issue: "the Council shall take into account that important national interests connected with a Member State's foreign policy are placed in jeopardy when it imposes a duty".
101 Reg. 4057/86, Art. 2(2).
102 In the *Hyundai* case the duties only related to goods loaded because Hyundai did not discharge relevant cargo in the EU.
103 Reg. 4057/86, Art. 15(2).

Retroactivity of redressive duties

17.049 As a general rule, a redressive duty may not be imposed retrospectively. However, such a duty may be imposed when the Council determines that an undertaking[104] has been violated or withdrawn.

Review of redressive duties

17.050 The Commission may carry out a review at any time, either on its own initiative or at the request of an EU Member State. Any interested party may ask the Commission to review the duty, provided that at least one year has elapsed since its imposition.

Refunds of redressive duties

17.051 The regulation lays down procedures for examining applications for refunds of redressive duties.[105] The non-EU shipowner can obtain a refund when the duty collected exceeds the difference between the freight rate actually charged by it and the "normal freight rate" imposed by the Commission.[106] In practice, such a refund might be paid after a considerable delay, if at all.

Appeals

17.052 In dumping cases generally, it has been recognised that complainants, exporters and importers have the right to bring a regulation imposing anti-dumping duties before the European Court so as to test its validity under EU law. The same right would apply in this context.[107]

Practice to date

17.053 Action was taken against Hyundai Merchant Marine Company Limited on 20 October 1988 on the basis of Regulation 4057/86[108] when the Commission proposed the imposition of redressive duties on container cargoes shipped from the EU to Australia by Hyundai Merchant Marine Company of Seoul in the Republic of Korea. This followed a complaint made in August 1987 by the Committee of European Community Shipowners ("CAACE")[109] regarding the alleged dumping of freight rates by Hyundai Merchant Marine on the EU–Australian route. The CAACE was acting on behalf of liner shipping companies from Denmark, France, Germany, Italy, the Netherlands, Spain and the UK operating in the liner shipping trade between the EU and Australia and organised in Europe/UK to Australia Conferences.[110] These companies were all the EU shipowners

---

104 On undertakings, see para. 13.040.
105 Reg. 4057/86, Art. 16.
106 Ibid.
107 See *Hyundai*, below, in para. 17.053.
108 OJ 1989 L4/1.
109 I.e. the Comité des Associations d'Armateurs des Communautes Europeénnes.
110 A Belgian shipowner (i.e. an outsider) later joined the proceedings.

engaged in that particular trade.[111] The CAACE alleged that Hyundai were benefiting from non-commercial advantages offered by the South Korean government and could thus charge rates 25% to 30% lower than the normal rates charged by CAACE companies. The Commission opened the proceedings.[112] It was the first case to be opened under Regulation 4057/86. The Commission investigated the matter over a period of 16 months and made visits to Antwerp, Crawley, Hamburg, Ipswich, London, Paris, Rotterdam, Seoul and Trieste. The service operated by Hyundai was compared by the Commission to a service operated by the Eagle Container Line, a Swiss company operating out of Ipswich in the UK,[113] but the basis of this comparison has been challenged by Hyundai which wanted to be compared to a Norwegian company.[114] The Commission rejected the comparison to the Norwegian company because "*inter alia*, [the Norwegian company] entered the trade only in 1985/86 and does not operate a fixed fleet and often calls only at one major Australian port" and was not thus an "appropriate choice".[115] Some shippers argued the case on behalf of Hyundai: (a) they argued that it was an inappropriate use of the regulation which was aimed at dumping by governments (particularly, the then USSR) and not low-cost carriers; (b) they argued that any action would damage trade between Europe and Australia for low-value cargoes; and (c) they argued that non-conference lines would be affected. The Commission conducted an investigation under Article 7 of the regulation. In October, 1988, the Commission held that the complaint was justified: Hyundai had, according to the Commission, been engaged in unfair pricing practices on the Europe to Australia route, thereby causing serious disruption of the freight pattern to the detriment of EU shipowners. The Commission concluded that Hyundai was benefiting from a number of non-commercial advantages. The first of these related to the cargo reservation scheme under Article 16 of the Korean Maritime Transportation Fostering Act and the second related to the Shipping Industry Rationalisation Plan ("SIRP") operated by the Korean government since 1984. According to the Commission, Hyundai was undercutting the normal freight rate by an average of 26% or €450 per 20 ft container during the ten-month period investigated by the Commission. Hyundai was, according to the Commission, benefiting from a cargo reservation scheme and a rationalisation plan for the shipping industry both operated by the Korean government. The Council of Ministers then imposed on 4 January 1989, by way of Regulation 15/89,[116] a redressive duty on containerised cargo loaded on to any vessel operated directly or indirectly by Hyundai at any EU port for Australia. The duty was €450 for a 20 ft container and €900 for a 40 ft container with no regard for the contents of the container – pro rata rates would apply for containers of other sizes. Hyundai then suspended its service. No duty was imposed on bulk cargo. Hyundai has appealed to the CJEU and a judgment was not to hand when completing this edition.[117] The Commission, in its Report to the Council of Ministers on 1 August 1990 on the Implementation of the Four Regulations in the Field of Maritime Transport,[118] stated:

---

111 See Reg. 15/89.
112 OJ 1987 C308/3.
113 See Reg. 15/89, para. 10.
114 Reg. 15/89, para. 12.
115 Ibid.
116 OJ 1989 L4/1.
117 Case 136/89.
118 SEC(90)1594 final, p. 19.

"82. The following conclusions can be drawn from the first case under the Regulation on unfair pricing practices:

- the legal instrument is adequate for its intended purpose;
- a proceeding can be carried out sufficiently quickly to offer relief where this is justified;
- national customs authorities can efficiently implement a specific regulation;
- maritime transport appears to lend itself to attempts to circumvent a redressive duty. Although the current legislation seems to be sufficient for the institutions to cope with this problem where anticipated, it would appear preferable to discourage such attempts from the outset. A clarification of the current legislation therefore appears desirable;
- a small number of points with regard in particular to customs rules and the procedural rights should be updated to keep up with post-1986 developments in EC customs and anti-dumping legislation on which latter a substantial part of Regulation No. 4057/86 has been modelled."

The Commission continued:

"84. Market reports seem to indicate that certain third country shipowners against whom complaints were being prepared have changed their rate policies subsequent to the imposition of the duty against HMM. Such reaction can only be welcomed: the value of Regulation 4057/86 is to be seen as much as a deterrent as a tool to take redressive action."

It has been stated that

"during the period under investigation (1 January to 31 October 1987), the average rate of undercutting being 26%. The increase of Hyundai's market share was from 0.3% for 1996 to 4% during the period of investigation. At the same time, the Community shipowners' share fell from 54% to 53.6%. This was not in itself considered as a major injury, but there were additional factors, amongst them, the fact that the revenue generated by the Community shipowners decreased by 7.5% as the result of a largely equivalent reduction in the average freight rate."[119]

Due to the subsequent transfer of the Korean interests to a French company, no duties were imposed.[120] It has thus been commented that because no duties were imposed in this case,

"some European shipowners have advocated towards the necessity of making this Regulation more watertight. However, it should also be mentioned ... that the Regulation has, in a number of cases, been effectively used by the Commission on a 'threat' against 'potential' dumping."[121]

There is little doubt that the Commission will have to utilise the regulation sparingly: its mere existence and its potency[122] to date has meant that it may well prove to be a strong deterrent rather than a weapon used in battle. It is ironic that Regulation 4057/86 which was adopted primarily to address dumping by the then USSR and Eastern bloc countries was never used against them but was used against South Korean interests. It is also ironic that the regulation was used only once but that one investigation demonstrated the difficulties associated with pursuing a case under the regulation. The fact that it has been used only once is not a sign of failure but a combination of its potency and the market

---

119 Lovett, *United States Shipping Policies and the Wider World* (1996), fn. 68.
120 See Haralambides, "Current Challenges in European Shipping Policy", *BIMCO Bukehn*, 91(1), February 1996.
121 Ibid.
122 This presumes no overturning of the Commission's decision by the ECJ.

conditions. However, the regulation has shortcomings in that it can be easily circumvented by establishing a shipping company in the EU and thereby becoming a EU shipowner. Indeed, it may now be more of a relic of the past but changing market conditions could change all of that. The fact that it was outdated was clear to the Commission over a decade ago[123] but it still remains in force and available for use.

---

[123] Commission, *Towards a New Maritime Strategy* COM(96)81 final, 13 March 1996, p. 23.

CHAPTER 18

Regulation 4058/86: co-ordinated action to safeguard free access to cargoes in ocean trade

A. INTRODUCTION

18.001 Council Regulation 4058/86[1] enables co-ordinated action to be taken by the European Union ("EU") to safeguard free access to cargoes in ocean trade.

18.002 The regulation was another element in the December 1986 package of shipping measures adopted by the Council under its then UK Presidency.[2] It provides a procedure to be used where certain trade practices by a third country[3] or its agents threaten to restrict free market access by Member States' shipping companies to ocean trade. In essence, it establishes a procedure for Member States to join together so as to resist cargo-reservation or other trade impediments by non-EU Member States.

18.003 The regulation was adopted because Member States believed that there was a need to ensure a free competitive environment, particularly in the dry and liquid bulk trades. As Heldring commented: "[t]he [Union] champions freedom of the seas, so it is very unusual for it to take countermeasures in shipping. However, it [was] clear that there were deficiencies in the EU's arsenal which put freedom of the sea at risk."[4] It is therefore another expression[5] of the EU's commitment to free market economics and, moreover, ensuring such freedom where it would not otherwise occur.

B. APPLICATION OF REGULATION 4058/86

18.004 The regulation applies, in essence, to all types of shipping services and all types of cargo in international trades. The markets principally concerned are: (a) liner cargoes in codist trades (except in the case of restrictions from the United Nations Code of Conduct on Liner Conferences ("UNCTAD Code")); (b) liner cargoes in non-codist trades; (c) bulk cargoes and any other cargo on tramp services; (d) passengers; as well as (e) persons and goods to or between offshore installations.

---

1 OJ L378/21, 31 December 1986. The regulation is usually referred to in this chapter as the "Regulation". See Heldring, "Free Access to Ocean Trades" (1988) 25(3) ETL 600 and Vermote, "The Application of the United Nations Liner Code within the European Communities" (1988) 25(3) ETL 571. See also Aspinwall, *Moveable Feast* (1985), pp. 124–125 and 164–165; and Ortiz Blanco, *Shipping Conferences under EC Antitrust Law* (2007), p. 119.

2 On the 1986 package of measures, see chap. 5 above. Agreement was reached on 16 December 1986 but it was not put into legal form on 22 December 1986 hence it is known as the 22 December 1986 package.

3 I.e. a non-EU Member State.

4 Op. cit. at fn. 1, p. 600.

5 Other expressions include Reg. 4055/86.

C. LEGAL BASES OF REGULATION 4058/86

18.005 The legal bases of the regulation were what are now the Treaty on the Functioning of the European Union ("TFEU") and Article 100(2) of the TFEU.

D. BACKGROUND TO REGULATION 4058/86

18.006 The recitals to the regulation are instructive and provide as follows:

"Whereas an increasing number of countries[6] resort to protecting their merchant fleets either unilaterally, through legislation or administrative measures, or through bilateral agreement with other countries;

Whereas certain countries, by virtue of measures they have adopted or practices they have imposed, have distorted the application of the principle of fair and free competition in shipping trade with one or more [Union][7] Member States;

Whereas in respect of liner trades the United Nations Convention on a Code of Conduct for Liner Conferences, which entered into force on 6 October 1983, grants certain rights to shipping companies which are members of a conference operating a pool;

Whereas, increasingly, third countries which are contracting parties or signatories to that Convention interpret its provisions in such a way as effectively to expand the rights given under the Convention to their companies both in liner and tramp trades, to the disadvantage of [Union][8] companies or companies of other OECD countries, whether conference members or not;

Whereas in respect of bulk trades there is an increasing tendency on the part of third countries to restrict access to bulk cargoes, which poses a serious threat to the freely competitive environment broadly prevailing in the bulk trades; whereas the Member States affirm their commitment to a freely competitive environment as being an essential feature of the dry and liquid bulk trades and are convinced that the introduction of cargo-sharing in these trades will have a serious effect on the trading interests of all countries by substantially increasing transportation costs;

Whereas the restriction of access to bulk cargoes would adversely affect the merchant fleets of the Member States, as well as substantially increasing the transportation costs of such cargoes, and would thereby have a serious effect on the trading interests of the [Union];

Whereas the [Union] should be enabled to provide for coordinated action by Member States if the competitive position of Member States' merchant fleets or Member States' trading interests are adversely affected by cargo reservation to shipping companies of third countries or if required by an international agreement;

Whereas Council Decision 77/587/EEC[9] provides, *inter alia*, for consultation on the various aspects of developments which have taken place in relations between Member States and third countries in shipping matters;

Whereas Council Decision 83/573/EEC[10] provides, *inter alia*, for concertation by Member States of any countermeasures they may take in relation to third countries and for the possibility of a decision on the joint application by Member States of appropriate countermeasures forming part of their national legislation;

Whereas it is necessary to elaborate and refine the machinery provided for in these Decisions with a view to providing for coordinated action by Member States in certain circumstances at the request of a Member State or Member States or on the basis of an international agreement…"

---

6 Ed., this refers to non-EU Member States.
7 Ed., i.e. EU Member States.
8 Ed., i.e. EU companies.
9 OJ No L239/23, 17.9.1977.
10 OJ No L332/37, 28.11.1983.

Before the regulation was adopted, most Member States had national countermeasures legislation to enable those States to react when their interests were affected.[11] The then EC was aware that some problems had been experienced on routes to certain parts of Africa by the then EC's non-conference lines (i.e. independents).

18.007 Heldring, after recalling the adoption of the UNCTAD Code,[12] observed:

"it was the pressure from the United States directed towards making a joint stand against increasing protectionism by developing countries which galvanized Europe and Japan into stopping a gap in this field. It irked the Americans that the Code, which they had categorically opposed from the outset, had been interpreted and applied by the developing countries in such a way that there seemed little chance of any element of free competition remaining. The USA had voted against the Code at the time because it legalized the closed Conference system, in opposition to US legislation which prohibited closed Conferences. By allowing the Code to be used to exclude outsiders from the market, Europe and Japan ... were helping to give Conferences a monopoly...

On 16 February 1983 Germany had submitted a draft Regulation to the Council concerning countermeasures in the field of international merchant shipping. The Germans gave two reasons for this move:

(i) the results of the 'monitoring system'[13] had shown that the competitive position of Community shipping companies was being increasingly undermined by measures taken by third countries which were incompatible with the principles of the Community market;
(ii) it was necessary to have an instrument which the Member States could use to ensure that the Code of Conduct for Liner Conferences and the accompanying Resolution on outsiders was applied correctly.

This required a provision which would form the framework within which Member States suffering as a result of discriminatory practices could take joint countermeasures on the basis of the 1977 consultation procedure.[14]

It was striking therefore that the German proposal was, in the first place, based on the harmful practices of specific shipping companies from third countries, and in particular the dumping practices by shipping lines from state-trading countries. ... Some Member States did not want dumping practices by shipping companies to be mentioned specifically as a possible reason for countermeasures, but wanted reference only to governmental measures (e.g., laws). The scope of the German proposal was broader and that was also the reason why the countermeasures proposed included both a system of permits (for loading or discharging cargoes) and the imposition of taxes or duties; the latter would perhaps have been a more appropriate punishment for freight prices or dumping rates.

It was also striking that the German proposal said nothing about the competence of the *Council* to take decisions on the possibility of imposing coordinated countermeasures. Many Member States felt that it was still too early to allow the Council that kind of competence in the area of shipping policy. On 26 October 1983 the Council adopted[15] the proposal, although it still seems to leave considerable latitude. If a Member State has adopted or intends to adopt countermeasures in international merchant shipping 'in relation to third countries' (and it is still open to

---

11 Greece, Ireland, Luxembourg and Portugal were the only Member States which did not have such countermeasures legislation at the time when the regulation was adopted.

12 Op. cit. at fn.1, pp. 601–605 in particular.

13 Council Decision 78/774/EEC of 19 September 1978 concerning the activities of certain third countries in the field of cargo shipping.

14 Council Decision 77/587/EEC of 13 September 1977 which required Member States to consult each other whenever problems arose with third countries in shipping matters and if it was necessary to take coordinated action in international organizations.

15 Council Decision 83/573/EEC of 26 October 1983 concerning countermeasures in the field of international merchant shipping.

question whether this includes shipping companies who offer freight rates at dumping levels), it is required to consult the other Member States and the Commission. The Member States must then *endeavour* to concert any countermeasures they may take. The Council may, *acting unanimously*, decide on the joint application by Member States of appropriate countermeasures forming part of their national legislation.

Consultations then make clear the reason for the countermeasures, the shipping area concerned and the nature of the countermeasures which should be taken. (In the latter connection, care is taken to avoid any mention of a system of permits or taxes and duties.)

Because this Decision leaves far too much latitude it has never been used but it did constitute one more step towards the ultimate recognition of [Union] competence in the area of countermeasures as provided for in Council Regulation 4058/86…

Regulation … 4058/86 is based more or less on Council Decision 83/537/EEC but carries much more weight because of the provisions on [Union] competence contained in it. The procedure also imposes time restrictions and leaves open the possibility of coordinating action with OECD [Organisation for Economic Co-operation and Development] countries, a clear gesture towards the USA, which for so long had been pressing for legal competence for the [EU] as one entity, which would make it easier for the two sides to work together."[16]

E. LEGAL HISTORY OF REGULATION 4058/86

18.008 The legislative history of the regulation commenced with a draft submitted by the Commission and was opined on by the European Parliament in 1986[17] as well as the Economic and Social Committee in 1985.[18] The regulation was well-supported by the Member States and the various pressure groups. This was despite the fact that the regulation could be harmful to cross-traders such as Denmark and the UK. Both carriers and shippers supported its adoption. The shippers succeeded in widening the type of non-Member State action which could be targeted under the regulation.

F. ENTRY INTO FORCE OF REGULATION 4058/86

18.009 The regulation entered into force on 1 July 1987.[19]

G. CONCEPTS IN REGULATION 4058/86

18.010 Article 2 of the regulation sets out the definition of the two key concepts in the regulation, namely, (a) the "home-trader" and (b) the "cross-trader". A "home-trader" is a "shipping company of a third country which operates a service between its own country and one or more Member States". A "cross-trader" is a "shipping company of a third country which operates a service between another third country and one or more Member States".

---

16 Op. cit. at fn. 1, pp. 605–608.
17 OJ C255/169, 15 October 1986.
18 OJ C344/31, 31 December 1985.
19 Reg. 4058/86, Art. 9.

H. TRIGGERING EVENT

18.011 Article 1 of the regulation provides:

"The procedure provided for by this Regulation shall be applicable when action by a third country or by its agents restricts or threatens to restrict free access by shipping companies of Member States or by ships registered in a Member State in accordance with its legislation to the transport of:

- liner cargoes in Code trades, except where such action is taken in accordance with the United Nations Convention on a Code of Conduct for Liner Conferences;
- liner cargoes in non-Code trades;
- bulk cargoes and any other cargo on tramp services;
- passengers;
- persons or goods to or between offshore installations.

This procedure shall be without prejudice to the obligations of the [EU] and its Member States under international law."

The regulation applies to both liner and bulk cargoes. The agents could be freight booking offices. A *threat* to restrict free access is sufficient. The obligations of the EU and its Member States under international law include obligations under, for example, the Lomé Convention. Heldring has commented that:

"Article 1 ... establishes a *norm*, namely that the [UNCTAD] Code of Conduct, which recognises a certain amount of cargo-sharing in order to help developing counties, has to be respected by the [EU] but only as far as it is applicable, of course (i.e., in traffic between parties who have acceded to the Code). However, action over and above this norm, e.g., applying the 40:40:20 formula to all liner shipping, shall not be tolerated."[20]

He also commented that the:

"important point [with Article 1] is that there should be action by a third *country* or by its agents (e.g., freight booking offices) which restricts or *threatens to restrict* free access. This is very important because joint action against third countries is possible even if legislation which is *intended* to restrict free access is under preparation but has not yet been adopted or not yet implemented."[21]

I. REQUESTS BY A MEMBER STATE FOR CO-ORDINATED ACTION

Introduction

18.012 Article 3 of the regulation provides that co-ordinated action may be requested by a Member State – it is not open to the injured shipping company to seek the assistance of the Commission but it would presumably call on the Member State to act. The request is to be made to the Commission which will then make the appropriate recommendation or proposal of recommendation to the Council within one month of the Member State's request. In considering the response, the Council must consider the external trade policy considerations as well as the port interests and the shipping policy considerations of the Member States concerned.

---

20 Op. cit. at fn. 1, p. 608.
21 Op. cit. at fn. 1, p. 608.

Text of Article 3

18.013 Article 3 of the regulation provides:

"Coordinated action may be requested by a Member State.
The request shall be made to the Commission; the latter shall make the appropriate recommendations or proposals to the Council within four weeks.

The Council, acting in accordance with the voting procedure laid down in Article [100(2)] of the [TFEU], may decide on the coordinated action provided for in Article 4.

In deciding on coordinated action, the Council shall also take due account of the external trade policy considerations as well as the port interests and the shipping policy considerations of the Member States concerned."

It is worth bearing in mind that only a Member State may request co-ordinated action. The requirement of unanimity under Article 100(2) was insisted upon by Greece which was concerned about any retaliatory reaction by the then USSR. The Single European Act – which coincidentally entered into force on 1 July 1987 (the same day as Regulation 4055/86) – meant that unanimity was no longer legally necessary. Despite the change from unanimity to a qualified majority, the use of the term "unanimity" in the regulation means that decisions should be adopted by way of "de fact unanimity".[22] Since the TFEU entered into force on 1 December 2009, Article 100(2) reads that the "European Parliament and the Council, acting in accordance with the ordinary legislative procedure, may lay down appropriate provisions for sea and air transport. They shall act after consulting the Committee of the Regions and the Economic and Social Committee."

18.014 It has been written that

"non-domiciled and [flag of convenience] vessels are considered beneficiaries, reflecting the wide variety of investment locations of EU companies. The internal market and anti-dumping regulations are treated the same way, contrary to what [labour] had demanded. Organised [labour] again had little impact in these negotiations, even though if carriers were correct in assuming it would mean more business for them, [labour] may also have gained."[23]

J. CO-ORDINATED ACTION

Introduction

18.015 Co-ordinated action by the EU may consist of countermeasures such as the imposition of quotas or taxes or duties. They must only be used however after diplomatic representations have been made. Diplomatic complaints must precede countermeasures.

Text of Article 4

18.016 Article 4 of the regulation provides:

"1. Coordinated action may consist of:

(a) diplomatic representation to the third countries concerned, in particular where their actions threaten to restrict access to trade;

---

22 See Bredima-Savopoulou and Tzoannos, *The Common Shipping Policy of the EC* (1990), pp. 202–203.
23 Aspinwall, op. cit. at fn. 1, p. 125.

(b) countermeasures directed at the shipping company or companies of the third countries concerned or at the shipping company or companies of other countries which benefit from the action taken by the countries concerned, whether operating as a hometrader or as a cross-trader in Community trades.

Those countermeasures may consist, separately or in combination, of:

(i) the imposition of an obligation to obtain a permit to load, carry or discharge cargoes; such a permit may be subject to conditions or obligations;
(ii) the imposition of a quota;
(iii) the imposition of taxes or duties.

2. Diplomatic representations shall be made before countermeasures are taken.

Such countermeasures shall be without prejudice to the obligations of the European [Union] and its Member States under international law, shall take into consideration all the interests concerned and shall neither directly nor indirectly lead to deflection of trade within the [Union]."

Diplomatic representations

18.017 In advance of any countermeasures being taken, diplomatic representations must however be made to the non-Member State concerned. This is in accordance with the normal rules of international relations and was included in the regulation to assuage the concerns of Greece which feared damage to trading relationships.

K. PROCEDURE

18.018 Article 5 of Regulation 4058/86 provides that:

"1. When deciding upon one or more of the countermeasures referred to in Article 4(1)(b) the Council shall specify, as appropriate, the following:

(a) the developments, which have caused countermeasures to be taken;
(b) the trade or range of ports to which the countermeasures are to apply;
(c) the flag or shipping company of the third country whose cargo reservation measures restrict free access to cargoes in the shipping area concerned;
(d) maximum volume (percentage weight in tonnes, containers) or value of cargo which may be loaded or discharged in ports of Member States;
(e) maximum number of sailings from and to ports of Member States;
(f) amount or percentage and basis of the taxes and duties to be levied and the manner in which they will be collected;
(g) the duration of the countermeasures.

2. Where the countermeasures envisaged by paragraph 1 are not provided for by the national legislation of a Member State they may be taken in accordance with the Council Decision referred to in the third paragraph of Article 3 by the Member State concerned on the basis of this Regulation."

18.019 Heldring has commented that

"[t]he latter part of ... Article [5] contains one of the most interesting provisions in the Regulation, namely that where the national legislation of a Member State does not contain any provisions on the basis of which a countermeasure, like the imposition of a levy for example, can be taken, such a measure may nevertheless be taken once the Council has taken the requisite decision on the basis of this Regulation. In some quarters this has been referred to as a 'legal innovation' but some Member States, whose legislation contains no provisions on countermeasures, or only partial provisions, found this a good solution, since a Regulation is directly applicable in each Member State and since Article 4 of the Regulation does in fact contain a list of possible countermeasures."[24]

L. ACTION BY MEMBER STATES IN DEFAULT OF COUNCIL ACTION

Individual or group action

18.020 Article 6(1) of the regulation provides that if the Council has not adopted the proposal on co-ordinated action within two months then Member States may apply national measures unilaterally or as a group, if the situation so requires. It is to be presumed that the situation must *objectively* require the action: any other interpretation would be a nonsense.

Urgent action

18.021 Article 6(2) of the regulation contemplates national urgent action. It provides that Member States may, in cases of urgency, take the necessary national measures on a provisional basis, unilaterally or as a group, even within the two-month period referred to in Article 6(1) of the regulation.

Report to the Commission

18.022 All national measures must be notified immediately to the Commission.[25]

M. CONSULTATION

18.023 Article 7 of the regulation provides that during the period in which the countermeasures are to apply, the Member States and the Commission shall consult each other in accordance with the consultation procedure established in Decision 77/587[26] every three months or earlier if the need arises, in order to discuss the effects of the countermeasures in force.

N. OECD MEMBER STATES

Introduction

18.024 Interestingly, co-ordinated action may be taken where other OECD States (i.e. OECD Member States which are not EU Member States) are restricted and, on the basis of reciprocity, that OECD State and the EU agree to resort to co-ordinated resistance. Aspinwall has written:

"[the] benefits of the market access regulation may be extended to the fleets of other OECD countries, provided there has been agreement to co-ordinate responses on a reciprocal basis. This

---

24 Op. cit. at fn. 1, p. 610.
25 Reg. 4058/86, Art. 6 (3).
26 OJ No L239/23, 17 November 1977.

is in response to the dialogue between the United States and the Consultative Shipping Group (an informal intergovernmental group comprising 13 west European and Japanese members[27]) in which agreement was sought on ways to counter growing flag discrimination in shipping; the terms of regulation 4058 are a response to the demands of the US that the EU provide a means of so doing."[28]

Article 8 of the regulation

18.025 Article 8 provides that the procedure provided for by the regulation may be applied when action by a third country or its agents restricts or threatens to restrict the access of shipping companies of another OECD country where, on a basis of reciprocity, it has been agreed between that country and the EU to resort to co-ordinated resistance in the case of restriction of access to cargoes. Such a country may make a request for co-ordinated action and join in such co-ordinated action in accordance with the regulation.

O. APPLICATION AND OBSERVATIONS

18.026 Regulation 4058/86 has been almost dormant. It appears to have been used formally only once. It has been used in relation to some States in West and Central Africa in regard to the Europe–West Africa and Central Africa trades. Denmark brought a complaint in 1987 against a number of activities in the Europe–West Africa trade. It alleged that some of the West African states were engaging in cargo reservation practices which excluded the Danish lines. The complaint was supported by the Greek and Italian governments as well as the European Shippers' Council. Belgium, France and Germany were somewhat sympathetic to the cause of the West African states. The Council decided that diplomatic representations would be made within the framework of the Lomé Convention. The matter then escalated into a three-pronged attack on the bases of Regulations 4055/86, 4056/86 and 4058/86. Belgium, Germany and the Netherlands were reticent about taking action; their reluctance was due to a special arrangement which they had under the so-called "Kinshasa Accord". The EU was seeking to open up liner trades to independents but it was not easy. The matter became more difficult because the Commission found breaches of competition law in 1992. The Council's Decision of 20 October 1987 on the issue has not been published. There was an expectation that similar problems are and will be experienced around the world[29] but, if they have, the regulation has not been invoked. Greaves also makes the connection between this complaint under Regulation 4058/86 and the Commission's decision in the *French West African Shipowners' Committees* case when she observes that the competition decision in that case under Regulation 4056/86 was the result of a complaint under Regulation 4058/86:

"[t]he investigation [in the *French West African Shipowners' Committees* case] arose out of complaints submitted by the Danish Shipowners' Association relying on the Competition Regulation [i.e. then Regulation 4056/86] and by the Danish Government relying on Council Regulation

---

27 The members of the Consultative Shipping Group are Belgium, Denmark, Finland, France, Germany, Greece, Italy, Japan, the Netherlands, Norway, Spain, Sweden and the UK.
28 Op. cit. at fn. 1, p. 125.
29 See the Report from the Commission to the Council of Ministers on the Implementation of the Four Regulations in the Field of Maritime Transport adopted by the Council on 22 December 1986, SEC (90) 1594 final.

4058/86,[30] concerning co-ordinated action to safeguard free access to cargoes in ocean trades. Council Regulation 4056/86 is directed at non-Member States and not at shipping companies. Thus, the Regulation provides a procedure for co-ordinated action. The complaint is initially addressed to the Commission, which then has a duty to recommend to the Council the appropriate measure that should be taken. The Regulation specifies the type of counter-measures that may be taken. The whole procedure, being targeted at a foreign state itself, follows diplomatic rather than legal channels."[31]

18.027 Strati has observed that Regulation 4058/86 (alongside Regulation 4055/86) was a victory for Greece in terms of the negotiations of the December 1986 package while Regulation 4056/86 and Regulation 4057/86 represented the majority view.[32]

18.028 Regulation 4058/86 allows the Member State affected to benefit from the collective muscle of the EU as a whole. It is therefore a potent but a blunt weapon. Its potency is derived in no small measure from the fact that it is the EU, with its large cargo base, which is brandishing the weapon.[33] It is however, as Heldring concluded, "no paper tiger".[34]

18.029 It is useful, in this context, to have regard to Decision 167/2006 of the European Parliament and of the Council of 18 January 2006 concerning the activities of certain third countries in the field of cargo shipping.[35] It was a measure based on what is now Article 100(2) of the TFEU. The background is clear from the recitals to the decision:

"(1) Council Decision 78/774/EEC of 19 September 1978 concerning the activities of certain third countries in the field of cargo shipping[36] has been substantially amended. In the interests of clarity and rationalisation the said Decision should be codified.
(2) Information systems should be established to enable the Community institutions to be kept informed of the activities of the fleets of third countries whose practices are harmful to the shipping interests of the Member States and in particular in so far as those activities adversely affect the competitive participation of the fleets of Member States in international maritime trade. Those information systems must facilitate consultation at Community level.
(3) The possibility should be provided for the necessary measures to be adopted at Community level for the joint exercise by Member States of their powers to adopt counter-measures in respect of the cargo shipping activities of certain third countries."[37]

18.030 Under Article 1 of the decision, each Member State must take all the necessary measures to institute a system allowing it to collect information on the activities of the fleets of third countries whose practices are harmful to the shipping interests of the Member States and in particular in so far as those activities adversely affect the competitive participation of the fleets of Member States in international maritime trade. That system must enable each Member State, to the extent necessary to attain the objectives referred to in the first paragraph, to collect information on: (a) the level of cargo shipping services offered; (b) the nature, volume, value, origin and destination of goods loaded or

---

30 O.J. 1986 L378/21.
31 Greaves, "EC Competition Rules and Maritime Transport" [1992] LMCLQ 459 at 464.
32 In Kariotis, *Aegean Institute of the Law of the Sea and Maritime Law* (1997), p. 266.
33 See Honka in Lovett (ed.), *United States Shipping Policies and World Markets* (1996) generally.
34 Op. cit. at fn.1, p. 611.
35 OJ 2006 L33/18.
36 OJ L258, 21.9.1978, p. 35. Decision as amended by Decision 89/242/EEC (OJ L97, 11.4.1989, p. 47).
37 Some footnotes omitted.

unloaded in the Member States concerned by the ships engaged in these services; and (c) the level of tariffs charged for such services.

18.031 Article 2 provides:

"1. The Council, acting by qualified majority, shall decide to which third countries' fleets the information system is to be jointly applied.
2. The decision referred to in paragraph 1 shall specify the type of cargo shipping to which the information system is to apply, the date of its introduction, the intervals at which the information is to be provided and which of the types of information listed in the second paragraph of Article 1 are to be collected.
3. Each Member State shall forward to the Commission, periodically or at the request of the latter, the information produced by its information system.
4. The Commission shall collate the information for the Community as a whole. Article 4 of Council Decision 77/587/EEC of 13 September 1977 setting up a consultation procedure on relations between Member States and third countries in shipping matters and on action relating to such matters in international organisations ... shall apply to that information."

18.032 Article 3 provides:

"The Member States and the Commission shall examine regularly, within the framework of the consultation procedure established by Decision 77/587/EEC and on the basis inter alia of the information produced by the information system referred to in Article 1, the activities of the fleets of the third countries specified in the decisions referred to in Article 2(1)."

18.033 Article 4 provides:

"The Council, acting unanimously, may decide on the joint application by Member States, in their relations with a third country or group of third countries regarding which a decision referred to in Article 2(1) has been adopted, of appropriate counter-measures forming part of their national legislation."

18.034 Article 5 provides that the Member States must retain the right to apply unilaterally their national information systems and countermeasures.

18.035 Article 6 provides that Decision 78/774 was repealed by the decision, without prejudice to the obligations of the Member States with regard to time-limits for implementing that decision. References made to the repealed decision are to be construed as being made to this decision and should be read in accordance with the correlation table in Annex II.

18.036 On 18 January 2006, the European Parliament and the Council adopted Decision 167/2006 of 18 January 2006 concerning the activities of certain third countries in the field of cargo shipping.[38]

P. CONCLUSIONS

18.037 Regulation 4056/86 was a significant measure to ensure that the EU's shipping sector was not damaged by the action of third States. It has not been used much and has not been considered by the CJEU in any judgment but its pressure – and the threat that it might be used – may have been sufficient.

---

38 OJ L33/21, 4 February 2006.